ACCESS REGULAR TEXT UPDATES, ONLINE STUDY MATERIALS, AND A COLLECTION OF INTERNET RESOURCES AT

www.mhhe.com/hill

- **Online Learning Center**–Review and apply text concepts with interactive practice quizzes, PowerPoint slides, Internet exercises, and more.

- **This Week in Global News**–Check out news briefs relating the latest international business news stories to chapter concepts.

- **International Business Web Directory**–Jump to a number of other Web sites of interest to students of international business.

- **Newsroom**–Research current events by linking to national and international news sources on the Internet.

- **Much more!**

A password-protected portion of the site is also available to instructors, offering updates related to cases in the text, downloadable supplements, an international business bulletin board service, and a complete selection of online teaching resources.

INTERNATIONAL BUSINESS

Competing in the
Global Marketplace:
Postscript 2002

Third Edition

Charles W. L. Hill
University of Washington

McGraw-Hill
Irwin

Boston   Burr Ridge, IL   Dubuque, IA   Madison, WI   New York   San Francisco   St. Louis
Bangkok   Bogotá   Caracas   Kuala Lumpur   Lisbon   London   Madrid   Mexico City
Milan   Montreal   New Delhi   Santiago   Seoul   Singapore   Sydney   Taipei   Toronto

McGraw-Hill Higher Education

*A Division of The **McGraw-Hill** Companies*

INTERNATIONAL BUSINESS:
COMPETING IN THE GLOBAL MARKETPLACE, POSTSCRIPT 2002

Published by McGraw-Hill/Irwin, an imprint of The McGraw-Hill Companies, Inc. 1221 Avenue of the Americas, New York, NY, 10020. Copyright © 2002, by The McGraw-Hill Companies, Inc. All rights reserved. No part of this publication may be reproduced or distributed in any form or by any means, or stored in a database or retrieval system, without the prior written consent of The McGraw-Hill Companies, Inc., including, but not limited to, in any network or other electronic storage or transmission, or broadcast for distance learning.

Some ancillaries, including electronic and print components, may not be available to customers outside the United States.

This book is printed on acid-free paper.

domestic 1 2 3 4 5 6 7 8 9 0 VNH/VNH 0 9 8 7 6 5 4 3 2 1
international 1 2 3 4 5 6 7 8 9 0 VNH/VNH 0 9 8 7 6 5 4 3 2 1

ISBN 0-07-239202-9

Executive editor: *John E. Biernat*
Senior developmental editor: *Laura Hurst Spell*
Marketing manager: *Lisa Nicks*
Project manager: *Laura Griffin*
Production supervisor: *Debra R. Sylvester*
Senior designer: *Jennifer McQueen*
Media technology producer: *Jenny R. Williams*
Interior and cover photos: *Copyright © 1999 PhotoDisc, Inc. All rights reserved.*
Back cover photographer: *Donna Day*
Compositor: *Precision Graphics*
Typeface: *10.5/12 Goudy*
Printer: *Von Hoffmann Press, Inc.*

Library of Congress Cataloging-in-Publication Data

Library of Congress Control Number: 2001088510

INTERNATIONAL EDITION ISBN 0-07-112084-X

Copyright © 2002. Exclusive rights by The McGraw-Hill Companies, Inc. for manufacture and export. This book cannot be re-exported from the country to which it is sold by McGraw-Hill. The International Edition is not available in North America.

www.mhhe.com

Introduction

One key task of any author of an international business text is to keep the content as current as possible. This is a difficult job given that the world around us is constantly changing, often in ways that are important for the global economy and international business. In this postscript, we review some important developments that have occurred since the manuscript for this edition of the book was sent to the publisher, and we discuss the implications of these developments for international business. One development has been the continuing globalization of the world economy. A second development, which represents a countertrend to the first development, was the breakdown of the World Trade Organization meetings in Seattle in December 1999 in the face of protests from various groups opposed to globalization. A third development was the decision to allow China to enter the World Trade Organization. A fourth development was the January 1999 birth of the euro, the currency unit now used by 11 of the 15 nations of the European Union. Since January 1999, the euro has failed to live up to expectations. This postscript examines why. To mark the first year of a new millennium, the postscript closes with a review of the economic and political achievements of the 20th century and a discussion of the outlook for the early years of the 21st century.

Globalization of the World Economy

As discussed in Chapter 1, for half a century global trade has expanded much faster than global output. Between 1950 and 1999 the volume of world trade increased twentyfold, while the inflation-adjusted value of world gross domestic product (GDP) increased a little over 6.3 times. The late 1990s and the first part of 2000 were no exception to this long-term trend. In 1998 and 1999, the volume of global trade in merchandised products expanded at 5 percent a year compounded, while world GDP grew at 2 percent in 1998 and 2.5 percent in 1999.[1]

For the first nine months of 2000, the volume of world trade surged to a near record 12 percent annual growth rate. While a slowdown in the last quarter of 2000 was expected to bring the total growth in the volume of world trade to about 10 percent for all of 2000, this is still well above historic norms and far in excess of the 4.5 percent expansion estimated for 2000. There are three reasons for this particularly strong growth. First, robust economic growth in the world's largest economy, the United States, resulted in high demand in the United States for imports, which grew at an annual rate of 20 percent during the first nine months of 2000. By comparison, US exports grew at an annual rate of 14 percent over the same period. As a result, in mid-2000, the US trade deficit hit a record $400 billion, amounting to about 4.5 percent of US GDP. Second, the continuing recovery of Asian countries from the 1997–98 financial crisis fueled growth in world trade. The value of Asia's imports and exports rose at a 27 percent annual rate in the first nine months of 2000 (these figures exclude China and Japan). Third, spurred by continued rapid economic growth, the value of China's trade expanded by more than one-third in the first nine months of 2000. Japan also registered a large expansion in international trade, which increased by 23 percent over the same period.[2]

The strong continuation of the long-term growth in the volume of international trade signals that the global economy is continuing to become ever more tightly integrated. As global trade grows faster than global GDP, national economies are becoming increasingly intertwined, depending on each other for an ever-larger percentage of goods and services. As this development unfolds, globalization is accelerating; global markets and global production systems are replacing national markets and national production systems. The economic theories reviewed in Chapter 4 suggest that this development is beneficial, with greater trade translating into an increase in the efficiency of the world economy, income gains in countries involved in the global trading system, and greater global economic growth.

A similar trend toward globalization can be seen in the data on foreign direct investment (FDI) flows. According to the most recent figures from the United Nations, foreign direct investment outflows hit record levels in 1999.[3] Enterprises resident in one country invested some $860 billion in productive assets in another country. This was up from $732 billion in 1998. Provisional data suggest foreign direct investment outflows will exceed $1 trillion in 2000. In comparison, the value of foreign direct investment in 1980 was just $60 billion, and in 1990 it was $210 billion.[4]

The rapid expansion of FDI suggests two things. First, individual enterprises are increasingly building global production systems, dispersing activities to those locations in the world where they can be produced most efficiently. Second, the data imply that enterprises are entering each other's markets in an attempt to create and exploit emerging global markets for the goods and services they produce. The most recent data also suggest a sharp rise in the volume and value of cross-border mergers and acquisitions. Mergers and acquisitions, rather than building operations from the ground up, are becoming the favored mode for entering foreign markets. In 1999, for example, the value of completed cross-border mergers and acquisitions rose to $720 billion and involved about 6,000 transactions, up from $100 billion in 1987.[5]

As a result of foreign direct investment activity, there are now some 63,000 multinational companies in the world with about 700,000 foreign affiliates. Their growing importance in the world economy can be measured by their share of foreign direct investment stock in world GDP, which increased from 2 percent in 1980 to 14 percent at the start of 2000.[6]

Despite this rapid growth, recent data show that foreign direct investment remains highly concentrated, with most of the flows taking place between a limited group of nations. In 1999, 10 developed countries received 70 percent of all FDI inflows, and 10 developing nations accounted for 80 percent of all the inflows into developing nations. The usual suspects figured prominently among this select group including the United States (the largest recipient of FDI and the second largest source), the United Kingdom (the largest source), France, Germany, the Netherlands, China, and Mexico. A similar though less dramatic pattern can be seen in the trade data, where 10 countries accounted for 58 percent of the value of world trade in 1999.

In sum, both the trade and foreign direct investment data suggest that we are witnessing not so much the globalization of the world economy, but the rapid integration of the economies of a select club of developed and developing nations. The poorer nations of the world continue to be left on the sidelines in the headlong rush toward global economic integration. Africa, for example, accounted for a little over 1 percent of all FDI in 1999 and about 2 percent of all international trade flows. In a recent report, the World Bank focused on this issue, noting that one-sixth of the world's people produce 78 percent of the world's goods and services and receive 78 percent of the world's income, an average of $70 a day. In contrast, three-fifths of the world's people in the 61 poorest countries receive 6 percent of the world's income, or less than $2 a day.[7]

This continuing disparity suggests that one of the biggest challenges facing global economic institutions such as the World Trade Organization, the World Bank, the International Monetary Fund, and the United Nations is to bring the poorer nations of the world into the global economic system of the 21st century. The exclusion of the majority of the world's population from the global economic system represents an enormous waste of resources, to say nothing of the suffering implied by the continued existence of extreme poverty. If the condition of the poor does not improve, the growing division between the rich and poor nations of the world could lead to geopolitical conflicts that impinge on the economic prosperity of the developed world.

The critical question is how to engage the world's poorer nations in the global economic system. The material contained in Chapters 2, 4, 6, and 10 suggests introducing democratic political institutions, reducing corruption, protecting property rights, deregulating markets, privatizing state-owned enterprises, and liberalizing regulations governing foreign trade and foreign direct investment will all help the poorer nations of the world to raise their economic growth rates and promote engagement in the world economy. However, many in the developed and developing world disagree with this assessment. Those who hold this contrary view made their presence felt in November 1999, when they helped to derail talks sponsored by the World Trade Organization that were aimed at initiating a new round of negotiations to reduce barriers to international trade and foreign direct investment.

The World Trade Organization: Recent Developments

The World Trade Organization (WTO) is the multinational institution that polices the global trading system, resolving trade disputes between member nations (see Chapter 5 for details). The WTO also coordinates efforts to further reduce barriers to cross-border trade and investment. With 140 countries in its membership roster as of November 30, 2000, and another 29—including China, the Russian Federation, and Saudi Arabia—negotiating their membership, the WTO is at the forefront of efforts to promote global free trade. Established in 1995, the WTO replaced the General Agreement on Tariffs and Trade (GATT), which had been overseeing world trade since 1947. The experience of the past few years suggests that the policing and enforcement mechanisms of the WTO are working well. Between 1995 and late 2000, 213 trade disputes between member countries were brought to the WTO.[8] This record compares with a total of 196 cases that were handled by the GATT over almost half a century. Of the cases brought to the WTO, three-quarters had been resolved by late 2000 following informal consultations between the countries in dispute. Resolving the remainder has involved more formal dispute resolution procedures, but these have been largely successful. In general, the countries involved have adopted the WTO's recommendations. Only a handful of cases so far have yet to be resolved by the WTO.

The fact that countries are using the WTO represents an important vote of confidence in the organization's procedures. Reflecting this success, in its 1999 annual report the WTO noted:

> The state of the world trading system is generally sound . . . there were no major trade policy reversals in 1998 and 1999 and . . . there is no evidence of a return to protectionist measures. On the contrary, a number of countries have undertaken concrete measures to further liberalize their economic and trade regimes.[9]

However, the tone of this report, released in November 1999, was to sound overly optimistic given events that occurred in Seattle just a few days latter.

The World Trade Organization in Seattle

At the end of November 1999, representatives from the WTO's member states met in Seattle. The goal of the meeting was to launch a new round of talks—dubbed "the millennium round"—aimed at further reducing barriers to cross-border trade and investment. This round of talks was to be the ninth since 1947, when the forerunner of the WTO, the General Agreement on Tariffs and Trade (GATT), was established (see Chapter 5 for details). Since 1947, the GATT and then the WTO have substantially lowered barriers to cross-border trade. Under the auspices of the GATT and WTO, the average tariff rate on manufactured products imported into developed nations has fallen from over 20 percent of value in 1950 to 3.4 percent today. As barriers tumbled, the volume of international trade expanded dramatically, increasing twentyfold between 1950 and 1999. Many economists argued that this surge in trade was one of the engines of world economic growth in the second half of the 20th century. As explained in Chapter 4, free trade allows countries to specialize in the production of goods and services that they can produce most efficiently, while importing those goods and services that they produce less efficiently. By increasing the efficiency of resource utilization, economic theory predicts that free trade will boost economic growth and real incomes in all countries that participate in a free trade agreement. The experience of the last 50 years seems to bear this theory out.

Given this background, when the WTO convened in Seattle, expectations were high that after the normal amount of haggling, posturing, and last-minute brinkmanship, the talks would yield agreement on major goals for the next round of talks, which were scheduled to begin shortly thereafter. Prominent on the agenda was an attempt to get the assembled countries to agree to work toward the reduction of barriers to trade in agricultural products and trade and investment in services. These expectations were dashed on the rocks of a hard and unexpected reality. On December 3, 1999, the talks ended without any agreement being reached. Inside the meeting rooms, the problem was an inability to reach consensus on the primary goals for the next round of talks. A major stumbling block was friction between the United States and the European Union over whether to endorse the aim of ultimately eliminating subsidies to farm exporters. The United States wanted the elimination of such subsidies to be a priority. The EU, with its politically powerful farm lobby and long history of farm subsidies, was unwilling to take this step. Another stumbling block was related to efforts by the United States to write "basic labor rights" into the law of the world trading system. The United States wanted the WTO to allow governments to impose tariffs on goods imported from countries that did not abide by what the United States saw as fair labor practices. Representatives from developing nations reacted angrily to this proposal, suggesting that it was simply an attempt by the United States to find a legal way of restricting imports from poorer nations.

However, while the disputes inside the meeting rooms were acrimonious, it was events outside that captured the attention of the world press. Originally, the choice of Seattle as the host city for the WTO meetings seemed auspicious. The Seattle region was one of the export powerhouses of the United States and was home to two of the largest multinationals in the country: Boeing and Microsoft. Surely there were few cities in the world that would be more open to the idea of free trade.

The calculation went spectacularly amiss. The WTO talks proved to be a lightning rod for a diverse collection of organizations from environmentalists and human rights groups to labor unions. For various reasons, these groups are opposed to free trade. All these organizations argue that the WTO is an undemocratic institution that was usurping the national sovereignty of member states and making important decisions behind closed doors. They took advantage of the Seattle meetings to voice their opposition, which the world press duly recorded. Environmentalists express concern about the impact that free trade in agricultural products might have on the rate of global deforestation. They argue that lower tariffs on imports of lumber from developing nations will stimulate demand and accelerate the rate at which virgin forests are logged, particularly in nations such as Malaysia and Indonesia. They also point to the adverse impact that some WTO rulings have had on environmental policies. For example, the WTO recently blocked a US rule that ordered fisherman to equip shrimp nets with a device that allows endangered sea turtles to escape. The WTO found the rule discriminated against foreign importers who lacked such nets.[10] Environmentalists argued that the rule was necessary to protect the turtles from extinction.

Human rights activists see WTO rules as outlawing the ability of nations to stop imports from countries where child labor is used or working conditions are hazardous. Similarly, labor unions oppose trade laws that allow imports from low-wage countries and result in a loss of jobs in high-wage countries. They buttress their position by arguing that American workers are losing their jobs to imports from developing nations that do not have adequate labor standards.

Supporters of the WTO and free trade are quick to dismiss these concerns. They have repeatedly pointed out that the WTO exists to serve the interests of its member states, not subvert them. The WTO lacks the ability to force any member nation to take an action that it is opposed to. The WTO can allow member nations to impose retaliatory tariffs on countries that do not abide by WTO rules, but that is the limit of its power. Furthermore, the supporters argue, it is rich countries that pass strict environmental laws and laws governing labor standards, not poor ones. In their view, free trade, by raising living standards in developing nations, will be followed by the passage of such laws in these nations. Using trade regulations to try to impose such practices on developing nations, they believe, will produce a self-defeating backlash.

Many representatives from developing nations, who make up about 105 of the WTO's 140 members, also reject the position taken by environmentalists and advocates of human and labor rights. Poor countries, which depend on exports to boost their economic growth rates and climb their way out of poverty, fear that rich countries will use environmental concerns, human rights, and labor-related issues to erect barriers to the products of the developing world. They believe that attempts to incorporate language about the environment or labor standards in future trade agreements will amount to little more than trade barriers by another name.[11] If this were to occur, they argue that the effect would be to trap developing nations in a grinding cycle of poverty and debt.

However, such pro-trade arguments fell on deaf ears. As the WTO representatives gathered in Seattle, environmentalists, human rights activists, and labor unions marched in the streets. Some of the more radical elements in these organizations, together with anarchists who were philosophically opposed to "global capitalism" and "the rape of the world by multinationals," succeeded not only in shutting down the opening ceremonies of the WTO but also in sparking violence in the normally peaceful streets of Seattle. Against the wishes of the vast majority of protesters, a number of demonstrators engaged in property damage and looting. The police responded with tear gas, rubber bullets, pepper spray, and baton charges. When it was over, 600 demonstrators had been arrested, millions of dollars in property damage had been done to downtown Seattle, and the global news media had their headline: WTO talks collapse amid violent demonstrations.

The question that now must be asked is whether the events in Seattle portray an end to half a century of trade liberalization or whether they represent nothing more than a bump in the road. On the one hand, history suggests that the WTO will ultimately get the next round of talks under way. After all, the last round of global trade talks—the Uruguay Round—also took several years to initiate.

On the other hand, there is a sense that Seattle may have been a watershed. Previous trade talks had been pursued in relative obscurity with only interested economists, politicians, and businesspeople paying much attention. Seattle demonstrated, however, that the issues surrounding the global trend toward free trade have suddenly moved to center stage in the popular consciousness. The debate on the merits of free trade and globalization has become mainstream. Whether further liberalization occurs, therefore, may depend on the importance that popular opinion in countries such as the United States attaches to issues such as human rights and labor standards, job security, environmental policies, and national sovereignty.

It will also depend on the ability of free trade advocates to articulate the argument that, in the long run, free trade is the best way of promoting adequate labor standards, of providing more jobs, and of protecting the environment. Much of the media coverage surrounding the Seattle conference made it clear that the merits of free trade are not well understood, while the perceived drawbacks are easy to identify and make for good press copy. Exactly how this debate will play out remains to be seen, but given recent trends it would not be surprising if labor rights and environmental considerations played a much larger role than hitherto in the next round of global trade talks when they finally get started.

China and the World Trade Organization

China has been trying to join the WTO, and the GATT before it, for 14 years. Within China, membership in the WTO is seen as a necessary component of the country's long march toward a fully functioning market economy. Over the past 20 years the value of China's exports to the rest of the world has climbed by 15 percent per year on average, while imports have grown at an annual rate of 13 percent.[12] The growth in international trade has helped China to expand its economy at 8 percent annually for the past decade. China is now the world's seventh largest economy and with the addition of Hong Kong, its fourth largest exporter.

China's leaders believe that further gains from trade will require membership in the WTO. They understand that this will not be a painless process. Joining the WTO will require China to dismantle many trade barriers that currently protect local industry from foreign competition. They calculate that such short-term pain will be quickly outweighed by long-term gains as foreign competition forces China's producers to become more efficient and as trade with other nations expands.

Historically, one of the biggest roadblocks standing in the way of China's accession to the WTO has been the United States. The United States is China's largest trading partner, accounting for $70 billion of exports in 1999. With its large population and rapid economic growth, China also holds the promise of being a very important market for US producers. For years, however, influential political forces in the United States have opposed China's entry into the WTO on the grounds that the country has scant respect for human rights, labor standards, and intellectual property rights (China is one of the largest consumers of pirated computer software).

Despite domestic opposition, in general the Clinton administration in the United States was a supporter of greater economic engagement with China. This administration repeatedly argued that greater economic freedom in China would be followed by greater political freedom and greater respect for human rights. Accordingly, in November 1999, after a difficult series of negotiations, the Clinton administration and China signed a bilateral trade agreement. The agreement resolved a series of outstanding trade issues between the two countries and set down schedules for phasing out tariff and nontariff barriers. In return for Chinese cooperation, the United States agreed to support China's application to join the WTO. China's bid to enter the WTO was further strengthened in mid-2000, when the European Union negotiated a bilateral trade agreement with China, effectively removing EU objections to China's entry into the WTO. A further signal of US support was given in September 2000, when the US Senate voted to normalize trade relations with China. By doing so, the United States signaled its intention to stop linking trade deals with China to human rights issues. This vote, coming as it did almost a year after the protests in Seattle, seems to indicate that political consensus in the United States is still in favor of pursuing a pro-trade agenda.

With these endorsements in hand, as of late 2000 China was in the final stages of negotiating entry into the WTO. Ironically, the process is now being held up not by forces outside of China, but by forces inside the country. There is unease in China about the impact WTO membership will have on farmers and workers in inefficient enterprises, particularly those based in state-supported industries. Entry into the WTO will hurt producers in inefficient sectors, although it will be a tremendous boon to producers in more efficient sectors. Although the objections from internal forces are not trivial, it still seems likely that China will join the World Trade Organization sometime in 2001.

The Birth of the Euro

The euro, born January 1, 1999, is the common currency unit now used by 11 of the 15 nations of the European Union (EU). The 11 states are members of what is often referred to as the euro zone. For now four EU countries, Britain, Denmark, Greece, and Sweden, are still sitting on the sidelines, although there are indications that Britain and Sweden may join before 2002.

The establishment of the euro was an amazing political feat. There are few historic precedents for what the Europeans are doing. Establishing the euro required the participating national governments not only to give up their own currencies, but also to give up control over monetary policy. Governments do not routinely give up control over important economic policy instruments—sacrifice national sovereignty for the greater good—so this demonstrates the importance the Europeans attach to the euro. By adopting the euro, the EU has created the second largest currency zone in the world after that of the US dollar.

Euro notes and coins will not actually be issued until January 1, 2002. In the interim, national currencies will continue to circulate in each of the 11 countries. However, in each participating state the national currency will stand for a defined amount of euros. Notes that now look like French francs or German deutsche marks or Italian lira are mere denominations of the euro. In each participating state, banks and businesses now keep two sets of accounts, one in the local currency and one in euros. Many prices are now posted in both euros and the local currency. Increasingly, many business transactions will be conducted in euros.

After January 1, 2002, euro notes and coins will be issued and the national currencies will start to be taken out of circulation. After about six months, only euros will be in circulation, and all prices and routine economic transactions within the euro zone will be in euros. In effect, after January 1, 2002, the euro will move from being a virtual currency to a real currency.

Benefits of the Euro

There are several reasons the Europeans decided to establish a single currency in the EU. First, they believe that businesses and individuals will realize significant savings from having to handle one currency, rather than many. The savings come from lower foreign exchange costs and lower hedging costs. For example, an individual going from Germany to France will no longer have to pay a commission to a bank to change deutsche marks into francs. Instead, travelers will be able to use euros. According to the European Commission, such savings could amount to 0.5 percent of the European Union's GDP, or about $40 billion per year.

Second, and perhaps more importantly, the adoption of a common currency will make it easier to compare prices across Europe. This should increase competition because it will be much easier for consumers to shop around. The resulting increase in competitive pressures should lead to lower prices within the euro zone, resulting in substantial gains for European consumers. Third, faced with increased competition and lower prices, European producers will be forced to look for ways to reduce their production costs to maintain their profit margins. To the extent that this occurs, the introduction of a common currency, by increasing competition, should ultimately produce long-run gains in the economic efficiency of European companies.

Fourth, the introduction of a common currency should give a strong boost to the development of a highly liquid pan-European capital market. The development of such a capital market should lower the cost of capital and lead to an increase in both the level of investment and the efficiency with which investment funds are allocated. This could be especially helpful to smaller companies that have historically had difficulty borrowing money from domestic banks.

Finally, the development of a pan-European, euro-denominated capital market will increase the range of investment options open to both individuals and institutions. For example, it will now be much easier for individuals and institutions based in, let's say Holland, to invest in Italian or French companies. This will enable European investors to better diversify their risk, which again lowers the cost of capital and should also increase the efficiency with which capital resources are allocated.[13]

Drawbacks of the Euro

The main drawback of a single currency is that national authorities within the euro zone have lost control over monetary policy. The European Central Bank (ECB) now manages monetary policy within the euro zone. Its prime objective is to ensure price stability. The major tool at its disposal is its ability to set interest rates for the euro. The implied loss of national sovereignty to the ECB underlay the decision by Britain, Denmark, and Sweden to stay out of the euro zone, at least initially. In these countries, many people are highly suspicious of the ECB's ability to remain free from political pressure and to keep price inflation under tight control.

In theory, the design of the ECB should ensure that it remains free of political pressure. The ECB is modeled on the German Bundesbank, which historically has been the most independent and successful central bank in Europe. The language contained in the Maastricht treaty prohibits the ECB from taking orders from politicians. The executive board of the bank, which consists of a president, vice president, and four other members, carries out policy by issuing instructions to national central banks. The policy itself is determined by the governing council, which consists of the executive board plus the central bank governors from the 11 euro zone countries. The governing council votes on interest rate changes. Members of the executive board are appointed for eight-year nonrenewable terms, insulating them from political pressures to get reappointed. Nevertheless, the jury is still out on the issue of the ECB's independence, and it will take some time for the bank to establish its inflation-fighting credentials.

According to critics, another drawback of the euro is that the EU is not what economists would call an optimal currency area. An optimal currency area is a region where similarities in the underlying structure of economic activity make it feasible to adopt a single currency and use one exchange rate as an instrument of macroeconomic policy. Many of the European economies in the euro zone, however, are very dissimilar. For example, Finland and Portugal have very different economies. They have different wage rates and tax regimes and different business cycles, and they may react very differently to external economic shocks. A change in the euro exchange rate that helps Finland may hurt Portugal. These differences complicate macroeconomic policy. For example, when euro economies are not growing in unison, a common monetary policy may mean that interest rates are too high in depressed regions and too low in booming regions. It will be interesting to see how the EU copes with the strains caused by such divergent economic performance.

One way of dealing with such divergent effects within the euro zone might be for the EU to engage in fiscal transfers, taking money from prosperous regions and pumping it into depressed regions. Such a move, however, would open a political can of worms. It is difficult, for example, to imagine the citizens of Germany forgoing their "fair share" of EU funds to create jobs for underemployed Portuguese workers.

Reflecting on these issues, several critics believe that the euro puts the economic cart before the political horse. In their view, a single currency should follow, not precede, political union. They argue that the euro will unleash enormous pressures for tax harmonization and fiscal transfers from the center, both policies that cannot be pursued without the appropriate political structure. The most apocalyptic vision that flows from these negative views is that far from stimulating economic growth, as its advocates claim, the euro will lead to lower economic growth and higher inflation within Europe.

The Early Experience

In the first 20 months of its existence, the euro did not live up to expectations of all its supporters. In January 1999, the euro was trading at 1 euro = $1.17. By late November of that year, the value of the euro had slumped to 1 euro = $1. Although it recovered slightly in December, by the end of the year the euro had still lost 15 percent of its value against the US dollar and was also down significantly against the Japanese yen. The slide continued in 2000, and by fall 2000 the euro was trading at 0.88 = $1, representing a decline against the dollar of more than 20 percent.

Critics were quick to claim that the fall in the euro demonstrated the lack of confidence the foreign exchange market has in the ability of the ECB to effectively manage monetary policy. However, there are no signs that the ECB is mismanaging monetary policy in the euro zone.[14] Inflationary pressures seem to be under control, the ECB seems to have managed interest rates with some skill, and there is no sign that the ECB is bowing to political pressure. Rather, the decline in the value of the euro can be attributed to two other factors: the growth differential and the interest rate differential between the United States and the European Union.[15]

With regard to the growth differential, while the US economy has continued to expand at a robust rate since January 1999, the EU economy showed more moderate growth. In 1999, the US economy grew at a 4.2 percent annual rate, while the EU economy grew at a slower 2.4 percent rate. A big drag on the EU economy in 1999 was Germany, the largest national economy in the euro zone, accounting for one-third of all output in the zone. Germany grew by 1.6 percent in 1999. The weakness in Germany can be partly attributed to inflexible labor markets, which have kept labor costs high and hindered the international competitiveness of German enterprises. In addition, Germany was more exposed than other EU nations to Eastern European economies. When Eastern Europe was hard hit in 1997–98, German industry suffered more than most. Although 2000 looks to have been better for Europe, with the EU nations expected to have grown by 3.5 percent over the full year, the US economy grew by an even stronger 5.2 percent. Yet again, Germany was the drag on the EU economy. Although Germany is coming to grips with its internal problems, and a recovery in Eastern Europe has helped, at 2.9 percent Germany still registered the lowest growth rate among all major EU economies in 2000.

With relatively slow growth in Europe, much of it attributable to problems in Germany, investors have been hesitant to hold euro-denominated assets, particularly when the returns to holding dollar-denominated assets, such as US stocks, have been so much greater. The healthy US economy and the long boom in the US stock market drew investment money away from Europe and into the United States. Also, the strong US economy led to a surge in foreign direct investment into the United States. Both of these factors have helped to bid up the price of the dollar relative to the euro.

The interest rate differential between the United States and the euro zone countries has exacerbated this trend. In a world where capital is internationally mobile, interest rate differentials can play a large role in explaining short-term exchange rate movements. In the United States, the Federal Reserve Board raised interest rates in 1999 and early 2000 in an attempt to slow down the rapidly expanding US economy, which was beginning to show signs of inflationary pressures. As a consequence, the differential between the long-term interest rates on dollar- and euro-denominated government bonds widened from 0.5 percent in January 1999 to 1.6 percent in August 2000. Not surprisingly, capital flowed to the United States and away from the euro zone to gain the benefits of higher US interest rates. As that occurred, the euro continued to depreciate against the dollar.

While this situation has created the impression that the euro has not been the success that was hoped for, there are some silver linings to these clouds. For one thing, the depreciation in the value of the euro against the dollar, and to a lesser extent the Japanese yen, has helped to make EU enterprises more competitive in the global marketplace. This has been translated into expanding exports and a growing surplus on the current account of the balance of payments in the euro zone (i.e., a trade surplus). According to the IMF, the current account surplus in the euro zone will amount to 0.9 percent of GDP in 2000 and is forecasted to reach 1.3 percent of GDP in 2001. In contrast, the United States has been running a current account deficit (a trade deficit) amounting to 4.2 percent of GDP in 2000 and is expected to run the same again in 2001.

There are now signs that the US economy is slowing, and the Federal Reserve Board has lowered interest rates in the United States. This reduced the interest rate differential between the United States and euro zone and should slow or reverse the flow of money from Europe to the United States. Furthermore, if the slowdown in the United States is steep enough, investors may start taking money out of US stocks, and foreign businesses may slow their rate of investment in the United States. If these trends occur, the euro may recover much of the ground that it has lost against the dollar. In sum, the recent weakness of the euro seems to owe more to short-term capital flows than it does to long-term problems in the euro zone or to any mismanagement by the ECB. It is certainly too early to write off the euro. It would not be surprising if the euro strengthened against the dollar in 2001.

International Business in the New Millennium

With the dawn of a new millennium, it seems worthwhile to reflect on how far the world has come over the last hundred years and what the next few years might hold for the global economy and for international business.

A Hundred Years of Progress

The last hundred years have in many ways seen remarkable progress. A person born at the beginning of the 1900s in the United States, then the world's richest country, entered a world in which few had access to running water, electricity, or the telephone. The automobile had only recently been invented and was still the plaything of the rich. Aircraft, radio, penicillin, television, computers, and the Internet all lay in the future. Average life expectancy was 47.3 years. Many people were infirm by the age of 40. There were 75 million people in the country and 1.65 billion people on the planet, up from 980 million in 1800. Income per capita was under $400. The United States was a continental economy in which international business and international trade played a limited role, but that role was starting to expand.

A person born at the beginning of 2000 in the United States entered a dramatically different world. Life expectancy had risen to 77 years, the consequence of a revolution in health care. Income per capita was $30,000. Automobiles, aircraft, antibiotics, computers, television, cell phones, and Internet connections were common. There were now over 6 billion people in the world and 270 million in the United States. There had been a dramatic expansion in both industrial output and in international trade. World trade had expanded twentyfold and world output sixfold since 1950.[16]

The world was a much more democratic place. In 1900, there were 55 sovereign nations, another 55 national entities that were governed by colonial and imperial systems, and 20 protectorates under the sway or protection of foreign powers. A mere 12.4 percent of the world's people lived under some form of democratic government, although suffrage was generally limited to males. By 2000, the great empires had disappeared and the world had 192 sovereign nations. Freedom House, an organization that tracks the spread of democratic freedoms, classified some 85 of these nations, or 44.3 percent, as "free." In 2000 55 percent of the world's population was living in democratic states, a greater proportion than at any other time in history.[17]

Market-based economic systems were also at a high-water mark around the globe. During the 20th century, rival philosophies of political economy, including fascism and communism, had fallen by the wayside. The "free world" had won a hot war against fascism (World War II) and a cold war against Communism. Liberal democracy with its emphasis on market-based economic systems was the ascendant ideology. Even the last great Communist state, China, had embraced market-based systems, making its claim to be a "Communist" country ring hollow. Clearly, this was a world in which international business could thrive, as indeed it has.

However, the 20th century was not one of smooth progress. There were two world wars and hundreds of minor ones that claimed some 37 million lives. Worse still, several Communist governments exhibited an appalling proclivity to murder their own people.

Some 62 million civilians were killed in the Soviet Union between 1917 and 1991, 35 million in China between 1949 and 1990, and 1.5 million in a spasm of brutality Cambodia. There was mass genocide in Turkey, Nazi Germany, Rwanda, and Bosnia. The Japanese killed some 6 million civilians in occupied territories during World War II. Overall, governments during the 20th century killed some 170 million civilians.[18] There was dropping of atomic bombs on Hiroshima and Nagasaki. There was the influenza pandemic of 1918, which left 20 million people dead around the world (in contrast, 8.5 million soldiers lost their lives during World War I). There was the still unfolding AIDS pandemic, which had claimed 16 million lives by 2000 and left 36 million infected with the HIV virus worldwide.[19] There was the great depression of the 1930s, during which the average American saw his income fall by more than half. For much of the 20th century most of the world lived under totalitarian dictatorships of one sort or another. Only in the last decade, since the 1989 collapse of Communism in Eastern Europe, has the balance of the world's population lived in democratic states. Moreover, for all of the progress of the 20th century, much of the world's population still lives in conditions that have more in common with the United States of 1900 than that of 2000. The GNP per capita of India with its 1 billion people, for example, is only about $400 per year. Despite dramatic economic growth, China's 1.2 billion people have a GNP per capita of under $900.

Reasons for Optimism

Looking forward, there are plenty of reasons for optimism, but the history of the 20th century also teaches us to expect reversals and uneven progress. Although predicting the future with certainty is impossible, one can argue that if current trends hold, living standards around the world will continue to improve. There are several reasons for expecting this. First, the prevailing economic ideology of the globe, with its emphasize on market-based systems, is likely to be supportive of the capitalist mode of production. In turn, as explained in Chapter 2, market-based systems beget innovations in products and processes, and innovations are the fuel of economic progress.

Second, the prevailing economic ideology is also supportive of removing barriers to cross-border trade and investment. Even without any further reductions in such barriers, the relatively low level of such barriers today seems likely to ensure that the trend toward the globalization of product and capital markets will continue. In turn, the efficiency gains that flow from global markets will constitute a rising tide that lifts all economic boats.

Third, as noted above, for the first time in history the majority of the world's population now lives in democratic states. The trend toward greater democracy seems to be firmly in place. Over the past 15 years, new democracies have sprung up throughout Latin America and Eastern Europe. There are signs that democracy may be gaining a foothold in parts of Africa, and several Asian countries, such as South Korea, have become far more democratic in recent decades. History teaches us that democracies rarely start wars, which bodes well for the future.

Fourth, current advances in computing and communications technology, if maintained for two more decades, promise to vastly improve the efficiency of global markets and global business. Communications technology has always been a major driver of economic progress. The Gutenberg press, postal services, the telegraph, the telephone, and the Internet have all lowered the costs of bringing together buyers and sellers—of making markets work—realizing substantial efficiency gains in the process. The Internet, because of its global reach, rapid growth, and potential for transmitting huge bundles of information at almost zero cost, will have a particularly dramatic impact in the near future.

Future Challenges

Having laid out the reasons for being optimistic about the near future, it would be naïve not to highlight some of the potential problems that might stall global economic growth in the coming decades, or at least present international businesses with some significant challenges. One possibility is that a combination of continued population growth, poverty in some less developed nations, and environmental degradation might lead to an ideological backlash against the global move toward free markets and the capitalist mode of production. One might argue that the protest against the World Trade Organization in Seattle might portend the leading edge of such a backlash.

Current estimates suggest that global population will continue to expand from 6 billion today to between 9 and 11 billion by 2100. Much of this growth is predicted to take place in the poorer nations of the world, many of which have yet to share in the economic benefits of global capitalism.[20] Environmentalists argue that population pressure puts stress on the environment, ranging from deforestation and soil erosion to air pollution and global warming.[21] As we saw at the recent World Trade Organization meetings, there will certainly be those who maintain that the adoption of free market economics and free trade are causes of such problems.

Naturally, one could counter that the relationship is not this simple. By creating wealth and incentives for enterprises to produce technological innovations, the free market system and free trade could make it easier for the world to cope with problems of pollution and population growth. While pollution levels are rising in the world's poorer countries, they have been falling in developed nations. In the United States, for example, the concentration of carbon monoxide and sulphur dioxide pollutants in the atmosphere decreased by 60 percent between 1978 and 1997, while lead concentrations decreased by 98 percent, and these reductions have occurred against a background of sustained economic expansion.[22] These figures are a testament to the ability of rich countries to take steps that limit the adverse environmental impact of economic development. However, this somewhat subtle argument is not an easy one for many to accept and often falls on deaf ears. The collapse of Communism has created something of an ideological vacuum into which political movement opposed to unfettered free markets might step; and a movement advocating greater regulation of markets and trade to protect the environment could fit the bill here.

If such a movement does arise, it may create many difficult challenges for international businesses, including limits to cross-border trade and investment, government regulation of business activities, consumer revolts, and the imposition of "pollution taxes." For a foretaste of what might come, one only has to look at the recent unhappy experience of Monsanto. Using recombinant DNA technology, Monsanto has genetically engineered certain types of seed corn so that they produce proteins that function as natural insecticides or so they are resistant to Roundup, a popular herbicide sold by Monsanto. Seeds engineered in this manner reduce the need to use insecticides and herbicides, thereby lowering farmers' costs and boosting crop yields. Monsanto thought the world would welcome its innovations, which it believed were environmentally beneficial. Its genetically altered seeds, such as soybeans, have become extremely popular among farmers not only in the United States but also in many other countries including Brazil, India, and China.

In Europe, however, environmentalists mounted a vigorous and largely successful campaign against Monsanto's products, arguing that genetically altered crops might lead to "genetic pollution." According to environmentalists, one possibility is that insects might soon become resistant to the "natural insecticides" produced by Monsanto's genetically modified seed corn. Thus, in the long run, Monsanto's products might actually end up creating "superbugs" that damage crop yields, not improve them. There is also a vague fear that genetic engineering, because it "upsets the natural order of things," might lead to serious problems that have yet to be identified, such as cancer. While these arguments lack scientific support, consumers and politicians across Europe have been receptive to them. Responding to pressure from consumers, many European supermarkets will no longer stock genetically modified foods. Also, the European Union has banned the importation of some genetically modified crops, even though this probably violates World Trade Organization rules. This backlash has effectively reduced Monsanto's ability to sell its products in a market of more than 350 million people, costing the company significant revenues.[23]

Another challenge to globalization and international business might arise from the fear that rapid globalization will drive down the wage rates of workers in developed nations, who will see their jobs "exported" to low-wage locations in the developing world. This fear has long underlay the opposition of labor unions to free trade. Populist politicians on both the left and right frequently articulate this argument. These politicians call for "fair trade"—meaning tariff barriers on imports from low-wage countries to protect inefficient domestic producers—as opposed to "free trade." If the argument gains wider support, it could lead to a partial retreat from free market ideology and an increase in trade barriers. To buttress their case, those who make this argument point to the evidence on growing wage inequality in developed nations. For example, a Federal Reserve study found that in the seven years up until 1996, the earnings of the best-paid 10 percent of US workers rose in real terms by 0.6 percent annually while the earnings of the 10 percent at the bottom of the heap fell by 8 percent. In some areas the fall was much greater. In New York City, the real wages of the worst-paid 10 percent dropped by 27 percent over this time period.[24] However, it seems unlikely that this growing inequality is due to globalization. In the United States, for example, only 13 percent of GNP can be attributed to international trade, and only one-fifth of that, or some 2.6 percent, is trade with developing nations. Most of America's trade is with high-wage countries such as Japan, Canada, and the nations of Europe. Given this, it is difficult to argue that international trade is the cause of growing income inequality.

It should also be noted that recent research suggests the evidence of growing income inequality may be suspect. Robert Lerman of the Urban Institute has taken a close look at the data. He believes that the finding of inequality is based on inappropriate calculations of wage rates. Reviewing the data using a different methodology, Lerman has found that far from increasing income inequality, an index of wage rate inequality for all workers actually fell by 5.5 percent between 1987 and 1994.[25] If future research supports Lerman's finding, the argument that globalization leads to growing income inequality may lose much of its punch. During the last few years of the 1990s, the income of the worst-paid 10 percent of the population has actually risen twice as fast as that of the average worker, suggesting that the high employment levels of these years have triggered a rise in the income of the lowest paid.[26]

A final challenge to globalization and international business might arise if the economic gap between the wealthy nations of the world and the poorest nations continues to widen. Despite all the benefits associated with globalization, over the last hundred years or so the gap between the rich and poor nations of the world has gotten wider. In 1870 the average income per capita in the world's 17 richest nations was 2.4 times that of all other countries. In 1990, the same group was 4.5 times as rich as the rest.[27] While recent history has shown that some of the world's poorer nations are capable of rapid periods of economic growth—witness the transformation that has occurred in some Southeast Asian nations such as South Korea, Thailand, and Malaysia—there also appear to be strong forces for stagnation among the world's poorest nations. A quarter of the countries with a GDP per capita of less than $1,000 in 1960 had growth rates of less than zero in the 1960–95 period, and a third had growth rates of less than 0.05 percent.[28]

Although the reasons for economic stagnation vary, several factors stand out. Many of the world's poorest countries have suffered from totalitarian governments, economic policies that destroyed wealth rather than facilitated its creation, scant protection for property rights, and war. Such factors certainly help explain why countries such as Afghanistan, Cambodia, Cuba, Haiti, Iraq, Libya, Nigeria, Sudan, Vietnam, and Zaire have failed to improve the economic lot of their citizens during recent decades. A complicating factor is that many of these countries have rapidly expanding populations. Without a major change in government, population growth may exacerbate their problems.

It is an open question as to whether such states will prove to be a destabilizing influence in the economy of the 21st century. They may lash out at their neighbors, as Iraq did in the 1991 Gulf War; export their people to other nations, as Haiti and Vietnam have done; or sponsor extensive terrorist activities, as Libya has done. If such geopolitical events do come to pass, there may be significant fallout for the global economy and international businesses. The task for the world community is to find ways to bring these countries into the global trading system so that they can share in the prosperity that has been and will be created.

Notes

1. World Trade Organization, *International Trade Statistics, 2000*, WTO Secretariat, November 30, 2000.

2. Ibid.

3. United Nations, *World Investment Report 2000*, October 2000.

4. United Nations, "Global Foreign Direct Investment to Exceed $1 Trillion," UN press release TAD/1926, October 3, 2000.

5. Ibid.

6. United Nations, *World Investment Report 2000*.

7. World Bank, *World Development Report, 2000–2001* (Oxford: Oxford University Press, 2000).

8. World Trade Organization, *Annual Report by the Director General: Overview of Developments in the International Trading Environment*, November 22, 2000.

9. *World Trade Organization 1999 Annual Report* (Geneva: WTO, 1999).

10. Jim Carlton, "Greens Target WTO Plan for Lumber," *The Wall Street Journal*, November 24, 1999, p. A2.

11. Kari Huus, "WTO Summit Leaves Only Discontent," MSNBC, December 3, 1999. (www.msnbc.com)

12. "China and the WTO: The Real Leap Forward," *The Economist*, November 20, 1999, pp. 25–26.

13. "The Confused Muddle," *The Economist*, December 11, 1999, pp. 44–45; and "Currency Crossroads," *The Economist*, December 4, 1999, pp. 17–18.

14. International Monetary Fund, *World Economic Outlook*.

15. *World Trade Organization 1999 Annual Report*.

16. Freedom House, "Freedom in the World: The Annual Survey of Political Rights and Civil Liberties, 1999–2000," http://freedomhouse.org.

17. These figures are from "Freedom's Journey: A Survey of the 20th Century. On the Yellow Brick Road," *The Economist*, September 11, 1999, p. 7.

18. D. Brown, "New Cases of HIV Decline in Africa for the First Time," *Washington Post*, November 29, 2000, p. A3.

19. Malcom Potts, "The Unmet Need for Family Planning," *Scientific American*, January 2000, pp. 88–93.

20. A. J. McMichael, *Planetary Overload* (Cambridge: Cambridge University Press, 1993).

21. These figures are from "Freedom's Journey: A Survey of the 20th Century. Our Durable Planet," *The Economist*, September 11, 1999, p. 30.

22. Tom Rhodes, "Bitter Harvest. The Real Story of Monsanto and GM Food," *Sunday Times*, August 22, 1999.

23. "A Survey of Pay. Winners and Losers," *The Economist*, May 8, 1999, pp. 5–8.

24. See Robert Lerman, *Is Earnings Inequality Really Increasing? Economic Restructuring and the Job Market*, Brief No. 1 (Washington, DC: Urban Institute, March 1997).

25. "A Survey of Pay."

26. Lant Pritchett, "Divergence, Big Time," *Journal of Economic Perspectives* 11, no. 3 (Summer 1997), pp. 3–18.

27. Ibid.

INTERNATIONAL BUSINESS

Competing in the
Global Marketplace

McGraw-Hill Advanced Topics in Global Management

United Kingdom (The INSÉAD Global Management Series)

Dutta/Manzoni
Process Re-Engineering, Organizational Change and Performance Improvement
© 1999

El Kahal
Business in Europe © 1998

Goddard/Demmirag
Financial Management for International Business, 2/e © 1994

Hayes
Principles of Auditing: An International Perspective © 1999

Lasserre
Strategy and Management in Asia Pacific
© 1999

Walter
Global Capital Markets and Banking © 1998

Canada

Beamish/Woodcock
Strategic Management: Text, Readings and Cases, 5/e © 1999

McShane
Canadian Organizational Behaviour © 1998

Australia

Clark
Human Resource Management © 2000

Deery
Industrial Relations: A Contemporary Analysis
© 1997

Hughes
Management Skills Series
  Managing Information © 1996
  Managing Operations: Customer Service © 1996
  Managing Operations: Productivity © 1996
  Managing Operations: Innovations © 1997
  Managing Operations: Change © 1997
  Managing Effective Working Relationships © 1996
  Managing and Developing Teams © 1996
  Managing and Organising Work for Goal Achievement © 1996
  Managing Performance and Goal Achievement © 1996
  Managing Grievances and Disputes © 1997
  Managing People: Workplace Practice © 1996
  Managing People: Recruitment, Selection and Induction © 1997
  Managing Group Problem Solving and Decision Making © 1996
  Managing People: Training and Development © 1997

McKenna
New Management © 1998

Meredith
Managing Finance © 1999

Page
Applied Business & Management Research
© 2000

Travaglione
Human Resource Strategies © 2000

United States

Ball/McCulloch
International Business: The Challenge of Global Competition, 7/e © 1999

Bartlett/Ghoshal
Transnational Management: Text Cases and Readings in Cross-Border Management, 4/e
© 2000

Beamish/Morrison/Rosenzweig/Inkpen
International Management, Text & Cases, 4/e
© 2000

de la Torre/Doz/Devinney
Managing the Global Corporation, 2/e © 2000

Hill
Global Business Today, 1/e © 1998

Hill
International Business: Competing in the Global Marketplace, 3/e © 2000

Hodgetts/Luthans
International Management: Culture, Strategy, and Behavior, 4/e © 2000

INTERNATIONAL BUSINESS

Competing in the Global Marketplace

Third Edition

Charles W. L. Hill
University of Washington

McGraw-Hill Irwin
McGraw-Hill

Boston Burr Ridge, IL Dubuque, IA Madison, WI New York San Francisco St. Louis
Bangkok Bogotá Caracas Lisbon London Madrid
Mexico City Milan New Delhi Seoul Singapore Sydney Taipei Toronto

McGraw-Hill Higher Education

*A Division of The **McGraw-Hill** Companies*

INTERNATIONAL BUSINESS: COMPETING IN THE GLOBAL MARKETPLACE

This book is printed on acid-free paper.

domestic   2 3 4 5 6 7 8 9 0 VNH/VNH 9 0 9 8 7 6 5 4 3 2 1 0 9
international   2 3 4 5 6 7 8 9 0 VNH/VNH 9 0 9 8 7 6 5 4 3 2 1 0 9

ISBN 0-07-365487-6

Vice president/Editor-in-chief: *Michael W. Junior*
Publisher: *Craig S. Beytien*
Senior sponsoring editor: *Jennifer Roche*
Senior developmental editor: *Laura Hurst Spell*
Marketing manager: *Kenyetta Giles Haynes*
Project manager: *Amy Hill*
Production supervisor: *Debra R. Benson*
Designer: *Jennifer McQueen Hollingsworth*
Photo research coordinator: *Sharon Miller*
Interior and cover photos: *Copyright © 1999 PhotoDisc, Inc. All rights reserved.*
Back cover photographer: *Donna Day*
Supplement coordinator: *Rose M. Range*
Compositor: *Precision Graphics Services, Inc.*
Typeface: *10.5/12 Goudy*
Printer: *Von Hoffmann Press, Inc.*

Library of Congress Cataloging-in-Publication Data
Hill, Charles W. L.
    International business: competing in the global marketplace /
Charles W. L. Hill. — 3rd ed.
     p. cm.
    Includes bibliographical references and index.
    ISBN 0-07-365487-6
    1. International business enterprises—Management.
2. Competition, International.   I. Title.
HD62.4.H55 1999
658'.049—dc21   98–49844

INTERNATIONAL EDITION

ISBN: 0-07-117584-9

http://www.mhhe.com

*For June Hill and
Mike Hill, my parents*

ABOUT THE AUTHOR

Charles W. L. Hill is the Hughes M. Blake Professor of International Business at the School of Business, University of Washington. Professor Hill received his Ph.D. from the University of Manchester's Institute of Science and Technology (UMIST) in Britain. In addition to the University of Washington, he has served on the faculties of UMIST, Texas A&M University, and Michigan State University.

Professor Hill has published over 40 articles in peer reviewed academic journals, including the *Academy of Management Journal*, *Academy of Management Review*, *Strategic Management Journal*, and *Organization Science*. He has also published two college texts, one on strategic management and the other on international business. Professor Hill has served on the editorial boards of several academic journals, including the *Strategic Manage-* *ment Journal* and *Organization Science*. Between 1993 and 1996 he was consulting editor at the *Academy of Management Review*.

Professor Hill teaches in the MBA, Executive MBA, Management, and Ph.D. programs at the University of Washington. He has received awards for teaching excellence in the MBA, Executive MBA, and Management programs. He has also taught customized executive programs.

Professor Hill works on a consulting basis with a number of organizations. His clients have included ATL, Boeing, BF Goodrich, Hexcel, House of Fraser, Microsoft, Seattle City Light, Tacoma City Light, Thompson Financial Services, and Wizards of the Coast. On occasion, Professor Hill serves as a guest commentator on National Public Radio.

BRIEF TABLE OF CONTENTS

CONTENTS

MAPS

PREFACE

International Business: Competing in the Global Market-place is intended for the first international business course at either the undergraduate or the MBA level. My goal in writing this book has been to set a new standard for international business textbooks: I have attempted to write a book that (1) is comprehensive and up-to-date, (2) goes beyond an uncritical presentation and shallow explanation of the body of knowledge, (3) maintains a tight, integrated flow between chapters, (4) focuses managerial implications, and (5) makes important theories accessible and interesting to students.

Comprehensive and Up-to-Date

To be comprehensive, an international business textbook must:

- Explain how and why the world's countries differ.
- Present a thorough review of the economics and politics of international trade and investment.
- Explain the functions and form of the global monetary system.
- Examine the strategies and structures of international businesses.
- Assess the special roles of an international business's various functions.

This textbook does all these things. Too many other textbooks pay scant attention to the strategies and structures of international businesses and to the implications of international business for firms' various functions. This omission is a serious deficiency, because the students in these international business courses will soon be international managers, and they will be expected to understand the implications of international business for their organization's strategy, structure, and functions. This book pays close attention to these issues.

Comprehensiveness and relevance also require coverage of the major theories. Although many international business textbooks do a reasonable job of reviewing long-established theories (e.g., the theory of comparative advantage and Vernon's product life-cycle theory) they tend to ignore such important newer work as:

- The new trade theory and strategic trade policy.
- Michael Porter's theory of the competitive advantage of nations.
- Robert Reich's work on national competitive advantage.
- The new growth theory championed by Paul Romer and Gene Grossman.
- The work of Douglas North and others on national institutional structures and the protection of property rights.
- The market imperfections approach to foreign direct investment that has grown out of Ronald Coase and Oliver Williamson's work on transaction cost economics.
- Bartlett and Ghoshal's research on the transnational corporation.
- The writings of C. K. Prahalad and Gary Hamel on core competencies, global competition, and global strategic alliances.

The failure of many books to discuss such work is a serious deficiency considering how influential these theories have become, not just in academic circles, but also in the world at large. A major proponent of strategic trade policy, Laura Tyson, served for a time as chairperson of President Clinton's Council of Economic Advisors. Robert Reich served as Secretary of Labor in the Clinton administration. Ronald Coase won the 1992 Nobel Prize in economics, giving the market imperfections approach new respectability. Two years later, Douglass North won the Nobel Prize in economics for his work showing how a nation's economic history influences its contemporary institutions and property rights regime. The work of Bartlett, Ghoshal, Hamel, and Prahalad is having an important impact on business practices.

I have incorporated all relevant state-of-the-art work at the appropriate points in this book. For example, in Chapter 2, "Country Differences in Political Economy," reference is made to the new growth theory and the work of North and others on national institutional structures and property rights. In Chapter 4, "International Trade Theory," in addition to such standard theories as the theory of comparative advantage and the Heckscher-Ohlin theory, there is detailed discussion of the new trade theory and Porter's theory of national competitive advantage. In Chapter 5, "The Political

Economy of International Trade," the pros and cons of strategic trade policy are discussed. In Chapter 6, "Foreign Direct Investment," the market imperfections approach is reviewed. Chapters 12, 13, and 14, which deal with the strategy and structure of international business, draw extensively on the work of Bartlett, Ghoshal, Hamel, and Prahalad.

In addition to including leading edge theory, in light of the fast-changing nature of the international business environment, every effort is being made to ensure that the book is as up-to-date as possible when it goes to press. A significant amount has happened in the world since the first edition of this book was published in 1993. The Uruguay Round of GATT negotiations was successfully concluded and the World Trade Organization was established. The European Union moved forward with its post-1992 agenda to achieve a closer economic and monetary union, including plans to establish a common currency by the end of the decade. The North American Free Trade Agreement passed into law, and Chile indicated its desire to become the next member of the free trade area. The Asian Pacific Economic Cooperation forum (APEC) emerged as the kernel of a possible future Asia Pacific free trade area. The former Communist states of Eastern Europe and Asia continued on the road to economic and political reform. As they did, the euphoric mood that followed the collapse of communism in 1989 was slowly replaced with a growing sense of realism about the hard path ahead for many of these countries. The global money market continued its meteoric growth. By 1995 over $1 trillion per day was flowing across national borders. The size of such flows fueled concern about the ability of short-term speculative shifts in global capital markets to destabilize the world economy. These fears were fanned by the well-publicized financial problems of a number of organizations that traded derivatives through the global money market, such as Baring's Bank. The World Wide Web emerged from nowhere to become the backbone of an emerging global network for electronic commerce. The world continued to become more global. Several Asian Pacific economies, including most notably China, continued to grow their economies at a rapid rate. New multinationals continued to emerge from developing nations in addition to the world's established industrial powers. And increasingly, the globalization of the world economy affected a wide range of firms of all sizes, from the very large to the very small.

Reflecting this rapid pace change, in this edition of the book I have tried to ensure that all material and statistics are as up-to-date as possible as of 1999. However, being absolutely up-to-date is impossible since change is always with us. What is current today may be outdated tomorrow. Accordingly, I have established a home page for this book on the World Wide Web at www.mhhe.com/hill. From this home page the reader can access regular updates of chapter material and reports on topical developments that are relevant to students of international business. I hope readers find this a useful addition to the support material for this book.

Beyond Uncritical Presentation and Shallow Explanation

Many issues in international business are complex and thus necessitate considerations of pros and cons. To demonstrate this to students, I have adopted a critical approach that presents the arguments for and against economic theories, government policies, business strategies, organizational structures, and so on.

Related to this, I have attempted to explain the complexities of the many theories and phenomena unique to international business so the student might fully comprehend the statements of a theory or the reasons a phenomenon is the way it is. These theories and phenomena are typically explained in more depth in this book than they are in competing textbooks, the rationale being that a shallow explanation is little better than no explanation. In international business, a little knowledge is indeed a dangerous thing.

Integrated Progression of Topics

Many textbooks lack a tight, integrated flow of topics from chapter to chapter. In this book students are told in Chapter 1 how the book's topics are related to each other. Integration has been achieved by organizing the material so that each chapter builds on the material of the previous ones in a logical fashion.

Part I Chapter 1 provides an overview of the key issues to be addressed and explains the plan of the book.

Part II Chapters 2 and 3 focus on national differences in political economy and culture. Most international business textbooks place this material at a later point, but I believe it is vital to discuss national differences first. After all, many of the central issues in international trade and investment, the global monetary system, international business strategy and structure, and international business operations arise out of national differences in political economy and culture. To fully understand these issues, students must first appreciate the differences in countries and cultures.

Part III Chapters 4 through 8 investigate the political economy of international trade and investment. The purpose of this part is to describe and explain the trade and investment environment in which international business occurs.

Part IV Chapters 9 through 11 describe and explain the global monetary system, laying out in detail the monetary framework in which international business transactions are conducted.

Part V In Chapters 12 through 14 attention shifts from the environment to the firm. Here the book examines the strategies and structures that firms adopt to compete effectively in the international business environment.

Part VI In Chapters 15 through 20 the focus narrows further to investigate business operations. These chapters explain how firms can perform their key functions—manufacturing, marketing, R&D, human resource management, accounting, and finance—in order to compete and succeed in the international business environment.

Throughout the book, the relationship of new material to topics discussed in earlier chapters is pointed out to the students to reinforce their understanding of how the material comprises an integrated whole.

Focus on Managerial Implications

Many international business textbooks fail to discuss the implications of the various topics for the actual practice of international business. This does not serve the needs of business school students who will soon be practicing managers. Accordingly, the usefulness of this book's material in the practice of international business is discussed explicitly. In particular, at the end of each chapter in Parts Two, Three, and Four—where the focus is on the environment of international business, as opposed to particular firms—there is a section titled *Implications for Business*. In this section, the managerial implications of the material discussed in the chapter are clearly explained. For example, Chapter 4, "International Trade Theory," ends with a detailed discussion of the various trade theories' implications for international business management.

In addition, each chapter begins with a case that illustrates the relevance of chapter material for the practice of international business. Chapter 2, "Country Differences in Political Economy," for example, opens with a case that describes Brazil's privatization efforts.

I have also added a closing case to each chapter. These cases are also designed to illustrate the relevance of chapter material for the practice of international business. The closing case to Chapter 2, for example, describes the problems General Electric has had trying to establish profitable operations in Hungary. As the case makes clear, these problems are rooted in the political economy of Hungary and in General Electric's initial failure to fully appreciate the impact that political economy has on business operations. Each closing case is followed by a list of discussion questions, which facilitates the use of these cases as a vehicle for in-class case discussion and analysis. Another tool that I have used to focus on managerial implications are Management Focus boxes. There is at least one Management Focus in each chapter. Like the opening case, the purpose of these boxes is to illustrate the relevance of chapter material for the practice of international business. The Management Focus in Chapter 2, for example, looks at Microsoft's battle against software piracy in China. This box fits in well with a section of the chapter that looks at the protection of intellectual property rights in different countries.

Accessible and Interesting

The international business arena is fascinating and exciting, and I have tried to communicate my enthusiasm for it to the student. Learning is easier and better if the subject matter is communicated in an interesting, informative, and accessible manner. One technique I have used to achieve this is weaving interesting anecdotes into the narrative of the text—stories that illustrate theory. The opening cases and focus boxes are also used to make the theory being discussed in the text both accessible and interesting.

Each chapter has two kinds of focus boxes—a Management Focus box (described above) and a Country Focus box. Country Focus boxes provide background on the political, economic, social, or cultural aspects of countries grappling with an international business issue. In Chapter 2, for example, the Country Focus box discusses the changing political economy in India. Moreover, the opening cases and boxed material are not free-floating. I continually refer to and utilize opening cases and boxed material in the main body of the text. The idea, once more, is to show students real-world examples of the issues being discussed in the text.

Just how accessible and interesting this book actually is will be revealed by time and student feedback. I am confident, however, that this book is far more accessible to students than its competitors. For those of you who view such a bold claim with skepticism, I urge you to read the sections in Chapter 1 on the globalization of the world economy, the changing nature of international business, and how international business is different.

What's New in the Third Edition

The success of the first two editions of International Business was based in part upon the incorporation of leading edge research into the text, the use of the up-to-date examples and statistics to illustrate global trends and enterprise strategy, and the discussion of current events within the context of the appropriate theory. Building on these strengths, my goals for the third revision have been threefold:

1. Incorporate new insights from recent scholarly research wherever appropriate.
2. Make sure the content of the text covers all appropriate issues.
3. Make sure the text is as up-to-date as possible with regard to current events, statistics, and examples.

Often these goals have overlapped. For example, the global financial crisis that started in Asia in 1997 and spread to Russia in 1998 is relevant both because it is a current event of great significance to international business and because it has sparked a furious debate between scholars as to the appropriate role of the IMF. Thus, in Chapter 10, I outline the causes and consequence of the recent Asian and Russian financial crises, and I discuss the current debate between scholars such as Jeffrey Sachs and Stanley Fisher over the role of the IMF in such crises.

As part of the revision process, *changes have been made to every chapter in the book*. The following are *examples* of the kind of changes that have been made in the text.

Chapter 1: Globalization. The chapter has been rewritten around the theme of globalization. All the statistics pertaining to globalization (such as the growth of world trade, output, and foreign direct investment) have been updated to incorporate the most recently available data. A new section deals with the debate between scholars on the merits and drawbacks of globalization. This debate is concerned with the impact of globalization on job security, income levels, labor policies, the environment, and national sovereignty.

Chapter 2: National Differences in Political Economy. A new section titled "States in Transition" has been added to the chapter. This section discusses the nature of the economic transformation, or liberalization, now being pursued by numerous states around the world, including many former Communist nations. The section discusses deregulation and privatization in greater depth than hitherto. Also new to this chapter is a discussion of Samuel Huntington's influential work on the *Clash of Civilizations and the New World Order*. Huntington rejects the popular view, best articulated by Francis Fukuyama in *The End of History*, that we are moving toward a universal global civilization based on Western liberal ideology. Instead, Huntington paints a picture of a world divided between different civilizations, some of which are potentially opposed to Western ideology. If Huntington is correct, the implications for international business are profound.

Chapter 5: The Political Economy of International Trade. The chapter has been significantly updated to reflect the recent activities of the World Trade Organization (WTO). This includes a discussion of the record of the WTO in resolving trade disputes between nations, as well as a discussion of recent multinational agreements, brokered by the WTO, to liberalize cross-border trade and investment in financial services and telecommunications.

Chapter 8: Regional Economic Integration. The chapter has been updated to reflect recent developments in the European Union, including the move toward monetary union, which began to take effect January 1, 1999. The chapter also contains an expanded and updated discussion of the effects of the 1993 North American Free Trade Agreement (NAFTA) and the South American free trade pact, MERCOSUR. Recent research has shed new light on the magnitude of the effects of NAFTA and MERCOSUR. The chapter also updates the evolution of other moves toward regional economic integration, including the Asian Pacific Economic Cooperation forum (APEC).

Chapter 10: The International Monetary System. New material has been added that reviews the causes and consequences of the recent financial crises in Asia and Russia. The response of the International Monetary Fund to these crises has been discussed in light of the debate between scholars such as Jeffrey Sachs and Stanley Fisher as to the appropriate role of the IMF.

Chapter 14: Entry Strategy and Strategic Alliances. A new section in this chapter discusses basic entry decisions, such as which foreign markets to enter first, the timing of entry, and the appropriate scale of entry and strategic commitments to a market. This section draws on recent research work pertaining to foreign market entry and strategic commitments.

Chapter 17: Global Marketing and R&D. This chapter has been extensively rewritten and extended to enhance its contribution to the text. A new section deals with market segmentation in global markets. The discussion of pricing strategy has been expanded to incorporate recent research on multipoint pricing by international businesses. The section on new product development has been significantly expanded to incorporate new research and discuss additional issues. Additional areas covered include how best to integrate different functions and manage cross-functional product development teams in a globally dispersed enterprise, and where to locate different R&D activities in a firm's global value chain.

Instructor Support Material

Instructor's Manual

The Instructor's Manual, prepared by Duane Helleloid of Towson University, contains chapter overviews, teaching suggestions, lecture notes, and video notes. New features in the third edition *Manual* include opening case discussion questions and answers, closing case solutions, Internet Exercises, and transparency masters.

Test Bank

This expanded edition of the Test Bank, prepared by Bruce R. Barringer of the University of Central Florida, contains approximately 100 true-false, multiple-choice, and essay questions per chapter.

Computest

A computerized version of the test bank allows the instructor to generate random tests and to add his or her own questions.

PowerPoint®

Prepared by Richard Hall of the University of Missouri-Kansas City, this edition of the PowerPoint program has been enhanced with the addition of original materials not found in the text. Reproductions of key text figures, tables, and maps are also included.

Videos

An improved video line-up, consisting of NBC News footage and original business documentaries, features programs based on examples and cases in the text, including "McDonald's Everywhere," "Eurodisney Attempts New Approach to Bring in Business," "Trade Off: Has NAFTA Hurt or Helped the U.S. Economy?" and "Hitting Home: How the World Financial Crisis Is Affecting the U.S."

Presentation CD-ROM

Much of the instructor's manual, the PowerPoint slides, video clips and more are compiled in electronic format on a CD for your convenience in customizing lecture presentations.

Website: www.mhhe.com/hill

A password-protected portion of the book website will be available to adopters of *International Business*, featuring a monthly case update service that provides coverage of the latest in online news and links relating to selected companies, countries, and situations referenced in the text, prepared by Jay H. Rhee, San Jose State University. Other online and downloadable teaching resources will be available for the instructor as well.

Student Resources

Global Business Plan Project and Resource CD

Designed to help students gain experience in conducting research and applying text concepts to the real world of international business, the resources on this CD are organized around a series of activities, created by Les Dlabay of Lake Forest College, which guide students step-by-step through the development of their own global business plan. As students work through the activities, they can link to hypertext chapters from the book, view related video clips, or launch to the book website and Internet.

Website: www.mhhe.com/hill

From the book website students can access bi-weekly updates of chapter material and commentary on topical issues, prepared by Jay H. Rhee, San Jose State University. Also available are chapter study questions and Internet applications; Internet exploration questions tied to each chapter's closing case; and an online Web directory containing links to websites of international organizations, news agencies, companies, and countries.

Rand McNally's *New Millennium World Atlas* Deluxe CD-ROM

By clicking on points of interest on this interactive world atlas, students can quickly access over 800 articles on world cultures, cities, and science, as well as 237 country profiles and links to specific Internet sites. Special tools such as Notebook, Map Customization, Global Find, Compare Maps, and Compare Facts allow you to access, manipulate, customize, organize, save, and print the content information.

Acknowledgments

Numerous people deserve to be thanked for their assistance in preparing this book. First, thank you to all the people at Irwin/McGraw-Hill who have worked with me on this project:

Craig Beytien, Publisher
Jennifer Roche, Senior Sponsoring Editor
Laura Hurst Spell, Senior Development Editor

Kenyetta Giles Haynes, Marketing Manager

Amy Hill, Project Manager

Jennifer Hollingsworth, Designer

Debra Benson, Production Supervisor

Sharon Miller, Photo Research Coordinator

Second, my thanks go to the reviewers, who provided good feedback that helped shape this book.

Gina Wilson Beckles, Bethune-Cookman College
Ingmar Bjorkman, INSEAD/Swedish School of Economics
Aruna Chandrasekaran, Ashland University
David L. Cleeton, Oberlin College
William B. Crawford, National Dong Hwa University
Les Dlabay , Lake Forest College
Golpira Eshghi, Bentley College
George Gresham, American University
Peggy F. Hayek, Pace University
Samuel B. Hinchey, University of Massachusetts
Veronica Horton, The University of Akron
Ralph Jagodka, Mt. San Antonio College
Lialian Lin, California State Polytechnic University
Joshua D. Martin, University of Delaware
Darryl J. Mitry, National University
Leslie C. Mueller, Central Washington University
Janet Y. Murray, Cleveland State University
Brian Peach, University of West Florida
Sandra Sutherland Rahman, Newbury College
Dinker Raval, Morgan State University
Russell T. Reston, George Mason University
Douglas N. Ross, Towson University
Bala Subramanian, Morgan State University
Xiaohua Yang, University of Redlands

Thank you also to reviewers who provided feedback on previous editions:

Suhail Abboushi, Duquesne University
Poul Andersen, The Aarhus School of Business
David Aviel, California State University
Thomas Bates, San Francisco State University
Thomas Becker, Florida Atlantic University
Dharma de Silva, Wichita State University
Gary Dicer, University of Tennessee
Robert Hopely, University of Massachusetts
C. Thomas Howard, University of Denver
Ben Kedia, Memphis State University
V.H. Kirpalani, Concordia University
Hermann Kopp, Norwegian School of Management
Jeffrey A. Krug, The University of Memphis
Morris Lamberson, University of Central Arkansas
Fran T. Lohrke, Louisiana State University
Kamlesh Mehta, St. Mary's University
Ron Meyer, Erasmus University
Hanne Norreklit, The Aarhus School of Business
Sam C. Okoroafo, University of Toledo
William Renforth, Florida International University
John Stanbury, Indiana University at Kokomo
Peter Wilamoski, Drake University

Third, I would like to thank my MBA research assistants, Maria Gonzalez and Maureen Kibelsted, for their assistance in preparing this manuscript. And last, but by no means least, I would like to thank my wife, Alexandra, and my daughters, Elizabeth, Charlotte, and Michelle, for their support and, indeed, for giving me the strength to write this book.

Charles W. L. Hill

INTRODUCTION AND OVERVIEW

Chapter One
Globalization

CHAPTER ONE

GLOBALIZATION

The Emerging Global Telecommunications Industry

A generation ago, telecommunications markets around the world shared many characteristics. In most nations, there was a dominant telecommunications provider—AT&T in the United States, British Telecom in Britain, Deutsche Telekom in Germany, NTT in Japan, Telebras in Brazil, and so on. The provider was often state-owned, and even when it wasn't, its operations were tightly regulated by the state. Cross-border competition between telecommunications providers was all but nonexistent. Typically, regulations prohibited foreign firms from entering a country's telecommunications market and competing head-to-head with the domestic carrier. Most of the traffic carried by telecommunications firms was voice traffic, almost all of it was carried over copper wires, and most telecommunications firms charged their customers a hefty premium to make long-distance and international calls.

A generation later, the landscape is radically different. Telecommunications markets around the world have been deregulated. This has allowed new competitors to emerge and compete with the dominant provider. State-owned monopolies have been privatized, including British Telecom and Deutsche Telekom. Several dominant telecommunications firms, state-owned or otherwise, have been broken up into smaller companies. For example, in 1998 Brazil's state-owned telecommunications monopoly, Telebras, was privatized and broken up into 12 smaller companies that will be allowed to compete with each other.

New wireless technologies have facilitated the emergence of new competitors, such as Orange and Vodfone in Britain, which now compete head-to-head with the former state monopoly, British Telecom. Thanks to the Internet, the volume of data traffic (e.g., Web graphics) is now growing much more rapidly than that of voice traffic. By 2005, the volume of data traffic may triple that of voice. Much of this data traffic is being transmitted over new digital networks that utilize fiber optics, Internet protocols, digital switches, and photons to send data around the world at the speed of light. Telecommunications firms are investing billions in digital networks to handle this traffic.

To cap it all, under a 1997 agreement brokered by the World Trade Organization, 68 countries accounting for more than 90 percent of the world's telecommunications revenues have agreed to open their telecommunications markets to foreign competition and to abide by common rules for fair competition in telecommunications. Most of the world's biggest markets, including the United States, European Union, and Japan, were fully liberalized and open to foreign competition on January 1, 1998.

The consequences of these changes are becoming apparent. A global market for telecommunications services is rapidly emerging. Telecommunications companies are starting to penetrate each other's markets. Prices are falling, both in the international market, where prices have long been kept artificially high by a lack of competition, and in the wireless market, which is rapidly becoming price competitive with traditional wire-line telecommunications services. Estimates from the World Trade Organization suggest that, following the deal that went into effect in 1998, the price for international telephone calls should fall 80 percent by 2001 as competition increases, saving consumers $1,000 billion. Soon it will cost no more to place a call halfway around the world than to call next door.

As competition intensifies, national telecommunications companies are entering into marketing alliances and joint ventures with each other to offer multinational companies a single global telecommunications provider for all their international voice and data needs. For example, in July 1998, AT&T and British Telecom announced they would merge most of their international operations into a jointly owned company that will have $10 billion in revenues. The venture will focus on serving the global telecommunications needs of multinational corporations, enabling workers in Manhattan to communicate as easily with computer systems in New Delhi, say, as with colleagues in New Jersey. AT&T and British Telecom estimate the market for providing international communications services to large and medium-sized business customers will expand from $36 billion in 1998 to $180 billion in 2007. Other companies that are working together on a global basis include MCI-WorldCom, the number two long-distance carrier in the United States, and Telefonica of Spain, which is also Latin America's biggest telecommunications carrier. The Sprint Corporation, the number three long-distance carrier in the United States, is partly owned by Deutsche Telekom and France Telecom. This trio is positioning itself to compete with the WorldCom/Telefonica and AT&T/BT ventures to gain the business of multinational customers in the brave new world of global telecommunications.

http://www.att.com

Sources: A. Kupfer, "The Big Switch," *Fortune*, October 13, 1997, pp. 105–16; S. Schiesel, "AT&T and British Telecom Merge Overseas Operations," *New York Times*, July 27, 1998, p. A1; and F. Cairncross, *The Death of Distance* (Boston: Harvard Business School Press, 1997).

Introduction

A fundamental shift is occurring in the world economy. We are moving progressively further away from a world in which national economies were relatively isolated from each other by barriers to cross-border trade and investment; by distance, time zones, and language; and by national differences in government regulation, culture, and business systems. And we are moving toward a world in which national economies are merging into an interdependent global economic system, commonly referred to as **globalization.** The trend toward a more integrated global economic system has been in place for many years. However, the rate at which this shift is occurring has been accelerating recently, and it looks set to continue to do so during the early years of the new millennium.

The global telecommunications industry, which was profiled in the opening case, is one industry at the forefront of this development. A decade ago most national telecommunications markets were dominated by state-owned monopolies and isolated from each other by substantial barriers to cross-border trade and investment. This is rapidly becoming a thing of the past. A global telecommunications market is emerging. In this new market, prices are being bargained down as telecommunications providers compete with each other around the world for residential and business customers. The big winners are the customers, who should see the price of telecommunications services plummet, saving them billions of dollars.

The rapidly emerging global economy raises a multitude of issues for businesses both large and small. It creates opportunities for businesses to expand their revenues, drive down their costs, and boost their profits. For example, companies can take advantage of the falling cost and enhanced functionality of global telecommunications services to more easily establish global markets for their products. Ten years ago no one would have thought that a small British company based in Stafford would have been able to build a global market for its products by utilizing the Internet, but that is exactly what Bridgewater Pottery has done.[1] Bridgewater has traditionally sold premium pottery through exclusive distribution channels, but the company found it difficult and laborious to identify new retail outlets. Since establishing an Internet presence in 1997, Bridgewater is now conducting a significant amount of business with consumers in other countries who could not be reached through existing channels of distribution or could not be reached cost effectively. Nor is Bridgewater alone; thousands of companies around the world are now taking advantage of the new global communications infrastructure to build new global markets for their products. As I sit in Seattle writing this book, I do so using an ergonomic computer mouse that was designed by a former farmer in Norway who found that repeated computer use gave him carpal tunnel syndrome. The farmer designed a mouse that alleviates his problem, started a company to manufacture it, and has now sold the mouse to consumers worldwide, using the Internet as his distribution channel.[2]

While the emerging global economy creates opportunities such as this for new entrepreneurs and established businesses around the world, it also gives rise to challenges and threats that yesterday's business managers did not have to deal with. For example, managers now routinely have to decide how best to expand into a foreign market. Should they export to that market from their home base; should they invest in productive facilities in that market, producing locally to sell locally; or should they produce in some third country where the cost of production is favorable and export from that base to other foreign markets and, perhaps, to their home market? Managers have to decide whether and how to customize their product offerings, marketing policies, human resource practices, and business strategies to deal with national differences in culture, language, business practices, and government regulations. And managers have to decide how best to deal with the threat posed by efficient foreign competitors entering their home marketplace.

Again, the opening case offers an example of how service providers in the telecommunications industry are positioning themselves to cope with this new global reality.

Companies such as AT&T and British Telecom, which for years had monopolies within their protected national markets, are now competing head-to-head with other telecommunications service providers. As the case tells us, to improve their chances of capturing the business of multinational corporations that prefer a single telecommunications provider for their worldwide operations (and most do), AT&T and British Telecom have formed a joint venture. Other competitors, such as MCI-WorldCom and Telefonica of Spain, have entered into more loosely structured marketing alliances in an attempt to achieve the same basic goal. These companies are experimenting with different strategies to better compete and prosper in the emerging global marketplace. Only time will tell which strategy makes the most sense. Such strategic experimentation, however, is occurring in a broad range of industries as firms struggle to come to grips with the new realities of global markets and global competition.

Against the background of rapid globalization, the goal of this book is to explain how and why globalization is occurring and to explore globalization's impact on the business firm and its management. In this introductory chapter, we discuss what we mean by globalization, review the main drivers of globalization, look at the changing profile of firms that do business outside their national borders, highlight concerns raised by critics of globalization, and explore the challenges that globalization holds for managers within an international business.

What is Globalization?

As used in this book, **globalization** refers to the shift toward a more integrated and interdependent world economy. Globalization has two main components: the globalization of markets and the globalization of production.

The Globalization of Markets

The **globalization of markets** refers to the merging of historically distinct and separate national markets into one huge global marketplace. It has been argued for some time that the tastes and preferences of consumers in different nations are beginning to converge on some global norm, thereby helping to create a global market.[3] The global acceptance of consumer products such as Citicorp credit cards, Coca-Cola, Levi's jeans, Sony Walkmans, Nintendo game players, and McDonald's hamburgers are all frequently held up as prototypical examples of this trend. Firms such as Citicorp, Coca-Cola, McDonald's, and Levi Strauss are more than just benefactors of this trend; they are also instrumental in facilitating it. By offering a standardized product worldwide, they are helping to *create* a global market. A company does not have to be the size of these multinational giants to facilitate, and benefit from, the globalization of markets. For example, the accompanying Management Focus describes how a small British enterprise with annual sales in 1997 of just £6.8 million ($10 million) is trying to build a global market for the traditional British fare of fish 'n' chips.

Despite the global prevalence of Citicorp credit cards, Coca-Cola, Levi blue jeans, McDonald's hamburgers, and (perhaps one day) Harry Ramsden's fish 'n' chips, it is important not to push too far the view that national markets are giving way to the global market. As we shall see in later chapters, *very* significant differences still exist between national markets along many relevant dimensions, including consumer tastes and preferences, distribution channels, culturally embedded value systems, and the like. In the case of many products, these differences frequently require that marketing strategies, product features, and operating practices be customized to best match conditions in a country. Thus, for example, automobile companies will promote different car models depending on a whole range of factors such as local fuel costs, income levels, traffic congestion, and cultural values.

The most global markets currently are not markets for consumer products—where national differences in tastes and preferences are still often important enough to act as a brake on globalization—but markets for industrial goods and materials that serve

MANAGEMENT FOCUS

Getting the World Hooked on Fish and Chips

Deep-fried fish and chips is a popular dish in England. Harry Ramsden's has long been considered one of the premium fish and chip "shops" in England, and it is one of only a few to have multiple locations. In the early 1990s, the company had a handful of highly profitable restaurants in Britain. Its busiest UK location, the resort town of Blackpool, generated annual sales of £1.5 million ($2.3 million). Harry Ramsden's managers, however, were not satisfied with this success. They wanted to turn Harry Ramsden's into a global enterprise.

In 1992, the company opened its first international operation in Hong Kong. The restaurant, which could seat 200 and also offered take-out food, was modeled after the original shop in Guiseley, Yorkshire, with the majority of the menu items, including the haddock, being exported from the United Kingdom. According to finance director Richard Taylor, "We marketed the product as Britain's fast food, and it's proved extremely successful." Within two years, the Hong Kong venture was generating annual sales equivalent to the Blackpool operation. While half of the initial customers in Hong Kong were British expatriates, now more than 80 percent are ethnic Chinese. Harry Ramsden's seems to be well on the way to broadening the tastes of Hong Kong Chinese.

Emboldened by this success, Harry Ramsden's has opened additional international branches in Dublin, Melbourne, Singapore, Jidda, Tenerife, and Tokyo. The company used a franchise arrangement to establish these foreign restaurants. It requires that the menu and design of each restaurant be based on the original Guiseley restaurant. Expatriate communities or other British connections helped to jump-start demand at all these locations, but in each case, local nationals have quickly become an important part of the business. All the restaurants except the one in Melbourne have quickly become profitable. By 1997, Harry Ramsden's had 33 stores, 7 of which were overseas, and generated profits of £1.5 million on annual sales of £6.8 million. However, the company is only getting started. John Barnes, the company's chairman, has set the goal of becoming the number one fish and chips brand in the world. "Not for us," he says, "the hamburger, pizza, and chicken playing fields of the big companies. We chose fish and chips as our pitch." Originally greeted with skepticism, Barnes's vision is starting to gain respect as the company continues to perform better than expected. The company now has plans to open additional restaurants in Thailand and Indonesia.

Sources: P. Abrahams, "Getting Hooked on Fish and Chips in Japan," *Financial Times*, May 17, 1994; R. Hobson, "Think Big, Act Small," *The Times*, February 12, 1998, p. 10; and D. Atkinson, "Harry Ramsden's Thinks Big." *The Guardian*, June 26, 1998, p. 3. Harry Ramsden's can be visited on the Internet at www.harryramsdens.co.uk.

a universal need the world over. These include the markets for commodities such as aluminum, oil, and wheat, the markets for industrial products such as microprocessors, DRAMs (computer memory chips), and commercial jet aircraft; and the markets for financial assets from US Treasury Bills to eurobonds and futures on the Nikkei index or the Mexican peso.

In many global markets, the same firms frequently confront each other as competitors in nation after nation. Coca-Cola's rivalry with Pepsi is a global one, as are the rivalries between Ford and Toyota, Boeing and Airbus, Caterpillar and Komatsu, and Nintendo and Sega. If one firm moves into a nation that is currently unserved by its rivals, those rivals are sure to follow lest their competitor gain an advantage.[4] These firms bring with them many of the assets that have served them well in other national markets—including their products, operating strategies, marketing strategies, and brand names—creating a certain degree of homogeneity across markets. Thus, diversity is replaced by greater uniformity. As rivals follow rivals around the world, these multinational enterprises emerge as an important driver of the convergence of different national markets into a single, and increasingly homogenous, global marketplace. Due to such developments, in an increasing number of industries it is no longer meaningful to talk about "the German market," "the American market," "the Brazilian market," or "the Japanese market"; for many firms there is only the global market.

The Globalization of Production

The **globalization of production** refers to the tendency among firms to source goods and services from locations around the globe to take advantage of national differences in the cost and quality of factors of production (such as labor, energy, land, and capital). By doing so, companies hope to lower their overall cost structure and/or improve the quality or functionality of their product offering, thereby allowing them to compete more effectively. Consider the Boeing Company's latest commercial jet airliner, the 777. The 777 contains 132,500 major component parts that are produced around the world by 545 suppliers. Eight Japanese suppliers make parts for the fuselage, doors, and wings; a supplier in Singapore makes the doors for the nose landing gear; three suppliers in Italy manufacture wing flaps; and so on.[5] Part of Boeing's rationale for outsourcing so much production to foreign suppliers is that these suppliers are the best in the world at performing their particular activity. The result of having a *global web* of suppliers is a better final product, which enhances the chances of Boeing winning a greater share of total orders for aircraft than its global rival, Airbus. Boeing also outsources some production to foreign countries to increase the chance that it will win significant orders from airliners based in that country.

The global dispersal of productive activities is not limited to giants such as Boeing. Many much smaller firms are also getting into the act. Consider Swan Optical, a US-based manufacturer and distributor of eyewear. With sales revenues of $20 to $30 million, Swan is hardly a giant, yet Swan manufactures its eyewear in low-cost factories in Hong Kong and China that it jointly owns with a Hong Kong-based partner. Swan also has a minority stake in eyewear design houses in Japan, France, and Italy. Swan has dispersed its manufacturing and design processes to different locations around the world to take advantage of the favorable skill base and cost structure found in foreign countries. Foreign investments in Hong Kong and then China have helped Swan lower its cost structure, while investments in Japan, France, and Italy have helped it produce designer eyewear for which it can charge a premium price. By dispersing its manufacturing and design activities, Swan has established a competitive advantage for itself in the global marketplace for eyewear, just as Boeing has tried to do by dispersing some of its activities to other countries.[6]

Robert Reich, the former secretary of labor in the Clinton administration, has argued that as a consequence of the trend exemplified by Boeing and Swan Optical, in many industries it is becoming irrelevant to talk about American products, Japanese products, German products, or Korean products. Increasingly, according to Reich, the outsourcing of productive activities to different suppliers results in the creation of products that are global in nature; that is, "global products."[7] But as with the globalization of markets, one must be careful not to push the globalization of production too far. As we will see in later chapters, substantial impediments still make it difficult for firms to achieve the optimal dispersion of their productive activities to locations around the globe. These impediments include formal and informal barriers to trade between countries, barriers to foreign direct investment, transportation costs, and issues associated with economic and political risk.

Nevertheless, we are traveling down the road toward a future characterized by the increased globalization of markets and production. Modern firms are important actors in this drama, fostering by their very actions increased globalization. These firms, however, are merely responding in an efficient manner to changing conditions in their operating environment—as well they should. In the next section, we look at the main drivers of globalization.

Drivers of Globalization

Two macro factors seem to underlie the trend toward greater globalization. The first is the decline in barriers to the free flow of goods, services, and capital that has occurred since the end of World War II. The second factor is technological change, particularly the dramatic developments in recent years in communications, information processing, and transportation technologies.

Declining Trade and Investment Barriers

During the 1920s and 30s, many of the nation-states of the world erected formidable barriers to international trade and foreign direct investment. **International trade** occurs when a firm exports goods or services to consumers in another country. **Foreign direct investment** occurs when a firm invests resources in business activities outside its home country. Many of the barriers to international trade took the form of high tariffs on imports of manufactured goods. The typical aim of such tariffs was to protect domestic industries from "foreign competition." One consequence, however, was "beggar thy neighbor" retaliatory trade policies with countries progressively raising trade barriers against each other. Ultimately, this depressed world demand and contributed to the Great Depression of the 1930s.

Having learned from this experience, after World War II, the advanced industrial nations of the West—under US leadership—committed themselves to removing barriers to the free flow of goods, services, and capital between nations.[8] This goal was enshrined in the treaty known as the **General Agreement on Tariffs and Trade** (GATT). Under the umbrella of GATT, there have been eight rounds of negotiations among member states—which now number over 130—designed to lower barriers to the free flow of goods and services. The most recent round of negotiations, known as the Uruguay Round, was completed in December 1993. The Uruguay Round further reduced trade barriers; extended GATT to cover services as well as manufactured goods; provided enhanced protection for patents, trademarks, and copyrights; and established the **World Trade Organization** (WTO) to police the international trading system.[9] Table 1.1 summarizes the impact of GATT agreements on average tariff rates for manufactured goods. As can be seen, average tariff rates have fallen significantly since 1950 and under the Uruguay agreement should hit 3.9 percent in 2000.

In addition to reducing trade barriers, many countries have also been progressively removing restrictions to foreign direct investment (FDI). According to the United Nations, between 1991 and 1996, more than 100 countries made 599 changes in legislation governing FDI. Some 95 percent of these changes involved liberalizing a country's foreign investment regulations to make it easier for foreign companies to enter their markets. The desire to facilitate FDI has also been reflected in a dramatic increase in the number of bilateral investment treaties designed to protect and promote investment between two countries. As of January 1, 1997, there were 1,330 such treaties in the world involving 162 countries, a threefold increase in five years.[10]

Table 1.1

Average Tariff Rates on Manufactured Products as Percent of Value

Source: "Who Wants to Be a Giant?" *The Economist: A Survey of the Multinationals*, June 24, 1995, pp. 3–4.

	1913	1950	1990	2000*
France	21	18	5.9	3.9
Germany	20	26	5.9	3.9
Italy	18	25	5.9	3.9
Japan	30	—	5.3	3.9
Holland	5	11	5.9	3.9
Sweden	20	9	4.4	3.9
Britain	—	23	5.9	3.9
United States	44	14	4.8	3.9

*Rates for 2000 based on full implementation of Uruguay agreement.

Figure 1.1

The Growth of World Trade and World Output

Source: World Trade Organization, *World Trade Growth Accelerated in 1997, Despite Turmoil in some Asian Financial Markets.* Press/98, 19 March 1998.

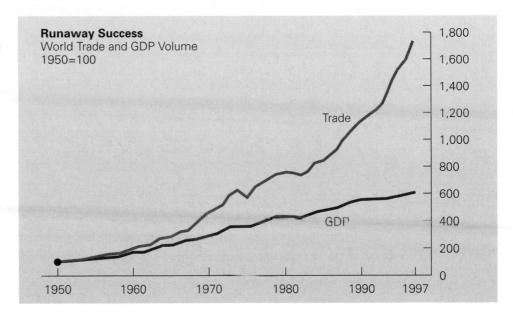

Such trends facilitate both the globalization of markets and the globalization of production. The lowering of barriers to international trade enables firms to view the world, rather than a single country, as their market. The lowering of trade *and* investment barriers also allows firms to base production at the optimal location for that activity, serving the world market from that location. Thus, a firm might design a product in one country, produce component parts in two other countries, assemble the product in yet another country, and then export the finished product around the world.

There is plenty of evidence that the lowering of trade barriers has facilitated the globalization of production. According to data from the World Trade Organization, the volume of world trade has grown consistently faster than the volume of world output since 1950.[11] Figure 1.1 gives data for 1950 to 1997. Over this period, world trade has expanded 16-fold, far outstripping world output, which has grown sixfold. As suggested by Figure 1.1, the growth in world trade seems to have accelerated in recent years.

The data summarized in Figure 1.1 imply two things. First, more firms are doing what Boeing does with the 777, dispersing parts of their overall production process to different locations around the globe to drive down production costs and increase product quality. Second, the economies of the world's nation-states are becoming more intertwined. As trade expands, nations are becoming increasingly dependent on each other for important goods and services.

The evidence also suggests that foreign direct investment is playing an increasing role in the global economy as firms ranging in size from Boeing to Swan Optical and Harry Ramsden's increase their cross-border investments. Between 1984 and 1997, the total annual flow of FDI from all countries increased tenfold from $42 billion to $430 billion, more than twice as fast as the growth rate in world trade.[12] The major investors have been US, Japanese, and Western European companies investing in Europe, Asia (particularly China), and the United States. For example, Japanese auto companies have been investing rapidly in Asian, European, and US-based auto assembly operations.

Finally, the globalization of markets and production and the resulting growth of world trade, foreign direct investment, and imports all imply that firms are finding their home markets under attack from foreign competitors. This is true in Japan, where US companies such as Kodak, Procter & Gamble, and Merrill Lynch are expanding their presence. It is true in the United States, where Japanese automobile firms have taken market share away from General Motors and Ford. And it is true in Europe, where the once-dominant Dutch company Philips has seen its market share in the consumer electronics industry taken by Japan's JVC, Matsushita, and Sony.

The bottom line is that the growing integration of the world economy into a single, huge marketplace is increasing the intensity of competition in a range of manufacturing and service industries.

Having said all this, declining trade barriers can't be taken for granted. As we shall see in the following chapters, demands for "protection" from foreign competitors are still often heard in countries around the world, including the United States. Although a return to the restrictive trade policies of the 1920s and 30s is unlikely, it is not clear whether the political majority in the industrialized world favors further reductions in trade barriers. If trade barriers decline no further, at least for the time being, a temporary limit may have been reached in the globalization of both markets and production.

The Role of Technological Change

The lowering of trade barriers made globalization of markets and production a theoretical possibility, and technological change has made it a tangible reality. Since the end of World War II, the world has seen major advances in communications, information processing, and transportation technology including, most recently, the explosive emergence of the Internet and World Wide Web. In the words of Renato Ruggiero, director general of the World Trade Organization,

> Telecommunications is creating a global audience. Transport is creating a global village. From Buenos Aires to Boston to Beijing, ordinary people are watching MTV, they're wearing Levi's jeans, and they're listening to Sony Walkmans as they commute to work.[13]

Microprocessors and Telecommunications

Perhaps the single most important innovation has been development of the microprocessor, which enabled the explosive growth of high-power, low-cost computing, vastly increasing the amount of information that can be processed by individuals and firms. The microprocessor also underlies many recent advances in telecommunications technology. Over the past 30 years, global communications have been revolutionized by developments in satellite, optical fiber, and wireless technologies, and now the Internet and the World Wide Web. These technologies rely on the microprocessor to encode, transmit, and decode the vast amount of information that flows along these electronic highways. The cost of microprocessors continues to fall, while their power increases (a phenomenon known as **Moore's Law,** which predicts that the power of microprocessor technology doubles and its cost of production falls in half every 18 months).[14] As this happens, the costs of global communications are plummeting, which lowers the costs of coordinating and controlling a global organization.

The Internet and World Wide Web

The phenomenal recent growth of the Internet and the associated World Wide Web (which utilizes the Internet to communicate between World Wide Web sites) is the latest expression of this development. In 1990, fewer than 1 million users were connected to the Internet. By mid-1998 the Internet had about 147 million users, of which some 70 million were in the United States. By the year 2000, the Internet may have over 330 million users.[15] In July 1993, some 1.8 million host computers were connected to the Internet (host computers host the Web pages of local users). By July 1998, the number of host computers had increased to 36.8 million, and the number is still growing rapidly.[16]

The Internet and World Wide Web (WWW) promise to develop into the information backbone of tomorrow's global economy. From virtually nothing in 1994, the value of Web-based transactions hit $7.5 billion in 1997. According to a recent report issued by the United States Department of Commerce, this figure could reach $300 billion in the United States alone by 2003.[17] Companies such as Dell Computer are booking over $4 million a day in Web-based sales, while Internet equipment giant Cisco Systems books more than $20 million per day in Web-based sales.

Included in this expanding volume of Web-based electronic commerce—or **e-commerce** as it is commonly called—is a growing percentage of cross-border transactions. Viewed globally, the Web is emerging as the great equalizer. It rolls back some of the constraints of location, scale, and time zones. The Web allows businesses, both small and large, to expand their global presence at a lower cost than ever before. One example is a small California-based start-up, Cardiac Science, which makes defibrillators and heart monitors. In 1996, Cardiac Science was itching to break into international markets but had little idea of how to establish an international presence. By 1998, the company was selling to customers in 46 countries and foreign sales accounted for 85 percent of its $1.2 million revenues. Although some of this business was developed through conventional export channels, a growing percentage of it came from "hits" to the company's Web site, which according to the company's CEO, "attracts international business people like bees to honey."[18] The Web makes it much easier for buyers and sellers to find each other, wherever they may be located, and whatever their size.

Transportation Technology

In addition to developments in communications technology, several major innovations in transportation technology have occurred since World War II. In economic terms, the most important are probably the development of commercial jet aircraft and superfreighters and the introduction of containerization, which simplifies transshipment from one mode of transport to another. The advent of commercial jet travel, by reducing the time needed to get from one location to another, has effectively shrunk the globe (see Figure 1.2). In terms of travel time, New York is now "closer" to Tokyo than it was to Philadelphia in the Colonial days.

Containerization has revolutionized the transportation business, significantly lowering the costs of shipping goods over long distances. Before the advent of containerization, moving goods from one mode of transport to another was very labor intensive, lengthy, and costly. It could take days and several hundred longshoremen to unload a ship and reload goods onto trucks and trains. With the advent of widespread containerization in the 1970s and 1980s, the whole process can be executed by a handful of longshoremen in a couple of days. Since 1980, the world's containership fleet has more than quadrupled, reflecting in part the growing volume of international trade and in part the switch to this mode of transportation. As a result of the efficiency gains associated with containerization, transportation costs have plummeted, making it much more economical to ship goods around the globe, thereby helping to drive the globalization of markets and production. In the United States, for example, the cost of shipping freight per ton mile on railroads has fallen from 3 cents in 1985 to 2.4 cents in 1997, largely as a result of efficiency gains from the widespread use of containers.[19]

Implications for the Globalization of Production

Due to containerization, the transportation costs associated with the globalization of production have declined. Plus, as a result of the technological innovations discussed above, the real costs of information processing and communication have fallen dramatically in the past two decades. This makes it possible for a firm to manage a globally dispersed production system, further facilitating the globalization of production. A worldwide communications network has become essential for many international businesses. For example, Texas Instruments (TI), the US electronics firm, has approximately 50 plants in 19 countries. A satellite-based communications system allows TI to coordinate, on a global scale, its production planning, cost accounting, financial planning, marketing, customer service, and personnel management. The system consists of more than 300 remote job-entry terminals, 8,000 inquiry terminals, and 140 mainframe computers. The system enables managers of TI's worldwide operations to send vast amounts of information to each other instantaneously and to coordinate the firm's different plants and activities.[20]

Another US electronics firm, Hewlett-Packard, uses satellite communications and information processing technologies to link its worldwide operations. Hewlett-

Figure 1.2

The Shrinking Globe

Source: P. Dicken, *Global Shift* (New York: Guilford Press, 1992), p. 104.

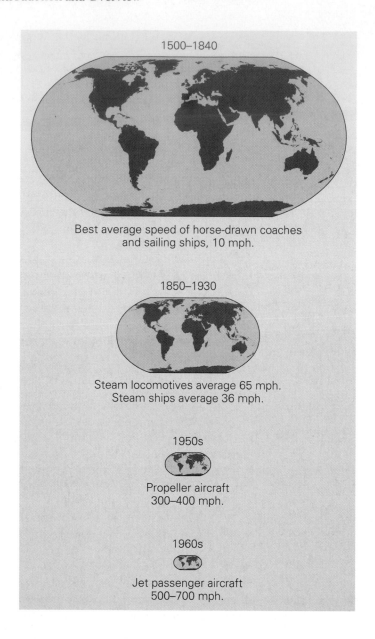

1500–1840

Best average speed of horse-drawn coaches and sailing ships, 10 mph.

1850–1930

Steam locomotives average 65 mph.
Steam ships average 36 mph.

1950s

Propeller aircraft
300–400 mph.

1960s

Jet passenger aircraft
500–700 mph.

Packard has new-product development teams composed of individuals based in different countries (e.g., Japan, the United States, Great Britain, and Germany). When developing new products, these individuals use videoconferencing to "meet" on a weekly basis. They also communicate with each other daily via telephone, electronic mail, and fax. Communication technologies have enabled Hewlett-Packard to increase the integration of its globally dispersed operations and to reduce the time needed for developing new products.[21]

The development of commercial jet aircraft has also helped knit together the worldwide operations of many international businesses. Using jet travel, an American manager need spend a day at most traveling to her firm's European or Asian operations. This enables her to oversee a globally dispersed production system.

Implications for the Globalization of Markets

In addition to the globalization of production, technological innovations have also facilitated the globalization of markets. As noted above, low-cost transportation has made it more economical to ship products around the world, thereby helping to create global markets. Low-cost global communications networks such as the World Wide

Web are helping to create electronic global marketplaces. In addition, low-cost jet travel has resulted in the mass movement of people between countries. This has reduced the cultural distance between countries and is bringing about some convergence of consumer tastes and preferences. At the same time, global communications networks and global media are creating a worldwide culture. US television networks such as CNN, MTV, and HBO are now received in many countries around the world, and Hollywood films are shown the world over. In any society, the media are primary conveyers of culture; as global media develop, we must expect the evolution of something akin to a global culture. A logical result of this evolution is the emergence of global markets for consumer products. The first signs of this are already apparent. It is now as easy to find a McDonald's restaurant in Tokyo as it is in New York, to buy a Sony Walkman in Rio as it is in Berlin, and to buy Levi's jeans in Paris as it is in San Francisco.

We must be careful not to overemphasize this trend. While modern communications and transportation technologies are ushering in the "global village," very significant national differences remain in culture, consumer preferences, and business practices. A firm that ignores differences between countries does so at its peril. We shall stress this point repeatedly throughout this book and elaborate on it in later chapters.

The Changing Demographics of the Global Economy

Hand in hand with the trend toward globalization has been a fairly dramatic change in the demographics of the global economy over the past 30 years or so. As late as the 1960s, four stylized facts described the demographics of the global economy. The first was US dominance in the world economy and world trade picture. The second was US dominance in world foreign direct investment. Related to this, the third fact was the dominance of large, multinational US firms on the international business scene. The fourth was that roughly half the globe—the centrally planned economics of the Communist world—was off-limits to Western international businesses. As will be explained below, all four of these qualities either have changed or are now changing rapidly.

The Changing World Output and World Trade Picture

In the early 1960s, the United States was still by far the world's dominant industrial power. In 1963, for example, the United States accounted for 40.3 percent of world output. By 1996, the United States accounted for only 20.8 percent (see Table 1.2). Nor was the United States the only developed nation to see its relative standing slip.

Table 1.2

The Changing Pattern of World Output and Trade

Sources: Export data from World Trade Organization, *International Trade Trends and Statistics, 1996*; World Output data from *CIA Factbook*, 1996 (1995 world output figures are estimates).

Country	Share of World Output, 1963[†]	Share of World Output, 1996	Share of World Exports, 1997[‡]
United States	40.3%	20.8%	12.6%
Japan	5.5%	8.3%	7.76%
Germany*	9.7%	4.8%	9.9%
France	6.3%	3.5%	5.46%
United Kingdom	6.5%	3.2%	4.94%
Italy	3.4%	3.2%	4.76%
Canada	3%	1.7%	3.81%
China[§]	NA	11.3%	2.85%
South Korea	NA	1.7%	2.45%

* 1963 figure for Germany refers to the former West Germany.

[†] Output is measured by gross national product.

[‡] The 1997 estimates are based on purchasing power parity (PPP) statistics that adjust GNP for differences in prices (the cost of living) between countries.

[§] The Chinese figures are somewhat suspect. When calculated using unadjusted GNP data, China's share of world output shrinks to 3.1%. Thus, China's high share of world output on a PPP basis is partly due to the relatively low cost of living in China.

The same occurred to Germany, France, and the United Kingdom, all nations that were among the first to industrialize. This decline in the US position was not an absolute decline, since the US economy grew at a relatively robust average annual rate of close to 3.0 percent in the 1963–96 time period (the economies of Germany, France, and the United Kingdom also grew over this time period). Rather, it was a relative decline, reflecting the faster economic growth of several other economies, particularly in Asia. For example, as can be seen from Table 1.2, over the 1963–96 time period, Japan's share of world output increased from 5.5 percent to 8.3 percent. Other countries that markedly increased their share of world output included China, Thailand, Malaysia, Taiwan, and South Korea. By virtue of its huge population and rapid industrialization, China in particular is emerging as an economic colossus.

Reflecting the relative decline in US dominance, by the end of the 1980s its position as the world's leading exporter was threatened. Over the past thirty years, US dominance in export markets has waned as Japan, Germany, and a number of newly industrialized countries such as South Korea and China have taken a larger share of world exports. During the 1960s, the United States routinely accounted for 20 percent of world exports of manufactured goods. Table 1.2 also reports manufacturing exports as a percentage of the world total in 1997. As can be seen, the US share of world exports of manufactured goods had slipped to 12.6 percent by 1997. But despite the fall, the United States still remained the world's largest exporter, ahead of Germany and Japan.

In 1997 and 1998 the dynamic economies of the Asian Pacific region were hit by a serious financial crisis that threatened to slow their economic growth rates for several years. Despite this, their powerful growth may continue over the long run, as will that of several other important emerging economies in Latin America (e.g., Brazil) and Eastern Europe (e.g., Poland). Thus, a further *relative* decline in the share of world output and world exports accounted for by the United States and other long-established developed nations seems likely. By itself, this is not a bad thing. The relative decline of the United States reflects the growing economic development and industrialization of the world economy, as opposed to any absolute decline in the health of the US economy, which in the late 1990s was stronger than it had ever been.

Notwithstanding the financial crisis that is gripping some Asian economies, if we look 20 years into the future, most forecasts now predict a rapid rise in the share of world output accounted for by developing nations such as China, India, Indonesia, Thailand, South Korea, and Brazil, and a commensurate decline in the share enjoyed by rich industrialized countries such as Britain, Germany, Japan, and the United States. The World Bank, for example, has estimated that if current trends continue for the next quarter of a century, by 2020 the Chinese economy could be 40 percent larger than that of the United States, while the economy of India will be larger than that of Germany. Moreover, the bank estimates that today's developing nations may account for over 60 percent of world economic activity by 2020, while today's rich nations, which currently account for over 55 percent of world economic activity, may account for only about 38 percent by 2020.[22] These forecasts suggest that a dramatic shift in the economic geography of the world is now under way. For international businesses, the implications of this changing economic geography are clear; many of tomorrow's economic opportunities may be found in the developing nations of the world, and many of tomorrow's most capable competitors will probably also emerge from these regions.

The Changing Foreign Direct Investment Picture

Reflecting the dominance of the United States in the global economy, US firms accounted for 66.3 percent of worldwide foreign direct investment flows in the 1960s. British firms were second, accounting for 10.5 percent, while Japanese firms were a distant eighth, with only 2 percent. The dominance of US firms was so great that in Europe, books were written about the economic threat posed to Europe by US corporations.[23] Several European governments, most notably that of France, talked of limiting inward investment by US firms in their economies.

However, as the barriers to the free flow of goods, services, and capital fell, and as other countries increased their shares of world output, non-US firms increasingly

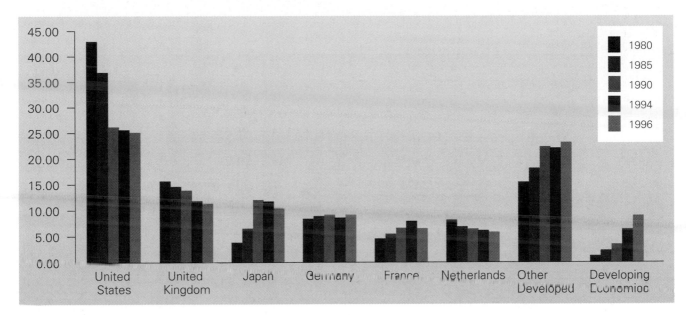

Figure 1.3

Percentage Share of Total FDI Stock, 1980–1996

Source: Data are taken from the United Nations, *World Investment Report, 1997* (New York: United Nations, 1997).

began to invest across national borders. The motivation for much of this foreign direct investment by non-US firms was the desire to disperse production activities to optimal locations and to build a direct presence in major foreign markets. Thus, during the 1970s and 80s, European and Japanese firms began to shift labor-intensive manufacturing operations from their home markets to developing nations where labor costs were lower. In addition, many Japanese firms have invested in North America and Europe— often as a hedge against unfavorable currency movements and the possible imposition of trade barriers. For example, Toyota, the Japanese automobile company, rapidly increased its investment in automobile production facilities in the United States and Britain during the late 1980s and early 1990s. Toyota executives believed that an increasingly strong Japanese yen would price Japanese automobile exports out of foreign markets; therefore, production in the most important foreign markets, as opposed to exports from Japan, made sense. Toyota also undertook these investments to head off growing political pressures in the United States and Europe to restrict Japanese automobile exports into those markets.

One consequence of these developments is illustrated in Figure 1.3, which shows how the stock of foreign direct investment by the world's six most important national sources—the United States, Britain, Japan, Germany, France, and the Netherlands— changed between 1980 and 1996. (The **stock of foreign direct investment** refers to the total cumulative value of foreign investments.) Figure 1.3 also shows the stock accounted for by firms from other developed nations and from developing economies. As can be seen, the share of the total stock accounted for by US firms declined substantially from around 44 percent in 1980 to 25 percent in 1996. Meanwhile, the shares accounted for by Japan, France, other developed nations, and the world's developing nations increased markedly. The rise in the share for developing nations reflects a small but growing trend for firms from these countries, such as South Korea, to invest outside their borders. In 1996 firms based in developing nations accounted for 8.9 percent of the stock of foreign direct investment, up from only 1.2 percent in 1980.

Figure 1.4 illustrates another important trend—the increasing tendency for cross-border investments to be directed at developing rather than rich industrialized nations. Figure 1.4 details recent changes in the annual inflows of foreign direct investment (the **flow of foreign direct investment** refers to amounts invested across

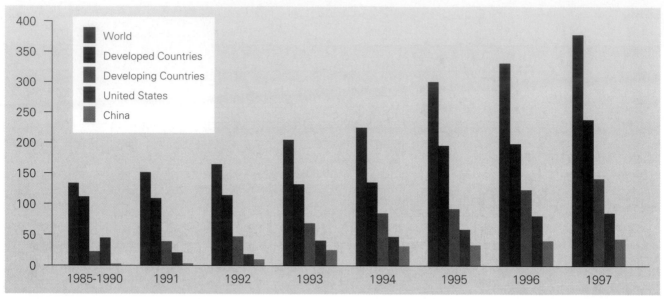

Figure 1.4

FDI Inflows, 1985–1997 (in US$ billions)

Source: United Nations, *World Investment Report*, various issues.

national borders each year). What stands out in Figure 1.4 is the increase in the share of foreign direct investment inflows accounted for by developing countries during the 1990s, and the commensurate decline in the share of inflows directed at developed nations. In 1997, foreign direct investment inflows into developing nations hit a record $149 billion, or 37 percent of the total, up from just $42 billion in 1991, or 26 percent of the total. Among developing nations, China has received the greatest volume of inward FDI in recent years. China took a record $45 billion out of the investment that went to developing nations in 1997. Other developing nations receiving a large amount of FDI in 1997 were Indonesia, Malaysia, the Philippines, Thailand, and Mexico. At the other end of the spectrum, the smallest 100 recipient countries accounted for just 1 percent of all FDI inflows.[24] Foreign investment into developing nations is focused on a relatively small group of countries experiencing rapid industrialization and economic growth. Businesses investing in these nations are positioning themselves to be active participants in those areas of the world that are expected to grow most rapidly over the next quarter of a century.

The Changing Nature of the Multinational Enterprise

A **multinational enterprise** is any business that has productive activities in two or more countries. Since the 1960s, there have been two notable trends in the demographics of the multinational enterprise: (1) the rise of non-US multinationals, particularly Japanese multinationals, and (2) the growth of mini-multinationals.

Non-US Multinationals

In the 1960s, global business activity was dominated by large US multinational corporations. With US firms accounting for about two-thirds of foreign direct investment during the 1960s, one would expect most multinationals to be US enterprises. According to the data presented in Table 1.3, in 1973, 48.5 percent of the world's 260 largest multinationals were US firms. The second-largest source country was Great Britain, with 18.8 percent of the largest multinationals. Japan accounted for only 3.5 percent of the world's largest multinationals at the time. The large number of US

Table 1.3

The National Composition
of the Largest Multinationals

Sources: Figures for 1973 from Neil
Hood and John Young, *The Economics
of the Multinational Enterprise* (New
York: Longman, 1979). Figures for
1997 from "The Global 500," *Fortune*,
August 4, 1997, pp. 130–31.

	Of the Top 260 in 1973	Of the Top 500 in 1997
United States	126 (48.5%)	162 (32.4%)
Japan	9 (3.5%)	126 (25.2%)
Britain	49 (18.8%)	34 (6.8%)
France	19 (7.3%)	42 (8.4%)
Germany	21 (8.1%)	41 (8.3%)

multinationals reflected US economic dominance in the three decades after World
War II, while the large number of British multinationals reflected that country's
industrial dominance in the early decades of the 20th century.

By 1997, however, things had shifted significantly. US firms accounted for 32.4 percent of the world's 500 largest multinationals, followed closely by Japan with 25.2 percent. France was a distant third with 8.4 percent. Although the two sets of figures in
Table 1.3 are not strictly comparable (the 1973 figures are based on the largest 260
firms, whereas the 1997 figures are based on the largest 500 firms), they illustrate the
trend. The globalization of the world economy together with Japan's rise to the top
rank of economic powers has resulted in a relative decline in the dominance of US
(and, to a lesser extent, British) firms in the global marketplace. Table 1.4 adds detail
to this picture by listing the largest 25 multinational corporations ranked by foreign
assets in 1996. Six of the top 25 are US enterprises, four are Japanese, five are German,
three are French, three are Swiss, two are jointly incorporated in the United Kingdom
and the Netherlands. The remainder are accounted for by the Netherlands and Italy.

Looking to the future, we can reasonably expect growth of new multinational
enterprises from the world's developing nations. As the accompanying Country Focus
(see page 20) demonstrates, South Korean firms are starting to invest outside their
national borders. The South Koreans may soon be followed by firms from countries
such as Mexico, China, Russia, and Brazil.

The Rise of Mini-Multinationals

Another trend in international business has been the growth of medium-sized and
small multinationals (mini-multinationals). When people think of international
businesses they tend to think of firms such as Exxon, General Motors, Ford, Fuji,
Kodak, Matsushita, Procter & Gamble, Sony, and Unilever—large, complex multinational corporations with operations that span the globe. Although it is certainly true
that most international trade and investment is still conducted by large firms, it is also
true that many medium-sized and small businesses are becoming increasingly
involved in international trade and investment. We have already discussed several
examples in this chapter—Swan Optical, Harry Ramsden's, and Cardiac Science—
and we have noted how the rise of the Internet is lowering the barriers that small
firms face in building international sales.

For another example, consider Lubricating Systems, Inc., of Kent, Washington.
Lubricating Systems, which manufactures lubricating fluids for machine tools,
employs 25 people and generates sales of $6.5 million. Hardly a large, complex multi-
national, yet more than $2 million of the company's sales are generated by exports to
a score of countries from Japan to Israel and the United Arab Emirates. Lubricating
Systems also has set up a joint venture with a German company to serve the European
market.[25] Consider also Lixi, Inc., a small US manufacturer of industrial X-ray equipment; 70 percent of Lixi's $4.5 million in revenues comes from exports to Japan.[26] Or
take G. W. Barth, a manufacturer of cocoa-bean roasting machinery based in Lud-
wigsburg, Germany. Employing just 65 people, this small company has captured 70

Ranking by:					Assets		Sales		Employment		
For. assets	Index	Corporation	Economy	Industry	Foreign	Total	Foreign	Total	Foreign	Total	Index
1	17	Shell, Royal Dutch	United Kingdom/ Netherlands	Oil, gas, coal and rel. services	79.7	117.6	80.6	109.9	81,000	104,000	73.0
2	83	Ford Motor Company	United States	Automotive	69.2	238.5	41.9	137.1	103,334	346,990	29.8
3	87	General Electric Company	United States	Electronics	69.2	228.0	17.1	70.0	72,000	222,000	29.1
4	22	Exxon Corporation	United States	Oil, gas, coal and rel. services	66.7	91.3	96.9	121.8	44,000	82,000	68.8
5	86	General Motors	United States	Automotive	54.1	217.1	47.8	163.9	252,699	745,000	29.3
6	27	Volkswagen AG	Germany	Automotive	49.8	58.7	37.4	61.5	114,000	257,000	63.4
7	43	IBM	United States	Computers	41.7	80.3	45.1	71.9	112,944	225,347	54.9
8	78	Toyota Motor Corporation	Japan	Automotive	36.0	118.2	50.4	111.7	33,796	146,855	32.9
9	1	Nestlé SA	Switzerland	Food	33.2	38.2	47.8	48.7	213,637	220,172	94.0
10	71	Mitsubishi Corporation	Japan	Diversified	...	79.3	51.0	124.9	3859	9241	39.5
11	18	Bayer AG	Germany	Chemicals	28.1	31.3	19.7	31.1	78,000	142,900	69.3
12	6	ABB Asea Brown Boveri Ltd.	Switzerland	Electrical equipment	27.2	32.1	29.4	33.7	196,937	209,637	88.6
13	66	Nissan Motor Co., Ltd.	Japan	Automotive	26.9	63.0	24.9	56.3	60,795	139,856	43.5
14	40	Elf Aquitaine SA	France	Oil, gas, coal and rel. services	26.9	49.4	27.8	42.5	40,650	85,500	55.8
15	32	Mobil Corporation	United States	Oil, gas, coal and rel. services	26.0	42.1	48.4	73.4	26,300	50,400	60.0
16	70	Daimler-Benz AG	Germany	Automotive	26.0	66.3	45.6	72.1	68,907	310,993	41.5
17	8	Unilever	United Kingdom/ Netherlands	Food	25.8	30.1	42.7	49.7	276,000	307,000	87.1
18	9	Philips Electronics N.V.	Netherlands	Electronics	25.2	32.7	38.4	40.1	221,000	265,100	85.4
19	10	Roche Holding AG	Switzerland	Pharmaceuticals	24.5	30.9	12.0	12.5	40,422	50,497	85.1
20	54	Fiat Spa	Italy	Automotive	24.4	59.1	26.3	40.6	95,930	248,180	48.2
21	59	Siemens AG	Germany	Electronics	24.0	57.7	35.5	62.0	162,000	373,000	47.4
22	33	Sony Corporation	Japan	Electronics	47.6	47.6	30.3	43.3	90,000	151,000	59.1
23	30	Alcatel Alsthom	France	Electronics	22.7	51.2	24.2	32.1	117,400	191,830	60.3
24	53	Hoechst	Germany	Chemicals	21.9	36.7	13.4	36.3	100,035	161,618	48.3
25	68	Renault SA	France	Automotive	21.2	44.6	19.1	36.8	40,066	139,950	42.7

Table 1.4

The Top 25 Multinational Businesses in 1996 (ranked by foreign assets)

Source: Adapted from Table 1.7 in United Nations, *World Investment Report, 1997* (New York and Geneva: United Nations, 1997).

percent of the global market for cocoa-bean roasting machines.[27] The point is, international business is conducted not just by large firms but also by medium-sized and small enterprises.

The Changing World Order

Between 1989 and 1991 a series of remarkable democratic revolutions swept the communist world. For reasons that are explored in more detail in Chapter 2, in country after country throughout Eastern Europe and eventually in the Soviet Union itself, Communist governments collapsed like the shells of rotten eggs. The Soviet Union is now history, having been replaced by 15 independent republics. Czechoslovakia has divided itself into two states, while Yugoslavia has dissolved into a bloody civil war among its five successor states.

Many of the former communist nations of Europe and Asia seem to share a commitment to democratic politics and free market economics. If this continues, the opportunities for international businesses may be enormous. For the best part of half a century, these countries were essentially closed to Western international businesses. Now they present a host of export and investment opportunities. Just how this will play out over the next 10 to 20 years is difficult to say. The economies of most of the former communist states are in very poor condition, and their continued commitment to democracy and free market economics cannot be taken for granted. Disturbing signs of growing unrest and totalitarian tendencies are seen in many Eastern European states. Thus, the risks involved in doing business in such countries are very high, but then, so may be the returns.

In addition to these changes, more quiet revolutions have been occurring in China and Latin America. Their implications for international businesses may be just as profound as the collapse of communism in Eastern Europe. China suppressed its own prodemocracy movement in the bloody Tiananmen Square massacre of 1989. Despite this, China seems to be moving progressively toward greater free market reforms. The southern Chinese province of Guangdong, where these reforms have been pushed the furthest, now frequently ranks as the fastest-growing economy in the world.[28] If what is now occurring in southern China continues, and particularly if it spreads throughout the country, China may move from Third World to industrial superpower status even more rapidly than Japan did. If China's GDP per capita grows by an average of 6 percent to 7 percent, which is slower than the 8 percent growth rate achieved during the last decade, then by 2020 this nation of 1.2 billion people could boast an average income per capita of about $13,000, roughly equivalent to that of Spain today.

The potential consequences for Western international business are enormous. On the one hand, with 1.2 billion people, China represents a huge and largely untapped market. Reflecting this, between 1983 and 1997, annual foreign direct investment in China increased from less than $2 billion to $45 billion. On the other hand, China's new firms are proving to be very capable competitors, and they could take global market share away from Western and Japanese enterprises. Thus, the changes in China are creating both opportunities and threats for established international businesses.

As for Latin America, here too both democracy and free market reforms seem to have taken hold. For decades, most Latin American countries were ruled by dictators, many of whom seemed to view Western international businesses as instruments of imperialist domination. Accordingly, they restricted direct investment by foreign firms. In addition, the poorly managed economies of Latin America were characterized by low growth, high debt, and hyperinflation—all of which discouraged investment by international businesses. Now all this seems to be changing. Throughout most of Latin America, debt and inflation are down, governments are selling state-owned enterprises to private investors, foreign investment is welcomed, and the region's economies are growing rapidly. These changes have increased the attractiveness of Latin America, both as a market for exports and as a site for foreign direct investment. At the same time, given the long history of eco-

COUNTRY FOCUS
South Korea's New Multinationals

In the forefront of South Korea's emergence as a modern industrial economy over the past 25 years have been the diversified business groups known as the *chaebol*. Samsung, the largest of the *chaebol*, had 1997 revenues of $96.1 billion and is involved in a wide range of industries including electronics (it is the world's largest manufacturer of memory chips for computers), automobiles, shipbuilding, aerospace, and machinery. Samsung is closely followed in size by three other major *chaebol*, Hyundai, LG (formerly Lucky Goldstar), and Daewoo. Together with six smaller *chaebol*, these large diversified industrial groups collectively account for about one-quarter of South Korea's gross national product.

Historically, South Korea's *chaebol* took advantage of low labor costs to export a wide range of goods to industrialized countries. In recent years, however, the costs of both land and labor in South Korea have risen sharply, nullifying important sources of the *chaebol's* competitive advantage in the global economy. A recent analysis of national competitiveness by the Swiss-based International Institute of Management Development ranked South Korea 24th out of 41 developed and developing nations, just behind Thailand and Chile, and just ahead of Spain and Mexico (the three top countries were the United States, Singapore, and Japan).

Unlike Japanese enterprises, with whom the South Koreans are so often compared, several of the *chaebol* suffer from relatively poor product quality and inferior product design. Thus, they have been unable to respond to higher costs by moving their exported products upmarket and raising prices (as did many Japanese enterprises). Rather, in an attempt to maintain their competitive position, the *chaebol* have responded to rising costs at home by expanding overseas, establishing factories in countries where direct labor costs are lower and employee productivity is higher than in South Korea. In 1996, for example, Daewoo expanded its investment in a videotape recorder plant in Northern Ireland partly to take advantage of lower labor costs. Daewoo had found that the average $1,300 monthly wage at its videotape recorder plant in Kumi, South Korea, was higher than the $1,200 it paid workers at a similar factory in Antrim, Northern Ireland, while the output per employee was 20 percent higher at the Irish plant.

Another reason for foreign investment by the *chaebol* has been to acquire foreign-owned entities that have the quality, design, engineering know-how, or market presence that the *chaebol* lack. For example, in early 1995 Samsung acquired 40 percent of AST, one of the largest manufacturers of personal computers in the United States, for $378 million. Similarly, Hyundai Electronics Industries, a subsidiary of Hyundai, the second-largest *chaebol*, recently acquired US computer diskmaker Maxtor for $165 million and a semiconductor division of AT&T for $340 million. Daewoo,

nomic mismanagement in Latin America, there is no guarantee that these favorable trends will continue. As in the case of Eastern Europe, substantial opportunities are accompanied by substantial risks.

The Global Economy of the 21st Century

In sum, the last quarter of century has seen rapid changes in the global economy. Barriers to the free flow of goods, services, and capital have been coming down. The volume of cross-border trade and investment has been growing more rapidly than global output, indicating that national economies are become more closely integrated into a single, interdependent, global economic system. As their economies advance, more nations are joining the ranks of the developed world. A generation ago, South Korea and Taiwan were viewed as second-tier developing nations. Now they boast powerful economies, and their firms are major players in many global industries from shipbuilding and steel to electronics and chemicals. The move toward a global economy has been further strengthened by the widespread adoption of liberal economic policies by countries that for two generations or more were firmly opposed to them. Thus, follow-

http://www.Kimsoft.com/Korea.htm

meanwhile, has been acquiring automobile plants in Eastern Europe, Vietnam, and Brazil as part of its strategy to become a major supplier of automobiles to developing nations, and to use that low-cost base to export to the developed world.

A third rationale for foreign expansion by South Korea's *chaebol* has been to placate foreign governments that have expressed concerns about the rising tide of Korean imports into their economies. This has been particularly notable in Western Europe, where lawsuits have been filed with the European Commission claiming that Korean firms have been dumping products in the European market—selling them at a price below their cost of production—in an attempt to gain market share and drive European firms out of business. Korean firms are increasingly trying to sidestep such charges by setting up production facilities in Europe. For example, a complaint against Samsung and Hyundai by European manufacturers of earthmoving equipment triggered direct investments by both *chaebol* in facilities to manufacture the equipment in Europe.

Spurred on by such forces, foreign direct investment by South Korea's *chaebol* has accelerated rapidly in recent years. In 1987 South Korean firms invested a little over $300 million in foreign establishments. By 1990 the figure had risen to $1.5 billion, in 1994 the figure hit $2.5 billion, and in 1997 it reached a record $4.19 billion. Since 1985, about 50 percent of

this investment has been directed at other Asian countries, 30 percent at North America, and 15 percent at Europe. However, the 1997–98 financial crisis, which hit South Korea hard, will probably lead to a temporary slowdown in this foreign investment activity. For now, many of the *chaebol* find themselves with too much debt and too much excess capacity to contemplate further investments on the scale of those undertaken in the mid-1990s. However, many of the largest *chaebol* are now true multinationals. In 1996, for example, the United Nations ranked Daewoo as the 52nd largest multinational in the world. Samsung now has over 390 foreign subsidiaries in 63 countries. Although South Korea's foreign investment drive will probably slow down over the next few years, most observers expect the country's economy to recover, and when it does, it seems likely that the drive to invest outside of the country's borders will accelerate again.

Sources: L. Nakarmi, "A Flying Leap toward the 21st Century," *Business Week,* March 20, 1995, pp. 78–80; J. Burton, "Samsung Drives on toward Globalization," *Financial Times,* October 25, 1994, p. 21; G. de Jonquieres and J. Burton, "Big Gamble on a European Thrust," *Financial Times,* October 2, 1995, p. 13; and United Nations, *World Investment Report, 1998.*

ing the normative prescriptions of liberal economic ideology, in country after country we are seeing state-owned businesses privatized, widespread deregulation, markets being opened to more competition, and increased commitment to removing barriers to cross-border trade and investment. This suggests that over the next few decades, countries such as the Czech Republic, Poland, Brazil, China, and South Africa may build powerful market-oriented economies. In short, current trends suggest that the world is moving rapidly toward an economic system that is more favorable for the practice of international business.

On the other hand, it is always hazardous to take established trends and use them to predict the future. The world may be moving toward a more global economic system, but globalization is not inevitable. Countries may pull back from the recent commitment to liberal economic ideology if their experiences do not match their expectations. There are signs, for example, of a retreat from liberal economic ideology in Russia. Russia has experienced considerable economic pain as it tries to shift from a centrally planned economy to a market economy. If Russia's hesitation were to become more permanent and widespread, the liberal vision of a more prosperous global economy based on free market principles might not come to pass as quickly as many hope. Clearly, this would be a tougher world for international businesses to compete in.

Moreover, greater globalization brings with it risks of its own. This was starkly demonstrated in 1997 and 1998 when a financial crisis in Thailand spread first to other East Asian nations and then in 1998 to Russia and Brazil. Ultimately the crisis threatened to plunge the economies of the developed world, including the United States, into a recession. We explore the causes and consequences of this and other similar global financial crises later in this book (see Chapters 10 and 11). For now it is simply worth noting that even from a purely economic perspective, globalization is not all good. The opportunities for doing business in a global economy may be significantly enhanced, but as we saw in 1997–98, the risks associated with global financial contagion are also greater. Still, as explained later in this book, there are ways for firms to exploit the opportunities associated with globalization, while at the same time reducing the risks through appropriate hedging strategies.

The Globalization Debate: Prosperity or Impoverishment?

Is the shift toward a more integrated and interdependent global economy a good thing? Many influential economists, politicians, and business leaders seem to think so. They argue that falling barriers to international trade and investment are the twin engines that are driving the global economy toward greater prosperity. They argue that increased international trade and cross-border investment will result in lower prices for goods and services. They believe that globalization stimulates economic growth, raises the incomes of consumers, and helps to create jobs in all countries that choose to participate in the global trading system.

The arguments of those who support globalization are covered in detail in Chapters 4, 5, 6, and 8 of this book. As we shall see, there are good theoretical reasons for believing that declining barriers to international trade and investment do stimulate economic growth, create jobs, and raise income levels. Moreover, as described in Chapters 5 to 7, empirical evidence lends support to the predictions of this theory. However, despite the existence of a compelling body of theory and evidence, globalization has its critics.[29] Here we briefly review the main themes of the debate. In later chapters we shall elaborate on many of the points mentioned below.

Globalization, Jobs, and Incomes

One frequently voiced concern is that far from creating jobs, falling barriers to international trade actually destroy manufacturing jobs in wealthy advanced economies such as the United States and United Kingdom. The critics argue that falling trade barriers allow firms to move their manufacturing activities offshore to countries where wage rates are much lower.[30] D. L. Bartlett and J. B. Steele, two journalists for the *Philadelphia Inquirer* who have gained notoriety for their attacks on free trade, cite the case of Harwood Industries, a US clothing manufacturer that closed its US operations, where it paid workers $9 per hour, and shifted manufacturing to Honduras, where textile workers receive 48 cents per hour.[31] Because of moves like this, argue Bartlett and Steele, the wage rates of poorer Americans have fallen significantly over the last quarter of a century.

Supporters of globalization reply that critics such as Bartlett and Steele miss the essential point about free trade—the benefits outweigh the costs.[32] They argue that free trade results in countries specializing in the production of those goods and services that they can produce most efficiently, while importing goods that they cannot produce as efficiently. When a country embraces free trade, there is always some dislocation—lost textile jobs at Harwood Industries, for example—but the whole economy is better off as a result. According to this view, it makes little sense for the United

States to produce textiles at home when they can be produced at a lower cost in Honduras or China (which, unlike Honduras, is a major source of US textile imports). Importing textiles from China leads to lower prices for clothes in the United States, which enables consumers to spend more of their money on other items. At the same time, the increased income generated in China from textile exports increases income levels in that country, which helps the Chinese to purchase more products produced in the United States, such as Boeing jets, Intel-based computers, Microsoft software, and Motorola cellular telephones. In this manner, supporters of globalization argue that free trade benefits all countries that adhere to a free trade regime.

Supporters of globalization do concede that the wage rate enjoyed by unskilled workers in many advanced economies has declined in recent years.[33] For example, data for the Organization for Economic Cooperation and Development suggest that since 1980 the lowest 10 percent of American workers have seen a drop in their real wages (adjusted for inflation) of about 20 percent, while the top 10 percent have enjoyed a real pay increase of around 10 percent.[34] Similar trends can be seen in many other countries. However, while globalization critics argue that the decline in unskilled wage rates is due to the migration of low-wage manufacturing jobs offshore and a corresponding reduction in demand for unskilled workers, supporters of globalization see a more complex picture. They maintain that the declining real wage rates of unskilled workers owes far more to a technology-induced shift within advanced economies away from jobs where the only qualification was a willingness to turn up for work every day and toward jobs that require significant education and skills. They point out that many advanced economies report a shortage of highly skilled workers and an excess supply of unskilled workers. Thus, growing income inequality is a result of the wages for skilled workers being bid up by the labor market, and the wages for unskilled workers being discounted. If one agrees with this logic, a solution to the problem of declining incomes is to be found not in limiting free trade and globalization, but in increasing society's investment in education to reduce the supply of unskilled workers.[35]

Globalization, Labor Policies, and the Environment

A second source of concern is that free trade encourages firms from advanced nations to move manufacturing facilities offshore to less developed countries that lack adequate regulations to protect labor and the environment from abuse by the unscrupulous.[36] Globalization critics often argue that adhering to labor and environmental regulations significantly increases the costs of manufacturing enterprises and puts them at a competitive disadvantage in the global marketplace vis-à-vis firms based in developing nations that do not have to comply with such regulations. Firms deal with this cost disadvantage, the theory goes, by moving their production facilities to nations that do not have such burdensome regulations, or by failing to enforce the regulations they have on their books. If this is the case, one might expect free trade to lead to an increase in pollution and result in firms from advanced nations exploiting the labor of less developed nations.[37] This argument was used repeatedly by those who opposed the 1994 formation of the North American Free Trade Agreement (NAFTA) between Canada, Mexico, and the United States. They painted a picture of US manufacturing firms moving to Mexico in droves so that they would be free to pollute the environment, employ child labor, and ignore workplace safety and health issues, all in the name of higher profits.[38]

Supporters of free trade and greater globalization express serious doubts about this scenario. They point out that tougher environmental regulations and stricter labor standards go hand in hand with economic progress. In general, as countries get richer, they enact tougher environmental and labor regulations. Because free trade enables developing countries to increase their economic growth rates and become richer, this should lead to tougher environmental and labor laws. In this view, the critics of free trade have got it backward—free trade does not lead to more pollution and labor exploitation, it leads to less. Supporters of free trade also point out that it is possible to tie free trade agreements to the implementation of tougher environmental and labor laws in less developed countries. NAFTA, for example, was passed only after side agreements had been negotiated that committed Mexico to tougher enforcement of environmental protection regulations. Thus, supporters of free trade argue that factories based in Mexico are now cleaner than they would have been without the passage of NAFTA.[39]

Supporters of free trade also argue that business firms are not the amoral organizations that critics suggest. While there may be a few rotten apples, the vast majority of business enterprises are staffed by managers who are committed to behave in an ethical manner and would be unlikely to move production offshore just so they could pump more pollution into the atmosphere or exploit labor. Furthermore, the relationship between pollution, labor exploitation, and production costs may not be that suggested by critics. In general, a well-treated labor force is productive, and it is productivity rather than base wage rates that often has the greatest influence on costs. Given this, in the vast majority of cases, the vision of greedy managers who shift production to low-wage companies to "exploit" their labor force may be misplaced.

Globalization and National Sovereignty

A final concern voiced by critics of globalization is that in today's increasingly interdependent global economy, economic power is shifting away from national governments and toward supranational organizations such as the World Trade Organization, the European Union, and the United Nations. As perceived by critics, unelected bureaucrats are now able to impose policies on the democratically elected governments of nation-states, thereby undermining the sovereignty of those states. In this manner, claim critics, the national state's ability to control its own destiny is being limited.[40]

The World Trade Organization is a favorite target of those who attack the world's headlong rush toward a global economy. The WTO was founded in 1994 to police the world trading system established by the General Agreement on Tariffs and Trade. The WTO arbitrates trade disputes between the 120 or so states that are signatories to the GATT. The WTO arbitration panel can issue a ruling instructing a member state to change trade policies that violate GATT regulations. If the violator refuses to comply with the ruling, the WTO allows other states to impose appropriate trade sanctions on the transgressor. As a result, according to one prominent critic, the US environmentalist and consumer rights advocate Ralph Nader:

> Under the new system, many decisions that affect billions of people are no longer made by local or national governments but instead, if challenged by any WTO member nation, would be deferred to a group of unelected bureaucrats sitting behind closed doors in Geneva (which is where the headquarters of the WTO are located). The bureaucrats can decide whether or not people in California can prevent the destruction of the last virgin forests or determine if carcinogenic pesticides can be banned from their foods; or whether European countries have the right to ban dangerous biotech hormones in meat . . . At risk is the very basis of democracy and accountable decision making.[41]

In contrast to Nader's inflammatory rhetoric, many economists and politicians maintain that the power of supranational organizations such as the WTO is limited to that which nation-states collectively agree to grant. They argue that bodies such as the United Nations and the WTO exist to serve the collective interests of member states, not to subvert those interests. Moreover, supporters of supranational organizations point out that in reality, the power of these bodies rests largely on their ability to *persuade* member states to follow a certain action. If these bodies fail to serve the collective interests of member states, those states will withdraw their support and the supranational organization will quickly collapse. In this view then, real power still resides with individual nation-states, not supranational organizations.

Managing in the Global Marketplace

Much of this book is concerned with the challenges of managing in an international business. An **international business** is any firm that engages in international trade or investment. A firm does not have to become a multinational enterprise, investing directly in operations in other countries, to engage in international business, although multinational enterprises are international businesses. All a firm has to do is export or import products from other countries. As the world shifts toward a truly integrated global economy, more firms, both large and small, are becoming international businesses. What does this shift toward a global economy mean for managers within an international business?

As their organizations increasingly engage in cross-border trade and investment, it means managers need to recognize that the task of managing an international business differs from that of managing a purely domestic business in many ways. At the most fundamental level, the differences arise from the simple fact that countries are different. Countries differ in their cultures, political systems, economic systems, legal systems, and levels of economic development. Despite all the talk about the emerging global village, and despite the trend toward globalization of markets and production, as we shall see in this book, many of these differences are very profound and enduring.

Differences between countries require that an international business vary its practices country by country. Marketing a product in Brazil may require a different approach than marketing the product in Germany; managing US workers might require different skills than managing Japanese workers; maintaining close relations with a particular level of government may be very important in Mexico and irrelevant in Great Britain; the business strategy pursued in Canada might not work in South Korea; and so on. Managers in an international business must not only be sensitive to these differences, but they must also adopt the appropriate policies and strategies for coping with them. Much of this book is devoted to explaining the sources of these differences and the methods for coping with them successfully. The accompanying Management Focus, which reviews Procter & Gamble's experiences in Japan, shows what happens when managers don't consider country differences.

A further way in which international business differs from domestic business is the greater complexity of managing an international business. In addition to the problems that arise from the differences between countries, a manager in an international business is confronted with a range of other issues that the manager in a domestic business never confronts. An international business must decide where in the world to site its production activities to minimize costs and to maximize value added. Then it must decide how best to coordinate and control its globally dispersed production activities (which, as we shall see later in the book, is not a trivial problem). An international business also must decide which foreign markets to enter and which to avoid. It also must choose the appropriate mode for entering a particular foreign country. Is it best to export its product to the foreign country? Should the firm allow a local company to produce its product under license in that country? Should the firm enter into a joint venture with a local firm to produce its product in that country? Or should the firm set up a wholly owned subsidiary to serve the market in that country? As we shall see, the choice of entry mode is critical, because it has major implications for the long-term health of the firm.

Conducting business transactions across national borders requires understanding the rules governing the international trading and investment system. Managers in an international business must also deal with government restrictions on international trade and investment. They must find ways to work within the limits imposed by specific governmental interventions. As this book explains, even though many governments are nominally committed to free trade, they often intervene to regulate cross-border trade and investment. Managers within international businesses must develop strategies and policies for dealing with such interventions.

MANAGEMENT FOCUS
Procter & Gamble in Japan

http://www.pg.com

Procter & Gamble entered the Japanese market in 1972, was the first company to introduce disposable diapers into Japan, and soon commanded 80 percent of the market. This had all the makings of a great success story, but it didn't work out that way. By 1985 P&G's share of the diaper market had slipped to 8 percent, the company had failed repeatedly to establish a strong position in the Japanese laundry detergent and personal care product markets, and its Japanese subsidiary was reportedly losing $40 million per year. The central problem: P&G had simply transferred its marketing strategies and products wholesale to Japan, without customizing them to account for local cultural differences. The American managers who headed P&G's Japanese subsidiary failed to appreciate that what worked in America would not work in Japan.

When it launched its bath soap in Japan, P&G used TV advertising that showed a Japanese woman relaxing in a luxurious bath of soap bubbles, while her husband walked in and asked her about the soap. This same advertisement had worked well in the United States and Europe, but in Japan, where it was culturally frowned on for a man to walk in on a woman having a bath, even if she was his wife, it was a huge flop.

P&G's Japanese competitors soon took advantage of P&G's cultural myopia. In the disposable diaper market, for example, Kao developed a line of trim-fit diapers that were more in tune with the tastes of Japanese consumers and was quickly rewarded with a 30 percent share of the market, all taken at P&G's expense.

Realizing that a lack of international business literacy among many of the Americans that worked in its Japanese operation had contributed to the debacle in that country, P&G has started to appoint local nationals to key management positions in many foreign subsidiaries.

Sources: "Perestroika in Soapland," *The Economist,* June 10, 1989, p. 69–71; and C. Bartlett and S. Ghoshal, *Managing Across Borders: The Transnational Solution* (Boston: Harvard Business School Press, 1989).

Cross-border transactions also require that money be converted from the firm's home currency into a foreign currency and vice versa. Since currency exchange rates vary in response to changing economic conditions, an international business must develop policies for dealing with exchange rate movements. A firm that adopts a wrong policy can lose large amounts of money, while a firm that adopts the right policy can increase the profitability of its international transactions.

In sum, managing an international business is different from managing a purely domestic business for at least four reasons: (1) countries are different, (2) the range of problems confronted by a manager in an international business is wider, and the problems themselves more complex than those confronted by a manager in a domestic business, (3) an international business must find ways to work within the limits imposed by government intervention in the international trade and investment system, and (4) international transactions involve converting money into different currencies.

In this book we examine all these issues in depth, paying close attention to the different strategies and policies that managers pursue in order to deal with the various challenges created when a firm becomes an international business. Chapters 2 and 3 explore how countries differ from each other with regard to their political, economic, legal, and cultural institutions. Chapters 4 to 8 look at the international trade and investment environment within which international businesses must operate. Chapters 9 through 11 review the international monetary system. These chapters focus on the nature of the foreign exchange market and the emerging global monetary system. Chapters 12 to 14 explore the strategies and structures of international businesses. Then Chapters 15 to 20 look at the management of various functional operations within an international business, including production, marketing, human relations, finance, and accounting. By the time you complete this book, you should have a good grasp of the issues that managers working within international business have to grapple with on a daily basis, and you should be familiar with the range of strategies and operating policies available to compete more effectively in today's rapidly emerging global economy.

Chapter Summary

This chapter sets the scene for the rest of the book. We have seen how the world economy is becoming more global, and we have reviewed the main drivers of globalization and argued that they seem to be thrusting nation-states toward a more tightly integrated global economy. We have looked at how the nature of international business is changing in response to the changing global economy; we have discussed some concerns raised by rapid globalization; and we have reviewed implications of rapid globalization for individual managers. These major points were made in the chapter:

1. Over the past two decades, we have witnessed the globalization of markets and production.

2. The globalization of markets implies that national markets are merging into one huge marketplace. However, it is important not to push this view too far.

3. The globalization of production implies that firms are basing individual productive activities at the optimal world locations for the particular activities. As a consequence, it is increasingly irrelevant to talk about American products, Japanese products, or German products, since these are being replaced by "global" products.

4. Two factors seem to underlie the trend toward globalization: declining trade barriers and changes in communication, information, and transportation technologies.

5. Since the end of World War II, there has been a significant lowering of barriers to the free flow of goods, services, and capital. More than anything else, this has facilitated the trend toward the globalization of production and has enabled firms to view the world as a single market.

6. As a consequence of the globalization of production and markets, in the last decade world trade has grown faster than world output, foreign direct investment has surged, imports have penetrated more deeply into the world's industrial nations, and competitive pressures have increased in industry after industry.

7. The development of the microprocessor and related developments in communications and information processing technology have helped firms link their worldwide operations into sophisticated information networks. Jet air travel, by shrinking travel time, has also helped to link the worldwide operations of international businesses. These changes have enabled firms to achieve tight coordination of their worldwide operations and to view the world as a single market.

8. Over the past three decades, a number of dramatic changes have occurred in the nature of international business. In the 1960s, the US economy was dominant in the world, US firms accounted for most of the foreign direct investment in the world economy, US firms dominated the list of large multinationals, and roughly half the world—the centrally planned economies of the communist world—was closed to Western businesses.

9. By the mid-1990s, the US share of world output had been cut in half, with major shares now being accounted for by Western European and Southeast Asian economies. The US share of worldwide foreign direct investment had also fallen, by about two-thirds. US multinationals were now facing competition from a large number of Japanese and European multinationals. In addition, the emergence of mini-multinationals was noted.

10. The most dramatic environmental trend has been the collapse of communist power in Eastern Europe, which has created enormous long-run opportunities for international businesses. In addition, the move toward free market economies in China and Latin America is creating opportunities (and threats) for Western international businesses.

11. The benefits and costs of the emerging global economy are being hotly debated among business people, economists, and politicians. The debate focuses on the impact of globalization on jobs,

wages, the environment, working conditions, and national sovereignty.

12. Managing an international business is different from managing a domestic business for at least four reasons: (i) countries are different, (ii) the range of problems confronted by a manager in an international business is wider and the problems themselves more complex than those confronted by a manager in a domestic business, (iii) managers in an international business must find ways to work within the limits imposed by governments' intervention in the international trade and investment system, and (iv) international transactions involve converting money into different currencies.

Critical Discussion Questions

1. Describe the shifts in the world economy over the past 30 years. What are the implications of these shifts for international businesses based in Britain? North America? Hong Kong?

2. "The study of international business is fine if you are going to work in a large multinational enterprise, but it has no relevance for individuals who are going to work in small firms." Evaluate this statement.

3. How have changes in technology contributed to the globalization of markets and production? Would the globalization of production and markets have been possible without these technological changes?

4. How might the Internet and the associated World Wide Web affect international business activity and the globalization of the world economy?

5. If current trends continue, China may emerge as the world's largest economy by 2020. Discuss the possible implications for such a development for

   - The world trading system.
   - The world monetary system.
   - The business strategy of today's European and US-based global corporations.

6. "Ultimately, the study of international business is no different from the study of domestic business. Thus, there is no point in having a separate course on international business." Evaluate this statement.

CLOSING CASE   Citigroup—Building a Global Financial Services Giant

In the largest merger ever in the financial services business, Citicorp joined forces with Travelers Group in the autumn of 1998. The combined group has revenues of close to $50 billion, assets in excess of $700 billion, and global reach.

Before the merger, Travelers Group was the largest property-casualty and life insurance business in the United States. In addition, Travelers had considerable investment banking, retail brokerage, and asset management operations. Travelers' insurance operations were almost exclusively domestic in their focus, although its investment banking and asset management business had some foreign exposure.

Citicorp was one of the world's most global banks. Citicorp had two main legs to its business, its corporate banking activities and its consumer banking activities. The corporate banking side of Citicorp focused on providing a wide range of financial services to 20,000 corporations in 75 emerging

economies and 22 developed economies. This business, which always had an international focus, generated revenues of $8.0 billion in 1997, over half of which came from activities in the world's emerging economies. What captured the attention of many observers, however, was the rapid growth of Citicorp's global consumer banking business. The consumer banking business focuses on providing basic financial services to individuals, including checking accounts, credit cards, and personal loans. In 1997 this business served 50 million consumers in 56 countries through a global network of 1,200 retail branches and generated revenues of $15 billion.

The merger talks were initiated by Travelers CEO Sandy Weill. Given the rapid globalization of the world economy, Weill felt it was important for Travelers to start selling its insurance products in foreign countries. Until recently, the barriers to cross-border trade and investment in financial services were such that this would have been difficult. However, under the terms of a deal brokered by the World Trade Organization in December 1997, over 100 countries agreed to open their banking, insurance, and securities markets to foreign competition. The deal, which was scheduled to take effect on March 1, 1999, included all developed nations and many developing nations. The deal would allow insurance companies such as Travelers to sell their products in foreign markets for the first time. To take advantage of this opportunity, however, Travelers needed a global retail distribution system, which is where Citicorp came in. For the past 20 years, the central strategy of Citicorp has been to build just such a distribution channel.

The architect of Citicorp's global retail banking strategy was its longtime CEO, John Reed (Reed is now co-CEO of Travelers, a position he shares with Weill). Reed has been on a quest to establish "Citicorp" as a global brand, positioning the bank as the Coca-Cola or McDonald's of financial services. The basic belief underpinning Reed's consumer banking strategy is that people everywhere have the same financial needs—needs that broaden as they pass through various life stages and levels of affluence. At the outset customers need the basics—a checking account, a credit card, and perhaps a loan for college. As they mature financially, customers add a mortgage, car loan, and investments (and insurance). As they accumulate wealth, portfolio management and estate planning become priorities. Citicorp aimed to provide these services to customers around the globe in a standardized fashion, in much the same way as McDonald's provides the same basic menu of fast food to consumers everywhere. With the merger with Travelers, the company will be able to push this concept further than ever, cross-selling insurance products and asset management services through its global retail distribution system.

Reed believes that global demographic, economic, and political forces strongly favor such a strategy. In the developed world, aging populations are buying more financial services. In the rapidly growing economies of many developing nations, Citigroup is targeting the emerging middle classes, whose needs for consumer banking services and insurance are rising with their affluence. This world view got Citicorp into many developing economies years ahead of its slowly awakening rivals. As a result, Citigroup is today the largest credit card issuer in Asia and Latin America, with 7 million cards issued in Asia and 9 million in Latin America. As for political forces, the worldwide movement toward greater deregulation of financial services allowed Citigroup to set up consumer banking operations in countries that only a decade ago did not allow foreign banks into their markets. Examples in the fast-growing Asian region include India, Indonesia, Japan, Taiwan, Vietnam, and the biggest potential prize of them all, China.

A key element of Citigroup's global strategy for its consumer bank is the standardization of operations around the globe. This has found its most visible expression in the so-called model branch. Originally designed in Chile and refined in Athens, the idea is to give the company's mobile customers the same retail experience everywhere in the world, from the greeter by the door to the standard blue sign overhead to the ATM machine to the gilded doorway through which the retail-elite "Citi-Gold" customers pass to meet with their "personal financial executives." By the end of 1997 this model branch was in place at 600 of Citicorp's 1,200 retail locations, and it is being rapidly introduced elsewhere. Another element of standardization, less obvious to customers, is Citigroup's emphasis on the uniformity of a range of back-office systems throughout its branches, including the systems to manage checking and savings accounts, mutual fund investments, and so on. According to Citigroup, this emphasis on uniformity makes it much easier for the company to roll out branches in a new market. Citigroup has also taken advantage of its global reach to centralize certain aspects of its operations to realize savings from economies of scale. For example, in Citigroup's fast-growing European credit card business, all credit cards are manufactured in Nevada; printing and mailing are done in the Netherlands; and data processing is done in South Dakota. Within each country, credit card operations are limited to marketing people and two staff units, customer service and collections.

Case Discussion Questions

1. What is the rationale for the merger between Travelers and Citicorp? How will this merger create value for (a) the stockholders of Citigroup and (b) the customers of Citigroup's global retail bank?

2. In 1997 the World Trade Organization brokered an agreement to liberalize cross-border trade and investment in global financial services. What will be the impact of this deal on competition in national markets? What would you expect to see occur?

3. Does the 1997 WTO agreement represent an opportunity for Citigroup or a threat?

4. How is Citigroup trying to build a global retail brand in financial services? What assumptions is this strategy based on? Do you think the assumptions and strategy make sense?

http://www.citicorp.com

Sources: C. J. Loomis, "Citicorp: John Reed's Second Act," *Fortune*, April 29, 1996, pp. 89–98; K. Klee, "Brand Builders," *Institutional Investor*, March 1997, pp. 89–101; M. Siconolfi, "Big Umbrella," *The Wall Street Journal*, April 7, 1998, pp. A1, A6; and L. N. Spiro and G. Silverman, "Will Citigroup's Parade Get Rained On?" *Business Week*, September 28, 1998, pp. 111–114.

Notes

1. A. Stewart, "Easier Access to World Markets," *Financial Times*, December 3, 1997, p. 8.

2. The product is the Anir ergonomic mouse.

3. T. Levitt, "The Globalization of Markets," *Harvard Business Review*, May–June 1983, pp. 92–102.

4. See F. T. Knickerbocker. *Oligopolistic Reaction and Multinational Enterprise* (Boston: Harvard Business School Press, 1973), and R. E. Caves, "Japanese Investment in the US: Lessons for the Economic Analysis of Foreign Investment," *The World Economy* 16 (1993), pp. 279–300.

5. I. Metthee, "Playing a Large Part," *Seattle Post-Intelligencer*, April 9, 1994, p. 13.

6. C. S. Tranger, "Enter the Mini-Multinational," *Northeast International Business*, March 1989, pp. 13–14.

7. R. B. Reich. *The Work of Nations* (New York: A. A. Knopf, 1991).

8. J. Bhagwati, *Protectionism* (Cambridge, MA: MIT Press, 1989).

9. F. Williams, "Trade Round Like This May Never Be Seen Again," *Financial Times*, April 15, 1994, p. 8.

10. United Nations, *World Investment Report, 1997* (New York & Geneva: United Nations, 1997).

11. World Trade Organization, *International Trade Trends and Statistics, 1998*.

12. United Nations, *World Investment Report, 1997*, and G. de Jonquieres, "Foreign Direct Investment Worldwide Figures to Reach $430 Billion," *Financial Times*, November 11, 1998, p. 6.

13. World Trade Organization, "Beyond Borders: Managing a World of Free Trade and Deep Interdependence," press release 55, September 10, 1996.

14. Moore's Law is named after Intel founder Gorden Moore.

15. Data compiled from various sources and listed at *http://www.euromktg.com/globstats*.

16. Data on the number of host computers can be found at *http://www.nw.com/zone/WWW/report.html*.

17. V. Houlder, "Fear and Enterprise As the Net Closes In," *Financial Times*, May 20, 1998, p. 18.

18. M. Dickerson, "All Those Inflated Expectations Aside, Many Firms Are Finding the Internet Invaluable in Pursuing International Trade," *Los Angeles Times*, October 14, 1998, p. 10. The company's Web site is *http://www.cardiacscience.com*.

19. "Delivering the Goods," *The Economist*, November 15, 1997, pp. 85–86.

20. Dicken, *Global Shift* (New York: Guilford Press, 1992).

21. Interviews with Hewlett-Packard personnel by the author.

22. "War of the Worlds," *The Economist: A Survey of the Global Economy*, October 1, 1994, p. 3–4.

23. One of the classics being J. J. Servan-Schreiber, *The American Challenge* (New York: Atheneum, 1968).

24. United Nations Press Release TAD/1861, November 8, 1998.

25. R. A. Mosbacher, "Opening Up Export Doors for Smaller Firms," *Seattle Times*, July 24, 1991, p. A7.

26. "Small Companies Learn How to Sell to the Japanese," *Seattle Times*, March 19, 1992.

27. W. J. Holstein, "Why Johann Can Export but Johnny Can't," *Business Week*, November 4, 1991, pp. 64–65.

28. P. Engardio and L. Curry, "The Fifth Tiger Is on China's Coast," *Business Week*, April 6, 1992, pp. 42–43.

29. See, for example, Ravi Batra, *The Myth of Free Trade*, (New York: Touchstone Books, 1993); William Greider, *One World, Ready or Not: The Manic Logic of Global Capitalism* (New York: Simon and Schuster, 1997); and D. Radrik *Has Globalization Gone Too Far?* (Washington, DC: Institution for International Economics, 1997).

30. James Goldsmith, "The Winners and the Losers," in *The Case Against the Global Economy*, ed. J. Mander and E. Goldsmith (San Francisco: The Sierra Book Club, 1996).

31. D. L. Bartlett and J. B. Steele, "America: Who Stole the Dream," *Philadelphia Inquirer*, September 9, 1996.

32. For example, see Paul Krugman, *Pop Internationalism* (Cambridge, MA: MIT Press, 1996).

33. Peter Gottschalk and Timothy M. Smeeding, "Cross-National Comparisons of Earnings and Income Inequality," *Journal of Economic Literature* 35 (June 1997), pp. 633–87, and Susan M. Collins, *Exports, Imports, and the American Worker* (Washington, DC: Brooking Institute, 1998).

34. Organization for Economic Cooperation and Development, *Income Distribution in OECD Countries*, OECD Policy Studies, no. 18 (October 1995).

35. See, Paul Krugman, *Pop Internationalism* (Cambridge, MA: MIT Press, 1996), and D. Belman and T. M. Lee, "International Trade and the Performance of US Labor Markets," in *U.S. Trade Policy and Global Growth*, ed. R. A. Blecker (New York: Economic Policy Institute, 1996).

36. E. Goldsmith, "Global Trade and the Environment."

37. Batra, *The Myth of Free Trade*.

38. P Choate, *Jobs at Risk: Vulnerable U.S. Industries and Jobs under NAFTA* (Washington, DC: Manufacturing Policy Project, 1993).

39. Krugman, *Pop Internationalism*.

40. R. Kuttner, "Managed Trade and Economic Sovereignty," in *U.S. Trade Policy and Global Growth*, ed. R. A. Blecker (New York: Economic Policy Institute, 1996).

41. Ralph Nader and Lori Wallach, "GATT, NAFTA, and the Subversion of the Democratic Process," in *US Trade Policy and Global Growth*, ed. R. A. Blecker (New York: Economic Policy Institute, 1996), p. 93–94.

COUNTRY FACTORS

Chapter Two
National Differences in Political Economy

Chapter Three
Differences in Culture

CHAPTER TWO

NATIONAL DIFFERENCES IN POLITICAL ECONOMY

Brazilian Privatization

In the middle years of the 20th century, many Latin American governments took a large number of private companies into state ownership. This wave of nationalizations reflected a populist ideology that was interlaced with socialist, nationalist, and, on occasion, fascist rhetoric. Supported by strong trade unions, particularly in Argentina and to some extent Brazil, many politicians advocated taking private enterprises into public ownership so they could be run "for the benefit of the state and its citizens, rather than the enrichment of a small capitalist elite."

However, by the early 1990s, inefficient management, political manipulation, and corruption had turned many state-owned enterprises into national liabilities. An example was Brazil's Embraer, the only manufacturer of jet aircraft in Latin America. Founded by a military regime in 1969, Embraer developed a reputation for solid engineering. Unfortunately, protected by public ownership from the need to account for its performance to private investors, no one at Embraer seemed to care about costs or customers. As a result, in 1994 Embraer lost $310 million on sales of only $253 million.

At the same time, the winds of change were also blowing through many other economies. Communism was collapsing in Eastern Europe, socialism was in retreat throughout much of the rest of the world, and free market economics was clearly on the ascendancy. Against this background, during the early 1990s there was a sharp move among the Latin American political establishment toward free market economics. This shift in political and economic ideology expressed itself through adoption of programs and plans to privatize many state-owned enterprises.

In Brazil, the privatization program began slowly and quietly but has recently accelerated. Around 70 state-owned enterprises were sold to private investors between 1990 and 1996 for a total take of $14.9 billion. In 1997, Brazil sold over $20 billion of state-owned assets, including Companhia Vale do Rio Doce (CVRD), the world's largest iron ore producer. Plans called for sales of a further $30 billion worth of state assets in 1998, including the sale of Telebras, Brazil's telecommunications company, which was to be broken up into four companies.

Early evidence suggests these privatizations are having the desired effects on the companies involved. Following its privatization in December 1994, Embraer reduced its payroll from 12,700 to 3,600 in 1996 as the new management team struggled to turn the company around. Today new orders are flowing in; production, sales, and profits are all projected to increase, and in 1997 the company added 1,100 employees to handle increased sales. Another example concerns Brazil's formerly state-owned steel industry, which between 1991 and 1993 was sold as six separate companies for a total of $8.2 billion. In 1990 the state-owned monopoly employed 115,000 people and produced 22.6 million tons of steel, or 196 tons per employee. In 1996 the six successor private companies produced 25.2 million tons of steel with only 65,000 employees, or 388 tons per employee, a striking increase in employee productivity. Along similar lines, the new private owners of CVRD think they can cut operating costs by at least 20 percent over the next few years.

The benefits of privatization are not limited to improved efficiency of former state-owned enterprises, important as that is. The Brazilian government is also opening the sale of state-owned assets to foreign investors and allowing foreign companies to set up enterprises in industries formerly controlled by state monopolies, such as steel, electric power generation, and telecommunications. The result has been a surge in private investment, much from foreign sources and much of it targeted toward basic infrastructure. Excluding telecommunications, infrastructure projects worth $190 billion were planned between 1997 and 2000. This compares to total spending of only $10 billion between 1993 and 1996. If this investment is made, it will have a significant impact on the growth rate of Brazil's economy.

http://www.cvrd.com.br

Sources: "Let the Party Begin," *The Economist*, April 26, 1997, pp. 57–58; and "A Very Big Deal. A Survey of Business in Latin America," *The Economist*, December 6, 1997, pp. S9–S12.

CHAPTER OUTLINE

BRAZILIAN PRIVATIZATION

INTRODUCTION

POLITICAL SYSTEMS
Collectivism and Individualism
Democracy and Totalitarianism

ECONOMIC SYSTEMS
Market Economy
Command Economy
Mixed Economy
State-Directed Economy

LEGAL SYSTEMS
Property Rights
The Protection of Intellectual
  Property
Product Safety and Product Liability
Contract Law

THE DETERMINANTS OF ECONOMIC DEVELOPMENT
Differences in Economic
  Development
Political Economy and Economic
  Progress
Other Determinants of Development:
  Geography and Education

STATES IN TRANSITION
The Spread of Democracy
Universal Civilization or a Clash of
  Civilizations?
The Spread of Market-Based
  Systems
The Nature of Economic
  Transformation
Implications

IMPLICATIONS FOR BUSINESS
Attractiveness
Ethical Issues

CHAPTER SUMMARY

CRITICAL DISCUSSION QUESTIONS

GENERAL ELECTRIC IN HUNGARY

Introduction

As noted in Chapter 1, international business is much more complicated than domestic business because countries differ in many ways. Countries have different political systems, economic systems, and legal systems. Cultural practices can vary dramatically from country to country, as can the education and skill level of the population, and countries are at different stages of economic development. All of these differences can and do have major implications for the practice of international business. They have a profound impact on the benefits, costs, and risks associated with doing business in different countries; the way in which operations in different countries should be managed; and the strategy international firms should pursue in different countries. A main function of this chapter and the next is to develop an awareness of and appreciation for the significance of country differences in political systems, economic systems, legal systems, and national culture. Another function of this chapter and the next is to describe how the political, economic, legal, and cultural systems of many of the world's nation-states are evolving and to draw out the implications of these changes for the practice of international business.

The opening case illustrates the changes occurring in the political and economic systems of one nation, Brazil. As in many other countries, over the last decade, political and economic ideology in Brazil has shifted toward a more free market orientation. One consequence of this shift in ideology has been adoption of an aggressive privatization program that is transforming Brazil's economy. Another has been the opening of the Brazilian economy to foreign investors. These changes are creating enormous opportunities for foreign investors, who for the first time in recent history can invest in many sectors of Brazil's expanding economy. For example, in 1997 the U.S.-based telecommunications company BellSouth paid $2.45 billion to the Brazilian government for a license that will enable it to install and market a wireless phone network in Brazil's largest city, Sao Paulo. Since there are only 12 telephone lines per 100 people in Sao Paulo, BellSouth believes that a huge untapped market exists here.[1]

This chapter focuses on how the political, economic, and legal systems of countries differ. Collectively we refer to these systems as constituting the **political economy** of a country. The political, economic, and legal systems of a country are not independent of each other. As we shall see, they interact and influence each other, and in doing so they affect the level of economic well-being in a country. In addition to reviewing these systems, we also explore how differences in political economy influence the benefits, costs, and risks associated with doing business in different countries, and how they impact on management practice and strategy. In the next chapter we will look at how differences in culture influence the practice of international business. Bear in mind, however, that the political economy and culture of a nation are not independent of each other. As will become apparent in Chapter 3, culture can exert an impact on political economy, and the converse can also hold true.

Political Systems

The economic and legal systems of a country are often shaped by its political system.[2] As such, it is important that we understand the nature of different political systems before discussing the nature of economic and legal systems. By **political system** we mean the system of government in a nation. Political systems can be assessed according to two *related* dimensions. The first is the degree to which they emphasize collectivism as opposed to individualism. The second dimension is the degree to which they are democratic or totalitarian. These dimensions are interrelated; systems that emphasize collectivism tend to be totalitarian, while systems that place a high value on individualism tend to be democratic. However, there is a gray area in the middle. It is possible to have democratic societies that emphasize a mix of collectivism and individualism. Similarly, it is possible to have totalitarian societies that are not collectivist.

Collectivism and Individualism

The term **collectivism** refers to a system that stresses the primacy of collective goals over individual goals.[3] When collectivism is emphasized, the needs of society as a whole are generally viewed as being more important than individual freedoms. In such circumstances, an individual's right to do something may be restricted on the grounds that it runs counter to "the good of society" or to "the common good." Advocacy of collectivism can be traced to the ancient Greek philosopher Plato (427–347 BC), who in the *Republic* argued that individual rights should be sacrificed for the good of the majority and that property should be owned in common. In modern times the collectivist mantle has been picked up by socialists.

Socialism

Socialists trace their intellectual roots back to Karl Marx (1818–1883). Marx argued that the few benefit at the expense of the many in a capitalist society where individual freedoms are not restricted. While successful capitalists accumulate considerable wealth, Marx postulated that the wages earned by the majority of workers in a capitalist society would be forced down to subsistence levels. Marx argued that capitalists expropriate for their own use the value created by workers, while paying workers only subsistence wages in return. Put another way, according to Marx, the pay of workers does not reflect the full value of their labor. To correct this perceived wrong, Marx advocated state ownership of the basic means of production, distribution, and exchange (i.e., businesses). His logic was that if the state owned the means of production, the state could ensure that workers were fully compensated for their labor. Thus, the idea is to manage state-owned enterprise to benefit society as a whole, rather than individual capitalists.[4]

In the early 20th century, the socialist ideology split into two broad camps. The **communists** believed that socialism could be achieved only through violent revolution and totalitarian dictatorship, while the **social democrats** committed themselves to achieving socialism by democratic means and turned their backs on violent revolution and dictatorship. Both versions of socialism have waxed and waned during the 20th century.

The communist version of socialism reached its high point in the late 1970s, when the majority of the world's population lived in communist states. The countries under Communist rule at that time included the former Soviet Union; its Eastern European client nations (e.g., Poland, Czechoslovakia, Hungary); China, the Southeast Asian nations of Cambodia, Laos, and Vietnam; various African nations (e.g., Angola, Mozambique); and the Latin American nations of Cuba and Nicaragua. By the mid-1990s, however, communism was in retreat worldwide. The Soviet Union had collapsed and had been replaced with a collection of 15 republics, most of which were at least nominally structured as democracies. Communism was swept out of Eastern Europe by the largely bloodless revolutions of 1989. Many believe it is now only a matter of time before communism collapses in China, the last major Communist power left. Although China is still nominally a communist state with substantial limits to individual political freedom, in the economic sphere the country has recently moved away from strict adherence to communist ideology.[5]

Social democracy also seems to have passed its high-water mark, although the ideology may prove to be more enduring than communism. Social democracy has had perhaps its greatest influence in a number of democratic Western nations including Australia, Britain, France, Germany, Norway, Spain, and Sweden, where social democratic parties have from time to time held political power. Other countries where social democracy has had an important influence include India and Brazil. Consistent with their Marxists roots, many social democratic governments nationalized private companies in certain industries, transforming them into state-owned enterprises to be run for the "public good rather than private profit." In Britain, for example, by the end of the 1970s, state-owned companies had a monopoly in the telecommunications, electricity, gas, coal, railway, and shipbuilding industries, as well as having substantial interests in the oil, airline, auto, and steel industries.

However, experience has demonstrated that far from being in the public interest, state ownership of the means of production often runs counter to the public interest. In many countries, state-owned companies have performed poorly (see the opening case on Brazil). Protected from significant competition by their monopoly position and guaranteed government financial support, many state-owned companies became increasingly inefficient. In the end, individuals found themselves paying for the luxury of state ownership through higher prices and higher taxes. As a consequence, a number of Western democracies voted many social democratic parties out of office in the late 1970s and early 1980s. They were succeeded by political parties, such as Britain's Conservative Party and Germany's Christian Democratic Party, that were more committed to free market economics. These parties devoted considerable effort to selling state-owned enterprises to private investors (a process referred to as privatization). Thus, in Britain the Conservative government sold the state's interests in telecommunications, electricity, gas, shipbuilding, oil, airlines, autos, and steel to private investors. Moreover, even when social democratic parties have regained the levers of power, as in Britain in 1997 when the left-leaning Labor party won control of the government, they now seem to be committed to greater private ownership.

Individualism

Individualism is the opposite of collectivism. In a political sense, **individualism** refers to a philosophy that an individual should have freedom in his or her economic and political pursuits. In contrast to collectivism, individualism stresses that the interests of the individual should take precedence over the interests of the state. Like collectivism, however, individualism can be traced back to an ancient Greek philosopher, in this case Plato's disciple Aristotle (384–322 BC). In contrast to Plato, Aristotle argued that individual diversity and private ownership are desirable. In a passage that might have been taken from a speech by Margaret Thatcher or Ronald Reagan, he argued that private property is more highly productive than communal property and will thus stimulate progress. According to Aristotle, communal property receives little care, whereas property that is owned by an individual will receive the greatest care and therefore be most productive.

After sinking into oblivion for the best part of two millennia, individualism was reborn as an influential political philosophy in the Protestant trading nations of England and the Netherlands during the 16th century. The philosophy was refined in the work of a number of British philosophers including David Hume (1711–1776), Adam Smith (1723–1790), and John Stuart Mill (1806–1873). The philosophy of individualism exercised a profound influence on those in the American colonies who sought independence from Britain. Individualism underlies the ideas expressed in the Declaration of Independence. In more recent years, the philosophy has been championed by several Nobel prize-winning economists, including Milton Friedman, Friedrich von Hayek, and James Buchanan.

Individualism is built on two central tenets. The first is an emphasis on the importance of guaranteeing individual freedom and self-expression. As John Stuart Mill put it,

> The sole end for which mankind are warranted, individually or collectively, in interfering with the liberty of action of any of their number is self-protection . . . The only purpose for which power can be rightfully exercised over any member of a civilized community, against his will, is to prevent harm to others. His own good, either physical or moral, is not a sufficient warrant. . . .

The only part of the conduct of any one, for which he is amenable to society, is that which concerns others. In the part which merely concerns himself, his independence is, of right, absolute. Over himself, over his own body and mind, the individual is sovereign.[6]

The second tenet of individualism is that the welfare of society is best served by letting people pursue their own economic self-interest, as opposed to some collective body (such as government) dictating what is in society's best interest. Or as Adam Smith put it in a famous passage from the *Wealth of Nations*, an individual who intends his own gain is

led by an invisible hand to promote an end which was no part of his intention. Nor is it always worse for the society that it was no part of it. By pursuing his own interest he frequently promotes that of the society more effectually than when he really intends to promote it. I have never known much good done by those who effect to trade for the public good.[7]

The central message of individualism, therefore, is that individual economic and political freedoms are the ground rules on which a society should be based. This puts individualism in direct conflict with collectivism. Collectivism asserts the primacy of the collective over the individual, while individualism asserts just the opposite. This underlying ideological conflict has shaped much of the recent history of the world. The Cold War, for example, was essentially a war between collectivism, championed by the now-defunct Soviet Union, and individualism, championed by the United States.

In practical terms, individualism translates into an advocacy for democratic political systems and free market economics. Viewed this way, we can see that since the late 1980s the waning of collectivism has been matched by the ascendancy of individualism. A wave of democratic ideals and free market economics is sweeping away socialism and communism worldwide. The changes of the past few years go beyond the revolutions in Eastern Europe and the former Soviet Union to include a move toward greater individualism in Latin America and in some of the social democratic states of the West (e.g., Britain and Sweden). This is not to claim that individualism has finally won a long battle with collectivism—it has not—but as a guiding political philosophy, individualism is on the ascendancy. This represents good news for international business, since in direct contrast to collectivism, the pro-business and pro-free trade values of individualism create a favorable environment within which international business can thrive.

Democracy and Totalitarianism

Democracy and totalitarianism are at different ends of a political dimension. **Democracy** refers to a political system in which government is by the people, exercised either directly or through elected representatives. **Totalitarianism** is a form of government in which one person or political party exercises absolute control over all spheres of human life and opposing political parties are prohibited. The democratic–totalitarian dimension is not independent of the collectivism–individualism dimension. Democracy and individualism go hand in hand, as do the communist version of collectivism and totalitarianism. However, gray areas exist; it is possible to have a democratic state where collective values predominate, and it is possible to have a totalitarian state that is hostile to collectivism and in which some degree of individualism—particularly in the economic sphere—is encouraged. For example, Chile in the 1980s was ruled by a totalitarian military dictatorship that encouraged economic freedom but not political freedom.

Democracy

The pure form of democracy, as originally practiced by several city-states in ancient Greece, is based on a belief that citizens should be directly involved in decision making. In complex, advanced societies with populations in the tens or hundreds of millions this is impractical. Most modern democratic states practice what is commonly referred to as **representative democracy**. In a representative democracy, citizens periodically elect individuals to represent them. These elected representatives then form a government, whose function is to make decisions on behalf of the electorate. A representative democracy rests on the assumption that if elected representatives fail to perform this job adequately, they will be voted down at the next election.

To guarantee that elected representatives can be held accountable for their actions by the electorate, an ideal representative democracy has a number of safeguards that are typically enshrined in constitutional law. These include (1) an individual's right to freedom of expression, opinion, and organization; (2) a free media; (3) regular elections in which all eligible citizens are allowed to vote; (4) universal adult suffrage; (5) limited terms for elected representatives; (6) a fair court system that is independent from the political system; (7) a nonpolitical state bureaucracy; (8) a nonpolitical police force and armed service; and (9) relatively free access to state information.[8]

Totalitarianism

In a totalitarian country, all the constitutional guarantees on which representative democracies are built—such as an individual's right to freedom of expression and organization, a free media, and regular elections—are denied to the citizens. In most totalitarian states, political repression is widespread and those who question the right of the rulers to rule find themselves imprisoned, or worse.

Four major forms of totalitarianism exist in the world today. Until recently the most widespread was **communist totalitarianism**. As discussed earlier, communism is a version of collectivism that advocates that socialism can be achieved only through totalitarian dictatorship. Communism, however, is in decline worldwide and many of the old Communist dictatorships have collapsed since 1989. The major exceptions to this trend (so far) are China, Vietnam, Laos, North Korea, and Cuba, although all of these states exhibit clear signs that the Communist Party's monopoly on political power is under attack.

A second form of totalitarianism might be labeled **theocratic totalitarianism**. Theocratic totalitarianism is found in states where political power is monopolized by a party, group, or individual that governs according to religious principles. The most common form of theocratic totalitarianism is based on Islam and is exemplified by states such as Iran and Saudi Arabia. These states restrict not only freedom of political expression but also freedom of religious expression, while the laws of the state are based on Islamic principles.

A third form of totalitarianism might be referred to as **tribal totalitarianism**. Tribal totalitarianism is found principally in African countries such as Zimbabwe, Tanzania, Uganda, and Kenya. The borders of most African states reflect the administrative boundaries drawn by the old European colonial powers, rather than tribal realities. Consequently, the typical African country contains a number of different tribes. Tribal totalitarianism occurs when a political party that represents the interests of a particular tribe (and not always the majority tribe) monopolizes power. Such one-party states still exist in Africa.

A fourth major form of totalitarianism might be described as **right-wing totalitarianism**. Right-wing totalitarianism generally permits individual economic freedom but restricts individual political freedom on the grounds that it would lead to the rise of communism. One common feature of most right-wing dictatorships is an overt hostility to socialist or communist ideas. Many right-wing totalitarian governments are backed by the military, and in some cases the government may be made up of military officers. Until the early 1980s, right-wing dictatorships, many of which were military dictatorships, were common throughout Latin America. They were also found in several Asian countries, particularly South Korea, Taiwan, Singapore, Indonesia, and the Philippines. Since the early 1980s, however, this form of government has been in retreat. The majority of Latin American countries are now genuine multiparty democracies, while significant political freedoms have been granted to the political opposition in countries such as South Korea, Taiwan, and the Philippines.

Economic Systems

It should be clear from the previous section that there is a connection between political ideology and economic systems. In countries where individual goals are given primacy over collective goals, we are more likely to find free market economic systems. In contrast, in countries where collective goals are given preeminence, the state may have taken control over many enterprises, while markets in such countries are likely to be restricted rather than free. More specifically, we can identify four broad types of economic systems—a market economy, a command economy, a mixed economy, and a state-directed economy.

Market Economy

In a pure **market economy** all productive activities are privately owned, as opposed to being owned by the state. The goods and services that a country produces, and the quantity in which they are produced, are not planned by anyone. Rather, production is determined by the interaction of supply and demand and signaled to producers through the price system. If demand for a product exceeds supply, prices will rise, signaling producers to produce more. If supply exceeds demand, prices will fall, signaling producers to produce less. In this system consumers are sovereign. The purchasing patterns of consumers, as signaled to producers through the mechanism of the price system, determine what is produced and in what quantity.

For a market to work in this manner there must be no restrictions on supply. A restriction on supply occurs when a market is monopolized by a single firm. In such circumstances, rather than increase output in response to increased demand, a monopolist might restrict output and let prices rise. This allows the monopolist to take a greater profit margin on each unit it sells. Although this is good for the monopolist, it is bad for the consumer, who has to pay higher prices. Moreover, it is probably bad for the welfare of society. Since, by definition, a monopolist has no competitors, it has no incentive to search for ways of lowering its production costs. Rather, it can simply pass on cost increases to consumers in the form of higher prices. The net result is that the monopolist is likely to become increasingly inefficient, producing high-priced, low-quality goods, while society suffers as a consequence.

Given the dangers inherent in monopoly, the role of government in a market economy is to encourage vigorous competition between private producers. Governments do this by outlawing monopolies and restrictive business practices designed to monopolize a market (antitrust laws serve this function in the United States). Private ownership also encourages vigorous competition and economic efficiency. Private ownership ensures that entrepreneurs have a right to the profits generated by their own efforts. This gives entrepreneurs an incentive to search for better ways of serving consumer needs. That may be through introducing new products, by developing more efficient production processes, by better marketing and after-sale service, or simply through managing their businesses more efficiently than their competitors. In turn, the constant improvement in product and process that results from such an incentive has been argued to have a major positive impact on economic growth and development.[9]

Command Economy

In a pure **command economy**, the goods and services that a country produces, the quantity in which they are produced, and the prices at which they are sold are all *planned* by the government. Consistent with the collectivist ideology, the objective of a command economy is for government to allocate resources for "the good of society." In addition, in a *pure* command economy, all businesses are state owned, the rationale being that the government can then direct them to make investments that are in the best interests of the nation as a whole, rather than in the interests of private individuals.

Historically, command economies were found in communist countries where collectivist goals were given priority over individual goals. Since the demise of communism in the late 1980s, the number of command economies has fallen dramatically. Some elements of a command economy were also evident in a number of democratic nations led by socialist-inclined governments. France and India both experimented with extensive government planning and state ownership, although government planning has fallen into disfavor in both countries.

While the objective of a command economy is to mobilize economic resources for the public good, just the opposite seems to have occurred. In a command economy, state-owned enterprises have little incentive to control costs and be efficient, because they cannot go out of business. Moreover, the abolition of private ownership means there is no incentive for individuals to look for better ways to serve consumer needs; hence, dynamism and innovation are absent from command economies. Instead of growing and becoming more prosperous, such economies tend to be characterized by stagnation.

Mixed Economy

Between market economies and command economies can be found mixed economies. In a **mixed economy**, certain sectors of the economy are left to private ownership and free market mechanisms, while other sectors have significant state ownership and government planning. Mixed economies are relatively common in Western Europe; although they are becoming less so. France, Italy, and Sweden can all be classified as mixed economies. In these countries the governments intervene in those sectors where they believe that private ownership is not in the best interests of society. For example, Britain and Sweden both have extensive state-owned health systems that provide free universal health care to all citizens (it is paid for through higher taxes). In both countries it is felt that government has a moral obligation to provide for the health of its citizens. One consequence is that private ownership of health care operations is very restricted in both countries.

In mixed economies, governments also tend to take into state ownership troubled firms whose continued operation is thought to be vital to national interests. The French automobile company Renault was state owned until recently. The government took over the company when it ran into serious financial problems. The French government reasoned that the social costs of the unemployment that might result if Renault collapsed were unacceptable, so it nationalized the company to save it from bankruptcy. Renault's competitors weren't thrilled by this move, since they had to compete with a company whose costs were subsidized by the state.

State-Directed Economy

A **state-directed economy** is one in which the state plays a significant role in directing the investment activities of private enterprise through "industrial policy" and in otherwise regulating business activity in accordance with national goals. Japan and South Korea are frequently cited as examples of state-directed economies. A state-directed economy differs from a mixed economy in so far as the state does not routinely take private enterprises into public ownership. Instead, it nurtures private enterprise but proactively directs investments made by private firms in accordance with the goals of its industrial policy. For example, in the early 1970s, the Japanese Ministry of International Trade and Industry (MITI) targeted the semiconductor industry as one in which it would like to see Japanese firms have a major presence.[10] Industrial policy often takes the form of state subsidies to private enterprises to encourage them to build significant sales in industries deemed to be of strategic value for the nation's economic development. Thus, the Japanese government subsidized research and development (R&D) investments made by Japanese semiconductor companies. It also used direct administrative pressure to persuade several companies to enter the industry. To help targeted industries develop, the state may also protect them from foreign competition by erecting barriers to imports and foreign direct investment. Accordingly, Japanese semiconductor companies were protected from foreign competition by barriers to imports and restrictions on the ability of foreigners to establish operations in Japan.

The intellectual foundation for a state-directed economy is based on the so-called *infant industry argument* (which we shall review in greater depth in Chapter 5). This argument suggests that in some industries, economies of scale are so large and incumbent firms from developed nations have such an advantage that it is difficult for new firms from developing nations to establish themselves. Industrial policy is seen as a means of overcoming this economic disadvantage. Moreover, it is argued that state-directed industrial policy may allow a country to establish a leading position in an emerging industry where scale economies will ultimately be of great importance (this argument is at the core of the *new trade theory*, which we review in Chapter 4).

One criticism of state-directed economies is that government bureaucrats don't necessarily make better decisions about the allocation of investment capital than the market mechanism would. For a long time, the economic success of countries such as Japan and South Korea allowed advocates of state involvement to dismiss such criticisms.[11] However, a decade of stagnant growth in Japan coupled with the 1997 implosion of the South Korean economy have added legitimacy to these criticisms. The South Korean collapse, in particular, has been widely attributed to uneconomic investments by Korean companies in industries that the government deemed to be of national importance, such as semiconductors.

Legal System

The **legal system** of a country refers to the rules, or laws, that regulate behavior along with the processes by which the laws are enforced and through which redress for grievances is obtained. The legal system of a country is of immense importance to international business. A country's laws regulate business practice, define the manner in which business transactions are to be executed, and set down the rights and obligations of those involved in business transactions. The legal environments of countries differ in significant ways. As we shall see, differences in legal systems can affect the attractiveness of a country as an investment site and/or market.

Like the economic system of a country, the legal system is influenced by the prevailing political system. The government of a country defines the legal framework within which firms do business—and often the laws that regulate business reflect the rulers' dominant political ideology. For example, collectivist-inclined totalitarian states tend to enact laws that severely restrict private enterprise, while the laws enacted by governments in democratic states where individualism is the dominant political philosophy tend to be pro-private enterprise and pro-consumer.

The variances in the structure of law among countries is a massive topic that warrants its own textbook. We do not attempt to give a full description of the variations; rather, we will focus on three issues that illustrate how legal systems can vary—and how such variations can affect international business. First, we look at the laws governing property rights with particular reference to patents, copyrights, and trademarks. Second, we look at laws covering product safety and product liability. Third, we look at country differences in contract law.

Property Rights

In a legal sense the term *property* refers to a resource over which an individual or business holds a legal title; that is, a resource that they own. **Property rights** refer to the bundle of legal rights over the *use* to which a resource is put and over the *use* made of any income that may be derived from that resource.[12] Countries differ significantly in the extent to which their legal system protects property rights. Although almost all countries have laws on their books that protect property rights, the reality is that in many countries these laws are not well enforced by the authorities and property rights are routinely violated. Property rights can be violated in two ways—through private action and through public action.

Private Action

Private action refers to theft, piracy, blackmail, and the like by private individuals or groups. While theft occurs in all countries, in some countries a weak legal system allows for a much higher level of criminal action than in others. An example much in the news of late is Russia where the chaotic legal system of the post-Communist era, coupled with a weak police force and judicial system, offers both domestic and foreign businesses scant protection from blackmail by the "Russian Mafia." Often successful business owners in Russia must pay "protection money" to the Mafia or face violent retribution, including bombings and assassinations (there were around 500 contract killings of businessmen in 1995 and again in 1996).[13] In one example, Ivan Kivelidi, a banker and founder of the Russian Business Roundtable, was murdered by poison applied to the rim of his coffee cup. In another, Vladislav Listiev, the head of Channel 1, Russia's largest nationwide TV network, announced in 1996 that he was going to remove unsavory elements (i.e., Mafia) from the network. Soon afterward he was gunned down by professional assassins outside of his apartment building.[14] And in perhaps the most disturbing case, American businessman Paul Tatum was assassinated in late 1996 after a Moscow hotel joint venture that he was involved in turned sour.[15]

Of course, Russia is not alone in having Mafia problems. The Mafia has a long history in the United States. In Japan, the local version of the Mafia, known as the *yakuza*, runs protection rackets, particularly in the food and entertainment industries.[16] However, there is an enormous difference between the magnitude of such activity in Russia and its limited impact in Japan and the United States. This difference arises because the legal enforcement apparatus, such as the police and court system, is so weak in Russia. Many other countries have problems similar to or even greater than those currently being experienced by Russia. In Somalia during 1993–1994, for example, the breakdown of law and order was so complete that even United Nations food relief convoys proceeding to famine areas under armed guard were held up by bandits.

Public Action

Public action to violate property rights occurs when public officials, such as politicians and government bureaucrats, extort income or resources from property holders. This can be done through a number of mechanisms including levying excessive taxation, requiring expensive licenses or permits from property holders, taking assets into state ownership without compensating the owners (as occurred to the assets of numerous US firms in Iran after the 1979 Iranian revolution), or by demanding bribes from businesses in return for the rights to operate in a country, industry, or location.[17] For example, the government of the late Ferdinand Marcos in the Philippines was famous for demanding bribes from foreign businesses wishing to set up operations in that country.[18]

Another example of such activity surfaced in mid-February 1994 when the British paper *The Sunday Times* ran an article that alleged a 1 billion sterling ($750 million) sale of defense equipment by British companies to Malaysia was secured only after bribes had been paid to Malaysian government officials and after the British Overseas Development Administration (ODA) had agreed to approve a 234 million sterling grant to the Malaysian government for a hydroelectric dam of (according to *The Sunday Times*) dubious economic value. The clear implication was that UK officials, in their enthusiasm to see British companies win a large defense contract, had yielded to pressures from "corrupt" Malaysian officials for bribes—both personal and in the form of the development grant.[19]

The Protection of Intellectual Property

Intellectual property refers to property, such as computer software, a screenplay, a music score, or the chemical formula for a new drug, that is the product of intellectual activity. It is possible to establish ownership rights over intellectual property through patents, copyrights, and trademarks. A **patent** grants the inventor of a new product or process exclusive rights to the manufacture, use, or sale of that invention. **Copyrights** are the exclusive legal rights of authors, composers, playwrights, artists, and publishers to publish and disperse their work as they see fit. **Trademarks** are designs and names, often officially registered, by which merchants or manufacturers designate and differentiate their products (e.g., Christian Dior clothes).

The philosophy behind intellectual property laws is to reward the originator of a new invention, book, musical record, clothes design, restaurant chain, and the like, for his or her idea and effort. Such laws are a very important stimulus to innovation and creative work. They provide an incentive for people to search for novel ways of doing things and they reward creativity. For example, consider innovation in the pharmaceutical industry. A patent will grant the inventor of a new drug a 17-year monopoly in production of that drug. This gives pharmaceutical firms an incentive to undertake the expensive, difficult, and time-consuming basic research required to generate new drugs (on average it costs $150 million in R&D and takes 12 years to get a new drug on the market). Without the guarantees provided by patents, it is unlikely that companies would commit themselves to extensive basic research.[20]

The protection of intellectual property rights differs greatly from country to country. While many countries have stringent intellectual property regulations on their books, the *enforcement* of these regulations has often been lax. This has been the case even among some countries that have signed important international agreements to protect intellectual property, such as the **Paris Convention for the Protection of Industrial Property**, which 96 countries are party to. Weak enforcement encourages the piracy of intellectual property. China and Thailand have recently been among the worst offenders in Asia. Local bookstores in China commonly maintain a section that is off-limits to foreigners; it ostensibly is reserved for sensitive political literature, but it more often displays illegally copied textbooks. Pirated computer software is also widely available in China. Similarly, the streets of Bangkok, the capital of Thailand, are lined with stands selling pirated copies of Rolex watches, Levi blue jeans, videotapes, and computer software.

The computer software industry suffers more than most from lax enforcement of intellectual property rights. Estimates suggest that violations of intellectual property rights cost computer software companies revenues equal to $12.3 billion in 1994, $13.3 billion in 1995, and $11.2 billion in 1996.[21] According to the Business Software Alliance, a software industry association, in 1996 43 percent of all software applications used in the world were pirated. The worst region was Eastern Europe, where the piracy rate was 80 percent. This was followed by piracy rates of 79 percent in the Middle East, 68 percent in Latin America, 55 percent in Asia, 43 percent in Western Europe, and 28 percent in North America. One of the worst countries was China, where the piracy rate in 1996 ran 96 percent and cost the industry $704 million in lost sales, up from $444 million in 1995.[22]

Music recordings represent another area where piracy is rampant. According to one estimate, nearly 200 million illegal compact disks are stamped each year, almost 60 percent of them in China. The International Federation of the Phonographic Industry claims that its members lose $2.2 billion annually to pirates.[23]

International businesses have a number of possible responses to such violations. Firms can lobby their respective governments to push for international agreements to ensure that intellectual property rights are protected and that the law is enforced. An example of such lobbying is given in the next Management Focus, which looks at how Microsoft prompted the US government to start insisting that other countries abide by stricter intellectual property laws.

MANAGEMENT FOCUS
Microsoft Battles Software Piracy in China

Microsoft, the world's biggest personal computer software company, developed MS-DOS and then Windows, respectively, the operating system and graphical user interface that now reside on over 90 percent of the world's personal computers. In addition, Microsoft has a slew of best-selling applications software, including its word processing program (Microsoft Word), spreadsheet program (Excel), and presentation program (PowerPoint). An integral part of Microsoft's international strategy has been expansion into mainland China, where 3.2 million personal computers were sold in 1997, a number that was expected to grow by at least 1 million per year through the rest of the decade. With a population of 1.5 billion, China represents a potentially huge market for Microsoft.

Microsoft's initial goal is to build up Chinese sales from nothing in 1994 to $100 million by 2000. However, before the company can achieve this goal, it has to overcome a very serious obstacle: software piracy. Over 96 percent of the software used in China in 1996 was pirated. Microsoft is a prime target of this activity. Most Microsoft products used in China are illegal copies. China's government is believed to be one of the worst offenders. Microsoft's lawyers complain that Beijing doesn't budget for software purchases, forcing its cash-strapped bureaucracy to find cheap software

solutions. Thus, Microsoft claims, much of the government ends up using pirated software.

To make matters worse, China is becoming a mass exporter of counterfeit software. Microsoft executives don't have to go far to see the problem. Just a few blocks from the company's Hong Kong office is a tiny shop that offers CD-ROMs, each crammed with dozens of computer programs that collectively are worth about $20,000. The asking price is about 500 Hong Kong dollars, or $52! In further evidence of the problem, Hong Kong customs seized a shipment of 2,200 such disks en route from China to Belgium.

Microsoft officials are quick to point out the problem arises because Chinese judicial authorities do not enforce their own laws. Microsoft found this out when it first tried to use China's judicial system to sue software pirates. Microsoft pressed officials in China's southern province of Guangdong to raid a manufacturer that was producing counterfeit holograms that Microsoft used to authenticate its software manuals. The Chinese authorities prosecuted the manufacturer, acknowledged that a copyright violation had occurred, but awarded Microsoft only $2,600 and fined the pirate company $3,000! Microsoft is appealing the verdict and is requesting $20 million in damages.

Partly as a result of such actions, international laws are being strengthened. As we shall see in Chapter 5, the most recent world trade agreement, which was signed in 1994 by 117 countries, for the first time extends the scope of the **General Agreement on Tariffs and Trade (GATT)** to cover intellectual property. Under the new agreement, as of 1995 a council of the newly created **World Trade Organization (WTO)** is overseeing enforcement of much stricter intellectual property regulations. These regulations oblige WTO members to grant and enforce patents lasting at least 20 years and copyrights lasting 50 years. Rich countries had to comply with the rules within a year. Poor countries, in which such protection generally was much weaker, had 5 years' grace, and the very poorest have 10 years.[24] (For further details, see Chapter 5.)

One problem with these new regulations, however, is that the world's biggest violator—China—is not yet a member of the WTO and is therefore not obliged to adhere to the agreement. However, following pressure from the US government, which included the threat of substantial trade sanctions, in 1996 the Chinese government agreed to enforce its existing intellectual property rights regulations (in China, as in many countries, the problem is not a lack of laws; the problem is that existing laws are not enforced). During 1996 Chinese officials closed 19 counterfeit

http://www.microsoft.com

Another Microsoft response to the problem has been to reduce the price on its software in order to compete with pirated versions. In October 1994 Microsoft reduced the price on its Chinese software by as much as 200 percent. However, this action may have little impact, for the programs are still priced at $100 to $200, compared to $5 to $20 for an illegal copy of the same software.

Yet another tactic adopted by the company has been to lobby the US government to pressure Chinese authorities to start enforcing their own laws. As part of its lobbying effort, Microsoft has engaged in its own version of "guerrilla warfare," digging through trash bins, paying locals to spy, even posing as money-grubbing businessmen to collect evidence of piracy, which they have then passed on to US trade officials. The tactic has worked because the US government currently has some leverage over China. China wishes to join the World Trade Organization and views US support as crucial. The United States has said it will not support Chinese membership unless China starts enforcing its intellectual property laws. This demand was backed up by a threat to impose tariffs of $1.08 billion on Chinese exports unless China agreed to stricter enforcement. After a tense period during which both countries were at loggerheads, the Chinese backed down and acquiesced to US demands in February 1995. The Chinese government agreed to start enforcing its intellectual property rights laws, to crack down on factories that the United States identified as pirating US goods, to respect US trademarks including Microsoft's, and to instruct Chinese government ministries to stop using pirated software.

Whether this agreement will make a difference remains to be seen. Microsoft, however, is taking no chances. The company announced it would work with the Chinese Ministry of Electronics to develop a Chinese version of the Windows 95 operating system. Microsoft's logic is that the best way to stop the Chinese government from using pirated software is to go into business with it. Once the government has a stake in maximizing sales of legitimate Microsoft products, the company reckons it will also have a strong incentive to crack down on sales of counterfeit software.*

*Sources: S. Bilello, "US Wages War on China's Pirates," *Newsday*, February 7, 1995, p. A41; (2) C. S. Smith, "Microsoft May Get Help in China from its Uncle Sam," *Wall Street Journal*, November 21, 1994, p. B4; "Making War on China's Pirates," *The Economist*, February 11, 1995, pp. 33–34; interviews with Microsoft officials; M. O'Neill, "Microsoft Chairman Says China Has Key Future Role," *South China Morning Post*, December 12, 1997, p. 1; and "Intellectual Property: Bazaar Software," *The Economist*, March 8, 1997, pp. 77–78.

CD-ROM factories with a capacity of 30 to 50 million units a year. Still, according to the Business Software Alliance, a further 21 counterfeit CD-ROM factories were operating in China as of late 1996.[25]

In addition to lobbying their governments, firms may want to stay out of countries where intellectual property laws are lax, rather than risk having their ideas stolen by local entrepreneurs (such reasoning partly underlay decisions by Coca-Cola and IBM to pull out of India in the early 1970s). Firms also need to be on the alert to ensure that pirated copies of their products produced in countries where intellectual property laws are lax do not turn up in their home market or in third countries. The US computer software giant Microsoft, for example, discovered that pirated Microsoft software, produced illegally in Thailand, was being sold worldwide as the real thing (including in the United States). In addition, Microsoft has encountered significant problems with pirated software in China, the details of which are discussed in the Management Focus.

Product Safety and Product Liability

Product safety laws set certain safety standards to which a product must adhere. Product liability involves holding a firm and its officers responsible when a product causes injury, death, or damage. Product liability can be much greater if a product does not conform to required safety standards. There are both civil and criminal product liability laws. Civil laws call for payment and money damages. Criminal liability laws result in fines or imprisonment. Both civil and criminal liability laws are probably more extensive in the United States than in any other country, although many other Western nations also have comprehensive liability laws. Liability laws are typically least extensive in less developed nations.

In the United States a boom in product liability suits and awards resulted in a dramatic increase in the cost of liability insurance. In turn, many business executives argue that the high costs of liability insurance are making American businesses less competitive in the global marketplace. This view was supported by the Bush administration. Former Vice President Dan Quayle once argued that the United States has too many lawyers and that product liability awards are too large. According to Quayle, the result is that product liability insurance rates are typically much lower overseas, thereby giving foreign firms a competitive advantage. In the United States, tort costs amount to about 2.4 percent of gross national product (GNP), three times as much as in any other industrialized country. So the cost of lawsuits does seem to put America at a competitive disadvantage.[26]

In addition to the competitiveness issue, country differences in product safety and liability laws raise an important ethical issue for firms doing business abroad. When product safety laws are tougher in a firm's home country than in a foreign country and/or when liability laws are more lax, should a firm doing business in that foreign country follow the more relaxed local standards or should it adhere to the standards of its home country? While the ethical thing to do is undoubtedly to adhere to home-country standards, firms have been known to take advantage of lax safety and liability laws to do business in a manner that would not be allowed back home.

Contract Law

A contract is a document that specifies the conditions under which an exchange is to take place and details the rights and obligations of the parties involved. Many business transactions are regulated by some form of contract. Contract law is the body of law that governs contract enforcement. The parties to an agreement normally resort to contract law when one party feels the other has violated either the letter or the spirit of an agreement.

Contract law can differ significantly across countries, and as such it affects the kind of contracts an international business will want to use to safeguard its position should a contract dispute arise. The main differences can be traced to differences in legal tradition. Two main legal traditions are found in the world today—the **common law system** and the **civil law system**. The common law system evolved in England over hundreds of years. It is now found in most of Britain's former colonies, including the United States. Common law is based on tradition, precedent, and custom. When law courts interpret common law, they do so with regard to these characteristics. Civil law is based on a very detailed set of laws organized into codes. Among other things, these codes define the laws that govern business transactions. When law courts interpret civil law, they do so with regard to these codes. Over 80 countries, including Germany, France, Japan, and Russia, operate with a civil law system. Since common law tends to be relatively ill-specified, contracts drafted under a common law framework tend to be very detailed with all contingencies spelled out. In civil law systems, however, contracts tend to be much shorter and less specific, because many of the issues typically covered in a common law contract are already covered in a civil code.

The Determinants of Economic Development

The political, economic, and legal systems of a country can have a profound impact on the level of economic development and hence on the attractiveness of a country as a possible market and/or production location for a firm. Here we look first at how countries differ in their level of development. Then we look at how political economy affects economic progress.

Differences in Economic Development

Different countries have dramatically different levels of economic development. One common measure of economic development is a country's gross national product per head of population. GNP is often regarded as a yardstick for the economic activity of a country; it measures the total value of the goods and services produced annually. Map 2.1 summarizes the GNP per capita of the world's nations in 1997. As can be seen, countries such as Japan, Sweden, Switzerland, and the United States are among the richest on this measure, while the large countries of China and India are among the poorest. Japan, for example, had a 1997 GNP per head of $37,850, whereas China achieved only $860, and India $390. The world's poorest country, Mozambique, had a GNP per head of only $90, while the world's richest, Switzerland, came in at $44,320.[27]

However, GNP per head figures can be misleading because they don't take into account differences in the cost of living. For example, although the 1997 GNP per head of Switzerland, at $44,320, exceeded that of the United States, which was $28,740, the higher cost of living in Switzerland meant that American citizens could actually afford more goods and services than Swiss citizens. To account for differences in the cost of living, one can adjust GNP per capita to account for differences in purchasing power. Referred to as a purchasing power parity (PPP) adjustment, this adjustment allows for a more direct comparison of living standards in different countries. The base for the adjustment is the cost of living in the United States. Table 2.1 gives the GNP per capita measured at PPP in 1997 for a selection of countries, along with their GNP per capita and their growth rate in GNP over the 1990–1997 time period. Map 2.2 summarizes the GNP per capita in 1997 for the nations of the world.

As can be seen, there are striking differences between the standard of living in different countries. Table 2.1 suggests that the average Indian citizen can afford to consume only 5.9 percent of the goods and services consumed by the average US citizen. Given this, one might conclude that, despite having a population of close to one billion, India is unlikely to be a very lucrative market for the consumer products produced by many Western international businesses. However, this is not quite the correct conclusion to draw, for India has a fairly wealthy middle class, despite its large number of very poor people.

Table 2.1:

PPP Index and GNP Data for Selected Countries

Country	GNP per Capita 1997 (US $)	GNP per Capita, Measured at PPP, 1997 (US $)	Annual Average Growth in GDP, 1990–97 (%)
Mozambique	90	520	6.9%
India	390	1,650	5.9%
China	860	3,570	11.9%
Indonesia	1,110	3,450	7.5%
Romania	1,420	4,290	0.0%
Russia	2,740	4,190	−9.0%
Mexico	3,680	8,120	1.8%
Brazil	4,720	6,240	3.1%
S. Korea	10,550	13,500	7.2%
United Kingdom	20,710	20,520	1.9%
Australia	20,540	20,170	3.7%
Canada	19,290	21,860	2.1%
Singapore	32,940	29,000	8.5%
United States	28,740	28,740	2.5%
Japan	37,850	23,400	1.4%
Switzerland	44,320	26,320	−0.1%

Source: World Bank. *World Development Report 1998/99.* Tables 1, 11. Oxford: Oxford University Press, 1999.

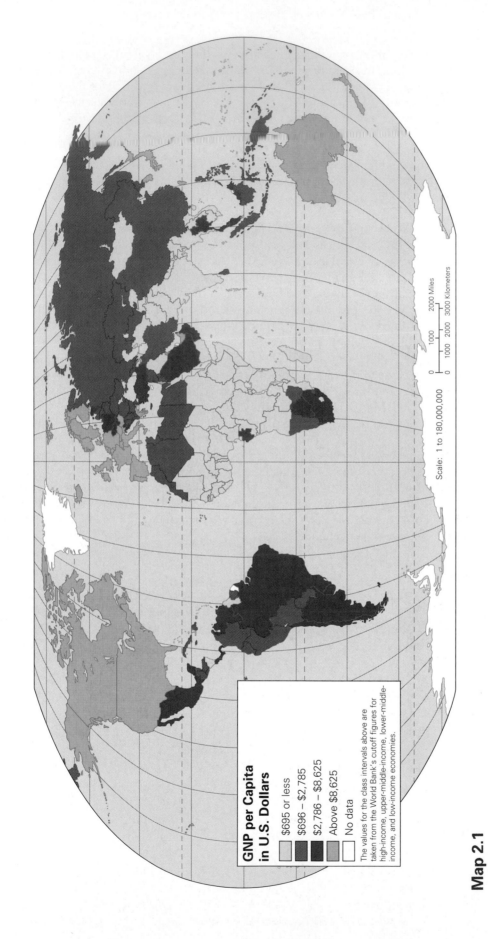

Map 2.1

Gross National Product per Capita, 1997

GNP per Capita in U.S. Dollars

- $695 or less
- $696 – $2,785
- $2,786 – $8,625
- Above $8,625
- No data

The values for the class intervals above are taken from the World Bank's cutoff figures for high-income, upper-middle-income, lower-middle-income, and low-income economies.

Scale: 1 to 180,000,000

0   1000   2000 Miles
0 1000 2000 3000 Kilometers

Source: GNP per Head 1995. Map 30, "Gross National Product per Capita," John L. Allen, *Student Atlas of World Geography*, Dushkin/McGraw-Hill, 1999, p. 49.

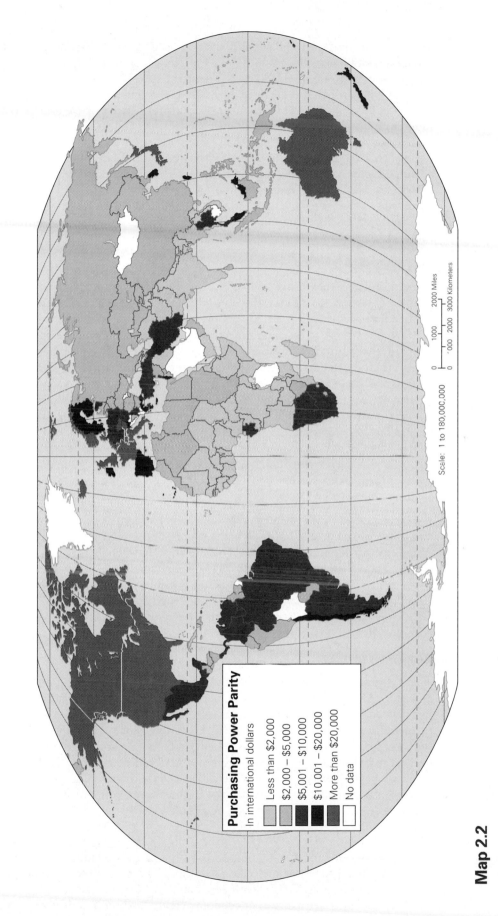

Purchasing Power Parity

In international dollars

- Less than $2,000
- $2,000 – $5,000
- $5,001 – $10,000
- $10,001 – $20,000
- More than $20,000
- No data

Scale: 1 to 180,000,000

Map 2.2

Purchasing Power Parity in 1997

Source: Purchasing Power Parity. Map 38, John Allen, *Student Atlas of World Geography*, Dushkin/McGraw-Hill, 1999, p. 57.

A problem with the GNP and PPP data discussed so far is that they give a static picture of development. They tell us, for example, that China is much poorer than the US, but they do not tell us if China is closing the gap. To assess this, we have to look at the economic growth rates achieved by different countries. Table 2.1 gives the rate of growth in GNP achieved by a number of countries between 1990 and 1997. Map 2.3 summarizes the growth rate in GNP over the 1990–97 time period. Although countries such as China and India are currently very poor, their economies are growing more rapidly than those of many advanced nations. Thus, in time they may become advanced nations themselves and be huge markets for the products of international businesses. Given their future potential, it may well be good advice for international businesses to start getting a foothold in these markets now. Even though their current contributions to an international firm's revenues might be small, their future contributions could be much larger. One might also note, however, that Table 2.1 tells us that the economy of Russia shrank substantially over the 1990–97 time period.

A number of other indicators can also be used to assess a country's economic development and its likely future growth rate. These include literacy rates, the number of people per doctor, infant mortality rates, life expectancy, calorie (food) consumption per head, car ownership per 1,000 people, and education spending as a percentage of GNP. In an attempt to estimate the impact of such factors upon the quality of life in a country, the United Nations has developed a **Human Development Index**. This index is based upon three measures: life expectancy, literacy rates, and whether average incomes, based on PPP estimates, are sufficient to meet the basic needs of life in a country (adequate food, shelter, and health care). The Human Development Index is scaled from 0 to 100. Countries scoring less than 50 are classified as having low human development (the quality of life is poor), those scoring from 50–80 are classified as having medium human development, while those countries that score above 80 are classified as having high human development. Map 2.4 summarizes the Human Development Index scores for 1995, the most recent year for which data is available.

Political Economy and Economic Progress

It is often argued that a country's economic development is a function of its economic and political systems. What then is the nature of the relationship between political economy and economic progress? This question has been the subject of a vigorous debate among academics and policymakers for some time. Despite the long debate, this remains a question for which it is not possible to give an unambiguous answer. However, it is possible to untangle the main threads of the academic arguments and make a few broad generalizations as to the nature of the relationship between political economy and economic progress.

Innovation Is the Engine of Growth

There is general agreement now that innovation is the engine of long-run economic growth.[28] Those who make this argument define **innovation** broadly to include not just new products, but also new processes, new organizations, new management practices, and new strategies. Thus, Toys "R" Us's strategy of establishing large warehouse-style toy stores and then engaging in heavy advertising and price discounting to sell the merchandise can be classified as an innovation because Toys "R" Us was the first company to pursue this strategy. One can conclude that if a country's economy is to sustain long-run economic growth, the business environment within that country must be conducive to the production of innovations.

Innovation Requires a Market Economy

This leads logically to a further question—What is required for the business environment of a country to be conducive to innovation? Those who have considered this issue highlight the advantages of a market economy.[29] It has been argued that the economic freedom associated with a market economy creates greater incentives for innovation

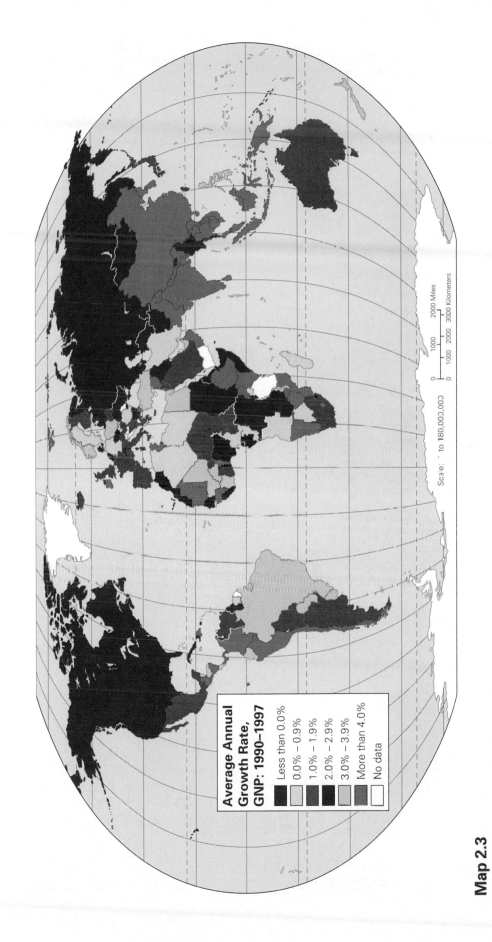

Map 2.3

Growth in Gross National Product, 1990–97

Source: Economic Growth. Map 31, John L. Allen, *Student Atlas of World Geography*, Dushkin/McGraw-Hill. 1999, p. 50.

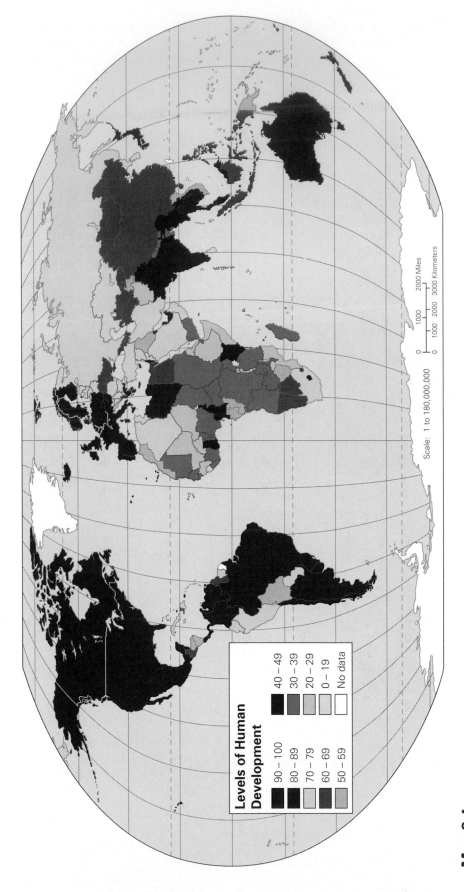

Legend (Levels of Human Development):
- 90 – 100
- 80 – 89
- 70 – 79
- 60 – 69
- 50 – 59
- 40 – 49
- 30 – 39
- 20 – 29
- 0 – 19
- No data

Scale: 1 to 180,000,000

Map 2.4

The Human Development Index, 1995

Source: Quality of Life: The Human Development Index. Map 28, John Allen, *Student Atlas of World Geography*, Dushkin/McGraw-Hill, 1999, p. 46. Data are from "Human Development Report 1998" by the United Nations Development Programme. Copyright 1998 by the United Nations Development Programme. Used by permission of Oxford University Press, Inc.

than either a planned or a mixed economy. In a market economy, any individual who has an innovative idea is free to try to make money out of that idea by starting a business (by engaging in entrepreneurial activity). Similarly, existing businesses are free to improve their operations through innovation. To the extent that they are successful, both individual entrepreneurs and established businesses can reap rewards in the form of high profits. Thus, in market economies there are enormous incentives to develop innovations.

In contrast, in a planned economy the state owns all means of production. Consequently there is no opportunity for entrepreneurial individuals to develop valuable new innovations, since it is the state, rather than the individual, that captures all the gains. The lack of economic freedom and incentives for innovation was probably a main factor in the economic stagnation of so many former communist states and led ultimately to their collapse at the end of the 1980s. A similar stagnation phenomenon occurred in many mixed economies in those sectors where the state had a monopoly (such as health care and telecommunications in Britain). This stagnation provided the impetus for the widespread privatization of state-owned enterprises that we witnessed in many mixed economies during the mid-1980s and is still going on today (**privatization** refers to the process of selling state-owned enterprises to private investors).

A recent study of 102 countries over a 20-year period provided compelling evidence of a strong relationship between economic freedom (as provided by a market economy) and economic growth.[30] The study found that the more economic freedom a country had between 1975 and 1995, the more economic growth it achieved and the richer its citizens became. The six countries that had persistently high ratings of economic freedom during the 1975–1995 period (Hong Kong, Switzerland, Singapore, the United States, Canada, and Germany) were also all in the top 10 in terms of economic growth rates. In contrast, no country with a persistently low rating achieved a respectable growth rate. For the 16 countries for which the index of economic freedom declined the most during the 1975–95 period, average annual gross domestic product *fell* at an annual rate of 0.6 percent.

Innovation Requires Strong Property Rights

Strong legal protection of property rights is another requirement for a business environment to be conducive to innovation and economic growth.[31] Both individuals and businesses must be given the opportunity to profit from innovative ideas. Without strong property rights protection, businesses and individuals run the risk that the profits from their innovative efforts will be expropriated, either by criminal elements, or by the state itself. The state can expropriate the profits from innovation through legal means, such as excessive taxation, or through illegal means, such as demands from state bureaucrats for kickbacks in return for granting an individual or firm a license to do business in a certain area. According to the Nobel prize-winning economist Douglass North, throughout history many governments have displayed a tendency to engage in such behavior. Inadequately enforced property rights reduce the incentives for innovation and entrepreneurial activity—since the profits from such activity are "stolen"—and hence reduce the rate of economic growth.

The Required Political System

There is a great deal of debate as to the kind of political system that best achieves a functioning market economy where there is strong protection for property rights.[32] We in the West tend to associate a representative democracy with a market economic system, strong property rights protection, and economic progress. Building on this, we tend to argue that democracy is good for growth.[33] However, some totalitarian regimes have fostered a market economy and strong property rights protection and have experienced rapid economic growth. Four of the fastest-growing economies of the last 30 years—South Korea, Taiwan, Singapore, and Hong Kong—all have grown faster than the Western democracies. All these economies had one thing in common at the start of their economic growth: undemocratic governments! At the same time, there are examples of countries with stable democratic governments, such as India, where economic growth remained sluggish for long periods.

In 1992, Lee Kuan Yew, Singapore's leader for many years, told an audience, "I do not believe that democracy necessarily leads to development. I believe that a country needs to develop discipline more than democracy. The exuberance of democracy leads to undisciplined and disorderly conduct which is inimical to development."[34] Others have argued that many of the current problems in Eastern Europe and the states of the former Soviet Union arose because democracy arrived before economic reform, making it more difficult for elected governments to introduce the policies that, while painful in the short run, were needed to promote rapid economic growth. It has become something of a cliché to argue that Russia got its political and economic reforms in the wrong order—unlike China, which maintains a totalitarian government but has moved rapidly toward a market economy.

However, those who argue for the value of a totalitarian regime miss an important point: if dictators made countries rich, then much of Africa, Asia, and Latin America should have been growing rapidly for the past 40 years, and this has not been the case. Only a certain kind of totalitarian regime is capable of promoting economic growth. It must be a dictatorship that is committed to a free market system and strong protection of property rights. Moreover, there is no guarantee that a dictatorship will continue to pursue such progressive policies. Dictators are rarely so benevolent. Many are tempted to use the apparatus of the state to further their own private ends, violating property rights and stalling economic growth. Given this, it seems likely democratic regimes are far more conducive to long-term economic growth than are dictatorships, even benevolent ones. Only in a well-functioning, mature democracy are property rights truly secure.[35]

Economic Progress Begets Democracy

While it is possible to argue that democracy is not a necessary precondition for establishment of a free market economy in which property rights are protected, subsequent economic growth often leads to establishment of a democratic regime. Several of the fastest-growing Asian economies have recently adopted more democratic governments, including South Korea and Taiwan. Thus, while democracy may not always be the cause of initial economic progress, it seems to be one consequence of that progress.

A strong belief that economic progress leads to adoption of a democratic regime underlies the fairly permissive attitude that many Western governments have adopted toward human rights violations in China. Although China has a totalitarian government in which human rights are abused, many Western countries have been hesitant to criticize the country too much for fear that this might hamper the country's march toward a free market system. The belief is that once China has a free market system, democracy will follow. Whether this optimistic vision comes to pass remains to be seen. Nevertheless, such a vision was an important factor in the US government's 1996 decision to grant China most favored nation trading status (which makes it easier for Chinese firms to sell products in the United States) despite reports of widespread human rights abuses in China.

Other Determinants of Development: Geography and Education

While a country's political and economic system is probably the big locomotive driving its rate of economic development, other factors are also important. One that has received attention recently is geography.[36] But the belief that geography can influence economic policy, and hence economic growth rates, goes back to Adam Smith. The influential Harvard University economist Jeffrey Sachs argues that

Throughout history, coastal states, with their long engagements in international trade, have been more supportive of market institutions than landlocked states, which have tended to organize themselves as hierarchical (and often military) societies. Mountainous states, as a result of physical isolation, have often neglected market-based trade. Temperate climes have generally supported higher densities of population and thus a more extensive division of labor than tropical regions.[37]

Sachs's point is that by virtue of favorable geography, certain societies were more likely to engage in trade than others and were thus more likely to be open to and develop market-based economic systems, which in turn would promote faster economic growth. He also argues that, irrespective of the economic and political institutions a country adopts, adverse geographical conditions, such as the high rate of disease, poor soils, and hostile climate that afflict many tropical countries, can have a negative impact on development.

Together with colleagues at Harvard's Institute for International Development, Sachs tested for the impact of geography on a country's economic growth rate between 1965 and 1990. He found that landlocked countries grew more slowly than coastal economies and that being entirely landlocked reduced a country's annual growth rate by roughly 0.7 percent per year. He also found that tropical countries grew 1.3 percent more slowly each year than countries in the temperate zone.

Education emerges as another important determinant of economic development. The general assertion is that nations that invest more in education will have higher growth rates because an educated population is a more productive population. Some rather striking anecdotal evidence suggests this is the case. In 1960 Pakistanis and South Koreans were on equal footing economically. However, just 30 percent of Pakistani children were enrolled in primary schools, while 94 percent of South Koreans were. By the mid-1980s, South Korea's GNP per person was three times that of Pakistan's.[38] More generally, a survey of 14 statistical studies that looked at the relationship between a country's investment in education and its subsequent growth rates concluded investment in education did have a positive and statistically significant impact on a country's rate of economic growth.[39] Similarly, the recent work by Sachs discussed above suggests that investments in education help explain why some countries in Southeast Asia, such as Indonesia, Malaysia, and Singapore, have been able to overcome the disadvantages associated with their tropical geography and grow far more rapidly than tropical nations in Africa and Latin America.

States in Transition

Since the late 1980s there have been major changes in the political economy of many of the world's nation-states. Two trends have been evident. First, during the late 1980s and early 1990s, a wave of democratic revolutions swept the world. Totalitarian governments collapsed and were replaced by democratically elected governments that were typically more committed to free market capitalism than their predecessors had been. The change was most dramatic in Eastern Europe, where the collapse of communism bought an end to the Cold War and led to the breakup of the Soviet Union, but similar changes were occurring throughout the world during the same period. Across much of Asia, Latin America, and Africa there was a marked shift toward greater democracy. Second, there has been a strong move away from centrally planned and mixed economies and toward a more free market economic model. We shall look first at the spread of democracy and then turn our attention to the spread of free market economics.

The Spread of Democracy

One notable development of the past 15 years has been the spread of democracy (and by extension, the decline of totalitarianism). Map 2.5 reports data on the extent of totalitarianism in the world as determined by Freedom House.[40] This map charts political freedom in 1997, on a scale from 1 for the highest degree of political freedom to 7 for the lowest. Among the criteria that Freedom House uses to determine ratings for political freedom are the following:

- Free and fair elections of the head of state and legislative representatives.
- Fair electoral laws, equal campaigning opportunities, and fair polling.
- The right to organize into different political parties.
- A parliament with effective power.
- A significant opposition that has a realistic chance of gaining power.
- Freedom from domination by the military, foreign powers, totalitarian parties, religious hierarchies, or any other powerful group.
- A reasonable amount of self-determination for cultural, ethnic, and religious minorities.

Factors contributing to a low rating (i.e., to totalitarianism) include military or foreign control, the denial of self-determination to major population groups, a lack of decentralized political power, and an absence of democratic elections.

The number of democracies in the world has increased from 69 nations in 1987 to 118 today, the highest total in history. Almost 55 percent of the world's population now lives under democratic rule. Many of these new democracies are to be found in Eastern Europe and Latin America, although there have also been some notable gains in Africa during this time period, such as in South Africa.

There are three main reasons for the spread of democracy.[41] First, many totalitarian regimes failed to deliver economic progress to the vast bulk of their populations. The collapse of communism in Eastern Europe, for example, was precipitated by the growing gulf between the vibrant and wealthy economies of the West and the stagnant economies of the Communist East. In looking for alternatives to the socialist model, the populations of these countries could not have failed to notice that most of the world's strongest economies were governed by representative democracies. Today, the economic success of many of the newer democracies, such as Poland and the Czech Republic in the former Communist bloc, the Philippines and Taiwan in Asia, and Chile in Latin America, has helped strengthen the case for democracy as a key component of successful economic advancement.

Second, new information and communications technologies, including shortwave radio, satellite television, fax machines, desktop publishing, and now the Internet, have broken down the ability of the state to control access to uncensored information. These technologies have created new conduits for the spread of democratic ideals and information from free societies. The 1989 collapse of East Germany's Communist government was in part due to unrest among a population who for years had been exposed via TV to the affluent lifestyles of West Germans. Today the Internet is allowing democratic ideals to penetrate closed societies as never before. In response, some governments have tried to restrict citizens' access to the Internet; for example, China limits access to government employees and those affiliated with universities.[42]

Third, in many countries the economic advances of the last quarter century have led to the emergence of increasingly prosperous middle and working classes who have pushed for democratic reforms. This was certainly a factor in the democratic transformation of South Korea. Entrepreneurs and other business leaders, eager to protect their property rights and ensure the dispassionate enforcement of contracts, are another force pressing for more accountable and open government.

Having said this, it would be naive to conclude that the global spread of democracy will continue unchallenged. There have been several reversals. In the former Soviet republic of Belarus, for example, the president, Alexander Lukashenko, dissolved a democratically elected parliament and harassed the press. In the African nation of Niger, a military coup deposed a democratically elected government. In

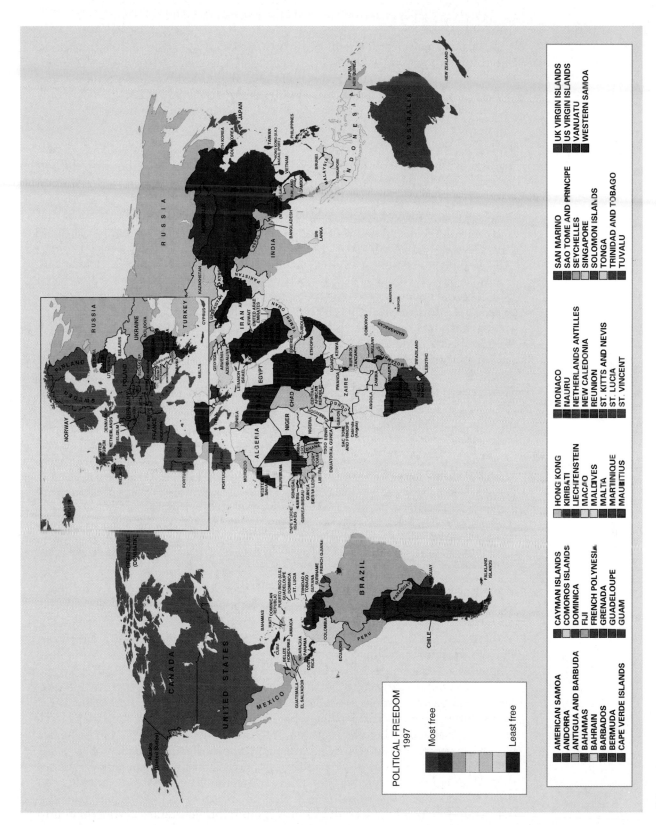

Map 2.5

Political Freedom in 1997

Source: Map data from *Freedom Review 28*, no. 1, p. 26.

Asia, Singapore's Lee Kuan Yew and China's Marxist–Leninist leaders continue to advocate the virtues of authoritarian paths to democracy and to denounce Western democracies as an unacceptable model.

Also, democracy is still rare in large parts of the world. In Africa, just 18 nations, one-third of those on the continent, are electoral democracies. Among the 12 countries that are full or associated members of the Commonwealth of Independent States (i.e., the republics of the former Soviet Union minus the Baltic states) there are only four electoral democracies. And there are no democracies in the Arab world.

Universal Civilization or a Clash of Civilizations?

The end of the Cold War and the "new world order" that followed the collapse of communism in Eastern Europe and the former Soviet Union, taken together with the collapse of many authoritarian regimes in Latin America, have given rise to intense speculation about the future shape of global geopolitics. Authors such as Francis Fukuyama have argued that "we may be witnessing . . . the end of history as such: that is, the end point of mankind's ideological evolution and the universalization of Western liberal democracy as the final form of human government."[43] Fukuyama goes on to argue that the war of ideas may be at an end and that liberal democracy has triumphed.

Others have questioned Fukuyama's vision of a more harmonious world dominated by a universal civilization characterized by democratic regimes and free market capitalism. In a controversial book, the influential political scientist Samuel Huntington argues that there is no "universal" civilization based on widespread acceptance of Western liberal democratic ideals.[44] Huntington maintains that while many societies may be modernizing—they are adopting the material paraphernalia of the modern world, from automobiles to Coca-Cola and MTV—they are not becoming more Western. On the contrary, Huntington theorizes that modernization in non-Western societies can result in a retreat toward the traditional, such as the resurgence of Islam in many traditionally Muslim societies:

> The Islamic resurgence is both a product of and an effort to come to grips with modernization. Its underlying causes are those generally responsible for indigenization trends in non-Western societies: urbanization, social mobilization, higher levels of literacy and education, intensified communication and media consumption, and expanded interaction with Western and other cultures. These developments undermine traditional village and clan ties and create alienation and an identity crisis. Islamist symbols, commitments, and beliefs meet these psychological needs, and Islamist welfare organizations, the social, cultural and economic needs of Muslims caught in the process of modernization. Muslims feel a need to return to Islamic ideas, practices, and institutions to provide the compass and the motor of modernization.[45]

Thus, the rise of Islamic fundamentalism is portrayed as a response to the alienation produced by modernization.

In contrast to Fukuyama, Huntington sees a world that is split into different civilizations, each of which has its own value systems and ideology. In addition to Western civilization, Huntington sees the emergence of strong Islamic and Sinic (Chinese) civilizations, as well as civilizations based on Japan, Africa, Latin America, Eastern Orthodox Christianity (Russian), and Hinduism (Indian). Moreover, Huntington sees the civilizations as headed for conflict, particularly along the "fault lines" that separate them, such as Bosnia (where Muslims and Orthodox Christians have clashed), Kashmir (where Muslims and Hindus clash), and the Sudan (where a bloody war between Christians and Muslims has persisted for decades). Figure 2.1 summarizes his views as to which civilizations are most likely to come into conflict in the future. Huntington predicts conflict between the West and Islam, and between the West and China. He bases his predictions on an analysis of the different value systems and ideology of these civilizations, which in his view tend to bring them into conflict with each other.

Figure 2.1

The Global Politics
of Civilizations

Source: Reprinted with permission
from Simon & Schuster, Inc. from
*The Clash of Civilizations and the New
World Order*, by Samuel P.
Huntington (New York) p. 245.
Copyright © 1996 by Samuel P.
Huntington. Reprinted by
permission of Georges Borchardt,
Inc. for the author.

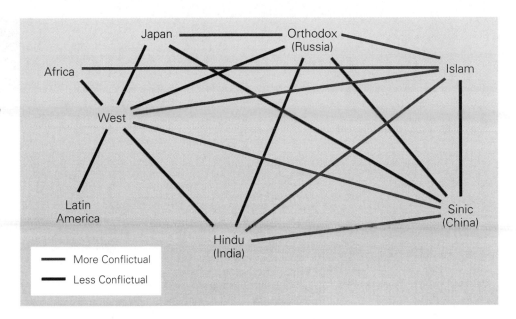

If Huntington's views are even partly correct, they have important implications for international business. They suggest many countries may be increasingly difficult places in which to do business, either because they are shot through with violent conflicts or because they are part of a civilization that is in conflict with an enterprise's home country. Bear in mind, however, that Huntington's views are speculative. It is by no means a sure thing that his predictions will come to pass. More likely is the evolution of a global political system that is positioned somewhere between Fukuyama's universal global civilization based on liberal democratic ideals and Huntington's vision of a fractured world. That would still be a world, however, in which geopolitical forces periodically limit the ability of business enterprises to operate in certain foreign countries.

The Spread of Market-Based Systems

Paralleling the spread of democracy since the 1980s has been the transformation from centrally planned command economies to market-based economies. More than 30 countries that were in the former Soviet Union or the Eastern European Communist bloc are now engaged in changing their economic systems. A complete list of countries would also include Asian states such as China and Vietnam, as well as African countries such as Angola, Ethiopia, and Mozambique.[46] There has been a similar shift away from a mixed economy. Many states in Asia, Latin America, and Western Europe have sold state-owned businesses to private investors (privatization) and deregulated their economies to promote greater competition. India's experience is detailed in the next Country Focus.

The underlying rationale for economic transformation has been the same the world over. In general, command and mixed economies failed to deliver the kind of sustained economic performance that was achieved by countries adopting market-based systems, such as the United States, Switzerland, Hong Kong, and Taiwan. As a consequence, even more states have gravitated toward the market-based model.

Map 2.6, based on data from the Heritage Foundation, a conservative United States research foundation, gives some idea of the degree to which the world has shifted toward market-based economic systems. The Heritage Foundation has constructed an index of economic freedom that is based on 10 indicators such as the extent to which the government intervenes in the economy, trade policy, the degree to which property

COUNTRY FOCUS
The Changing Political Economy of India

After gaining independence from Britain in 1947, India adopted a democratic system of government. However, the economic system that developed in India was a mixed economy characterized by a heavy dose of state enterprise and planning. This system placed major constraints around the growth of the private sector. Private companies could expand only with government permission. Under this system, derisively dubbed the "License Raj," private companies often had to wait months for government approval of routine business activities, such as expanding production or hiring a new director. It could take years to get permission to diversify into a new product. Moreover, much of heavy industry, such as auto, chemical, and steel production, was reserved for state-owned enterprises. The development of a healthy private sector was also stunted by production quotas and high tariffs on imports. Access to foreign exchange was limited, investment by foreign firms was restricted, land use was strictly controlled, and prices were routinely managed by the government, as opposed to being determined by market forces.

By the early 1990s, it was clear that after 40 years of near stagnation, this system was incapable of delivering the kind of economic progress that many Southeastern Asian nations had started to enjoy. By 1994 India's economy was still smaller than Belgium's,

despite having a population of 950 million. Its GDP per head was a paltry $310; less than half the population could read; only 6 million had access to telephones; only 14 percent had access to clean sanitation; the World Bank estimated that some 40 percent of the world's desperately poor lived in India; and only 2.3 percent of the population had a household income in excess of $2,484.

In 1991 the lack of progress led the government of Prime Minister P. V. Narasimha Rao to embark on an ambitious economic reform program. Much of the industrial licensing system was dismantled, and several areas once closed to the private sector were opened up including electricity generation, parts of the oil industry, steelmaking, air transport, and some areas of the telecommunications industry. Foreign investment, formerly allowed in only grudgingly and subject to arbitrary ceilings, was suddenly welcomed. Approval is now automatic for foreign equity stakes of up to 51 percent in an Indian enterprise, and 100 percent foreign ownership is now allowed under certain circumstances. The government announced plans to privatize many of India's state-owned businesses. Raw materials and many industrial goods can now be freely imported, and the maximum tariff that can be levied upon imports has been reduced from 400 percent to 65 percent. The top rate of

rights are protected, foreign investment regulations, and taxation rules. A country can score between 1 (most free) and 5 (least free) on each of these indicators. The lower a country's average score across all 10 indicators, the more closely its economy represents the pure market model. According to the 1998 index, which is summarized in Map 2.3, the world's freest economies are (in rank order) Hong Kong, Singapore, Bahrain, New Zealand, Switzerland, the United States, Luxembourg, Taiwan, and the United Kingdom. By way of comparison, Japan is ranked at 12, France at 34, Indonesia at 65, Poland at 65, Brazil at 90, Russia at 106, India at 120, China at 124, while the command economies of Cuba, Laos, and North Korea prop up the bottom of the rankings.[47]

Economic freedom does not necessarily equate with political freedom, as detailed in Map 2.5. For example, the top three countries in the Heritage Foundation index, Hong Kong, Singapore, and Bahrain, cannot be classified as politically free. Hong Kong was reabsorbed into Communist China in 1997, and the first thing Beijing did was shut down Hong Kong's freely elected legislature. Singapore is ranked as only "partly free" on Freedom House's index of political freedom due to practices such as widespread press censorship, while Bahrain is classified as "least free" due to the monopolization of political power by a hereditary monarchy (see Map 2.2).

http://www.ib-net.com

income tax has also been reduced, and corporate tax has come down from 57.5 percent to 46 percent in 1994 and then to 35 percent in 1997.

Judged by some measures, the response has been impressive. The economy has been expanding at an annual rate of almost 5 percent between 1992 and 1996; exports have begun to grow at a respectable pace (they were up 20 percent between 1993 and 1994); and corporate profits have jumped. Delivery trucks loaded with once-banned foreign products, such as Ruffles potato chips and Nestlé Crunch bars, rumble over India's potholed highways. Advertisements for AT&T's communications solutions can be seen on New Delhi streets, signs of an upcoming liberalization of the telecommunications industry. Moreover, foreign investment, which is a good indicator of foreign companies' perceptions about the health of the Indian economy, has surged from $150 million in 1991 to an estimated $3.5 billion in 1998.

However, India is still short of achieving the kind of free market economic system now found in many Western states. The reform process is being fought by many bureaucrats and politicians. Several Western companies now investing in India have painful memories of the 1970s when India nationalized the assets of foreign companies on terms that were tantamount to confiscation. Such memories are one reason

companies such as IBM, Coca-Cola, and Mobil have kept their investment modest. Other foreign companies have made major investment commitments to India only after securing special guarantees. For example, AES Corporation, a power generating company based in Virginia, concluded a deal to build power stations in India, but only after the Indian government agreed to give guarantees that it would pay for power delivered to Indian electric utilities if the utilities defaulted.

Despite ambitious plans, India's privatization program has proceeded slowly. By 1997 the government had sold equity stakes in about 40 companies to private investors, including state-owned telecommunications, steel, and electronics enterprises. However, India still has around 245 state-owned companies that are engaged in activities ranging from baking bread to making railway carriages. Many outside observers feel that the government needs to accelerate its privatization program if it is to continue to attract foreign capital.

Sources: S. Moshavi, and P. Endarido. "India Shakes off Its Shackles," *Business Week*, January 30, 1995, pp. 48–49; "A Survey of India: The Tiger Steps Out," *The Economist*, January 21, 1995, J. F. Burns, "India Now Winning US Investment," *New York Times*, February 3, 1995, pp. C1, C5; "Tarnished Silver," *The Economist*, September 6, 1997, pp. 64–65; and P. Moore, "Three Steps Forward," *Euromoney*, September 1997, pp. 190–95

The Nature of Economic Transformation

The shift toward a market-based economic system typically entails a number of steps: deregulation, privatization, and creation of a legal system to safeguard property rights. We shall review each before looking at the track record of states engaged in economic transformation.

Deregulation

Deregulation involves removing legal restrictions to the free play of markets, the establishment of private enterprises, and the manner in which private enterprises operate. For example, before the collapse of communism, the governments in most command economies exercised tight control over prices and outputs, setting both through detailed state planning. They also prohibited private enterprises from operating in most sectors of the economy. Deregulation in these cases involved removing price controls, thereby allowing prices to be set by the interplay between demand and supply, and abolishing laws regulating the establishment and operation of private enterprises.

In mixed economies, deregulation has involved abolishing laws that either prohibited private enterprises from competing in certain sectors of the economy or regulated the manner in which they operated. For example, as outlined in the Country Focus

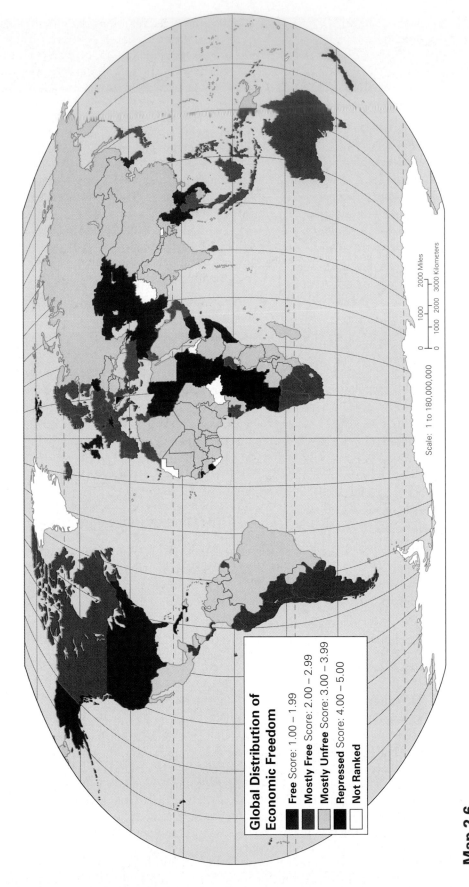

Map 2.6

Global Distribution of Economic Freedom

Scale: 1 to 180,000,000

Global Distribution of Economic Freedom

- Free Score: 1.00 – 1.99
- Mostly Free Score: 2.00 – 2.99
- Mostly Unfree Score: 3.00 – 3.99
- Repressed Score: 4.00 – 5.00
- Not Ranked

Source: Heritage Foundation. *1999 Index of Economic Freedom*. http://www.heritage.org:so/index/countries/maps&charts/list1.gif.

feature on India, deregulation there has involved reforming the industrial licensing system that made it difficult to establish private enterprises, opening up areas that were once closed to the private sector such as electricity generation, parts of the oil industry, steelmaking, air transport, and some areas of the telecommunications industry; and removing restrictions to foreign investment. In another case, the Japanese government is trying to abolish some of the 11,000 regulations and 10,000 administrative guidelines that regulate and restrict private enterprise in that economy. Some of these regulations are very restrictive. For example, if a private enterprise wants to open a retail store with floor space of more than 1,000 square meters, it must first gain the consent of a government advisory panel charged with limiting the influence on the local shops against which the new retail store wants to compete! In addition, the average large retailer must file over 150 documents to gain permission to sell everyday items such as meat, tofu, and electronic appliances. In an effort to unravel such restrictions, the Japanese government plans to deregulate a diverse range of industries including power generation, gasoline retailing, financial services, retail, telecommunications, and transportation.[48] How quickly this can be achieved, however, depends on the ability of a weak government to impose its wishes on Japan's traditionally powerful civil service bureaucracies, which can be expected to resist any attempt to diminish their influence on the economy.

Privatization

Hand in hand with deregulation has come a sharp increase in privatization activity during the 1990s. **Privatization** transfers the ownership of state property into the hands of private individuals, frequently by the sale of state assets through an auction.[49] Privatization is seen as a way to unlock gains in economic efficiency by giving new private owners a powerful incentive—the reward of greater profits—to search for increases in productivity, to enter new markets, and to exit losing ones.

The privatization movement started in Britain in the early 1980s when then-Prime Minister Margaret Thatcher started to sell state-owned assets, such as the British telephone company, British Telecom (BT). In a pattern that has been repeated around the world, this sale was linked with the deregulation of the British telecommunications industry. By allowing other firms to compete head-to-head with BT, deregulation ensured that privatization did not simply replace a state-owned monopoly with a private monopoly.

The opening case to this chapter details the extent of privatization activity in Brazil, and the Country Focus feature discusses privatization in India. As these two examples suggest, privatization has become a worldwide movement. In Africa, for example, Mozambique and Zambia are leading the way with very ambitious privatization plans. Zambia has put over 145 state-owned companies up for sale, while Mozambique has already sold scores of enterprises, ranging from tea plantations to a chocolate factory. The most dramatic privatization programs, however, have occurred in the economies of the former Soviet Union and its Eastern European satellite states. In the Czech Republic, three-quarters of all state-owned enterprises were privatized between 1989 and 1996, helping to push the share of gross domestic product (GDP) accounted for by the private sector up from 11 percent in 1989 to 60 percent in 1995. In Russia, where the private sector had been almost completely repressed before 1989, 50 percent of GDP was in private hands by 1995, again much as a result of privatization. And in Poland the private sector accounted for 59 percent of GDP in 1995, up from 20 percent in 1989.[50] However, Poland also illustrates how far some of these countries still have to travel. Despite an aggressive privatization program, Poland still had 4,000 state-owned enterprises that dominate the heavy industry, mining, and transportation sectors.

Legal Systems

As noted earlier in this chapter, laws protecting private property rights and providing mechanisms for contract enforcement are required for a well-functioning market economy. Without a legal system that protects property rights, and without the machinery to enforce that system, the incentive to engage in economic activity can be reduced substantially by private and public entities—including organized crime—that expropriate the profits generated by the efforts of private-sector entrepreneurs. As noted earlier, this has become a problem in many former Communist states, such as Russia, where organized crime has penetrated deeply into the fabric of many business enterprises. When communism collapsed, many of these countries lacked the legal structure required to protect property rights, all property having been held by the state. Although many states have made big strides toward instituting the required system, it will be many more years before the legal system is functioning as smoothly as it does in the West. For example, in most East European nations, the title to urban and agricultural property is often uncertain because of incomplete and inaccurate records, multiple pledges on the same property, and unsettled claims resulting from demands for restitution from owners in the pre-Communist era. Also, while most countries have improved their commercial codes, institutional weaknesses still undermine contract enforcement. Court capacity is often inadequate, and procedures for resolving contract disputes out of court are often inadequate or poorly developed.[51]

The Rocky Road

In practice, the road that must be traveled to reach a market-based economic system has often turned out to be rocky.[52] This has been particularly true for the states of Eastern Europe in the post-Communist era. In this region, the move toward greater political and economic freedom has sometimes been accompanied by economic and political chaos.[53] Most East European states began to liberalize their economies in the heady days of the early 1990s. They dismantled decades of price controls, allowed widespread private ownership of businesses, and permitted much greater competition. Most also planned to sell state-owned enterprises to private investors. However, given the vast number of such enterprises and how inefficient many were, making them unappealing to private investors, most privatization efforts moved forward slowly. In this new environment, many inefficient state-owned enterprises found that they could not survive without a guaranteed market. The newly democratic governments often continued to support these money-losing enterprises in an attempt to stave off massive unemployment. The resulting subsidies to state-owned enterprises led to ballooning budget deficits that were typically financed by printing money. Printing money, along with the lack of price controls, often led to hyperinflation. In 1993 the inflation rate was 21 percent in Hungary, 38 percent in Poland, 841 percent in Russia, and a staggering 10,000 percent in the Ukraine.[54] Since then, however, many governments have instituted tight monetary policies and brought down their inflation rates.

Another consequence of the shift toward a market economy was collapsing output as inefficient state-owned enterprises failed to find buyers for their goods. Real gross domestic product fell dramatically in many post-Communist states between 1990 and 1994. However, the corner has been turned in several countries. Poland, the Czech Republic, and Hungary now all boast growing economies and relatively low inflation. But some countries, such as Russia and the Ukraine, still find themselves grappling with major economic problems.

A study by the World Bank suggests that the post-Communist states that have been most successful at transforming their economies were those that followed an economic policy best described as "shock therapy." In these countries—which include the Czech Republic, Hungary, and Poland—prices and trade were liberated fast, inflation was held in check by tight monetary policy, and the privatization of state-owned industries was implemented quickly. Among the 26 economies of Eastern Europe and the former Soviet Union, the World Bank found a strong positive correlation between the imposition of such shock therapy and subsequent economic growth. Speedy reformers suffered smaller falls in output and returned to growth more quickly than those such as Russia and the Ukraine that moved more slowly.[55]

Implications

The global changes in political and economic systems discussed above have several implications for international business. The ideological conflict between collectivism and individualism that so defined the 20th century is winding down. The free market ideology of the West has won the Cold War and has never been more widespread than it was at the beginning of the millennium. Although command economies still remain and totalitarian dictatorships can still be found around the world, the tide is running in favor of free markets and democracy.

The implications for business are enormous. For the best part of 50 years, half of the world was off-limits to Western businesses. Now all that is changing. Many of the national markets of Eastern Europe, Latin America, Africa, and Asia may still be undeveloped and impoverished, but they are potentially enormous. With a population of 1.2 billion, the Chinese market alone is potentially bigger than that of the United States, the European Union, and Japan combined! Similarly India, with its 930 million people, is a potentially huge future market. Latin America has another 400 million potential consumers. It is unlikely that China, Russia, Poland, or any of the other states now moving toward a free market system will attain the living standards of the West anytime soon. Nevertheless, the upside potential is so large that companies need to consider making inroads now.

However, just as the potential gains are large, so are the risks. There is no guarantee that democracy will thrive in the newly democratic states of Eastern Europe, particularly if these states have to grapple with severe economic setbacks. Totalitarian dictatorships could return, although they are unlikely to be of the communist variety. Moreover, although the bipolar world of the Cold War era has vanished, it may be replaced by a multi-polar world dominated by a number of civilizations. In such a world, much of the economic promise inherent in the global shift toward market-based economic systems may evaporate in the face of conflicts between civilizations. While the long-term potential for economic gain from investment in the world's new market economies is large, the risks associated with any such investment are also substantial. It would be foolish to ignore these.

IMPLICATIONS FOR BUSINESS

The implications for international business of the material discussed in this chapter fall into two broad categories. First, the political, economic, and legal environment of a country clearly influences the *attractiveness* of that country as a market and/or investment site. The benefits, costs, and risks associated with doing business in a country are a function of that country's political, economic, and legal systems. Second, the political, economic, and legal systems of a country can raise important *ethical issues* that have implications for the practice of international business. Here we consider each of these issues.

Attractiveness

The overall attractiveness of a country as a market and/or investment site depends on balancing the likely long-term benefits of doing business in that country against the likely costs and risks. Below we consider the determinants of benefits, costs, and risks.

Benefits

In the most general sense, the long-run monetary benefits of doing business in a country are a function of the size of the market, the present wealth (purchasing power) of consumers in that market, and the likely future wealth of consumers. While some markets are very large when measured by number of consumers (e.g., China and India), low living standards may imply limited purchasing power and, therefore, a relatively small market when measured in economic terms. While international businesses need to be aware of this distinction, they also need to keep in mind the likely future prospects of a country. In 1960, for example, South Korea was viewed as just another impoverished Third World nation. By 1996 it was the world's 11th largest economy, measured in terms of GDP. International firms that recognized South Korea's potential in 1960 and began to do business in that country may have reaped greater benefits than those that wrote off South Korea.

By identifying and investing early in a potential future economic star, international firms may build brand loyalty and gain experience in that country's business practices. These will pay back substantial dividends if that country achieves sustained high economic growth rates. In contrast, late entrants may find that they lack the brand loyalty and experience necessary to achieve a significant presence in the market. In the language of business strategy, early entrants into potential future economic stars may be able to reap substantial **first-mover advantages**, while late entrants may fall victim to **late-mover disadvantages**.[56] (First-mover advantages are the advantages that accrue to early entrants into a market. Late-mover disadvantages are the handicap that late entrants might suffer from.)

A country's economic system and property rights regime are reasonably good predictors of economic prospects. Countries with free market economies in which property rights are well protected tend to achieve greater economic growth rates than command economies and/or economies where property rights are poorly protected. It follows that a country's economic system and property rights regime, when taken together with market size (in terms of population), probably constitute reasonably good indicators of the potential long-run benefits of doing business in a country.[57]

Costs

A number of political, economic, and legal factors determine the costs of doing business in a country. With regard to political factors, the costs of doing business in a country can be increased by a need to pay off the politically powerful in order to be allowed by the government to do business. The need to pay what are essentially bribes is greater in closed totalitarian states than in open democratic societies where politicians are held accountable by the electorate (although this is not a hard-and-fast distinction). Whether a company should actually pay bribes in return for market access should be determined on the basis of the legal and ethical implications of such action. We discuss this consideration below.

With regard to economic factors, one of the most important variables is the sophistication of a country's economy. It may be more costly to do business in relatively primitive or undeveloped economies because of the lack of infrastructure and supporting businesses. At the extreme, an international firm may have to provide its own infrastructure and supporting business if it wishes to do business in a country, which obviously raises costs. When McDonald's decided to open its first restaurant in Moscow, it found that in order to serve food and drink indistinguishable from that served in McDonald's restaurants elsewhere, it had to vertically integrate backward to supply its own needs. The quality of Russian-grown potatoes and meat was too poor. Thus, to protect the quality of its product, McDonald's set up its own dairy farms, cattle ranches, vegetable plots, and food processing plants within Russia. This raised the cost of doing business in Russia, relative to the cost in more sophisticated economies where high-quality inputs could be purchased on the open market.

As for legal factors, it can be more costly to do business in a country where local laws and regulations set strict standards with regard to product safety, safety in the workplace, environmental pollution, and the like (since adhering to such regulations is costly). It can also be more costly to do business in a country like the United States, where the absence of a cap on damage awards has meant spiraling liability insurance rates. Moreover, it can be more costly to do business in a country that lacks well-established laws for regulating business practice (as is the case in many of the former Communist nations). In the absence of a well-developed body of business contract law, international firms may find that there is no satisfactory way to resolve contract disputes and, consequently, routinely face large losses from contract violations. Similarly, when local laws fail to adequately protect intellectual property, this can lead to the "theft" of an international business's intellectual property, and lost income (see the Management Focus on Microsoft).

Risks

As with costs, the risks of doing business in a country are determined by a number of political, economic, and legal factors. On the political front, there is the issue of **political risk**. Political risk has been defined as *the likelihood that political forces will cause drastic changes in a country's business environment that adversely affect the profit and other goals of a particular business enterprise.*[58] So defined, political risk tends to be greater in countries experiencing social unrest and disorder or in countries where the underlying nature of a society increases the likelihood of social unrest. Social unrest typically finds expression in strikes, demonstrations, terrorism, and violent conflict. Such unrest is more likely to be found in countries that contain more than one ethnic nationality, in countries where competing ideologies are battling for political control, in countries where economic mismanagement has created high inflation and falling living standards, or in countries that straddle the "fault lines" between civilizations, such as Bosnia.

Social unrest can result in abrupt changes in government and government policy or, in some cases, in protracted civil strife. Such strife tends to have negative economic implications for the profit goals of business enterprises. For example, in the aftermath of the 1979 Islamic revolution in Iran, the Iranian assets of numerous US companies were seized by the new Iranian government without compensation. Similarly, the violent disintegration of the Yugoslavian federation into warring states, including Bosnia, Croatia, and Serbia, precipitated a collapse in the local economies and in the profitability of investments in those countries.

On the economic front, **economic risks** arise from economic mismanagement by the government of a country. Economic risks can be defined as *the likelihood that economic mismanagement will cause drastic changes in a country's business environment that adversely affect the profit and other goals of a particular business enterprise.* Economic risks are not independent of political risk. Economic mismanagement may give rise to significant social unrest and hence political risk. Nevertheless, economic risks are worth emphasizing as a separate category because there is not always a one-to-one relationship between economic mismanagement and social unrest. One visible indicator of economic mismanagement tends to be a country's inflation rate. Another tends to be the level of business and government debt in the country.

In Asian states such as Indonesia, Thailand, and South Korea, businesses increased their debt rapidly during the 1990s, often at the bequest of the government, which was encouraging them to invest in industries deemed to be of "strategic importance" to the country. The result was overinvestment, with more industrial (factories) and commercial capacity (office space) being built than could be justified by demand conditions. Many of these investments turned out to be uneconomic.

The borrowers failed to generate the profits required to meet their debt payment obligations. In turn, the banks that had lent money to these businesses suddenly found that they had rapid increases in nonperforming loans on their books. Foreign investors, believing that many local companies and banks might go bankrupt, pulled their money out of these countries, selling local stocks, bonds, and currency. This action precipitated the 1997–1998 financial crisis in Southeast Asia. The crisis included a precipitous decline in the value of Asian stocks markets, which in some cases exceeded 70 percent; a similar collapse in the value of many Asian currencies against the US dollar; an implosion of local demand; and a severe economic recession that will affect many Asian countries for years to come. In short, economic risks were rising throughout Southeast Asia during the 1990s. Astute foreign businesses and investors, seeing this situation, limited their exposure in this part of the world. More naive businesses and investors lost their shirts!

On the legal front, risks arise when a country's legal system fails to provide adequate safeguards in the case of contract violations or to protect property rights. When legal safeguards are weak, firms are more likely to break contracts and/or steal intellectual property if they perceive it as being in their interests to do so. Thus, **legal risks** might be defined as *the likelihood that a trading partner will opportunistically break a contract or expropriate property rights.* When legal risks in a country are high, an international business might hesitate entering into a long-term contract or joint-venture agreement with a firm in that country. For example, in the 1970s when the Indian government passed a law requiring all foreign investors to enter into joint ventures with Indian companies, US companies such as IBM and Coca-Cola closed their investments in India. They believed that the Indian legal system did not provide for adequate protection of intellectual property rights, creating the very real danger that their Indian partners might expropriate the intellectual property of the American companies—which for IBM and Coca-Cola amounted to the core of their competitive advantage.

Overall Attractiveness

The overall attractiveness of a country as a potential market and/or investment site for an international business depends on balancing the benefits, costs, and risks associated with doing business in that country. Generally, the costs and risks associated with doing business in a foreign country are typically lower in economically advanced and politically stable democratic nations and greater in less developed and politically unstable nations. The calculus is complicated, however, by the fact that the potential *long-run* benefits bear little relationship to a nation's current stage of economic development or political stability. Rather, the benefits depend on likely future economic growth rates. Economic growth appears to be a function of a free market system and a country's capacity for growth (which may be greater in less developed nations). This leads one to conclude that, other things being equal, the benefit, cost, risk trade-off is likely to be most favorable in the case of politically stable developed and developing nations that have free market systems and no dramatic upsurge in either inflation rates or private-sector debt. It is likely to be least favorable in the case of politically unstable developing nations that operate with a mixed or command economy or in developing nations where speculative financial bubbles have led to excess borrowing.

Ethical Issues

Country differences give rise to some important and contentious ethical issues. Three important issues that have been the focus of much debate in recent years are (1) the ethics of doing business in nations that violate human rights, (2) the ethics of doing business in countries with very lax labor and environmental regulations, and (3) the ethics of corruption.

Ethics and Human Rights

One major ethical dilemma facing firms from democratic nations is whether they should do business in totalitarian countries that routinely violate the human rights of their citizens (such as China). There are two sides to this issue. Some argue that investing in totalitarian countries provides comfort to dictators and can help prop up repressive regimes that abuse basic human rights. For instance, Human Rights Watch, an organization that promotes the protection of basic human rights around the world, has argued that the progressive trade policies adopted by Western nations toward China has done little to deter human rights abuses.[59] According to Human Rights Watch, the Chinese government stepped up its repression of political dissidents in 1996 after the Clinton administration removed human rights as a factor in determining China's trade status with the United States. Without investment by Western firms and the support of Western governments, many repressive regimes would collapse and be replaced by more democratically inclined governments, critics such as Human Rights Watch argue. Firms that have invested in Chile, China, Iraq, and South Africa have all been the direct targets of such criticisms. The 1994 dismantling of the apartheid system in South Africa has been credited to economic sanctions by Western nations, including a lack of investment by Western firms. This, say those who argue against investment in totalitarian countries, is proof that investment boycotts can work (although decades of US-led investment boycotts against Cuba and Iran, among other countries, have failed to have a similar impact).

In contrast, some argue that Western investment, by raising the level of economic development of a totalitarian country, can help change it from within. They note that economic well-being and political freedoms often go hand in hand. Thus when arguing against attempts to apply trade sanctions to China in the wake of the violent 1989 government crackdown on prodemocracy demonstrators, the Bush administration claimed that US firms should continue to be allowed to invest in mainland China because greater political freedoms would follow the resulting economic growth. The Clinton administration used similar logic as the basis for its 1996 decision decoupling human rights issues from trade policy considerations.

Since both positions have some merit, it is difficult to arrive at a general statement of what firms should do. Unless mandated by government (as in the case of investment in South Africa) each firm must make its own judgments about the ethical implications of investing in totalitarian states on a case-by-case basis. The more repressive the regime, however, and the less amenable it seems to be to change, the greater the case for not investing.

Ethics and Regulations

A second important ethical issue is whether an international firm should adhere to the same standards of product safety, work safety, and environmental protection that are required in its home country. This is of particular concern to many firms based in Western nations, where product safety, worker safety, and environmental protection laws are among the toughest in the world. Should Western firms investing in less developed countries adhere to tough Western standards, even though local regulations don't require them to do so? This issue has taken on added importance in recent years following revelations that Western enterprises have been using child labor or very poorly paid "sweat-shop" labor in developing nations. Companies criticized for using sweatshop labor include the Gap, Disney, Wal-Mart, and Nike.[60]

Again there is no easy answer. While on the face of it the argument for adhering to Western standards might seem strong, on closer examination the issue becomes more complicated. What if adhering to Western standards would make the foreign investment unprofitable, thereby denying the foreign country much-needed jobs? What is the ethical thing to do? To adhere to Western standards and not invest, thereby denying people jobs, or to adhere to local standards and invest, thereby providing jobs and income? As with many ethical dilemmas, there is no easy answer. Each case needs to be assessed on its own merits.

Ethics and Corruption

A final ethical issue concerns bribes and corruption. Should an international business pay bribes to corrupt government officials to gain market access to a foreign country? To most Westerners, bribery seems to be a corrupt and morally repugnant way of doing business, so the answer might initially be no. Some countries have laws on their books that prohibit their citizens from paying bribes to foreign government officials in return for economic favors. In the United States, for example, the **Foreign Corrupt Practices Act** of 1977 prohibits US companies from making "corrupt" payments to foreign officials to obtain or retain business, although many other developed nations lack similar laws. Trade and finance ministers from the member states of the Organization for Economic Cooperation and Development (the OECD), an association of the world's 20 or so most powerful economies, are working on a convention that would oblige member states to make the bribery of foreign public officials a criminal offense.

However, in many parts of the world, payoffs to government officials are a part of life. One can argue that not investing ignores the fact that such investment can bring substantial benefits to the local populace in terms of income and jobs. Given this, from a pragmatic standpoint, perhaps the practice of giving bribes, although a little evil, is the price that must be paid to do a greater good (assuming the investment creates jobs where none existed before and assuming the practice is not illegal). This kind of reasoning has been advocated by several economists, who suggest that in the context of pervasive and cumbersome regulations in developing countries, corruption may actually improve efficiency and help growth! These economists theorize that in a country where preexisting political structures distort or limit the workings of the market mechanism, corruption in the form of black marketeering, smuggling, and side payments to government bureaucrats to "speed up" approval for business investments may actually enhance welfare.[61]

However, other economists have argued that corruption can reduce the returns on business investment.[62] In a country where corruption is common, the profits from a business activity may be siphoned off by unproductive bureaucrats who demand side payments for granting the enterprise permission to operate. This reduces the incentive that businesses have to invest and may hurt a country's economic growth rate. One economist's study of the connection between corruption and growth in 70 countries found that corruption had a significant negative impact on a country's economic growth rate.[63]

Given the debate and the complexity of this issue, one again might conclude that generalization is difficult. Yes, corruption is bad, and yes, it may harm a country's economic development, but yes, there are also cases where side payments to government officials can remove the bureaucratic barriers to investments that create jobs. What this pragmatic stance ignores, however, is that corruption tends to "corrupt" both the bribe giver and the bribe taker. Corruption feeds on itself, and once an individual has started to walk down the road of corruption, pulling back may be difficult if not impossible. If this is so, it strengthens the moral case for never engaging in corruption, no matter how compelling the benefits might seem.

Chapter Summary

This chapter has reviewed how the political, economic, and legal systems of different countries vary. The potential benefits, costs, and risks of doing business in a country are a function of its political, economic, and legal systems. More specifically:

1. Political systems can be assessed according to two dimensions: the degree to which they emphasize collectivism as opposed to individualism, and the degree to which they are democratic or totalitarian.

2. Collectivism is an ideology that views the needs of society as being more important than the needs of the individual. Collectivism translates into an advocacy for state intervention in economic activity and, in the case of communism, a totalitarian dictatorship.

3. Individualism is an ideology that is built upon an emphasis of the primacy of individual's freedoms in the political, economic, and cultural realms. Individualism translates into an advocacy for democratic ideals and free market economics.

4. Democracy and totalitarianism are at different ends of the political spectrum. In a representative democracy, citizens periodically elect individuals to represent them and political freedoms are guaranteed by a constitution. In a totalitarian state, political power is monopolized by a party, group, or individual, and basic political freedoms are denied to citizens of the state.

5. There are four broad types of economic systems: a market economy, a command economy, a mixed economy, and a state-directed economy. In a market economy, prices are free of controls and private ownership is predominant. In a command economy, prices are set by central planners, productive assets are owned by the state, and private ownership is forbidden. A mixed economy has elements of both a market economy and a command economy. A state-directed economy is one in which the state plays a significant role in directing the investment activities of private enterprise through "industrial policy" and in otherwise regulating business activity in accordance with national goals.

6. Differences in the structure of law between countries can have important implications for the practice of international business. The degree to which property rights are protected can vary dramatically from country to country, as can product safety and product liability legislation and the nature of contract law.

7. The rate of economic progress in a country seems to depend on the extent to which that country has a well-functioning market economy in which property rights are protected.

8. Many country are now in a state of transition. There is a marked shift away from totalitarian governments and command or mixed economic systems and toward democratic political institutions and free market economic systems.

9. It is not clear, however, that we are witnessing the emergence of a universal global civilization based on democratic institutions and free market capitalism. The bipolar world of the Cold War era may ultimately be replaced by a multi-polar world of ideologically divergent civilizations.

10. The attractiveness of a country as a market and/or investment site depends on balancing the likely long-run benefits of doing business in that country against the likely costs and risks.

11. The benefits of doing business in a country are a function of the size of the market (population), its present wealth (purchasing power), and its future growth prospects. By investing early in countries that are currently poor but are nevertheless growing rapidly, firms can gain first-mover advantages that will pay back substantial dividends in the future.

12. The costs of doing business in a country tend to be greater where political payoffs are required to gain market access, where supporting infrastructure is lacking or underdeveloped, and where adhering to local laws and regulations is costly.

13. The risks of doing business in a country tend to be greater in countries that are (1) politically unstable, (2) subject to economic mismanagement, and (3) lacking a legal system to provide adequate safeguards in the case of contract or property rights violations.

14. Country differences give rise to several ethical dilemmas. These including (1) should a firm do business in a repressive totalitarian state, (2) should a firm conform to its home product, workplace, and environmental standards when they are not required by the host country, and (3) should a firm pay bribes to government officials to gain market access?

Critical Discussion Questions

1. Free market economies stimulate greater economic growth, whereas state-directed economies stifle growth! Discuss.

2. A democratic political system is an essential condition for *sustained economic progress*. Discuss.

3. During the late 1980s and early 1990s, China was routinely cited by various international organizations such as Amnesty International and Freedom Watch for major human rights violations, including torture, beatings, imprisonment, and executions of political dissidents. Despite this, in the mid-1990s China received record levels of foreign direct investment, mainly from firms based in democra-

tic societies such as the United States, Japan, and Germany. Evaluate this trend from an ethical perspective. If you were the CEO of a firm that had the option of making a potentially very profitable investment in China, what would you do?

4. You are the CEO of a company that has to choose between making a $100 million investment in Russia or the Czech Republic. Both investments promise the same long-run return, so your choice is driven by risk considerations. Assess the various risks of doing business in each of these nations. Which investment would you favor and why?

CLOSING CASE   General Electric in Hungary

In the heady days of late 1989 when Communist regimes were disintegrating across Eastern Europe, the General Electric Company (GE) launched a major expansion in Hungary with the $150 million acquisition of a 51 percent interest in Tungsram. A manufacturer of lighting products, Tungsram was widely regarded as one of Hungary's industrial gems. GE was attracted to Tungsram by Hungary's low wage rates and by the possibility of using the company to export lighting products to Western Europe. Like many other Western companies, GE believed that Hungary's shift from a totalitarian Communist country with a state-owned and planned economic system to a politically democratic country with a largely free market economic system would create enormous long-run business opportunities.

At the time, many observers believed that General Electric would show other Western companies how to turn enterprises once run by Communist party hacks into capitalist moneymakers. GE promptly transferred some of its best management talent to Tungsram and waited for the miracle to happen. The miracle was slow in coming. As losses mounted, General Electric faced the reality of what happens when grand expectations collide with the grim realities of an embedded culture of waste, inefficiency, and indifference about customers and quality.

The American managers complained that the Hungarians were lackadaisical; the Hungarians thought the Americans pushy. The company's aggressive management system depended on communication between workers and managers; the old Communist system had forbidden this, and changing attitudes at Tungsram proved difficult. The Americans wanted strong sales and marketing functions that would pamper customers; used to life in a centrally planned economy, the Hungarians believed that these things took care of themselves. The Hungarians expected GE to deliver Western-style wages, but GE came to Hungary to take advantage of the country's low wage structure.

In retrospect, GE managers admit they underestimated how long it would take to turn Tungsram around—and how much it would cost. As Charles Pipper, Tungsram's American general manager, says, "Human engineering was much more difficult than product engineering." GE now believes it has turned the corner. However, getting to this point has meant laying off half of Tungsram's 20,000 employees, including two out of every three managers. It has also meant an additional $440 million investment in new plant and equipment and in retraining the employees and managers that remained. By 1997 the investment finally seemed to be paying off. Despite a 50 percent cut in the work force, production volume is now double the 1989 level. Although some large Eastern European customers are no longer on Tungsram's books, many of those were themselves poorly run state-owned enterprises.

Sources: J. Perlez, "GE Finds Tough Going in Hungary," *New York Times*, July 25, 1994, pp. C1, C3; C. R. Whitney, "East Europe's Hard Path to New Day," *New York Times*, September 30, 1994, pp. A1, A4; and T. Agassi, "Hungary for Capitalism," *The Jerusalem Post*, June 18, 1997, p. 8.

http://www.ge.com

Case Discussion Questions

1. What does GE's experience in Hungary tell you about the relationship among economic systems, political systems, and national culture?

2. Given the problems GE experienced with Tungsram, in retrospect might it have chosen a better strategy to attack the Western European lighting products market?

3. How important to the economic development of Hungary are investments such as GE's? What are the benefits that GE brings to Hungary?

4. If Tungsram had continued under local ownership, what do you think would have been its fate?

Notes

1. M. Kreinin, "Brazil: the Land of Telecom Opportunity: US Firms Profit from Privatization," *USA Today*, December 1, 1997, p. B12.

2. Although as we shall see, there is not a strict one-to-one correspondence between political systems and economic systems. A. O. Hirschman, "The On-and-Off Again Connection between Political and Economic Progress," *American Economic Review* 84, no. 2 (1994), pp. 343–348.

3. For a discussion of the roots of collectivism and individualism see H. W. Spiegel, *The Growth of Economic Thought* (Durham, NC: Duke University Press, 1991). An easily assessable discussion of collectivism and individualism can be found in M. Friedman and R. Friedman, *Free to Choose* (London: Penguin Books, 1980).

4. For a classic summary of the tenets of Marxism details, see A. Giddens, *Capitalism and Modern Social Theory* (Cambridge: Cambridge University Press, 1971).

5. For details see "A Survey of China," *The Economist*, March 18, 1995.

6. J. S. Mill, *On Liberty* (London: Longman's, 1865), p.6.

7. A. Smith, *The Wealth of Nations*, Vol. 1 (London: Penguin Books), p. 325.

8. R. Wesson, *Modern Government—Democracy and Authoritarianism*, 2nd ed. (Englewood Cliffs, NJ: Prentice Hall, 1990).

9. For a detailed but accessible elaboration of this argument see M. Friedman and R. Friedman, *Free to Choose* (London: Penguin Books, 1980). Also see P. M. Romer, "The Origins of Endogenous Growth," *Journal of Economic Perspectives* 8, no. 1 (1994), pp. 2–32.

10. M. Borrus, L. A. Tyson and J. Zysman, "Creating Advantage: How Government Policies Created Trade in the Semiconductor Industry," in *Strategic Trade Policy and the New International Economics*, ed. P. Krugman (Cambridge, MA: MIT Press, 1986).

11. See Lester Thurow, *Head to Head* (New York: Warner Books, 1993).

12. D. North, *Institutions, Institutional Change, and Economic Performance* (Cambridge: Cambridge University Press, 1991).

13. P. Klebnikov, "Russia's Robber Barons," *Forbes*, November 21, 1994, pp 74–84; C. Mellow, "Russia: Making Cash from Chaos," *Fortune*, April 17, 1995, pp. 145–151; and "Mr Tatum Checks Out," *The Economist*, November 9, 1996, p. 78.

14. "Godfather of the Kremlin?" *Fortune*, December 30, 1996, pp. 90–96.

15. "Mr Tatum Checks Out."

16. K. van Wolferen, *The Enigma of Japanese Power* (New York: Vintage Books, 1990), pp. 100–05.

17. P. Bardhan, "Corruption and Development: A Review of the Issues," *Journal of Economic Literature*, September 1997, pp. 1320–46.

18. K. M. Murphy, A. Shleifer, and R. Vishny, "Why Is Rent Seeking So Costly to Growth," *American Economic Review* 83, no. 2 (1993), pp. 409–14.

19. Keiran Cooke, "Honeypot of as Much as $4 Billion Down the Drain," *Financial Times*, February 26, 1994, p. 4.

20. Douglass North has argued that the correct specification of intellectual property rights is one factor that lowers the cost of doing business and, thereby, stimulates economic growth and development. See D. North, *Institutions, Institutional Change, and Economic Performance* (Cambridge: Cambridge University Press, 1991).

21. Business Software Alliance, *Global Software Piracy Report: Facts and Figures, 1994–1996*. Available from http://www.bsa.org.

22. Ibid.

23. S. Greenberger and C. S. Smith, "CD Piracy Flourishes in China and the West Supplies Equipment," *Wall Street Journal*, April 27, 1997, pp. A1, A4.

24. "Trade tripwires," *The Economist*, August 27, 1994, p. 61.

25. *Business Software Alliance*, "Software Piracy in China," press release, November 18, 1996.

26. "A Survey of the Legal Profession," *The Economist*, July 18, 1992, pp. 1–18.

27. The World Bank, *World Development Report, 1998/99: Knowledge for Development* (Oxford: Oxford University Press, 1999).

28. G. M. Grossman and E. Helpman, "Endogenous Innovation in the Theory of Growth," *Journal of Economic Perspectives* 8, no. 1 (1994), pp. 23–44; and P. M. Romer, "The Origins of Endogenous Growth," *Journal of Economic Perspectives*, 8, no. 1 (1994), pp. 3–22.

29. F. A. Hayek, *The Fatal Conceit: Errors of Socialism* (Chicago: University of Chicago Press, 1989).

30. James Gwartney, Robert Lawson, and Walter Block, *Economic Freedom of the World: 1975–1995* (London: Institute of Economic Affairs, 1996).

31. North, *Institutions, Institutional Change and Economic Performance*. See also Murphy, Shleifer, and Vishny, "Why Is Rent Seeking so Costly to Growth?"

32. Hirschman, "The On-and-Off Again Connection between Political and Economic Progress"; A. Przeworski and F. Limongi, "Political Regimes and Economic Growth," *Journal of Economic Perspectives* 7, no. 3 (1993), pp. 51–59.

33. As an example, see "Why Voting Is Good for You," *The Economist*, August 27, 1994, pp. 15–17.

34. Ibid.

35. For details of this argument see M. Olson, "Dictatorship, Democracy, and Development," *American Political Science Review*, September 1993.

36. For example see Jarad Diamond, *Guns, Germs, and Steel* (New York: W. W. Norton, 1997). Also see J. Sachs, "Nature, Nurture and Growth," *The Economist*, June 14, 1997, pp. 19–22.

37. Ibid.

38. "What Can the Rest of the World Learn from the Classrooms of Asia?" *The Economist*, September 21, 1996, p. 24.

39. J. Fagerberg, "Technology and International Differences in Growth Rates," *Journal of Economic Literature*, 32 (September 1994), pp. 1147–75.

40. See "1997 Freedom Around the World," *Freedom Review*, January–February 1997, pp. 5–29.

41. Ibid.

42. L. Conners, "Freedom to Connect," *Wired*, August 1997, pp. 105–06.

43. F. Fukuyama, "The End of History," *The National Interest* 16 (Summer 1989), p. 18.

44. S. P. Huntington, *The Clash of Civilizations and the Remaking of World Order* (New York: Simon & Schuster, 1996).

45. Ibid., p. 116.

46. S. Fisher, R. Sahay, and C. A. Vegh, "Stabilization and the Growth in Transition Economies: the Early Experience," *Journal of Economic Perspectives* 10 (Spring 1996), pp. 45–66.

47. B. T. Johnson, K. R. Holmes, and M. Kirpatrick, *1999 Index of Economic Freedom* (Heritage Foundation, 1998).

48. N. Weinberg, "First the Pain, Then the Gain," *Forbes*, May 5, 1997, pp. 134–37.

49. J. C. Brada, "Privatization Is Transition—Is It?" *Journal of Economic Perspectives*, Spring 1996, pp. 67–86.

50. M. S. Borish and M. Noel, "Private Sector Development in the Visegrad Countries," *World Bank*, March 1997.

51. Ibid.

52. Fischer, Sahay, and Vegh, "Stabilization and Growth in Transition Economies."

53. M. Bleaney, "Economic Liberalization in Eastern Europe: Problems and Prospects," *The World Economy* 17, no. 4 (1994), pp. 497–507.

54. M. Wolf and C. Freeland, "The Long Day's Journey to Market," *Financial Times*, March 7, 1995, p. 15.

55. "Lessons of Transition," *The Economist*, June 29, 1996, p. 81.

56. For a discussion of first-mover advantages, see M. Liberman and D. Montgomery, "First-Mover Advantages," *Strategic Management* Journal 9 (Summer Special Issue, 1988), pp. 41–58.

57. "Of Liberty and Prosperity," *The Economist*, January 13, 1996, pp. 21–23.

58. S. H. Robock, "Political Risk: Identification and Assessment," *Columbia Journal of World Business*, July/August 1971, pp. 6–20.

59. Steven L. Myers, "Report Says Business Interests Overshadow Rights," *New York Times*, December 5, 1996, p. A8.

60. Jo-Ann Mort, "Sweated Shopping," *The Guardian*, September 8, 1997, p. 11.

61. Bardhan Pranab, "Corruption and Development," *Journal of Economic Literature* 36 (September 1997), pp. 1320–46.

62. A. Shleifer and R. W. Vishny, "Corruption," *Quarterly Journal of Economics*, no. 108 (1993), pp. 599–617.

63. P. Mauro, "Corruption and Growth," *Quarterly Journal of Economics*, no. 110 (1995), pp. 681–712.

CHAPTER THREE

DIFFERENCES IN CULTURE

A Scotsman at Mazda

In 1996, a small earthquake hit Japan—Henry Wallace, a Scotsman, was appointed head of Hiroshima-based Mazda, Japan's fifth largest auto manufacturer. Although Mazda had a proud history as one of Japan's more innovative automobile manufacturers, the company seemed to have lost its way in the 1990s. With Japan mired in a prolonged recession, Mazda saw its domestic sales shrink. At the same time, the company was unable to expand its international sales to make up for the shortfall. From the peak of 1.4 million units in 1990, Mazda's sales had slumped to 770,000 units in 1995. In the two fiscal years before March 1995, the company lost the equivalent of $710 million, and in the year ending March 1996 it managed a razor-thin profit of $2.7 million. This poor performance was too much for its major shareholder, the Ford Motor Company of the United States. Ford responded by increasing its stake in Mazda to 33.4 percent with a $500 million investment and placing one of its own, Wallace, as president.

Wallace, who before moving to Mazda had been the president of Ford's Venezuela operation, was the first foreigner to head a major Japanese company. The appointment was greeted with some trepidation in Hiroshima. Like many Japanese companies, Mazda's organizational practices and business relationships had been influenced by the country's cultural traditions. The company honored the practice of lifetime employment. Internal promotions were based primarily on seniority. Decision making was consensus based, and there was an emphasis on harmony and a reluctance to create discord within the management group. Also, Mazda had long-standing "family-like" relationships with an extensive network of local suppliers.

The fear among many in Hiroshima was that Wallace's appointment would signal an end to all this. How would Wallace's decisions affect a community where 40 percent of the work force depended directly or indirectly on Mazda? Would lifetime employment be replaced by American style layoffs? How would Wallace function in a society and company that valued long-term relationships, trust, and reciprocal obligations? Would Wallace break decadeslong commitments to local suppliers and purchase more parts from overseas? The head of one small Hiroshima supplier noted, "If the president were Japanese he would have some sympathy towards us. He would think, 'you have been working hard for Mazda, even in times of difficulties, so we will support you.' He would take care so that as many companies as possible would survive."

Others worried about what would happen to Mazda's consensus-based decision making. When Japanese have a meeting, "only those who are opposed to a proposal speak," noted the president of Mazda's workers union, Takeshi Morikawa, in an interview. "If you are for an idea, you keep quiet. But Ford people speak, even if they are for an idea. They ask questions, or they speak about why they are for the idea. So at some meetings, the Japanese think that foreigners are dominating the floor too much . . . In Japan, asking about details can seem to be an attack on the integrity of the person. Just look into my eyes and then you will know. So the questioning process to a Japanese is a problem. They don't understand it."

Another concern centered on how a man whose command of Japanese was highly imperfect could possibly understand the cultural context within which business decisions were made in Japan. Wallace also admitted to having concerns, particularly with regard to the language issue. As he observed in a 1996 interview: "In the West we have this direct communication. But in Japan it's indirect communication. Very often you are left to draw your own conclusions . . . It's particularly difficult to have brainstorming sessions. When you have to go through an interpreter, all you get back is the answer to your question. You don't get back the wider view."

Eighteen months into his job, Wallace seemed to be making progress improving Mazda's performance, while simultaneously easing some fears that surfaced following his appointment. A clear strategy has been articulated where none existed before. The work force has been reduced through attrition rather than layoffs, and the lifetime employment system remains intact. Some suppliers have been cut as orders for parts have shifted to lower-cost sources overseas, but the shift has not been as dramatic as many feared. Wallace repeatedly emphasizes that he is not trying to dismantle the traditional supplier network, or *keiretsu*. Several unprofitable models have been discontinued, and more attention has been focused on marketing and market research than has historically been the case at Mazda. There have also been big changes in the internal management structure and decision-making processes. Merit has become a much more important basis for promotions, while decision making has shifted away from the old consensus-based system and toward a system that is characterized by more spirited debate.

Wallace also notes that being Western has some advantages in this situation. Since foreigners are always expected to act differently, Wallace has been able to cross the lines of Japan's hierarchical business world in ways that would be more difficult for a Japanese president. For example, the day after he was appointed president, Wallace asked the leaders of Mazda's union to talk with him, an action that was unprecedented at Mazda. Wallace also took the unusual step of sharing confidential strategic information with the union leaders in order to win their cooperation—a move that so far has been successful.

http://www.mazda.com

Sources: S. Sugawara, S. "Odd Man In," *Washington Post*, October 10, 1996, p. C1; M. A. Lev, "Ford Exec Retools Mazda," *Chicago Tribune*, March 31, 1997, p. 1; M. Nakamoto, "New Driver Takes the Wheel," *Financial Times*, April 22, 1996, p. 18; I. Morton, "The Height of Mazda's Empire," *The Times*, June 7, 1997; and Y. Kageyama, "West Meets East," *Chicago Tribune*, November 24, 1996, p. 3.

Introduction

International business is different because countries are different. In Chapter 2 we saw how national differences in political, economic, and legal systems influence the benefits, costs, and risks associated with doing business in different countries. In this chapter, we will explore how differences in culture across and within countries can affect international business. Two themes run through this chapter.

The first theme is that business success in a variety of countries requires cross-cultural literacy. By cross-cultural literacy, we mean an understanding of how cultural differences across *and* within nations can affect the way in which business is practiced. In these days of global communications, rapid transportation, and global markets, when the era of the global village seems just around the corner, it is easy to forget just how different various cultures really are. Underneath the veneer of modernism, deep cultural differences often remain. Westerners in general, and Americans in particular, are quick to conclude that because people from other parts of the world also wear blue jeans, listen to Western popular music, eat at McDonald's, and drink Coca-Cola, they also accept the basic tenets of Western (or American) culture. But this is not true. Many of the "Islamic militants" that invaded the American Embassy in Iran after the Iranian revolution that ousted the pro-Western Shah of Iran wore blue jeans, but they certainly showed no love of American values.

Japan is a case in point. The Japanese have embraced the products of modern society, but as the opening case demonstrates, the country's long-standing cultural traditions continue to have an important impact on many aspects of Japanese life, including the organization and management principles of enterprises such as Mazda. However, the opening case also illustrates that a sophisticated manager who is willing to work within the constraints of traditional values can change some of those management principles. Despite his lack of Japanese-language skills, Henry Wallace has displayed a sensitivity for important, culturally grounded institutions in Japan, such as lifetime employment and reciprocal relationships with suppliers. A less sophisticated Western manager might have pushed for large-scale "American-style" layoffs or cut all local suppliers to source components from lower-cost Asian countries. Such actions might have provoked a counterproductive backlash. Wallace seems to have understood the importance of honoring traditional commitments. At the same time, he has used his position as a foreigner to push for some important changes. He appears to be changing the consensus-based decision making within Mazda, and he has been able to cross some barriers that a native-born Japanese might find difficult, such as the barrier between management and labor. Wallace illustrates how cross-cultural literacy can be a valuable asset in a foreign country.

A second theme of this chapter is that a relationship may exist between culture and the costs of doing business in a country or region. The culture of some countries (or regions) is supportive of the capitalist mode of production and lowers the costs of doing business there. Cultural factors can help firms based in such countries achieve a competitive advantage in the world economy. For example, some observers have argued that cultural factors have lowered the costs of doing business in Japan,[1] giving some Japanese businesses a competitive advantage in the world economy. By the same token, cultural factors can sometimes raise the costs of doing business. Historically a culture that emphasized class conflict, British firms found it difficult to achieve cooperation between management and labor. Such conflict has been reflected in a high level of industrial disputes, and this raised the costs of doing business in Britain relative to the costs in countries such as Switzerland, Norway, Germany, or Japan, where class conflict was historically less prevalent.

We open this chapter with a general discussion of what culture is. Then we focus on how differences in social structure, religion, language, and education influence the culture of a country. The implications for business practice will be highlighted throughout the chapter and summarized in a section at the end.

What Is Culture?

Scholars have never been able to agree on a simple definition of culture. In the 1870s, the anthropologist Edward Tylor defined culture as *that complex whole which includes knowledge, belief, art, morals, law, custom, and other capabilities acquired by man as a member of society.*[2] Since then hundreds of other definitions have been offered. Geert Hofstede, an expert on cross-cultural differences and management, defined culture as *the collective programming of the mind which distinguishes the members of one human group from another . . . Culture, in this sense, includes systems of values; and values are among the building blocks of culture.*[3] Another definition of culture comes from sociologists Zvi Namenwirth and Robert Weber who see culture as *a system of ideas* and argue that these ideas constitute *a design for living.*[4]

Here we follow both Hofstede and Namenwirth and Weber by viewing **culture** as *a system of values and norms that are shared among a group of people and that when taken together constitute a design for living*. By **values** we mean abstract *ideas* about what a group believes to be good, right, and desirable. Put differently, values are shared assumptions about how things ought to be.[5] By **norms** we mean the social rules and guidelines that prescribe appropriate behavior in particular situations. We shall use the term **society** to refer to a group of people who share a common set of values and norms. While a *society* may be equivalent to a country, some countries harbor several "societies" (i.e., they support multiple cultures) and some societies embrace more than one country.

Values and Norms

Values form the bedrock of a culture. They provide the context within which a society's norms are established and justified. They may include a society's attitudes toward such concepts as individual freedom, democracy, truth, justice, honesty, loyalty, social obligations, collective responsibility, the role of women, love, sex, marriage, and so on. Values are not just abstract concepts; they are invested with considerable emotional significance. People argue, fight, and even die over values such as freedom. Values also often are reflected in the political and economic systems of a society. As we saw in Chapter 2, democratic free market capitalism is a reflection of a philosophical value system that emphasizes individual freedom.

Norms are the social rules that govern people's actions toward one another. Norms can be subdivided further into two major categories: *folkways* and *mores*. **Folkways** are the routine conventions of everyday life. Generally, folkways are actions of little *moral* significance. Rather, folkways are social conventions concerning things such as the appropriate dress code in a particular situation, good social manners, eating with the correct utensils, neighborly behavior, and the like. While folkways define the way people are expected to behave, violation of folkways is not normally a serious matter. People who violate folkways may be thought of as eccentric or ill-mannered, but they are not usually considered to be evil or bad. In many countries, foreigners may initially be excused for violating folkways.

A good example of folkways concerns attitudes toward time in different countries. People are very time conscious in the United States. Americans tend to arrive a few minutes early for business appointments. When invited for dinner to someone's home, it is considered polite to arrive on time or just a few minutes late. The concept of time can be very different in other countries. It is not necessarily a breach of etiquette to arrive a little late for a business appointment; it might even be considered more impolite to arrive early. As for dinner invitations, arriving on time for a dinner engagement can be very bad manners. In Britain, for example, when someone says, "Come for dinner at 7:00 PM," what he means is "come for dinner at 7:30 to 8:00 PM." The guest who arrives at 7:00 PM is likely to find an unprepared and embarrassed host. Similarly, when an Argentinean says, "Come for dinner anytime after 8:00 PM," what she means is don't come at 8:00 PM—it's far too early!

Mores are norms that are seen as central to the functioning of a society and to its social life. They have much greater significance than folkways. Accordingly, violating mores can bring serious retribution. Mores include such factors as indictments against theft, adultery, incest, and cannibalism. In many societies, certain mores have been enacted into law. Thus, all advanced societies have laws against theft, incest, and cannibalism. However, there are also many differences between cultures as to what is perceived as mores. In America, for example, drinking alcohol is widely accepted, whereas in Saudi Arabia the consumption of alcohol is viewed as violating important social mores and is punishable by imprisonment (as some Western citizens working in Saudi Arabia have found out).

Culture, Society, and the Nation-State

We have defined a society as a group of people that share a common set of values and norms; that is, people who are bound together by a common culture. However, there is *not* a strict one-to-one correspondence between a society and a nation-state. Nation-states are political creations. They may contain a single culture or several cultures. While the French nation can be thought of as the political embodiment of French culture, the nation of Canada has at least three cultures—an Anglo culture, a French-speaking "Quebecois" culture, and a Native American culture. Similarly, in many African nations there are important cultural differences between tribal groups, a fact that was driven home in the early 1990s when the nation of Rwanda dissolved into a bloody civil war between two tribes, the Tutsis and Hutus. Africa is not alone in this regard. India is composed of many distinct cultural groups. During the Gulf War, the prevailing view presented to Western audiences was that Iraq was a homogenous Arab nation. But the chaos that followed the war revealed several different societies within Iraq, each with its own culture. The Kurds in the North do not view themselves as Arabs at all and have their own distinct history and traditions. Then there are two Arab societies, the Shiites in the South and the Sunnis who populate the middle of the country and who rule Iraq (the terms *Shiites* and *Sunnis* refer to different sects within the religion of Islam). Among the southern Sunnis is another distinct society of 500,000 "Marsh Arabs" who live at the confluence of the Tigris and Euphrates rivers, pursuing a way of life that dates back 5,000 years.[6]

At the other end of the scale, we can speak of cultures that embrace several nations. Several scholars, for example, argue that we can speak of an Islamic society or culture that is shared by the citizens of many different nations in the Middle East, Asia, and Africa. As you will recall from the last chapter, this view of expansive cultures that embrace several nations underpins Samuel Huntington's view of a world that is fragmented into different civilizations including Western, Islamic, and Sinic (Chinese) civilizations.[7]

To complicate things further, it is also possible to talk about culture at different levels. It is reasonable to talk about "American society" and "American culture," but there are several societies within America, each with its own culture. One can talk about Afro-American culture, Cajun culture, Chinese-American culture, Hispanic culture,

Figure 3.1

The Determinants of Culture

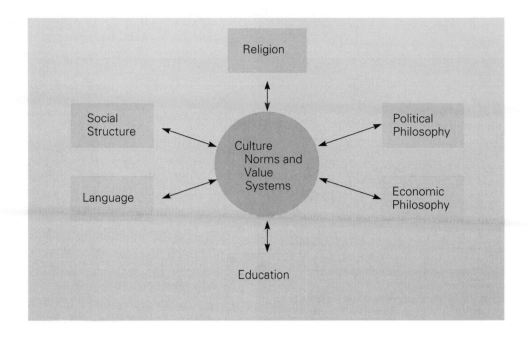

Indian culture, Irish-American culture, and Southern culture. The point is that the relationship between culture and country is often ambiguous. One cannot always characterize a country as having a single homogenous culture, and even when one can, one must also often recognize that the national culture is a mosaic of subcultures.

The Determinants of Culture

The values and norms of a culture do not emerge fully formed. They are the evolutionary product of a number of factors at work in a society. These factors include the prevailing political and economic philosophy, the social structure of a society, and the dominant religion, language, and education (see Figure 3.1). We discussed political and economic philosophy at length in Chapter 2. Such philosophy clearly influences the value systems of a society. For example, the values found in the former Soviet Union toward freedom, justice, and individual achievement were clearly different from the values found in the United States, precisely because each society operated according to a different political and economic philosophy. Below we will discuss the influence of social structure, religion, language, and education. Remember that the chain of causation runs both ways. While factors such as social structure and religion clearly influence the values and norms of a society, it is also true that the values and norms of a society can influence social structure and religion.

Social Structure

A society's "social structure" refers to its basic social organization. Although there are many different aspects of social structure, two dimensions stand out as being of particular importance when explaining differences between cultures. The first is the degree to which the basic unit of social organization is the individual, as opposed to the group. Western societies tend to emphasize the primacy of the individual, while groups tend to figure much larger in many other societies. The second dimension is the degree to which a society is stratified into classes or castes.

Some societies are characterized by a relatively high degree of social stratification and relatively low mobility between strata (e.g., Indian), while other societies are characterized by a low degree of social stratification and high mobility between strata (e.g., American).

Individuals and Groups

A group is an association of two or more individuals who have a shared sense of identity and who interact with each other in structured ways on the basis of a common set of expectations about each other's behavior.[8] Human social life is group life. Individuals are involved in families, work groups, social groups, recreational groups, and so on. However, while groups are found in all societies, societies differ according to the degree to which the group is viewed as the primary means of social organization.[9] In some societies, individual attributes and achievements are viewed as being more important than group membership, while in other societies the reverse is true.

The Individual

In Chapter 2, we discussed individualism as a political philosophy. However, individualism is more than just an abstract political philosophy. In many Western societies, the individual is the basic building block of social organization. This is reflected not just in the political and economic organization of society, but also in the way people perceive themselves and relate to each other in social and business settings. The value systems of many Western societies, for example, place a high emphasis on individual achievement. The social standing of individuals is not so much a function of whom they work for, as of their individual performance in whatever work setting they choose.

The emphasis on individual performance in many Western societies has both beneficial and harmful aspects. In the United States, the emphasis on individual performance finds expression in an admiration of "rugged individualism" and entrepreneurship. One benefit of this is the high level of entrepreneurial activity in the United States and other Western societies. New products and new ways of doing business (e.g. personal computers, photocopiers, computer software, biotechnology, supermarkets, and discount retail stores) have repeatedly been created in the United States by entrepreneurial individuals. One can argue that the dynamism of the US economy owes much to the philosophy of individualism.

Individualism also finds expression in a high degree of managerial mobility between companies, and this is not always a good thing. While moving from company to company may be good for individual managers, who are trying to build impressive resumes, it is not necessarily a good thing for American companies. The lack of loyalty and commitment to an individual company, and the tendency to move on when a better offer comes along, can result in managers that have good general skills but lack the knowledge, experience, and network of interpersonal contacts that come from years of working within the same company. An effective manager draws on company-specific experience, knowledge, and a network of contacts to find solutions to current problems, and American companies may suffer if their managers lack these attributes.

The emphasis on individualism may also make it difficult to build teams within an organization to perform collective tasks. If individuals are always competing with each other on the basis of individual performance, it may prove difficult for them to cooperate. A recent study of US competitiveness by MIT concluded that US firms are being hurt in the global economy by a failure to achieve cooperation both within a company (e.g., between functions; between management and labor) and between companies (e.g., between a firm and its suppliers). Given the emphasis on individualism in the American value system, this failure is not surprising.[10] So the emphasis on individualism in the United States, while helping to create a dynamic entrepreneurial economy, may raise the costs of doing business due to its adverse impact on managerial mobility and cooperation.

One positive aspect of high managerial mobility is that executives are exposed to different ways of doing business. The ability to compare business practices helps US executives identify how good practices and techniques developed in one firm might be profitably applied to other firms.

The Group

In contrast to the Western emphasis on the individual, the group is the primary unit of social organization in many other societies. In Japan, the social status of an individual is determined as much by the standing of the group to which he or she belongs as by his or her individual performance.[11] In traditional Japanese society, the group was the family or village to which an individual belonged. Today the group has frequently come to be associated with the work team or business organization to which an individual belongs. In a now classic study of Japanese society, Nakane has noted how this expresses itself in everyday life:

> When a Japanese faces the outside (confronts another person) and affixes some position to himself socially he is inclined to give precedence to institution over kind of occupation. Rather than saying, "I am a typesetter" or "I am a filing clerk," he is likely to say, "I am from B Publishing Group" or "I belong to S company".[12]

Nakane goes on to observe that the primacy of the group to which an individual belongs often evolves into a deeply emotional attachment in which identification with the group becomes all important in one's life. One of the central values of Japanese culture is the importance attached to group membership. This may have beneficial implications for business firms. Strong identification with the group is argued to create pressures for mutual self-help and collective action. If the worth of an individual is closely linked to the achievements of the group (e.g., firm), as Nakane maintains is the case in Japan, this creates a strong incentive for individual members of the group to work together for the common good. The failures of cooperation that the MIT study found in many American firms may not be a problem in Japanese firms. Some argue that the competitive advantage of Japanese enterprises in the global economy is based partly on their ability to achieve close cooperation between individuals within a company and between companies. This finds expression in the widespread diffusion of self-managing work teams within Japanese organizations, the close cooperation between different functions within Japanese companies (e.g., between manufacturing, marketing, and R&D), and the cooperation between a company and its suppliers on issues such as design, quality control, and inventory reduction.[13] In all of these cases, cooperation is driven by the need to improve the performance of the group (i.e., the business firm).

The primacy of the value of group identification also discourages managers and workers from moving from company to company. This is the case in Japan where lifetime employment in a particular company is the norm in certain sectors of the economy (estimates suggest that between 20 and 40 percent of all Japanese employees have formal or informal lifetime employment guarantees). Over the years, managers and workers build up knowledge, experience, and a network of interpersonal business contacts. All these things can help managers perform their jobs more effectively and achieve cooperation with others.

However, the primacy of the group is not always beneficial. Just as US society is characterized by a great deal of dynamism and entrepreneurship, reflecting the primacy of values associated with individualism, some argue that Japanese society is characterized by a corresponding lack of dynamism and entrepreneurship. Although it is not clear how this will play itself out in the long run, it is possible that due to the cultural emphasis on individualism, the United States could continue to create more new industries than Japan and continue to be more successful at pioneering radically new products and new ways of doing business.

Social Stratification

All societies are stratified on a hierarchical basis into social categories—that is, into **social strata.** These strata are typically defined on the basis of characteristics such as family background, occupation, and income. Individuals are born into a particular stratum. They become a member of the social category to which their parents belong. Individuals born into a stratum toward the top of the social hierarchy tend to have better *life chances* than individuals born into a stratum toward the bottom of the hierarchy. They are likely to have a better education, better health, a better standard of living, and better work opportunities. Although all societies are stratified to some degree, they differ in two related ways that are of interest to us here. First, they differ from each other with regard to the degree of *mobility* between social strata, and second, they differ with regard to the *significance* attached to social strata in business contexts.

Social Mobility

The term **social mobility** refers to the extent to which individuals can move out of the strata into which they are born. Social mobility varies significantly from society to society. The most rigid system of stratification is a caste system. A **caste system** is a *closed system of stratification* in which social position is determined by the family into which a person is born, and change in that position is usually not possible during an individual's lifetime. Often a caste position carries with it a specific occupation. Members of one caste might be shoemakers, members of another caste might be butchers, and so on. These occupations are embedded in the caste and passed down through the family to succeeding generations. Although the number of societies with caste systems has diminished rapidly during the 20th century, one major example still remains. India has four main castes and several thousand subcastes. Even though the caste system was officially abolished in 1949, two years after India became independent, it is still a powerful force in rural Indian society where occupation and marital opportunities are still partly related to caste.

A **class system** is a less rigid form of social stratification in which social mobility is possible. A class system is a form of *open stratification* in which the position a person has by birth can be changed through their own achievements and/or luck. Individuals born into a class at the bottom of the hierarchy can work their way upwards, while individuals born into a class at the top of the hierarchy can slip down.

While many societies have class systems, social mobility within a class system varies from society to society. For example, some sociologists have argued that Britain has a more rigid class structure than certain other Western societies, such as the United States.[14] Historically, British society was divided into three main classes; the *upper class,* which was made up of individuals whose families had wealth, prestige, and occasionally power for generations; the *middle class,* whose members were involved in professional, managerial, and clerical occupations; and the *working class,* whose members earn their living from manual occupations. The middle class was further subdivided into the *upper-middle class,* whose members are involved in important managerial occupations and the prestigious professions (e.g. lawyers, accountants, doctors), and the *lower-middle class,* whose members were involved in clerical work (e.g. bank tellers) and the less prestigious professions (e.g. school teachers).

What was significant about the British class system was the extent of divergence between the life chances of members of different classes. The upper and upper-middle classes typically send their children to a select group of private schools, where they don't mix with lower-class children, and where they pick up many of the speech accents and social norms that mark them as being from the higher strata of society. These same private schools also have close ties with the most prestigious universities, such as Oxford and Cambridge. Indeed, until recently Oxford and Cambridge guaranteed to reserve a certain number of places for the graduates of these private schools. Having been to a prestigious university, the offspring of the upper and upper-middle classes then had an excellent chance of being offered a prestigious job in companies, banks, brokerage firms, and law firms that are themselves run by members of the upper and upper-middle classes.

In contrast, the members of the British working and lower-middle classes typically go to state schools. The majority left at 16, and those that went on to higher education found it more difficult to get accepted at the best universities. When they did, they found that their lower-class accent and lack of social skills marked them as being from a lower social stratum, which made it more difficult for them to get access to the most prestigious jobs.

As a result of these factors, the class system in Britain tended to perpetuate itself from generation to generation, and mobility was limited. Although upward mobility was possible, it is something that could not normally be achieved in one generation. While an individual from a working class background may have succeeded in establishing an income level that was consistent with membership of the upper-middle class, he or she may not have been accepted as such by others of that class due to accent and background. However, by sending his or her offspring to the "right kind of school," the individual can ensure that his or her children were accepted.

Accordingly to many politicians and popular commentators, modern British society is now rapidly leaving this class structure behind and moving towards a *classless* society. However, sociologists continue to dispute this finding and present evidence that this is not the case. For example, a recent study reported that in 1994, state schools in the London suburb of Islington, which has a population of 175,000, had only 79 candidates for university, while one prestigious private school alone, Eton, sent more than that number to Oxford and Cambridge.[15] This, according to the authors, implies that "money still begets money." They argue that a good school means a good university, a good university means a good job, and "merit" only has a limited chance of elbowing its way into this tight little circle.

The class system in the United States is less extreme than in Britain and mobility is greater. Like Britain, the United States has its own upper, middle, and working classes. However, class membership is determined principally by individual economic achievements, as opposed to background and schooling. Thus, an individual can, by their own economic achievement, move smoothly from the working class to the upper class in their own lifetime. Indeed, in American society successful individuals from humble origins are highly respected.

Significance

From a business perspective, the stratification of a society is significant if it affects the operation of business organizations. In American society, the high degree of social mobility and the extreme emphasis upon individualism limits the impact of class background on business operations. The same is true in Japan, where the majority of the population perceive themselves to be middle-class. In a country such as Britain, however, the relative lack of class mobility and the differences between classes has resulted in the emergence of class consciousness. **Class consciousness** refers to a condition where people tend to perceive themselves in terms of their class background, and this shapes their relationships with members of other classes.

One way in which this has been played out in British society is in terms of the traditional hostility between upper-middle class managers and their working class employees. Mutual antagonism and lack of respect historically made it difficult to achieve cooperation between management and labor in many British companies, and resulted in a relatively high level of industrial disputes. However, the last two decades have seen a dramatic reduction in industrial disputes in Britain, which bolsters the arguments of those who claim that Britain is moving towards a classless society. In any event, an antagonistic relationship between management and labor, and the resulting lack of cooperation and high level of industrial disruption, tends to raise the costs of production in countries characterized by significant class divisions. In turn, this can make it more difficult for companies based in such countries to establish a competitive advantage in the global economy.

Religious and Ethical Systems

Religion may be defined as a system of shared beliefs and rituals that are concerned with the realm of the sacred.[16] **Ethical systems** refer to a set of moral principles, or values, that are used to guide and shape behavior. Most of the world's ethical systems are the product of religions. Thus, we can talk about Christian ethics and Islamic ethics. However, there is a major exception to the principle that ethical systems are grounded in religion. Confucianism and Confucian ethics influence behavior and shape culture in parts of Asia, yet, as we shall see, it is incorrect to characterize Confucianism as a religion.

The relationship between religion, ethics, and society is subtle, complex, and profound. While there are thousands of religions in the world today, four dominate— Christianity, Islam, Hinduism, and Buddhism (see Map 3.1). We review each of these, along with Confucianism, focusing on their business implications. Perhaps the most important business implications of religion center on the extent to which different religions shape attitudes toward work and entrepreneurship and the degree to which the religious ethics affect the costs of doing business in a country.

Christianity

Christianity is the most widely practiced religion in the world. About 1 billion people, approximately 20 percent of the world's population, identify themselves as Christians. The vast majority of Christians live in Europe and the Americas, although their numbers are growing rapidly in Africa. Christianity grew out of Judaism. Like Judaism, it is a monotheistic religion (monotheism is the belief in one god). A religious division in the 11th century led to the establishment of two major Christian organizations—the Roman Catholic church and the Orthodox church. Today the Roman Catholic church accounts for over half of all Christians, most of whom are found in Southern Europe and Latin America. The Orthodox church, while less influential, is still of major importance in several countries (e.g., Greece and Russia). In the 16th century, the Reformation led to a further split with Rome; the result was Protestantism. The nonconformist nature of Protestantism has facilitated the emergence of numerous denominations under the Protestant umbrella (e.g., Baptist, Methodist, Calvinist).

Economic Implications of Christianity: The Protestant Work Ethic

Some sociologists have argued that of the two main branches of Christianity—Catholicism and Protestantism—the latter has the most important economic implications. In 1904, a German sociologist, Max Weber, made a connection between Protestant ethics and "the spirit of capitalism" that has since become famous.[17] Weber noted that capitalism emerged in Western Europe. He also noted that in Western Europe:

> Business leaders and owners of capital, as well as the higher grades of skilled labor, and even more the higher technically and commercially trained personnel of modern enterprises, are overwhelmingly Protestant.[18]

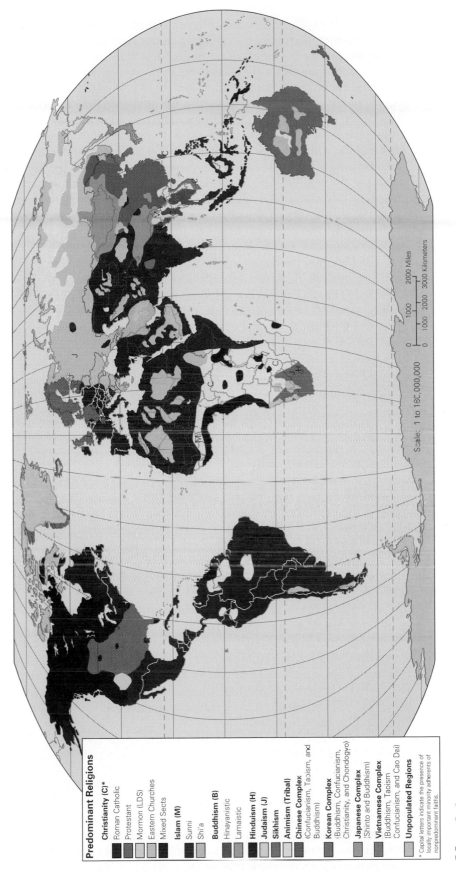

Predominant Religions

Christianity (C)*
- Roman Catholic
- Protestant
- Mormon (LDS)
- Eastern Churches
- Mixed Sects

Islam (M)
- Sunni
- Shi'a

Buddhism (B)
- Hinayanistic
- Lamaistic

Hinduism (H)
Judaism (J)
Sikhism
Animism (Tribal)
Chinese Complex
(Confucianism, Taoism, and Buddhism)

Korean Complex
(Buddhism, Confucianism, Christianity, and Chondogyo)

Japanese Complex
(Shinto and Buddhism)

Vietnamese Complex
(Buddhism, Taoism, Confucianism, and Cao Dai)

Unpopulated Regions

* Capital letters indicate the presence of locally important minority adherents of nonpredominant faiths.

Scale: 1 to 180,000,000

0   1000   2000 Miles
0   1000   2000   3000 Kilometers

Map 3.1

World Religions

Source: Map 17, John L. Allen, *Student Atlas of World Geography*, Dushkin/McGraw-Hill, 1999, p. 34.

According to Weber, there was a relationship between Protestantism and the emergence of modern capitalism. Weber argued that Protestant ethics emphasize the importance of hard work and wealth creation (for the glory of God) and frugality (abstinence from worldly pleasures). According to Weber, this was the kind of value system needed to facilitate the development of capitalism. Protestants worked hard and systematically to accumulate wealth. However, their ascetic beliefs suggested that rather than consuming this wealth by indulging in worldly pleasures, they should invest it in the expansion of capitalist enterprises. Thus, the combination of hard work and the accumulation of capital, which could be used to finance investment and expansion, paved the way for the development of capitalism in Western Europe and subsequently in the United States. In contrast, Weber argued that the Catholic promise of salvation in the next world, rather than this world, did not foster the same kind of work ethic among members of the Catholic religion.

There is also another way in which Protestantism may have encouraged capitalism's development. By breaking away from the hierarchical domination of religious and social life that characterized the Catholic church for much of its history, Protestantism gave individuals significantly more freedom to develop their own relationship with God. The right to freedom of form of worship was central to the nonconformist nature of early Protestantism. This emphasis on individual religious freedom may have paved the way for the subsequent emphasis on individual economic and political freedoms and the development of individualism as an economic and political philosophy. As we saw in Chapter 2, such a philosophy forms the bedrock on which entrepreneurial free market capitalism is based.

Islam

With close to 1 billion adherents, Islam is the second largest of the world's major religions. Islam dates back to 610 AD when the prophet Mohammed began spreading the word. Adherents of Islam are referred to as Muslims. Muslims constitute a majority in more than 35 countries and inhabit a nearly contiguous stretch of land from the northwest coast of Africa, through the Middle East, to China and Malaysia in the Far East.

Islam has roots in both Judaism and Christianity (Islam views Jesus Christ as one of God's prophets). Like Christianity and Judaism, Islam is a monotheistic religion. The central principle of Islam is that there is but the one true omnipotent God. Islam requires unconditional acceptance of the uniqueness, power, and authority of God and the understanding that the objective of life is to fulfill the dictates of his will in the hope of admission to paradise. According to Islam, worldly gain and temporal power are an illusion. Those who pursue riches on earth may gain them, but those who forgo worldly ambitions to seek the favor of Allah may gain the greater treasure—entry into paradise. Other major principles of Islam include: (1) honoring and respecting parents, (2) respecting the rights of others, (3) being generous but not a squanderer, (4) avoiding killing except for justifiable causes, (5) not committing adultery, (6) dealing justly and equitably with others, (7) being of pure heart and mind, (8) safeguarding the possessions of orphans, and (9) being humble and unpretentious.[19] There are obvious parallels here with many of the central principles of both Judaism and Christianity.

Islam is an all-embracing way of life governing the totality of a Muslim's being.[20] As God's surrogate in this world, a Muslim is not a totally free agent but is circumscribed by religious principles—by a code of conduct for interpersonal relations—in social and economic activities. Religion is paramount in all areas of life. The Muslim lives in a social structure that is shaped by Islamic values and norms of moral conduct. The ritual nature of everyday life in a Muslim country is striking to a Western visitor. Among other things, Muslim ritual requires prayer five times a day (it is not unusual for business meetings to be put on hold while the Muslim participants engage in their daily prayer ritual), demands that women should be dressed in a certain manner and subordinate to men, and forbids the consumption of either pig meat or alcohol.

Islamic Fundamentalism

The past two decades have witnessed a surge in what is often referred to as "Islamic fundamentalism."[21] In the West, Islamic fundamentalism is often associated in the media with militants, terrorists, and violent upheavals, such as the bloody conflict occurring in Algeria or the killing of foreign tourists in Egypt. This characterization is at best a half-truth. Just as "Christian fundamentalists" in the West are motivated by sincere and deeply held religious values firmly rooted in their faith, so are "Islamic fundamentalists." The violence that the Western media associates with Islamic fundamentalism is perpetrated by a very small minority of "fundamentalists" and explicitly repudiated by many.

The rise of fundamentalism has no one cause. In part it is a response to the social pressures created in traditional Islamic societies by the move toward modernization and by the influence of Western ideas, such as liberal democracy, materialism, equal rights for women, and by Western attitudes toward sex, marriage, and alcohol. In many Muslim countries, modernization has been accompanied by a growing gap between a rich urban minority and an impoverished urban and rural majority. For the impoverished majority, modernization has offered little in the way of tangible economic progress, while threatening the traditional value system. Thus, for a Muslim who cherishes his traditions and feels that his identity is jeopardized by the encroachment of alien Western values, Islamic fundamentalism has become a cultural anchor.

Fundamentalists demand a rigid commitment to traditional religious beliefs and rituals. The result has been a marked increase in the use of symbolic gestures that confirm Islamic values. Women are once again wearing floor-length, long-sleeved dresses and covering their hair; religious studies have increased in universities; the publication of religious tracts has increased; and more religious orations are heard in public.[22] Also, the sentiments of some fundamentalist groups are increasingly anti-Western. Rightly or wrongly, Western influence is blamed for a whole range of social ills, and many fundamentalists' actions are directed against Western governments, cultural symbols, businesses, and even individuals.

In several Muslim countries, fundamentalists have gained political power and have used this to try to make Islamic law (as set down in the Koran—the bible of Islam) the law of the land. There are good grounds for this in Islam. There is technically no distinction between church and state in Islam. Islam is not just a religion; it is also the source of law, a guide to statecraft, and an arbiter of social behavior. Muslims believe that every human endeavor is within the purview of the faith—and this includes political activity—because the only purpose of any activity is to do God's will.[23] (Muslims are not unique in this view; it is also shared by some Christian fundamentalists.)

The fundamentalists have been most successful in Iran, where a fundamentalist party has held power since 1979, but they also have a growing influence in many other countries, such as Algeria, Egypt, Pakistan, and Saudi Arabia. The accompanying Country Focus profiles the rise of Islamic fundamentalism in Saudi Arabia. The concern is that fundamentalist forces in Saudi Arabia may gain power and turn their back to the West in general and the United States in particular, which has been a long-standing ally of the country. Given the importance of Saudi Arabia as a source for oil, the economic ramifications of such a shift in geopolitics are serious.

Economic Implications of Islam

Some explicit economic principles are set down in the Koran.[24] Many of the economic principles of Islam are pro-free enterprise. The Koran speaks approvingly of free enterprise and of earning *legitimate* profit through trade and commerce (the prophet Mohammed was once a trader). The protection of the right to private property is also embedded within Islam, although Islam asserts that all property is a favor from Allah (God), who created and so owns everything. Those who hold property are regarded as trustees who are entitled to receive profits from it, rather than owners in the Western

COUNTRY FOCUS
Islamic Dissent in Saudi Arabia

The desert kingdom of Saudi Arabia is a new nation. This state of 7 million was a loosely governed area inhabited by numerous Bedouin tribes until King Abdel-Aziz unified the country by conquest and intermarriage in 1935. His descendants—the House of Saudi—still rule what remains a monarchy with few democratic institutions. The majority of Saudis are Sunnis, although a Shiite minority lives on the eastern coast. Saudi Arabia has long been thought of as a close ally of the West. Western governments have gone out of their way to curry the favor of Saudi Arabia, a cynic might say because the country sits on more than a quarter of the world's oil reserves—oil that the West needs to keep its industrial machinery humming. In the 1970s and early 1980s, high oil prices turned Saudi Arabia into one of the richest countries when measured by GDP per capita. This oil wealth supported a spending spree on basic infrastructure that gave the country all the trappings of a modern state. Nevertheless, traditional tribal values remained just below the surface.

The spending spree is now over. The high oil prices that sustained Saudi spending collapsed in 1985 and have yet to recover. While Saudi Arabia was on the winning side in the Gulf War, the cost of financing the war drained the Saudi treasury. As a consequence, government spending has been declining sharply since 1991. In 1994, the Saudi government cut spending by 20 percent.

As oil revenues and government spending shrunk, the Saudis began to experience unemployment and social unrest. This has led Islamic fundamentalists to question the legitimacy of the rule of the House of Saudi. The irony of the current Saudi predicament is that the House of Saudi has always seen itself as the guardian of traditional Islamic values. The legitimacy of the royal family has been based in part on the backing of the *ulema,* an influential group of Islamic scholars. The laws of Saudi Arabia have always been based on Islamic principles. Still, dissident members of the *ulema* have united with hard-line Islamic radicals—a group that includes preachers, professors, students, and marginalized city dwellers—to criticize the ruling family. These radicals tend to be anti-Western, anti-Shiite, and highly critical of the ruling family. Their opposition is based not just on economic problems, but also on a perception that the House of Saudi has been cor-

sense of the word, and they are admonished to use it in a righteous, socially beneficial, and prudent manner. This reflects Islam's concern with social justice. Islam is critical of those who earn profit through the exploitation of others. In the Islamic view of the world, humans are part of a collective in which the wealthy and successful have obligations to help the disadvantaged. Put simply, in Muslim countries, it is fine to earn a profit, so long as that profit is justly earned and not based on the exploitation of others for one's own advantage. It also helps if those making profits undertake charitable acts to help the poor. Furthermore, Islam stresses the importance of living up to contractual obligations, of keeping one's word, and of abstaining from deception.

Given the Islamic proclivity to favor market-based systems, Muslim countries are likely to be receptive to international businesses so long as those businesses behave in a manner that is consistent with Islamic ethics. Businesses that are perceived as making an unjust profit through the exploitation of others, by deception, or by breaking contractual obligations are unlikely to be welcomed in an Islamic state. In addition, in Islamic states where fundamentalism is on the rise, it is likely that hostility to Western-owned businesses will increase.

One economic principle of Islam prohibits the payment or receipt of interest, which is considered usury. To the devout Muslim, acceptance of interest payments is seen as a very grave sin. Practitioners of the black art of usury are warned on the pain of hellfire to abstain; the giver and the taker are equally damned. This is not just a matter of theology, in several Islamic states, it is also becoming a matter of law. In 1992, for example, Pakistan's Federal Shariat Court, the highest Islamic law-making

http://www.saudinf.com/index.htm

rupted by its wealth and has monopolized political power in the country.

The sermons of radical preachers denounce a Judeo-Christian conspiracy against Islam and criticize Western values and lifestyles. In September 1994, one of the best-known radical preachers, Sheik Salman al-Audah, was asked by the government to sign a gag order. He refused, published the order, and was arrested. Hundreds of his followers were also arrested when they protested by taking to the streets of Buraida, a fundamentalist stronghold. Harassing, arresting, and sometimes torturing fundamentalist opponents may prove to be a costly error for the government. As the governments of Algeria and Egypt have recently discovered, fundamentalists seem to draw strength from repression.

Another source of dissent has been lingering resentment among the radicals to the government's decision to allow 500,000 Western troops onto Saudi soil during the Gulf War. The fact that Saudi Arabia was on the winning side during the war apparently matters less to the fundamentalists than the "dishonor" associated with having to rely on outsiders, and Western ones at that, to protect Saudi sovereignty.

In November 1995, the dissent became violent when a car bomb stuffed with 250 pounds of high explosives blew up at a base in Riyadh where US military personnel helped train their Saudi counterparts. The blast killed 5 Americans and wounded 34. In May 1996, the Saudi government beheaded four "Muslim extremists" that the government claimed confessed to the bombing, though no trial was held and Saudi officials denied US investigators access to the men. Less than a month later, a huge truck bomb tore out the face of a US military apartment tower outside of Dhahran, killing 19 more US military personnel and wounding 200 others. Since then things have quieted down in Saudi Arabia, but there is growing concern that underneath the surface, dissent is growing and may come to a head.

Sources: "The Cracks in the Kingdom," *The Economist,* March 18, 1995, pp. 21–25; B. Deans, "Saudi–US Ties Shows New Strains," *Atlanta Constitution,* August 18, 1996, p. 16A; and J. Keen, "Winds Shifting in Saudi Arabia," *USA Today* June 26, 1996, p. 3A.

body in the country, pronounced interest to be un-Islamic and therefore illegal and demanded that the government amend all financial laws accordingly.[25]

On the face of it, rigid adherence to this particular Islamic law could wreak havoc with a country's financial and banking system, raising the costs of doing business and scaring away international businesses and international investors. To skirt the ban on interest, Islamic banks have been experimenting with a profit-sharing system to replace interest on borrowed money. When an Islamic bank lends money to a business, rather than charging that business interest on the loan, it takes a share in the profits that are derived from the investment. Similarly, when a business (or individual) deposits money at an Islamic bank in a savings account, the deposit is treated as an equity investment in whatever activity the bank uses the capital for. Thus, the depositor receives a share in the profit from the bank's investment (as opposed to interest payments). Some Muslims claim this is a more efficient system than the Western banking system, since it encourages both long-term savings and long-term investment. However, there is no hard evidence of this, and many believe that an Islamic banking system is less efficient than a conventional Western banking system.

Hinduism

Hinduism has approximately 500 million adherents, most of whom are on the Indian subcontinent. Hinduism began in the Indus Valley in India over 4,000 years ago, making it the world's oldest major religion. Unlike Christianity and Islam, its founding is not linked to a particular person. Nor does it have an officially sanctioned sacred book such as the Bible or the Koran. Hindus believe that there is a moral force in society that requires the acceptance of certain responsibilities, called *dharma*. Hindus believe in *reincarnation*, or rebirth into a different body after death. Hindus also believe in *karma*, the spiritual progression of each person's soul. A person's *karma* is affected by the way he or she lives. The moral state of an individual's *karma* determines the challenges they will face in their next life. By perfecting the soul in each new life, Hindus believe that an individual can eventually achieve *nirvana*, a state of complete spiritual perfection that renders reincarnation no longer necessary. Many Hindus believe that the way to achieve nirvana is to lead a severe ascetic lifestyle of material and physical self-denial, devoting life to a spiritual rather than material quest.

Economic Implications of Hinduism

Max Weber, who is famous for expounding on the Protestant work ethic, also argued that the ascetic principles embedded in Hinduism do not encourage the kind of entrepreneurial activity in pursuit of wealth creation that we find in Protestantism.[26] According to Weber, traditional Hindu values emphasize that individuals should not be judged by their material achievements, but by their spiritual achievements. Indeed, Hindus perceive the pursuit of material well-being as making the attainment of *nirvana* more difficult. Given the emphasis on an ascetic lifestyle, Weber thought that devout Hindus would be less likely to engage in entrepreneurial activity than devout Protestants.

Mahatma Gandhi, the famous Indian nationalist and spiritual leader, was certainly the embodiment of Hindu asceticism. It has been argued that the values of Hindu asceticism and self-reliance that Gandhi advocated had a negative impact on the economic development of post-independence India.[27] But one must be careful not to read too much into Weber's arguments. Today, millions of hardworking entrepreneurs form the economic backbone of India's rapidly growing economy.

Hinduism also supports India's caste system. The concept of mobility between castes within an individual's lifetime makes no sense to Hindus. Hindus see mobility between castes as something that is achieved through spiritual progression and reincarnation. An individual can be reborn into a higher caste in his next life if he achieves spiritual development in this life. In so far as the caste system limits individuals' opportunities to adopt positions of responsibility and influence in society, the economic consequences of this religious belief are bound to be negative. For example, within a business organization, the most able individuals may find their route to the higher levels of the organization blocked simply because they come from a lower caste. By the same token, individuals may get promoted to higher positions within a firm as much because of their caste background as because of their ability.

Buddhism

Buddhism was founded in India in the sixth century BC by Siddhartha Gautama, an Indian prince who renounced his wealth to pursue an ascetic lifestyle and spiritual perfection. Siddhartha achieved *nirvana* but decided to remain on Earth to teach his followers how they too could achieve this state of spiritual enlightenment. Siddhartha became known as the Buddha (which means "the awakened one"). Today Buddhism has 250 million followers, most of whom are found in Central and Southeast Asia, China, Korea, and Japan. According to Buddhism, life is comprised of suffering. Misery is everywhere and originates in people's desires for pleasure. These desires can be curbed by systematically following the *Noble Eightfold Path*, which emphasizes right seeing, thinking, speech, action, living, effort, mindfulness, and meditation. Unlike Hinduism, Buddhism does not support the caste system. Nor does Buddhism advocate the kind of extreme ascetic behavior that is encouraged by Hinduism. Nevertheless, like Hindus, Buddhists stress the afterlife and spiritual achievement rather than involvement in this world.

Because Buddhists, like Hindus, stress spiritual achievement rather than involvement in this world, the emphasis on wealth creation that is embedded in Protestantism is not found in Buddhism. Thus, in Buddhist societies, we do not see the same kind of cultural stress on entrepreneurial behavior that we see in the Protestant West. But unlike Hinduism, the lack of support for the caste system and extreme ascetic behavior suggests that a Buddhist society may represent a more fertile ground for entrepreneurial activity than a Muslim culture.

Confucianism

Confucianism was founded in the fifth century BC by K'ung-Fu-tzu, more generally known as Confucius. For more than 2,000 years until the 1949 communist revolution, Confucianism was the official ethical system of China. While observance of Confucian ethics has been weakened in China since 1949, over 150 million people still follow the teachings of Confucius, principally in China, Korea, and Japan. Confucianism teaches the importance of attaining personal salvation through right action. Confucianism is built around a comprehensive ethical code that sets down guidelines for relationships with others. The need for high moral and ethical conduct and loyalty to others are central to Confucianism. Unlike religions, Confucianism is not concerned with the supernatural and has little to say about the concept of a supreme being or an afterlife.

Economic Implications of Confucianism

There are those who maintain that Confucianism may have economic implications that are as profound as those found in Protestantism, although they are of a somewhat different nature.[28] Their basic thesis is that the influence of Confucian ethics on the culture of Japan, South Korea, and Taiwan, by lowering the costs of doing business in those countries, may help explain their economic success. In this regard, three values central to the Confucian system of ethics are of particular interest—*loyalty, reciprocal obligations*, and *honesty* in dealings with others.

In Confucian thought, loyalty to one's superiors is regarded as a sacred duty—an absolute obligation that is necessary for religious salvation. In modern organizations based in Confucian cultures, the loyalty that binds employees to the heads of their organization can reduce the conflict between management and labor that we find in class-conscious societies such as Britain. Cooperation between management and labor can be achieved at a lower cost in a culture where the virtue of loyalty is emphasized in the value systems.

However, in a Confucian culture, loyalty to one's superiors, such as a worker's loyalty to management, is not blind loyalty. The concept of reciprocal obligations also comes into play. Confucian ethics stress that superiors are obliged to reward the loyalty of their subordinates by bestowing blessings on them. If these "blessings" are not forthcoming, then neither will be the loyalty. This Confucian ethic exhibits itself in Japanese organizations in the concept of lifetime employment. The employees of a Japanese company are loyal to the leaders of the organization, and in return the leaders bestow on them the "blessing" of lifetime employment. The business implications of this cultural practice have been touched on earlier in this chapter. Specifically, the lack of mobility between companies implied by the lifetime employment system suggests that over the years managers and workers build up knowledge, experience, and a network of interpersonal business contacts. All of these can help managers and workers perform their jobs more effectively and cooperate with others in the organization. One result is improved economic performance of the company.

A third concept found in Confucian ethics is the importance attached to honesty. Confucian thinkers emphasize that, although dishonest behavior may yield short-term benefits for the transgressor, in the long run dishonesty does not pay. The importance attached to honesty has major economic implications. When companies can trust each other not to break contractual obligations, the costs of doing business are lowered. Expensive lawyers are not needed to resolve contract disputes. In a Confucian society, there may be less hesitation to commit substantial resources to cooperative ventures than in a society where honesty is less pervasive. When companies adhere to Confucian ethics, they can trust each other not to violate the terms of cooperative agreements. Thus, the costs of achieving cooperation between companies may be lowered in societies such as Japan relative to societies where trust is less pervasive.

For example, it has been argued that the close ties between the automobile companies and their component parts suppliers in Japan are facilitated by a combination of trust and reciprocal obligations. These close ties allow the auto companies and their suppliers to work together on a range of issues, including inventory reduction, quality control, and design. It is claimed that the competitive advantage of Japanese auto companies can in part be explained by such factors.[29]

Language

One of the most obvious ways in which countries differ is language. By language, we mean both the spoken and the unspoken means of communication. Language is one of the defining characteristics of a culture.

Spoken Language

Language does far more than just enable people to communicate with each other. The nature of a language also structures the way we perceive the world. The language of a society can direct the attention of its members to certain features of the world rather than others. The classic illustration of this phenomenon is that whereas the English language has but one word for snow, the language of the Inuit (Eskimos) lacks a general term for it. Instead, because distinguishing different forms of snow is so important in the lives of the Inuit, they have 24 words that describe different types of snow (e.g., powder snow, falling snow, wet snow, drifting snow).[30]

Because language shapes the way people perceive the world, it also helps define culture. In countries with more than one language, one also often finds more than one culture. Canada has an English-speaking culture and a French-speaking culture. Tensions between the two run quite high, with a substantial proportion of the French-speaking minority demanding independence from a Canada "dominated by English speakers." The same phenomenon can be observed in many countries. For example, Belgium is divided into Flemish and French speakers, and tensions between the two groups exist; in Spain, a Basque-speaking minority with its own distinctive culture has been agitating for independence from the Spanish-speaking majority for decades; on the Mediterranean island of Cyprus, the culturally diverse Greek- and Turkish-speaking populations of the island engaged in open conflict in the 1970s, and the island is now partitioned into two parts. While it does not necessarily follow that language differences create differences in culture and, therefore, separatist pressures (e.g., witness the harmony in Switzerland, where four languages are spoken) there certainly seems to be a tendency in this direction.

Chinese is the "mother tongue" of the largest number of people, followed by English and Hindi, which is spoken in India (see Figure 3.2). However, the most widely spoken language in the world is English, followed by French, Spanish, and Chinese (i.e., many people speak English as a second language). English is increasingly becoming the language of international business. When a Japanese and a German businessperson get together to do business, it is almost certain that they will communicate in English. However, while English is widely used, learning the local language yields considerable advantages. Most people prefer to converse in their own language and being able to speak the local language can build rapport, which may be very important for a business deal.

Figure 3.2

Mother Tongues

Language	Percentage of the World Population for Whom This Is a First Language
Chinese	20.0
English	6.0
Hindi	4.5
Russian	3.5
Spanish	3.0
Portuguese	2.0
Japanese	2.0
Arabic	2.0
French	1.5
German	1.5
Other	54.0

Source: *The Economist Atlas* (London: The Economist Books, 1991), p. 116. Copyright © 1989 and © 1991 The Economist Books, Ltd.

International businesses that do not understand the local language can make some major blunders through improper translation. For example, the Sunbeam Corporation used the English words for its "Mist-Stick" mist-producing hair curling iron when it entered the German market, only to discover after an expensive advertising campaign that *mist* means *excrement* in German. General Motors was troubled by the lack of enthusiasm among Puerto Rican dealers for its new Chevrolet Nova. When literally translated into Spanish, *Nova* meant star. However, when spoken it sounded like "no va," which in Spanish means "it doesn't go." General Motors changed the name of the car to Caribe.[31]

Unspoken Language

Unspoken language refers to nonverbal communication. We all communicate with each other by a host of nonverbal cues. The raising of eyebrows, for example, is a sign of recognition in most cultures, while a smile is a sign of joy. Many nonverbal cues, however, are culturally bound. A failure to understand the nonverbal cues of another culture can lead to a failure of communication. For example, making a circle with the thumb and the forefinger is a friendly gesture in the US, but it is a vulgar sexual invitation in Greece and Turkey. Similarly, while most Americans and Europeans use the thumbs-up gesture to indicate that "it's all right," in Greece the gesture is obscene.

Another aspect of nonverbal communication is personal space, which is the comfortable amount of distance between you and someone you are talking to. In the United States, the customary distance apart adopted by parties in a business discussion is five to eight feet. In Latin America, it is three to five feet. Consequently, many North Americans unconsciously feel that Latin Americans are invading their personal space and can be seen backing away from them during a conversation. In turn, the Latin American may interpret such backing away as aloofness. The result can be a regrettable lack of rapport between two businesspeople from different cultures.

Education

Formal education plays a key role in a society. Formal education is the medium through which individuals learn many of the language, conceptual, and mathematical skills that are indispensable in a modern society. Formal education also supplements the family's role in socializing the young into the values and norms of a society. Values and norms are taught both directly and indirectly. Schools generally teach basic facts about the social and political nature of a society. They also focus on the fundamental obligations of citizenship. Cultural norms are also taught indirectly at school. Respect for others, obedience to authority, honesty, neatness, being on time, and so on, are all part of the "hidden curriculum" of schools. The use of a grading system also teaches children the value of personal achievement and competition.[32]

From an international business perspective, perhaps one of the most important aspects of education is its role as a determinant of national competitive advantage.[33] The availability of a pool of skilled and educated workers seems to be a major determinant of the likely economic success of a country. In analyzing the competitive success of Japan since 1945, for example, Michael Porter notes that after the war Japan had almost nothing except for a pool of skilled and educated human resources.

> With a long tradition of respect for education that borders on reverence, Japan possessed a large pool of literate, educated, and increasingly skilled human resources . . . Japan has benefited from a large pool of trained engineers. Japanese universities graduate many more engineers per capita than in the United States . . . A first-rate primary and secondary education system in Japan operates based on high standards and emphasizes math and science. Primary and secondary education is highly competitive . . . Japanese education provides most students all over Japan with a sound education for later education and training. A Japanese high school graduate knows as much about math as most American college graduates.[34]

Porter's point is that Japan's excellent education system was an important factor explaining the country's postwar economic success. Not only is a good education system a determinant of national competitive advantage, but it is also an important factor guiding the location choices of international businesses. It would make little sense to base production facilities that require highly skilled labor in a country where the education system was so poor that a skilled labor pool wasn't available, no matter how attractive the country might seem on other dimensions. It might make sense to base production operations that require only unskilled labor in such a country.

The general education level of a country is also a good index of the kind of products that might sell in a country and of the type of promotional material that should be used. For example, a country such as Pakistan where 73.8 percent of the population is illiterate is unlikely to be a good market for popular books. Promotional material containing written descriptions of mass-marketed products is unlikely to have an effect in a country where almost three-quarters of the population cannot read. It is far better to use pictorial promotions in such circumstances.

Maps 3.2 and 3.3 provide some important data on education worldwide. Map 3.2 shows the percentage of a country's GNP that is devoted to education. Map 3.3 shows illiteracy rates. Although there is not a perfect one-to-one correspondence between the percentage of GNP devoted to education and the quality of education, the overall level of spending indicates a country's commitment to education. Note that the United States spends more of its GNP on education than many other advanced industrialized nations, including Germany and Japan. Despite this, the *quality* of US education is often argued to be inferior to that offered in many other industrialized countries.

Culture and the Workplace

For an international business with operations in different countries, a question of considerable importance is *how does a society's culture affect the values found in the workplace?* The question points to the need to vary management process and practices according to culturally determined work-related values. For example, if the cultures of

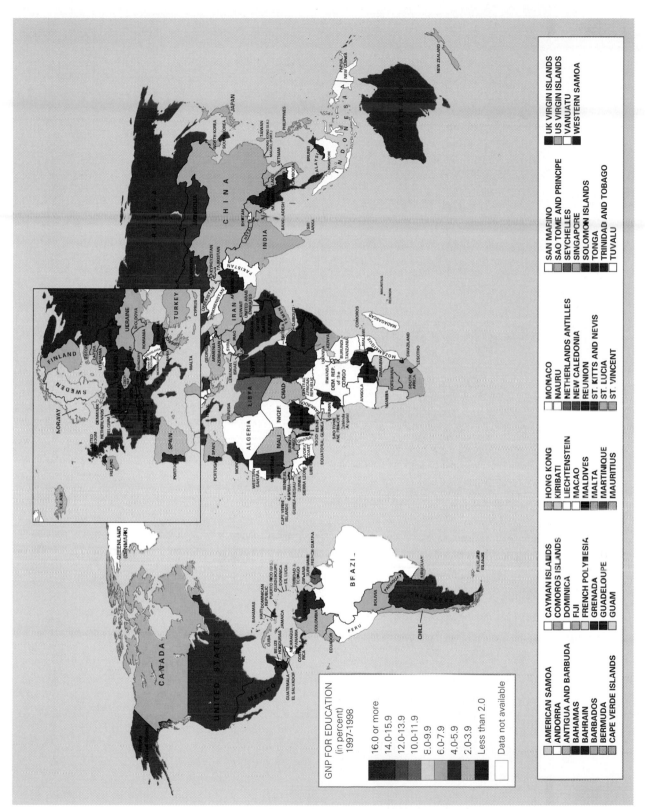

Map 3.2

Percentage of Gross National Product (GNP) Spent on Education

Source: Map data are from World Bank, *World Development Report 1998–99*, pp. 202–01.

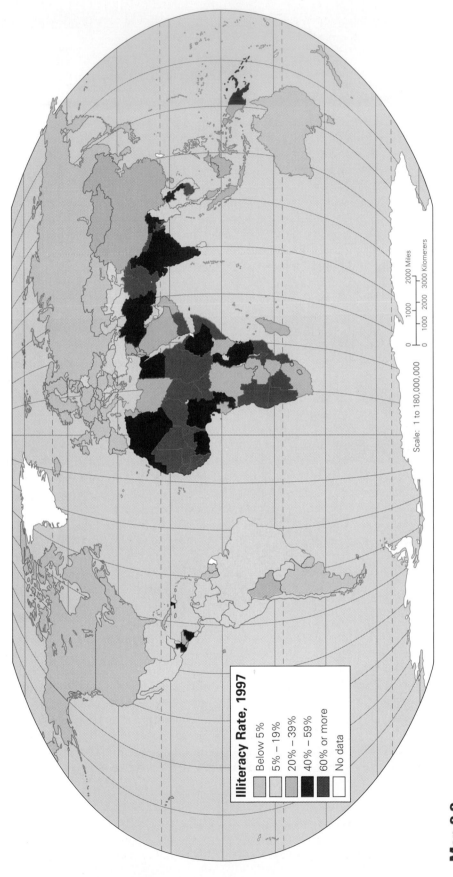

Map 3.3

Illiteracy Rates

Source: Map 26, John L. Allen, *Student Atlas of World Geography*, Dushkin/McGraw-Hill, 1999, p. 44.

the United States and France result in different work-related values, an international business with operations in both countries should vary its management process and practices to take these differences into account.

Hofstede's Model

Probably the most famous study of how culture relates to values in the workplace was undertaken by Geert Hofstede.[35] As part of his job as a psychologist working for IBM, Hofstede collected data on employee attitudes and values for over 100,000 individuals from 1967 to 1973. This data enabled him to compare dimensions of culture across 40 countries. Hofstede isolated four dimensions that he claimed summarized different cultures—power distance, uncertainty avoidance, individualism versus collectivism, and masculinity versus femininity.

Hofstede's **power distance** dimension focused on how a society deals with the fact that people are unequal in physical and intellectual capabilities. According to Hofstede, high power distance cultures were found in countries that let inequalities grow over time into inequalities of power and wealth. Low power distance cultures were found in societies that tried to play down such inequalities as much as possible.

The **individualism versus collectivism** dimension focused on the relationship between the individual and his or her fellows. In individualistic societies, the ties between individuals were loose and individual achievement and freedom were highly valued. In societies where collectivism was emphasized, the ties between individuals were tight. In such societies, people were born into collectives, such as extended families, and everyone was supposed to look after the interest of his or her collective.

Hofstede's **uncertainty avoidance** dimension measured the extent to which different cultures socialized their members into accepting ambiguous situations and tolerating uncertainty. Members of high uncertainty avoidance cultures placed a premium on job security, career patterns, retirement benefits, and so on. They also had a strong need for rules and regulations; the manager was expected to issue clear instructions, and subordinates' initiatives were tightly controlled. Lower uncertainty avoidance cultures were characterized by a greater readiness to take risks and less emotional resistance to change.

Hofstede's **masculinity versus femininity** dimension looked at the relationship between gender and work roles. In masculine cultures, sex roles were sharply differentiated and traditional "masculine values," such as achievement and the effective exercise of power, determined cultural ideals. In feminine cultures, sex roles were less sharply distinguished, and little differentiation was made between men and women in the same job.

Hofstede created an index score for each of these four dimensions that ranged from 0 to 100 and scored high for high individualism, high power distance, high uncertainty avoidance, and high masculinity. He averaged the score for all employees from a given country. Table 3.1 summarizes this data for 20 selected countries. Among other things, this data tell us that Western nations such as the United States, Canada, and Britain score high on the individualism scale and low on the power distance scale. At the other extreme are a group of Latin American and Asian countries that emphasize collectivism over individualism and score high on the power distance scale. Table 3.1 also tells us that Japan is a country with a culture of strong uncertainty avoidance and high masculinity. This characterization fits the standard stereotype of Japan as a country that is male dominant, and where uncertainty avoidance exhibits itself in the institution of lifetime employment. Sweden and Denmark stand out as countries that have both low uncertainty avoidance and low masculinity (high emphasis on "feminine" values).

Evaluating Hofstede's Model

Hofstede's results are interesting for what they tell us in a general way about differences between cultures. Many of Hofstede's findings are consistent with standard Western stereotypes about cultural differences. For example, many people believe

Table 3.1

Work-Related Values for 20
Selected Countries

	Power Distance	Uncertainty Avoidance	Individualism	Masculinity
Argentina	49	86	46	56
Australia	36	51	90	61
Brazil	69	76	38	49
Canada	39	48	80	52
Denmark	18	23	74	16
France	68	86	71	43
Germany (F.R.)	35	65	67	66
Great Britain	35	35	89	66
Indonesia	78	48	14	46
India	77	40	48	56
Israel	13	81	54	47
Japan	54	92	46	95
Mexico	81	82	30	69
Netherlands	38	53	80	14
Panama	95	86	11	44
Spain	57	86	51	42
Sweden	31	29	71	5
Thailand	64	64	20	34
Turkey	66	85	37	45
United States	40	46	91	62

Source: G. Hofstede, *Culture's Consequences*. Copyright 1980 by Sage Publications. Reprinted by permission of Sage Publications. Cited in G. Hofstede, "The Cultural Relativity of Organizational Practices and Theories." *Journal of International Business Studies*, 14 (Fall), 1983, pp. 75–89.

Americans are more individualistic and egalitarian than the Japanese (they have a lower power distance), who in turn are more individualistic and egalitarian than Mexicans. Similarly, many might agree that Latin countries such as Mexico place a higher emphasis on masculine value—they are machismo cultures—than the Nordic countries of Denmark and Sweden.

However, one should be careful about reading too much into Hofstede's research. It is deficient in a number of important respects.[36] First, Hofstede assumes there is a one-to-one correspondence between culture and the nation-state, but as we saw earlier, many countries have more than one culture. Hofstede's results do not capture this distinction. Second, the research may have been culturally bound. The research team was composed of Europeans and Americans. The questions they asked of IBM employees and their analysis of the answers may have been shaped by their own cultural biases and concerns. So it is not surprising that Hofstede's results confirm Western stereotypes, since it was Westerners who undertook the research!

Third, Hofstede's informants worked not only within a single industry, the computer industry, but also within one company, IBM. At the time, IBM was renowned for its own strong corporate culture and employee selection procedures, making it possible that the employees' values were different in important respects from the values of the cultures from which those employees came. Also, certain social classes (such as unskilled manual workers) were excluded from Hofstede's sample. A final caution is that Hofstede's work is now beginning to look dated. Cultures do not stand still; they evolve over time, albeit slowly. What was a reasonable characterization in the 1960s and 1970s may not be so today.

Still, just as it should not be accepted without question, Hofstede's work should not be dismissed entirely either. It represents a starting point for managers trying to figure out how cultures differ and what that might mean for management practices. Also, it is worth noting that several other scholars have found strong evidence that differences in culture affect values and practices in the workplace.[37] But managers should use the results with caution, for they are not necessarily accurate.

Cultural Change

Culture is not a constant; it evolves over time. Changes in value systems can be slow and painful for a society. In the 1960s, for example, American values toward the role of women, love, sex, and marriage underwent significant changes. Much of the social turmoil of that time reflected these changes. Similarly, today the value systems of many ex-communist states, such as Russia, are undergoing significant changes as those countries move away from values that emphasize collectivism and toward those that emphasize individualism. Social turmoil is an inevitable outcome.

Some claim that a major cultural shift is occurring in Japan, with a move toward greater individualism.[38] The model Japanese office worker, or "salaryman," is pictured as being loyal to his boss and the organization to the point of giving up evenings, weekends, and vacations in order to serve the organization, which is the collective of which he is a member. However, a new generation of office workers does not seem to fit this model. It is claimed that an individual from the new generation

> is more direct than the traditional Japanese. He acts more like a Westerner, a *gaijian*. He does not live for the company, and will move on if he gets the offer of a better job. He is not keen on overtime, especially if he has a date with a girl. He has his own plans for his free time, and they may not include drinking or playing golf with the boss.[39]

A more detailed example of the changes occurring in Japan is given in the Management Focus, which looks at the impact of Japan's changing culture on Hitachi.

The Hitachi example in the Management Focus points to two forces that may result in cultural change—economic advancement and globalization. Several studies have suggested that both these forces may be important factors in societal change.[40] For example, there is evidence that economic progress is accompanied by a shift in values away from collectivism and towards individualism.[41] Thus, as Japan has become richer, the cultural emphasis on collectivism has declined and greater individualism is being witnessed. One reason for this shift may be that richer societies exhibit less need for social and material support structures built on collectives, whether the collective is the extended family or the paternalistic company. People are better able to take care of their own needs. As a result, the importance attached to collectivism declines, while greater economic freedoms lead to an increase in opportunities for expressing individualism.

The culture of societies may also change as they become richer because economic progress affects a number of other factors, which in turn impact on culture. For example, increased urbanization and improvements in the quality and availability of education are both a function of economic progress, and both can lead to declining emphasis on the traditional values associated with poor rural societies.

As for globalization, some have argued that advances in transportation and communications technologies, the dramatic increase in trade that we have witnessed since World War II, and the rise of global corporations such as Hitachi, Disney, Microsoft, and Levi Strauss, whose products and operations can be found around the globe, are creating the conditions for the merging of cultures.[42] With McDonald's hamburgers in China, Levi's in India, Sony Walkmans in South Africa, and MTV everywhere helping to foster a ubiquitous youth culture, some argue that the

MANAGEMENT FOCUS
Hitachi and Japan's Changing Culture

http://www.hitachi.com

Hitachi was founded in 1911 by Namihei Odaira, who named his company after the town in which it was based. By 1965 Hitachi was a giant of Japanese industry; its sales accounted for over 1 percent of Japan's gross national product. In many ways, Hitachi was a typical Japanese company. New recruits were lectured on Odaira's reverence for *wa*, or harmony. Managers and workers, dressed in identical uniforms, were tirelessly punctual and trusted each other like brothers. Decision making was characterized by the consensus model, so typical of Japanese corporations, where managers consulted juniors exhaustively before making a decision. And the lifetime employment system was instituted at Hitachi.

According to old Hitachi hands, the harmony and togetherness owed as much to poverty as it did to anything else. Many employees and their families were housed in company dormitories because they could afford nothing else. Younger employees slept two to a room, and all ate their meals communally in the company cafeteria. Because public facilities were few, everyone went to the company bathhouse. In the evenings, employees saw the same colleagues in the same company bars. Their wives shopped at the company store. The company even provided a wedding hall and funeral parlor.

Today two forces are affecting Japan's culture—prosperity and globalization. Both are leading to changes at Hitachi. Over the last four decades, Japan has become one of the world's richest countries. At Hitachi, prosperity means nobody sleeps two to a room in the company dormitory anymore. Since the 1960s, employees have been moving

"outside the fence," away from the company dormitories. Prosperity has brought more entertainment and leisure options. The company bathhouse has given way to private bathhouses. The choice between a French restaurant and an Indian restaurant divides one employee from the next. Hobbies are more diverse. There are cars, drinking, bonsai gardening, bands. Employees spend more time with their families; the biological family is replacing the company family as the anchor of social life. Companies such as Hitachi used to provide for all aspects of employees' lives. Now leisure is an opportunity for individualism, not a prop for workplace harmony.

Then there is globalization. Like many other Japanese companies, Hitachi is now a global enterprise with worldwide operations. Japanese society also has become more international in recent years. In this new environment, top management states bluntly that monoculture firms will not survive. In 1991, Hitachi set up a department to educate executives about other cultures. This department downplays the old notions of harmony and consensus decision making. Hitachi is also sending increasing numbers of its executives for prolonged postings overseas, and it is starting to bring foreign managers back to Japan. The foreign experience has encouraged senior managers to seek firmer leadership in Japan—to shift away from the old consensus decision making—and Hitachi's top executives have encouraged this trend.

Sources: "The Long March from Harmony," *The Economist*, July 9, 1994, pp. 6–10; and L. Swanson, "Meeting Global Business Challenges the Japanese Way," CMA *Magazine*, February 1997, pp. 23–25.

conditions for less cultural variation have been created. At the same time, one must not ignore important countertrends, such as the shift toward Islamic fundamentalism in several countries; the separatist movement in Quebec, Canada; or the continuing ethnic strains and separatist movements in Russia. Such countertrends in many ways are a reaction to the pressures for cultural convergence. In an increasingly modern and materialistic world, some societies are trying to reemphasize their cultural roots and uniqueness.

IMPLICATIONS FOR BUSINESS

International business is different from national business because countries and societies are different. In this chapter, we have seen just how different societies can be. Societies differ because their cultures vary. Their cultures vary because of profound differences in social structure, religion, language, education, economic philosophy, and political philosophy. Two important implications for international business flow from these differences. The first is the need to develop cross-cultural literacy. There is a need to appreciate not only that cultural differences exist, but also to appreciate what such differences mean for international business. A second implication for international business centers on the connection between culture and national competitive advantage. In this section, we will explore both of these issues in greater detail.

Cross-Cultural Literacy

One of the biggest dangers confronting a company that goes abroad for the first time is the danger of being ill-informed. International businesses that are ill-informed about the practices of another culture are likely to fail. Doing business in different cultures requires adaptation to conform with the value systems and norms of that culture. Adaptation can embrace all aspects of an international firm's operations in a foreign country. The way in which deals are negotiated, the appropriate incentive pay systems for salespeople, the structure of the organization, the name of a product, the tenor of relations between management and labor, the manner in which the product is promoted, and so on, are all sensitive to cultural differences. What works in one culture might not work in another.

To combat the danger of being ill-informed, international businesses should consider employing local citizens to help them do business in a particular culture. They must also ensure that home-country executives are cosmopolitan enough to understand how differences in culture affect the practice of international business. Transferring executives overseas at regular intervals to expose them to different cultures will help build a cadre of cosmopolitan executives. Hitachi is now taking this approach as it transforms itself from a Japanese into a global company (see the Management Focus for details).

An international business must also be constantly on guard against the dangers of **ethnocentric behavior.** Ethnocentrism is a belief in the superiority of one's own ethnic group or culture. Hand in hand with ethnocentrism goes a disregard or contempt for the culture of other countries. Unfortunately, ethnocentrism is all too prevalent; many Americans are guilty of it, as are many French people, Japanese people, British people, and so on. Ugly as it is, ethnocentrism is a fact of life, one that international businesses must be on continual guard against.

Culture and Competitive Advantage

One theme that continually surfaced in this chapter is the relationship between culture and national competitive advantage. Put simply, the value systems and norms of a country influence the costs of doing business in that country. The costs of doing business in a country influence the ability of firms to establish a competitive advantage in the global marketplace. We have seen how attitudes toward cooperation between management and labor, toward work, and toward the payment of interest are influenced by social structure and religion. It can be argued that the class-based conflict between workers and management found in British society, when it leads to industrial disruption, raises the costs of doing business in that culture. Similarly, we have seen how the ascetic "other worldly" ethics of Hinduism may not be as supportive of capitalism as the ethics embedded in Protestantism and Confucianism. Also, Islamic laws banning interest payments may raise the costs of doing business by constraining a country's banking system.

Japan presents us with an interesting example of how culture can influence competitive advantage. Some scholars have argued that the culture of modern Japan lowers the costs of doing business relative to the costs in most Western nations. Japan's emphasis on group affiliation, loyalty, reciprocal obligations, honesty, and education all boost the competitiveness of Japanese companies. The emphasis on group affiliation and loyalty encourages individuals to identify strongly with the companies in which they work. This tends to foster an ethic of hard work and cooperation between management and labor "for the good of the company." Similarly, reciprocal obligations and honesty help foster an atmosphere of trust between companies and their suppliers. This encourages them to enter into long-term relationships with each other to work on factors such as inventory reduction, quality control, and joint design—all of which have been shown to improve an organization's competitiveness. This level of cooperation has often been lacking in the West, where the relationship between a company and its suppliers tends to be a short-term one structured around competitive bidding, rather than one based on long-term mutual commitments. In addition, the availability of a pool of highly skilled labor, particularly engineers, has helped Japanese enterprises develop cost-reducing process innovations that have boosted their productivity.[43] Thus, cultural factors may help explain the competitive advantage enjoyed by many Japanese businesses in the global marketplace. The rise of Japan as an economic power during the second half of the 20th century may be in part attributed to the economic consequences of its culture.

It can also be argued that the Japanese culture is less supportive of entrepreneurial activity than, say, American society. In many ways, entrepreneurial activity is a product of an individualistic mind-set, not a classic characteristic of the Japanese. This may explain why American enterprises, rather than Japanese corporations, dominate industries where entrepreneurship and innovation are highly valued, such as computer software and biotechnology. Of course, there are obvious exceptions to this generalization. Masayoshi Son recognized the potential of software far faster than any of Japan's corporate giants, set up his company, Softbank, in 1981, and has since built it into Japan's top software distributor. But individuals such as Son are the exception that proves the rule, for there has been no surge in entrepreneurial high-technology enterprises in Japan equivalent to what has occurred in the United States.

For the international business, the connection between culture and competitive advantage is important for two reasons. First, the connection suggests which countries are likely to produce the most viable competitors. For example, US enterprises are likely to see continued growth in aggressive, cost-efficient competitors from those Pacific Rim nations where a combination of free market economics, Confucian ideology, group-oriented social structures, and advanced education systems can all be found (e.g., South Korea, Taiwan, Japan, and increasingly China).

Second, the connection between culture and competitive advantage has important implications for the choice of countries in which to locate production facilities and do business. Consider a hypothetical case when a company has to choose between two countries, A and B, for locating a production facility. Both countries are characterized by low labor costs and good access to world markets. Both countries are of roughly the same size (in terms of population) and both are at a similar stage of economic development. In country A, the education system is undeveloped, the society is characterized by a marked stratification between the upper and lower classes, the dominant religion stresses the importance of reincarnation, and there are three major linguistic groups. In country B, the education system is well developed, there is a lack of social stratification, group identification is valued by the culture, the dominant religion stresses the virtue of hard work, and there is only one linguistic group. Which country makes the best investment site?

Country B does. The culture of country B is supportive of the capitalist mode of production and social harmony, whereas the culture of country A is not. In country A, conflict between management and labor, and between different language groups, can be expected to lead to social and industrial disruption, thereby raising the costs of doing business. The lack of a good education system and the dominance of a religion that stresses ascetic behavior as a way of achieving advancement in the next life can also be expected to work against the attainment of business goals.

The same kind of comparison could be made for an international business trying to decide where to push its products, country A or B. Again, country B would be the logical choice because cultural factors suggest that in the long run, country B is the nation most likely to achieve the greatest level of economic growth. In comparison, the culture of country A may produce economic stagnation.

Chapter Summary

We have looked at the nature of social culture and drawn out some of the implications for business practice. The following points have been made in the chapter:

1. Culture is that complex whole that includes knowledge, beliefs, art, morals, law, customs, and other capabilities acquired by people as members of society.

2. Values and norms are the central components of a culture. Values are abstract ideals about what a society believes to be good, right, and desirable. Norms are social rules and guidelines that prescribe appropriate behavior in particular situations.

3. Values and norms are influenced by political and economic philosophy, social structure, religion, language, and education.

4. The social structure of a society refers to its basic social organization. Two main dimensions along which social structures differ are the individual–group dimension and the stratification dimension.

5. In some societies, the individual is the basic building block of social organization. These societies emphasize individual achievements above all else. In other societies, the group is the basic building block of social organization. These societies emphasize group membership and group achievements above all else.

6. All societies are stratified into different classes. Class-conscious societies are characterized by low social mobility and a high degree of stratification. Less class-conscious societies are characterized by high social mobility and a low degree of stratification.

7. Religion may be defined as a system of shared beliefs and rituals that are concerned with the realm of the sacred. Ethical systems refer to a set of moral principles, or values, that are used to guide and shape behavior. The world's major religions are Christianity, Islam, Hinduism, and Buddhism. Although not a religion, Confucianism has an impact upon behavior that is as profound as that of many religions. The value systems of different religious and ethical systems have different implications for business practice.

8. Language is one defining characteristic of a culture. It has both a spoken and an unspoken dimension. In countries with more than one spoken language, we tend to find more than one culture.

9. Formal education is the medium through which individuals learn skills and are socialized into the values and norms of a society. Education plays an important role in the determination of national competitive advantage.

10. Geert Hofstede studied how culture relates to values in the workplace. Hofstede isolated four dimensions that he claimed summarized different cultures: power distance, uncertainty avoidance, individualism versus collectivism, and masculinity versus femininity.

11. Culture is not a constant; it evolves over time. Economic progress and globalization seem to be two important engines of cultural change.

12. One danger confronting a company that goes abroad for the first time is being ill-informed. To develop cross-cultural literacy, international businesses need to employ host-country nationals, build a cadre of cosmopolitan executives, and guard against the dangers of ethnocentric behavior.

13. The value systems and norms of a country can affect the costs of doing business in that country.

Critical Discussion Questions

1. Outline why the culture of a country might influence the costs of doing business in that country. Illustrate your answer with examples.

2. Do you think that business practices in an Islamic country are likely to differ from business practices in the United States, and if so how?

3. What are the implications for international business of differences in the dominant religion and/or ethical system of a country?

4. Choose two countries that appear to be culturally diverse. Compare the culture of those countries and then indicate how cultural differences influence (*a*) the costs of doing business in each country, (*b*) the likely future economic development of that country, and (*c*) business practices.

CLOSING CASE   Disney in France

Until 1992, the Walt Disney Company had experienced nothing but success in the theme park business. Its first park, Disneyland, opened in Anaheim, California, in 1955. Its theme song, "It's a Small World After All," promoted "an idealized vision of America spiced with reassuring glimpses of exotic cultures all calculated to promote heartwarming feelings about living together as one happy family. There were dark tunnels and bumpy rides to scare the children a little but none of the terrors of the real world . . . The Disney characters that everyone knew from the cartoons and comic books were on hand to shepherd the guests and to direct them to the Mickey Mouse watches and Little Mermaid records."[44] The Anaheim park was an instant success.

In the 1970s, the triumph was repeated in Florida, and in 1983, Disney proved the Japanese also have an affinity for Mickey Mouse with the successful opening of Tokyo Disneyland. Having wooed the Japanese, Disney executives in 1986 turned their attention to France and, more specifically, to Paris, the self-proclaimed capital of European high culture and style. "Why did they pick France?" many asked. When word first got out that Disney wanted to build another international theme park, officials from more than 200 locations all over the world descended on Disney with pleas and cash inducements to work the Disney magic in their hometowns. But Paris was chosen because of demographics and subsidies. About 17 million Europeans live less than a two-hour drive from Paris. Another 310 million can fly there in the same time or less. Also, the French government was so eager to attract Disney that it offered the company more than $1 billion in various incentives, all in the expectation that the project would create 30,000 French jobs.

From the beginning, cultural gaffes by Disney set the tone for the project. By late 1986, Disney was deep in negotiations with the French government. To the exasperation of the Disney team, headed by Joe Shapiro, the talks were taking far longer than expected. Jean-Rene Bernard, the chief French negotiator, said he was astonished when Mr. Shapiro, his patience depleted, ran to the door of the room and, in a very un-Gallic gesture, began kicking it repeatedly, shouting, "Get me something to break!"

There was also snipping from Parisian intellectuals who attacked the transplantation of Disney's dream world as an assault on French culture; "a cultural Chernobyl," one prominent intellectual called it. The minister of culture announced he would boycott the opening, proclaiming it to be an unwelcome symbol of American clichés and a consumer society. Unperturbed, Disney pushed ahead with the planned summer 1992 opening of the $5 billion park. Shortly after Euro-Disneyland opened, French farmers drove their tractors to the entrance and blocked it. This globally televised act of protest was aimed not at Disney but at the US government, which had been demanding that French agricultural subsidies be cut. Still, it focused world attention upon the loveless marriage of Disney and Paris.

Then there were the operational errors. Disney's policy of serving no alcohol in the park, since reversed, caused astonishment in a country where a glass of wine for lunch is a given. Disney thought that Monday would be a light day for visitors and Friday a heavy one and allocated staff accordingly, but the reality was the reverse. Another unpleasant surprise was the hotel breakfast debacle. "We were told that Europeans 'don't take breakfast,' so we downsized the restaurants," recalled one Disney executive. "And guess what? Everybody showed up for breakfast. We were trying to serve 2,500 breakfasts in a 350-seat restaurant at some of the hotels. The lines were horrendous. Moreover, they didn't want the typical French breakfast of croissants and coffee, which was our assumption. They wanted bacon and eggs." Lunch turned out to be another problem. "Everybody wanted lunch at 12:30. The crowds were huge. Our smiling cast members had to calm down surly patrons and engage in some 'behavior modification' to teach them that they could eat lunch at 11:00 AM or 2:00 PM."

There were major staffing problems too. Disney tried to use the same teamwork model with its staff that had worked so well in America and Japan, but it ran into trouble in France. In the first nine weeks of Euro-Disneyland's operation, roughly 1,000 employees, 10 percent of the total, left. One former employee was a 22-year-old medical student from a nearby town who signed up for a weekend job. After two days of "brainwashing," as he called Disney's training, he left following a dispute with his supervisor over the timing of his lunch hour. Another former employee noted, "I don't think that they realize what Europeans are like . . . that we ask questions and don't think all the same way."

One of the biggest problems, however, was that Europeans didn't stay at the park as long as Disney expected. While Disney succeeded in getting close to 9 million visitors a year through the park gates, in line with its plans, most stayed only a day or two. Few stayed the four to five days that Disney had hoped for. It seems that most Europeans regard theme parks as places for day excursions. A theme park is just not seen as a destination for an extended vacation. This was a big shock for Disney. The company had invested billions in building luxury hotels next to the park—hotels that the day-trippers didn't need and that stood half empty most of the time. To make matters worse, the French didn't show up in the expected numbers. In 1994, only 40 percent of the park's visitors were French. One puzzled executive noted that many visitors were Americans living in Europe or, stranger still, Japanese on a European vacation! As a result, by the end of 1994 Euro-Disneyland had cumulative losses of $2 billion.

At this point, Euro-Disney changed its strategy. First, the company changed the name to Disneyland Paris in an attempt to strengthen the park's identity. Second, food and fashion offerings changed. To quote one manager, "We opened with restaurants providing French-style food service, but we found that customers wanted self-service like in the US parks. Similarly, products in the boutiques were initially toned down for the French market, but since then the range has changed to give it a more definite Disney image." Third, the prices for day tickets and hotel rooms were cut by one-third. The result was an attendance of 11.7 million in 1996, up from a low of 8.8 million in 1994.

http://www.disney.com

Sources: P. Gumble and R. Turner, "Mouse Trap: Fans Like Euro Disney But Its Parent's Goofs Weigh the Park Down," *The Wall Street Journal*, March 10, 1994, p. A1; R. J. Barnet and J. Cavanagh, *Global Dreams* (New York: Touchstone Books, 1994), pp. 33–34; J. Huey, "Eisner Explains Everything," *Fortune*, April 17, 1995, pp. 45–68; R. Anthony, "Euro: Disney: The First 100 days," *Harvard Business School Case* # 9-693-013; and Charles Masters, "French Fall for the Charms of Disney," *Sunday Telegraph*, April 13, 1997, p. 21.

Case Discussion Questions

1. What assumptions did Disney make about the tastes and preferences of French consumers? Which of these assumptions were correct? Which were not?

2. How might Disney have had a more favorable initial experience in France? What steps might it have taken to reduce the mistakes associated with the launch of Euro-Disney?

3. In retrospect, was France the best choice for the location of Euro-Disney?

Notes

1. See R. Dore, *Taking Japan Seriously* (Stanford, CA: Stanford University Press, 1987).

2. E. B. Tylor, *Primitive Culture* (London: Murray, 1871).

3. Geert Hofstede, *Culture's Consequences: International Differences in Work Related Values* (Beverly Hills, CA: Sage Publications, 1984), p. 21.

4. J. Z. Namenwirth and R. B. Weber, *Dynamics of Culture* (Boston: Allen & Unwin, 1987), p. 8.

5. R. Mead, *International Management: Cross Cultural Dimensions* (Oxford: Blackwell Business, 1994), p. 7.

6. "Iraq: Down But Not Out," *The Economist*, April 8, 1995, pp. 21–23.

7. S. P. Huntington, *The Clash of Civilizations* (New York, Simon & Schuster, 1996).

8. M. Thompson, R. Ellis, and A. Wildavsky, *Cultural Theory* (Boulder, CO: Westview Press, 1990).

9. M. Douglas, "Cultural Bias," *In the Active Voice* (London: Routledge, 1982), pp. 183–254.

10. M. L. Dertouzos, R. K. Lester, and R. M. Solow, *Made in America* (Cambridge, MA: MIT Press, 1989).

11. C. Nakane, *Japanese Society* (Berkeley, CA: University of California Press, 1970).

12. Ibid.

13. For details, see M. Aoki, *Information, Incentives, and Bargaining in the Japanese Economy* (Cambridge: Cambridge University Press, 1988); and Dertouzos, Lester, and Solow, *Made in America*.

14. For an excellent historical treatment of the evolution of the English class system see E. P. Thompson, *The Making of the English Working Class* (London: Vintage Books, 1966). See also R. Miliband, *The State in Capitalist Society*. (New York: Basic Books, 1969), especially chapter 2. For more recent studies of class in British societies see (1) Stephen Brook, *Class: Knowing Your Place in Modern Britain* (London: Victor Gollancz, 1997). (2) A. Adonis and S. Pollard, *A Class Act: The Myth of Britain's Classless Society* (London, 1997). (3) J. Gerteis and M. Savage, "The Salience of Class in Britain and America: A Comparative Analysis," *British Journal of Sociology*, June, 1998.

15. A. Adonis and S. Pollard, *A Class Act: The Myth of Britain's Classless Society* (London, 1997).

16. N. Goodman, *An Introduction to Sociology* (New York: Harper Collins, 1991).

17. M. Weber, *The Protestant Ethic and the Spirit of Capitalism* (New York: Scribner's Sons, 1958 (original 1904–1905). For an excellent review of Weber's work see A. Giddens, *Capitalism and Modern Social Theory* (Cambridge: Cambridge University Press, 1971).

18. M. Weber, *The Protestant Ethic and the Spirit of Capitalism*, p. 35.

19. See S. M. Abbasi, K. W. Hollman, and J. H. Murrey, "Islamic Economics; Foundations and Practices," *International Journal of Social Economics* 16, no. 5 (1990), pp. 5–17; and R. H. Dekmejian, *Islam in Revolution: Fundamentalism in the Arab World* (Syracuse: Syracuse University Press, 1995).

20. T. W. Lippman, *Understanding Islam* (New York: Meridian Books, 1995).

21. Dekmejian, *Islam in Revolution: Fundamentalism in the Arab World*.

22. M. K. Nydell, *Understanding Arabs* (Yarmouth, ME: Intercultural Press, 1987).

23. Lippman, *Understanding Islam*.

24. The material in this section is based largely on Abbasi, Hollman, and Murrey, "Foundations and Practices."

25. "Islam's Interest," *The Economist*, January 18, 1992, pp. 33–34.

26. For details of Weber's work and views, see A. Giddens, *Capitalism and Modern Social Theory*.

27. See, for example, the views expressed in "A Survey of India: The Tiger Steps Out," *The Economist*, January 21, 1995.

28. See R. Dore, R. *Taking Japan Seriously* (Stanford, CA: Stanford University Press, 1987); and C. W. L. Hill, "Transaction Cost Economizing as a Source of Comparative Advantage: The Case of Japan," *Organization Science* 6 (1995).

29. See M. Aoki, *Information, Incentives, and Bargaining in the Japanese Economy* (Cambridge: Cambridge University Press, 1988), and J. P. Womack, D T. Jones, and D. Roos, *The Machine That Changed the World* (New York: Rawson Associates, 1990).

30. This hypothesis dates back to two anthropologists, Edward Sapir and Benjamin Lee Whorf. See E. Sapir, "The Status of Linguistics as a Science," *Language* 5 (1929), pp. 207–14, and B. L. Whorf, *Language, Thought, and Reality* (Cambridge, MA: MIT Press, 1956).

31. D. A. Ricks, *Big Business Blunders: Mistakes in Multinational Marketing* (Homewood IL: Dow Jones-Irwin, 1983).

32. N. Goodman, *An Introduction to Sociology* (New York: HarperCollins, 1991).

33. M. E. Porter, *The Competitive Advantage of Nations* (New York: Free Press, 1990).

34. Ibid., pp. 395–97.

35. G. Hofstede, "The Cultural Relativity of Organizational Practices and Theories," *Journal of International Business Studies*, Fall 1983, pp. 75–89.

36. For more a detailed critique, see R. Mead, *International Management: Cross-Cultural Dimensions* (Oxford: Blackwell, 1994), pp. 73–75.

37. For example, see W. J. Bigoness, and G. L. Blakely, "A Cross-National Study of Managerial Values," *Journal of International Business Studies*, December 1996, p. 739; D. H. Ralston, D. H. Holt, R. H. Terpstra, and Y. Kai-Cheng, "The Impact of National Culture and Economic Ideology on Managerial Work Values," *Journal of International Business Studies* 28, no. 1 (1997), pp. 177–208; and P. B. Smith, M. F. Peterson, and Z. Ming Wang, "The Manager as a Mediator of Alternative Meanings," *Journal of International Business Studies* 27, no. 1 (1996), pp. 115–137.

38. R. Mead, *International Management: Cross-Cultural Dimensions*, chap. 17.

39. "Free, Young, and Japanese," *The Economist*, December 21, 1991.

40. J. Z. Namerwirth and R. P. Weber, *Dynamics of Culture*.

41. G. Hofstede, "National Cultures in Four Dimensions," *International Studies of Management and Organization* 13, no. 1, pp. 46–74.

42. R. J. Barnet and J. Cavanagh, *Global Dreams: Imperial Corporations and the New World Order* (New York: Touchstone Books, 1994).

43. See M. Aoki, *Information, Incentives, and Bargaining in the Japanese Economy*; Dertouzos, Lester, and Solow, *Made in America*; and Porter, *The Competitive Advantage of Nations*, pp. 395–97.

44. R. J. Barnet and J. Cavanagh, *Global Dreams*, p. 33.

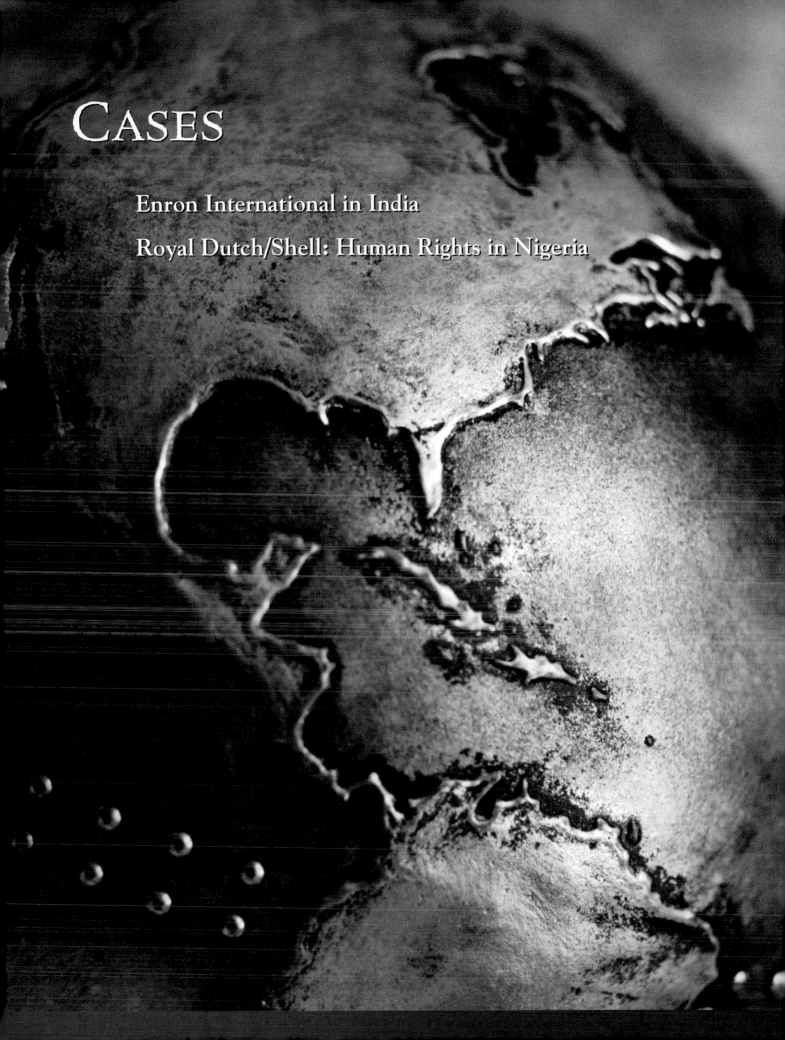

CASES

Enron International in India

Royal Dutch/Shell: Human Rights in Nigeria

Enron International in India

Introduction

In 1990, Enron, a Houston-based independent power company, established a subsidiary, Enron International, and gave it the mission of building and running power generation projects in the developing world. Enron's chairman appointed one of his protégés, Rebecca Mark, then only 36 years old, as CEO of the new unit. By 1997, the outspoken and photogenic Mark, who was fast gaining a reputation as one of the most dynamic businesswomen in America, had built Enron International into a global operation with sales of $1.1 billion, annual profits of $220 million, and a backlog of international energy projects worth over $20 billion. The potential jewel in Enron International's crown was a growing presence in India. By the end of 1997, Enron International had plans to invest $20 billion in India. Getting to this point, however, had severely tested Mark's diplomatic skills and political acumen.

Enron's India Strategy

Enron's interests in India date back to 1991, when the country's former prime minister, Narasimha Rao, visited the United States to seek help with India's economic development. Rao asked Enron if it was interested in independent power projects in the country. This request signaled a shift of policy in India. Since independence from Britain in 1947, political opinion in India had by and large opposed significant foreign direct investment on anything other than highly favorable terms to the host country. For almost half a century, Indian politics had been strongly influenced by Gandhi's doctrine of *swadeshi*, or self-reliance from foreign influence. This had been translated into a presumption against foreign investment and a desire to see India build its own domestic industries under the protection of restrictions on foreign investment and high import tariffs.

However, by the 1990s, the winds of ideological change were blowing through India. The national government seemed to be embracing a free market approach that included substantial deregulation and the loosening of rules on foreign direct investment. Consistent with this, in October 1991, Rao's government liberalized India's domestic power producing sector, allowing private developers, both Indian and foreign, to build and operate independent power projects with no restrictions on foreign equity ownership.

India's need for power was obvious. A plentiful supply of electric power is a key requirement for economic development, but India was suffering from chronic power shortages. At peak periods, demand for electricity often exceeded available power supply by more than 20 percent. The installed capacity in the early 1990s, which amounted to around 80,000 megawatts, was working at only about 60 percent efficiency. Forecasts suggested that an extra 140,000 megawatts of capacity would be needed by 2005, but public money to finance such massive investments in infrastructure was scarce. In the mid-1990s, about 70 percent of India's electricity supply was being produced by state-owned electricity generation and distribution boards, which collectively were running up losses of over $2 billion per year. They could not afford to fund the required expansions in capacity.

Mark jumped on Rao's offer, but quickly discovered that India's energy problems involved more than a simple lack of generating capacity. The country also lacked adequate supplies of fuel. To help solve these problems, Mark articulated a strategic vision that was audacious in scope. The vision called for Enron to invest up to $20 billion to become the largest distributor and consumer of liquefied natural gas (LNG) in India by 2010. Under the plan, Enron would set up two LNG terminals and regassification units in India, one at Dabhol in the state of Maharashtra, and one at Ennore in the state of Tamil Nadu. The company would construct two gas-based power generating plants near the terminals. Enron would also build a network of pipelines to pipe the gas to its LNG terminals from oil and gas fields near Bombay, and then onward to its own and other power plants around the country. The Bombay fields, however, were not large enough to supply India's projected LNG needs, so the company also planned to import LNG from a facility it was building in the Gulf state of Qatar. The Qatar facility would cost $4 billion to complete and was being funded by a group of investors including the state-owned Qatar Gas & Pipeline Co., Enron International's parent company, and Royal Dutch/Shell. Enron International had promised investors in the Qatar facility a 15 percent annual growth in shareholders' income. Achieving this goal, however, was highly dependent on the success of Mark's India strategy. Without India, Enron might lack sufficient customers to absorb the LNG output from its Qatar facility.

The Dabhol Project

By mid-1992, Mark was moving forward with the first stage of her plan. She was deep in negotiations with the Indian federal government and the government of the state of Maharashtra where Enron's Dabhol power plant was to be constructed. The Dabhol project was bold; Enron was to develop a 2,015 megawatt power plant that would be fired by LNG. The total cost for the project was well over $2 billion, making the Dabhol project the largest foreign investment ever committed to India and the biggest independent power project in the world.

The choice of Dabhol for Enron's first investment in India was dictated by a number of factors. Located on India's western seaboard, the state of Maharashtra and its capital Bombay were enjoying a sustained period of political stability and economic growth. This had enabled the state to attract industry from other areas of India, such as the traditional industrial heartlands of Calcutta and eastern India. Economic growth in these regions had suffered under successive communist governments at the state level. The western seaboard was also closer to the Gulf states, and Qatar in particular, which would lower the costs of shipping LNG. Also, the state of Maharashtra was then governed by the Congress Party, the same party that governed the nation. Rebecca Mark reasoned that Prime Minister Rao would be able to pressure the local state government to approve the project.

Mark was alert to the basic political realities in India. While the federal government in Delhi might in principle approve the project, she realized that Enron would also have to win approval from the Maharashtra state government and cultivate the approval of key players in India's extensive civil service. To get the Dabhol project approved, the company needed to get 170 different state and federal permits, sort through 50 complicated legal questions, and deal with a complex web of state and federal taxes. Reflecting on this process, Mark reported:

> I've had tea with every bureaucrat in India . . . . People (foreigners) don't understand how to get things done in India. Politicians lay out a plan, but that's different from working through the system. There's only one political level approval—that of the foreign investment board. But then there are all sorts of channels and procedures needed. Politicians will never intervene and force a bureaucrat to make a decision when an issue of process is at stake. This is where companies mess up and are confused.[1]

By early 1995, Enron had received full approval for the project and was proceeding with the initial construction. However, storm clouds were gathering on the political horizon of Maharashtra, and they spelled trouble for Enron. Throughout the negotiations, Maharashtra had been controlled by the Congress Party. Its local leader, Sharad Pawar, was a big supporter of Enron's Dabhol project. Unfortunately, during 1994 and early 1995, the popularity of the Congress Party started to decline. In 1994, a series of ethnic riots swept through

Bombay. Anti-Muslim hysteria had been whipped up by Shiv Sena, a local militant Hindu nationalist party. The party was led by Bal Thackery, a former political cartoonist and an admirer of Adolf Hitler. To fight upcoming state elections in February 1995, Shiv Sena formed an alliance with a less extreme Hindu nationalist party, the BJP. If the alliance won the state elections, Shiv Sena would control the local administration in Maharashtra, while the BJP would occupy any seats won by the alliance in the national parliament.

During the election campaign, Shiv Sena seized on the Dabhol project and used it to attack the Congress Party and its leader, Sharad Pawar. Shiv Sena claimed that Pawar had been bribed by Enron to support the Dabhol project. This played well in the court of public opinion in India, where in the words of one observer, "The popular belief is that any dealings with foreigners are bound to be either crooked or disadvantageous. Maybe 9 times out of 10 this is correct."[2] The BJP also warmed to this theme as the election campaign progressed and began to champion the Gandhi doctrine of *swadeshi* (self-reliance). Both the BJP and Shiv Sena successfully contrasted their defense of Indian rights and Indian self-reliance against what they depicted as the corrupt machinations of Enron, Pawar, and the Congress Party.

Fuel was added to this fire when an Enron official, in testimony before a committee of the US Congress that was dealing with foreign aid allocations, revealed that Enron had spent $20 million to educate Indians about the benefits of its various power projects in the country. (The Enron official made the apparently innocent suggestion that the US government might want to use its foreign aid help with such educational campaigns.) Elements of the Indian press, in concert with Shiv Sena, seized on this "revelation" to claim that the $20 million had been used primarily to "educate" corrupt officials such as Pawar to win approval for the Dabhol project; in other words, that much of the $20 million had been in the form of bribes. In the heat of the election campaign, it apparently mattered little that there was no evidence that Enron had bribed anyone. Mud sticks, and the charges proved to be powerful ammunition. As a result, in February 1995, Pawar and the Congress Party were swept from power in the state of Maharashtra to be replaced by Shiv Sena and its new chief minister, Manohar Joshi.

After the election, the new government set up a committee, under the leadership of Gopinath Munde, the BJP deputy minister in the coalition, to review the Dabhol project. The committee was to review the charges of corruption and abuse that had been leveled at Enron during the election campaign. However, Rebecca Mark felt she was on solid ground. Enron had not done anything wrong, contracts had been signed, construction work on the project was under way, India clearly needed the power, and the agreements protected Enron from any unilateral breach of contract. If the state canceled the project, it would be hit with a $200 million cancellation fee.

In mid-1995, the state government committee reviewing the Dabhol project finished its report. The report was never published, although excerpts in which Enron was accused of deception and cost padding were leaked to the press. Enron vigorously denied these charges. On the cost padding charges, Rebecca Mark later noted,

> In India you are supposed to have a 20 percent import duty on equipment. But when it comes right down to it, very common in a project is that it doesn't end up being 20 percent but whatever the customs inspector wants it to be on the day you get there. So you have to price that risk in.[3]

The implication was that there was a risk premium built into Enron's contract with the state of Maharashtra.

The report also criticized the previous administration for not putting the Dabhol project out to competitive bids. Privately, Enron officials noted that this was an absurd charge. After all, Enron had been invited to the country by Prime Minister Rao, it was Enron that had suggested the Dabhol project, and Enron was the only foreign power producer apparently willing to shoulder the risk associated with such a large investment in the country. Reflecting this, Bob Pender, an independent lawyer who specializes in financing energy projects, noted that the lack of competitive bidding "was the opportunity cost of getting a company to come and create an industry."[4]

Significantly though, the committee was not able to uncover any evidence of corruption by either Enron or Indian political officials. However, after having made such an issue of the project during the election, the Shiv Sena/BJP coalition was not yet ready to back down. On August 3, 1995, the state government issued a work stoppage order on the deal, after Enron had already spent $100 million.

Two days later, Enron served the state government with legal notice that it would pursue arbitration in London. The Maharashtra state government was now facing damages of at least $300 million, with the possibility of another $500 million on top of that. On August 12, Little & Co., which had acted as the lawyers for the Maharashtra state government for the last 20 years, resigned and stated "off the record" that the state's position was indefensible. Top civil servants in the state also reportedly told Munde and Joshi that the government's position was untenable.

Simultaneously, Enron mounted a public relations campaign of its own. Enron ran full-page advertise- ments in Indian newspapers publicizing the benefits to India of its Dabhol project. It also prevailed on US President Bill Clinton to call the Indian premier to try to get the project started again. By September public opinion polls showed that 80 percent of the people in Maharashtra and 60 percent of those in India wanted the project restarted.

Despite rising pressure to restart the project, the Shiv Sena/BJP coalition government was unwilling to back off without getting something in return. By this point, however, it was clear that the best interests of all parties would be served by a compromise. Enron wanted to get the project back on track. It still had big plans for India, and then there was that plant in Qatar whose output was projected for India. The Maharashtra government, for its part, was facing the potential of heavy damages and was rapidly losing support for its position. At the same time, the government needed evidence that its efforts had not been for naught; it needed to save face.

That fall Rebecca Mark returned to the bargaining table, and a settlement was worked out. Enron agreed to cut the price it charged for power generated by the Dabhol project by 22.6 percent. In return, Enron walked away with a deal for a 2,450 megawatt plant, 450 megawatts bigger than the initial plant. According to Enron, the larger plant would realize much greater scale economies and allow Enron to maintain its projected rate of return on investment while simultaneously cutting prices.

Aftermath

Reflecting on her Indian experience, Mark suggests that the key to Enron's success was its intentions to help India solve a problem and to stay engaged in the country for the long term. She and her colleagues have spent six years coming to India, meeting with the same people, talking about the same projects. Says Mark, "I don't think that anyone who works with us doubts our intentions, goodwill, or long-term commitment to India. We've earned a place on the list of friendlies."[5] Mark also believes that Enron's appeal to the people of India ultimately served the company well. She concludes:

> Our experience tells us that India's a good environment for foreign investment, and a market where foreign investors are seen as necessary. If anything, our experience proves the strength of the system in India to withstand a lot of assaults from different places. Even though the political system is shaky, the judiciary and the business system work.[6]

In February 1997, Enron reaffirmed its commitment to India when it submitted a proposal to build five to seven more power plants in the country for a total cost of $10 billion. As for the Dabhol plant, the first phase of the project, which will generate 740 megawatts of power, was completed in December 1998, three months ahead of schedule.

For India's part, there is little doubt that Enron's experience with the Dabhol project was a public relations setback. Although ultimately the outcome reaffirmed the country's commitment to encouraging foreign direct investment, the perception has been created that the shifting political landscape, bureaucratic rules, and the crosscurrents between national and state governments, make India a difficult place in which to invest. As noted by former US Ambassador to India William Clark, the Dabhol incident "sends the right signals, but unfortunately it sent off the wrong signals for awhile. Just like a retraction in a newspaper, it will take a long time for people to notice."[7]

Discussion Questions

1. Why do you think Enron was willing to shoulder the risk of making such a significant investment in India? What long-run benefits did the company foresee? Do you think these benefits compensated for the risks involved?

2. Do you think Enron was correct to build a risk premium into its original pricing of the Dabhol project? Should the company have foreseen that this might have been perceived as cost padding?

3. What lessons about the requirements for successful investment in India can other foreign companies draw from Enron's experience with the Dabhol project?

4. Is former US Ambassador William Clark right when he claims that, in the end, the Dabhol

incident sent the right kind of signals about foreign investment in India? What kind of signals do you think it sends about investment in India?

Notes

1. From C. Hill, "How Rebecca Mark Solved India," *Institutional Investor,* January 1998, p. 28G.

2. B. Edwards and M. Shukla, "The Mugging of Enron," *Euromoney,* October 1995, p. 28–33.

3. "You Have to Be Pushy and Aggressive," *Business Week,* February 24, 1997, p. 56.

4. B. Edwards and M. Shukla, "The Mugging of Enron," *Euromoney,* October 1995, p. 28 33.

5. C. Hill, "How Rebecca Mark Solved India."

6. "It's a Done Deal," *Journal of Commerce,* December 20, 1996, p. 7B.

7. Ibid.

Sources

1. Edwards, B., and M. Shukla. "The Mugging of Enron." *Euromoney,* October 1995, pp. 28–33.

2. Hill, C. "How Rebecca Mark Solved India." *Institutional Investor,* January 1998, p. 28G.

3. "It's a Done Deal." *Journal of Commerce,* December 20, 1996, p. 7B.

4. Mack, T. "High Finance with a Touch of Theater." *Forbes,* May 18, 1998, pp. 140–54.

5. Williams, G. "More Power to India." *Business Week,* January 22, 1996, p. 62.

6. Nicholson, M. "Dabhol Plant Finally Gets Green Light." *Financial Times,* January 9, 1996, p. 6.

7. Sibbald, P. "You Have to Be Pushy and Aggressive." *Business Week,* February 24, 1997, p. 56.

ROYAL DUTCH/SHELL: HUMAN RIGHTS IN NIGERIA

Introduction

In 1995, a Nigerian military tribunal, in what most observers decried as a sham trial, ordered the execution of noted author and playwright Ken Saro-Wiwa and eight other members of the Movement for the Survival of the Ogoni People. The Ogoni are a 500,000-member ethnic group of farmers and fishermen that live in Nigeria's coastal plain. For several years, the Ogoni had been waging a vigorous political campaign against Nigeria's military rulers and the giant oil company Royal Dutch/Shell. They had been seeking greater self-determination, rights to the revenue stemming from oil

exploration on traditional Ogoni lands, and compensation for the environmental degradation to their land caused by frequent oil spills from fractured pipelines. Shell had been pumping oil from Ogoni lands since the late 1950s. In 1994, four Ogoni chiefs who advocated cooperation rather than confrontation with Nigeria's military government were lynched by a mob of Ogoni youth. Though he was not present, Saro-Wiwa, a leader of the protest movement, was arrested and subsequently sentenced to death along with eight other Ogoni activists.

Despite intensive international pressure that included appeals to Shell to use its influence in the country to gain clemency for the convicted, the executions went ahead as scheduled on November 10, 1995. After the executions, Shell was criticized in the Western media for its apparent unwillingness to pressure Nigeria's totalitarian regime. The incident started some soul-searching at Shell about the social and environmental responsibility of a multinational corporation in societies such as Nigeria that fall short of Western standards for the protection of human rights and the environment.

Background

In 1961, the African nation of Nigeria won independence from Britain. At that time, many believed that Nigeria had the potential to become one of the engines of economic growth in Africa. The country was blessed with abundant natural resources, particularly oil and gas; was a net exporter of foodstuffs; and had a large population that by African standards was well educated (today Nigeria has the largest population in Africa, with over 110 million people). By the mid-1990s, it was clear that much of that potential was still to be realized. Thirty-five years after winning independence, Nigeria was still heavily dependent on the oil sector. Oil production accounted for 30 percent of GDP, 95 percent of foreign exchange earnings, and about 80 percent of the government's budget revenues. The largely subsistence agricultural sector had failed to keep up with rapid population growth, and Nigeria, once a large net exporter of food, now had to import food. GDP per capita was a paltry $230, one-quarter of what it was in 1981, and the country was creaking under $40 billion of external debt. Nigeria had been unable to garner financial assistance from institutions such as the International Monetary Fund because of the government's unwillingness to account for how it used the revenues from oil taxes.

Political problems partly explained Nigeria's economic malaise. The country has suffered from internal strife among some of the more than 250 ethnic groups that constitute the nation. In the 1960s, the country was racked by a particularly nasty civil war. In December 1983, the civilian government of the country was replaced in a coup by a military regime that proceeded to rule by decree. In 1993, democratic elections were held in Nigeria, but the military government nullified the results, declaring there had been widespread ballot fraud.

Royal Dutch/Shell is the main foreign oil producer operating in Nigeria. The company was formed at the turn of the century when Holland's Royal Dutch Company, which had substantial oil operations in Indonesia, merged with Britain's Shell Transport and Trading to create one of the world's first multinational oil companies. Shell is now the world's largest oil company with annual revenues that exceed $130 billion. The company has been operating in Nigeria since 1937, and by the mid-1990s was pumping about half of Nigeria's oil. Nigerian oil accounts for about 11 to 12 percent of the company's global output and generates net income for Shell of around $200 million per year.

Problems in the Ogoni Region

In 1958, Royal Dutch/Shell struck oil on Ogoni lands. By some estimates, the company has extracted some $30 billion worth of oil from the region since then. Despite this, the Ogoni remain desperately poor. Most live in palm-roofed mud huts and practice subsistence agriculture. Of Shell's 5,000 employees in Nigeria, in 1995 only 85 were Ogoni. Because they are a powerless minority among Nigeria's 110 million people, the Ogoni are often overlooked when it comes to the allocation of jobs either in government or the private sector.

Starting in 1982, the Nigerian government supposedly directed 1.5 percent of the oil revenue it received back to the communities where the oil was produced. In 1992, the percentage was increased to 3 percent. The Ogoni, however, claim they have seen virtually none of this money. Most appears to have been spent in the tribal lands of the ruling majority or has vanished in corrupt deals. Although there were 96 oil wells, two refineries, a petrochemical complex, and a fertilizer plant in the Ogoni region in 1994, the lone hospital was an unfinished concrete husk and the government schools, unable to pay teachers, were rarely open.

In addition to the lack of returns from oil production in their region, the Ogoni claim that their lands have suffered from environmental degradation, much of which could be laid at the feet of Shell. Ogoni activists claim that Shell's poor environmental safeguards have resulted in numerous oil spills and widespread contamination of the soil and groundwater. A Shell spokesman, interviewed in 1994, seemed to acknowledge there might be some basis to these complaints. He stated, "Some of the facilities installed during the last 30 years, whilst acceptable at the time, aren't as we would build them today. Given the age of some of these lines (oil pipelines), regrettably oil spills have occurred from time to time."[1] However, the same spokesman also blamed many of the more recent leaks in the Ogoni region on deliberate sabotage. The sabotage, he stated, had one of two motives—to back up claims for compensation and to support claims of environmental degradation.

On hearing of these claims, Ken Saro-Wiwa called them preposterous. Saro-Wiwa argued that although uneducated youths, frustrated and angry, may have damaged some Shell installations in one or two incidents, "the people would never deliberately spill oil on their land because they know the so-called compensation is paltry and the land is never restored."[2] To support his position, Saro-Wiwa pointed to a spill from the 1960s near a settlement called Ebubu that still had not been cleaned up. In response, Shell stated that the spill occurred during the civil war in the 1960s, and cleanup work was completed in 1990. Subsequently, sunken oil reappeared at the surface, but Shell claims it was unable to do anything about this because of threats made against its employees in the region. In January 1993, out of concern for their safety, Shell barred its employees from entering the region.

In April 1993, the Ogoni organized their first protests against Shell and the government. Ogoni farmers stood in front of earthmoving equipment that was laying a pipeline for Shell through croplands. Although Shell stated that the land had been acquired by legal means and that full compensation had been paid to the farmers and the local community, some of the locals remained unhappy about what they viewed as continuing exploitation of their land. Seeing a threat to the continuity of its oil operations, Shell informed the Nigerian government about the protest. Units from the Nigerian military soon arrived and shots were fired into the crowd of protesters, killing one Ogoni man and wounding several others.

Subsequently, in a series of murky incidents, Nigerian soldiers stormed Ogoni villages, saying they were quelling unrest between neighboring Ogoni tribes. The Ogoni claimed the raids were punishment for obstructing Shell. They stated that the military had orders to use minor land disputes, which had long been settled with little violence, as an excuse to lay entire villages to waste. A feared unit of the mobile police with the nickname "Kill and Go" conducted some of the raids. Although details are sketchy, it has been reported that hundreds of people lost their lives in the violence. The cycle of violence ultimately culminated in the killing of the Ogoni chiefs who argued for compromise with the Nigerian government. This provided the government with the justification they needed to arrest Ken Saro-Wiwa and eight associates in the Movement for the Survival of the Ogoni People.

Nigeria and Shell under Pressure

Saro-Wiwa's arrest achieved the goal that the protests and bloodshed had not; it focused international attention on the plight of the Ogoni people, the heavy-handed policies of the Nigerian government, and Shell's activities in Nigeria. Several human rights organizations immediately pressured Shell to use its influence to gain the release of Saro-Wiwa. They also urged Shell to put on hold plans to start work on a $3.5 billion liquefied natural gas project in Nigeria. The project was structured as a

joint venture with the Nigerian government. Shell's central role in the project gave it considerable influence over the government, or so human rights activists believed.

Shell stated that it deplored the heavy-handed approach taken by the Nigerian government to the Ogoni people and regretted pain and loss suffered by Ogoni communities. The company also indicated it was using "discreet diplomacy" to try to bring influence to bear on the Nigerian government. Nigeria's military leadership, however, was in no mood to listen to discreet diplomacy from Shell or anyone else. After a trial by a military tribunal that was derided as nothing more than a kangaroo court, Saro-Wiwa and his associates were sentenced to death by hanging. The sentence was carried out shortly after sunrise on November 10, 1995.

Aftermath

In the wake of Saro-Wiwa's hanging, a storm of protest erupted around the world. The heads of state of the 52-nation British Commonwealth, meeting in New Zealand at the time of Saro-Wiwa's execution, suspended Nigeria and stated they would expel the country if it did not return to democratic rule within two years. US President Bill Clinton recalled the US ambassador to Nigeria and banned the sale of military equipment, on top of aid cuts made in protest at Saro-Wiwa's arrest. British Prime Minister John Major banned arms sales to Nigeria and called for the widest possible embargo. Ambassadors from the 15-nation European Union were recalled, and the EU suspended all aid to Nigeria.

But no country halted purchases of Nigerian oil or sales of oil service equipment to Nigeria. The United States, which imports 40 percent of Nigeria's daily output of 2 million barrels, was silent on the question of an oil embargo. Similarly, no Western country—many of which had national companies working in the Nigerian oil industry—indicated they would impose an embargo on sales to, or purchase from, the Nigerian oil industry. Alone among major public figures, South African President Nelson Mandela called for a ban on Shell. The call was echoed by several environmental groups, including Greenpeace and Friends of the Earth, both of which urged their supporters to boycott Shell products. However, South Africa never enacted a formal ban, and the boycott calls met with only limited success.

For its part, Shell indicated it would go ahead with its plans for a liquefied natural gas operation in Nigeria in partnership with the Nigerian government. In a public notice published in British newspapers, Shell stated, "It has been suggested that Shell should pull out of Nigeria's liquefied natural gas project. But if we do so now, the project will collapse. Maybe forever. So let's be clear who gets hurt if the project gets cancelled. A cancellation would certainly hurt the thousands of Nigerians who will be working on the project, and the tens of thousands benefiting in the local economy."[3]

In November 1996, the Center for Constitutional Rights filed a federal lawsuit in the US District Court in Manhattan on behalf of relatives of Saro-Wiwa who were now residing in the United States. The lawsuit accused Royal Dutch/Shell of being part of a conspiracy that led to Saro-Wiwa's hanging. Shell denied the allegations and stated that they would be refuted in court.

In May 1997, at the annual general meeting of Shell Transport and Trading in London, a group of 18 institutional investors tabled a resolution that would have required Shell to establish an independent external body to monitor its environmental and human rights policies. John Jennings, the outgoing chairman of the company, told reporters after the meeting that proxy votes from shareholders were running 10 to 1 against the resolution.

One reason for the defeat of the shareholder resolution was that the company had already indicated it was taking steps to reform its culture and improve its own monitoring of environmental and human rights policies. Before the shareholder meeting, the company issued its own report on its policies in Nigeria, in which the company admitted that it needed to improve its monitoring of environmental and human rights policies. Under the leadership of its new head, Mark Moody-Stuart, Shell subsequently stated that it expected its companies to express support for fundamental human rights in line with the legitimate role of business and to give proper regard to health, safety, and the environment consistent with their commitment to sustainable development. The company also embraced the UN Universal Declaration of Human Rights, pledged to set up socially responsible management systems, and to develop training procedures to help management deal with human rights dilemmas.

Commenting on these steps, a spokesman for Human Rights Watch stated, "I'm prepared to give them some credit that they realized they had to look at what their own operations were and how to respond. They acknowledged that big companies have social responsibility, and that's a pretty big step for the multinational corporations."[4]

Discussion Questions

1. Does Shell bear some responsibility for the problems in the Ogoni region of Nigeria?
2. What steps might Shell have taken to nip some of the protests against it in the bud, or even preempt them?

3. Could the company have done more to gain clemency for Ken Saro-Wiwa? What? Should it have done more?
4. Was the response of Western governments to the execution of Ken Saro-Wiwa about right, too excessive, or too mild? What should have been the appropriate response?
5. In the wake of Saro-Wiwa's execution, was Shell correct to push ahead with the liquefied natural gas project in Nigeria?
6. Do you think it is possible for a company such as Shell to reform itself from within, or would it have been better for Shell to establish an external body to monitor its human rights and environmental policies?

Notes

1. G. Brooks, "Slick Alliance," *The Wall Street Journal*, May 6, 1994, p. A1.
2. Ibid.
3. P. Beckett, "Shell Boldly Defends Its Role in Nigeria," *The Wall Street Journal*, November 27, 1995, p. A9.

Sources

1. Beckett, P. "Shell Boldly Defends Its Role in Nigeria." *The Wall Street Journal*, November 27, 1995, p. A9.
2. Brooks, G. "Slick Alliance." *The Wall Street Journal*, May 6, 1994, p. A1.
3. Corzine, R. "Shell Discovers Time and Tide Wait for No Man." *Financial Times*, March 10, 1998, p. 17.
4. Corzine, R., and Boulton. "Shell Defends Its Ethics on Eve of General Meeting." *Financial Times*, May 14, 1997, p. 29.
5. Hamilton, H. "Shell's New Worldview." *Washington Post*, August 2, 1998, p. H1.
6. Hoagland, J. "Shell's Game in Nigeria." *Washington Post*, November 5, 1995, p. C7.
7. Hudson, R., and M. Rose. "Shell Is Pressured to Scrap Its Plans for a New Plant in Nigeria amid Protests." *The Wall Street Journal*, November 14, 1995, p. A11.
8. Kamm, T. "Executions Raise Sanction Threat." *The Wall Street Journal*, November 13, 1995, p. A10.
9. "Multinationals and Their Morals." *The Economist*, December 2, 1995, p. 18.

THE GLOBAL TRADE AND INVESTMENT ENVIRONMENT

Chapter Four
International Trade Theory

Chapter Five
The Political Economy of International Trade

Chapter Six
Foreign Direct Investment

Chapter Seven
The Political Economy of Foreign Direct Investment

Chapter Eight
Regional Economic Integration

INTERNATIONAL TRADE THEORY

The Gains from Trade: Ghana and South Korea

In 1970, living standards in Ghana and South Korea were roughly comparable. Ghana's 1970 gross national product (GNP) per head was $250, and South Korea's was $260. By 1995, the situation had changed dramatically. South Korea had a GNP per head of $9,700, while Ghana's was only $390, reflecting vastly different economic growth rates. Between 1968 and 1995, the average annual growth rate in Ghana's GNP was under 1.4 percent. In contrast, South Korea achieved a growth rate of about 9 percent annually between 1968 and 1995.

What explains the difference between Ghana and South Korea? There is no simple answer, but the attitudes of both countries toward international trade could provide part of the explanation. A study by the World Bank suggests that whereas the South Korean government implemented policies that encouraged companies to engage in international trade, the actions of the Ghanaian government discouraged domestic producers from becoming involved in international trade. In 1980, international trade accounted for 18 percent of Ghana's GNP, by value, compared to 74 percent of South Korea's GNP.

Ghana was the first of Great Britain's West African colonies to become independent, in 1957. Its first president, Kwame Nkrumah, influenced the rest of the continent with his theories of pan-African socialism. For Ghana this meant high tariffs on many imports, an import substitution policy aimed at fostering Ghana self-sufficiency in certain manufactured goods, and policies that discouraged Ghana's enterprises from exporting. The results were an unmitigated disaster that transformed one of Africa's most prosperous nations into one of the world's poorest.

The Ghanaian government's involvement in the cocoa trade is an example of how antitrade policies destroyed the Ghanaian economy. Favorable climate, good soils, and ready access to world shipping routes have given Ghana an absolute advantage in cocoa production. It is one of the best places in the world to grow cocoa. As a consequence,

Ghana was the world's largest producer and exporter of cocoa in 1957. Then the government of the newly independent nation created a state-controlled cocoa marketing board. The board was given the authority to fix prices for cocoa and was designated the sole buyer of all cocoa grown in Ghana. The board held down the prices that it paid farmers for cocoa, while selling the cocoa on the world market at world prices. It might buy cocoa from farmers at 25 cents a pound and sell it on the world market for 50 cents a pound. In effect, the board was taxing exports by paying farmers considerably less for their cocoa than it was worth on the world market and putting the difference into government coffers. This money was used to fund the government policy of nationalization and industrialization.

One result of the cocoa policy was that between 1963 and 1979 the price paid by the cocoa marketing board to Ghana's farmers increased by a factor of 6, while the price of consumer goods in Ghana increased by a factor of 22, and the price of cocoa in neighboring countries increased by a factor of 36! In real terms, the Ghanaian farmers were paid less every year for their cocoa by the cocoa marketing board, while the world price increased significantly. Ghana's farmers responded by switching to the production of subsistence foodstuffs that could be sold within Ghana, and the country's production and exports of cocoa plummeted by more than one-third in seven years. At the same time, the Ghanaian government's attempt to build an industrial base through state-run enterprises failed. The resulting drop in Ghana's export earnings plunged the country into recession, led to a decline in its foreign currency reserves, and limited its ability to pay for necessary imports.

Ghana's inward-oriented trade policy resulted in a shift of resources away from the profitable activity of growing cocoa—where it had an absolute advantage in the world economy—and toward growing subsistence foods and manufacturing, where it had no advantage. This inefficient use of the country's resources severely damaged the Ghanaian economy and held back the country's economic development.

In contrast, consider the trade policy adopted by the South Korean government. The World Bank has characterized the trade policy of South Korea as "strongly outward-oriented." Unlike in Ghana, the policies of the South Korean government emphasized low import barriers on manufactured goods (but not on agricultural goods) and incentives to encourage South Korean firms to export. Beginning in the late 1950s, the South Korean government progressively reduced import tariffs from an average of 60 percent of the price of an imported good to less than 20 percent in the mid-1980s. On most nonagricultural goods, import tariffs were reduced to zero. In addition, the number of imported goods subject to quotas was reduced from more than 90 percent in the late 1950s to zero by the early 1980s. Over the same period, South Korea progressively reduced the subsidies given to South Korean exporters from an average of 80 percent of their sales price in the late 1950s to an average of less than 20 percent in 1965, and down to zero in 1984. With the exception of the agricultural sector (where a strong farm lobby maintained import controls), South Korea moved progressively toward a free trade stance.

South Korea's outward-looking orientation has been rewarded by a dramatic transformation of its economy. Initially, South Korea's resources shifted from agriculture to the manufacture of labor-intensive goods, especially textiles, clothing, and footwear. An abundant supply of cheap but well-educated labor helped form the basis of South Korea's comparative advantage in labor-intensive manufacturing. More recently, as labor costs have risen, the growth areas in the economy have been in the more capital-intensive manufacturing sectors, especially motor vehicles, semiconductors, consumer electronics, and advanced materials. As a result of these developments, South Korea has gone through some dramatic changes. In the late 1950s, 77 percent of the country's employment was in the agricultural sector; today the figure is less than 20 percent. Over the same period, the percentage of its GNP accounted for by manufacturing increased from less than 10 percent to more than 30 percent, while the overall GNP grew at an annual rate of more than 9 percent.

http://www.ghanaweb.com/GhanaHomePage/ghana.htm

Sources: "Poor Man's Burden: A Survey of the Third World," *The Economist*, September 23, 1989; World Bank, *World Development Report, 1997* (Oxford: Oxford University Press, 1997) Tables 1 and 2; and J. Wha-Lee, International Trade, Distortions, and Long-Run Economic Growth," *International Monetary Fund Staff Papers 40*, No. 2, (June 1993), p. 299.

Introduction

The opening case illustrates the gains that come from international trade. For a long time the economic policies of the Ghanaian government discouraged trade with other nations. The result was a shift in Ghana's resources away from productive uses (growing cocoa) and toward unproductive uses (subsistence agriculture). The economic policies of the South Korean government encouraged trade with other nations. The result was a shift in South Korea's resources away from uses where it had no comparative advantage in the world economy (agriculture) and toward more productive uses (labor-intensive manufacturing). As a direct result of their policies toward international trade, Ghana's economy declined while South Korea's grew.

This chapter has two goals that are related to the story of Ghana and South Korea. The first is to review a number of theories that explain why it is beneficial for a country to engage in international trade. The second goal is to explain the pattern of international trade that we observe in the world economy. We will be primarily concerned with explaining the pattern of exports and imports of products between countries. The pattern of foreign direct investment between countries will be discussed in Chapter 7.

An Overview of Trade Theory

We open this chapter with a discussion of mercantilism. Propagated in the 16th and 17th centuries, mercantilism advocated that countries should simultaneously encourage exports and discourage imports. Although mercantilism is an old and largely discredited doctrine, its echoes remain in modern political debate and in the trade policies of many countries. Next we will look at Adam Smith's theory of absolute advantage. Proposed in 1776, Smith's theory was the first to explain why unrestricted free trade is beneficial to a country. **Free trade** occurs when a government does not attempt to influence through quotas or duties what its citizens can buy from another country or what they can produce and sell to another country. Smith argued that the invisible hand of the market mechanism, rather than government policy, should determine what a country imports and what it exports. His arguments implied that such a *laissez-faire* stance toward trade was in the best interests of a country. Building on Smith's work are two additional theories that we shall review. One is the theory of comparative advantage, advanced by the 19th century English economist David Ricardo. This theory is the intellectual basis of the modern argument for unrestricted free trade. In the 20th century, Ricardo's work was refined by two Swedish economists, Eli Heckscher and Bertil Ohlin, whose theory is known as the Heckscher-Ohlin theory.

The Benefits of Trade

The great strength of the theories of Smith, Ricardo, and Heckscher-Ohlin is that they identify with precision the specific benefits of international trade. Common sense suggests that some international trade is beneficial. For example, nobody would suggest that Iceland should grow its own oranges. Iceland can benefit from trade by exchanging some of the products it can produce at low cost (fish) for some products it cannot produce at all (oranges). Thus, by engaging in international trade, Icelanders are able to add oranges to their diet of fish.

The theories of Smith, Ricardo, and Heckscher-Ohlin go beyond this common-sense notion, however, to show why it is beneficial for a country to engage in international trade *even for products it can produce for itself*. This is a difficult concept for people to grasp. Many people in the United States believe that American consumers should buy products produced in the United States by American companies whenever possible to help save American jobs from foreign competition. Such thinking apparently underlay a recent decision by the International Trade Commission to protect the Louisiana crawfish industry from inexpensive Chinese imports (see the accompanying Country Focus).

The same kind of nationalistic sentiments can be observed in many other countries. However, the theories of Smith, Ricardo, and Heckscher-Ohlin tell us that a country's economy may gain if its citizens buy from other nations certain products that could be produced at home. The gains arise because international trade allows a country to specialize in the manufacture and export of products that can be produced most efficiently in that country, while importing products that can be produced more efficiently in other countries. So it may make sense for the United States to specialize in the production and export of commercial jet aircraft, since the efficient production of commercial jet aircraft requires resources that are abundant in the United States, such as a highly skilled labor force and cutting-edge technological know-how. On the other hand, it may make sense for the United States to import textiles from India since the efficient production of textiles requires a relatively cheap labor force—and cheap labor is not abundant in the United States.

This economic argument is often difficult for segments of a country's population to accept. With their future threatened by imports, American textile companies and their employees have tried hard to persuade the US government to impose quotas and tariffs to restrict importation of textiles. Similarly, as the Country Focus illustrates, the Louisiana crawfish industry succeeded in persuading the government to limit imports of crawfish from China. Although such import controls may benefit particular groups, such as American textile businesses and their employees or Louisiana crawfish farmers, the theories of Smith, Ricardo, and Heckscher-Ohlin suggest that the economy as a whole is hurt by this action. Limits on imports are often in the interests of domestic producers, but not domestic consumers.

The Pattern of International Trade

The theories of Smith, Ricardo, and Heckscher-Ohlin also help to explain the pattern of international trade that we observe in the world economy. Some aspects of the pattern are easy to understand. Climate and natural resources explain why

COUNTRY FOCUS
Crawfish Wars

Once upon a time, Louisiana was owned by the French. Napoleon sold the territory to the United States when Thomas Jefferson was president, but many of the French stayed on. Their descendants developed the distinctive Cajun culture that today is celebrated in the United States for its unique cuisine and music. At the heart of that cuisine can be found the venerable crawfish, as Louisianians call the crayfish. The crawfish is a fresh-water crustacean native to the bayous of Louisiana. A central ingredient of crawfish pie, bisque, etouffee, and gumbo, the crawfish is to Cajun Louisiana what wine is to France, a culinary symbol of its culture. It is also a major industry that generates $300 million per year in revenues for Louisiana crawfish farmers—or at least it did until the Chinese appeared.

In the early 1990s, development of the Chinese industry was encouraged by Louisiana importers to meet the growing demand for crawfish. In China, the crawfish industry proved to be attractive for entrepreneurial farmers. Chinese crawfish first started to appear on the Louisiana scene in 1991. Although old-time Cajuns were quick to claim that the Chinese craw-

fish had an inferior taste, consumers didn't seem to notice the difference. More importantly perhaps, they liked the price, which ran between $2 and $3 per pound, depending on the season, compared to $5 to $8 per pound for native Louisiana crawfish. With a significant price advantage on their side, sales of Chinese imports skyrocketed from 353,000 pounds in 1992 to 5.5 million pounds in 1996. By 1996, Louisiana state officials estimated that 3,000 jobs had been lost in the local industry, mostly minimum-wage crawfish peelers, due to market share gains made by the Chinese.

This was too much for the Louisiana industry to stomach. In 1996, Louisiana's Crawfish Promotion and Research Board filed a petition with the International Trade Commission, an arm of the US government, requesting an antidumping action. The petition claimed that Chinese crawfish producers were dumping their product, selling at below cost in order to drive Louisiana producers out of business. The industry requested that a 200 to 300 percent import tax be placed on Chinese crawfish. The State of Louisiana appropriated $350,000 from state funds to support the action.

Ghana exports cocoa, Brazil exports coffee, Saudi Arabia exports oil, and China exports crawfish. But much of the observed pattern of international trade is more difficult to explain. For example, why does Japan export automobiles, consumer electronics, and machine tools? Why does Switzerland export chemicals, watches, and jewelry? David Ricardo's theory of comparative advantage offers an explanation in terms of international differences in labor productivity. The more sophisticated Heckscher-Ohlin theory emphasizes the interplay between the proportions in which the factors of production (such as land, labor, and capital) are available in different countries and the proportions in which they are needed for producing particular goods. This explanation rests on the assumption that different countries have different endowments of the various factors of production. Tests of this theory, however, suggest that it is a less powerful explanation of real-world trade patterns than once thought.

One early response to the failure of the Heckscher-Ohlin theory to explain the observed pattern of international trade was the *product life-cycle theory*. Proposed by Raymond Vernon, this theory suggests that early in their life cycle, most new products are produced in and exported from the country in which they were developed. As a new product becomes widely accepted internationally, production starts in other countries. As a result, the theory suggests, the product may ultimately be exported back to the country of its innovation.

http://www.ita.doc.gov

Lawyers representing the Chinese crawfish industry claimed that lower production costs in China were the reason for the low prices—not dumping. One Louisiana-based importer of Chinese crawfish pointed out that 27 processing plants in China supplied his company. Workers at these plants were given housing and other amenities and paid 15 cents per hour, or $9 for a 60-hour week. Moreover, claimed these lawyers, Chinese crawfish have been good for American consumers, who have been able to save money and have benefited from a steadier supply, and good for Louisiana cuisine, because it is has become less expensive to cook. The lawyers pointed out that the action is not in the interests of American consumers, since it is nothing more than an attempt by Louisiana producers to reestablish their lucrative monopoly on the production of crawfish, a monopoly that would enable them to extract higher prices from consumers.

However, the International Trade Commission turned out to be deaf to such arguments. The commission deemed that China is a "nonmarket economy" because it is not yet a member of the World Trade Organization. The commission then used prices in a

"market economy," Spain, to establish a benchmark for a fair market value for crawfish. Since Spanish crawfish sell for approximately twice the price of Chinese crawfish, about the same price as Louisiana crawfish, the commission concluded that the Chinese were dumping (selling below costs of production). In August 1997, the commission levied a 110 to 123 percent duty on imports of Chinese crawfish, negating the price advantage enjoyed by Chinese producers. In the interests of protecting American jobs, the commission had sided with Louisiana producers and against American consumers, who would now have to pay higher prices for crawfish.

Sources: Donna St. George, "Crawfish Wars: Cajun Country vs China," *New York Times*, May 7, 1997, pp. B1, B10; P Passell, "Protecting America's Shores from Those Chinese Crawfish," *New York Times*, August 28, 1997, p. D2; and N. Dunne, "Shellfish Imports Stick in the Cajun Craw," *Financial Times*, August 21, 1997, p. 16.

In a similar vein, during the 1980s, economists such as Paul Krugman of the Massachusetts Institute of Technology developed what has come to be known as the *new trade theory*. New trade theory stresses that in some cases countries specialize in the production and export of particular products not because of underlying differences in factor endowments, but because in certain industries the world market can support only a limited number of firms. (This is argued to be the case for the commercial aircraft industry.) In such industries, firms that enter the market first build a competitive advantage that is difficult to challenge. Thus, the observed pattern of trade between nations may in part be due to the ability of firms to capture first-mover advantages. The United States dominates in the export of commercial jet aircraft because American firms such as Boeing were first movers in the world market. Boeing built a competitive advantage that has subsequently been difficult for firms from countries with equally favorable factor endowments to challenge.

In a work related to the new trade theory, Michael Porter of the Harvard Business School has developed a theory, referred to as the theory of national competitive advantage, that attempts to explain why particular nations achieve international success in particular industries. Like the new trade theorists, in addition to factor endowments, Porter points out the importance of country factors such as domestic demand and domestic rivalry in explaining a nation's dominance in the production and export of particular products.

Trade Theory and Government Policy

Although all these theories agree that international trade is beneficial to a country, they lack agreement in their recommendations for government policy. Mercantilism makes a crude case for government involvement in promoting exports and limiting imports. The theories of Smith, Ricardo, and Heckscher-Ohlin form part of the case for unrestricted free trade. The argument for unrestricted free trade is that both import controls and export incentives (such as subsidies) are self-defeating and result in wasted resources. Both the new trade theory and Porter's theory of national competitive advantage can be interpreted as justifying some limited and selective government intervention to support the development of certain export-oriented industries. We will discuss the pros and cons of this argument, known as strategic trade policy, as well as the pros and cons of the argument for unrestricted free trade in Chapter 5.

Mercantilism

The first theory of international trade emerged in England in the mid-16th century. Referred to as *mercantilism*, its principle assertion was that gold and silver were the mainstays of national wealth and essential to vigorous commerce. At that time, gold and silver were the currency of trade between countries; a country could earn gold and silver by exporting goods. By the same token, importing goods from other countries would result in an outflow of gold and silver to those countries. The main tenent of **mercantilism** was that it was in a country's best interests to maintain a trade surplus, to export more than it imported. By doing so, a country would accumulate gold and silver and increase its national wealth and prestige. As the English mercantilist writer Thomas Mun put it in 1630:

> The ordinary means therefore to increase our wealth and treasure is by foreign trade, wherein we must ever observe this rule: to sell more to strangers yearly than we consume of theirs in value.[1]

Consistent with this belief, the mercantilist doctrine advocated government intervention to achieve a surplus in the balance of trade. The mercantilists saw no virtue in a large volume of trade. Rather, they recommended policies to maximize exports and minimize imports. To achieve this, imports were limited by tariffs and quotas, and exports were subsidized.

An inherent inconsistency in the mercantilist doctrine was pointed out by the classical economist David Hume in 1752. According to Hume, if England had a balance-of-trade surplus with France (it exported more than it imported) the resulting inflow of gold and silver would swell the domestic money supply and generate inflation in England. In France, however, the outflow of gold and silver would have the opposite effect. France's money supply would contract, and its prices would fall. This change in relative prices between France and England would encourage the French to buy fewer English goods (because they were becoming more expensive) and the English to buy more French goods (because they were becoming cheaper). The result would be a deterioration in the English balance of trade and an improvement in France's trade balance, until the English surplus was eliminated. Hence, according to Hume, in the long run, no country could sustain a surplus on the balance of trade and so accumulate gold and silver as the mercantilists had envisaged.

The flaw with mercantilism was that it viewed trade as a zero-sum game. (A **zero-sum game** is one in which a gain by one country results in a loss by another.) It was left to Adam Smith and David Ricardo to show the shortsightedness of this approach and to demonstrate that trade is a **positive-sum game,** in which all countries can benefit. The mercantilist doctrine is by no means dead.[2] For example, Jarl Hagelstam, a director at the Finnish Ministry of Finance, has observed that in most trade negotiations:

> The approach of individual negotiating countries, both industrialized and developing, has been to press for trade liberalization in areas where their own comparative competitive advantages are the strongest, and to resist liberalization in areas where they are less competitive and fear that imports would replace domestic production.[3]

Hagelstam attributes this strategy by negotiating countries to a neomercantilist belief held by the politicians of many nations. This belief equates political power with economic power and economic power with a balance-of-trade surplus. Thus, the trade strategy of many nations is designed to simultaneously boost exports and limit imports. For example, many American politicians claim that Japan is a neomercantilist nation because its government, while publicly supporting free trade, simultaneously seeks to protect certain segments of its economy from more efficient foreign competition (see the next Country Focus feature for further details).

Absolute Advantage

In his 1776 landmark book *The Wealth of Nations*, Adam Smith attacked the mercantilist assumption that trade is a zero-sum game. Smith argued that countries differ in their ability to produce goods efficiently. In his time, the English, by virtue of their superior manufacturing processes, were the world's most efficient textile manufacturers. Due to the combination of favorable climate, good soils, and accumulated expertise, the French had the world's most efficient wine industry. The English had an *absolute advantage* in the production of textiles, while the French had an *absolute advantage* in the production of wine. Thus, a country has an **absolute advantage** in the production of a product when it is more efficient than any other country in producing it.

According to Smith, countries should specialize in the production of goods for which they have an absolute advantage and then trade these goods for the goods produced by other countries. In Smith's time, this suggested that the English should specialize in the production of textiles while the French should specialize in wine. England could get all the wine it needed by selling its textiles to France and buying wine in exchange. Similarly, France could get all the textiles it needed by selling wine to England and buying textiles in exchange. Smith's basic argument is that you should never produce goods at home that you can buy at a lower cost from other countries. Moreover, Smith demonstrates that by specializing in the production of goods in which each has an absolute advantage, both countries benefit by engaging in trade.

Consider the effects of trade between Ghana and South Korea. The production of any good (output) requires resources (inputs) such as land, labor, and capital. Assume that Ghana and South Korea both have 200 units of resources and that these resources can be used to produce either rice or cocoa. Imagine that in Ghana it takes 10 resources to produce one ton of cocoa and 20 resources to produce one ton of rice. Thus, Ghana could produce 20 tons of cocoa and no rice, 10 tons of rice and no cocoa, or some combination of rice and cocoa in between these two extremes. The different combinations that Ghana could produce are represented by the line GG' in Figure 4.1. This is referred to as Ghana's production possibility frontier (PPF). Similarly, imagine that in South Korea it takes 40 resources to produce one ton of cocoa and 10 resources to produce one ton of rice. Thus, South Korea could produce 5 tons of cocoa and no rice, 20 tons of rice and no cocoa, or some combination in between these two extremes. The different combinations available to South Korea are represented by the line KK' in Figure 4.1, which is South Korea's PPF. Clearly, Ghana has an absolute advantage in the production of cocoa (more resources are needed to produce a ton of cocoa in South Korea than in Ghana), and South Korea has an absolute advantage in the production of rice.

COUNTRY FOCUS
Is Japan a Neomercantilist Nation?

In the international arena, Japan has long been a strong supporter of free trade agreements. However, the US government has repeatedly suggested that the Japanese approach is a cynical neomercantilist one. The Japanese, US officials say, are all too happy to sign international agreements that open foreign markets to the products of Japanese companies, but at the same time they protect their home market from foreign competition. As evidence, US officials point to the large trade imbalance between America and Japan, which in 1994 ran out at over $80 billion (meaning that the United States imported $80 billion more in goods from Japan than it exported to Japan).

The US government recently received support from an unlikely source—three Japanese economists. In a study published in 1994, the three economists cited food products, cosmetics, and chemical production as areas where the Japanese government protected Japanese industry from more efficient foreign competition through import restrictions, such as quotas (lim-

its) on the amount of a product that can be imported into Japan. According to the economists, without barriers protecting these areas from foreign competition, imports would have more than doubled and prices in Japan would have fallen substantially.

The study suggested that falling prices would have saved the average Japanese consumer about $890 per year in 1989. At the same time, however, there would have been a drop in Japanese production of more than 20 percent in certain areas including wheat, oilseeds, leaf tobacco, canned fruit and vegetables, and cosmetics. Trade liberalization would also have resulted in the loss of more than 180,000 Japanese jobs. It would seem, therefore, that Japan's government protects these areas from more efficient foreign competition to save jobs, even though the average Japanese consumer has to pay for this action through higher prices. Protection of the food products area in particular may be motivated by the fact that Japanese farmers, who benefit most from this protec-

Now consider a situation in which neither country trades with any other. Each country devotes half of its resources to the production of rice and half to the production of cocoa. Each country must also consume what it produces. Ghana would be able to produce 10 tons of cocoa and 5 tons of rice (point A in Figure 4.1), while South Korea would be able to produce 10 tons of rice and 2.5 tons of cocoa. Without trade, the combined production of both countries would be 12.5 tons of cocoa (10 tons in Ghana plus 2.5 tons in South Korea) and 15 tons of rice (5 tons in Ghana and 10 tons in South Korea). If each country were to specialize in producing the good for which it had an absolute advantage and then trade with the other for the good it lacks, Ghana could produce 20 tons of cocoa, and South Korea could produce 20 tons of rice. Thus, by specializing, the production of both goods could be increased. Production of cocoa would increase from 12.5 tons to 20 tons, while production of rice would increase from 15 tons to 20 tons. The increase in production that would result from specialization is therefore 7.5 tons of cocoa and 5 tons of rice. Table 4.1 summarizes these figures.

By engaging in trade and swapping one ton of cocoa for one ton of rice, producers in both countries could consume more of both cocoa and rice. Imagine that Ghana and South Korea swap cocoa and rice on a one-to-one basis; that is, the price of one ton of cocoa is equal to the price of one ton of rice. If Ghana decided to export 6 tons of cocoa to South Korea and import 6 tons of rice in return, its final consumption after trade would be 14 tons of cocoa and 6 tons of rice. This is four tons more cocoa than it could have consumed before specialization and trade and one ton more rice. Similarly, South Korea's final consumption after trade would be 6 tons of cocoa and 14 tons of rice. This is 3.5 tons more cocoa than it could have consumed before specialization and trade and 4

http://www.jinjapan.org

tion, are a powerful political force within Japanese society.

The US government claims that another area where Japan has taken a neomercantilist stance is in the importation of automobiles and automobile parts. Japan is a major exporter of autos and auto parts to the United States and Europe, but historically it has imported only 3 percent of its autos and 2 percent of its auto components. Other developed countries import between 22 percent and 78 percent of their autos and 16 to 60 percent of their auto parts. According to US trade negotiators, the Japanese government limits imports by requiring stringent safety inspections that are designed to raise the costs to foreigners trying to sell in Japan. For example, the US Commerce Department claims that the addition of front brush guards to a recreational vehicle, a safety feature required only in Japan, necessitates a complete reinspection that costs up to $3,000 per vehicle.

The Japanese government rejects such charges. Government officials argue that the main reason US auto companies have not been successful in Japan is that they do not make cars suited to the Japanese market. They point out that while 80 percent of the autos sold in the Japanese market have engines under 2,000cc, no US auto company sells cars in Japan in that range. They also point out that imported autos and auto parts are increasing their share of the Japanese market. Between 1990 and 1994, for example, the share of the Japanese market accounted for by imported cars increased from 5.1 percent to 8.1 percent.

Sources: Y. Sazanami, S. Urata, and H. Kawai, *Measuring the Costs of Protection in Japan (Washington DC: Institute for International Economics, 1994)*; M. Nakamoto, "All Action and No Talk," Financial Times, March 17, 1995, p. 5; and N. Dunne, "US Threatens WTO Complaint Against Japan," *Financial Times*, March 29, 1995, p. 6.

Figure 4.1

The Theory of Absolute Advantage

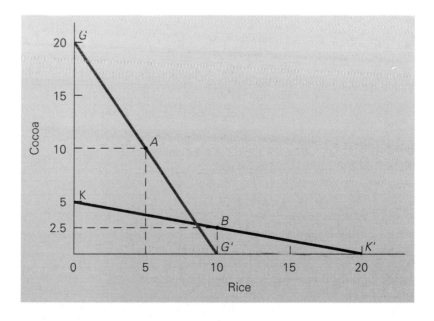

Table 4.1

Absolute Advantage and the Gains from Trade

	Resources Required to Produce 1 Ton of Cocoa and Rice	
	Cocoa	Rice
Ghana	10	20
South Korea	40	10
	Production and Consumption without Trade	
	Cocoa	Rice
Ghana	10.0	5.0
South Korea	2.5	10.0
Total production	12.5	15.0
	Production with Specialization	
	Cocoa	Rice
Ghana	20.0	0.0
South Korea	0.0	20.0
Total production	20.0	20.0
	Consumption After Ghana Trades 6 Tons of Cocoa for 6 Tons of South Korean Rice	
	Cocoa	Rice
Ghana	14.0	6.0
South Korea	6.0	14.0
	Increase in Consumption as a Result of Specialization and Trade	
	Cocoa	Rice
Ghana	4.0	1.0
South Korea	3.5	4.0

tons more rice. Thus, as a result of specialization and trade, output of both cocoa and rice would be increased, and consumers in both nations would be able to consume more. Thus, we can see that trade is a positive-sum game; it produces net gains for all involved.

Comparative Advantage

David Ricardo took Adam Smith's theory one step further by exploring what might happen when one country has an absolute advantage in the production of all goods.[4] Smith's theory of absolute advantage suggests that such a country might derive no benefits from international trade. In his 1817 book *Principles of Political Economy*, Ricardo showed that this was not the case. According to Ricardo's theory of **comparative advantage,** it makes sense for a country to specialize in the production of those goods that it produces most efficiently and to buy the goods that it produces less efficiently from other countries, even if this means buying goods from other countries that it could produce more efficiently itself.[5] While this may seem counterintuitive, the logic can be explained with a simple example.

Assume that Ghana is more efficient in the production of both cocoa and rice; that Ghana has an absolute advantage in the production of both products. In Ghana, it takes 10 resources to produce one ton of cocoa and $13\frac{1}{3}$ resources to produce one

Figure 4.2

The Theory of Comparative Advantage

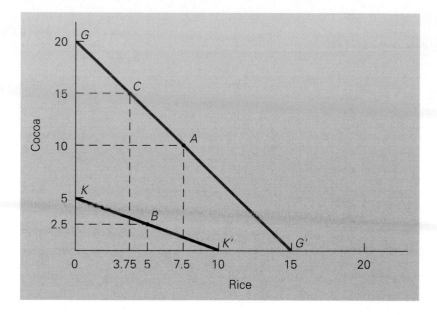

ton of rice. Thus, given its 200 units of resources, Ghana can produce 20 tons of cocoa and no rice, 15 tons of rice and no cocoa, or any combination in between on its PPF (the line GG' in Figure 4.2). In South Korea, it takes 40 resources to produce one ton of cocoa and 20 resources to produce 1 ton of rice. Thus, South Korea can produce 5 tons of cocoa and no rice, 10 tons of rice and no cocoa, or any combination on its PPF (the line KK' in Figure 4.2). Again assume that without trade, each country uses half of its resources to produce rice and half to produce cocoa. Thus, without trade, Ghana will produce 10 tons of cocoa and 7.5 tons of rice (point A in Figure 4.2), while South Korea will produce 2.5 tons of cocoa and 5 tons of rice (point B in Figure 4.2).

In light of Ghana's absolute advantage in the production of both goods, why should it trade with South Korea? Although Ghana has an absolute advantage in the production of both cocoa and rice, it has a comparative advantage only in the production of cocoa: Ghana can produce 4 times as much cocoa as South Korea, but only 1.5 times as much rice. Ghana is *comparatively* more efficient at producing cocoa than it is at producing rice.

Without trade, the combined production of cocoa will be 12.5 tons (10 tons in Ghana and 2.5 in South Korea), and the combined production of rice will also be 12.5 tons (7.5 tons in Ghana and 5 tons in South Korea). Without trade, each country must consume what it produces. By engaging in trade, the two countries can increase their combined production of rice and cocoa, and consumers in both nations can consume more of both goods.

The Gains from Trade

Imagine that Ghana exploits its comparative advantage in the production of cocoa to increase its output from 10 tons to 15 tons. This uses up 150 units of resources, leaving the remaining 50 units of resources to use in producing 3.75 tons of rice (point C in Figure 4.2). Meanwhile, South Korea specializes in the production of rice, producing 10 tons. The combined output of both cocoa and rice has now increased. Before specialization, the combined output was 12.5 tons of cocoa and 12.5 tons of rice. Now it is 15 tons of cocoa and 13.75 tons of rice (3.75 tons in Ghana and 10 tons in South Korea). Table 4.2 summarizes the source of the increase in production.

Not only is output higher, but also both countries can now benefit from trade. If Ghana and South Korea swap cocoa and rice on a one-to-one basis, with both countries choosing to exchange four tons of their export for four tons of the import, both

Table 4.2

Comparative Advantage
and the Gains from Trade

	Resources Required to Produce 1 Ton of Cocoa and Rice	
	Cocoa	Rice
Ghana	10	13.33
South Korea	40	20
	Production and Consumption without Trade	
	Cocoa	Rice
Ghana	10.0	7.5
South Korea	2.5	5.0
Total production	12.5	12.5
	Production with Specialization	
	Cocoa	Rice
Ghana	15.0	3.75
South Korea	0.0	10.0
Total production	15.0	13.75
	Consumption After Ghana Trades 4 Tons of Cocoa for 4 Tons of South Korean Rice	
	Cocoa	Rice
Ghana	11.0	7.75
South Korea	4.0	6.0
	Increase in Consumption as a Result of Specialization and Trade	
	Cocoa	Rice
Ghana	1.0	0.25
South Korea	1.5	1.0

countries are able to consume more cocoa and rice than they could before specialization and trade (see Table 4.2). Thus, if Ghana exchanges 4 tons of cocoa with South Korea for 4 tons of rice, it is still left with 11 tons of rice, which is 1 ton more than it had before trade. Moreover, the 4 tons of rice it gets from South Korea in exchange for its 4 tons of cocoa, when added to the 3.75 tons it now produces domestically, gives it a total of 7.75 tons of rice, which is .25 of a ton more than it had before trade. Similarly, after swapping four tons of rice with Ghana, South Korea still ends up with 6 tons of rice, which is more than it had before trade. In addition, the 4 tons of cocoa it receives in exchange is 1.5 tons more than it produced before trade. Thus, consumption of cocoa and rice can increase in both countries as a result of specialization and trade.

Generalizing from this example, the basic message of the theory of comparative advantage is that *potential world production is greater with unrestricted free trade than it is with restricted trade*. Ricardo's theory suggests that consumers in all nations can consume more if there are no trade restrictions. This occurs even in countries that lack an absolute advantage in the production of any good. To an even greater degree than the theory of absolute advantage, the theory of comparative advantage suggests that trade is a positive-sum game in which all gain. As such, this theory provides a strong rationale for encouraging free trade. Ricardo's theory is so powerful that it remains a major intellectual weapon for those who argue for free trade.

Qualifications and Assumptions

The conclusion that free trade is universally beneficial is a rather bold one to draw from such a simple model. Our simple model includes many unrealistic assumptions:

1. We have assumed a simple world in which there are only two countries and two goods. In the real world, there are many countries and many goods.
2. We have assumed away transportation costs between countries.
3. We have assumed away differences in the prices of resources in different countries. We have said nothing about exchange rates and simply assumed that cocoa and rice could be swapped on a one-to-one basis.
4. We have assumed that while resources can move freely from the production of one good to another within a country, they are not free to move internationally. In reality, some resources are somewhat internationally mobile. This is true of capital and, to a lesser extent, labor.
5. We have assumed constant returns to scale; that is, that specialization by Ghana or South Korea has no effect on the amount of resources required to produce one ton of cocoa or rice. In reality, both diminishing and increasing returns to specialization exist. The amount of resources required to produce a good might decrease or increase as a nation specializes in production of that good.
6. We have assumed that each country has a fixed stock of resources and that free trade does not change the efficiency with which a country uses its resources. This static assumption makes no allowances for the dynamic changes in a country's stock of resources and in the efficiency with which the country uses its resources that might result from free trade.
7. We have assumed away the effects of trade on income distribution within a country.

Given these assumptions, can the conclusion that free trade is mutually beneficial be extended to the real world of many countries, many goods, transportation costs, volatile exchange rates, internationally mobile resources, nonconstant returns to specialization, and dynamic changes? Although a detailed extension of the theory of comparative advantage is beyond the scope of this book, economists have shown that the basic result derived from our simple model can be generalized to a world composed of many countries producing many different goods.[6] Despite all of the shortcomings of the Ricardian model, research suggests that the basic proposition that countries will export the goods that they are most efficient at producing is borne out by the data.[7] However, once all the assumptions are dropped, the case for unrestricted free trade, while still positive, has been argued by some economists associated with the "new trade theory" to lose some of its strength.[8] We return to this issue later in this chapter and in the next.

Simple Extensions of the Ricardian Model

Let us explore the effect of relaxing two of the assumptions identified above in the simple comparative advantage model. Below we relax the assumption of constant returns to specialization and the static assumption that trade does not change a country's stock of resources or the efficiency with which it utilizes those resources.

Diminishing Returns

The simple comparative advantage model developed in the preceding subsection assumes constant returns to specialization. By **constant returns to specialization,** we mean that the units of resources required to produce a good (cocoa or rice) are assumed to remain constant no matter where one is on a country's production possibility frontier (PPF). Thus, we assumed that it always took Ghana 10 units of resources to produce one ton of cocoa. However, it is more realistic to assume diminishing returns to specialization. **Diminishing returns to specialization** occur when more units of resources are required to produce each additional unit. Whereas 10 units of resources

Figure 4.3

Ghana's PPF under Diminishing Returns

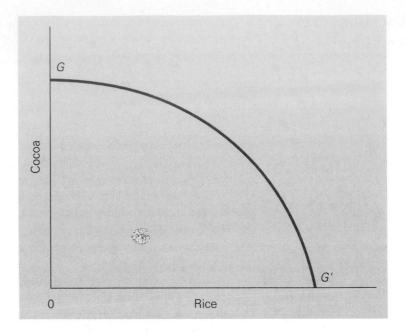

may be sufficient to increase Ghana's output of cocoa from 12 tons to 13 tons, 11 units of resources may be needed to increase output from 13 to 14 tons, 12 units to increase output from 14 tons to 15 tons, and so on. Diminishing returns imply a convex PPF for Ghana (see Figure 4.3), rather than the straight line depicted in Figure 4.2.

There are two reasons why it is more realistic to assume diminishing returns. First, not all resources are of the same quality. As a country tries to increase output of a certain good, it is increasingly likely to draw on more marginal resources whose productivity is not as great as those initially employed. The end result is that it requires more resources to produce an equal increase in output. For example, some land is more productive (fertile) than other land. As Ghana tries to expand its output of cocoa, it might have to utilize increasingly marginal land that is less fertile than the land it originally used. As yields per acre decline, Ghana must use more land to produce one ton of cocoa.

A second reason for diminishing returns is that different goods use resources in different proportions. For example, imagine that growing cocoa uses more land and less labor than growing rice, and that Ghana tries to transfer resources from rice production to cocoa production. The rice industry will release proportionately too much labor and too little land for efficient cocoa production. To absorb the additional resources of labor and land, the cocoa industry will have to shift toward more labor-intensive production methods. The effect is that the efficiency with which the cocoa industry uses labor will decline; and returns will diminish.

The significance of diminishing returns is that it is not feasible for a country to specialize to the degree suggested by the simple Ricardian model outlined earlier. Diminishing returns to specialization suggest that the gains from specialization are likely to be exhausted before specialization is complete. In reality, most countries do not specialize, but produce a range of goods. However, the theory predicts that it is worthwhile to specialize until that point where the resulting gains from trade are outweighed by diminishing returns. Thus, the basic conclusion that unrestricted free trade is beneficial still holds, although due to diminishing returns, the gains may not be as great as suggested in the constant returns case.

Dynamic Effects and Economic Growth

Our simple comparative advantage model assumed that trade does not change a country's stock of resources or the efficiency with which it utilizes those resources. This static assumption makes no allowances for the dynamic changes that might result from

Figure 4.4

The Influence of Free Trade
on the PPF

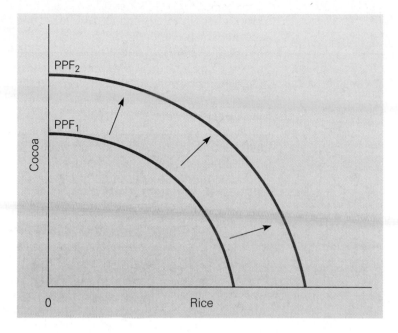

trade. If we relax this assumption, it becomes apparent that opening an economy to trade is likely to generate dynamic gains.[9] These dynamic gains are of two sorts. First, free trade might increase a country's stock of resources as increased supplies of labor and capital from abroad become available for use within the country. This is occurring right now in Eastern Europe, where many Western businesses are investing large amounts of capital in the former Communist bloc countries.

Second, free trade might also increase the efficiency with which a country uses its resources. For example, economies of large-scale production might become available as trade expands the size of the total market available to domestic firms. Trade might make better technology from abroad available to domestic firms. In turn, better technology can increase labor productivity or the productivity of land. (The so-called green revolution had this effect on agricultural outputs in developing countries.) Also, opening an economy to foreign competition might stimulate domestic producers to look for ways to increase the efficiency of their operations. Again, this phenomenon is occurring currently in the once-protected markets of Eastern Europe, where many former state monopolies must increase the efficiency of their operations to survive in the competitive world market.

Dynamic gains in both the stock of a country's resources and the efficiency with which resources are utilized will cause a country's PPF to shift outward. This is illustrated in Figure 4.4, where the shift from PPF_1 to PPF_2 results from the dynamic gains that arise from free trade. Because of this outward shift, the country in Figure 4.4 can produce more of both goods than it did before free trade. The theory suggests that opening an economy to free trade not only results in static gains of the type discussed earlier, but also results in dynamic gains that stimulate economic growth. If this is so, the case for free trade becomes stronger, and the World Bank has assembled evidence that suggests a free trade stance does have these kind of beneficial effects on economic growth.[10]

Heckscher-Ohlin Theory

Ricardo's theory stresses that comparative advantage arises from differences in productivity. Thus, whether Ghana is more efficient than South Korea in the production of cocoa depends on how productively it uses its resources. Ricardo particularly stressed labor productivity and argued that differences in labor productivity between nations underlie the notion of comparative advantage. Swedish economists Eli

Heckscher (in 1919) and Bertil Ohlin (in 1933) put forward a different explanation of comparative advantage. They argued that comparative advantage arises from differences in national factor endowments.[11] By factor endowments, they meant the extent to which a country is endowed with such resources as land, labor, and capital. Different nations have different factor endowments, and different factor endowments explain differences in factor costs. The more abundant a factor, the lower its cost. The Heckscher-Ohlin theory predicts that countries will export those goods that make intensive use of those factors that are locally abundant, while importing goods that make intensive use of factors that are locally scarce. Thus, the Heckscher-Ohlin theory attempts to explain the pattern of international trade that we observe in the world economy. Like Ricardo's theory, the Heckscher-Ohlin theory argues that free trade is beneficial. Unlike Ricardo's theory, however, the Heckscher-Ohlin theory argues that the pattern of international trade is determined by differences in factor endowments, rather than differences in productivity.

The Heckscher-Ohlin theory also has commonsense appeal. For example, the United States has long been a substantial exporter of agricultural goods, reflecting in part its unusual abundance of large tracts of arable land. In contrast, South Korea has excelled in the export of goods produced in labor-intensive manufacturing industries, such as textiles and footwear. This reflects South Korea's relative abundance of low-cost labor. The United States, which lacks abundant low-cost labor, has been a primary importer of these goods. It is relative, not absolute, endowments that are important; a country may have larger absolute amounts of land and labor than another country, but be relatively abundant in one of them.

The Leontief Paradox

The Heckscher-Ohlin theory has been one of the most influential theoretical ideas in international economics. Most economists prefer the Heckscher-Ohlin theory to Ricardo's theory because it makes fewer simplifying assumptions. It has been subjected to many empirical tests. Beginning with a famous study published in 1953 by Wassily Leontief (winner of the Nobel prize in economics in 1973), many of these tests have raised questions about the validity of the Heckscher-Ohlin theory.[12] Using the Heckscher-Ohlin theory, Leontief postulated that since the United States was relatively abundant in capital compared to other nations, the United States would be an exporter of capital-intensive goods and an importer of labor-intensive goods. To his surprise, however, he found that US exports were less capital intensive than US imports. Since this result was at variance with the predictions of the theory, it has become known as the Leontief paradox.

Why do we observe the Leontief paradox? No one is quite sure. One possible explanation is that the United States has a special advantage in producing new products or goods made with innovative technologies. Such products may be less capital intensive than products whose technology has had time to mature and become suitable for mass production. Thus, the United States may be exporting goods that use skilled labor and innovative entrepreneurship, while importing manufactures that use large amounts of capital. More recent empirical studies tend to confirm this.[13] Recent tests of the Heckscher-Ohlin theory using data for a large number of countries tend to confirm the existence of the Leontief paradox.[14]

This leaves economists with a difficult dilemma. They prefer Heckscher-Ohlin on theoretical grounds, but it is a relatively poor predictor of real-world international trade patterns. The theory they regard as being too limited, Ricardo's theory of comparative advantage, actually predicts trade patterns with greater accuracy. The best solution to this dilemma may be to return to the Ricardian idea that trade patterns are largely driven by international differences in productivity. Thus, one might argue that the United States exports commercial aircraft and imports automobiles not because its factor endowments are especially suited to aircraft manufacture and not suited to automobile manufacture, but because the United States is more efficient at producing aircraft than automobiles.

The Product Life-Cycle Theory

Raymond Vernon initially proposed the product life-cycle theory in the mid-1960s.[15] Vernon's theory was based on the observation that for most of the 20th century, a very large proportion of the world's new products had been developed by US firms and sold first in the United States (e.g., mass-produced automobiles, televisions, instant cameras, photocopiers, personal computers, and semiconductor chips). To explain this, Vernon argued that the wealth and size of the US market gave US firms a strong incentive to develop new consumer products. In addition, the high cost of US labor gave firms an incentive to develop cost-saving process innovations.

Just because a new product is developed by a US firm and first sold in the United States, it does not follow that the product must be produced in the United States. It could be produced abroad at some low-cost location and then exported back into the United States. However, Vernon argued that most new products were initially produced in America. Apparently, pioneering firms believed it was better to keep production facilities close to the market and to the firm's center of decision making, given the uncertainty and risks inherent in new-product introduction. Because the demand for most new products tends to be based on nonprice factors, firms can charge relatively high prices for new products, which obviates the need to look for low-cost production sites in other countries.

Vernon went on to argue that early in the life cycle of a typical new product, while demand is starting to grow rapidly in the United States, demand in other advanced countries is limited to high-income groups. The limited initial demand in other advanced countries does not make it worthwhile for firms in those countries to produce the new product, but it does necessitate some exports from the United States to those countries.

Over time, demand for the new product starts to grow in other advanced countries (e.g., Great Britain, France, Germany, and Japan). As it does, it becomes worthwhile for foreign producers to begin producing for their home markets. In addition, US firms might set up production facilities in those advanced countries where demand is growing. Consequently, production within other advanced countries begins to limit the potential for exports from the United States.

As the market in the United States and other advanced nations matures, the product becomes more standardized, and price becomes the main competitive weapon. As this occurs, cost considerations play a greater role in the competitive process. One result is that producers based in advanced countries where labor costs are lower than in the United States (e.g., Italy, Spain) might now be able to export to the United States.

If cost pressures become intense, the process might not stop there. The cycle might be repeated once more, as developing countries (e.g., Thailand) begin to acquire a production advantage over advanced countries. Thus, the locus of global production initially switches from the United States to other advanced nations, and then from those nations to developing countries.

Over time, the United States switches from being an exporter of the product to an importer of the product as production becomes concentrated in lower-cost foreign locations. These dynamics are illustrated in Figure 4.5, which shows the growth of production and consumption over time in the United States, other advanced countries, and developing countries.

Figure 4.5

The Product Life-Cycle Theory

Source: Adapted from R. Vernon and L. T. Wells, *The Economic Environment of International Business*, 4th ed. (Englewood Cliffs, NJ: Prentice-Hall, 1986).

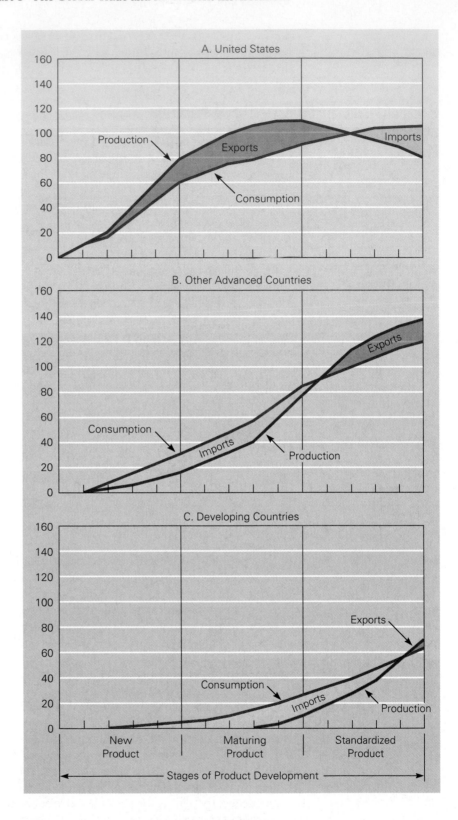

Evaluating the Product Life-Cycle Theory

Historically, the product life-cycle theory is an accurate explanation of international trade patterns. Consider photocopiers; the product was first developed in the early 1960s by Xerox in the United States and sold initially to US users. Originally Xerox exported photocopiers from the United States, primarily to Japan and the advanced countries of Western Europe. As demand began to grow in those countries, Xerox entered into joint ventures to set up production in Japan (Fuji-Xerox) and Great Britain (Rank-Xerox). In addition, once Xerox's patents on the photocopier process expired, other foreign competitors began to enter the market (e.g., Canon in Japan, Olivetti in Italy). As a consequence, exports from the United States declined, and US users began to buy some of their photocopiers from lower-cost foreign sources, particularly from Japan. More recently, Japanese companies have found that manufacturing costs are too high in their own country, so they have begun to switch production to developing countries such as Singapore and Thailand. As a result, the United States and several other advanced countries (e.g., Japan and Great Britain) have switched from being exporters of photocopiers to being importers. This evolution in the pattern of international trade in photocopiers is consistent with the predictions of the product life-cycle theory. The product life-cycle theory clearly explains the migration of mature industries out of the United States and into low-cost assembly locations.

However, the product life-cycle theory is not without weaknesses. Viewed from an Asian or European perspective, Vernon's argument that most new products are developed and introduced in the United States seems ethnocentric. Although it may be true that most new products were introduced in the United States from 1945 to 1975, there have always been important exceptions. In recent years, these exceptions have become more common. Many new products are now introduced in Japan (e.g., high-definition television or digital audiotapes). With the increased globalization and integration of the world economy that we discussed in Chapter 1, a growing number of new products are now introduced simultaneously in the United States, Japan, and the advanced European nations (e.g., laptop computers, compact disks, and electronic cameras). This may be accompanied by globally dispersed production, with particular components of a new product being produced in those locations around the globe where the mix of factor costs and skills is most favorable (as predicted by the theory of comparative advantage).

Consider laptop computers, which were introduced simultaneously into a number of major national markets by Toshiba. Although various components for Toshiba laptop computers are manufactured in Japan (e.g., display screens, memory chips), other components are manufactured in Singapore and Taiwan, and still others (e.g., hard drives and microprocessors) are manufactured in the United States. All the components are shipped to Singapore for final assembly, and the completed product is then shipped to the major world markets (the United States, Western Europe, and Japan). The pattern of trade associated with this new product is both different from and more complex than the pattern predicted by Vernon's model. Trying to explain this pattern using the product life-cycle theory would be very difficult. The theory of comparative advantage might better explain why certain components are produced in certain locations and why the final product is assembled in Singapore. In short, although Vernon's theory may be useful for explaining the pattern of international trade during the brief period of American global dominance, its relevance in the modern world is limited.

The New Trade Theory

The new trade theory began to emerge in the 1970s. At that time, a number of economists were questioning the assumption of diminishing returns to specialization used in international trade theory.[16] They argued that many industries experience increasing returns to specialization because of the presence of substantial economies of scale. As output expands with specialization, the ability to realize economies of scale increases and so the unit costs of production should decrease. Economies of scale are primarily derived by spreading fixed costs (such as the costs of developing a new product) over a larger output. Consider the commercial jet aircraft industry. The fixed costs of developing a new commercial jet airliner are astronomical. For example, Boeing spent an estimated $5 billion to develop its new 777. The company will have to sell at least 350 of the 777s just to recoup these development costs and break even. Thus, due to the high fixed costs of developing a new jet aircraft, the economies of scale in this industry are substantial.

The new trade theorists further argue that due to the presence of substantial scale economies, world demand will support only a few firms in many industries. This is the case in the commercial jet aircraft industry; estimates suggest that world demand can profitably support only three major manufacturers. For example, the total world demand for 300-seat commercial jet aircraft similar to Boeing's 777 model will probably be only 1,500 aircraft between 1995 and 2005. If we assume that firms must sell at least 500 aircraft to get an acceptable return on their investment (which is reasonable, given the break-even point of 300 aircraft), we can see that the world market can profitably support only three firms!

The new trade theorists argue that countries may export certain products simply because they have a firm that was an early entrant into an industry that will support only a few firms because of substantial economies of scale. Underpinning this argument is the notion of **first-mover advantages,** which are the economic and strategic advantages that accrue to early entrants into an industry.[17] Because they can gain economies of scale, the early entrants into an industry may get a lock on the world market that discourages subsequent entry. The ability of first movers to reap economies of scale creates a barrier to entry. In the commercial aircraft industry, for example, the presence of Boeing and Airbus Industrie and their economies of scale effectively discourage new entries.

This theory has profound implications. It suggests that a country may predominate in the export of a good simply because it was lucky enough to have one or more firms among the first to produce that good. This is at variance with the Heckscher-Ohlin theory, which suggests that a country will predominate in the export of a product when it is particularly well endowed with those factors used intensively in its manufacture. Thus, the new trade theorists argue that the United States leads in exports of commercial jet aircraft not because it is better endowed with the factors of production required to manufacture aircraft, but because two of the first movers in the industry, Boeing and McDonnell Douglas, were US firms. However, the new trade theory is not at variance with the theory of comparative advantage. Since economies of scale result in an increase in the efficiency of resource utilization, and hence in productivity, the new trade theory identifies an important source of comparative advantage.

How useful is this theory in explaining trade patterns? It is too early to say; the theory is so new that little supporting empirical work has been done. Consistent with the theory, however, a study by Harvard business historian Alfred Chandler suggests that first-mover advantages are important in explaining the dominance of firms from certain nations in certain industries.[18] Also, many global industries have a very limited number of firms. This is the case with the commercial aircraft industry, the chemical industry, the heavy construction-equipment industry, the heavy truck industry, the tire industry, the consumer electronics industry, and the jet engine industry, to name but a few.

Perhaps the most contentious implication of the new trade theory is the argument that it generates for government intervention and strategic trade policy.[19] New trade theorists stress the role of luck, entrepreneurship, and innovation in giving a firm first-mover advantages. According to this argument, the reason Boeing was the first mover in commercial jet aircraft manufacture—rather than firms such as Great Britain's DeHavilland and Hawker Siddely, or Holland's Fokker, all of which could have been—was that Boeing was both lucky and innovative. One way Boeing was lucky is that DeHavilland's Comet jet airliner, introduced two years earlier than Boeing's first jet airliner, the 707, was full of serious technological flaws. Had DeHavilland not made some serious technological mistakes, Great Britain might now be the world's leading exporter of commercial jet aircraft! Boeing's innovativeness was demonstrated by its independent development of the technological know-how required to build a commercial jet airliner. Several new trade theorists have pointed out, however, that Boeing's R&D was largely paid for by the US government; the 707 was a spinoff from a government-funded military program. Herein lies a rationale for government intervention. By the sophisticated and judicious use of subsidies, a government may increase the chances of domestic firms becoming first movers in newly emerging industries. If this is possible, and the new trade theory suggests it might be, then we have an economic rationale for a proactive trade policy that is at variance with the free trade prescriptions of the trade theories we have reviewed so far. We will consider the policy implications of this issue in Chapter 5.

National Competitive Advantage: Porter's Diamond

In 1990, Michael Porter of Harvard Business School published the results of an intensive research effort that attempted to determine why some nations succeed and others fail in international competition.[20] Porter and his team looked at 100 industries in 10 nations. The book that contains the results of this work, *The Competitive Advantage of Nations*, has made an important contribution to thinking about trade. Like the work of the new trade theorists, Porter's work was driven by a feeling that the existing theories of international trade told only part of the story. For Porter, the essential task was to explain why a nation achieves international success in a particular industry. Why does Japan do so well in the automobile industry? Why does Switzerland excel in the production and export of precision instruments and pharmaceuticals? Why do Germany and the United States do so well in the chemical industry? These questions cannot be answered easily by the Heckscher-Ohlin theory, and the theory of comparative advantage offers only a partial explanation. The theory of comparative advantage would say that Switzerland excels in the production and export of precision instruments because it uses its resources very productively in these industries. Although this may be correct, this does not explain why Switzerland is more productive in this industry than Great Britain, Germany, or Spain. It is this puzzle that Porter tries to solve.

Porter's thesis is that four broad attributes of a nation shape the environment in which local firms compete, and these attributes promote or impede the creation of competitive advantage (see Figure 4.6). These attributes are

- *Factor endowments*—a nation's position in factors of production such as skilled labor or the infrastructure necessary to compete in a given industry.
- *Demand conditions*—the nature of home demand for the industry's product or service.
- *Relating and supporting industries*—the presence or absence in a nation of supplier industries and related industries that are internationally competitive.
- *Firm strategy, structure, and rivalry*—the conditions in the nation governing how companies are created, organized, and managed and the nature of domestic rivalry.

Figure 4.6

Determinants of National Competitive Advantage: Porter's Diamond

Reprinted by permission of the *Harvard Business Review.* "The Competitive Advantage of Nations" by Michael E. Porter, March–April 1990, p. 77. Copyright © 1990 by the President and Fellows of Harvard College; all rights reserved.

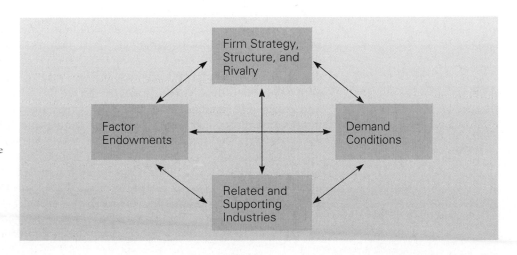

Porter speaks of these four attributes as constituting the *diamond*. He argues that firms are most likely to succeed in industries or industry segments where the diamond is most favorable. He also argues that the diamond is a mutually reinforcing system. The effect of one attribute is contingent on the state of others. For example, Porter argues, favorable demand conditions will not result in competitive advantage unless the state of rivalry is sufficient to cause firms to respond to them.

Porter maintains that two additional variables can influence the national diamond in important ways: chance and government. Chance events, such as major innovations, create discontinuities that can unfreeze or reshape industry structure and provide the opportunity for one nation's firms to supplant another's. Government, by its choice of policies, can detract from or improve national advantage. For example, regulation can alter home demand conditions, antitrust policies can influence the intensity of rivalry within an industry, and government investments in education can change factor endowments.

Factor Endowments

Factor endowments lie at the center of the Heckscher-Ohlin theory. While Porter does not propose anything radically new, he does analyze the characteristics of factors of production in some detail. He recognizes hierarchies among factors, distinguishing between basic factors (e.g., natural resources, climate, location, and demographics) and advanced factors (e.g., communications infrastructure, sophisticated and skilled labor, research facilities, and technological know-how). He argues that advanced factors are the most significant for competitive advantage. Unlike basic factors (which are naturally endowed), advanced factors are a product of investment by individuals, companies, and governments. Thus, government investments in basic and higher education, by improving the general skills and knowledge of the population and by stimulating advanced research at higher education institutions, can upgrade a nation's advanced factors.

The relationship between advanced and basic factors is complex. Basic factors can provide an initial advantage that is subsequently reinforced and extended by investment in advanced factors. Conversely, disadvantages in basic factors can create pressures to invest in advanced factors. The most obvious example of this phenomenon is Japan, a country that lacks much in the way of arable land or mineral deposits and yet through investment has built a substantial endowment of advanced factors. Porter notes that Japan's large pool of engineers (reflecting a much higher number of engineering graduates per capita than almost any other nation) has been vital to Japan's success in many manufacturing industries.

Demand Conditions

Porter emphasizes the role home demand plays in providing the impetus for upgrading competitive advantage. Firms are typically most sensitive to the needs of their closest customers. Thus, the characteristics of home demand are particularly important in shaping the attributes of domestically made products and in creating pressures for innovation and quality. Porter argues that a nation's firms gain competitive advantage if their domestic consumers are sophisticated and demanding. Sophisticated and demanding consumers pressure local firms to meet high standards of product quality and to produce innovative products. Porter notes that Japan's sophisticated and knowledgeable buyers of cameras helped stimulate the Japanese camera industry to improve product quality and to introduce innovative models. A similar example can be found in the cellular phone equipment industry, where sophisticated and demanding local customers in Scandinavia helped push Nokia of Finland and Ericsson of Sweden to invest in cellular phone technology long before demand for cellular phones took off in other developed nations. As a result, Nokia and Ericsson, together with Motorola, are dominant players in the global cellular telephone equipment industry. The case of Nokia is detailed in the next Management Focus.

Related and Supporting Industries

The third broad attribute of national advantage in an industry is the presence of internationally competitive suppliers or related industries. The benefits of investments in advanced factors of production by related and supporting industries can spill over into an industry, thereby helping it achieve a strong competitive position internationally. Swedish strength in fabricated steel products (e.g., ball bearings and cutting tools) has drawn on strengths in Sweden's specialty steel industry. Technological leadership in the US semiconductor industry until the mid-1980s provided the basis for US success in personal computers and several other technically advanced electronic products. Similarly, Switzerland's success in pharmaceuticals is closely related to its previous international success in the technologically related dye industry.

One consequence of this is that successful industries within a country tend to be grouped into clusters of related industries. This was one of the most pervasive findings of Porter's study. One such cluster is the German textile and apparel sector, which includes high-quality cotton, wool, synthetic fibers, sewing machine needles, and a wide range of textile machinery.

Firm Strategy, Structure, and Rivalry

The fourth broad attribute of national competitive advantage in Porter's model is the strategy, structure, and rivalry of firms within a nation. Porter makes two important points here. His first is that nations are characterized by different "management ideologies," which either help them or do not help them to build national competitive advantage. For example, Porter notes the predominance of engineers on the top-management teams of German and Japanese firms. He attributes this to these firms' emphasis on improving manufacturing processes and product design. In contrast, Porter notes a predominance of people with finance backgrounds on the top-management teams of many US firms. He links this to the lack of attention by many US firms to improving manufacturing processes and product design, particularly during the 1970s and 80s. He also argues that the dominance of finance has led to a corresponding overemphasis on maximizing short-term financial returns. According to Porter, one consequence of these different management ideologies has been a relative loss of US competitiveness in those engineering-based industries where manufacturing processes and product design issues are all-important (e.g., the automobile industry).

Porter's second point is that there is a strong association between vigorous domestic rivalry and the creation and persistence of competitive advantage in an industry. Vigorous domestic rivalry induces firms to look for ways to improve efficiency, which makes them better international competitors. Domestic rivalry creates pressures to innovate, to improve quality, to reduce costs, and to invest in upgrading advanced factors. All of this helps to create world-class competitors. Porter cites the case of Japan:

> Nowhere is the role of domestic rivalry more evident than in Japan, where it is all-out warfare in which many companies fail to achieve profitability. With goals that stress market share, Japanese companies engage in a continuing struggle to outdo each other. Shares fluctuate markedly. The process is prominently covered in the business press. Elaborate rankings measure which companies are most popular with university graduates. The rate of new product and process development is breathtaking.[21]

Strong domestic competition also stimulated the rise of Nokia of Finland to global preeminence in the market for cellular telephone equipment. For details, see the accompanying Management Focus.

Evaluating Porter's Theory

In sum, Porter's argument is that the degree to which a nation is likely to achieve international success in a certain industry is a function of the combined impact of factor endowments, domestic demand conditions, related and supporting industries, and domestic rivalry. He argues that the presence of all four components is usually required for this diamond to positively impact competitive performance (although there are some exceptions). Porter also contends that government can influence each

MANAGEMENT FOCUS
The Rise of Finland's Nokia

The cellular telephone equipment industry is one of the great growth stories of the 1990s. The number of cellular subscribers has been expanding rapidly. By the end of 1997, there were over 100 million cellular subscribers worldwide, up from under 10 million in 1990. Three firms currently dominate the global market for cellular equipment (e.g., cellular phones, base station equipment, digital switches): Motorola, Nokia, and Ericsson. Of the three, the dramatic rise of Nokia has perhaps been the most surprising.

Nokia's roots are in Finland, not normally a country that comes to mind when one talks about leading-edge technology companies. In the 1980s, Nokia was a rambling Finnish conglomerate with activities that embraced tire manufacturing, paper production, consumer electronics, and telecommunications equipment. Today it is a focused $10 billion telecommunications equipment manufacturer with a global reach second only to that of Motorola and with sales and earnings that are growing in excess of 30 percent annually. How has this former conglomerate emerged to

take a global leadership position in cellular equipment? Much of the answer lies in the history, geography, and political economy of Finland and its Nordic neighbors.

The story starts in 1981 when the Nordic nations created the world's first international cellular telephone network. They had good reason to become pioneers; in the sparsely populated and inhospitably cold areas, it cost far too much to lay a traditional wireline telephone service. Yet the same features make telecommunications all the more valuable; people driving through the Arctic winter and owners of remote northern houses need a telephone to summon help if things go wrong. As a result, Sweden, Norway, and Finland became the first nations in the world to take cellular telecommunications seriously. They found, for example, that while it cost up to $800 per subscriber to bring a traditional wireline service to remote locations in the far north, the same locations could be linked by wireless cellular service for only $500 per person. As a consequence, by 1994, 12 percent of people in Scandinavia owned cellular phones,

of the four components of the diamond either positively or negatively. Factor endowments can be affected by subsidies, policies toward capital markets, policies toward education, and the like. Government can shape domestic demand through local product standards or with regulations that mandate or influence buyer needs. Government policy can influence supporting and related industries through regulation and influence firm rivalry through such devices as capital market regulation, tax policy, and antitrust laws.

If Porter is correct, we would expect his model to predict the pattern of international trade that we observe in the real world. Countries should be exporting products from those industries where all four components of the diamond are favorable, while importing in those areas where the components are not favorable. Is he correct? We do not yet know. Porter's theory is so new that it has not yet been subjected to independent empirical testing. Much about the theory rings true, but the same can be said for the new trade theory, the theory of comparative advantage, and the Heckscher-Ohlin theory. It may be that each of these theories explains something about the pattern of international trade. In many respects, these theories complement each other.

IMPLICATIONS FOR BUSINESS

Why does all this matter for business? Three main implications of the material discussed in this chapter for international businesses are (1) location implications, (2) first-mover implications, and (3) policy implications.

http://www.nokia.com

compared with less than 6 percent in the United States, the world's second most developed market.

Nokia, as a long-time telecommunications equipment supplier, was well-positioned to take advantage of this development, but other forces were also at work in Finland that helped Nokia develop its competitive edge. Unlike virtually every other developed nation, Finland has never had a national telephone monopoly. Instead, the country's telephone services have long been provided by about 50 or so autonomous local telephone companies, whose elected boards set prices by referendum (which naturally means low prices). This army of independent and cost-conscious telephone service providers have prevented Nokia from taking anything for granted in its home country. With typical Finnish pragmatism, they have been willing to buy from the lowest-cost supplier, whether that was Nokia, Ericsson, Motorola, or someone else. This situation contrasted sharply with that prevailing in most developed nations up until the late 1980s and early 1990s, where domestic telephone monopolies typically purchased equipment from a dominant local supplier or

made it themselves. Nokia has responded to this competitive pressure by doing everything possible to drive down its manufacturing costs while still staying at the leading edge of cellular technology.

The consequences of these forces are clear. While Motorola remains the number one firm in cellular equipment, Nokia is snapping at its heels. Nokia, not Motorola, is the leader in digital cellular technology, which seems to be the wave of the future. Nokia has the lead because Scandinavia started switching over to digital technology five years before the rest of the world. Moreover, spurred on by its cost-conscious Finnish customers, Nokia now has the lowest cost structure of any cellular phone equipment manufacturer in the world, making it a more profitable enterprise than Motorola. Nokia's operating margins in 1996 were 8.3 percent, compared with 4.1 percent at Motorola.

Sources: "Lessons from the Frozen North," *The Economist*, October 8, 1994, pp. 76–77; G. Edmondson, "Grabbing Markets from the Giants," *Business Week, Special Issue: 21st Century Capitalism*, 1995, p. 156; and company news releases.

Location Implications

Underlying most of the theories we have discussed is the notion that different countries have particular advantages in different productive activities. Thus, from a profit perspective, it makes sense for a firm to disperse its productive activities to those countries where, according to the theory of international trade, they can be performed most efficiently. If design can be performed most efficiently in France, that is where design facilities should be located; if the manufacture of basic components can be performed most efficiently in Singapore, that is where they should be manufactured; and if final assembly can be performed most efficiently in China, that is where final assembly should be performed. The result is a global web of productive activities, with different activities being performed in different locations around the globe depending on considerations of comparative advantage, factor endowments, and the like. If the firm does not do this, it may find itself at a competitive disadvantage relative to firms that do.

Consider the production of a laptop computer, a process with four major stages: (1) basic research and development of the product design, (2) manufacture of standard electronic components (e.g., memory chips), (3) manufacture of advanced components (e.g., flat-top color display screens and microprocessors), and (4) final assembly. Basic R&D and design require a pool of highly skilled and educated workers with backgrounds in microelectronics. The two countries with a comparative advantage in basic microelectronics R&D and design are Japan and the United States, so most producers of laptop computers locate their R&D facilities in one, or both, of these countries. (Apple, IBM, Motorola, Texas Instruments, Toshiba, and Sony all have major R&D facilities in both Japan and the United States.)

The manufacture of standard electronic components is a capital-intensive process requiring semiskilled labor, and cost pressures are intense. The best locations for such activities today are places such as Singapore, Taiwan, Malaysia, and South Korea. These countries have pools of relatively skilled, low-cost labor. Thus, many producers of laptop computers have standard components, such as memory chips, produced at these locations.

The manufacture of advanced components such as microprocessors and display screens is a capital-intensive process requiring skilled labor, and cost pressures are less intense. Since cost pressures are not so intense at this stage, these components are manufactured in countries with high labor costs that also have pools of highly skilled labor (primarily Japan and the United States).

Finally, assembly is a relatively labor-intensive process requiring only low-skilled labor, and cost pressures are intense. As a result, final assembly may be carried out in a country such as Mexico, which has an abundance of low-cost, low-skilled labor.

When we look at a laptop computer produced by a US manufacturer, we may find that it was designed in California, its standard components were produced in Taiwan and Singapore, its advanced components were produced in Japan and the United States, its final assembly occurred in Mexico, and the finished product was sold in the United States or elsewhere in the world. By dispersing production activities to different locations around the globe, the US manufacturer is taking advantage of the differences between countries identified by the various theories of international trade.

First-Mover Implications

The new trade theory suggests the importance of first-mover advantages. According to the new trade theory, firms that establish a first-mover advantage in the production of a new product may dominate global trade in that product. This is particularly true in those industries where the global market can profitably support only a limited number of firms, such as the aerospace market, but early commitments also seem to be important in less concentrated industries such as the market for cellular telephone equipment (see the Management Focus on Nokia). For the individual firm, the clear message is that it pays to invest substantial financial resources in building a first-mover, or early-mover, advantage, even if that means several years of substantial losses before a new venture becomes profitable. Although the precise details of how to achieve this are beyond the scope of this book, much has been written on strategies for exploiting first-mover advantages.[22] In recent years, Japanese firms, rather than their European or North American competitors, seem to have undertaken the vast investments and years of losses required to build a first-mover advantage. This has been true in the production of liquid crystal display (LCD) screens for laptop computers. While firms such as Toshiba and NEC invested heavily in this technology during the 1980s, many large European and American firms exited the market. As a result, Japanese firms dominate global trade in LCD screens, even though the technology was invented in the United States.

Policy Implications

The theories of international trade also matter to international businesses because business firms are major players on the international trade scene. Business firms produce exports, and business firms import the products of other countries. Because of their pivotal role in international trade, business firms exert a strong influence on government trade policy. By lobbying government, firms can help promote free trade or trade restrictions. The theories of international trade tell businesses that promoting free trade is generally in the best interests of their home country, although it may not always be in the best interest of an individual firm. Many firms recognize this and lobby for open markets.

For example, in 1991, when the US government announced its intention to place a tariff on Japanese imports of liquid crystal display screens, IBM and Apple Computer protested strongly. Both IBM and Apple pointed out that (1) Japan was the lowest-cost source of LCD screens, (2) they used these screens in their laptop computers, and (3) the proposed tariff, by increasing the cost of LCD screens, would increase the cost of laptop computers produced by IBM and Apple, thus making them less competitive in the world market. In other words, the tariff, designed to protect US firms, would be self-defeating. In response to these pressures, the US government reversed its posture on this issue.

Unlike IBM and Apple, however, businesses do not always lobby for free trade. In the United States, for example, "voluntary" restrictions on imports on automobiles, machine tools, textiles, and steel are the result of direct pressures by US firms in these industries on the government. The government has responded by getting foreign companies to agree to "voluntary" restrictions on their imports, using the threat of more comprehensive formal trade barriers to get them to adhere to these agreements. As predicted by international trade theory, many of these agreements have been self-defeating. Take the voluntary restriction on machine-tool imports agreed to in 1985 as an example. Due to limited import competition from more-efficient foreign suppliers, the prices of machine tools in the United States have risen to higher levels than would have prevailed under a free trade scenario. Since machine tools are used throughout the manufacturing industry, the result has been an increase in the costs of US manufacturing in general and a corresponding loss in world market competitiveness. Shielded from international competition by import barriers, the US machine tool industry has had no incentive to increase its efficiency. Consequently, it has lost many of its export markets to more efficient foreign competitors. Thus, the US machine tool industry is now smaller than it was in 1985. For anyone schooled in international trade theory, these events are not surprising.[23]

Finally, Porter's theory of national competitive advantage also contains policy implications. Porter's theory suggests that it is in a firm's best interests to upgrade advanced factors of production; for example, to invest in better training for its employees and to increase its commitment to research and development. It is also in the best interests of business to lobby the government to adopt policies that have a favorable impact on each component of the national "diamond." Thus, according to Porter, businesses should urge government to increase its investment in education, infrastructure, and basic research (since all of these enhance advanced factors) and to adopt policies that promote strong competition within domestic markets (since this makes firms stronger international competitors, according to Porter's findings).

Chapter Summary

This chapter has reviewed a number of theories that explain why it is beneficial for a country to engage in international trade and has explained the pattern of international trade that we observe in the world economy. We have seen how the theories of Smith, Ricardo, and Heckscher-Ohlin all make strong cases for unrestricted free trade. In contrast, the mercantilist doctrine and, to a lesser extent, the new trade theory can be interpreted to support government intervention to promote exports through subsidies and to limit imports through tariffs and quotas.

In explaining the pattern of international trade, the second objective of this chapter, we have seen that with the exception of mercantilism, which is silent on this issue, the different theories offer largely complementary explanations. Although no one theory may explain the apparent pattern of international trade, taken together, the theory of comparative advantage, the Heckscher-Ohlin theory, the product life-cycle theory, the new trade theory, and Porter's theory of national competitive advantage do suggest which factors are important. Comparative advantage tells us that productivity differences are important; the Heckscher-Ohlin theory tells us that factor endowments matter; the product life-cycle theory tells us that where a new product is introduced is important; the new trade theory tells us that increasing returns to specialization and first-mover advantages matter; and Porter tells us that all these factors may be important insofar as they affect the four components of the national diamond.

The following points have been made in this chapter:

1. Mercantilists argued that it was in a country's best interests to run a balance-of-trade surplus. They viewed trade as a zero-sum game, in which one country's gains cause losses for other countries.

2. The theory of absolute advantage suggests that countries differ in their ability to produce goods efficiently. The theory suggests that a country should specialize in producing goods in areas where it has an absolute advantage and import goods in areas where other countries have absolute advantages.

3. The theory of comparative advantage suggests that it makes sense for a country to specialize in producing those goods that it can produce most efficiently, while buying goods that it can produce relatively less efficiently from other countries—even if that means buying goods from other countries that it could produce more efficiently itself.

4. The theory of comparative advantage suggests that unrestricted free trade brings about increased world production; that is, that trade is a positive-sum game.

5. The theory of comparative advantage also suggests that opening a country to free trade stimulates economic growth, which in turn creates dynamic gains from trade.

6. The Heckscher-Ohlin theory argues that the pattern of international trade is determined by differences in factor endowments. It predicts that countries will export those goods that make intensive use of locally abundant factors and will import goods that make intensive use of factors that are locally scarce.

7. The product life-cycle theory suggests that trade patterns are influenced by where a new product is introduced. In an increasingly integrated global economy, the product life-cycle theory seems to be less predictive than it was between 1945 and 1975.

8. The new trade theory argues that a country may predominate in the export of a certain product simply because it had a firm that was a first mover in an industry that will profitably support only a few firms because of substantial economies of scale.

9. Some new trade theorists have promoted the idea of strategic trade policy. The argument is that government, by the sophisticated and judicious use of subsidies, might be able to increase the chances of domestic firms becoming first movers in newly emerging industries.

10. Porter's theory of national competitive advantage suggests that the pattern of trade is influenced by four attributes of a nation: (*i*) factor endowments, (*ii*) domestic demand conditions, (*iii*) related and supporting industries, and (*iv*) firm strategy, structure, and rivalry.

11. Theories of international trade are important to an individual business firm primarily because they can help the firm decide where to locate its various production activities.

12. Firms involved in international trade exert a strong influence on government policy toward trade. By lobbying government bodies, firms can help promote free trade or trade restrictions.

Critical Discussion Questions

1. Mercantilism is a bankrupt theory that has no place in the modern world. Discuss.

2. One Country Focus in this chapter reviews the arguments of those who suggest that Japan is a neomercantilist nation. Do you agree with this assessment? Can you think of cases in which your country has taken a neomercantilist stance to foreign competition?

3. Using the theory of comparative advantage to support your arguments, outline the case for free trade.

4. Using the new trade theory and Porter's theory of national competitive advantage, outline the case for government policies that would build national competitive advantage in a particular industry. What kind of policies would you recommend that

the government adopt? Are these policies at variance with the basic free trade philosophy?

5. You are the CEO of a textile firm that designs and manufactures mass-market clothing products in the United States. Your manufacturing process is labor-intensive and does not require highly skilled employees. You have design facilities in Paris and New York and manufacturing facilities in North Carolina. Drawing on the theory of international trade, decide whether these are optimal locations for these activities.

6. In general, policies designed to limit competition from low-cost foreign competitors do not help a country achieve greater economic growth. Discuss this statement.

CLOSING CASE The Rise of the Indian Software Industry

As a relatively poor country, India is not normally thought of as a nation that is capable of building a major presence in a high-technology industry, such as computer software. In a little over a decade, however, the Indian software industry has astounded its skeptics and emerged from obscurity into an important force in the global software industry. Between 1991–92 and 1996–97, sales of Indian software companies grew at a compound rate of 53 percent annually. In 1991–92, the industry had sales totaling $388 million. By 1996–97 sales were around $1.8 billion. By 1997, there were over 760 software companies in India employing 160,000 software engineers, the third-largest concentration of such talent in the world. Much of this growth was powered by exports. In 1985, Indian software exports were worth less than $10 million. Exports hit $1.1 billion in 1996–97 and are projected to reach $4 billion by 2000–01. As a testament to this growth, many foreign software companies are now investing heavily in Indian software development operations, including Microsoft, IBM, Oracle, and Computer Associates, the four largest US-based software houses.

Most of the growth of the Indian software industry has been based on contract or project-based work for foreign clients. Many Indian companies, for example, maintain applications for their clients, convert code, or migrate software from one platform to another. Increasingly, Indian companies are also involved in important development projects for foreign clients. For example, TCS, India's largest software company, has an alliance with Ernst & Young under which TCS will develop and maintain customized software for Ernst & Young's global clients. TCS also has a development alliance with Microsoft under which the company developed a paperless National Share Depositary system for the Indian stock market based on Microsoft's Windows NT operating system and SQL Server database technology.

The Indian software industry has emerged despite a poor information technology infrastructure. The installed base of personal computers in India stood at just 1.8 million in 1997, and this in a nation of 1 billion people. Moreover, with just 1.5 telephone lines per 100 people, India has one of the lowest penetration

rates for fixed telephone lines in Asia, if not the world. Internet connections numbered just 45,000 in 1997, compared to 30 million in the United States. Sales of personal computers are starting to take off; over 500,000 were expected to be sold in 1998. The rapid growth of mobile telephones in India's main cities is to some extent compensating for the lack of fixed telephone lines.

In explaining the success of their industry, India's software entrepreneurs point to a number of factors. Although the general level of education in India is low, India's important middle class is highly educated and its top educational institutions are world class. Also, there has always been an emphasis on engineering in India. Another great plus from an international perspective is that English is the working language throughout much of middle-class India—a remnant from the days of the British raja. Then there is the wage rate. In America, software engineers are increasingly scarce, and the basic salary has been driven up to one of the highest for any occupational group in the country, with entry-level programmers earning $70,000 per year. An entry-level programmer in India, in contrast, starts at around $5,000 per year, which is very low by international standards but high by Indian standards. Still, salaries for programmers are rising rapidly in India, but so is productivity. In 1992, productivity was around $21,000 per software engineer. By 1996, the figure had risen to $45,000. Many Indian firms now feel that they have approached the critical mass required to realize scale economies in software development and to achieve legitimacy in the eyes of important global partners and clients.

Another factor playing to India's hand is that satellite communications have removed distance as an obstacle to doing business for foreign clients. Since software is nothing more than a stream of zeros and ones, it can be transported at the speed of light and negligible cost to any point in the world. In a world of instant communications, India's geographical position has given it a time zone advantage. Indian companies have exploited the rapidly expanding international market for outsourced software services including the expanding market for remote maintenance. Indian engineers can fix software bugs, upgrade systems, or process data overnight while their users in Western companies are asleep.

To maintain their competitive position, Indian software companies are now investing heavily in training and leading-edge programming skills. They have also been enthusiastic adopters of international quality standards, particularly ISO 9000 certification. Indian companies are also starting to make forays into the application and shrink-wrapped software business, primarily with applications aimed at the domestic market. It may only be a matter of time, however, before Indian companies start to compete head-to-head with companies such as Microsoft, Oracle, PeopleSoft, and SAP in the applications business.

http://www.tcs.co.in/index.html

Sources: P. Taylor, "Poised for Global Growth," *Financial Times: India's Software Industry*, December 3, 1997, pp. 1, 8; P. Taylor, "An Industry on the Up and Up," *Financial Times: India's Software Industry*, December 3,

1997, p. 3; and Krishna Guha, "Strategic Alliances with Global Partners," *Financial Times: India's Software Industry*, December 3, 1997, p. 6.

Case Discussion Questions

1. To what extent does the theory of comparative advantage explain the rise of the Indian software industry?

2. To what extent does the Heckscher-Ohlin theory explain the rise of the Indian software industry?

3. Use Michael Porter's diamond to analyze the rise of the Indian software industry. Does this analysis help explain the rise of this industry?

4. Which of the above theories—comparative advantage, Heckscher-Ohlin, or Porter's—gives the best explanation of the rise of the Indian software industry? Why?

Notes

1. H. W. Spiegel, *The Growth of Economic Thought* (Durham, NC: Duke University Press, 1991).

2. G. de Jonquieres, "Mercantilists Are Treading on Thin Ice," *Financial Times*, July 3, 1994, p. 16.

3. Jarl Hagelstam, "Mercantilism Still Influences Practical Trade Policy at the End of the Twentieth Century," *Journal of World Trade*, 1991, pp. 95–105.

4. S. Hollander, *The Economics of David Ricardo* (Buffalo, NY: The University of Toronto Press, 1979).

5. D. Ricardo, *The Principles of Political Economy and Taxation* (Homewood, IL: Irwin, 1967, first published in 1817).

6. For example, R. Dornbusch, S. Fischer, and P. Samuelson, "Comparative Advantage: Trade and Payments in a Ricardian Model with a Continuum of Goods," *American Economic Review* 67 (December 1977), pp. 823–39.

7. B. Balassa, "An Empirical Demonstration of Classic Comparative Cost Theory," *Review of Economics and Statistics*, 1963, pp. 231–38.

8. See P. R. Krugman, "Is Free Trade Passé? *Journal of Economic Perspectives* 1 (Fall 1987), pp. 131–44.

9. P. Samuelson, "The Gains from International Trade Once Again," *Economic Journal* 72 (1962), pp. 820–29.

10. For a summary see "The Gains from Trade," *The Economist*, September 23, 1989, pp. 25–26.

11. B. Ohlin, *Interregional and International Trade* (Cambridge, MA: Harvard University Press, 1933). For a summary, see R. W. Jones and J. P.Neary, "The Positive Theory of International Trade," in *Handbook of International Economics*, ed. R. W. Jones and P. B. Kenen (Amsterdam: North Holland, 1984).

12. W. Leontief, "Domestic Production and Foreign Trade: The American Capital Position Re-Examined," *Proceedings of the American Philosophical Society* 97 (1953), pp. 331–49.

13. R. M. Stern and K. Maskus, "Determinants of the Structure of US Foreign Trade," *Journal of International Economics* 11 (1981), pp. 207–44.

14. See H. P. Bowen, E. E. Leamer, and L. Sveikayskas, "Multicountry, Multifactor Tests of the Factor Abundance Theory," *American Economic Review* 77, (1987), pp. 791–809.

15. R. Vernon, "International Investments and International Trade in the Product Life Cycle," *Quarterly Journal of Economics*, May 1966, pp. 190–207; and R. Vernon and L. T. Wells, *The Economic Environment of International Business*, 4th ed. (Englewood Cliffs, NJ: Prentice Hall, 1986).

16. For a good summary of this literature, see E. Helpman and P. Krugman, *Market Structure and Foreign Trade: Increasing Returns, Imperfect Competition, and the International Economy* (Boston: MIT Press, 1985). Also see, P. Krugman, "Does the New Trade Theory Require a New Trade Policy?" *World Economy* 15, no. (4), (1992), pp. 423–41.

17. M. B. Lieberman and D. B. Montgomery, "First-Mover Advantages," *Strategic Management Journal*, 9 (Summer 1988), pp. 41–58.

18. A. D. Chandler, *Scale and Scope*. (New York: Free Press, 1990).

19. Krugman, "Does the New Trade Theory Require a New Trade Policy?"

20. M. E. Porter, *The Competitive Advantage of Nations* (New York: Free Press, 1990). For a good review of this book, see R. M. Grant, "Porter's Competitive Advantage of Nations: An Assessment," *Strategic Management Journal* 12 (1991), pp. 535–48.

21. Porter, *Competitive Advantage*, p. 121.

22. Lieberman and Montgomery, "First-Mover Advantages."

23. C. A. Hamilton, "Building Better Machine Tools," *The Journal of Commerce*, October 30, 1991, p. 8; and "Manufacturing Trouble," *The Economist*, October 12, 1991, p. 71.

CHAPTER FIVE

THE POLITICAL ECONOMY OF INTERNATIONAL TRADE

Trade in Hormone-Treated Beef

In the 1970s, scientists discovered how to synthesize certain hormones and use them to promote the growth of livestock animals, reduce the fat content of meat, and increase milk production. Bovine somatotropin (BST), a growth hormone produced by beef cattle was first synthesized by the biotechnology firm Genentech. Injections of BST could be used to supplement an animal's own hormone production and increase its growth rate. These hormones soon became popular among farmers, who found that they could cut costs and help satisfy consumer demands for leaner meat. Although several of these hormones occurred naturally in animals, consumer groups in several countries soon raised concerns about the practice. They argued that the use of hormone supplements was unnatural and that the health consequences of consuming hormone-treated meat were unknown but might include hormonal irregularities and cancer.

In 1989, the European Union (EU) responded to these concerns by banning the use of growth-promoting hormones in the production of livestock and the importation of hormone-treated meat. The ban was controversial because a reasonable consensus existed among scientists that the hormones posed no health risk. Before the ban, a number of these hormones had already passed licensing procedures in several EU countries. As part of this process, research had been assembled that appeared to show that consuming hormone-treated meat had no effects on human health. Although the EU banned hormone-treated meat, many other countries did not, including big meat-producing countries such as Australia, Canada, New Zealand, and the United States. The use of hormones soon became widespread in these countries.

According to trade officials outside the EU, the European ban constituted an unfair restraint on trade. As a result of this ban, exports of meat to the EU fell. For example, US red meat exports to the EU declined from $231 million in 1988 to $98 million in 1994. The complaints of meat exporters were bolstered in 1995 when Codex Alimentarius, the international food standards body of the UN's Food and Agriculture Organization and the World Health Organization approved the use of growth hormones. In making this decision, Codex reviewed the scientific literature and found no evidence of a link between the consumption of hormone-treated meat and human health problems, such as cancer.

Fortified by such decisions, in 1995 the United States pressed the EU to drop the ban on the import of hormone-treated beef. The EU refused, citing "consumer concerns about food safety." In response, both Canada and the United States independently filed formal complaints with the World Trade Commission. The United States was joined in its complaint by a number of other countries, including Australia and New Zealand. Created in 1995, the World Trade Organization (WTO) has powers to enforce fair trading practices between its member states, which include all the parties to this particular dispute.

The WTO created a trade panel comprising three independent experts. After reviewing copious evidence and hearing from a wide range of experts, as well as from representatives of both parties, the panel issued a preliminary ruling in May 1997. In a stunning decision, the panel ruled that the EU ban on hormone-treated beef was illegal because it had no scientific justification. Moreover, the panel noted that the EU was inconsistent in its application of the ban. The EU takes a very strict view on the use of growth-promoting hormones in the beef sector, where it has a substantial surplus and is not internationally competitive, while it still allows the use of some growth hormones for pork production where the EU has no substantial surplus and does not compete on international markets.

The EU immediately indicated that it would appeal the finding to the WTO court of appeals. The WTO court heard the appeal in November 1997 and in February 1998 issued its decision agreeing with the findings of the trade panel that the EU had not presented any scientific evidence to justify the hormone ban.

This ruling left the EU in a difficult position. Legally, the EU now has to lift the ban, but the ban has wide support among the public in Europe, and lifting it might produce a consumer backlash. Most observers now expect the EU to seek a negotiated solution to the problem that would allow it to keep the ban intact. Under WTO rules, a country can choose to maintain its restriction if it gives up something of comparable value—by cutting tariffs on other products, for example.

The WTO's precedent-setting ruling could have a direct bearing on potential disputes over genetically engineered crops, which raise many of the same political issues as hormone-treated beef. American companies such as Monsanto are already marketing genetically engineered corn that resists root worms and soybeans that are impervious to powerful pesticides. Both products have generated intense political opposition in Europe. The ruling could also be used to attack scores of other trade barriers—from Japanese certification of apples to European rules for poultry inspection—that are based on health concerns.

http://www.wto.org

Sources: C. Southey, "Hormones Fuel a Meaty EU Row," *Financial Times*, September 7, 1995, p. 2; E. L. Andrews, "In Victory for US, European Ban on Treated Beef Is Ruled Illegal," *New York Times*, May 9, 1997, p. A1; F. Williams and G. de Jonquieres, "WTO's Beef Rulings Give Europe Food for Thought," *Financial Times*, February 13, 1998, p. 5; and World Trade Organization, *EC Measures Concerning Meat and Meat Products*, August 18, 1997, Geneva.

CHAPTER OUTLINE

TRADE IN HORMONE-TREATED BEEF

INTRODUCTION

INSTRUMENTS OF TRADE POLICY
Tariffs
Subsidies
Import Quotas and Voluntary
  Export Restraints
Local Content Requirements
Antidumping Policies
Administrative Policies

THE CASE FOR GOVERNMENT INTERVENTION
Political Arguments for Intervention
Economic Arguments for Intervention

THE REVISED CASE FOR FREE TRADE
Retaliation and Trade War
Domestic Politics

DEVELOPMENT OF THE WORLD TRADING SYSTEM
From Smith to the Great Depression
1947–1979: GATT, Trade
  Liberalization, and
  Economic Growth
1980–1993: Disturbing Trends
The Uruguay Round and
  the World Trade Organization
WTO: Early Experience
The Future: Unresolved Issues

IMPLICATIONS FOR BUSINESS
Trade Barriers and Firm Strategy
Policy Implications

CHAPTER SUMMARY

CRITICAL DISCUSSION QUESTIONS

SHRIMPS, TURTLES, AND THE WTO

Introduction

Our review of the classical trade theories of Smith, Ricardo, and Heckscher-Ohlin in Chapter 4 showed us that in a world without trade barriers, trade patterns will be determined by the relative productivity of different factors of production. Countries will specialize in the production of products that they can produce most efficiently, while importing products that they can produce less efficiently. Chapter 4 also laid out the intellectual case for free trade. Remember, *free trade* refers to a situation where a government does not attempt to restrict what its citizens can buy from another country or what they can sell to another country. As we saw in Chapter 4, the theories of Smith, Ricardo, and Heckscher-Ohlin predict that the consequences of free trade include both static economic gains (because free trade supports a higher level of domestic consumption and more efficient utilization of resources) and dynamic economic gains (because free trade stimulates economic growth and the creation of wealth).

In this chapter, we look at the political reality of international trade. While many nations are nominally committed to free trade, in practice nations tend to intervene in international trade. The nature of these political realities are amply illustrated in the case that opens this chapter. The case describes how the decision by the European Union (EU) to ban hormone-treated beef in Europe has given rise to a contentious trade dispute between the EU and several beef-producing countries such as Canada and the United States. The EU banned the sale of hormone-treated beef for political reasons—it wanted to soothe concerns in Europe about the potential health effects of such meat, even though such concerns have no basis in scientific fact. However, the EU is also a member of the World Trade Organization and has to abide by its rules if it wants to enjoy the benefits of membership. Unfortunately for the EU, the WTO ruled that the EU ban is illegal. This decision has placed the EU between a rock and a hard place. On the one hand, the EU is under considerable political pressure from consumer groups within Europe to maintain the ban. On the other, it wants to play by the rules of the WTO—rules that have brought significant benefits to the EU (as we shall discuss later in this chapter). Exactly how the EU will solve this dilemma remains to be seen. For the time being, it looks like it will keep the ban, pay a penalty for violating WTO rules, and continue to search for scientific evidence to support its position.

In this chapter, we explore the political and economic reasons for intervening in international trade. When governments intervene, they often do so by restricting imports of goods and services into their nation, while adopting policies that promote exports. Normally their motives for intervention are to protect domestic producers and jobs from foreign competition, while increasing the foreign market for domestic products. However, as the opening case illustrates, in recent years "social" issues have tended to intrude in the decision making. The decision by the EU to ban imports of hormone-treated beef, for example, was only tangentially influenced by a desire to protect the jobs of beef producers in Europe. Rather, it was a political response to social concerns about the health consequences of hormone-treated beef. Social issues are also entering into the trade calculus in other countries. In the United States, for example, there is a movement to ban imports of goods from countries that do not abide by the same labor, health, and environmental regulations as the United States does.

We start this chapter by describing the range of policy instruments that governments use to intervene in international trade. This is followed by a detailed review of the various political and economic motives that governments have for intervention. In the third section, we consider how the case for free trade stands up in view of the various justifications given for government intervention in international trade. Then we look at the emergence of the modern international trading system, which is based on the General Agreement on Tariffs and Trade (GATT) and its successor, the World Trade Organization. The GATT and WTO are the creations of a series of multinational treaties. The most recent was completed in 1995, involved over 120 countries, and resulted in creation of the WTO. The purpose of these treaties has been to lower barriers to the free flow of goods and services between nations. Like the GATT before it, the WTO promotes free trade by limiting the ability of national governments to adopt policies that restrict imports into their nations. In the final section of this chapter, we discuss the implications for business practice.

Instruments of Trade Policy

We review seven main instruments of trade policy in this section: tariffs, subsidies, import quotas, voluntary export restraints, local content requirements, antidumping policies, and administrative policies. Tariffs are the oldest and simplest instrument of trade policy. As we shall see later in this chapter, they are also the instrument that GATT and WTO have been most successful in limiting. But a fall in tariff barriers in recent decades has been accompanied by a rise of nontariff barriers such as subsidies, quotas, voluntary export restraints, and antidumping policies.

Tariffs

A **tariff** is a tax levied on imports. The oldest form of trade policy, tariffs fall into two categories. **Specific tariffs** are levied as a fixed charge for each unit of a good imported (for example, $3 per barrel of oil). **Ad valorem tariffs** are levied as a proportion of the value of the imported good. An example of an ad valorem tariff is the 25 percent tariff the American government placed on imported light trucks (pickup trucks, four-wheel-drive vehicles, and minivans) in the late 1980s.

A tariff raises the cost of imported products relative to domestic products. Thus, the 25 percent tariff on light trucks imported into the United States increased the price of European and Japanese light truck imports relative to US-produced light trucks. This tariff has afforded some protection for the market share of US auto manufacturers (although a cynic might note that all the tariff did was speed up the plans of European and Japanese automobile companies to build light trucks in the United States). While the principal objective of most tariffs is to protect domestic producers and employees against foreign competition, they also raise revenue for the government. Until the introduction of the income tax, for example, the US government raised most of its revenues from tariffs.

The important thing to understand about a tariff is who suffers and who gains. The government gains, because the tariff increases government revenues. Domestic producers gain, because the tariff gives them some protection against foreign competitors by increasing the cost of imported foreign goods. Consumers lose because they must pay more for certain imports. Whether the gains to the government and domestic producers exceed the loss to consumers depends on various factors such as the amount of the tariff, the importance of the imported good to domestic consumers, the number of jobs saved in the protected industry, and so on.

Although detailed consideration of these issues is beyond the scope of this book, two conclusions can be derived from a more advanced analysis.[1] First, tariffs are unambiguously pro-producer and anti-consumer. While they protect producers from foreign competitors, this supply restriction also raises domestic prices. Thus, as noted in Chapter 4, a recent study by Japanese economists calculated that in 1989 restrictions on imports of foodstuffs, cosmetics, and chemicals into Japan cost the average Japanese consumer about $890 per year in the form of higher prices.[2] Almost all studies of this issue have concluded that import tariffs impose significant costs on domestic consumers in the form of higher prices.[3] For another example, see the accompanying Country Focus, which looks at the cost to consumers of tariffs on imports into the United States.

A second point worth emphasizing is that tariffs reduce the overall efficiency of the world economy. They reduce efficiency because a protective tariff encourages domestic firms to produce products at home that, in theory, could be produced more efficiently abroad. The consequence is inefficient utilization of resources. For example, tariffs on the importation of rice into South Korea has meant that the land of South Korean rice farmers has been used in an unproductive manner. It would make more sense for the South Koreans to purchase their rice from lower-cost foreign producers and to use the land now employed in rice production in some other way, such as growing foodstuffs that cannot be produced more efficiently elsewhere or for residential and industrial purposes.

Subsidies

A **subsidy** is a government payment to a domestic producer. Subsidies take many forms including cash grants, low-interest loans, tax breaks, and government equity participation in domestic firms. By lowering costs, subsidies help domestic producers in two ways: they help them compete against low-cost foreign imports and they help them gain export markets.

According to official national figures, government subsidies in most industrialized countries amount to between 2 percent and 3.5 percent of the value of industrial output. (These figures exclude subsidies to agriculture and public services.) The average rate of subsidy in the United States was 0.5 percent; in Japan it was 1 percent; and in Europe it ranged from just below 2 percent in Great Britain and West Germany to as much as 6 to 7 percent in Sweden and Ireland.[4] These figures, however, almost certainly underestimate the true value of subsidies, since they are based only on cash grants and ignore other kinds of subsidies (e.g., equity participation or low-interest loans). A more detailed study of subsidies within the European Union was undertaken by the EU Commission. This study found that subsidies to manufacturing enterprises in the early 1990s ranged from a low of 2 percent of total value added in Great Britain to a high of 14.6 percent in Greece. Among the four largest EU countries, Italy was the worst offender; its subsidies are three times those of Great Britain, twice those of Germany, and 1.5 times those of France.[5]

The main gains from subsidies accrue to domestic producers, whose international competitiveness is increased as a result. Advocates of strategic trade policy (which is an outgrowth of the new trade theory) favor the use of subsidies as a way of helping domestic firms achieve a dominant position in those industries where economies of scale are important and the world market is not large enough to profitably support more than a few firms (e.g., aerospace, semiconductors). According to this argument, subsidies can help a firm achieve a first-mover advantage in an emerging industry (just as US government subsidies, in the form of substantial R&D grants, allegedly helped Boeing). If this is achieved, further gains to the domestic economy arise from the employment and tax revenues that a major global company can generate.

But subsidies must be paid for. Governments typically pay for subsidies by taxing individuals. Therefore, whether subsidies generate national benefits that exceed their national costs is debatable. In practice, many subsidies are not that successful at increasing the international competitiveness of domestic producers. They tend to protect the inefficient, rather than promoting efficiency.

COUNTRY FOCUS
The Costs of Protectionism in the United States

http://www.iie.com

The United States likes to think of itself as a nation that is committed to unrestricted free trade. In their negotiations with trading partners, such as China, the European Union, and Japan, US trade representatives can often be heard claiming that the US economy is an open one with few import tariffs. However, while it is true that US import tariffs are low when compared to those found in many other industrialized nations, they still exist. A recent study concluded that during the 1980s these tariffs cost US consumers about $32 billion per year.

The study, by Gary Hufbauer and Kim Elliott of the Institute for International Economics, looked at the effect of import tariffs upon economic activity in 21 industries with annual sales of $1 billion or more that the United States protected most heavily from foreign competition. The industries included apparel, ceramic tiles, luggage, and sugar. In most of these industries import tariffs had originally been imposed to protect US firms and employees from the effects of low-cost foreign competitors. The typical reasoning behind the tariffs was that without such protection, US firms in these industries would go out of business and substantial unemployment would result. So the tariffs were presented as having positive effects for the economy, not to mention the US Treasury, which benefited from the revenues.

The study found, however, that while these import tariffs saved around 200,000 jobs in the protected industries that would otherwise have been lost to foreign competition, they also cost American consumers about $32 billion per year in the form of higher prices. Even when the proceeds from the tariffs that accrued to the US Treasury were added into the equation, the total cost to the nation of this protectionism still amounted to $10.2 billion per year, or over $50,000 per job saved.

The two economists who undertook the study also argued that these figures understated the true cost of the tariffs. They maintained that by making imports less competitive with American-made products, tariffs allowed domestic producers to charge more than they might otherwise because they did not have to compete with low-priced imports. By dampening competition, these tariffs removed an incentive for firms in the protected industries to become more efficient, thereby retarding economic progress. Further, the study's authors noted that if the tariffs had not been imposed, some of the $32 billion freed up every year would have been spent on other goods and services, and growth in these areas would have created additional jobs, thereby offsetting the loss of 200,000 jobs in the protected industries.

Sources: C. Hufbauer, and K. A. Elliott, *Measuring the Costs of Protectionism in the United States* (Washington, DC: Institute for International Economics, 1993); and S. Nasar, "The High Costs of Protectionism," *New York Times*, November 12, 1993, pp. C1, C2.

Import Quotas and Voluntary Export Restraints

An **import quota** is a direct restriction on the quantity of some good that may be imported into a country. The restriction is normally enforced by issuing import licenses to a group of individuals or firms. For example, the United States has a quota on imports of cheese. The only firms allowed to import cheese are certain trading companies, each of which is allocated the right to import a maximum number of pounds of cheese each year. In some cases, the right to sell is given directly to the governments of exporting countries. This is the case for sugar and textile imports in the United States.

A variant on the import quota is the voluntary export restraint (VER). A **voluntary export restraint** is a quota on trade imposed by the exporting country, typically at the request of the importing country's government. One of the most famous examples was the limitation on auto exports to the United States enforced by Japanese automobile producers in 1981. A response to direct pressure from the US government, this VER limited Japanese imports to no more than 1.68 million vehicles per year. The agreement was revised in 1984 to allow Japanese producers to import 1.85 million vehicles per year. In 1985 the agreement was allowed to lapse, but the Japanese government indicated its intentions at that time to continue to restrict exports to the United States to 1.85 million vehicles per year.[6]

Foreign producers agree to VERs because they fear far more damaging punitive tariffs or import quotas might follow if they do not. Agreeing to a VER is seen as a way of making the best of a bad situation by appeasing protectionist pressures in a country.

As with tariffs and subsidies, both import quotas and VERs benefit domestic producers by limiting import competition. Quotas do not benefit consumers. An import quota or VER always raises the domestic price of an imported good. When imports are limited to a low percentage of the market by a quota or VER, this bids the price up for that limited foreign supply. In the case of the automobile industry, for example, the VER increased the price of the limited supply of Japanese imports into the United States. As a result, according to a study by the US Federal Trade Commission, the automobile industry VER cost US consumers about $1 billion per year between 1981 and 1985. That $1 billion per year went to Japanese producers in the form of higher prices.[7]

Local Content Requirements

A **local content requirement** calls for some specific fraction of a good to be produced domestically. The requirement can be expressed either in physical terms (e.g., 75 percent of component parts for this product must be produced locally) or in value terms (e.g., 75 percent of the value of this product must be produced locally). Local content regulations have been widely used by developing countries as a device for shifting their manufacturing base from the simple assembly of products whose parts are manufactured elsewhere, to the local manufacture of component parts. More recently, the issue of local content has been raised by several developed countries. In the United States, for example, pressure is building to insist that 75 percent of the component parts that go into cars built in the United States by Japanese companies such as Toyota and Honda be manufactured in the United States. Both Toyota and Honda have reacted to such pressures by announcing their intention to buy more American-manufactured parts.

For a domestic producer of component parts, local content regulations provide protection in the same way an import quota does: by limiting foreign competition. The aggregate economic effects are also the same; domestic producers benefit, but the restrictions on imports raise the prices of imported components. In turn, higher prices for imported components are passed on to consumers of the final product in the form of higher prices. As with all trade policies, local content regulations tend to benefit producers and not consumers.

Antidumping Policies

In the context of international trade, **dumping** is variously defined as selling goods in a foreign market at below their costs of production, or as selling goods in a foreign market at below their "fair" market value. There is a difference between these two definitions, since the "fair" market value of a good is normally judged to be greater than the costs of producing that good (since the former includes a "fair" profit margin). Dumping is viewed as a method by which firms unload excess production in foreign markets. Alternatively, some dumping may be the result of predatory behavior, with producers using substantial profits from their home markets to subsidize prices in a foreign market with a view to driving indigenous competitors out of that market. Once this has been achieved, so the argument goes, the predatory firm can raise prices and earn substantial profits. An alleged example of dumping occurred in 1997, when two Korean manufacturers of semiconductors, LG Semicon and Hyundai Electronics, were accused of selling dynamic random access memory chips (DRAMs) in the US market at below their costs of production. This action occurred in the middle of a worldwide glut of chip making capacity. It was alleged that the Korean firms were trying to unload their excess production in the United States.

Antidumping policies are policies designed to punish foreign firms that engage in dumping. The ultimate objective is to protect domestic producers from "unfair" foreign competition. Although antidumping policies vary somewhat from country to country, the majority are similar to the policies used in the United States. In the case of the United States, if a domestic producer believes that a foreign firm is dumping production in the US market, it can file a petition with two government agencies, the Commerce Department and the International Trade Commission. In the Korean DRAM case, the petition was filed by Micron Technology, a US manufacturer of DRAMs. The government agencies then investigate the complaint. If they find it has merit, the Commerce Department may impose an antidumping duty on the offending foreign imports. These duties, which in effect represent a special tariff, can be fairly substantial. For example, after reviewing Micron's complaint, the Commerce Department imposed 9 percent and 4 percent dumping duties on LG Semicon- and Hyundai-made DRAM chips respectively.

Administrative Policies

In addition to the formal instruments of trade policy, governments of all types sometimes use a range of informal or administrative policies to restrict imports and boost exports. **Administrative trade policies** are bureaucratic rules designed to make it difficult for imports to enter a country. Some would argue that the Japanese are the masters of this kind of trade barrier. In recent years, Japan's formal tariff and nontariff barriers have been among the lowest in the world. However, critics charge that their informal administrative barriers to imports more than compensate for this. One example is that of tulip bulbs; the Netherlands exports tulip bulbs to almost every country in the world except Japan. Japanese customs inspectors insist on checking every tulip bulb by cutting it vertically down the middle, and even Japanese ingenuity cannot put them back together! Another example concerns the US express delivery service, Federal Express. Federal Express has had a tough time expanding its global services into Japan, primarily because Japanese customs inspectors insist on opening a large proportion of express packages to check for pornography—a process that can delay an "express" package for days. Japan is not the only country that engages in such policies. France required that all imported videotape recorders arrive through a small customs entry point that was both remote and poorly staffed. The resulting delays kept Japanese VCRs out of the French market until a VER agreement was negotiated.[8] As with all instruments of trade policy, administrative instruments benefit producers and hurt consumers, who are denied access to possibly superior foreign products.

The Case for Government Intervention

Now that we have reviewed the various instruments of trade policy, it is time to take a more detailed look at the case for government intervention in international trade. In general, there are two types of argument for government intervention, political and economic. Political arguments for intervention are concerned with protecting the interests of certain groups within a nation (normally producers), often at the expense of other groups (normally consumers). Economic arguments for intervention are typically concerned with boosting the overall wealth of a nation (to the benefit of all, both producers and consumers).

Political Arguments for Intervention

Political arguments for government intervention cover a range of issues including protecting jobs, protecting industries deemed important for national security, retaliating to unfair foreign competition, protecting consumers from "dangerous" products, furthering the goals of foreign policy, and protecting the human rights of individuals in exporting countries.

Protecting Jobs and Industries

Perhaps the most common political argument for government intervention is that it is necessary for protecting jobs and industries from foreign competition. Antidumping policies are frequently justified on such grounds. The voluntary export restraints that offered some protection to the US automobile, machine tool, and steel industries during the 1980s were motivated by such considerations. Similarly, Japan's quotas on rice imports are aimed at protecting jobs in that country's agricultural sector. The same motive underlay the establishment of the Common Agricultural Policy (CAP) by the European Union. The CAP was designed to protect the jobs of Europe's politically powerful farmers by restricting imports and guaranteeing prices. However, the higher prices that resulted from the CAP have cost Europe's consumers dearly. This is true of most attempts to protect jobs and industries through government intervention. As we saw earlier in the chapter, all that the VER in the automobile industry did was raise the price of Japanese imports, at a cost of $1 billion per year to US consumers.

In addition to trade controls hurting consumers, evidence also indicates they may sometimes hurt the producers they are intended to protect. In Chapter 4, for example, we noted how the VER agreement in the US machine tool industry has been self-defeating. By limiting Japanese and Taiwanese machine tool imports, the VER raised the prices of machine tools purchased by US manufacturers to levels above those prevailing in the world market. In turn, this raised the capital costs of the US manufacturing industry, thereby decreasing its international competitiveness.

National Security

Countries sometimes argue that it is necessary to protect certain industries because they are important for national security. Defense-related industries often get this kind of attention (e.g., aerospace, advanced electronics, semiconductors, and so on). Although not as common as it used to be, this argument is still made. Those in favor of protecting the US semiconductor industry from foreign competition, for example, argue that semiconductors are now such important components of defense products that it would be dangerous to rely primarily on foreign producers for them. In 1986, this argument helped convince the federal government to support Sematech, a consortium of 14 US semiconductor companies that accounts for 90 percent of the US industry's revenues. Sematech's mission is to conduct joint research into manufacturing techniques that can be parceled out to members. The government saw the venture as so critical that Sematech was specially protected from antitrust laws. Initially, the US government provided Sematech with $100 million per year subsidies. By the mid-1990s, however, the US semiconductor industry had regained its leading market position, largely through the personal computer boom and demand for microprocessor chips made by Intel. In 1994, the consortium's board voted to seek an end to federal funding, and since 1996 the consortium has been funded entirely by private money.[9]

Retaliation

Some argue that governments should use the threat to intervene in trade policy as a bargaining tool to help open foreign markets and force trading partners to "play by the rules of the game." Successive US governments have been among those that adopted this get-tough approach. The US government has used the threat of punitive trade sanctions to get the Chinese government to enforce its intellectual property laws. As you will recall from Chapter 2, lax enforcement of these laws had given rise to massive copyright infringements in China that have been costing US companies such as Microsoft hundreds of millions of dollars per year in lost sales revenues. After the United States threatened to impose 100 percent tariffs on a range of Chinese imports, and after harsh words between officials from the two countries, the Chinese backed down and agreed to tighter enforcement of intellectual property regulations.[10]

If it works, such a politically motivated rationale for government intervention may liberalize trade and bring with it resulting economic gains. It is a risky strategy, however, because a country that is being pressured might not back down and instead may respond to the punitive tariffs by raising trade barriers of its own. This is exactly what the Chinese government threatened to do when pressured by the United States, although the Chinese ultimately did back down. If a government does not back down, however, the results could be higher trade barriers all around and an economic loss to all involved.

Protecting Consumers

The opening case describes how the European Union banned the sale and importation of hormone-treated beef. The ban was motivated by a desire to protect European consumers from the possible health consequences of meat treated with growth hormones. It was motivated by concerns for the safety and health of consumers, as opposed to economic considerations. Many governments have long had regulations to protect consumers from "unsafe" products. Often, the indirect effect of such regulations is to limit or ban the importation of such products. Another example concerns the 1998 decision by the Clinton administration to permanently ban imports into the United States of 58 types of military-style assault weapons (the United States already prohibits the sale of such weapons by US-based firms). The ban was motivated by a desire to increase public safety. It followed a rash of random and deadly shootings by deranged individuals using such weapons, including one in the president's home state of Arkansas that left four children and a schoolteacher dead.[11]

The conflict over the importation of hormone-treated beef into the European Union may prove to be a taste of things to come. In addition to the use of hormones to promote animal growth and meat production, biotechnology has made it possible to genetically alter many crops so that they are resistant to common herbicides, produce proteins that are natural insecticides, have dramatically improved yields, or can withstand inclement weather. One example is a new breed of genetically modified tomatoes that have an antifreeze gene inserted into their genome and can be grown in colder climates than hitherto possible. Another example is a genetically engineered cotton seed produced by Monsanto. The seed has been engineered to express a protein that provides protection against three common insect pests—the cotton bollworm, tobacco budworm, and pink bollworm. Use of this seed reduces or eliminates the need for traditional pesticide applications for these pests. As enticing as such innovations sound, they have met with intense resistance from consumer groups, particularly in Europe. The fear is that the widespread use of genetically altered seed corn could have unanticipated and harmful effects on human health and may result in "genetic pollution." (An example of genetic pollution would be when the widespread use of crops that produce "natural pesticides" stimulates the evolution of "super-bugs" that are resistant to those pesticides.) Such concerns have led Austria and Luxembourg to outlaw the importation, sale, or use of genetically altered organisms. Strong sentiment against genetically altered organisms also exists in several other European countries, most notably Germany and Switzerland. It seems increasingly likely, therefore, that the World Trade Organization will be drawn into the conflict between those that want to expand the global market for genetically altered organisms, such as Monsanto, and those that want to limit it, such as Austria and Luxembourg.[12]

Furthering Foreign Policy Objectives

Governments will use trade policy to support their foreign policy objectives.[13] A government may grant preferential trade terms to a country with which it wants to build strong relations. Trade policy has also been used several times as an instrument for pressuring or punishing "rogue states" that do not abide by international law or norms. The most obvious recent example is Iraq, which has labored under extensive trade sanctions ever since the UN coalition defeated the country in the 1991 Gulf War. The theory is that such pressure might persuade the rogue state to mend its ways, or perhaps hasten a change of government. In the case of Iraq, the sanctions are seen as a way of forcing that country to comply with several UN resolutions. In another example, the United States has maintained long-running trade sanctions against Cuba. Their principal function is to impoverish Cuba in the hope that the resulting economic hardship will ultimately lead to the downfall of Cuba's Communist government and its replacement with a more democratically inclined (and pro-US) regime. The United States also has long-running trade sanctions in place against Libya and Iran, both of which it accuses of supporting terrorist action against US interests.

A serious problem with using trade as an instrument of foreign policy is that other countries can undermine any unilateral trade sanctions. The US sanctions against Cuba, for example, have not stopped other Western countries from trading with Cuba. The US sanctions have done little more than create a vacuum into which other trading nations, such as Canada and Germany, can and have stepped. In an attempt to halt this and further tighten the screws on Cuba, in 1996 Congress passed the **Helms-Burton Act.** This act allows Americans to sue foreign firms that use Cuban property confiscated from them after the 1959 revolution. A similar act, the **D'Amato Act,** aimed at Libya and Iran was also passed that year. The passage of Helms-Burton elicited howls of protest from America's trading partners—including the European Union, Canada, and Mexico—all of whom claim that the law violates their sovereignty and is illegal under World Trade Organization rules. For example, Canadian companies that have been doing business in Cuba for years see no reason why they should suddenly be sued in US courts when Canada has not and does not restrict trade with Cuba. They are not violating Canadian law and they are not US companies, so why should they be subject to US law? Despite such protests, the law is still on the books in the United States, although the Clinton administration has been less than enthusiastic about enforcing it—probably because it is unenforceable. The fuss over Helms-Burton illustrates that trade policy is a rather blunt and sometimes counterproductive instrument of foreign policy.

Protecting Human Rights

Protecting and promoting human rights in other countries is an important element of foreign policy for many democracies. Governments sometimes use trade policy to try to improve the human rights policies of trading partners. In recent years, the most obvious example of this has been the annual debate in the United States over whether to grant most favored nation (MFN) status to China. MFN status allows countries to exports goods to the United States under favorable terms. Under MFN rules, the average tariff on Chinese goods imported into the United States is 8 percent. If China's MFN status were rescinded, tariffs would probably rise to around 40 percent. Trading partners who are signatories of the World Trade Organization—as most are—automatically receive MFN status. However, China is not yet a member of the WTO. The decision of whether to grant MFN status to China is made more difficult by the perception that China has a poor human rights record. Critics of China often point to the 1989 Tiananmen Square massacre, China's continuing subjugation of Tibet (which China occupied in the 1950s), and the quashing of political dissent in China (there are an estimated 1,700 political prisoners in China).[14] These critics argue that the United States should withhold MFN status until China shows measurable improvement in its human rights record. They argue that trade policy should be used as a political weapon to force China to change its internal policies toward human rights.

On the other hand, some argue that limiting trade with countries such as China where human rights abuses are widespread makes matters worse, not better. The best way to change the internal human rights stance of a country is to engage it in international trade, they argue. At its core, the argument is simple: Growing bilateral trade raises the income levels of both countries, and as a state becomes richer, so its people begin to demand—and generally receive—better treatment with regard to their human rights. This is a variant of the argument touched on in Chapter 2 that economic progress begets political progress (if political progress is measured by the adoption of a democratic government that respects human rights). This argument has currently won the day in the United States. In 1997, President Clinton announced he would grant MFN status to China and in doing so argued that trade and human rights issues should be decoupled. The United States is not alone in taking such a position. Europe is close behind. For example, in March 1996, France, eager for China to sign a $1.5 billion contract for Airbus planes, argued within the European Union against a resolution in the UN Commission on Human Rights urging improvement of Chinese human rights practices.

Economic Arguments for Intervention

With the development of the new trade theory and strategic trade policy (see Chapter 4), the economic arguments for government intervention have undergone something of a renaissance in recent years. Until the early 1980s, most economists saw little benefit in government intervention and strongly advocated a free trade policy. This position has changed somewhat with the development of strategic trade policy, although as we will see in the next section, there are still strong economic arguments for sticking to a free trade stance.

The Infant Industry Argument

The infant industry argument is by far the oldest economic argument for government intervention. It was proposed by Alexander Hamilton in 1792. According to this argument, many developing countries have a potential comparative advantage in manufacturing, but new manufacturing industries there cannot initially compete with well-established industries in developed countries. To allow manufacturing to get a toehold, the argument is that governments should temporarily support new industries (with tariffs, import quotas, and subsidies) until they have grown strong enough to meet international competition.

This argument has appealed to the governments of developing nations during the past 40 years. Also, the infant industry argument has been recognized as a legitimate reason for protectionism by the WTO. Nevertheless, many economists remain very critical of this argument. They make two main points. First, protection from foreign competition does no good unless the protection helps make the industry efficient. In case after case, however, protection seems to have done little more than foster the development of inefficient industries that have little hope of ever competing in the world market. Brazil, for example, built up the world's 10th largest auto industry behind tariff barriers and quotas. Once those barriers were removed in the late 1980s, foreign imports soared and the industry was forced to face up to the fact that after 30 years of protection, the Brazilian industry was one of the world's most inefficient.[15]

A second point is that the infant industry argument relies on an assumption that firms are unable to make efficient long-term investments by borrowing money from the domestic or international capital market. Consequently, governments have been required to subsidize long-term investments. Given the development of global capital markets over the past 20 years, this assumption no longer looks as valid as it once did (see Chapter 11 for details). Today, if a developing country has a potential comparative advantage in a manufacturing industry, firms in that country should be able to borrow money from the capital markets to finance the required investments. Given financial support, firms based in countries with a potential comparative advantage have an incentive to go through the initial losses in order to make long-run gains without requiring government protection. This is what many Taiwanese and South Korean firms did in industries such as textiles, semiconductors, machine tools, steel, and shipping. Thus, given efficient global capital markets, the only industries that would require government protection would be those that are not worthwhile.

Strategic Trade Policy

The strategic trade policy argument has been proposed by the new trade theorists.[16] We reviewed the basic argument in Chapter 4 when we considered the new trade theory, which argues that countries may predominate in the export of certain products simply because they had firms that were able to capture first-mover advantages in industries that would support only a few firms because of substantial economies of scale. The dominance of Boeing in the commercial aircraft industry is attributed to such factors.

There are two components to the strategic trade policy argument. First, a government can help raise national income if it can somehow ensure that the firm or firms to gain first-mover advantages in such an industry are domestic rather than foreign enterprises. Thus, according to the strategic trade policy argument, a government should use subsidies to support promising firms in emerging industries. Advocates of this argument point out that the substantial R&D grants the US government gave Boeing in the 1950s and 60s probably helped tilt the field of competition in the newly emerging market for jet passenger planes in Boeing's favor. (Boeing's 707 jet airliner was derived from a military plane.) Similar arguments are now made with regard to Japan's dominance in the production of liquid crystal display screens (used in laptop computers). Although these screens were invented in the United States, the Japanese government, in cooperation with major electronics companies, targeted this industry for research support in the late 1970s and early 80s. The result was that Japanese firms, not US firms, captured the first-mover advantages in this market.

The second component of the strategic trade policy argument is that it might pay government to intervene in an industry if it helps domestic firms overcome the barriers to entry created by foreign firms that have already reaped first-mover advantages. This argument underlies government support of Airbus Industrie, Boeing's major competitor. Airbus, a consortium of four companies from Great Britain, France, Germany, and Spain, was formed in 1966. When it began production in the mid-1970s, it had less than 5 percent of the world commercial aircraft market. By the late 1990s, it had increased its share to around 40 percent and was threatening Boeing's dominance. How has Airbus achieved this? According to the US government, the answer is a $13.5 billion subsidy from the governments of Great Britain, France, Germany, and Spain.[17] Without this subsidy, Airbus would have never been able to break into the world market. In another example, the rise to dominance of the Japanese semiconductor industry, despite the first-mover advantages enjoyed by US firms, is attributed to intervention by the Japanese government. In this case, the government did not subsidize the costs of domestic manufacturers. Rather, it protected the Japanese home market while pursuing policies that ensured Japanese companies got access to the necessary manufacturing and product know-how.

If these arguments are correct, they clearly suggest a rationale for government intervention in international trade. Specifically, governments should target technologies that may be important in the future and use subsidies to support development work aimed at commercializing those technologies. Furthermore, government should provide export subsidies until the domestic firms have established first-mover advantages in the world market. Government support may also be justified if it can help domestic firms overcome the first-mover advantages enjoyed by foreign competitors and emerge as viable competitors in the world market (as in the Airbus and semiconductor examples). In this case, a combination of home-market protection and export-promoting subsidies may be called for.

The Revised Case for Free Trade

The strategic trade policy arguments of the new trade theorists suggest an economic justification for government intervention in international trade. This justification challenges the rationale for unrestricted free trade found in the work of classic trade theorists such as Adam Smith and David Ricardo. In response to this challenge to economic orthodoxy, a number of economists, including some of those responsible for the development of the new trade theory, such as Paul Krugman of MIT, have been quick to point out that although strategic trade policy looks nice in theory, in practice it may be unworkable. This response to the strategic trade policy argument constitutes the revised case for free trade.[18]

Retaliation and Trade War

Krugman argues that strategic trade policy aimed at establishing domestic firms in a dominant position in a global industry are beggar-thy-neighbor policies that boost national income at the expense of other countries. A country that attempts to use such policies will probably provoke retaliation. In many cases, the resulting trade war between two or more interventionist governments will leave all countries involved worse off than if a hands-off approach had been adopted. If the US government were to respond to the Airbus subsidy by increasing its own subsidies to Boeing, for example, the result might be that the subsidies would cancel each other out. In the process, both European and US taxpayers would end up supporting an expensive and pointless trade war, and both Europe and the United States would be worse off.

Krugman may be right about the danger of a strategic trade policy leading to a trade war. The problem, however, is how to respond when one's competitors are being supported by government subsidies; that is, how should Boeing and the United States respond to the subsidization of Airbus? According to Krugman, the answer is not to engage in retaliatory action, but to help establish rules of the game that minimize the use of trade-distorting subsidies. This is what the WTO seeks to do.

Domestic Politics

Governments do not always act in the national interest when they intervene in the economy. Instead, they are influenced by politically important interest groups. The European Union's support for the Common Agricultural Policy (CAP), which arose because of the political power of French and German farmers, is an example. The CAP benefited inefficient farmers and the politicians who relied on the farm vote, but no one else. Thus, a further reason for not embracing strategic trade policy, according to Krugman, is that such a policy is almost certain to be captured by special interest groups within the economy, who will distort it to their own ends. Krugman concludes that in the United States:

> To ask the Commerce Department to ignore special interest politics while formulating detailed policy for many industries is not realistic; to establish a blanket policy of free trade, with exceptions granted only under extreme pressure, may not be the optimal policy according to the theory but may be the best policy that the country is likely to get.[19]

Development of the World Trading System

We have read in this chapter and the previous one about strong economic arguments for supporting unrestricted free trade. While many governments have recognized the value of these arguments, they have been unwilling to unilaterally lower their trade barriers for fear that other nations might not follow suit. Consider the problem that two neighboring countries, say France and Italy, face when considering whether to lower barriers to trade between them. The government of Italy might be in favor of lowering trade barriers, but it might be unwilling to do so for fear that France will not do the same. Italian officials might fear that the French will take advantage of Italy's low barriers to enter the Italian market, while continuing to shut Italian products out of France through high trade barriers. The French government might feel that it faces the same dilemma. The essence of the problem is a lack of trust between the governments of France and Italy. Both governments recognize that their respective nations will benefit from lower trade barriers between them, but neither government is willing to lower barriers for fear that the other might not follow.[20]

Such a deadlock can be resolved if both countries negotiate rules that will govern cross-border trade and lower trade barriers. But who is to monitor the governments to make sure they are playing by the trade rules? And who is to impose sanctions on a government that cheats? Both governments could set up an independent body whose function is to act as a referee. This referee could monitor trade between the countries, make sure that no side cheats, and impose sanctions on a country if it does cheat.

While it might sound unlikely that any government would compromise its national sovereignty by submitting to such an arrangement, since World War II an international trading framework has evolved that has exactly these features. For its first 50 years, this framework was known as the General Agreement on Tariffs and Trade (the GATT). Since 1995, it has been known as the World Trade Organization (WTO). Here we look at the evolution and workings of the GATT and the WTO. We begin, however, with a brief discussion of the pre-GATT history of world trade, since this helps set the scene.

From Smith to the Great Depression

As we saw in Chapter 4, the intellectual case for free trade goes back to the late 18th century and the work of Adam Smith and David Ricardo. Free trade as a government policy was first officially embraced by Great Britain in 1846, when the British Parliament repealed the Corn Laws. The Corn Laws placed a high tariff on corn imports. The objectives of the Corn Law tariff were to raise government revenues and to protect British corn producers. There had been annual motions in Parliament in favor of free trade since the 1820s when David Ricardo was a member of Parliament. However, agricultural protection was withdrawn only after a protracted debate when the effects of a harvest failure in Britain were compounded by the imminent threat of famine in Ireland. Faced with considerable hardship and suffering, among the populace, Parliament narrowly reversed its long-held position.

During the next 80 years or so, Great Britain, as one of the world's dominant trading powers, pushed the case for trade liberalization; but the British government was a voice in the wilderness. Its policy of unilateral free trade was not reciprocated by its major trading partners. The only reason Britain kept this policy for so long was that, as the world's largest exporting nation, it had far more to lose from a trade war than did any other country.

By the 1930s, however, the British attempt to stimulate free trade was buried under the economic rubble of the Great Depression, which had roots in the world economy's failure to mount a sustained economic recovery after the end of World War I in 1918. Things got worse in 1929 with the US stock market collapse and the subsequent run on the US banking system. Economic problems were compounded in 1930 when Congress passed the Smoot-Hawley tariff. Aimed at avoiding rising unemployment by protecting domestic industries and diverting consumer demand away from foreign products, the Smoot-Hawley tariff erected an enormous wall of tariff barriers. Almost every industry was rewarded with its "made-to-order" tariff. A particularly odd aspect of the Smoot-Hawley tariff-raising binge was that the United States was running a balance-of-payment surplus at the time and it was the world's largest creditor nation. The Smoot-Hawley tariff had a damaging effect on employment abroad. Other countries reacted to the US action by raising their own tariff barriers. US exports tumbled in response, and the world slid further into the Great Depression.[21]

1947–1979: GATT, Trade Liberalization, and Economic Growth

The economic damage caused by the beggar-thy-neighbor trade policies that the Smoot-Hawley Act ushered in influenced the economic institutions and ideology of the post-World War II world. The United States emerged from the war not only victorious but also economically dominant. After the debacle of the Great Depression, opinion in the US Congress had swung strongly in favor of free trade. As a consequence, under US leadership, GATT was established in 1947.

The GATT was a multilateral agreement whose objective was to liberalize trade by eliminating tariffs, subsidies, import quotas, and the like. From its foundation in 1947 until it was superseded by the WTO, the GATT's membership grew from 19 to more than 120 nations. The GATT did not attempt to liberalize trade restrictions in one fell swoop; that would have been impossible. Rather, tariff reduction was spread over eight rounds. The most recent, the Uruguay Round, was launched in 1986 and completed in December 1993. In these rounds, mutual tariff reductions were negotiated among all members, who then committed themselves not to raise import tariffs above negotiated rates. GATT regulations were enforced by a mutual monitoring mechanism. If a country felt that one of its trading partners was violating a GATT regulation, it could ask the Geneva-based bureaucracy that administered the GATT to investigate. If GATT investigators found the complaints to be valid, member countries could be asked to pressure the offending party to change its policies. In general, such pressure was always sufficient to get an offending country to change its policies. If it were not, the offending country could have been expelled from the GATT.

In its early years, the GATT was by most measures very successful. In the United States, for example, the average tariff declined by nearly 92 percent between the Geneva Round of 1947 and the Tokyo Round of 1973–79 (see Figure 5.1). Consistent with the theoretical arguments first advanced by Ricardo and reviewed in Chapter 4, the move toward free trade under the GATT appeared to stimulate economic growth. From 1953 to 1963, world trade grew at an annual rate of 6.1 percent, and world income grew at an annual rate of 4.3 percent. Performance from 1963 to 1973 was even better; world trade grew at 8.9 percent annually, and world income grew at 5.1 percent.[22]

1980–1993: Disturbing Trends

During the 1980s and early 1990s, the world trading system erected by the GATT began to come under strain as pressures for greater protectionism increased around the world. Three main reasons caused the rise in such pressures during the 1980s.

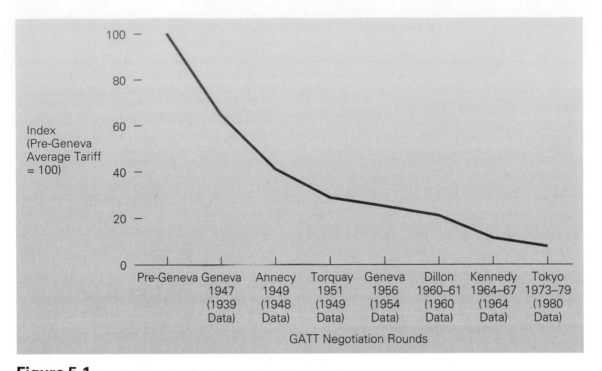

Figure 5.1

Average Reductions in US Tariffs Rates, 1947–1979

Note: Indexes are calculated from percentage reductions in average weighted tariff rates given in Finger, 1979 (Table 1, p. 425), World Bank, *World Development Report* (New York: Oxford University Press, 1987), (Table 8.1, p. 136); and World Bank, *World Development Report* (New York: Oxford University Press, 1994). Weighted average US tariff rate after Tokyo Round was 4.6 percent (World Bank, 1987).

First, the economic success of Japan strained the world trading system. Japan was in ruins when the GATT was created. By the early 1980s, however, it had become the world's second largest economy and its largest exporter. Japan's success in the automobile and semiconductor industries by themselves might have been enough to strain the world trading system. Things were made worse, however, by the widespread perception in the West that despite low tariff rates and subsidies, Japanese markets were closed to imports and foreign investment by administrative trade barriers.

Second, the world trading system was further strained by the persistent trade deficit in the world's largest economy, the United States. Although the deficit peaked in 1987 at over $170 billion, by the end of 1992 the annual rate was still running about $80 billion. From a political perspective, the matter was worsened by the fact that in 1992 the United States also ran a $45 billion deficit in its trade with Japan—a country perceived as not playing by the rules. The consequences of the US deficit included painful adjustments in industries such as automobiles, machine tools, semiconductors, steel, and textiles, where domestic producers steadily lost market share to foreign competitors. The resulting unemployment gave rise to renewed demands in the US Congress for protection against imports.

A third reason for the trend toward greater protectionism was that many countries found ways to get around GATT regulations. Bilateral voluntary export restraints circumvented GATT agreements because neither the importing country nor the exporting country complained to the GATT bureaucracy in Geneva—and without a complaint, the GATT bureaucracy could do nothing. Exporting countries agreed to VERs to avoid more damaging punitive tariffs. One of the best-known examples is the VER between Japan and the United States, under which Japanese producers promised to limit their auto imports into the United States to defuse growing trade tensions. According to a World Bank study, 13 percent of the imports of industrialized countries in 1981 were subjected to nontariff trade barriers such as VERs. By 1986, this figure had increased to 16 percent. The most rapid rise was in the United States, where the value of imports affected by nontariff barriers (primarily VERs) increased by 23 percent between 1981 and 1986.[23]

The Uruguay Round and the World Trade Organization

Against the background of rising pressures for protectionism, in 1986 the members of the GATT embarked upon their eighth round of negotiations to reduce tariffs, the Uruguay Round (so named because they occurred in Uruguay). This was the most difficult round of negotiations yet, primarily because it was also the most ambitious. Until then, GATT rules had applied only to trade in manufactured goods and commodities. In the Uruguay Round, member countries sought to extend GATT rules to cover trade in services. They also sought to write rules governing the protection of intellectual property, to reduce agricultural subsidies, and to strengthen the GATT's monitoring and enforcement mechanisms.

The Uruguay Round dragged on for seven years. For a time, it looked as if an agreement might not be possible, raising fears that the world might slip into a trade war. The main impediment to an agreement was a long-standing dispute between the United States and the European Union on agricultural subsidies. An agreement had to be reached before December 16, 1993, which was when the "fast-track negotiating authority" granted to President Clinton by Congress was to expire. Without this authority, any agreement would have to have been approved by Congress rather than just the president, a much more difficult proposition. An 11th hour compromise on agricultural subsidies—which reduced the level of subsidies significantly, but not by as much as the United States had wanted—saved the day, and an agreement was reached on December 15, 1993. The agreement was formally signed by member states at a meeting in Marrakech, Morocco, on April 15, 1994. It took effect July 1, 1995.

The most important components of the Uruguay Round agreement are detailed in Table 5.1. The Uruguay Round contained the following provisions: Tariffs on industrial goods were to be reduced by more than one-third; agricultural subsidies were to be substantially reduced; fair trade and market access rules were to be extended to cover a wide range of services; GATT rules were also to be extended to protect patents, copyrights, and trademarks (intellectual property); barriers on trade in textiles were to be significantly reduced over 10 years; and a World Trade Organization was to be created to implement the GATT agreement.

Services and Intellectual Property

In the long run, the extension of GATT rules to cover services and intellectual property may be particularly significant. In 1997, world trade in services amounted to $1,295 billion (compared to world trade in goods of $5,295).[24] Extending GATT rules to this important trading arena could significantly increase both the total share of world trade accounted for by services and the overall volume of world trade. Having GATT rules cover intellectual property will make it much easier for high-technology companies to do business in developing nations where intellectual property rules have historically been poorly enforced (see Chapter 2 for details). High-technology companies will now have a mechanism to force countries to prohibit the piracy of intellectual property.

The World Trade Organization

The clarification and strengthening of GATT rules and the creation of the World Trade Organization also hold out the promise of more effective policing and enforcement of GATT rules in the future. This should have a beneficial effect on overall

Up to 1993	The 1993 Agreement	Main Impact
Industrial Tariffs		
Backbone of previous GATT rounds. Tariffs on industrial goods average 5% in industrialized countries, down from 40% in the late 1940s.	Rich countries will cut tariffs on industrial goods by more than one-third. Tariffs will be scrapped on over 40% of manufactured goods.	Easier access to world markets for exports of industrial goods. Lower prices for consumers.
Agriculture		
High farm subsidies and protected markets in United States and EC lead to overproduction and dumping.	Subsidies and other barriers to trade in agricultural products will be cut over six years. Subsidies cut by 20%. All import barriers will be converted to tariffs and cut by 36%.	Better market opportunities for efficient food producers. Lower prices for consumers. Restraint of farm subsidies war.
Services		
GATT rules do not extend to services. Many countries protect service industries from international competition.	GATT rules on fair trade principles extended to cover many services. Failure to reach agreement on financial services and telecommunications. Special talks will continue.	Increase in trade services. Further liberalization of trade in services now seems likely.
Intellectual Property		
Standards of protection for patents, copyrights, and trademarks vary widely. Ineffective enforcement of national laws a growing source of trade friction.	Extensive agreements on patents, copyrights, and trademarks. International standards of protection, and agreements for effective enforcement, established.	Increased protection and reduction of intellectual property piracy will benefit producers of intellectual property (e.g., computer software firms, performing artists). Will increase technology transfer.
Textiles		
Rich countries have restricted imports of textiles and clothing through bilateral quotas under Multi-Fiber Arrangement	MFA quotas progressively dismantled over 10 years and tariffs reduced. Normal GATT rules will apply at end of 10 years.	Increased trade in textiles should benefit developing countries. Reduced prices for consumers worldwide.
GATT Rules		
GATT remains the same as when drafted in 1947, even though many more countries have entered the world trading community and trade patterns have shifted.	Many GATT rules revised and updated. They include codes on customs valuation and import licensing, customs unions and free trade areas, and rules dealing with waivers from GATT regulations.	Greater transparency, security, and predictability in trading policies.
World Trade Organization		
GATT original envisioned as part of an International Trade Organization. ITO never ratified and GATT applied provisionally.	GATT becomes a permanent world trade body covering goods, services, and intellectual property with a common disputes procedure. WTO to implement results of Uruguay Round.	More effective advocacy and policing of the international trading system.

Source: "The GATT Deal," *Financial Times*, December 16, 1993, pp. 4–7.

Table 5.1

Main Features of the Uruguay Round Agreement

economic growth and development by promoting trade. The WTO will act as an umbrella organization that which will encompass the GATT along with two new sister bodies, one on services and the other on intellectual property. The WTO will take over responsibility for arbitrating trade disputes and monitoring the trade policies of member countries. While the WTO will operate as GATT now does—on the basis of consensus—in the area of dispute settlement, member countries will no longer be able to block adoption of arbitration reports. Arbitration panel reports on trade disputes between member countries will be automatically adopted by the WTO unless there is a consensus to reject them. Countries that have been found by the arbitration panel to violate GATT rules may appeal to a permanent appellate body, but its verdict will be binding. If offenders then fail to comply with the recommendations of the arbitration panel, trading partners will have the right to compensation or, in the last resort, to impose (commensurate) trade sanctions. Every stage of the procedure will be subject to strict time limits. Thus, the WTO will have something that the GATT never had—teeth.[25]

Implications of the Uruguay Round

The world is better off with a GATT deal than without it. Without the deal, the world might have slipped into increasingly dangerous trade wars, which might have triggered a recession. With a GATT deal concluded, the current world trading system looks secure, and there is a good possibility that the world economy will now grow faster than would otherwise have been the case. Estimates as to the overall impact of the GATT agreement, however, are not that dramatic. Three studies undertaken in mid-1993 (before the agreement was finalized) estimated the deal will add between $213 billion and $274 billion in 1992 US dollars to aggregate world income by 2002—or about 0.75 percent to 1 percent of gross global income by that time.[26] Others argue that these figures underestimate the potential gain because they do not factor in gains from the liberalization of trade in services, stronger trade rules, and greater business confidence. Taking such factors into account, it is claimed that global economic output could be as much as 8 percent higher by 2002 than it would have been without the agreement.[27] Whatever figure is closer to the truth, it is best to keep in mind what a successful GATT agreement helps avoid: the risk of a trade war that might reduce global economic growth and raise prices for consumers around the globe.

WTO: Early Experience

When the WTO was established, its creators hoped the WTO's enforcement mechanisms would make it a more effective policeman of global trade rules than the GATT had been. The expectation was that the WTO would emerge as an effective advocate and facilitator of future trade deals, particularly in areas such as services. The experience so far has been encouraging.

WTO as a Global Policeman

The first three years in the life of the WTO suggest its policing and enforcement mechanisms are having a positive effect. As of July 31, 1997, 104 trade disputes had been brought to the WTO for arbitration.[28] This compares with a total of 196 cases handled by the GATT over almost half a century. Countries' use of the WTO represents an important vote of confidence in the organization's dispute resolution.

The backing of the leading trading powers has been crucial to the early success of the WTO. Initially, some feared that the United States might undermine the system by continuing to rely on unilateral measures when it suited or by refusing to accept WTO verdicts. These fears were enhanced in 1995 when the United States refused to bring a dispute with Japan over trade in autos and auto parts to the WTO (that dispute was settled bilaterally). Since then, however, the United States has emerged as the biggest user of the WTO, bringing 34 complaints on everything from food inspection in South Korea to taxation of foreign film revenues in Turkey. The top four trading entities—the United States, the European Union, Japan, and Canada—dominated the dispute settlement process.

Of the cases filed by the United States, five led to outright US victories and another seven yielded favorable results. The rest of the cases are still under review, but WTO analysts figure that the United States will win 80 to 85 percent of its cases, about the same percentage as under the GATT.[29] In 1997, the European Union lost two major cases brought by the United States, a complaint on EU restrictions limiting the import of hormone-treated US beef (see the opening case) and a protest against the EU's discriminatory banana import policy. The United States lost a major case to Japan when the WTO rejected every element of a US claim that Japan should reorganize its commercial economy so that Kodak could better compete there against its global rival, Fuji. Kodak claimed that its access to Japanese markets was unfairly restricted because of the close relationships between Japanese manufacturing companies, banks, and retail outlets. There is little question that these exist, but they are neither unique to Japan nor, the WTO observed, were they created to keep Kodak out of the Japanese markets: they were there long before Kodak came along. Besides, Fuji holds no larger share of the Japanese market than Kodak does of the US market.

Encouraged perhaps by the tougher system, developing countries are also starting to use the settlement procedures more than they did under the GATT. Developing countries had launched over 30 complaints by July 1997, many targeted at developed nations. When Costa Rica complained that US regulations discriminated against its textile exports, the WTO ruled in favor of the Central American nation.

So far the United States has proved willing to accept WTO rulings that go against it. The United States agreed to implement a WTO judgment that called for the country to remove discriminatory antipollution regulations that were applied to gasoline imports. In a dispute with India over textile imports, the United States rescinded quotas before a WTO panel could start work. And in June 1996, the United States preempted the establishment of a WTO panel by revoking punitive tariffs placed on EU food and drink exports that were imposed in 1988 in retaliation for the EU's ban on hormone-treated beef.

Despite its early success, questions still remain as to how effective the WTO's dispute resolution procedures will be. The first real test of the procedures will arise when the WTO has to arbitrate a politically sensitive case, particularly one that involves the United States or the European Union, where a significant and vocal minority of politicians argues that the WTO infringes on national sovereignty. The WTO rulings on Kodak and hormone-treated beef produced complaints from vocal minorities in the United States and EU, respectively.

WTO Telecommunications Agreement

As explained above, the Uruguay Round of GATT negotiations extended global trading rules to cover services. The WTO was given the role of brokering future agreements to open global trade in services. The WTO was also encouraged to extend its reach to encompass regulations governing foreign direct investment—something the GATT had never done. Two of the first industries targeted for reform were the global telecommunications and financial services industries. The WTO came close to reaching an agreement to liberalize global telecommunications services in early 1996, but ultimately failed to close a deal when the United States declined to sanction the draft agreement, arguing that it did not do enough to open national telecommunications markets to foreign investment.

The WTO tried again to reach an agreement in February 1997. Many observers felt that the negotiations represented a major test of the WTO's credibility as a facilitator of future global trade and investment deals. In 1995, the global telecommunications services market was worth just over $600 billion—or 2.5 percent of global GDP—only 20 percent of which was open to competition. Given its importance in the global economy, the telecommunications services industry was a very important target for reform. The WTO's goal was to get countries to open their telecommunications markets to competition, allowing foreign operators to purchase ownership stakes in domestic telecommunications providers and establishing a set of common rules for fair competition in the telecommunications sector. Three benefits were cited.

First, advocates argued that inward investment and increased competition would stimulate the modernization of telephone networks around the world and lead to higher-quality service. Second, supporters maintained that the increased competition would benefit customers through lower prices. Estimates suggested that a deal would soon reduce the average cost of international telephone calls by 80 percent and save consumers $1,000 billion over three years.[30] Third, the WTO argued that trade in other goods and services invariably depends on flows of information matching buyers to sellers. As telecommunications service improves in quality and declines in price, international trade increases in volume and becomes less costly for traders. Telecommunications reform, therefore, should promote cross-border trade in other goods and services. In sum, Renato Ruggiero, the director general of the WTO, argued:

> Telecommunications liberalization could mean global income gains of some $1 trillion over the next decade or so. This represents about 4 percent of world GDP at today's prices.[31]

After some last-minute hedging by the United States, a deal was reached on February 15, 1997. Under the pact, 68 countries accounting for more than 90 percent of world telecommunications revenues pledged to open their markets to foreign competition and to abide by common rules for fair competition in telecommunications. Most of the world's biggest markets, including the United States, European Union, and Japan, were fully liberalized by January 1, 1998, when the pact took effect. All forms of basic telecommunications service are covered, including voice telephony, data and fax transmissions, and satellite and radio communications. Many telecommunications companies responded positively to the deal, pointing out that it would give them a much greater ability to offer their business customers "one-stop shopping"—a global, seamless service for all of their corporate needs and a single bill.[32]

WTO Financial Services Agreement

Fresh from its success in brokering a telecommunications agreement, in April 1997 the WTO embarked on negotiations to liberalize the global financial services industry. Under the negotiating schedule, an agreement had to be reached by December 31, 1997. The financial services industry includes banking, securities businesses, insurance, asset management services, and the like. As with telecommunications, the first attempt at reaching a global deal in 1995 failed when the United States refused to join a pact. The negotiations stalled because the United States felt developing countries were not prepared to make enough concessions.

The global financial services industry is enormous. The sector executes $1.2 trillion a day in foreign exchange transactions. International financing extended by banks around the world reporting to the Bank for International Settlements is estimated at $6.4 trillion, including $4.6 trillion net international lending. Total world banking assets are put at more than $20 trillion, insurance premiums at $2 trillion, stock market capitalization at over $10 trillion, and market value of listed bonds at about $10 trillion. In addition, practically every international trade deal in goods or services requires credit, capital, foreign exchange, and insurance.[33]

Participants in the negotiations wanted to see more competition in the sector both to allow firms greater opportunities abroad and to encourage greater efficiency. Developing countries need the capital and financial infrastructure for their development. But governments also have to ensure that the system is sound and stable because of the economic shocks that can be caused by exchange rates, interest rates, or other market conditions fluctuating excessively. They also have to avoid economic crisis caused by bank failures. Therefore, government intervention in the interest of prudential safeguards is an important condition underpinning financial market liberalization.

An agreement was finally reached December 14, 1997.[34] The deal covers more than 95 percent of the world's financial services market. Under the agreement, which was to take effect in March 1999, 102 countries have pledged to open to varying degrees their banking, securities, and insurance sectors to foreign competition. Just as in the telecommunications deal, the accord covers not just cross-border trade, but also foreign direct investment. Seventy countries have agreed to dramatically lower or eradicate barriers to FDI in their financial services sector. The United States and the European Union will, with minor exceptions, be fully open to inward investment by foreign banks, insurance, and securities companies. As part of the deal, many Asian countries made important concessions that will allow significant foreign participation in their financial services sectors for the first time.

The Future: Unresolved Issues

The 1994 GATT deal still leaves a lot to be done on the international trade front. Substantial trade barriers still remain in areas such as financial services and broadcast entertainment, although these seem likely to be reduced eventually. More significantly perhaps, WTO has yet to deal with the areas of environmentalism, worker rights, foreign direct investment, and dumping.[35]

High on the list of the WTO's future concerns will be the interaction of environmental and trade policies and how best to promote sustainable development and ecological well-being without resorting to protectionism. The WTO will have to deal with environmentalists' claims that expanded international trade encourages companies to locate factories in areas of the world where they are freer to pollute and degrade the environment.

Paralleling environmental concerns are concerns that free trade encourages firms to shift their production to countries with low labor rates where worker rights are routinely violated. The United States has repeatedly and unsuccessfully pressed for discussion of common international standards on workers rights—an idea strongly opposed by poorer nations who fear that it is just another excuse for protectionism by the rich.

GATT regulations have never been extended to embrace foreign direct investment (investment by a firm based in one country in productive facilities in another country). Given the globalization of production that we are now witnessing, barriers to foreign direct investment seem antiquated, and yet they are still widespread (we will discuss these in detail in Chapter 7). Currently many countries limit investment by foreign companies in their economies (e.g., local content requirements, local ownership rules, and even outright prohibition).

A final issue of concern has been the proliferation of antidumping actions in recent years. WTO rules allow countries to impose antidumping duties on foreign goods that are being sold cheaper than at home, or below their cost of production, when domestic producers can show that they are being harmed. Unfortunately, the rather vague definition of what constitutes "dumping" has proved to be something of a loophole which many countries are exploiting to pursue protectionism. In the United States, for example, 26 antidumping cases were launched in 1998, up from 16 cases in the prior year. There has also been a rise in cases filed by the European Union. Increasingly, it seems to be that whenever an industry faces strong foreign competition, the first response of some firms in that industry is to cry foul and accuse the foreign producers of dumping. The process can then become politicized, as representatives of businesses and their employees lobby government officials to "protect domestic jobs from unfair foreign competition." If this trend continues, it is likely that the WTO will try to strengthen the regulations governing the imposition of antidumping duties.

IMPLICATIONS FOR BUSINESS

Why should the international manager care about the political economy of free trade, about the relative merits of arguments for free trade and protectionism? There are two answers to this question. The first concerns the impact of trade barriers on a firm's strategy. The second concerns the role that business firms can play in promoting free trade and/or trade barriers.

Trade Barriers and Firm Strategy

To understand how trade barriers affect a firm's strategy, consider the material we covered in Chapter 4. Drawing on the theories of international trade, we discussed how it may make sense for the firm to disperse its production activities to countries where they can be performed most efficiently. It may make sense for a firm to design and engineer its product in one country, to manufacture components in another, to perform final assembly operations in yet another country, and then export the finished product to the rest of the world.

Trade barriers constrain a firm's ability to disperse its productive activities in such a manner. First, and most obviously, tariff barriers raise the costs of exporting products to a country (or of exporting partly finished products between countries). This may put the firm at a competitive disadvantage vis-à-vis indigenous competitors in that country. In response, the firm may then find it economical to locate production facilities in that country so it can compete on an even footing with indigenous competitors. Second, voluntary export restraints may limit a firm's ability to serve a country from locations outside of that country. The firm's response might be to set up production facilities in that country—even though it may result in higher production costs. Such reasoning underlay the rapid expansion of Japanese automaking capacity in the United States during the 1980s. This followed the establishment of a VER agreement between the United States and Japan that limited imports of Japanese automobiles. For details, see the accompanying Management Focus, which describes how Toyota responded to threats of greater protectionism by opening auto assembly plants in the United States and Europe.

Third, to conform with local content regulations, a firm may have to locate more production activities in a given market than it would otherwise. From the firm's perspective, the consequence might be to raise costs above the level that could be achieved if each production activity was dispersed to the optimal location for that activity. And fourth, even when trade barriers do not exist, the firm may still want to locate some production activities in a given country to reduce the threat of trade barriers being imposed in the future.

All the above effects are likely to raise the firm's costs above the level that could be achieved in a world without trade barriers. The higher costs that result need not translate into a significant competitive disadvantage, however, if the countries imposing trade barriers do so to the imported products of all foreign firms, irrespective of their national origin. But when trade barriers are targeted at exports from a particular nation, firms based in that nation are at a competitive disadvantage vis-à-vis the firms of other nations (VERs are targeted trade barriers). The firm may deal with such targeted trade barriers by moving production into the country imposing barriers. Another strategy may be to move production to countries whose exports are not targeted by the specific trade barrier.

MANAGEMENT FOCUS
Toyota's Response to Rising Protectionist Pressures in Europe and the United States

In many respects, Toyota has been a victim of its own success. Until the 1960s, Toyota was viewed as little more than an obscure Japanese automobile company. In 1950, Toyota produced a mere 11,700 vehicles. In 1970, it was producing 1.6 million vehicles, and by 1990, the figure had increased to 4.12 million. In the process, Toyota rose to become the third largest automobile company and the largest automobile exporter in the world. Most analysts credited Toyota's dramatic rise to the company's world-class manufacturing and design skills. These made Toyota not only the most productive automobile company in the world, but also the one that consistently produced the highest-quality and best-designed automobiles.

For most of its history, Toyota has exported automobiles to the world market from its plants in Japan. However, by the early 1980s, political pressures and talk of local content regulations in the United States and Europe were forcing an initially reluctant Toyota to rethink its exporting strategy. Toyota had already agreed to "voluntary" export restraints with the United States in 1981. The consequence for Toyota was stagnant export growth between 1981 and 1984. In the early 1980s, Toyota began to think seriously about setting up manufacturing operations overseas.

Toyota's first overseas operation was a 50/50 joint venture with General Motors established in February 1983 under the name New United Motor Manufacturing Inc. (NUMMI). NUMMI, which is based in Fremont, California, began producing Chevrolet Nova cars for GM in December 1984. The maximum capacity of the Fremont plant is about 250,000 cars per year.

For Toyota, the joint venture provided a chance to find out whether it could build quality cars in the United States using American workers and American suppliers. It also provided Toyota with experience dealing with an American union (the United Auto Workers Union) and with a means of circumventing voluntary import restrictions. By fall 1986, the NUMMI plant was running at full capacity and early indications were that the NUMMI plant was achieving productivity and quality levels close to those achieved at Toyota's major Takaoka plant in Japan.

Encouraged by its success at NUMMI, Toyota announced in December 1985 that it would build an automobile manufacturing plant in Georgetown, Kentucky. The plant, which came on stream in May 1988, officially had the capacity to produce 200,000 Toyota Camrys a year. However, by early 1990, it was producing the equivalent of 220,000 cars per year. This success was followed by an announcement in December 1990 that Toyota would build a second plant in Georgetown with a capacity to produce a further 200,000 vehicles per year. The two plants and NUMMI

Policy Implications

As noted in Chapter 4, business firms are major players on the international trade scene. Because of their pivotal role in international trade, business firms exert a strong influence on government policy toward trade. This influence can encourage protectionism or it can encourage the government to support the WTO and push for open markets and freer trade. Government policies with regard to international trade also can have a direct impact on business.

Consistent with strategic trade policy, examples can be found of government intervention in the form of tariffs, quotas, and subsidies helping firms and industries to establish a competitive advantage in the world economy. In general, however, the arguments contained in this chapter suggest that a policy of government intervention has three drawbacks. Intervention can be self-defeating, since it tends to protect the inefficient rather than help firms become efficient global competitors. Intervention is dangerous because it may invite retaliation and trigger a trade war. Finally, intervention is unlikely to be well-executed, given the opportunity for such a policy to be captured by special interest groups. Does this mean that business should simply encourage government to adopt a *laissez-faire* free trade policy?

http://www.toyota.com

gave Toyota the capacity to build 660,000 vehicles per year in North America.

In addition to its North American operations, Toyota moved to set up production facilities in Europe. This move was also in response to growing protectionist pressures. Toyota was also anticipating the 1992 lowering of trade barriers among the member states of the European Union. In 1989, the company announced it would build a plant in England with the capacity to manufacture 200,000 cars per year by 1997. The clear implication was that after 1992, much of this plant's output would be exported to the rest of the EU. This decision prompted the French prime minister to describe Britain as "a Japanese aircraft carrier, sitting off the coast of Europe waiting to attack." Fearing that the EU would limit its expansion, Toyota joined other Japanese automobile companies in agreeing to keep their share of the European auto market to under 11 percent, at least until 2000.

Despite Toyota's apparent commitment to expand its US and European assembly operations, it has not all been smooth sailing. A major problem has been building an overseas supplier network that is comparable to Toyota's Japanese network. For example, in a 1990 meeting of Toyota's North American suppliers' association, Toyota executives informed their North American suppliers that the defect ratio for parts produced by 75

North American and European suppliers was 100 times greater than the defect ratio for parts supplied by 147 Japanese suppliers. Toyota executives also pointed out that parts manufactured by North American and European suppliers tended to be significantly more expensive than comparable parts manufactured in Japan.

Because of these problems, Toyota initially imported many parts from Japan for its European and US assembly operations. However, the increase in imports of automobile components from Japan only heightened trade tensions between the two countries. The high volume of such imports became a major sticking point in trade negotiations between the United States and Japan. In an attempt to diffuse the situation, Toyota worked to increase the local content of cars assembled in North America and Europe. By 1996, 70 percent of the value of Toyota cars assembled in Europe and the United States was produced locally, up from less than 40 percent in 1990. To achieve this, Toyota embarked on an aggressive supplier education drive in both Europe and the United States aimed at familiarizing its local suppliers with Japanese production methods.

Source: C. W. L. Hill, "The Toyota Corporation in 1994," in C. W. L. Hill and G. R. Jones, *Strategic Management: An Integrated Approach* (Boston: Houghton Mifflin, 1995).

Most economists would probably argue that the best interests of international business are served by a free trade stance, but not a *laissez-faire* stance. It is probably in the best long-run interests of the business community to encourage the government to aggressively promote greater free trade by, for example, strengthening the WTO. Business probably has much more to gain from government efforts to open protected markets to imports and foreign direct investment than from government efforts to support certain domestic industries in a manner consistent with the recommendations of strategic trade policy.

This conclusion is reinforced by a phenomenon that we touched on in Chapter 1, the increasing integration of the world economy and internationalization of production that has occurred over the past two decades. We live in a world where many firms of all national origins increasingly depend for their competitive advantage on globally dispersed production systems. Such systems are the result of free trade. Free trade has brought great advantages to firms that have exploited it and to consumers who benefit from the resulting lower prices. Given the danger of retaliatory action, business firms that lobby their governments to engage in protectionism must realize that by doing so they may be denying themselves the opportunity to build a competitive advantage by constructing a globally dispersed production system. Also, by encouraging their governments to engage in protectionism, their own activities and sales overseas may be jeopardized if other governments retaliate.

Chapter Summary

This chapter described how the reality of international trade deviates from the theoretical ideal of unrestricted free trade that we reviewed in Chapter 4. In this chapter, we reviewed the various instruments of trade policy, reviewed the political and economic arguments for government intervention in international trade, reexamined the economic case for free trade in light of the strategic trade policy argument, and looked at the evolution of the world trading framework. We concluded that, while a policy of free trade may not always be the theoretically optimal policy (given the arguments of the new trade theorists), in practice it is probably the best policy for a government to pursue. The long-run interests of businesses and consumers may be best served by strengthening international institutions such as the WTO and the GATT. Given the danger that isolated protectionism might escalate into a trade war, business probably has far more to gain from government efforts to open protected markets to imports and foreign direct investment (through the WTO) than from government efforts to protect domestic industries from foreign competition.

This chapter made the following points:

1. The effect of a tariff is to raise the cost of imported products. Gains accrue to the government (from revenues) and to producers (who are protected from foreign competitors). Consumers lose because they must pay more for imports.

2. By lowering costs, subsidies help domestic producers compete against low-cost foreign imports and gain export markets. However, subsidies must be paid for by taxpayers. They also tend to be captured by special interests who use them to protect the inefficient.

3. An import quota is a direct restriction imposed by an importing country on the quantity of some good that may be imported. A voluntary export restraint (VER) is a quota on trade imposed from the exporting country's side. Both import quotas and VERs benefit domestic producers by limiting import competition, but they result in higher prices, which hurts consumers.

4. A local content requirement demands that some specific fraction of a good be produced domestically. Local content requirements benefit the producers of component parts, but they raise prices of imported components, which hurts consumers.

5. An administrative policy is an informal instrument or bureaucratic rule that can be used to restrict imports and boost exports. Such policies benefit producers but hurt consumers, who are denied access to possibly superior foreign products.

6. There are two types of arguments for government intervention in international trade: political and economic. Political arguments for intervention are concerned with protecting the interests of certain groups, often at the expense of other groups, or with promoting goals with regard to foreign policy, human rights, consumer protection, and the like. Economic arguments for intervention are about boosting the overall wealth of a nation.

7. The most common political argument for intervention is that it is necessary to protect jobs. However, political intervention often hurts consumers and it can be self-defeating.

8. Countries sometimes argue that it is important to protect certain industries for reasons of national security.

9. Some argue that government should use the threat to intervene in trade policy as a bargaining tool to open foreign markets. This can be a risky policy; if it fails the result can be higher trade barriers.

10. The infant industry argument for government intervention is that governments should temporarily support new industries to let manufacturing get a toehold. In practice, however, governments often end up protecting the inefficient.

11. Strategic trade policy suggests that with subsidies, governments can help domestic firms gain first-mover advantages in global industries where economies of scale are important. Government subsidies may also help domestic firms overcome barriers to entry into such industries.

12. The problems with strategic trade policy are twofold: (*i*) Such a policy may invite retaliation, in which case all will lose, and (*ii*) strategic trade policy may be captured by special interest groups, who will distort it to their own ends.

13. The Smoot-Hawley tariff, introduced in 1930, erected an enormous wall of barriers to US imports. Other countries responded by adopting similar tariffs, and the world slid further into the Great Depression.

14. The GATT was a product of the post-war free trade movement. The GATT was successful in lowering trade barriers on manufactured goods and commodities. The move toward greater free trade under the GATT appeared to stimulate economic growth.

15. The completion of the Uruguay Round of GATT talks and the establishment of the World Trade Organization have strengthened the world trading system by extending GATT rules to services, increasing protection for intellectual property, reducing agricultural subsidies, and enhancing monitoring and enforcement mechanisms.

16. Trade barriers constrain a firm's ability to disperse its various production activities to optimal locations around the globe. One response to trade barriers is to establish more production activities in the protected country.

17. Business may have more to gain from government efforts to open protected markets to imports and foreign direct investment than from government efforts to protect domestic industries from foreign competition.

Critical Discussion Questions

1. Do you think the US government should take human rights considerations into account when granting most favored nation trading status to China? What are the arguments for and against taking such a position?

2. Whose interests should be the paramount concern of government trade policy—the interests of producers (businesses and their employees) or of consumers?

3. Given the arguments relating to the new trade theory and strategic trade policy, what kind of trade policy should business be pressuring government to adopt?

4. You are an employee of a US firm that produces personal computers in Thailand and then exports them to the United States and other countries for sale. The personal computers were originally produced in Thailand to take advantage of relatively low labor costs and a skilled work force. Other possible locations considered at the time were Malaysia and Hong Kong. The US government decides to impose punitive 100 percent ad valorem tariffs on imports of computers from Thailand to punish the country for administrative trade barriers that restrict US exports to Thailand. How do you think your firm should respond? What does this tell you about the use of targeted trade barriers?

CLOSING CASE Shrimps, Turtles, and the WTO

There are seven species of sea turtles in the world; six of them are on the US list of endangered species. A major cause of the decline of sea turtles has been poor fishing practices, particularly by shrimp boats. An estimated 150,000 sea turtles per year are trapped and drown in the nets of shrimp boats. In an effort to limit this carnage, the US Congress in 1989 passed a law that required shrimp boats to be equipped with a turtle-excluder device, a simple grate that fits over the mouth of shrimp trawling nets and prevents sea turtles from becoming trapped. The law also banned the importation of shrimp from countries that fail to mandate the use of turtle excluder devices by their shrimp fleets.

As with many such laws, the US government dragged its heels on enforcing the import ban. It wasn't until 1996 that the United States placed an embargo on the importation of shrimp from countries that failed to mandate the use of excluder devices. Even then, it did so only because environmental groups in the United States had sued the government to compel it to enforce its own law. Three countries were targeted by the 1996 ban—India, Pakistan, and Malaysia. The three responded to the ban by filing a complaint with the World Trade Organization. They were joined by Thailand, which decided as a matter of principle to pursue the WTO case (Thailand had already satisfied the United States that its turtle protection methods were adequate).

The WTO formed an independent arbitration panel composed of three experts from countries not involved in the dispute. The panel was charged with reviewing the

US position to see whether it conflicted with WTO rules. In its defense, the United States claimed there are provisions in the WTO rules for using restrictive measures if they are related "to the conservation of exhaustible natural resources and if such measures are made effective in conjunction with restrictions on domestic production or consumption." The United States was supported by a number of environmental organizations, including the World Wildlife Fund (WWF). In a brief submitted to the panel, the WWF argued that marine turtles are migratory animals, a global resource that should be subject to stewardship by international society. Even though no multilateral body or resolution had authorized the United States to enact its ban, the WWF claimed that the United States acted in a manner consistent with its obligations and took reasonable measures that reflected the will of the international community.

The four countries that brought the complaint argued that the US ban represented an unfair restraint on trade that was illegal under WTO rules. According to these countries, the United States was violating WTO rules by applying domestic legislation outside its boundaries and by applying it in a discriminatory manner. Influential voices in all these countries accused the United States of hypocrisy. An article in *The Hindu*, an Indian newspaper, stated

> Compared to what the US as a nation is doing to other global shared resources, the world's climate and atmosphere, what complainant nations like India are doing to the marine turtle is a contemptuously small problem . . . . The US leadership has, unfortunately, always put its national interests before global concerns in its global environmental policies. Its behavior on the climate change issue is one example. Its refusal to sign the biodiversity treaty is another. Its refusal to pay dues to the United Nations is yet another.

The World Trade Organization panel issued its ruling on April 6, 1998. The WTO ruled that the United States was wrong to prohibit shrimp imports from countries that failed to protect sea turtles from entrapment in the nets of shrimp boats. The WTO stated that while

environmental considerations were important, the primary aim of international agreements on trade remained the promotion of economic development through unfettered free trade. Further, the WTO stated that even under WTO treaty provisions that allow environmental exceptions, the United States would not be allowed to force other nations to adopt policies to protect an endangered species such as the turtle.

While the WTO has no power to overturn US law, the United States must pay a penalty to the WTO if it keeps its law and the import ban in place. Environmental groups responded with outrage to the WTO's ruling. A Sierra Club spokesman noted, "This is the clearest slap at environmental protection to come out of the WTO to date." Similarly, a spokeswoman for the Washington, DC-based Center for Marine Conservation stated, "It is unthinkable that we should not be allowed to mitigate the impacts of our own shrimp markets on endangered sea turtles. This entire life form is threatened with extinction."

http://www.worldwildlife.org

Sources: A. Aggarwal and S. Narain, "Politics of Conservation," *The Hindu*, October 26, 1997, p. 26; J. H. Cushman, "Trade Group Strikes a Blow at US Environmental Law," *New York Times*, April 7, 1998, p. D1; "WTO Ruling in Turtle Protection Dispute," *Bangkok Post*, March 18, 1998; and J. Maggs, "WTO Shrimp Ruling Heightens Environment vs Trade Debate," *Journal of Commerce*, April 7, 1998, p. 3A.

Case Discussion Questions

1. Do you think the United States is correct to try to use its law and trade policy to force other countries to adopt environmental policies that it perceives to be sound?

2. Does the WTO decision have implications for US national sovereignty? If so, what?

3. Do you think that it is correct for the WTO to decouple trade policy from environmental policy? Why?

4. Do you think that other countries are correct to accuse the United States of hypocrisy on the environmental issue?

5. How should the United States react to the WTO decision in this case?

Notes

1. For a detailed welfare analysis of the effect of a tariff, see P. R. Krugman and M. Obstfeld, *International Economics: Theory and Policy* (New York: Harper Collins, 1994), chap. 9.

2. Y. Sazanami, S. Urata, and H. Kawai, *Measuring the Costs of Protection in Japan* (Washington, DC: Institute for International Economics, 1994).

3. See J. Bhagwati, *Protectionism* (Cambridge, MA: MIT Press, 1988); and "Costs of Protection," *Journal of Commerce*, September 25, 1991, p. 8A.

4. "From the Sublime to the Subsidy," *The Economist*, February 24, 1990, p. 71.

5. "Aid Addicts," *The Economist*, August 8, 1992, p. 61, and "State Aid: The Addicts in Europe," *The Economist*, November 22, 1997, p. 75.

6. R. W. Crandall, *Regulating the Automobile* (Washington, DC: Brookings Institute, 1986).

7. Quoted in Krugman and Obstfeld, *International Economics*.

8. Bhagwati, *Protectionism*; and "Japan to Curb VCR Exports," *New York Times*, November 21, 1983, p. D5.

9. Alan Goldstein, "Sematech Members Facing Dues Increase; 30% Jump to Make up for Loss of Federal Funding," *Dallas Morning News*, July 27, 1996, p. 2F.

10. N. Dunne and R. Waters, "US Waves a Big Stick at Chinese Pirates," *Financial Times*, January 6, 1995, p. 4.

11. John Broder, "Clinton to Impose Ban on 58 Types of Imported Guns," *New York Times*, April 6, 1998, sect. A; p. 1.

12. Bill Lambrecht, "Monsanto Softens Its Stance on Labeling in Europe," *St. Louis Post-Dispatch*, March 15, 1998, p. E1.

13. Peter S. Jordan, "Country Sanctions and the International Business Community," *American Society of International Law Proceedings of the Annual Meeting* 20, no. 9 (1997), p. 333–42.

14. "Waiting for China; Human Rights and International Trade," March 11, 1994; and "China: The Cost of Putting Business First," *Human Rights Watch*, July 1996.

15. "Brazil's Auto Industry Struggles to Boost Global Competitiveness," *Journal of Commerce*, October 10, 1991, p. 6A.

16. For reviews, see J. A. Brander, "Rationales for Strategic Trade and Industrial Policy," in *Strategic Trade Policy and the New International Economics*, ed. P. R. Krugman (Cambridge, MA: MIT Press, 1986); P. R. Krugman, "Is Free Trade Passé?" *Journal of Economic Perspectives* 1 (1987), pp. 131–44; and P. R. Krugman, "Does the New Trade Theory Require a New Trade Policy?" *World Economy* 15, no. 4 (1992), pp. 423–441.

17. "Airbus and Boeing: The Jumbo War," *The Economist*, June 15, 1991, pp. 65–66.

18. For details see Krugman, "Is Free Trade Passé?" and Brander, "Rationales for Strategic Trade."

19. Krugman, "Is Free Trade Passé?"

20. This dilemma is a variant of the famous Prisoner's Dilemma, which has become a classic metaphor for the difficulty of achieving cooperation between self-interested and mutually suspicious entities. For a good general introduction, see A. Dixit and B. Nalebuff, *Thinking Strategically: The Competitive Edge in Business, Politics, and Everyday Life* (New York: W. W. Norton & Co., 1991).

21. Note that the Smoot-Hawley tariff did not cause the Great Depression. However, the beggar-thy-neighbor trade policies that it ushered in certainly made things worse. See J. Bhagwati, *Protectionism* (Cambridge, MA: MIT Press, 1989).

22. Bhagwati, *Protectionism*.

23. World Bank, *World Development Report* (New York: Oxford University Press, 1987).

24. World Trade Organization, *World Trade Growth Accelerated in 1997*, WTO press release, March 19, 1998.

25. Frances Williams, "WTO—New Name Heralds New Powers," *Financial Times*, December 16, 1993, p. 5; and Frances Williams, "Gatt's Successor to Be Given Real Clout," *Financial Times*, April 4, 1994, p. 6.

26. The studies are OECD and the World Bank, *Trade Liberalization: The Global Economic Implications* (Paris and Washington; 1993); OECD, *Assessing the Effects of the Uruguay Round* (Paris, 1993); and "GATT Secretariat," *Background Paper: The Uruguay Round* (GATT, 1993).

27. Martin Wolf, "Doing Good Despite Themselves," *Financial Times*, December 16, 1993, p. 15.

28. World Trade Organization, *Annual Report, 1997*.

29. L. Abruzzese, "In Defense of the WTO," *Journal of Commerce*, October 21, 1997, p. 8A.

30. Alan Cane, "Getting Through: Why Telecommunications Talks Matter," *Financial Times*, February 14, 1997.

31. "Ruggiero Congratulates Governments on Landmark Telecommunications Agreement," *World Trade Organization* press release, February 17, 1997.

32. Francis Williams, "Telecoms: World Pact Set to Slash Costs of Calls," *Financial Times*, February 17, 1997.

33. "Financial Services," *WTO Press Brief*, September 1996.

34. G. De Jonquieres, Happy End to a Cliff Hanger," *Financial Times*, December 15, 1997, p. 15.

35. A Disquieting New Agenda for Trade," *The Economist*, July 16, 1994, pp. 55–56; and Frances Williams, "Trade Round Like This May Never Be Seen Again," *Financial Times*, December 16, 1993, p. 7.

CHAPTER SIX

FOREIGN DIRECT INVESTMENT

Electrolux's Global Investment Strategy

With 1998 sales of over SKr110 billion ($14 billion), Electrolux is the world's largest manufacturer of household appliances (washing machines, dishwashers, refrigerators, vacuum cleaners, and so on). A Swedish company with a small home market, Electrolux has always had to look to other markets for its growth. By 1997, the company was generating over 85 percent of its sales outside of Sweden. A little over 52 percent of sales are in Western Europe, with another 27 percent in North America. In recent years, the most rapid growth has come from Asia (which accounted for 5.1 percent of 1997 revenues), Eastern Europe (7 percent of revenues), and Latin America (6.4 percent of revenues). As of early 1998, the company employed over 100,000 people worldwide, had 150 factories and 300 warehouses located in 60 countries, and sold about 55 million products per year in 150 countries.

Electrolux's expansion into Asia, Eastern Europe, and Latin America dates from an early 1990s planning review, which concluded that demand for household appliances was mature in Western Europe and North America. The company conjectured that growth in these regions would be limited to replacement demand and the growth in population, and would be unlikely to exceed 2 to 3 percent annually. Leif Johansson, then the CEO of Electrolux, decided the company was too dependent on these mature markets. He reasoned that the company would have to expand aggressively into the emerging markets of the developing world if it was to maintain its historic growth rate. The company estimated that demand for household appliances in Asia, Eastern Europe, and Latin America could grow at 20 percent annually for at least the next decade, and probably beyond. In 1994, he set an ambitious goal for Electrolux; the company would have to double its sales in these emerging markets from the $1.35 billion it achieved in 1994 to $2.7 billion by 1997 (this target was exceeded). As an additional goal, he stated that Electrolux should become one of the top three suppliers of household goods in Southeast Asia by the year 2000.

In addition to the obvious growth potential, another consideration for Electrolux was that its main global competitors, General Electric and Whirlpool of the United States and Germany's Bosch-Siemans, had recently announced similar plans. Electrolux felt that it better move quickly so as not to be left out in the race to profit from these emerging markets.

Having committed itself to expansion, Electrolux had to decide how to achieve its ambitious goals. A combination of cost considerations and import barriers made direct exporting from its Western European and North American plants uneconomical. Instead, various approaches were adopted for different regions and countries. Acquisitions of going concerns, green-field developments, joint ventures, and enhanced marketing were all considered. Electrolux stated that it was prepared to spend $200 million per year to increase its presence in these emerging markets.

Electrolux made its first move into Eastern Europe in 1991 when it acquired Lehel, Hungary's largest manufacturer of household appliances. In addition, Electrolux decided to establish wholly owned operating companies in Russia, Poland, and the Czech Republic. Each of these operating subsidiaries was a green-field development. Asia demands a much greater need to adapt to local conditions. Regulations concerning foreign ownership in India and China, for example, virtually compel Electrolux to work through joint ventures with local partners. In China, the world's fastest-growing market, the company already had joint ventures in compressors, vacuum cleaners, and water purification equipment in 1994. Between 1994 and 1997, the company spent another $300 million to build five manufacturing plants in the country. In Southeast Asia, the emphasis is on the marketing of goods imported from China, rather than on local production. In Latin America, the company expanded through acquisitions, including its 1996 acquisition of Refripar, the largest producer of refrigerator products in Brazil. Electrolux's goal is to turn Refripar, which had 1995 sales of about $600 million, into its Latin American base for the production of household products.

Although Electrolux has been largely successful in its attempt to globalize its production and sales base, the expansion has not been without its problems. In 1997, the company suffered a significant drop in profit due to deteriorating market conditions in Brazil and the Asian Pacific region. The profit slump exposed serious weaknesses that had developed in Electrolux's global production system. Although the company had expanded rapidly via acquisitions since the early 1990s, it had not rationalized its production operations. Consequently, there was often considerable duplication of facilities within regions. In early 1998, the company's new CEO, Michael Treschow, announced a restructuring plan that called for the loss of 12,000 jobs and the closure of 25 factories and 50 warehouses worldwide. At the same time, however, Treschow reaffirmed Electrolux's commitment to building a global corporation with significant operations in the world's developing markets.

http://www.electrolux.se

Sources: C. Brown-Humes, "Electrolux Plugs into Households All over Asia," *Financial Times*, April 27, 1995, p. 15; C. Brown-Humes, "Electrolux Buys Control of Brazilian Group," *Financial Times*, January 11, 1996, p. 30; G. McIvor, "Electrolux Comes under the Scalpel," *Financial Times*, October 29, 1997, p. 27; and Electrolux's Web site, http://www.electrolux.com.

CHAPTER OUTLINE

ELECTROLUX'S GLOBAL INVESTMENT STRATEGY

INTRODUCTION

FOREIGN DIRECT INVESTMENT IN THE WORLD ECONOMY
The Growth of FDI
The Direction of FDI
The Source of FDI

HORIZONTAL FOREIGN DIRECT INVESTMENT
Transportation Costs
Market Imperfections (Internalization Theory)
Strategic Behavior
The Product Life Cycle
Location-Specific Advantages

VERTICAL FOREIGN DIRECT INVESTMENT
Strategic Behavior
Market Imperfections

IMPLICATIONS FOR BUSINESS

CHAPTER SUMMARY

CRITICAL DISCUSSION QUESTIONS

HONDA IN NORTH AMERICA

Introduction

This chapter is concerned with the phenomenon of foreign direct investment (FDI). **Foreign direct investment** occurs when a firm invests directly in facilities to produce and/or market a product in a foreign country. The 1991 purchase of Hungary's Lehel by Electrolux and its 1996 acquisition of Brazil's Refripar are examples of FDI, as are the company's investments in joint ventures to manufacture products in China and in green-field (new) wholly owned production facilities in Russia, Poland, and the Czech Republic (for details, see the opening case). The U.S. Department of Commerce has come up with a more precise definition of FDI. According to the department, FDI occurs whenever a US citizen, organization, or affiliated group takes an interest of 10 percent or more in a foreign business entity. Once a firm undertakes FDI it becomes a **multinational enterprise** (the meaning of multinational being "more than one country").

There is an important distinction between FDI and **foreign portfolio investment** (FPI). Foreign portfolio investment is investment by individuals, firms, or public bodies (e.g., national and local governments) in foreign financial instruments (e.g., government bonds, foreign stocks). FPI does not involve taking a significant equity stake in a foreign business entity. FPI is determined by different factors than FDI and raises different issues. Accordingly, we discuss FPI in Chapter 11 in our review of the international capital market.

In Chapter 4, we considered several theories that sought to explain the pattern of trade between countries. These theories focus on why countries export some products and import others. None of these theories address why a firm might decide to invest directly in production facilities in a foreign country, rather than exporting its domestic production to that country. The theories we reviewed in Chapter 4 do not explain the pattern of foreign direct investment between countries. The theories we explore in this chapter seek to do just this.

Our central objective will be to identify the economic rationale that underlies foreign direct investment. Firms often view exports and FDI as "substitutes" for each other. In the opening case, we saw how Electrolux considered and then ruled out serving emerging markets through exports from Western Europe. Instead, the company decided to invest directly in production facilities in those markets. One question this chapter attempts to answer is, *Under what conditions do firms such as Electrolux prefer FDI to exporting?* The opening case hints at some of the answers (e.g., trade barriers, access to markets, cost considerations). Here we will review various theories that attempt to provide a comprehensive explanation for this question.

This is not the only question these theories need to address. They also need to explain why it is preferable for a firm to engage in FDI rather than licensing. Licensing occurs when a domestic firm, the licensor, licenses to a foreign firm, the licensee, the right to produce its product, to use its production processes, or to use its brand name or trademark. In return for giving the licensee these rights, the licensor collects a royalty fee on every unit the licensee sells. The great advantage claimed for licensing over FDI is that the licensor does not have to pay for opening a foreign market; the licensee does that. For example, why did Electrolux acquire Lehel of Hungary, when it could have simply allowed Lehel to build Electrolux products under license and collected a royalty fee on each product that Lehel subsequently sold? Why did Electrolux prefer to bear the substantial risks and costs associated with purchasing Lehel, when in theory it could have earned a good return by licensing? The theories reviewed here attempt to provide an answer to this puzzle.

In the remainder of the chapter, we first look at the growing importance of FDI in the world economy. Next we look at the theories that have been used to explain horizontal foreign direct investment. **Horizontal foreign direct investment** is FDI in the same industry as a firm operates in at home. Electrolux's investments in Eastern Europe and Asia are examples of horizontal FDI. Having reviewed horizontal FDI, we consider the theories that help to explain vertical foreign direct investment. **Vertical foreign direct investment** is FDI in an industry that provides inputs for a firm's domestic operations, or it may be FDI in an industry abroad that sells the outputs of a firm's domestic operations. Finally, we review the implications of these theories for business practice.

Foreign Direct Investment in the World Economy

When discussing foreign direct investment, it is important to distinguish between the *flow* of FDI and the *stock* of FDI. The **flow of FDI** refers to the amount of FDI undertaken over a given time period (normally a year). The **stock of FDI** refers to the total accumulated value of foreign-owned assets at a given time. We also talk of **outflows of FDI,** meaning the flow of FDI out of a country, and **inflows of FDI,** meaning the flow of FDI into a country.

The Growth of FDI

The past 20 years there have seen a marked increase in both the *flow* and *stock* of FDI in the world economy. The average yearly *outflow* of FDI increased from about $25 billion in 1975 to a record $430 billion in 1998 (see Figure 6.1).[1] The flow of FDI not only accelerated during the 1980s and 1990s, but it also accelerated faster than the growth in world trade. Between 1984 and 1998, the total flow of FDI from all countries increased by over 900 percent, while world trade grew by 121 percent, and world output by 34 percent (see Figure 6.2).[2] As a result of the strong FDI flow, by 1998 the global stock of FDI exceeded $4.0 trillion. In total, 45,000 parent companies had

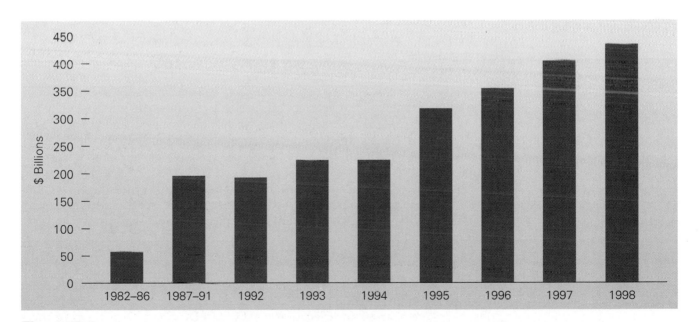

Figure 6.1

FDI Outflows 1982–1998 ($ billions)*

*Note: 1998 data based on preliminary estimates.

Source: United Nations, *World Investment Report, 1998* (New York and Geneva: United Nations, 1997).

Figure 6.2

Growth of FDI, World Trade, and World Output 1984–1998 (Index = 100 in 1984)*

*Note: 1998 data based on preliminary estimates.

Source: World Trade Organization, *Annual Report, 1998* (Geneva: WTO, 1998); and United Nations, *World Investment Report, 1998* (New York and Geneva: United Nations, 1998).

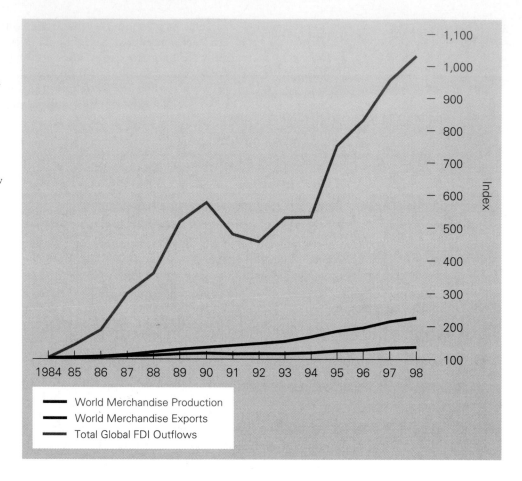

280,000 affiliates in foreign markets that collectively produced an estimated $7 trillion in global sales.[3]

FDI is growing more rapidly than world trade and world output for several reasons. Despite the general decline in trade barriers that we have witnessed over the past 30 years, business firms still fear protectionist pressures. Business executives see FDI as a way of circumventing future trade barriers. Much of the Japanese automobile companies' investment in the United States during the 1980s and early 1990s was driven by a desire to reduce exports from Japan, thereby alleviating trade tensions between the two nations.

Second, much of the recent increase in FDI is being driven by the dramatic political and economic changes that have been occurring in many of the world's developing nations. The general shift toward democratic political institutions and free market economics that we discussed in Chapter 2 has encouraged FDI. Across much of Asia, Eastern Europe, and Latin America, economic growth, economic deregulation, privatization programs that are open to foreign investors, and the removal of many restrictions on FDI have all made these countries more attractive to foreign investors. According to the United Nations, between 1991 and 1996 over 100 countries made 599 changes in legislation governing FDI. Some 95 percent of these changes involved liberalizing a country's foreign investment regulations to make it easier for foreign companies to enter their markets. The desire of governments to facilitate FDI has also been reflected in a dramatic increase in the number of bilateral investment treaties designed to protect and promote investment between two countries. As of January 1, 1997, there were 1,330 such treaties in the world involving 162 countries, a threefold increase in five years.[4]

We saw in the opening case how Electrolux has responded to these trends by investing in Eastern Europe and Asia. The acquisition of Lehel of Hungary, for example, was the result of a privatization program that allowed foreign investors to purchase state-owned enterprises.

The globalization of the world economy, a phenomenon that we first discussed in Chapter 1, is also having a positive impact on the volume of FDI. Firms such as Electrolux now see the whole world as their market, and they are undertaking FDI in an attempt to make sure they have a significant presence in every region of the world. For reasons that we shall explore later in this book, many firms now believe it is important to have production facilities based close to their major customers. This, too, is creating pressures for greater FDI.

The Direction of FDI

Not only has there been rapid growth in the flow of FDI, but there has also been an important shift in the direction of FDI. Historically, most FDI has been directed at the developed nations of the world as firms based in advanced countries invested in the others' markets. The United States has often been the favorite target for FDI inflows. This trend continued in 1996 when $84.6 billion was invested in the country (see Figure 6.3).[5] The United States is attractive because of its large and wealthy domestic markets, its dynamic and stable economy, a favorable political environment, and the openness of the country to FDI. Investors have included firms based in the United Kingdom, Japan, Germany, Holland, and France.

While developed nations in general, and the United States in particular, still account for the largest share of FDI inflows, there has been a surge of FDI into the world's developing nations (see Figure 6.3). From 1985 to 1990, the annual inflow of FDI into developing nations averaged $27.4 billion, or 17.4 percent of the total global flow. By 1997, the inflow into developing nations had risen to $149 billion, or 37 percent of the total. The lion's share of the 1997 inflow into developing nations was targeted at the emerging economies of South, East, and Southeast Asia, which collectively accounted for $87 billion of the 1997 total. Driving much of the increase

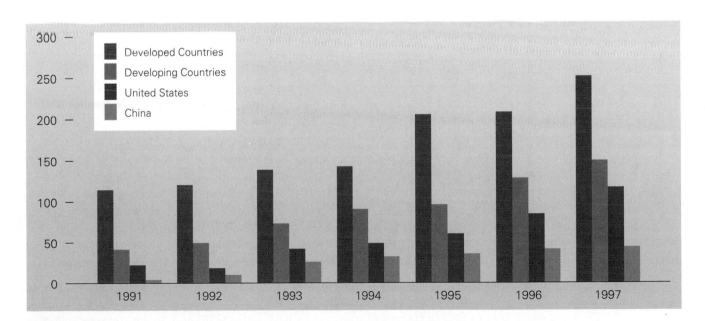

Figure 6.3

FDI Inflows, 1991–1997 ($ billions)

Source: United Nations, *World Investment Report, 1998* (New York and Geneva: United Nations, 1998).

COUNTRY FOCUS
Foreign Direct Investment in China

Beginning in late 1978, China's leadership decided to move the economy away from a centrally planned system to one that was more market driven, while still maintaining the rigid political framework of Communist party control. The strategy had a number of key elements, including a switch to household responsibility in agriculture instead of the old collectivization, increases in the authority of local officials and plant managers in industry, establishment of small-scale private enterprises in services and light manufacturing, and increased foreign trade and investment. The result has been a quadrupling of GDP since 1978. Agricultural output doubled in the 1980s, and industry posted major gains, especially in coastal areas near Hong Kong and opposite Taiwan, where foreign investment helped spur output of both domestic and export goods.

Starting from a tiny base, foreign investment surged to an annual average rate of $2.7 billion between 1985 and 1990 and then exploded to reach a record $45.2 billion in 1997, making China the second biggest recipient of FDI inflows in the world after the United States. About 80 percent of that investment has come from other Asian countries, such as Hong Kong (which is now part of China), Singapore, Korea, and Japan, with the balance coming from the United States and Western European nations. Over the past 20 years, this inflow has resulted in establishment of 145,000 foreign-funded enterprises in China, which realized capital investments of $216 billion. According to some estimates, this investment might have provided 20 to 30 percent of China's economic growth during the late 1980s and 1990s. By 1996, firms with foreign ownership accounted for 12 percent of industrial production, with manufacturing concentrated in toys, shoes, electrical appliances, and other labor-intensive sectors.

The reasons for the rise in investment are fairly obvious. With a population of 1.2 billion people, China represents the largest potential market in the world. Import tariffs make it difficult to serve this market via exports, so FDI is required if a company wants to tap into the huge potential of the country. Also, a combination of cheap labor and tax incentives, particularly for enterprises that establish themselves in special economic zones, makes China an attractive base from which to serve Asian or world markets with exports.

Less obvious, at least to begin with, was how difficult it would be for foreign firms to do business in China. Blinded by the size and potential of China's market, many firms have paid scant attention to the complexities of operating a business in this country until after the investment has been made. China may have a huge population, but despite two decades of rapid growth, it is still a poor country where the average income is little more than $700 per year. This lack of purchasing power translates into a weak market for many Western consumer goods from automobiles to household appliances. Another problem is the lack of a well-developed transportation infrastructure or distribution system. Pepsi discovered this problem at its subsidiary in Chongqing. Perched above the Yangtze River in southwest Sichuan province, Chongqing lies at the heart of China's massive hinterland. The Chongqing municipality, which includes the city and its surrounding regions, contains over 30 million people, but according to Steve Chen, the manager of the Pepsi subsidiary, the lack of well-developed road and distribution systems means he can reach only about half of this population with his product.

Other problems include a highly regulated environment that can make it problematic to conduct business transactions and shifting tax and regulatory regimes. For example, in 1997, the Chinese government suddenly scrapped a tax credit scheme that had made it attractive to import capital equipment into China.

has been the growing importance of China as a recipient of FDI. In 1997, China received direct investments valued at $45 billion, making it the second largest recipient of FDI in the world after the United States. The reasons for the strong flow of investment into China are discussed in the accompanying Country Focus. Singapore was the second largest investment recipient in the Asian region, with inflows valued at $9 billion.

http://www.asiasociety.org

This immediately made it more expensive to set up operations in the country.

There are also difficulties finding qualified personnel to staff operations. The cultural revolution produced a generation of people who lack the basic educational background that is taken for granted in the West. Because of the country's past, few local people understand the complexities of managing a modern industrial enterprise.

There are also problems with local joint venture partners who are inexperienced, opportunistic, or simply operate according to different goals. One United States manager explained that when he laid off 200 people to reduce costs, his Chinese joint venture partner hired them all back the next day. When he inquired why they had been hired back, the Chinese partner, which was government owned, explained that as an agency of the government, it had an "obligation" to reduce unemployment.

Increased investment in China's coastal regions has raised another source of concern. Serious overcapacity now looms in certain sectors, with negative implications for prices and profits.

Reflecting the growing awareness of these problems, Western enterprises' rate of investment into China slowed in late 1997 and early 1998. In July 1997, Chrysler said that it would close its sales office in Beijing, citing overcapacity in the automobile market and lower than expected demand for cars. Chrysler also announced that, while it will maintain its joint venture in Shanghai to make Jeeps, it will not be looking for new investments in China. Similarly, in August 1997, Chicago-based Ameritech Corp. stated that because of regulatory problems it would drop out of its telecommunications joint venture and pull out of China. Around the same time, Caterpillar Inc. stated it would be closing a joint venture in China because there was little demand

for the engines produced by the venture. To compound matters further, the financial crisis that swept through Asia in late 1997 and early 1998 seemed likely to drastically curtail the flow of investment money from other Asian countries, a source that historically had been of major importance. Because of these factors, initial projections call for FDI inflows into China to decline in 1998 to $35 billion, down $10 billion from 1997.

What all this means for long-term inflows of FDI into China, and for the country's long-term growth rate, remains to be seen. Chinese officials have tried a number of tactics to drum up support for FDI. The government has committed itself to invest over $800 billion in infrastructure projects over the next 10 years, which should improve the nation's poor highway system. By giving preferential tax breaks to companies that invest in special regions, such as that around Chongqing, the Chinese have created incentives for foreign companies to invest in China's vast interior where markets are underserved. They have been pursuing a macroeconomic policy that includes an emphasis on maintaining steady economic growth, low inflation, and a stable currency, all of which are attractive to foreign investors. And to deal with the lack of qualified personnel, in 1997 the government instructed universities to establish 30 business schools to train Chinese in basic skills such as accounting, finance, and human resource management. Although the bloom may be coming off China's current boom in FDI inflows, it seems likely that the country will continue to be an important magnet for foreign investors well into the next century.

Sources: Interviews by the author while in China, March 1998; L. Sly, "China Losing Its Golden Glow," *Chicago Tribune,* September 15, 1997, p. 1; M. Miller, "Search for Fresh Capital Widens," *South China Morning Post,* April 9, 1998, p. 1; and S. Mufson, "China Says Asian Crisis Will Have an Impact," *Washington Post,* March 8, 1998, p. A27.

After South, East, and Southeast Asia, Latin America emerged as the next most important region in the developing world for FDI inflows. In 1997, total inward investments into this region reached a record $58 billion. About $16 billion of this total was invested in Brazil, with another $12 billion targeted at Mexico. Much of this investment was a response to pro-market reforms in the region, including privatization, the liberalization of regulations governing FDI, and the growing importance of

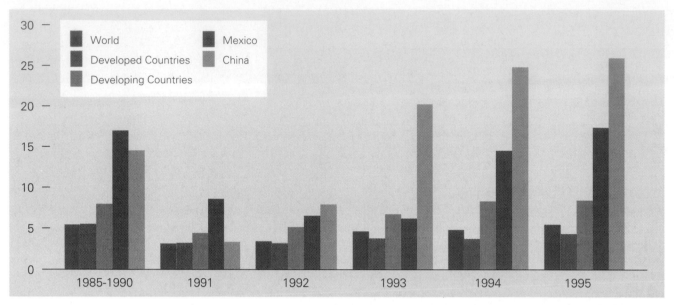

Figure 6.4

Inward FDI Flows as a Percentage of Gross Fixed Capital Formation, 1985–1995

Source: Data from United Nations, *World Investment Report, 1998* (New York and Geneva: United Nations, 1998).

regional free trade areas such as MERCOSUR and NAFTA (which will be discussed in Chapter 8). At the other end of the scale, Africa received the smallest amount of inward investment, $5 billion in 1997. The inability of Africa to attract greater investment is in part a reflection of the political unrest, armed conflict, and frequent changes in economic policy that have long held the region down.

Another way of looking at the importance of FDI inflows in an economy is to express them as a percentage of gross fixed capital formation. **Gross fixed capital formation** summarizes the total amount of capital invested in factories, stores, office buildings, and the like. Other things being equal, the greater the capital investment in an economy, the more favorable its future growth prospects are likely to be. Viewed this way, FDI can be seen as an important source of capital investment and a determinant of the future growth rate of an economy. Figure 6.4 provides some summary statistics on inward flows of FDI as a percentage of gross fixed capital formation from 1985 to 1995. In general, FDI accounts for between 3 percent and 5.4 percent of worldwide gross fixed capital formation. In 1995, the latest year for which figures are available, the percentage was 5.2 percent. As Figure 6.4 illustrates, however, when expressed as a percentage of total gross fixed capital formation, FDI is more important to the developing nations of the world. In 1995, for example, 8.2 percent of all capital investment in developed nations took the form of FDI inflows. These average figures disguise the importance of FDI for certain nations. In 1995, FDI inflows accounted for 25.7 percent of all gross fixed capital formation in China and 17.1 percent in Mexico. In comparison, FDI inflows accounted for only 5.9 percent of all capital investment in the United States. It follows that FDI is far more important as a source of investment capital to countries such as China and Mexico than it is to the United States, even though the United States accounts for a larger absolute amount of FDI inflows.

There are many developed nations other than the United States for which FDI is far more important as a source of capital. Examples include the United Kingdom, where FDI inflows accounted for 13.2 percent of all capital investment in 1995, Sweden (42.8 percent in 1995), and Australia (20 percent in 1995). But FDI inflows accounted for less than 0.1 percent of all gross fixed capital formation in the Japanese economy in 1995—a figure that reflects not only the prolonged economic recession in that country, but also the host of formal regulations and informal barriers that make it difficult for foreign companies to invest in and do business in this nation. South Korea, which historically modeled itself on Japan, also has a low level of FDI as a percentage of capital formation (1.1 percent in 1995). To the extent that capital inflows allow a country to achieve higher future growth rates, countries such as Japan and South Korea may be hurting themselves by adopting restrictive regulations with regard to FDI inflows. We shall return to this issue in the next chapter.

The Source of FDI

Since World War II, the United States has traditionally been by far the largest source country for FDI. During the late 1970s the United States was still accounting for about 47 percent of all FDI *outflows* from industrialized countries, while the second-place United Kingdom accounted for about 18 percent. US firms so dominated the growth of FDI in the 1960s and 70s, that the words *American* and *multinational* became almost synonymous. As a result, by 1980, 178 of the world's largest 382 multinationals were US firms, and 40 of them were British.[6] However, during the 1985–90 period, the United States slipped to third place behind Japan and the United Kingdom. Since then, as Figure 6.5 illustrates, the United States has regained its dominant position, accounting for $116.5 billion of FDI outflows, or 29 percent of the global total, in 1997. After a surge during the 1980s, FDI by Japanese firms has slipped, accounting for only 6.4 percent of the global total in 1997, down from 21 percent in 1990.

The increase in Japanese FDI outflows during the 1980s and the subsequent stagnation during the 1990s reflect the strong Japanese economy during the 1980s and the prolonged recession that gripped the economy during the 1990s. During the 1980s,

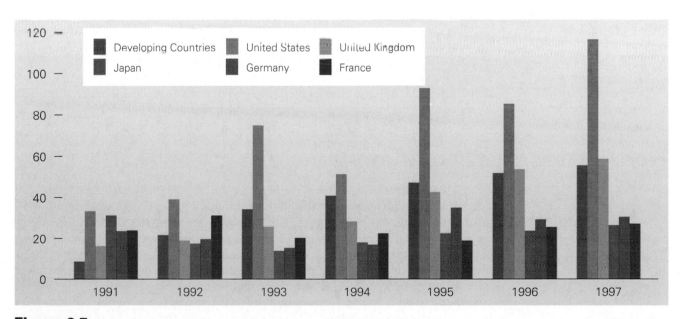

Figure 6.5

FDI Outflows, 1991–1997 ($ billions)

Japanese firms were making market share gains in industry after industry. This yielded strong growth in profits and cash flows. In addition, the Japanese currency increased in value against many other currencies during this period, including the US dollar. Data from J. P. Morgan suggest that an index measuring the value of the Japanese yen against 44 other currencies increased from 89.2 in January 1980 to a high of 130.4 in August 1993 (the index was set to 100 in 1990).[7] As the yen became more valuable, it became progressively cheaper to acquire assets in countries whose currencies were not as strong, such as the United States. Thus, the combination of strong growth in corporate profits and cash flows and a strong currency made it both easy and relatively inexpensive for Japanese firms to purchase the assets—including factories, land, office buildings, and often whole firms—in countries whose economic performance was less robust and whose currency was weaker. Also, in many countries there was an increased threat that trade barriers might be put in place to hold back the growing flood of Japanese exports (this was certainly true in the United States). This gave many Japanese firms a strong incentive to invest in production facilities overseas and serve foreign markets from those facilities, as opposed to exporting from Japan. In sum, a strong corporate performance, a strong currency, and the threat that foreign countries might erect trade barriers against Japanese exports all created a climate that helped propel Japanese FDI outflows to record levels from 1985 to 1991. The slowdown in the growth of Japanese FDI outflows since 1991 simply reflects the poor corporate performance in Japan that is the result of the country's economic malaise.

The growth of FDI outflows from the United States has been driven by a combination of favorable factors including a strong US economy, strong corporate profits and cash flow—which have given US firms the capital to invest abroad—and a relatively strong currency, particularly since 1995. Similar factors explain the continued growth of FDI outflows from the United Kingdom during the 1990s.

The other notable trend in the statistics summarized in Figure 6.5 has been the rise of FDI outflows from developing nations. These have increased from an annual average of $10.5 billion from 1985 to 1990 to a record $55 billion in 1997. The biggest investors among developing nations in 1996-97 were Hong Kong, Singapore, and South Korea. Much of the Hong Kong and Singapore investment was targeted at China and other Southeast Asian nations. While Korean firms also invested in these regions, they also targeted the United States and Europe. Such investments in 1996 propelled Daewoo of South Korea to number 52 on the list of the 100 largest multinational corporations in the world, as measured by asset value. Although the 1997/98 financial crisis in Southeast Asia caused a near-term slowdown in the investment outflow from these nations, in the long run the flow of FDI from developing nations will likely keep pace with the underlying growth in their economies.

Horizontal Foreign Direct Investment

Horizontal FDI is FDI in the same industry abroad as a firm operates in at home. We need to understand why firms go to all of the trouble of acquiring or establishing operations abroad, when the alternatives of exporting and licensing are available. Why, for example, did Electrolux choose FDI in Hungary over exporting from an existing Western European plant or licensing a Hungarian firm to build its appliances in Hungary? Other things being equal, FDI is expensive and risky compared to exporting or licensing. FDI is expensive because a firm must bear the costs of establishing production facilities in a foreign country or of acquiring a foreign enterprise. FDI is risky because of the problems associated with doing business in another culture where the "rules of the game" may be very different. Relative to firms native to a culture, there is a greater probability that a firm undertaking FDI in a foreign culture will make costly mistakes due to ignorance. When a firm exports, it need not bear the costs of FDI, and the risks associated with selling abroad can be reduced by using a native sales agent. Similarly, when a firm licenses its know-how, it need not bear the costs or risks of FDI, since these are born by the native firm that licenses the know-how. So why do so many firms apparently prefer FDI over either exporting or licensing?

The quick answer is that other things are not equal! A number of factors can alter the relative attractiveness of exporting, licensing, and FDI. We will consider these factors: (1) transportation costs, (2) market imperfections, (3) following competitors, (4) the product life cycle, and (5) location advantages.

Transportation Costs

When transportation costs are added to production costs, it becomes unprofitable to ship some products over a large distance. This is particularly true of products that have a low value-to-weight ratio and can be produced in almost any location (e.g., cement, soft drinks, etc.). For such products, relative to either FDI or licensing, the attractiveness of exporting decreases. For products with a high value-to-weight ratio, however, transport costs are normally a very minor component of total landed cost (e.g., electronic components, personal computers, medical equipment, computer software, etc.). In such cases, transportation costs have little impact on the relative attractiveness of exporting, licensing, and FDI.

Market Imperfections (Internalization Theory)

Market imperfections provide a major explanation of why firms may prefer FDI to either exporting or licensing. **Market imperfections** are factors that inhibit markets from working perfectly. The market imperfections explanation of FDI is the one favored by most economists.[8] In the international business literature, the marketing imperfection approach to FDI is typically referred to as **internalization theory.**

With regard to horizontal FDI, market imperfections arise in two circumstances: when there are impediments to the free flow of products between nations, and when there are impediments to the sale of know-how. (Licensing is a mechanism for selling know-how.) Impediments to the free flow of products between nations decrease the profitability of exporting, relative to FDI and licensing. Impediments to the sale of know-how increase the profitability of FDI relative to licensing. Thus, the market imperfections explanation predicts that FDI will be preferred whenever there are impediments that make both exporting and the sale of know-how difficult and/or expensive. We will consider each situation.

Impediments to Exporting

Governments are the main source of impediments to the free flow of products between nations. By placing tariffs on imported goods, governments can increase the cost of exporting relative to FDI and licensing. Similarly, by limiting imports through the imposition of quotas, governments increase the attractiveness of FDI and licensing. For example, the wave of FDI by Japanese auto companies in the United States during the 1980s was partly driven by protectionist threats from Congress and by quotas on the importation of Japanese cars. For Japanese auto companies, these factors have decreased the profitability of exporting and increased the profitability of FDI.

Impediments to the Sale of Know-How

The competitive advantage that many firms enjoy comes from their technological, marketing, or management know-how. Technological know-how can enable a company to build a better product; for example, Xerox's technological know-how enabled it to build the first photocopier, and Motorola's technological know-how has given it a strong competitive position in the global market for cellular telephone equipment. Alternatively, technological know-how can improve a company's production process vis-á-vis competitors; for example, many claim that Toyota's competitive advantage comes from its superior production system. Marketing know-how can enable a company to better position its products in the marketplace vis-á-vis competitors; the competitive advantage of such companies as Kellogg, H. J. Heinz, and Procter & Gamble seems to come from superior marketing know-how. Management know-how with regard to factors such as organizational structure, human relations, control systems, planning systems, inventory management, and so on can enable a company to manage its assets more efficiently than competitors. The competitive advantage of Wal-Mart, which is profiled in the next Management Focus, seems to come from its management know-how.

If we view know-how (expertise) as a competitive asset, it follows that the larger the market in which that asset is applied, the greater the profits that can be earned from the asset. Motorola can earn greater returns on its know-how by selling its cellular telephone equipment worldwide than by selling it only in North America. However, this alone does not explain why Motorola undertakes FDI (the company has production locations around the world). For Motorola to favor FDI, two conditions must hold. First, transportation costs and/or impediments to exporting must rule out exporting as an option. Second, there must be some reason Motorola cannot sell its cellular know-how to foreign producers. Since licensing is the main mechanism by which firms sell their know-how, there must be some reason Motorola is not willing to license a foreign firm to manufacture and market its cellular telephone equipment. Other things being equal, licensing might look attractive to such a firm, since it would not have to bear the costs and risks associated with FDI yet it could still earn a good return from its know-how in the form of royalty fees.

According to economic theory, there are three reasons the market does not always work well as a mechanism for selling know-how, or why licensing is not as attractive as it initially appears. First, *licensing may result in a firm's giving away its know-how to a potential foreign competitor.* For example, in the 1960s, RCA licensed its leading-edge color television technology to a number of Japanese companies, including Matsushita and Sony. At the time RCA saw licensing as a way to earn a good return from its technological know-how in the Japanese market without the costs and risks associated with FDI. However, Matsushita and Sony quickly assimilated RCA's technology and used it to enter the US market to compete directly against RCA. As a result, RCA is now a minor player in its home market, while Matsushita and Sony have a much bigger market share.

Second, *licensing does not give a firm the tight control over manufacturing, marketing, and strategy in a foreign country that may be required to profitably exploit its advantage in know-how.* With licensing, control over production, marketing, and strategy is granted to a licensee in return for a royalty fee. However, for both strategic and operational reasons, a firm may want to retain control over these functions. For example, a firm might want its foreign subsidiary to price and market very aggressively to keep a foreign competitor in check. Kodak is pursuing this strategy in Japan. The competitive attacks launched by Kodak's Japanese subsidiary are keeping its major global competitor, Fuji, busy defending its competitive position in Japan. Consequently, Fuji has pulled back from its earlier strategy of attacking Kodak aggressively in the United States. Unlike a wholly owned subsidiary, a licensee would be unlikely to accept such an imposition, since such a strategy would allow the licensee to make only a low profit or even take a loss.

Or a firm may want control over the operations of a foreign entity to take advantage of differences in factor costs among countries, producing only part of its final product in a given country, while importing other parts from where they can be produced at lower cost. Again, a licensee would be unlikely to accept such an arrangement because it would limit the licensee's autonomy. For these reasons, when tight control over a foreign entity is desirable, horizontal FDI is preferable to licensing.

Third, *a firm's know-how may not be amenable to licensing.* This is particularly true of management and marketing know-how. It is one thing to license a foreign firm to manufacture a particular product, but quite another to license the way a firm does business—how it manages its process and markets its products. Consider Toyota, a company whose competitive advantage in the global auto industry is acknowledged to come from its superior ability to manage the overall process of designing, engineering, manufacturing, and selling automobiles; that is, from its management and organizational know-how. Toyota is credited with pioneering the development of a new production process, known as lean production, that enables it to produce higher-quality automobiles at a lower cost than its global rivals.[9] Although Toyota has certain products that can be licensed, its real competitive advantage comes from its management and process know-how. These kinds of skills are difficult to articulate or codify; they cannot be written down in a simple licensing contract. They are organizationwide and have been developed over years. They are not embodied in any one individual, but instead are widely dispersed throughout the company. Toyota's skills are embedded in its organizational culture, and culture is something that cannot be licensed. Thus, as Toyota moves away from its traditional exporting strategy, it has increasingly pursued a strategy of FDI, rather than licensing foreign enterprises to produce its cars. The same is true of Wal-Mart, which is profiled in the accompanying Management Focus. Wal-Mart considered expanding internationally via franchising but decided that its culture would be difficult to replicate in franchisees. (Franchising is the market-based mechanism by which firms "sell" or "license" the right to use their brand name, subject to the franchisee adhering to certain strict requirements regarding the way it operates its business.)

All of this suggests that when one or more of the following conditions holds, markets fail as a mechanism for selling know-how and FDI is more profitable than licensing: (1) when the firm has valuable know-how that cannot be adequately protected by a licensing contract, (2) when the firm needs tight control over a foreign entity to maximize its market share and earnings in that country, and (3) when a firm's skills and know-how are not amenable to licensing.

Strategic Behavior

Another theory used to explain FDI is based on the idea that FDI flows are a reflection of strategic rivalry between firms in the global marketplace. An early variant of this argument was expounded by F. T. Knickerbocker, who looked at the relationship between FDI and rivalry in oligopolistic industries.[10] An oligopoly is an industry composed of a limited number of large firms (e.g., an industry in which four firms control 80 percent of a domestic market would be defined as an oligopoly). A critical competitive feature of such industries is interdependence of the major players: What one firm does can have an immediate impact on the major competitors, forcing a response in kind. If one firm in an oligopoly cuts prices, this can take market share away from its competitors, forcing them to respond with similar price cuts to retain their market share.

This kind of imitative behavior can take many forms in an oligopoly. One firm raises prices, the others follow; someone expands capacity, and the rivals imitate lest they be left in a disadvantageous position in the future. Building on this, Knickerbocker argued that the same kind of imitative behavior characterizes FDI. Consider an oligopoly in the United States in which three firms—A, B, and C—dominate the market. Firm A establishes a subsidiary in France. Firms B and C reflect that if this investment is successful, it may knock out their export business to France and give Firm A a first-mover advantage. Furthermore, Firm A might discover some competitive asset in France that it could repatriate to the United States to torment Firms B and C on their native soil. Given these possibilities, Firms B and C decide to follow Firm A and establish operations in France.

There is evidence that such imitative behavior does lead to FDI. Studies that looked at FDI by US firms during the 1950s and 60s show that firms based in

MANAGEMENT FOCUS
Wal-Mart's International Expansion

http://www.wal-mart.com

Founded by Sam Walton in the 1960s, Wal-Mart had grown to become the largest discount retailer in the United States with annual sales of $32.6 billion by the early 1990s. Wal-Mart's spectacular growth from a small Arkansas retailer to a national powerhouse was based on a first-class management team that pursued a number of innovative operations strategies that backed up the company's commitment to deliver a large selection of high-value merchandise at a low cost to consumers.

The firm pioneered the development of a "hub and spoke" distribution system, where central distribution warehouses were strategically located to serve clusters of stores. This helped drive down inventory and logistics costs. The firm was also one of the first to utilize computer-based information systems to track in-store sales and transmit this information to suppliers. The information provided by these systems was used to determine pricing and stocking strategy and to better manage inventories. Today Wal-Mart is still a leader in information systems. All Wal-Mart stores, distribution centers, and suppliers are linked via sophisticated information systems and satellite-based communications systems that allow for daily adjustments to orders, inventory, and prices. In addition, the company is famous for a dynamic and egalitarian culture that grants major decision-making authority to store managers, department managers, and individual employees (referred to as "associates"). Wal-Mart is renowned for treating its employees extremely well, but at the same time, for demanding commitment and excellent performance from them. This culture is backed up with a generous profit-sharing plan and stock ownership plan for all employees, including associates. By such means, Wal-Mart has developed a culture and control system that creates incentives for associates and managers to give their best for the company.

Despite its success, by 1991 Wal-Mart was encountering significant problems. With 1,568 stores nationwide its growth prospects in the United States were looking more limited. Wal-Mart decided to try to expand its operations outside the United States and build a global brand. The company debated a number of options for expansion, including licensing its brand name to franchisees, but soon decided that it would be best to expand via wholly owned subsidiaries in foreign countries where that was permitted by local regulations. The company concluded that its competitive advantage was based on the combination of culture and supporting information and logistics systems, and that such a culture and systems would be difficult to transfer to franchisees. It felt that the management know-how that underlay its culture and systems was not amenable to franchising. In 1992, Wal-Mart began its foreign adventure by establishing six stores in Mexico. By the end of 1997, it had 402 stores in that country, along with 144 in Canada, 13 in Puerto Rico, 9 in Argentina, 8 in Brazil, 3 in China, and 3 in Indonesia. It had also announced the decision to purchase 21 Wertkauf hypermarket stores in Germany, its first venture in Europe. As part of its entry strategy, once it has established or acquired a store in a foreign country, Wal-Mart transfers some of its US associates to that store for two to three years to help establish the back-office systems and transfer the Wal-Mart culture to the new associates.

The strategy seems to be working. Wal-Mart's international stores contributed over $5 billion in sales to the company's $120 billion revenues in 1997, and they are already posting profits.

Source: *Wal-Mart Annual Reports,* 1996 and 1997, and news releases and other information posted on the company's Web site, http://www.wal-mart.com.

oligopolistic industries tended to imitate each other's FDI.[11] The same phenomenon has been observed with regard to FDI undertaken by Japanese firms during the 1980s.[12] For example, Toyota and Nissan responded to investments by Honda in the United States and Europe by undertaking their own FDI in the United States and Europe.

It is possible to extend Knickerbocker's theory to embrace the concept of multi-point competition. **Multipoint competition** arises when two or more enterprises encounter each other in different regional markets, national markets, or industries. Economic theory suggests that rather like chess players jockeying for advantage, firms will try to match each other's moves in different markets to try to hold each other in check. The idea is to ensure that a rival does not gain a commanding position in one market and then use the profits generated there to subsidize competitive attacks in other markets. Kodak and Fuji Photo Film Co., for example, compete against each other around the world. If Kodak enters a particular foreign market, Fuji will not be far behind. Fuji feels compelled to follow Kodak to ensure that Kodak does not gain a dominant position in the foreign market that it could then leverage to gain a competitive advantage elsewhere. The converse also holds, with Kodak following Fuji when the Japanese firm is the first to enter a foreign market. Similarly, in the opening case we saw how Electrolux's expansion into Eastern Europe, Latin America, and Asia was in part being driven by similar moves by its global competitors, such as Whirlpool and General Electric. The FDI behavior of Electrolux, Whirlpool, and General Electric might be explained in part by multipoint competition and rivalry in a global oligopoly.

Although Knickerbocker's theory and its extensions can help to explain imitative FDI behavior by firms in oligopolistic industries, it does not explain why the first firm in an oligopoly decides to undertake FDI, rather than to export or license. In contrast, the market imperfections explanation addresses this phenomenon. The imitative theory also does not address the issue of whether FDI is more efficient than exporting or licensing for expanding abroad. Again, the market imperfections approach addresses the efficiency issue. For these reasons, many economists favor the market imperfections explanation for FDI, although most would agree that the imitative explanation tells part of the story.

The Product Life Cycle

We considered Raymond Vernon's product life-cycle theory in Chapter 4, but what we did not dwell on was Vernon's contention that his theory also explains FDI. Vernon argued that often the same firms that pioneer a product in their home markets undertake FDI to produce a product for consumption in foreign markets. Thus, Xerox introduced the photocopier in the United States, and it was Xerox that set up production facilities in Japan (Fuji-Xerox) and Great Britain (Rank-Xerox) to serve those markets.

Vernon's view is that firms undertake FDI at particular stages in the life cycle of a product they have pioneered. They invest in other advanced countries when local demand in those countries grows large enough to support local production (as Xerox did). They subsequently shift production to developing countries when product standardization and market saturation give rise to price competition and cost pressures. Investment in developing countries, where labor costs are lower, is seen as the best way to reduce costs.

Vernon's theory has merit. Firms do invest in a foreign country when demand in that country will support local production, and they do invest in low-cost locations (e.g., developing countries) when cost pressures become intense.[13] However, Vernon's theory fails to explain why it is profitable for a firm to undertake FDI at such times, rather than continuing to export from its home base and rather than licensing a foreign firm to produce its product. Just because demand in a foreign country is large enough to support local production, it does not necessarily follow that local production is the most profitable option. It may still be more profitable to produce at home and export to that country (to realize the scale economies that arise from serving the global market from one location). Alternatively, it may be more profitable for the firm to license a foreign firm to produce its product for sale in that country. The product life-cycle theory ignores these options and, instead, simply argues that once a foreign market is large enough to support local production, FDI will occur. This limits its explanatory power and its usefulness to business in that it fails to identify when it is profitable to invest abroad.

Location-Specific Advantages

The British economist John Dunning has argued that in addition to the various factors discussed above, location-specific advantages can help explain the nature and direction of FDI.[14] By **location-specific advantages,** Dunning means the advantages that arise from using resource endowments or assets that are tied to a particular foreign location and that a firm finds valuable to combine with its own unique assets (such as the firm's technological, marketing, or management know-how). Dunning accepts the internalization argument that market failures make it difficult for a firm to license its own unique assets (know-how). Therefore, he argues that combining location-specific assets or resource endowments *and* the firm's own unique assets often requires FDI. It requires the firm to establish production facilities where those foreign assets or resource endowments are located (Dunning refers to this argument as the **eclectic paradigm).**

An obvious example of Dunning's arguments are natural resources, such as oil and other minerals, which are by their character specific to certain locations. Dunning suggests that a firm must undertake FDI to exploit such foreign resources. This explains the FDI undertaken by many of the world's oil companies, which have to invest where oil is located to combine their technological and managerial knowledge with this valuable location-specific resource. Another example is valuable human resources, such as low-cost highly-skilled labor. The cost and skill of labor varies from country to country. Since labor is not internationally mobile, according to Dunning it makes sense for a firm to locate production facilities where the cost and skills of local labor are most suited to its particular production processes. One reason Electrolux is building factories in China is because China has an abundant supply of low-cost but well-educated and skilled labor. Thus, other factors aside, China is a good location for producing household appliances both for the Chinese market and for export elsewhere.

However, Dunning's theory has implications that go beyond basic resources such as minerals and labor. Consider Silicon Valley, which is the world center for the computer and semiconductor industry. Many of the world's major computer and semiconductor companies, such as Apple Computer, Silicon Graphics, and Intel, are located close to each other in the Silicon Valley region of California. As a result, much of the cutting-edge research and product development in computers and semiconductors occurs here. According to Dunning's arguments, knowledge being generated in Silicon Valley with regard to the design and manufacture of computers and semiconductors is available nowhere else in the world. As it is commercialized, that knowledge diffuses throughout the world, but the leading edge of knowledge generation in the computer and semiconductor industries is to be found in Silicon Valley. In Dunning's language, this means Silicon Valley has a *location-specific advantage* in the generation of knowledge related to the computer and semiconductor industries. In part, this advantage comes from the sheer concentration of intellectual talent in this area, and in part it arises from a network of informal contacts that allow firms to benefit from each other's knowledge generation. Economists refer to such knowledge "spillovers" as **externalities,** and one well-established theory suggests that firms can benefit from such externalities by locating close to their source.[15]

In so far as this is the case, it makes sense for foreign computer and semiconductor firms to invest in research and (perhaps) production facilities so they too can learn about and utilize valuable new knowledge before those based elsewhere, thereby giving them a competitive advantage in the global marketplace. Evidence suggests that European, Japanese, South Korean, and Taiwanese computer and semiconductor firms are investing in the Silicon Valley region, precisely because they wish to benefit from the externalities that arise there.[16] In a similar vein, others have argued that direct investment by foreign firms in the US biotechnology industry has been motivated by desires to gain access to the unique location-specific technological knowledge of US biotechnology firms.[17] Dunning's theory, therefore, seems to be a useful addition to those outlined above, for it helps explain like no other how location factors affect the direction of FDI.

Vertical Foreign Direct Investment

Vertical FDI takes two forms. First, there is backward vertical FDI into an industry abroad that provides inputs for a firm's domestic production processes. Historically, most backward vertical FDI has been in extractive industries (e.g., oil extraction, bauxite mining, tin mining, copper mining). The objective has been to provide inputs into a firm's downstream operations (e.g., oil refining, aluminum smelting and fabrication, tin smelting and fabrication). Firms such as Royal Dutch Shell, British Petroleum (BP), RTZ, Consolidated Gold Field, and Alcoa are among the classic examples of such vertically integrated multinationals.

A second form of vertical FDI is forward vertical FDI. Forward vertical FDI is FDI into an industry abroad that sells the outputs of a firm's domestic production processes. Forward vertical FDI is less common than backward vertical FDI. For example, when Volkswagen entered the US market, it acquired a large number of dealers rather than distribute its cars through independent US dealers.

With both horizontal and vertical FDI, the question that must be answered is why would a firm go to all the trouble and expense of setting up operations in a foreign country? Why, for example, did petroleum companies such as BP and Royal Dutch Shell vertically integrate backward into oil production abroad? Clearly, the location-specific advantages argument that we reviewed in the previous section helps explain the *direction* of such FDI; vertically integrated multinationals in extractive industries invest where the raw materials are. However, this argument does not clarify why they did not simply import raw materials extracted by local producers. And why do companies such as Volkswagen feel it is necessary to acquire their own dealers in foreign markets, when in theory it might seem less costly to rely on foreign dealers? There are two basic answers to these kinds of questions. The first is a strategic behavior argument, and the second draws on the market imperfections approach.

Strategic Behavior

According to economic theory, by vertically integrating backward to gain control over the source of raw material, a firm can raise entry barriers and shut new competitors out of an industry.[18] Such strategic behavior involves vertical FDI if the raw material is found abroad. An example occurred in the 1930s, when commercial smelting of aluminum was pioneered by North American firms such as Alcoa and Alcan Aluminum Ltd. Aluminum is derived by smelting bauxite. Although bauxite is a common mineral, the percentage of aluminum in bauxite is typically so low that it is not economical to mine and smelt. During the 1930s, only one large-scale deposit of bauxite with an economical percentage of aluminum had been discovered, and it was on the Caribbean island of Trinidad. Alcoa and Alcan vertically integrated backward and acquired ownership of the deposit. This action created a barrier to entry into the aluminum industry. Potential competitors were deterred because they could not get access to high-grade bauxite—it was all owned by Alcoa and Alcan. Those that did enter the industry had to use lower-grade bauxite than Alcan and Alcoa and found themselves at a cost disadvantage. This situation persisted until the 1950s and 1960s, when new high-grade deposits were discovered in Australia and Indonesia.

However, despite the bauxite example, the opportunities for barring entry through vertical FDI seem far too limited to explain the incidence of vertical FDI among the world's multinationals. In most extractive industries, mineral deposits are not as concentrated as in the case of bauxite in the 1930s, while new deposits are constantly being discovered. Consequently, any attempt to monopolize all viable raw material deposits is bound to prove very expensive if not impossible.

Another strand of the strategic behavior explanation of vertical FDI sees such investment not as an attempt to build entry barriers, but as an attempt to circumvent the barriers established by firms already doing business in a country. This may explain Volkswagen's decision to establish its own dealer network when it entered the North American auto market. The market was then dominated by GM, Ford, and Chrysler. Each firm had its own network of independent dealers. Volkswagen felt that the only way to get quick access to the United States market was to promote its cars through independent dealerships.

Market Imperfections

As in the case of horizontal FDI, a more general explanation of vertical FDI can be found in the market imperfections approach.[19] The market imperfections approach offers two explanations for vertical FDI. As with horizontal FDI, the first explanation revolves around the idea that there are impediments to the sale of know-how through the market mechanism. The second explanation is based upon the idea that investments in specialized assets expose the investing firm to hazards that can be reduced only through vertical FDI.

Impediments to the Sale of Know-How

Consider the case of oil refining companies such as British Petroleum and Royal Dutch Shell. Historically, these firms pursued backward vertical FDI to supply their British and Dutch oil refining facilities with crude oil. When this occurred in the early decades of this century, neither Great Britain nor the Netherlands had domestic oil supplies. However, why did these firms not just import oil from firms in oil-rich countries such as Saudi Arabia and Kuwait?

Originally there were no Saudi Arabian or Kuwaiti firms with the technological expertise for finding and extracting oil. BP and Royal Dutch Shell had to develop this know-how themselves to get access to oil. This alone does not explain FDI, however, for once BP and Shell had developed the necessary know-how they could have licensed it to Saudi Arabian or Kuwaiti firms. However, as we saw in the case of horizontal FDI, licensing can be self-defeating as a mechanism for the sale of know-how. If the oil refining firms had licensed their prospecting and extraction know-how to Saudi Arabian or Kuwaiti firms, they would have risked giving away their technological know-how to those firms, creating future competitors in the process. Once they had the know-how, the Saudi and Kuwaiti firms might have gone prospecting for oil in other parts of the world, competing directly against BP and Royal Dutch Shell. Thus, it made more sense for these firms to undertake backward vertical FDI and extract the oil themselves instead of licensing their hard-earned technological expertise to local firms.

Generalizing from this example, the prediction is that backward vertical FDI will occur when a firm has the knowledge and the ability to extract raw materials in another country and there is no efficient producer in that country that can supply raw materials to the firm.

Investment in Specialized Assets

Another strand of the market imperfections argument predicts that vertical FDI will occur when a firm must invest in specialized assets whose value depends on inputs provided by a foreign supplier. In this context, a specialized asset is an asset designed to perform a specific task and whose value is significantly reduced in its next-best use.

Consider the case of an aluminum refinery, which is designed to refine bauxite ore and produce aluminum. Bauxite ores vary in content and chemical composition from deposit to deposit. Each type of ore requires a different type of refinery. Running one type of bauxite through a refinery designed for another type increases production costs by 20 percent to 100 percent.[20] Thus, the value of an investment in an aluminum refinery depends on the availability of the desired kind of bauxite ore.

Imagine that a US aluminum company must decide whether to invest in an aluminum refinery designed to refine a certain type of ore. Assume further that this ore is available only through an Australian mining firm at a single bauxite mine. Using a different type of ore in the refinery would raise production costs by at least 20 percent. Therefore, the value of the US company's investment depends on the price it must pay the Australian firm for this bauxite. Recognizing this, once the US company has invested in a new refinery, what is to stop the Australian firm from raising bauxite prices? Absolutely nothing; and once it has made the investment, the US firm is locked into its relationship with the Australian supplier. The Australian firm can increase bauxite prices, secure in the knowledge that as long as the increase in the total production costs is less than 20 percent, the US firm will continue to buy from it. (It would become economical for the US firm to buy from another supplier only if total production costs increased by more than 20 percent.)

The US firm can reduce the risk of the Australian firm opportunistically raising prices in this manner by buying out the Australian firm. If the US firm can buy the Australian firm, or its bauxite mine, it need no longer fear that bauxite prices will be increased after it has invested in the refinery. In other words, it would make economic sense for the US firm to engage in vertical FDI. In practice, these kinds of considerations have driven aluminum firms to pursue vertical FDI to such a degree that in 1976, 91 percent of the total volume of bauxite was transferred within vertically integrated firms.[21]

IMPLICATIONS FOR BUSINESS

The implications of the theories of horizontal and vertical FDI for business practice are relatively straightforward. First, the location-specific advantages argument associated with John Dunning does help explain the *direction* of FDI, both with regard to horizontal and vertical FDI. However, the argument does not explain *why* firms prefer FDI to licensing or to exporting. In this regard, from both an explanatory and a business perspective, perhaps the most useful theory is the market imperfections approach. With regard to horizontal FDI, this approach identifies with some precision how the relative rates of return associated with horizontal FDI, exporting, and licensing vary with circumstances. The theory suggests that exporting is preferable to licensing and horizontal FDI as long as transport costs are minor and tariff barriers are trivial. As transport costs and/or tariff barriers increase, exporting becomes unprofitable, and the choice is between horizontal FDI and licensing. Since horizontal FDI is more costly and more risky than licensing, other things being equal, the theory argues that licensing is preferable to horizontal FDI. Other things are seldom equal, however. Although licensing may work, it is not an attractive option when one or more of the following conditions exist: (*a*) the firm has valuable know-how that cannot be adequately protected by a licensing contract, (*b*) the firm needs tight control over a foreign entity to maximize its market share and earnings in that country, and (*c*) a firm's skills and know-how are not amenable to licensing. Figure 6.6 presents these considerations as a decision tree.

Figure 6.6

A Decision Framework

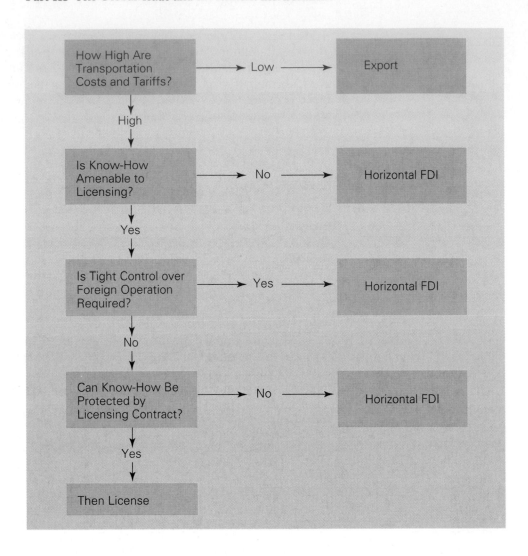

Firms for which licensing is not a good option tend to be clustered in three types of industries:

1. High-technology industries where protecting firm-specific expertise is of paramount importance and licensing is hazardous.
2. Global oligopolies, where competitive interdependence requires that multinational firms maintain tight control over foreign operations so that they have the ability to launch coordinated attacks against their global competitors (as Kodak has done with Fuji).
3. Industries where intense cost pressures require that multinational firms maintain tight control over foreign operations (so they can disperse manufacturing to locations around the globe where factor costs are most favorable to minimize costs).

Although empirical evidence is limited, the majority of the evidence seems to support these conjectures.[22]

Firms for which licensing is a good option tend to be in industries whose conditions are opposite to those specified above. Licensing tends to be more common (and more profitable) in fragmented, low-technology industries in which globally dispersed manufacturing is not an option. A good example is the fast food industry. McDonald's has expanded globally by using a franchising strategy. Franchising is essentially the service-industry version of licensing—although it normally involves much longer-term commitments than licensing. With franchising, the firm licenses its brand name to a foreign firm in return for a percentage of the franchisee's profits. The franchising contract specifies the conditions that the franchisee must fulfill if it is to use the franchisor's brand name. Thus, McDonald's allows foreign firms to use its brand name as long as they agree to run their restaurants on exactly the same lines as McDonald's restaurants elsewhere in the world. This strategy makes sense for McDonald's because (a) like many services, fast food cannot be exported, (b) franchising economizes the costs and risks associated with opening foreign markets, (c) unlike technological know-how, brand names are relatively easy to protect using a contract, (d) there is no compelling reason for McDonald's to have tight control over franchisees, and (e) McDonald's know-how, in terms of how to run a fast food restaurant, is amenable to being specified in a written contract (e.g., the contract specifies the details of how to run a McDonald's restaurant).

In contrast to the market imperfections approach, the product life-cycle theory and Knickerbocker's theory of horizontal FDI tend to be less useful from a business perspective. These two theories are descriptive rather than analytical. They do a good job of describing the historical pattern of FDI, but they do a relatively poor job of identifying the factors that influence the relative profitability of FDI, licensing, and exporting. The issue of licensing as an alternative to FDI is ignored by both of these theories.

Finally, with regard to vertical FDI, both the market imperfections approach and the strategic behavior approach have some useful implications for business practice. The strategic behavior approach points out that vertical FDI may be a way of building barriers to entry into an industry. The strength of the market imperfections approach is that it points out the conditions under which vertical FDI might be preferable to the alternatives. Most importantly, the market imperfections approach points to the importance of investments in specialized assets and imperfections in the market for know-how as factors that increase the relative attractiveness of vertical FDI.

Chapter Summary

This chapter reviewed theories that attempt to explain the pattern of FDI between countries. This objective takes on added importance in light of the expanding volume of FDI in the world economy. As we saw early in the chapter, the volume of FDI has grown more rapidly than the volume of world trade in recent years. We also noted that any theory seeking to explain FDI must explain why firms go to the trouble of acquiring or establishing operations abroad when the alternatives of exporting and licensing are available.

We reviewed a number of theories that attempt to explain horizontal and vertical FDI. With regard to horizontal FDI, it was argued that the market imperfections and location-specific advantages approaches might have the greatest explanatory power and therefore be most useful for business practice. This is not to belittle the explanations for horizontal FDI put forward by Vernon and Knickerbocker, since these theories also

have value in explaining the pattern of FDI in the world economy. Still, both theories are weakened by their failure to explicitly consider the factors that drive the choice among exporting, licensing, and FDI. Finally, with regard to vertical FDI, it was argued that the strategic behavior and market imperfections approaches both have a certain amount of explanatory power.

This chapter made the following points:

1. Foreign direct investment occurs when a firm invests directly in facilities to produce a product in a foreign country. It also occurs when a firm buys an existing enterprise in a foreign country.

2. Horizontal FDI is FDI in the same industry abroad as a firm operates at home. Vertical FDI is FDI in an industry abroad that provides inputs into a firm's domestic operations.

3. Any theory seeking to explain FDI must explain why firms go to the trouble of acquiring or establishing operations abroad when the alternatives of exporting and licensing are available.

4. Several factors characterized FDI trends over the past 20 years; (1) there has been a rapid increase in the total volume of FDI undertaken; (2) there has been some decline in the *relative* importance of the United States as a source for FDI, while several other countries, most notably Japan, have increased their share of total FDI outflows; (3) an increasing share of FDI seems to be directed at the developing nations of Asia and Eastern Europe, while the United States has become a major recipient of FDI; and (4) there has been a notable increase in the amount of FDI undertaken by firms based in developing nations.

5. High transportation costs and/or tariffs imposed on imports help explain why many firms prefer horizontal FDI or licensing over exporting.

6. Impediments to the sale of know-how explain why firms prefer horizontal FDI to licensing. These impediments arise when: (*a*) a firm has valuable know-how that cannot be adequately protected by a licensing contract, (*b*) a firm needs tight control over a foreign entity to maximize its market share and earnings in that country, and (*c*) a firm's skills and know-how are not amenable to licensing.

7. Knickerbocker's theory suggests that much FDI is explained by imitative strategic behavior by rival

firms in an oligopolistic industry. However, this theory does not address the issue of whether FDI is more efficient than exporting or licensing for expanding abroad.

8. Vernon's product life-cycle theory suggests that firms undertake FDI at particular stages in the life cycle of products they have pioneered. However, Vernon's theory does not address the issue of whether FDI is more efficient than exporting or licensing for expanding abroad.

9. Dunning has argued that location-specific advantages are of considerable importance in explaining the nature and direction of FDI. According to Dunning, firms undertake FDI to exploit resource endowments or assets that are location-specific.

10. Backward vertical FDI may be explained as an attempt to create barriers to entry by gaining control over the source of material inputs into the downstream stage of a production process. Forward vertical FDI may be seen as an attempt to circumvent entry barriers and gain access to a national market.

11. The market imperfections approach suggests that vertical FDI is a way of reducing a firm's exposure to the risks that arise from investments in specialized assets.

12. From a business perspective, the most useful theory is probably the market imperfections approach, because it identifies how the relative profit rates associated with horizontal FDI, exporting, and licensing vary with circumstances.

Critical Discussion Questions

1. In recent years, Japanese FDI in the United States has grown far more rapidly than US FDI in Japan. Why do you think this is the case? What are the implications of this trend?

2. Compare and contrast these explanations of horizontal FDI: the market imperfections approach, Vernon's product life-cycle theory, and Knickerbocker's theory of FDI. Which theory do you think offers the best explanation of the historical pattern of horizontal FDI? Why?

3. Compare and contrast these explanations of vertical FDI: the strategic behavior approach and the market imperfections approach. Which theory do you think offers the better explanation of the historical pattern of vertical FDI? Why?

4. You are the international manager of a US business that has just developed a revolutionary new personal computer that can perform the same functions as IBM and Apple computers and their clones but costs only half as much to manufacture. Your CEO has asked you to formulate a recommendation for how to expand into Western Europe. Your options are (*a*) to export from the United States, (*b*) to license a European firm to manufacture and market the computer in Europe, and (*c*) to set up a wholly owned subsidiary in Europe. Evaluate the pros and cons of each alternative and suggest a course of action to your CEO.

CLOSING CASE   Honda in North America

One of the most dramatic trends during the 1980s was the surge in Japanese direct investment in the United States. Leading this trend were the Japanese automobile companies, particularly Honda, Mazda, Nissan, and Toyota. Collectively these companies invested $5.3 billion in North American-based automobile assembly plants between 1982 and 1991. The early leader in this trend was Honda, which by 1991 had invested $1.13 billion in three North American auto assembly plants—two major plants in central Ohio and a smaller one in Ontario, Canada. Honda has invested an additional $500 million in an engine plant in Ohio that supplies its Ohio assembly plants. The company has also established major R&D and engineering facilities at its Ohio plants and has purchased an existing automotive test center—adjacent to the assembly plants—from the state of Ohio for $31 million.

As a result of these investments, Honda now employs 10,000 workers in its central Ohio plants and pumps a payroll of $7.3 million per week into the local economy. Of the 854,879 cars that Honda sold in the United States during 1990, nearly two-thirds were built at its three North American assembly plants—the vast majority of them in Ohio. Honda says the domestic content of its American-built cars is 75 percent, meaning that three-fourths of the final cost of a car is accounted for by North American labor, components, and other costs. The remaining 25 percent of the cost is accounted for by imported parts.

Honda had considered establishing auto assembly operations in North America as early as 1974 but ruled out investment then because of the high cost of North American labor. In 1977, Honda announced it had selected a site in the small town of Marysville, Ohio, for a motorcycle assembly plant. Motorcycle production would test the ground for the possible manufacture of automobiles. This experiment was deemed necessary because Honda's internal feasibility studies still predicted that high labor costs and poor productivity would make North American-based automobile production unprofitable. However, Honda quickly realized that its assumptions about US workers' poor productivity were unfounded, and in 1979 it announced plans to construct an automobile assembly plant adjacent to its Marysville motorcycle plant. Two years later, in

November 1982, the first US-built Honda was assembled, and by 1984 the plant was producing 150,000 automobiles per year.

Throughout the 1980s, Honda's direct investment in North America produced complementary investments by many of its Japanese suppliers of component parts. By 1989, at least 29 major Japanese supplier companies had established transplant manufacturing facilities in Ohio to supply Honda with component parts. In addition, 33 other Japanese firms had invested in the United States to supply Honda and several other Japanese and US automobile manufacturers. Honda required many of these companies to build their plants close to its Ohio complex so they could introduce a just-in-time production system, in which parts are delivered to the assembly plants just as they are needed. This technique virtually eliminates the need to hold in-process inventories and is regarded as a major cost savings. In addition, Honda wanted major suppliers close by so they could conveniently collaborate on the design of major components and on techniques for reducing costs and boosting quality.

A number of concerns seem to underlie Honda's decision to invest in North America. First, it is widely assumed that many Japanese firms, including Honda, did this largely to circumvent the threat of protectionist trade legislation, which seemed very real following the rapid increase in Japanese automobile exports to North America during the 1970s and early 80s. The threat of protectionism—especially the 1981 Voluntary Restraint Agreement under which Japanese companies agreed not to further increase their imports into the United States—may have accelerated Honda's late-1980s investments in Ohio. A second concern was probably the sharp rise in the value of the Japanese yen against the US dollar during 1987. This dramatically increased the cost of exporting both finished automobiles and component parts from Japan to North America. This also may have accelerated Honda's investments in the late 1980s.

However, it is also necessary to consider Honda's investment in North America in the context of its long-term corporate strategy. As a latecomer to automobile production in Japan, Honda had always struggled to be profitable in the intensely competitive Japanese auto industry. Against this background, Honda's North American assembly plants can be seen as part of a strategy designed to circumvent Toyota and Nissan and to make major inroads in the United States market ahead of its Japanese rivals. Underlying this strategy was Honda's strong belief that products need to be customized to the requirements of local markets. To paraphrase Hideo Sugiura, the former chairman of Honda, there are subtle differences, from country to country and from region to region, in the ways a product is used and what customers expect of it. If a corporation believes that simply because a product has succeeded in a certain market it will sell well throughout the world, it is likely destined for large and expensive errors or even failure. To produce products that account for local differences in customer tastes and preferences, Sugiura claimed that a company needed to establish top-to-bottom engineering, design, and production facilities in each major market in which it competed. Thus, in the late 1970s, Honda decided to invest in North America. Its success can be judged by the fact that although it was only the fourth largest automobile manufacturer in Japan in 1990 (with 9.3 percent of the market, compared to Toyota's 32.5 percent), it was the second largest Japanese automobile manufacturer in the United States (with 6.14 per-

cent of the market, compared to first-place Toyota's 7.6 percent).

http://www.honda.com

Sources: A. Mair, R. Florida, and M. Kenney, "The New Geography of Automobile Production: Japanese Transplants in North America," *Economic Geography* 64 (1988), pp. 352–73; H. Sugiura, "How Honda Localizes Its Global Strategy," *Sloan Management Review*, Fall 1990, pp. 77–82; S. Toy, N. Gross, and J. B. Treece, "The Americanization of Honda," *Business Week*, April 25, 1988, pp. 90–96; and P. Magnusson, J. B. Treece, and W. C. Symonds, "Honda: Is It an American Car?" *Business Week*, November 18, 1991, pp. 105–9.

Case Discussion Questions

1. Drawing on the market imperfections approach to FDI, explain why Honda chose to invest in production facilities in the United States, as opposed to contracting with an established US auto company to produce its cars under licensing in the United States?

2. Which of the theories of FDI reviewed in this chapter best explain Honda's FDI into the United States?

3. Are there aspects of Honda's investment in the United States that are not explained by the theories of FDI reviewed in this chapter? What are these aspects and how would you explain them?

Notes

1. United Nations, *World Investment Report, 1997* (New York and Geneva, United Nations, 1998).

2. World Trade Organization, *Annual Report, 1998* (Geneva, WTO, 1998) and United Nations, *World Investment Report, 1997* (New York and Geneva, United Nations, 1997).

3. United Nations, *World Investment Report*.

4. Ibid.

5. Ibid.

6. M. Kidron and R. Segal, *The New State of the World Atlas* (New York: Simon & Schuster, 1987).

7. The data can be found on J. P. Morgan's Web site, http://www.jpmorgan.com.

8. For example, see S. H. Hymer, *The International Operations of National Firms: A Study of Direct Foreign Investment* (Cambridge, MA: MIT Press, 1976); A. M. Rugman, *Inside the Multinationals: The Economics of Internal Markets* (New York: Columbia University Press, 1981); D. J. Teece, "Multinational Enterprise, Internal Governance, and Industrial Organization," *American Economic Review* 75 (May 1983), pp. 233–38; and C. W. L. Hill and W. C. Kim, "Searching for a Dynamic Theory

of the Multinational Enterprise: A Transaction Cost Model," *Strategic Management Journal* (special issue) 9 (1988), pp. 93–104.

9. J. P. Womack, D. T. Jones, and D. Roos, *The Machine That Changed the World* (New York: Rawson Associates, 1990).

10. The argument is most often associated with F. T. Knickerbocker, *Oligopolistic Reaction and Multinational Enterprise* (Boston: Harvard Business School Press, 1973).

11. The studies are summarized in R. E. Caves, *Multinational Enterprise and Economic Analysis*, 2nd ed. (Cambridge, UK: Cambridge University Press, 1996).

12. See R. E. Caves, "Japanese Investment in the US: Lessons for the Economic Analysis of Foreign Investment," *The World Economy*, 16 (1993), pp. 279–300; B. Kogut, and S. J. Chang, "Technological Capabilities and Japanese Direct Investment in the United States," *Review of Economics and Statistics*, 73 (1991), pp. 401–43; and J. Anand and B. Kogut, "Technological Capabilities of Countries, Firm Rivalry, and Foreign Direct Investment," *Journal of International Business Studies*, Third Quarter (1997), 445–65.

13. For the use of Vernon's theory to explain Japanese direct investment in the United States and Europe, see S. Thomsen, "Japanese Direct Investment in the European Community," *The World Economy*, 16 (1993), pp. 301–15.

14. J. H. Dunning, *Explaining International Production*, (London: Unwin Hyman, 1988).

15. P. Krugman, "Increasing Returns and Economic Geography, *Journal of Political Economy*, 99, no. 3 (1991), pp. 483–99.

16. J. H. Dunning and R. Narula, "Transpacific Foreign Direct Investment and the Investment Development Path," *South Carolina Essays in International Business*, 10 (May 1995).

17. W. Shan and J. Song, "Foreign Direct Investment and the Sourcing of Technological Advantage: Evidence from the Biotechnology Industry, *Journal of International Business Studies*, Second Quarter (1997), pp. 267–84.

18. R. E. Caves, *Multinational Enterprise and Economic Analysis*.

19. J. F. Hennart, "Upstream Vertical Integration in the Aluminum and Tin Industries," *Journal of Economic Behavior and Organization*, 9 (1988), pp. 281–99; and O. E. Williamson, *The Economic Institutions of Capitalism* (New York: Free Press, 1985).

20. Hennart, "Upstream Vertical Integration."

21. Ibid.

22. See R. E. Caves, *Multinational Enterprise and Economic Analysis* (Cambridge, UK: Cambridge University Press, 1982).

CHAPTER SEVEN

THE POLITICAL ECONOMY OF FOREIGN DIRECT INVESTMENT

Toyota in France

The French have always been somewhat ambivalent toward foreign direct investment. In the 1960s and 1970s, successive French governments used a mixture of socialist and nationalist rhetoric to spurn foreign investment proposals by companies such as General Motors. These governments took the view that direct investment by foreign multinational enterprises would damage the French economy. Government officials believed strongly in the need for France to build its own indigenous enterprises. They argued that the economic power enjoyed by foreign multinationals gave them the ability to dominate any markets they entered, at the expense of locally grown enterprises. Successive socialist governments in France expressed a desire to control economic activity through extensive planning and the nationalization of private businesses. Letting foreign multinationals into the country was thought to be inconsistent with this goal.

France's policy toward inward foreign direct investment began to change in the early 1980s. Although France's socialist president, Francois Mitterrand, remained suspicious of direct investment by foreign firms, his successive administrations reduced the bureaucratic obstacles to foreign investment and created a more coherent mechanism for luring inward investment. The change in policy reflected the growing realization that inward investment could have substantial benefits for the French economy, including the creation of jobs, the transfer of valuable technology, and the increase of exports that would bolster France's balance-of-payments position. The shift toward a more liberal attitude accelerated under Mitterrand's successor, Gaullist president Jacques Chirac. Chirac, who espouses a free market philosophy with a unique French twist, has made encouraging inward investment a priority. The results have been striking. According to recent UN data, in 1996 France attracted $21 billion in inward investment, coming in fourth behind the United States, China, and the United Kingdom. Between 1991 and 1996, the cumulative total for France stood at $119 billion, forcing the United Kingdom into second place within Europe. Among the foreign companies that have undertaken major investments in France are Toyota, IBM, Motorola, and Federal Express Corp.

One noteworthy inward investment in recent years was Toyota's December 1997 decision to invest $656.8 million in a car plant in France to produce 150,000 vehicles per year. The investment represents the Japanese company's second major commitment to Europe. Toyota already has extensive operations in the United Kingdom. The decision to locate in France was taken despite intense lobbying from British government officials, who wanted Toyota to expand its UK operations. The investment represents a continuation of Toyota's strategy to replace exports from Japan with direct production in important regional markets. This strategy was originally undertaken to reduce European demands for trade barriers to limit the "flood" of Japanese automobile imports.

The car to be produced at Toyota's French plant will initially have 60 percent European content, thus qualifying it to be classified as European and allowing Toyota to circumvent import duties. Estimates suggest that 2,000 people will be employed at the new plant by the time it reaches full operation in 2001. An additional 2,000 jobs may be created among suppliers. Toyota's plans call for the plant to export its output to other countries within the European Union, which will help France's balance-of-trade position.

A number of factors motivated Toyota's choice of France as a location for the plant. First, the company hopes that its new plant will help it to increase its market share in France from 1.1 percent in 1997 to around 5 percent. Second, Toyota picked France because the country has long had an indigenous automobile industry, which yields an adequate supply of trained labor and technical expertise, along with a network of experienced subcontractors. Third, the French government reportedly offered considerable subsidies to induce Toyota to invest in the country. These included tax breaks, the waiving of some social security contributions, and financial aid for training the work force. In addition, the city of Valenciennes, where the plant is to be located, is expected to waive or significantly reduce the annual property tax on the site. These subsidies are estimated to reach 10 percent of the value of the investment. Fourth, one of the most important attractions of France was the priority of establishing a presence not only within Europe's single market, but also within the euro single currency zone. The United Kingdom's continued ambivalence to monetary (and currency) union with other European Union countries was a big hindrance to Toyota investing further in the United Kingdom. As of January 1999, the exchange rate for the French franc was locked against that of several other currencies—including that of Germany—in advance of full monetary union and currency union in 2002.

http://www.toyota.com

Sources: A. Jack, "French Consider Takeover Defences," *Financial Times,* November 15, 1997, p. 2; R. Graham and H. Simonian, "Toyota Picks France for New Plant," *Financial Times,* December 10, 1997, p. 6; and A. Jack, "French Go into Overdrive to Win Investors," *Financial Times,* December 10, 1997, p. 6.

CHAPTER OUTLINE

TOYOTA IN FRANCE

INTRODUCTION

POLITICAL IDEOLOGY AND FOREIGN DIRECT INVESTMENT
The Radical View
The Free Market View
Pragmatic Nationalism
Summary

THE BENEFITS OF FDI TO HOST COUNTRIES
Resource-Transfer Effects
Employment Effects
Balance-of-Payments Effects
Effect on Competition and Economic Growth

THE COSTS OF FDI TO HOST COUNTRIES
Adverse Effects on Competition
Adverse Effects on the Balance of Payments
National Sovereignty and Autonomy

THE BENEFITS AND COSTS OF FDI TO HOME COUNTRIES
Benefits of FDI to the Home Country
Costs of FDI to the Home Country
International Trade Theory and Offshore Production

GOVERNMENT POLICY INSTRUMENTS AND FDI
Home-Country Policies
Host-Country Policies
International Institutions and the Liberalization of FDI

IMPLICATIONS FOR BUSINESS
The Nature of Negotiation
Bargaining Power

CHAPTER SUMMARY

CRITICAL DISCUSSION QUESTIONS

FDI IN RUSSIA

Introduction

Chapter 6 looked at the phenomenon of foreign direct investment (FDI) and reviewed several theories that attempt to explain the economic rationale for FDI, but it did not discuss the role of governments in FDI. Through their choice of policies, governments can both encourage and restrict FDI. Host governments can encourage FDI by providing incentives for foreign firms to invest in their economies, and they can restrict FDI through a variety of laws and policies. The opening case illustrated how the French government provided incentives that helped induce Toyota to set up an automobile plant in that country.

The government of a source country for FDI also can encourage or restrict FDI by domestic firms. In recent years, the Japanese government has pressured many Japanese firms to undertake FDI. The Japanese government sees FDI as a substitute for exporting and thus as a way of reducing Japan's politically embarrassing balance of payments surplus. In contrast, the US government has, for political reasons, from time to time restricted FDI by domestic firms. For example, in response to a belief that the Iranian government actively supports terrorist organizations, the US government has prohibited US firms from investing in or exporting to Iran.

Historically, one important determinant of a government's policy toward FDI has been its political ideology. Accordingly, this chapter opens with a discussion of how political ideology influences government policy. To a greater or lesser degree, the officials of many governments tend to be pragmatic nationalists who weigh the benefits and costs of FDI and vary their stated policy on a case-by-case basis. After discussing political ideology, we will consider the benefits and costs of FDI. Then we will look at the various policies home and host governments adopt to encourage and/or restrict FDI. The chapter closes with a detailed discussion of the implications of government policy for the business firm. In this closing section, we examine the factors that determine the relative bargaining strengths of a host government and a firm contemplating FDI. We will look at how the negotiations between firm and government are often played out and at how firms can use this knowledge to their advantage.

Political Ideology and Foreign Direct Investment

Historically, ideology toward FDI has ranged from a dogmatic radical stance that is hostile to all FDI at one extreme to an adherence to the noninterventionist principle of free market economics at the other. Between these two extremes is an approach that might be called pragmatic nationalism. The spectrum is shown in Figure 7.1, and we will review each of these approaches in turn.

The Radical View

The radical view traces its roots to Marxist political and economic theory. Radical writers argue that the multinational enterprise (MNE) is an instrument of imperialist domination. They see the MNE as a tool for exploiting host countries to the exclusive benefit of their capitalist-imperialist home countries. They argue that MNEs extract profits from the host country and take them to their home country, giving nothing of value to the host country in exchange. They note, for example, that key technology is tightly controlled by the MNE, and that important jobs in the foreign subsidiaries of MNEs go to home-country nationals rather than to citizens of the host country. Because of this, according to the radical view, FDI by the MNEs of advanced capitalist nations keeps the less developed countries of the

Figure 7.1

The Spectrum of Political
Ideology toward FDI

world relatively backward and dependent on advanced capitalist nations for
investment, jobs, and technology. Thus, according to the extreme version of this
view, no country should ever permit foreign corporations to undertake FDI, since
they can never be instruments of economic development, only of economic domination. Where MNEs already exist in a country, they should be immediately
nationalized.[1]

From 1945 until the 1980s, the radical view was very influential in the world
economy. Until the collapse of communism between 1989 and 1991, the countries
of Eastern Europe were opposed to FDI. Similarly, communist countries elsewhere,
such as China, Cambodia, and Cuba, were all opposed in principle to FDI
(although in practice the Chinese started to allow FDI in mainland China in the
1970s). The radical position was also embraced by many socialist countries, particularly in Africa where one of the first actions of many newly independent states was
to nationalize foreign-owned enterprises. The radical position was further embraced
by countries whose political ideology was more nationalistic than socialistic. This
was true in Iran and India, for example, both of which adopted tough policies
restricting FDI and nationalized many foreign-owned enterprises. Iran is a particularly interesting case because its Islamic government, while rejecting Marxist theory, has essentially embraced the radical view that FDI by MNEs is an instrument of
imperialism.

By the end of the 1980s, however, the radical position was in retreat almost everywhere. There seem to be three reasons for this: (1) the collapse of communism in
Eastern Europe; (2) the generally abysmal economic performance of those countries
that embraced the radical position, and a growing belief by many of these countries
that FDI can be an important source of technology and jobs and can stimulate economic growth; and (3) the strong economic performance of those developing countries that embraced capitalism rather than radical ideology (e.g., Singapore, Hong
Kong, and Taiwan).

**The Free Market
View**

The free market view traces its roots to classical economics and the international
trade theories of Adam Smith and David Ricardo (see Chapter 4). The intellectual
case for this view has been strengthened by the market imperfections explanation of
horizontal and vertical FDI that we reviewed in Chapter 6. The free market view
argues that international production should be distributed among countries according
to the theory of comparative advantage. Countries should specialize in the production of those goods and services that they can produce most efficiently. Within this
framework, the MNE is an instrument for dispersing the production of goods and services to the most efficient locations around the globe. Viewed this way, FDI by the
MNE increases the overall efficiency of the world economy.

Consider a well-publicized decision by IBM in the mid-1980s to move assembly
operations for many of its personal computers from the United States to Guadalajara,
Mexico. IBM invested about $90 million in an assembly facility with the capacity to
produce 100,000 PCs per year, 75 percent of which were exported back to the United
States.[2] According to the free market view, moves such as this can be seen as increasing the overall efficiency of resource utilization in the world economy. Mexico, due to

MANAGEMENT FOCUS
Makro's Investment in South Korea

In the early 1990s, the government of South Korea decided to start liberalizing the country's restrictive regulations governing foreign direct investment. The move was motivated by a desire to gain access to the capital, management skills, and technology that foreign companies might bring to Korea. Some also believed that foreign investment would provide a much-needed stimulus to competition in Korea. In January 1996, the South Korean government lifted almost all legal restrictions on foreign investment in its retail trade industry.

In response, growth in foreign investment inflows into Korea has been on a steep incline since 1993. The year-on-year gains in foreign direct investment in Korea stood at 16.8 percent in 1993, 26.2 percent in 1994, 47.4 percent in 1995, and 65 percent in 1996. In the first six months of 1997, foreigners invested a record

$4.46 billion in South Korea, which exceeded by 34 percent the $3.32 billion total for the whole of 1996.

One of the first companies to take advantage of the relaxation of regulations was Makro, a Dutch-based retailer. Makro operates membership-only warehouse discount stores. Makro's retailing formula is to sell a wide variety of products at near wholesale prices to small businesses such as restaurants, catering businesses, hospitals, and professional firms. The warehouse stores reduce expenditures on advertising, interior design, and staff, enabling the company to drive down its operating costs and charge low prices for its goods. The typical Makro store carries about 15,000 different products, compared to the 3,000 to 4,000 items in the typical South Korean discount store, and prices its products 5 to 10 percent below those of

its low labor costs, has a comparative advantage in the assembly of PCs. According to the free market view, by moving the production of PCs from the United States to Mexico, IBM frees US resources for use in activities in which the United States has a comparative advantage (e.g., the design of computer software, the manufacture of high-value-added components such as microprocessors, or basic R&D). Also, consumers benefit because the PCs cost less than they would if they were produced domestically. In addition, Mexico gains from the technology, skills, and capital that IBM transfers with its FDI. Contrary to the radical view, the free market view stresses that such resource transfers benefit the host country and stimulate its economic growth. Thus, the free market view argues that FDI is a benefit to both the source country and the host country.

For reasons explored earlier in this book (see Chapter 2), in recent years, the free market view has been ascendant worldwide, spurring a global move toward the removal of restrictions on inward and outward foreign direct investment. An example is South Korea, which started dismantling its restrictive regulations governing inward FDI in the mid-1990s. As described in the accompanying Management Focus, foreign firms are starting to affect competition in certain sectors of the Korean economy.

According to the United Nations, between 1991 and 1996 over 100 countries made 599 changes in legislation governing FDI. Some 95 percent of these changes involved liberalizing a country's foreign investment regulations to make it easier for foreign companies to enter markets.[3] However, in practice no country has adopted the free market view in its pure form (just as no country has adopted the radical view in its pure form). Countries such as Britain and the United States are among the most open to FDI, but the governments of both countries have a tendency to intervene. Britain does so by reserving the right to block foreign takeovers of domestic firms if the takeovers are seen as "contrary to national security interests" or if they have the

http://www.costco.com

Korean discount stores. Before its entry into South Korea, Makro had already built substantial operations in Asia, with stores in Taiwan, Thailand, and Malaysia. The company has about 150 stores around the world.

To facilitate its entry into South Korea, Makro set up a joint venture with local investors called Makro-Korea. The venture opened its first store in Inchon in mid-1997. The company's expansion plans called for 10 stores in South Korea by the end of 2000. Makro's great hope was that its retailing formula would prove compelling to South Korean consumers, who had not been exposed to the warehouse discount store concept until Makro's entry. Makro's entry into South Korea was quickly followed by the entry of a number of other foreign discount retailers, including the American companies Price Costco and Wal-Mart and the French

discount retailer Carrefour. Several South Korean companies responded to Makro's entry by developing their own version of the warehouse discount store, including Shinsegae Group's E-Mart. Consequently, competitive pressures have increased significantly in the South Korean discount store retail market, depressing prices and profits for all involved. The primary beneficiaries of the relaxation of foreign direct investment regulations will not be foreign entrants such as Marko, but South Koreans who benefit from lower prices and significantly greater choice.

Sources: *Korean Herald,* "Korean Makro Plans to Set up Operations in Seoul by 2000," May 31, 1997; Yoo Cheong-mo, "Foreign Direct Investments in First Half Total $4.46 Billion," *Korean Herald,* July 24, 1997; and Y. J. Sohn, "Survival Game: Defeat or Be Defeated," *Business Korea,* February 1996, pp. 23–26.

potential for "reducing competition." (In practice this right is rarely exercised.) US controls on FDI are more limited and largely informal. As noted earlier, for political reasons, the United States will occasionally restrict US firms from undertaking FDI in certain countries (e.g., Cuba and Iran). In addition, there are some limited restrictions on inward FDI. For example, foreigners are prohibited from purchasing more than 25 percent of any US airline or from acquiring a controlling interest in a US television broadcast network. Since 1989, the government has had the right to review foreign investment on the grounds of "national security."

Pragmatic Nationalism

In practice, many countries have adopted neither a radical policy nor a free market policy toward FDI, but instead a policy that can best be described as pragmatic nationalism. The pragmatic nationalist view is that FDI has both benefits and costs. FDI can benefit a host country by bringing capital, skills, technology, and jobs, but those benefits often come at a cost. When products are produced by a foreign company rather than a domestic company, the profits from that investment go abroad. Many countries are also concerned that a foreign-owned manufacturing plant may import many components from its home country, which has negative implications for the host country's balance-of-payments position.

Recognizing this, countries adopting a pragmatic stance pursue policies designed to maximize the national benefits and minimize the national costs. According to this view, FDI should be allowed only if the benefits outweigh the costs. Japan offers one of the more extreme examples of pragmatic nationalism. Until the 1980s, Japan's policy was probably one of the most restrictive among countries adopting a pragmatic nationalist stance. This was due to Japan's perception that direct entry of foreign (especially US) firms with ample managerial resources into the Japanese markets could hamper the development and growth of their own industry and technology.[4] This belief led Japan to block the majority of applications to invest in Japan. However, there were always exceptions to this policy. Firms that had important technology were often permitted to undertake FDI if they insisted that they would neither license their technology to a Japanese firm nor enter into a joint venture with a Japanese enterprise. IBM and Texas Instruments were able to set up wholly owned subsidiaries in Japan by adopting this negotiating position. From the perspective of the Japanese government, the benefits of FDI in such cases—the stimulus that these firms might impart to the Japanese economy—outweighed the perceived costs.

Another aspect of pragmatic nationalism is the tendency to aggressively court FDI believed to be in the national interest by, for example, offering subsidies to foreign MNEs in the form of tax breaks or grants. As we saw in the opening case, subsidies in the form of tax breaks were one factor that helped persuade Toyota to build an assembly plant in France as opposed to the United Kingdom. The countries of the European Union often seem to be competing with each other to attract US and Japanese FDI by offering large tax breaks and subsidies. Britain has been the most successful at attracting Japanese investment in the automobile industry. Nissan, Toyota, and Honda now have major assembly plants in Britain and use the country as their base for serving the rest of Europe—with obvious employment and balance-of-payments benefits for Britain.

Summary

The three main ideological positions regarding FDI are summarized in Table 7.1. Recent years have seen a marked decline in the number of countries that adhere to a radical ideology. Although no countries have adopted a *pure* free market policy stance, an increasing number of countries are gravitating toward the free market end of the spectrum and have liberalized their foreign investment regime. This includes many countries that only a few years ago were firmly in the radical camp (e.g., the former communist countries of Eastern Europe and many of the socialist countries of Africa) and several countries that until recently could best be described as pragmatic nationalists with regard to FDI (e.g., Japan, South Korea, Italy, Spain, and most Latin American countries). One result has been the surge in the volume of FDI worldwide, which, as we noted in Chapter 6, has been growing twice as fast as the growth in world trade. Another result has been a dramatic increase in the volume of FDI directed at countries that have recently liberalized their FDI regimes, such as China, India, and Vietnam.

Table 7.1

Political Ideology toward FDI

Ideology	Characteristics	Host-Government Policy Implications
Radical	Marxist roots Views the MNE as an instrument of imperialist domination	Prohibit FDI Nationalize subsidiaries of foreign-owned MNEs
Free market	Classical economic roots (Smith) Views the MNE as an instrument for allocating production to most efficient locations	No restrictions on FDI
Pragmatic nationalism	Views FDA as having both benefits and costs	Restrict FDI where costs outweigh benefits Bargain for greater benefits and fewer costs Aggressively court beneficial FDI by offering incentives

The Benefits of FDI to Host Countries

In this section, we explore the four main benefits of FDI for a host country: the resource-transfer effect, the employment effect, the balance-of-payments effect, and the effect on competition and economic growth. In the next section, we will explore the costs of FDI to host countries. Economists who favor the free market view argue that the benefits of FDI to a host country so outweigh the costs that pragmatic nationalism is a misguided policy. According to the free market view, in a perfect world the best policy would be for all countries to forgo intervening in the investment decisions of MNEs.[5]

Resource-Transfer Effects

Foreign direct investment can make a positive contribution to a host economy by supplying capital, technology, and management resources that would otherwise not be available and thus boost that country's economic growth rate. The accompanying Country Focus describes how the Venezuelan government has been encouraging FDI in its petroleum industry in an attempt to benefit from resource-transfer effects.

Capital

Many MNEs, by virtue of their large size and financial strength, have access to financial resources not available to host-country firms. These funds may be available from internal company sources, or, because of their reputation, large MNEs may find it easier to borrow money from capital markets than host-country firms would. This consideration was a factor in the Venezuelan government's decision to invite foreign oil companies to enter into joint ventures with PDVSA, the state-owned Venezuelan oil company, to develop Venezuela's oil industry.

Technology

As we saw in Chapter 2, the crucial role played by technological progress in economic growth is now widely accepted.[6] Technology can stimulate economic development and industrialization. It can take two forms, both of which are valuable. Technology can be incorporated in a production process (e.g., the technology for discovering, extracting, and refining oil) or it can be incorporated in a product (e.g., personal computers). However, many countries lack the research and development resources and skills required to develop their own indigenous product and process technology. This is particularly true of the world's less developed nations. Such countries must rely on advanced industrialized nations for much of the technology required to stimulate economic growth, and FDI can provide it. As we see in the Country Focus on Venezuela, a lack of relevant technological know-how with regard to the discovery, extraction, and refining of oil was one factor behind the Venezuelan government's decision to invite foreign oil companies into Venezuela.

FDI is not the only way to access advanced technology. Another option is to license that technology from foreign MNEs. The Japanese government, in particular, has long favored this strategy. The Japanese government believes that, in the case of FDI, the technology is still ultimately controlled by the foreign MNE. Consequently, it is difficult for indigenous Japanese firms to develop their own, possibly better, technology because they are denied access to the basic technology. With this in mind, the Japanese government has insisted in the past that technology be transferred to Japan through licensing agreements, rather than through FDI. The advantage of licensing is that in return for royalty payments, host-country firms are given direct access to valuable technology. The licensing option is generally less attractive to the MNE, however. By licensing its technology to foreign companies, an MNE risks creating a future competitor—as many US firms have learned at great cost in Japan.

COUNTRY FOCUS
Foreign Direct Investment in Venezuela's Petroleum Industry

In 1976, Venezuela nationalized its oil industry, effectively closing the sector to foreign investors. The stated goal at the time was to control this important natural resource for the benefit of Venezuela, as opposed to foreign oil companies. The results, however, fell short of expectations. The country's state-owned oil monopoly, Petroleos de Venezuela SA (PDVSA), failed to develop new oil fields to replace the depletion of existing reserves, and the country's oil output was falling by the mid-1980s.

Faced with the prospect of declining export revenues from oil, Venezuela reversed its policy in 1991 and began to open its oil industry to foreign investors. The Venezuelan government turned to foreign investors for three reasons. First, it recognized that PDVSA did not have the capital required to undertake the investment alone. Second, it realized that PDVSA lacked the technological resources and

skills of many of the world's major oil companies, particularly in the areas of oil exploration, oil field development, and sophisticated refining. The government understood that if PDVSA was to develop many of Venezuela's oil fields in a timely fashion, it had no alternative but to turn to foreign companies for help. Third, the government believed that PDVSA would be able to use joint ventures with foreign oil companies as a vehicle for learning about modern management techniques in the industry. PDVSA could then use this knowledge to improve the efficiency of its own operations.

Current plans call for the investment of $73 billion in the oil industry. The plan, as outlined by Gustavo Roosen, president of PDVSA, is to develop a crude oil production potential of 4 million barrels per day by 2002 and 7 million barrels per day by 2007 (the country produced about 2.6 million barrels per day in 1991). Of

Given this tension, the mode for transferring technology—licensing or FDI—can be a major negotiating point between an MNE and a host government. Whether the MNE gets its way depends on the relative bargaining powers of the MNE and the host government. Such was the bargaining power of IBM in Japan that it was able to get around Japan's preference for licensing arrangements and establish a wholly owned subsidiary.

Management

Foreign management skills acquired through FDI may also produce important benefits for the host country. Beneficial spin-off effects arise when local personnel who are trained to occupy managerial, financial, and technical posts in the subsidiary of a foreign MNE leave the firm and help to establish indigenous firms. Similar benefits may arise if the superior management skills of a foreign MNE stimulate local suppliers, distributors, and competitors to improve their own management skills.

The benefits may be considerably reduced if most management and highly skilled jobs in the subsidiaries are reserved for home-country nationals. The percentage of management and skilled jobs that go to citizens of the host country can be a major negotiating point between an MNE wishing to undertake FDI and a potential host government. In recent years, most MNEs have responded to host-government pressures on this issue by agreeing to reserve a large proportion of management and highly skilled jobs for citizens of the host country.

Employment Effects

The beneficial employment effect claimed for FDI is that it brings jobs to a host country that would otherwise not be created there. As we saw in the opening case on Toyota in France, employment effects are both direct and indirect. Direct effects arise when a foreign MNE employs a number of host-country citizens. Indirect effects arise

http://www.exxon.com

the $73 billion in projected capital spending, PDVSA plans to invest around $45 billion, while foreign oil companies will supply the remaining $28 billion. The first FDI agreement was signed in 1992 with British Petroleum (BP). BP agreed to invest $60 million by 1995 to develop a marginal oil field that it would then be given the rights to for 20 years. Using a BP study, PDVSA has also identified sectors in eastern Venezuela with strong prospects for large discoveries of crude oil and has entered into several ventures with other foreign partners to develop these zones. If commercial quantities of oil are discovered, PDVSA will share future production with its partners. Under the terms of most agreements, PDVSA will receive 35 percent of the earnings from any successful exploration venture. Also, with foreign investors such as Conoco and Total, PDVSA is investing in state-of-the-art refining facilities that can be used to convert heavy crude oil into a

lighter, high-value crude oil for export. Finally, PDVSA, Shell, Exxon, and Mitsubishi have entered into a $5.6 billion joint venture to produce liquefied natural gas for export.

By 1997, over 40 development projects were under way in Venezuela involving cooperation between PDVSA and foreign oil companies. Almost all of the world's major oil companies now had some activities in the country, compared to none before 1991. The country's oil output was also expanding, reaching 3.5 million barrels per day in 1997, up from a low of 1.7 million barrels per day in 1985.

Sources: J. Mann, "A Little Help from Their Friends, " *Financial Times,* November 10, 1993, p. 28; "Venezuela: A Survey," *The Economist,* October 14, 1994; and E. Luce, "Oil: Foreign Investment: Finding a Balanced Approach," *Financial Times,* October 21, 1997, p. 6.

when jobs are created in local suppliers as a result of the investment and when jobs are created because of increased local spending by employees of the MNE. The indirect employment effects are often as large as, if not larger than, the direct effects. The opening case revealed that Toyota's investment in France created 2,000 direct jobs and perhaps another 2,000 jobs in support industries.

Cynics note that not all the "new jobs" created by FDI represent net additions in employment. In the case of FDI by Japanese auto companies in the United States, some argue that the jobs created by this investment have been more than offset by the jobs lost in US-owned auto companies, which have lost market share to their Japanese competitors. As a consequence of such substitution effects, the net number of new jobs created by FDI may not be as great as initially claimed by an MNE. The issue of the likely net gain in employment may be a major negotiating point between an MNE wishing to undertake FDI and the host government.

Balance-of-Payments Effects

FDI's effect on a country's balance-of-payments accounts is an important policy issue for most host governments. To understand this concern, we must first familiarize ourselves with balance-of-payments accounting. Then we will examine the link between FDI and the balance-of-payments accounts.

Balance-of-Payments Accounts

A country's **balance-of-payments accounts** keep track of both its payments to and its receipts from other countries. A summary copy of the US balance-of-payments accounts for 1995 is given in Table 7.2. Any transaction resulting in a payment to other countries is entered in the balance-of-payments accounts as a debit and given a negative (−) sign. Any transaction resulting in a receipt from other countries is entered as a credit and given a positive (+) sign.

Table 7.2

US Balance-of-Payments Accounts for 1995 (figures in $ millions)

Current Account	Credits	Debits
Exports of goods, services, and income:	$969,189	
Merchandise	575,940	
Services	210,590	
Income receipts on investments	182,659	
Imports of goods, services, and income:		$−1,082,268
Merchandise		−749,364
Services		−142,230
Income payments on investments		−190,674
Unilateral transfers		−35,075
Balance of current account		−113,079
Capital Account		
US assets abroad (net):		−307,856
US official reserve assets		−9,742
Other government assets		−280
US private assets		−297,834
Foreign assets in United States	424,462	
Foreign official assets	109,757	
Other foreign assets	314,705	
Balance on capital account	116,606	
Statistical discrepancy	31,548	

Source: US Department of Commerce, *Survey of Current Business*, December 1996, p. D-56.

Balance-of-payments accounts are divided into two main sections: the current account and the capital account. The **current account** records transactions that pertain to three categories, all of which can be seen in Table 7.2. The first category, *merchandise trade*, refers to the export or import of goods (e.g., autos, computers, chemicals). The second category is the export or import of *services* (e.g., intangible products such as banking and insurance services). The third category, *investment income*, refers to income from foreign investments and payments that have to be made to foreigners investing in a country. For example, if a US citizen owns a share of a Finnish company and receives a dividend payment of $5, that payment shows up on the US current account as the receipt of $5 of investment income.

A **current account deficit** occurs when a country imports more goods, services, and income than it exports. A **current account surplus** occurs when a country exports more goods, services, and income than it imports. In recent years, the United States has run a persistent trade deficit. Table 7.2 shows that in 1995 the current account deficit was $113,079.

The **capital account** records transactions that involve the purchase or sale of assets. Thus, when a Japanese firm purchases stock in a US company, the transaction enters the US balance of payments as a credit on the capital account. This is because capital is flowing into the country. When capital flows out of the United States, it enters the capital account as a debit.

A basic principle of balance-of-payments accounting is double-entry bookkeeping. Every international transaction automatically enters the balance of payments twice—once as a credit and once as a debit. Imagine that you purchase a car produced in Japan by Toyota for $12,000. Since your purchase represents a payment to another country for goods, it will enter the balance of payments as a debit on the current account. Toyota now has the $12,000 and must do something with it. If Toyota deposits the money at a US bank, Toyota has purchased a US asset—a bank deposit worth $12,000—and the transaction will show up as a $12,000 credit on the capital account. Or Toyota might deposit the cash in a Japanese bank in return for Japanese yen. Now the Japanese bank must decide what to do with the $12,000. Any action that it takes will ultimately result in a credit for the US balance of payments. For example, if the bank lends the $12,000 to a Japanese firm that uses it to import personal computers from the United States, then the $12,000 must be credited to the US balance-of-payments current account. Or the Japanese bank might use the $12,000 to purchase US government bonds, in which case it will show up as a credit on the US balance-of-payments capital account.

Thus, any international transaction automatically gives rise to two offsetting entries in the balance of payments. Because of this, the current account balance and the capital account balance should always add up to zero. (In practice, this does not always occur due to the existence of statistical discrepancies which need not concern us here.)

Governments normally are concerned when their country is running a deficit on the current account of their balance of payments.[7] When a country runs a current account deficit, the money that flows to other countries is then used by those countries to purchase assets in the deficit country. Thus, when the United States runs a trade deficit with Japan, the Japanese use the money that they receive from US consumers to purchase US assets such as stocks, bonds, and the like. Put another way, a deficit on the current account is financed by selling assets to other countries; that is, by a surplus on the capital account. Thus, the US current account deficit during the 1980s and 90s was financed by a steady sale of US assets (stocks, bonds, real estate, and whole corporations) to other countries. Countries that run current account deficits become net debtors.

For example, as a result of financing its current account deficit through asset sales, the United States must deliver a stream of interest payments to foreign bondholders, rents to foreign landowners, and dividends to foreign stockholders. Such payments to foreigners drain resources from a country and limit the funds available for investment within the country. Since investment within a country is necessary to stimulate economic growth, a persistent current account deficit can choke off a country's future economic growth.

FDI and the Balance of Payments

Given the concern about current account deficits, the balance-of-payments effects of FDI can be an important consideration for a host government. There are three potential balance-of-payments consequences of FDI. First, when an MNE establishes a foreign subsidiary, the capital account of the host country benefits from the initial capital inflow. (A debit will be recorded in the capital account of the home country, since capital is flowing out of the home country.) However, this is a one-time-only effect. Set against this must be the outflow of earnings to the foreign parent company, which will be recorded as a debit on the current account of the host country.

Second, if the FDI is a substitute for imports of goods or services, it can improve the current account of the host country's balance of payments. Much of the FDI by Japanese automobile companies in the United States and United Kingdom, for example, can be seen as substituting for imports from Japan. Thus, the current account of the US balance of payments has improved somewhat because many Japanese companies are now supplying the US market from production facilities in the United States, as opposed to facilities in Japan. Insofar as this has reduced the need to finance a current account deficit by asset sales to foreigners, the United States has clearly benefited from this. A third potential benefit to the host country's balance-of-payments position arises when the MNE uses a foreign subsidiary to export goods and services to other countries.

Effect on Competition and Economic Growth

Economic theory tells us that the efficient functioning of markets depends on an adequate level of competition between producers. By increasing consumer choice, foreign direct investment can help to increase the level of competition in national markets, thereby driving down prices and increasing the economic welfare of consumers. Increased competition tends to stimulate capital investments by firms in plant, equipment, and R&D as they struggle to gain an edge over their rivals. The long-term results may include increased productivity growth, product and process innovations, and greater economic growth. FDI's impact on competition in domestic markets may be particularly important in the case of services, such as telecommunications, retailing, and many financial services, where exporting is often not an option because the service has to be produced where it is delivered.[8]

As we saw in the Management Focus, foreign direct investment has helped increase competition in the South Korean retail sector. The increase in choices, and the resulting fall in prices, clearly benefits South Korean consumers. Under a 1997 agreement sponsored by the World Trade Organization, 68 countries accounting for more than 90 percent of world telecommunications revenues pledged to start opening their markets to foreign investment and competition and to abide by common rules for fair competition in telecommunications. Before this agreement, most of the world's telecommunications markets were closed to foreign competitors, and in most countries the market was monopolized by a single carrier, which was often a state-owned enterprise. The agreement will dramatically increase the level of competition in many national telecommunications markets. Three benefits from this agreement were touted. First, advocates argued that inward investment and increased competition will stimulate investment in the modernization of telephone networks around the world and lead to better service. Second, supporters maintained that the increased competition will benefit customers through lower prices. Estimates suggested that a deal will soon reduce the average cost of international telephone calls by 80 percent and save consumers $1,000 billion over three years.[9] Third, the WTO argued that trade in other goods and services invariably depends upon flows of information matching buyers to sellers. As telecommunications service improves in quality and declines in price, international trade increases in volume and becomes less costly for traders. Telecommunications reform, therefore, should promote cross-border trade in other goods and services. In sum, although it is difficult to be precise about these matters, Renato Ruggiero, the director general of the WTO, argued:

> Telecommunications liberalization could mean global income gains of some $1 trillion over the next decade or so. This represents about 4 percent of world GDP at today's prices.[10]

The Costs of FDI to Host Countries

Three costs of FDI concern host countries. They arise from possible adverse effects on competition within the host nation, adverse effects on the balance of payments, and the perceived loss of national sovereignty and autonomy.

Adverse Effects on Competition

Although we have just outlined in the previous section how foreign direct investment can boost competition, host governments sometimes worry that the subsidiaries of foreign MNEs may have greater economic power than indigenous competitors. If it is part of a larger international organization, the foreign MNE may be able to draw on funds generated elsewhere to subsidize its costs in the host market, which could drive indigenous companies out of business and allow the firm to monopolize the market. (Once the market was monopolized, the foreign MNE could raise prices above those that would prevail in competitive markets, with harmful effects on the economic welfare of the host nation.) This concern tends to be greater in countries that have few large firms of their own (generally less developed countries). It tends to be a relatively minor concern in most advanced industrialized nations.

Another variant of the competition argument is related to the infant industry concern that we discussed in Chapter 6. We explained that import controls may be motivated by a desire to let a local industry develop to a stage where it can compete in world markets. The same logic suggests that FDI should be restricted. If a country with a potential comparative advantage in a particular industry allows FDI in that industry, indigenous firms may never have a chance to develop.

In practice, the above arguments are often used by inefficient indigenous competitors when lobbying their government to restrict direct investment by foreign MNEs. Although a host government may state publicly in such cases that its restrictions on inward FDI are designed to protect indigenous competitors from the market power of foreign MNEs, they may have been enacted to protect inefficient but politically powerful indigenous competitors from foreign competition.

Adverse Effects on the Balance of Payments

The possible adverse effects of FDI on a host country's balance-of-payments position have been hinted at earlier. There are two main areas of concern with regard to the balance of payments. First, as mentioned earlier, set against the initial capital inflow that comes with FDI must be the subsequent outflow of earnings from the foreign subsidiary to its parent company. Such outflows show up as a debit on the capital account. Some governments have responded to such outflows by restricting the amount of earnings that can be repatriated to a foreign subsidiary's home country.

A second concern arises when a foreign subsidiary imports a substantial number of its inputs from abroad, which results in a debit on the current account of the host country's balance of payments. One criticism leveled against Japanese-owned auto assembly operations in the United States, for example, is that they tend to import many component parts from Japan. Because of this, the favorable impact of this FDI on the current account of the US balance-of-payments position may not be as great as initially supposed. The Japanese auto companies have responded to these criticisms by pledging to purchase 75 percent of their component parts from US-based manufacturers (but not necessarily US-owned manufacturers). In the case of Nissan's investment in the United Kingdom, Nissan responded to concerns about local content by pledging to increase the proportion of local content to 60 percent, and by subsequently raising it to over 80 percent.

National Sovereignty and Autonomy

Many host governments worry that FDI is accompanied by some loss of economic independence. The concern is that key decisions that can affect the host country's economy will be made by a foreign parent that has no real commitment to the host country, and over which the host country's government has no real control. A quarter of a century ago this concern was expressed by several European countries, who feared that FDI by US MNEs was threatening their national sovereignty. The same concerns are now surfacing in the United States with regard to European and Japanese FDI. The main fear seems to be that if foreigners own assets in the United States, they can somehow "hold the country to economic ransom." Twenty-five years ago when officials in the French government were making similar complaints about US investments in France, many US politicians dismissed the charge as silly. Now that the shoe is on the other foot, many US politicians no longer think the notion is silly. However, most economists dismiss such concerns as groundless and irrational. Political scientist Robert Reich recently spoke of such concerns as the product of outmoded thinking because they fail to account for the growing interdependence of the world economy.[11] In a world where firms from all advanced nations are increasingly investing in each other's markets, it is not possible for one country to hold another to "economic ransom" without hurting itself.

The Benefits and Costs of FDI to Home Countries

FDI also produces costs and benefits to the home (or source) country. Does the US economy benefit or lose from investments by its firms in foreign markets? Does the Japanese economy lose or gain from Toyota's investment in France? Some argue that

FDI is not always in the home country's national interest and should be restricted. Others argue that the benefits far outweigh the costs and any restrictions would be contrary to national interests. To understand why people take these positions, let us look at the benefits and costs of FDI to the home (source) country.[12]

Benefits of FDI to the Home Country

The benefits of FDI to the home country arise from three sources. First, and perhaps most important, the capital account of the home country's balance of payments benefits from the inward flow of foreign earnings. Thus, one benefit to Japan from Toyota's investment in France are the earnings that are subsequently repatriated to Japan from France. FDI can also benefit the current account of the home country's balance of payments if the foreign subsidiary creates demands for home-country exports of capital equipment, intermediate goods, complementary products, and the like.

Second, benefits to the home country from outward FDI arise from employment effects. As with the balance of payments, positive employment effects arise when the foreign subsidiary creates demand for home-country exports of capital equipment, intermediate goods, complementary products, and the like. Thus, Toyota's investment in auto assembly operations in Europe has benefited both the Japanese balance-of-payments position and employment in Japan, because Toyota imports some component parts for its European-based auto assembly operations directly from Japan.

Third, benefits arise when the home-country MNE learns valuable skills from its exposure to foreign markets that can subsequently be transferred back to the home country. This amounts to a reverse resource-transfer effect. Through its exposure to a foreign market, an MNE can learn about superior management techniques and superior product and process technologies. These resources can then be transferred back to the home country, contributing to the home country's economic growth rate.[13] For example, one reason General Motors and Ford invested in Japanese automobile companies (GM owns part of Isuzu, and Ford owns part of Mazda) was to learn about their production processes. If GM and Ford are successful in transferring this know-how back to their US operations, the result may be a net gain for the US economy.

Costs of FDI to the Home Country

Against these benefits must be set the apparent costs of FDI for the home (source) country. The most important concerns center around the balance-of-payments and employment effects of outward FDI. The home country's balance of payments may suffer in three ways. First, the capital account of the balance of payments suffers from the initial capital outflow required to finance the FDI. This effect, however, is usually more than offset by the subsequent inflow of foreign earnings. Second, the current account of the balance of payments suffers if the purpose of the foreign investment is to serve the home market from a low-cost production location. Third, the current account of the balance of payments suffers if the FDI is a substitute for direct exports. Thus, insofar as Toyota's assembly operations in the United States are intended to substitute for direct exports from Japan, the current account position of Japan will deteriorate.

With regard to employment effects, the most serious concerns arise when FDI is seen as a substitute for domestic production. This was the case with Toyota's investments in Europe. One obvious result of such FDI is reduced home-country employment. If the labor market in the home country is already very tight, with little unemployment (as was the case in both Japan and the United States during the 1980s), this concern may not be that great. However, if the home country is suffering from unemployment, concern about the export of jobs may arise. For example, one objection frequently raised by US labor leaders to the free trade pact between the United States, Mexico, and Canada (see the next chapter) is that the United States will lose hundreds of thousands of jobs as US firms invest in Mexico to take advantage of cheaper labor and then export back to the United States market.[14]

International Trade Theory and Offshore Production

When assessing the costs and benefits of FDI to the home country, keep in mind the lessons of international trade theory (see Chapter 4). International trade theory tells us that home-country concerns about the negative economic effects of offshore production may be misplaced. The term *offshore production* refers to FDI undertaken to serve the home market. Far from reducing home-country employment, such FDI may actually stimulate economic growth (and hence employment) in the home country by freeing up home-country resources to concentrate on activities where the home country has a comparative advantage. In addition, home-country consumers benefit if the price of the particular product falls as a result of the FDI. Also, if a company were prohibited from making such investments on the grounds of negative employment effects while its international competitors reaped the benefits of low-cost production locations, it would undoubtedly lose market share to its international competitors. Under such a scenario, the adverse long-run economic effects for a country would probably outweigh the relatively minor balance-of-payments and employment effects associated with offshore production.

Government Policy Instruments and FDI

Before tackling the important issue of bargaining between the MNE and the host government, we need to discuss the policy instruments that governments use to regulate FDI activity by MNEs. Both home (source) countries and host countries have a range of policy instruments that they can use. We will look at each in turn.

Home-Country Policies

Through their choice of policies, home countries can both encourage and restrict FDI by local firms. We look at policies designed to encourage outward FDI first. These include foreign risk insurance, capital assistance, tax incentives, and political pressure. Then we will look at policies designed to restrict outward FDI.

Encouraging Outward FDI

Many investor nations now have government-backed insurance programs to cover major types of foreign investment risk. The types of risks insurable through these programs include the risks of expropriation (nationalization), war losses, and the inability to transfer profits back home. Such programs are particularly useful in encouraging firms to undertake investments in politically unstable countries.[15] In addition, several advanced countries also have special funds or banks that make government loans to firms wishing to invest in developing countries. As a further incentive to encourage domestic firms to undertake FDI, many countries have eliminated double taxation of foreign income (i.e., taxation of income in both the host country and the home country). Last, and perhaps most significant, a number of investor countries (particularly the United States) have used their political influence to persuade host countries to relax their restrictions on inbound FDI. For example, in response to direct US pressure, Japan relaxed many of its formal restrictions on inward FDI in the early 1980s. Now, in response to further US pressure, Japan is moving toward relaxing its informal barriers to inward FDI. One notable beneficiary of this trend has been Toys "R" Us, which, after five years of intensive lobbying by company and US government officials, opened its first retail stores in Japan in December 1991. By the end of 1997, Toys "R" Us had 51 stores in Japan.

Restricting Outward FDI

Virtually all investor countries, including the United States, have exercised some control over outward FDI from time to time. One common policy has been to limit capital outflows out of concern for the country's balance of payments. From the early 1960s until 1979, for example, Britain had exchange-control regulations that limited the amount of capital a firm could take out of the country. Although the main intent of such policies was to improve the British balance of payments, an important secondary intent was to make it more difficult for British firms to undertake FDI.

In addition, countries have occasionally manipulated tax rules to try to encourage their firms to invest at home. The objective behind such policies is to create jobs at home rather than in other nations. At one time these policies were also adopted by Britain. The British advanced corporation tax system taxed British companies' foreign earnings at a higher rate than their domestic earnings. This tax code created an incentive for British companies to invest at home.

Finally, countries sometimes prohibit national firms from investing in certain countries for political reasons. Such restrictions can be formal or informal. For example, formal US rules prohibited US firms from investing in countries such as Cuba, Libya, and Iran, whose political ideology and actions are judged to be contrary to US interests. Similarly, during the 1980s, informal pressure was applied to dissuade US firms from investing in South Africa. In this case, the objective was to put pressure on South Africa to change its apartheid laws, which occurred during the early 1990s. Thus, this policy was successful.

Host-Country Policies

Host countries adopt policies designed both to restrict and to encourage inward FDI. As noted earlier in this chapter, political ideology has determined the type and scope of these policies in the past. In the last decade of the 20th century, we seemed to be moving quickly away from a situation where many countries adhered to some version of the radical stance and prohibited much FDI, and toward a situation where a combination of free market objectives and pragmatic nationalism seemed to be taking hold.

Encouraging Inward FDI

It is increasingly common for governments to offer incentives to foreign firms to invest in their countries. Such incentives take many forms, but the most common are tax concessions, low-interest loans, and grants or subsidies. Incentives are motivated by a desire to gain from the resource-transfer and employment effects of FDI. They are also motivated by a desire to capture FDI away from other potential host countries. For example, as we saw in the opening case, the governments of Britain and France competed with each other on the incentives they offered Toyota to invest in their respective countries. In the United States, state governments often compete with each other to attract FDI. For example, Kentucky offered Toyota an incentive package worth $112 million to persuade it to build its US automobile assembly plants there. The package included tax breaks, new state spending on infrastructure, and low-interest loans.[16]

Restricting Inward FDI

Host governments use a wide range of controls to restrict FDI in one way or another. The two most common are ownership restraints and performance requirements. Ownership restraints can take several forms. In some countries, foreign companies are excluded from specific fields. For example, they are excluded from tobacco and mining in Sweden and from the development of certain natural resources in Brazil, Finland, and Morocco. In other industries, foreign ownership may be permitted although a significant proportion of the equity of the subsidiary must be owned by local investors. For example, foreign ownership is restricted to 25 percent or less of a airline in the United States.

The rationale underlying ownership restraints seems to be twofold. First, foreign firms are often excluded from certain sectors on the grounds of national security or competition. Particularly in less developed countries, the feeling seems to be that local firms might not be able to develop unless foreign competition is restricted by a combination of import tariffs and controls on FDI. This is really a variant of the infant industry argument that we discussed in Chapter 5.

Second, ownership restraints seem to be based on a belief that local owners can help to maximize the resource-transfer and employment benefits of FDI for the host country. Until the early 1980s, the Japanese government prohibited most FDI but allowed joint ventures between Japanese firms and foreign MNEs if the MNE had a valuable technology. The Japanese government clearly believed such an arrangement would speed up the subsequent diffusion of the MNE's valuable technology throughout the Japanese economy.

Performance requirements can also take several forms. Performance requirements are controls over the behavior of the MNE's local subsidiary. The most common performance requirements are related to local content, exports, technology transfer, and local participation in top management. As with certain ownership restrictions, the logic underlying performance requirements is that such rules help to maximize the benefits and minimize the costs of FDI for the host country. Virtually all countries employ some form of performance requirements when it suits their objectives. However, performance requirements tend to be more common in less developed countries than in advanced industrialized nations. For example, one study found that some 30 percent of the affiliates of US MNEs in less developed countries were subject to performance requirements, while only 6 percent of the affiliates in advanced countries were faced with such requirements.[17]

International Institutions and the Liberalization of FDI

Until recently there has been no consistent involvement by multinational institutions in the governing of FDI. This is now changing rapidly with the formation of the World Trade Organization in 1995. As noted in Chapter 5, the role of the WTO embraces the promotion of international trade in services. Since many services have to be produced where they are sold, exporting is not an option (for example, one cannot export McDonald's hamburgers or consumer banking services). Given this, the WTO has become involved in regulations governing FDI. As might be expected for an institution created to promote free trade, the thrust of the WTO's efforts has been to push for the liberalization of regulations governing FDI, particularly in services. Under the auspices of the WTO, two extensive multinational agreements were reached in 1997 to liberalize trade in telecommunications and financial services. Both these agreements contained detailed clauses that require signatories to liberalize their regulations governing inward FDI, essentially opening their markets to foreign telecommunications and financial services companies.

However, the WTO has had less success trying to initiate talks aimed at establishing a universal set of rules designed to promote the liberalization of FDI. Led by Malaysia and India, developing nations have so far rejected any attempts by the WTO to start such discussions. In an attempt to make some progress on this issue, the **Organization for Economic Cooperation and Development** (OECD) in 1995 initiated talks between its members. (The OECD is a Paris-based intergovernmental organization of "wealthy" nations whose purpose is to provide its 29 member states with a forum in which governments can compare their experiences, discuss the problems they share, and seek solutions that can then be applied within their own national contexts. The members include most European Union countries, the United States, Canada, Japan, and South Korea). The aim of the talks was to draft a **Multilateral Agreement on Investment** (MAI) that would make it illegal for signatory states to discriminate against foreign investors. This would liberalize rules governing FDI between OECD states. Unfortunately for those promoting the agreement, the talks broke down in early 1998, primarily because the United States refused to sign the agreement. According to the United States, the proposed agreement contained too many exceptions that would weaken its powers. For example, the proposed agreement would not have barred discriminatory taxation of foreign-owned companies, and it would have allowed countries to restrict foreign television programs and music in the name of preserving culture. Also campaigning against the MAI were environmental and labor groups, who criticized the proposed agreement on the grounds that it contained no binding environmental or labor agreements. Despite these problems, there is still a good chance that negotiations on a revised MAI treaty will restart soon.[18]

IMPLICATIONS FOR BUSINESS

There are a number of fairly obvious implications for business in the material discussed in this chapter. For a start, a host government's attitude toward FDI should be an important variable in deciding where to locate foreign production facilities and where to make a foreign direct investment. Other things being equal, investing in countries that have permissive policies toward FDI is clearly preferable to investing in countries that restrict FDI.

Generally, however, the issue is not this straightforward. Despite the move toward a free market stance in recent years, many countries still have a rather pragmatic stance toward FDI. In such cases, a firm considering FDI usually must negotiate the specific terms of the investment with the country's government. Such negotiations center on two broad issues. If the host government is trying to attract FDI, the central issue is likely to be the kind of incentives the host government is prepared to offer to the MNE and what the firm will commit in exchange. If the host government is uncertain about the benefits of FDI and might restrict access, the central issue is likely to be the concessions that the firm must make to go forward with a proposed investment. In the remainder of this section, we will focus on negotiating with a host government.

The Nature of Negotiation

The objective of any negotiation is to reach an agreement that benefits both parties. Negotiation is both an art and a science. The science of it requires analyzing the relative bargaining strengths of each party and the different strategic options available to each party and assessing how the other party might respond to various bargaining ploys.[19] The art of negotiation incorporates "interpersonal skills, the ability to convince and be convinced, the ability to employ a basketful of bargaining ploys, and the wisdom to know when and how to use them."[20] In the context of international business, the art of negotiation also includes understanding the influence of national norms, value systems, and culture on the approach and likely negotiating tactics of the other party as well as sensitivity to such factors in shaping a firm's approach to negotiations with a foreign government. For example, negotiating with the Japanese government for access is likely to be very different from negotiating with the British government. Consequently, it requires different interpersonal skills and bargaining ploys. We discussed the importance of national differences in society and culture in Chapter 3. It would be well to keep these differences in mind at this juncture.

The negotiation process has been characterized as occurring within the context of "the four Cs": common interests, conflicting interests, compromise, and criteria (see Figure 7.2).[21] To explore this concept, consider the negotiation between IBM and Mexico that occurred in 1984 and 1985 when IBM tried to get permission to establish a facility to manufacture personal computers in Guadalajara, Mexico. At that time, Mexican law required foreign investors to agree to a minimum of 51 percent local ownership of any production facilities they established in Mexico (the law was repealed as part of the 1994 North American Free Trade Agreement). The rationale for this law was Mexico's desire to reduce its economic dependence on foreign-owned enterprises, thereby preserving its national sovereignty. As with many such laws, in practice it was used as a bargaining chip by the Mexican government to extract concessions from foreign firms wishing to establish production facilities in Mexico. The government was often willing to waive the 51 percent ownership requirement if a foreign firm would make concessions that increased the beneficial impact of its investment on the Mexican economy.

IBM proposed to invest about $40 million in a state-of-the-art production facility with the capacity to produce 100,000 PCs per year, 75 percent of which would be exported (primarily to the United States). IBM's objective was to take advantage of

Figure 7.2

The Context of
Negotiation—the Four Cs

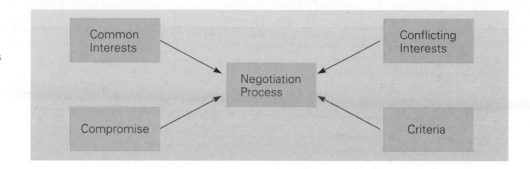

Mexico's low labor costs to reduce the cost of manufacturing PCs. Given the proprietary nature of the product and process technology involved in the design and manufacture of PCs, IBM wanted to maintain 100 percent ownership of the Guadalajara facility. IBM felt that if it entered into a joint venture with a Mexican firm to produce PCs, as required under Mexican law, it would risk giving away valuable technology to a potential future competitor. When presenting its case to the Mexican government, IBM stressed the benefits of the proposed investment for the Mexican economy. These included the creation of 80 direct jobs and 800 indirect ones, the transfer of high-technology job skills to Mexico, new direct investment of $7 million (the remaining $33 million required to finance the investment would be raised from the Mexican capital market), and exports of 75,000 personal computers per year. The Mexican government rejected the proposal on the grounds that IBM did not propose to use sufficient local content in the plant and would thus be importing too many parts and materials. IBM twice resubmitted its proposal. Maintaining its insistence on 100 percent ownership, IBM with each proposal increased its commitment to purchase local parts, increased the level of its direct investment, and raised its planned level of exports. The Mexican government agreed to the third proposal, which had extracted significant concessions from IBM. The final agreement required IBM to invest $91 million (up from $40 million). This money was distributed among expansion of the Guadalajara plant ($7 million), investment in local R&D ($35 million), development of local part suppliers ($20 million), expansion of its purchasing and distribution network ($13 million), contributions to a Mexican government-sponsored semiconductor technology center ($12 million), and various other minor investments. In addition, IBM agreed to achieve 82 percent local content by the fourth year of operation and to export 92 percent of the PCs produced in Mexico. In exchange, the Mexican government waived its 51 percent local ownership requirement and allowed IBM to maintain 100 percent control.[22]

In this example, the common interest of both IBM and Mexico is establishing a new enterprise in Mexico. Conflicting interests arise from such issues as the proportion of component parts that will be procured locally rather than imported, the total amount of investment, the total number of jobs created, and the proportion of output that will be exported. Compromise involves reaching a decision that brings benefits to both parties, even though neither will get all of what it wants. IBM's criteria or objectives are to achieve satisfactory profits and to maintain 100 percent ownership. Mexico's criteria are to achieve satisfactory net benefits from the resource-transfer, employment, and balance-of-payments effects of the investment.

Bargaining Power

The outcome of any negotiated agreement depends on the relative bargaining power of both parties. Each side's bargaining power depends on three factors (see Table 7.3):

- The value each side places on what the other has to offer.
- The number of comparable alternatives available to each side.
- Each party's time horizon.

From the perspective of a firm negotiating the terms of an investment with a host government, the firm's bargaining power is high when the host government places a high value on what the firm has to offer, the number of comparable alternatives open to the firm is great, and the firm has a long time in which to complete the negotiations. The converse also holds. The firm's bargaining power is low when the host government places a low value on what the firm has to offer, few comparable alternatives are open to the firm, and the firm has a short time in which to complete the negotiations.

To see how this plays out in practice, consider again the case of IBM and Mexico. IBM was in a fairly strong bargaining position, primarily because Mexico was suffering from a flight of capital out of the country at the time (1985 and 86), which made the government eager to attract new foreign investment. But IBM's bargaining power was moderated somewhat by three things. First, despite its symbolic importance, the size of the proposed investment was unlikely to have more than a marginal impact on the Mexican economy, so the economic value placed by Mexico on the investment was not that great. Second, IBM was looking for a low-labor-cost, politically stable location close to the United States. Mexico was obviously the most desirable location given these criteria. Greater distance and higher transportation costs made alternative low-labor-cost locations, such as Taiwan or Singapore, relatively less attractive, while other potential locations in Central America were ruled out by political instability. Third, given the profusion of low-cost competitors moving into the US personal computer market during the mid-1980s, IBM probably felt it needed to move quickly to establish its own low-cost production facilities. But there was no compelling reason for Mexico to close a deal quickly. Due to all these factors, the Mexican government also held some bargaining power in the negotiations and was able to extract some concessions from IBM. On the other hand, IBM's strong position allowed it to insist that it maintain 100 percent ownership of its Mexican subsidiary. This represented a significant concession from the Mexican government; IBM was the first major company for which Mexico waived its prohibition of majority ownership.

In a similar case during the 1960s, IBM was one of the few firms to get the Japanese government to waive the restriction on FDI that would allow it to establish a wholly owned subsidiary in Japan. IBM was able to do this because it was the only major source of mainframe computer technology at the time, and numerous Japanese companies needed that technology for data processing. The lack of comparable alternatives available to the Japanese enabled IBM to pry open the Japanese market. Similarly, during the 1980s, Toyota extracted significant concessions from the state of Kentucky in the form of tax breaks, low-interest loans, and grants, and Honda received similar concessions from the state of Ohio. At that time, both states were suffering from high unemployment, and the proposed auto assembly plants promised to have a substantial impact on employment. Also, both companies had a number of states from which to choose. Thus, the high value placed by state governments on the proposed investment and the number of comparable alternatives open to each company considerably strengthened the bargaining power of both companies relative to that of the state governments.

Table 7.3

Determinants of
Bargaining Power

	Bargaining Power of Firm	
	High	**Low**
Firm's time horizon	Long	Short
Comparable alternatives open to firm	Many	Few
Value placed by host government on investment	High	Low

Chapter Summary

This chapter examined governments' influence on firms' decisions to invest in foreign countries. By their choice of policies, both host-country and home-country governments encourage and restrict FDI. We also explored the factors that influence negotiations between a host-country government and a firm contemplating FDI. The chapter made the following points:

1. An important determinant of government policy toward FDI is political ideology. Political ideology ranges from a radical stance that is hostile to FDI to a noninterventionist, free market stance. Between the two extremes is an approach best described as pragmatic nationalism.

2. The radical view sees the MNE as an imperialist tool for exploiting host countries. According to this view, no country should allow FDI. Due to the collapse of communism, the radical view was in retreat everywhere by the end of the 1990s.

3. The free market view sees the MNE as an instrument for increasing the overall efficiency of resource utilization in the world economy. FDI can be viewed as a way of dispersing the production of goods and services to those locations around the globe where they can be produced most efficiently. This view is embraced in principle by a number of nations; in practice, however, most are pragmatic nationalists.

4. Pragmatic nationalism views FDI as having both benefits and costs. Countries adopting a pragmatic stance pursue policies designed to maximize the benefits and minimize the costs of FDI.

5. The benefits of FDI to a host country arise from resource-transfer effects, employment effects, balance-of-payments effects, and its ability to promote competition.

6. FDI can make a positive contribution to a host economy by supplying capital, technology, and management resources that would otherwise not be available. Such resource transfers can stimulate the economic growth of the host economy.

7. Employment effects arise from the direct and indirect creation of jobs by FDI.

8. Balance-of-payments effects arise from the initial capital inflow to finance FDI, from import substitution effects, and from subsequent exports by the new enterprise.

9. By increasing consumer choice, foreign direct investment can help to increase the level of competition in national markets, thereby driving down prices and increasing the economic welfare of consumers.

10. The costs of FDI to a host country include adverse effects on competition and balance of payments and a perceived loss of national sovereignty.

11. Host governments are concerned that foreign MNEs may have greater economic power than indigenous companies and that they may be able to monopolize the market.

12. Adverse effects on the balance of payments arise from the outflow of a foreign subsidiary's earnings and from the import of inputs from abroad.

13. National sovereignty concerns are raised by FDI because key decisions that affect the host country will be made by a foreign parent that may have no real commitment to the host country and the host government will have no control over them.

14. The benefits of FDI to the home (source) country include improvement in the balance of payments as a result of the inward flow of foreign earnings, positive employment effects when the foreign subsidiary creates demand for home-country exports, and benefits from a reverse resource-transfer effect. A reverse resource-transfer effect arises when the foreign subsidiary learns valuable skills abroad that can be transferred back to the home country.

15. The costs of FDI to the home country include adverse balance-of-payments effects that arise from the initial capital outflow and from the export substitution effects of FDI. Costs also arise when FDI exports jobs abroad.

16. Home countries can adopt policies designed to both encourage and restrict FDI. Host countries try to attract FDI by offering incentives and try to restrict FDI by dictating ownership restraints and requiring that foreign MNEs meet specific performance requirements.

17. A firm considering FDI usually must negotiate the terms of the investment with the host government. The object of any negotiation is to reach an agreement that benefits both parties. Negotiation inevitably involves compromise.

18. The outcome of negotiation is typically determined by the relative bargaining powers of the foreign MNE and the host government. Bargaining power depends on the value each side places on what the other has to offer, the number of comparable alternatives available to each side, and each party's time horizon.

Critical Discussion Questions

1. Explain how the political ideology of a host government might influence the negotiations between the host government and a foreign MNE.

2. Under what circumstances is an MNE in a powerful negotiating position vis-à-vis a host government? What kind of concessions is a firm likely to win in such situations?

3. Under what circumstances is an MNE in a weak negotiating position vis-à-vis a host government? What kind of concessions is a host government likely to win in such situations?

4. Inward FDI is bad for (*i*) a developing economy and (*ii*) a developed economy and should be subjected to strict controls! Discuss.

5. Firms should not be investing abroad when there is a need for investment to create jobs at home! Discuss.

6. Do you think the successful conclusion of a multilateral agreement to liberalize regulations governing FDI will benefit the world economy? Why?

CLOSING CASE   FDI in Russia

Five years after the launch of economic reforms designed to transform Russia's lumbering state-directed economy into a modern market system, Russia was experiencing unprecedented capital flight. In 1996, some $22.3 billion left the country, most of it illegally. In contrast, a mere $2.2 billion in foreign investment flowed into the country. According to data from the European Bank for Reconstruction and Development, between 1989 and 1996, foreigners invested just $5.3 billion in Russia, compared to foreign investment of about $11.5 billion in another much smaller former Communist state, Hungary.

Russia consistently tops the charts as the riskiest investment destination tracked by the Economist Intelligence Unit. The risks include a complex tax code that is ever-changing and randomly enforced, often at the expense of foreign companies. Weak and untested property and contract safeguards, endless regulations, and a playing field made uneven by trading and tax favors granted by the Russian government to Russian companies are also frequently cited as contributing to the high risks associated with investment in Russia.

Russia's privatization laws have also tended to discriminate against foreign investors. Most privatization schemes in Russia favor incumbent management and/or local companies. For example, a "shares for loans" scheme in 1995 saw a dozen large companies sold for a fraction of their market value to several large Moscow banks. Foreign investors were not given an opportunity to bid on these assets. Similarly, the privatization of several large-scale companies has seen the majority of stock sold to incumbent managers and employees for a fraction of the price the stock could fetch on the open market.

The failure of the Russian government to capitalize on the sale of state-owned assets is self-defeating given that the country desperately needs capital resources to upgrade its crumbling infrastructure, which is suffering from years of neglect and mismanagement under communism. The Russian oil and gas industry is an example. Russia has the largest oil and gas reserves in the world, but increasingly it is finding it difficult to get these reserves out of the ground and to the international market. Russian oil output plummeted after the collapse of the Soviet Union from 569 million tons in 1988 to 305 million tons in 1996. The problems include leaking pipelines, aging oil wells, a lack of new drilling, and conflict between the various states of the former Soviet Union as to who actually owns much of the oil and gas infrastructure. According to estimates by the World Bank, Russia needs to spend between $40 billion and $50 billion per year just to maintain oil and gas production at its current levels. Boosting produc-

tion back to the levels achieved in the 1980s could require investments of $80 to $100 billion per year—money that Russia does not have.

In an attempt to reverse this slide, the government of Boris Yeltsin in November 1997 announced that Russia's oil and gas industries were open to foreign investment. Among other things, the decree signed by Yeltsin allowed foreign investors to buy 100 percent of Russian oil companies. Within days, Royal Dutch Shell had teamed up with RAO Gazprom, Russia's giant gas monopoly, to bid for Rosneft, the last big state-owned oil group to be privatized. This was quickly followed by a deal under which British Petroleum announced it would purchase 10 percent of another Russian company, Sidanco, giving it a stake in a huge oil field near the Chinese border. The benefits that flow to Russia from such investments could be substantial. In a report prepared for the Russian parliament, Western oil companies said foreign development of just six identified oil and gas fields could create more than 550,000 jobs and earn about $450 billion over their operating lives.

However, before they are prepared to make further large-scale investments, many Western companies say they need stronger legal and tax guarantees. Their preferred method of operation would be to sign internationally recognizable production sharing agreements, which leave the ownership of natural resources with the state but allow foreign developers a defined share of future revenues. Although the Russian government has tried to enact such legislation, the Communist-dominated parliament has so far resisted any attempt to pass such laws.

http://www.gazprom.ru

Sources: C. S. Nicandros, "The Russian Investment Dilemma," *Harvard Business Review,* May–June 1994, p. 40; T. Carrington, "World Bank President Says Economists Were Too Optimistic on Soviet Block," *The Wall Street Journal,* October 14, 1994, p. 13; R. Holman, "Russia to Lift Oil Restrictions," *The Wall Street Journal,* December 6, 1994, p. 24A; R. Corzine, "The Beginning of Russia's Oil Rush," *Financial Times,* November 19, 1997, p. 18; and M. Kaminski, "Russia: Foreign Direct Investment," *Financial Times,* April 9, 1997, p. 6.

Case Discussion Questions

1. What are the benefits to the Russian economy from foreign direct investment in general and in the oil industry in particular?

2. What are the risks that foreign companies must bear when making investments in Russia? What is the source of these risks? How substantial are they?

3. How can foreign companies reduce these risks?

Notes

1. For elaboration see S. Hood and S. Young, *The Economics of the Multinational Enterprise* (London: Longman, 1979), and P. M. Sweezy and H. Magdoff, "The Dynamics of U.S. Capitalism," New York: *Monthly Review Press,* 1972.

2. S. Weiss, "The Long Path to the IBM-Mexico Agreement: An Analysis of Micro-Computer Investment Decisions," working paper 3, NYU School of Business, 1989.

3. United Nations, *World Investment Report, 1998* (New York and Geneva: United Nations, 1997).

4. M. Itoh and K. Kiyono, "Foreign Trade and Direct Investment," in *Industrial Policy of Japan,* ed. R. Komiya, M. Okuno, and K. Suzumura (Tokyo: Academic Press, 1988).

5. Most of the material for this section is drawn from Hood and Young, *Economics of the Multinational Enterprise.*

6. P. M. Romer, "The Origins of Endogenous Growth," *Journal of Economic Perspectives,* 8, no. 1 (1994), pp. 3–22.

7. P. Krugman, *The Age of Diminished Expectations* (Cambridge, MA: MIT Press, 1990).

8. United Nations, *World Investment Report, 1998* (New York and Geneva, United Nations, 1997).

9. A. Cane, "Getting Through: Why Telecommunications Talks Matter," *Financial Times,* February 14, 1997.

10. "Ruggiero Congratulates Governments on Landmark Telecommunications Agreement," World Trade Organization Press Release, February 17, 1997.

11. R. B. Reich, *The Work of Nations: Preparing Ourselves for the 21st Century* (New York: Alfred A. Knopf, 1991).

12. For a recent review, see J. H. Dunning, "Re-Evaluating the Benefits of Foreign Direct Investment," *Transnational Corporations,* 3, no. 1 (February 1994), pp. 23–51.

13. This idea has recently been articulated, although not quite in this form, by C. A. Bartlett and S. Ghoshal, *Managing across Borders: The Transnational Solution* (Boston: Harvard Business School Press, 1989).

14. P. Magnusson, "The Mexico Pact: Worth the Price?" *Business Week,* May 27, 1991, pp. 32–35.

15. C. Johnston, "Political Risk Insurance," in *Assessing Corporate Political Risk,* ed. D. M. Raddock (Totowa, NJ: Rowan & Littlefield, 1986).

16. M. Tolchin and S. Tolchin, *Buying into America: How Foreign Money Is Changing the Face of Our Nation* (New York: Times Books, 1988).

17. J. Behrman and R. E. Grosse, *International Business and Government: Issues and Institutions* (Columbia: University of South Carolina Press, 1990).

18. G. De Jonquiers and S. Kuper, "Push to Keep Alive Effort to Draft Global Investment Rules," *Financial Times,* April 29, 1988, p. 5.

19. For a good introduction, see M. H. Bazerman, *Negotiating Rationally* (New York: Free Press, 1997); and A. Dixit and B. Nalebuff, *Thinking Strategically: The Competitive Edge in Business, Politics, and Everyday Life* (New York: W. W. Norton, 1991).

20. H. Raiffa, *The Art and Science of Negotiation* (Cambridge, MA: Harvard University Press, 1982).

21. J. Fayerweather and A. Kapoor, *Strategy and Negotiation for the International Corporation* (Cambridge, MA: Ballinger, 1976).

22. J. Behrman and R. E. Grosse, *International Business and Government: Issues and Institutions.* (Columbia: University of South Carolina Press, 1990); and S. Weiss, "The Long Path to the IBM-Mexico Agreement: An Analysis of Microcomputer Investment Negotiations, 1983-1986," working paper 3, NYU School of Business, 1989.

CHAPTER EIGHT

REGIONAL ECONOMIC INTEGRATION

Consolidation in the European Insurance Market

Between 1996 and 1998, a wave of mergers swept through the insurance industry in the European Union. The mergers were the results of a process begun on January 1, 1993, when the Single European Act became law among the member states of the European Union. The goal of the Single European Act was to remove barriers to cross-border trade and investment within the confines of the EU, thereby creating a single market instead of a collection of distinct national markets.

Under the act, the EU insurance industry was deregulated and liberalized in mid-1994. Before that, wide variations in competitive conditions, regulations, and prices existed among the different national insurance markets. For example, in early 1994, a simple 10-year life insurance policy in Portugal cost three times more than the same policy in France, while automobile insurance for an experienced driver cost twice as much in Ireland as in Italy and four times as much as in Britain. The new rules did two main things. First, they made genuine cross-border trade possible by allowing insurance companies to sell their products anywhere in the EU on the basis of regulations in their home state, the so-called single license. Second, insurers throughout the EU were allowed to set their own rates for all classes of insurance policy. They no longer needed to submit policy wordings to local officials for approval, thereby dismantling the highly regulated regime behind which much of the industry had sheltered. Among the expected outcomes of these changes were an increase in competition and downward pressure on prices.

By mid-1997, it looked as if the move toward a single market in the EU was going to be given a further push by the impending adoption of a common currency, the euro, among a majority of the EU's member states. The first stage in the adoption of a common currency occurred on January 1, 1999, when 11 of the EU's 15 member states locked in their currency exchange rates against each other and begin handing over responsibility for monetary policy to the newly created European Central Bank. The second stage will occur January 1, 2002, when the currencies of the participating states will be formally abolished and replaced by a common monetary unit, the euro. The coming of the euro will make it much easier for consumers to compare the insurance products offered by companies based in different EU states. This should increase competition and lower prices.

The initial response to these changes in the competitive environment was muted. However, by mid-1996, insurance companies were beginning to realize they needed to reposition themselves to compete more effectively in a single market dominated by a single currency. This realization resulted in a wave of mergers between firms within nations as they tried to attain the scale economies necessary to compete on a larger European playing field. In 1996, Axa and UAP, two French insurance companies, merged to create the largest European insurance company. As part of the deal, Axa gained control over several subsidiary companies that UAP had acquired in Germany in 1994, allowing Axa to increase its presence in this important market. Two large British insurance companies, Royal Insurance and Sun Alliance, also joined forces in 1996.

This was followed in 1997 and early 1998 by a number of cross-border mergers, the most notable of which was between Germany's Allianz and AGF, a large French insurance company. The merger between Allianz and AGF was prompted by a takeover bid for AGF launched by the large Italian insurance company Generali. Generali wanted to acquire AGF to expand its presence in France. The bid spurred Allianz into action. Allianz, which dominates the German insurance market, had been feeling threatened by increased competition in its home market arising in part from a merger between Munich-based Hamburg–Mannheimer and Britain's Victoria Insurance and in part from the increased strength of the Axa–UAP combination. Displaying a sensitivity for French sentiments that Generali lacked, Allianz promised that AGF's management would remain French and that Allianz executives would be in the minority on the board of the merged company. Unwilling to make such concessions, Generali eventually withdrew its counter-bid for AGF, but not before it had won a significant concession from Allianz and AGF. In return for withdrawing its bid, the German and French companies agreed to sell several important subsidiaries to the Italian insurer, boosting Generali's premiums by more than half and giving it a sizable presence in both Germany and Italy.

As a result of these developments, the shape of the EU insurance industry had been substantially altered by mid-1998. Allianz had emerged as the largest pan-European insurer, with $64 billion in total premium income. In addition to its leading position in Germany, Allianz had become one of the top five insurers in Beligum, Spain, and France. The Axa–UAP combination had become the second largest European insurer with significant activities in France and Germany, while Italy's Generali with premium income of $31 billion was now the third largest pan-European insurance company.

http://www.allianz.com

Sources: R. Lapper, "Hard Work to Be Free and Single,"*Financial Times*, July 1, 1994, p. 19; "A Singular Market. In the European Union: A Survey," *The Economist*, October 22, 1994, pp. 10–16; "Insurance: Can the Empire Strike Back?" *The Economist*, April 25, 1998, p. 76; and C. Adams, A. Jack and A. Fisher, "Allianz Bid Mirrors Its Global Ambitions," *Financial Times*, November 11, 1997, p. 20.

Introduction

One of the most notable trends in the global economy in recent years has been the accelerated movement toward regional economic integration. By **regional economic integration,** we mean agreements among countries in a geographic region to reduce, and ultimately remove, tariff and nontariff barriers to the free flow of goods, services, and factors of production between each other. The last decade has witnessed an unprecedented proliferation of regional arrangements. Between 1947 and mid-1997, 163 regional trade agreements were notified to the GATT or its successor, the WTO. Between 1986 and 1991, only five agreements were notified to the GATT, but in the five years between 1992 and 1996, 77 agreements were reported. Of these 163 agreements, about 60 percent are currently in force. Thus, over three-quarters of the operational regional agreements in existence today were established in the 1992–1996 period.[1]

Consistent with the predictions of international trade theory, particularly the theory of comparative advantage (see Chapter 4), the belief has been that agreements designed to promote freer trade within regions will produce gains from trade for all member countries. As we saw in Chapter 5, the General Agreement on Tariffs and Trade and its successor, the World Trade Organization, also seek to reduce trade barriers. However, with over 120 member-states the WTO has a worldwide perspective. By entering into regional agreements, groups of countries aim to reduce trade barriers more rapidly than can be achieved under the auspices of the WTO.

Nowhere has the movement toward regional economic integration been more successful than in Europe. As noted in the opening case, on January 1, 1993, the European Union effectively became a single market with 340 million consumers. But the EU is not stopping there. The member-states of the EU are launching a single currency, they are moving toward a closer political union, and they are discussing enlarging the EU from the current 15 countries to ultimately include another 15 Eastern European states.

Similar moves toward regional integration are being pursued elsewhere in the world. Canada, Mexico, and the United States have implemented the North American Free Trade Agreement (NAFTA). This promises to ultimately remove all barriers to the free flow of goods and services between the three countries. Argentina, Brazil, Paraguay, and Uruguay have implemented a 1991 agreement to start reducing barriers to trade between themselves. Known as MERCOSUR, this free trade area is viewed by some as the first step in a move toward creation of a South American Free Trade Area (SAFTA). There is also talk of establishing a hemispherewide Free Trade Agreement of the Americas (FTAA). Along similar lines, 18 Pacific Rim countries, including the NAFTA member states, Japan, and China, have been discussing a possible pan-Pacific free trade area under the auspices of the Asian Pacific Economic Cooperation forum

(APEC). There are also active attempts at regional economic integration in Central America, the Andean Region of South America, Southeast Asia, and parts of Africa.

As the opening case on the European Insurance industry demonstrates, a move toward greater regional economic integration can deliver important benefits to consumers and present firms with new challenges. In the European insurance industry, the creation of a single EU insurance market opened formerly protected national markets to increased competition, resulting in lower prices for insurance products. This benefits consumers, who now have more money to spend on other goods and services. As for insurance companies, the increase in competition and greater price pressure that has followed the creation of a single market have forced them to look for cost savings from economies of scale. They have also sought to increase their presence in different nations. The mergers occurring in the European insurance industry are seen as a way of achieving both these goals.

The rapid spread of regional trade agreements raises the fear among some of a world in which regional trade blocs compete against each other. In this scenario of the future, free trade will exist within each bloc, but each bloc will protect its market from outside competition with high tariffs. The specter of the EU and NAFTA turning into "economic fortresses" that shut out foreign producers with high tariff barriers is particularly worrisome to those who believe in unrestricted free trade. If such a scenario were to materialize, the resulting decline in trade between blocs could more than offset the gains from free trade within blocs.

With these issues in mind, the main objectives of this chapter are as follows: (1) to explore the economic and political debate surrounding regional economic integration, paying particular attention to the economic and political benefits and costs of integration; (2) to review progress toward regional economic integration around the world; and (3) to map the important implications of regional economic integration for the practice of international business. Before tackling these objectives, however, we first need to examine the levels of integration that are theoretically possible.

Levels of Economic Integration

Several levels of economic integration are possible in theory (see Figure 8.1). From least integrated to most integrated, they are a free trade area, a customs union, a common market, an economic union, and, finally, a full political union.

Free Trade Area

In a free trade area, all barriers to the trade of goods and services among member countries are removed. In the theoretically ideal free trade area, no discriminatory tariffs, quotas, subsidies, or administrative impediments are allowed to distort trade between members. Each country, however, is allowed to determine its own trade policies with regard to nonmembers. Thus, for example, the tariffs placed on the products of nonmember countries may vary from member to member.

The most enduring free trade area in the world is the European Free Trade Association (EFTA). Established in January 1960, EFTA currently joins four countries—Norway, Iceland, Liechtenstein, and Switzerland—down from seven in 1995 (three EFTA members, Austria, Finland, and Sweden, joined the EU on January 1, 1996). EFTA was founded by those Western European countries that initially decided not to be part of the European Community (the forerunner of the EU). Its original members included Austria, Britain, Denmark, Finland, and Sweden, all of whom are now members of the EU. The emphasis of EFTA has been on free trade in industrial goods. Agriculture was left out of the arrangement, each member being allowed to determine its own level of support. Members are also free to determine the level of protection applied to goods coming from outside EFTA. Other free trade areas include the North American Free Trade Agreement.

Figure 8.1

Levels of Economic Integration

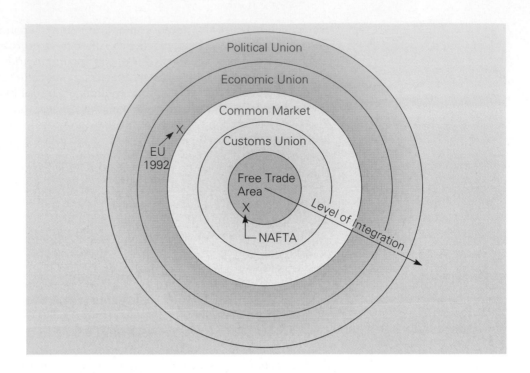

Customs Union

The customs union is one step further along the road to full economic and political integration. A customs union eliminates trade barriers between member countries and adopts a common external trade policy. Establishment of a common external trade policy necessitates significant administrative machinery to oversee trade relations with nonmembers. Most countries that enter into a customs union desire even greater economic integration down the road. The EU began as a customs union and has moved beyond this stage. Other customs unions around the world include the current version of the Andean Pact (between Bolivia, Colombia, Ecuador, and Peru). The Andean Pact established free trade between member countries and imposes a common tariff, of 5 to 20 percent, on products imported from outside.[2]

Common Market

Like a customs union, the theoretically ideal common market has no barriers to trade between member countries and a common external trade policy. Unlike a customs union, a common market also allows factors of production to move freely between members. Labor and capital are free to move because there are no restrictions on immigration, emigration, or cross-border flows of capital between member countries. The EU is currently a common market, although its goal is full economic union. The EU is the only successful common market ever established, although several regional groupings have aspired to this goal. Establishing a common market demands a significant degree of harmony and cooperation on fiscal, monetary, and employment policies. Achieving this degree of cooperation has proven very difficult. Currently, MERCOSUR, the South America grouping of Argentina, Brazil, Paraguay, and Uruguay, hopes to eventually establish itself as a common market.

Economic Union

An economic union entails even closer economic integration and cooperation than a common market. Like the common market, an economic union involves the free flow of products and factors of production between member countries and the adoption of a common external trade policy. Unlike a common market, a full economic union also requires a common currency, harmonization of members' tax rates, and a common monetary and fiscal policy. Such a high degree of integration demands a coordinating bureaucracy and the sacrifice of significant amounts of national sovereignty to that bureaucracy. There are no true economic unions in the world today, but the EU is clearly moving in this direction, particularly given the plans to create a single EU currency, the euro, by January 1, 2002.

Political Union

The move toward economic union raises the issue of how to make a coordinating bureaucracy accountable to the citizens of member nations. The answer is through political union. The EU is on the road toward political union. The European Parliament, which is playing an ever more important role in the EU, has been directly elected by citizens of the EU countries since the late 1970s. In addition, the Council of Ministers (the controlling, decision-making body of the EU) is composed of government ministers from each EU member. Canada and the United States provide examples of even closer degrees of political union; in each country, independent states were effectively combined into a single nation. Ultimately, the EU may move toward a similar federal structure.

The Case for Regional Integration

The case for regional integration is both economic and political. The case for integration is typically not accepted by many groups within a country, which explains why most attempts to achieve regional economic integration have been contentious and halting. In this section, we examine the economic and political cases for integration and two impediments to integration. In the next section, we look at the case against integration.

The Economic Case for Integration

The economic case for regional integration is relatively straightforward. We saw in Chapter 4 how economic theories of international trade predict that unrestricted free trade will allow countries to specialize in the production of goods and services that they can produce most efficiently. The result is greater world production than would be possible with trade restrictions. We also saw in that chapter how opening a country to free trade stimulates economic growth in the country, which creates dynamic gains from trade. Further, we saw in Chapter 6 how foreign direct investment (FDI) can transfer technological, marketing, and managerial know-how to host nations. Given the central role of knowledge in stimulating economic growth, opening a country to FDI also is likely to stimulate economic growth. In sum, economic theories suggest that free trade and investment is a positive-sum game, in which all participating countries stand to gain.

Given this, the theoretical ideal is a total absence of barriers to the free flow of goods, services, and factors of production among nations. However, as we saw in Chapters 5 and 7, a case can be made for government intervention in international trade and FDI. Because many governments have accepted part or all of the case for intervention, unrestricted free trade and FDI have proved to be only an ideal. Although international institutions such as GATT and the WTO have been moving the world toward a free trade regime, success has been less than total. In a world of many nations and many political ideologies, it is very difficult to get all countries to agree to a common set of rules.

Against this background, regional economic integration can be seen as an attempt to achieve additional gains from the free flow of trade and investment between countries beyond those attainable under international agreements such as GATT and the WTO. It is easier to establish a free trade and investment regime among a limited number of adjacent countries than among the world community. Problems of coordination and policy harmonization are largely a function of the number of countries that seek agreement. The greater the number of countries involved, the greater the number of perspectives that must be reconciled, and the harder it will be to reach agreement. Thus, attempts at regional economic integration are motivated by a desire to exploit the gains from free trade and investment.

The Political Case for Integration

The political case for regional economic integration has also loomed large in most attempts to establish free trade areas, customs unions, and the like. By linking neighboring economies and making them increasingly dependent on each other, incentives are created for political cooperation between the neighboring states. In turn, the potential for violent conflict between the states is reduced. In addition, by grouping their economies, the countries can enhance their political weight in the world.

These considerations underlay establishment of the European Community (EC) in 1957 (the EC was the forerunner of the EU). Europe had suffered two devastating wars in the first half of the century, both arising out of the unbridled ambitions of nation-states. Those who have sought a united Europe have always had a desire to make another outbreak of war in Europe unthinkable. Many Europeans also felt that after World War II the European nation-states were no longer large enough to hold their own in world markets and world politics. The need for a united Europe to deal with the United States and the politically alien Soviet Union certainly loomed large in the minds of many of the EC's founders.[3]

Impediments to Integration

Despite the strong economic and political arguments for integration, it has never been easy to achieve or sustain. There are two main reasons for this. First, although economic integration benefits the majority, it has its costs. While a nation as a whole may benefit significantly from a regional free trade agreement, certain groups may lose. Moving to a free trade regime involves some painful adjustments. For example, as a result of the 1994 establishment of NAFTA, some Canadian and US workers in such industries as textiles, which employ low-cost, low-skilled labor, will certainly lose their jobs as Canadian and US firms move production to Mexico. The promise of significant net benefits to the Canadian and US economies as a whole is little comfort to those who will lose as a result of NAFTA. It is understandable then, that such groups were in the forefront of opposition to NAFTA and will continue to oppose any widening of the agreement.

A second impediment to integration arises from concerns over national sovereignty. For example, Mexico's concerns about maintaining control of its oil interests resulted in an agreement with Canada and the United States to exempt the Mexican oil industry from any liberalization of foreign investment regulations achieved under NAFTA. Concerns about national sovereignty arise because close economic integration demands that countries give up some degree of their control over such key policy issues as monetary policy, fiscal policy (e.g., tax policy), and trade policy. This has been a major stumbling block in the EU. To achieve full economic union, the EU is trying to introduce a common currency to be controlled by a central EU bank. Although most member states have signed on to such a deal, Britain remains an important holdout. A politically important segment of public opinion in that country opposes a common currency on the grounds that it would require relinquishing control of the country's monetary policy to the EU—which many British perceive as a bureaucracy run by foreigners. In 1992, the British won the right to opt out of any single currency agreement, and as of 1998, there was little sign that the British government would reverse its decision.

The Case Against Regional Integration

Although the tide has been running strongly in favor of regional free trade agreements in recent years, some economists have expressed concern that the benefits of regional integration have been oversold, while the costs have often been ignored.[4] They point out that the benefits of regional integration are determined by the extent of trade creation, as opposed to trade diversion. **Trade creation** occurs when high-cost domestic producers are replaced by low-cost producers within the free trade area. It may also occur when higher-cost external producers are replaced by lower-cost external producers within the free trade area (see the accompanying Country Focus for an example). **Trade diversion** occurs when lower-cost external suppliers are replaced by higher-cost suppliers within the free trade area. A regional free trade agreement will benefit the world only if the amount of trade it creates exceeds the amount it diverts.

Suppose the United States and Mexico imposed tariffs on imports from all countries, and then they set up a free trade area, scrapping all trade barriers between themselves but maintaining tariffs on imports from the rest of the world. If the United States began to import textiles from Mexico, would this change be for the better? If the United States previously produced all its own textiles at a higher cost than Mexico, then the free trade agreement has shifted production to the cheaper source. According to the theory of comparative advantage, trade has been created within the regional grouping, and there would be no decrease in trade with the rest of the world. Clearly, the change would be for the better. If, however, the United States previously imported textiles from South Korea, which produced them more cheaply than either Mexico or the United States, then trade has been diverted from a low-cost source—a change for the worse.

In theory, WTO rules should ensure that a free trade agreement does not result in trade diversion. These rules allow free trade areas to be formed only if the members set tariffs that are not higher or more restrictive to outsiders than the ones previously in effect. However, as we saw in Chapter 5, a wide range of nontariff barriers are not covered by GATT and the WTO. As a result, regional trade blocs could emerge whose markets are protected from outside competition by high nontariff barriers. In such cases, the trade diversion effects might well outweigh the trade creation effects. The only way to guard against this possibility, according to those concerned about this potential, is to increase the scope of the WTO so it covers nontariff barriers to trade. There is no sign that this is going to occur anytime soon, however; so the risk remains that regional economic integration will result in trade diversion.

Regional Economic Integration in Europe

Europe has two trade blocs—the European Union and the European Free Trade Association. Of the two, the EU is by far the more significant, not just in terms of membership (the EU has 15 members, and EFTA has 4), but also in terms of economic and political influence in the world economy. Many now see the EU as an emerging economic and political superpower of the same order as the United States and Japan. Accordingly, we will concentrate our attention on the EU.[5]

Evolution of the European Union

The EU is the product of two political factors: (1) the devastation of two world wars on Western Europe and the desire for a lasting peace, and (2) the European nations' desire to hold their own on the world's political and economic stage. In addition, many Europeans were aware of the potential economic benefits of closer economic integration of the countries.

COUNTRY FOCUS
The Impact of NAFTA on the US Textile Industry

When the North American Free Trade Agreement went into effect in 1994, many expressed fears that one consequence would be large job losses in the US textile industry as companies moved production from the United States to Mexico. Oopponents of NAFTA argued passionately, but unsuccessfully, that the treaty should not be adopted because of the negative impact it would have on employment in the United States, particularly in industries such as textiles.

A glance at the data four years after the passage of NAFTA suggests the critics had a point. Between 1994 and mid-1997, about 149,000 US apparel workers lost their jobs, over 15 percent of all employment in the industry. Much of this job loss has occurred because producers have moved production to Mexico. Between 1994 and 1997, Mexico's apparel exports to the United States trebled to $3.3 billion. In 1993, the US jeans maker, Guess?, sourced 95 percent of its product domestically. Now it gets about 60 percent of its clothing from outside the United States, with Mexico as one of the biggest suppliers. Similarly, in 1995, Fruit of the Loom Inc., the largest manufacturer of underwear in the United States, said it would close six of its domestic plants and cut back operations at two others, laying off about 3,200 workers, or 12 percent of

its US work force. The company announced the closures were part of its drive to move its operations to cheaper plants abroad, particularly in Mexico. Before the closures less than 30 percent of its sewing was done outside the United States, but Fruit of the Loom planned to move the majority of that work to Mexico.

However, the issue becomes more complicated when one takes a closer look at the data. To be sure, there have been job losses in the US textile industry, but clothing prices in the United States have also fallen since 1994 as textile production shifted from high-cost US producers to lower-cost Mexican producers. This obviously benefits US consumers, who now have more money to spend on other items. The cost of a typical pair of designer jeans, for example, fell from $55 in 1994 to $48 in 1997. Nor is the fall in prices simply a result of the movement of production from the United States to Mexico. NAFTA has also resulted in textile production being moved from Asia to Mexico. In 1980, 83 percent of all US textile imports came from Asia. By 1997, Asia accounted for 41 percent of US textile imports as companies switched their source of textiles from Asia to Mexico. An example of this trend is the US clothing retailer The Limited Inc., which in 1997 switched its source for textile products from Sri Lanka to Mexico.

The original forerunner of the EU, the European Coal and Steel Community, was formed in 1951 by Belgium, France, West Germany, Italy, Luxembourg, and the Netherlands. Its objective was to remove barriers to intragroup shipments of coal, iron, steel, and scrap metal. With the signing of the Treaty of Rome in 1957, the European Community was established. The name changed again in 1994 when the *European Community* became the *European Union* following the ratification of the Maastricht Treaty (discussed later).

The Treaty of Rome provided for the creation of a common market. This is apparent in Article 3 of the treaty, which laid down the key objectives of the new community. Article 3 called for the elimination of internal trade barriers and the creation of a common external tariff and required member states to abolish obstacles to the free movement of factors of production among the members. To facilitate the free movement of goods, services, and factors of production, the treaty provided for any necessary harmonization of the member states' laws. Furthermore, the treaty committed the EC to establish common policies in agriculture and transportation.

The community grew in 1973, when Great Britain, Ireland, and Denmark joined. These three were followed in 1981 by Greece, in 1986 by Spain and Portugal, and in

http://iepnt1.itaiep.doc.gov/nafta/nafta2.htm

According to a spokesman for The Limited, although wages in Mexico are three times the $60 per month that apparel workers make in Sri Lanka, it's cheaper and faster to move goods from Mexico to the United States than from Sri Lanka. Under NAFTA there are no tariffs on imports from Mexico, but there is a 19 percent tariff levied on textile imports from Sri Lanka. When all these factors are considered, it becomes cheaper to produce textiles in Mexico than Sri Lanka. Thus, as a result of NAFTA, production has been shifted to a lower external cost source. The Limited plans to pass on its cost savings to US consumers in the form of lower prices.

In addition to lower prices, the shift in textile production to Mexico has also benefited the US economy in other ways. First, it has helped produce a surge in exports from US fabric and yarn makers—many of whom are in the chemical industry. Before the passage of NAFTA, US yarn producers, such as Burlington Industries and E.I. du Pont, supplied only small amounts of fabric and yarn to Asian producers. However, as apparel production has moved from Asia to Mexico, exports of fabric and yarn to that country have surged. US producers supply 70 percent of the raw material going to Mexican sewing shops. Between 1994 and 1997, fabric and yarn exports to Mexico,

mostly in the form of cut pieces ready for sewing, nearly doubled to around $2.5 billion per year. In addition, US manufacturers of textile equipment have also seen an increase in their sales as apparel factories in Mexico order textile equipment. Exports of textile equipment to Mexico nearly doubled in 1995 over the 1994 level to $35.5 million.

Although there have been job losses in the US textile industry, advocates of NAFTA argue that there have been net benefits to the US economy in the form of lower clothing prices and an increase in exports from fabric and yarn producers and from producers of textile machinery. Trade has been created as a result of NAFTA. The gains from trade are being captured by US consumers and by producers in certain sectors. As always, the establishment of a free trade area creates winners and losers, but advocates argue that the gains easily outweigh the losses.

Sources: C. Palmeri and J. Aguayo, "Good-bye Guangdong, Hello Jalisco," *Forbes,* February 10, 1997, pp. 76–77; "NAFTA Open Market Bolsters Mexican Textile Industry," *Journal of Commerce,* December 6, 1996, p. 4A; B. J. Feder, "Fruit of the Loom to Close Six U.S. Plants," *New York Times,* October 31, 1995, p. 6; and P. Green, "US Textile Machinery Sector Battles Deficit as Exports Inch Up," *Journal of Commerce,* March 23, 1995, p. 8B.

1996 by Austria, Finland, and Sweden (see Map 8.1) bringing the total membership to 15 (East Germany became part of the EC after the reunification of Germany in 1990). With a population of 350 million and a GDP greater than that of the United States, these enlargements made the EU a potential global superpower.

Political Structure of the European Union

The economic policies of the EU are formulated and implemented by a complex and still-evolving political structure. The five main institutions in this structure are the European Council, the Council of Ministers, the European Commission, the European Parliament, and the Court of Justice.[6]

The European Council

The European Council is composed of the heads of state of the EU's member nations and the president of the European Commission. Each head of state is normally accompanied by a foreign minister to these meetings. The European Council meets at least twice a year and often resolves major policy issues and sets policy directions.

Map 8.1

The European Union

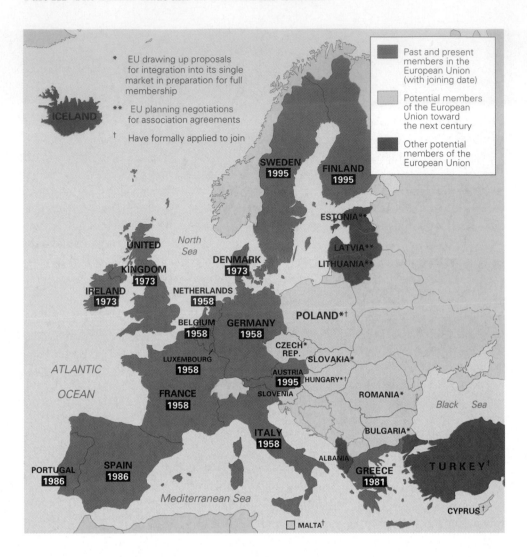

The European Commission

The European Commission is responsible for proposing EU legislation, implementing it, and monitoring compliance with EU laws by member states. Headquartered in Brussels, Belgium, the commission has more than 10,000 employees. It is run by a group of 20 commissioners appointed by each member country for four-year renewable terms. Most countries appoint only one commissioner, although the most populated states—Britain, France, Germany, Italy, and Spain—appoint two each. A president and six vice presidents are chosen from among these commissioners for two-year renewable terms. Each commissioner is responsible for a portfolio that is typically concerned with a specific policy area. For example, there is a commissioner for agricultural policy and another for competition policy. Although they are appointed by their respective governments, commissioners are meant to act independently and in the best interests of the EU, as opposed to being advocates for a particular national interest.

The commission has a monopoly in proposing European Union legislation. The commission starts the legislative ball rolling by making a proposal, which goes to the Council of Ministers and then to the European Parliament. The Council of Ministers cannot legislate without a commission proposal in front of it. The Treaty of Rome gave the commission this power in an attempt to limit national infighting by taking the right to propose legislation away from nationally elected political representatives, giving it to "independent" commissioners.

The commission is also responsible for implementing aspects of EU law, although in practice much of this must be delegated to member states. Another responsibility of the commission is to monitor member states to make sure they are complying with EU laws. In this policing role, the commission will normally ask a state to comply with any EU laws that are being broken. If this persuasion is not sufficient, the commission can refer a case to the Court of Justice.

The Council of Ministers

The interests of member states are represented in the Council of Ministers. It is clearly the ultimate controlling authority within the EU since draft legislation from the commission can become EU law only if the council agrees. The council is composed of one representative from the government of each member state. The membership, however, varies depending on the topic being discussed. When agricultural issues are being discussed, the agriculture ministers from each state attend council meetings; when transportation is being discussed transportation ministers attend, and so on. Before 1993, all council issues had to be decided by unanimous agreement between member states. This often led to marathon council sessions and a failure to make progress or reach agreement on proposals submitted from the commission. In an attempt to clear the resulting logjams, the Single European Act formalized the use of majority voting rules on issues "which have as their object the establishment and functioning of a single market." Most other issues, however, such as tax regulations and immigration policy, still require unanimity among council members if they are to become law.

The European Parliament

The European Parliament, which now has about 630 members, is directly elected by the populations of the member states. The parliament, which meets in Strasbourg, France, is primarily a consultative rather than legislative body. It debates legislation proposed by the commission and forwarded to it by the council. It can propose amendments to that legislation, which the commission (and ultimately the council) are not obliged to take up but often will. The power of the parliament recently has been increasing, although not by as much as parliamentarians would like. The European Parliament now has the right to vote on the appointment of commissioners, as well as veto power over some laws (such as the EU budget and single-market legislation). One major debate now being waged in Europe is whether the council or the parliament should ultimately be the most powerful body in the EU. There is concern in Europe over the democratic accountability of the EU bureaucracy. Some think the answer to this apparent democratic deficit lies in increasing the power of the parliament, while others think that true democratic legitimacy lies with elected governments, acting through the Council of Ministers.[7]

The Court of Justice

The Court of Justice, which is comprised of one judge from each country, is the supreme appeals court for EU law. Like commissioners, the judges are required to act as independent officials, rather than as representatives of national interests. The commission or a member country can bring other members to the court for failing to meet treaty obligations. Similarly, member countries, companies, or institutions can bring the commission or council to the court for failure to act according to an EU treaty.

The Single European Act

Two revolutions occurred in Europe in the late 1980s. The first was the collapse of communism in Eastern Europe. The second revolution was much quieter, but its impact on Europe and the world may have been just as profound as the first. It was the adoption of the Single European Act by the member nations of the EC in 1987. This act committed the EC countries to work toward establishment of a single market by December 31, 1992.

The Stimulus for the Single European Act

The Single European Act was born of a frustration among EC members that the community was not living up to its promise. By the early 1980s, it was clear that the EC had fallen short of its objectives to remove barriers to the free flow of trade and investment between member countries and to harmonize the wide range of technical and legal standards for doing business. At the end of 1982, the European Commission found itself inundated with 770 cases of intra-EC protectionism to investigate. In addition, some 20 EC directives setting common technical standards for a variety of products ranging from cars to thermometers were deadlocked.

Many companies considered the EC's main problem was the disharmony of the members' technical, legal, regulatory, and tax standards. The "rules of the game" differed substantially from country to country, which stalled the creation of a true single internal market. Consider the European automobile industry. In the mid-1980s, there was no single EC-wide automobile market analogous to the US automobile market. Instead, the EC market remained fragmented into 12 national markets. There were four main reasons for this:

- Different technical standards required cars to be customized to national requirements (e.g., the headlights and sidelights of cars sold in Great Britain must be wired in a significantly different way than those of cars sold in Italy, and the standards for car windshields in France are very different from those in Germany).

- Different tax regimes created price differentials across countries that would not be found in a single market.

- An agreement to allow automobile companies to sell cars through exclusive dealer networks allowed auto companies and their dealers to adapt their model ranges and prices on a country-by-country basis with little fear that these differences would be undermined by competing retailers.

- In violation of Article 3 of the Treaty of Rome, each country had adopted its own trade policy with regard to automobile imports (e.g., whereas Japanese imports were not restricted in Belgium, they were limited to 11 percent of the car market in Great Britain and to less than 2 percent in France and Italy). These divisions resulted in substantial price differentials between countries. In 1989, the prices of the same model of car were, on average, 31 percent higher in the United Kingdom and 11 percent higher in Germany than in Belgium.[8]

In addition to such considerations, many member countries were subsidizing national firms, thereby distorting competition. For example, the French government in 1990 decided to pump FFr 6 billion into Groupe Bull, a state-owned computer maker, and Thomson, a defense and electronics group. This brought protests from ICL, a British computer maker, on the grounds that such a subsidy would allow Groupe Bull to capture more of the EC computer market.[9]

Against this background, many of the EC's prominent business people mounted an energetic campaign in the early 1980s to end the EC's economic divisions. The EC responded by creating the Delors Commission. Under the chairmanship of Jacques Delors, the former French finance minister and president of the EC Commission, the Delors Commission produced a discussion paper in 1985. This proposed that all impediments to the formation of a single market be eliminated by December 31, 1992. Two more years passed before the EC persuaded all member countries to accept the proposals contained in the discussion paper. The result was the Single European Act, which was independently ratified by the parliaments of each member country and became EC law in 1987.

The Objectives of the Act

The purpose of the Single European Act was to have a single market in place by December 31, 1992. The act proposed the following changes:[10]

1. Remove all frontier controls between EC countries, thereby abolishing delays and reducing the resources required for complying with trade bureaucracy.

2. Apply the principle of "mutual recognition" to product standards. A standard developed in one EC country should be accepted in another, provided it meets basic requirements in such matters as health and safety.

3. Open public procurement to nonnational suppliers, reducing costs directly by allowing lower-cost suppliers into national economies and indirectly by forcing national suppliers to compete.

4. Lift barriers to competition in the retail banking and insurance businesses, which should drive down the costs of financial services, including borrowing, throughout the EC.

5. Remove all restrictions on foreign exchange transactions between member countries by the end of 1992.

6. Abolish restrictions on cabotage—the right of foreign truckers to pick up and deliver goods within another member state's borders—by the end of 1992. This could reduce the cost of haulage within the EC by 10 to 15 percent.

7. All those changes should lower the costs of doing business in the EC, but the single-market program was also expected to have more complicated supply-side effects. For example, the expanded market should give EC firms greater opportunities to exploit economies of scale. In addition, the increase in competitive intensity brought about by removing internal barriers to trade and investment should force EC firms to become more efficient.

To signify the importance of the Single European Act, the European Community also decided to change its name to the European Union once the act took effect.

Implications

The implications of the Single European Act are potentially enormous. We discuss the implications for business practice in more detail in the Implications for Business section at the end of the chapter. For now it should be noted that, as long as the EU is successful in establishing a single market, the member countries can expect significant gains from the free flow of trade and investment. These gains may be greater than those predicted by standard trade theory that accrue when regions specialize in producing those goods and services that they produce most efficiently. The lower costs of doing business implied by the Single European Act will benefit EU firms, as will the potential economies of scale inherent in serving a single market of 360 million consumers. On the other hand, as a result of the Single European Act, many EU firms are facing increased competitive pressure. Countries such as France and Italy have long used administrative trade barriers and subsidies to protect their home markets from foreign competition. Removal of these barriers has increased competition, and some firms may go out of business. Ultimately, however, both consumers and EU firms will benefit from this. Consumers will benefit from the lower prices implied by a more competitive market. EU firms will benefit if the increased competitive pressure forces them to become more efficient, thereby transforming them into more effective international competitors capable of going head-to-head with US and Asian rivals in the world marketplace.

But the shift toward a single market has not been as rapid as many would like. Six years after the Single European Act became EU law, there have been a number of delays in applying the act to certain industries, often because countries have appealed to the Council of Ministers for more time. The insurance industry, for example, was exempt until July 1994 (see the opening case for details). Investment services were not liberalized until January 1996, and there was no compulsion to liberalize basic telephone services until 1998 (and until 2003 in poorer countries such as Greece to protect local telephone companies from being "crushed" by the likes of Britain's BT or America's AT&T).[11] Also, many European countries have found their dreams of a single market dashed by the realities of deep and enduring cultural and language barriers between countries, which still separate many national markets, although not as effectively as formal barriers to trade once did. Still, the long-run prognosis remains very strong, and despite all the short-term setbacks, the EU will probably have a reasonably well-functioning single market by the early years of the next century.

European Monetary Union (EMU): The Adoption of a Single Currency

In December 1991, leaders of the EC member states met in Maastricht, the Netherlands, to discuss the next steps for the EC. The results of the Maastricht meeting surprised both Europe and the rest of the world. The EC countries had been fighting for months over a common currency. Although many economists believed a common currency was required to cement a closer economic union, deadlock had been predicted. The British in particular had opposed any attempt to establish a common currency. Instead of a deadlock, the 12 members signed a treaty that not only committed them to adopting a common EC currency by January 1, 1999, but also paved the way for closer political cooperation.

The treaty laid down the main elements, if only in embryo, of a future European government: a single currency, the euro; a common foreign and defense policy; a common citizenship; and an EU parliament with teeth. It is now just a matter of waiting, some believe, for history to take its course and a "United States of Europe" to emerge. Of more immediate interest are the implications for business of the plans to establish a single currency.[12]

Benefits of EMU

As with many of the provisions of the Single European Act, the move to a single currency should significantly lower the costs of doing business in the EU. The gains come from reduced exchange costs and reduced risk.[13] The EU has calculated that EU businesses convert roughly $8 trillion from one EU currency to another every year, which necessitates about $12 billion in exchange costs. A single currency would avoid these costs and help firms in other ways, as fewer resources would be required for accounting, treasury management, and the like. As for reduced risk, a single currency would reduce the risks that arise from currency fluctuations. The values of currencies fluctuate against each other continually. As we will see in Chapter 9, this introduces risks into international transactions. For example, if a British firm builds a factory in Greece, and the value of the Greek currency subsequently declines against the British pound, the value of the British firm's Greek assets will also decline. A single currency would eliminate such risks, thus reducing the cost of capital. Interest rates would fall, and investment and output would increase as a consequence.

In addition to these gains, advocates argue that a single currency will make it difficult for companies to charge different prices in different EU countries.[14] If the price for a car in euros is 20 percent higher in Germany than it is in France, so the argument goes, many German consumers will simply go to France to buy their cars. This will force down the price for cars in Germany until they are equal to the price for the same car in neighboring states, resulting in significant gains for German consumers. The introduction of the euro should result in a significant increase in price competition across a wide range of industries (for another example, see the opening case on the European insurance industry). The resulting fall in prices will give European consumers more money to spend on other items, raising their economic welfare. In addition, the increase in price competition will force business to respond by becoming more efficient. This too should be good for the EU economy.

Costs of EMU

The drawback, for some, of a single currency is that national authorities would lose control over monetary policy. Thus, the EU's monetary policy must be well managed. The Maastricht Treaty called for establishment of an independent European Central Bank (ECB), similar in some respects to the US Federal Reserve, with a clear mandate to manage monetary policy so as to ensure price stability. Like the US Federal Reserve, the ECB, based in Frankfurt, is meant to be independent from political pressure—although critics question this. Among other things, the ECB will set interest rates and determine monetary policy across the euro zone. Critics fear that the ECB will respond to political pressure by pursuing a lax monetary policy, which in turn will raise average inflation rates across the euro zone, hampering economic growth.

Several nations were concerned about the effectiveness of such an arrangement and the implied loss of national sovereignty. Reflecting these concerns, Britain, Denmark, and Sweden won the right from other members to stay out of the monetary union if they chose. According to some critics, European monetary union represents putting the economic cart before the political horse. In their view, a single currency should follow, not precede, political union. They argue that the euro will unleash enormous pressures for tax harmonization and fiscal transfers, both policies that cannot be pursued without the appropriate political structure. Some critics also argue that the EMU will result in the imposition of a single interest rate regime on national economies that are not truly convergent and are experiencing divergent economic growth rates.

The most apolitical vision that flows from these negative views is that the euro will lead to lower economic growth and higher inflation within Europe. To quote one critic:

> Imposing a single exchange rate and an inflexible exchange rate on countries that are characterized by different economic shocks, inflexible wages, low labor mobility, and separate national fiscal systems without significant cross-border fiscal transfers will raise the overall level of cyclical unemployment among EMU members. The shift from national monetary policies dominated by the (German) Bundesbank within the European Monetary System to a European Central Bank governed by majority voting with a politically determined exchange rate policy will almost certainly raise the average future rate of inflation.[15]

The Road Toward EMU

According to the Maastricht Treaty, to achieve monetary union by 1999, member countries must have achieved low inflation rates, low long-term interest rates, a stable exchange rate, public debt limited to no more than 60 percent of a country's GDP, and current budget deficits of no more than 3 percent of GDP. Initially there was considerable skepticism that this would be possible. However, by mid-1998, of the 12 countries that had singled their intention to join the euro zone, only Greece would not make the criteria. For now three EU countries, Britain, Denmark and Sweden, are still sitting on the sidelines, although there is speculation that Britain and Sweden may join before 2002. Under the current timetable, the 11 countries that made the grade and agreed to EMU locked their exchange rates against each other on January 1, 1999, and the ECB then took over management of monetary policy in those countries. The financial markets began to trade euro-dominated assets on January 4, 1999, effectively creating the world's second largest currency after the US dollar. Notes and coins denominated in euros will go into circulation at the beginning of 2002, and national currencies will be withdrawn in July 2002. Between 1999 and 2002, shops and restaurants in the euro zone will display prices in both euros and the local currency. Prior to its introduction, the theoretical value of the euro was estimated to be around one US dollar. In late January 1999, the euro was trading at 1 euro = $1.17.

Enlargement of the European Union

The other big issue the EU must now grapple with is enlargement. After a bitter dispute among the existing 12 members, they agreed in March 1994 to enlarge the EU to include Austria, Finland, Sweden, and Norway. Most of the opposition to enlargement came from Britain, which worried that enlargement and a subsequent reduction in its voting power in the EU's top decision-making body, the Council of Ministers, would limit its ability to block EU developments that it did not like. Britain backed down in the face of strong opposition from other EU members and agreed to enlargement.

Voters in the four countries went to the polls in late 1994. Austria, Finland, and Sweden all voted to join the EU, but Norway voted to stay out. Thus, the EU of 12 became the EU of 15 on January 1, 1996. Next the EU had to deal with membership applications from Hungary, Poland, the Czech Republic, Estonia, Slovenia, Malta, Cyprus, and Turkey.[16] In 1997, the EU responded by formally inviting five former communist states, Estonia, Poland, the Czech Republic, Slovenia, and Hungary, to join. However, the timetable for this event is uncertain, and any additional expansion unlikely until after completion of EMU in 2002. All these countries still have a long way to go before their economies reach the level enjoyed by current EU members. For example, according to the European Commission, Poland, the country with the largest population among the five, needs to modernize its agricultural sector, speed up its sluggish privatization efforts, and bring its inflation rate down from around 20 percent to about 3 percent.[17]

Fortress Europe?

One of the main concerns of the United States and Asian countries is that the EU will at some point impose new barriers on imports from outside the EU. The fear is that the EU might increase external protection as weaker member states attempt to offset their loss of protection against other EU countries by arguing for limitations on outside competition.

In theory, given the free market philosophy that underpins the Single European Act, this should not occur. In October 1988, the European Commission debated external trading policy and published a detailed statement of the EC's trading intentions in the post-1992 era.[18] The commission stressed the EC's interests in vigorous external trade. It noted that exports by EC countries to non-EC countries are equivalent to 20 percent of total world exports, compared to 15 percent for the United States and 9 percent for Japan. These external exports are equivalent to 9 percent of its own GDP, compared to 6.7 percent for the United States and 9.7 percent for Japan. In short, it is not in the EU's interests to adopt a protectionist stance, given the EU's reliance on external trade. The commission has also promised loyalty to GATT and WTO rules on international trade. As for the types of trade not covered by the WTO, the EU states it will push for reciprocal access. The EU has stated that in certain cases it might replace individual national trade barriers with EU protection against imports, but it also has promised that the overall level of protection would not rise.

Despite such reassurances, there is no guarantee that the EU will not adopt a protectionist stance toward external trade, and there are indications that has occurred in two industries, agriculture and automobiles. The EU has continued the Common Market Agricultural Policy, which limits many food imports. In autos, the EU reached an agreement with the Japanese to limit the Japanese market share of the EU auto market. Between 1993 and 1998, those countries that had quotas on Japanese car imports lifted them gradually until the end of 1998, when they were abolished. Meanwhile, Japanese producers committed themselves to voluntarily restraining sales so that by the end of the century they hold no more than 17 percent of the European market. After that, all restrictions are to be abolished. These examples of protectionism, however, are not the norm, and the EU countries generally have adopted a relatively liberal trade policy with regard to third parties, such as Japan and the United States. In a published report on the issue, the WTO has stated that the growth of regional trade groups such as the EU has not impeded the growth of freer world trade, as some fear, and may have helped to promote it.[19]

Regional Economic Integration in the Americas

No other attempt at regional economic integration comes close to the EU in its boldness or its potential implications for the world economy, but regional economic integration is on the rise in the Americas. The most significant attempt is the North American Free Trade Agreement. In addition to NAFTA, several other trade blocs are in the offing in the Americas (see Map 8.2), the most significant of which appear to be the Andean Group and MERCOSUR. There are also plans to establish a hemispherewide Free Trade Area of the Americas by 2005.

The North American Free Trade Agreement

The governments of the United States and Canada in 1988 agreed to enter into a free trade agreement, which took effect January 1, 1989. The goal of the agreement was to eliminate all tariffs on bilateral trade between Canada and the United States by 1998. This was followed in 1991 by talks among the United States,

Map 8.2

Economic Integration in the Americas

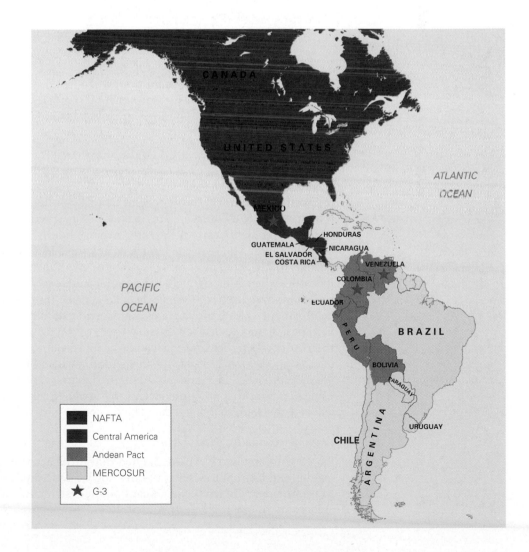

Canada, and Mexico aimed at establishing a North American Free Trade Agreement for the three countries. The talks concluded in August 1992 with an agreement in principle.

Both Canada and Mexico committed themselves to NAFTA by the fall of 1993, leaving only the US government to signal its intention to go forward with the agreement. The Clinton administration had already committed itself to NAFTA, and passage by the Senate looked likely, but the agreement faced stiff opposition in the House of Representatives. A last-minute round of lobbying by President Clinton helped the bill pass the House by a comfortable margin on November 17, 1993.

NAFTA's Contents

The agreement became law January 1, 1994.[20] The contents of NAFTA include the following:

- Abolition within 10 years of tariffs on 99 percent of the goods traded between Mexico, Canada, and the United States.
- Removal of most barriers on the cross-border flow of services, allowing financial institutions, for example, unrestricted access to the Mexican market by 2000.
- Protection of intellectual property rights.
- Removal of most restrictions on foreign direct investment between the three member countries, although special treatment (protection) will be given to Mexican energy and railway industries, American airline and radio communications industries, and Canadian culture.
- Application of national environmental standards, provided such standards have a scientific basis. Lowering of standards to lure investment is described as being inappropriate.
- Establishment of two commissions with the power to impose fines and remove trade privileges when environmental standards or legislation involving health and safety, minimum wages, or child labor are ignored.

Arguments for NAFTA

Opinions remain divided as to the consequences of NAFTA. Proponents argue that NAFTA should be viewed as an opportunity to create an enlarged and more efficient productive base for the entire region. One likely short-term effect of NAFTA will be that many US and Canadian firms will move some production to Mexico to take advantage of lower labor costs. In 1991, the average hourly labor cost in Mexico was $2.32, compared with $14.31 in the United States and $14.71 in Canada. Movement of production to Mexico is most likely to occur in low-skilled, labor-intensive manufacturing industries where Mexico might have a comparative advantage (e.g., textiles). Many will benefit from such a trend. Mexico benefits because it gets much-needed investment and employment. The United States and Canada should benefit because the increased incomes of the Mexicans will allow them to import more US and Canadian goods, thereby increasing demand and making up for the jobs lost in industries that moved production to Mexico. US and Canadian consumers will benefit from the lower prices of products produced in Mexico. In addition, the international competitiveness of US and Canadian firms that move production to Mexico to take advantage of lower labor costs will be enhanced, enabling them to better compete with Asian and European rivals.

Arguments against NAFTA

Those who opposed NAFTA claimed that ratification would be followed by a mass exodus of jobs from the United States and Canada into Mexico as employers sought to profit from Mexico's lower wages and less strict environmental and labor laws. According to one extreme opponent, Ross Perot, up to 5.9 million US jobs would be lost to Mexico after NAFTA. Most economists, however, dismiss these numbers as being absurd and alarmist. They point out that Mexico would have to run a bilateral trade surplus with the United States of close to $300 billion for job loss on such a scale to occur—and $300 billion is about the size of Mexico's present GDP. In other words, such a scenario is implausible.

More sober estimates of the impact of NAFTA ranged from a net creation of 170,000 jobs in the United States (due to increased Mexican demand for US goods and services) and an increase of $15 billion per year to the US and Mexican GDP, to a net loss of 490,000 US jobs. To put these numbers in perspective, employment in the US economy was predicted to grow by 18 million from 1993 to 2003. As most economists repeatedly stress, NAFTA will have a small impact on both Canada and the United States. It could hardly be any other way, since the Mexican economy is only 5 percent of the size of the US economy. Signing NAFTA required the largest leap of economic faith from Mexico rather than Canada or the United States. Falling trade barriers are exposing Mexican firms to highly efficient US and Canadian competitors that, when compared to the average Mexican firm, have far greater capital resources, access to highly educated and skilled work forces, and much greater technological sophistication. The short-run outcome is bound to be painful economic restructuring and unemployment in Mexico. But if economic theory is any guide, there should be dynamic gains in the long run in the efficiency of Mexican firms as they adjust to the rigors of a more competitive marketplace. To the extent that this happens, an acceleration of Mexico's long run rate of economic growth will follow, and Mexico might yet become a major market for Canadian and US firms.[21]

Environmentalists have also voiced concerns about NAFTA. They point to the sludge in the Rio Grande River and the smog in the air over Mexico City and warn that Mexico could degrade clean air and toxic-waste standards across the continent. Already, they claim, the lower Rio Grande is the most polluted river in the United States, increasing in chemical waste and sewage along its course from El Paso, Texas, to the Gulf of Mexico.

There is also continued opposition in Mexico to NAFTA from those who fear a loss of national sovereignty. Mexican critics argue that their country will be dominated by US firms that will not really contribute to Mexico's economic growth, but instead will use Mexico as a low-cost assembly site, while keeping their high-paying, high-skilled jobs north of the border.

The Early Experience

The first year after NAFTA turned out to be a largely positive experience for all three countries. US trade with Canada and Mexico expanded at about twice the rate of trade with non-NAFTA countries in the first nine months of 1994, compared with the same period in 1993. US exports to Mexico grew by 22 percent, while Mexican exports to the United States grew by 23 percent. Anti-NAFTA campaigners had warned of doom for the US auto industry, but exports of autos to Mexico increased by nearly 500 percent in the first nine months of 1993. The US Commerce Department estimated that the surge in exports to Mexico secured about 130,000 US jobs, while only 13,000 people applied for aid under a program designed to help workers displaced by the movement of jobs to Mexico, suggesting that job losses from NAFTA had been small.[22]

However, the early euphoria over NAFTA was snuffed out in December 1994 when the Mexican economy was shaken by a financial crisis. Through 1993 and 1994, Mexico's trade deficit with the rest of the world had grown sharply, while Mexico's inflation rate had started to accelerate. This put increasing pressure on the Mexican currency, the peso. Traders in the foreign exchange markets, betting that there would be a large decline in the value of the peso against the dollar, began to sell pesos and buy dollars. As a result, in December 1994, the Mexican government was forced to devalue the peso by about 35 percent against the dollar. This effectively increased the cost of imports from the United States by 35 percent. The devaluation of the peso was followed quickly by a collapse in the value of the Mexican stock market, and the country suddenly and unexpectedly appeared to be in the midst of a major economic crisis. Shortly afterward, the Mexican government introduced an austerity program designed to rebuild confidence in the country's financial institutions and reign in growth and inflation. The program was backed by a $20 billion loan guarantee from the US government.[23]

One result of this turmoil has been a sharp decline in Canadian and US exports to Mexico. Many companies have also reduced or put on hold their plans to expand into Mexico. NAFTA critics seized on Mexico's financial crisis to crow that they had been right. But in reality, just as the celebrations of NAFTA's success were premature, so are claims of its sudden demise. Early studies of NAFTA's impact suggest that so far at least, its effects have been at best muted.[24] The most comprehensive study to date was undertaken by researchers at the University of California, Los Angeles, and funded by various departments of the US government.[25] Their findings are enlightening. First, they conclude that the growth in trade between Mexico and the United States began to change nearly a decade before the implementation of NAFTA when Mexico unilaterally started to liberalize its own trade regime to conform with GATT standards. The period since NAFTA took effect has had little impact on trends already in place. The study found that trade growth in those sectors that underwent tariff liberalization in the first two and a half years of NAFTA was only marginally higher than trade growth in sectors not yet liberalized. For example, between 1993 and 1996, US exports to Mexico in sectors liberalized under NAFTA grew by 5.83 percent annually, while exports in sectors not liberalized under NAFTA grew by 5.35 percent. In short, the authors argue that NAFTA has so far had only a marginal impact on the level of trade between the United States and Mexico.

As for NAFTA's much-debated impact on jobs in the United States, the study concluded that the impact was positive but very small. The study found that while NAFTA created 31,158 new jobs in the United States, 28,168 jobs were also lost due to imports from Mexico, for a net job gain of around 3,000 in the first two years of the NAFTA regime.

However, as the authors of the report point out, trade flows and employment in 1995 and 1996 were significantly affected by the consequences of the peso devaluation and subsequent economic crisis that gripped Mexico in early 1995. Given this, it is probably too early to draw conclusions about the true impact of NAFTA on trade flows and employment. It will be a decade or more before any meaningful conclusions can be stated. The most that can be said at this juncture is that while the optimistic picture of job creation painted by NAFTA's advocates has not yet come to pass, neither has the apocalyptic vision of widespread job losses in the United States and Canada propagated by NAFTA's opponents.

Enlargement

One big issue now confronting NAFTA is that of enlargement. A number of other Latin American countries have indicated their desire to eventually join NAFTA. The governments of both Canada and the United States are adopting a wait-and-see attitude with regard to most countries. Getting NAFTA approved was a bruising political experience, and neither government is eager to repeat the process soon. Nevertheless, the Canadian, Mexican, and US governments began talks in May 1995 regarding Chile's possible entry into NAFTA. So far, however, these talks have yielded little progress, primarily because of political opposition to expanding NAFTA in the US Congress.

The Andean Pact

The Andean Pact was formed in 1969 when Bolivia, Chile, Ecuador, Colombia, and Peru signed the Cartagena Agreement. The Andean Pact was largely based on the EU model, but it has been far less successful at achieving its stated goals. The integration steps begun in 1969 included an internal tariff reduction program, a common external tariff, a transportation policy, a common industrial policy, and special concessions for the smallest members, Bolivia and Ecuador.

By the mid-1980s, the Andean Pact had all but collapsed, and had failed to achieve any of its stated objectives. There was no tariff-free trade between member countries, no common external tariff, and no harmonization of economic policies. The attempt to achieve cooperation between member countries seems to have been hindered by political and economic problems. The countries of the Andean Pact have had to deal with low economic growth, hyperinflation, high unemployment, political unrest, and crushing debt burdens. In addition, the dominant political ideology in many of the Andean countries during this period tended toward the radical/socialist end of the political spectrum. Since such an ideology is hostile to the free market economic principles on which the Andean Pact was based, progress toward closer integration could not be expected.

The tide began to turn in the late 1980s when, after years of economic decline, the governments of Latin America began to adopt free market economic policies. In 1990, the heads of the five current members of the Andean Pact—Bolivia, Ecuador, Peru, Colombia, and Venezuela—met in the Galápagos Islands. The resulting Galápagos Declaration effectively relaunched the Andean Pact. The declaration's objectives included the establishment of a free trade area by 1992, a customs union by 1994, and a common market by 1995.

While this last milestone has not been reached, there are some grounds for cautious optimism. For the first time, the controlling political ideology of the Andean countries is at least consistent with the free market principles underlying a common market. In addition, since the Galápagos Declaration, internal tariff levels have been reduced by all five members, and a customs union with a common external tariff was established in mid-1994, six months behind schedule.

Significant differences between member countries still exist that may make harmonization of policies and close integration difficult. For example, Venezuela's GNP per person is four times that of Bolivia's, and Ecuador's tiny production-line industries cannot compete with Colombia's and Venezuela's more advanced industries. Such differences are a recipe for disagreement and suggest that many of the adjustments required to achieve a true common market will be painful, even though the net benefits will probably outweigh the costs.[26] To complicate matters even further, in recent years Peru and Ecuador have fought a border war, Venezuela has remained aloof during a banking crisis, and Colombia has suffered from domestic political turmoil and problems related to its drug trade. This has led some to argue that the pact is more "formal than real."[27] However, the outlook for the Andean Pact started to change in 1998 when the group entered into negotiations with MERCOSUR to establish a South American free trade area.

MERCOSUR

MERCOSUR originated in 1988 as a free trade pact between Brazil and Argentina. The modest reductions in tariffs and quotas accompanying this pact reportedly helped bring about an 80 percent increase in trade between the two countries in the late 1980s.[28] Encouraged by this success, the pact was expanded in March 1990 to include Paraguay and Uruguay. The initial aim was to establish a full free trade area by the end of 1994 and a common market sometime thereafter. The four countries of MERCOSUR have a combined population of 200 million. With a market of this size, MERCOSUR could have a significant impact on the economic growth rate of the four economies.

In December 1995, MERCOSUR's members agreed to a five-year program under which they hoped to perfect their free trade area and move toward a full customs union. Also, the four member states of MERCOSUR have now formally committed themselves to establishing a wider free trade area, the South American Free Trade

Area (SAFTA). The goal is to bring other South American countries into the agreement, including the nations of the Andean Pact, and to have internal free trade for not less of 80 percent of goods produced in the region by 2005.[29]

MERCOSUR seems to be making a positive contribution to the economic growth rates of its member states. Trade between MERCOSUR's four core members grew from $4 billion in 1990 to $16.9 billion in 1996. Moreover, the combined GDP of the four member states grew at an annual average rate of 3.5 percent between 1990 and 1996, a performance that is significantly better than the four attained during the 1980s.[30]

However, MERCOSUR has its critics, including Alexander Yeats, a senior economist at the World Bank, who wrote a stinging critique of MERCOSUR that was "leaked" to the press in October 1996.[31] According to Yeats, the trade diversion effects of MERCOSUR outweigh its trade creation effects. Yeats points out that the fastest-growing items in intra-MERCOSUR trade are cars, buses, agricultural equipment, and other capital-intensive goods that are produced relatively inefficiently in the four member countries. In other words, MERCOSUR countries, insulated from outside competition by tariffs that run as high as 70 percent of value on motor vehicles, are investing in factories that build products that are too expensive to sell to anyone but themselves. The result, according to Yeats, is that MERCOSUR countries might not be able to compete globally once the group's external trade barriers come down. In the meantime, capital is being drawn away from more efficient enterprises. In the near term, countries with more efficient manufacturing enterprises lose because MERCOSUR's external trade barriers keep them out of the market.

The leak of Yeats's report caused a storm at the World Bank, which typically does not release reports that are critical of member states (the MERCOSUR countries are members of the World Bank). It also drew strong protests from Brazil, which was one of the primary targets of Yeats's critique. Still, in tacit admission that at least some of Yeats's arguments have merit, a senior MERCOSUR diplomat let it be known that external trade barriers will gradually be reduced, forcing member countries to compete globally. Many external MERCOSUR tariffs, which average 14 percent, are lower than they were before the group's creation, and there are plans for a hemispheric Free Trade Area of the Americas to be established by 2005 (which will combine MERCOSUR, NAFTA, and other American nations). If that occurs, MERCOSUR will have no choice but to reduce its external tariffs further.

Central American Common Market and CARICOM

There are two other trade pacts in the Americas, although neither has made much progress as yet. In the early 1960s, Costa Rica, El Salvador, Guatemala, Honduras, and Nicaragua attempted to set up a Central American common market. It collapsed in 1969 when war broke out between Honduras and El Salvador after a riot at a soccer match between teams from the two countries. Now the five countries are trying to revive their agreement, although no definite progress has been made.

Then there is the customs union that was to have been created in 1991 between the English-speaking Caribbean countries under the auspices of the Caribbean Community. Referred to as **CARICOM,** it was originally established in 1973. However, it has repeatedly failed to progress toward economic integration. A formal commitment to economic and monetary union was adopted by CARICOM's member states in 1984, but since then little progress has been made. In October 1991, the CARICOM governments failed, for the third consecutive time, to meet a deadline for establishing a common external tariff.

Free Trade Area of the Americas

At a hemispherewide "Summit of the Americas" in December 1994 a proposal was made to establish a Free Trade Area of the Americas (FTAA). It took over three years for talks to be begin, but in April 1998, 34 heads of state traveled to Santiago, Chile, for the second Summit of the Americas where they formally inaugurated talks to establish an FTAA by 2005. The talks will continue for seven years and will address a wide range of economic, political, and environmental issues related to cross-border trade and investment. Although the United States was an early advocate of an FTAA, at this point support from the United States seems to be mixed. Since the United States has by far the largest economy in the region, strong US support is a precondition for establishment of an FTAA.

Canada is chairing the crucial first stage of negotiations and will host the next Summit of the Americas, either in 2001 or 2002. If an FTAA is established, it will have major implications for cross-border trade and investment flows within the hemisphere, but at this point it is a long way off.

Regional Economic Integration Elsewhere

Outside of Western Europe and the Americas, there have been few significant attempts at regional economic integration. Although there are a number of groupings throughout Asia and Africa, few exist in anything other than name. Perhaps the most significant is the Association of Southeast Asian Nations (ASEAN). In addition, the Asian Pacific Economic Cooperation (APEC) forum has recently emerged as the seed of a potential free trade region.

Association of Southeast Asian Nations

Formed in 1967, ASEAN includes Brunei, Indonesia, Laos, Malaysia, Myanmar, Philippines, Singapore, Thailand, and Vietnam. Laos, Myanmar, and Vietnam have all joined recently, and their inclusion complicates matters because their economies are a long way behind those of the original members. The basic objectives of ASEAN are to foster freer trade between member countries and to achieve cooperation in their industrial policies. Progress has been very limited, however. For example, only 5 percent of intra-ASEAN trade currently consists of goods whose tariffs have been reduced through an ASEAN preferential trade arrangement. Future progress seems limited because the financial crisis that swept through Southeast Asia in 1997 hit several ASEAN countries particularly hard, most notably Indonesia, Malaysia, and Thailand. Until these countries can get back on their economic feet, it is unlikely that much progress will be made.

Asia Pacific Economic Cooperation

Asia Pacific Economic Cooperation (APEC) was founded in 1990 at the suggestion of Australia. APEC currently has 18 member states including such economic powerhouses as the United States, Japan, and China (see Map 8.3). Collectively the 18 member states account for half of the world's GNP, 40 percent of world trade, and most of the growth in the world economy. The stated aim of APEC is to increase multilateral cooperation in view of the economic rise of the Pacific nations and the growing interdependence within the region. US support for APEC was also based on the belief that it might prove a viable strategy for heading off any moves to create Asian groupings from which it would be excluded.

Interest in APEC was heightened considerably in November 1993 when the heads of APEC member states met for the first time at a two-day conference in Seattle. Debate before the meeting speculated on the likely future role of APEC. One view was that APEC should commit itself to the ultimate formation of a free trade area. Such a move would transform the Pacific Rim from a geographical expression into the world's largest free trade area. Another view was that APEC would produce no more than hot air and lots of photo opportunities for the leaders involved. As it turned out, the APEC meeting produced little more than some vague commitments from member states to work closely together for greater economic integration and a general lowering of trade barriers. However, significantly, member states did not rule out the possibility of closer economic cooperation in the future.[32]

The heads of state met again in November 1994 in Jakarta, Indonesia. This time they agreed to take more concrete steps, and the joint statement at the end of the

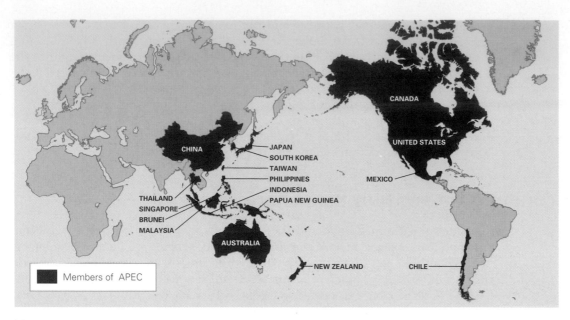

Map 8.3

Asia Pacific Economic Cooperation

meeting formally committed APEC's industrialized members to remove their trade and investment barriers by 2010 and for developing economies to do so by 2020. They also called for a detailed blueprint charting how this might be achieved. This blueprint was presented and discussed at the next APEC summit, held in Osaka, Japan, in November 1995.[33] This was followed by further meetings in 1996 and 1997. At the 1997 meeting, member states formally endorsed proposals designed to remove trade barriers in 15 sectors, ranging from fish to toys. However, the plan is vague and commits APEC to doing no more than holding further talks. Commenting on the vagueness of APEC pronouncements, the influential Brookings Institute, a US-based economic policy institution, noted that APEC "is in grave danger of shrinking into irrelevance as a serious forum." Despite the slow progress, APEC is worth watching. If it eventually does transform itself into a free trade area, it will probably be the world's largest.[34]

 # IMPLICATIONS FOR BUSINESS

Currently the most significant developments in regional economic integration are occurring in the EU, NAFTA, and MERCOSUR groups. Although some of the other Latin American trade blocs and APEC may have greater economic significance in the future, at present the EU, NAFTA, and MERCOSUR have more profound and immediate implications for business practice. Accordingly, in this section we will concentrate on the business implications of those three groups. Similar conclusions, however, could be drawn with regard to the creation of a single market anywhere in the world.

Opportunities

The creation of a single market offers significant opportunities because markets that were formerly protected from foreign competition are opened. For example, in Europe before 1992 the large French and Italian markets were among the most protected. These markets are now much more open to foreign competition in the form of both exports and direct investment. Nonetheless, the specter of

"Fortress Europe" suggests that to fully exploit such opportunities, it will pay non-EU firms to set up EU subsidiaries. Many major US firms have long had subsidiaries in Europe. Those that do not would be advised to consider establishing them now, lest they run the risk of being shut out of the EU by nontariff barriers. In fact, non-EU firms rapidly increased their direct investment in the EU in anticipation of the creation of a single market. Between 1985 and 1989, for example, approximately 37 percent of the FDI inflows into industrialized countries was directed at the EC. By 1991, this figure had risen to 66 percent.[35]

Additional opportunities arise from the inherent lower costs of doing business in a single market—as opposed to 15 national markets in the case of the EU or 3 national markets in the case of NAFTA. Free movement of goods across borders, harmonized product standards, and simplified tax regimes make it possible for firms based in the EU and the NAFTA countries to realize potentially enormous cost economies by centralizing production in those EU and NAFTA locations where the mix of factor costs and skills is optimal. Rather than producing a product in each of the 15 EU countries or the 3 NAFTA countries, a firm may be able to serve the whole EU or North American market from a single location. This location must be chosen carefully, of course, with an eye on local factor costs and skills.

For example, in response to the changes created by EU after 1992, the Minneapolis-based company 3M has been consolidating its European manufacturing and distribution facilities to take advantage of economies of scale. Thus, a plant in Great Britain now produces 3M's printing products and a German factory its reflective traffic control materials for all of the EU. In each case, 3M chose a location for centralized production after carefully considering the likely production costs in alternative locations within the EU. The ultimate goal of 3M is to dispense with all national distinctions, directing R&D, manufacturing, distribution, and marketing for each product group from an EU headquarters.[36] Similarly, Unilever, one of Europe's largest companies, began rationalizing its production in advance of 1992 to attain scale economies. Unilever concentrated its production of dishwashing powder for the EU in one plant, toilet soap in another, and so on.[37]

Even after the removal of barriers to trade and investment, enduring differences in culture and competitive practices often limit the ability of companies to realize cost economies by centralizing production in key locations and producing a standardized product for a single multicountry market. Consider the case of Atag Holdings NV, a Dutch maker of kitchen appliances that is profiled in the accompanying Management Focus. Due to enduring differences between nations within the EU's single market, Atag still has to produce various "national brands," which clearly limits the company's ability to attain scale economies.

Threats

Just as the emergence of single markets in the EU and the Americas creates opportunities for business, it also presents a number of threats. For one thing, the business environment within each grouping will become more competitive. The lowering of barriers to trade and investment between countries is likely to lead to increased price competition throughout the EU, NAFTA, and MERCOSUR. For example, before 1992 a Volkswagen Golf cost 55 percent more in Great Britain than in Denmark and 29 percent more in Ireland than in Greece.[38] Such price differentials will vanish in a single market. This is a direct threat to any firm doing business in EU, NAFTA, or MERCOSUR countries. To survive in the tougher single-market environment, firms must take advantage of the opportunities offered by the creation of a single market to rationalize their production and reduce their costs. Otherwise, they will be severely disadvantaged.

A further threat to firms outside these trading blocs arises from the likely long-term improvement in the competitive position of many firms within the areas.

MANAGEMENT FOCUS
Atag Holdings

http://www.atagholding.com/
english/news.htm

Atag Holdings NV is a Dutch company whose main business is kitchen appliances. Atag thought it was well placed to benefit from the single market, but so far it has found it tough going. Atag's plant is just one mile from the German border and near the center of the EU's population. The company thought that it could cater to both the "potato" and "spaghetti" belts—marketers' terms for consumers in Southern and Northern Europe—by producing two main product lines and selling these standardized "euro-products" to "euro-consumers." The main benefits of doing so is the economy of scale derived from mass production of a standardized range of products.

Unfortunately, Atag quickly discovered that the "euro-consumer" is a myth. Consumer preferences vary much more across nations than Atag had thought. Consider ceramic stove tops; Atag planned to market just 2 varieties throughout the EU but has found it needs 11. Belgians, who cook in huge pots, require extra-large burners. Germans like oval pots and burners to fit. The French need small burners and very low temperatures for simmering sauces and broths. Germans like oven knobs on the top; the

French want them on the front. Most Germans and French prefer black and white cookers; the British demand a vast range of different colors including peach, pigeon blue, and mint green. Despite these problems, foreign sales of Atag's kitchenware have increased from 4 percent of total revenues in 1985 to 25 percent in 1994. But the company now has a much more realistic assessment of the benefits of a single market among a group of countries whose cultures and traditions still differ in deep and often profound ways. Atag now believes its range of designs and product quality, rather than the magic bullet of a "euro-product" designed for a "euro-consumer," will keep the company competitive. At the same time, Atag has to cope with higher costs than would have been the case were it possible to pursue greater product standardization.

Sources: T. Horwitz, "Europe's Borders Fade," *The Wall Street Journal,* May 18, 1993, pp. A1, A12; "A Singular Market," *The Economist,* October 22, 1994, pp. 10–16; and "Something Dodgy in Europe's Single Market," *The Economist,* May 21, 1994, pp. 69–70.

This is particularly relevant in the EU, where many firms are currently limited by a high cost structure in their ability to compete globally with North American and Asian firms. The creation of a single market and the resulting increased competition in the EU is beginning to produce serious attempts by many EU firms to reduce their cost structure by rationalizing production. This could transform many EU companies into efficient global competitors. The message for non-EU businesses is that they need to prepare for the emergence of more capable European competitors by reducing their own cost structures.

A final threat to firms outside of trading areas is the threat of being shut out of the single market by the creation of a "Trade Fortress." The charge that regional economic integration might lead to a fortress mentality is most often leveled at the EU. As noted earlier in the chapter, although the free trade philosophy underpinning the EU theoretically argues against the creation of any "fortress" in Europe, there are signs that the EU may raise barriers to imports and investment in certain "politically sensitive" areas, such as autos. Non-EU firms might be well advised, therefore, to set up their own EU operations as quickly as possible. This could also occur in the NAFTA countries, but it seems less likely.

Chapter Summary

This chapter pursued three main objectives: to examine the economic and political debate surrounding regional economic integration; to review the progress toward regional economic integration in Europe, the Americas, and elsewhere; and to distinguish the important implications of regional economic integration for the practice of international business. This chapter made the following points:

1. A number of levels of economic integration are possible in theory. In order of increasing integration, they include a free trade area, a customs union, a common market, an economic union, and full political union.

2. In a free trade area, barriers to trade between member countries are removed, but each country determines its own external trade policy. In a customs union, internal barriers to trade are removed and a common external trade policy is adopted. A common market is similar to a customs union, except that a common market also allows factors of production to move freely between countries. An economic union involves even closer integration, including the establishment of a common currency and the harmonization of tax rates. A political union is the logical culmination of attempts to achieve ever-closer economic integration.

3. Regional economic integration is an attempt to achieve economic gains from the free flow of trade and investment between neighboring countries.

4. Integration is not easily achieved or sustained. Although integration brings benefits to the majority, it is never without costs for the minority. Furthermore, concerns over national sovereignty often slow or stop integration attempts.

5. Regional integration will not increase economic welfare if the trade creation effects in the free trade area are outweighed by the trade diversion effects.

6. The Single European Act sought to create a true single market by abolishing administrative barriers to the free flow of trade and investment between EU countries.

7. The Maastricht Treaty aims to take the EU even further along the road to economic union by establishing a common currency. The economic gains from a common currency come from reduced exchange costs, reduced risk associated with currency fluctuations, and increased price competition within the EU.

8. Although no other attempt at regional economic integration comes close to the EU in terms of potential economic and political significance, various other attempts are being made in the world. The most notable include NAFTA in North America, the Andean Pact and MERCOSUR in Latin America, ASEAN in Southeast Asia, and (perhaps) APEC.

9. The creation of single markets in the EU and North America means that many markets that were formerly protected from foreign competition are now more open. This creates major investment and export opportunities for firms within and outside these regions.

10. The free movement of goods across borders, the harmonization of product standards, and the simplification of tax regimes make it possible for firms based in a free trade area to realize potentially enormous cost economies by centralizing production in those locations within the area where the mix of factor costs and skills is optimal.

11. The lowering of barriers to trade and investment between countries within a trade group will probably be followed by increased price competition.

Critical Discussion Questions

1. NAFTA is likely to produce net benefits for the US economy. Discuss.

2. What are the economic and political arguments for regional economic integration? Given these arguments, why don't we see more integration in the world economy?

3. What is the effect of creation of a single market and a single currency within the EU likely to be on competition within the EU? Why?

4. How should a US firm that currently exports only to Western Europe respond to the creation of a single market?

5. How should a firm with self-sufficient production facilities in several EU countries respond to the creation of a single market? What are the constraints on its ability to respond in a manner that minimizes production costs?

CLOSING CASE   Martin's Textiles

August 12, 1992, was a really bad day for John Martin. That was the day Canada, Mexico, and the United States announced an agreement in principle to form the North American Free Trade Agreement. Under the plan, all tariffs between the three countries would be eliminated within the next 10 to 15 years, with most being cut in 5 years. What disturbed John most was the plan's provision that all tariffs on trade of textiles among the three countries were to be removed within 10 years. Under the proposed agreement, Mexico and Canada would also be allowed to ship a specific amount of clothing and textiles made from foreign materials to the United States each year, and this quota would rise slightly over the first five years of the agreement. "My God!" thought John. "Now I'm going to have to decide about moving my plants to Mexico."

John is the CEO of a New York-based textile company, Martin's Textiles. The company has been in the Martin family for four generations, having been founded by his great-grandfather in 1910. Today the company employs 1,500 people in three New York plants that produce cotton-based clothes, primarily underwear. All production employees are union members, and the company has a long history of good labor relations. The company has never had a labor dispute, and John, like his father, grandfather, and great-grandfather before him, regards the work force as part of the "Martin family." John prides himself not only on knowing many of the employees by name, but also on knowing a great deal about the family circumstances of many of the longtime employees.

Over the past 20 years, the company has experienced increasingly tough competition, both from overseas and at home. The mid-1980s were particularly difficult. The strength of the dollar on the foreign exchange market during that period enabled Asian producers to enter the US market with very low prices. Since then, although the dollar has weakened against many major currencies, the Asian producers have not raised their prices in response to the falling dollar. In a low-skilled, labor-intensive business such as clothing manufacture, costs are driven by wage rates and labor productivity. Not surprisingly, most of John's competitors in the northeastern United States responded to the intense cost competition by moving production south, first to states such as South Carolina and Mississippi, where nonunion labor could be hired for significantly less than in the unionized Northeast, and then to Mexico, where labor costs for textile workers were less than $2 per hour. In contrast, wage rates are $12.50 per hour at John's New York plant and $8 to $10 per hour at nonunion textile plants in the southeastern United States.

The last three years have been particularly tough at Martin's Textiles. The company has registered a small loss each year, and John knows the company cannot go on like this. His major customers, while praising the quality of Martin's products, have warned him that his prices are getting too high and they may not be able to continue to do business with him. His longtime banker has told him that he must get his labor costs down. John agrees, but he knows of only one surefire way to do that, to move production south—way south, to Mexico. He has always been reluctant to do that, but now he seems to have little choice. He fears that in five years the US market will be flooded with cheap imports from Asian, US, and Mexican companies, all producing in Mexico. It looks like the only way for Martin's Textiles to survive is to close the New York plants and move production to Mexico. All that would be left in the United States would be the sales force.

John's mind was spinning. How could something that throws good honest people out of work be good for the country? The politicians said it would be good for trade, good for economic growth, good for the three countries. John could not see it that way. What about Mary Morgan, who has worked for Martin's for 30 years? She is now 54 years old. How will she and others like her find another job? What about his moral obligation to his workers? What about the loyalty his workers have shown his family over the years? Is this a good way to repay it? How would he break the news to his employees, many of whom have worked for the company 10 to 20 years? And what about the Mexican workers; could they be as loyal and productive as his present employees? From other US textile companies that had set up production in Mexico he had heard stories of low productivity, poor workmanship, high turnover, and high absenteeism. If this was true, how could he ever cope with that? John has always felt that the success of Martin's Textiles is partly due to the family atmosphere, which encourages worker loyalty, productivity, and attention to quality, an atmosphere that has been built up over four generations. How could he replicate that in Mexico with a bunch of foreign workers who speak a language that he doesn't even understand?

http://iepnt1.itaiep.doc.gov/nafta/nafta2.htm

Case Discussion Questions

1. What are the economic costs and benefits to Martin's Textiles of shifting production to Mexico?

2. What are the social costs and benefits to Martin's Textiles of shifting production to Mexico?

3. Are the economic and social costs and benefits of moving production to Mexico independent of each other?

4. What seems to be the most ethical action?

5. What would you do if you were John Martin?

Notes

1. From a speech given by R. Ruggiero, director general of the World Trade Organization, "Regional Initiatives, Global Impact: Cooperation and the Multinational System," to the third conference of the Transatlantic Business Dialogue in Rome, November 7, 1997.

2. The Andean Pact has been through a number of changes since its inception. The latest version was established in 1991. See "Free-Trade Free for All," *The Economist*, January 4, 1991, p. 63.

3. D. Swann, *The Economics of the Common Market*, 6th ed. (London: Penguin Books, 1990).

4. See J. Bhagwati, "Regionalism and Multilateralism: An Overview," Columbia University discussion paper 603, Department of Economics, Columbia University, New York; A. de la Torre and M. Kelly, "Regional Trade Arrangements," occasional paper 93, Washington, DC: International Monetary Fund, March 1992; and J. Bhagwati, "Fast Track to Nowhere," *The Economist*, October 18, 1997, pp. 21–24.

5. N. Colchester and D. Buchan, *Europower: The Essential Guide to Europe's Economic Transformation in 1992* (London: The Economist Books, 1990); and Swann, *Economics of the Common Market*.

6. Swann, *Economics of the Common Market*; N. Colchester and D. Buchan, *Europower: The Essential Guide to Europe's Economic Transformation in 1992* (London: The Economist Books, 1990); "The European Union: A Survey," *The Economist*, October 22, 1994; and "The European Community: A Survey," *The Economist*, July 3, 1993.

7. "The European Community: A Survey," *The Economist*, July 3, 1993.

8. Colchester and Buchan, *Europower*.

9. "The Aid Plague: Business in Europe, A Survey," *The Economist*, June 8, 1991, pp. 12–18.

10. "One Europe, One Economy," *The Economist*, November 30, 1991, pp. 53–54; "Market Failure: A Survey of Business in Europe," *The Economist*, June 8, 1991, pp. 6–10.

11. "A Singular Market. In The European Union: A Survey," *The Economist*, October 22, 1994, pp. 10–16.

12. See C. Wyploze, "EMU: Why and How It Might Happen," *Journal of Economic Perspectives*, 11 (1997), pp. 3–22; and M. Feldstein, "The Political Economy of the European Economic and Monetary Union," *Journal of Economic Perspectives*, 11 (1997), pp. 23–42.

13. "One Europe, One Economy," and Feldstein, "The Political Economy of the European Economic and Monetary Union."

14. Feldstein, "The Political Economy of the European Economic and Monetary Union," and "When the Walls Come Down," *The Economist*, July 5, 1997, pp. 61–62.

15. Feldstein, "The Political Economy of the European Economic and Monetary Union," p. 41.

16. "From the Arctic to the Mediterranean," *The Economist*, March 5, 1994, pp. 52, 57; L. Barber, "More Does Not Mean Merrier," *Financial Times*, March 14, 1994, p. 13; and L. Barber, "Hopes of Wider Union Turn to Fear of No Union," *Financial Times*, December 9, 1994, p. 2.

17. J. Perles., "Europe Invites 5 Ex-Communist Nations to Join," *The New York Times*, July 17, 1997, p. A6.

18. "What Are They Building? Survey of Europe's Internal Market," *The Economist*, July 8, 1989, pp. 5–7; and Colchester and Buchan, *Europower*.

19. World Trade Organization, *Regionalism and the World Trading System* (Geneva: World Trade Organization, 1995).

20. "What Is NAFTA?" *Financial Times*, November 17, 1993, p. 6, and S. Garland, "Sweet Victory," *Business Week*, November 29, 1993, pp. 30–31.

21. "NAFTA: The Showdown," *The Economist*, November 13, 1993, pp. 23–36.

22. "Happy Ever NAFTA?" *The Economist*, December 10, 1994, pp. 23–24; and D. Harbrecht, "What Has NAFTA Wrought? Plenty of Trade?" *Business Week*, November 21, 1994, pp. 48–49.

23. P. B. Carroll and C. Torres, "Mexico Unveils Program of Harsh Fiscal Medicine," *The Wall Street Journal*, March 3, 1995, pp. A1, A6.

24. N. C. Lustog, "NAFTA: Setting the Record Straight," *The World Economy*, 1997, pp. 605–14.

25. R. H. Ojeda, C. Dowds, R. McCleery, S. Robinson, D. Runsten, C. Wolff, and G. Wolff, "NAFTA—How Has It Done? North American Integration Three Years after NAFTA," North American Integration and Development Center at UCLA, December 1996.

26. "NAFTA Is Not Alone," *The Economist*, June 18, 1994, pp. 47–48; Sweeney, "First Latin American Customs Union Looms over Venezuela," *Journal of Commerce*, September 26, 1991, p. 5A; and "The Business of the American Hemisphere," *The Economist*, August 24, 1991, pp. 37–38.

27. The comment was made by the Colombian ambassador. See K. G. Hall, "Andean Pact Nations to Work Together at Talks," *Journal of Commerce*, April 8, 1998, p. 2A.

28. "Business of the American Hemisphere."

29. "NAFTA Is Not Alone."

30. "Murky MERCOSUR," *The Economist*, July 26, 1997, pp. 66–67.

31. See M. Philips, "South American Trade Pact Under Fire," *The Wall Street Journal*, October 23, 1996, p. A2; A. J. Yeats, *Does MERCOSUR's Trade Performance Justify Concerns about the Global Welfare-Reducing Effects of Free Trade Arrangements? Yes!* (Washington, DC: World Bank, 1996); and D. M. Leipziger et al., "MERCOSUR: Integration and Industrial Policy," *The World Economy*, 1997, pp. 585–604.

32. "Aimless in Seattle," *The Economist*, November 13, 1993, pp. 35–36.

33. G. de Jonquieres, "Different Aims, Common Cause," *Financial Times*, November 18, 1995, p. 14.

34. G. de Jonquieres, "APEC Grapples with Market Turmoil," *Financial Times*, November 21, 1997, p. 6; and G. Baker, "Clinton Team Wins Most of the APEC Tricks," *Financial Times*, November 27, 1997, p. 5.

35. "World Economic Survey," *The Economist*, September 19, 1992, p. 17.

36. P. Davis, "A European Campaign: Local Companies Rush for a Share of EC Market While Barriers Are Down," *Minneapolis-St. Paul City Business*, January 8, 1990, p. 1.

37. "The Business of Europe," *The Economist*, December 7, 1991, pp. 63–64.

38. E. G. Friberg, "1992: Moves Europeans Are Making," *Harvard Business Review*, May–June 1989, pp. 85–89.

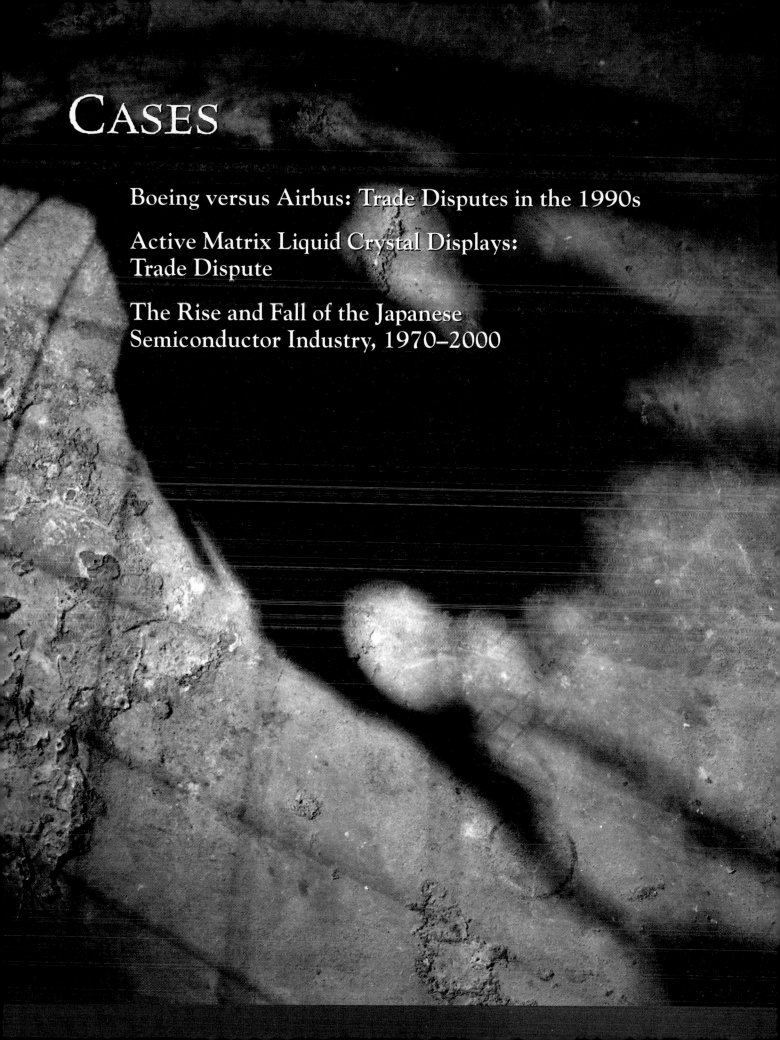

CASES

Boeing versus Airbus: Trade Disputes in the 1990s

Active Matrix Liquid Crystal Displays:
Trade Dispute

The Rise and Fall of the Japanese
Semiconductor Industry, 1970–2000

BOEING VERSUS AIRBUS: TRADE DISPUTES IN THE 1990S

Introduction

For years the commercial aircraft industry has been an American success story. Until 1980, US manufacturers held a virtual monopoly. Despite the rise of the European-based Airbus Industrie, this persisted through to the mid-1990s, when two US firms, Boeing and McDonnell Douglas, accounted for over two-thirds of world market share. In late 1996, many analysts thought that US dominance in this industry would be further strengthened when Boeing announced a decision to acquire McDonnell Douglas for $13.3 billion, creating an aerospace behemoth nearly twice the size of its nearest competitor.

The industry is routinely the largest net contributor to the US balance of trade and Boeing is the largest US exporter. In the 1990s, the US commercial aircraft industry regularly ran a substantial positive trade balance with the rest of the world of $12 to $15 billion per year. The impact of the industry on US employment is also enormous. In 1998, Boeing directly employed over 120,000 people in the Seattle area alone, and another 100,000 elsewhere in the nation. The company also indirectly supported a further 600,000 jobs nationwide in related industries (e.g., subcontractors) and through the impact of Boeing wages on the general level of economic activity.

Despite Boeing's formidable reach, since the mid-1980s US dominance in the commercial aerospace industry has been threatened by the rise of Airbus Industrie. Airbus is a consortium of four European aircraft manufacturers: one British (20.0 percent ownership stake), one French (37.9 percent ownership), one German (37.9 percent ownership), and one Spanish (4.2 percent ownership). Founded in 1970, Airbus was initially a marginal competitor and was regarded as unlikely to challenge US dominance. Since 1981, however, Airbus has confounded its critics and emerged as the world's second largest aircraft manufacturer. By the early 1990s, Airbus's share of aircraft orders in any one year stood between 20 percent and 30 percent, up from 14 percent in 1981. In 1994, Airbus captured more orders than Boeing for the first time in history (Airbus garnered 122 orders against Boeing's 121). However, most analysts point out that this was an aberration, given the extremely low level of aircraft orders in that year. In 1995, Boeing captured over 70 percent of all new aircraft orders, leaving Airbus with less than a 25 percent share. Nevertheless, Airbus set its sights on gaining a 50 percent share of all new orders for commercial jet aircraft of more than 100 seats by 2000. In 1998,

Airbus moved closer to attaining this goal when it snagged 46 percent of the record 1,212 large commercial jet aircraft ordered that year, leaving Boeing with 54 percent of the market.

Over the years, many in the United States have responded to the success of Airbus by crying foul. It has been repeatedly claimed that Airbus is heavily subsidized by the governments of Great Britain, France, Germany, and Spain. Airbus has responded by pointing out that both Boeing and McDonnell Douglas have benefited for years from hidden US government subsidies. In 1992, the two sides appeared to reach an agreement that put to rest their long-standing trade dispute. However, the dispute erupted again in 1997, when the European Union decided to challenge the merger between Boeing and McDonnell Douglas on the grounds that it limited competition. In this case, we examine the debate between the two sides in this on-again, off-again trade dispute. First, however, let us look at the competitive structure of the commercial aircraft industry.

Industry Competitive Dynamics

Competitive dynamics in the commercial aircraft industry are driven by a number of key factors. Perhaps foremost among these is that the costs of developing a new airliner are enormous. Boeing spent a reported $5 billion developing and tooling up to produce the 777 wide-bodied jetliner that it introduced in 1994. The development cost for Airbus's next aircraft, the 555-seat A3XX "super-jumbo," are estimated to be anywhere between $10 billion and $15 billion. (The A3XX is being touted by Airbus as a direct competitor to Boeing's profitable 747 model line).

Given such enormous development costs, a company must capture a significant share of world demand to break even. In the case of the 777, for example, Boeing needed to sell more than 200 aircraft to break even, a figure that represented about 15 percent of predicted industry sales for this class of aircraft between 1994 and 2004. Given the volume of sales required to break even, it can take up to 10 to 14 years of production for an aircraft model to turn a profit and this on top of the 5 to 6 years of negative cash flows during development.

On the manufacturing side, a significant experience curve exists in aircraft production. Due to learning effects, on average, unit cost falls by about 20 percent with each doubling of accumulated output. A company that fails to move along the experience curve faces a significant unit-cost disadvantage. A company that achieves only half of the market share required to break even will suffer a 20 percent unit-cost disadvantage.

Another feature of the industry is that demand for aircraft is highly volatile. This makes long-run planning difficult and raises the risks involved in producing aircraft. The commercial airline business is prone to boom-and-bust cycles. During the early 1990s, many major airlines experienced financial trouble. Pan Am, Eastern, Braniff, and TWA were all either in Chapter 11 bankruptcy protection or had recently folded. Many other airlines were losing money. In response, airlines slowed their ordering of new aircraft, pushed back delivery dates for aircraft already on firm order, and decided not to convert their options on future aircraft deliveries to firm orders. Thus, although both Boeing and Airbus both entered the 1990s with record orders, the troubles in the airline business spread to them. The low point was reached in 1994 when 260 large (100-seat plus) commercial jet aircraft were ordered worldwide. A significant recovery occurred in 1995, with close to 500 aircraft orders. The growth in demand continued during the next three years. In 1998, 1,212 large commercial jet aircraft were ordered, a record. However, underlining the cyclical nature of the economy, both Boeing and Airbus stated that they thought orders would decrease in 1999, partly because of the lingering effects of the Asian financial crisis, which resulted in a sharp decline in orders from this once fast-growing region.

The combination of high development costs, break-even levels that constitute a significant percentage of world demand, substantial experience curve levels, and volatile demand makes for an industry that can support only a few major players. Analysts seem to agree that the large jet commercial aircraft market can profitably support only two, or possibly three, major producers. By 1998, there were only two major players in the industry, McDonnell Douglas having been absorbed by Boeing. This, combined with the strong production and order levels reached that year, should have boded well for productivity. However, Boeing's profits were poor during 1997 and 1998 as it struggled to cope with a poorly managed ramp up of its aircraft production rates, the effects of unexpectedly high manufacturing costs, and intense price competition from an increasingly aggressive Airbus.

Trade Frictions before 1992

In the 1980s and early 1990s, both Boeing and McDonnell Douglas argued that Airbus had an unfair competitive advantage due to the level of subsidy it received from the governments of Great Britain, France, Germany, and Spain. They argued that the subsidies allow Airbus to set unrealistically low prices, to offer concessions and attractive financing terms to airlines, to write off development costs, and to use state-owned airlines to obtain orders. In making these claims, Boeing and McDonnell Douglas had the support of the US government. According to a study by the Department of Commerce, Airbus received more than $13.5 billion in government subsidies between 1970 and 1990 ($25.9 billion if commercial interest rates are applied). Most of these subsidies were in the form of loans at below-market interest rates and tax breaks. The subsidies financed research and development and provided attractive financing terms for Airbus's customers. For most of its customers, Airbus is believed to have financed 80 percent of the cost of aircraft for a term of 8 to 10 years at an annual interest rate of approximately 7 percent. In contrast, the US Export–Import Bank required 20 percent down payments from Boeing and McDonnell Douglas customers, financed only 40 percent of the cost of an aircraft directly, and guaranteed the financing of the remaining 40 percent by private banks at an average interest rate of 8.4 percent to 8.5 percent for a period of 10 years.

Airbus's response to these charges was to point out that its success is not due to subsidies but to a good product and a good strategy. Most observers agree that Airbus's aircraft incorporate state-of-the-art technology, particularly in materials applications, systems for flight control and safety, and aerodynamics. Airbus gained ground initially by targeting market segments not served by new aircraft or not served at all. Thus, Airbus has taken the initiative in targeting two segments of the market with wide-bodied twin-engined aircraft, then in developing a new generation of aircraft for the 150-seat market, and most recently in going after the market below the 747 for a 250- to 300-seat airliner with its A330 and A340 models (to which Boeing's 777 is a belated but apparently successful competitive response).

Airbus also argued that both Boeing and McDonnell Douglas have benefited from US government aid for a long time and that the aid it has received has merely leveled the playing field. In the United States, planes were built under government contract during World War I, and the construction of mail planes was subsidized between the world wars. Almost all production was subsidized during World War II, and subsidies continued at a high level after the war. The Boeing 707, for example, is a derivative of a military transport program that was subsidized by the US government. Boeing's subsidized programs include the B-17, B-29, B-47, B-52, and K-135, just to name a few. Its nonairline programs have included the Minuteman missile, Apollo-Saturn, and space station programs.

A 1991 European Commission study attempted to estimate the amount of subsidies received by the US industry. The study contends that Boeing and McDonnell Douglas received $18 billion to $22 billion in indirect government aid between 1976 and 1990. The report claims that commercial aircraft operations benefited through Defense Department contracts by as much as $6.34 billion during the 1976–90 period. In addition, the report claims that NASA has pumped at least $8 billion into commercial aircraft production over the same period, and that tax exemptions have given an additional $1.7 billion to Boeing and $1.4 billion to McDonnell Douglas.

Boeing rejected the claims of the European Commission report. The company pointed out that the report's assumption that Boeing receives direct government grants in the form of an additional 5 percent for commercial work with every military or space contract it receives was false. Moreover, the company argued that during the 1980s only 3 percent of Boeing's R&D spending came from Department of Defense funding and only 4 percent from NASA funding. Boeing also argued that since the four companies in the Airbus consortium do twice as much miliary and space work as Boeing, they must receive much larger indirect subsidies.

The 1992 Agreement and Its Aftermath

In mid-1992, the United States and the four European governments involved agreed to a pact that seemed likely to end the long-standing dispute. The 1992 pact, which was negotiated by the European Union on behalf of the four member states, limited direct European government subsidies to each Airbus partner to 33 percent of new development costs and specified that future subsidies must be repaid with interest. The agreement also limited indirect subsidies, such as military research that has applications to commercial aircraft, to 5 percent of development costs for commercial aircraft. Although Airbus officials say the controversy has been resolved, Boeing officials say they will be competing for years against subsidized products.

In February 1993, it looked as if the trade dispute was about to reemerge. The newly elected President Clinton repeatedly blasted the European Union for allowing subsidies of Airbus to continue, blamed job losses in the US aerospace industry on the subsidies, and called for the EU to renegotiate the 1992 deal.

To the surprise of the administration, however, this renewed attack on Airbus subsidies was greeted with conspicuous silence from the US industry. Many analysts theorized that this was because a renewed dispute could prompt damaging retaliation from Europe. For one thing, Airbus equips its aircraft with engines made by two US companies—Pratt & Whitney and General Electric—and with avionics made by US companies. In addition, many state-owned airlines in Europe purchase aircraft from Boeing and McDonnell Douglas. Many in the US industry apparently felt that this lucrative business would be put at risk if the government reopened the trade dispute so soon after the 1992 agreement.

A similar cool response from the US industry greeted attempts by two US senators, John C. Danforth of Missouri and Max Baucus of Montana, to reopen the trade dispute with Airbus. In early 1993, Danforth and Baucus cosponsored legislation requiring the US government to launch a trade case against Airbus on charges of unfair subsidies. They also sponsored a bill to create an aerospace industry consortium called Aerotech that would finance aerospace research, with half of the funds coming from industry and half from the US government. Vice President Al Gore called the establishment of Aerotech "an administration priority," but a Boeing spokesman said the company was "very guarded about Aerotech" because it could violate the 1992 accord. Both Danforth/Baucus bills died in committee hearings, and the Clinton administration quietly dropped all talk of reopening the trade dispute.

The Boeing–McDonnell Douglas Merger

In December 1996, Boeing stunned the aerospace industry by announcing it would merge with longtime rival McDonnell Douglas in a deal estimated to be worth $13.3 billion. The merger was scheduled to be completed by the end of July 1997. The merger was driven by Boeing's desire to strengthen its presence in the defense and space side of the aerospace business areas where McDonnell Douglas was traditionally strong. On the commercial side of the aerospace business, Douglas had been losing market share since the 1970s. By 1996, Douglas accounted for less than 10 percent of production in the large commercial jet aircraft market and only 3 percent of new orders placed that year. The dearth of new orders meant the long-term outlook for Douglas's commercial business was increasingly murky. With or without the merger, many analysts felt that it was only a matter of time before McDonnell Douglas would be forced to exit from the commercial jet aircraft business. In their view, the merger with Boeing merely accelerated that process. Because the merger would reduce the number of players in the commercial aerospace industry from three to two, it was expected that the antitrust authorities would review the merger.

Boeing and McDonnell Douglas officials expected both the US Federal Trade Commission (FTC) and the Competition Commission of the European Union to investigate the merger to assess its effects on competition. Boeing executives believed that the FTC would approve the proposed merger. Boeing's argument was that the Boeing-McDonnell Douglas combination was necessary to create a strong US competitor in a competitive global marketplace. This is an argument that US antitrust authorities have been sympathetic to in recent years. Moreover, Boeing executives pointed out that since the end of the Cold War, the US government had been arguing for consolidation in the defense industry to eliminate excess capacity. The Boeing-McDonnell Douglas merger helped to achieve that goal and thus should receive government support.

As for the Europeans, here too Boeing executives believed there would be little opposition to the merger. In the words of Harry Stonecipher, CEO of McDonnell Douglas, "My good friend Jean Pierson, head of Airbus, has been saying at airshows lately, 'Douglas is not a factor in the commercial industry' so the deal is apparently a non-event."[1] Initially, Airbus officials seemed to indicate they agreed with this assessment and would not oppose the merger. However, within days of the merger announcement, Karl Van Miert, the EU competition commissioner, signaled that the EU would launch a probe of the merger. Van Miert stated that the EU would oppose the merger if it thought doing so was necessary to preserve competition. In justifying the probe, he expressed the concern that if the number of players in the market for large commercial jet aircraft was reduced to two, they might engage in tacit collusion, raising prices above the level that would prevail in more competitive market situations.

Van Miert's statements raised hackles in the United States. Government officials and Boeing executives were heard wondering out loud what authority a European body would have over a merger between two US companies that did almost all their manufacturing in the United States and had few assets in Europe. Van Miert stated that EU law required him to evaluate the merger and entitled the EU to block the merger if it was found to be anticompetitive. While Van Miert acknowledged that the EU could not actually stop the merger, under EU competition law the commission could declare the merger illegal, restrict its business in Europe, and fine it up to 10 percent of its estimated $48 billion annual sales. Boeing executives argued that if this were the outcome, it would provoke a trade war between the United States and the EU. Some US politicians claimed that the stance adopted by the EU amounted to nothing less than a flagrant violation of US national sovereignty.

Complicating the issue further was Boeing's success in inking long-term exclusive supply contracts with three major US-based airlines: American Airlines, Delta, and Continental. The American Airlines deal was signed in late 1996 and the two others in the first half of 1997. All three deals named Boeing the exclusive supplier of each airlines' aircraft needs for 20 years. Van Miert argued that these agreements were anticompetitive and reinforced his concerns about the market power of a Boeing–McDonnell Douglas combination. These agreements seemed to promote a change of heart among Airbus executives. After originally stating that they had no objections to the merger, Airbus executives became increasingly vocal in their opposition to the merger. In March 1997, Jean Pierson, the head of the consortium, warned that the proposed merger could give Boeing a "structural hold" on the industry, spanning the supply of aircraft, servicing, and spare parts. Similarly, commenting on the exclusive supplier deals, Airbus spokesman David Venz argued that the Boeing–McDonnell Douglas combination would "have a locked-in captive customer for 29 years. They have effectively removed choice from the airline who signs those contracts."[2]

In mid-May 1997, the European Commission gave Boeing and McDonnell Douglas its official statement of objections to the planned merger and asked the two US groups to respond before June 12, when hearings on the subject were scheduled to take place in Brussels. The commission stated that the merger raised three principal concerns. First, it would restrict competition in the market for large commercial jet aircraft. Second, McDonnell Douglas's extensive defense and space activities raised the possibility that US government funding for defense and space programs would be used to fund the development of commercial jet aircraft. Third, the sole supplier agreements with American Airlines, Delta, and Continental restricted competition in the commercial aerospace market.

In commenting on these concerns, Boeing CEO Phil Condit noted that since McDonnell Douglas accounted for only 3 percent of commercial sales in 1996, one could hardly argue that the merger would have a restrictive effect on competition. Condit stated that there was no question of defense research funding being used for civil programs, since the issue was already regulated by the 1992 bilateral trade agreement. As for the sole supplier agreements, Condit noted that the deals were struck at the initiative of the airlines.

On June 30, 1997, the Federal Trade Commission issued its own ruling on the merger. In a 4-to-1 decision, an FTC panel recommended that the merger be given unconditional approval. Before reaching its decision, the FTC interviewed 40 executives of airlines to find out whether they thought the merger would cause higher prices from Boeing. While some airlines expressed a preference that McDonnell Douglas remain in the bidding, they were virtually unanimous in acknowledging that they were unlikely to buy from that company because it appeared not to be making the investment required to remain viable. In short, the FTC concluded that McDonnell Douglas was no longer a viable competitor in the large commercial jet market, and therefore, the merger would not have a detrimental effect on competition. At the same time, the FTC did note that the sole supplier agreements that Boeing had reached were "potentially troubling." Although the three agreements reached by July 1997 accounted for only 11 percent of the global market, the FTC signaled that it would be concerned if more occurred.

On July 18, senior EU officials stated publicly that they planned to declare the merger illegal, insisting that it would harm competition in Europe. In announcing this intention, Van Miert stated that he was particularly concerned about the exclusive supplier contracts, which unfairly closed Airbus out of an important segment of the global market.

In a last-minute bid to stop the European Commission from declaring the merger illegal, Boeing blinked and stated it would not enforce provisions in the 20-year supplier contracts with American, Delta, and Continental. With this concession in hand, on July 23, a triumphant Van Miert announced that the European Commission would now approve the merger. Across Europe, newspapers sang Van Miert's praise, depicting him as the man who had taken on the American colossus and won. "You have to hand it to him," stated one EU official, "he took them on and won. He showed them that the European Commission is a force to be reckoned with."[3]

The Future

With the merger approved, EU officials switched their attentions to another potentially damaging issue, allegations that the United States was violating the 1992 accord limiting government subsidies to the aerospace industry. The 1992 accord limits direct government subsidies to one-third of the development costs of a new commercial jet aircraft and curbs indirect handouts, including research grants, to 3 percent of a manufacturer's revenues. The EU now claims that the United States is openly flouting this accord and is channeling significant support to its aerospace firms through the Department of Defense and NASA. An EU official claimed that the aid exceeds the agreed limits by a factor of three to five. European aerospace executives claim that while EU government loans have to be repaid, US government research expenditure does not have to be

repaid. US officials argued that the charges were incorrect and motivated by a desire to get out of the 1992 agreement so that the EU could increase subsidies to Airbus, allowing the consortium to profitably fund the development of its next generation "super-jumbo" aircraft, the 550-seat A3XX.

Discussion Questions

1. Do you believe Airbus could have become a viable competitor without subsidies?

2. Why do you think the four European governments agreed to subsidize the establishment of Airbus?

3. Is Airbus's position with regard to the dispute over subsidies reasonable?

4. Given the 1992 agreement, what additional action (if any) should the US government take with respect to Airbus?

5. Why do you think that the US industry reacted with caution to attempts by politicians to reopen the trade dispute in 1993?

6. In an era of global competition, what is the case for antitrust authorities to permit the formation of large domestic firms through mergers and acquisitions?

7. Was the threat by EU authorities to declare the Boeing–McDonnell Douglas merger illegal a violation of US national sovereignty?

8. Do you think the EU Commission had a strong case in its attempts to wring concessions from Boeing regarding the merger with McDonnell Douglas? Was Boeing right to make significant concessions to the EU? What might have occurred if the concessions were not made?

Notes

1. John Mintz, "Boeing to Buy McDonnell Douglas," *Washington Post*, December 16, 1996, p. A1.

2. M. Kayal, "Boeing May Be Flying into Antitrust Territory," *Journal of Commerce*, March 25, 1997, p. 3A.

3. Emma Tucker, "Van Miert's Finest Hour," *Financial Times*, July 24, 1997, p. 23.

Sources

1. Barnard, B. "Battle over Boeing Shifts to Subsidies." *Journal of Commerce*, July 25, 1997, p. 1A.

2. Cohen, R. "France Pledges Subsidy to Aerospace Group." *New York Times*, February 3, 1994, p. 5.

3. Coleman, B. "GATT to Rule against German Aid to Airbus." *The Wall Street Journal*, January 16, 1992, p. 5.

4. Core, O. C. "Airbus Arrives." *Seattle Times,* July 21, 1992, pp. C1–C3.

5. Davis, B., and B. Ingersoll. "Cloudy Issue." *The Wall Street Journal,* March 8, 1993, p. A1.

6. De Jonquieres, G. "Storm over the Atlantic." *Financial Times,* May 22, 1997, p. 17.

7. Dertouzos, M. L.; R. K. Lester; and R. M. Solow. *Made in America.* Cambridge, MA: MIT Press, 1989.

8. "Dissecting Airbus." *The Economist,* February 16, 1991, pp. 51–52.

9. Gow, D. "Airbus Warns on Sales." *The Guardian,* January 14, 1999, p. 22.

10. Grimaldi, J. "FTC Approves Boeing Merger." *Seattle Times,* July 1, 1997, p. A1.

11. "The Jumbo War." *The Economist,* June 15, 1991, pp. 65–66.

12. Kayal, M. "Boeing May Be Flying into Antitrust Territory." *Journal of Commerce,* March 25, 1997, p. 3A.

13. Kayal, M. "The Boeing-McDonnell Merger Looks Very Different through European Eyes." *Journal of Commerce,* July 21, 1997, p. 1A.

14. Klepper, G. "Entry into the Market for Large Transport Aircraft." *European Economic Review* 34 (1990), pp. 775–803.

15. Lane, P. "Study Complains of Alleged Subsidies." *Seattle Times,* December 4, 1991, p. G2.

16. Mintz, J. "Boeing to Buy McDonnell Douglas." *Washington Post,* December 16, 1996, p. A1.

17. Skapinker, M. "EU Sets out Objections to Boeing Merger." *Financial Times,* May 23, 1997, p. 6.

18. Stroud, M. "Worries over a Technology Shift Follow McDonnell-Taiwan Accord." *Investor's Business Daily,* November 21, 1991, p. 36.

19. Toy, S., et al. "Zoom! Airbus Comes on Strong." *Business Week,* April 22, 1991, pp. 48–50.

20. Tucker, E. "Van Miert's Finest Hour." *Financial Times,* July 24, 1997, p. 23.

ACTIVE MATRIX LIQUID CRYSTAL DISPLAYS: TRADE DISPUTE

Introduction

The active matrix liquid crystal display screen (AM-LCD) is seen as a technology of the future. These flat display screens offer several advantages over the monochromatic, passive matrix liquid crystal display screens (PM-LCD) used in laptop computers and digital watches. Compared to PM-LCDs, AM-LCDs are light, use little electricity, do not emit radiation, are easy on the eyes, and respond quickly to electrical inputs. These features make high-quality color, text, graphic, and video possible when the screens are integrated into laptop computers. In addition to computer displays, the screens are also critical components in camcorders, medical instruments, high-definition television, auto dashboards, aerospace instruments, factory control devices, and instrumentation for the military. Sales were just $250 million worldwide in 1990, but forecasts suggest worldwide sales of more than $10 billion by 2000.

The Market

The technology was pioneered in the United States during the 1960s. In recent years, however, the Japanese have emerged as the major producers of AM-LCDs and now account for 95 percent of worldwide production. Sharp, NEC, and Toshiba dominate the market. Unlike their major US competitors, these Japanese firms made massive investments in AM-LCD research and production facilities during the 1980s. Sharp reportedly spent more than $1 billion on developing the technology during the 1980s and spent $640 million more in the 1991–95 period.

Although a number of small US companies are involved in this business, they tend to focus on highly specialized niches (e.g., supplying the Defense Department) and have made investments only to support their limited production. With the exception of IBM, which has a joint venture with Toshiba in Japan to manufacture AM-LCDs, no major US company has a presence in the industry, and no US company is capable of mass production. There are a number of reasons for this. First, the massive capital expenditures required to produce AM-LCD screens have deterred many US firms, as have the high risks involved. The risks are judged to be particularly acute, given the Japanese lead in the technology and the long payback period for any investments. (Japanese executives regard five or six years of losses as the cost of entering this business.) Few American companies are willing to invest in an industry where Japanese companies are already well ahead. In addition, the production process is particularly difficult to master, since even the smallest contaminant (such as dust) can damage a display. It is estimated that 80 percent of AM-LCDs coming off Japanese production lines are defective and must be scrapped. Thus, the combination of high capital costs, high risks, and a difficult production process have deterred many major US firms from entering the market.

The Imposition of Antidumping Duties

Against this background, in July 1990, a group of small US manufacturers of AM-LCDs filed an "antidumping" action with the US Department of Commerce. They claimed that the Japanese suppliers of AM-LCDs were selling their screens below market value and at less than half of their production cost—in other words, dumping them—in the United States. The International Trade Commission (ITC), a branch of the Department of Commerce, investigated the charges. In August 1991, the ITC reported that the Japanese producers had been selling AM-LCDs below cost and imposed a 62.67 percent duty on AM-LCDs imported from Japan in an effort to shelter small US manufacturers from unfair foreign competition. The ITC acknowledged that the Japanese competition was killing small US companies, but it warned that the duties would not guarantee the US industry's success. US success would require significant investments, investments that the government was not prepared to subsidize.

The decision to impose an antidumping tariff on AM-LCD screens imported from Japan followed a 1987 US government decision to impose a 100 percent tariff on laptop computers imported from Japan. Both of these tariffs are country specific; they target imports from Japan only.

The Response of US Computer Makers

The response by American computer manufacturers to the imposition of duties took the Department of Commerce by surprise. Most US manufacturers of laptop computers were already importing LCD screens from Japanese suppliers. IBM, for example, was importing screens made in Japan by its joint venture with Toshiba. AM-LCD screens are the most costly component for

laptops, accounting for 50 percent of their total cost. Thus, the duty increased the cost of manufacturing a laptop computer in the United States by about 30 percent. Not surprisingly, US computer companies felt that this placed them at a significant disadvantage vis-á-vis companies that manufactured laptops in other countries.

The response of US computer manufacturers was twofold. First, they lodged formal protests with the US government for imposing the duties and filed appeals with the Court of International Trade for a reversal of the decision. IBM, Apple, Compaq, and Tandy all argued that the government's decision to protect small AM-LCD makers via antidumping duties was possible only at their expense. Second, they began to move their assembly of laptop computers out of the United States. Apple abandoned its plans to manufacture its notebook computers in Colorado and decided to move production to Ireland; Compaq announced plans to produce laptops in Scotland. Their logic was that these third countries do not levy tariffs on imports of AM-LCDs from Japan and that the United States does not levy tariffs on imports of finished laptops from these countries. By pursuing such a strategy, Apple and Compaq could maintain their competitive cost structure, but only at the cost of lost jobs in the United States.

The Japanese Reaction

Some analysts believe that behind the antidumping duty was a cynical attempt by the Commerce Department to encourage Japanese manufacturers to move their production of AM-LCDs to the United States, which would benefit the United States with job creation and technology transfer. If this is true, the Commerce Department badly miscalculated. Few if any Japanese companies seemed to have any intention of switching AM-LCD production to the United States. Mass production of AM-LCDs had barely begun in Japan, and it would be years before the capital costs of their investments are recouped, so additional investments in the United States were unlikely. Instead, seven Japanese manufacturers, including Sharp, Toshiba, and Hitachi, joined the US computer manufacturers in lodging appeals with the Court of International Trade. They charged that the decision to impose duties was illogical because there were virtually no US manufacturers capable of producing AM-LCDs commercially. Moreover, they noted that the dumping charge was misplaced. While it was true that no Japanese manufacturers were making profits on AM-LCDs, they contended that this was due to the enormous capital expenditure required to start production. They argued that production costs would decline and profits would follow once the production process was perfected, output built, and scale economies realized. Japan's Ministry of International Trade and Industry was also investigating the possibility the Department of Commerce's decision violated the General Agreement on Tariffs and Trade (GATT).

Can the U.S. Industry Be Saved?

Many people believe that the decision to impose antidumping duties came too late to save the US LCD industry. They point out that Japanese companies had been investing heavily in AM-LCD technology for years and that US companies lacked the capacity to sell commercially. Instead, US manufacturers sold most of their screens to the Pentagon. It is believed that a minimum investment of $300 million would be required to set up a commercial manufacturing operation—a figure that is probably beyond the reach of most US firms currently in the industry. In addition, US firms would have to support five to six years of losses to enter the market and would have to solve the production problems that bedevil AM-LCD production in Japan, the world capital of precision manufacturing.

While all of this seems unlikely, some government experts remain convinced that the United States is still capable of catching up with Japan. Having toured AM-LCD plants in Japan, these experts believe that US companies can obtain enough government and private funds not only to reproduce AM-LCD technology, but also to improve on the manufacturing processes in use. Against this background, the US Air Force has proposed to fund AM-LCD production. The Air Force is interested because it uses AM-LCD screens for cockpit instrumentation and flight-simulation devices. The US Army also needs the screens for its battle tanks, and the Navy uses them in its shipboard command centers. The Pentagon says the AM-LCD project meets its criteria for the "selective production" program. This program allows the Pentagon to commit funds for purchasing critical defense materials from selected contractors when projects meet certain standards. Firms obtaining contracts for AM-LCD production would be expected to find commercial buyers for the screens to keep their manufacturing cost effective and to avoid high-priced

products. A Pentagon commitment to AM-LCD production may be enough to encourage other US investors to finance AM-LCD production to cultivate a customer base for the screens.

Discussion Questions

1. Evaluate the Commerce Department's decision to impose duties on Japanese-manufactured AM-LCDs. Has this decision helped or harmed US industry? What is the likely impact on the US consumer?

2. What, if anything, could the US government do to keep US computer manufacturers from moving their manufacturing operations offshore? Should the government take such action?

3. What criteria should the US government apply in targeting industries for antidumping protection?

4. If you were the CEO of a small US firm interested in AM-LCD manufacturing, what factors would be important in your decision to enter the AM-LCD market? Under what conditions might you enter the market?

5. Should the US government urge the Pentagon to support production of AM-LCDs? Explain the reasoning behind your answer.

Sources

1. Department of Commerce, International Trade Administration. "High Information Content of Flat Panel Displays and Display Glass Therefore from Japan: Anti-Dumping Duty Orders." September 4, 1992.

2. "Flat Out in Japan." *The Economist*, February 1, 1992, pp. 79–80.

3. "Flat Screens Come to Life." *Far Eastern Economic Review*, August 15, 1991, p. 58.

4. "Imported Japanese Flat Panel Displays Injure U.S. Industry, ITC Says." *International Trade Reporter*, August 21, 1991.

5. Johnson, R. "Flat Out for Profits." *Far Eastern Economic Review*, April 19, 1990.

6. "LCD Makers Appeal against U.S. Anti-Dumping Ruling." Kyodo News Service, October 9, 1991.

7. Magnusson, P. "Did Washington Lose Sight of the Big Picture?" *Business Week*, December 2, 1991.

8. Nomura, H. "IBM, Apple Fight LCD Screen Tariffs: U.S. Decision Forcing Assembly Offshore." *The Nikkei Weekly*, October 26, 1992.

9. Tanzer, A. "The New Improved Color Computer." *Forbes*, July 23, 1990, pp. 276–80.

THE RISE AND FALL OF THE JAPANESE SEMICONDUCTOR INDUSTRY, 1970–2000

Introduction

The semiconductor industry was born with the invention of the transistor at Bell Telephone laboratories in 1947. The transistor was first commercialized in the 1950s by US firms and it soon became a major component of electronic products. In the 1960s, the transistor was replaced by the integrated circuit. Like the transistor, the integrated circuit was first developed and commercialized by US firms. Today, semiconductors are the main components of numerous electronic products including computers, photocopiers, and telecommunications equipment. In addition, they are increasingly finding their way into a host of other products from automobiles to machine tools.

Semiconductors can be divided into several broad product groups, the most important of which are *memory devices*, such as DRAMs (dynamic random access memory chips), and *logic chips*, such as the microprocessors and microcontrollers. The total world market for semiconductors stood at $35 billion in 1988, reached $91.5 billion in 1994, increased to $122 billion in 1998, and is predicted to total $182 billion by the year 2001.

US enterprises dominated the world market from the 1950s until the early 1980s. At the height of US success in the mid-1970s, US firms held close to 70 percent of the world market. During the 1980s, however, the market share of US firms plummeted, falling to 29 percent by 1990, while the share held by Japanese producers rose from 24 percent at the end of the 1970s to 49 percent by 1990. By the end of the 1980s, the US was a net importer of semiconductors, while 5 of the 10 largest semiconductor producers were Japanese. More significantly still, by 1988 Japanese firms had captured more than 80 percent of the world market for the most widely used integrated circuit in digital equipment, the DRAM. Invented by Intel and once produced exclusively by US firms, as of 1988 there were only two US firms in the DRAM market, Micron Technologies and Texas Instruments, and Texas Instruments was manufacturing most of its DRAMs in Japan.

However, the late 1980s may have ben something of a high water mark in the global success of Japanese semiconductor firms. By the mid-1990s, the US industry was again gaining global market share. By 1994, US manufacturers had increased their share of the world semiconductor market to 42 percent, while the share taken by Japanese firms stood at 41 percent, down almost ten percentage points from their high. Also, foreign firms held 22.4 percent of the Japanese semiconductor market in 1994, up from about 14 percent in 1990. As the 1990s progressed, Japan's share of the global market continued to decline. In this case we explore some reasons for the rise of Japan's semiconductor industry and for the subsequent decline in its growth in global market share.

Japan's Industrial Policy

Why were the Japanese so successful in the global semiconductor industry between the 1970s and late 1980s? One argument is that the industrial policy of the Japanese government was the driving force behind Japan's success in semiconductors. During the 1960s and 1970s, the Japanese government, principally through the Ministry of International Trade and Industry (MITI), sought to build a competitive semiconductor industry by limiting foreign competition in the domestic market and acquiring foreign technology and know-how. The foreign investment laws created after World War II (ironically by the US occupation government) required the Japanese government to review for approval all applications for foreign direct investment in Japan. MITI consistently rejected all applications by US semiconductor firms to set up wholly owned subsidiaries in Japan, to set up joint ventures in which the US partner would have a majority stake, or to acquire equity in Japanese semiconductor firms. At the same time, the government limited foreign import penetration of the Japanese market through a combination of high tariffs and restrictive quotas. Import penetration of the Japanese market was also limited by requirements that Japanese companies get permission from MITI before buying advanced integrated circuits from foreign companies. For example, until 1974, integrated circuits that contained more than 200 circuit elements could not be imported without special permission.

Because US producers were denied direct access to the Japanese semiconductor market, they typically sought indirect access by licensing their product and process know-how to Japanese enterprises. This too was regulated by MITI. MITI's policy was to insist that if a foreign firm was going to license technology in Japan, that technology had to be licensed to all Japanese firms that requested access. In other words, US firms were not able to discriminate between licensees. MITI also conditioned approval of certain deals on the willingness of the involved Japanese firms to diffuse their technological developments, through sublicensing agreements, to other Japanese firms. The net result of these policies was to encourage the rapid diffusion of advanced semiconductor product and process technology throughout the Japanese semiconductor industry.

US firms went along with this policy because it was their only way to get access to the Japanese market. Initially, licensing was a very lucrative arrangement for US firms. By the end of the 1960s, Japanese semiconductor firms were reportedly paying at least 10 percent of their sales revenues as royalties to US firms: 2 percent to General Electric, 4.5 percent to Fairchild, and 3.5 percent to Texas Instruments. The most notable long-run consequence, however, was a transfer of US technological know-how to a number of emerging Japanese competitors. Shielded from foreign competition by import barriers and restrictions on foreign direct investment and armed with state-of-the-art technological know-how, the Japanese firms had only each other to compete with for a share of the rapidly growing Japanese semiconductor market. Stimulated by MITI's insistence that technology be shared among all Japanese semiconductor firms, this competition was intense and based primarily on cost (since everyone had the same technology). The firms that rose to the top in this tough environment, such as NEC, were more than capable of going head-to-head with US semiconductor firms by the mid-1970s.

Trade Agreements

By the mid-1980s, the changing fortunes of the Japanese and US semiconductor industries had given birth to a bitter trade dispute between the two countries. After incurring heavy losses, US firms claimed they were facing unfair competition from Japan. They accused the Japanese of selling semiconductors, and especially DRAMs, in the United States for less than their fair market value while simultaneously shutting US firms out of the important and lucrative Japanese semiconductor market. The dispute was settled by a 1986 trade agreement between the United States and Japan. The agreement specified a fair market value for semiconductors. Japanese companies were not supposed to sell their semiconductors for less than this price outside of Japan. The agreement also sought to increase foreign access to Japan's domestic semiconductor market. In a nonbinding side letter, the Japanese government agreed to help ensure that foreign manufacturers gained more than 20 percent of the Japanese market by the end of 1991, a significant increase from the 8.6 percent share held in 1986.

Although the agreement led to an increase in prices for semiconductors in the United States, foreign producers were still not able to capture a major share of Japan's semiconductor market. By early 1991 when the 1986 agreement was close to expiration, the American Semiconductor Industry Association claimed that foreigners held only a 12 percent share of the Japanese market (the Japanese claimed the foreign share was closer to 17 percent).

In June 1991, the United States and Japan signed a new five-year pact to replace the 1986 agreement. Unlike the previous agreement, this pact formally committed the Japanese to ensuring that foreign producers gained a 20 percent share of their semiconductor market by the end of 1992. In return, the United States agreed to abolish the fair market value system created under the 1986 pact.

This new agreement was greeted with a mixed reception on both sides. While most US semiconductor manufacturers approved of the agreement, some analysts and politicians argued that the government should not have abolished the fair market value system. House Democratic Leader Richard Gephardt, for example, criticized the agreement for its lack of specific commitments by Japan to widen its chip market to foreign sellers. Similarly, Clyde Prestowitz, a former US trade official who helped to craft the 1986 agreement, called the pact "a step backwards," primarily because it abolished the fair market value system. The Japanese, in contrast, expressed pleasure that the fair market value system had been removed, but many criticized the formal commitment to a 20 percent market share for foreign companies. For example, a senior official at Toshiba, one of Japan's largest semiconductor manufacturers, noted, "We believe that the agreement infringes the principles of free trade, which shouldn't be limited by an agreement of any kind." Similarly, a senior official from the NEC Corporation said, "As you know, the semiconductor was invented in the US and the US was number one in the world for a long time in semiconductors. The US might be a little complacent about what it has achieved. There has been a lack of effort."

Despite such misgivings, the pact seemed to deliver what it promised. The foreign share of the Japanese semiconductor market reached 20 percent in the fourth quarter of 1992. Although it fell back somewhat in the first half of 1993, foreign producers again gained share in the fourth quarter, pushing their total share for the year to 19.4 percent, up from an average of 16.7 percent for all of 1992. The performance of foreigners was even better in 1994, when they captured over 22 percent of the Japanese market. In the fourth quarter of 1994, foreign producers gained a record 23.7 percent market share. However, some analysts wondered whether the pact had much to do with the foreign success. They pointed out that the value of the Japanese yen had strengthened by about 40 percent against the US dollar since 1991. With the yen this high, the terms of trade in the Japanese semiconductor market had swung sharply toward foreign producers, who now had a distinct cost advantage over their Japanese rivals.

Moreover, critics note that in the important DRAM market there has been only a limited US resurgence (in contrast to the market for logic chips, where Intel, Motorola, and other continue to dominate). While both Micron Technology and Texas Instruments—the lone two US DRAM manufacturers—did extremely well during 1994 and 1995, much of the DRAM market share gain in Japan has been made by Korean firms, particularly Samsung. Samsung, which didn't even produce DRAMs in 1988, accounted for 12.7 percent of the world DRAM market in 1994, ahead of Japan's Hitachi Corp. and NEC, which accounted for 9.7 percent and 9.2 percent, respectively. The Japanese share of the world DRAM market was cut in half between 1988 and 1994 as customers switched to low-cost producers such as market leader Samsung and Micron Technology (which enjoyed a 4.5 percent market share in 1994). As of 1995, these trends showed no sign of slowing down. One 1995 estimate suggested that South Korean firms were reinvesting 30 percent to 55 percent of their semiconductor revenues in new plants and equipment, the Americans were reinvesting 22 percent, while the Japanese were reinvesting only 15 percent. Also, a number of Taiwanese firms had announced aggressive plans to expand their presence in the DRAM business. In the face of this rapid investment in capacity by non-Japanese firms and the apparent reluctance of Japanese firms to invest many thought it would be difficult for the Japanese producers to hold onto their 37 percent share of the global DRAM market.

In the summer of 1996, representatives from Japan and the United States met again to renegotiate the 1991 semiconductor agreement, which was due to expire July 31, 1996. This time, the Japanese were determined to oppose any attempt by the US side to continue to impose numerical targets or otherwise interfere in the market mechanism. In making their case, the Japanese pointed out that during the first six months of 1996, the foreign share of the Japanese semiconductor market had risen to over 30 percent and that two-thirds of that share had been taken by American firms. In the wider global market, Japanese producers were seeing their share being taken by aggressive competitors from South Korea and now Taiwan. In the DRAM sector in particular, the rise in the value of the Japanese yen had made it increasingly difficult for Japanese firms to compete against the Koreans and Taiwanese.

Publicly, the Americans declared that they would push for another agreement, and they voiced concerns that without some kind of deal, the Japanese market would once more be closed to foreign competition. Privately, however, government officials admitted that Japan's semiconductor industry seemed to be on the wane, and that it would be difficult to renew the agreement, particularly given the rise of new competitors and the profit boom being enjoyed by some of America's own semiconductor companies.

After the customary hard bargaining, which went down to the wire as so many trade deals seem to, an agreement was reached that enabled the American side to save face while basically giving the Japanese what they wanted. Under the deal, US and Japanese industry associations agreed to create an entity to collect data about the sector and deliver it to their governments, which would meet annually to discuss the industry. In the worlds of one observer, the deal represented "the tiniest of fig leaves . . . .The idea that there will be government meetings yearly to review semiconductor trade but with no power to do anything about it means that everyone has decided to smile and go home."[1]

Aftermath

The years after the 1996 agreement were not kind to the semiconductor industry. A glut of new capacity in South Korea and Taiwan produced excess capacity in memory chips. Prices for DRAMs fell by as much as 70 percent, and most of the world's major producers of memory chips posted significant losses. Among those worst hit were the big five Japanese semiconductor companies NEC, Toshiba, Hitachi, Fujitsu, and Mitsubishi Electric. Throughout 1997–98, the yen continued to gain strength against the currencies of South Korea and Taiwan (the former collapsed in value in late 1997), effectively pricing Japanese firms out of the DRAM market. By late 1998, Japan's share of the global market for DRAMs had shrunk to 30 percent, down from a peak of 80 percent 10 years earlier, and Japan's share was forecasted to fall to 20 percent by 2000. New reports suggested that Hitachi, Fujitsu, and Mitsubishi Electric were contemplating leaving the DRAM market and focusing on niches within the market for logic chips. The big gainers had been Taiwanese companies in the DRAM market, although American companies continued to hold onto their share, both in the DRAM market and in the logic market, where companies such as Intel continued to post record profits.

Discussion Questions

1. What factors account for the rise of Japan's semiconductor manufacturers during the 1970s and 1980s?

2. Does the rise of Japanese semiconductor companies during the 1970s and 1980s indicate that government industrial policy can play an important role in facilitating national competitiveness in industries targeted by that policy?

3. What explains the relative decline of Japanese semiconductor firms since 1988? Can it be attributed to the 1991 semiconductor pact or to other economic factors?

4. What are the implications of your answer to Question 3 for national trade policy?

Notes

1. M. Nakamoto, "Tough Poker Game for Barshefsky," *Financial Times*, August 5, 1996, p. 3.

Sources

1. "And Then There Were Two." *The Economist*, January 23, 1999, p. 58–59.

2. Borrus, M., L. A. Tyson, and J. Zysman. "Creating Advantage: How Government Policies Created Trade in the Semiconductor Industry." In *Strategic Trade Policy and the New International Economics*, ed. P. Krugman. Cambridge, MA: MIT Press, 1986.

3. Chao, J., and D. Hamilton. "Bad Times Are Just a Memory for DRAM Chip Makers." *The Wall Street Journal*, August 28, 1995, p. B4.

4. Davis, B. "Chip Report Eases U.S.-Japan Conflict." *The Wall Street Journal*, March 21, 1994, p. A2.

5. Darlin, D. "South Korean Chip Firms Play Catch-Up." *The Wall Street Journal*, July 29, 1991, p. A5.

6. Dertouzos, M. L., R. K. Lester, and R. M. Solow. *Made in America*. Cambridge, MA: MIT Press, 1989.

7. Dunne, N. "US and Japan in Agreement on Chips." *Financial Times*, August 3, 1996, p. 3.

8. "Global Sales Heading for 9% Growth Next Year." *Financial Times*, November 13, 1998, p. 6.

9. Nakamoto, M. "Tough Poker Game for Barshefsky." *Financial Times*, August 5, 1996, p. 3.

10. Schlesinger, J. "As U.S. Firms Hail Semiconductor Pact, Some Japan Concerns Have Reservations." *The Wall Street Journal*, June 6, 1991, p. A14.

11. "Semiconductor Trade: A Wafer Thin Case." *The Economist*, July 27, 1996, p. 53.

12. "Standard & Poors Industry Surveys." *Electronics*, August 3, 1995.

13. Yamamura, K. "Caveat Emptor: The Industrial Policy of Japan." In *Strategic Trade Policy and the New International Economics*, ed. P. Krugman. Cambridge, MA: MIT Press, 1986.

THE GLOBAL MONETARY SYSTEM

Chapter Nine
The Foreign Exchange Market

Chapter Ten
The International Monetary System

Chapter Eleven
The Global Capital Market

CHAPTER NINE

THE FOREIGN EXCHANGE MARKET

Foreign Exchange Losses at JAL

One of the world's largest airlines, Japan Airlines (JAL), is also one of the best customers of Boeing, the world's biggest manufacturer of commercial airplanes. Every year JAL needs to raise about $800 million to purchase aircraft from Boeing. Boeing aircraft are priced in US dollars, with prices ranging from about $35 million for a 737 to $160 million for a top-of-the-line 747-400. JAL orders an aircraft two to six years before the plane is actually needed. JAL normally pays Boeing a 10 percent deposit when ordering, and the bulk of the payment is made when the aircraft is delivered.

The long lag between placing an order and making a final payment presents a conundrum for JAL. Most of JAL's revenues are in Japanese yen, not US dollars (which is not surprising for a Japanese airline). When purchasing Boeing aircraft, JAL must change its yen into dollars to pay Boeing. In the interval between placing an order and making final payment, the value of the yen against the dollar may change. This can increase or decrease the cost of an aircraft. Consider an order placed in 1985 for a 747 aircraft that was to be delivered in 1990. In 1985, the dollar value of this order was $100 million. The prevailing exchange rate in 1985 was $1 = ¥240 (i.e., one dollar was worth 240 yen), so the price of the 747 was ¥2.4 billion. When final payment was due in 1990, however, the dollar–yen exchange rate might have changed. The yen might have declined in value against the dollar. For example, by 1990 the dollar–yen exchange rate might have been $1=¥300. If this had come to pass, the price of the 747 would have gone from ¥2.4 billion to ¥3.0 billion, an increase of 25 percent. Another (more favorable) scenario is that the yen might have risen in value against the dollar to $1=¥200. If this had occurred, the yen price of the 747 would have fallen 16.7 percent to ¥2.0 billion.

In 1985, JAL has no way of knowing what the value of the yen will be against the dollar by 1990. However, JAL can enter into a contract with foreign exchange traders in 1985 to purchase dollars in 1990 based on the assessment of those traders as to what they think the dollar–yen exchange rate will be in 1990. This is called entering into a *forward exchange contract*. The advantage of entering into a forward exchange contract is that JAL knows in 1985 what it will have to pay for the 747 in 1990. For example, if the value of the yen is expected to increase against the dollar between 1985 and 1990, foreign exchange traders might offer a forward exchange contract that allows JAL to purchase dollars at a rate of $1=¥185 in 1990, instead of the $1=¥240 rate that prevailed in 1985. At this forward exchange rate, the 747 would only cost ¥1.85 billion, a 23 percent saving over the yen price implied by the 1985 exchange rate.

JAL was confronted with just this scenario in 1985 when it entered into a 10-year forward exchange contract with a total value of about $3.6 billion. This contract gave JAL the right to buy US dollars from a consortium of foreign exchange traders at various points during the next 10 years for an average exchange rate of $1=¥185. This looked like a great deal to JAL given the 1985 exchange rate of $1=¥240. However, by September 1994 when the bulk of the contract had been executed, it no longer looked like a good deal. To everyone's surprise, the value of the yen had surged against the dollar. By 1992 the exchange rate stood at $1=¥120, and by 1994 it was $1=¥99. Unfortunately, JAL could not take advantage of this more favorable exchange rate. Instead, JAL was bound by the terms of the contract to purchase dollars at the contract rate of $1=¥185, a rate that by 1994 looked outrageously expensive. This misjudgment cost JAL dearly. In 1994, JAL was paying 86 percent more than it needed to for each Boeing aircraft bought with dollars purchased via the forward exchange contract! In October 1994, JAL admitted publicly that the loss in its most recent financial year from this misjudgment amounted to $450 million, or ¥45 billion. Furthermore, foreign exchange traders speculated that JAL had probably lost a total of ¥155 billion ($1.5 billion) on this contract since 1988.

http://www.boeing.com

Sources: W. Dawkins, "JAL to Disclose Huge Currency Hedge Loss," *Financial Times*, October 4, 1994, p. 19; and W. Dawkins, "Tokyo to Lift Veil on Currency Risks," *Financial Times*, October 5, 1994, p. 23.

CHAPTER OUTLINE

FOREIGN EXCHANGE LOSSES AT JAL

INTRODUCTION

THE FUNCTIONS OF THE FOREIGN EXCHANGE MARKET
Currency Conversion
Insuring against Foreign
   Exchange Risk

THE NATURE OF THE FOREIGN EXCHANGE MARKET

ECONOMIC THEORIES OF EXCHANGE RATE DETERMINATION
Prices and Exchange Rates
Interest Rates and Exchange Rates
Investor Psychology
   and Bandwagon Effects
Summary

EXCHANGE RATE FORECASTING
The Efficient Market School
The Inefficient Market School
Approaches to Forecasting

CURRENCY CONVERTIBILITY
Convertibility and Government Policy
Countertrade

IMPLICATIONS FOR BUSINESS

CHAPTER SUMMARY

CRITICAL DISCUSSION QUESTIONS

THE COLLAPSE OF THE THAI BAHT IN 1997

Introduction

This chapter has three main objectives. The first is to explain how the foreign exchange market works. The second is to examine the forces that determine exchange rates and to discuss the degree to which it is possible to predict future exchange rate movements. The third objective is to map the implications for international business of exchange rate movements and the foreign exchange market. This chapter is the first of three that deal with the international monetary system and its relationship to international business. In Chapter 10, we will explore the institutional structure of the international monetary system. The institutional structure is the context within which the foreign exchange market functions. As we shall see, changes in the institutional structure of the international monetary system can exert a profound influence on the development of foreign exchange markets. In Chapter 11, we will look at the recent evolution of global capital markets and discuss the implications of this development for international businesses.

The **foreign exchange market** is a market for converting the currency of one country into that of another country. An **exchange rate** is simply the rate at which one currency is converted into another. We saw in the opening case how JAL used the foreign exchange market to convert Japanese yen into US dollars. Without the foreign exchange market, international trade and international investment on the scale that we see today would be impossible; companies would have to resort to barter. The foreign exchange market is the lubricant that enables companies based in countries that use different currencies to trade with each other.

We know from earlier chapters that international trade and investment have their risks. As the opening case illustrates, some of these risks exist because future exchange rates cannot be perfectly predicted. The rate at which one currency is converted into another typically changes over time. One function of the foreign exchange market is to provide some insurance against the risks that arise from changes in exchange rates, commonly referred to as foreign exchange risk. Although the foreign exchange market offers some insurance against foreign exchange risk, it cannot provide complete insurance. JAL's loss of $1.5 billion on foreign exchange transactions is an extreme example of what can happen, but it is not unusual for international businesses to suffer losses because of unpredicted changes in exchange rates. Currency fluctuations can make seemingly profitable trade and investment deals unprofitable, and vice versa. The opening case contains an example of this as it relates to trade. For an example that deals with investment, consider the case of Mexico. Between 1976 and 1987, the value of the Mexican peso dropped from 22 per US dollar to 1,500 per US dollar. As a result, a US company with an investment in Mexico that yielded an income of 100 million pesos per year would have seen the dollar value of that income shrink from $4.55 million in 1976 to $66,666 by 1987!

In addition to altering the value of trade deals and foreign investments, currency movements can also open or close export opportunities and alter the attractiveness of imports. In 1984, for example, the US dollar was trading at an all-time high against most other currencies. At that time, one dollar could buy one British pound or 250 Japanese yen, compared to 0.55 of a British pound and about 85 yen in early 1995. In the 1984 US presidential campaign, then-President Ronald Reagan boasted about how good the strong dollar was for the United States. Many US companies did not see it that way. Companies such as Caterpillar that earned their living by exporting to other countries were being priced out of foreign markets by the strong dollar. In 1980 when the dollar-to-pound exchange rate was $1 = £0.63, a $100,000 Caterpillar earthmover cost a British buyer £63,000. In 1984, with the exchange rate at $1 = £0.99, it cost close to £99,000—a 60 percent increase in four years! At that exchange rate Caterpillar's products were overpriced in comparison to those of its foreign competitors, such as Japan's Komatsu. At the same time, the strong dollar reduced the price of the earthmovers Komatsu imported into the United States, which allowed the Japanese company to take US market share away from Caterpillar.

While the existence of foreign exchange markets is a necessary precondition for large-scale international trade and investment, the movement of exchange rates introduces many risks into international trade and investment. Some of these risks can be insured against by using instruments offered by the foreign exchange market, such as the forward exchange contracts discussed in the opening case; others cannot be.

We begin this chapter by looking at the functions and the form of the foreign exchange market. This includes distinguishing among spot exchanges, forward exchanges, and currency swaps. Then we will consider the factors that determine exchange rates. We will also look at how foreign trade is conducted when a country's currency cannot be exchanged for other currencies; that is, when its currency is not convertible. The chapter closes with a discussion of these things in terms of their implications for business.

The Functions of the Foreign Exchange Market

The foreign exchange market serves two main functions. The first is to convert the currency of one country into the currency of another. The second is to provide some insurance against **foreign exchange risk,** by which we mean the adverse consequences of unpredictable changes in exchange rates. We consider each function in turn.[1]

Currency Conversion

Each country has a currency in which the prices of goods and services are quoted. In the United States, it is the dollar ($); in Great Britain, the pound (£); in France, the French franc (FFr); in Germany, the deutsche mark (DM); in Japan, the yen (¥); and so on. In general, within the borders of a particular country, one must use the national currency. A US tourist cannot walk into a store in Edinburgh, Scotland, and use US dollars to buy a bottle of Scotch whisky. Dollars are not recognized as legal tender in Scotland; the tourist must use British pounds. Fortunately, the tourist can go to a bank and exchange her dollars for pounds. Then she can buy the whisky.

When a tourist changes one currency into another, she is participating in the **foreign exchange market.** The **exchange rate** is the rate at which the market converts one currency into another. For example, an exchange rate of $1 = ¥85 specifies that one US dollar has the equivalent value of 85 Japanese yen. The exchange rate allows us to compare the relative prices of goods and services in different countries. Returning to our example of the US tourist wishing to buy a bottle of Scotch whisky in Edinburgh, she may find that she must pay £25 for the bottle, knowing that the same bottle costs $40 in the United States. Is this a good deal? Imagine the current dollar/pound exchange rate is $1 = £0.50. Our intrepid tourist takes out her calculator and converts £25 into dollars. (The calculation is 25/0.50.) She finds that the bottle of Scotch costs the equivalent of $50. She is surprised that a bottle of Scotch whisky could cost less in the United States than in Scotland. (This is true; alcohol is taxed heavily in Great Britain.)

Tourists are minor participants in the foreign exchange market; companies engaged in international trade and investment are major ones. International businesses have four main uses of foreign exchange markets. First, the payments a company receives for its exports, the income it receives from foreign investments, or the income it receives from licensing agreements with foreign firms may be in foreign currencies. To use those funds in its home country, the company must convert them to its home country's currency. Consider the Scotch distillery that exports its whisky to the United States. The distillery is paid in dollars, but since those dollars cannot be spent in Great Britain, they must be converted into British pounds.

Second, international businesses use foreign exchange markets when they must pay a foreign company for its products or services in its country's currency. For example, our friend Michael runs a company called NST, a large British travel service for school groups. Each year Michael's company arranges vacations for thousands of British schoolchildren and their teachers in France. French hotel proprietors demand payment in francs, so Michael must convert large sums of money from pounds into francs to pay them.

Third, international businesses use foreign exchange markets when they have spare cash that they wish to invest for short terms in money markets. For example, consider a US company that has $10 million it wants to invest for three months. The best interest rate it can earn on these funds in the United States may be 8 percent. Investing in a French money market account, however, may earn 12 percent. Thus, the company may change its $10 million into francs and invest it in France. Note, however, that the rate of return it earns on this investment depends not only on the French interest rate, but also on the changes in the value of the franc against the dollar in the intervening period.

Finally, currency speculation is another use of foreign exchange markets. **Currency speculation** typically involves the short-term movement of funds from one currency to another in the hopes of profiting from shifts in exchange rates. Consider again the US company with $10 million to invest for three months. Suppose the company suspects that the US dollar is overvalued against the French franc. That is, the company expects the value of the dollar to depreciate against that of the franc. Imagine the current dollar/franc exchange rate is $1 = FFr 6. The company exchanges its $10 million into francs, receiving FFr 60 million. Over the next three months, the value of the dollar depreciates until $1 = FFr 5. Now the company exchanges its FFr 60 million back into dollars and finds that it has $12 million. The company has made a $2 million profit on currency speculation in three months on an initial investment of $10 million.

One of the most famous currency "speculators" is George Soros, whose Quantum Group of "hedge funds" controls about $15 billion in assets. The activities of Soros, who has been spectacularly successful, are profiled in the accompanying Management Focus. In general, however, companies should beware of speculation for it is by definition a very risky business. The company cannot know for sure what will happen to exchange rates. While a speculator may profit handsomely if his speculation about future currency movements turns out to be correct, he can also lose vast amounts of money if it turns out to be wrong. For example, in 1991, Clifford Hatch, the finance director of the British food and drink company Allied-Lyons, bet large amounts of the company's funds on the speculation that the British pound would rise in value against the US dollar. Over the previous three years, Hatch had made over $25 million for Allied-Lyons by placing similar currency bets. His 1991 bet, however, went spectacularly wrong when the British pound plummeted in value against the US dollar. In February 1991, one pound bought $2; by April it bought less than $1.75. The total loss to Allied-Lyons from this speculation was a staggering $269 million, more than the company was to earn from all of its food and drink activities during 1991![2]

Insuring against Foreign Exchange Risk

A second function of the foreign exchange market is to provide insurance to protect against the possible adverse consequences of unpredictable changes in exchange rates (foreign exchange risk). To explain how the market performs this function, we must first distinguish among spot exchange rates, forward exchange rates, and currency swaps.

Spot Exchange Rates

When two parties agree to exchange currency and execute the deal immediately, the transaction is referred to as a spot exchange. Exchange rates governing such "on the

Currency Last Trade	U.S. $ N/A	Aust $ Jan 15	U.K. £ Jan 15	Can $ Jan 15	DMark Jan 15	FFranc Jan 15	¥en Jan 15	SFranc Jan 15	Euro Jan 15
U.S. $	1	0.635	1.652	0.6546	0.5925	0.1767	0.00877	0.07264	1.159
Aust $	1.575	1	2.602	1.031	0.9331	0.2782	0.01381	1.144	1.825
U.K. £	0.6053	0.3843	1	0.3962	0.3586	0.1069	0.005308	0.4397	0.7015
Can $	1.528	0.9701	2.524	1	0.9051	0.2699	0.0134	1.11	1.771
DMark	1.688	1.072	2.789	1.105	1	0.2982	0.0148	1.226	1.956
FFranc	5.66	3.594	9.352	3.705	3.354	1	0.04964	4.112	6.561
¥en	114	72.41	188.4	74.64	67.56	20.14	1	82.83	132.2
SFranc	1.377	0.8742	2.275	0.9012	0.8157	0.2432	0.01207	1	1.596
Euro	0.8627	0.5478	1.425	0.5647	0.5112	0.1524	0.007566	0.6267	1

Table 9.1

Foreign Exchange Quotations

spot" trades are referred to as spot exchange rates. The **spot exchange rate** is the rate at which a foreign exchange dealer converts one currency into another currency on a particular day. Thus, when our US tourist in Edinburgh goes to a bank to convert her dollars into pounds, the exchange rate is the spot rate for that day.

Although it is necessary to use a spot rate to execute a transaction immediately, it may not be the most attractive rate. The value of a currency is determined by the interaction between the demand and supply of that currency relative to the demand and supply of other currencies. For example, if lots of people want US dollars and dollars are in short supply, and few people want French francs and francs are in plentiful supply, the spot exchange rate for converting dollars into francs will change. The dollar is likely to appreciate against the franc (or, conversely, the franc will depreciate against the dollar). Imagine the spot exchange rate is $1 = FFr 5 when the market opens. As the day progresses, dealers demand more dollars and fewer francs. By the end of the day, the spot exchange rate might be $1 = FFr 5.3. The dollar has appreciated, and the franc has depreciated.

Table 9.1 lists spot exchange rate quotes for several currencies on May 14, 1998, at 11:48 AM Eastern US time (note that the quotes can change by the minute). As can be seen, on this day at this time $1 could be exchanged for Australian $ 1.594, UK£ 0.6134, and so on. Table 9.1 also tells us what other currencies would purchase. For example, FFr 1 could be exchanged for DMark 0.298, the Germany currency.

Forward Exchange Rates

The fact that spot exchange rates change continually as determined by the relative demand and supply for different currencies can be problematic for an international business. One example was given in the opening case; here is another. A US company that imports laptop computers from Japan knows that in 30 days it must pay yen to a Japanese supplier when a shipment arrives. The company will pay the Japanese supplier ¥200,000 for each laptop computer, and the current dollar/yen spot exchange rate is $1 = ¥120. At this rate, each computer costs the importer $1,667 (i.e., 1667 = 200,000/120). The importer knows she can sell the computers the day they arrive for $2,000 each, which yields a gross profit of $333 on each computer ($2,000 – $1667). However, the importer will not have the funds to pay the Japanese supplier until the computers have been sold. If over the next 30 days the dollar unexpectedly depreciates against the yen, say to $1 = ¥95, the importer will still have to pay the Japanese company ¥200,000 per computer, but in dollar terms that would be equivalent to $2,105 per computer, which is more than she can sell the computers

MANAGEMENT FOCUS
George Soros—The Man Who Can Move Currency Markets

George Soros, a 68-year-old Hungarian-born financier, is the principal partner of the Quantum Group, which controls a series of hedge funds with assets of about $15 billion. A **hedge fund** is an investment fund that not only buys financial assets (such as stocks, bonds, and currencies) but also sells them short. **Short selling** occurs when an investor places a speculative bet that the value of a financial asset will decline, and profits from that decline. A common variant of short selling occurs when an investor borrows stock from his broker and sells that stock. The short seller has to ultimately pay back that stock to his broker. However, he hopes that in the intervening period the value of the stock will decline so that the cost of repurchasing the stock to pay back the broker is significantly less than the income he received from the initial sale of the stock. For example, imagine that a short seller borrows 100 units of IBM stock and sells it in the market at $150 per share, yielding a total income of $15,000. In one year, the short seller has to give the 100 units of IBM stock back to his broker. In the intervening period, the value of the IBM stock falls to $50. Consequently, it now costs the short seller only $5,000 to repurchase the 100 units of IBM stock for his broker. The difference between the initial sales price ($150) and the repurchase price ($50) represents the short seller's

profit, which in this case is $100 per unit of stock for a total profit of $10,000. Short selling was originally developed as a means of reducing risk (of hedging), but it is often used for speculation.

Along with other hedge funds, Soros's Quantum fund often takes a short position in currencies that he expects to decline in value. For example, if Soros expects the British pound to decline against the US dollar, he may borrow one billion pounds from a currency trader and immediately sell those for US dollars. Soros will then hope that the value of the pound will decline against the dollar, so that when he has to repay the one billion pounds it will cost him considerably less (in US dollars) than he received from the initial sale.

Since the 1970s, Soros has consistently earned huge returns by making such speculative bets. His most spectacular triumph came in September 1992. He believed the British pound was likely to decline in value against major currencies, particularly the German deutsche mark. The prevailing exchange rate was £1=DM2.80. The British government was obliged by a European Union agreement on monetary policy to try to keep the pound above DM2.77. Soros doubted that the British could do this, so he shorted the pound, borrowing billions of pounds (using the $12 billion assets

for. A depreciation in the value of the dollar against the yen from $1 = ¥120 to $1 = ¥95 would transform a profitable deal into an unprofitable one.

To avoid this risk, the US importer might want to engage in a forward exchange. A **forward exchange** occurs when two parties agree to exchange currency and execute the deal at some specific date in the future. Exchange rates governing such future transactions are referred to as forward exchange rates. For most major currencies, **forward exchange rates** are quoted for 30 days, 90 days, and 180 days into the future. (An example of forward exchange rate quotations appears in Table 9.2.) In some cases, it is possible to get forward exchange rates for several years into the future. The opening case, for example, reported how JAL entered into a contract that predicted forward exchange rates up to 10 years in the future. Returning to our computer importer example, let us assume the 30-day forward exchange rate for converting dollars into yen is $1 = ¥110. The importer enters into a 30-day forward exchange transaction with a foreign exchange dealer at this rate and is guaranteed that she will have to pay no more than $1,818 for each computer (1,818 = 200,000/110). This guarantees her a profit of $182 per computer ($2,000 – $1,818). She also insures herself against the possibility that an unanticipated change in the dollar/yen exchange rate will turn a profitable deal into an unprofitable one.

http://www.lib.berkeley.edu/GSSI/eu.html

of the Quantum Fund as collateral) and immediately began selling them for German deutsche marks. His simultaneous sale of pounds and purchase of marks were so large that it helped drive down the value of the pound against the mark. Other currency traders, seeing Soros's market moves and knowing his reputation for making successful currency bets, jumped on the bandwagon and started to sell pounds short and buy deutsche marks. The resulting *bandwagon effect* put enormous pressure on the pound. The British Central Bank, at the request of the British government, spent about 20 billion pounds on September 16 to try to prop up the value of the pound against the deutsche mark (by selling marks and buying pounds), but to no avail. The pound continued to fall and on September 17, the British government gave up and let the pound decline (it actually fell to £1=DM2.00). Soros made a $1 billion profit in four weeks!

Like all currency speculators, however, George Soros has had his losses. In February 1994, he bet that the Japanese yen would decline in value against the US dollar and promptly shorted the yen. However, the yen defied his expectations and continued to rise, costing his Quantum Fund $600 million. Similarly, a series of incorrect bets in 1987 resulted in losses of over $800 million for Quantum. Despite such defeats, how-

ever, the Quantum Fund has earned an average annual rate of return of over 40 percent since 1970.

Soros has gained a reputation for being able to move currency markets by his actions. This is the consequence not so much of the money that Soros puts into play, but of the bandwagon effect that results when other speculators follow his lead. This reputation has resulted in Soros being depicted as the archvillain of the 1997 Asian currency crisis. In 1997, the currencies of Thailand, Malaysia, South Korea, and Indonesia all lost between 50 percent and 70 percent of their value against the US dollar. While the reasons for the crisis are complex, a common feature was excessive borrowing by firms based in these countries. Several Asian leaders, however, most notably Mahathir bin Mohamad, the prime minister of Malaysia, instead blamed the crisis on "criminal speculation" by Soros, who had been intent on impoverishing Asian nations. Soros denied that his fund had been involved in shorting Asian currencies.

Sources: P. Harverson, "Billion Dollar Man the Money Markets Fear," *Financial Times,* September 30, 1994, p. 10; "A Quantum Dive," *The Economist,* March 15, 1994, pp. 83–84; B. J. Javetski, "Europe's Money Mess," *Business Week,* September 28, 1992, pp. 30–31; "Meltdown," *The Economist,* September 19, 1992, p. 69, and I. L. Friedman, "Mahathir's Wrath," *New York Times,* December 18, 1997, p. 27.

In this example, the spot exchange rate ($1 = ¥120) and the 30-day forward rate ($1 = ¥110) differ. Such differences are normal; they reflect the expectations of the foreign exchange market about future currency movements. In our example, the fact that $1 bought more yen with a spot exchange than with a 30-day forward exchange indicates foreign exchange dealers expected the dollar to depreciate against the yen in the next 30 days. When this occurs, we say the dollar is selling at a *discount* on the 30-day forward market (i.e., it is worth less than on the spot market). Of course, the opposite can also occur. If the 30-day forward exchange rate were $1 = ¥130, for example, $1 would buy more yen with a forward exchange than with a spot exchange. In such a case, we say the dollar is selling at a *premium* on the 30-day forward market. This reflects the foreign exchange dealers' expectations that the dollar will appreciate against the yen over the next 30 days.

Currency Swaps

The above discussion of spot and forward exchange rates might lead you to conclude that the option to buy forward is very important to companies engaged in international trade—and you would be right. But Figure 9.1, which shows the nature of foreign exchange transactions in April 1995 for a sample of US banks surveyed by the

CURRENCY TRADING

Friday, January 15, 1999
EXCHANGE RATES

The New York foreign exchange mid-range rates below apply to trading among banks in amounts of $1 million and more, as quoted at 4 p.m. Eastern time by Telerate and other sources. Retail transactions provide fewer units of foreign currency per dollar. Rates for the 11 Euro currency countries are derived from the latest dollar-euro rate using the exchange ratios set 1/1/99.

Country	U.S. $ equiv. Fri	U.S. $ equiv. Thu	Currency per U.S. $ Fri	Currency per U.S. $ Thu
Argentina (Peso)....	1.0011	1.0002	.9990	.9998
Australia (Dollar)....	.6315	.6330	1.5835	1.5798
Austria (Schilling) ...	.08406	.08503	11.896	11.760
Bahrain (Dinar)	2.6525	2.6525	.3770	.3770
Belgium (Franc)	.02867	.02901	34.875	34.476
Brazil (Real)........	.6993	.7576	1.4300	1.3200
Britain (Pound)	1.6515	1.6569	.6055	.6035
1-month forward ...	1.6500	1.6554	.6061	.6041
3-months forward..	1.6484	1.6537	.6066	.6047
6-months forward..	1.6472	1.6525	.6071	.6052
Canada (Dollar)	.6555	.6521	1.5255	1.5336
1-month forward ..	.6547	.6521	1.5275	1.5336
3-months forward..	.6549	.6520	1.5270	1.5337
6-months forward..	.6577	.6523	1.5205	1.5329
Chile (Peso)........	.002094	.002102	477.50	475.75
China (Renminbi) ...	.1208	.1208	8.2790	8.2789
Colombia (Peso)	.0006311	.0006294	1584.42	1588.80
Czech. Rep. (Koruna)				
Commercial rate...	.03252	.03269	30.753	30.586
Denmark (Krone) ...	.1558	.1576	6.4170	6.3437
Ecuador (Sucre)				
Floating rate	.0001406	.0001406	7113.00	7113.00
Finland (Markka)....	.1945	.1968	5.1403	5.0814
France (Franc)......	.1763	.1784	5.6709	5.6060
1-month forward ..	.1766	.1787	5.6623	5.5975
3-months forward..	.1771	.1792	5.6454	5.5811
6-months forward..	.1780	.1800	5.6182	5.5548
Germany (Mark)	.5914	.5983	1.6909	1.6715
1-month forward ..	.5923	.5992	1.6882	1.6690
3-months forward..	.5941	.6009	1.6832	1.6641
6-months forward..	.5971	.6038	1.6747	1.6563
Greece (Drachma) ..	.003597	.003602	278.00	277.60
Hong Kong (Dollar)..	.1291	.1291	7.7482	7.7479
Hungary (Forint)	.004582	.004615	218.26	216.67
India (Rupee)	.02353	.02353	42.500	42.498
Indonesia (Rupiah) ..	.0001132	.0001153	8835.00	8675.00
Ireland (Punt)	1.4695	1.4857	.6805	.6731
Israel (Shekel)......	.2442	.2446	4.0953	4.0877
Italy (Lira)	.0005974	.0006043	1673.96	1654.79

Country	U.S. $ equiv. Fri	U.S. $ equiv. Thu	Currency per U.S. $ Fri	Currency per U.S. $ Thu
Japan (Yen).........	.008787	.008802	113.81	113.61
1-month forward ...	.008787	.008802	113.81	113.61
3-months forward ..	.008788	.008803	113.80	113.60
6-months forward...	008789	.008804	113.78	113.58
Jordan (Dinar).......	1.4094	1.4114	.7095	.7085
Kuwait (Dinar).......	3.3167	3.3167	.3015	.3015
Lebanon (Pound)	.0006631	.0006629	1508.00	1508.50
Malaysia (Ringgit-b)..	.2632	.2632	3.8000	3.7998
Malta (Lira)	2.6110	2.6110	.3830	.3830
Mexico (Peso)				
Floating rate	.09785	.09421	10.220	10.615
Netherland (Guilder) .	.5249	.5310	1.9052	1.8834
New Zealand (Dollar).	.5414	.5395	1.8471	1.8536
Norway (Krone)	.1336	.1343	7.4862	7.4463
Pakistan (Rupee)	.02002	.02038	49.950	49.070
Peru (new Sol)	.3051	.3175	3.2775	3.1500
Philippines (Peso) ...	.02587	.02600	38.655	38.455
Poland (Zloty)	.2820	.2809	3.5460	3.5600
Portugal (Escudo) ...	.005773	.005839	173.23	171.25
Russia (Ruble) (a)....	.04570	.04662	21.880	21.450
Saudi Arabia (Riyal) ..	.2664	.2666	3.7535	3.7506
Singapore (Dollar) ...	.5958	.5951	1.6785	1.6805
Slovak Rep. (Koruna) .	.02720	.02740	36.762	36.492
South Africa (Rand) ..	.1642	.1623	6.0910	6.1600
South Korea (Won) ..	.0008449	.0008432	1183.60	1186.00
Spain (Peseta)	.006952	.007032	143.85	142.20
Sweden (Krona).....	.1275	.1284	7.8452	7.7875
Switzerland (Franc) ..	.7230	.7366	1.3831	1.3575
1-month forward ...	.7255	.7392	1.3785	1.3529
3-months forward...	.7297	.7435	1.3705	1.3450
6-months forward...	.7362	.7502	1.3584	1.3330
Taiwan (Dollar).......	.03105	.03100	32.204	32.255
Thailand (Baht)	.02699	.02710	37.050	36.905
Turkey (Lira)	.00000311	.00000311	321253.00	321179.00
United Arab (Dirham).	.2723	.2723	3.6730	3.6730
Uruguay (New Peso) .				
Financial	.09183	.09217	10.890	10.850
Venezuela (Bolivar) ..	.001755	.001758	569.75	568.75
SDR...............	1.4073	1.4041	.7106	.7122
Euro...............	1.1567	1.1701	.8645	.8546

Special Drawing Rights (SDR) are based on exchange rates for the U.S., German, British, French, and Japanese currencies. Source: International Monetary Fund.

a-Russian Central Bank rate. Trading band lowered on 8/17/98. b-Government rate.

The Wall Street Journal daily foreign exchange data from 1996 forward may be purchased through the Readers' Reference Service (413) 592-3600.

Source: *The Wall Street Journal*, January 18, 1999. Reprinted by permission of the *Wall Street Journal*, © 1999 Dow Jones & Company, Inc. All rights reserved worldwide.

Table 9.2

Spot and Forward Rates

Federal Reserve Board, reveals that the majority (55 percent) of foreign exchange transactions were spot exchanges, followed by swaps (34 percent). Forward exchanges accounted for only 11 percent of all foreign exchange transactions that month, but swaps are a sophisticated kind of forward exchange.

A **currency swap** is the simultaneous purchase and sale of a given amount of foreign exchange for two different value dates. Swaps are transacted between international

Figure 9.1

Foreign Exchange
Transactions, April 1995

Source: Summary of results of US
Foreign Exchange Market Survey
conducted April 1995 by Federal
Reserve Bank of New York.

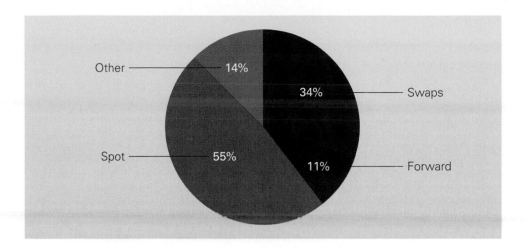

businesses and their banks, between banks, and between governments when it is desirable to move out of one currency into another for a limited period without incurring foreign exchange risk. A common kind of swap is spot against forward. Consider a company such as Apple Computer. Apple assembles laptop computers in the United States, but the screens are made in Japan. Apple also sells some of the finished laptops in Japan. So, like many companies, Apple both buys from and sells to Japan. Imagine Apple needs to change $1 million into yen to pay its supplier of laptop screens today. Apple knows that in 90 days it will be paid ¥120 million by the Japanese importer that buys its finished laptops. It will want to convert these yen into dollars for use in the United States. Let us say today's spot exchange rate is $1 = ¥120 and the 90-day forward exchange rate is $1 = ¥110. Apple sells $1 million to its bank in return for ¥120 million. Now Apple can pay its Japanese supplier. At the same time, Apple enters into a 90-day forward exchange deal with its bank for converting ¥120 million into dollars. Thus, in 90 days Apple will receive $1.09 million (¥120 million/110 = $1.09 million). Since the yen is trading at a premium on the 90-day forward market, Apple ends up with more dollars than it started with (although the opposite could also occur). The swap deal is just like a conventional forward deal in one important respect: It enables Apple to insure itself against foreign exchange risk. By engaging in a swap, Apple knows today that the ¥120 million payment it will receive in 90 days will yield $1.09 million.

The Nature of the Foreign Exchange Market

So far we have dealt with the foreign exchange market only as an abstract concept. It is now time to take a closer look at the nature of this market. The foreign exchange market is not located in any one place. It is a global network of banks, brokers, and foreign exchange dealers connected by electronic communications systems. When companies wish to convert currencies, they typically go through their own banks rather than entering the market directly. The foreign exchange market has been growing at a rapid pace, reflecting a general growth in the volume of cross-border trade and investment (see Chapter 1). In March 1986, for example, the average total value of global foreign exchange trading was about $200 billion per day. By April 1989, it had soared to over $650 billion per day, and by 1995 it was over $1,200 billion per day.[3] The most important trading centers are London, New York, and Tokyo. In April 1995, over $450 billion was traded through London each day, $240 billion through New York, and $150 billion through Tokyo.[4] Major secondary trading centers include Zurich, Frankfurt, Paris, Hong Kong, Singapore, San Francisco, and Sydney (see Figure 9.2).

London's dominance in the foreign exchange market is due to both history and geography. As the capital of the world's first major industrial trading nation, London had become the world's largest center for international banking by the end of the last

Figure 9.2

Reported Foreign Exchange Market Turnover in Major Centers in April 1989, April 1992, and April 1995

Source: *Central Bank Survey of Foreign Exchange and Derivatives Market Activity* (Basle, Switzerland: BIS, May 1996), Graph F-4.

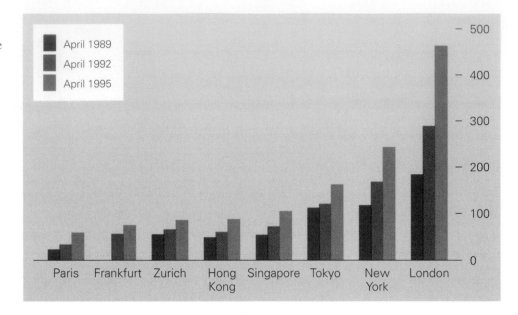

century, a position it has retained. Today London's central position between Tokyo to the east and New York to the west has made it the critical link between the Tokyo and New York markets. Due to the particular differences in time zones, London opens soon after Tokyo closes for the night and is still open for the first few hours of trading in New York. However, some now argue that the failure of Britain to join the first round of the European monetary union might lead to the demise of London as the center of global foreign exchange trading. This is particularly likely to occur if the euro emerges as a major currency unit after 2002, and if Britain stays out of the euro zone (see Chapter 8 for details of EMU).

Two features of the foreign exchange market are of particular note. The first is that the market never sleeps. There are only 3 hours out of every 24 that Tokyo, London, and New York are all shut down. During these three hours, trading continues in a number of minor centers, particularly San Francisco and Sydney, Australia.

The second feature of the market is the extent of integration of the various trading centers. Direct telephone lines, fax, and computer linkages between trading centers around the globe have effectively created a single market. The integration of financial centers implies there can be no significant difference in exchange rates quoted in the trading centers. For example, if the dollar/franc exchange rate quoted in London at 3 PM is $1 = FFr 5.0, the dollar/franc exchange rate quoted in New York at the same time (10 AM New York time) will be identical. If the New York dollar/franc exchange rate were $1 = FFr 5.5, a dealer could make a profit through **arbitrage,** buying a currency low and selling it high. For example, if the prices differed in London and New York as given, a dealer could purchase FFr 550,000 for $100,000 in New York and immediately sell them in London for $110,000, making a quick profit of $10,000. If all dealers tried to cash in on the opportunity, however, the demand for francs in New York would result in an appreciation of the franc against the dollar, while the increase in the supply of francs in London would result in their depreciation there. The discrepancy in the New York and London exchange rates would disappear very quickly. Since foreign exchange dealers are continually watching their computer screens for arbitrage opportunities, the few that arise tend to be small, and they disappear in minutes.

Another feature of the foreign exchange market is the important role played by the US dollar. Although a foreign exchange transaction can in theory involve any two currencies, most transactions involve dollars. This is true even when a dealer wants to sell one nondollar currency and buy another. A dealer wishing to sell Dutch guilders

Table 9.3

Use of Currencies on One Side of a Foreign Exchange Transaction as a Percentage of Global Gross Foreign Exchange Market Turnover

	(Percentage shares)		
Currency	April 1989	April 1992	April 1995
US dollar	90	82	83
Deutsche mark	27	40	37
Japanese yen	27	23	24
Pound sterling	15	14	10
French franc	2	4	8
Swiss franc	10	9	7
Canadian dollar	1	3	3
Australian dollar	2	2	3
ECU	1	3	2
Other EMS currencies	3	9	13
Currencies of other reporting countries	3	3	2
Other currencies	19	8	8
All currencies	**200**	**200**	**200**

Source: Bank for International Settlements, *Central Bank Survey of Foreign Exchange and Derivatives Market Activity* (Basle, Switzerland: BIS, May 1996), Table F-3.

for Italian lira, for example, will usually sell the guilders for dollars and then use the dollars to buy lira. Although this may seem a roundabout way of doing things, it is actually cheaper than trying to find a holder of lira who wants to buy guilders. Because the volume of international transactions involving dollars is so great, it is not hard to find dealers who wish to trade dollars for guilders or lira.

Due to its central role in so many foreign exchange deals, the dollar is a vehicle currency. Table 9.3 tells us that in April 1995, 83 percent of all foreign exchange transactions involved dollars. After the dollar, the most important vehicle currencies are the German mark, the Japanese yen, and the British pound in that order—reflecting the importance of these trading nations in the world economy (see Table 9.3). The British pound used to be second in importance to the dollar as a vehicle currency, but its importance has diminished in recent years. Despite this, London has retained its leading position in the global foreign exchange market, which suggests that the introduction of the euro might not have the negative impact suggested by critics of Britain's decision to stay out of EMU.

Economic Theories of Exchange Rate Determination

At the most basic level, exchange rates are determined by the demand and supply of one currency relative to the demand and supply of another. For example, if the demand for dollars outstrips the supply of them and if the supply of German deutsche marks is greater than the demand for them, the dollar/mark exchange rate will change. The dollar will appreciate against the mark (or the mark will depreciate against the dollar). However, while differences in relative demand and supply explain the determination of exchange rates, they do so only in a superficial sense. This simple explanation does not tell us what factors underlie the demand for and supply of a currency. Nor does it tell us when the demand for dollars will exceed the supply (and vice versa) or when the supply of German marks will exceed demand for them (and vice versa). Neither does it tell us under what conditions a currency is in demand or under what conditions it is not demanded. In this section, we will review economic theory's answers to these questions. This will give us a deeper understanding of how exchange rates are determined.

If we understand how exchange rates are determined, we may be able to forecast exchange rate movements. Since future exchange rate movements influence export opportunities, the profitability of international trade and investment deals, and the price competitiveness of foreign imports, this is valuable information for an international business. Unfortunately, there is no simple explanation. The forces that determine exchange rates are complex, and no theoretical consensus exists, even among academic economists who study the phenomenon every day. Nonetheless, most economic theories of exchange rate movements seem to agree that three factors have an important impact on future exchange rate movements in a country's currency: the country's price inflation, its interest rate, and market psychology.[5]

Prices and Exchange Rates

To understand how prices are related to exchange rate movements, we first need to discuss an economic proposition known as the law of one price. Then we will discuss the theory of purchasing power parity (PPP), which links changes in the exchange rate between two countries' currencies to changes in the countries' price levels.

The Law of One Price

The **law of one price** states that in competitive markets free of transportation costs and barriers to trade (such as tariffs), identical products sold in different countries must sell for the same price when their price is expressed in terms of the same currency.[6] For example, if the exchange rate between the dollar and the French franc is $1 = FFr 5, a jacket that retails for $50 in New York should retail for FFr 250 (50×5) in Paris. Consider what would happen if the jacket cost FFr 300 in Paris ($60 in US currency). At this price, it would pay a company to buy jackets in New York and sell them in Paris (an example of arbitrage). The company initially could make a profit of $10 on each jacket by purchasing them for $50 in New York and selling them for FFr 300 in Paris. (We are assuming away transportation costs and trade barriers.) However, the increased demand for jackets in New York would raise their price in New York, and the increased supply of jackets in Paris would lower their price there. This would continue until prices were equalized. Thus, prices might equalize when the jacket cost $55 in New York and FFr 275 in Paris (assuming no change in the exchange rate of $1 = FFr 5).

Purchasing Power Parity

If the law of one price were true for all goods and services, the purchasing power parity (PPP) exchange rate could be found from any individual set of prices. By comparing the prices of identical products in different currencies, it would be possible to determine the "real" or PPP exchange rate that would exist if markets were efficient. (An **efficient market** has no impediments to the free flow of goods and services, such as trade barriers.)

A less extreme version of the PPP theory states that given **relatively efficient markets**—that is, markets in which few impediments to international trade and investment exist—the price of a "basket of goods" should be roughly equivalent in each country. To express the PPP theory in symbols, let $P_\$$ be the US dollar price of a basket of particular goods and P_{DM} be the price of the same basket of goods in German deutsche marks. The PPP theory predicts that the dollar/DM exchange rate should be equivalent to:

$$\$/DM \text{ exchange rate} = P_\$/P_{DM}$$

Thus, if a basket of goods costs $200 in the United States and DM 600 in Germany, PPP theory predicts that the dollar/DM exchange rate should be $200/DM600 or $0.33 per DM (i.e., $1 = DM 3).

The next step in the PPP theory is to argue that the exchange rate will change if relative prices change. For example, imagine there is no price inflation in the United

States, while prices in Germany are increasing by 20 percent a year. At the beginning of the year, a basket of goods costs $200 in the United States and DM 600 in Germany, so the dollar/DM exchange rate, according to PPP theory, should be $0.33 = DM 1. At the end of the year, the basket of goods still costs $200 in the United States, but it costs DM 720 in Germany. PPP theory predicts that the exchange rate should change as a result. More precisely, by the end of the year, $0.27 = DM 1 (i.e., $1 = DM 3.6). Because of price inflation, the DM has depreciated against the dollar. One dollar should buy more marks at the end of the year than at the beginning.

Money Supply and Price Inflation

In essence, PPP theory predicts that changes in relative prices will result in a change in exchange rates. Theoretically, a country in which price inflation is running wild should expect to see its currency depreciate against that of countries in which inflation rates are lower. Because the growth rate of a country's money supply and its inflation rates are closely correlated,[7] we can predict a country's likely inflation rate. Then we can use this information to forecast exchange rate movements.

Inflation is a monetary phenomenon. It occurs when the quantity of money in circulation rises faster than the stock of goods and services; that is, when the money supply increases faster than output increases. Imagine what would happen if everyone in the country was suddenly given $10,000 by the government. Many people would rush out to spend their extra money on those things they had always wanted—new cars, new furniture, better clothes, and so on. There would be a surge in demand for goods and services. Car dealers, department stores, and other providers of goods and services would respond to this upsurge in demand by raising prices. The result would be price inflation.

A government increasing the money supply is analogous to giving people more money. An increase in the money supply makes it easier for banks to borrow from the government and for individuals and companies to borrow from banks. The resulting increase in credit causes increases in demand for goods and services. Unless the output of goods and services is growing at a rate similar to that of the money supply, the result will be inflation. This relationship has been observed time after time in country after country.

So now we have a connection between the growth in a country's money supply, price inflation, and exchange rate movements. Put simply, when the growth in a country's money supply is faster than the growth in its output, price inflation is fueled. The PPP theory tells us that a country with a high inflation rate will see a depreciation in its currency exchange rate. Consider the case of Bolivia. In the mid-1980s, Bolivia experienced hyperinflation—an explosive and seemingly uncontrollable price inflation in which money loses value very rapidly. Table 9.4 presents data on Bolivia's money supply, inflation rate, and its peso's exchange rate with the US dollar during the period of hyperinflation. The exchange rate is actually the "black market" exchange rate, as the Bolivian government prohibited converting the peso to other currencies during the period. The data show that the growth in money supply, the rate of price inflation, and the depreciation of the peso against the dollar all moved in step with each other. This is just what PPP theory and monetary economics predict. Between April 1984 and July 1985, Bolivia's money supply increased by 17,433 percent, prices increased by 22,908 percent, and the value of the peso against the dollar fell by 24,662 percent! In October 1985, the Bolivian government instituted a dramatic stabilization plan—which included the introduction of a new currency and tight control of the money supply—and by 1987 the country's annual inflation rate was down to 16 percent.[8]

Another way of looking at the same phenomenon is that an increase in a country's money supply, which increases the amount of currency available, changes the relative demand and supply conditions in the foreign exchange market. If the US money supply is growing more rapidly than US output, dollars will be relatively more

Table 9.4

Macroeconomic Data
for Bolivia,
April 1984–October 1985

Month	Money Supply (billions of pesos)	Price Level Relative to 1982 (average = 1)	Exchange Rate (pesos per dollar)
1984			
April	270	21.1	3,576
May	330	31.1	3.512
June	440	32.3	3,342
July	599	34.0	3,570
August	718	39.1	7,038
September	889	53.7	13,685
October	1,194	85.5	15,205
November	1,495	112.4	18,469
December	3,296	180.9	24,515
1985			
January	4,630	305.3	73,016
February	6,455	863.3	141,101
March	9,089	1,078.6	128,137
April	12,885	1,205.7	167,428
May	21,309	1,635.7	272,375
June	27,778	2,919.1	481,756
July	47,341	4,854.6	885,476
August	74,306	8,081.0	1,182,300
September	103,272	12,647.6	1,087,440
October	132,550	12,411.8	1,120,210

Source: Juan-Antino Morales, "Inflation Stabilization in Bolivia," in *Inflation Stabilization: The Experience of Israel, Argentina, Brazil, Bolivia, and Mexico,* ed. Michael Bruno et al. (Cambridge, MA: MIT Press, 1988).

plentiful than the currencies of countries where monetary growth is closer to output growth. As a result of this relative increase in the supply of dollars, the dollar will depreciate on the foreign exchange market against the currencies of countries with slower monetary growth.

Government policy determines whether the rate of growth in a country's money supply is greater than the rate of growth in output. A government can increase the money supply simply by telling the country's central bank to print more money. Governments tend to do this to finance public expenditure (building roads, paying government workers, paying for defense, etc.). A government could finance public expenditure by raising taxes, but since nobody likes paying more taxes and since politicians do not like to be unpopular, they have a natural preference for printing money. Unfortunately, there is no magic money tree. The inevitable result of excessive growth in money supply is price inflation. However, this has not stopped governments around the world from printing money, with predictable results. If an international business is attempting to predict future movements in the value of a country's currency on the foreign exchange market, it should examine that country's policy toward monetary growth. If the government seems committed to controlling the rate of growth in money supply, the country's future inflation rate may be low (even if the current rate is high) and its currency should not depreciate too much on the foreign exchange market. If the government seems to lack the political will to control the rate of growth in money supply, the future inflation rate may be high, which is likely to cause its currency to depreciate. Historically, many Latin American governments have fallen into this latter category, including Argentina, Bolivia, and Brazil. There are signs that many of the newly democratic states of Eastern Europe might be making the same mistake.

Empirical Tests of PPP Theory

PPP theory predicts that changes in relative prices will result in a change in exchange rates. A country in which price inflation is running wild should expect to see its currency depreciate against that of countries with lower inflation rates. This is intuitively appealing, but is it true in practice? There are several good examples of the connection between a country's price inflation and exchange rate position (such as Bolivia). However, extensive empirical testing of PPP theory has yielded mixed results.[9] While PPP theory seems to yield relatively accurate predictions in the long run, it does not appear to be a strong predictor of short-run movements in exchange rates covering time spans of five years or less. In addition, the theory seems to best predict exchange rate changes for countries with high rates of inflation and underdeveloped capital markets. The theory is less useful for predicting short-term exchange rate movements between the currencies of advanced industrialized nations that have relatively small differentials in inflation rates.

Several factors may explain the failure of PPP theory to predict exchange rates more accurately. PPP theory assumes away transportation costs and barriers to trade and investment. In practice, these factors are significant, and they tend to create price differentials between countries. As we saw in Chapters 5 and 7, governments routinely intervene in international trade and investment. Such intervention, by violating the assumption of efficient markets, weakens the link between relative price changes and changes in exchange rates predicted by PPP theory.

Another factor of some importance is that governments also intervene in the foreign exchange market in attempting to influence the value of their currencies. We will look at why and how they do this in Chapter 10. For now, the important thing to note is that governments regularly intervene in the foreign exchange market, and this further weakens the link between price changes and changes in exchange rates.

Perhaps the most important factor explaining the failure of PPP theory to predict short-term movements in foreign exchange rates, however, is the impact of investor psychology and other factors on currency purchasing decisions and exchange rate movements. We will discuss this issue in more detail later in this chapter.

Interest Rates and Exchange Rates

Economic theory tells us that interest rates reflect expectations about likely future inflation rates. In countries where inflation is expected to be high, interest rates also will be high, because investors want compensation for the decline in the value of their money. This relationship was first formalized by economist Irvin Fisher and is referred to as the Fisher effect. The Fisher effect states that a country's "nominal" interest rate (i) is the sum of the required "real" rate of interest (r) and the expected rate of inflation over the period for which the funds are to be lent (I). More formally,

$$i = r + I$$

For example, if the real rate of interest in a country is 5 percent and annual inflation is expected to be 10 percent, the nominal interest rate will be 15 percent. As predicted by the Fisher effect, a strong relationship seems to exist between inflation rates and interest rates.[10]

We can take this one step further and consider how it applies in a world of many countries and unrestricted capital flows. When investors are free to transfer capital between countries, real interest rates will be the same in every country. If differences in real interest rates did emerge between countries, arbitrage would soon equalize them. For example, if the real interest rate in Germany was 10 percent and only 6 percent in the United States, it would pay investors to borrow money in the United States and invest it in Germany. The resulting increase in the demand for money in the United States would raise the real interest rate there, while the increase in the supply of foreign money in Germany would lower the real interest rate there. This would continue until the two sets of real interest rates were equalized. (In practice, differences in real interest rates may persist due to government controls on capital flows; investors are not always free to transfer capital between countries.)

It follows from the Fisher effect that if the real interest rate is the same worldwide, any difference in interest rates between countries reflects differing expectations about inflation rates. Thus, if the expected rate of inflation in the United States is greater than that in Germany, US nominal interest rates will be greater than German nominal interest rates.

Since we know from PPP theory that there is a link (in theory at least) between inflation and exchange rates, and since interest rates reflect expectations about inflation, it follows that there must also be a link between interest rates and exchange rates. This link is known as the International Fisher Effect (IFE). The **International Fisher Effect** states that for any two countries, the spot exchange rate should change in an equal amount but in the opposite direction to the difference in nominal interest rates between the two countries. Stated more formally,

$$(S_1 - S_2)/S_2 \times 100 = i_\$ - i_{DM}$$

where $i_\$$ and i_{DM} are the respective nominal interest rates in the United States and Germany (for the sake of example), S_1 is the spot exchange rate at the beginning of the period, and S_2 is the spot exchange rate at the end of the period.

If the US nominal interest rate is higher than Germany's, reflecting greater expected inflation rates, the value of the dollar against the deutsche mark should fall by that interest rate differential in the future. So if the interest rate in the United States is 10 percent, and in Germany it is 6 percent, reflecting 4 percent higher expected inflation in the United States, we would expect the value of the dollar to depreciate by 4 percent against the mark.

Do interest rate differentials help predict future currency movements? The evidence is mixed; as in the case of PPP theory, in the long run, there seems to be a relationship between interest rate differentials and subsequent changes in spot exchange rates. However, considerable short-run deviations occur. Like PPP, the International Fisher Effect is not a good predictor of short-run changes in spot exchange rates.[11]

Investor Psychology and Bandwagon Effects

Empirical evidence suggests that neither PPP theory nor the International Fisher Effect are particularly good at explaining short-term movements in exchange rates. One reason may be the impact of investor psychology on short-run exchange rate movements. Increasing evidence reveals that various psychological factors play an important role in determining the expectations of market traders as to likely future exchange rates.[12] In turn, expectations have a tendency to become self-filling prophecies. We discussed a good example of this mechanism in the Management focus about George Soros. When George Soros shorted the British pound in September 1992, many foreign exchange traders jumped on the bandwagon and did likewise, selling British pounds and purchasing German marks. As the bandwagon effect gained momentum, with more traders selling British pounds and purchasing deutsche marks in expectation of a decline in the pound, their expectations became a self-fulfilling prophecy with massive selling forcing down the value of the pound against the deutsche mark. In other words, the pound declined in value not because of any major shift in macroeconomic fundamentals, but because investors moved in a herd in response to a bet placed by a major speculator, George Soros.

According to a number of recent studies, investor psychology and bandwagon effects play a major role in determining short-run exchange rate movements.[13] However, these effects can be hard to predict. Investor psychology can be influenced by political factors and by microeconomic events, such as the investment decisions of individual firms, many of which are only loosely linked to macroeconomic fundamentals, such as relative inflation rates. Moreover, bandwagon effects can be both triggered and exacerbated by the idiosyncratic behavior of politicians. Something like this seems to have occurred in Southeast Asia during 1997 when one after another, the currencies of Thailand, Malaysia, South Korea, and Indonesia lost between 50 percent and 70 percent of their value against the US dollar in a few months. For a detailed look at what occurred in South Korea, see the accompanying Country Focus. The collapse in the value of the Korean currency did not occur because South Korea had a higher inflation rate than the United States. It occurred because of an excessive buildup of dollar-denominated debt among South Korean firms. By mid-1997 it was clear that these companies were having trouble servicing this debt. Foreign investors, fearing a wave of corporate bankruptcies, took their money out of the country, exchanging won for US dollars. As this began to depress the exchange rate, currency traders jumped on the bandwagon and speculated against the won (selling it short).

Summary

Relative monetary growth, relative inflation rates, and nominal interest rate differentials are all moderately good predictors of long-run changes in exchange rates. They are poor predictors of short-run changes in exchange rates, however, perhaps because of the impact of psychological factors, investor expectations, and bandwagon effects on short-term currency movements. This information is useful for an international business. Insofar as the long-term profitability of foreign investments, export opportunities, and the price competitiveness of foreign imports are all influenced by long-term movements in exchange rates, international businesses would be advised to pay attention to countries' differing monetary growth, inflation, and interest rates. International businesses that engage in foreign exchange transactions on a day-to-day basis could benefit by knowing some predictors of short-term foreign exchange rate movements. Unfortunately, short-term exchange rate movements are difficult to predict.

Exchange Rate Forecasting

A company's need to predict future exchange rate variations raises the issue of whether it is worthwhile for the company to invest in exchange rate forecasting services to aid decision making. Two schools of thought address this issue. The efficient market school argues that forward exchange rates do the best possible job of forecasting future spot exchange rates, and, therefore, investing in forecasting services would be a waste of money. The other school of thought, the inefficient market school, argues that companies can improve the foreign exchange market's estimate of future exchange rates (as contained in the forward rate) by investing in forecasting services. In other words, this school of thought does not believe the forward exchange rates are the best possible predictors of future spot exchange rates.

The Efficient Market School

Forward exchange rates represent market participants' collective predictions of likely spot exchange rates at specified future dates. If forward exchange rates are the best possible predictor of future spot rates, it would make no sense for companies to spend additional money trying to forecast short-run exchange rate movements. Many economists believe the foreign exchange market is efficient at setting forward rates.[14] An **efficient market** is one in which prices reflect all available public information. (If forward rates reflect all available information about likely future changes in exchange rates, there is no way a company can beat the market by investing in forecasting services.)

If the foreign exchange market is efficient, forward exchange rates should be unbiased predictors of future spot rates. This does not mean the predictions will be accurate in any specific situation. It means inaccuracies will not be consistently above or below future spot rates; they will be random. Many empirical tests have addressed the efficient market hypothesis. Although most of the early work seems to confirm the

COUNTRY FOCUS
Why Did the Korean Won Collapse?

In early 1997, South Korea could look back with pride on a 30-year "economic miracle" that had raised the country from the ranks of the poor and given it the world's 11th largest economy. By the end of 1997, the Korean currency, the won, had lost a staggering 67 percent of its value against the US dollar, the South Korean economy lay in tatters, and the International Monetary Fund was overseeing a $55 billion rescue package. This sudden turn of events had its roots in investments made by South Korea's large industrial conglomerates, or *chaebol,* during the 1990s, often at the bequest of politicians. In 1993, Kim Young-Sam, a populist politician, became president of South Korea. Mr. Kim took office during a mild recession and promised to boost economic growth by encouraging investment in export-oriented industries. He urged the *chaebol* to invest in new factories. South Korea enjoyed an investment-led economic boom in 1994–95, but at a cost. The *chaebol,* always reliant on heavy borrowing, built up massive debts that were equivalent, on average, to four times their equity.

As might be expected, as the volume of investments ballooned during the 1990s, the *quality* of many of these investments declined significantly. The investments often were made on the basis of unrealistic projections about future demand conditions. This resulted in significant excess capacity and falling prices. An example is investments made by South Korean *chaebol* in semiconductor factories. Investments in such facilities surged in 1994 and 1995 when a temporary global shortage of dynamic random access memory chips (DRAMs) led to sharp price

increases for this product. However, supply shortages had disappeared by 1996 and excess capacity was beginning to make itself felt, just as the South Koreans started to bring new DRAM factories on stream. The results were predictable; prices for DRAMs plunged through the floor and the earnings of South Korean DRAM manufacturers fell by 90 percent, which meant it was difficult for them to make scheduled payments on the debt they had taken on to build the extra capacity. The risk of corporate bankruptcy increased significantly, and not just in the semiconductor industry. South Korean companies were also investing heavily in a wide range of other industries, including automobiles and steel.

Matters were complicated further because much of the borrowing had been in US dollars, as opposed to Korean won. This had seemed like a smart move at the time. The dollar/won exchange rate had been stable at around $1=W850. Interest rates on dollar borrowings were two to three percentage points lower than rates on borrowings in Korean won. Much of this borrowing was in the form of short-term dollar-denominated debt that had to be paid back to the lending institution within one year. While the borrowing strategy seemed to make sense, there was a risk here. If the won were to depreciate against the dollar, this would increase the size of the debt burden that South Korean companies would have to service, when measured in the local currency. Currency depreciation would raise borrowing costs, depress corporate earnings, and increase the risk of bankruptcy. This is exactly what happened.

By mid-1997, foreign investors had become

---

hypothesis (suggesting that companies should not waste their money on forecasting services), more recent studies have challenged it.[15] There is some evidence that forward rates are not unbiased predictors of future spot rates, and that more accurate predictions of future spot rates can be calculated from publicly available information.[16]

The Inefficient Market School

Citing evidence against the efficient market hypothesis, some economists believe the foreign exchange market is inefficient. An **inefficient market** is one in which prices do not reflect all available information. In an inefficient market, forward exchange rates will not be the best possible predictors of future spot exchange rates.

If this is true, it may be worthwhile for international businesses to invest in forecasting services (as many do). The belief is that professional exchange rate forecasts

http://www.cftech.com/BrainBank/FINANCE/IMFHistory.html

alarmed at the rising debt levels of South Korean companies, particularly given the emergence of excess capacity and plunging prices in several areas where the companies had made huge investments, including semiconductors, automobiles, and steel. Given increasing speculation that many South Korean companies would not be able to service their debt payments, foreign investors began to withdraw their money from the Korean stock and bond markets. In the process, they sold Korean won and purchased US dollars. The selling of won accelerated in mid-1997 when two of the smaller *chaebol* filed for bankruptcy, citing their inability to meet scheduled debt payments. The increased supply of won and the increased demand for US dollars pushed down the price of won in dollar terms from around won 840=$1 to won 900=$1.

At this point, the South Korean central bank stepped into the foreign exchange market to try to keep the exchange rate above won 1,000=$1. It used dollars that it held in reserve to purchase won. The idea was to try to push up the price of the won in dollar terms and restore investor confidence in the stability of the exchange rate. This action, however, did not address the underlying debt problem faced by South Korean companies. Against a backdrop of more corporate bankruptcies in South Korea, and the government's stated intentions to take some troubled companies into state ownership, Standard & Poor's, the US credit rating agency, downgraded South Korea's sovereign debt. This caused the Korean stock market to plunge 5.5 percent, and the Korean won to fall to won930 = $1. According to S&P, "the downgrade of...ratings

reflects the escalating cost to the government of supporting the country's ailing corporate and financial sectors."

The S&P downgrade triggered a sharp sale of the Korean won. In an attempt to protect the won against what was fast becoming a classic bandwagon effect, the South Korean central bank raised short-term interest rates to over 12 percent, more than double the inflation rate. The bank also stepped up its intervention in the currency exchange markets, selling dollars and purchasing won in an attempt to keep the dollar/won exchange rate above $1=W1,000. The main effect of this action, however, was to rapidly deplete South Korea's foreign exchange reserves. These stood at $30 billion on November 1, but fell to only $15 billion two weeks later. With its foreign exchange reserves almost exhausted, the South Korean central bank gave up its defense of the won on November 17. Immediately, the price of won in dollars plunged to around won 1,500=$1, effectively increasing by 60 to 70 percent the amount of won heavily indebted Korean companies had to pay to meet scheduled payments on their dollar-denominated debt. These losses, due to adverse changes in foreign exchange rates, depressed the profits of many firms. South Korean firms suffered foreign exchange losses of more than $15 billion in 1997.

Sources: J. Burton and G. Baker, "The Country That Invested Its Way into Trouble," *Financial Times*, January 15, 1998, p. 8; J. Burton, "South Korea's Credit Rating is Lowered," *Financial Times*, October 25, 1997, p. 3; J. Burton, "Currency Losses Hit Samsung Electronics," *Financial Times*, March 20, 1998, p. 24; and "Korean Firms' Foreign Exchange Losses Exceed US $15 Billion," *Business Korea*, February 1998, p. 55.

might provide better predictions of future spot rates than forward exchange rates do. It should be pointed out, however, that the track record of professional forecasting services is not that good. An analysis of the forecasts of 12 major forecasting services between 1978 and 1982 concluded the forecasters in general did not provide better forecasts than the forward exchange rates.[17] Also, forecasting services did not predict the 1997 currency crisis that swept through Southeast Asia.

Approaches to Forecasting

Assuming the inefficient market school is correct that the foreign exchange market's estimate of future spot rates can be improved, on what basis should forecasts be prepared? Here again, there are two schools of thought. One adheres to fundamental analysis, while the other uses technical analysis.

Fundamental Analysis

Fundamental analysis draws on economic theory to construct sophisticated econometric models for predicting exchange rate movements. The variables contained in these models typically include those we have discussed, such as relative money supply growth rates, inflation rates, and interest rates. In addition, they may include variables related to balance-of-payments positions.

Running a deficit on a balance-of-payments current account (a country is importing more goods and services than it is exporting), creates pressures that result in the depreciation of the country's currency on the foreign exchange market.[18] (For background on the balance of payments, see Chapter 7.) Consider what might happen if the United States was running a persistent current account balance-of-payments deficit. Since the United States would be importing more than it was exporting, people in other countries would be increasing their holdings of US dollars. If these people were willing to hold their dollars, the dollar's exchange rate would not be influenced. However, if these people converted their dollars into other currencies, the supply of dollars in the foreign exchange market would increase (as would demand for the other currencies). This shift in demand and supply would create pressures that could lead to the depreciation of the dollar against other currencies.

This argument hinges on whether people in other countries are willing to hold dollars. This depends on such factors as US interest rates and inflation rates. So, in a sense, the balance-of-payments position is not a fundamental predictor of future exchange rate movements. For example, between 1981 and 1985, the US dollar appreciated against most major currencies despite a growing balance-of-payments deficit. Relatively high real interest rates in the United States made the dollar very attractive to foreigners, so they did not convert their dollars into other currencies. Given this, we are back to the argument that the fundamental determinants of exchange rates are monetary growth, inflation rates, and interest rates.

Technical Analysis

Technical analysis uses price and volume data to determine past trends, which are expected to continue into the future. This approach does not rely on a consideration of economic fundamentals. Technical analysis is based on the premise that there are analyzable market trends and waves and that previous trends and waves can be used to predict future trends and waves. Since there is no theoretical rationale for this assumption of predictability, many economists compare technical analysis to fortune-telling. Despite this skepticism, technical analysis has gained favor in recent years.[19]

Currency Convertibility

Until this point we have assumed that the currencies of various countries are freely convertible into other currencies. This assumption is invalid. Many countries restrict the ability of residents and nonresidents to convert the local currency into a foreign currency, making international trade and investment more difficult. Many international businesses have used "countertrade" practices to circumvent problems that arise when a currency is not freely convertible.

Convertibility and Government Policy

Due to government restrictions, a significant number of currencies are not freely convertible into other currencies. A country's currency is said to be **freely convertible** when the country's government allows both residents and nonresidents to purchase unlimited amounts of a foreign currency with it. A currency is said to be **externally convertible** when only nonresidents may convert it into a foreign currency without any limitations. A currency is **nonconvertible** when neither residents nor nonresidents are allowed to convert it into a foreign currency.

Free convertibility is the exception rather than the rule. Many countries place some restrictions on their residents' ability to convert the domestic currency into a foreign currency (a policy of external convertibility). Restrictions range from the relatively minor (such as restricting the amount of foreign currency they may take with them out of the country on trips) to the major (such as restricting domestic businesses' ability to take foreign currency out of the country). External convertibility restrictions can limit domestic companies' ability to invest abroad, but they present few problems for foreign companies wishing to do business in that country. For example, even if the Japanese government tightly controlled the ability of its residents to convert the yen into US dollars, all US businesses with deposits in Japanese banks may at any time convert all their yen into dollars and take them out of the country. Thus, a US company with a subsidiary in Japan is assured that it will be able to convert the profits from its Japanese operation into dollars and take them out of the country.

Serious problems arise, however, when a policy of nonconvertibility is in force. This was the practice of the former Soviet Union, and it continued to be the practice in Russia until recently. When strictly applied, nonconvertibility means that although a US company doing business in a country such as Russia may be able to generate significant ruble profits, it may not convert those rubles into dollars and take them out of the country. Obviously this is not desirable for international business.

Governments limit convertibility to preserve their foreign exchange reserves. A country needs an adequate supply of these reserves to service its international debt commitments and to purchase imports. Governments typically impose convertibility restrictions on their currency when they fear that free convertibility will lead to a run on their foreign exchange reserves. This occurs when residents and nonresidents rush to convert their holdings of domestic currency into a foreign currency— a phenomenon generally referred to as capital flight. Capital flight is most likely to occur when the value of the domestic currency is depreciating rapidly because of hyperinflation, or when a country's economic prospects are shaky in other respects. Under such circumstances, both residents and nonresidents tend to believe that their money is more likely to hold its value if it is converted into a foreign currency and invested abroad. Not only will a run on foreign exchange reserves limit the country's ability to service its international debt and pay for imports, but it will also lead to a precipitous depreciation in the exchange rate as residents and nonresidents unload their holdings of domestic currency on the foreign exchange markets (thereby increasing the market supply of the country's currency). Governments fear that the rise in import prices resulting from currency depreciation will lead to further increases in inflation. This fear provides another rationale for limiting convertibility.

Countertrade

Companies can deal with the nonconvertibility problem by engaging in countertrade. Countertrade is discussed in detail in Chapter 15, so we will merely introduce the concept here. **Countertrade** refers to a range of barterlike agreements by which goods and services can be traded for other goods and services. Countertrade can make sense when a country's currency is nonconvertible. For example, consider the deal that General Electric struck with the Romanian government in 1984, when that country's currency was nonconvertible. When General Electric won a contract for a $150 million generator project in Romania, it agreed to take payment in the form of Romanian goods that could be sold for $150 million on international markets. In a similar case, the Venezuelan government negotiated a contract with Caterpillar in 1986 under which Venezuela would trade 350,000 tons of iron ore for Caterpillar heavy construction equipment. Caterpillar subsequently traded the iron ore to Romania in exchange for Romanian farm products, which it then sold on international markets for dollars.[20]

How important is countertrade? One estimate is that 20 to 30 percent of world trade in 1985 involved some form of countertrade agreements. Since then, however, more currencies have become freely convertible, and the percentage of world trade that involves some form of countertrade has fallen to between 10 percent and 20 percent.[21] Since countertrade apparently remains an important method for conducting international trade, we discuss it again in Chapter 15.

 # IMPLICATIONS FOR BUSINESS

This chapter contains a number of clear implications for business. First, it is critical that international businesses understand the influence of exchange rates on the profitability of trade and investment deals. Adverse changes in exchange rates can make apparently profitable deals unprofitable. The risk introduced into international business transactions by changes in exchange rates is referred to as foreign exchange risk. Means of hedging against foreign exchange risk are available. Forward exchange rates and currency swaps allow companies to insure against this risk.

International businesses must also understand the forces that determine exchange rates. This is particularly true in light of the increasing evidence that forward exchange rates are not unbiased predictors. If a company wants to know how the value of a particular currency is likely to change over the long term on the foreign exchange market, it should look closely at those economic fundamentals that appear to predict long-run exchange rate movements (i.e., the growth in a country's money supply, its inflation rate, and its nominal interest rates). For example, an international business should be very cautious about trading with or investing in a country with a recent history of rapid growth in its domestic money supply. The upsurge in inflation that is likely to follow such rapid monetary growth could lead to a sharp drop in the value of the country's currency on the foreign exchange market, which could transform a profitable deal into an unprofitable one. This is not to say that an international business should not trade with or invest in such a country. Rather, it means an international business should take some precautions before doing so, such as buying currency forward on the foreign exchange market or structuring the deal around a countertrade arrangement.

Complicating this picture is the issue of currency convertibility. The proclivity that many governments seem to have to restrict currency convertibility suggests that the foreign exchange market does not always provide the lubricant necessary to make international trade and investment possible. Given this, international businesses need to explore alternative mechanisms for facilitating international trade and investment that do not involve currency conversion. Countertrade seems the obvious mechanism. We return to the topic of countertrade and discuss it in depth in Chapter 15.

Chapter Summary

This chapter explained how the foreign exchange market works, examined the forces that determine exchange rates, and then discussed the implications of these factors for international business. Given that changes in exchange rates can dramatically alter the profitability of foreign trade and investment deals, this is an area of major interest to international business. This chapter made the following points:

1. One function of the foreign exchange market is to convert the currency of one country into the currency of another.

2. International businesses participate in the foreign exchange market to facilitate international trade and investment, to invest spare cash in short-term money market accounts abroad, and to engage in currency speculation.

3. A second function of the foreign exchange market is to provide insurance against foreign exchange risk.

4. The spot exchange rate is the exchange rate at which a dealer converts one currency into another currency on a particular day.

5. Foreign exchange risk can be reduced by using forward exchange rates. A forward exchange rate is an exchange rate governing future transactions.

6. Foreign exchange risk can also be reduced by engaging in currency swaps. A swap is the simultaneous purchase and sale of a given amount of foreign exchange for two different value dates.

7. The law of one price holds that in competitive markets that are free of transportation costs and barriers to trade, identical products sold in different countries must sell for the same price when their price is expressed in the same currency.

8. Purchasing power parity (PPP) theory states the price of a basket of particular goods should be roughly equivalent in each country. PPP theory predicts that the exchange rate will change if relative prices change.

9. The rate of change in countries' relative prices depends on their relative inflation rates. A country's inflation rate seems to be a function of the growth in its money supply.

10. The PPP theory of exchange rate changes yields relatively accurate predictions of long-term trends in exchange rates, but not of short-term movements. The failure of PPP theory to predict exchange rate changes more accurately may be due to the existence of transportation costs, barriers to trade and investment, and the impact of psychological factors such as bandwagon effects on market movements and short-run exchange rates.

11. Interest rates reflect expectations about inflation. In countries where inflation is expected to be high, interest rates also will be high.

12. The International Fisher Effect states that for any two countries, the spot exchange rate should change in an equal amount but in the opposite direction to the difference in nominal interest rates.

13. The most common approach to exchange rate forecasting is fundamental analysis. This relies on variables such as money supply growth, inflation rates, nominal interest rates, and balance-of-payments positions to predict future changes in exchange rates.

14. In many countries, the ability of residents and nonresidents to convert local currency into a foreign currency is restricted by government policy. A government restricts the convertibility of its currency to protect the country's foreign exchange reserves and to halt any capital flight.

15. Particularly bothersome for international business is a policy of nonconvertibility, which prohibits residents and nonresidents from exchanging local currency for foreign currency. A policy of nonconvertibility makes it very difficult to engage in international trade and investment in the country.

16. One way of coping with the nonconvertibility problem is to engage in countertrade—to trade goods and services for other goods and services.

Critical Discussion Questions

1. The interest rate on South Korean government securities with one-year maturity is 4 percent, and the expected inflation rate for the coming year is 2 percent. The interest rate on US government securities with one-year maturity is 7 percent, and the expected rate of inflation is 5 percent. The current spot exchange rate for Korean won is $1 = W1,200. Forecast the spot exchange rate one year from today. Explain the logic of your answer.

2. Two countries, Britain and the United States, produce just one good: beef. Suppose the price of beef in the United States is $2.80 per pound and in Britain it is £3.70 per pound.

   a. According to PPP theory, what should the $/£ spot exchange rate be?

   b. Suppose the price of beef is expected to rise to $3.10 in the United States, and to £4.65 in Britain. What should the one-year forward $/£ exchange rate be?

   c. Given your answers to parts a and b, and given that the current interest rate in the United States is 10 percent, what would you expect the current interest rate to be in Britain?

3. You manufacture wine goblets. In mid-June you receive an order for 10,000 goblets from Japan. Payment of ¥400,000 is due in mid-December. You expect the yen to rise from its present rate of $1 = ¥130 to $1 = ¥100 by December. You can borrow yen at 6 percent per annum. What should you do?

CLOSING CASE   The Collapse of the Thai Baht in 1997

During the 1980s and 1990s, Thailand emerged as one of Asia's most dynamic tiger economies. From 1985 to 1995, Thailand achieved an annual average economic growth rate of 8.4 percent, while keeping its annual inflation rate at only 5 percent (comparable figures for the United States over this period were 1.3 percent for economic growth and 3.2 percent for inflation). Much of Thailand's economic growth was powered by exports. Over the 1990–1996 period, for example, the value of exports from Thailand grew by 16 percent per year compounded. The wealth created by export-led growth fueled an investment boom in commercial and residential property, industrial assets, and infrastructure. As demand for property increased, the value of commercial and residential real estate in Bangkok soared. This fed a building boom the likes of which had never been seen in Thailand. Office and apartment buildings were going up all over the city. Heavy borrowing from banks financed much of this construction, but as long as property values continued to rise, the banks were happy to lend to property companies.

By early 1997, however, it was clear that the boom had produced excess capacity in residential and commercial property. There were an estimated 365,000 apartment units unoccupied in Bangkok in late 1996. With another 100,000 units scheduled to be completed in 1997, years of excess demand in the Thai property market had been replaced by excess supply. By one estimate, Bangkok's building boom by 1997 had produced enough excess space to meet its residential and commercial needs for at least five years.

At the same time, Thailand's investments in infrastructure, industrial capacity, and commercial real estate were sucking in foreign goods at unprecedented rates. To build infrastructure, factories, and office buildings, Thailand was purchasing capital equipment and materials from America, Europe, and Japan. As a consequence, the current account of the balance of payments shifted strongly into the red during the mid-1990s. Despite strong export growth, imports grew faster. By 1995, Thailand was running a current account deficit equivalent to 8.1 percent of its GDP.

Things started to fall apart February 5, 1997, when Somprasong Land, a Thai property developer, announced it had failed to make a scheduled $3.1 million interest payment on an $80 billion eurobond loan, effectively entering into default. Somprasong Land was the first victim of speculative overbuilding in the Bangkok property market. The Thai stock market had already declined by 45 percent since its high in early 1996, primarily on concerns that several property companies might be forced into bankruptcy. Now one had been. The stock market fell another 2.7 percent on the news, but it was only the beginning.

In the aftermath of Somprasong's default, it became clear that, along with several other property developers, many of the country's financial institutions, including Finance One, were also on the brink of default. Finance One, the country's largest financial institution, had pioneered a practice that had become widespread among Thai institutions—issuing bonds denominated in US dollars and using the proceeds to finance lending to the country's booming property developers. In theory, this practice made sense because Finance One was able to exploit the interest rate differential between dollar-denominated debt and Thai debt (i.e., Finance One borrowed in US dollars at a low interest rate and lent in Thai baht at high interest rates). The only problem with this financing strategy was that when the Thai property market began to unravel in 1996 and 1997, the property developers could no longer pay back the cash they had borrowed from Finance One. This made it difficult for Finance One to pay back its creditors. As the effects of overbuilding became evident in 1996, Finance One's nonperforming loans doubled, then doubled again in the first quarter of 1997.

In February 1997, trading in the shares of Finance One was suspended while the government tried to arrange for the troubled company to be acquired by a small Thai bank, in a deal sponsored by the Thai central bank. It didn't work, and when trading resumed in Finance One shares in May, they fell 70 percent in a single day. By this time bad loans in the Thai property market were swelling daily and had risen to over $30 billion. Finance One was bankrupt, and it was feared that others would follow.

It was at this point that currency traders began a concerted attack on the Thai currency. For the previous 13 years, the Thai baht had been pegged to the US dollar at an exchange rate of about $1=Bt25. This peg, however, had become increasingly difficult to defend. Currency traders looking at Thailand's growing current account deficit and dollar-denominated debt burden, reasoned that demand for dollars in Thailand would rise while demand for baht would fall. (Businesses and financial institutions would be exchanging baht for dollars to service their debt payments and purchase imports.) There were several attempts to force a devaluation of the baht in late 1996 and early 1997. These speculative attacks typically involved traders selling baht short to profit from a future decline in the value of the baht against the dollar. In this context, short selling involves a currency trader borrowing baht from a financial institution and immediately reselling those baht in the foreign exchange market for dollars. The theory is that if the value of the baht subsequently falls against the dollar, then when the trader has to buy the baht back to repay the financial institution, it will cost her fewer dollars than she received from the initial sale of baht. For example, a trader might borrow Bt100 from a bank for six months. The trader then exchanges the Bt100 for $4 (at an exchange rate of $1=Bt25). If the exchange rate subsequently declines to $1=Bt50 it will cost the trader only $2 to repurchase the Bt100 in six months

and pay back the bank, leaving the trader with a 100 percent profit!

In May 1997, short sellers were swarming over the Thai baht. In an attempt to defend the peg, the Thai government used its foreign exchange reserves (which were denominated in US dollars) to purchase baht. It cost the Thai government $5 billion to defend the baht, which reduced its "officially reported" foreign exchange reserves to a two-year low of $33 billion. In addition, the Thai government raised key interest rates from 10 percent to 12.5 percent to make holding baht more attractive, but because this also raised corporate borrowing costs it exacerbated the debt crisis. What the world financial community did not know at this point, was that with the blessing of his superiors, a foreign exchange trader at the Thai central bank had locked up most of Thailand's foreign exchange reserves in forward contracts.

The reality was that Thailand had only $1.14 billion in available foreign exchange reserves left to defend the dollar peg. Defending the peg was now impossible.

On July 2, 1997, the Thai government bowed to the inevitable and announced it would allow the baht to float freely against the dollar. The baht immediately lost 18 percent of its value and started a slide that would bring the exchange rate down to $1=Bt55 by January 1998. As the baht declined, the Thai debt bomb exploded. A 50 percent decline in the value of the baht against the dollar doubled the amount of baht required to serve the dollar-denominated debt commitments taken on by Thai financial institutions and businesses. This made more bankruptcies and further pushed down the battered Thai stock market. The Thailand Set stock market index ultimately declined from 787 in January 1997 to a low of 337 in December of that year, and this on top of a 45 percent decline in 1996!

http://www.tat.or.th/index-shock.htm

Sources: "Bitter Pill for the Thais," *The Straits Times*, July 5, 1997, p. 46; World Bank, *1997 World Development Report* (New York: World Bank), Table 2; T. Bardacke, "Somprasong Defaults on $80 Million Eurobond," *Financial Times*, February 6, 1997, p. 25; and T. Bardacke, "The Day the Miracle Came to an End," *Financial Times*, January 12, 1998, pp. 6–7.

Case Discussion Questions

1. Identify the main factors that led to the collapse of the Thai baht in 1997?

2. Do you think the sudden collapse of the Thai baht can be explained by the purchasing power parity theorem?

3. What role did speculators play in the fall of the Thai baht? Did they cause its fall?

4. What steps might the Thai government have taken to preempt the financial crisis that swept the nation in 1997?

5. How will the collapse of the Thai baht affect businesses in Thailand, particularly those that purchase inputs from abroad or export finished products?

6. Do you notice any similarities between the collapse of the Thai baht in 1997 and the collapse of the Korean won around the same time (see the Country Focus in this chapter)? What are these similarities? Do you think these two events were related? How?

Notes

1. For a good general introduction to the foreign exchange market, see R. Weisweiller, *How the Foreign Exchange Market Works* (New York: New York Institute of Finance, 1990). A detailed description of the economics of foreign exchange markets can be found in P. R. Krugman and M. Obstfeld, *International Economics: Theory and Policy* (New York: Harper-Collins, 1994).

2. C. Forman, "Allied-Lyons to Post $269 Million Loss from Foreign Exchange as Dollar Soars," *The Wall Street Journal*, March 20, 1991, p. A17.

3. Data from Bank for International Settlements, *Central Bank Survey of Foreign Exchange and Derivatives Market Activity, 1995*. (Basle, Switzerland: BIS, May 1996).

4. Federal Reserve Bank of New York, *Summary of Results of U.S. Foreign Exchange Market Survey*, conducted April 1992 (New York: Federal Reserve Bank of New York, 1992).

5. For a recent comprehensive review see M. Taylor, "The Economics of Exchange Rates," *Journal of Economic Literature* 33, (1995), pp. 13–47.

6. Krugman and Obstfeld, *International Economics: Theory and Policy.*

7. M. Friedman, *Studies in the Quantity Theory of Money* (Chicago: University of Chicago Press, 1956). For an accessible explanation, see M. Friedman and R. Friedman, *Free to Choose* (London: Penguin Books, 1979), chap. 9.

8. Juan-Antino Morales, "Inflation Stabilization in Bolivia," in *Inflation Stabilization: The Experience of Israel, Argentina, Brazil, Bolivia, and Mexico*, ed. Michael Bruno et al. (Cambridge, MA: MIT Press, 1988); and The Economist, *World Book of Vital Statistics* (New York: Random House, 1990).

9. For reviews and recent articles, see L. H. Officer, "The Purchasing Power Parity Theory of Exchange Rates: A Review Article," International Monetary Fund staff papers, March 1976, pp. 1–60; Taylor, "The Economics of Exchange Rates"; H. J. Edison, J. E. Gagnon, and W. R. Melick, "Understanding the Empirical Literature on Purchasing Power Parity," *Journal of International Money and Finance* 16 (February 1997), pp. 1–18; J. R. Edison, "Multi-Country Evidence on the Behavior of Purchasing Power Parity under the Current Float," *Journal of International Money and Finance* 16 (February 1997), pp. 19–36; and K. Rogoff, "The Purchasing Power Parity Puzzle," *Journal of Economic Literature* 34 (1996), pp. 647–68.

10. For a summary of the evidence, see the survey by Taylor, "The Economics of Exchange Rates."

11. R. E. Cumby and M. Obstfeld, "A Note on Exchange Rate Expectations and Nominal Interest Differentials: A Test of the Fisher Hypothesis," *Journal of Finance*, June 1981, pp. 697–703.

12. Taylor, "The Economics of Exchange Rates."

13. See, H. L. Allen and M. P. Taylor, "Charts, Noise, and Fundamentals in the Foreign Exchange Market," *Economic Journal* 100 (1990), pp. 49–59; and T. Ito, "Foreign Exchange Rate Expectations: Micro Survey Data," *American Economic Review* 80 (1990), pp. 434–49.

14. For example, see E. Fama, "Forward Rates as Predictors of Future Spot Rates," *Journal of Financial Economics*, October 1976, pp. 361–77.

15. R. M. Levich, "The Efficiency of Markets for Foreign Exchange," in *International Finance*, ed. G. D. Gay and R. W. Kold (Richmond, VA: Robert F. Dane, Inc., 1983).

16. J. Williamson, *The Exchange Rate System* (Washington, DC: Institute for International Economics, 1983).

17. R. M. Levich, "Currency Forecasters Lose Their Way," *Euromoney*, August 1983, p. 140.

18. Rogoff, "The Purchasing Power Parity Puzzle."

19. C. Engel and J. D. Hamilton, "Long Swings in the Dollar: Are They in the Data and Do Markets Know It?"

American Economic Review, September 1990, pp. 689–713.

20. J. R. Carter and J. Gagne, "The Do's and Don'ts of International Countertrade," *Sloan Management Review*, Spring 1988, pp. 31–37.

21. D. S. Levine, "Got a Spare Destroyer Lying Around?" *World Trade* 10 (June 1997), pp. 34–35.

Chapter Ten

The International Monetary System

The Tragedy of the Congo (Zaire)

The Democratic Republic of the Congo, formerly known as Zaire, gained its independence from Belgium in 1960. The central African nation, rich in natural resources such as copper, seemed to have a promising future. If the country had simply sustained its pre-independence economic growth rate, its gross national product (GNP) would have been $1,400 per capita by 1997, making it one of the richest countries in Africa. Instead, by 1997, the country was a wreck. Battered by a brutal civil war that led to the ousting of the country's longtime dictator, Mobutu Sese Seko, the economy had shrunk to its 1958 level with a GNP per capita below $100. The annual inflation rate was in excess of 750 percent, an improvement from the 9,800 percent inflation rate recorded in 1994. Consequently, the local currency is almost worthless. Most transactions are made by barter or, for the lucky few, with US dollars. Infant mortality stood at a dismal 106 per thousand live births, and life expectancy stood at 47 years, roughly comparable to that of Europe in the Middle Ages.

What were the underlying causes of the economic, political, and social collapse of Zaire? While the story is a complex one, according to several influential critics, some of the blame must be placed at the feet of two multinational lending institutions, the International Monetary Fund (IMF) and the World Bank. Both institutions were established in 1944 at the famous Bretton Woods conference, which paved the way for the post-World War II international monetary system. The IMF was given the task of maintaining order in the international monetary system, while the role of the World Bank was to promote general economic development, particularly among the world's poorer nations. The IMF typically provides loans to countries whose currencies are losing value due to economic mismanagement. In return for these loans, the IMF imposes on debtor countries strict financial policies that are designed to rein in inflation and stabilize their economies. The World Bank has historically provided low interest rate loans to help countries build basic infrastructure. Both institutions are funded by subscriptions from member states, including significant contributions from all of the world's developed nations.

The IMF and the World Bank were major donors to post-independence Zaire. The IMF's involvement with Zaire dates to 1967, when the IMF approved Zaire's first economic stabilization plan, backed by a $27 million line of credit. Around the same time the World Bank began to make low interest rate infrastructure loans to the government of Mobutu Sese Seko. This was followed by a series of further plans and loans between 1976 and 1981. At the urging of the IMF, Zaire's currency was devalued five times during this period to help boost exports and reduce imports, while taxes were raised in an effort to balance Zaire's budget. IMF and other Western officials were also placed in key positions at the Zairian central bank, finance ministry, and office of debt management.

Despite all this help, Zaire's economy continued to deteriorate. By 1982, after 15 years of IMF assistance, Zaire had a lower GNP than in 1967 and faced default on its debt. Some critics, including Jeffery Sachs, the noted development economist from Harvard University, claim that this poor performance could in part be attributed to the policies imposed by the IMF, which included tax hikes, cuts in government subsidies, and periodic competitive currency devaluations. These policies, claim critics, were ill-suited to such a poor country and created a vicious cycle of economic decline. The tax hikes simply drove work into the "underground economy" or created a disincentive to work. As a consequence, government tax revenues dwindled and the budget deficit expanded, making it difficult for the government to service its debt obligations. By raising import prices, the devaluations helped fuel the phenomenon the IMF was trying to control: inflation. In turn, high inflation of both prices and wages soon brought ordinary Zairians into high tax brackets, which drove even more work into the underground economy and further shrank government tax revenues.

When explaining Zaire's malaise, others point to endemic corruption. In 1982, a senior IMF official in Zaire reported that President Mobutu Sese Seko and his cronies were systematically stealing IMF and World Bank loans. Later news reports suggest that Mobutu accumulated a personal fortune of $4 billion by the mid-1980s, making him one of the richest men in the world at that time.

In 1982, Zaire was initially suspended from further use of its IMF credit line. However, the position was reversed in 1983 when a new agreement was negotiated that included an additional $356 million in IMF loans. The loans were linked to a further devaluation of the

Zairian currency, more tax hikes, and cuts in government subsidies. The IMF's decision to turn a blind eye to the corruption problem and extend new loans was influenced by pressure from Western politicians who saw Mobutu's pro-Western regime as a bulwark against the spread of Marxism in Africa. By ignoring the corruption, the IMF could claim it was abiding by IMF rules, which stated the institution should offer only economic advice and stay out of internal political issues. The IMF's decision lent credence to Mobutu Sese Seko's government and enabled Zaire to attract more foreign loans. As a consequence, the country's overall foreign debt increased to $5 billion by the mid-1980s, up from $3 billion in 1978.

Unfortunately, the new loans and IMF policies did little to improve Zaire's economic performance, which continued to deteriorate. In 1987, Zaire was forced to abandon its agreement with the IMF due to food riots. The IMF negotiated another agreement for the 1989–1991 period, which included a further currency devaluation. This also failed to produce any tangible progress. The Zairian economy continued to implode while the country's civil war flared. In 1993, Zaire suspended its debt repayments, effectively going into default. In 1994, the World Bank announced it would shut down its operations in the country. About the same time, the IMF suspended Zaire's membership in the institution, making Zaire ineligible for further loans.

In 1997, after a long civil war, Mobutu Sese Seko was deposed from power. The new government inherited $14.6 billion of external debt, including debt arrears exceeding $1 billion. At a formal meeting chaired by the World Bank to discuss rescheduling of the country's debt, delegates from the new government claimed that the World Bank, IMF, and other institutions acted irresponsibly by lending money to Mobutu's regime despite evidence of both substantial corruption and Zaire's inability to service such a high level of debt. In an implicit acknowledgment that this may have been the case, the IMF and World Bank began telling debtor countries to stamp out corruption or lose access to IMF and World Bank loans.

http://www.sas.upenn.edu/African_Studies/Home_Page/WWW_Links.html

Sources: G. Fossedal, "The IMF's Role in Zaire's Decline," *The Wall Street Journal*, May 15, 1997, p. 22; J. Burns and M. Holman, "Mobutu Built a Fortune of $4 Billion from Looted Aid," *Financial Times*, May 12, 1997, p. 1; J. D. Sachs and R. I. Rotberg, "Help Congo Now," *New York Times*, May 29, 1997, p. 21; H. Dunphy, "IMF, World Bank Now Make Political Judgements," *Journal of Commerce*, August 21, 1997, p. 3A; and *CIA Annual Fact Book* (Washington, DC: CIA, 1998).

Introduction

Although we discussed the workings of the foreign exchange market in some depth in Chapter 9, we did not mention the international monetary system's role in determining exchange rates. Rather, we assumed that currencies were free to "float" against each other; that is, that a currency's relative value on the foreign exchange market is determined primarily by the impersonal market forces of demand and supply. In turn, we explained, the demand and supply of currencies is influenced by their respective countries' relative inflation rates and interest rates. Only at the end of the chapter, in our discussion of currency convertibility, did we admit the possibility that the foreign exchange market might not work as we had depicted.

Our explanation in Chapter 9 of how exchange rates are determined is oversimplified. Contrary to our implicit assumption, many currencies are not free to float against each other. Rather, exchange rates are determined within the context of an international monetary system in which the ability of many currencies to float against other currencies is limited by their respective governments or by intergovernmental arrangements. In 1997, only 51 of the world's viable currencies were freely floating; this includes the currencies of many of the world's larger industrial nations such as the United States, Canada, Japan, and Britain. A further 50 currencies were "pegged" to the exchange rates of certain major currencies—particularly the US dollar and the French franc—or to "baskets" of other currencies, while another 45 currencies were allowed by their governments to float as long as they stayed within a broad range relative to another currency, such as the US dollar.[1]

This chapter will explain how the international monetary system works and point out its implications for international business. To understand how the international monetary system works, we must review the system's evolution. We will begin with a discussion of the gold standard and its breakup during the 1930s. Then we will discuss the Bretton Woods conference, which took place in 1944. This established the basic framework for the post–World War II international monetary system. The Bretton Woods system called for fixed exchange rates against the US dollar. Under this **fixed exchange rate** system, the value of most currencies in terms of US dollars was fixed for long periods and allowed to change only under a specific set of circumstances. The Bretton Woods conference also created two major international institutions, both of which are discussed in the opening case, the International Monetary Fund (IMF) and the World Bank. The IMF was given the task of maintaining order in the international monetary system; the World Bank's role was to promote development.

Today, both these institutions continue to play major roles in the world economy. In 1997 and 1998, for example, the IMF helped several Asian countries deal with the dramatic decline in the value of their currencies that occurred during the Asian financial crisis that started in 1997. By early 1998, the IMF had programs in 75 countries. As the opening case on Zaire illustrates, however, there is a growing debate about the role of the IMF and to a lesser extent the World Bank and the appropriateness of their policies for many developing nations. In the case of Zaire, several prominent critics claim that IMF policy contributed to the country's economic misery, rather than curing it. The debate over the role of the IMF has taken on new urgency given the institution's extensive involvement in the economies of Asia and Eastern Europe during the latter part of the 1990s. Accordingly, we shall discuss the issue in depth.

The Bretton Woods system of fixed exchange rates collapsed in 1973. Since then, the world has operated with a mixed system in which some currencies are allowed to float freely, but many are either managed by government intervention or pegged to another currency. We will explain the reasons for the failure of the Bretton Woods system as well as the nature of the present system. We will also discuss how pegged exchange rate systems work.

Two decades after the breakdown of the Bretton Woods system, the debate continues over what kind of exchange rate regime is best for the world. Some economists advocate a system in which major currencies are allowed to float against each other. Others argue for a return to a fixed exchange rate regime similar to the one established at Bretton Woods. This debate is intense and important, and we will examine the arguments of both sides.

Finally, we will discuss the implications of all this material for international business. We will see how the exchange rate policy adopted by a government can have an important impact on the outlook for business operations in a given country. If government exchange rate policies result in a currency devaluation, for example, exporters based in that country may benefit as their products become more price competitive in foreign markets. Alternatively, importers will suffer from an increase in the price of their products. We will also look at how the policies adopted by the IMF can have an impact on the economic outlook for a country and, accordingly, on the costs and benefits of doing business in that country.

The Gold Standard

The gold standard had its origin in the use of gold coins as a medium of exchange, unit of account, and store of value—a practice that dates to ancient times. When international trade was limited in volume, payment for goods purchased from another country was typically made in gold or silver. However, as the volume of international trade expanded in the wake of the Industrial Revolution, a more convenient means of financing international trade was needed. Shipping large quantities of gold and silver around the world to finance international trade seemed impractical. The solution adopted was to arrange for payment in paper currency and for governments to agree to convert the paper currency into gold on demand at a fixed rate.

Nature of the Gold Standard

Pegging currencies to gold and guaranteeing convertibility is known as the **gold standard.** By 1880, most of the world's major trading nations, including Great Britain, Germany, Japan, and the United States, had adopted the gold standard. Given a common gold standard, the value of any currency in units of any other currency (the exchange rate) was easy to determine.

For example, under the gold standard, one US dollar was defined as equivalent to 23.22 grains of "fine" (pure) gold. Thus, one could, in theory, demand that the US government convert that one dollar into 23.22 grains of gold. Since there are 480 grains in an ounce, one ounce of gold cost \$20.67 (480/23.22). The amount of a currency needed to purchase one ounce of gold was referred to as the gold par value. The British pound was defined as containing 113 grains of fine gold. In other words, one ounce of gold cost £4.25 (480/113). From the gold par values of pounds and dollars, we can calculate what the exchange rate was for converting pounds into dollars; it was £1 = \$4.87 (i.e., \$20.67/£4.25).

The Strength of the Gold Standard

The great strength claimed for the gold standard was that it contained a powerful mechanism for achieving balance-of-trade equilibrium by all countries.[2] A country is said to be in balance-of-trade equilibrium when the income its residents earn from exports is equal to the money its residents pay to people in other countries for imports (i.e., the current account of its balance of payments is in balance).

Suppose there are only two countries in the world, Japan and the United States. Imagine Japan's trade balance is in surplus because it exports more to the United States than it imports from the United States. Japanese exporters are paid in US dollars, which they exchange for Japanese yen at a Japanese bank. The Japanese bank submits the dollars to the US government and demands payment of gold in return. (This is a simplification of what would occur, but it will make our point.)

Under the gold standard, when Japan has a trade surplus, there will be a net flow of gold from the United States to Japan. These gold flows automatically reduce the US money supply and swell Japan's money supply. As we saw in Chapter 9, there is a close connection between money supply growth and price inflation. An increase in money supply will raise prices in Japan, while a decrease in the US money supply will push US prices downward. The rise in the price of Japanese goods will decrease demand for these goods, while the fall in the price of US goods will increase demand for these goods. Thus, Japan will start to buy more from the United States, and the United States will buy less from Japan, until a balance-of-trade equilibrium is achieved.

This adjustment mechanism seems so simple and attractive that even today, more than half a century after the final collapse of the gold standard, there are people who believe the world should return to a gold standard.

The Period between the Wars, 1918–1939

The gold standard worked reasonably well from the 1870s until the start of World War I in 1914, when it was abandoned. During the war, several governments financed part of their massive military expenditures by printing money. This resulted in inflation, and by the war's end in 1918, price levels were higher everywhere. The United States returned to the gold standard in 1919, Great Britain in 1925, and France in 1928.

Great Britain returned to the gold standard by pegging the pound to gold at the prewar gold parity level of £4.25 per ounce, despite substantial inflation between 1914 and 1925. This priced British goods out of foreign markets, which pushed the country into a deep depression. When foreign holders of pounds lost confidence in Great Britain's commitment to maintaining its currency's value, they began converting their holdings of pounds into gold. The British government saw that it could not satisfy the demand for gold without seriously depleting its gold reserves, so it suspended convertibility in 1931.

The United States followed suit and left the gold standard in 1933 but returned to it in 1934, raising the dollar price of gold from $20.67 per ounce to $35 per ounce. Since more dollars were needed to buy an ounce of gold than before, the implication was that the dollar was worth less. This effectively amounted to a devaluation of the dollar relative to other currencies. Thus, before the devaluation the pound/dollar exchange rate was £1 = $4.87, but after the devaluation it was £1 = $8.24. By reducing the price of US exports and increasing the price of imports, the government was trying to create employment in the United States by boosting output. However, a number of other countries adopted a similar tactic, and in the cycle of competitive devaluations that soon emerged, no country could win.

The net result was the shattering of any remaining confidence in the system. With countries devaluing their currencies at will, one could no longer be certain how much gold a currency could buy. Instead of holding onto another country's currency, people often tried to change it into gold immediately, lest the country devalue its currency in the intervening period. This put pressure on the gold reserves of various countries, forcing them to suspend gold convertibility. By the start of World War II in 1939, the gold standard was dead.

The Bretton Woods System

In 1944, at the height of World War II, representatives from 44 countries met at Bretton Woods, New Hampshire, to design a new international monetary system. With the collapse of the gold standard and the Great Depression of the 1930s fresh in their minds, these statesmen were determined to build an enduring economic order that would facilitate postwar economic growth. There was general consensus that fixed exchange rates were desirable. In addition, the conference participants wanted to avoid the senseless competitive devaluations of the 1930s, and they recognized that the gold standard would not assure this. The major problem with the gold standard as previously constituted was that there was no multinational institution that could stop countries from engaging in competitive devaluations.

The agreement reached at Bretton Woods established two multinational institutions—the International Monetary Fund (IMF) and the World Bank. The task of the IMF would be to maintain order in the international monetary system, and that of the World Bank would be to promote general economic development. The Bretton Woods agreement also called for a system of fixed exchange rates that would be policed by the IMF. Under the agreement, all countries were to fix the value of their currency in terms of gold but were not required to exchange their currencies for gold. Only the dollar remained convertible into gold—at a price of $35 per ounce. Each country decided what it wanted its exchange rate to be vis-à-vis the dollar and then calculated the gold par value of the currency based on that selected dollar exchange rate. All participating countries agreed to try to maintain the value of their currencies within 1 percent of the par value by buying or selling currencies (or gold) as needed. For example, if foreign exchange dealers were selling more of a country's currency than they demanded, the government of that country would intervene in the foreign exchange markets, buying its currency in an attempt to increase demand and maintain its gold par value.

Another aspect of the Bretton Woods agreement was a commitment not to use devaluation as a weapon of competitive trade policy. However, if a currency became too weak to defend, a devaluation of up to 10 percent would be allowed without any formal approval by the IMF. Larger devaluations required IMF approval.

The Role of the IMF

The IMF Articles of Agreement were heavily influenced by the worldwide financial collapse, competitive devaluations, trade wars, high unemployment, hyperinflation in Germany and elsewhere, and general economic disintegration that occurred between the two world wars. The aim of the Bretton Woods agreement, of which the IMF was the main custodian, was to try to avoid a repetition of that chaos through a combination of discipline and flexibility.

Discipline

A fixed exchange rate regime imposes discipline in two ways. First, the need to maintain a fixed exchange rate puts a brake on competitive devaluations and brings stability to the world trade environment. Second, a fixed exchange rate regime imposes monetary discipline on countries, thereby curtailing price inflation. For example, consider what would happen under a fixed exchange rate regime if Great Britain rapidly increased its money supply by printing pounds. As explained in Chapter 9, the increase in money supply would lead to price inflation. Given fixed exchange rates, inflation would make British goods uncompetitive in world markets, while the prices of imports would become more attractive in Great Britain. The result would be a widening trade deficit in Great Britain, with the country importing more than it exports. To correct this trade imbalance under a fixed exchange rate regime, Great Britain would be required to restrict the rate of growth in its money supply to bring price inflation back under control. Thus, fixed exchange rates are seen as a mechanism for controlling inflation and imposing economic discipline on countries.

Flexibility

Although monetary discipline was a central objective of the Bretton Woods agreement, it was recognized that a rigid policy of fixed exchange rates would be too inflexible. It would probably break down just as the gold standard had. In some cases, a country's attempts to reduce its money supply growth and correct a persistent balance-of-payments deficit could force the country into recession and create high unemployment. The architects of the Bretton Woods agreement wanted to avoid high unemployment, so they built some limited flexibility into the system. Two major features of the IMF Articles of Agreement fostered this flexibility: IMF lending facilities and adjustable parities.

The IMF stood ready to lend foreign currencies to members to tide them over during short periods of balance-of-payments deficits, when a rapid tightening of monetary or fiscal policy would hurt domestic employment. A pool of gold and currencies contributed by IMF members provided the resources for these lending operations. A persistent balance-of-payments deficit can lead to a depletion of a country's reserves of foreign currency, forcing it to devalue its currency. By providing deficit-laden countries with short-term foreign currency loans, IMF funds would buy time for countries to bring down their inflation rates and reduce their balance-of-payments deficits. The belief was that such loans would reduce pressures for devaluation and allow for a more orderly and less painful adjustment.

Countries were to be allowed to borrow a limited amount from the IMF without adhering to any specific agreements. However, extensive drawings from IMF funds would require a country to agree to increasingly stringent IMF supervision of its macroeconomics policies. Heavy borrowers from the IMF must agree to monetary and fiscal conditions set down by the IMF, which typically included IMF-mandated targets on domestic money supply growth, exchange rate policy, tax policy, government spending, and so on.

The system of adjustable parities allows for the devaluation of a country's currency by more than 10 percent if the IMF agrees that the country's balance of payments is in "fundamental disequilibrium." The term *fundamental disequilibrium* was not defined in the IMF's Articles of Agreement, but it was intended to apply to countries that have suffered permanent adverse shifts in the demand for their products. Without a devaluation, such a country would experience high unemployment and a persistent trade deficit until the domestic price level had fallen far enough to restore a balance-of-payments equilibrium. The belief was that devaluation could help sidestep a painful adjustment process in such circumstances.

The Role of the World Bank

The official name for the World Bank is the International Bank for Reconstruction and Development (IBRD). When the Bretton Woods participants established the World Bank, the need to reconstruct the war-torn economies of Europe was foremost in their minds. The bank's initial mission was to help finance the building of Europe's economy by providing low-interest loans. As it turned out, the World Bank was overshadowed in this role by the Marshall Plan, under which the United States lent money directly to European nations to help them rebuild. So the bank turned its attention to "development" and began lending money to the nations of the Third World. In the 1950s, the bank concentrated on public-sector projects. Power station projects, road building, and other transportation investments were much in favor. During the 1960s, the bank also began to lend heavily in support of agriculture, education, population control, and urban development.

The bank lends money under two schemes. Under the IBRD scheme, money is raised through bond sales in the international capital market. Borrowers pay what the bank calls a market rate of interest—the bank's cost of funds plus a margin for expenses. This "market" rate is lower than commercial banks' market rate. Under the IBRD scheme, the bank offers low-interest loans to risky customers whose credit rating is often poor.

A second scheme is overseen by the International Development Agency (IDA), an arm of the bank created in 1960. Resources to fund IDA loans are raised through subscriptions from wealthy members such as the United States, Japan, and Germany. IDA loans go only to the poorest countries. (In 1991, those were defined as countries with annual incomes per capita of less than $580.) Borrowers have 50 years to repay at an interest rate of 1 percent a year.

The Collapse of the Fixed Exchange Rate System

The system of fixed exchange rates established at Bretton Woods worked well until the late 1960s, when it began to show signs of strain. The system finally collapsed in 1973, and since then we have had a managed-float system. To understand why the system collapsed, one must appreciate the special role of the US dollar in the system. As the only currency that could be converted into gold, and as the currency that served as the reference point for all others, the dollar occupied a central place in the system. Any pressure on the dollar to devalue could wreak havoc with the system, and that is what occurred.

Most economists trace the breakup of the fixed exchange rate system to the US macroeconomic policy package of 1965–1968.[3] To finance both the Vietnam conflict and his welfare programs, President Johnson backed an increase in US government spending that was not financed by an increase in taxes. Instead, it was financed by an increase in the money supply, which led to a rise in price inflation from less than 4 percent in 1966 to close to 9 percent by 1968. At the same time, the rise in government spending had stimulated the economy. With more money in their pockets, people spent more—particularly on imports—and the US trade balance began to deteriorate.

The increase in inflation and the worsening of the US foreign trade position gave rise to speculation in the foreign exchange market that the dollar would be devalued. Things came to a head in the spring of 1971 when US trade figures showed that for the first time since 1945, the United States was importing more than it was exporting. This set off massive purchases of deutsche marks in the foreign exchange market by speculators who guessed that the mark would be revalued against the dollar. On a single day, May 4, 1971, the Bundesbank (Germany's central bank) had to buy $1 billion to hold the dollar/deutsche mark exchange rate at its fixed exchange rate given the great demand for deutsche marks. On the morning of May 5, the Bundesbank purchased another $1 billion during the first hour of foreign exchange trading! At that point, the Bundesbank faced the inevitable and allowed its currency to float.

In the weeks following the decision to float the deutsche mark, the foreign exchange market became increasingly convinced that the dollar would have to be devalued. However, devaluation of the dollar was no easy matter. Under the Bretton Woods provisions, any other country could change its exchange rates against all currencies simply by fixing its dollar rate at a new level. But as the key currency in the system, the dollar could be devalued only if all countries agreed to simultaneously revalue against the dollar. And many countries did not want this, because it would make their products more expensive relative to US products.

To force the issue, President Nixon announced in August 1971 that the dollar was no longer convertible into gold. He also announced that a new 10 percent tax on imports would remain in effect until US trading partners agreed to revalue their currencies against the dollar. This brought the trading partners to the bargaining table, and in December 1971 an agreement was reached to devalue the dollar by about 8 percent against foreign currencies. The import tax was then removed.

The problem was not solved, however. The US balance-of-payments position continued to deteriorate throughout 1972, while the US money supply continued to expand at an inflationary rate. Speculation continued to grow that the dollar was still overvalued and that a second devaluation would be necessary. In anticipation, foreign exchange dealers began converting dollars to deutsche marks and other currencies. After a massive wave of speculation in February 1972, which culminated with European central banks spending $3.6 billion on March 1 to try to prevent their currencies from appreciating against the dollar, the foreign exchange market was closed. When the foreign exchange market reopened March 19, the currencies of Japan and most European countries were floating against the dollar, although many developing countries continued to peg their currency to the dollar, and many do to this day. At that time, the switch to a floating system was viewed as a temporary response to unmanageable speculation in the foreign exchange market. But it is now almost 30 years since the Bretton Woods system of fixed exchange rates collapsed, and the temporary solution looks permanent.

The Bretton Woods system had an Achilles' heel: The system could not work if its key currency, the US dollar, was under speculative attack. The Bretton Woods system could work only as long as the US inflation rate remained low and the United States did not run a balance-of-payments deficit. Once these things occurred, the system soon became strained to the breaking point.

The Floating Exchange Rate Regime

The floating exchange rate regime that followed the collapse of the fixed exchange rate system was formalized in January 1976 when IMF members met in Jamaica and agreed to the rules for the international monetary system that are in place today. We will discuss the Jamaica agreement before looking at how the floating exchange rate regime has operated.

The Jamaica Agreement

The Jamaica meeting revised the IMF's Articles of Agreement to reflect the new reality of floating exchange rates. The main elements of the Jamaica agreement include the following:

1. Floating rates were declared acceptable. IMF members were permitted to enter the foreign exchange market to even out "unwarranted" speculative fluctuations.
2. Gold was abandoned as a reserve asset. The IMF returned its gold reserves to members at the current market price, placing the proceeds in a trust fund to help poor nations. IMF members were permitted to sell their own gold reserves at the market price.
3. Total annual IMF quotas—the amount member countries contribute to the IMF—were increased to $41 billion. (Since then they have been increased to $195 billion while the membership of the IMF has been expanded to include 182 countries.) Non-oil-exporting, less developed countries were given greater access to IMF funds.

After Jamaica, the IMF continued its role of helping countries cope with macroeconomic and exchange rate problems, albeit within the context of a radically different exchange rate regime.

Exchange Rates since 1973

Since March 1973, exchange rates have become much more volatile and less predictable than they were between 1945 and 1973.[4] This volatility has been partly due to a number of unexpected shocks to the world monetary system, including:

1. The oil crisis in 1971, when the Organization of Petroleum Exporting Countries (OPEC) quadrupled the price of oil. The harmful effect of this on the US inflation rate and trade position resulted in a further decline in the value of the dollar.
2. The loss of confidence in the dollar that followed the rise of US inflation in 1977 and 1978.
3. The oil crisis of 1979, when OPEC once again increased the price of oil dramatically—this time it was doubled.
4. The unexpected rise in the dollar between 1980 and 1985, despite a deteriorating balance-of-payments picture.
5. The rapid fall of the US dollar against the Japanese yen and German deutsche mark between 1985 and 1987, and against the yen between 1993 and 1995.
6. The partial collapse of the European Monetary System in 1992.
7. The 1997 Asian currency crisis, when the Asian currencies of several countries, including South Korea, Indonesia, Malaysia, and Thailand, lost between 50 percent and 80 percent of their value against the US dollar in a few months.

COUNTRY FOCUS
The Rise and Fall of the Japanese Yen

In 1971, before the collapse of the Bretton Woods system of fixed exchange rates, one US dollar purchased 350 Japanese yen. In 1985, the exchange rate was $1=¥250; in 1990, it stood at $1=¥150; in 1993, it was $1=¥125; by March 1995 the exchange rate stood at $1=¥85. Much of the decline in the value of the dollar against the yen between 1971 and the 1995 can be explained by differences in relative inflation rates. Between 1983 and 1989, for example, inflation in Japan averaged 1.1 percent annually, whereas US price inflation ran at an average annual rate of 3.6 percent. Between 1988 and 1993, inflation in Japan ran at an average annual rate of 2 percent, compared to 4.1 percent in the United States. However, between 1993 and early 1995, the yen appreciated by 50 percent against the dollar. On a purchasing power parity basis, by mid-1995 the yen looked to be overvalued against the dollar by about 30 percent. This overvaluation suggested that differences in US and Japanese inflation rates were not sufficient to explain the rise of the yen during this period.

One explanation for the dramatic rise in the dollar value of the yen between 1993 and 1995 can be found in the behavior of Japanese financial institutions (particularly banks and insurance companies). Japan has long run a large balance-of-trade surplus with the United States. One consequence of this surplus is that many Japanese companies have found themselves holding lots of dollars (earned from the sale of products to US consumers). During the 1980s, Japanese financial institutions helped recycle these dollars by purchasing them from Japanese companies and reinvesting them in US stocks and bonds.

As long as Japanese financial institutions reinvested dollars in the United States, as opposed to selling them for yen, the dollar/yen exchange rate was relatively stable. However, in the early 1990s, Japan entered its worst recession since 1945. The severity of this recession was compounded by a collapse in Japanese stock and property prices, both of which fell more than 50 percent. This deflation hit Japanese financial institutions hard. Most Japanese financial institutions held many of their assets in the form of Japanese stock and property investments. With stock and property prices plunging, Japanese financial institutions saw their balance sheets deteriorate. Their weak balance sheets reduced the appetite of the financial institutions for risky investments, so they reduced their purchases of US assets and increased their investments in Japanese government bonds. In short, the financial institutions stopped recycling dollars earned from exports back to the United States. From 1993 onwards, they changed many of these dollars into yen and reinvested them in Japan. To make matters worse, many financial institutions started liquidating their holdings of US stocks and bonds to increase the funds available for investment in low-risk Japanese government bonds. Thus, after having doubled the value of their US investments in the two years before 1989, Japanese financial institutions reduced their foreign assets by 20 percent over the next four years.

Figure 10.1 summarizes the volatility of four major currencies—the German mark, Japanese yen, British pound, and US dollar—from 1970 to 1998. The Morgan Guaranty Index, the basis for Figure 10.1, represents the exchange rate of each of these currencies against a weighted basket of the currencies of 19 industrial countries (the index was set equal to 100 in 1990). All four currencies have been quite volatile over the period. The index value of the Japanese yen, for example, has ranged from a low of 44 in 1970 to a high of 170 in June 1995. Similarly, the US dollar index has been as low as 89.3 in 1995 and as high as 158 in 1985.

Perhaps the most interesting phenomena in Figure 10.1 are the rapid rise in the value of the dollar between 1980 and 1985 and its subsequent fall between 1985 and 1988, and the similar rise and fall in the value of the Japanese yen between 1990 and

http://www.accj.or.jp

The net effect of these developments was to reduce the demand for dollars and increase the demand for yen; hence the appreciation of the yen against the dollar. As the value of the yen accelerated in 1993, US assets began to look even less attractive (their valuation in yen declined). This increased the reluctance of Japanese institutions to invest in US stocks and bonds. Thus, by 1995 a self-fulfilling bandwagon effect had led to a massive rise in the value of the yen as Japanese investors held back from investing in US assets lest they see the value of those assets reduced by appreciation in the value of the yen.

By 1996, however, this process had reversed itself, and the yen started a slide against the dollar that would take it down to $1=¥140 by June 1998. As with the rise of the yen, much of the momentum for its subsequent fall can be laid at the feet of Japanese financial institutions. Throughout the 1990s, Japan remained mired in a persistent economic malaise characterized by weak domestic demand. The Japanese government repeatedly cut interest rates in an attempt to stimulate the domestic economy, but to no avail. Japan's economic situation deteriorated even further in 1997 when the collapse of several Asian economies reduced demand for Japanese goods and services. This event also threatened to push several Japanese banks with heavy loan exposure to troubled Asian economies into bankruptcy, and the Japanese stock market tumbled to the lowest levels in a decade. The Japanese government responded by further reducing interest rates, which by mid-1998 stood at a record low of 0.5

percent. At the same time, the US economy was entering its seventh year of robust economic expansion characterized by steady growth and inflation rates that were the lowest since the 1960s. In an attempt to rein in the US economy and keep inflation in check, the US Federal Reserve maintained relatively high interest rates in the United States.

As a consequence of these divergent interest rate policies, a significant interest rate differential had emerged between the United States and Japan by the late 1990s. US Treasury bonds offered a yield of 5.8 percent, while Japanese government bonds provided a yield of 1.4 percent. The US stock market continued its robust performance, while the Japanese stock market continued to flirt with its decadelong lows. Given these factors, Japanese financial institutions reversed their stance of the early 1990s and started plowing money into US bonds and stocks. The reduced demand for yen and increased demand for dollars naturally led to a decline in the value of the yen. As the yen declined against the dollar, the process began once more to take on a bandwagon effect, with many Japanese institutions investing in dollar-denominated bonds not only to exploit interest rate differentials, but also to profit from the continued decline of the yen against the dollar.

Sources: S. Brittan, "Tragi-comedy of the Rising Yen," *Financial Times,* March 3, 1994, p. 16; G. Baker, "Stay at Home Investors Drive the Yen's Rise," *Financial Times,* April 21, 1995, p. 5; "Dial C for Chaos," *The Economist,* March 11, 1995, pp. 69–70; and P. Abrahams, "Dreaming of a Way to Curb Slide," *Financial Times,* June 5, 1998, p. 2.

1998. We will briefly discuss the rise and fall of the dollar, since this tells us something about how the international monetary system has operated in recent years. The rise and recent fall of the yen are profiled in the accompanying Country Focus.[5]

The rise in the value of the dollar between 1980 and 1985 is particularly interesting because it occurred when the United States was running a large and growing trade deficit, importing substantially more than it exported. Conventional wisdom would suggest that the increased supply of dollars in the foreign exchange market as a result of the deficit should lead to a reduction in the value of the dollar, but it increased in value. Why? A number of favorable factors temporarily overcame the unfavorable effect of a trade deficit. Strong economic growth in the United States attracted heavy inflows of capital from foreign investors seeking high returns on capital assets. High

Figure 10.1

Long-Term Exchange
Rate Trends

Source: JP Morgan, Effective
Exchange Rate Index, 1970–98.
(1990=100.)

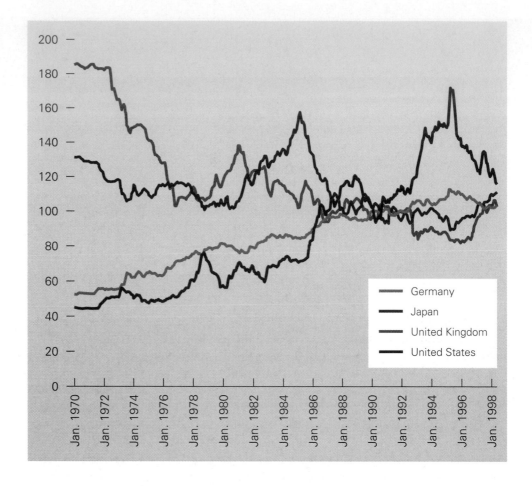

real interest rates attracted foreign investors seeking high returns on financial assets. At the same time, political turmoil in other parts of the world, along with relatively slow economic growth in the developed countries of Europe, helped create the view that the United States was a good place to invest. These inflows of capital increased the demand for dollars in the foreign exchange market, which pushed the value of the dollar upward against other currencies.

The fall in the value of the dollar between 1985 and 1988 was caused by a combination of government intervention and market forces. The rise in the dollar, which priced US goods out of foreign markets and made imports relatively cheap, had contributed to a dismal trade picture. In 1985, the United States posted a record-high trade deficit of over $160 billion. This led to growth in demands for protectionism in the United States. In September 1985, the finance ministers and central bank governors of the so-called Group of Five major industrial countries (Great Britain, France, Japan, Germany, and the United States) met at the Plaza Hotel in New York and reached what was later referred to as the Plaza Accord. They announced that it would be desirable for most major currencies to appreciate vis-à-vis the US dollar and pledged to intervene in the foreign exchange markets, selling dollars, to encourage this objective. The dollar had already begun to weaken in the summer of 1985, and this announcement further accelerated the decline.

The dollar continued to decline until early 1987. The governments of the Group of Five even began to worry that the dollar might decline too far, so the finance ministers of the Group of Five met in Paris in February 1987 and reached a new agreement known as the Louvre Accord. They agreed that exchange rates had been realigned sufficiently and pledged to support the stability of exchange rates around their current levels by intervening in the foreign exchange markets when necessary to buy and sell currency. Although the dollar continued to decline for a few months after the Louvre Accord, the rate of decline slowed, and by early 1988 the decline had ended. Except for a brief speculative flurry around the time of the Persian Gulf War in 1991, the dollar has been relatively stable since then against most major currencies with the notable exception of the Japanese yen.

Thus, we see that in recent history the value of the dollar has been determined by both market forces and government intervention. Under a floating exchange rate regime, market forces have produced a volatile dollar exchange rate. Governments have responded by intervening in the market—buying and selling dollars—in attempting to limit the market's volatility and to correct what they see as overvaluation (in 1985) or potential undervaluation (in 1987) of the dollar. The frequency of government intervention in the foreign exchange markets explains why the current system is often referred to as a **managed-float system** or a **dirty float system.**

Fixed versus Floating Exchange Rates

The breakdown of the Bretton Woods system has not stopped the debate about the relative merits of fixed versus floating exchange rate regimes. Disappointment with the system of floating rates in recent years has led to renewed debate about the merits of fixed exchange rates. In this section we review the arguments for fixed and floating exchange rate regimes.[6] We will discuss the case for floating rates before discussing why many commentators are disappointed with the experience under floating exchange rates and yearn for a system of fixed rates.

The Case for Floating Exchange Rates

The case for floating exchange rates has two main elements: monetary policy autonomy and automatic trade balance adjustments.

Monetary Policy Autonomy

It is argued that under a fixed system, a country's ability to expand or contract its money supply as it sees fit is limited by the need to maintain exchange rate parity. Monetary expansion can lead to inflation, which puts downward pressure on a fixed exchange rate (as predicted by PPP theory; see Chapter 9). Similarly, monetary contraction requires high interest rates (to reduce the demand for money). Higher interest rates lead to an inflow of money from abroad, which puts upward pressure on a fixed exchange rate. Thus, to maintain exchange rate parity under a fixed system, countries were limited in their ability to use monetary policy to expand or contract their economies.

Advocates of a floating exchange rate regime argue that removal of the obligation to maintain exchange rate parity would restore monetary control to a government. If a government faced with unemployment wanted to increase its money supply to stimulate domestic demand and reduce unemployment, it could do so unencumbered by the need to maintain its exchange rate. While monetary expansion might lead to inflation, this would lead to a depreciation in the country's currency. If PPP theory is correct, the resulting currency depreciation on the foreign exchange markets should offset the effects of inflation. Although under a floating exchange rate regime domestic inflation would have an impact on the exchange rate, it should have no impact on businesses' international cost competitiveness due to exchange rate depreciation. The rise in domestic costs should be exactly offset by the fall in the value of the country's currency on the foreign exchange markets. Similarly, a government could use monetary policy to contract the economy without worrying about the need to maintain parity.

Trade Balance Adjustments

Under the Bretton Woods system, if a country developed a permanent deficit in its balance of trade (importing more than it exported) that could not be corrected by domestic policy, this would require the IMF to agree to a currency devaluation. Critics of this system argue that the adjustment mechanism works much more smoothly under a floating exchange rate regime. They argue that if a country is running a trade deficit, the imbalance between the supply and demand of that country's currency in the foreign exchange markets (supply exceeding demand) will lead to depreciation in its exchange rate. In turn, by making its exports cheaper and its imports more expensive, an exchange rate depreciation should correct the trade deficit.

The Case for Fixed Exchange Rates

The case for fixed exchange rates rests on arguments about monetary discipline, speculation, uncertainty, and the lack of connection between the trade balance and exchange rates.

Monetary Discipline

We have already discussed the nature of monetary discipline inherent in a fixed exchange rate system when we discussed the Bretton Woods system. The need to maintain a fixed exchange rate parity ensures that governments do not expand their money supplies at inflationary rates. While advocates of floating rates argue that each country should be allowed to choose its own inflation rate (the monetary autonomy argument), advocates of fixed rates argue that governments all too often give in to political pressures and expand the monetary supply far too rapidly, causing unacceptably high price inflation. A fixed exchange rate regime will ensure that this does not occur.

Speculation

Critics of a floating exchange rate regime also argue that speculation can cause fluctuations in exchange rates. They point to the dollar's rapid rise and fall during the 1980s, which they claim had nothing to do with comparative inflation rates and the US trade deficit, but everything to do with speculation. They argue that when foreign exchange dealers see a currency depreciating, they tend to sell the currency in the expectation of future depreciation regardless of the currency's longer-term prospects. As more traders jump on the bandwagon, the expectations of depreciation are realized. Such destabilizing speculation tends to accentuate the fluctuations around the exchange rate's long-run value. It can damage a country's economy by distorting export and import prices. Thus, advocates of a fixed exchange rate regime argue that such a system will limit the destabilizing effects of speculation.

Uncertainty

Speculation also adds to the uncertainty surrounding future currency movements that characterizes floating exchange rate regimes. The unpredictability of exchange rate movements in the post-Bretton Woods era has made business planning difficult, and it makes exporting, importing, and foreign investment risky activities. Given a volatile exchange rate, international businesses do not know how to react to the changes—and often they do not react. Why change plans for exporting, importing, or foreign investment after a 6 percent fall in the dollar this month, when the dollar may rise 6 percent next month? This uncertainty, according to the critics, dampens the growth of international trade and investment. They argue that a fixed exchange rate, by eliminating such uncertainty, promotes the growth of international trade and investment. Advocates of a floating system reply that the forward exchange market insures against the risks associated with exchange rate fluctuations (see Chapter 9) so the adverse impact of uncertainty on the growth of international trade and investment has been overstated.

Trade Balance Adjustments

Those in favor of floating exchange rates argue that floating rates help adjust trade imbalances. Critics question the closeness of the link between the exchange rate and the trade balance. They claim trade deficits are determined by the balance between savings and investment in a country, not by the external value of its currency.[7] They argue that depreciation in a currency will lead to inflation (due to the resulting increase in import prices). This inflation will wipe out any apparent gains in cost competitiveness that come from currency depreciation. In other words, a depreciating exchange rate will not boost exports and reduce imports, as advocates of floating rates claim; it will simply boost price inflation. In support of this argument, those who favor floating rates point out that the 40 percent drop in the value of the dollar between 1985 and 1988 did not correct the US trade deficit. In reply, advocates of a floating exchange rate regime argue that between 1985 and 1992, the US trade deficit fell from over $160 billion to about $70 billion, and they attribute this in part to the decline in the value of the dollar.

Who Is Right?

Which side is right in the vigorous debate between those who favor a fixed exchange rate regime and those who favor a floating exchange rate regime? Economists cannot agree on this issue. From a business perspective, this is unfortunate because business, as a major player on the international trade and investment scene, has a large stake in the resolution of the debate. Would international business be better off under a fixed regime, or are flexible rates better? The evidence is not clear.

We do, however, know that a fixed exchange rate regime modeled along the lines of the Bretton Woods system will not work. Speculation ultimately broke the system, a phenomenon that advocates of fixed rate regimes claim is associated with floating exchange rates! Nevertheless, a different kind of fixed exchange rate system might be more enduring and might foster the kind of stability that would facilitate more rapid growth in international trade and investment. In the next section, we look at potential models for such a system and the problems with such systems.

Exchange Rate Regimes in Practice

A number of different exchange rate policies are pursued by governments around the world. These range from a pure "free float" where the exchange rate is determined by market forces to a pegged system that has some aspects of the pre-1973 Bretton Woods system of fixed exchange rates. Figure 10.2 summarizes the different exchange rate policies adopted by member states of the IMF in 1987. While over half of IMF members allow their currencies to float freely or intervene in only a limited way (the so-called managed float), a significant minority use a more inflexible system under which they peg their currencies to other currencies, such as the US dollar or the French franc. Still other countries have adopted a somewhat more flexible system under which their exchange rate is allowed to fluctuate against other currencies within a target zone. In this section, we will look more closely at the mechanics and implications of exchange rate regimes that rely on a currency peg or target zone.

Pegged Exchange Rates and Currency Boards

Under a pegged exchange rate regime a country will peg the value of its currency to that of a major currency so that, for example, as the US dollar rises in value, its own currency rises too. Pegged exchange rates are popular among many of the world's smaller nations. As with a full fixed exchange rate regime, the great virtue claimed for a pegged exchange rate regime is that it imposes monetary discipline on a country and leads to low inflation. For example, if Mexico pegs the value of the peso to that of the US dollar so that $1 is equal to 8.80 Mexican pesos, then the Mexican government must make sure the inflation rate in Mexico is similar to that in the United States. If

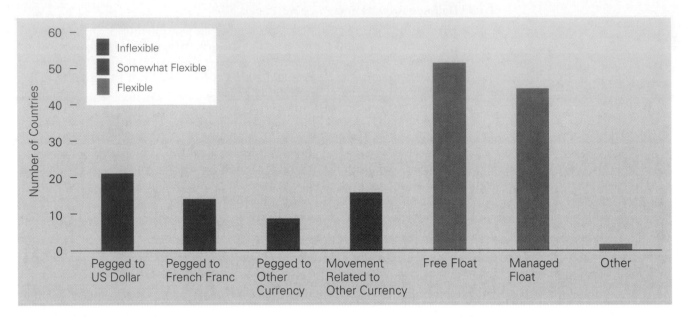

Figure 10.2

How IMF Members Determine Exchange Values

Source: IMF data.

the Mexican inflation rate is greater than the US inflation rate, this will lead to pressure to devalue the Mexican peso (i.e., to alter the peg). To maintain the peg, the Mexican government would be required to rein in inflation. Of course, for a pegged exchange rate to impose monetary discipline on a country, the country whose currency is chosen for the peg must also pursue sound monetary policy.

There is some evidence that adopting a pegged exchange rate regime does moderate inflationary pressures in a country. A recent IMF study concluded that countries with pegged exchange rates regimes had an average annual inflation rate of 8 percent, compared with 14 percent for intermediate regimes and 16 percent for floating regimes.[8] However, many countries operate with only a nominal peg and in practice are willing to devalue their currency rather than pursue a tight monetary policy. It can be very difficult for a smaller country to maintain a peg against another currency if capital is flowing out of the country and foreign exchange traders are speculating against the currency. Something like this occurred in 1997 when a combination of adverse capital flows and currency speculation forced several Asian countries, including Thailand and Malaysia, to abandon pegs against the US dollar and let their currencies float freely. Malaysia and Thailand would not have been in this position had they dealt with a number of problems that began to arise in their economies during the 1990s, including the excessive private-sector debt and expanding current account trade deficits.

Hong Kong's experience during the 1997 Asian currency crisis, however, has added a new dimension to the debate over how to manage a pegged exchange rate. During late 1997 when other Asian currencies were collapsing, Hong Kong maintained the value of its currency against the US dollar at around $1=HK$7.8 despite several concerted speculative attacks. Hong Kong's **currency board** has been given credit for this success. A country that introduces a currency board commits itself to converting its domestic currency on demand into another currency at a fixed exchange rate. To make this commitment credible, the currency board holds reserves of foreign currency equal at the fixed exchange rate to at least 100 percent of the domestic currency issued. The system used in Hong Kong means its currency must be fully backed by the US dollar at the specified exchange rate. This is still not a true fixed exchange rate regime, because the US dollar, and by extension the Hong Kong dollar, floats against other currencies, but it has some features of a fixed exchange rate regime.

Under this arrangement, the currency board can issue additional domestic notes and coins only when there are foreign exchange reserves to back it. This limits the ability of the government to print money and, thereby, create inflationary pressures. Under a strict currency board system, interest rates adjust automatically. If investors want to switch out of domestic currency into, for example, US dollars, the supply of domestic currency will shrink. This will cause interest rates to rise until it eventually becomes attractive for investors to hold the local currency again. In the case of Hong Kong, the interest rate on three-month deposits climbed as high as 20 percent in late 1997, as investors switched out of Hong Kong dollars and into US dollars. The dollar peg, however, held, and interest rates declined again.

Since its establishment in 1983, the Hong Kong currency board has weathered several storms, including the latest. This success seems to be persuading other countries in the developing world to consider a similar system. Argentina introduced a currency board in 1991, and Bulgaria, Estonia, and Lithuania have all gone down this road in recent years. Despite growing interest in the arrangement, however, critics are quick to point out that currency boards have their drawbacks.[9] If local inflation rates remain higher than the inflation rate in the country to which the currency is pegged, the currencies of countries with currency boards can become uncompetitive and overvalued. Also, under a currency board system, government lacks the ability to set interest rates. Interest rates in Hong Kong, for example, are effectively set by the US Federal Reserve. Despite these drawbacks, Hong Kong's success in avoiding the currency collapse that afflicted its Asian neighbors suggests that other developing countries may adopt a similar system.

Target Zones: The European Monetary System

An exchange rate system based on target zones involves a group of countries trying to keep their currencies within a predetermined range, or zone, of other currencies in the group. The exchange rate mechanism (ERM) that was a central part of the European Monetary System (EMS) of the European Union between 1979 and 1999 is the most famous example of this kind of system.

In our discussion of the European Union (EU) in Chapter 8, we noted that the EU is committed to monetary union, including establishment of a single currency. The process began January 1, 1999, and it should be completed by January 1, 2002.[10] A formal commitment to a common currency dates back only to the Maastricht Treaty in December 1991, but it has been an underlying theme in the EU and a subject of debate for some time. To establish a common currency, the EU needed to achieve convergence between the inflation rates and interest rates of its member states. The European Monetary System (EMS) was a mechanism for attaining this goal.[11]

When the EMS was created in March 1979, it was entrusted with three main objectives: (1) to create a zone of monetary stability in Europe by reducing exchange rate volatility and converging national interest rates; (2) to control inflation through the imposition of monetary discipline; (3) to coordinate exchange rate policies versus non-EU currencies such as the US dollar and the yen. In 1991, the objective of paving the way for introduction of a common currency in 1999 was added to this list. Two instruments were used to achieve these objectives, the European currency unit (ecu) and the exchange rate mechanism.

The Ecu and the ERM

The **ecu** was a basket of the EU currencies that served as the unit of account for the EMS. One ecu comprised a defined percentage of national currencies. The share of each country's currency in the ecu depended on the country's relative economic weight within the EC. Thus, for example, 30.1 percent of the ecu's value was established by the value of the German deutsche mark in 1989 because that was the estimate of Germany's relative strength and size within the EU economy at the time.

Until 1992, the exchange rate mechanism worked as follows: Each national currency in the EU was given a central rate vis-à-vis the ecu. For example, in September 1989, one ecu was equal to DM2.05853, to FFr6.90404, or to £0.739615. This central rate could be changed only by a commonly agreed realignment. From these central rates flowed a series of bilateral rates—the French franc against the Italian lira, the German deutsche mark against the British pound, and so on. For example, the given figures vis-à-vis the ecu indicate that the bilateral rate for exchanging deutsche marks into francs was DM1 = FFr3.3539 (i.e., FFr6.90404/DM2.05853). The bilateral rates formed a cat's cradle known as the ERM parity grid, which was the system's operational component. Before 1992, the rule was that a currency must not depart by more than 2.25 percent from its bilateral central rate with another ERM participating currency.

Intervention in the foreign exchange markets was compulsory whenever one currency hit its outer margin of fluctuation relative to another. The central banks of the countries issuing both currencies were supposed to intervene to keep their currencies within the 2.25 percent band. The central bank of the country with the stronger currency was supposed to buy the weaker currency, and vice versa. It tended to be left to the country with the weaker currency to take action.

To defend its currency against speculative pressure, each member could borrow almost unlimited amounts of foreign currency from other members for up to three months. A second line of defense included loans that could be extended for up to nine months, but the total amount available was limited to a pool of credit—originally about 14 billion ecus—and the size of the member's quota in the pool. Additional funds were available for maturities from two to five years from a second pool of about 11 billion ecus (originally). However, as a condition of using these funds, the borrowing member had to commit itself to correcting the economic policies causing its currency to deviate.

Performance of the System

Underlying the ERM were all the standard beliefs about the virtues of fixed rate regimes that we have discussed. EU members believed the system imposed monetary discipline, removed uncertainty, limited speculation, and promoted trade and investment within the EU. For most of the EMS's existence, it achieved these objectives. When the ERM was established, wide variations in national interest rates and inflation rates made its prospects seem shaky. For example, in early 1979, inflation was running at 2.7 percent in Germany and 12.1 percent in Italy. By 1992, however, both inflation rates and interest rates had converged somewhat. As this occurred, the need for intervention and realignments declined, and the system appeared to become more stable.

However, there had long been concern within the EU about the vulnerability of a fixed system to speculative pressures. Many of these concerns were realized dramatically in September 1992, when two of the major EMS currencies—the British pound and the Italian lira—were hit by waves of speculative pressure. Dealers in the foreign exchange market, believing a realignment of the pound and the lira within the ERM was imminent, started to sell pounds and lira and to purchase German deutsche marks. This led to a fall in the value of the pound and the lira against the mark on the foreign exchange markets. Although the central banks of Great Britain and Italy tried to defend their currencies by raising interest rates and buying back pounds and lira, they were unable to keep the values of their currencies within their respective ERM bands. As a consequence, first Great Britain and then Italy pulled out of the ERM, leaving the EMS on the brink of collapse.

The speculative pressures and subsequent withdrawal of Britain and Italy from the ERM led the EU countries to make two major changes to the EMS in August 1993.

First, the 2.25 percent fluctuation bands were widened to 15 percent. The idea was to loosen the rigidities in the system and hence reduce the scope for speculation. Second, the EMS no longer obligated the central banks of countries with strong currencies to intervene in the foreign exchange market to purchase weaker currencies. This change essentially recognized what had already occurred. In the crisis of September 1992, for example, the German central bank did not intervene aggressively to help keep the value of the British pound within the prescribed fluctuation bands.[12]

After 1993 this modified system again performed fairly well. The biggest strain occurred in March 1995 when speculative pressures again forced devaluations of two EMS currencies, this time the Spanish peseta and Portuguese escudo. This was a relatively minor crisis compared with that of September 1992.[13] By mid-1998, the system appeared to have delivered what it was designed to do—low and convergent inflation rates among the EU's member states. In 1998, the average annual rate fell to 1.6 percent (1993 = 4 percent), with the differential between the lowest and the highest rates at 1.7 percent (1993 = 5 percent). On January 1, 1999, the exchange rates of 11 EU states were fixed against national currencies and the euro became a full-fledged currency for commercial purposes, replacing the ecu basket of currencies. Until 2002, the euro will be used in financial markets only. On January 1, 2002, the single currency will become part of daily life, as euro notes and coins finally come into circulation.

Recent Activities and the Future of the IMF

Many observers initially believed that the collapse of the Bretton Woods system in 1973 would diminish the role of the IMF within the international monetary system. The IMF's original function was to provide a pool of money from which members could borrow, short term, to adjust their balance-of-payments position and maintain their exchange rate. Some believed the demand for short-term loans would be considerably diminished under a floating exchange rate regime. A trade deficit would presumably lead to a decline in a country's exchange rate, which would help reduce imports and boost exports. No temporary IMF adjustment loan would be needed. Consistent with this, after 1973 most industrialized countries tended to let the foreign exchange market determine exchange rates in response to demand and supply. No major industrial country has borrowed funds from the IMF since the mid-1970s, when Great Britain and Italy did. Since the early 1970s, the rapid development of global capital markets has allowed developed countries such as Great Britain and the United States to finance their deficits by borrowing private money, as opposed to drawing on IMF funds.

Despite these developments, the activities of the IMF have expanded over the past 30 years. By 1997, the IMF had 182 members, 75 of which had IMF programs in place, and the institution was implementing its largest rescue packages, committing over $110 billion in short-term loans to three troubled Asian countries—South Korea, Indonesia, and Thailand. The IMF's activities have expanded because periodic financial crises have continued to hit many economies in the post-Bretton Woods era, particularly among the world's developing nations. The IMF has repeatedly lent money to nations experiencing financial crises, requesting in return that the governments enact certain macroeconomic policies. As in the case of Zaire, which was profiled in the opening case, critics of the IMF claim these policies have not always been as beneficial as the IMF might have hoped and in some cases may have made things worse. With the recent extension of IMF loans to several Asian economies, these criticisms have reached new levels and a vigorous debate is under way as to the appropriate role of the IMF. In this section, we shall discuss some of the main challenges the IMF has had to deal with over the last quarter of a century and review the ongoing debate over the role of the IMF.

Financial Crises in the Post-Bretton Woods Era

A number of broad types of financial crisis have occurred over the last quarter of a century, many of which have required IMF involvement. A **currency crisis** occurs when a speculative attack on the exchange value of a currency results in a sharp depreciation in the value of the currency or forces authorities to expend large volumes of international currency reserves and sharply increase interest rates to defend the prevailing exchange rate. A **banking crisis** refers to a loss of confidence in the banking system that leads to a run on banks, as individuals and companies withdraw their deposits. A **foreign debt crisis** is a situation in which a country cannot service its foreign debt obligations, whether private-sector or government debt. These crises tend to have common underlying macroeconomic causes: high relative price inflation rates, a widening current account deficit, excessive expansion of domestic borrowing, and asset price inflation (such as sharp increases in stock and property prices).[14] At times, elements of currency, banking, and debt crises may be present simultaneously, as in the 1997 Asian crisis.

To assess the frequency of financial crises, the IMF recently looked at the macroeconomic performance of a group of 53 countries from 1975 to 1997 (22 of these countries were developed nations, and 31 were developing countries).[15] The IMF found there were 158 currency crises, including 55 episodes in which a country's currency declined by more than 25 percent. There were also 54 banking crises. The IMF's data, which are summarized in Figure 10.3, suggest that developing nations were more than twice as likely to experience currency and banking crises than developed nations. It is not surprising, therefore, that most of the IMF's loan activities since the mid-1970s have been targeted toward developing nations.

Four crises have been of particular significance: in terms of IMF involvement, the Third World debt crisis of the 1980s, the crisis experienced by Russia as it moved toward a market-based economic system, the 1995 Mexican currency crisis, and the 1997 Asian financial crisis. All four of these crises were the result of excessive foreign borrowings, a weak or poorly regulated banking system, and high inflation rates. These factors came together to trigger simultaneous debt and currency crises. Checking the resulting crises required IMF involvement.

Third World Debt Crisis

The Third World debt crisis had its roots in the OPEC oil price hikes of 1973 and 1979. These resulted in massive flows of funds from the major oil-importing nations (Germany, Japan, and the United States) to the oil-producing nations of OPEC. Commercial banks stepped in to recycle this money, borrowing from OPEC countries and lending to governments and businesses around the world. Much of the recycled money ended up in the form of loans to the governments of various Latin American and African nations. The loans were made on the basis of optimistic assessments about these nations' growth prospects, which did not materialize. Instead, Third World economic growth was choked off in the early 1980s by a combination of factors, including high inflation, rising short-term interest rates (which increased the costs of servicing the debt), and recession conditions in many industrialized nations (which were the markets for Third World goods).

The consequence was a Third World debt crisis of huge proportions. At one point it was calculated that commercial banks had over $1 trillion of bad debts on their books, debts that the debtor nations had no hope of paying off. Against this background, Mexico announced in 1982 that it could no longer service its $80 billion in international debt without an immediate new loan of $3 billion. Brazil quickly followed, revealing it could not meet the required payments on its borrowed $87 billion.

Figure 10.3

Incidence of Currency and
Banking Crises, 1975–1997

Source: International Monetary
Fund, *World Economic Outlook, 1998*
(Washington, DC: IMF, May 1998),
p. 77.

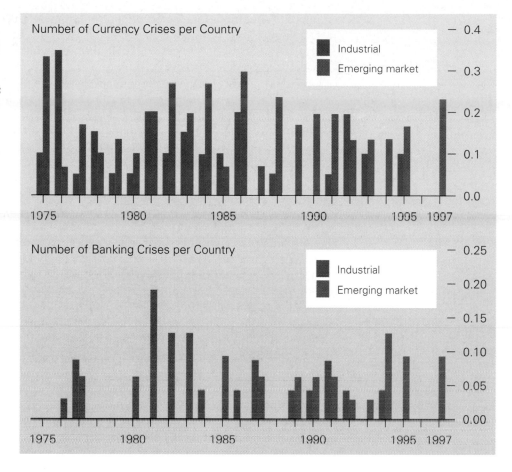

Then Argentina and several dozen other countries of lesser credit standings followed suit. The international monetary system faced a crisis of enormous dimensions.

Into the breach stepped the IMF. Together with several Western governments, particularly that of the United States, the IMF emerged as the key player in resolving the debt crisis. The deal with Mexico involved three elements: (1) rescheduling of Mexico's old debt, (2) new loans to Mexico from the IMF, the World Bank, and commercial banks, and (3) the Mexican government's agreement to abide by a set of IMF-dictated macroeconomic prescriptions for its economy, including tight control over the growth of the money supply and major cuts in government spending.

However, the IMF's solution to the debt crisis contained a major weakness: It depended on the rapid resumption of growth in the debtor nations. If this occurred, their capacity to repay debt would grow faster than their debt itself, and the crisis would be resolved. By the mid-1980s, it was clear this was not going to happen. The IMF-imposed macroeconomic policies did bring the trade deficits and inflation rates of many debtor nations under control, but it created sharp contractions in their economic growth rates.

It was apparent by 1989 that the debt problem was not going to be solved merely by rescheduling debt. In April of that year, the IMF endorsed a new approach that had been proposed by Nicholas Brady, the US Treasury secretary. The Brady Plan, as it became known, stated that debt reduction, as distinguished from debt rescheduling, was a necessary part of the solution and the IMF and World Bank would assume roles in financing it. The essence of the plan was that the IMF, the World Bank, and the Japanese government would each contribute $10 billion toward debt reduction. To gain access to these funds, a debtor nation would once again have to submit to imposed conditions for macroeconomic policy management and debt repayment. The first application of the Brady Plan was the Mexican debt reduction of 1989. The deal reduced Mexico's 1989 debt of $107 billion by about $15 billion and until 1995 was widely regarded as a success.[16]

Mexican Currency Crisis of 1995

The Mexican peso had been pegged to the dollar since the early 1980s when the International Monetary Fund had made it a condition for lending money to the Mexican government to help bail the country out of a 1982 financial crisis. Under the IMF-brokered arrangement, the peso had been allowed to trade within a tolerance band of plus or minus 3 percent against the dollar. The band was also permitted to "crawl" down daily, allowing for an annual peso depreciation of about 4 percent against the dollar. The IMF believed that the need to maintain the exchange rate within a fairly narrow trading band would force the Mexican government to adopt stringent financial policies to limit the growth in the money supply and contain inflation.

Until the early 1990s, it looked as if the IMF policy had worked. However, the strains were beginning to show by 1994. Since the mid-1980s, Mexican producer prices had risen 45 percent more than prices in the United States, and yet there had not been a corresponding adjustment in the exchange rate. By late 1994 , Mexico was running a $17 billion trade deficit, which amounted to some 6 percent of the country's gross domestic product and there had been an uncomfortably rapid expansion in the countries public and private-sector debt. Despite these strains, Mexican government officials had been stating publicly that they would support the peso's dollar peg at around $1 = 3.5 pesos by adopting appropriate monetary policies and by intervening in the currency markets if necessary. Encouraged by such public statements, $64 billion of foreign investment money poured into Mexico between 1990 and 1994 as corporations and mutual fund money managers sought to take advantage of the booming economy.

However, many currency traders concluded that the peso would have to be devalued, and they began to dump pesos on the foreign exchange market. The government tried to hold the line by buying pesos and selling dollars, but it lacked the foreign currency reserves required to halt the speculative tide (Mexico's foreign exchange reserves fell from $6 billion at the beginning of 1994 to under $3.5 billion at the end of the year). In mid-December 1994, the Mexican government abruptly announced a devaluation. Immediately, much of the short-term investment money that had flowed into Mexican stocks and bonds over the previous year reversed its course, as foreign investors bailed out of peso-denominated financial assets. This exacerbated the sell-off of the peso and contributed to the rapid 40 percent drop in its value.

The IMF stepped in again, this time arm in arm with the US government and the Bank for International Settlements. Together the three institutions pledged close to $50 billion to help Mexico stabilize the peso and to redeem $47 billion of public and private-sector debt that was set to mature in 1995. Of this amount, $20 billion came from the US government and another $18 billion came from the IMF (which made Mexico the largest recipient of IMF aid up until that point). Without the aid package, Mexico would probably have defaulted on its debt obligations, and the peso would have gone into free fall. As is normal in such cases, the IMF insisted on tight monetary policies and further cuts in public spending, both of which helped push the country into a deep recession. However, the recession was relatively short-lived, and by 1997 the country was once more on a growth path, had pared down its debt, and had paid back the $20 billion borrowed from the US government ahead of schedule.[17] (The accompanying Management Focus details how this crisis affected the US automobile industry, which before the crisis, was experiencing booming sales in Mexico.)

MANAGEMENT FOCUS   http://www.ford.com

The 1995 Mexican Peso Crisis and the Automobile Industry

In the euphoria that followed the January 1, 1994, implementation of the North American Free Trade Agreement (NAFTA) no industry looked set to gain more than the auto industry. Because of falling trade barriers and booming demand in Mexico, between January and October of 1994, US car exports to Mexico increased 500 percent. For all of 1994, Ford shipped 30,000 vehicles to Mexico, up from 6,000 in 1993. The company planned to ship 50,000 in 1995. General Motors and Chrysler also saw their shipments to Mexico surge in 1994 and were planning for even greater increases in 1995. Forecasts suggested that the number of vehicles sold in Mexico would rise to 1.2 million by 1999, up from 600,000 in 1994. With this growth in mind, not only had auto companies been exporting more to Mexico, but they also had been investing in Mexican-based production capacity both for serving the Mexican market and for exporting elsewhere. Among the biggest foreign investors were Chrysler, Ford, General Motors, Nissan, Mercedes-Benz, and Volkswagen.

In a few short days in December 1994, the euphoric bubble of the post-NAFTA boom was rudely burst by an unexpected decision on the part of the Mexican government to abandon a system of pegging the value of the peso at 3.5 to the dollar. Instead, the government decided to allow the peso to float freely against the dollar. In the weeks that followed this decision, the peso plummeted 40 percent, and by mid-January 1995 it was trading at 5.6 to the dollar.

As with many other industries, the impact on the auto industry was dramatic and immediate. By February 1995, the price of imported autos had risen by 40 percent. There had also been a substantial rise in the price of most autos assembled in Mexico, such as those coming off Ford's Cuautitlan plant, because many of these operations depended on parts imported from the United States and Canada. Demand for autos was further depressed by the Mexican government's economic austerity plan, introduced in March 1995 at the IMF's insistence. The plan tightened credit and raised interest rates.

Demand for autos slumped. Demand for the whole of 1995 was expected to come in between 30 and 50 percent below 1994 levels. Volkswagen, Nissan, Mercedes-Benz, and Ford temporarily closed their Mexican factories in January in expectation of the drop in demand. In other developments, Fiat of Italy pulled out of plans to build a new auto factory in Mexico, while Nissan announced plans to cut its 1995 production in Mexico from 210,000 to 180,000 vehicles. However, while the short-term outlook was grim, many auto companies may benefit from the fall in the value of the peso in the longer run. Although Volkswagen closed its Mexican plant for two weeks in January 1995, it estimated it would ship 175,000 Mexican-made vehicles to the US in 1995, 25,000 more than in 1994. Similarly, the big three United States automakers planned to keep their Mexican plants operating at full capacity in the second half of 1995 by boosting exports to the United States.

Sources: J. Darling and D. Nauss, "Stall in the Fast Lane," *Los Angeles Times*, February 19, 1995, p. 1; "Mexico Drops Efforts to Prop up Peso," *The Wall Street Journal*, December 23, 1994, p. A3; and R. Dornbusch, "We Have Salinas to Thank for the Peso Debacle," *Business Week*, January 16, 1995, p. 20.

Russian Ruble Crisis

The IMF's involvement in Russia came about as the result of a persistent decline in the value of the Russian ruble, which was the product of high inflation rates and growing public-sector debt. Between January 1992 and April 1995, the value of the ruble against the US dollar fell from $1=R125 to $1=R5130. This fall occurred while Russia was implementing an economic reform program designed to transform the country's crumbling centrally planned economy into a dynamic market economy. The reform program involved a number of steps, including the removal of price controls on January 1, 1992. Prices surged immediately and inflation was soon running at a *monthly* rate of about 30 percent. For the whole of 1992, the inflation rate in Russia was 3,000 percent. The annual rate for 1993 was approximately 900 percent.

Several factors contributed to Russia's high inflation. Prices had been held at artificially low levels by state planners during the Communist era. At the same time there was a shortage of many basic goods, so with nothing to spend their money on, many Russians simply hoarded rubles. After the liberalization of price controls, the country was suddenly awash in rubles chasing a still limited supply of goods. The result was to rapidly bid up prices. The inflationary fires that followed price liberalization were stoked by the Russian government itself. Unwilling to face the social consequences of the massive unemployment that would follow if many state-owned enterprises quickly were privatized, the government continued to subsidize the operations of many money-losing establishments. The result was a surge in the government's budget deficit. In the first quarter of 1992 the budget deficit amounted to 1.5 percent of the country's GDP. By the end of 1992 it had risen to 17 percent. Unable or unwilling to finance this deficit by raising taxes, the government found another solution—it printed money, which added fuel to the inflation fire.

With inflation rising, the ruble tumbled. By the end of 1992, the exchange rate was $1=R480. By the end of 1993 it was $1=R1,500. As 1994 progressed, it became increasingly evident that due to vigorous political opposition, the government would not be able to bring down its budget deficit as quickly as had been thought. By September the monthly inflation rate was accelerating. October started badly, with the ruble sliding more than 10 percent in value against the US dollar in the first ten days of the month. Then on October 11, the ruble plunged 21.5 percent against the dollar, reaching a value of $1=R3926 by the time the foreign exchange market closed!

Despite the announcement of a tough budget plan that placed tight controls on the money supply, the ruble continued to slide and by April 1995 the exchange rate stood at $1=R5120. However, by mid-1995 inflation was again on the way down. In June 1995 the monthly inflation rate was at a yearly low of 6.7 percent. Moreover, the ruble had recovered to stand at $1=R4559 by July 6. On that day the Russian government announced that it would intervene in the currency market to keep the ruble in a trading range of R4,3000 to R4,900 against the dollar. The Russian government felt that it was essential to maintain a relatively stable currency. They announced that the central bank would be able to draw upon $10 billion in foreign exchange reserves to defend the ruble against any speculative selling in Russia's relatively small foreign exchange market.

In the world of international finance, $10 billion is small change and it wasn't long before Russia found that its foreign exchange reserves were being depleted. It was at this point that the Russian government requested IMF loans. In February 1996, the IMF obliged with its second largest rescue effort after Mexico, a loan of $10 billion. In return for the loan, Russia agreed to limit the growth in its money supply, reduce public sector debt, increase government tax revenues, and peg the ruble to the dollar.

Initially the package seemed to have the desired effect. Inflation declined from nearly 50 percent in 1996 to about 15 percent in 1997; the exchange rate stayed within its predetermined band; and the balance of payments situation remained broadly favorable. And in 1997, the Russian economy grew for the first time since the breakup of the former Soviet Union, if only by a modest half of 1 percent of GDP. However, the public sector debt situation did not improve. The Russian government continued to spend more than it agreed to under IMF targets, while government tax revenues were much lower than projected. Low tax revenues were in part due to falling oil prices (the government collected tax on oil sales), in part due to the difficulties of collecting tax in an economy where so much economic activity was in the "underground economy," and partly due to a complex tax system that was peppered with loopholes. Currently available estimates indicate that in 1997, Russian federal government spending amounted to 18.3 percent of GDP, while revenues were only

10.8 percent of GDP, implying a deficit of 7.5 percent of GDP, which was financed by an expansion in public debt.

The IMF responded by suspending its scheduled payment to Russia in early 1998 pending reform of Russia's complex tax system, and a sustained attempt by the Russian government to cut public spending. This put further pressure on the Russian ruble, forcing the Russian central bank to raise interest rates on overnight loans to 150 percent. In June 1998, the US government indicated that it would support a new IMF bailout . The IMF was more circumspect, insisting instead that the Russian government push through a package of corporate tax increases and public spending cuts in order to balance the budget. The Russian government indicated that it would do so, and the IMF released a tranche of $640 million that had been suspended. The IMF followed this with an additional $11.2 billion loan designed to preserve the ruble's stability.

Almost as soon as the funding was announced, however, it began to unravel. The IMF loan required the Russian government to take concrete steps to raise personal tax rates, improve tax collections, and cut government spending. A bill containing the required legislative changes was sent to the Russian parliament, where it was emasculated by antigovernment forces. The IMF responded by withholding $800 million of its first $5.6 billion tranche, undermining the credibility of its own program. The Russian stock market plummeted on the news, closing 6.5 percent down. Selling of rubles accelerated. The central bank began hemorrhaging foreign exchange reserves as it tried to maintain the value of the ruble. Foreign exchange reserves fell by $1.4 billion in the first week of August alone, to $17 billion, while interest rates surged again.

Against this background, on the weekend of August 15–16, top Russian officials huddled together to develop a response to the most recent crisis. Their options were severely limited. The patience of the IMF had been exhausted. Foreign currency reserves were being rapidly depleted. Social tensions in the country were running high. Moreover, the government faced upcoming redemptions on $18 billion of domestic bonds, with no idea of where the money would come from.

On Monday, August 17, prime minister Kiriyenko announced the results of the weekend's conclave. Russia, he said, would restructure the domestic debt market, unilaterally transforming short-term debt into long-term debt. In other words, the government had decided to default on its debt commitments. The government also announced a 90-day moratorium on the repayment of private foreign debt, and stated that it would allow the ruble to decline by 34 percent against the U.S. dollar. In short, Russia had in effect turned its back on the IMF plan.

The effect on Russia was immediate. Overnight, shops marked up the price of goods by 20 percent. As the ruble plummeted, currency exchange points were only prepared to sell dollars at a rate of 9 rubles per dollar, rather than the new official exchange rate of 6.43 rubles to the dollar. As for Russian government debt, it lost 85 percent of its value in a matter of hours, leaving foreign and Russian holders of debt alike suddenly gaping at a huge black hole in their financial assets.[18]

The Asian Crisis

The financial crisis that erupted across Southeast Asia during the fall of 1997 has emerged as the biggest challenge ever. Holding the crisis in check required IMF loans to help the shattered economies of Indonesia, Thailand, and South Korea stabilize their currencies. In addition, although they did not request IMF loans, the economies of Japan, Malaysia, Singapore, and the Philippines were also badly hurt by the crisis.

The seeds of this crisis were sown during the previous decade when these countries were experiencing unprecedented economic growth. Although there were and remain important differences between the individual countries, a number of elements were common to most. Exports had long been the engine of economic growth in these countries. From 1990 to 1996, the value of exports from Malaysia had grown by 18 percent annually, Thai exports had grown by 16 percent per year, Singapore's by 15 percent, Hong Kong's by 14 percent, and those of South Korea and Indonesia by 12 percent annually.[19] The nature of these exports had also shifted in recent years from basic materials and products such as textiles to complex and increasingly high-technology products, such as automobiles, semiconductors, and consumer electronics.

The Investment Boom

The wealth created by export-led growth helped fuel an investment boom in commercial and residential property, industrial assets, and infrastructure. The value of commercial and residential real estate in cities such as Hong Kong and Bangkok started to soar. This fed a building boom the likes of which had never been seen in Asia. Heavy borrowing from banks financed much of this construction. As for industrial assets, the success of Asian exporters encouraged them to make bolder investments in industrial capacity. This was exemplified most clearly by South Korea's giant diversified conglomerates, or *chaebol*, many of which had ambitions to build a major position in the global automobile and semiconductor industries.

An added factor behind the investment boom in most Southeast Asian economies was the government. In many cases, the governments had embarked on huge infrastructure projects. In Malaysia, for example, a new government administrative center was being constructed in Putrajaya for M$20 billion (US$8 billion at the pre-July 1997 exchange rate), and the government was funding the development of a massive high-technology communications corridor and the huge Bakun dam, which at a cost of M$13.6 billion was to be the most expensive power generation plant in the country.[20]

Throughout the region, governments also encouraged private businesses to invest in certain sectors of the economy in accordance with "national goals" and "industrialization strategy." In South Korea, long a country where the government played a proactive role in private-sector investments, President Kim Young-Sam urged the *chaebol* to invest in new factories as a way of boosting economic growth. South Korea enjoyed an investment-led economic boom in the 1994–95 period, but at a cost. The *chaebol*, always reliant on heavy borrowings, built up massive debts that were equivalent, on average, to four times their equity.[21]

In Indonesia, President Suharto had long supported investments in a network of an estimated 300 businesses owned by his family and friends in a system known as "crony capitalism." Many of these businesses were granted lucrative monopolies by the president. For example, Suharto announced in 1995 that he had decided to build a national car and the car would be built by a company owned by one of his sons, Hutomo Mandala Putra, in association with Kia Motors of South Korea. To support the venture, a consortium of Indonesian banks was "ordered" by the government to offer almost $700 million in start-up loans to the company.[22]

By the mid-1990s, Southeast Asia was in the grips of an unprecedented investment boom, much of it financed with borrowed money. Between 1990 and 1995, gross domestic investment grew by 16.3 percent annually in Indonesia, 16 percent in Malaysia, 15.3 percent in Thailand, and 7.2 percent in South Korea. By comparison, investment grew by 4.1 percent annually over the same period in the United States and 0.8 percent in all high-income economies.[23] And the rate of investment accelerated in 1996. In Malaysia, for example, spending on investment accounted for a remarkable 43 percent of GDP in 1996.[24]

Excess Capacity

As the volume of investments ballooned during the 1990s, often at the bequest of national governments, the *quality* of many of these investments declined significantly. The investments often were made on the basis of unrealistic projections about future demand conditions. The result was significant excess capacity. For example, Korean *chaebol's* investments in semiconductor factories surged in 1994 and 1995 when a temporary global shortage of dynamic random access memory chips (DRAMs) led to sharp price increases for this product. However, supply shortages had disappeared by 1996 and excess capacity was beginning to make itself felt, just as the South Koreans started to bring new DRAM factories on stream. The results were predictable; prices for DRAMs plunged through the floor, and the earnings of South Korean DRAM manufacturers fell by 90 percent, which meant it was difficult for them to make scheduled payments on the debt they had taken on to build the extra capacity.[25]

In another example, a building boom in Thailand resulted in excess capacity in residential and commercial property. By early 1997, an estimated 365,000 apartment units were unoccupied in Bangkok. With another 100,000 units scheduled to be completed in 1997, years of excess demand in the Thai property market had been replaced by excess supply. By one estimate, by 1997 Bangkok's building boom had produced enough excess space to meet its residential and commercial needs for five years.[26]

The Debt Bomb

By early 1997 what was happening in the South Korean semiconductor industry and the Bangkok property market was being played out elsewhere in the region. Massive investments in industrial assets and property had created excess capacity and plunging prices, while leaving the companies that had made the investments groaning under huge debt burdens that they were now finding it difficult to service.

To make matters worse, much of the borrowing had been in US dollars, as opposed to local currencies. This had originally seemed like a smart move. Throughout the region, local currencies were pegged to the dollar, and interest rates on dollar borrowings were generally lower than rates on borrowings in domestic currency. Thus, it often made economic sense to borrow in dollars if the option was available. However, if the governments could not maintain the dollar peg and their currencies started to depreciate against the dollar, this would increase the size of the debt burden, when measured in the local currency. Currency depreciation would raise borrowing costs and could result in companies defaulting on their debt obligations.

Expanding Imports

A final complicating factor was that by the mid-1990s, although exports were still expanding across the region, imports were too. The investments in infrastructure, industrial capacity, and commercial real estate were sucking in foreign goods at unprecedented rates. To build infrastructure, factories, and office buildings, Southeast Asian countries were purchasing capital equipment and materials from America, Europe, and Japan. Many Southeast Asian states saw the current accounts of their balance of payments shift strongly into the red during the mid-1990s. By 1995, Indonesia was running a current account deficit that was equivalent to 3.5 percent of its GDP, Malaysia's was 5.9 percent, and Thailand's was 8.1 percent.[27] With deficits like these, it was increasingly difficult for the governments of these countries to maintain their currencies against the US dollar. If that peg could not be held, the local currency value of dollar-dominated debt would increase, raising the specter of large-scale default on debt service payments. The scene was now set for a potentially rapid economic meltdown.

The Crisis

The Asian meltdown began in mid-1997 in Thailand when it became clear that several key Thai financial institutions were on the verge of default (see the closing case to Chapter 9 for more details). These institutions had been borrowing dollars from international banks at low interest rates and lending Thai baht at higher interest rates to local property developers. However, due to speculative overbuilding, these developers could not sell their commercial and residential property, forcing them to default on their debt obligations. In turn, the Thai financial institutions seemed increasingly likely to default on their dollar-denominated debt obligations to international banks. Sensing the beginning of the crisis, foreign investors fled the Thai stock market, selling their positions and converting them into US dollars. The increased demand for dollars and increased supply of Thai baht, pushed down the dollar/Thai baht exchange rate, while the stock market plunged.

Seeing these developments, foreign exchange dealers and hedge funds started speculating against the baht, selling it short. For the previous 13 years, the Thai baht had been pegged to the US dollar at an exchange rate of about $1=Bt25. The Thai government tried to defend the peg, but only succeeded in depleting its foreign exchange reserves. On July 2, 1997, the Thai government abandoned its defense and announced it would allow the baht to float freely against the dollar. The baht started a slide that would bring the exchange rate down to $1=Bt55 by January 1998. As the baht declined, the Thai debt bomb exploded. The 55 percent decline in the value of the baht against the dollar doubled the amount of baht required to serve the dollar-denominated debt commitments taken on by Thai financial institutions and businesses. This increased the probability of corporate bankruptcies and further pushed down the battered Thai stock market. The Thailand Set stock market index ultimately declined from 787 in January 1997 to a low of 337 in December of that year, on top of a 45 percent decline in 1996.

On July 28, the Thai government called in the International Monetary Fund. With its foreign exchange reserves depleted, Thailand lacked the foreign currency needed to finance its international trade and service debt commitments and desperately needed of the capital the IMF could provide. It also needed to restore international confidence in its currency and needed the credibility associated with gaining access to IMF funds. Without IMF loans, the baht likely would increase its free fall against the US dollar, and the whole country might go into default. The IMF agreed to provide the Thai government with $17.2 billion in loans, but the conditions were restrictive.[28] The IMF required the Thai government to increase taxes, cut public spending, privatize several state-owned businesses, and raise interest rates—all steps designed to cool Thailand's overheated economy. The IMF also required Thailand to close illiquid financial institutions. In December 1997, the government shut 56 financial institutions, laying off 16,000 people, and further deepening the recession that now gripped the country.

Following the devaluation of the Thai baht, wave after wave of speculation hit other Asian currencies. One after another in a period of weeks, the Malaysian ringgit, Indonesian rupiah, and the Singapore dollar were all marked sharply lower. With its foreign exchange reserves down to $28 billion, Malaysia let the ringgit float on July 14, 1997. Before the devaluation, the ringgit was trading at $1=2.525 ringgit. Six months later it had declined to $1=4.15 ringgit. Singapore followed on July 17, and the Singapore dollar quickly dropped in value from $1=S$1.495 before the devaluation to $1=S$2.68 a few days later. Next up was Indonesia, whose rupiah was allowed to float August 14. For Indonesia, this was the beginning of a precipitous decline in the value of its currency, which was to fall from $1=2,400 rupiah in August 1997 to $1=10,000 rupiah on January 6, 1998, a loss of 75 percent.

With the exception of Singapore, whose economy is probably the most stable in the region, these devaluations were driven by factors similar to those behind the earlier devaluation of the Thai baht—a combination of excess investment, high borrowings, much of it in dollar-denominated debt, and a deteriorating balance-of-payments position. Although both Malaysia and Singapore were able to halt the slide in their currencies and stock markets without the help of the IMF, Indonesia was not. Indonesia was struggling with a private-sector, dollar-denominated debt of close to $80 billion. With the rupiah sliding precipitously almost every day, the cost of servicing this debt was exploding, pushing more Indonesian companies into technical default.

On October 31, 1997, the IMF announced that it had put together a $37 billion rescue deal for Indonesia in conjunction with the World Bank and the Asian Development Bank. In return, the Indonesian government agreed to close a number of troubled banks, reduce public spending, remove government subsidies on basic foodstuffs and energy, balance the budget, and unravel the crony capitalism that was so widespread in Indonesia. But the government of President Suharto appeared to backtrack several times on commitments made to the IMF. This precipitated further declines in the Indonesian currency and stock markets. Ultimately, Suharto caved in and removed costly government subsidies, only to see the country dissolve into chaos as the populace took to the streets to protest the resulting price increases. This unleashed a chain of events that led to Suharto's removal from power in May 1998.

The final domino to fall was South Korea (for further details, see the Country Focus in Chapter 9). During the 1990s, South Korean companies had built up huge debt loads as they invested heavily in new industrial capacity. Now they found they had too much industrial capacity and could not generate the income required to service their debt. South Korean banks and companies had also made the mistake of borrowing in dollars, much of it in the form of short-term loans that would come due within a year. Thus, when the Korean won started to decline in the fall of 1997 in sympathy with the problems elsewhere in Asia, South Korean companies saw their debt obligations balloon. Several large companies were forced to file for bankruptcy. This triggered a decline in the South Korean currency and stock market that was difficult to halt. The South Korean central bank tried to keep the dollar/won exchange rate above $1 = W1,000 but found that this only depleted its foreign exchange reserves. On November 17, the Korean central bank gave up the defense of the won, which quickly fell to $1 = W1,500.

With its economy of the verge of collapse, the South Korean government on November 21 requested $20 billion in standby loans from the IMF. As the negotiations progressed, it became apparent that South Korea was going to need far more than $20 billion. Among other problems, the country's short-term foreign debt was found to be twice as large as previously thought at close to $100 billion, while the country's foreign exchange reserves were down to less than $6 billion. On December 3, the IMF and South Korean government reached a deal to lend $55 billion to the country. The agreement with the IMF called for the South Koreans to open their economy and banking system to foreign investors. South Korea also pledged to restrain the *chaebol* by reducing their share of bank financing and requiring them to publish consolidated financial statements and undergo annual independent external audits. On trade liberalization, the IMF said South Korea will comply with its commitments to the World Trade Organization to eliminate trade-related subsidies and restrictive import licensing and will streamline its import certification procedures, all of which should open the South Korean economy to greater foreign competition.[29]

Evaluating the IMF's Policy Prescriptions

By early 1998, the IMF was committing over $110 billion in short-term loans to three Asian countries: South Korea, Indonesia, and Thailand. This was on top of the $20 billion package the IMF gave to Mexico in 1995 and the $10 billion loan to Russia. All these loan packages came with conditions attached. In general, the IMF insists on a combination of tight macroeconomic policies, including cuts in public spending, higher interest rates, and tight monetary policy. It also often pushes for the deregulation of sectors formerly protected from domestic and foreign competition, privatization of state-owned assets, and better financial reporting from the banking sector. In general, these policies are designed to cool overheated economies by reining in inflation and reducing government spending and debt. Recently, this set of policy prescriptions has come in for tough criticisms from many Western observers.[30]

One criticism is that the IMF's "one-size-fits-all" approach to macroeconomic policy is inappropriate for many countries. This point was made in the opening case when we looked at how the IMF's policies toward Zaire may have made things worse rather than better. In the recent Asian crisis, critics argue that the tight macroeconomic policies imposed by the IMF are not well suited to countries that are suffering not from excessive government spending and inflation, but from a private-sector debt crisis with deflationary undertones.[31] In South Korea, for example, the government has been running a budget surplus for years (it was 4 percent of South Korea's GDP in the 1994–1996 period) and inflation is low at about 5 percent. South Korea has the second strongest financial position of any country in the Organization for Economic Cooperation and Development. Despite this, say critics, the IMF is insisting on applying the same policies that it applies to countries suffering from high inflation. The IMF is requiring South Korea to maintain an inflation rate of 5 percent. However, given the collapse in the value of its currency and the subsequent rise in price for imports such as oil, inflationary pressures will inevitably increase in South Korea. So to hit a 5 percent inflation rate, the South Koreans are being forced to apply an unnecessarily tight monetary policy. Short-term interest rates in South Korea jumped from 12.5 percent to 21 percent immediately after the country signed its initial deal with the IMF. Increasing interest rates make it even more difficult for companies to service their already excessive short-term debt obligations, so the cure prescribed by the IMF may actually increase the probability of widespread corporate defaults, not reduce them.

The IMF rejects this criticism. According to the IMF, the critical task is to rebuild confidence in the won. Once this has been achieved, the won will recover from its oversold levels. This will reduce the size of South Korea's dollar-denominated debt burden when expressed in won, making it easier for companies to service their dollar-denominated debt. The IMF also argues that by requiring South Korea to remove restrictions on foreign direct investment, foreign capital will flow into the country to take advantage of cheap assets. This, too, will increase demand for the Korean currency and help to improve the dollar/won exchange rate.

A second criticism of the IMF is that its rescue efforts are exacerbating a problem known to economists as **moral hazard.** Moral hazard arises when people behave recklessly because they know they will be saved if things go wrong. Critics point out that many Japanese and Western banks were far too willing to lend large amounts of capital to over-leveraged Asian companies during the boom years of the 1990s. These critics argue that the banks should now be forced to pay the price for their rash lending policies, even if that means some banks must shut down.[32] Only by taking such drastic action, the argument goes, will banks learn the error of their ways and not engage in rash lending in the future. By providing support to these countries, the IMF is reducing the probability of debt default and in effect bailing out the banks whose loans gave rise to this situation.

This argument ignores two critical points. First, if some Japanese or Western banks with heavy exposure to the troubled Asian economies were forced to write off their loans due to widespread debt default, the impact would be difficult to contain. The failure of large Japanese banks, for example, could trigger a meltdown in the Japanese financial markets. This would almost inevitably lead to a serious decline in stock markets around the world. That is the very risk the IMF was trying to avoid by stepping in with financial support. Second, it is incorrect to imply that some banks have not had to pay the price for rash lending policies. The IMF has insisted on the closure of banks in South Korea, Thailand, and Indonesia. Foreign banks with short-term loans outstanding to South Korean enterprises have been forced by circumstances to reschedule those loans at interest rates that do not compensate for the extension of the loan maturity.

The final criticism of the IMF is that it has become too powerful for an institution that lacks any real mechanism for accountability.[33] By the end of 1997, the IMF was engaged in loan programs in 75 developing countries that collectively contain 1.4 billion people. The IMF was determining macroeconomic policies in those countries, yet according to critics such as noted Harvard economist Jeffery Sachs, the IMF, with a staff of under 1,000, lacks the expertise required to do a good job. Evidence of this, according to Sachs, can be found in the fact that the IMF was singing the praises of the Thai and South Korean governments only months before both countries lurched into crisis. Then the IMF put together a draconian program for South Korea without having deep knowledge of the country. Sachs's solution to this problem is to reform the IMF so it makes greater use of outside experts and its operations are open to great outside scrutiny.

As with many debates about international economics, it is not clear which side has the winning hand about the appropriateness of IMF policies. There are cases where one can argue that IMF policies have been counterproductive, such as Zaire, which we discussed in the opening case. But the IMF can point to some notable accomplishments, including its success in containing the Asian crisis, which could have rocked the global international monetary system to its core. Similarly, many observers give the IMF credit for its deft handling of politically difficult situations, such as the Russian ruble crisis, and for successfully promoting a free market philosophy.

IMPLICATIONS FOR BUSINESS

The implications for international businesses of the material discussed in this chapter fall into three main areas: currency management, business strategy, and corporate–government relations.

Currency Management

An obvious implication with regard to currency management is that companies must recognize that the foreign exchange market does not work quite as depicted in Chapter 9. The current system is a mixed system in which a combination of government intervention and speculative activity can drive the foreign exchange market. Companies engaged in significant foreign exchange activities need to be aware of this and to adjust their foreign exchange transactions accordingly. For example, the currency management unit of Caterpillar claims it made millions of dollars in the hours following the announcement of the Plaza Accord by selling dollars and buying currencies that it expected to appreciate on the foreign exchange market following government intervention.

We have seen how under the present system, speculative buying and selling of currencies can create very volatile movements in exchange rates (as exhibited by the rise and fall of the dollar during the 1980s). Contrary to the predictions of the purchasing power parity theory (see Chapter 9), we have seen that exchange rate movements during the 1980s, at least with regard to the dollar, did not seem to be strongly influenced by relative inflation rates. Insofar as volatile exchange rates increase foreign exchange risk, this is not good news for business. On the other hand, as we saw in Chapter 9, the foreign exchange market has developed a number of instruments, such as the forward market and swaps, that can help to insure against foreign exchange risk. Not surprisingly, use of these instruments has increased markedly since the breakdown of the Bretton Woods system in 1973.

Business Strategy

The volatility of the present global exchange rate regime presents a conundrum for international businesses. Exchange rate movements are difficult to predict, and yet their movement can have a major impact on a business's competitive position. Faced with uncertainty about the future value of currencies, firms can utilize the forward exchange market. However, the forward exchange market is far from perfect as a predictor of future exchange rates (see Chapter 9). It is also difficult if not impossible to get adequate insurance coverage for exchange rate changes that might occur several years in the future. The forward market tends to offer coverage for exchange rate changes a few months—not years—ahead. Given this, it makes sense to pursue strategies that will increase the company's strategic flexibility in the face of unpredictable exchange rate movements.

Maintaining strategic flexibility can take the form of dispersing production to different locations around the globe as a hedge against currency fluctuations. Consider the case of Daimler-Benz, Germany's export-oriented automobile and aerospace company. In June 1995, the company stunned the German business community when it announced it expected to post a severe loss in 1995 of about $720 million. The cause was Germany's strong currency, which had appreciated by 4 percent against a basket of major currencies since the beginning of 1995 and had risen by over 30 percent against the US dollar since late 1994. By mid-1995, the exchange rate against the dollar stood at $1=DM1.38. Daimler's management believed it could not make money with an exchange rate under $1=DM1.60. Daimler's senior managers concluded that the appreciation of the mark against the dollar was probably permanent, so they decided to move substantial production outside of Germany and increase purchasing of foreign components. The idea was to reduce the vulnerability of the company to future exchange rate movements. The Mercedes-Benz division has begun to implement this move. Even before its acquisition of Chrysler Corporation in 1998, Mercedes planned to produce 10 percent of its cars outside of Germany by 2000, mostly in the United States.[34] Similarly, the move by Japanese automobile companies to expand their productive capacity in the United States and Europe can be seen in the context of the increase in the value of the yen between 1985 and 1995, which increased the price of Japanese exports. For the Japanese companies, building production capacity overseas is a hedge against continued appreciation of the yen (as well as against trade barriers).

Another way of building strategic flexibility involves contracting out manufacturing. This allows a company to shift suppliers from country to country in response to changes in relative costs brought about by exchange rate movements. However, this kind of strategy works only for low-value-added manufacturing (e.g., textiles), in which the individual manufacturers have few if any firm-specific skills that contribute to the value of the product. It is inappropriate for high-value-added manufacturing, in which firm-specific technology and skills add significant value to the product (e.g., the heavy equipment industry) and in which switching costs are correspondingly high. For high-value-added manufacturing, switching suppliers will lead to a reduction in the value that is added, which may offset any cost gains arising from exchange rate fluctuations.

The roles of the IMF and the World Bank in the present international monetary system also have implications for business strategy. Increasingly, the IMF has been acting as the macroeconomic policeman of the world economy, insisting that countries seeking significant borrowings adopt IMF-mandated macroeconomic policies. These policies typically include anti-inflationary monetary policies and reductions in government spending. In the short run, such policies usually result in a sharp contraction of demand. International businesses selling or producing in such countries need to be aware of this and plan accordingly. In the long run, the kind of policies imposed by the IMF can promote economic growth and an expansion of demand, which create opportunities for international business.

Corporate–Government Relations

As major players in the international trade and investment environment, businesses can influence government policy toward the international monetary system. For example, intense government lobbying by US exporters helped convince the US government that intervention in the foreign exchange market was necessary. Similarly, much of the impetus behind establishment of the exchange rate mechanism of the European monetary system came from European business-people, who understood the costs of volatile exchange rates.

With this in mind, business can and should use its influence to promote an international monetary system that facilitates the growth of international trade and investment. Whether a fixed or floating regime is optimal is a subject for debate. However, exchange rate volatility such as the world experienced during the 1980s and 1990s creates an environment less conducive to international trade and investment than one with more stable exchange rates. Therefore, it would seem to be in the interests of international business to promote an international monetary system that minimizes volatile exchange rate movements, particularly when those movements are unrelated to long-run economic fundamentals.

Chapter Summary

This chapter explained the workings of the international monetary system and pointed out its implications for international business. This chapter made the following points:

1. The gold standard is a monetary standard that pegs currencies to gold and guarantees convertibility to gold.

2. It was thought that the gold standard contained an automatic mechanism that contributed to the simultaneous achievement of a balance-of-payments equilibrium by all countries.

3. The gold standard broke down during the 1930s as countries engaged in competitive devaluations.

4. The Bretton Woods system of fixed exchange rates was established in 1944. The US dollar was the central currency of this system; the value of every other currency was pegged to its value. Significant exchange rate devaluations were allowed only with the permission of the IMF.

5. The role of the IMF was to maintain order in the international monetary system (*i*) to avoid a repetition of the competitive devaluations of the 1930s and (*ii*) to control price inflation by imposing monetary discipline on countries.

6. To build flexibility into the system, the IMF stood ready to lend countries funds to help protect their currency on the foreign exchange market in the face of speculative pressure, and to assist countries in correcting a fundamental disequilibrium in their balance-of-payments position.

7. The fixed exchange rate system collapsed in 1973, primarily due to speculative pressure on the dollar following a rise in US inflation and a growing US balance-of-trade deficit.

8. Since 1973 the world has operated with a floating exchange rate regime, and exchange rates have become more volatile and far less predictable. Volatile exchange rate movements have helped reopen the debate over the merits of fixed and floating systems.

9. The case for a floating exchange rate regime claims: (*i*) that such a system gives countries autonomy regarding their monetary policy and (*ii*) that floating exchange rates facilitate smooth adjustment of trade imbalances.

10. The case for a fixed exchange rate regime claims: (*i*) that the need to maintain a fixed exchange rate imposes monetary discipline on a country, (*ii*) that floating exchange rate regimes are vulnerable to speculative pressure, (*iii*) that the uncertainty that accompanies floating exchange rates dampens the growth of international trade and investment, and (*iv*) that far from correcting trade imbalances, depreciating a currency on the foreign exchange market tends to cause price inflation.

11. In today's international monetary system, some countries have adopted floating exchange rates, some have pegged their currency to another currency, such as the US dollar, and some have pegged their currency to a basket of other currencies, allowing their currency to fluctuate within a zone around the basket.

12. In the post-Bretton Woods era, the IMF has continued to play an important role in helping countries navigate their way through financial crises by lending significant capital to embattled governments and by requiring them to adopt certain macroeconomic policies.

13. There is an important debate taking place over the appropriateness of IMF-mandated macroeconomic policies. Critics charge that the IMF often imposes inappropriate conditions on developing nations that are the recipients of its loans.

14. The present managed-float system of exchange rate determination has increased the importance of currency management in international businesses.

15. The volatility of exchange rates under the present managed-float system creates both opportunities and threats. One way of responding to this volatility is for companies to build strategic flexibility by dispersing production to different locations around the globe by contracting out manufacturing (in the case of low-value-added manufacturing) and other means.

Critical Discussion Questions

1. Why did the gold standard collapse? Is there a case for returning to some type of gold standard? What is it?

2. What opportunities might current IMF lending policies to Third World nations create for international businesses? What threats might they create?

3. Do you think the standard IMF policy prescriptions of tight monetary policy and reduced government spending are always appropriate for developing nations experiencing a currency crisis? How might the IMF change its approach? What would the implications be for international businesses?

4. Debate the relative merits of fixed and floating exchange rate regimes. From the perspective of an international business, what are the most important criteria in a choice between the systems? Which system is the more desirable for an international business?

5. Imagine that Canada, the United States, and Mexico decide to adopt a fixed exchange rate system similar to the ERM of the European Monetary System. What would be the likely consequences of such a system for (a) international businesses and (b) the flow of trade and investment among the three countries?

CLOSING CASE   Caterpillar Inc.

Caterpillar Inc. (Cat) is the world's largest manufacturer of heavy earthmoving equipment. Earthmoving equipment typically represents about 70 percent of the annual dollar sales of construction equipment worldwide. In 1980, Cat held 53.3 percent of the global market for earthmoving equipment. Its closest competitor was Komatsu of Japan, with 60 percent of the Japanese market but only 15.2 percent worldwide.

In 1980, Caterpillar was widely considered one of the premier manufacturing and exporting companies in the United States. The company had enjoyed 50 consecutive years of profits and returns on shareholders equity as high as 27 percent. In 1981, 57 percent of its sales were outside the United States, and roughly two-thirds of these orders were filled by exports. Cat was the third largest US exporter. Reflecting this underlying strength, Cat recorded record pretax profits of $579 million in 1981. However, the next three years were disastrous. Caterpillar lost a total of $1 billion and saw its market share slip to as low as 40 percent in 1985, while Komatsu increased its share to 25 percent. Three factors explain this startling turn of events: the higher productivity of Komatsu, the rise in the value of the dollar, and the Third World debt crisis.

In retrospect, Komatsu had been creeping up on Cat for a long time. In the 1960s, the company had a minuscule presence outside of Japan. By 1974, it had increased its global market share of heavy earthmoving equipment to 9 percent, and by 1980 it was over 15 percent. Part of Komatsu's growth was due to its superior labor productivity; throughout the 1970s, it had been able to price its machines 10 to 15 percent below Caterpillar's. However, Komatsu lacked an extensive dealer network outside of Japan, and Cat's worldwide dealer network and superior after-sale service and support functions were seen as justifying a price premium for Cat machines. For these reasons, many industry observers believed Komatsu would not increase its share much beyond its 1980 level.

An unprecedented rise in the value of the dollar against most major world currencies changed the picture. Between 1980 and 1987, the dollar rose an average of 87 percent against the currencies of 10 other industrialized countries. The dollar was driven up by strong economic growth in the United States, which attracted heavy inflows of capital from foreign investors seeking high returns on capital assets. High real interest rates attracted foreign investors seeking high returns on financial assets. At the same time, political turmoil in other parts of the world and relatively slow economic growth in Europe helped create the view that the United States was a good place in which to invest. These inflows of capital increased the demand for dollars in the foreign exchange market, which pushed the value of the dollar upward against other currencies.

The strong dollar substantially increased the dollar price of Cat's machines. At the same time, the dollar price of Komatsu products imported into the United States fell. Because of the shift in the relative values of the dollar and the yen, Komatsu priced its machines as much as 40 percent below Caterpillar's prices by 1985. In light of this enormous price difference, many consumers chose to forgo Caterpillar's superior after-sale service and support and bought Komatsu machines.

The third factor, the Third World debt crisis, became apparent in 1982. During the early 1970s, the nations of OPEC quadrupled the price of oil, which resulted in a massive flow of funds into these nations. Commercial banks borrowed this money from the OPEC countries and lent it to the governments of many Third World nations to finance massive construction projects—which led to a global boom in demand for heavy earthmoving equipment. Caterpillar benefited from this development. By 1982, however, it became apparent that the commercial banks had lent too much money to risky and unproductive investments, and the governments of several countries (including Mexico, Brazil, and Argentina) threatened to suspend debt payments. The International Monetary Fund stepped in and arranged for new loans to indebted Third World countries, on the condition that they adopt deflationary macroeconomic policies. For Cat, the party was over; orders for heavy earthmoving equipment dried up almost overnight, and those that were placed went to the lowest bidder, which often was Komatsu.

As a result of these factors, Caterpillar was in deep trouble by late 1982. The company responded quickly and between 1982 and 1985 cut costs by more than 20 percent. This was achieved by a 40 percent reduction in work force, the closure of nine plants, and a $1.8 billion investment in flexible manufacturing technologies designed to boost quality and lower cost. The company also pressed the government to lower the value of the dollar on foreign exchange markets. By 1984, Cat was a leading voice among US exporters trying to get the Reagan administration to intervene in the foreign exchange market.

Things began to go Caterpillar's way in early 1985. Prompted by Cat and other exporters, representatives of the US government met with representatives of Japan, Germany, France, and Great Britain at the Plaza Hotel in New York. In the resulting communiqué—known as the Plaza Accord—the five governments acknowledged that the dollar was overvalued and pledged to take actions that would drive down its price on the foreign exchange market. The central bank of each country intervened in the foreign exchange market, selling dollars and buying other currencies (including its own). The dollar had already begun to fall in early 1985 in response to a string of record US trade deficits. The Plaza Accord accelerated this trend, and over the next three years the dollar fell back to its 1980 level.

The effect for Caterpillar was almost immediate. Like any major exporter, Caterpillar had its own foreign exchange unit. Suspecting that an adjustment in the dollar would come soon, Cat had increased its holdings of foreign currencies in early 1985, using the strong dollar to purchase them. As the dollar fell, the company was able to convert these currencies back into dollars for a healthy profit. In 1985, Cat had pretax profits of $32 million; without foreign exchange gains of $89 million, it would have lost money. In 1986, foreign exchange gains of $100 million accounted for nearly two-thirds of its pretax profits of $159 million.

More significant for Cat's long-term position, the fall in the dollar against the yen and Caterpillar's cost-cutting efforts by 1988 had helped to eradicate the 10 percent cost advantage that Komatsu had enjoyed over Caterpillar four years earlier. After trying to hold its prices down, Komatsu had to raise its prices that year by 18 percent, while Cat was able to hold its price increase to 3 percent. With the terms of trade no longer handicapping Caterpillar, the company regained some of its lost market share. By 1989, it reportedly held 47 percent of the world market for heavy earthmoving equipment, up from a low of 40 percent three years earlier, while Komatsu's share had slipped to below 20 percent.

http://www.caterpillar.com

Sources: R. S. Eckley, "Caterpillar's Ordeal: Foreign Competition in Capital Goods," *Business Horizons*, March–April 1989, pp. 80–86; H. S. Byrne, "Track of the Cat: Caterpillar Is Bulldozing Its Way Back to Higher Profits," *Barron's*, April 6, 1987, pp. 13, 70–71; R. Henkoff, "This Cat Is Acting like a Tiger," *Fortune*, December 19, 1988, pp. 71–76; and "Caterpillar and Komatsu," in *Transnational Management: Text, Cases, and Readings in Cross-Border Management*, ed. C. A. Bartlett and S. Ghosal (Homewood, IL: Richard D. Irwin, 1992).

Case Discussion Questions

1. To what extent is the competitive position of Caterpillar against Komatsu dependent on the dollar/yen exchange rate? Between mid-1996 and early 1998, the dollar appreciated by over 40 percent against the yen. How do you think this would have affected the relatively competitive position of Caterpillar and Komatsu?

2. If you were the CEO of Caterpillar, what actions would you take now to make sure there is no repeat of the early 1980s experience?

3. What potential impact can the actions of the IMF and World Bank have on Caterpillar's business? Is there anything Cat can do to influence the actions of the IMF and World Bank?

4. As the CEO of Caterpillar, would you prefer a fixed exchange rate regime or a continuation of the current managed-float regime? Why?

Notes

1. D. Driscoll, *What is the International Monetary Fund?* (Washington, DC: IMF, July 1997).

2. The argument goes back to 18th century philosopher David Hume. See D. Hume, "On the Balance of Trade," reprinted in *The Gold Standard in Theory and in History*, ed. B. Eichengreen. (London: Methuen, 1985).

3. R. Solomon, *The International Monetary System, 1945–1981.* (New York: Harper & Row, 1982).

4. International Monetary Fund, *World Economic Outlook, 1998* (Washington, DC: IMF, May 1998).

5. For an extended discussion of the dollar exchange rate in the 1980s, see B. D. Pauls, "US Exchange Rate Policy: Bretton Woods to the Present," *Federal Reserve Bulletin*, November 1990, pp. 891–908.

6. For a feel for the issues contained in this debate, see P. Krugman, *Has the Adjustment Process Worked?* (Washington, DC: Institute for International Economics, 1991); "Time to Tether Currencies," *The Economist*, January 6, 1990, pp. 15–16; P. R. Krugman and M. Obstfeld, *International Economics: Theory and Policy* (New York: Harper Collins, 1994); J. Shelton, *Money Meltdown* (New York: Free Press, 1994); and S. Edwards, "Exchange Rates and the Political Economy of Macroeconomic Discipline," *American Economic Review* 86, no. 2 (May 1996), pp. 159–63.

7. The argument is made by several prominent economists, particularly Stanford's Robert McKinnon. See R. McKinnon, "An International Standard for Monetary Stabilization," *Policy Analyses in International Economics* 8 (1984). The details of this argument are beyond the scope of this book. For a relatively accessible exposition, see P. Krugman, *The Age of Diminished Expectations* (Cambridge, MA: MIT Press, 1990).

8. A. R. Ghosh and A. M. Gulde, "Does the Exchange Rate Regime Matter for Inflation and Growth?" *Economic Issues*, no. 2, (1997).

9. "The ABC of Currency Boards," *The Economist*, November 1, 1997, p. 80.

10. For a time, the plan was to introduce a common currency by 1997, but in July 1995 this was changed to 1999, and many think this date cannot be attained. L. Barber, "EU Leaders Plan 1999 Launch Date of Single Currency," *Financial Times*, June 27, 1995, p. 1.

11. N. Colchester and D. Buchan, *Europower* (New York: Random House, 1990), and D. Swann, *The Economics of the Common Market* (London: Penguin Books, 1990).

12. M. Wolf, "Emu May Not Be Dead After All." *Financial Times*, August 1, 1994, p. 13.

13. P. Norman, "A Test for the ERM and a Warning for the Emu," *Financial Times*, March 7, 1995, p. 2.

14. International Monetary Fund, *World Economic Outlook, 1998.*

15. Ibid.

16. For a summary of the arguments for debt reductions, see "And Forgive Us Our Debts: A Survey of the IMF and the World Bank," *The Economist*, October 12, 1991, pp. 23–33; and Krugman, *Age of Diminished Expectations*.

17. See P. Carroll and C. Torres, "Mexico Unveils Program of Harsh Fiscal Medicine," *The Wall Street Journal*, March 10, 1995, pp. A1, A6; and "Putting Mexico Together Again," *The Economist*, February 4, 1995, p. 65.

18. S. Erlanger, "Russia Will Test a Trading Band for the Ruble," *New York Times*, July 7, 1995, p. 1; C. Freeland, "Russian to Introduce a Trading Band for Ruble against Dollar," *Financial Times*, July 7, 1995, p. 1; J. Thornhill, "Russians Bemused by 'Black Tuesday,'" *Financial Times*, October 12, 1994, p. 4; R. Sikorski, "Mirage of Numbers," *The Wall Street Journal*, May 18, 1994, p. 14; "Can Russia Fight Back?", *The Economist*, June 6, 1998, pp. 47–48; J. Thornhill, "Russia's Shrinking Options," *Financial Times*, August 19, 1998, page 19.

19. World Trade Organization, *Annual Report, 1997*, vol. II, table III. 69.

20. J. Ridding and J. Kynge, "Complacency Gives Way to Contagion," *Financial Times*, January 13, 1998, p. 8.

21. J. Burton and G. Baker, "The Country That Invested Its Way into Trouble," *Financial Times*, January 15, 1998, p. 8.

22. P. Shenon, "The Suharto Billions," *New York Times*, January 16, 1998, p. 1.

23. World Bank, *1997 World Development Report* (Oxford: Oxford Univ. Press, Table 11).

24. Ridding and Kynge, "Complacency Gives Way to Contagion."

25. Burton and Baker. "The Country That Invested Its Way into Trouble."

26. "Bitter Pill for the Thais," *The Straits Times*, July 5, 1997, p. 46.

27. World Bank, *1997 World Development Report*, Table 2.

28. *International Monetary Fund*, press release no. 97/37, August 20, 1997.

29. T. S. Shorrock, "Korea Starts Overhaul; IMF Aid Hits $60 Billion," *Journal of Commerce*, December 8, 1997, p. 3A.

30. Particularly Jeffery Sachs. See J. Sachs, "Economic Transition and Exchange Rate Regime," *American Economic Review* 86, no. 92 (May 1996), pp. 147–52; and J. Sachs, "Power unto Itself," *Financial Times*, December 11, 1997, p. 11.

31. Sachs, "Power unto Itself."

32. Martin Wolf, "Same Old IMF Medicine," *Financial Times*, December 9, 1997, p. 12.

33. Sachs, "Power unto Itself."

34. P. Gumbel and B. Coleman, "Daimler Warns of Severe 95 Loss Due to Strong Mark," *New York Times*, June 29, 1995, pp. 1, 10; and M. Wolf, "Daimler-Benz Announces Major Losses," *Financial Times*, June 29, 1995, p. 1.

CHAPTER ELEVEN

THE GLOBAL CAPITAL MARKET

Deutsche Telekom Taps the Global Capital Market

Based in the world's third largest industrial economy, Deutsche Telekom is one of the world's largest telephone companies. Until late 1996, the company was wholly owned by the German government. However, in the mid-1990s, the German government formulated plans to privatize the utility, selling shares to the public. The privatization effort was driven by two factors: (1) a realization that state-owned enterprises tend to be inherently inefficient, and (2) the impending deregulation of the European Union telecommunications industry in 1998, which promised to expose Deutsche Telekom to foreign competition for the first time. Deutsche Telekom realized that, to become more competitive, it needed massive investments in new telecommunications infrastructure, including fiber optics and wireless, lest it start losing share in its home market to more efficient competitors such as AT&T and British Telecom after 1998. Financing such investments from state sources would have been difficult even under the best of circumstances and almost impossible in the late 1990s, when the German government was trying to limit its budget deficit to meet the criteria for membership in the European monetary union. With the active encouragement of the government, Deutsche Telekom hoped to finance its investments in capital equipment through the sale of shares to the public.

From a financial perspective, the privatization looked anything but easy. In 1996, Deutsche Telekom was valued at about $60 billion. If it maintained this valuation as a private company, it would dwarf all others listed on the German stock market. However, many analysts doubted there was anything close to $60 billion available in Germany for investment in Deutsche Telekom stock. One problem was that there was no tradition of retail stock investing in Germany. In 1996, only 1 in 20 German citizens owned shares, compared with 1 in every 4 or 5 in the United States and Britain. This lack of retail interest in stock ownership makes for a relatively illiquid stock market. Nor did banks, the traditional investors in company stocks in Germany, seem enthused about underwriting such a massive privatization effort. A further problem was that a wave of privatizations was already sweeping through Germany and the rest of Europe, so Deutsche Telekom would have to compete with many other state-owned enterprises for investors' attention. Given these factors, probably the only way that Deutsche Telekom could raise $60 billion through the German capital market would have been by promising investors a dividend yield that would raise the company's cost of capital above levels that could be serviced profitably.

Deutsche Telekom managers concluded they had to privatize the company in stages and sell a substantial portion of Deutsche Telekom stock to foreign investors. The company's plans called for an initial public offering (IPO) of 713 million shares of Deutsche Telekom stock, representing 25 percent of the company's total value, for about $18.50 per share. With a total projected value in excess of $13 billion, even this "limited" sale of Deutsche Telekom represented the largest IPO in European history and the second largest in the world after the 1987 sale of shares in Japan's telephone monopoly, NTT, for $15.6 billion. Concluding there was no way the German capital market could absorb even this partial sale of Deutsche Telekom equity, the managers of the company decided to simultaneously list shares and offer them for sale in Frankfurt (where the German stock exchange is located), London, New York, and Tokyo, attracting investors from all over the world. The IPO was successfully executed in November 1996 and raised $13.3 billion for the company.

http://www.dtag.de

Sources: J. O. Jackson, "The Selling of the Big Pink," *Time*, December 2, 1996, p. 46; S. Ascarelli, "Privatization Is Worrying Deutsche Telekom," *The Wall Street Journal*, February 3, 1995, p. A1; "Plunging into Foreign Markets, *The Economist*, September 17, 1994, pp. 86–87; and A. Raghavan and M. R. Sesit, "Financing Boom: Foreign Firms Raise More and More Money in the U.S. Market," *The Wall Street Journal*, October 5, 1993, p. A1.

Introduction

The opening case describes how Deutsche Telekom overcame the financing constraints imposed by a relatively illiquid German capital market and raised $13.3 billion by simultaneously listing its shares for sale on stock exchanges in Frankfurt, London, New York, and Tokyo. Deutsche Telekom tapped the international capital market to finance its capital spending needs because the German capital market alone was too small to supply the requisite funds at a reasonable cost. This illustrates a primary benefit of the global capital market—the increased liquidity relative to a purely domestic capital market enables a borrower to lower its cost of capital (that is, to borrow funds at a lower cost).

Although Deutsche Telekom's initial public offering represents one of the more notable examples of the use of the global capital market to finance capital spending needs, it is not unique. In recent years, many companies have sought to raise capital by selling shares and bonds to foreign investors or by borrowing money from foreign banks. In 1994, Daimler-Benz, Germany's largest industrial company, raised $300 million by issuing new shares not in Germany, but in Singapore.[1] In 1997, Yukos, a large Russian oil company, raised $1 billion in loans from Western banks.[2] Also in 1997, three other national telecommunications companies, Telecom Italia, Ente Nazionale Idrocarburi, and France Telecom, made international equity offerings of $11 billion, $7.8 billion, and $7.1 billion, respectively. According to data from the Bank for International Settlements, by late 1997 the stock of cross-border loans stood at $5,285 billion, there were $3,515 billion in outstanding international bonds, and international equity offerings were on target to exceed $100 billion.[3] All figures were records and represented steep increases from a decade earlier.

We begin this chapter by looking at the benefits associated with the globalization of capital markets. This is followed by a more detailed look at the growth of the international capital market and the risks associated with such growth. Next, there is a detailed review of three important segments of the global capital market: the Eurocurrency market, the international bond market, and the international equity market. As usual, we close the chapter by pointing out some of the implications for the practice of international business.

Benefits of the Global Capital Market

Although this section is about the global capital market, we open it by discussing the functions of a generic capital market. Then we will look at the limitations of domestic capital markets and discuss the benefits of using global capital markets.

The Functions of a Generic Capital Market

Why do we have capital markets? What is their function? A capital market brings together those who want to invest money and those who want to borrow money (see Figure 11.1). Those who want to invest money include corporations with surplus cash, individuals, and nonbank financial institutions (e.g., pension funds, insurance companies). Those who want to borrow money include individuals, companies, and governments. Between these two groups are the market makers. Market makers are the financial service companies that connect investors and borrowers, either directly or indirectly. They include commercial banks (e.g., Citibank, U.S. Bank) and investment banks (e.g., Merrill Lynch, Goldman Sachs).

Commercial banks perform an indirect connection function. They take cash deposits from corporations and individuals and pay them a rate of interest in return. They then lend that money to borrowers at a higher rate of interest, making a profit from the difference in interest rates (commonly referred to as the *interest rate spread*). Investment banks perform a direct connection function. They bring investors and

Figure 11.1

The Main Players in a Generic Capital Market

borrowers together and charge commissions for doing so. For example, Merrill Lynch may act as a stockbroker for an individual who wants to invest some money. Its personnel will advise her as to the most attractive purchases and buy stock on her behalf, charging a fee for the service.

Capital market loans to corporations are either equity loans or debt loans. An equity loan is made when a corporation sells stock to investors. The money the corporation receives in return for its stock can be used to purchase plants and equipment, fund R&D projects, pay wages, and so on. A share of stock gives its holder a claim to a firm's profit stream. The corporation honors this claim by paying dividends to the stockholders. The amount of the dividends is not fixed in advance. Rather, it is determined by management based on how much profit the corporation is making. Investors purchase stock both for their dividend yield and in anticipation of gains in the price of the stock. Stock prices increase when a corporation is projected to have greater earnings in the future, which increases the probability that it will raise future dividend payments.

A debt loan requires the corporation to repay a predetermined portion of the loan amount (the sum of the principal plus the specified interest) at regular intervals regardless of how much profit it is making. Management has no discretion as to the amount it will pay investors. Debt loans include cash loans from banks and funds raised from the sale of corporate bonds to investors. When an investor purchases a corporate bond, he purchases the right to receive a specified fixed stream of income from the corporation for a specified number of years (i.e., until the bond maturity date).

Attractions of the Global Capital Market

Why do we need a global capital market? Why are domestic capital markets not sufficient? A global capital market benefits both borrowers and investors. It benefits borrowers by increasing the supply of funds available for borrowing and by lowering the cost of capital. It benefits investors by providing a wider range of investment opportunities, thereby allowing them to build portfolios of international investments that diversify their risks.

The Borrower's Perspective: A Lower Cost of Capital

In a purely domestic capital market, the pool of investors is limited to residents of the country. This places an upper limit on the supply of funds available to borrowers. In other words, the liquidity of the market is limited. (Deutsche Telekom faced this problem in the opening case.) A global capital market, with its much larger pool of investors, provides a larger supply of funds for borrowers to draw on.

Perhaps the most important drawback of the limited liquidity of a purely domestic capital market is that the cost of capital tends to be higher than it is in an international market. The cost of capital is the rate of return that borrowers must pay investors (the price of borrowing money). This is the interest rate on debt loans and the dividend yield and expected capital gains on equity loans. In a purely domestic market, the limited pool of investors implies that borrowers must pay more to persuade investors to lend them their money. The larger pool of investors in an international market implies that borrowers will be able to pay less.

Figure 11.2

Market Liquidity and the
Cost of Capital

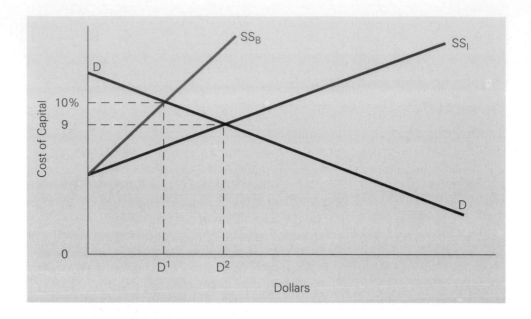

The argument is illustrated in Figure 11.2, using the Deutsche Telekom example. The vertical axis in the figure is the cost of capital (the price of borrowing money) and the horizontal axis, the amount of money available at varying interest rates. DD is the Deutsche Telekom demand curve for borrowings. Note that the Deutsche Telekom demand for funds varies with the cost of capital; the lower the cost of capital, the more money Deutsche Telekom will borrow. (Money is just like anything else; the lower its price, the more of it people can afford.) SS_B is the supply curve of funds available in the German capital market, and SS_I represents the funds available in the global capital market. Note that Deutsche Telekom can borrow more funds more cheaply on the global capital market. As Figure 11.2 illustrates, the greater pool of resources in the global capital market both lowers the cost of capital and increases the amount Deutsche Telekom can borrow. Thus, the advantage of a global capital market to borrowers is that it lowers the cost of capital.

Problems of limited liquidity are not restricted to less developed nations, which naturally tend to have smaller domestic capital markets. As illustrated in the opening case and discussed in the introduction, in recent years even very large enterprises based in some of the world's most advanced industrialized nations have tapped the international capital markets in their search for greater liquidity and a lower cost of capital.[4] Another example of a company that tapped the global capital market to lower its cost of capital is profiled in the accompanying Management Focus.

The Investor's Perspective: Portfolio Diversification

By using the global capital market, investors have a much wider range of investment opportunities than in a purely domestic capital market. The most significant consequence of this choice is that investors can diversify their portfolios internationally, thereby reducing their risk to below what could be achieved in a purely domestic capital market. We will consider how this works in the case of stock holdings, although the same argument could be made for bond holdings.

Consider an investor who buys stock in a biotech firm that has not yet produced a new product. Imagine the price of the stock is very volatile—investors are buying and selling the stock in large numbers in response to information about the firm's prospects. Such stocks are risky investments; investors may win big if the firm

MANAGEMENT FOCUS
BioGenetics

http://www.sec.gov

BioGenetics is a small Danish biotechnology company. The company began exploratory biotechnology research in the mid-1980s. By the early 1990s, it had isolated and genetically engineered several human proteins that seemed to have promise in the treatment of autoimmune diseases, such as rheumatoid arthritis. Production of a commercially viable biotechnology product, however, would take at least six to eight years. To proceed, BioGenetics needed to raise large sums of capital to fund research and product development, including extensive human clinical trials. The most obvious thing for BioGenetics to do would have been to arrange for a new issue of shares on the Danish stock market. Unfortunately, Denmark's stock market is small, lacks liquidity, and is segmented from international markets. Consequently, it would have been very difficult for BioGenetics to float successfully a new equity issue of the size needed. Even if an equity issue of the required size could have been floated successfully, the rate of return demanded by Danish stockholders would have made BioGenetic's cost of capital significantly higher than its international competitors'. In other words, the limited liquidity and conservative nature of Denmark's capital market would have made it very costly for BioGenetics to raise the capital in its own country.

Faced with this dilemma, BioGenetics contacted Morgan Grenfell, a London-based commercial bank with major international banking operations. Morgan Grenfell advised BioGenetics to issue Eurobonds to foreign investors. In 1995, Morgan Grenfell successfully organized a syndicate to underwrite and sell an issue of convertible Eurobonds that would raise $35 million for BioGenetics. In addition, Morgan Grenfell arranged for BioGenetics to list its shares on the London Stock Exchange to facilitate conversion and gain visibility.

At this time, biotechnology was attracting the interest of the US investment community. Stock issues by a number of US start-up biotechnology firms had been oversubscribed. BioGenetics, needing additional funds, decided to explore the potential of a US stock offering. With the assistance of Morgan Grenfell and Goldman Sachs, a major US investment bank, BioGenetics prepared a prospectus for Securities Exchange Commission (SEC) registration of its US stock offering and listing on the over-the-counter market (NASDAQ). To comply with the SEC's regulations, BioGenetics had to prepare financial statements consistent with US accounting principles. This was no small task, since its existing accounting systems—tailored to Danish law—did not supply data in the form required by the SEC.

By June 1996, BioGenetics was ready to announce its new share issue, which would increase the number of BioGenetics shares outstanding by 20 percent. Immediately after the new issue, BioGenetics shares lost 15 percent of their value on the Danish stock exchange. This reaction is typical in an illiquid, conservative stock market. Many Danish investors, worried about the dilution from the new share issue, sold their stock. When the market opened in the United States six hours later, however, BioGenetics shares quickly rose to above their previous value. The demand for BioGenetics stock in the United States reflected US investors' belief that a greater supply of BioGenetics stock following the new issue would create a more liquid market for the stock. This attracted many institutional investors that had previously held off buying out of fear that they may not be able to sell the stock subsequently without depressing the price. The broader market in BioGenetics stock that would exist after the new issue made this less likely—hence the surge in US demand for BioGenetics stock. The new issue was a huge success, raising an additional $50 million for BioGenetics.

Source: BioGenetics is a fictitious company. The case is based on information contained in a case on a Danish firm, Nova, that faced similar problems. See A. Stonehill and K. B. Dullum, *Internationalizing the Cost of Capital in Theory and in Practice: The Nova Experience and National Policy Implications* (New York: Wiley, 1983).

produces a marketable product, but investors may also lose all their money if the firm fails to come up with a product that sells. Investors can guard against the risk associated with holding this stock by buying other firms' stocks, particularly those weakly or negatively correlated with the biotech stock. By holding a variety of stocks in a diversified portfolio, the losses incurred when some stocks fail to live up to their promises are offset by the gains enjoyed when other stocks exceed their promise.

As an investor increases the number of stocks in her portfolio, the portfolio's risk declines. At first this decline is rapid. Soon, however, the rate of decline falls off and asymptotically approaches the systematic risk of the market. **Systematic risk** refers to movements in a stock portfolio's value that are attributable to macroeconomic forces affecting all firms in an economy, rather than factors specific to an individual firm. The systematic risk is the level of nondiversifiable risk in an economy. Figure 11.3a illustrates this relationship for the United States. It suggests that a fully diversified US portfolio is only about 27 percent as risky as a typical individual stock.

By diversifying a portfolio internationally, an investor can reduce the level of risk even further because the movements of stock market prices across countries are not perfectly correlated. For example, one recent study looked at the correlation between three stock market indexes. The Standard & Poor's 500 (S&P 500) summarized the movement of large US stocks. The Morgan Stanley Capital International Europe, Australia, and Far East Index (EAFE) summarized stock market movements in other developed nations. The third index, the International Finance Corporation Global Emerging Markets Index (IFC) summarized stock market movements in less developed "emerging economies." From 1981 to 1994, the correlation between the S&P 500 and EAFE indexes was 0.45, suggesting they moved together only about 20 percent of the time (i.e., $0.45 \times 0.45 = 0.2025$). The correlation between the S&P 500 and IFC indexes was even lower at 0.32, suggesting they moved together only a little over 10 percent of the time.[5]

The relatively low correlation between the movement of stock markets in different countries reflects two basic factors. First, countries pursue different macroeconomic policies and face different economic conditions, so their stock markets respond to different forces and can move in different ways. For example, in 1997, the stock markets of several Asian countries, including South Korea, Malaysia, Indonesia, and Thailand, lost over 50 percent of their value in response to the Asian financial crisis, while at the same time the S&P 500 increased in value by over 20 percent. Second, different stock markets are still somewhat *segmented* from each other by **capital controls**—that is, by restrictions on cross-border capital flows (although such restrictions are declining rapidly). The most common restrictions include limits on the amount of a firm's stock that a foreigner can own and limits on the ability of a country's citizens to invest their money outside that country. For example, until recently it was difficult for foreigners to own more than 30 percent of the equity of South Korean enterprises. Tight restrictions on capital flows make it very hard for Chinese citizens to take money out of their country and invest it in foreign assets. Such barriers to cross-border capital flows limit the ability of capital to roam the world freely in search of the highest risk-adjusted return. Consequently, at any one time, there may be too much capital invested in some markets and too little in others. This will tend to produce differences in rates of return across stock markets.[6] The implication is that by diversifying a portfolio to include foreign stocks, an investor can reduce the level of risk below that incurred by holding just domestic stocks.

Figure 11.3b illustrates the relationship between international diversification and risk found by a now classic study.[7] According to the figure, a fully diversified portfolio that contains stocks from many countries is less than half as risky as a fully diversified portfolio that contains only US stocks. A fully diversified portfolio of international stocks is only about 12 percent as risky as a typical individual stock, whereas a fully

Figure 11.3

Risk Reduction through Portfolio Diversification

Source: B. Solnik, "Why Not Diversify Internationally Rather than Domestically?" Adapted with permission from *Financial Analysts Journal,* July/August 1974, p. 17, Copyright 1974, Financial Analysts Federation. Charlottesville, VA. All rights reserved.

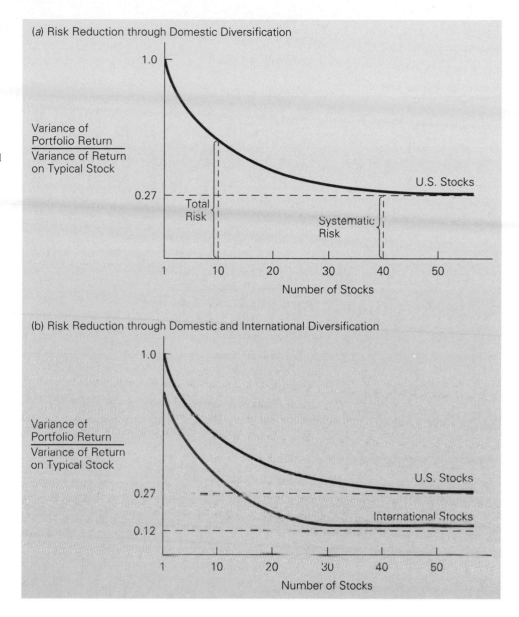

diversified portfolio of US stocks is about 27 percent as risky as a typical individual stock. More recent studies have tended to confirm the relationship summarized in Figure 11.3b. A 1994 study of portfolio diversification in Europe found that a diversified portfolio of stocks held within a single country was on average about 38 percent as risky as a typical individual stock, whereas a portfolio of stocks that was diversified across 12 European countries was only 18 percent as risky as a typical individual stock.[8] Such data suggest a strong case for investing internationally as a means of diversifying risk.

The risk-reducing effects of international portfolio diversification would be greater were it not for the volatile exchange rates associated with the current floating exchange rate regime. Floating exchange rates introduce an additional element of risk into investing in foreign assets. As we have said repeatedly, adverse exchange rate movements can transform otherwise profitable investments into unprofitable investments. The uncertainty engendered by volatile exchange rates may be acting as a brake on the otherwise rapid growth of the international capital market.

Figure 11.4

Net International Bank
Lending ($ billions)

Source: Bank for International
Settlements database.

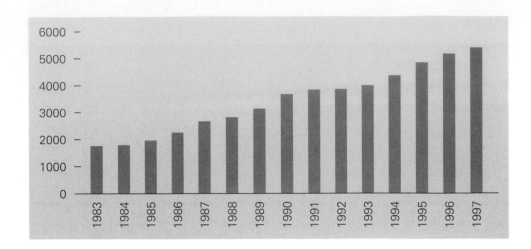

Growth of the Global Capital Market

In the introduction, we noted that there has been rapid growth in the size of the global capital market in recent years. The following figures add some substance to this claim.[9] Figure 11.4 shows the growth in international bank lending from 1983 to the end of 1997. As can be seen, international bank lending increased rapidly over this period, hitting a record $5.3 trillion by the end of 1997. Figure 11.5 shows the quarter-by-quarter increase in international bond issuance, from 1994 through 1997. By 1997, international bond issues were running at over $250 billion per quarter, up from $110 to $150 billion a quarter in 1994. Figure 11.5 also gives details of the currency in which most international bonds were issued. The US dollar has been the favored currency for issuing international bonds. Figure 11.6 shows the volume of international equity offerings between 1985 and 1997. Again, there has been a steep increase, with international equity issues closing in on $100 billion in 1997, up from about $4 billion in 1985. Figure 11.6 also shows details of the Morgan Stanley Capital Market International World Stock Market Index. As can be seen, the value of world stock markets has also increased substantially. It is easier to raise capital from new stock issue in a climate where stock markets are rising than in one where stock markets are declining in value. A decline in the value of world stock markets, such as occurred toward the end of 1987, makes it more difficult for companies to raise additional funds from international equity issues.

The data contained in Figures 11.4 to 11.6 clearly illustrate the rapid growth in the size of the global capital market in recent years. What factors allowed the international capital market to bloom in the 1980s and 1990s? There seem to be two answers—advances in information technology and deregulation by governments.

Information Technology

Financial services is an information-intensive industry. It draws on large volumes of information about markets, risks, exchange rates, interest rates, creditworthiness, and so on. It uses this information to make decisions about what to invest where, how much to charge borrowers, how much interest to pay to depositors, and the value and riskiness of a range of financial assets including corporate bonds, stocks, government securities, and currencies.

Because of this information intensity, the financial services industry has been revolutionized more than any other industry by advances in information technology since the 1970s. The growth of international communications technology has facilitated instantaneous communication between any two points on the globe. At the same time, rapid advances in data processing capabilities have allowed market makers to

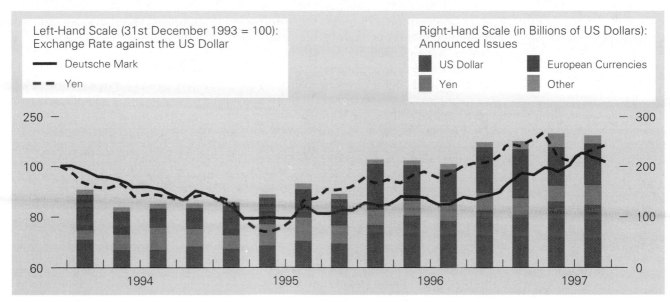

Figure 11.5

International Bond Issues and the US Dollar Exchange Rate

Sources: Bank for International Settlements database; Euromoney data; Bank of England data.

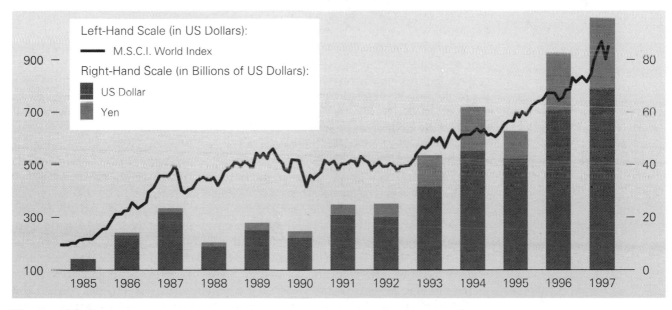

Figure 11.6

International Equity Offerings and Equity Price Developments

Sources: Bank for International Settlements database; Euromoney data.

absorb and process large volumes of information from around the world. According to one study, because of these technological developments, the real cost of recording, transmitting, and processing information has fallen by 95 percent since 1964.[10]

Such developments have facilitated the emergence of an integrated international capital market. It is now technologically possible for financial services companies to engage in 24-hour-a-day trading, whether it is in stocks, bonds, foreign exchange, or any other financial asset. Due to advances in communications and data processing technology, the international capital market never sleeps. San Francisco closes one hour before Tokyo opens, but during this period trading continues in New Zealand.

The integration facilitated by technology has a dark side.[11] "Shocks" that occur in one financial center now spread around the globe very quickly. The collapse of US stock prices on the notorious Black Monday of October 19, 1987, immediately triggered similar collapses in all the world's major stock markets, wiping billions of dollars off the value of corporate stocks worldwide. However, most market participants would argue that the benefits of an integrated global capital market far outweigh any potential costs.

Deregulation

In country after country, financial services have been the most tightly regulated of all industries. Governments around the world have traditionally kept other countries' financial service firms from entering their capital markets. In some cases, they have also restricted the overseas expansion of their domestic financial services firms. In many countries, the law has also segmented the domestic financial services industry. In the United States, for example, commercial banks are prohibited from performing the functions of investment banks, and vice versa. Historically, many countries have limited the ability of foreign investors to purchase significant equity positions in domestic companies. They have also limited the amount of foreign investment that their citizens could undertake. In the 1970s, for example, capital controls made it very difficult for a British investor to purchase American stocks and bonds.

Many of these restrictions have been crumbling since the late 1970s. In part, this has been a response to the development of the Eurocurrency market, which from the beginning was outside of national control. (This is explained later in the chapter.) It has also been a response to pressure from financial services companies, which have long wanted to operate in a less regulated environment. Increasing acceptance of the free market ideology associated with an individualistic political philosophy also has a lot to do with the global trend toward the deregulation of financial markets (see Chapter 2). Whatever the reason, deregulation in a number of key countries has undoubtedly facilitated the growth of the international capital market.

The trend began in the United States in the late 1970s and early 80s with a series of changes that allowed foreign banks to enter the US capital market and domestic banks to expand their operations overseas. In Great Britain, the so-called Big Bang of October 1986 removed barriers that had existed between banks and stockbrokers and allowed foreign financial service companies to enter the British stock market. Restrictions on the entry of foreign securities houses have been relaxed in Japan, and Japanese banks are now allowed to open international banking facilities. In France, the "Little Bang" of 1987 is gradually opening the French stock market to outsiders and to foreign and domestic banks. In Germany, foreign banks are now allowed to lend and manage foreign deutsche mark issues, subject to reciprocity agreements.[12] All of this has enabled financial services companies to transform themselves from primarily domestic companies into global operations with major offices around the world—a prerequisite for the development of a truly international capital market. As we saw in Chapter 5, in late 1997 the World Trade Organization brokered a deal that removed many of the restrictions on cross-border trade in financial services. This deal should encourage further growth in the size of the global capital market.

In addition to the deregulation of the financial services industry, many countries beginning in the 1970s started to dismantle capital controls, loosening both restrictions on inward investment by foreigners and outward investment by their own citizens and corporations. By the 1980s, this trend spread from developed nations to the emerging economies of the world as countries across Latin America, Asia, and Eastern Europe started to dismantle decades-old restrictions on capital flows. Figure 11.7 illustrates the consequences. Since 1985, an index of capital controls in emerging markets that is com-

Figure 11.7

Index of Capital Controls in Emerging Markets

Note: Index ranges from 0 to 1. 0 = No capital controls, 1 = Tight capital controls.

Source: IMF database.

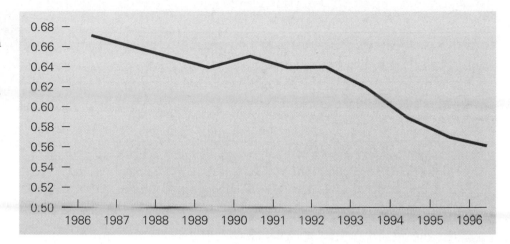

puted by the IMF has declined from a high of 0.66 to around 0.56 (the index would be 1.0 if all emerging economies had tight capital controls, and 0.0 if they had no controls). According to the World Bank, capital flows into the emerging economies of the world went from less than $50 billion in 1990 to over $336 billion in 1997.[13]

As of 1998, the trends toward deregulation of financial services and removal of capital controls were still firmly in place. Given the benefits associated with the globalization of capital, the growth of the global capital market mapped out in Figures 11.4 to 11.6 can be expected to continue for the foreseeable future. While most commentators see this as a positive development, there are those who believe that there are serious risks inherent in the globalization of capital.

Global Capital Market Risks

Some analysts are concerned that due to deregulation and reduced controls on cross-border capital flows, individual nations are becoming more vulnerable to speculative capital flows. They see this as having a destabilizing effect on national economies.[14] Harvard economist Martin Feldstein, for example, has argued that most of the capital that moves internationally is pursuing temporary gains, and it shifts in and out of countries as quickly as conditions change.[15] He distinguishes between this short-term capital, or "hot money," and "patient money" that would support long-term cross-border capital flows. To Feldstein, patient money is still relatively rare, primarily because although capital is free to move internationally, its owners and managers still prefer to keep most of it at home. Feldstein supports his arguments with statistics that demonstrate that although $1.2 trillion flows through the foreign exchange markets every day, "when the dust settles, most of the savings done in each country stays in that country."[16] Feldstein argues that the lack of patient money is due to the relative paucity of information that investors have about foreign investments. In his view, if investors had better information about foreign assets, the global capital market would work more efficiently and be less subject to short-term speculative capital flows. Feldstein claims that Mexico's economic problems in the mid-1990s were the result of too much hot money flowing in and out of the country and too little patient money. This example is reviewed in detail in the accompanying Country Focus.

A lack of information about the fundamental *quality* of foreign investments may encourage speculative flows in the global capital market. Faced with a lack of quality information, investors may react to dramatic news events in foreign nations and pull their money out too quickly. Despite advances in information technology, it is still difficult for an investor to get access to the same quantity and quality of information about foreign investment opportunities that he can get about domestic investment opportunities. This information gap is exacerbated by different accounting conventions in different countries, which makes the direct comparison of cross-border

COUNTRY FOCUS
Did the Global Capital Market Fail Mexico?

In early 1994, soon after passage of the North American Free Trade Agreement (NAFTA), Mexico was widely admired among the international community as a shining example of a developing country with a bright economic future. Since the late 1980s, the Mexican government had pursued sound monetary, budget, tax, and trade policies. By historical standards, inflation was low, the country was experiencing solid economic growth, and exports were booming. This robust picture attracted capital from foreign investors; between 1991 and 1993, foreigners invested over $75 billion in the Mexican economy, more than in any other developing nation.

If there was a blot on Mexico's economic report card, it was the country's growing current account (trade) deficit. Mexican exports were booming, but so were its imports. In the 1989–1990 period, the current account deficit was equivalent to about 3 percent of Mexico's gross domestic product. In 1991 it increased to 5 percent, and by 1994 it was running at an annual rate of over 6 percent. Bad as this might seem, it is not unsustainable and should not bring an economy crashing down. The United States has been running a current account deficit for decades with apparently little in the way of ill effects. A current account deficit will not be a problem for a country as long as foreign

investors take the money they earn from trade with that country and reinvest it within the country. This has been the case in the United States for years, and during the early 1990s, it was occurring in Mexico too. Thus, companies such as Ford took the pesos they earned from exports to Mexico and reinvested those funds in productive capacity in Mexico, building auto plants to serve the future needs of the Mexican market and to export elsewhere.

Unfortunately for Mexico, much of the $25 billion annual inflow of capital it received during the early 1990s was not the kind of patient long-term money that Ford was putting into Mexico. Rather, according to economist Martin Feldstein, much of the inflow was short-term capital that could flee if economic conditions changed for the worst. This is what seems to have occurred. In February 1994, the US Federal Reserve began to increase US interest rates. This led to a rapid fall in US bond prices. At the same time, the yen began to appreciate sharply against the US dollar. These events resulted in large losses for many managers of short-term capital, such as hedge fund managers and banks, who had been betting on exactly the opposite happening. Many hedge funds had been betting that interest rates would fall, bond prices would rise, and the dollar would appreciate against the yen.

investment opportunities difficult for all but the most sophisticated investor (see Chapter 19 for details). For example, German accounting principles are very different from those found in the United States and can present quite a different picture of the health of a company. Thus, when the Germany company Daimler-Benz translated its German financial accounts into US-style accounts in 1993, as it had to do to be listed on the New York Stock Exchange, it found that while it had made a profit of $97 million under German rules, under US rules it had lost $548 million![17]

Given the problems created by differences in the quantity and quality of information, many investors have yet to venture into the world of cross-border investing, and those that do are prone to reverse their decision on the basis of limited (and perhaps inaccurate) information. However, if the international capital market continues to grow, financial intermediaries likely will increasingly provide quality information about foreign investment opportunities. Better information should increase the sophistication of investment decisions and reduce the frequency and size of speculative capital flows. Although concerns about the volume of "hot money" sloshing around in the global capital market have recently increased as a result of the Asian financial crisis, IMF research suggests there has not been an increase in the volatility of financial markets over the past 25 years.[18]

http://www.mexonline.com/websites.htm

Faced with large losses, money managers tried to reduce the riskiness of their portfolios by pulling out of risky situations. About the same time, events took a turn for the worse in Mexico. An armed uprising in the southern state of Chiapas, the assassination of the leading candidate in the presidential election campaign, and an accelerating inflation rate all helped produce a feeling that Mexican investments were riskier than had been assumed. Money managers began to pull many of their short-term investments out of the country.

As hot money flowed out, the Mexican government realized it could not continue to count on capital inflows to finance its current account deficit. The government had assumed the inflow was mainly composed of patient, long-term money. In reality, much of it appeared to be short-term money. As money flowed out of Mexico, the Mexican government had to commit more foreign reserves to defending the value of the peso against the US dollar, which was pegged at 3.5 to the dollar. Currency speculators entered the picture and began to bet against the Mexican government by selling pesos short. Events came to a head in December 1994 when the Mexican government was essentially forced by capital flows to abandon its support for the peso. Over the next month,

the peso lost 40 percent of its value against the dollar, the government was forced to introduce an economic austerity program, and the Mexican economic boom came to an abrupt end.

According to Martin Feldstein, the Mexican economy was brought down not by currency speculation on the foreign exchange market, but by a lack of long-term patient money. He argued that Mexico offered, and still offers, many attractive long-term investment opportunities, but because of the lack of information on long-term investment opportunities in Mexico, most of the capital flowing into the country from 1991 to 1993 was short-term, speculative money, the flow of which could quickly be reversed. If foreign investors had better information, Feldstein argued, Mexico should have been able to finance its current account deficit from inward capital flows because patient capital would naturally gravitate toward attractive Mexican investment opportunities.

Sources: Martin Feldstein, "Global Capital Flows: Too Little, Not Too Much," *The Economist*, June 24, 1995, pp. 72–73; R. Dornbusch, "We Have Salinas to Thank for the Peso Debacle," *Business Week*, January 16, 1995, p. 20; P. Carroll and C. Torres, "Mexico Unveils Program of Harsh Fiscal Medicine," *The Wall Street Journal*, March 10, 1995, pp. A1, A6. See also, Martin Feldstein and Charles Horioka, "Domestic Savings and International Capital Flows," *Economic Journal* 90 (1980), pp. 314–29.

The Eurocurrency Market

A **eurocurrency** is any currency banked outside of its country of origin. **Eurodollars**, which account for about two-thirds of all eurocurrencies, are dollars banked outside of the United States. Other important eurocurrencies include the euro-yen, the euro-deutsche mark, the euro-franc, and the euro-pound. The term *eurocurrency* is actually a misnomer because a eurocurrency can be created anywhere in the world; the persistent euro- prefix reflects the European origin of the market. As we shall see, the eurocurrency market is an important, relatively low-cost source of funds for international businesses.

Genesis and Growth of the Market

The eurocurrency market was born in the mid-1950s when Eastern European holders of dollars, including the former Soviet Union, were afraid to deposit their holdings of dollars in the United States lest they be seized by the US government to settle US residents' claims against business losses resulting from the Communist takeover of Eastern Europe. These countries deposited many of their dollar holdings in Europe, particularly in London. Additional dollar deposits came from various Western European central banks and from companies that earned dollars by exporting to the United States. These two groups deposited their dollars in London banks, rather than US banks, because they were able to earn a higher rate of interest (which will be explained).

The eurocurrency market received a major push in 1957 when the British government prohibited British banks from lending British pounds to finance non-British trade, a business that had been very profitable for British banks. British banks began financing the same trade by attracting dollar deposits and lending dollars to companies engaged in international trade and investment. Because of this historical event, London became, and has remained, the leading center of eurocurrency trading.

The eurocurrency market received another push in the 1960s when the US government enacted regulations that discouraged US banks from lending to non-US residents. Would-be dollar borrowers outside the United States found it increasingly difficult to borrow dollars in the United States to finance international trade, so they turned to the eurodollar market to obtain the necessary dollar funds.

The US government changed its policies after the 1973 collapse of the Bretton Woods system (see Chapter 10), removing an important impetus to the growth of the eurocurrency market. However, another political event, the oil price increases engineered by OPEC in the 1973–74 and 1979–80 periods, gave the market another big shove. As a result of the oil price increases, the Arab members of OPEC accumulated huge amounts of dollars. They were afraid to place their money in US banks or their European branches, lest the US government attempt to confiscate them. (Iranian assets in US banks and their European branches were frozen by President Carter in 1979 after Americans were taken hostage at the US embassy in Tehran; their fear was not unfounded.) Instead, these countries deposited their dollars with banks in London, further increasing the supply of eurodollars.

Although these various political events contributed to the growth of the eurocurrency market, they alone were not responsible for it. The market grew because it offered real financial advantages—initially to those who wanted to deposit dollars or borrow dollars and later to those who wanted to deposit and borrow other currencies. We now look at the source of these financial advantages.

Attractions of the Eurocurrency Market

The main factor that makes the eurocurrency market so attractive to both depositors and borrowers is its lack of government regulation. This allows banks to offer higher interest rates on eurocurrency deposits than on deposits made in the home currency, making eurocurrency deposits attractive to those who have cash to deposit. The lack of regulation also allows banks to charge borrowers a lower interest rate for eurocurrency borrowings than for borrowings in the home currency, making eurocurrency loans attractive for those who want to borrow money. In other words, the spread between the eurocurrency deposit rate and the eurocurrency lending rate is less than the spread between the domestic deposit and lending rates (see Figure 11.8). To understand why this is so, we must examine how government regulations raise the costs of domestic banking.

Domestic currency deposits are regulated in all industrialized countries. Such regulations ensure that banks have enough liquid funds to satisfy demand if large numbers of domestic depositors should suddenly decide to withdraw their money. All countries operate with certain reserve requirements. For example, each time a US bank accepts a deposit in dollars, it must place some fraction of that deposit in a non-interest-bearing account at a Federal Reserve bank as part of its required reserves. Similarly, each time a British bank accepts a deposit in pounds sterling, it must place a certain fraction of that deposit with the Bank of England.

Banks are given much more freedom in their dealings in foreign currencies, however. For example, the British government does not impose reserve requirement restrictions on deposits of foreign currencies within its borders. Nor are the London

Figure 11.8

Interest Rate Spreads in
Domestic and Eurocurrency
Markets

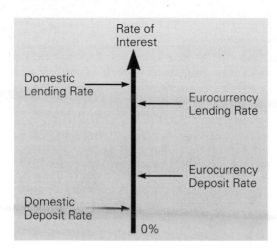

branches of US banks subject to US reserve requirement regulations, provided those deposits are payable only outside the United States. This gives eurobanks a competitive advantage.

For example, suppose a bank based in New York faces a 10 percent reserve requirement. According to this requirement, if the bank receives a $100 deposit, it can lend out no more than $90 of that and it must place the remaining $10 in a non-interest-bearing account at a Federal Reserve bank. Suppose the bank has annual operating costs of $1 per $100 of deposits and that it charges 10 percent interest on loans. The highest interest the New York bank can offer its depositors and still cover its costs is 8 percent per year. Thus, the bank pays the owner of the $100 deposit $(0.08 \times \$100 =)$ $8, earns $(0.10 \times \$90 =)$ $9 on the fraction of the deposit it is allowed to lend, and just covers its operating costs.

In contrast, a eurobank can offer a higher interest rate on dollar deposits and still cover its costs. The eurobank, with no reserve requirements regarding dollar deposits, can lend out all of a $100 deposit. Therefore, it can earn $0.10 \times \$100 = \$10$ at a loan rate of 10 percent. If the eurobank has the same operating costs as the New York bank ($1 per $100 deposit), it can pay its depositors an interest rate of 9 percent, a full percentage point higher than that paid by the New York bank, and still cover its costs. That is, it can pay out $0.09 \times \$100 = \$9$ to its depositor, receive $10 from the borrower, and be left with $1 to cover operating costs. Alternatively, the eurobank might pay the depositor 8.5 percent (which is still above the rate paid by the New York bank), charge borrowers 9.5 percent (still less than the New York bank charges), and cover its operating costs even better. Thus, the eurobank has a competitive advantage vis-à-vis the New York bank in both its deposit rate and its loan rate.

Clearly, there are very strong financial motivations for companies to use the eurocurrency market. By doing so, they receive a higher interest rate on deposits and pay less for loans. Given this, the surprising thing is not that the euromarket has grown rapidly but that it hasn't grown even faster. Why do any depositors hold deposits in their home currency when they could get better yields in the eurocurrency market?

Drawbacks of the Eurocurrency Market

The eurocurrency market has two drawbacks. First, when depositors use a regulated banking system, they know that the probability of a bank failure that would cause them to lose their deposits is very low. Regulation maintains the liquidity of the banking system. In an unregulated system such as the eurocurrency market, the probability of a bank failure that would cause depositors to lose their money is greater (although in absolute terms, still low). Thus, the lower interest rate received on home-country deposits reflects the costs of insuring against bank failure. Some depositors are more comfortable with the security of such a system and are willing to pay the price.

Second, borrowing funds internationally can expose a company to foreign exchange risk. For example, consider a US company that uses the eurocurrency market to borrow euro-pounds—perhaps because it can pay a lower interest rate on euro-pound loans than on dollar loans. Imagine, however, that the British pound subsequently appreciates against the dollar. This would increase the dollar cost of repaying the euro-pound loan and thus the company's cost of capital. This possibility can be insured against by using the forward exchange market (as we saw in Chapter 9) but the forward exchange market does not offer perfect insurance. Consequently, many companies borrow funds in their domestic currency to avoid foreign exchange risk, even though the eurocurrency markets may offer more attractive interest rates.

The Global Bond Market

The global bond market grew rapidly during the 1980s and 1990s (see Figure 11.5). Bonds are an important means of financing for many companies. The most common kind of bond is a fixed-rate bond. The investor who purchases a **fixed-rate bond** receives a fixed set of cash payoffs. Each year until the bond matures, the investor gets an interest payment and then at maturity he gets back the face value of the bond.

International bonds are of two types: foreign bonds and eurobonds. **Foreign bonds** are sold outside of the borrower's country and are denominated in the currency of the country in which they are issued. Thus, when Dow Chemical issues bonds in Japanese yen and sells them in Japan, it is issuing foreign bonds. Many foreign bonds have nicknames; foreign bonds sold in the United States are called Yankee bonds, foreign bonds sold in Japan are Samurai bonds, and foreign bonds sold in Great Britain are bulldogs.

Eurobonds are normally underwritten by an international syndicate of banks and placed in countries other than the one in whose currency the bond is denominated. For example, a bond may be issued by a German corporation, denominated in US dollars, and sold to investors outside of the United States by an international syndicate of banks. Eurobonds are routinely issued by multinational corporations, large domestic corporations, sovereign governments, and international institutions. They are usually offered simultaneously in several national capital markets, but not in the capital market of the country, nor to residents of the country, in whose currency they are denominated. Eurobonds account for the lion's share of international bond issues.

Attractions of the Eurobond Market

Three features of the eurobond market make it an appealing alternative to most major domestic bond markets; specifically,

- An absence of regulatory interference.
- Less stringent disclosure requirements than in most domestic bond markets.
- A favorable tax status.

Regulatory Interference

National governments often impose tight controls on domestic and foreign issuers of bonds denominated in the local currency and sold within their national boundaries. These controls tend to raise the cost of issuing bonds. However, government limitations are generally less stringent for securities denominated in foreign currencies and sold to holders of those foreign currencies. Eurobonds fall outside of the regulatory domain of any single nation. As such, they can often be issued at a lower cost to the issuer.

Disclosure Requirements

Eurobond market disclosure requirements tend to be less stringent than those of several national governments. For example, if a firm wishes to issue dollar-denominated bonds within the United States, it must first comply with SEC disclosure requirements. The firm must disclose detailed information about its activities, the salaries and other compensation of its senior executives, stock trades by its senior executives, and the like. In addition, the issuing firm must submit financial accounts that conform to US accounting standards. For non-US firms, redoing their accounts to make them consistent with US standards can be very time consuming and expensive. Therefore, many firms have found it cheaper to issue eurobonds, including those denominated in dollars, than to issue dollar-denominated bonds within the United States.

Favorable Tax Status

Before 1984, US corporations issuing eurobonds were required to withhold for US income tax up to 30 percent of each interest payment to foreigners. This did not encourage foreigners to hold bonds issued by US corporations. Similar tax laws were operational in many countries at that time, and they limited market demand for eurobonds. US laws were revised in 1984 to exempt from any withholding tax foreign holders of bonds issued by US corporations. As a result, US corporations found it feasible for the first time to sell eurobonds directly to foreigners. Repeal of the US laws caused other governments—including those of France, Germany, and Japan—to liberalize their tax laws likewise to avoid outflows of capital from their markets. The consequence was an upsurge in demand for eurobonds from investors who wanted to take advantage of their tax benefits.

The Global Equity Market

Although we have talked about the growth of the global equity market, strictly speaking there is no international equity market in the sense that there are international currency and bond markets. Rather, many countries have their own domestic equity markets in which corporate stock is traded. The largest of these domestic equity markets are to be found in the United States, Britain, Japan, and Germany. Although each domestic equity market is still dominated by investors who are citizens of that country and companies incorporated in that country, developments are internationalizing the world equity market. Investors are investing heavily in foreign equity markets to diversify their portfolios. By 1994, individuals and institutions had invested more than $1.3 trillion in stocks outside their home markets.[19] This figure continued to increase through 1997. Facilitated by deregulation and advances in information technology, this trend seems to be here to stay.

An interesting consequence of the trend toward international equity investment is the internationalization of corporate ownership. Today it is still generally possible to talk about US corporations, British corporations, and Japanese corporations, primarily because the majority of stockholders (owners) of these corporations are of the respective nationality. However, this is changing. Increasingly, US citizens are buying stock in companies incorporated abroad, and foreigners are buying stock in companies incorporated in the United States. Looking into the future, Robert Reich has mused about "the coming irrelevance of corporate nationality."[20]

A second development internationalizing the world equity market is that companies with historic roots in one nation are broadening their stock ownership by listing their stock in the equity markets of other nations. The reasons are primarily financial. Listing stock on a foreign market is often a prelude to issuing stock in that market to raise capital. The idea is to tap into the liquidity of foreign markets, thereby increasing the funds available for investment and lowering the firm's cost of capital. (The relationship between liquidity and the cost of capital was discussed earlier in the chapter.) Firms also often list their stock on foreign equity markets to facilitate future acquisitions of foreign companies. Other reasons for listing a company's stock on a foreign equity market are that the company's stock and stock options can be used to compensate local management and employees, it satisfies the desire for local ownership, and it increases the company's visibility with local employees, customers, suppliers, and bankers.

Foreign Exchange Risk and the Cost of Capital

We have emphasized repeatedly that a firm can borrow funds at a lower cost on the global capital market than on the domestic capital market. However, we have also mentioned that under a floating exchange rate regime, foreign exchange risk complicates this picture. Adverse movements in foreign exchange rates can substantially increase the cost of foreign currency loans, which is what happened to many Asian companies during the 1997–98 Asian financial crisis.

Consider a South Korean firm that wants to borrow 1 billion Korean won for one year to fund a capital investment project. The company can borrow this money from a Korean bank at an interest rate of 10 percent, and at the end of the year pay back the loan plus interest, for a total of W1.10 billion. Or the firm could borrow dollars from an international bank at a 6 percent interest rate. At the prevailing exchange rate of $1=W1,000, the firm would borrow $1 million and the total loan cost would be $1.06 million, or W1.06 billion. By borrowing dollars, the firm could reduce its cost of capital by 4 percent, or W40 million. However, this saving is predicated on the assumption that during the year of the loan, the dollar/won exchange rate stays constant. Instead, imagine that the won depreciates sharply against the US dollar during the year and ends the year at $1=W1,500. (This occurred in late 1997 when the won declined in value from $1=W1,000 to $1=W1,500 in two months.) The firm still has to pay the international bank $1.06 million at the end of the year, but now this costs the company W1.59 billion (i.e., $1.06 × 1,500). As a result of the depreciation in the value of the won, the cost of borrowing in US dollars has soared from 6 percent to 59 percent, a huge rise in the firm's cost of capital. Although this may seem like an extreme example, it happened to many South Korean firms in 1997 at the height of the Asian financial crisis. Not surprisingly, many of them were pushed into technical default on their loans.

Unpredictable movements in exchange rates can inject risk into foreign currency borrowing, making something that initially seems less expensive ultimately much more expensive. The borrower can hedge against such a possibility by entering into a forward contract to purchase the required amount of the currency being borrowed at a predetermined exchange rate when the loan comes due (see Chapter 9 for details). Although this will raise the borrower's cost of capital, the added insurance limits the risk involved in such a transaction. Unfortunately, many Asian borrowers did not hedge their dollar-denominated short-term debt, so when their currencies collapsed against the dollar in 1997, many saw a sharp increase in their cost of capital.

When a firm borrows funds from the global capital market, it must weigh the benefits of a lower interest rate against the risks of an increase in the real cost of capital due to adverse exchange rate movements. Although using forward exchange markets may lower foreign exchange risk with short-term borrowings, it cannot remove the risk. Most importantly, the forward exchange market does not provide adequate coverage for long-term borrowings.

IMPLICATIONS FOR BUSINESS

The implications of the material discussed in this chapter for international business are quite straightforward but no less important for being obvious. The growth of the global capital market has created opportunities for international businesses that wish to borrow and/or invest money. On the borrowing side, by using the global capital market, firms can often borrow funds at a lower cost than is possible in a purely domestic capital market. This conclusion holds no matter what form of borrowing a firm uses—equity, bonds, or cash loans. The lower cost of capital on the global market reflects their greater liquidity and the general absence of government regulation. Government regulation tends to raise the cost of capital in most domestic capital markets. The global market, being transnational, escapes regulation. Balanced against this, however, is the foreign exchange risk associated with borrowing in a foreign currency.

On the investment side, the growth of the global capital market is providing opportunities for firms, institutions, and individuals to diversify their investments to limit risk. By holding a diverse portfolio of stocks and bonds in different nations, an investor can reduce total risk to a lower level than can be achieved in a purely domestic setting. Once again, however, foreign exchange risk is a complicating factor.

The trends noted in this chapter seem likely to continue, with the global capital market continuing to increase in both importance and degree of integration over the next decade. Perhaps the most significant development will be the emergence of a unified capital market and common currency within the EU by the end of the decade as those countries continue toward economic and monetary union. Since Europe's capital markets are currently fragmented and relatively introspective (with the major exception of Britain's capital market), such a development could pave the way for even more rapid internationalization of the capital market in the early years of the next century. If this occurs, the implications for business are likely to be positive.

Chapter Summary

This chapter explained the functions and form of the global capital market and defined the implications of these for international business practice. This chapter made the following points:

1. The function of a capital market is to bring those who want to invest money together with those who want to borrow money.

2. Relative to a domestic capital market, the global capital market has a greater supply of funds available for borrowing, and this makes for a lower cost of capital for borrowers.

3. Relative to a domestic capital market, the global capital market allows investors to diversify portfolios of holdings internationally, thereby reducing risk.

4. The growth of the global capital market during recent decades can be attributed to advances in information technology, the widespread deregulation of financial services, and the relaxation of regulations governing cross-border capital flows.

5. A eurocurrency is any currency banked outside its country of origin. The lack of government regulations makes the eurocurrency market attractive to both depositors and borrowers. Due to the absence of regulation, the spread between the eurocurrency deposit and lending rates is less than the spread between the domestic deposit and lending rates. This gives eurobanks a competitive advantage.

6. The global bond market has two classifications: the foreign bond market and the eurobond market. Foreign bonds are sold outside of the borrower's country and are denominated in the currency of the country in which they are issued. A eurobond issue is normally underwritten by an international

syndicate of banks and placed in countries other than the one in whose currency the bond is denominated. Eurobonds account for the lion's share of international bond issues.

7. The eurobond market is an attractive way for companies to raise funds due to the absence of regulatory interference, less stringent disclosure requirements, and eurobonds' favorable tax status.

8. Foreign investors are investing in other countries' equity markets to reduce risk by diversifying their stock holdings among nations.

9. Many companies are now listing their stock in the equity markets of other nations, primarily as a prelude to issuing stock in those markets to raise additional capital. Other reasons for listing stock in another country's exchange are to facilitate future stock swaps; to enable the company to use its stock and stock options for compensating local manage-

ment and employees; to satisfy local ownership desires; and to increase the company's visibility among its local employees, customers, suppliers, and bankers.

10. When borrowing funds from the global capital market, companies must weigh the benefits of a lower interest rate against the risks of greater real costs of capital due to adverse exchange rate movements.

11. One major implication of the global capital market for international business is that companies can often borrow funds at a lower cost of capital in the international capital market than they can in the domestic capital market.

12. The global capital market provides greater opportunities for businesses and individuals to build a truly diversified portfolio of international investments in financial assets, which lowers risk.

Critical Discussion Questions

1. Why has the global capital market grown so rapidly in recent decades? Do you think this growth will continue throughout the 2000s? Why?

2. A firm based in Mexico has found that its growth is restricted by the limited liquidity of the Mexican capital market. List the firm's options for raising money on the global capital market. Discuss the pros and cons of each option, and make a recommendation. How might your recommended options be affected if the Mexican peso depreciates significantly on the foreign exchange markets over the next two years?

3. Happy Company wants to raise $2 million with debt financing. The funds are needed to finance working capital, and the firm will repay them with interest in one year. Happy Company's treasurer is considering three options:

a. Borrowing US dollars from Security Pacific Bank at 8 percent.

b. Borrowing British pounds from Midland Bank at 14 percent.

c. Borrowing Japanese yen from Sanwa bank at 5 percent.

If Happy borrows foreign currency, it will not cover it; that is, it will simply change foreign currency for dollars at today's spot rate and buy the same foreign currency a year later at the spot rate then in effect. Happy Company estimates the pound will depreciate by 5 percent relative to the dollar and the yen will appreciate 3 percent relative to the dollar in the next year. From which bank should Happy Company borrow?

CLOSING CASE   The Search for Capital in the Czech Republic

Following the collapse of communism and the shift toward a more market-oriented system, the Czech Republic initially emerged as one of the more vibrant and market-driven economies in Eastern Europe. By early 1998, however, the economic development of the Czech Republic was being held back by a shortage of capital. The problem was rooted in macroeconomic conditions and institutional problems.

On the macroeconomic front, 1997 saw a combination of adverse developments, including a rise in inflation, a growing government deficit, and a speculative attack on the Czech currency that forced the government to abandon its fixed exchange rate policy for a floating exchange rate system. After the shift to a floating exchange rate system, the Czech currency declined by about 10 percent against the German deutsche mark and over 15 percent against the US dollar. Since many internationally traded commodities, such as oil, are traded in dollars, this devaluation added fuel to the Czech Republic's inflation rate fire. The government responded by tightening monetary policy, raising interest rates to around 16 percent.

These macroeconomic problems had a predictably negative effect on the Prague stock market. The PX50, the key index of Czech shares listed on the Prague exchange, declined from around 520 to a low of 430 by June 1998. Much of the decline was due to foreign investment capital leaving the country for more attractive investment opportunities in neighboring Hungary and Poland, where macroeconomic conditions were more favorable and where local stock markets were performing better.

But that wasn't the only problem for the Prague stock market. Many Western investors had been discouraged from investing in Czech stocks by the poor reputation of the Prague stock exchange. That institution is reportedly rife with stock manipulation by insiders, insider trading that would be illegal in more developed markets, a lack of protection for minority stockholders, poor corporate reporting, and fraud. Also, most state-owned enterprises in the Czech Republic were privatized through a voucher scheme that has left the majority of shareholdings in the hands of institutions and groups that are preoccupied with maintaining control over their companies and opposed to any attempt to raise capital through new equity issues. Consequently, the Prague stock market is small and liquidity is very limited.

These factors have combined to increase the cost of capital for individual Czech enterprises. Traditionally, many Czech firms forged tight relationships with banks and borrowed money from them. However, with interest rates at 16 percent and many banks reining in credit to make up for past largesse, it was increasingly expensive for Czech companies to raise capital through borrowings. As for the Czech stock market, its poor reputation and low liquidity made it almost impossible to raise capital by issuing new shares. In mid-1997, one of the Czech Republic's most dynamic and profitable new enterprises, Bonton, a film and music company, attempted to raise $30 to $40 million through an initial public offering on the Prague exchange. This would have been only the second IPO in the history of the Prague exchange, and the only one of any significance. A successful IPO would have helped to legitimize the market, but Bonton canceled the IPO when the Prague market declined to yearlong lows in the wake of the Asian financial crisis.

Despite all these problems, most agree that the Czech economy has a bright future. However, this future cannot be realized unless Czech companies can raise the capital to invest in the necessary plants and equipment. A number of prominent Czech companies in 1998 announced their intentions to make international equity issues. At the beginning of 1997, only two Czech companies had foreign listings, both of them large banks. However, another five significant companies sought listings on the London stock exchange in 1998. In a sign that this strategy may work, the first to list was Ceske Radiokomunikace, a state-owned radio, television, and telecommunications company that successfully raised $134 million in equity by listing Global Depository Receipts on the London exchange, increasing its equity by 36 percent and decreasing the state holding in the company to around 51 percent.

http://www.henge.com/~vspina/index.shtml

Sources: R. Anderson, "Czech Groups Cast Their Net Abroad in Search of Funds," *Financial Times*, May 26, 1997, p. 27; V. Boland, "The Czech Stockmarket: Looking Beyond Recent Turmoil," *Financial Times*, December 1, 1997, p. 4; and "Ceske Radiokomunikace Equity Offer Raises $134 million," *Financial Times*, May 27, 1998, p. 38.

Case Discussion Questions

1. What are the causes and likely consequences of the capital shortage faced by Czech firms? How does the capital shortage affect the cost of capital in the Czech Republic?

2. How will selling equity to foreign investors benefit Czech firms and the Czech economy? What would happen to the Czech economy if Czech firms were prohibited from accessing the global capital market? Can you see any drawbacks with the strategy of selling equity to foreign investors?

3. Why is it easier for Czech firms to execute an IPO in London than in Prague?

4. If Czech firms continue to raise capital through foreign equity issues, ultimately more than 50 percent of the equity of these firms will be owned by investors based outside the Czech republic. If and when this occurs, will these still be Czech firms?

Notes

1. D. Waller, "Daimler in $250m Singapore Placing," *Financial Times*, May 10, 1994, p. 17.

2. C. Freeland, "Russian Oil Company Raises $1 Billion from Western Banks," *Financial Times*, December 15, 1997, p. 17.

3. Bank for International Settlements, *International Banking and Financial Market Developments* (Basle, Switzerland: BIS, November 1997).

4. Waller, "Daimler in $250m Singapore Placing."

5. C. G. Luck and R. Choudhury, "International Equity Diversification for Pension Funds," *Journal of Investing* 5, no. 2 (1996), pp. 43–53.

6. Ian Domowitz, Jack Glen, and Ananth Madhavan, "Market Segmentation and Stock Prices: Evidence from an Emerging Market," *Journal of Finance* 3, no. 3 (1997), pp. 1059–68.

7. B. Solnik, "Why Not Diversify Internationally Rather than Domestically?" *Financial Analysts Journal*, July 1974, p. 17.

8. S. L. Heston and K. G. Rouwenhorst, "Does Industrial Structure Explain the Benefits of International Diversification?" *Journal of Financial Economics* 36, pp. 3–27.

9. All raw data come from the Bank for International Settlements and can be accessed from its Web site at http://www.bis.org.

10. T. F. Huertas, "U.S. Multinational Banking: History and Prospects," in *Banks as Multinationals*, ed. G. Jones (London: Routledge, 1990).

11. G. J. Millman, *The Vandals' Crown* (New York: Free Press, 1995).

12. P. Dicken, *Global Shift: The Internationalization of Economic Activity* (London: The Guilford Press, 1992).

13. "Capital Goes Global," *The Economist*, October 25, 1997, pp. 87–88.

14. Ibid.

15. Martin Feldstein, "Global Capital Flows: Too Little, Not Too Much," *The Economist*, June 24, 1995, pp. 72–73.

16. Ibid., p. 73.

17. D. Duffy and L. Murry, "The Wooing of American Investors," *The Wall Street Journal*, February 25, 1994, p. A14.

18. International Monetary Fund, *World Economic Outlook* (Washington, DC: IMF, 1998).

19. B. Javetski and W. Glasgall, "Borderless Finance: Fuel for Growth," *Business Week*, November 18, 1994, pp. 40–50.

20. R. Reich, *The Work of Nations* (New York: Alfred A. Knopf, 1991).

CASES

Defending the Brazilian Real

Risky Business: Nick Leeson, Global Derivatives
Trading, and the Fall of Barings Bank

DEFENDING THE BRAZILIAN REAL

Introduction

Since the early 1990s, Brazil has been a story of steady economic improvement. Once the home of perennial hyperinflation, Brazil has pursued economic policies that have been designed to transform Latin America's largest economy into a dynamic market-based system. These policies have included the privatization of state-owned enterprises, such as the onetime local telephone monopoly, Telebras; substantial deregulation to open the economy to greater domestic and foreign competition; the pursuit of regional and multinational free trade agreements; and the dismantling of barriers to foreign direct investment. The centerpiece of these policies, however, was the *Plano Real* (Real Plan) introduced in mid-1994.

The Real Plan

The *real* (pronounced ray-ahl) is the Brazilian currency. In 1994, it replaced the old currency, the cruzeiro, whose value had been significantly debased by years of high inflation. The *real* plan was the brainchild of Fernando Henrique Cardoso, then the finance minister and now the president. Cardoso's real plan was designed to drive inflation out of the Brazilian economy. When implemented in 1994, the annual inflation rate was running at over 1,000 percent. This hyperinflation disrupted economic activity and discouraged foreign investment. The *real* plan was based on tight monetary policy. To help enforce this, the value of the *real* was pegged to that of the US dollar and allowed to depreciate against the dollar by no more than 7.5 percent per year. To keep depreciation within these bounds, Brazilian authorities had to raise interest rates repeatedly to maintain the value of the real against the dollar. The high cost of credit helped reduce the expansion of the money supply and brought inflation under control in Brazil.

By all accounts, the *real* plan was a major success. In 1996, inflation had already fallen to 10 percent, and it fell to an annual rate of 4 percent by early 1998 and 2 percent by late 1998. At the same time, the Brazilian economy continued to grow at the relatively robust rate of 3 to 4 percent a year, while foreign direct investment soared to a record $16 billion in 1997 and $22 billion in 1998.

Brazil's Economic Straitjacket

Despite the defeat of inflation and several years of robust economic activity, not all was well within Brazil's economy. By mid-1998, the trade deficit on the current account was running at about 4 percent of GDP. Also, the Brazilian government was spending in excess of its tax receipts and running a fiscal deficit that amounted to 7 percent of GDP. According to critics of the government, the trade deficit was the result of an overvalued real, which was hindering exports while sucking imports into the country. By most estimates, the real was overvalued against the US dollar by between 15 and 20 percent. Some economists argued that the Brazilian government should devalue the real to help correct the trade imbalance. The Cardoso government, however, was reluctant to abandon its commitment to maintaining the dollar peg. After all, this policy had defeated decades of hyperinflation and stabilized the economy.

The causes of Brazil's fiscal deficit was more complex. Government spending had exceeded tax revenues for years. Financing the public-sector deficit required government borrowing, which had pushed up interest rates and made it more difficult for private businesses to get access to credit. The root cause of the deficit was the rigid structure of government spending in Brazil. In all, Brazil collected some 30 percent of GDP in taxes, but only two-thirds of this, some 18.4 percent of GDP, went to the federal government (the rest going to state and local governments). Also, four *constitutionally mandated* budget items were eating up 90 percent of the government's tax revenues. These were (*i*) transfers to other branches and tiers of government, (*ii*) civil service pay, (*iii*) pensions and other welfare spending, and (*iv*) interest payments on federal debt. In the years of hyperinflation, making huge future commitments to pensions or welfare spending mattered little. Inflation would rapidly reduce the value of such commitments when measured in constant currency units. However, with inflation under control, the government could no longer rely on inflation to reduce the value of its public-sector commitments.

The deficit problem was exacerbated by the fact that government employees were overpaid, earning about 30 percent more than their private-sector counterparts. Their pension privileges were even larger. The 3 million public service pensioners got about as much as nearly 18 million private sector ones. The public-sector pension system had allowed many civil servants to retire in their mid-40s on pensions higher than their last salary. The cost of servicing these pensions had soared because high inflation ended, a bulge of people who entered the labor force during the 1960s and 1970s had retired during the 1990s, and pensioners were living longer.

Cardoso's approach to solving the structural deficit problem was to try to amend the Brazilian constitution to reform the pension, civil service, and tax systems. However, pushing constitutional changes through Brazil's parliament required a 60 percent majority in both houses, and despite repeated attempts, by mid-1998 Cardoso had made only limited progress in reforming Brazil's constitution to gain greater control over fiscal spending.

The Real under Pressure

The first sign that Brazil's economic progress might be starting to unravel came in late 1997, when the Asian financial crisis was unfolding. The Asian crisis triggered panic selling in all emerging markets. Money started to flow out of Brazil, putting pressure on the *real*. Cardoso's government responded by raising interest rates to 43 percent and announced an $18 billion package of tax increases and spending cuts to stabilize the economy and reduce the budget deficit to 2.5 percent of GDP. These actions helped to stem the flow of capital and stabilize the *real*, but at the cost of slowing the economy and exacerbating the budget deficit as government tax receipts declined. While Cardoso gained parliamentary approval for the tax increases in November 1997, the legislature balked at the cuts in social spending. As a consequence, the public-sector borrowing requirement climbed to 7 percent of GDP, up from 4.5 percent the year earlier. In October 1998, federal government tax receipts were 4 percent lower than in the same month in 1997.

The next financial shock came in August 1998, when the Russian government announced it would default on its debt obligations and devalue the Russian ruble by a third. The debt default by the Russian government sent a shock wave throughout the emerging markets around the world. If Russia could default on its debt, who else might? Acting in dreadful unison, financial institutions reacted by indiscriminately pulling out of emerging market debt and equity positions, triggering a global collapse in stock and bond prices. Across Latin America, widely viewed as one of the most vulnerable regions, stock markets fell by 25 to 30 percent, bond prices slumped, and interest rates soared as investors fled to the security of high-quality US Treasury bonds. This global "flight to quality" pushed the yield on 30-year US T-bills to an all-time low of less than 5 percent, while the interest rate spreads between US and emerging market sovereign debt widened alarmingly. The spread between yields on Brazilian government bonds and US government bonds, for example, surged from 4 percent to 12 percent in a matter of days. The flight to US government debt, however, did not save the US stock market, which tumbled in sympathy with stock markets around the world, losing nearly 20 percent of its value in a few short, sharp trading sessions.

With money flowing out of emerging markets like a riptide, the currencies of several nations came under strong selling pressure. The nation of most concern to foreign investors was Brazil, which many feared would be the next to crumble. If Brazil collapsed, taking the rest of Latin America down with it, the United States would suffer major adverse consequences. Latin America absorbed over 20 percent of all exports from the United States, and American multinationals had major investments across the region.

Defending the Real

To defend the Brazilian *real* against this latest round of selling, the Brazilian government took a number of steps. First, the Brazilian central bank entered the foreign exchange market, using its foreign exchange reserves to purchase *reals* in the open market. As a result, between early August and mid-September 1998, Brazil lost about one-third of its foreign exchange reserves, reducing them to less than $50 billion. At one point, the central bank was spending $1 billion a day to defend the *real*. Second, the government announced $10.8 billion in budget cuts. However, after having failed to follow through with budget cuts announced the previous November, the international markets viewed this announcement with some skepticism and traders continued to sell the *real*. Third, the Brazilian government repeatedly raised interest rates in order to increase the attractiveness of holding the *real*. By late September, Brazilian interest rates stood at 39 percent, the highest interest rates in the world. While the interest rate hikes helped to slow down the fall in the currency, they also increased the costs of servicing government debt while depressing economic activity, thereby reducing government tax receipts and raising the specter of further deterioration in the fiscal deficit. To complicate matters further, Brazil was in the middle of a presidential election campaign and the resulting political uncertainty put further pressure on the *real*.

By late September, the government revealed that it was negotiating with the International Monetary Fund (IMF) for financial support. This, coupled with polls suggesting that Cardoso would win the upcoming presidential election campaign, helped to bring some calm back to the foreign exchange markets. On October 4, Cardoso was reelected president, getting a majority of all votes cast in the first round of elections, an outcome that was widely interpreted as a vote in support of his proposals for tough fiscal medicine to help defend the real and correct Brazil's fiscal deficit. Cardoso's election victory had bought the country time, but not much.

With Cardoso reelected, the government continued to negotiate with the IMF. On October 8, 1998, in a joint statement with the Cardoso government, the IMF promised support in return for a number of actions from Brazil. These included stiff reductions in government spending, accompanied by associated reforms in the social security, civil service, pension, and tax systems. The goals of the actions included a budget surplus before interest payments of around 2.5 percent of GDP in 1999 and stabilization of the ratio of debt to GDP by 2000.

On October 28, the Brazilian government followed up the joint statement by announcing a $23.5 billion austerity package for 1999. The plan contained $11 billion worth of tax increases and $12.5 billion in budget cuts and major structural reforms. Further proposed retrenchments, if implemented, would make it an $84 billion program over three years. The austerity package singled out the pension system with an 11 percent tax on pensions collected by retired civil servants and on retirement contributions by active public employees. An additional 20 percent tax would be imposed on the highest pensions. Another feature of the package would raise the tax on corporate earnings from 2 percent to 3 percent and levy a tax on banks as well. With the announcement of this package, the Cardoso government hoped to be able to unlock funds from the IMF.

The IMF, however, had been struggling with problems of its own. The institution had been widely criticized for its handling of the Asian financial crisis. Some argued that the stiff monetary and fiscal policy measures that the IMF had recently imposed on three Asian clients, South Korea, Thailand, and Indonesia, were inappropriate given the price deflation those nations were experiencing. The IMF, critics charged, had helped to exacerbate the economic troubles of Asian nations, not solve them. Seizing on such criticisms, opponents of the IMF in the US Congress held up requests by the executive branch to replenish the IMF's coffers. It was only after intense lobbying and significant concessions that Congress backed down. On October 16, 1997, it agreed to approve $3.4 billion toward a new emergency credit line, as well as $14.5 billion in new capital. The concessions extracted from the IMF by the Congress included a requirement that IMF loans to troubled countries would come with an interest rate at least three percentage points above broader market rates and would be repaid within 30 months. It was widely expected that once the US government stepped up to the plate and funded the IMF, a further $74 billion would be forthcoming from other IMF member states.

The IMF Package

On November 13, 1998, a Friday, the IMF announced that Brazil would receive loans of $41.5 billion. Of this amount, $14.5 billion would come from the world's richest countries, led by the United States (which put up $5 billion). The loan was to support the Brazilian economy

while it implemented the austerity package unveiled October 28. After the announcement, capital flight diminished to a trickle and the real stabilized. Brazil's stock market even staged a small rally.

However, not everyone was satisfied that the IMF rescue package was the right approach to take in the case of Brazil. According to some influential economists, such as Jeffrey Sachs, director of Harvard's Institute for International Development, attempts by the IMF and Cardoso to defend the *real* were folly. According to Sachs, Brazil would be better served by bowing to market forces and letting the *real* float freely. In making his case, Sachs pointed to the relative success of Mexico in handling external shocks since it was forced to float the peso in December 1994. Allowing the real to float, according to Sachs, would help Brazil keep its exports competitive. It would also reduce the need for the country to raise interest rates to levels that severely depressed economic activity and dramatically increased the costs of servicing government debt. Critics of this approach argued that if Brazil were to let the real float, the decision would trigger panic among international investors and undermine the credibility of a government that had hitched its wagon to a pegged exchange rate policy. For a country with a long history of inflation, a floating exchange rate would be widely viewed as rekindling the inflationary fires.

Others argued that far from going to a floating system, Brazil should try to strengthen its commitment to maintaining a stable real by adopting a currency board system for managing the exchange rate and locking the real into the US dollar. The currency board system would require that all real issued be backed by US dollars held by the Brazilian central bank. New real could be issued only if the country could gain additional US dollars to back them up. Gaining additional dollars would require Brazil to make itself an attractive investment location for holders of US dollars, which cannot be achieved without a sound economic policy. It would also require that Brazil cede control over interest rates to the US Federal Reserve. Although several countries have adopted a currency board, including Hong Kong and Argentina, both of which have arguably benefited from the system, it might be culturally difficult to implement such a system in Brazil, implying as it does the loss of some national sovereignty.

Aftermath

If anyone thought the IMF announcement would bring an end to Brazil's troubles, they were disappointed. Cardoso's government did push several elements of the austerity package through the Brazilian Congress. However, despite having the nominal support of three-quarters of the members of Congress, in early December 1998, the government's proposal to raise pension contributions for civil servants and raise taxes on the pensions of retired government employees was defeated. Although recent constitutional reforms meant the government had to get only a simple majority to force the measure through Congress, it failed to do so. After intense lobbying by public-sector workers, about 100 nominal supporters of the government voted against the measure. Another 100 finessed the issue by failing to turn up for the vote. Despite this setback, Cardoso remained confident that the measure would be passed early in the new year.

However, Cardoso's political problems were not over. Claiming a lack of funds due to economic hardship, on January 10, 1999, the Brazilian state of Minas Gerais declared a 90-day moratorium on debt payments owed to the central government. This would make it more difficult for the federal government to meet its own debt service obligations. The decision to declare a moratorium was made by the state's Governor and former Brazilian President Itamar Franco. Although the amount of money involved was not huge—$67 million a month—the action raised concerns that other cash-strapped states would follow. The Brazilian stock market plunged 6 percent on the news and a further 7 percent the following day. On January 12, the US stock market dropped 2 percent in sympathy. Brazil and the global financial system were not out of the woods yet.

Discussion Questions

1. Explain the mechanism by which the *real* plan helped to defeat hyperinflation in Brazil.

2. What actions does the Brazilian government need to take to defend the peg of the real against the US dollar?

3. Do you think the Brazilian government was correct to place a high value on defending the peg of the *real* against the US dollar? What were the costs to Brazil of this policy? What were the benefits?

4. What do you think might happen to the value of the *real*, and the Brazilian economy in general, if the Brazilian government abandoned its defense of the real and decided to let it float against the dollar?

5. What would be the implications of allowing the *real* to float for the rest of Latin America and for the economy of the United States?

Sources

1. Balls, A. "IMF Leads $41 Billion Gamble on Fiscal Adjustment Plan." *Financial Times*, December 21, 1998, p. 2.

2. "The Battle Royal for Brazil's Real." *The Economist*, September 12, 1998, p. 35.

3. "Brazil's Last Stand?" *The Economist*, September 19, 1998, p. 98.

4. "Can Cardoso Use Financial Chaos to Reform Brazil?" *The Economist*, September 26, 1998, p. 33.

5. Druckerman, P., and P. Beckett. "Foreign Banks Turn More Cautious on Brazil." *The Wall Street Journal*, January 11, 1999, p. A10.

6. Dyer, J. "Make or Break Time for President." *Financial Times*, December 21, 1998, p. 3.

7. Feldstein, M., and K. Feldstein. "It's Imperative to Save Latin America's Largest Economy." *Boston Globe*, November 10, 1998, p. D4.

8. Fidler, S. "Last Tango in Rio." *Financial Times*, November 18, 1998, p. 23.

9. Fritsch, P. "Brazil Jolted as Governor Balks on Federal Debt." *The Wall Street Journal*, January 8, 1999, p. A15.

10. "The IMF and Brazil: A Deal at Last." *The Economist*, October 17, 1998, p. 93.

11. Katz, I. "Brazil's Ill Winds." *Business Week*, September 21, 1998, p. 34.

12. Rotella, S. "Brazil Unveils Plan to Stave Off Economic Crisis." *Los Angeles Times*, October 29, 1998, p. A1.

RISKY BUSINESS: NICK LEESON, GLOBAL DERIVATIVES TRADING, AND THE FALL OF BARINGS BANK

"Derivatives need to be well controlled and understood, but we believe we do that here."

Peter Baring, chairman, Barings Brothers, October 1993.

"I'm sorry."

Note left by Nick Leeson, February 1995

Introduction

In February 1995, the financial world was shaken by the revelation that unauthorized derivatives trading by a 27-year-old Englishman, Nick Leeson, employed at the Singapore office of Britain's oldest bank, Barings Plc, had amassed losses of at least $950 million (the figure was later revised upward to $1.33 billion). The debacle resulted in the collapse of Barings and its purchase, for the princely sum of £1, by a Dutch bank, International Nederlanden Groep NV (ING). So ended the history of a 233-year-old "aristocratic" bank whose clients at the time of its collapse included Queen Elizabeth II of England.

To many critics, the collapse of Barings offered more proof that the rapid rise of derivatives trading in global financial markets was a dangerous and potentially destabilizing influence in the world economy. Barings joined a growing list of organizations that had lost vast sums of money on derivatives trading, including Metallgesellschaft AG of Germany (lost $1.3 billion), Procter & Gamble (lost $102 million), Kidder Peabody & Co. (lost $350 million), and Orange County of California (lost $1.7 billion). These critics used the collapse of Barings to intensify their calls for tighter regulation of global derivatives trading.

But there were those who argued that when employed correctly, derivatives can be used to reduce risk, not increase it. They attributed the losses at Barings to the actions of a rogue financial trader who was engaged in risky speculation and to poor internal management controls at Barings. Further, they argued that the ease with which the world's financial markets absorbed the shock of the Barings collapse is proof that the world financial system is sound and should not be encumbered by unnecessary government regulations.

Financial Derivatives

A *derivatives transaction* is a contract whose value depends on ("derives from") the value of an underlying asset, reference rate, or index. Derivatives include forward, future, swap, and option transactions that are based on interest rates, currencies, equities, and commodities (for a detailed exposition of the mechanics of forward and swap transactions based on currencies, see Chapter 9). Derivatives have been in use for at least 100 years, although their popularity in recent years has grown rapidly. In 1986, derivative contracts with a notional value of about $1 trillion were traded annually. By 1990, this figure had risen to $5 trillion, and it approached $20 trillion by 1994. This rapid growth in the volume of derivative trading has raised fears that derivatives might destabilize the world financial system.

A major factor leading to the growth of derivatives trading in currencies was the collapse of the Bretton Woods agreement in 1971 and the resulting shift from a fixed to a floating exchange rate regime (see Chapter 10 for details). Under a floating exchange rate regime,

exporters and importers hedged (insured against) adverse currency changes by purchasing foreign currency through forward exchanges or by engaging in currency swaps. During the 1970s and 1980s, corporations and traders increasingly turned to derivatives contracts to insure against possibly adverse future changes in a wide range of other assets such as commodities, bonds, or stocks.

For an example of a derivative contract for a commodity, consider a company that knows it will need to purchase 1 million barrels of oil in six months. Imagine that the current price of oil is $15 per barrel, but the company fears that the price may rise substantially over the next six months because of turmoil in Saudi Arabia, the world's largest oil exporting nation. The company can either wait and bear the risk that the price of oil might rise in six months, or it can enter into a *futures contract* today. Under this contract, it might agree to purchase the price of oil in six months at $16 per barrel. The $1 difference between the price of oil today and the price specified in the contract represents an insurance, or hedge, against a possible rise in the future price of oil. By entering into the contract, the company has reduced its exposure to future rises in oil prices; it has reduced its risk.

Another common form of derivative is a stock option. A stock option is a contract that gives the owner the right to purchase or sell a specific number of shares at a fixed price within a definite time. For example, imagine that you hold 1,000 shares of Compaq Computer, which is trading at $50 per share (the market value of your holding is $50,000). You fear that due to a temporary slowdown in the growth rate of personal computer sales, the price of Compaq might fall in the near future, but you don't want to sell the stock because you like Compaq's long-term prospects. You know that it is by no means a sure thing that sales are slowing, and Compaq could continue to do well even if sales do slow. You might decide to take out insurance against the possibility that the stock will fall by purchasing a *put option*. The put option contract might give you the right but not the obligation to sell 1,000 shares of Compaq in three months at $50 per share to the *writer of the option*. The put option might cost you $1 per share, or $1,000.

If the price of Compaq shares does not fall, the put option contract might expire worthless in three months. However, if Compaq shares fall to $40, the put option contract will rise to about $10 per share. You can either sell the shares for $50 each to the writer of the put option, or your could sell the option contract for $10,000 (1,000 shares at $10 per share) and pocket the $9,000 profit while holding onto the shares. Whatever action you choose, although the value of your Compaq stock has fallen from $50,000 to $40,000 over the three months, your actual loss is limited to just $1,000, the price of the put option contract. By purchasing a put option contract, you have limited your exposure to a fall in the price of Compaq shares.

In addition to put options, one can also purchase *call options*. Call options are simply the reverse of put options. They are an option that gives you the right to purchase a certain number of shares *from the option writer* at a fixed price within a specified time. For example, if you think that Compaq's price might rise from $50 to $80 per share, but you are unwilling to purchase another 1,000 shares for $50,000 at this time, you could enter into a call option contract that gives you the right to purchase 1,000 shares from the call option writer in three months at $50 per share. Again, the option contract might cost you $1 per share. If the price of shares goes up to $80, you will make a large profit. If the price falls, your loss is limited to the $1,000 cost of the call option contract.

You might be wondering why anyone would want to *write* an option contract. The option writer pockets the price of the option contract if it expires worthless, which happens enough to make the practice worthwhile. To increase their potential returns further, many option writers write "uncovered" or "naked" options. For example, consider a trader who writes a call option that gives the buyer the right to purchase 1,000 shares of Compaq at $50 per share in three months. If the option writer deposited 1,000 shares of Compaq with her stockbroker, this would be termed a *covered call*, because the writer (or seller) has enough shares in her account to pay the buyer if he exercises his call option to purchase 1,000 shares at $50. An *uncovered call* occurs when the option writer does not deposit enough shares to cover the eventuality that the buyer of the option will exercise his call option. An option writer can write such an uncovered call option in a *margin account*, which is an account where the broker lends the money to the option writer (at an appropriate rate of interest) to cover the cost of meeting the call obligation. Brokers will do this if the option writer can show that she has sufficient funds elsewhere to cover the cost of meeting her potential call obligations and/or servicing any interest payments that must be incurred on funds borrowed to meet call obligations. Writing uncovered calls (or uncovered puts) is a risky strategy, but it does have the advantage of *leverage*. For a relatively small deposit in a margin account, the option writer can write a relatively large volume of options and potentially earn substantial returns on this relatively small deposit.

Option contracts are not limited to stock equities. They can also be written for many other financial assets. One popular form of options are index options, where the value of an option is linked to the value of a basket of stocks that make up a popular stock index, such as the Dow Jones Industrials, the S&P 500, or the Nikkei 225 stock market index.

Barings Bank

Although a relatively small player in the investment banking world with about 4,000 employees and assets of $10 billion in 1994, Barings was a widely respected bank that was considered a strong niche player in the emerging markets of Asia, Latin America, and Eastern Europe. Its money management arm managed about $46 billion for a variety of individual and corporate clients, including the Queen of England. The bank was also considered to have a talented corporate finance team with good connections in British industry.

The bank was established in 1762 by two sons of German immigrants, and it flourished. Barings was the first bank to reopen trade with America after the Revolutionary War; it helped the US government finance the Louisiana purchase from France; and it played a major role in financing Britain's wars against Napoleon. For its help in the Napoleonic wars, a grateful British government bestowed five noble titles on the Baring family. The family became prominent members of the British ruling class. The family continued to maintain close ties with the bank, and in 1995 the chairman was Peter Baring.

For most of its 233 years, Barings concentrated on the old-fashioned business of investment banking, taking in deposits and lending money to corporations and governments. In a departure from this focus, Barings in 1984 established a securities trading arm, Barings Securities, to take advantage of and profit from the trading opportunities presented by the rapid growth of international financial markets. The trading arm quickly established itself as a profitable operation.

However, a clash of cultures soon began to emerge between the investment banking and securities operations. Part of the problem seems to have been linked to the different backgrounds and attitudes of the personalities involved. The investment banking arm, known as Barings Brothers, was staffed by products of the British establishment, but many of the traders came from a different class background. In distinct contrast to the "blue-blooded" investment bankers typified by Peter Baring, Nick Leeson, whose unauthorized trades sunk the bank, was the son of a North London working-class family. A securities trader who once worked for Barings Securities in Tokyo had the following recollections:

> There was always an uneasy tension between Barings Brothers and Barings Securities. "We're the bankers," they seemed to say, "heirs to a 200-year tradition, and you're the

jumped up guys from Liverpool." What seemed to make things worse was that Barings Securities was phenomenally profitable for a while. But the attitude persisted: "OK you guys did great for five years, but we've been here for 200. Don't tell us how to run the business . . . When Peter Baring came to Tokyo to visit the securities department, it was like a visit from the queen."

The British newsmagazine *The Economist* had a similar view of the relationship between Barings Brothers and Barings Securities:

> The old-style bankers who dominated Barings' senior management have long looked down their aristocratic noses at the traders who run the bank's security operations.

Things came to a head in 1992 when tumbling stock prices in Tokyo pushed the normally profitable Barings Securities into a $20 million loss. In an attempt to turn things around, Christopher Heath, the head of Barings Securities, lobbied for more capital to boost proprietary trading (trading on the firm's own account). Andrew Tuckey, the deputy chairman of Barings, objected that this would leave the group too exposed to volatile financial markets. In response, Heath resigned, and he was followed by a number of other key directors at Barings Securities. According to one former Barings Securities employee,

> It was effectively a takeover of the securities operation by the (investment) bank. You had the unworkable situation of investment bankers supposedly overseeing investment traders.

Barings employees refer to the period that following 1993 coup as "The Turbulence." In Asia, it led to a confusing series of personnel moves that ultimately left management dangerously weakened. In Tokyo, for example, the longtime Barings Securities branch manager, Richard Greer, was replaced by Henry Anstey, who was also soon replaced. Barings Securities in Hong Kong lost a team of seven from its proprietary trading and derivatives desk to the start-up operation New China Hong Kong Securities. The Hong Kong operation suffered another blow when Willie Phillips, formerly head of all security business in Asia outside of Japan, left for Salomon Brothers. Also important was the loss of Richard Johnson, who had headed Barings derivative operations in Tokyo until he was transferred to London in 1992. Johnson, who left Barings in May 1993, was "the brains of the group," according to a former colleague. "His departure opened a large hole in the region."

As a result of these management changes, in 1995 a former Barings employee observed:

> There has been no continuity of management for the past two years. It was difficult to say who was in charge of what

and where from one month to the next . . . The team that had been built up from the late 1980s (in the Asian securities operations) was scattered to the four winds . . . The pool of derivatives-based knowledge in the region virtually disappeared.

Another former employee had similar observations:

> You had a situation where the securities side was still at loggerheads with the banking side. On top of that, the derivatives side was little understood by either... Working in derivatives was a little like working in a vacuum. To most of the senior guys on both the securities side and the merchant bank, it was like we were talking a foreign language. They just let us get on with it. We did our own controls and regulated ourselves to all intents and purposes. In hindsight, there wasn't anyone for us to report to.

Nick Leeson's Little Trades

It was against this chaotic background in Barings Asian securities operations that Nick Leeson arrived in Singapore in 1991 to help unravel some backroom trading problems. Within a year, Leeson had joined the trading team on the floor of the Singapore International Monetary Exchange (SIMEX). By day he executed trades in the Nikkei Stock Averages futures contracts under the direction of Barings traders in Japan. By night he partied in the yuppie bars along the Singapore River. According to a former colleague:

> He was your average English guy who likes to go out for a beer after work, and sometimes has a few too many. I wouldn't have said anything negative about him.

Leeson's primary job at Barings was to arbitrage Nikkei Index futures contracts that were traded on both the Singapore and Osaka exchanges (trading of Nikkei futures in Singapore began in the 1980s when the Japanese government tried to curtail futures trading in Osaka). Such arbitrage involves buying futures contracts on one market and simultaneously selling them on another. Profits are made by exploiting small price differentials for the same contract between the two exchanges. Because the margins are small, the volumes traded by arbitrageurs tend to be very large. However, the strategy is associated with very little risk.

Leeson was a successful arbitrage trader. By September 1994, he was viewed as the senior trader for Barings in Singapore, even though he was only 27 years old. At this point Leeson departed from the low-risk arbitrage strategy and started to speculate on the volatility of the Nikkei 225 stock index. Leeson's motives for speculation aren't entirely clear, although maximizing the size of his bonus, which could have easily run into seven figures had his strategy been successful, was a factor. Leeson's strategy involved simultaneously writing uncovered put and call options on Nikkei 225 futures. Known as a straddle strategy, the procedures will make money for the option writer provided the market stays within a relatively narrow trading range. However, the strategy required Barings to sell the Nikkei 225 index when it crossed 19,500 and to buy it when it fell below 18,500. Leeson's strategy made Barings money as long as the Nikkei stayed within this relatively narrow range. Once the Nikkei went outside this range, Barings started to lose large amounts of money—about $70 million for every 1 percent move above or below these limits. The loss was exacerbated by Leeson's aggressive use of leverage (he was writing options from a margin account).

At first the strategy seemed to be working. Traders at other banks reckon that Leeson may have earned as much as $150 million for Barings from this strategy by the end of 1994. However, the strategy started to fall apart when the Kobe earthquake struck January 17, 1995. In response to the economic devastation caused by the earthquake, the Nikkei started to plunge. Worried that the market would fall well below 18,500, Leeson seems to have entered the market and purchased Nikkei futures on a huge scale in an attempt to push the market up above 18,500. This is not an easy thing to do; the Tokyo stock market is the second biggest in the world.

Leeson's position deteriorated further on January 23 when the Tokyo stock market plunged 1,000 points to under 17,800. An increasingly desperate Nick Leeson responded to the crisis by drawing on a margin account to continue purchasing Nikkei futures in what was to prove to be a futile attempt to prop up the Nikkei index. By late February 1995, Barings had accumulated index positions that effectively amounted to a $7 billion bet on the Tokyo stock market. At the height of Leeson's trades, Barings accounted for about half of the open positions in Nikkei 225 futures contracts.

Such financial excess did not go unnoticed by other traders in Singapore or by executives at Barings Bank in London. However, Barings executives and other traders were all under the impression that Leeson was acting on behalf of a major client, perhaps a big hedge fund. No one could conceive that the positions belonged to Barings. Apparently much of the cash required to purchase Nikkei futures came from an account for a fictitious client that Leeson had set up as early as 1992. This account contained some of Barings' own cash, along with all the proceeds of Leeson's option sales and some fictitious profits from falsified arbitrage deals. He used this fictitious account to pay margin calls on his growing futures position. When the account was exhausted, Leeson turned to Barings in London, saying he was executing trades on behalf of a major client who would settle

up in a few days. Barings proved only too willing to send more money to its star trader in Singapore.

Bolstered by the arrival of additional funds from London, Leeson kept up the charade until February 23, when the cash flowing out to cover margin payments exceeded Barings's limits. With the Nikkei continuing to decline, Leeson apparently realized that he could no longer carry on with the game. He hurriedly faxed a letter to Barings in London tendering his resignation, adding that he was sorry for the trouble he had caused and along with his wife boarded a plane out of Singapore. The next day shocked Barings executives informed the Bank of England that they were technically bankrupt. The liabilities from Leeson's trades already exceeded $800 million and were growing by the hour as the Nikkei index continued to fall.

Aftermath

Over the weekend of February 25 and 26, the stunned management of Barings tried to arrange for a bailout by the Bank of England. Several investment banks were summoned to the Bank of England's offices to discuss the possibility of raising enough private money to recapitalize Barings before the Tokyo market reopened on Monday morning. However, the attempt failed because of the size of Barings's positions in Japanese derivatives contracts, many of them still open and liable to incur still bigger losses. No bank was willing to take on these contracts without a large fee or a guarantee from the Bank of England that it would cover these losses. The Bank of England, which stated later that such a fee might have amounted to $700 million, decided it was not prepared to put the British taxpayers' money at risk.

On March 3, the Dutch financial group ING stepped in and offered to purchase Barings for £1 in exchange for taking on all of the Barings liabilities. With no other offers on the table, Barings directors were obliged to accept the ING offer. In the following weeks, ING moved quickly to replace virtually all of Barings' top management, including Chairman Peter Baring, and to tighten controls within the group.

Nick Leeson's whereabouts were a mystery for several days. Then on March 3, Leeson was detained by German immigration authorities as he tried to board a plane back to Britain. Leeson was eventually deported back to Singapore, where he faced charges for securities fraud. Among other things, it was alleged that he falsified trading data to create paper profits that were then funneled into accounts attributed to fictitious clients. It was from these accounts that Leeson executed many of his trades in the run up to the collapse of Barings. In December 1995, he was sentenced to six and a half years in prison.

As for the global financial system, initially there were worries that the revelations about Barings might lead to a loss of confidence in the global financial system and in the financial position of many banks engaged in derivatives trading. But there was no evidence of a negative effect from the Barings collapse. Rather, the financial community soon viewed the collapse of Barings as having little to do with derivatives trading per se and much more to do with the lack of internal management controls at Barings. This lack of controls allowed Leeson to speculate using financial instruments that were designed to reduce risk, not increase it. According to the prevailing view among other traders, the problem lay not in the tool Leeson used—derivatives—but in the way Leeson used that tool and the poor monitoring of his activities.

In July of 1995, the Bank of England issued a report on the collapse of Barings. The bank also expressed the view that Barings suffered from poor internal management controls. According to the report:

> Significant amounts were regularly remitted to BFS without any clear understanding on the part of Barings' management on whose behalf these monies were to be applied, and without any real demur.

The Bank of England's report also cited a number of senior managers at Barings, including Andrew Tuckey and Peter Baring, for failing to apply proper controls.

In an interview given to BBC Television's David Frost in September, Nick Leeson, then in a German jail awaiting deportation to Singapore, also gave more insight into the collapse of Barings. According to Leeson, he got away with his trading for so long because of the failure of key executives at Barings' London headquarters to understand the business he was engaged in and to look more closely into his activities.

> The first day that I asked for funding (to meet margin calls) there should have been massive alarm bells ringing. But senior people in London that were arranging these payments didn't understand the basic administration of futures and options . . . They wanted to believe in the profits being reported, and therefore they weren't willing to question.

Discussion Questions

1. Why do you think critics are worried that the rapid growth in the use of derivatives might destabilize global financial markets?

2. Do you think derivatives are risky and speculative financial instruments or instruments that can be used to reduce an investor's risk?

3. Does the collapse of Barings expose a fundamental flaw in the global financial system? If so, how might this flaw be fixed?

4. What is your view on the basic causes of the collapse of Barings Bank?

Sources

1. Bray, N., and G. Whitney. "Barings Collapse Tied to Wide Cast." *The Wall Street Journal*, July 19, 1995, p. A5.

2. Bray, N. "Leeson Says Losses at Barings Started with Bailout of Errors by Colleagues." *The Wall Street Journal*, September 11, 1995, p. A16.

3. "A Fallen Star." *The Economist*, March 4, 1995, pp. 19–21.

4. Mark, J., and M. Sesit. "Losses at Barings Grow to $1.24 Billion." *The Wall Street Journal*, February 28, 1995, p. A3.

5. Melloan, G. "Leeson's Law." *The Wall Street Journal*, March 6, 1995, p. A15.

6. Nusbaum, D., and J. Reerink. "BoE Report Details Barings' Guiles and Goofs." *Futures*, September 1995, pp. 12–22.

7. "A Royal Mess." *The Wall Street Journal*, February 27, 1995, p. A1.

8. Shale, T. "Why Barings Was Doomed." *Euromoney*, March 1995, pp. 38–41.

9. United States General Accounting Office; Report to Congress. *Financial Derivatives*, May 1994, GOA GGD-94-133.

10. Whitney, G. "Dutch Giant Offers to Buy All of Barings." *The Wall Street Journal*, March 3, 1995, p. A3.

THE STRATEGY AND STRUCTURE OF INTERNATIONAL BUSINESS

Chapter Twelve
The Strategy of International Business

Chapter Thirteen
The Organization of International Business

Chapter Fourteen
Entry Strategy and Strategic Alliances

CHAPTER TWELVE

THE STRATEGY OF INTERNATIONAL BUSINESS

Global Strategy at General Motors

General Motors is one of the oldest multinational corporations in the world. Founded in 1908, GM established its first international operations in the 1920s. General Motors is now the world's largest industrial corporation and full-line automobile manufacturer with annual revenues of over $100 billion. The company sells 8 million vehicles per year, 3.2 million of which are produced and marketed outside of its North American base. In 1997, GM had a 31 percent share of the North American market and an 8.9 percent share of the market in the rest of the world.

Historically, the bulk of GM's foreign operations have been concentrated in Western Europe. Local brand names, such as Opel, Vauxhall, Saab, and Holden, helped the company sell 1.7 million vehicles in 1997 and gain an 11.3 percent market share, second only to that of Ford in Western Europe. Although GM has long had a presence in Latin America and Asia, until recently sales there accounted for only a small fraction of the company's total international business. However, GM's plans call for this to change rapidly over the next few years. Sensing that Asia, Latin America, and Eastern Europe may be the automobile industry's growth markets early in the 21st century, GM has embarked on ambitious plans to invest $2.2 billion in four new manufacturing facilities in Argentina, Poland, China, and Thailand. This expansion goes hand in hand with a sea change in GM's philosophy toward the management of its international operations.

Traditionally, GM saw the developing world as a dumping ground for obsolete technology and outdated models. Just a few years ago, for example, GM's Brazilian factories were churning out US-designed Chevy Chevettes that hadn't been produced in North America for years. GM's Detroit-based executives saw this as a way of squeezing the maximum cash flow from the company's investments in aging technology. GM managers in the developing world, however, took it as an indication that the center did not view developing world operations as being of great significance. This feeling was exacerbated by the fact that most operations in the developing world were instructed to carry out manufacturing and marketing plans formulated in the company's Detroit headquarters, rather than being trusted to develop their own.

In contrast, GM's European operations were traditionally managed on an arm's-length basis, with the company's national operations often being allowed to design their own cars and manufacturing facilities and formulate their own marketing strategies. This regional and national autonomy allowed GM's European operations to produce vehicles that were tailored to the needs of local customers. However, it also led to the costly duplication of effort in design and manufacturing operations and to a failure to share valuable technology, skills, and practices across different national subsidiaries. Thus, while General Motors exerted tight control over its operations in the developing world, its control over operations in Europe was perhaps too lax. The result was a company whose international operations lacked overall strategic coherence.

Now GM is trying to change this. GM is switching from its Detroit-centric view of the world to a philosophy that centers of excellence may reside anywhere in the company's global operations. The company is trying to tap these centers of excellence to provide its global operations with the latest technology. The four new manufacturing plants being constructed in the developing world are an embodiment of this new approach. Each is identical, each incorporates state-of-the-art technology, and each has been designed not by Americans, but by a team of Brazilian and German engineers. By building identical plants, GM should be able to mimic Toyota, whose plants are so alike that a change in a car in Japan can be quickly replicated around the world. The GM plants are modeled after its Eisenach facility in Germany, which is managed by the company's Opel subsidiary. It was at the Eisenach plant that GM figured out how to implement the lean production system pioneered by Toyota. The plant is now the most efficient auto-manufacturing operation in Europe and the best within GM, with a productivity rate at least twice that of most North American assembly operations. When completed, each of these new plants will produce state-of-the-art vehicles for local consumption.

To realize scale economies, GM is also trying to design and build vehicles that share a common global platform. Engineering teams in Germany, Detroit, South America, and Australia are designing these common vehicle platforms. Local plants will be allowed to customize certain features of these vehicles to match the tastes and preferences of local customers. At the same time, adhering to a common global platform will enable the company to spread its costs of designing a car over greater volume and to realize scale economies in the manufacture of shared components—which should help GM to lower its overall cost structure. The first fruits of this effort include the 1998 Cadillac

Seville, which was designed to be sold in more than 40 countries. GM's family of front-wheel-drive minivans was also designed around a common platform that will allow the vehicles to be produced in multiple locations around the globe, as was the 1998 Opel Astra, which is GM's best-selling car in Europe.

Despite making bold moves in the direction of greater global integration, numerous problems can still be seen on GM's horizon. Compared to Ford, Toyota, or the new Mercedes/Chrysler combination, GM still suffers from high costs, low perceived quality, and a profusion of brands. Moreover, while its aggressive move into emerging markets may be based on the reasonable assumption that demand will be strong in these areas, other automobile companies are also expanding their production facilities in the same markets, raising the specter of global excess capacity and price wars. Finally, and perhaps most significantly, there are those within GM who argue that the push toward "global cars" is misconceived. In particular, the German-based engineering staff at Opel's Russelsheim design facility, which takes the lead on design of many key global models, has voiced concerns that distinctively European engineering features they deem essential to local success may be left by the wayside in a drive to devise what they see as blander "global" cars.

http://www.gm.com

Sources: R. Blumenstein, "GM Is Building Plants in Developing Nations to Woo New Markets," *The Wall Street Journal*, August 4, 1997, p. A1; Haig Simonian, "GM Hopes to Turn Corner with New Astra," *Financial Times*, November 29, 1997, p. 15; and D. Howes, "GM, Ford Play for Keeps Abroad," *Detroit News*, March 8, 1998, p. D1.

Introduction

Our primary concern thus far in this book has been with aspects of the larger environment in which international businesses compete. This environment has included the different political, economic, and cultural institutions found in different nations, the international trade and investment framework, and the international monetary system. Now our focus shifts from the environment to the firm, and in particular, to the actions that managers can take to compete more effectively as an international business. In this chapter, we look at how firms can increase their profitability by expanding their operations in foreign markets. We discuss the different strategies that firms pursue when competing internationally, consider the pros and cons of these strategies, discuss the various factors that affect a firm's choice of strategy, and look at the tactics firms adopt when competing head to head across various national markets. In subsequent chapters, we shall build on the framework established here to discuss a variety of topics including the design of organization structures and control systems for international businesses, the use and misuse of strategic alliances, strategies for exporting, and the various manufacturing, marketing, R&D, human resource, accounting, and financial strategies that are pursued by international businesses.

General Motors, which was profiled in the opening case, gives us a preview of some issues we will deal with in the current chapter. As described in the case, General Motor's international expansion is being driven by a belief that emerging markets offer the greatest potential for future demand growth. GM is not alone in this belief. Not only are many other automobile firms also pursuing a similar expansion strategy, but so are firms based in a wide range of industries. Although GM has long had operations overseas, until recently these took second place in the company's Detroit-centric view of the world. Now GM is recognizing that if it is to compete successfully in emerging markets, it is no longer enough to transfer outdated technology and designs from Detroit. It must build a globally integrated corporation that draws on centers of excellence wherever they may reside in the world to engineer "global" cars and state-of-the-art production systems. But for all its economic benefits, the trend toward greater integration of its global operations is raising concerns within GM's European units. They fear that an ability to respond to local market needs may be lost in the process. As we shall see in this chapter, GM's struggle with this issue is not unique. Many multinational enterprises are struggling to find the right balance between global integration and local responsiveness.

Strategy and the Firm

The fundamental purpose of any business firm is to make a profit. A firm makes a profit if the price it can charge for its output is greater than its costs of producing that output. To do this, a firm must produce a product that is valued by consumers. Thus, we say that business firms engage in value creation. The price consumers are prepared to pay for a product is a measure of the value of the product to consumers.

Firms can increase their profits in two ways: by adding value to a product so that consumers are willing to pay more for it and by lowering the costs of value creation (i.e., the costs of production). A firm adds value to a product when it improves the product's quality, provides a service to the consumer, or customizes the product to consumer needs in such a way that consumers will pay more for it; that is, when the firm *differentiates* the product from that offered by competitors. For example, consumers will pay more for a Mercedes-Benz car than a Hyundai car because they value the superior quality of the Mercedes. Firms lower the costs of value creation when they find ways to perform value creation activities more efficiently. Thus, there are two basic strategies for improving a firm's profitability—a *differentiation strategy* and a *low-cost strategy*.[1]

The Firm as a Value Chain

It is useful to think of the firm as a value chain composed of a series of distinct value creation activities including production, marketing, materials management, R&D, human resources, information systems, and the firm infrastructure. We can categorize these value creation activities as primary activities and support activities (see Figure 12.1).[2]

Primary Activities

The primary activities of a firm have to do with creating the product, marketing and delivering the product to buyers, and providing support and after-sale service to the buyers of the product. We consider the activities involved in the physical creation of

Figure 12.1

The Firm as a Value Chain

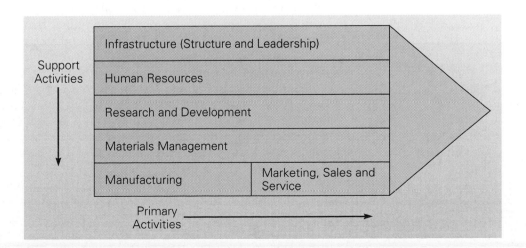

the product as production and those involved in marketing, delivery, and after-sale service as marketing. Efficient production can reduce the costs of creating value (e.g., by realizing scale economies) and can add value by increasing product quality (e.g., by reducing the number of defective products), which facilitates premium pricing. Efficient marketing also can help the firm reduce its production costs (e.g., by generating the volume sales necessary to realize scale economies) and can add value by helping the firm customize its product to consumer needs and differentiate its product from competitors' products—both of which facilitate premium pricing.

Support Activities

Support activities provide the inputs that allow the primary activities of production and marketing to occur. The materials management function controls the transmission of physical materials through the value chain—from procurement through production and into distribution. The efficiency with which this is carried out can significantly reduce the cost of creating value. In addition, an effective materials management function can monitor the quality of inputs into the production process. This results in improved quality of the firm's outputs, which adds value and thus facilitates premium pricing.

The R&D function develops new product and process technologies. Technological developments can reduce production costs and can result in the creation of more useful and more attractive products that can demand a premium price. Thus, R&D can affect primary production and marketing activities and, through them, value creation.

An effective human resource function ensures that the firm has an optimal mix of people to perform its primary production and marketing activities, that the staffing requirements of the support activities are met, and that employees are well trained for their tasks and compensated accordingly. The information systems function makes certain that management has the information it needs to maximize the efficiency of its value chain and to exploit information-based competitive advantages in the marketplace. Firm infrastructure—consisting of such factors as organizational structure, general management, planning, finance, and legal and government affairs—embraces all other activities of the firm and establishes the context for them. An efficient infrastructure helps both to create value and to reduce the costs of creating value.

The Role of Strategy

A firm's **strategy** can be defined as the actions managers take to attain the goals of the firm. For most firms, a principal goal is to be highly profitable. To be profitable in a competitive global environment, a firm must pay continual attention to both reducing the costs of value creation and to differentiating its product offering so that consumers are willing to pay more for the product than it costs to produce it. Thus, strategy is often concerned with identifying and taking actions that will *lower the costs* of value creation and/or will *differentiate* the firm's product offering through superior design, quality, service, functionality, and the like.

Consider the case of Clear Vision, which is profiled in the accompanying Management Focus. A US-based manufacturer of eyeglasses, Clear Vision found its survival threatened by low-cost foreign competitors. To deal with this threat, Clear Vision adopted a strategy intended to lower its cost structure: shifting its production from a high-cost location, the United States, to a low-cost location, Hong Kong. Clear Vision later adopted a strategy intended to differentiate its basic product so it could charge a premium price. Reasoning that premium pricing in eyewear depended on superior design, its strategy involved investing capital in French, Italian, and Japanese factories that had reputations for superior design. In sum, Clear Vision's strategies included some actions intended to reduce its costs of creating value and other actions intended to add value to its product through differentiation.

MANAGEMENT FOCUS
Strategy at Clear Vision

Clear Vision is a manufacturer and distributor of eyewear. Started in the 1970s by David Glassman, the firm today generates annual gross revenues of more than $60 million. Not exactly small, but no corporate giant either, Clear Vision is also a multinational firm with production facilities on three continents and customers around the world. Clear Vision began its move toward becoming a multinational in the early 1980s. The strong dollar at that time made US-based manufacturing very expensive. Low-priced imports were taking a larger share of the US eyewear market, and Clear Vision realized it could not survive unless it also began to import. Initially, the firm bought from independent overseas manufacturers, primarily in Hong Kong. However, the firm became dissatisfied with these suppliers' product quality and delivery. As Clear Vision's volume of imports increased, Glassman decided the best way to guarantee quality and delivery was to set up Clear Vision's own manufacturing operation overseas. Clear Vision found a Chinese partner, and together they opened a manufacturing facility in Hong Kong, with Clear Vision being the majority shareholder.

The choice of the Hong Kong location was influenced by its combination of low labor costs, a skilled work force, and tax breaks given by the Hong Kong government. By 1986, however, the increasing industrialization of Hong Kong and a growing labor shortage had pushed up wage rates so it was no longer a low-cost location. In response, Glassman and his Chinese partner moved part of their manufacturing to a plant in mainland China to take advantage of the lower wage rates there. The parts manufactured at this plant are shipped to the Hong Kong factory for final assembly and then distributed to markets in North and South America. The Hong Kong factory now employs 80 people and the China plant between 300 and 400.

At the same time, Clear Vision had begun to look for opportunities to invest in foreign eyewear firms with reputations for fashionable design and high quality. Its objective was not to reduce manufacturing costs but to launch a line of high-quality, "designer" eyewear. Clear Vision did not have the design capability in-house to support such a line, but Glassman knew that certain foreign manufacturers had the capability. Clear Vision invested in factories in Japan, France, and Italy, taking a minority shareholding in each case. These factories now supply eyewear for Clear Vision's Status Eye division, which markets high-priced designer eyewear.

Source: Based on C. S. Trager, "Enter the Mini-Multinational," *Northeast International Business*, March 1989, pp. 13–14.

Profiting from Global Expansion

Expanding globally allows firms to increase their profitability in ways not available to purely domestic enterprises.[3] Firms that operate internationally are able to:

1. Earn a greater return from their distinctive skills or core competencies.
2. Realize location economies by dispersing particular value creation activities to those locations where they can be performed most efficiently.
3. Realize greater experience curve economies, which reduces the cost of value creation.

As we will see, however, a firm's ability to increase its profitability by pursuing these strategies is constrained by the need to customize its product offering, marketing strategy, and business strategy to differing national conditions.

Transferring Core Competencies

The term **core competence** refers to skills within the firm that competitors cannot easily match or imitate.[4] These skills may exist in any of the firm's value creation activities—production, marketing, R&D, human resources, general management, and so on. Such skills are typically expressed in product offerings that other firms find difficult to match or imitate; thus, the core competencies are the bedrock of a firm's competitive advantage. They enable a firm to reduce the costs of value creation and/or to create value in such a way that premium pricing is possible. For example, Toyota has a core competence in the production of cars. It can produce high-quality, well-designed cars at a lower delivered cost than any other firm in the world. The skills that enable Toyota to do this seem to reside primarily in the firm's production and materials management functions.[5] McDonald's has a core competence in managing fast-food operations (it seems to be one of the most skilled firms in the world in this industry); Toys "R" Us has a core competence in managing high-volume, discount toy stores (it is perhaps the most skilled firm in the world in this business); Procter & Gamble has a core competence in developing and marketing name brand consumer products (it is one of the most skilled firms in the world in this business); Wal-Mart has a core competence in information systems and logistics; and so on.

For such firms, global expansion is a way to further exploit the value creation potential of their skills and product offerings by applying those skills and products in a larger market. The potential for creating value from such a strategy is greatest when the skills and products of the firm are most unique, when the value placed on them by consumers is great, and when there are very few capable competitors with similar skills and/or products in foreign markets. Firms with unique and valuable skills can often realize enormous returns by applying those skills, and the products they produce, to foreign markets where indigenous competitors lack similar skills and products. For example, as we saw in the opening case, General Motors is trying to create value by leveraging the production skills developed at its Eisenach plant in Germany to new plants being built in Argentina, Poland, China, and Thailand. McDonald's, as detailed in the Management Focus later in the chapter, has profited by leveraging its core competence in running fast-food restaurants to foreign markets where indigenous competitors either did not exist or lacked similar skills.

In earlier eras, US firms such as Kellogg, Coca-Cola, H. J. Heinz, and Procter & Gamble expanded overseas to exploit their skills in developing and marketing name brand consumer products. These skills and the resulting products, which were developed in the United States market during the 1950s and 60s, yielded enormous returns when applied to European markets, where most indigenous competitors lacked similar marketing skills and products. Their near-monopoly on consumer marketing skills allowed these US firms to dominate many European consumer product markets during the 1960s and 1970s. Similarly, in the 1970s and 1980s, many Japanese firms expanded globally to exploit their skills in production, materials management, and new product development—skills that many of their North American and European competitors seemed to lack at the time. Today, retail companies such as Wal-Mart and financial companies such as Citicorp, Merrill Lynch, and American Express are transferring the valuable skills they developed in their core home markets to other developed and emerging markets where indigenous competitors lack those skills.

Realizing Location Economies

We know from earlier chapters that countries differ along a whole range of dimensions, including the economic, political, legal, and cultural, and that these differences can either raise or lower the costs of doing business. We also know from the theory of international trade that because of differences in factor costs, certain countries have a comparative advantage in the production of certain products. For example, Japan excels in the production of automobiles and consumer electronics. The United States excels in the production of computer software, pharmaceuticals, biotechnology products, and financial services. Switzerland excels in the production of precision instruments and pharmaceuticals.[6]

What does all this mean for a firm that is trying to survive in a competitive global market? It means that, *trade barriers and transportation costs* permitting, the firm will benefit by basing each value creation activity it performs at that location where economic, political, and cultural conditions, including relative factor costs, are most conducive to the performance of that activity. Thus, if the best designers for a product live in France, a firm should base its design operations in France. If the most productive labor force for assembly operations is in Mexico, assembly operations should be based in Mexico. If the best marketers are in the United States, the marketing strategy should be formulated in the United States. And so on.

Firms that pursue such a strategy can realize what we refer to as location economies. We can define **location economies** as the economies that arise from performing a value creation activity in the optimal location for that activity, wherever in the world that might be (transportation costs and trade barriers permitting). Locating a value creation activity in the optimal location for that activity can have one or two effects. *It can lower the costs of value creation and help the firm to achieve a low-cost position, and/or it can enable a firm to differentiate its product offering from those of competitors.* Both of these considerations were at work in the case of Clear Vision, which was profiled in the earlier Management Focus. Clear Vision moved its manufacturing operations out of the United States, first to Hong Kong and then to mainland China, to take advantage of low labor costs, thereby lowering the costs of value creation. At the same time, Clear Vision shifted some of its design operations from the United States to France and Italy. Clear Vision reasoned that skilled Italian and French designers could probably help the firm better differentiate its product. In other words, Clear Vision thinks the optimal location for performing manufacturing operations is China, whereas the optimal locations for performing design operations are France and Italy. The firm has configured its value chain accordingly. By doing so, Clear Vision hopes to simultaneously lower its cost structure and differentiate its product offering. In turn, differentiation should allow Clear Vision to charge a premium price for its product.

Creating a Global Web

One result of Clear Vision's kind of thinking is the creation of a **global web** of value creation activities, with different stages of the value chain being dispersed to those locations around the globe where value added is maximized or where the costs of value creation are minimized. Consider the case of General Motors' (GM) Pontiac Le Mans cited in Robert Reich's *The Work of Nations*.[7] Marketed primarily in the United States, the car was designed in Germany; key components were manufactured in Japan, Taiwan, and Singapore; assembly was performed in South Korea; and the advertising strategy was formulated in Great Britain. The car was designed in Germany because GM believed the designers in its German subsidiary had the skills most suited to the job. (They were the most capable of producing a design that added value.) Components were manufactured in Japan, Taiwan, and Singapore because favorable factor conditions there—relatively low-cost, skilled labor—suggested that those locations had a comparative advantage in the production of components (which helped reduce the costs of value creation). The car was assembled in South Korea because GM believed that due to its low labor costs, the costs of assembly could be minimized there (also helping to minimize the costs of value creation). Finally, the advertising strategy was formulated in Great Britain because GM believed a particular advertising agency there was the most able to produce an advertising campaign that would help sell the car. (This decision was consistent with GM's desire to maximize the value added.)

In theory, a firm that realizes location economies by dispersing each of its value creation activities to its optimal location should have a competitive advantage vis-à-vis a firm that bases all its value creation activities at a single location. It should be able to better differentiate its product offering and lower its cost structure than its single-location competitor. In a world where competitive pressures are increasing, such a strategy may become an imperative for survival (as it seems to have been for Clear Vision).

Some Caveats

Introducing transportation costs and trade barriers complicates this picture somewhat. Due to favorable factor endowments, New Zealand may have a comparative advantage for automobile assembly operations, but high transportation costs would make it an uneconomical location for them. Transportation costs and trade barriers explain why many US firms are shifting their production from Asia to Mexico. Mexico has three distinct advantages over many Asian countries. First, low labor costs make it a good location for labor-intensive production processes. In recent years, wage rates have increased significantly in Japan, Taiwan, and Hong Kong, but they have remained low in Mexico. Second, Mexico's proximity to the United States reduces transportation costs. This is particularly important for products with high weight-to-value ratios (e.g., automobiles). And third, the North American Free Trade Agreement (see Chapter 8) has removed many trade barriers between Mexico, the United States, and Canada, increasing Mexico's attractiveness as a production site for the North American market. Although value added and the costs of value creation are important, transportation costs and trade barriers also must be considered in location decisions.

Another caveat concerns the importance of assessing political and economic risks when making location decisions. Even if a country looks very attractive as a production location when measured against all the standard criteria, if its government is unstable or totalitarian, a firm might be advised not to base production there. (Political risk is discussed in Chapter 2.) Similarly, if the government appears to be pursuing inappropriate economic policies, production at that location might be ill-advised, even if other factors look favorable.

Realizing Experience Curve Economies

The **experience curve** refers to the systematic reductions in production costs that have been observed to occur over the life of a product.[8] A number of studies have observed that a product's production costs decline by some characteristic each time accumulated output doubles. The relationship was first observed in the aircraft industry, where each time accumulated output of airframes was doubled, unit costs typically declined to 80 percent of their previous level.[9] Thus, production cost for the fourth airframe would be 80 percent of production cost for the second airframe, the eighth airframe's production cost 80 percent of the fourth's, the sixteenth's 80 percent of the eighth's, and so on. Figure 12.2 illustrates this experience curve relationship between production costs and output. Two things explain this: learning effects and economies of scale.

Learning Effects

Learning effects refer to cost savings that come from learning by doing. Labor, for example, learns by repetition how to carry out a task, such as assembling airframes, most efficiently. Labor productivity increases over time as individuals learn the most efficient ways to perform particular tasks. Equally important, in new production facilities, management typically learns how to manage the new operation more efficiently over time. Hence, production costs eventually decline due to increasing labor productivity and management efficiency.

Learning effects tend to be more significant when a technologically complex task is repeated because there is more that can be learned about the task. Thus, learning effects will be more significant in an assembly process involving 1,000 complex steps than in one of only 100 simple steps. No matter how complex the task, however, learning effects typically die out after a time. It has been suggested that they are important only during the start-up period of a new process and that they cease after

Figure 12.2

The Experience Curve

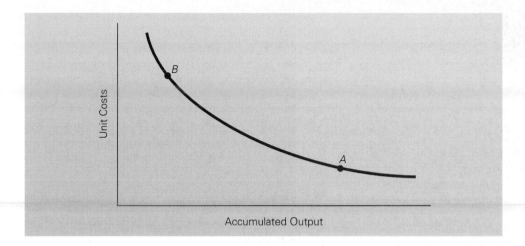

two or three years.[10] Any decline in the experience curve after such a point is due to economies of scale.

Economies of Scale

The term **economies of scale** refers to the reductions in unit cost achieved by producing a large volume of a product. Economies of scale have a number of sources, one of the most important of which seems to be the ability to spread fixed costs over a large volume.[11] Fixed costs are the costs required to set up a production facility, develop a new product, and the like, and they can be substantial. For example, establishing a new production line to manufacture semiconductor chips costs about $1 billion. According to one estimate, developing a new drug costs about $250 million and takes about 12 years.[12] The only way to recoup such high fixed costs is to sell the product worldwide, which reduces unit costs by spreading them over a larger volume. Also, the more rapidly that cumulative sales volume is built up, the more rapidly fixed costs can be amortized, and the more rapidly unit costs fall.

Another source of scale economies arises from the ability of large firms to employ increasingly specialized equipment or personnel. This theory goes back over 200 years to Adam Smith, who argued that the division of labor is limited by the extent of the market. In simple terms, this means that as a firm's output expands, it is better able to make full use of specialized equipment, and has the output required to justify the hiring of specialized personnel. Consider a metal stamping machine that is used in the production of automobile body parts. The machine can be purchased in a customized form, which is optimized for the production of a particular type of body part, or a general purpose form, which will produce any kind of body part. The general form is less efficient and costs more to purchase than the customized form, but it is more flexible. Since these machines cost millions of dollars each, they have to be used continually to recoup a return on their costs. Fully utilized, a machine can turn out about 200,000 units a year. If an automobile company sells only 100,000 cars a year, it will not be worthwhile purchasing the specialized equipment, and it will have to purchase general purpose machines. This will give it a higher cost structure than a firm that sells 200,000 cars per year and for which it is economical to purchase a specialized stamping machine. Thus, because a firm with a large output can more fully utilize specialized equipment (and personnel), it should have a lower unit cost for its products than a firm that must use generalized equipment.

Strategic Significance

The strategic significance of the experience curve is clear. Moving down the experience curve allows a firm to reduce its cost of creating value. The firm that moves down the experience curve most rapidly will have a cost advantage vis-à-vis its competitors. Thus, Firm A in Figure 12.2, because it is further down the experience curve, has a clear cost advantage over Firm B.

Many of the underlying sources of experience-based cost economies are plant based. This is true for most learning effects as well as for the economies of scale derived by spreading the fixed costs of building productive capacity over a large output. Thus, the key to progressing downward on the experience curve as rapidly as possible is to increase the volume produced by a single plant as rapidly as possible. Since global markets are larger than domestic markets, a firm that serves a global market from a single location is likely to build accumulated volume more quickly than a firm that serves only its home market or that serves multiple markets from multiple production locations. Thus, serving a global market from a single location is consistent with moving down the experience curve and establishing a low-cost position. In addition, to get down the experience curve rapidly, a firm must price and market very aggressively so demand will expand rapidly. It will also need to build sufficient production capacity for serving a global market. Also, the cost advantages of serving the world market from a single location will be all the more significant if that location is the optimal one for performing the particular value creation activity.

Once a firm has established a low-cost position, it can act as a barrier to new competition. An established firm that is well down the experience curve, such as Firm A in Figure 12.2, can price so that it is making a profit while new entrants, which are further up the curve, such as Firm B in the figure, are suffering losses.

One firm that has excelled in the pursuit of such a strategy is Matsushita. Along with Sony and Philips, Matsushita was in the race to develop a commercially viable videocassette recorder in the 1970s. Although Matsushita initially lagged behind Philips and Sony, it got its VHS format accepted as the world standard and reaped enormous experience-curve-based cost economies. This cost advantage constituted a formidable barrier to new competition. Matsushita's strategy was to build global volume as rapidly as possible. To ensure it could accommodate worldwide demand, the firm increased its production capacity 33-fold from 205,000 units in 1977 to 6.8 million units by 1984. By serving the world market from a single location in Japan, Matsushita realized significant learning effects and economies of scale. These allowed Matsushita to drop its prices 50 percent within five years of selling its first VHS-formatted VCR. As a result, Matsushita was the world's major VCR producer by 1983, accounting for approximately 45 percent of world production and enjoying a significant cost advantage over its competitors. The next largest firm, Hitachi, accounted for only 11.1 percent of world production in 1983.[13]

Pressures for Cost Reductions and Local Responsiveness

Firms that compete in the global marketplace typically face two types of competitive pressure. They face *pressures for cost reductions* and *pressures to be locally responsive* (see Figure 12.3). These competitive pressures place conflicting demands on a firm. Responding to pressures to reduce costs requires that a firm try to minimize its unit costs. Attaining such a goal may necessitate that a firm base its productive activities at the most favorable low-cost location, wherever in the world that might be. It may also necessitate that a firm offer a standardized product to the global marketplace to ride down the experience curve as quickly as possible. In contrast, responding to pressures to be locally responsive requires that a firm differentiate its product offering and marketing strategy from country to country in an attempt to accommodate the diverse demands that arise from national differences in consumer tastes and preferences, business practices, distribution channels, competitive conditions, and government policies. Because customizing product offerings to different national

Figure 12.3

Pressures for Cost Reduction
and Local Responsiveness

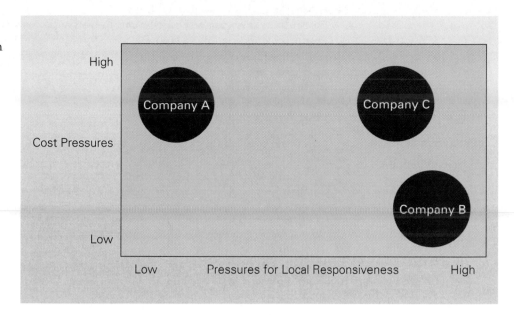

requirements can involve significant duplication and a lack of product standardization, the result may be to raise costs.

While some firms, such as Firm A in Figure 12.3, face high pressures for cost reductions and low pressures for local responsiveness, and others, such as Firm B, face low pressures for cost reductions and high pressures for local responsiveness, many firms are in the position of Firm C. They face high pressures for cost reductions and high pressures for local responsiveness. Dealing with these conflicting and contradictory pressures is a difficult strategic challenge for a firm, primarily because being locally responsive tends to raise costs. In the remainder of this section, we will look at the source of pressures for cost reductions and local responsiveness. In the next section, we look at the strategies firms adopt to deal with these pressures.

Pressures for Cost Reductions

Increasingly, international businesses face pressures for cost reductions. This requires a firm to try to lower the costs of value creation by mass producing a standardized product at the optimal location in the world to try to realize location and experience curve economies. Pressures for cost reductions can be particularly intense in industries producing commodity products where meaningful differentiation on nonprice factors is difficult and price is the main competitive weapon. This tends to be the case for products that serve universal needs. Universal needs exist when the tastes and preferences of consumers in different nations are similar. This is the case for conventional commodity products such as bulk chemicals, petroleum, steel, sugar, and the like. It also tends to be the case for many industrial and consumer products (for example, handheld calculators, semiconductor chips, personal computers, liquid crystal display screens). Pressures for cost reductions are also intense in industries where major competitors are based in low-cost locations, where there is persistent excess capacity, and where consumers are powerful and face low switching costs. Many commentators have also argued that the liberalization of the world trade and investment environment in recent decades, by facilitating greater international competition, has generally increased cost pressures.[14]

Cost pressures have been intense in the global tire industry in recent years. Tires are essentially a commodity product where meaningful differentiation is difficult and price is the main competitive weapon. The major buyers of tires, automobile firms, are powerful and face low switching costs, so they play tire firms against each other to get lower prices. And the decline in global demand for automobiles in the early 1990s created excess capacity in the tire industry, with as much as 25 percent of world capacity standing idle. The result was a worldwide price war with almost all tire firms suffering heavy losses in the early 1990s. In response to the resulting cost pressures, most tire firms are trying to attain a low-cost position. This includes moving production facilities to low-cost facilities and offering globally standardized products to realize experience curve economies.[15]

Pressures for Local Responsiveness

Pressures for local responsiveness arise from a number of sources including (a) differences in consumer tastes and preferences, (b) differences in infrastructure and traditional practices, (c) differences in distribution channels, and (d) host government demands.

Differences in Consumer Tastes and Preferences

Strong pressures for local responsiveness emerge when consumer tastes and preferences differ significantly between countries—as they may for historic or cultural reasons. In such cases, product and/or marketing messages have to be customized to appeal to the tastes and preferences of local consumers. This typically prompts delegating production and marketing functions to national subsidiaries.

For example, there is a strong demand among North American consumers for pickup trucks, particularly in the South and West where many families have a pickup truck as a second or third car. In contrast, in European countries, pickup trucks are seen purely as utility vehicles and are purchased primarily by firms rather than individuals. As a consequence, the marketing message needs to be tailored to the different nature of demand in North America and Europe.

But Harvard Business School Professor Theodore Levitt has argued that consumer demands for local customization are declining worldwide.[16] According to Levitt, modern communications and transportation technologies have created the conditions for a convergence of the tastes of consumers from different nations. The result is the emergence of enormous global markets for standardized consumer products. Levitt cites worldwide acceptance of McDonald's hamburgers, Coca-Cola, Levi Strauss jeans, and Sony television sets, all of which are sold as standardized products, as evidence of the increasing homogeneity of the global marketplace.

Levitt's argument, however, has been characterized as extreme by many commentators. For example, Christopher Bartlett and Sumantra Ghoshal have observed that in the consumer electronics industry, consumers reacted to an overdose of standardized global products by showing a renewed preference for products that are differentiated to local conditions.[17] They note that Amstrad, the fast-growing British computer and electronics firm, got its start by recognizing and responding to local consumer needs. Amstrad captured a major share of the British audio player market by moving away from the standardized, inexpensive stereo systems marketed by global firms such as Sony and Matsushita. Amstrad's product is encased in teak rather than metal and has a control panel tailor-made to appeal to British consumers' preferences. In response, Matsushita had to reverse its earlier bias toward standardized global design and place more emphasis on local customization.

Differences in Infrastructure and Traditional Practices

Pressures for local responsiveness emerge when there are differences in infrastructure and/or traditional practices between countries. In such circumstances, customizing the product to the distinctive infrastructure and practices of different nations may necessitate delegating manufacturing and production functions to foreign subsidiaries. For example, North American consumer electrical systems are based on 110 volts, while in some European countries, 240 volt systems are standard. Thus, domestic electrical appliances have to be customized for this difference in infrastructure. Traditional practices also often vary across nations. For example, people drive on the left side of the road in Britain, creating a demand for right-hand drive cars, but in neighboring France, people drive on the right side of the road, creating a demand for left-hand drive cars. Automobiles have to be customized to meet this difference in traditional practices.

Differences in Distribution Channels

A firm's marketing strategies may have to be responsive to differences in distribution channels between countries. This may necessitate the delegation of marketing functions to national subsidiaries. In laundry detergents, for example, five retail chains control 65 percent of the market in Germany, but no chain controls more than 2 percent of the market in neighboring Italy. Thus, retail chains have considerable buying power in Germany, but relatively little in Italy. Dealing with these differences requires detergent firms to use varying marketing approaches. In the pharmaceutical industry, the British and Japanese distribution systems are radically different from the US system. British and Japanese doctors will not accept or respond favorably to an American-style high pressure sales force. Thus, pharmaceutical firms have to adopt different marketing practices in Britain and Japan compared to the United States (soft sell versus hard sell).

Host Government Demands

Economic and political demands imposed by host-country governments may necessitate local responsiveness. For example, the politics of health care around the world requires that pharmaceutical firms manufacture in multiple locations. Pharmaceutical firms are subject to local clinical testing, registration procedures, and pricing restrictions, all of which demand that the manufacturing and marketing of a drug meet local requirements. Also, because governments and government agencies control a significant portion of the health care budget in most countries, they can demand a high level of local responsiveness.

Threats of protectionism, economic nationalism, and local content rules (which require that a certain percentage of a product be manufactured locally) all dictate that international businesses manufacture locally. Consider Bombardier, the Canadian-based manufacturer of railcars, aircraft, jet boats, and snowmobiles. Bombardier has 12 railcar factories across Europe. Some argue that the duplication of manufacturing facilities leads to high costs and lowers profit margins, but Bombardier managers say that informal rules in Europe favor companies that use local workers. To sell railcars in Germany, they claim, you must manufacture in Germany. The same goes for Belgium, Austria, and France. To address its cost structure in Europe, Bombardier has centralized its engineering and purchasing functions, but it has no plans to centralize manufacturing.[18]

Implications

Pressures for local responsiveness imply that it may not be possible for a firm to realize the full benefits from experience curve and location economies. For example, it may not be possible to serve the global marketplace from a single low-cost location, producing a globally standardized product and marketing it worldwide to achieve experience curve cost economies. The need to customize the product to local conditions may work against such a strategy. Automobile firms, for example, have found that Japanese, American, and European consumers demand different kinds of cars, and this necessitates producing products that are customized for local markets. In response, firms such as Honda, Ford, and Toyota are establishing top to bottom design and production facilities in each of these regions so they can better serve local demands. While such customization brings benefits, it also limits a firm's ability to realize significant experience curve economies and location economies.

In addition, pressures for local responsiveness imply that it may not be possible to transfer the skills and products associated with a firm's core competencies whole-

MANAGEMENT FOCUS
McDonald's Everywhere

Established in 1955, McDonald's faced a problem by the early 1980s: After three decades of rapid growth, the US fast-food market was beginning to show signs of market saturation. McDonald's response to the slowdown was to expand abroad rapidly. In 1980, 28 percent of the chain's new restaurant openings were abroad; in 1986, the figure was 40 percent; in 1990, it was close to 60 percent; and in 1997, it was over 70 percent. Since the early 1980s, the firm's foreign revenues and profits have grown at 22 percent a year. By 1997, the firm had 10,752 restaurants in 108 countries outside of the United States. They generated $16.5 billion (53 percent) of the firm's $31 billion in revenues. And McDonald's shows no signs of slowing down. Management notes that there is still only one McDonald's restaurant for every 500,000 people in the foreign countries in which it currently does business. This compares to one McDonald's restaurant for every 25,000 people in the United States. The firm's plans call for this foreign expansion to continue at a rapid rate. The firm opened 500 more restaurants in England, France, and Germany combined between 1995 and 1997, for a total gain of 37 percent. In 1997, McDonald's stated it would open 2,000 restaurants per year for the foreseeable future, the majority of them outside the United States. This includes major expansion plans for Latin America, where the company plans to invest $2 billion over the next few years.

One key to the firm's successful foreign expansion is detailed planning. When McDonald's enters a foreign country, it does so only after careful preparation. In what is a fairly typical pattern, before McDonald's opened its first Polish restaurant in 1992, the firm spent 18 months establishing essential contacts and getting to know the local culture. Locations, real estate, construction, supply, personnel, legal, and government relations were all worked out in advance. In June 1992, a team of 50 employees from the United States, Russia, Germany, and Britain went to Poland to help with the opening of the first four restaurants. A primary objective was to hire and train local personnel. By mid-1994, all these employees except one had returned to their home country. They were replaced by Polish nationals who had been brought up to the skill level required to run a McDonald's operation.

Another key to the firm's international strategy is the export of the management skills that spurred its growth in the United States—not just its fast-food products. McDonald's US success was built on a formula of close relations with suppliers, nationwide marketing might, tight control over store-level operating procedures, and a franchising system that encourages entrepreneurial franchisees. Although this system has worked flawlessly in the United States, some modifications must be made in other countries. One of the firm's biggest challenges has been to infuse each store with the same gung-ho culture and standardized operating procedures that have been the hallmark of its success in the United States. To aid in this task, McDonald's has enlisted the help of large partners through joint ventures in many countries. The

sale from one nation to another. Concessions often have to be made to local conditions. Despite being depicted as "poster boy" for the proliferation of standardized global products, even McDonald's has customized its product (i.e., its menu) to account for national differences in tastes and preferences (see the accompanying Management Focus for details).

Strategic Choice

Firms use four basic strategies to compete in the international environment: an international strategy, a multidomestic strategy, a global strategy, and a transnational strategy.[19] Each strategy has its advantages and disadvantages. The appropriateness of each strategy varies with the extent of pressures for cost reductions and local responsiveness.

http://www.mcdonalds.com

partners play a key role in learning and transplanting the organization's values to local employees.

Foreign partners have also played a key role in helping McDonald's adapt its marketing methods and menu to local conditions. Although US-style fast food remains the staple fare on the menu, local products have been added. In Brazil, for example, McDonald's sells a soft drink made from the guarana, an Amazonian berry. Patrons of McDonald's in Malaysia, Singapore, and Thailand savor shakes flavored with durian, a foul-smelling (to US tastes, at least) fruit considered an aphrodisiac by the locals. In Arab countries, McDonald's restaurants maintain "Halal" menus, which signify compliance with Islamic laws on food preparation, especially beef. In 1995, McDonald's opened the first kosher restaurant in suburban Jerusalem. The restaurant does not serve dairy products. And in India, the Big Mac is made with lamb and called the "Maharaja Mac."

McDonald's biggest problem has been to replicate its US supply chain in other countries. US suppliers are fiercely loyal to McDonald's; they must be, because their fortunes are closely linked to those of McDonald's. McDonald's maintains very rigorous specifications for all the raw ingredients it uses—the key to its consistency and quality control. Outside the United States, however, McDonald's has found suppliers far less willing to make the investments required to meet its specifications. In Great Britain, for example, McDonald's had problems getting local bakeries to produce the hamburger bun. After experiencing quality

problems with two local bakeries, McDonald's built its own bakery to supply its stores there. In a more extreme case, when McDonald's decided to open a store in Russia, it found that local suppliers lacked the capability to produce goods of the quality it demanded. The firm was forced to vertically integrate through the local food industry on a heroic scale, importing potato seeds and bull semen and indirectly managing dairy farms, cattle ranches, and vegetable plots. It also had to construct the world's largest food-processing plant, at a cost of $40 million. The restaurant itself cost only $4.5 million.

Now that it has a successful foreign operation, McDonald's is experiencing benefits that go beyond the immediate financial ones. The firm is finding that its foreign franchisees are a source for valuable new ideas. The Dutch operation created a prefabricated modular store that can be moved over a weekend and is now widely used to set up temporary restaurants at big outdoor events. The Swedes came up with an enhanced meat freezer that is now used firmwide. And satellite stores, or low-overhead mini-McDonald's, which are now appearing in hospitals and sports arenas in the United States, were invented in Singapore.

Sources: Kathleen Deveny et al., "McWorld?" *Business Week*, October 13, 1986, pp. 78–86; "Slow Food," *The Economist*, February 3, 1990, p. 64; Harlan S. Byrne, "Welcome to McWorld," *Barron's*, August 29, 1994, pp. 25–28; and Andrew E. Serwer, "McDonald's Conquers the World," *Fortune*, October 17, 1994, pp. 103–16.

Figure 12.4 illustrates when each of these strategies is most appropriate. In this section we describe each strategy, identify when it is appropriate, and discuss its pros and cons.

International Strategy

Firms that pursue an international strategy try to create value by transferring valuable skills and products to foreign markets where indigenous competitors lack those skills and products. Most international firms have created value by transferring differentiated product offerings developed at home to new markets overseas. They tend to centralize product development functions at home (e.g., R&D). However, they also tend to establish manufacturing and marketing functions in each major country in which they do business. But while they may undertake some local customization of products and marketing strategy, this tends to be limited. Ultimately, in most international firms, the head office retains tight control over marketing and product strategy.

Figure 12.4

Four Basic Strategies

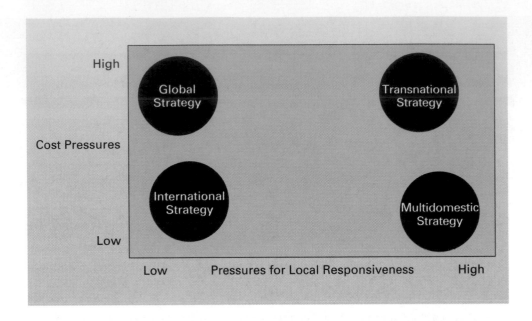

International firms include the likes of Toys "R" Us, McDonald's, IBM, Kellogg, Procter & Gamble, Wal-Mart, and Microsoft. Microsoft develops the core architecture underlying its products at its Redmond campus in Washington state and also writes the bulk of the computer code there. However, the company allows national subsidiaries to develop their own marketing and distribution strategies and to customize aspects of the product to account for such basic local differences as language and alphabet. Procter & Gamble, which is profiled in the accompanying Management Focus, has traditionally had production facilities in all its major markets outside the United States, including Britain, Germany, and Japan. These facilities, however, manufactured differentiated products that had been developed by the US parent firm and were often marketed using the marketing message developed in the United States. Historically, local responsiveness at P&G has been limited.

An international strategy makes sense if a firm has a valuable core competence that indigenous competitors in foreign markets lack, and if the firm faces relatively weak pressures for local responsiveness and cost reductions (as in the case of Microsoft). In such circumstances, an international strategy can be very profitable. However, when pressures for local responsiveness are high, firms pursuing this strategy lose out to firms that place a greater emphasis on customizing the product offering and market strategy to local conditions. Due to the duplication of manufacturing facilities, firms that pursue an international strategy tend to suffer from high operating costs. This makes the strategy inappropriate in manufacturing industries where cost pressures are high.

Multidomestic Strategy

Firms pursuing a multidomestic strategy orient themselves toward achieving maximum local responsiveness. Multidomestic firms extensively customize both their product offering and their marketing strategy to match different national conditions. They also tend to establish a complete set of value creation activities—including production, marketing, and R&D—in each major national market in which they do business. As a consequence, they generally fail to realize value from experience curve effects and location economies. Accordingly, many multidomestic firms have a high cost structure. They also tend to do a poor job of leveraging core competencies within the firm. General Motors, profiled in the opening case, is a good example of a company that has historically functioned as a multidomestic corporation, particularly with regard to its extensive European operations, which are largely self-contained entities.

A multidomestic strategy makes most sense when there are high pressures for local responsiveness and low pressures for cost reductions. The high-cost structure associated with the duplication of production facilities makes this strategy inappropriate in industries where cost pressures are intense (which is the case in the automobile industry, a fact that explains GM's current attempts to change its strategic orientation). Another weakness associated with this strategy is that many multidomestic firms have developed into decentralized federations in which each national subsidiary functions in a largely autonomous manner. This was exemplified by the failure of Philips NV to establish its V2000 format as the standard in the VCR industry during the late 1970s. Philips' US subsidiary refused to adopt the V2000 format; instead, it bought VHS-format VCRs produced by Matsushita and put its own label on them!

Global Strategy

Firms that pursue a global strategy focus on increasing profitability by reaping the cost reductions that come from experience curve effects and location economies. They are pursuing a low-cost strategy. The production, marketing, and R&D activities of firms pursuing a global strategy are concentrated in a few favorable locations. Global firms tend not to customize their product offering and marketing strategy to local conditions because customization raises costs (it involves shorter production runs and the duplication of functions). Instead, global firms prefer to market a standardized product worldwide so they can reap the maximum benefits from the economies of scale that underlie the experience curve. They also tend to use their cost advantage to support aggressive pricing in world markets.

This strategy makes most sense where there are strong pressures for cost reductions and where demands for local responsiveness are minimal. Increasingly, these conditions prevail in many industrial goods industries. For example, global standards have emerged in the semiconductor industry. Accordingly, firms such as Intel, Texas Instruments, and Motorola all pursue a global strategy. However, as we noted earlier, these conditions are not found in many consumer goods markets, where demands for local responsiveness remain high (e.g., audio players, automobiles, processed food products). The strategy is inappropriate when demands for local responsiveness are high.

Transnational Strategy

Christopher Bartlett and Sumantra Ghoshal have argued that in today's environment, competitive conditions are so intense that to survive in the global marketplace, firms *must exploit experience-based cost economies and location economies, they must transfer core competencies within the firm, and they must do all this while paying attention to pressures for local responsiveness.*[20] They note that in the modern multinational enterprise, core competencies do not reside just in the home country. They can develop in any of the firm's worldwide operations. Thus, they maintain that the flow of skills and product offerings should not be all one way, from home firm to foreign subsidiary, as in the case of firms pursuing an international strategy. Rather, the flow should also be from foreign subsidiary to home country, and from foreign subsidiary to foreign subsidiary—a process they refer to as **global learning** (for examples of such knowledge flows, see the opening case on General Motors and the Management Focus on McDonald's). Bartlett and Ghoshal refer to the strategy pursued by firms that are trying to achieve all these objectives simultaneously as a **transnational strategy**.

A transnational strategy makes sense when a firm faces high pressures for cost reductions and high pressures for local responsiveness. Firms that pursue a transnational strategy are trying to simultaneously achieve low-cost and differentiation advantages. As attractive as this sounds, the strategy is not an easy one to pursue. Pressures for local responsiveness and cost reductions place conflicting demands on a firm. Being locally responsive raises costs, which makes cost reductions difficult to achieve. How can a firm effectively pursue a transnational strategy?

MANAGEMENT FOCUS
Procter & Gamble's International Strategy

Procter & Gamble (P&G), the large US consumer products company, has a well-earned reputation as one of the world's best marketers. With over 80 major brands, P&G generates more than $20 billion in revenues worldwide. P&G is a dominant global force in laundry detergents, cleaning products, and personal care products. P&G expanded abroad after World War II by pursuing an international strategy—transferring brands and marketing policies developed in the United States to Western Europe, initially with considerable success. Over the next 30 years, this policy resulted in development of a classic international firm in which new-product development and marketing strategies were pioneered in the United States and then transferred to other countries. Although some adaptation of marketing policies to accommodate country differences was pursued, this adaptation was fairly minimal.

The first signs that this strategy was flawed began to emerge in the 1970s when P&G suffered a number of major setbacks in Japan. By 1985, after 13 years in Japan, P&G was still losing $40 million a year there. After introducing disposable diapers into Japan and at one time commanding an 80 percent share of the market, P&G had seen its share slip to a miserable 8

percent by the early 1980s. Three major Japanese consumer products firms dominated the market. P&G's problem was that its diapers, developed in America, were too bulky for the tastes of Japanese consumers. The Japanese consumer products firm Kao developed a line of trim-fit diapers that appealed more to the tastes of Japanese consumers. Kao supported the product introduction with a marketing blitz and was quickly rewarded with a 30 percent share of the market. Only belatedly did P&G realize that it had to modify its diapers to accommodate the tastes of Japanese consumers. Now the company has increased its share of the Japanese market to 30 percent. And in an example of global learning, P&G's trim-fit diapers, originally developed for the Japanese market, have now become a best-seller in the United States.

P&G's experience with disposable diapers in Japan prompted the company to rethink its new-product development and marketing philosophy. Since the late 1980s, P&G has been delegating far more responsibility for new-product development and marketing strategy to its major subsidiary firms in Japan and Europe. The result has been a company that is more

Some clues can be derived from Caterpillar Inc. In the late 1970s, the need to compete with low-cost competitors such as Komatsu and Hitachi of Japan forced Caterpillar to look for greater cost economies. At the same time, national variations in construction practices and government regulations meant that Caterpillar had to remain responsive to local demands. As illustrated in Figure 12.5, Caterpillar was confronted with significant pressures for cost reductions and for local responsiveness.

To deal with cost pressures, Caterpillar redesigned its products to use many identical components and invested in a few large-scale component manufacturing facilities, sited at favorable locations, to fill global demand and realize scale economics. The firm augmented the centralized manufacturing of components with assembly plants in each of its major global markets. At these plants, Caterpillar added local product features, tailoring the finished product to local needs. By pursuing this strategy, Caterpillar realized many of the benefits of global manufacturing while responding to pressures for local responsiveness by differentiating its product among national markets.[21] Caterpillar started to pursue this strategy in 1979 and by 1997 had doubled output per employee, significantly reducing its overall cost structure. Meanwhile, Komatsu and Hitachi, which are still wedded to a Japan-centric global strategy, have seen their cost advantages evaporate and have been steadily losing market share to Caterpillar. (General Motors is trying to pursue a similar strategy with its development of common global platforms for some of its vehicles; see the opening case for details.)

http://www.pg.com

responsive to local differences in consumer tastes and preferences and more willing to admit that good new products can be developed outside the United States.

Despite the apparent changes at P&G, the company's venture into the Polish shampoo market illustrates the company still had some way to go. In the summer of 1991, P&G entered the Polish market with its Vidal Sassoon Wash & Go, an all-in-one shampoo and conditioner that is a best-seller in America and Europe. The product launch was supported by an American-style marketing blitz on a scale never before seen in Poland. At first the campaign seemed to be working as P&G captured more than 30 percent of the market for shampoos in Poland, but in early 1992 sales suddenly plummeted. Then came the rumors—Wash & Go caused dandruff and hair loss-allegations that P&G strenuously denied. Next came the jokes: "I washed my car with Wash & Go and the tires went bald." And when President Lech Walesa proposed that he also become prime minister, critics derided the idea as a "two in one solution, just like Wash & Go."

Where did P&G go wrong? The most common theory is that it promoted Wash & Go too hard in a country that has little enthusiasm for brash American-style advertising. A poll by Pentor, a private market research company in Warsaw, found that almost three times more Poles disliked P&G's commercials than liked them. Pentor also argued that the high-profile marketing campaign backfired because years of Communist party propaganda had led Polish consumers to suspect that advertising is simply a way to sell goods that nobody wants. Some also believe that Wash & Go, which was developed for US consumers who shampoo daily, was too sophisticated for Polish consumers who are less obsessed with personal hygiene. Underlying all these criticisms was the idea that P&G once again stumbled because it had transferred a product and marketing strategy wholesale from the United States to another country without modification to accommodate the tastes and preferences of local consumers.

Sources: Guy de Jonquieres and C. Bobinski, "Wash and Get into a Lather in Poland," *Financial Times*, May 28, 1989, p. 2; "Perestroika in Soapland," *The Economist*, June 10, 1989, pp. 69–71; "After Early Stumbles P&G Is Making Inroads Overseas," *The Wall Street Journal*, February 6, 1989, p. B1; and C. A. Bartlett and S. Ghoshal, *Managing across Borders. The Transnational Solution* (Boston: Harvard Business School Press, 1989).

Figure 12.5

Cost Pressures and Pressures for Local Responsiveness Facing Caterpillar

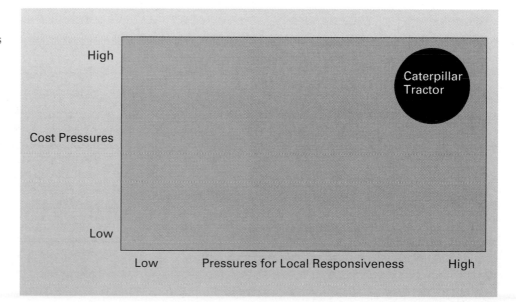

For another example consider Unilever. Once a classic multidomestic firm, Unilever has had to shift toward more of a transnational strategy. A rise in low-cost competition, which increased cost pressures, has forced Unilever to look for ways of rationalizing its detergents business. During the 1980s, Unilever had 17 different and largely self-contained detergent operations in Europe alone. The duplication in assets and marketing was enormous. Also, because Unilever was so fragmented it could take as long as four years for the firm to introduce a new product across Europe. Now Unilever is trying to weld its European operation into a single entity, with detergents being manufactured in a handful of cost-efficient plants, and standard packaging and advertising being used across Europe. According to company estimates, the result could be an annual cost saving of over $200 million. At the same time, however, due to national differences in distribution channels and brand awareness, Unilever recognizes that it must still remain locally responsive, even while it tries to realize economies from consolidating production and marketing at the optimal locations.[22]

Bartlett and Ghoshal admit that building an organization that can support a transnational strategic posture is complex and difficult. Simultaneously trying to achieve cost efficiencies, global learning, and local responsiveness places contradictory demands on an organization. Chapter 13 discusses how a firm can deal with the dilemmas posed by such difficult organizational issues. Firms that attempt to pursue a transnational strategy can become bogged down in an organizational morass that only leads to inefficiencies.

Bartlett and Ghoshal may be overstating the case for the transnational strategy when they present it as the only viable strategy. While no one doubts that in some industries the firm that can adopt a transnational strategy will have a competitive advantage, in other industries, global, multidomestic, and international strategies remain viable. In the semiconductor industry, for example, pressures for local customization are minimal and competition is purely a cost game, in which case a global strategy, not a transnational strategy, is optimal. This is the case in many industrial goods markets where the product serves universal needs. But the argument can be made that to compete in certain consumer goods markets, such as the automobile and consumer electronics industry, a firm has to try to adopt a transnational strategy.

Summary

The advantages and disadvantages of each of the four strategies discussed above are summarized in Figure 12.6. While a transnational strategy appears to offer the most advantages, implementing a transnational strategy raises difficult organiza-

Strategy	Advantages	Disadvantages
Global	• Exploit experience curve effects • Exploit location economies	• Lack of local responsiveness
International	• Transfer distinctive competencies to foreign markets	• Lack of local responsiveness • Inability to realize location economies • Failure to exploit experience curve effects
Multidomestic	• Customize product offerings and marketing in accordance with local responsiveness	• Inability to realize location economies • Failure to exploit experience curve effects • Failure to transfer distinctive competencies to foreign markets
Transnational	• Exploit experience curve effects • Exploit location economies • Customize product offerings and marketing in accordance with local responsiveness • Reap benefits of global learning	• Difficult to implement due to organizational problems

Figure 12.6

The Advantages and Disadvantages of the Four Strategies

tional issues. As shown in Figure 12.3, the appropriateness of each strategy depends on the relative strength of pressures for cost reductions and pressures for local responsiveness.

Chapter Summary

This chapter reviewed the various ways in which firms can profit from global expansion and the strategies that firms which compete globally can adopt, discussed the optimal choice of entry mode to serve a foreign market, and looked at the issue of strategic alliances. This chapter made the following points:

1. For some firms, international expansion represents a way of earning greater returns by transferring the skills and product offerings derived from their core competencies to markets where indigenous competitors lack those skills.

2. Due to national differences, it pays a firm to base each value creation activity it performs where factor conditions are most conducive to the performance of that activity. We refer to this strategy as focusing on the attainment of location economics.

3. By building sales volume more rapidly, international expansion can assist a firm moving down the experience curve.

4. The best strategy for a firm to pursue may depend on a consideration of the pressures for cost reductions and the pressures for local responsiveness.

5. Pressures for cost reductions are greatest in industries producing commodity-type products where price is the main competitive weapon.

6. Pressures for local responsiveness arise from differences in consumer tastes and preferences, national infrastructure and traditional practices, distribution channels, and from host government demands.

7. Firms pursuing an international strategy transfer the skills and products derived from distinctive competencies to foreign markets, while undertaking some limited local customization.

8. Firms pursuing a multidomestic strategy customize their product offering, marketing strategy, and business strategy to national conditions.

9. Firms pursuing a global strategy focus on reaping the cost reductions that come from experience curve effects and location economics.

10. Many industries are now so competitive that firms must adopt a transnational strategy. This involves a simultaneous focus on reducing costs, transferring skills and products, and being locally responsive. Implementing such a strategy may not be easy.

Critical Discussion Questions

1. In a world of zero transportation costs, no trade barriers, and nontrivial differences between nations with regard to factor conditions, firms must expand internationally if they are to survive. Discuss.

2. Plot the position of the following firms on Figure 12.3; Procter & Gamble, IBM, Coca-Cola, Dow Chemical, US Steel, McDonald's. In each case justify your answer.

3. Are the following global industries or multidomestic industries: bulk chemicals, pharmaceuticals, branded food products, movie making, television manufacture, personal computers, airline travel?

4. Discuss how the need for control over foreign operations varies with the strategy and core competencies of a firm. What are the implications of this for the choice of entry mode?

5. What do you see as the main organizational problems that are likely to be associated with a transnational strategy?

CLOSING CASE   Sweden's IKEA

Established in the 1940s in Sweden by Ingvar Kamprad, IKEA has grown rapidly in recent years to become one of the world's largest retailers of home furnishings. In its initial push to expand globally, IKEA largely ignored the retailing rule that international success involves tailoring product lines closely to national tastes and preferences. Instead, IKEA stuck with the vision, articulated by founder Kamprad, that the company should sell a basic product range that is "typically Swedish" wherever it ventures in the world. The company also remained primarily production oriented; that is, the Swedish management and design group decided what it was going to sell and then presented it to the worldwide public—often with little research as to what the public wanted. The company also emphasized its Swedish roots in its international advertising, even insisting on a "Swedish" blue and gold color scheme for its stores.

Despite breaking some key rules of international retailing, the formula of selling Swedish-designed products in the same manner everywhere seemed to work. Between 1974 and 1997, IKEA expanded from a company with 10 stores, only 1 of which was outside Scandinavia, and annual revenues of $210 million to a group with 138 stores in 28 countries and sales of close to $6 billion. Only 11 percent of its sales were generated in Sweden in 1997. Of the balance, 29.6 percent of sales came from Germany, 42.5 percent from the rest of Western Europe, and 14.4 percent from North America. IKEA is now expanding into Asia, with the opening of stores in mainland China.

The foundation of IKEA's success has been to offer consumers good value for their money. IKEA's approach starts with a global network of suppliers, which now numbers 2,400 firms in 65 countries. An IKEA supplier gains long-term contracts, technical advice, and leased equipment from the company. In return, IKEA demands an exclusive contract and low prices. IKEA's designers work closely with suppliers to build savings into the products from the outset by designing products that can be produced at a low cost. IKEA displays its enormous range of more than 10,000 products in out-of-town stores. It sells most of its furniture as kits for customers to assemble themselves. The firm reaps huge economies of scale from the size of each store and the big production runs made possible by selling the same products all over the world. This strategy allows IKEA to match its rivals on quality, while undercutting them by up to 30 percent on price and still maintaining a healthy after-tax return on sales of about 7 percent.

This strategy worked well until 1985 when IKEA decided to enter the North American market. Between 1985 and 1996 IKEA opened 26 stores in North America, but unlike the company's experience across Europe, the stores did not quickly become profitable. As early as 1990 it was clear that IKEA's North American operations were in trouble. Part of the problem was an adverse movement in exchange rates. In 1985, the exchange rate was $1=8.6 Swedish kronor; by 1990, it was $1=Skr5.8. At this exchange rate, many products imported from Sweden did not look inexpensive to American consumers.

But there was more to IKEA's problems than adverse movements in exchange rates. IKEA's unapologetically Swedish products, which had sold so well across Europe, jarred American tastes and sometimes physiques. Swedish beds were narrow and measured in centimeters. IKEA did not sell the matching bedroom suites that Americans liked. Its kitchen cupboards were too narrow for the large dinner plates. Its glasses were too small for a nation that adds ice to everything. The drawers in IKEA's bedroom chests were too shallow for American consumers, who tend to store sweaters in them. And the company made the mistake of selling European-sized curtains that did not fit American windows. As one senior IKEA manager joked later, "Americans just wouldn't lower their ceilings to fit our curtains."

By 1991, the company's top management realized that if it was going to succeed in North America, it would have to customize its product offering to North American tastes. The company set about redesigning its product range. The drawers in bedroom chests were made two inches deeper—and sales immediately increased by 30 to 40 percent. IKEA now sells American-style king and queen-sized beds, measured in inches, and it sells them as part of complete bedroom suites. It has redesigned its kitchen furniture and kitchenware to better appeal to American tastes. The company has also boosted the amount of products being sourced locally from 15 percent in 1990 to 45 percent in 1997, a move that makes the company far less vulnerable to adverse movements in exchange rates. By 1997, about one-third of IKEA's total product offerings were designed exclusively for the US market.

This break with IKEA's traditional strategy seems to be paying off. Between 1990 and 1994, IKEA's North American sales tripled to $480 million, and they nearly doubled again to about $900 million in 1997. The company claims it has been making a profit in North America since early 1993, although it does not release precise figures and does admit that its profit rate is lower in America than in Europe. Still, the company is pushing ahead with plans for further expansions in America, including the 1998 opening of a $50 million IKEA superstore in Illinois, which the company claims is the first of a new generation of larger stores.

http://www.ikea.com

Sources: "Furnishing the World," *The Economist*, November 19, 1994, pp. 79–80; H. Carnegy, "Struggle to Save the Soul of IKEA," *Financial Times*, March 27, 1995, p. 12; J. Flynn and L. Bongiorno, "IKEA's New Game Plan," *Business Week*, October 6, 1997, pp. 99–102; and IKEA's Web site at http://www.ikea.com.

Case Discussion Questions

1. What strategy was IKEA pursuing as it expanded throughout Europe during the 1970s and early 1980s—a multidomestic strategy, a global strategy, or an international strategy?

2. Why do you think this strategy did not work as well in North America as it did in Europe?

3. As of 1998, what strategy is IKEA pursuing? Does this strategy make sense? Can you see any drawbacks with this strategy?

Notes

1. M. E. Porter, *Competitive Strategy* (New York: Free Press, 1980).

2. M. E. Porter, *Competitive Advantage* (New York: Free Press, 1985).

3. Empirical evidence seems to indicate that, on average, international expansion is linked to greater firm profitability. For some recent examples, see M. A. Hitt, R. E. Hoskisson, and H. Kim, "International Diversification, Effects on Innovation and Firm Performance," *Academy of Management Journal* 40, no. 4 (1997), pp. 767–98; and S. Tallman and J. Li, "Effects of International Diversity and Product Diversity on the Performance of Multinational Firms," *Academy of Management Journal* 39, no. 1 (1996), pp. 179–96.

4. This concept has been popularized by G. Hamel and C. K. Prahalad, *Competing for the Future* (Boston: Harvard Business School Press, 1994). The concept is grounded in the resource-based view of the firm. For a summary, see J. B. Barney, "Firm Resources and Sustained Competitive Advantage," *Journal of Management* 17 (1991), pp. 99–120; and K. R. Conner, "A Historical Comparison of Resource Based Theory and Five Schools of Thought within Industrial Organization Economics: Do We Have a New Theory of the Firm?" *Journal of Management* 17 (1991), pp. 121–54.

5. J. P. Woomack, D. T. Jones, and D. Roos, *The Machine that Changed the World* (New York: Rawson Associates, 1990).

6. M. E. Porter, *The Competitive Advantage of Nations* (New York: Free Press, 1990).

7. R. B. Reich, *The Work of Nations* (New York: Alfred A. Knopf, 1991).

8. G. Hall and S. Howell, "The Experience Curve from an Economist's Perspective," *Strategic Management Journal* 6 (1985), pp. 197–212.

9. A. A. Alchain, "Reliability of Progress Curves in Airframe Production," *Econometrica* 31 (1963), pp. 697–93.

10. Hall and Howell, "The Experience Curve from an Economist's Perspective."

11. For a full discussion of the source of scale economies, see D. Besanko, D. Dranove, and M. Shanley, *Economics of Strategy* (New York, Wiley, 1996).

12. J. Main, "How to Go Global—and Why," *Fortune*, August 28, 1989, pp. 70–76.

13. "Matsushita Electrical Industrial in 1987," in *Transnational Management*, ed. C. A. Bartlett and S. Ghoshal (Homewood, IL: Richard D. Irwin, 1992).

14. C. K. Prahalad and Yves L. Doz, *The Multinational Mission: Balancing Local Demands and Global Vision* (New York: Free Press, 1987). Prahalad and Doz actually talk about local responsiveness rather than local customization.

15. "The Tire Industry's Costly Obsession with Size," *The Economist*, June 8, 1993, pp. 65–66.

16. T. Levitt, "The Globalization of Markets," *Harvard Business Review*, May–June 1983, pp. 92–102.

17. C. A. Bartlett and S. Ghoshal, *Managing across Borders* (Boston: Harvard Business School Press, 1989).

18. C. J. Chipello, "Local Presence Is Key to European Deals," *The Wall Street Journal*, June 30, 1998, p. A15.

19. This section is based on Bartlett and Ghoshal, *Managing across Borders*.

20. Bartlett and Ghoshal, *Managing across Borders*.

21. See P. Marsh and S. Wagstyle, "The Hungry Caterpillar," *Financial Times*, December 2, 1997, p. 22; and T. Hout, M. E. Porter, and E. Rudden, "How Global Firms Win Out," *Harvard Business Review*, September–October 1982, pp. 98–108.

22. Guy de Jonquieres, "Unilever Adopts a Clean Sheet Approach," *Financial Times*, October 21, 1991, p. 13.

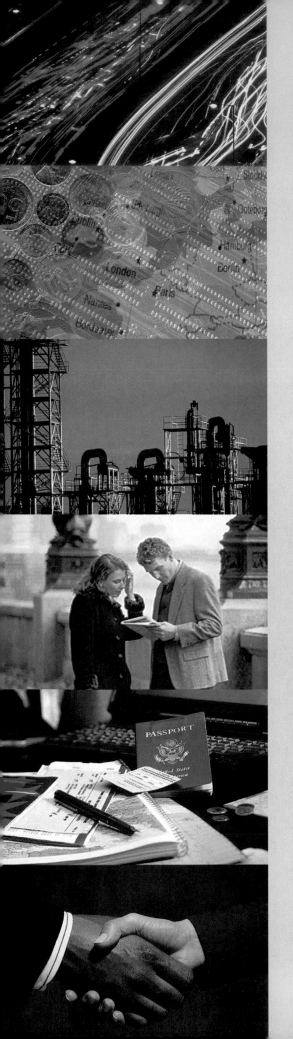

CHAPTER THIRTEEN

THE ORGANIZATION OF INTERNATIONAL BUSINESS

Organizational Change at Royal Dutch/Shell

The Anglo-Dutch company Royal Dutch/Shell is the world's largest non-state-owned oil company with activities in more than 130 countries and 1997 revenues of $128 billion. From the 1950s until 1994, Shell operated with a matrix structure invented for it by McKinsey & Company, a management consulting firm that specializes in organizational design. Under this matrix structure, the head of each operating company reported to two bosses. One boss was responsible for the geographical region or country in which the operating company was based, while the other was responsible for the business activity that the operating company was engaged in (Shell's business activities included oil exploration and production, oil products, chemicals, gas, and coal). For example, the head of the local Shell chemical company in Australia reported both to the head of Shell Australia and to the head of Shell's chemical division, who was based in London. In theory, both bosses had equal influence and status within the organization.

This matrix structure had two very visible consequences at Shell. First, because each operating company had two bosses to satisfy, decision making typically followed a pattern of consensus building, with differences of perspective between country (or regional) heads and the heads of business divisions being worked out through debate. Although this process could be slow and cumbersome, it was seen as a good thing in the oil industry where most big decisions are long-term ones that involve substantial capital expenditures and where informed debate can help to clarify the pros and cons of issues, rather than hinder decision making. Second, because the decision-making process was slow, it was reserved for only the most important decisions (such as major new capital investments). The result was substantial decentralization by default to the heads of the individual operating companies, who were largely left alone to run their own operations. This decentralization helped Shell respond to local differences in government regulations, competitive conditions, and consumer tastes. Thus, for example, the head of Shell's Australian chemical company was given the freedom to determine pricing practices and marketing strategy in the Australian market. Only if he wished to undertake a major capital investment, such as building a new chemical plant, would the consensus-building decision-making system be invoked.

As desirable as this matrix structure seemed, Shell announced in 1995 a radical plan to dismantle it. The primary reason given by top management was continuing slack demand for oil and weak oil prices, which had put pressure on Shell's profit margins. Although Shell had traditionally been among the most profitable oil companies in the world, its relative performance began to slip in the early 1990s as other oil companies, such as Exxon, adapted more rapidly to low oil prices by sharply cutting their overhead costs and consolidating production in efficient scale facilities. Consolidating production at these companies often involved serving the world market from a smaller number of large-scale refining facilities and shutting down smaller facilities. In contrast, Shell still operated with a large head office in London that contained 3,000 people, which was required to effect coordination within Shell's matrix structure, and substantial duplication of oil and chemical refining facilities across operating companies, each of which typically developed the facilities required to serve its own market.

In 1995, Shell's senior management decided that lowering operating costs required a sharp reduction in head office overhead and the elimination of any unnecessary duplication of facilities across countries. To achieve these goals, they decided to reorganize the company along divisional lines. Shell now operates with five main global product divisions: exploration and production, oil products, chemicals, gas, and coal. Each operating company reports to whichever global division is the most relevant. Thus, the head of the Australian chemical operation now reports directly to the head of the global chemical division. The thinking is that this will increase the power of the global chemical division and enable that division to eliminate any unnecessary duplication of facilities across countries. Eventually, production may be consolidated in larger facilities that serve an entire region, rather than a single country, enabling Shell to reap greater scale economies.

The country (or regional) chiefs remain but their roles and responsibilities have been reduced. Now their primary responsibility is coordination between operating companies within a country (or region) and relations with the local government. Also, there is a solid line of reporting and responsibility between the heads of operating companies and the global divisions and only a dotted line between the heads of operating companies and country chiefs. Thus, for example, the ability of the head of Shell Australia to shape the major capital investment decisions of Shell's Australian chemical operation has been substantially reduced as a result of these changes. Furthermore, the simplified reporting system has reduced the need for a large head office bureaucracy, and Shell announced plans to cut the work force of its London head office by 1,170, which should help drive down Shell's cost structure.

The early indications are that the changes are having the desired effect. For example, by looking at purchasing decisions on a global basis, the oil products division is paying significantly lower prices for inputs, such as gasoline additives, than when each national operating company purchased its own additives. In the chemical division, the changed perspective led the company to build a new polymer plant closer to customers in Louisiana instead of near the existing plant in Britain. Before the 1995 reorganization, the plant automatically would have been added to the UK fiefdom. The consequences of these changes are starting to show up in the company's financial reports. Return on capital increased to 12 percent in 1997, up from 7.9 percent in 1993.

http://www.shell.com

Sources: "Shell on the Rocks," *The Economist*, June 24, 1995, pp. 57–58; D. Lascelles, "Barons Swept out of Fiefdoms," *Financial Times*, March 30, 1995, p. 15; C. Lorenz, "End of a Corporate Era," *Financial Times*, March 30, 1995, p. 15; R. Corzine, "Shell Discovers Time and Tide Wait for No Man," *Financial Times*, March 10, 1998, p. 17; R. Corzine, "Oiling the Group's Wheels of Change," *Financial Times*, April 1, 1998, p. 12; and J. Guyon, "Why Is the World's Most Profitable Company Turning Itself Inside Out?" *Fortune*, August 4, 1997, pp. 120–25.

Introduction

The objective of this chapter is to identify the organizational structures and internal control mechanisms international businesses use to manage and direct their global operations. We will be concerned not just with formal structures and control mechanisms but also with informal structures and control mechanisms such as corporate culture and companywide networks. To succeed, an international business must have appropriate formal and informal organizational structure and control mechanisms. The strategy of the firm determines what is "appropriate." Firms pursuing a global strategy require different structures and control mechanisms than firms pursuing a multidomestic or a transnational strategy. To succeed, a firm's structure and control systems must match its strategy in discriminating ways.

The opening case illustrates this. From the 1960s to the late 1980s, the matrix structure utilized by Royal Dutch Shell served the company well. It enabled Shell to respond to national differences in consumer tastes and preferences, government regulations, and competitive conditions while giving the head office control over major strategic decisions and investments. The structure was consistent with the multidomestic strategy Shell was pursuing at the time. However, this structure made sense only as long as the firm did not have to worry about high overhead costs, slow decision making, and duplication of facilities that resulted from the structure. By the early 1990s, increasing cost pressures made it imperative for Shell to look for ways to drive down its cost structure. The matrix structure became a distinct drawback. The environment had become more cost competitive, and Shell had to respond by adopting a global strategy. Implementing this strategy required a change of structure, both to reduce overhead costs and to give the corporate center the power required to minimize operating costs by eliminating unnecessary duplication of operating facilities and consolidating production in large facilities that could reap scale economies. The structure that Shell chose to adopt, which was based on global product divisions, was consistent with this new emphasis on a global strategy.

Another example of the need for a fit between strategy and structure concerns the recent history of Philips Electronics NV. One of the largest industrial companies in the world (with operations in more than 60 countries), this Dutch company has long been a dominant force in the global electronics, consumer appliances, and lighting industries. However, its performance started to slip in the 1970s, and by the early 1990s, Philips was suffering a string of record financial losses. During the 1970s and 80s, Philips's markets were attacked by Japanese companies such as Matsushita and Sony. These companies were pursuing a global strategy, using their resulting low costs to undercut Philips. To compete on an equal footing with Matsushita and Sony, Philips had to realize experience curve and location economies (see Chapter 12). Unfortunately, its attempts to do this were hindered by an organization more suited to a multidomestic strategy. Most of Philips's foreign subsidiaries were self-contained operations with their own production facilities. Like Shell, Philips desperately needed to consolidate production in a few facilities to realize location and experience curve economies, but it was hindered by resistance from its national operations and by the sheer scale of the needed reorganization. As a consequence of this misfit of structure and strategy, Philips suffered a decade of financial trouble. The company began to get its financial act together in the mid-1990s, primarily because it changed its organizational structure, moving away from a structure based on national organizations and toward one based on worldwide product divisions. This new structure was much better suited to the global strategy Philips was now trying to pursue, and it allowed the company to start driving down its cost structure.[1]

To come to grips with issues of structure and control in international business, in the next four sections we consider the basic dimensions of structure and control: vertical differentiation, horizontal differentiation, integration, and control systems. Vertical differentiation is the distribution of decision-making authority within a hierarchy (i.e., centralized versus decentralized). Horizontal differentiation is the division of an organization into subunits (e.g., into functions, divisions, or subsidiaries). Integration refers to the body of mechanisms that coordinate and integrate the subunits. These mechanisms are formal and informal. Control systems are the systems that top management uses to direct and control subunits, and these also are formal and informal. Throughout these sections, we will focus on the implications of the four dimensions for the international firm. Then we will attempt to determine the optimal structures and controls for multidomestic, global, international, and transnational firms.

Vertical Differentiation

A firm's vertical differentiation determines where in its hierarchy the decision-making power is concentrated.[2] For example, are production and marketing decisions centralized in the offices of upper-level managers, or are they decentralized to lower-level managers? Where does the responsibility for R&D decisions lie? Are strategic and financial control responsibilities pushed down to operating units, or are they concentrated in the hands of top management? And so on. There are arguments for centralization and other arguments for decentralization.

Arguments for Centralization

There are four main arguments for centralization. First, centralization can facilitate coordination. For example, consider a firm that has a component-manufacturing operation in Taiwan and an assembly operation in Mexico. There may be a need to coordinate the activities of these two operations to ensure a smooth flow of products from the component operation to the assembly operation. This might be achieved by centralizing production scheduling decisions at the firm's head office. Second, centralization can help ensure that decisions are consistent with organizational objectives. When decisions are decentralized to lower-level managers, those managers may make decisions at variance with top management's goals. Centralization of important decisions minimizes the chance of this occurring.

Third, by concentrating power and authority in one individual or a top-management team, centralization can give top-level managers the means to bring about needed major organizational changes. Fourth, centralization can avoid the duplication of activities that occurs when similar activities are carried on by various subunits within the organization. For example, many international firms centralize their R&D functions at one or two locations to ensure that R&D work is not duplicated. Similarly, production activities may be centralized at key locations for the same reason.

Arguments for Decentralization

There are five main arguments for decentralization. First, top management can become overburdened when decision-making authority is centralized, and this can result in poor decisions. Decentralization gives top management the time to focus on critical issues by delegating more routine issues to lower-level managers. Second, motivational research favors decentralization. Behavioral scientists have long argued that people are willing to give more to their jobs when they have a greater degree of individual freedom and control over their work. Third, decentralization permits greater flexibility—more rapid response to environmental changes—because decisions do not have to be "referred up the hierarchy" unless they are exceptional. Fourth, decentralization can result in better decisions because decisions are made closer to the spot by individuals who (presumably) have better information than managers several levels up in a hierarchy. Fifth, decentralization can increase control. Decentralization can be used to establish relatively autonomous, self-contained subunits within an organization. Subunit managers can then be held accountable for subunit performance. The more responsibility subunit managers have for decisions that impact subunit performance, the fewer alibis they have for poor performance.

Strategy and Centralization in an International Business

The choice between centralization and decentralization is not absolute. It frequently makes sense to centralize some decisions and to decentralize others, depending on the type of decision and the firm's strategy. Decisions regarding overall firm strategy, major financial expenditures, financial objectives, and the like are typically centralized at the firm's headquarters. However, operating decisions—such as those relating to production, marketing, R&D, and human resource management—may or may not be centralized depending on the firm's international strategy.

Consider firms pursuing a global strategy. They must decide how to disperse the various value creation activities around the globe so location and experience economies can be realized. The head office must decide where to locate R&D, production, marketing, and so on. In addition, the globally dispersed web of value creation activities that facilitates a global strategy must be coordinated. All this creates pressures for centralizing some operating decisions.

In contrast, the emphasis on local responsiveness in multidomestic firms creates strong pressures for decentralizing operating decisions to foreign subsidiaries. Thus, in the classic multidomestic firm, foreign subsidiaries have autonomy in most production and marketing decisions. International firms tend to maintain centralized control over their core competency and to decentralize other decisions to foreign subsidiaries. This typically centralizes control over R&D and/or marketing in the home country and decentralizes operating decisions to the foreign subsidiaries. Microsoft Corporation, which fits the international mode, centralizes its product development activities (where its core competencies lie) at its Redmond, Washington, headquarters and decentralizes marketing activity to various foreign subsidiaries. Thus, while products are developed at home, managers in the various foreign subsidiaries have significant latitude for formulating strategies to market those products in their particular settings.[3]

The situation in transnational firms is more complex. The need to realize location and experience curve economies requires some degree of centralized control over global production centers (as it does in global firms). However, the need for local responsiveness dictates the decentralization of many operating decisions, particularly for marketing, to foreign subsidiaries. Thus, in transnational firms, some operating decisions are relatively centralized, while others are relatively decentralized. In addition, global learning based on the multidirectional transfer of skills between subsidiaries, and between subsidiaries and the corporate center, is a central feature of a firm pursuing a transnational strategy. The concept of global learning is predicated on the notion that foreign subsidiaries within a multinational firm have significant freedom to develop their own skills and competencies. Only then can these be leveraged to benefit other parts of the organization. A substantial degree of decentralization is required if subsidiaries are going to have the freedom to develop their own skills and competencies. So for this reason too, the pursuit of a transnational strategy requires a high degree of decentralization.[4]

Horizontal Differentiation

Horizontal differentiation is basically concerned with how the firm decides to divide itself into subunits.[5] The decision is typically made on the basis of function, type of business, or geographical area. In many firms, just one of these criteria predominates, but more complex solutions are adopted in others. This is particularly likely in the case of international firms, where the conflicting demands to organize the company around different products (to realize location and experience curve economies) and different national markets (to remain locally responsive) must be reconciled. One solution to this dilemma is to adopt a matrix structure that divides the organization on the basis of both products and national markets. In this section, we look at some different ways firms divide themselves into subunits.

The Structure of Domestic Firms

Most firms begin with no formal structure and as they grow, the demands of management become too great for one individual to handle. At this point, the organization is typically split into functions reflecting the firm's value creation activities (e.g., finance, production, marketing, R&D). These functions are typically coordinated and controlled by a top-management team (see Figure 13.1). Decision making in this functional structure tends to be centralized.

Further horizontal differentiation may be required if the firm significantly diversifies its product offering. For example, although Philips NV started as a lighting company, it now also has activities in consumer electronics (e.g., visual and audio

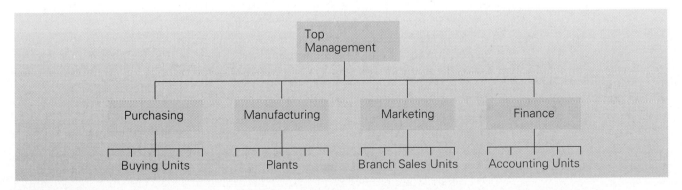

Figure 13.1

A Typical Functional Structure

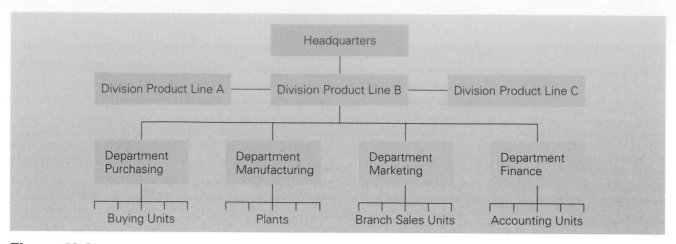

Figure 13.2

A Typical Product Division Structure

equipment), industrial electronics (integrated circuits and other electronic components), and medical systems (CT scanners and ultrasound systems). In such circumstances, a functional structure can be too clumsy. Problems of coordination and control arise when different business areas are managed within the framework of a functional structure.[6] It becomes difficult to identify the profitability of each distinct business area, and it is difficult to run a functional department, such as production or marketing, if it is supervising the value creation activities of several business areas.

To solve the problems of coordination and control, most firms switch to a product division structure at this stage (see Figure 13.2). With a product division structure, each division is responsible for a distinct product line (business area). Thus, Philips has divisions for lighting, consumer electronics, industrial electronics, and medical systems. Each product division is set up as a self-contained, largely autonomous entity with its own functions. The responsibility for operating decisions is typically decentralized to product divisions, which are then held accountable for their performance. Headquarters is responsible for the overall strategic development of the firm and for the financial control of the various divisions.

The International Division

Historically, when firms have expanded abroad they have typically grouped all their international activities into an international division. This has tended to be the case for firms organized on the basis of functions and for firms organized on the basis of product divisions. Regardless of the firm's domestic structure, its international division tends to be organized on geography. This is illustrated in Figure 13.3 for a firm whose domestic organization is based on product divisions.

Many manufacturing firms expanded internationally by exporting the product manufactured at home to foreign subsidiaries to sell. Thus, in the firm illustrated in Figure 13.3, the subsidiaries in Countries 1 and 2 would sell the products manufactured by Divisions A, B, and C. In time it might prove viable to manufacture the product in each country, and so production facilities would be added on a country-by-country basis. For firms with a functional structure at home, this might mean replicating the functional structure in every country in which the firm does business. For firms with a divisional structure, this might mean replicating the divisional structure in every country in which the firm does business.

This structure has been widely used; according to a Harvard study, 60 percent of all firms that have expanded internationally have initially adopted it. Nonetheless,

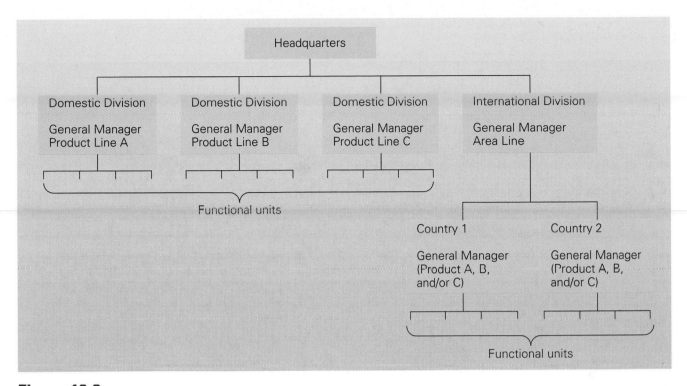

Figure 13.3

One Company's International Division Structure

it gives rise to problems.[7] The dual structure it creates contains inherent potential for conflict and coordination problems between domestic and foreign operations. The heads of foreign subsidiaries are not given as much voice in the organization as the heads of domestic functions (in the case of functional firms) or divisions (in the case of divisional firms). Rather, the head of the international division is presumed to be able to represent the interests of all countries to headquarters. This relegates each country's manager to the second tier of the firm's hierarchy, which is inconsistent with a strategy of trying to expand internationally and build a true multinational organization.

Another problem is the implied lack of coordination between domestic operations and foreign operations, which are isolated from each other in separate parts of the structural hierarchy. This can inhibit the worldwide introduction of new products, the transfer of core competencies between domestic and foreign operations, and the consolidation of global production at key locations so as to realize location and experience curve economies. An example of these problems is given in the accompanying Management Focus, which looks at the experience of Abbott Laboratories with an international division structure.

Because of such problems, most firms that continue to expand internationally abandon this structure and adopt one of the worldwide structures we discuss next. The two initial choices are a worldwide product division structure, which tends to be adopted by diversified firms that have domestic product divisions, and a worldwide area structure, which tends to be adopted by undiversified firms whose domestic structures are based on functions. These two alternative paths of development are illustrated in Figure 13.4. The model in the figure is referred to as the international structural stages model and it was developed by John Stopford and Louis Wells.[8]

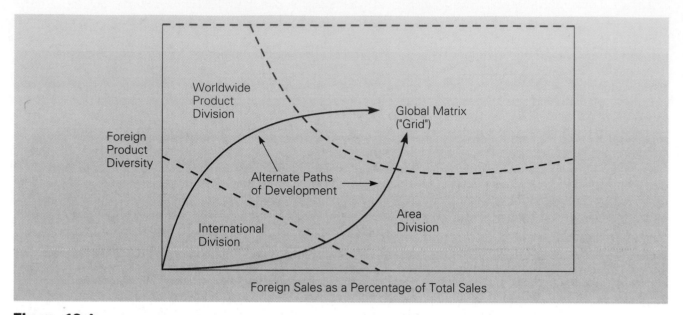

Figure 13.4

The International Structural Stages Model

Source: Adapted from John M. Stopford and Louis T. Wells, *Strategy and Structure of the Multinational Enterprise* (New York: Basic Books, 1972).

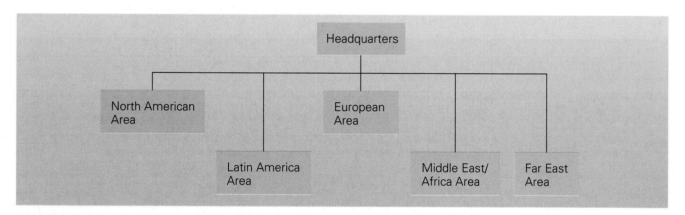

Figure 13.5

A Worldwide Area Structure

Worldwide Area Structure

A worldwide area structure tends to be favored by firms with a low degree of diversification and a domestic structure based on function (see Figure 13.5). This structure divides the world into areas. An area may be a country (if the market is large enough) or a group of countries. Each area tends to be a self-contained, largely autonomous entity with its own set of value creation activities (e.g., its own production, marketing, R&D, human resources, and finance functions). Operations authority and strategic decisions relating to each of these activities are typically decentralized to each area, with headquarters retaining authority for the overall strategic direction of the firm and overall financial control.

This structure facilitates local responsiveness. Because decision-making responsibilities are decentralized to each area, each area can customize product offerings, marketing strategy, and business strategy to the local conditions. The weakness of the

MANAGEMENT FOCUS
The International Division at Abbott Laboratories

http://www.abbott.com

With 1997 sales of over $12 billion, Abbott Laboratories is one of the world's largest health care companies. The company first split itself into three divisions—pharmaceuticals, hospital products, and nutritional products—in the 1960s. Each division operated as a profit center, and each was relatively autonomous and self-contained, with its own R&D, manufacturing, and marketing functions. By the late 1960s, Abbott's foreign sales were growing rapidly, so the company established an international division to handle all the firm's non-US operations on geographic rather than product lines.

Alongside these four divisions, however, a new business has grown up that is organized differently. Abbott's diagnostics business, which was established in the 1970s, is now a world leader with global sales of $2.4 billion. Unlike other businesses, the diagnostics business is organized on a global basis, operating in foreign countries through its own staff, rather than through the international division. Abbott uses two different ways of handling global sales—through an international division and through a global product division (the diagnostics business organization). And the company is debating the best way of organizing international operations.

This debate is being informed by two changes occurring in Abbott's environment that are pulling the company in different directions. One change has been a shift toward global product development in the health care industry. In an effort to quickly recapture the costs of developing new products, which for new pharmaceuticals can sometimes be over $100 million, pharmaceutical companies are trying to introduce new products as rapidly as possible worldwide. Abbott has found that developing products first for the US market and then modifying those products for foreign customers is a slow and expensive process.

Instead, across all four of the company's businesses, Abbott is trying to build global products and then launch those products simultaneously around the world. This change is pulling Abbott in the direction of adopting global product divisions for all four businesses. Only global product divisions would give Abbott the tight control over new-product development and product launch strategy that is deemed necessary.

The other change is the greater purchasing leverage in both the United States and elsewhere of bigger health care organizations. Large hospital groups and health maintenance organizations are coordinating their buying across a range of product lines. These powerful customers have expressed a preference to have a single contact point at Abbott, and Abbott has recognized that it is becoming increasingly important to develop stronger relations with key customers. The best way of doing this is to have a single marketing organization in each country in which Abbott does business. This organization would sell the products from each of Abbott's four product divisions. In 1994, Abbott established a separate marketing unit in the United States to do just this, while Abbott's international division adopts this approach in each country in which it operates.

Currently, Abbott is sticking with the status quo. Executives at Abbott's international division support this move, while the heads of the product divisions favor a shift toward four global product divisions. However, top management seems to have decided there is no perfect solution to the company's organizational problems and that, imperfect as the current structure is, it works too well to contemplate a major change now.

Sources: R. Walters, "Two's Company," *Financial Times,* July 7, 1995, p. 12; and *Abbott Laboratories 1997 Annual Report.*

structure is that it encourages fragmentation of the organization into highly autonomous entities. This can make it difficult to transfer core competencies between areas and to undertake the rationalization in value creation activities required for realizing location and experience curve economies. The structure is consistent with a multidomestic strategy but with little else. Thus, firms structured on this basis may encounter significant problems if local responsiveness is less critical than reducing

Figure 13.6

A Worldwide Area Product Division Structure

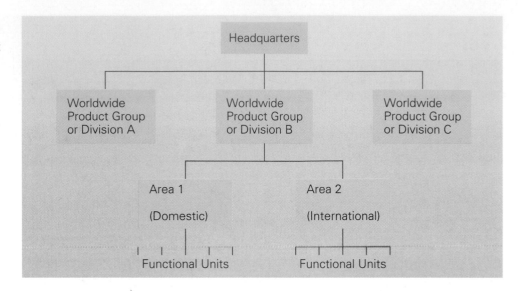

costs or transferring core competencies for establishing a competitive advantage in their industry. For an example of the nature of such problems, see the closing case about Unilever.

Worldwide Product Division Structure

A worldwide product division structure tends to be adopted by firms that are reasonably diversified and, accordingly, originally had domestic structures based on product divisions. As with the domestic product division structure, each division is a self-contained, largely autonomous entity with full responsibility for its own value creation activities. The headquarters retains responsibility for the overall strategic development and financial control of the firm (see Figure 13.6).

Underpinning the organization is a belief that the various value creation activities of each product division should be coordinated by that division worldwide. Thus, the worldwide product division structure is designed to help overcome the coordination problems that arise with the international division and worldwide area structures (see the Management Focus on Abbott Laboratories for a detailed example). This structure provides an organizational context in which it is easier to pursue the consolidation of value creation activities at key locations necessary for realizing location and experience curve economies. It also facilitates the transfer of core competencies within a division's worldwide operations and the simultaneous worldwide introduction of new products. The main problem with the structure is the limited voice it gives to area or country managers, since they are seen as subservient to product division managers. The result can be a lack of local responsiveness, which, as we saw in Chapter 12, can be a fatal flaw.

Global Matrix Structure

Both the worldwide area structure and the worldwide product division structure have strengths and weaknesses. The worldwide area structure facilitates local responsiveness, but it can inhibit the realization of location and experience curve economies and the transfer of core competencies between areas. The worldwide product division structure provides a better framework for pursuing location and experience curve economies and for transferring core competencies, but it is weak in local responsiveness. Other things being equal, this suggests that a worldwide area structure is more appropriate if the firm's strategy is multidomestic, whereas a worldwide product division structure is more appropriate for firms pursuing global or international strategies. However, as we saw in Chapter 12, other things are not equal; most important, as Bartlett and Ghoshal have argued, to survive in some industries, firms must adopt a transnational strategy. That is, they must focus simultaneously on realizing location

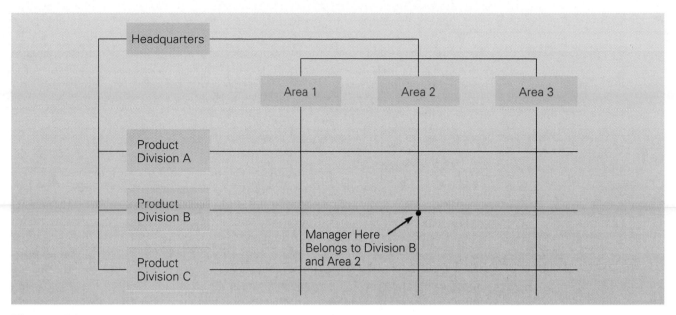

Figure 13.7

A Global Matrix Structure

and experience curve economies, on local responsiveness, and on the internal transfer of core competencies (worldwide learning).[9]

Many firms have attempted to cope with the conflicting demands of a transnational strategy by using a matrix structure. In the classic global matrix structure, horizontal differentiation proceeds along two dimensions: product division and geographical area (see Figure 13.7). The basic philosophy is that responsibility for operating decisions pertaining to a particular product should be shared by the product division and the various areas of the firm. Thus, the nature of the product offering, the marketing strategy, and the business strategy to be pursued in Area 1 for the products produced by Division A are determined by conciliation between Division A and Area 1 management. It is believed that this dual decision-making responsibility should enable the firm to simultaneously achieve its particular objectives. In most classic matrix structures, dual responsibility is reinforced by giving product divisions and geographical areas equal status within the organization. Individual managers belong to two hierarchies (a divisional hierarchy and an area hierarchy) and have two bosses (a divisional boss and an area boss).

Unfortunately, the global matrix structure often does not work as well as the theory predicts. In practice, the matrix often is clumsy and bureaucratic. It can require so many meetings that it is difficult to get any work done. Often, the need to get an area and a product division to reach a decision slows decision making and produces an inflexible organization unable to respond quickly to market shifts or to innovate. The dual-hierarchy structure can also lead to conflict and perpetual power struggles between the areas and the product divisions, catching many managers in the middle. To make matters worse, it can prove difficult to ascertain accountability in this structure. When all critical decisions are the product of negotiation between divisions and areas, one side can always blame the other when things go wrong. As a manager in one global matrix structure, reflecting on a failed product launch, said to the author, "Had we been able to do things our way, instead of having to accommodate those guys from the product division, this would never have happened." (A manager in the product division expressed similar sentiments.) Such finger pointing can compromise accountability, enhance conflict, and allow headquarters to lose control over the organization.

In light of these problems, many transnational firms are now trying to build "flexible" matrix structures based on firmwide networks and a shared culture and vision rather than on a rigid hierarchical arrangement. Dow Chemical, which is profiled in the accompanying Management Focus, is one such firm. Within such companies, the informal structure plays a greater role than the formal structure. We discuss this issue when we consider informal integrating mechanisms in the next section.

Integrating Mechanisms

In the previous section, we explained that firms divide themselves into subunits. Now we need to examine some means of coordinating those subunits. One way of achieving coordination is through centralization. If the coordination task is complex, however, centralization may not be very effective. Higher-level managers responsible for achieving coordination can soon become overwhelmed by the volume of work required to coordinate the activities of various subunits, particularly if the subunits are large, diverse, and/or geographically dispersed. When this is the case, firms look toward integrating mechanisms, both formal and informal, to help achieve coordination. In this section, we introduce the various integrating mechanisms that international businesses can use. Before doing so, however, let us explore the need for coordination in international firms and some impediments to coordination.

Strategy and Coordination in the International Business

The need for coordination between subunits varies with the strategy of the firm. The need for coordination is lowest in multidomestic companies, is higher in international companies, higher still in global companies, and highest of all in the transnational firms. Multidomestic firms are primarily concerned with local responsiveness. Such firms are likely to operate with a worldwide area structure in which each area has considerable autonomy and its own set of value creation functions. Since each area is established as a stand-alone entity, the need for coordination between areas is minimized.

The need for coordination is greater in firms pursuing an international strategy and trying to profit from the transfer of core competencies between the home country and foreign operations. Coordination is necessary to support the transfer of skills and product offerings from home to foreign operations. The need for coordination is greater still in firms trying to profit from location and experience curve economies; that is, in firms pursuing global strategies. Achieving location and experience economies involves dispersing value creation activities to various locations around the globe. The resulting global web of activities must be coordinated to ensure the smooth flow of inputs into the value chain, the smooth flow of semifinished products through the value chain, and the smooth flow of finished products to markets around the world.

The need for coordination is greatest in transnational firms. Recall that these firms simultaneously pursue location and experience curve economies, local responsiveness, and the multidirectional transfer of core competencies among all the firm's subunits (this is referred to as global learning). As in global companies, coordination is required to ensure the smooth flow of products through the global value chain. As in international companies, coordination is required for ensuring the transfer of core competencies to subunits. However, the transnational goal of achieving multidirectional transfer of competencies requires much greater coordination than in international firms. In addition, transnationals require coordination between foreign subunits and the firm's globally dispersed value creation activities (e.g., production, R&D, marketing) to ensure that any product offering and marketing strategy is sufficiently customized to local conditions.

Impediments to Coordination

Managers of the various subunits have different orientations, partly because they have different tasks. For example, production managers are typically concerned with production issues such as capacity utilization, cost control, and quality control, whereas

MANAGEMENT FOCUS
Dow Chemical's Matrix Structure

http://www.dow.com

The chemical industry is a global industry in which six major players compete head to head around the world. These companies are Dow Chemical and Du Pont of the United States, Great Britain's ICI, and the German trio of BASF, Hoechst AG, and Bayer. The barriers to the free flow of chemical products between nations largely disappeared in the 1970s. This along with the commodity nature of most bulk chemicals and a severe recession in the early 1980s ushered in a prolonged period of intense price competition. In such an environment, the company that wins the competitive race is the one with the lowest costs, and in recent years that has been Dow.

Dow's managers insist that part of the credit must be placed at the feet of its maligned "matrix" organization. Dow's organizational matrix has three interacting elements: functions (e.g., R&D, manufacturing, marketing), businesses (e.g., ethylene, plastics, pharmaceuticals), and geography (e.g., Spain, Germany, Brazil). Managers' job titles incorporate all three elements—for example, plastics marketing manager for Spain—and most managers report to at least two bosses. Thus, the plastics marketing manager in Spain might report to both the head of the worldwide plastics business and the head of the Spanish operations. The intent of the matrix was to make Dow operations responsive to both local market needs and corporate objectives. Thus, the plastics business might be charged with minimizing Dow's global plastics production costs, while the Spanish operation might be charged with determining how best to sell plastics in the Spanish market.

When Dow introduced this structure, the results were less than promising; multiple reporting channels led to confusion and conflict. The large number of bosses made for an unwieldy bureaucracy. The overlapping responsibilities resulted in turf battles and a lack of accountability. Area managers disagreed with managers overseeing business sectors about which plants should be built and where. In short, the structure didn't work. Instead of abandoning the structure,

however, Dow decided to see if it could be made more flexible.

Dow's decision to keep its matrix structure was prompted by its move into the pharmaceuticals industry. The company realized that the pharmaceutical business is very different from the bulk chemicals business. In bulk chemicals, the big returns come from achieving economies of scale in production. This dictates establishing large plants in key locations from which regional or global markets can be served. In pharmaceuticals, regulatory and marketing requirements for drugs vary so much from country to country that local needs are far more important than reducing manufacturing costs through scale economies. A high degree of local responsiveness is essential. Dow realized its pharmaceutical business would never thrive if it were managed by the same priorities as its mainstream chemical operations.

Instead of abandoning its matrix, Dow decided to make it more flexible so it could better accommodate the different businesses, each with its own priorities, within a single management system. A small team of senior executives at headquarters now helps set the priorities for each type of business. After priorities are identified for each business sector, one of the three elements of the matrix—function, business, or geographical area—is given primary authority in decision making. Which element takes the lead varies according to the type of decision and the market or location in which the company is competing. Such flexibility requires that all employees understand what is occurring in the rest of the matrix so they can cooperate rather than act individually. Although this may seem confusing, Dow claims this flexible system works well and credits much of its success to the quality of the decisions it facilitates.

Source: "Dow Draws Its Matrix Again, and Again, and Again," *The Economist,* August 5, 1989, pp. 55–56.

marketing managers are concerned with marketing issues such as pricing, promotions, distribution, and market share. These differences can inhibit communication between the managers. These managers often do not even "speak the same language." There may also be a lack of respect between subunits (e.g., marketing managers "looking down on" production managers, and vice versa), which further inhibits the communication required to achieve cooperation and coordination.

Differences in subunits' orientations also arise from their differing goals. For example, worldwide product divisions of a multinational firm may be committed to cost goals that require global production of a standardized product, whereas a foreign subsidiary may be committed to increasing its market share in its country, which will require a nonstandard product. In this case, these different goals can lead to conflict.

Such impediments to coordination are not unusual in any firm, but they can be particularly problematic in the multinational enterprise with its profusion of subunits at home and abroad. Also, differences in subunit orientation are often reinforced in multinationals by the separations of time zone, distance, and nationality between managers of the subunits.

For example, until recently, the Dutch company Philips had an organization comprising worldwide product divisions and largely autonomous national organizations. The company has long had problems getting its product divisions and national organizations to cooperate on such things as new-product introductions. When Philips developed a VCR format, the V2000 system, it could not get its North American subsidiary to introduce the product. Rather, the North American unit adopted the rival VHS format produced by Philip's global competitor Matsushita. Unilever has experienced a similar problem in its detergents business. The company has found that the need to resolve disputes between its many national organizations and its product divisions can extend the time necessary for introducing a new product across Europe to four years. This denies Unilever the first-mover advantage crucial to building a strong market position.[10]

Formal Integrating Mechanisms

The formal mechanisms used to integrate subunits vary in complexity from simple direct contact and liaison roles, to teams, to a matrix structure (see Figure 13.8). In general, the greater the need for coordination, the more complex the formal integrating mechanisms need to be.[11]

Direct contact between subunit managers is the simplest integrating mechanism. By this "mechanism," managers of the various subunits simply contact each other whenever they have a common concern. Direct contact may not be effective if the managers have differing orientations that act to impede coordination, as pointed out in the previous subsection.

Liaison roles are a bit more complex. When the volume of contacts between subunits increases, coordination can be improved by giving a person in each subunit responsibility for coordinating with another subunit on a regular basis. Through these roles, a permanent relationship is established between the people involved, which helps attenuate the impediments to coordination discussed in the previous subsection.

When the need for coordination is greater still, firms tend to use temporary or permanent teams composed of individuals from the subunits that need to achieve coordination. They are typically used to coordinate new-product development and introduction, but they are useful when any aspect of operations or strategy requires the cooperation of two or more subunits. New-product development and introduction teams are typically composed of personnel from R&D, production, and marketing. The resulting coordination aids the development of products that are tailored to consumer needs and that can be produced at a reasonable cost (design for manufacturing).

When the need for integration is very high, firms may institute some kind of matrix structure, in which all roles are viewed as integrating roles. The structure is designed to facilitate maximum integration among subunits. As explained earlier, the most common matrix in multinational firms is based on geographical areas and world-

Figure 13.8

Formal Integrating
Mechanisms

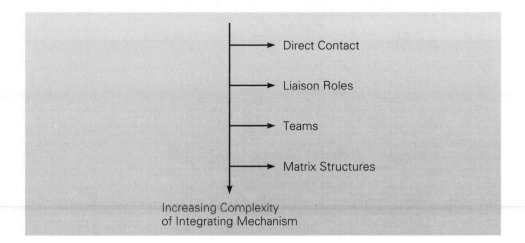

Direct Contact

Liaison Roles

Teams

Matrix Structures

Increasing Complexity
of Integrating Mechanism

wide product divisions. This achieves a high level of integration between the product divisions and the areas so that, in theory, the firm can pay close attention to both local responsiveness and the pursuit of location and experience curve economies.

In some multinationals the matrix is more complex still, structuring the firm into geographical areas, worldwide product divisions, and functions, all of which report directly to headquarters. Thus, within a company such as Dow Chemical (see the Management Focus) each manager belongs to three hierarchies (e.g., a plastics marketing manager in Spain is a member of the Spanish subsidiary, the plastics product division, and the marketing function). In addition to facilitating local responsiveness and location and experience curve economies, such a matrix fosters the transfer of core competencies within the organization. This occurs because core competencies tend to reside in functions (e.g., R&D, marketing). A structure such as Dow's facilitates the transfer of competencies existing in functions from division to division and from area to area.

However, as discussed earlier, such matrix solutions can quickly become bogged down in a bureaucratic tangle that creates as many problems as it solves. Matrix structures tend to be bureaucratic, inflexible, and characterized by conflict rather than cooperation. As in the case of Dow Chemical, such a structure needs to be somewhat flexible and supported by informal integrating mechanisms.

Informal Integrating Mechanisms

In attempting to alleviate or avoid the problems associated with formal integrating mechanisms in general, and matrix structures in particular, firms with a high need for integration have been experimenting with two informal integrating mechanisms: management networks and organization culture.[12]

Management Networks

A management network is a system of informal contacts between managers within an enterprise.[13] For a network to exist, managers at different locations within the organization must be linked to each other at least indirectly. For example, consider Figure 13.9, which shows the simple network relationships between seven managers within a multinational firm. Managers A, B, and C all know each other personally, as do Managers D, E, and F. Although Manager B does not know Manager F personally, they are linked through common acquaintances (Managers C and D). Thus, we can say that Managers A through F are all part of the network, and also that Manager G is not.

Imagine Manager B is a marketing manager in Spain and needs to know the solution to a technical problem to better serve an important European customer. Imagine further that Manager F, an R&D manager in the United States, has the solution to Manager B's problem. Manager B mentions her problem to all of her contacts, including Manager C, and asks them if they know of anyone who might provide a solution.

Figure 13.9

A Simple Management
Network

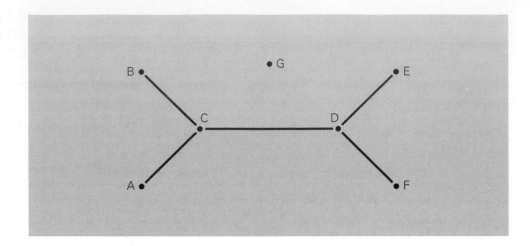

Manager C asks Manager D, who tells Manager F, who then calls Manager B with the solution. In this way, coordination is achieved informally through the network, rather than by formal integrating mechanisms such as teams or a matrix structure.

For such a network to function effectively, however, it must embrace as many managers as possible. For example, if Manager G had a problem similar to Manager B's, he would not be able to utilize the informal network to find a solution; he would have to resort to more formal mechanisms. Establishing firmwide networks is difficult, and although network enthusiasts speak of networks as the "glue" that binds multinational companies together, it is far from clear how successful firms have been at building companywide networks. Two techniques being used to establish firmwide networks are information systems and management development policies.

Firms are using their computer and telecommunications networks to provide the physical foundation for informal information systems networks.[14] Electronic mail, videoconferencing, and high-speed data systems make it much easier for managers scattered over the globe to get to know each other. Without an existing network of personal contacts, however, worldwide information systems are unlikely to meet a firm's need for integration. Firms are using their management development programs to build informal networks. Tactics include rotating managers through various subunits on a regular basis so they build their own informal networks and using management education programs to bring managers of subunits together in a single location so they can become acquainted.

Organization Culture

Management networks may not be sufficient to achieve coordination if subunit managers persist in pursuing subgoals that are at variance with firmwide goals. For a management network to function properly—and for a formal matrix structure to work—managers must share a strong commitment to the same goals. To appreciate the nature of the problem, consider again the case of Manager B and Manager F. As before, Manager F hears about Manager B's problem through the network. However, solving Manager B's problem would require Manager F to devote considerable time to the task. Insofar as this would divert Manager F away from his own regular tasks—and the pursuit of subgoals that differ from those of Manager B—he may be unwilling to do it. Thus, Manager F may not call Manager B, and the informal network would fail to provide a solution to Manager B's problem.

To eliminate this flaw, the organization's managers must adhere to a common set of norms and values; that is, the firm's culture should override differing subunit orientations.[15] When this is the case, a manager is willing and able to set aside the interests of his own subunit when doing so benefits the firm as a whole. If Manager B and Manager F are committed to the same organizational norms and value systems, and if these organizational norms and values place the interests of the firm as a whole above the interests of any individual subunit, Manager F should be willing to cooperate with Manager B on solving her subunit's problems.

The critical question then becomes, How can a firm build a common culture? The ability to establish a common vision for the company is critical.[16] Top management needs to determine the mission of the firm and how this should be reflected in the organization's norms and values. These determinations then need to be disseminated throughout the organization. As with building informal networks, this can be achieved in part through management education programs that "socialize" managers into the firm's norms and value system. Leadership by example is another important tool for building a common culture. Human relations policies also seem to play a critical role. There is a need to select managers who are team players. There is also a need to devise reward and incentive policies that encourage managers to cooperate for the good of the firm. Put simply, Manager F is more likely to cooperate with Manager B if he gets credit for doing so than if he is made to suffer in some way for spending time on problems not directly related to his immediate task.

Summary

The message contained in this section is crucial to understanding the problems of managing the multinational firm. Multinationals need integration—particularly if they are pursuing global, international, or transnational strategies—but it can be difficult to achieve due to the impediments to coordination we discussed. Traditionally, firms have tried to achieve coordination by adopting formal integrating mechanisms. These do not always work, however, since they tend to be bureaucratic and do not necessarily address the problems that arise from differing subunit orientations. This is particularly likely with a complex matrix structure, and yet, a complex matrix structure is required for simultaneously achieving location and experience curve economies, local responsiveness, and the multidirectional transfer of core competencies within the organization.

The solution to this dilemma seems twofold. First, the firm must try to establish an informal management network that can do much of the work previously undertaken by a formal matrix structure. Second, the firm must build a common culture. Neither of these partial solutions, however, is easy to achieve.[17]

Control Systems

A major task of a firm's leadership is to control the various subunits of the firm—whether they be defined on the basis of function, product division, or geographical area—to ensure their actions are consistent with the firm's overall strategic and financial objectives. Firms achieve this with various control systems. In this section, we review the various types of control systems used, and then we will see that appropriate control systems vary according to international strategies.

Types of Control Systems

Four main types of control systems are used in multinational firms: personal controls, bureaucratic controls, output controls, and cultural controls. In most firms, all four are used, but their relative emphasis tends to vary with the strategy of the firm.

Personal Controls

Personal control is control by personal contact with subordinates. This type of control tends to be most widely used in small firms, where it is seen in the direct supervision of subordinates' actions. However, it also structures the relationships between high-level managers in large multinational enterprises. The CEO may use a great deal of personal control to influence the behavior of his or her immediate subordinates, such as the heads of worldwide product divisions or major geographical areas. These heads may use personal control to influence the behavior of their subordinates, and so on down through the organization. For example, Jack Welch, CEO of General Electric, has regular one-on-one meetings with the heads of all of GE's major businesses (most of which are international). He uses these meetings to probe the managers about the strategy, structure, and financial performance of their operations. In doing so, he is essentially exercising personal control over these managers and over the strategies they favor.

Bureaucratic Controls

Bureaucratic control is control through a system of rules and procedures that direct the actions of subunits. The most important bureaucratic controls in subunits within multinational firms are budgets and capital spending rules. Budgets are essentially a set of rules for allocating a firm's financial resources. A subunit's budget specifies with some precision how much the subunit may spend. Headquarters uses budgets to influence the behavior of subunits. For example, the R&D budget normally specifies how much cash the R&D unit may spend on new-product development. R&D managers know that if they spend too much on one project, they will have less to spend on other projects. Hence, they modify their behavior to stay within the budget. Most budgets are set by negotiation between headquarters management and subunit management. Headquarters management can encourage the growth of certain subunits and restrict the growth of others by manipulating their budgets.

Capital spending rules require headquarters management to approve any capital expenditure by a subunit that exceeds a certain amount (at GE, $50,000). A budget allows headquarters to specify the amount a subunit can spend in a given year, and capital spending rules give headquarters additional control—control over how the money is spent. Top managers can be expected to deny approval for capital spending requests that are at variance with overall firm objectives and to approve those that are congruent with firm objectives.

Output Controls

Output controls involve setting goals for subunits to achieve; expressing those goals in terms of relatively objective criteria such as profitability, productivity, growth, market share, and quality; and then judging the performance of subunit management by their ability to achieve the goals.[18] The kinds of goals subunits are given depends on their role in the firm. Self-contained product divisions or national subsidiaries are typically given goals for profitability, sales growth, and market share. Functions are more likely to be given goals related to their particular activity. Thus, R&D will be given new-product development goals, production will be given productivity and quality goals, marketing will be given market share goals, and so on.

As with budgets, goals are normally established through negotiation between subunits and headquarters. Generally, headquarters tries to set goals that are challenging but realistic, so subunit managers look for ways to improve their operations but are not so pressured that they will resort to dysfunctional activities to do so (such as short-run profit maximization). Output controls foster a system of "management by exception"; as long as subunits meet their goals, they are left alone. If a subunit fails to attain its goals, headquarters management is likely to ask some tough questions. If they don't get satisfactory answers, they are likely to intervene in a subunit, replacing its top management and looking for ways to improve its efficiency.

Output controls are typically reinforced by linking management reward and incentive schemes. For example, if a worldwide product division achieves its profitability goals, its managers may receive a significant pay bonus. The size of the bonus might reflect the extent to which a subunit exceeds its goal so that subunit management has an incentive to optimize performance.

Cultural Controls

We touched on the issue of cultural controls in the previous section when we discussed organization culture as a means of facilitating cooperation. Cultural controls exist when employees "buy into" the norms and value systems of the firm. When this occurs, employees tend to control their own behavior, which reduces the need for direct supervision. In a firm with a strong culture, self-control can reduce the need for other control systems.

McDonald's is a good example of a firm that actively promotes organizational norms and values. McDonald's refers to its franchisees and suppliers as partners and emphasizes its long-term commitment to them. This commitment is not just a public relations exercise; it is backed up by actions, including a willingness to help suppliers and franchisees improve their operations by providing capital and/or management assistance when needed. In response, McDonald's franchisees and suppliers are integrated into the firm's culture and become committed to helping McDonald's succeed. One result is that McDonald's can devote less time than would otherwise be necessary to controlling its franchisees and suppliers.

Cultural control is very difficult to build. Substantial investments of time and money are required to cultivate organizationwide norms and value systems. As we saw earlier, this involves defining and clarifying the company mission or vision, disseminating the desired norms and value systems through management education programs, leading by example, and adopting appropriate human relations policies. Even with all these devices in place, it may take years to establish a common, cohesive culture in an organization.

Control Systems and Strategy in the International Business

The key to understanding the relationship between international strategy and control systems is the concept of performance ambiguity.

Performance Ambiguity

Performance ambiguity exists when the causes of a subunit's poor performance are ambiguous. This is not uncommon when a subunit's performance depends partly on the performance of other subunits; that is, when there is a high degree of interdependence between subunits within the organization. Consider the case of a French subsidiary of a US firm that depends on another subsidiary, a manufacturer based in Italy, for the products it sells. The French subsidiary is failing to achieve its sales goals, and the US management asks the managers to explain. They reply that they are receiving poor-quality goods from the Italian subsidiary. So the US management asks the managers of the Italian operation what the problem is. They reply that their product quality is excellent—the best in the industry—and that the French simply don't know how to sell a good product. Who is right, the French or the Italians? Without more information, top management cannot tell. Collecting this information will be expensive and time consuming, and it will divert attention away from other issues. Performance ambiguity raises the costs of control.

Consider how different things would be if the French operation were self-contained, with its own manufacturing, marketing, and R&D facilities. Then the French operation would lack a convenient alibi for its poor performance; the French managers would stand or fall on their own merits. They could not blame the Italians for their poor sales. The level of performance ambiguity is a function of the extent of interdependence of subunits in an organization.

Strategy, Interdependence, and Ambiguity

Now let us consider the relationship among international strategy, interdependence, and performance ambiguity. In multidomestic firms, each national operation is a stand-alone entity and can be judged on its own merits. The level of performance ambiguity is low. In an international firm, the level of interdependence is somewhat higher. Integration is required to facilitate the transfer of core competencies. Since the success of a foreign operation depends partly on the quality of the competency transferred from the home country, performance ambiguity can exist.

In global firms, the situation is still more complex. In a pure global firm, the pursuit of location and experience curve economies leads to the development of a global web

Table 13.1

Interdependence, Performance Ambiguity, and the Costs of Control for the Four International Business Strategies

Strategy	Interdependence	Performance Ambiguity	Costs of Control
Multidomestic	Low	Low	Low
International	Moderate	Moderate	Moderate
Global	High	High	High
Transnational	Very high	Very high	Very high

of value creation activities. Many of the activities in a global firm are interdependent. A French subsidiary's ability to sell a product depends on how well other operations in other countries perform their value creation activities. Thus, the levels of interdependence and performance ambiguity are high in global companies.

The level of performance ambiguity is highest of all in transnational firms. Transnational firms suffer from the same performance ambiguity problems that global firms do. In addition, because they emphasize the multidirectional transfer of core competencies, they also suffer from the problems of firms pursuing an international strategy. The extremely high level of integration within transnational firms implies a high degree of joint decision making, and the resulting interdependencies create plenty of alibis for poor performance. There is lots of room for finger-pointing in transnational firms.

Implications for Control

The arguments of the previous section and the implications for the costs of control are summarized in Table 13.1. The costs of control might be defined as the amount of time top management must devote to monitoring and evaluating subunits' performance. This will be greater when the amount of performance ambiguity is greater. When performance ambiguity is low, management can use output controls and a system of management by exception; when it is high, they have no such luxury. Output controls do not provide totally unambiguous signals of a subunit's efficiency when the performance of that subunit depends on the performance of another subunit within the organization. Thus, management must devote time to resolving the problems that arise from performance ambiguity, with a corresponding rise in the costs of control.

Table 13.1 reveals a paradox. We saw in Chapter 12 that a transnational strategy is desirable because it gives a firm more ways to profit from international expansion than do multidomestic, international, and global strategies. But now we see that due to the high level of interdependence, the costs of controlling transnational firms are higher than the costs of controlling firms that pursue other strategies. Unless there is some way of reducing these costs, the higher profitability associated with a transnational strategy could be canceled out by the higher costs of control. The same point, although to a lesser extent, can be made with regard to global firms. Although firms pursuing a global strategy can reap the cost benefits of location and experience curve economies, they must cope with a higher level of performance ambiguity, and this raises the costs of control (in comparison with firms pursuing an international or multidomestic strategy).

When we survey the control systems that corporations use to control their subunits, we find that irrespective of their strategy, multinational firms all use output and bureaucratic controls. However, in firms pursuing either global or transnational strategies, substantial performance ambiguities limit the usefulness of output controls. As a result, these firms place greater emphasis on cultural controls. Cultural control—by encouraging managers to want to assume the organization's norms and value systems—gives managers of interdependent subunits an incentive to look for ways to work out problems that arise between them. The result is a reduction in finger-pointing and, accordingly, in the costs of control. Development of cultural controls may be a precondition for the successful pursuit of a transnational strategy, and perhaps of a global strategy as well.[19]

Structure and Controls	Strategy			
	Multidomestic	**International**	**Global**	**Transnational**
Vertical differentiation	Decentralized	Core competency centralized; rest decentralized	Some centralized	Mixed centralized and decentralized
Horizontal differentiation	Worldwide area structure	Worldwide product division	Worldwide product division	Informal matrix
Need for coordination	Low	Moderate	High	Very high
Integrating mechanisms	None	Few	Many	Very many
Performance ambiguity	Low	Moderate	High	Very high
Need for cultural controls	Low	Moderate	High	Very high

Table 13.2

A Synthesis of Strategy, Structure, and Control Systems

Synthesis: Strategy and Structure

Chapter 12 identified four international business strategies: multidomestic, international, global, and transnational. So far in this chapter we have looked at four aspects of organizational structure—vertical differentiation, horizontal differentiation, integration, and control systems—and we have discussed the interrelationships between these dimensions and strategies. Now it is time to synthesize this material. Table 13.2 summarizes our synthesis.

Multidomestic Firms

Firms pursuing a multidomestic strategy focus on local responsiveness. Referring to Table 13.2, we can see that multidomestic firms tend to operate with worldwide area structures, within which operating decisions are decentralized to functionally self-contained foreign subsidiaries. The need for coordination between subunits (areas) is low, so multidomestic firms operate with few interarea integrating mechanisms, either formal or informal. The lack of interdependence implies that the level of performance ambiguity in multidomestic concerns is low, as (by extension) are the costs of control. Thus, headquarters can manage foreign operations by relying primarily on output and bureaucratic controls and a policy of management by exception. The need for cultural controls is low. If these firms were able to profit from the realization of location and experience curve economies or from the transfer of core competencies, their organizational simplicity would make this a very attractive strategy.

International Firms

Firms pursuing an international strategy attempt to create value by transferring core competencies from home to foreign markets. If they are diverse, as most of them are, these firms operate with a worldwide product division structure. Headquarters typically maintains centralized control over the source of the firm's core competency, which is most typically found in the R&D and/or marketing functions. All other operating decisions are decentralized within the firm to national operations (which in diverse firms report to worldwide product divisions). The need for coordination is moderate in such firms, reflecting the need to transfer core competencies. Thus, although such firms operate with some integrating mechanisms, they are not that extensive. The relatively low level of interdependence that results translates into a moderate level of performance ambiguity. Thus, these firms can generally get by with output and bureaucratic controls. Overall, although the organization of international firms is more complex than that of multidomestic firms, the increase in the level of complexity is not that great.

Global Firms

Firms pursuing a global strategy focus on the realization of location and experience curve economies. If they are diverse, as most of them are, these firms operate with a worldwide product division structure. To coordinate the firm's globally dispersed web of value creation activities, headquarters typically maintains ultimate control over most operating decisions. In general, global firms are more centralized than most multinational enterprises. Reflecting the need for coordination of the various stages of the firms' globally dispersed value chains, the need for integration in these firms also is high. Thus, these firms tend to operate with an array of formal and informal integrating mechanisms. The resulting interdependencies can lead to significant performance ambiguities. As a result, in addition to output and bureaucratic controls, global firms tend to stress cultural controls. On average, the organization of global firms is more complex than that of multidomestic and transnational firms.

Transnational Firms

Firms pursuing a transnational strategy focus on the simultaneous attainment of location and experience curve economies, local responsiveness, and global learning (the multidirectional transfer of core competencies). These firms tend to operate with matrix-type structures in which both product divisions and areas have significant influence. The needs to coordinate a globally dispersed value chain and to transfer core competencies create pressures for centralizing some operating decisions (particularly production and R&D). At the same time, the need to be locally responsive creates pressures for decentralizing other operating decisions to national operations (particularly marketing). Consequently, these firms tend to mix relatively high degrees of centralization for some operating decisions with relative high degrees of decentralization for other operating decisions.

The need for coordination is particularly high in transnational firms. This is reflected in the use of a wide array of formal and informal integrating mechanisms, including formal matrix structures and informal management networks. The high level of interdependence of subunits implied by such integration can result in significant performance ambiguities, which raise the costs of control. To reduce these, in addition to output and bureaucratic controls, transnational firms need to cultivate cultural controls.

Environment, Strategy, Structure, and Performance

Underlying the scheme outlined in Table 13.2 is the notion that a "fit" between strategy and structure is necessary for a firm to achieve high performance. For a firm to succeed, two conditions must be fulfilled. First, the firm's strategy must be consistent with the environment in which the firm operates. We discussed this issue in Chapter 12 and noted that in some industries a global strategy is most viable, in others an international or transnational strategy may be most viable, and in still others a multidomestic strategy may be best (although the number of multidomestic industries is on the decline). Second, the firm's organizational structure and control systems must be consistent with its strategy.

If the strategy does not fit the environment, the firm is likely to experience significant performance problems. If the structure does not fit the strategy, the firm is also likely to experience performance problems. Therefore, a firm must strive to achieve a *fit* of its environment, its strategy, its organizational structure, and its control systems. We saw the importance of this concept in the opening case. Shell switched in 1995 from a matrix structure to a structure based on global product divisions because its matrix structure was no longer consistent with the global strategy that Shell had to pursue, given the extreme cost pressures in Shell's operating environment.

Philips NV, the Dutch electronics firm, provides us with another illustration of the need for this fit. Philips operated until recently with an organization typical of a multidomestic enterprise. Operating decisions were decentralized to largely autonomous foreign subsidiaries. But the industry in which Philips competed was revolutionized by technological change and the emergence of low-cost Japanese competitors who utilized a global strategy. To survive, Philips needed to become a transnational. The firm tried to adopt a transnational posture, but it did little to change its organizational structure. The firm nominally adopted a matrix structure based on worldwide product divisions and national areas. In reality, however, the national areas continued to dominate the organization, and the product divisions had little more than an advisory role. Also, Philips lacked the informal management networks and strong unifying culture that transnationals need to succeed. As a result, the company's structure did not fit the strategy that it had to pursue to survive, and by the early 1990s, Philips was losing money. Only after four years of wrenching change and large losses was Philips finally able to tilt the balance of power in its matrix toward the product divisions. By 1995, the fruits of this effort to realign the company's strategy and structure with the demands of its operating environment were beginning to show up in improved financial performance.[20]

Chapter Summary

This chapter identified the organizational structures and internal control mechanisms, both formal and informal, that international businesses use to manage and direct their global operations. A central theme of the chapter was that different strategies require different structures and control systems. To succeed, a firm must match its structure and controls to its strategy in discriminating ways. Firms whose structure and controls do not fit their strategic requirements will experience performance problems. This chapter made the following points:

1. There are four main dimensions of organizational structure: vertical differentiation, horizontal differentiation, integration, and control systems.

2. Vertical differentiation is the centralization versus decentralization of decision-making responsibilities.

3. Operating decisions are generally decentralized in multidomestic firms, somewhat centralized in international firms, and more centralized still in global firms. The situation in transnational firms is more complex.

4. Horizontal differentiation refers to how the firm is divided into subunits.

5. Undiversified domestic firms are typically divided into subunits on the basis of functions. Diversified domestic firms typically adopt a product divisional structure.

6. When firms expand abroad, they often begin with an international division. However, this structure rarely serves satisfactorily very long because of its inherent potential for conflict and coordination problems between domestic and foreign operations.

7. Firms then switch to one of two structures: a worldwide area structure (undiversified firms) or a worldwide product division structure (diversified firms).

8. Since neither of these structures achieves a balance between local responsiveness and location and experience curve economies, many multinationals adopt matrix-type structures. However, global matrix structures have typically failed to work well, primarily due to bureaucratic problems.

9. Firms use integrating mechanisms to help achieve coordination between subunits.

10. The need for coordination (and hence integrating mechanisms) varies with firm strategy. This need is lowest in multidomestic firms, higher in international firms, higher still in global firms, and highest in transnational firms.

11. Integration is inhibited by a number of impediments to coordination, particularly by differing subunit orientations.

12. Integration can be achieved through formal integrating mechanisms. These vary in complexity from direct contact and simple liaison roles, to teams, to a matrix structure. A drawback of formal integrating mechanisms is that they can become bureaucratic.

13. To overcome the bureaucracy associated with formal integrating mechanisms, firms often use informal mechanisms, which include management networks and organization culture.

14. For a network to function effectively, it must embrace as many managers within the organization as possible. Information systems and management development policies (including job rotation and management education programs) can be used to establish firmwide networks.

15. For a network to function properly, subunit managers must be committed to the same goals. One

way of achieving this is to foster the development of a common organization culture. Leadership by example, management development programs, and human relations policies are all important in building a common culture.

16. A major task of a firm's headquarters is to control the various subunits of the firm to ensure consistency with strategic goals. Headquarters can achieve this through control systems.

17. There are four main types of controls: personal, bureaucratic, output, and cultural (which foster self-control).

18. The key to understanding the relationship between international strategy and control

systems is the concept of performance ambiguity. Performance ambiguity is a function of the degree of interdependence of subunits, and it raises the costs of control.

19. The degree of subunit interdependence—and, hence, performance ambiguity and the costs of control—is a function of the firm's strategy. It is lowest in multidomestic firms, higher in international firms, higher still in global firms, and highest in transnationals.

20. To reduce the high costs of control, firms with a high degree of interdependence between subunits (e.g., transnationals) must develop cultural controls.

Critical Discussion Questions

1. "The choice of strategy for a multinational firm to pursue must depend on a comparison of the benefits of that strategy (in terms of value creation) with the costs of implementing it (as defined by organizational requirements necessary for implementation). On this basis, it may be logical for some firms to pursue a multidomestic strategy, others a global or international strategy, and still others a transnational strategy." Is this statement correct?

2. Discuss this statement: "An understanding of the causes and consequences of performance ambiguity is central to the issue of organizational design in multinational firms."

3. Describe the organizational solutions a transnational firm might adopt to reduce the costs of control.

4. What actions must a firm take to establish a viable organizationwide management network?

CLOSING CASE　Organizational Change at Unilever

Unilever is a very old multinational with worldwide operations in the detergent and food industries. For decades, Unilever managed its worldwide detergents activities in an arm's-length manner. A subsidiary was set up in each major national market and allowed to operate largely autonomously, with each subsidiary carrying out the full range of value creation activities, including manufacturing, marketing, and R&D. The company had 17 autonomous national operations in Europe alone by the mid-1980s.

In the 1990s, Unilever began to transform its worldwide detergents activities from a loose confederation into a tightly managed business with a global strategy. The shift was prompted by Unilever's realization that its traditional way of doing business was no longer effective in an arena where it had become essential to realize substantial cost economies, to innovate, and to respond quickly to changing market trends.

The point was driven home in the 1980s when the company's archrival, Procter & Gamble, repeatedly stole

the lead in bringing new products to market. Within Unilever, "persuading" the 17 European operations to adopt new products could take four to five years. In addition, Unilever was handicapped by a high-cost structure from the duplication of manufacturing facilities from country to country and by the company's inability to enjoy the same kind of scale economies as P&G. Unilever's high costs ruled out its use of competitive pricing.

To change this situation, Unilever established product divisions to coordinate regional operations. The 17 European companies now report directly to Lever Europe. Implicit in this new approach is a bargain: The 17 companies are relinquishing autonomy in their traditional markets in exchange for opportunities to help develop and execute a unified pan-European strategy.

As a consequence of these changes, manufacturing is now being rationalized, with detergent production for the European market concentrated in a few key locations. The number of European plants manufacturing soap has been cut from 10 to 2, and some new products will be manufactured at only one site. Product sizing and packaging are being harmonized to cut purchasing costs and to pave the way for unified pan-European advertising. By taking these steps, Unilever estimates it may save as much as $400 million a year in its European operations.

Lever Europe is attempting to speed its development of new products and to synchronize the launch of new products throughout Europe. Its efforts seem to be paying off: A dishwasher detergent introduced in Germany in the early 1990s was available across Europe a year later—a distinct improvement.

But history still imposes constraints. Procter & Gamble's leading laundry detergent carries the same brand name across Europe, but Unilever sells its product under a variety of names. The company has no plans to change this. Having spent 100 years building these brand names, it believes it would be foolish to scrap them in the interest of pan-European standardization.

http://www.unilever.com

Sources: Guy de Jonguieres, "Unilever Adopts a Clean Sheet Approach," *Financial Times*, October 21, 1991, p. 13; and C. A. Bartlett and S. Ghoshal, *Managing across Borders* (Boston: Harvard Business School Press, 1989).

Case Discussion Questions

1. What strategy was Unilever pursuing before its early 1990s reorganization? What kind of structure did the company have? Were Unilever's strategy and structure consistent with each other? What were the benefits of this strategy and structure? What were the drawbacks?

2. By the 1990s, was there still a fit between Unilever's strategy and structure and the operating environment in which it competed? If not, why not?

3. What kind of strategy and structure did Unilever adopt in the 1990s? Is this appropriate given the environment in which Unilever now competes? What are the benefits of this organizational and strategic shift? What are the costs?

Notes

1. See F. J. Aguilar and M. Y. Yoshino, "The Philips Group: 1987," Harvard Business School Case, 388-050, 1987; and "Philips Fights the Flab," *The Economist*, April 7, 1990, pp. 73–74.

2. The material in this section draws on John Child, *Organizations* (London: Harper & Row, 1984).

3. Allan Cane, "Microsoft Reorganizes to Meet Market Challenges," *Financial Times*, March 16, 1994, p. 1.

4. For research evidence that is related to this issue, see J. Birkinshaw, "Entrepreneurship in Multinational Corporations: The Characteristics of Subsidiary Initiatives," *Strategic Management Journal* 18 (1997), pp. 207–29; and J. Birkinshaw, N. Hood, and S. Jonsson, "Building Firm Specific Advantages in Multinational Corporations: The Role of Subsidiary Initiatives," *Strategic Management Journal* 19 (1998), pp. 221–41.

5. For more detail, see S. M. Davis, "Managing and Organizing Multinational Corporations," reprinted in C. A. Bartlett and S. Ghoshal, *Transnational Management* (Homewood, IL: Richard D. Irwin, 1992).

6. A. D. Chandler, *Strategy and Structure: Chapters in the History of the Industrial Enterprise* (Cambridge, MA: MIT Press, 1962).

7. Davis, "Managing and Organizing Multinational Corporations."

8. J. M. Stopford and L. T. Wells, *Strategy and Structure of Multinational Enterprises* (New York: Basic Books, 1972).

9. C. A. Bartlett and S. Ghoshal, *Managing across Borders* (Boston: Harvard Business School Press, 1989).

10. Guy de Jonquieres, "Unilever Adopts a Clean Sheet Approach," *Financial Times*, October 21, 1991, p. 13.

11. See J. R. Galbraith, *Designing Complex Organizations* (Reading, MA: Addison-Wesley, 1977).

12. See Bartlett and Ghoshal, *Managing across Borders*; and F. V. Guterl, "Goodbye, Old Matrix," *Business Month*, February 1989, pp. 32–38.

13. M. S. Granovetter, "The Strength of Weak Ties," *American Journal of Sociology* 78 (1973), pp. 1360–80.

14. For examples, see W. H. Davidow and M. S. Malone, *The Virtual Corporation* (New York: Harper Collins, 1992).

15. W. G. Ouchi, "Markets, Bureaucracies, and Clans," *Administrative Science Quarterly* 25 (1980), pp. 129–44.

16. J. P. Kotter and J. L. Heskett, *Corporate Culture and Performance* (New York: Free Press, 1992).

17. Recent empirical work that addresses this issue includes T. P. Murtha, S. A. Lenway, and R. P. Bagozzi, "Global Mind Sets and Cognitive Shift in a Complex Multinational Corporation," *Strategic Management Journal* 19 (1998), pp. 97–114.

18. C. W. L. Hill., M. E. Hitt, and R. E. Hoskisson, "Cooperative versus Competitive Structures in Related and Unrelated Diversified Firms," *Organization Science* 3 (1992), pp. 501–21.

19. Murtha, Lenway, and Bagozzi, "Global Mind Sets and Cognitive Shift in a Complex Multinational Corporation."

20. See Aguilar and Yoshino, "The Philips Group"; "Philips Fights the Flab"; and R. Van de Krol, "Philips Wins back Old Friends," *Financial Times*, July 14, 1995, p. 14.

CHAPTER FOURTEEN

ENTRY STRATEGY AND STRATEGIC ALLIANCES

Merrill Lynch in Japan

Merrill Lynch is an investment banking titan. The US-based financial services institution is the world's largest underwriter of debt and equity and the third largest mergers and acquisitions advisor behind Morgan Stanley and Goldman Sachs. Merrill Lynch's investment banking operations have long had a global reach. The company has a dominant presence in London and Tokyo. However, Merrill Lynch's international presence was limited to the investment banking side of its business until recently. In contrast, its private client business, which offers banking, financial advice, and stockbrokerage services to individuals, has historically been concentrated in the United States. This is now changing rapidly. In 1995, Merrill Lynch purchased Smith New Court, the largest stockbrokerage in Britain. This was followed in 1997 by the acquisition of Mercury Asset Management, the United Kingdom's leading manager of mutual funds. Then in 1998, Merrill Lynch acquired Midland Walwyn, Canada's last major independent stockbrokerage. The company's boldest moves, however, have probably been in Japan.

Merrill Lynch started a private client business in Japan in the 1980s, but met with limited success. At the time, it was the first foreign firm to enter Japan's private client investment market. The company found it extremely difficult to attract employee talent and customers away from Japan's big four stockbrokerages, which traditionally had monopolized the Japanese market. Plus, restrictive regulations made it almost impossible for Merrill Lynch to offer its Japanese private clients the range of services it offered clients in the United States. For example, foreign exchange regulations meant it was very difficult to sell non-Japanese stocks, bonds, and mutual funds to Japanese investors. In 1993, Merrill Lynch admitted defeat, closed its six retail branches in Kobe and Kyoto, and withdrew from the private client market in Japan.

Over the next few years, however, things changed. In the mid-1990s, Japan embarked on a wide-ranging deregulation of its financial services industry. This led to the removal of many of the restrictions that had made it so difficult for Merrill to do business in Japan. For example, the relaxation of foreign exchange controls meant that by 1998, Japanese citizens could purchase foreign stocks, bonds, and mutual funds. Meanwhile, Japan's big four stockbrokerages continued to struggle with serious financial problems that resulted from the 1991 crash of that country's stock market. In November 1997, in what was a shock to many Japanese, one of these firms, Yamaichi Securities, declared it was bankrupt due to $2.2 billion in accumulated "hidden losses" and that it would shut its doors. Recognizing the country's financial system was strained and in need of fresh capital, know-how, and the stimulus of greater competition, the Japanese government signaled that it would adopt a more relaxed attitude to foreign entry into its financial services industry. This attitude underlay Japan's wholehearted endorsement of a 1997 deal brokered by the World Trade Organization to liberalize global financial services. Among other things, the WTO deal made it much easier for foreign firms to sell financial service products to Japanese investors.

By 1997, it had become clear to Merrill Lynch that the climate in Japan had changed significantly. The big attraction of the market was still the same: the financial assets owned by Japanese households are huge, amounting to a staggering ¥1,220 trillion in late 1997, only 3 percent of which were then invested in mutual funds (most are invested in low-yielding bank accounts and government bonds). In mid-1997, Merrill started to consider reentering the Japanese private client market.

The company initially considered a joint venture with Sanwa Bank to sell Merrill Lynch's mutual fund products to Japanese consumers through Sanwa's 400 retail branches. The proposed alliance would have allowed Merrill Lynch to leverage Sanwa's existing distribution system, rather than having to build a distribution system of its own. However, the long-run disadvantage of such a strategy was that it would not have given Merrill Lynch the presence that it felt it needed to build a solid financial services business in Japan. Top executives reasoned that it was important for them to make a major commitment to the Japanese market in order to establish the company's brand name as a premier provider of investment products and financial advice to individuals. This would enable Merrill Lynch to entrench itself as a major player before other foreign institutions entered the market—and before Japan's own stockbrokerages rose to the challenge. At the same time, given their prior experience in Japan, Merrill Lynch executives were hesitant to go down this road because of the huge costs and risks involved.

The problem of how best to enter the Japanese market was solved by the bankruptcy of Yamaichi Securities. Suddenly Yamaichi's nationwide network of offices and 7,000 employees were up for grabs. In late December 1997, Merrill Lynch announced it would hire 2,000 of Yamaichi's employees and acquire up to 50 of Yamaichi's branch offices. The deal, which was enthusiastically endorsed by the Japanese government, significantly lowered Merrill Lynch's costs of establishing a retail network in Japan. The goal for the new Merrill Lynch subsidiary is to have $20 billion under management by 2000. The company got off to a quick start. In February 1998, Merrill Lynch launched its first mutual fund in Japan and saw the value of its assets swell to $1 billion by April. The company now has a significant head start over other foreign financial service institutions contemplating building a private client network in Japan. Merrill Lynch's hope is that by the time other foreign institutions enter, it will already have a commanding presence in Japan that will be difficult to challenge.

http://www.ml.com

Sources: "Japan's Big Bang. Enter Merrill," *The Economist*, January 3, 1998, p. 72; J. P. Donlon, "Merrill Cinch," *Chief Executive*, March 1998, pp. 28–32; D. Holley, "Merrill Lynch to Open 31 Offices throughout Japan," *Los Angeles Times*, February 13, 1998, p. D1; and A. Rowley, "Merrill Thunders into Japan," *The Banker*, March 1998, p. 6.

Introduction

This chapter is concerned with three closely related topics: (1) The decision of which foreign markets to enter, when to enter them, and on what scale; (2) the choice of entry mode, and (3) the role of strategic alliances. Any firm contemplating foreign expansion must first struggle with the issue of which foreign markets to enter and the timing and scale of entry. The choice of which markets to enter should be driven by an assessment of relative long-run growth and profit potential. In the opening case, we saw how Merrill Lynch's entry into the Japanese private client financial services market was driven by a desire to participate in a market that is potentially huge. Japanese households have ¥1,220 trillion in financial assets, only a tiny fraction of which are invested in stocks. If Merrill Lynch can tap into even a small percentage of this savings pool, Japan will quickly become its second biggest market after the United States. Thus, it makes sense for the company to focus on Japan rather than a country with a much smaller savings pool, such as India.

The opening case also illustrates the issues involved in the timing and scale of entry. Merrill Lynch entered Japan's private client market on a small scale in the mid-1980s, only to exit in 1993 after admitting it was making no progress. The reasons for this lack of progress included an adverse regulatory environment that made it difficult for Merrill Lynch to expand and an inability to recruit sufficiently talented people away from Japan's domestic financial institutions. In other words, the company was too early. By 1997, however, the regulatory climate in Japan had changed significantly. This, coupled with the bankruptcy of Yamaichi Securities and the resulting availability of talented financial services people, made it feasible for Merrill Lynch to reenter the market on a much larger scale. The timing now seemed right. A significant feature of Merrill Lynch's reengagement in Japan's private client market is that the company is still an early mover among foreign financial services entering the market. It is also an early mover relative to Japanese financial service firms. This preemptive move, combined with the substantial scale of the commitment, bodes well for the firm's objective of establishing itself as a dominant player in Japan's potentially huge private client market.

The choice of mode for entering a foreign market is another major issue with which international businesses must wrestle. The various modes for serving foreign markets are exporting, licensing or franchising to host-country firms, establishing joint ventures with a host-country firm, and setting up a wholly owned subsidiary in a host country to serve its market. Each of these options has advantages and disadvantages. The magnitude of the advantages and disadvantages associated with each entry mode are determined by a number of factors, including transport costs, trade barriers, political risks, economic risks, and firm strategy. The optimal entry mode varies from situation to situation depending on these various factors. Thus, whereas some firms may best serve a given market by exporting, other firms may better serve the market by setting up a wholly owned subsidiary or by using some other entry mode. The opening case reported Merrill Lynch's consideration of a joint venture with Sanwa Bank to serve the Japanese private client market, although it ultimately chose to establish a wholly owned subsidiary.

We touched on the topic of entry modes when we examined foreign direct investment (FDI) in Chapter 6. There we related economic theory to exporting, licensing, and foreign direct investment as means of entering foreign markets. Here we integrate that material with the material we discussed in Chapter 12 on firm strategy to present a comprehensive picture of the factors that determine the optimal entry mode. We consider a wider range of modes in this chapter as well as mixed entry modes. (For example, establishing joint ventures and wholly owned subsidiaries in another country are both FDI, but we did not make a distinction in Chapter 6.)

The final topic of this chapter is that of strategic alliances. **Strategic alliances** are cooperative agreements between actual or potential competitors. The term *strategic alliances* is often used loosely to embrace a variety of arrangements between actual or potential competitors including cross-shareholding deals, licensing arrangements, formal joint ventures, and informal cooperative arrangements. The motives for entering strategic alliances are varied, but they often include market access; hence, the overlap with the topic of entry mode.

Strategic alliances have advantages and disadvantages and a firm must weigh these carefully before deciding whether to ally itself with an actual or potential competitor. Perhaps the biggest danger is that the firm will give away more to its ally than it receives. As we will see, firms can reduce this risk in the way they structure their strategic alliances. We will also see how firms can build alliances that benefit both partners.

The chapter opens with a look at how firms choose which foreign markets to enter and at the factors that are important in determining the best timing and scale of entry. Then we will review the various entry modes available, discussing the advantages and disadvantages of each option. Next, we will consider the factors that determine a firm's optimal entry mode and then look at the advantages and disadvantages of engaging in strategic alliances with competitors. Finally, we will consider how a firm should select an ally, structure the alliance, and manage it to maximize the advantages and minimize the disadvantages associated with alliances.

Basic Entry Decisions

In this section, we look at three basic decisions that a firm contemplating foreign expansion must make: which markets to enter, when to enter those markets, and on what scale.

Which Foreign Markets?

There are more than 160 nation-states in the world, but they do not all hold the same profit potential for a firm contemplating foreign expansion. Ultimately, the choice must be based on an assessment of a nation's long-run profit potential. This potential is a function of several factors, many of which we have already studied in earlier chapters. In Chapter 2, we looked in detail at the economic and political factors that influence the potential attractiveness of a foreign market. There we noted that the attractiveness of a country as a potential market for an international business depends on balancing the benefits, costs, and risks associated with doing business in that country.

Chapter 2 also noted that the long-run economic benefits of doing business in a country are a function of factors such as the size of the market (in terms of demographics), the present wealth (purchasing power) of consumers in that market, and the likely future wealth of consumers. While some markets are very large when measured by numbers of consumers (e.g., China and India), low living standards may imply limited purchasing power and a relatively small market when measured in economic terms. We also argued that the costs and risks associated with doing business in a foreign country are typically lower in economically advanced and politically stable democratic nations, and they are greater in less developed and politically unstable nations.

However, this calculus is complicated by the fact that the potential *long-run* benefits bear little relationship to a nation's current stage of economic development or political stability. Long-run benefits depend on likely future economic growth rates, and economic growth appears to be a function of a free market system and a country's capacity for growth (which may be greater in less developed nations). This leads one to the conclusion that, other things being equal, the benefit–cost–risk trade-off is likely to be most favorable in politically stable developed and developing nations that have free market systems, and where there is not a dramatic upsurge in either inflation rates or private-sector debt. The trade-off is likely to be least favorable in politically unstable developing nations that operate with a mixed or command economy or in developing nations where speculative financial bubbles have led to excess borrowing (see Chapter 2 for further details).

By applying the reasoning processes alluded to above and discussed in more detail in Chapter 2, a firm can rank countries in terms of their attractiveness and long-run profit potential. Preference is then given to entering markets that rank highly. In the case of Merrill Lynch, its recent international ventures in the private client business have been focused on the United Kingdom, Canada, and Japan (see the opening case). All three of these countries have a large pool of private savings and exhibit relatively low political and economic risks, so it makes sense that they would be attractive to Merrill Lynch. The company should be able to capture a large enough proportion of the private savings pool in each country to justify its investment in setting up business there. Of the three countries, Japan is probably the most risky given the rather fragile state of its financial system. However, the large size of the Japanese market and the fact that the government seems to be embarking on significant reform explain why Merrill has been attracted to this nation.

One other fact we have not yet discussed is the value an international business can create in a foreign market. This depends on the suitability of its product offering to that market and the nature of indigenous competition.[1] If the international business can offer a product that has not been widely available in that market and that satisfies an unmet need, the value of that product to consumers is likely to be much greater than if the international business simply offers the same type of product that indigenous competitors and other foreign entrants are already offering. Greater value translates into an ability to charge higher prices and/or to build sales volume more rapidly. Again, on this count, Japan is clearly very attractive to Merrill Lynch. Japanese households invest only 3 percent of their savings in individuals stocks and mutual funds (much of the balance being in low-yielding bank accounts or government bonds). In comparison, over 40 percent of US households invest in individual stocks and mutual funds. Japan's own financial institutions have been slow to offer stock-based mutual funds to retail investors, and other foreign firms have yet to establish a significant presence in the market. Merrill Lynch can create potentially enormous value by offering Japanese consumers a range of products they have previously not been offered and that satisfy unmet needs for greater returns from their savings.

Timing of Entry

Once attractive markets have been identified, it is important to consider the **timing of entry**. We say that entry is early when an international business enters a foreign market before other foreign firms and late when it enters after other international businesses have already established themselves. The advantages frequently associated with entering a market early are commonly known as **first-mover advantages**.[2] One first-mover advantage is the ability to preempt rivals and capture demand by establishing a strong brand name. A second advantage is the ability to build sales volume in that country and ride down the experience curve ahead of rivals, giving the early entrant a cost advantage over later entrants. This cost advantage may enable the early entrant to cut prices below the higher cost structure of later entrants, thereby driving them out of the market. A third advantage is the ability of early entrants to create switching costs that tie customers into their products or services. Such switching costs make it difficult for later entrants to win business.

By entering the private client market in Japan early, Merrill Lynch hopes to establish a brand name that later entrants will find difficult to match. And, by entering early with a valuable product offering, Merrill Lynch hopes to build its sales volume rapidly. This will enable the company to spread the fixed costs associated with setting up operations in Japan over a large volume, thereby realizing scale economies. These fixed costs include the costs of establishing a network of branches in Japan. In addition, as Merrill Lynch trains its Japanese employees, their productivity should rise due to learning economies, which again translates into lower costs. Thus, the company should be able to ride down the experience curve, giving it a lower cost structure than later entrants. Finally, Merrill Lynch's business philosophy is to establish close relationships between its financial advisors (i.e., stockbrokers) and private clients. The financial advisors are taught to get to know the needs of their clients and help manage their finances more effectively. Once established, people rarely change these relationships. In other words, due to switching costs, they are unlikely to shift their business to later entrants. This effect is likely to be particularly strong in a country like Japan, where long-term relationships have traditionally been very important in business and social settings. For all these reasons, Merrill Lynch may be able to capture first-mover advantages that will enable it to enjoy a strong competitive position in Japan for years.

There can also be disadvantages associated with entering a foreign market before other international businesses. These are often referred to as **first-mover disadvantages**.[3] These disadvantages may give rise to pioneering costs. **Pioneering costs** are costs that an early entrant has to bear that a later entrant can avoid. Pioneering costs arise when the business system in a foreign country is so different from that in a firm's home market that the enterprise has to devote considerable effort, time, and expense to learning the rules of the game. Pioneering costs include the costs of business failure if the firm, due to its ignorance of the foreign environment, makes some major mistakes. A certain liability is associated with being a foreigner, and this liability is greater for foreign firms that enter a national market early.[4] Recent research seems to confirm that the probability of survival increases if an international business enters a national market *after* several other foreign firms have already done so.[5] The late entrant may benefit by observing and learning from the mistakes made by early entrants.

Pioneering costs also include the costs of promoting and establishing a product offering, including the costs of educating customers. These costs can be particularly significant when the product being promoted is one that local consumers are not familiar with. In many ways, Merrill Lynch will have to bear such pioneering costs in Japan. Most Japanese are not familiar with the type of investment products and services that Merrill Lynch is selling, so the company will have to invest significant resources in customer education. In contrast, later entrants may be able to ride on an early entrant's investments in learning and customer education by watching how the early entrant proceeded in the market, by avoiding costly mistakes made by the early entrant, and by exploiting the market potential created by the early entrant's investments in customer education. For example, KFC introduced the Chinese to American-style fast food, but it has been a later entrant, McDonald's, that capitalized on the market in China.

An early entrant may be put at a severe disadvantage, relative to a later entrant, if regulations change in a way that diminishes the value of an early entrant's investments. This is a serious risk in many developing nations where the rules that govern business practices are still evolving. Early entrants can find themselves at a disadvantage if a subsequent change in regulations invalidates prior assumptions about the best business model for operating in that country. For an illustration of the potential difficulties and hazards, consider the experience of the Amway Corporation in China, which is described in the accompanying Management Focus.

Scale of Entry and Strategic Commitments

The final issue that an international business needs to consider when contemplating market entry is the scale of entry. Entering a market on a large scale involves the commitment of significant resources. Not all firms have the resources necessary to enter on a large scale, and even some large firms prefer to enter foreign markets on a small scale and then build slowly as they become more familiar with the market. Merrill Lynch's original entry into the private client market in Japan was on a small scale, involving only a handful of branches. In contrast, the company's reentry in 1997 was on a significant scale, as was Amway's entry into the Chinese market.

The consequences of entering on a significant scale are associated with the value of the resulting strategic commitments.[6] A **strategic commitment** is a decision that has a long-term impact and is difficult to reverse. Deciding to enter a foreign market on a significant scale is a major strategic commitment. Strategic commitments, such as large-scale market entry, can have an important influence on the nature of competition in a market. For example, by entering Japan's private client business on a significant scale, Merrill Lynch has signaled its commitment to the market. This will have several effects. On the positive side, it will make it easier for the company to attract clients. The scale of entry gives potential clients reason for believing that Merrill Lynch will remain in the market for the long run. The scale of entry may also give other foreign institutions considering entry into Japan pause; now they will have to compete not only against Japan's indigenous institutions, but also against an aggressive and successful US institution. On the negative side, the move may wake up Japan's financial institutions and elicit a vigorous competitive response from them. By committing itself heavily to Japan, Merrill Lynch may have fewer resources available to support expansion in other desirable markets. In other words, the commitment to Japan limits the company's strategic flexibility.

As suggested by this example, significant strategic commitments are neither unambiguously good nor bad. Rather, they tend to change the competitive playing field and unleash a number of changes, some of which may be desirable and some of which will not be. It is important for a firm to think through the implications of large-scale entry into a market and act accordingly. Of particular relevance is trying to identify how actual and potential competitors might react to large-scale entry into a market. Also, the large-scale entrant is more likely than the small-scale entrant to be able to capture first-mover advantages associated with demand preemption, scale economies, and switching costs.

The value of the commitments that flow from large-scale entry into a foreign market must be balanced against the resulting risks and lack of flexibility associated with significant commitments. But strategic inflexibility can also have value. A famous example from military history illustrates the value of inflexibility. When Hernán Cortés landed in Mexico, he ordered his men to burn all but one of his ships. Cortés reasoned that by eliminating their only method of retreat, his men had no choice but to fight hard to win against the Aztecs—and ultimately they did.[7]

Balanced against the value and risks of the commitments associated with large-scale entry are the benefits of a small-scale entry. Small-scale entry allows a firm to learn about a foreign market while limiting the firm's exposure to that market. Small-scale entry can be seen as a way to gather information about a foreign market before

MANAGEMENT FOCUS

Amway Goes Astray in China

http://www.amway.com

Amway is a US-based direct sales company that sells a wide variety of household and personal products using a grassroots marketing approach. The company signs up individual consumers as "distributors" who then earn a commission on sales of Amway products. Almost anyone can become an Amway distributor by purchasing for a few hundred dollars a "starter kit" that contains an assortment of Amway products and promotional literature and by attending a few meetings for training about the Amway system, products, and sales techniques. The distributors are taught to engage in door-to-door selling and are encouraged to sell to friends, relatives, and acquaintances. In 1997, the company racked up $7 billion in sales using this approach, more than half outside the United States.

Amway entered China in 1995, closely behind rival direct marketers Avon and Mary Kay. Several features attracted Amway to China. With a population of 1.2 billion people, the country offered a potentially huge consumer market. Given Amway's emphasis on direct selling, the lack of well-developed retail distribution systems in China seemed to play right into the company's hands. An Amway representative could offer a far broader range of products than could be found at most Chinese retail outlets and often at a lower price. Also, the strategy of selling to friends, relatives, and acquaintances seemed to make great sense in a society that emphasizes social relations and interpersonal networks.

From the outset, Amway was determined to be one of the first direct marketers to establish a significant presence in China. Accordingly, it entered the country on a significant scale, quickly surpassing Avon and Mary Kay to become the largest direct marketer in China. By early 1998, Amway seemed to be doing well. The company had signed up 80,000 distributors in 37 cities across mainland China. It had opened a major factory in Guangzhou and had plans to invest $30 million in a second factory in Shanghai. Sales had reached $178 million in 1997, an 80 percent increase from the previous year. Then, unexpectedly, on April 22, 1998, the Chinese government announced a ban on direct selling!

According to the Chinese government, direct selling practices such as those employed by Amway spawned "weird cults, triads, superstitious groups, and hooliganism." One problem was that the success of Amway and its American kin had encouraged thousands of local imitators, including a number of fraudulent enterprises and fly-by-night operators that sold everything from fake gold to potency pills. The government also objected to the motivational meetings used by Amway and others to reward top sellers and recruit new ones. The official Chinese media compared such gatherings-at which people sang and chanted company slogans-to "religious cults." The *People's Daily,* the mouthpiece of China's governing Communist party, complained that the meetings encouraged "excessive hugging" and references to "God."

Facing the loss of their Chinese investments, the US companies called in the heavy cavalry in the form of US Trade Representative Charlene Barshefsky. After intense pressure, the Chinese government agreed to a partial reversal of the ban. Under the new regulations, issued in July 1998, the ban on direct selling stays in place, but Amway, Avon, and Mary Kay will be allowed to sell their products through retail outlets. In addition, they can use their sales representatives for service and delivery but not for direct selling. The new regulations also state that only companies with an investment of more than $10 million may establish direct sales agents.

Amway restarted its business in China the day after the change in regulations was announced. However, the three-month shutdown had cost the company millions of dollars in lost sales. More significantly perhaps, the ban on direct selling made it impossible for Amway to follow its normal business model in China. Given this, the company might not grow as fast as planned. An unforeseen change in the regulations governing a critical element of business practice in China has significantly diminished the value of the company's investment in the country and negated much of its early-mover advantage.

Sources: L. Pappas, "Amway Sells Itself in China," *St. Petersburg Times,* March 15, 1998, p. 1H; M. Farley, "Avon and Amway Reopen in China," *Los Angeles Times,* July 25, 1998, p. D1; and Associated Press, "China Gives Amway Sales OK," *Minneapolis Star Tribune,* July 22, 1998, p. 3D.

deciding whether to enter on a significant scale and how best to enter. By giving the firm time to collect information, small-scale entry reduces the risks associated with a subsequent large-scale entry. But the lack of commitment associated with small-scale entry may make it more difficult for the small-scale entrant to build market share and to capture first-mover or early-mover advantages. The risk-averse firm that enters a foreign market on a small scale may limit its potential losses, but it may also miss the chance to capture first-mover advantages.

Summary

There are no "right" decisions here, just decisions that are associated with different levels of risk and reward. Entering a large developing nation such as China or India before most other international businesses in the firm's industry, and entering on a large scale, will be associated with high levels of risk. In such cases, the liability of being foreign is increased by the absence of prior foreign entrants whose experience can be a useful guide. At the same time, the potential long-term rewards associated with such a strategy are great. The early large-scale entrant into a major developing nation may be able to capture significant first-mover advantages that will bolster its long-run position in that market. In contrast, entering developed nations such as Australia or Canada after other international businesses in the firm's industry, and entering on a small scale to first learn more about those markets, will be associated with much lower levels of risk. However, the potential long-term rewards are also likely to be lower since the firm is essentially forgoing the opportunity to capture first-mover advantages and because the lack of commitment signaled by small-scale entry may limit its future growth potential.

Entry Modes

Once a firm decides to enter a foreign market, the question arises as to the best mode of entry. Firms use basically six different modes to enter foreign markets: exporting, turnkey projects, licensing, franchising, establishing joint ventures with a host-country firm, and setting up a wholly owned subsidiary in the host country. Each entry mode has advantages and disadvantages. Managers need to consider these carefully when deciding which to use.[8]

Exporting

Many manufacturing firms begin their global expansion as exporters and only later switch to another mode for serving a foreign market. We take a close look at the mechanics of exporting in the next chapter. Here we focus on the advantages and disadvantages of exporting as an entry mode.

Advantages

Exporting has two distinct advantages. First, it avoids the often-substantial costs of establishing manufacturing operations in the host country. Second, exporting may help a firm achieve experience curve and location economies (see Chapter 12). By manufacturing the product in a centralized location and exporting it to other national markets, the firm may realize substantial scale economies from its global sales volume. This is how Sony came to dominate the global TV market, how Matsushita came to dominate the VCR market, and how many Japanese auto firms made inroads into the US auto market.

Disadvantages

Exporting has a number of drawbacks. First, exporting from the firm's home base may not be appropriate if there are lower-cost locations for manufacturing the product abroad (i.e., if the firm can realize location economies by moving production elsewhere). Thus, particularly for firms pursuing global or transnational strategies, it may be preferable to manufacture where the mix of factor conditions is most favorable from a value creation perspective and to export to the rest of the world from that location. This is not so much an argument against exporting as an argument against exporting from the firm's home country. Many US electronics firms have moved some of their manufacturing to the Far East because of the availability of low-cost, highly skilled labor there. They then export from that location to the rest of the world, including the United States.

A second drawback to exporting is that high transport costs can make exporting uneconomical, particularly for bulk products. One way of getting around this is to manufacture bulk products regionally. This strategy enables the firm to realize some economies from large-scale production and at the same time to limit its transport costs. For example, many multinational chemical firms manufacture their products regionally, serving several countries from one facility.

Another drawback is that tariff barriers can make exporting uneconomical. Similarly, the threat of tariff barriers by the host-country government can make it very risky. An implicit threat by the US Congress to impose tariffs on imported Japanese autos led many Japanese auto firms to set up manufacturing plants in the United States. By 1990, almost 50 percent of all Japanese cars sold in the United States were manufactured locally—up from 0 percent in 1985.

A fourth drawback to exporting arises when a firm delegates its marketing in each country where it does business to a local agent. (This is common for firms that are just beginning to export.) Foreign agents often carry the products of competing firms and so have divided loyalties. In such cases, the foreign agent may not do as good a job as the firm would if it managed its marketing itself. There are ways around this problem, however. One way is to set up a wholly owned subsidiary in the country to handle local marketing. By doing this, the firm can exercise tight control over marketing in the country while reaping the cost advantages of manufacturing the product in a single location.

Turnkey Projects

Firms that specialize in the design, construction, and start-up of turnkey plants are common in some industries. In a **turnkey project**, the contractor agrees to handle every detail of the project for a foreign client, including the training of operating personnel. At completion of the contract, the foreign client is handed the "key" to a plant that is ready for full operation—hence, the term *turnkey*. This is a means of exporting process technology to other countries. Turnkey projects are most common in the chemical, pharmaceutical, petroleum refining, and metal refining industries, all of which use complex, expensive production technologies.

Advantages

The know-how required to assemble and run a technologically complex process, such as refining petroleum or steel, is a valuable asset. Turnkey projects are a way of earning great economic returns from that asset. The strategy is particularly useful where FDI is limited by host-government regulations. For example, the governments of many oil-rich countries have set out to build their own petroleum refining industries, so they restrict FDI in their oil and refining sectors. But because many of these countries lacked petroleum-refining technology, they gained it by entering into turnkey projects with foreign firms that had the technology. Such deals are often attractive to the selling firm because without them, they would have no way to earn a return on their valuable know-how in that country.

A turnkey strategy can also be less risky than conventional FDI. In a country with unstable political and economic environments, a longer-term investment might expose the firm to unacceptable political and/or economic risks (e.g., the risk of nationalization or of economic collapse).

Disadvantages

Three main drawbacks are associated with a turnkey strategy. First, the firm that enters into a turnkey deal will have no long-term interest in the foreign country. This can be a disadvantage if that country subsequently proves to be a major market for the output of the process that has been exported. One way around this is to take a minority equity interest in the operation.

Second, the firm that enters into a turnkey project with a foreign enterprise may inadvertently create a competitor. For example, many of the Western firms that sold oil refining technology to firms in Saudi Arabia, Kuwait, and other Gulf states now find themselves competing with these firms in the world oil market. Third, if the firm's process technology is a source of competitive advantage, then selling this technology through a turnkey project is also selling competitive advantage to potential and/or actual competitors.

Licensing

A **licensing agreement** is an arrangement whereby a licensor grants the rights to intangible property to another entity (the licensee) for a specified period, and in return, the licensor receives a royalty fee from the licensee.[9] Intangible property includes patents, inventions, formulas, processes, designs, copyrights, and trademarks. For example, as described in the accompanying Management Focus, to enter the Japanese market, Xerox, inventor of the photocopier, established a joint venture with Fuji Photo that is known as Fuji-Xerox. Xerox then licensed its xerographic know-how to Fuji-Xerox. In return, Fuji-Xerox paid Xerox a royalty fee equal to 5 percent of the net sales revenue that Fuji-Xerox earned from the sales of photocopiers based on Xerox's patented know-how. In the Fuji-Xerox case, the license was originally granted for 10 years, and it has been renegotiated and extended several times since. The licensing agreement between Xerox and Fuji-Xerox also limited Fuji-Xerox's direct sales to the Asian Pacific region (although Fuji-Xerox does supply Xerox with photocopiers that are sold in North America under the Xerox label).[10]

Advantages

In the typical international licensing deal, the licensee puts up most of the capital necessary to get the overseas operation going. Thus, a primary advantage of licensing is that the firm does not have to bear the development costs and risks associated with opening a foreign market. Licensing is very attractive for firms lacking the capital to develop operations overseas. In addition, licensing can be attractive when a firm is unwilling to commit substantial financial resources to an unfamiliar or politically volatile foreign market. Licensing is also often used when a firm wishes to participate in a foreign market but is prohibited from doing so by barriers to investment. This was one of the original reasons for the formation of the Fuji-Xerox joint venture (see the Management Focus for details). Xerox wanted to participate in the Japanese market but was prohibited from setting up a wholly owned subsidiary by the Japanese government. So Xerox set up the joint venture with Fuji and then licensed its know-how to the joint venture. Finally, licensing is frequently used when a firm possesses some intangible property that might have business applications, but it does not want to develop those applications itself. For example, Bell Laboratories at AT&T originally invented the transistor circuit in the 1950s, but AT&T decided it did not want to produce transistors, so it licensed the technology to a number of other companies, such as Texas Instruments. Similarly, Coca-Cola has licensed its famous trademark to clothing manufacturers, who have incorporated the design into their clothing (e.g., Coca-Cola T-shirts).

Disadvantages

Licensing has three serious drawbacks. First, it does not give a firm the tight control over manufacturing, marketing, and strategy that is required for realizing experience curve and location economies (as global and transnational firms must do; see Chapter

12). Licensing typically involves each licensee setting up its own production operations. This severely limits the firm's ability to realize experience curve and location economies by producing its product in a centralized location. When these economies are important, licensing may not be the best way to expand overseas.

Second, competing in a global market may require a firm to coordinate strategic moves across countries by using profits earned in one country to support competitive attacks in another (see Chapter 12). By its very nature, licensing limits a firm's ability to do this. A licensee is unlikely to allow a multinational firm to use its profits (beyond those due in the form of royalty payments) to support a different licensee operating in another country.

A third problem with licensing is one that we first encountered in Chapter 6 when we reviewed the economic theory of FDI. This is the risk associated with licensing technological know-how to foreign companies. Technological know-how constitutes the basis of many multinational firms' competitive advantage. Most firms wish to maintain control over how their know-how is used, and a firm can quickly lose control over its technology by licensing it. Many firms have made the mistake of thinking they could maintain control over their know-how within the framework of a licensing agreement. RCA Corporation, for example, once licensed its color TV technology to Japanese firms including Matsushita and Sony. The Japanese firms quickly assimilated the technology, improved on it, and used it to enter the US market. Now the Japanese firms have a bigger share of the US market than the RCA brand. Similar concerns surfaced over the 1989 decision by Congress to allow Japanese firms to produce the advanced FSX fighter plane under license from McDonnell Douglas. Critics of the decision fear the Japanese will use the FSX technology to support the development of a commercial airline industry that will compete with Boeing in the global marketplace.

There are ways of reducing the risks of this occurring. One way is by entering into a cross-licensing agreement with a foreign firm. Under a cross-licensing agreement, a firm might license some valuable intangible property to a foreign partner, but in addition to a royalty payment, the firm might also request that the foreign partner license some of its valuable know-how to the firm. Such agreements are believed to reduce the risks associated with licensing technological know-how, since the licensee realizes that if it violates the licensing contract (by using the knowledge obtained to compete directly with the licensor), the licensor can do the same to it. Cross-licensing agreements enable firms to hold each other hostage, which reduces the probability that they will behave opportunistically toward each other.[11] Such cross-licensing agreements are increasingly common in high-technology industries. For example, the US biotechnology firm Amgen has licensed one of its key drugs, Nuprogene, to Kirin, the Japanese pharmaceutical company. The license gives Kirin the right to sell Nuprogene in Japan. In return, Amgen receives a royalty payment, and in addition, through a licensing agreement, it gained the right to sell some of Kirin's products in the United States.

Another way of reducing the risk associated with licensing is to follow the Fuji-Xerox model and link an agreement to license know-how with the formation of a joint venture in which the licensor and licensee take an important equity stake. Such an approach aligns the interests of licensor and licensee, since both have a stake in ensuring that the venture is successful. Thus, the risk that Fuji Photo might appropriate Xerox's technological know-how, and then compete directly against Xerox in the global photocopier market, was reduced by the establishment of a joint venture in which both Xerox and Fuji Photo had an important stake.

Franchising

In many respects, franchising is similar to licensing, although franchising tends to involve longer-term commitments than licensing. **Franchising** is basically a specialized form of licensing in which the franchiser not only sells intangible property to the

MANAGEMENT FOCUS
Fuji-Xerox

Fuji-Xerox is one of the most enduring and reportedly successful alliances between two companies from different countries. Established in 1962, today Fuji-Xerox is structured as a as a 50/50 joint venture between the Xerox Group, the US maker of photocopiers, and Fuji Photo Film, Japan's largest manufacturer of film products. With sales of close to $10 billion, Fuji-Xerox provides Xerox with over 20 percent of its worldwide revenues.

A prime motivation to establish the joint venture was the Japanese government's refusal in the early 1960s to allow foreign companies to set up wholly owned subsidiaries in Japan. The joint venture was conceived as a marketing organization to sell xerographic products that would be manufactured by Fuji Photo under license from Xerox. However, when the Japanese government refused to approve the establishment of a joint venture intended solely as a sales company, the joint venture agreement was revised to give Fuji-Xerox manufacturing rights. Management of the venture was placed in the hands of Japanese managers who were given considerable autonomy to develop their own operations and strategy, subject to oversight by a board of directors that contained representatives from both Xerox and Fuji Photo.

Initially, Fuji-Xerox followed the lead of Xerox in manufacturing and selling the large high-volume copiers developed by Xerox in the United States. These machines were sold at a premium price to the high end of the market. However, Fuji-Xerox noticed that in the Japanese market new competitors, such as Canon and Ricoh, were making significant inroads by building small low-volume copiers and focusing on the mid- and low-priced segments of the market. This led to Fuji-Xerox's development of its first "homegrown" copier, the FX2200, which at the time was billed as the world's smallest copier. Introduced in 1973, the FX2200 hit the market just in time to allow Fuji-Xerox to hold its own against a blizzard of new competition in Japan that followed the expiration of many of Xerox's key patents.

About the same time, Fuji-Xerox also embarked on a total quality control (TQC) program. The aims of the program were to speed up the development of new products, reduce waste, improve quality, and lower manufacturing costs. The first fruit of this program was the FX3500. Introduced in 1977, the FX3500 by 1979 had broken the Japanese record for the number of copiers sold in one year. Partly because of the success of the FX3500, in 1980 the company won Japan's prestigious Deming Prize. The success of the FX3500 was all the more notable because at the same time Xerox was canceling programs to develop low- to mid-level copiers and reaffirming its commitment to serving the high end of the market. Because of these cancellations, Tony Kobayashi, the CEO of Fuji-Xerox, was initially told to stop work on development of the FX3500. He refused, arguing that the FX3500 was crucial for the survival of Fuji-Xerox in the Japanese market. Given the arm's-length relationship between Xerox and Fuji-Xerox, Kobayashi was able to prevail.

By the early 1980s, Fuji-Xerox was number two in the Japanese copier market with between 20 and 22 percent of the market, just behind that of market leader Canon. In contrast, Xerox was running into all sorts of problems in the United States. As Xerox's

franchisee (normally a trademark), but also insists that the franchisee agree to abide by strict rules as to how it does business. The franchiser will also often assist the franchisee to run the business on an ongoing basis. As with licensing, the franchiser typically receives a royalty payment, which amounts to some percentage of the franchisee's revenues. Whereas licensing is pursued primarily by manufacturing firms, franchising is employed primarily by service firms.[12] McDonald's is a good example of a firm that has grown by using a franchising strategy. McDonald's has strict rules as to how franchisees should operate a restaurant. These rules extend to control over the

http://www.xerox.com

patents had expired, a number of companies, including Canon, Ricoh, Kodak, and IBM, began to take market share from Xerox. Canon and Ricoh were particularly successful by focusing upon that segment of the market that Xerox had ignored: the low end. As a result, Xerox's market share in the Americas fell from 35 percent in 1975 to 25 percent in 1980, while its profitability slumped.

In an attempt to recapture market share, Xerox began to sell Fuji-Xerox's FX3500 copier in the United States. Not only did the FX3500 help Xerox to halt the rapid decline in its share of the US market; but it also opened Xerox's eyes to the benefits of Fuji-Xerox's TQC program. Xerox found that the reject rate for Fuji-Xerox parts was only a fraction of the reject rate for American-produced parts. Visits to Fuji-Xerox revealed another important truth: quality in manufacturing does not increase real costs—it reduces costs by reducing defective products and service costs.

These developments forced Xerox to rethink the way it did business. From being the main provider of products, technology, and management know-how to Fuji-Xerox, Xerox in the 1980s became the willing pupil of Fuji-Xerox. In 1983, Xerox introduced its leadership through quality program, which was based on Fuji-Xerox's TQC program. As part of this effort, Xerox launched a quality training effort with its suppliers and was rewarded when the number of defective parts from suppliers subsequently fell from 25,000 per million in 1983 to 300 per million by 1992.

In 1985 and 1986, Xerox began to focus on its new-product development process. One goal was to design products that, while customized to market conditions in different countries, also contained a large number of globally standardized parts. Another goal was to reduce the time it took to design new products and bring them to market. To achieve these goals, Xerox set up joint product development teams with Fuji-Xerox. Each team managed the design, component sources, manufacturing, distribution, and follow-up customer service on a worldwide basis. The use of design teams cut as much as one year from the overall product development cycle and saved millions of dollars.

One consequence of the new approach to product development was the 5100 copier. This was the first product designed jointly by Xerox and Fuji-Xerox for the worldwide market. The 5100 is manufactured in US plants. It was launched in Japan in November 1990 and in the United States the following February. The 5100's global design reportedly reduced the overall time to market and saved the company more than $10 million in development costs.

As a result of the skills and products acquired from Fuji-Xerox, Xerox's position improved markedly during the 1980s. Due to its improved quality, lower costs, shorter product development time, and more appealing product range, Xerox was able to gain market share back from its competitors and to boost its profits and revenues. Xerox's share of the US copier market increased from a low of 10 percent in 1985 to 18 percent in 1991.

Sources: R. Howard, "The CEO as Organizational Architect," *Harvard Business Review,* September–October, 1992, pp. 106–23; D. Kearns, "Leadership through Quality," *Academy of Management Executive* 4 (1990), pp. 86–89; K. McQuade and B. Gomes-Casseres, "Xerox and Fuji-Xerox," Harvard Business School Case #9-391-156; and E. Terazono and C. Lorenz, "An Angry Young Warrior," *Financial Times,* September 19, 1994, p. 11.

menu, cooking methods, staffing policies, and design and location of a restaurant. McDonald's also organizes the supply chain for its franchisees and provides management training and financial assistance.[13]

Advantages

The advantages of franchising as an entry mode are very similar to those of licensing. The firm is relieved of many of the costs and risks of opening a foreign market on its own. Instead, the franchisee typically assumes those costs and risks. This creates a good incentive for the franchisee to build profitable operation as quickly as possible. Thus, using a franchising strategy, a service firm can build up a global presence quickly and at a relatively low cost and risk, as McDonald's has.

Disadvantages

The disadvantages are less pronounced than in the case of licensing. Since franchising is often used by service companies, there is no reason to consider the need for coordination of manufacturing to achieve experience curve and location economies. But franchising may inhibit the firm's ability to take profits out of one country to support competitive attacks in another.

A more significant disadvantage of franchising is quality control. The foundation of franchising arrangements is that the firm's brand name conveys a message to consumers about the quality of the firm's product. Thus, a business traveler checking in at a Hilton International hotel in Hong Kong can reasonably expect the same quality of room, food, and service that she would receive in New York. The Hilton name is supposed to guarantee consistent product quality. This presents a problem in that foreign franchisees may not be as concerned about quality as they are supposed to be, and the result of poor quality can extend beyond lost sales in a particular foreign market to a decline in the firm's worldwide reputation. For example, if the business traveler has a bad experience at the Hilton in Hong Kong, she may never go to another Hilton hotel and may urge her colleagues to do likewise. The geographical distance of the firm from its foreign franchisees, however, can make poor quality difficult to detect. In addition, the sheer numbers of franchisees—in the case of McDonald's, tens of thousands—can make quality control difficult. Due to these factors, quality problems may persist.

One way around this disadvantage is to set up a subsidiary in each country in which the firm expands. The subsidiary might be wholly owned by the company or a joint venture with a foreign company. The subsidiary assumes the rights and obligations to establish franchises throughout the particular country or region. McDonald's, for example, establishes a master franchisee in many countries. Typically, this master franchisee is a joint venture between McDonald's and a local firm. The proximity and the smaller number of franchises to oversee reduce the quality control challenge. In addition, because the subsidiary (or master franchisee) is at least partly owned by the firm, the firm can place its own managers in the subsidiary to help ensure that it is doing a good job of monitoring the franchises. This organizational arrangement has proven very satisfactory for McDonald's, Kentucky Fried Chicken, Hilton International, and others.

Joint Ventures

A **joint venture** entails establishing a firm that is jointly owned by two or more otherwise independent firms. Fuji-Xerox, for example, was set up as a joint venture between Xerox and Fuji Photo (see the Management Focus). Establishing a joint venture with a foreign firm has long been a popular mode for entering a new market. The most typical joint venture is a 50/50 venture, in which there are two parties, each of which holds a 50 percent ownership stake (as is the case with the Fuji-Xerox joint venture) and contributes a team of managers to share operating control. Some firms, however, have sought joint ventures in which they have a majority share and thus tighter control.[14]

Advantages

Joint ventures have a number of advantages. First, a firm benefits from a local partner's knowledge of the host country's competitive conditions, culture, language, political systems, and business systems. Thus, for many US firms, joint ventures have involved the US company providing technological know-how and products and the local partner providing the marketing expertise and the local knowledge necessary for competing in that country. This was the case with the Fuji-Xerox joint venture. Second, when the development costs and/or risks of opening a foreign market are high, a firm might gain by sharing these costs and/or risks with a local partner. Third, in many countries, political considerations make joint ventures the only feasible entry mode. Again, this was a consideration in the establishment of the Fuji-Xerox venture. Research suggests joint ventures with local partners face a low risk of being subject to nationalization or other forms of government interference.[15] This appears to be because local equity partners, who may have some influence on host-government policy, have a vested interest in speaking out against nationalization or government interference.

Disadvantages

Despite these advantages, there are two major disadvantages with joint ventures. First, as with licensing, a firm that enters into a joint venture risks giving control of its technology to its partner. The joint venture between Boeing and a consortium of Japanese firms to build the 767 airliner raised fears that Boeing was unwittingly giving away its commercial airline technology to the Japanese. However, joint venture agreements can be constructed to minimize this risk. One option is to hold majority ownership in the venture. This allows the dominant partner to exercise greater control over its technology. The drawback with this is that it can be difficult to find a foreign partner who is willing to settle for minority ownership.

A second disadvantage is that a joint venture does not give a firm the tight control over subsidiaries that it might need to realize experience curve or location economies. Nor does it give a firm the tight control over a foreign subsidiary that it might need for engaging in coordinated global attacks against its rivals. Consider the entry of Texas Instruments (TI) into the Japanese semiconductor market. When TI established semiconductor facilities in Japan, it did so for the dual purpose of checking Japanese manufacturers' market share and limiting their cash available for invading TI's global market. In other words, TI was engaging in global strategic coordination. To implement this strategy, TI's subsidiary in Japan had to be prepared to take instructions from corporate headquarters regarding competitive strategy. The strategy also required the Japanese subsidiary to run at a loss if necessary. Few if any potential joint venture partners would have been willing to accept such conditions, since it would have necessitated a willingness to accept a negative return on their investment. Thus, to implement this strategy, TI set up a wholly owned subsidiary in Japan.

A third disadvantage with joint ventures is that the shared ownership arrangement can lead to conflicts and battles for control between the investing firms if their goals and objectives change or if they take different views as to what the strategy should be. This has apparently not been a problem with the Fuji-Xerox joint venture. According to Tony Kobayashi, the CEO of Fuji-Xerox, a primary reason is that both Xerox and Fuji Photo adopted an arm's-length relationship with Fuji-Xerox, giving the venture's management considerable freedom to determine its own strategy.[16] However, much research indicates that conflicts of interest over strategy and goals often arise in joint ventures, that these conflicts tend to be greater when the venture is between firms of different nationalities, and that they often end in the dissolution of the venture.[17] Such conflicts tend to be triggered by shifts in the relative bargaining power of venture partners. For example, in the case of ventures between a foreign firm and a local firm, as a foreign partner's knowledge about local market conditions increases, it depends less on the expertise of a local partner. This increases the bargaining power of the foreign partner and ultimately leads to conflicts over control of the venture's strategy and goals.[18]

Wholly Owned Subsidiaries

In a **wholly owned subsidiary**, the firm owns 100 percent of the stock. Establishing a wholly owned subsidiary in a foreign market can be done two ways. The firm can either set up a new operation in that country or it can acquire an established firm and use that firm to promote its products (as Merrill Lynch did when it acquired various assets of Yamaichi Securities).

Advantages

There are three clear advantages of wholly owned subsidiaries. First, when a firm's competitive advantage is based on technological competence, a wholly owned subsidiary will often be the preferred entry mode, because it reduces the risk of losing control over that competence. (See Chapter 6 for more details.) Many high-tech firms prefer this entry mode for overseas expansion (e.g., firms in the semiconductor, electronics, and pharmaceutical industries). Second, a wholly owned subsidiary gives a firm the tight control over operations in different countries that is necessary for engaging in global strategic coordination (i.e., using profits from one country to support competitive attacks in another). Third, a wholly owned subsidiary may be required if a firm is trying to realize location and experience curve economies (as firms pursuing global and transnational strategies try to do). As we saw in Chapter 12, when cost pressures are intense, it may pay a firm to configure its value chain in such a way that the value added at each stage is maximized. Thus, a national subsidiary may specialize in manufacturing only part of the product line or certain components of the end product, exchanging parts and products with other subsidiaries in the firm's global system. Establishing such a global production system requires a high degree of control over the operations of each affiliate. The various operations must be prepared to accept centrally determined decisions as to how they will produce, how much they will produce, and how their output will be priced for transfer to the next operation. Since licensees or joint venture partners are unlikely to accept such a subservient role, establishment of wholly owned subsidiaries may be necessary.

Disadvantages

Establishing a wholly owned subsidiary is generally the most costly method of serving a foreign market. Firms doing this must bear the full costs and risks of setting up overseas operations. The risks associated with learning to do business in a new culture are less if the firm acquires an established host-country enterprise. However, acquisitions raise additional problems, including those associated with trying to marry divergent corporate cultures. These problems may more than offset any benefits derived by acquiring an established operation.[19]

Selecting an Entry Mode

As the preceding discussion demonstrated, there are advantages and disadvantages associated with all the entry modes; they are summarized in Table 14.1. Due to these advantages and disadvantages, trade-offs are inevitable when selecting an entry mode. For example, when considering entry into an unfamiliar country with a track record for nationalizing foreign-owned enterprises, a firm might favor a joint venture with a local enterprise. Its rationale might be that the local partner will help it establish operations in an unfamiliar environment and will speak out against nationalization should the possibility arise. However, if the firm's core competence is based on proprietary technology, entering a joint venture might risk losing control of that technology to the joint venture partner, in which case the strategy may seem unattractive. Despite the existence of such trade-offs, it is possible to make some generalizations about the optimal choice of entry mode. That is what we do in this section.[20]

Core Competencies and Entry Mode

We saw in Chapter 12 that firms often expand internationally to earn greater returns from their core competencies, transferring the skills and products derived from their core competencies to foreign markets where indigenous competitors lack those skills. We say that such firms are pursuing an international strategy. The optimal entry mode

Table 14.1

Advantages and
Disadvantages
of Entry Modes

Entry Mode	Advantages	Disadvantages
Exporting	Ability to realize location and experience curve economies	High transport costs Trade barriers Problems with local marketing agents
Turnkey contracts	Ability to earn returns from process technology skills in countries where FDI is restricted	Creating efficient competitors Lack of long-term market presence
Licensing	Low development costs and risks	Lack of control over technology Inability to realize location and experience curve economies Inability to engage in global strategic coordination
Franchising	Low development costs and risks	Lack of control over quality Inability to engage in global strategic coordination
Joint ventures	Access to local partner's knowledge Sharing development costs and risks Politically acceptable	Lack of control over technology Inability to engage in global strategic coordination Inability to realize location and experience economies
Wholly owned subsidiaries	Protection of technology Ability to engage in global strategic coordination Ability to realize location and experience economies	High costs and risks

for these firms depends to some degree on the nature of their core competencies. A distinction can be drawn between firms whose core competency is in technological know-how and those whose core competency is in management know-how.

Technological Know-How

As was observed in Chapter 6, if a firm's competitive advantage (its core competence) is based on control over proprietary technological know-how, licensing and joint venture arrangements should be avoided if possible so that the risk of losing control over that technology is minimized. Thus, if a high-tech firm sets up operations in a foreign country to profit from a core competency in technological know-how, it will probably do so through a wholly owned subsidiary.

This rule should not be viewed as hard and fast, however. One exception is when a licensing or joint venture arrangement can be structured so as to reduce the risks of a firm's technological know-how being expropriated by licensees or joint venture partners. We will see how this might be achieved later in the chapter when we examine the structuring of strategic alliances. Another exception exists when a firm perceives its technological advantage to be only transitory, when it expects rapid imitation of its core technology by competitors. In such cases, the firm might want to license its technology as rapidly as possible to foreign firms to gain global acceptance for its technology before the imitation occurs.[21] Such a strategy has some advantages. By licensing its technology to competitors, the firm may deter them from developing their own, possibly superior, technology. Further, by licensing its technology, the firm may establish its technology as the dominant design in the industry (as Matsushita did with its VHS format for VCRs). This may ensure a steady stream of royalty payments. However, the attractions of licensing are probably outweighed by the risks of losing control over technology, and thus licensing should be avoided.

Management Know-How

The competitive advantage of many service firms is based on management know-how (e.g., McDonald's). For such firms, the risk of losing control over their management skills to franchisees or joint venture partners is not that great. These firms' valuable asset is their brand name, and brand names are generally well protected by international laws pertaining to trademarks. Given this, many of the issues arising in the case of technological know-how are of less concern here. As a result, many service firms favor a combination of franchising and subsidiaries to control the franchises within particular countries or regions. The subsidiaries may be wholly owned or joint ventures, but most service firms have found that joint ventures with local partners work best for the controlling subsidiaries. A joint venture is often politically more acceptable and brings a degree of local knowledge to the subsidiary.

Pressures for Cost Reductions and Entry Mode

The greater the pressures for cost reductions are, the more likely a firm will want to pursue some combination of exporting and wholly owned subsidiaries. By manufacturing in those locations where factor conditions are optimal and then exporting to the rest of the world, a firm may be able to realize substantial location and experience curve economies. The firm might then want to export the finished product to marketing subsidiaries based in various countries. These subsidiaries will typically be wholly owned and have the responsibility for overseeing distribution in their particular countries. Setting up wholly owned marketing subsidiaries is preferable to joint venture arrangements and to using foreign marketing agents because it gives the firm the tight control over marketing that might be required for coordinating a globally dispersed value chain. It also gives the firm the ability to use the profits generated in one market to improve its competitive position in another market. In other words, firms pursuing global or transnational strategies tend to prefer establishing wholly owned subsidiaries.

Strategic Alliances

Strategic alliances refer to cooperative agreements between potential or actual competitors. In this section, we are concerned specifically with strategic alliances between firms from different countries. Strategic alliances run the range from formal joint ventures, in which two or more firms have equity stakes (e.g., Fuji-Xerox), to short-term contractual agreements, in which two companies agree to cooperate on a particular task (such as developing a new product). Collaboration between competitors is fashionable; the 1980s and 1990s have seen an explosion in the number of strategic alliances.

The Advantages of Strategic Alliances

Firms ally themselves with actual or potential competitors for various strategic purposes.[22] First, as noted earlier in the chapter, strategic alliances may facilitate entry into a foreign market. For example, Motorola initially found it very difficult to gain access to the Japanese cellular telephone market. In the mid-1980s, the firm complained loudly about formal and informal Japanese trade barriers. The turning point for Motorola came in 1987 when it allied itself with Toshiba to build microprocessors. As part of the deal, Toshiba provided Motorola with marketing help, including some of its best managers. This helped Motorola in the political game of securing government approval to enter the Japanese market and getting radio frequencies assigned for its mobile communications systems. Motorola no longer complains about Japan's trade barriers. Although privately the company admits they still exist, with Toshiba's help Motorola has become skilled at getting around them.[23]

Strategic alliances also allow firms to share the fixed costs (and associated risks) of developing new products or processes. Motorola's alliance with Toshiba also was partly motivated by a desire to share the high fixed costs of setting up an operation to manufacture microprocessors. The microprocessor business is so capital intensive—Motorola and Toshiba each contributed close to $1 billion to set up their facility—that few firms can afford the costs and risks by themselves. Similarly, the alliance between Boeing and a number of Japanese companies to build the 767 was motivated by Boeing's desire to share the estimated $2 billion investment required to develop the aircraft.

Third, an alliance is a way to bring together complementary skills and assets that neither company could easily develop on its own. An example is the alliance between France's Thomson and Japan's JVC to manufacture videocassette recorders. JVC and Thomson are trading core competencies; Thomson needs product technology and manufacturing skills, while JVC needs to learn how to succeed in the fragmented European market. Both sides believe there is an equitable chance for gain. Similarly AT&T struck a deal in 1990 with NEC Corporation of Japan to trade technological skills. AT&T gave NEC some of its computer-aided design technology and NEC is giving AT&T access to the technology underlying its advanced logic computer chips. Such trading of core competencies seems to underlie many of the most successful strategic alliances.

Fourth, it can make sense to form an alliance that will help the firm establish technological standards for the industry that will benefit the firm. For example, in 1992, Philips NV allied with its global competitor, Matsushita, to manufacture and market the digital compact cassette (DCC) system Philips had developed. Philips's motive was that this linking with Matsushita would help it establish the DCC system as a new technological standard in the recording and consumer electronics industries. The issue was important because Sony had developed a competing "mini compact disk" technology that it hoped to establish as the new technical standard. Since the two technologies did very similar things, there was at most only room for one new standard. Philips saw its alliance with Matsushita as a tactic for winning the race.[24]

The Disadvantages of Strategic Alliances

The advantages we have discussed can be very significant. Despite this, some commentators have criticized strategic alliances on the grounds that they give competitors a low-cost route to new technology and markets. For example, Robert Reich and Eric Mankin have argued that strategic alliances between US and Japanese firms are part of an implicit Japanese strategy to keep higher-paying, higher-value-added jobs in Japan while gaining the project engineering and production process skills that underlie the competitive success of many US companies.[25] They argue that Japanese successes in the machine tool and semiconductor industries were largely built on US technology acquired through strategic alliances. And they argue that US managers are aiding the Japanese in achieving their goals by entering alliances that channel new inventions to Japan and provide a US sales and distribution network for the resulting products. Although such deals may generate short-term profits, Reich and Mankin argue, in the long run the result is to "hollow out" US firms, leaving them with no competitive advantage in the global marketplace.

Reich and Mankin have a point. Alliances have risks. Unless a firm is careful, it can give away more than it receives. But, there are so many examples of apparently successful alliances between firms—including alliances between US and Japanese firms—that their position seems more than a little extreme. It is difficult to see how the Motorola-Toshiba alliance or the Fuji-Xerox alliance fit Reich and Mankin's thesis. In these cases, both partners seem to have gained from the alliance. Why do some alliances benefit both firms while others benefit one firm and hurt the other? The next section provides an answer to this question.

Making Alliances Work

The failure rate for international strategic alliances seems to be quite high. For example, one study of 49 international strategic alliances found that two-thirds run into serious managerial and financial troubles within two years of their formation, and that although many of these problems are solved, 33 percent are ultimately rated as failures by the parties involved.[26] Below we argue that the success of an alliance seems to be a function of three main factors: partner selection, alliance structure, and the manner in which the alliance is managed.

Partner Selection

One key to making a strategic alliance work is to select the right ally. A good ally, or partner, has three principal characteristics. First, a good partner helps the firm achieve its strategic goals, whether they are market access, sharing the costs and risks of new-product development, or gaining access to critical core competencies. The partner must have capabilities that the firm lacks and that it values. Second, a good partner shares the firm's vision for the purpose of the alliance. If two firms approach an alliance with radically different agendas, the chances are great that the relationship will not be harmonious, will not flourish, and will end in divorce. Third, a good partner is unlikely to try to opportunistically exploit the alliance for its own ends; that is, to expropriate the firm's technological know-how while giving away little in return. In this respect, firms with reputations for "fair play" to maintain probably make the best allies. For example, IBM is involved in so many strategic alliances that it would not pay the company to trample roughshod over individual alliance partners. This would tarnish IBM's reputation of being a good ally and would make it more difficult for IBM to attract alliance partners. Since IBM attaches great importance to its alliances, it is unlikely to engage in the kind of opportunistic behavior that Reich and Mankin highlight. Similarly, their reputations make it less likely (but by no means impossible) that such Japanese firms as Sony, Toshiba, and Fuji, which have histories of alliances with non-Japanese firms, would opportunistically exploit an alliance partner.

To select a partner with these three characteristics, a firm needs to conduct comprehensive research on potential alliance candidates. To increase the probability of selecting a good partner, the firm should:

1. Collect as much pertinent, publicly available information on potential allies as possible.
2. Collect data from informed third parties. These include firms that have had alliances with the potential partners, investment bankers who have had dealings with them, and former employees.
3. Get to know the potential partner as well as possible before committing to an alliance. This should include face-to-face meetings between senior managers (and perhaps middle-level managers) to ensure that the chemistry is right.

Alliance Structure

Having selected a partner, the alliance should be structured so that the firm's risks of giving too much away to the partner are reduced to an acceptable level. Figure 14.1 depicts the four safeguards against opportunism by alliance partners that we discuss here. (Opportunism includes the theft of technology and/or markets that Reich and Mankin describe.) First, alliances can be designed to make it difficult (if not impossible) to transfer technology not meant to be transferred. The design, development, manufacture, and service of a product manufactured by an alliance can be structured so as to wall off sensitive technologies to prevent their leakage to the other participant. In the alliance between General Electric and Snecma to build commercial air-

Figure 14.1

Structuring Alliances to Reduce Opportunism

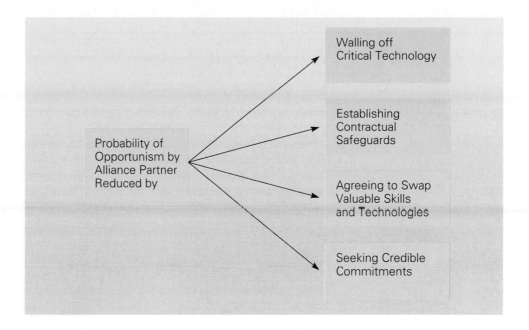

craft engines, for example, GE reduced the risk of excess transfer by walling off certain sections of the production process. The modularization effectively cut off the transfer of what GE regarded as key competitive technology, while permitting Snecma access to final assembly. Similarly, in the alliance between Boeing and the Japanese to build the 767, Boeing walled off research, design, and marketing functions considered central to its competitive position, while allowing the Japanese to share in production technology. Boeing also walled off new technologies not required for 767 production.[27]

Second, contractual safeguards can be written into an alliance agreement to guard against the risk of opportunism by a partner. For example, TRW, Inc., has three strategic alliances with large Japanese auto component suppliers to produce seat belts, engine valves, and steering gears for sale to Japanese-owned auto assembly plants in the United States. TRW has clauses in each of its alliance contracts that bar the Japanese firms from competing with TRW to supply US-owned auto companies with component parts. By doing this, TRW protects itself against the possibility that the Japanese companies are entering into the alliances merely as a means of gaining access to the North American market to compete with TRW in its home market.

Third, both parties to an alliance can agree in advance to swap skills and technologies that the other covets, thereby ensuring a chance for equitable gain. Cross-licensing agreements are one way to achieve this goal. For example, in the alliance between Motorola and Toshiba, Motorola has licensed some of its microprocessor technology to Toshiba, and in return, Toshiba has licensed some of its memory chip technology to Motorola.

Fourth, the risk of opportunism by an alliance partner can be reduced if the firm extracts a significant credible commitment from its partner in advance. The long-term alliance between Xerox and Fuji to build photocopiers for the Asian market perhaps best illustrates this. Rather than enter into an informal agreement or a licensing arrangement (which Fuji Photo initially wanted), Xerox insisted that Fuji invest in a 50/50 joint venture to serve Japan and East Asia. This venture constituted such a significant investment in people, equipment, and facilities that Fuji Photo was committed from the outset to making the alliance work in order to earn a return on its investment. By agreeing to the joint venture, Fuji essentially made a credible commitment to the alliance. Given this, Xerox felt secure in transferring its photocopier technology to Fuji (see the Management Focus for details).[28]

Managing the Alliance

Once a partner has been selected and an appropriate alliance structure has been agreed on, the task facing the firm is to maximize its benefits from the alliance. As in all international business deals, an important factor is sensitivity to cultural differences (see Chapter 3). Many differences in management style are attributable to cultural differences, and managers need to make allowances for these in dealing with their partner. Beyond this, maximizing the benefits from an alliance seems to involve building trust between partners and learning from partners.[29]

Building Trust

Managing an alliance successfully seems to require building interpersonal relationships between the firms' managers. This is one lesson that can be drawn from the successful strategic alliance between Ford and Mazda. Ford and Mazda have set up a framework of meetings within which their managers not only discuss matters pertaining to the alliance but also have time to get to know each other better. The belief is that the resulting friendships help build trust and facilitate harmonious relations between the two firms. Personal relationships also foster an informal management network between the firms. (Chapter 13 discusses informal management networks.) This network can then be used to help solve problems arising in more formal contexts (such as in joint committee meetings between personnel from the two firms).

Learning from Partners

After a five-year study of 15 strategic alliances between major multinationals, Gary Hamel, Yves Doz, and C. K. Prahalad concluded that a major determinant of how much a company gains from an alliance is its ability to learn from its alliance partner.[30] They focused on a number of alliances between Japanese companies and Western (European or American) partners. In every case in which a Japanese company emerged from an alliance stronger than its Western partner, the Japanese company had made a greater effort to learn. Few Western companies studied seemed to want to learn from their Japanese partners. They tended to regard the alliance purely as a cost-sharing or risk-sharing device, rather than as an opportunity to learn how a potential competitor does business.

For example, consider the 10-year alliance between General Motors and Toyota constituted in 1985 to build the Chevrolet Nova. This alliance was structured as a formal joint venture, called New United Motor Manufacturing, Inc., and each party had a 50 percent equity stake. The venture owned an auto plant in Fremont, California. According to one Japanese manager, Toyota quickly achieved most of its objectives from the alliance: "We learned about US supply and transportation. And we got the confidence to manage US workers."[31] All that knowledge was then transferred to Georgetown, Kentucky, where Toyota opened its own plant in 1988. On the other hand, possibly all GM got was a new product, the Chevrolet Nova. Some GM managers complained that the knowledge they gained through the alliance with Toyota has never been put to good use inside GM. They believe they should have been kept together as a team to educate GM's engineers and workers about the Japanese system. Instead, they were dispersed to various GM subsidiaries.

To maximize the learning benefits of an alliance, a firm must try to learn from its partner and then apply the knowledge within its own organization. It has been suggested that all operating employees should be well briefed on the partner's strengths and weaknesses and should understand how acquiring particular skills will bolster their firm's competitive position. Hamel, Doz, and Prahalad note that this is already standard practice among Japanese companies. For example, they made this observation:

We accompanied a Japanese development engineer on a tour through a partner's factory. This engineer dutifully took notes on plant layout, the number of production stages, the rate at which the line was running, and the number of employees. He recorded all this despite the fact that he had no manufacturing responsibility in his own company, and that the alliance did not encompass joint manufacturing. Such dedication greatly enhances learning.[32]

For such learning to be of value, it must be diffused throughout the organization (as was seemingly not the case at GM after the GM–Toyota joint venture). To achieve this, the managers involved in the alliance should be used to educate their colleagues in the firm about the skills of the alliance partner.

Chapter Summary

This chapter addressed two related topics: the optimal choice of entry mode to serve a foreign market and strategic alliances. The two topics are related in that several entry modes (e.g., licensing and joint ventures) are strategic alliances. Most strategic alliances, however, involve more than just issues of market access. This chapter made the following points:

1. Basic entry decisions include identifying which markets to enter, when to enter those markets, and on what scale.

2. The most attractive foreign markets tend to be found in politically stable developed and developing nations that have free market systems and where there is not a dramatic upsurge in either inflation rates or private-sector debt.

3. There are several advantages associated with entering a national market early, before other international businesses have established themselves. These advantages must be balanced against the pioneering costs that early entrants often have to bear including the greater risk of business failure.

4. Large-scale entry into a national market constitutes a major strategic commitment that is likely to change the nature of competition in that market and limit the entrant's future strategic flexibility. The firm needs to think through the implications of such commitments before embarking on a large-scale entry. Although making major strategic commitments can yield many benefits, there are also risks associated with such a strategy.

5. There are six modes of entering a foreign market: exporting, turnkey projects, licensing, franchising, establishing joint ventures, and setting up a wholly owned subsidiary.

6. Exporting has the advantages of facilitating the realization of experience curve economies and of avoiding the costs of setting up manufacturing operations in another country. Disadvantages include high transport costs and trade barriers and problems with local marketing agents. The latter can be overcome if the firm sets up a wholly owned marketing subsidiary in the host country.

7. Turnkey projects allow firms to export their process know-how to countries where FDI might be prohibited, thereby enabling the firm to earn a greater return from this asset. The disadvantage is that the firm may inadvertently create efficient global competitors in the process.

8. The main advantage of licensing is that the licensee bears the costs and risks of opening a foreign market. Disadvantages include the risk of losing technological know-how to the licensee and a lack of tight control over licensees.

9. The main advantage of franchising is that the franchisee bears the costs and risks of opening a foreign market. Disadvantages center on problems of quality control of distant franchisees.

10. Joint ventures have the advantages of sharing the costs and risks of opening a foreign market and of gaining local knowledge and political influence. Disadvantages include the risk of losing control over technology and a lack of tight control.

11. The advantages of wholly owned subsidiaries include tight control over technological know-how. The main disadvantage is that the firm must bear all the costs and risks of opening a foreign market.

12. The optimal choice of entry mode depends on the strategy of the firm.

13. When technological know-how constitutes a firm's core competence, wholly owned subsidiaries are preferred, since they best control technology.

14. When management know-how constitutes a firm's core competence, foreign franchises controlled by joint ventures seem to be optimal. This gives the firm the cost and risk benefits associated with franchising, while enabling it to monitor and control franchisee quality effectively.

15. When the firm is pursuing a global or transnational strategy, the need for tight control over operations in order to realize location and experience curve economies suggests wholly owned subsidiaries are the best entry mode.

16. Strategic alliances are cooperative agreements between actual or potential competitors.

17. The advantage of alliances are that they facilitate entry into foreign markets, enable partners to share the fixed costs and risks associated with new products and processes, facilitate the transfer of complementary skills between companies, and can help firms establish technical standards.

18. The disadvantage of a strategic alliance is that the firm risks giving away technological know-how and market access to its alliance partner in return for very little.

19. The disadvantages associated with alliances can be reduced if the firm selects partners carefully, paying close attention to the issue of reputation and structure of the alliance so as to avoid unintended transfers of know-how.

20. Two of the keys to making alliances work seem to be building trust and informal communications networks between partners and taking proactive steps to learn from alliance partners.

Critical Discussion Questions

1. Review Merrill Lynch's 1997 reentry into the Japanese private client market (see the opening case for details). Pay close attention to the timing and scale of entry and the nature of the strategic commitments Merrill Lynch is making in Japan. What are the potential benefits associated with this strategy? What are the costs and risks? Do you think the trade-off between benefits and risks and costs makes sense? Why?

2. Licensing proprietary technology to foreign competitors is the best way to give up a firm's competitive advantage. Discuss.

3. What kinds of companies stand to gain the most from entering into strategic alliances with potential competitors? Why?

4. Discuss how the need for control over foreign operations varies with firms' strategies and core competencies. What are the implications for the choice of entry mode?

5. A small Canadian firm that has developed some valuable new medical products using its unique biotechnology know-how is trying to decide how best to serve the European Community market. Its choices are:

- Manufacture the product at home and let foreign sales agents handle marketing.

- Manufacture the products at home and set up a wholly owned subsidiary in Europe to handle marketing.

- Enter into a strategic alliance with a large European pharmaceutical firm. The product would be manufactured in Europe by the 50/50 joint venture and marketed by the European firm.

The cost of investment in manufacturing facilities will be a major one for the Canadian firm, but it is not outside its reach. If these are the firm's only options, which one would you advise it to choose? Why?

CLOSING CASE   Anatomy of a Failed Alliance—General Motors and Daewoo

In June 1984, General Motors and the Daewoo Group of Korea signed an agreement that called for each to invest $100 million in a South Korean-based 50/50 joint venture, Daewoo Motor Company, that would manufacture a subcompact car, the Pontiac LeMans, based on GM's popular German-designed Opel Kadett (Opel is a wholly owned German subsidiary of GM). Much of the day-to-day management of the alliance was to be placed in the hands of Daewoo executives, with managerial and technical advice being provided by a limited number of GM executives. At the time, many hailed the alliance as a smart move for both companies. GM doubted that a small car could be built profitably in the United States because of high labor costs, and it saw enormous advantages in this marriage of German technology and South Korean cheap labor. At the time, Roger Smith, GM's chairman, told Korean reporters that GM's North American operation would probably end up importing 80,000 to 100,000 cars a year from Daewoo Motors. As for the Daewoo Group, it was getting access to the superior engineering skills of GM and an entrée into the world's largest car market—the United States.

Eight years of financial losses later the joint venture collapsed in a blizzard of mutual recriminations between Daewoo and General Motors. From the perspective of GM, things started to go seriously wrong in 1987, just as the first LeMans was rolling off Daewoo's production line. South Korea had lurched toward democracy, and workers throughout the country demanded better wages. Daewoo Motor was hit by a series of bitter strikes that repeatedly halted LeMans production. To calm the labor troubles, Daewoo Motor more than doubled workers' wages. Suddenly it was cheaper to build Opels in Germany than in South Korea. (German wages were still higher, but German productivity was also much higher, which translated into lower labor costs.)

Equally problematic was the poor quality of the cars rolling off the Daewoo production line. Electrical systems often crashed on the LeMans and the braking system had a tendency to fail after just a few thousand miles. The LeMans soon gained a reputation for poor quality, and US sales plummeted to 37,000 vehicles in 1991, down 86 percent from their 1988 high point. Hurt by the LeMans's reputation as a lemon, Daewoo's share of the rapidly growing Korean car market also slumped from a high of 21.4 percent in 1987 to 12.3 percent in 1991.

However, if General Motors was disappointed in Daewoo, that was nothing compared to Daewoo's frustration with GM. Daewoo Group Chairman Kim Woo-Choong complained publicly that GM executives were arrogant and treated him shabbily. Mr. Kim was angry that GM tried to prohibit him from expanding the market for Daewoo's cars. In late 1988, Mr. Kim negotiated a deal to sell 7,000 of Daewoo Motor's cars in Eastern Europe. GM executives immediately tried to kill the deal, telling Mr. Kim that Europe was the territory of GM's German subsidiary, Opel. Daewoo ultimately agreed to limit the sale to 3,000 cars and never sell again in Eastern Europe. To make matters worse, when Daewoo developed a new sedan car and asked GM to sell it in the US, GM said no. By this point, Mr. Kim was very frustrated at having his expansion plans in Eastern

Europe and the United States held back by GM. Daewoo management also believed that the poor sales of the LeMans in the United States were not due to quality problems but to GM's poor marketing efforts.

Things came to a head in 1991 when Daewoo asked GM to agree to expand the manufacturing facilities of the joint venture. The plan called for each partner to put in another $100 million and for Daewoo Motor to double its output. GM management refused on the grounds that increasing output would not help Daewoo Motor unless the venture could first improve its product quality. The matter festered until late 1991 when GM management delivered a blunt proposal to Daewoo—either GM would buy out Daewoo's stake, or Daewoo would buy out GM's stake in the joint venture. Much to GM's surprise, Daewoo agreed to buy out GM's stake. The divorce was completed in November 1992 with an agreement by Daewoo to pay GM $170 million over three years for its 50 percent stake in Daewoo Motor Company.

http://www.gm.com

Sources: D. Darlin, "Daewoo Will Pay GM $170 Million for Venture Stake," *The Wall Street Journal*, November 11, 1992, p. A6; and D. Darlin and J. B. White, "Failed Marriage," *The Wall Street Journal*, January 16, 1992, p. A1.

Case Discussion Questions

1. What were GM's motives for entering into the alliance with Daewoo? What were Daewoo's motives for entering into an alliance with GM? Do you think these different motivations ultimately contributed to the dissolution of the alliance? Why?

2. Did the relative bargaining power of General Motors and Daewoo change over the lifetime of the alliance? If so, do you think this helped contribute to the dissolution of the alliance? How?

3. How might GM and Daewoo have reduced the chances of the alliance dissolving? What might they have done differently?

Notes

1. This can be reconceptualized as the resource base of the entrant, relative to indigenous competitors. For work that focuses on this issue, see W. C. Bogenr, H. Thomas, and J. McGee, "A Longitudinal Study of the Competitive Positions and Entry Paths of European Firms in the U.S. Pharmaceutical Market," *Strategic Management Journal* 17 (1996), pp. 85–107; D. Collis, "A Resource-Based Analysis of Global Competition,"

Strategic Management Journal 12 (1991), pp. 49–68; S. Tallman, "Strategic Management Models and Resource-Based Strategies among MNEs in a Host Market," *Strategic Management Journal* 12 (1991), pp. 69–82.

2. For a discussion of first-mover advantages see M. Liberman and D. Montgomery, "First-Mover Advantages," *Strategic Management Journal* 9 (Summer Special Issue, 1988), pp. 41–58.

3. J. M. Shaver, W. Mitchell, and B. Yeung, "The Effect of Own Firm and Other Firm Experience on Foreign Direct Investment Survival in the United States, 1987–92," *Strategic Management Journal* 18 (1997), pp. 811–24.

4. S. Zaheer and E. Mosakowski, "The Dynamics of the Liability of Foreignness: A Global Study of Survival in the Financial Services Industry," *Strategic Management Journal* 18 (1997), pp. 439–64.

5. Shaver, Mitchell, and Yeung, "The Effect of Own Firm and Other Firm Experience on Foreign Direct Investment Survival in the United States, 1987–92."

6. P. Ghemawat, *Commitment: The Dynamics of Strategy* (New York: Free Press, 1991).

7. R. Luecke, *Scuttle Your Ships before Advancing* (Oxford: Oxford University Press, 1994).

8. This section draws on several studies including: C. W. L. Hill, P. Hwang, and W. C. Kim, "An Eclectic Theory of the Choice of International Entry Mode," *Strategic Management Journal* 11 (1990), pp. 117–28; C. W. L. Hill and W. C. Kim, "Searching for a Dynamic Theory of the Multinational Enterprise: A Transaction Cost Model," *Strategic Management Journal* 9 (Special Issue on Strategy Content, 1988), pp. 93–104; E. Anderson and H. Gatignon, "Modes of Foreign Entry: A Transaction Cost Analysis and Propositions," *Journal of International Business Studies* 17 (1986), pp. 1–26; F. R. Root, *Entry Strategies for International Markets* (Lexington, MA: D. C. Heath, 1980); and A. Madhok, "Cost, Value and Foreign Market Entry: The Transaction and the Firm," *Strategic Management Journal* 18 (1997), pp. 39–61.

9. For a general discussion of licensing, see F. J. Contractor, "The Role of Licensing in International Strategy," *Columbia Journal of World Business*, Winter 1982, pp. 73–83.

10. See E. Terazono and C. Lorenz, "An Angry Young Warrior," *Financial Times*, September 19, 1994, p. 11, and K. McQuade and B. Gomes-Casseres, "Xerox and Fuji-Xerox," Harvard Business School Case #9-391-156.

11. O. E. Williamson, *The Economic Institutions of Capitalism* (New York: Free Press, 1985).

12. J. H. Dunning and M. McQueen, "The Eclectic Theory of International Production: A Case Study of the International Hotel Industry," *Managerial and Decision Economics* 2 (1981), pp. 197–210.

13. Andrew E. Serwer, "McDonald's Conquers the World," *Fortune*, October 17, 1994, pp. 103–16.

14. For an excellent review of the literature of joint ventures, see B. Kogut, "Joint Ventures: Theoretical and Empirical Perspectives," *Strategic Management Journal* 9 (1988), pp. 319–32.

15. D. G. Bradley, "Managing against Expropriation," *Harvard Business Review*, July–August 1977, pp. 78–90.

16. Speech given by Tony Kobayashi at the University of Washington Business School, October 1992.

17. A. C. Inkpen and P. W. Beamish, "Knowledge, Bargaining Power, and the Instability of International Joint Ventures," *Academy of Management Review* 22 (1997), pp. 177–202; and S. H. Park and G. R. Ungson, "The Effect of National Culture, Organizational Complementarity, and Economic Motivation on Joint Venture Dissolution," *Academy of Management Journal* 40 (1997), pp. 279–307.

18. Inkpen and Beamish, "Knowledge, Bargaining Power, and the Instability of International Joint Ventures."

19. For a review of the kinds of problems encountered when making acquisitions, see Chapter 9 in C. W. L. Hill and G. R. Jones, *Strategic Management Theory* (Boston: Houghton Mifflin, 1995).

20. This section draws on Hill, Hwang, and Kim, "An Eclectic Theory of the Choice of International Entry Mode."

21. C. W. L. Hill, "Strategies for Exploiting Technological Innovations: When and When Not to License," *Organization Science* 3 (1992), pp. 428–41.

22. See K. Ohmae, "The Global Logic of Strategic Alliances," *Harvard Business Review*, March–April 1989, pp. 143–54; G. Hamel, Y. L. Doz, and C. K. Prahalad, "Collaborate with Your Competitors and Win!" *Harvard Business Review*, January–February 1989, pp. 133–39; and W. Burgers, C. W. L. Hill, and W. C. Kim, "Alliances in the Global Auto Industry," *Strategic Management Journal* 14 (1993), pp. 419–32.

23. "Asia Beckons," *The Economist*, May 30, 1992, pp. 63–64.

24. P. M. Reilly, "Sony's Digital Audio Format Pulls ahead of Philips's," *The Wall Street Journal*, August 6, 1993, p. B1.

25. R. B. Reich and E. D. Mankin, "Joint Ventures with Japan Give Away Our Future," *Harvard Business Review*, March–April 1986, pp. 78–90.

26. J. Bleeke and D. Ernst, "The Way to Win in Cross-Border Alliances," *Harvard Business Review*, November–December 1991, pp. 127–135.

27. W. Roehl and J. F. Truitt, "Stormy Open Marriages Are Better," *Columbia Journal of World Business*, Summer 1987, pp. 87–95.

28. K. McQuade and B. Gomes-Casseres, "Xerox and Fuji-Xerox," Harvard Business School Case #9-391-156.

29. T. Khanna, R. Gulati, and N. Nohria, "The Dynamics of Learning Alliances: Competition, Cooperation, and Relative Scope," *Strategic Management Journal* 19 (1998), pp. 193–210.

30. Hamel, Doz, and Prahalad, "Collaborate with Competitors."

31. B. Wysocki, "Cross-Border Alliances Become Favorite Way to Crack New Markets," *The Wall Street Journal*, March 4, 1990, p. A1.

32. Hamel, Doz, and Prahalad, "Collaborate with Competitors," p. 138.

CASES

Nestlé: Global Strategy

Ford 2000

Orient Foods Ltd.: Business Development in China

Kentucky Fried Chicken: Latin American Strategy

NESTLÉ: GLOBAL STRATEGY

Introduction

Nestlé is one of the oldest of all multinational businesses. The company was founded in Switzerland in 1866 by Heinrich Nestlé, who established Nestlé to distribute "milk food," a type of infant food he had invented that was made from powdered milk, baked food, and sugar. From its very early days, the company looked to other countries for growth opportunities, establishing its first foreign offices in London in 1868. In 1905, the company merged with the Anglo-Swiss Condensed Milk, thereby broadening the company's product line to include both condensed milk and infant formulas. Forced by Switzerland's small size to look outside its borders for growth opportunities, Nestlé established condensed milk and infant food processing plants in the United States and Britain in the late 19th century and in Australia, South America, Africa, and Asia in the first three decades of the 20th century.

In 1929, Nestlé moved into the chocolate business when it acquired a Swiss chocolate maker. This was followed in 1938 by the development of Nestlé's most revolutionary product, Nescafe, the world's first soluble coffee drink. After World War II, Nestlé continued to expand into other areas of the food business, primarily through a series of acquisitions that included Maggi (1947), Cross & Blackwell (1960), Findus (1962), Libby's (1970), Stouffer's (1973), Carnation (1985), Rowntree (1988), and Perrier (1992).

By the late 1990s, Nestlé had 500 factories in 76 countries and sold its products in a staggering 193 nations—almost every country in the world. In 1998, the company generated sales of close to SWF 72 billion ($51 billion), only 1 percent of which occurred in its home country. Similarly, only 3 percent of its 210,000 employees were located in Switzerland. Nestlé was the world's biggest maker of infant formula, powdered milk, chocolates, instant coffee, soups, and mineral waters. It was number two in ice cream, breakfast cereals, and pet food. Roughly 38 percent of its food sales were made in Europe, 32 percent in the Americas, and 20 percent in Africa and Asia.

A Growth Strategy for the 21st Century

Despite its undisputed success, Nestlé realized by the early 1990s that it faced significant challenges in maintaining its growth rate. The large Western European and North American markets were mature. In several countries, population growth had stagnated and in some there had been a small decline in food consumption. The retail environment in many Western nations had become increasingly challenging, and the balance of power was shifting away from the large-scale manufacturers of branded foods and beverages and toward nationwide supermarket and discount chains. Increasingly, retailers found themselves in the unfamiliar position of playing off against each other manufacturers of branded foods, thus bargaining down prices. Particularly in Europe, this trend was enhanced by the successful introduction of private-label brands by several of Europe's leading supermarket chains. The results included increased price competition in several key segments of the food and beverage market, such as cereals, coffee, and soft drinks.

At Nestlé, one response has been to look toward emerging markets in Eastern Europe, Asia, and Latin America for growth possibilities. The logic is simple and obvious—a combination of economic and population growth, when coupled with the widespread adoption of market-oriented economic policies by the governments of many developing nations, makes for attractive business opportunities. Many of these countries are still relatively poor, but their economies are growing rapidly. For example, if current economic growth forecasts occur, by 2010 there will be 700 million people in China and India that have income levels approaching those of Spain in the mid-1990s. As income levels rise, it is increasingly likely that consumers in these nations will start to substitute branded food products for basic foodstuffs, creating a large market opportunity for companies such as Nestlé.

In general, the company's strategy has been to enter emerging markets early—before competitors—and build a substantial position by selling basic food items that appeal to the local population base, such as infant formula, condensed milk, noodles, and tofu. By narrowing its initial market focus to just a handful of strategic brands, Nestlé claims it can simplify life, reduce risk, and concentrate its marketing resources and managerial effort on a limited number of key niches. The goal is to build a commanding market position in each of these niches. By pursuing such a strategy, Nestlé has taken as much as 85 percent of the market for instant coffee in Mexico, 66 percent of the market for powdered milk in the Philippines, and 70 percent of the markets for soups in Chile. As income levels rise, the company progressively moves out from these niches, introducing more upscale items, such as mineral water, chocolate, cookies, and prepared foodstuffs.

Although the company is known worldwide for several key brands, such as Nescafe, it uses local brands in many markets. The company owns 8,500 brands, but only 750 of them are registered in more than one country, and only 80 are registered in more than 10 countries. While the company will use the same "global brands" in multiple developed markets, in the developing world it focuses on trying to optimize ingredients and processing technology to local conditions and then using a brand name that resonates locally. Customization rather than globalization is the key to the company's strategy in emerging markets.

Executing the Strategy

Successful execution of the strategy for developing markets requires a degree of flexibility, an ability to adapt in often unforeseen ways to local conditions, and a long-term perspective that puts building a sustainable business before short-term profitability. In Nigeria, for example, a crumbling road system, aging trucks, and the danger of violence forced the company to rethink its traditional distribution methods. Instead of operating a central warehouse, as is its preference in most nations, the company built a network of small warehouses around the country. For safety reasons, trucks carrying Nestlé goods are allowed to travel only during the day and frequently under armed guard. Marketing also poses challenges in Nigeria. With little opportunity for typical Western-style advertising on television or billboards, the company hired local singers to go to towns and villages offering a mix of entertainment and product demonstrations.

China provides another interesting example of local adaptation and a long-term focus. After 13 years of talks, Nestlé was formally invited into China in 1987 by the government of Heilongjiang province. Nestlé opened a plant to produce powdered milk and infant formula there in 1990, but quickly realized that the local rail and road infrastructure was inadequate and inhibited the collection of milk and delivery of finished products. Rather than make do with the local infrastructure, Nestlé embarked on an ambitious plan to establish its own distribution network, known as milk roads, between 27 villages in the region and factory collection points, called chilling centers. Farmers brought their milk—often on bicycles or carts—to the centers where it was weighed and analyzed. Unlike the government, Nestlé paid the farmers promptly. Suddenly the farmers had an incentive to produce milk, and many bought a second cow, increasing the cow population in the district by 3,000, to 9,000, in 18 months. Area managers then organized a delivery system that used dedicated vans to deliver the milk to Nestlé's factory.

Although at first glance this might seem to be a very costly solution, Nestlé calculated that the long-term benefits would be substantial. Nestlé's strategy is similar to that undertaken by many European and American companies during the first waves of industrialization in those countries. Companies often had to invest in infrastructure that we now take for granted to get production off the ground. Once the infrastructure was in place in China, Nestlé's production took off. In 1990, 316 tons of powdered milk and infant formula were produced. By 1994, output exceeded 10,000 tons, and the company decided to triple capacity. Based on this experience, Nestlé decided to build another two powdered milk factories in China and was aiming to generate sales of $700 million by 2000.

Nestlé is pursuing a similar long-term bet in the Middle East, an area in which most multinational food companies have little presence. Collectively, the Middle East accounts for only about 2 percent of Nestlé's worldwide sales, and the individual markets are very small. However, Nestlé's long-term strategy is based on the assumption that regional conflicts will subside and intraregional trade will expand as trade barriers between countries in the region come down. Once that happens, Nestlé's factories in the Middle East should be able to sell throughout the region, thereby realizing scale economies. In anticipation of this development, Nestlé has established a network of factories in five countries in hopes that each will someday supply the entire region with different products. The company currently makes ice cream in Dubai, soups and cereals in Saudi Arabia, yogurt and bouillon in Egypt, chocolate in Turkey, and ketchup and instant noodles in Syria. For the present, Nestlé can survive in these markets by using local materials and focusing on local demand. The Syrian factory, for example, relies on products that use tomatoes, a major local agricultural product. Syria also produces wheat, which is the main ingredient in instant noodles. Even if trade barriers don't come down soon, Nestlé has indicated it will remain committed to the region. By using local inputs and focusing on local consumer needs, it has earned a good rate of return in the region, even though the individual markets are small.

Despite its successes in places such as China and parts of the Middle East, not all of Nestlé's moves have worked out so well. Like several other Western companies, Nestlé has had its problems in Japan, where a failure to adapt its coffee brand to local conditions meant the loss of a significant market opportunity to another Western company, Coca-Cola. For years, Nestlé's instant coffee brand was the dominant coffee product in Japan. In the 1960s, cold canned coffee (which can be purchased from soda vending machines) started to gain a following in Japan. Nestlé dismissed the product as just a coffee-flavored drink, rather than the real thing, and declined to enter the market. Nestlé's local partner at the time, Kirin Beer, was so incensed at Nestlé's refusal to enter the canned coffee market that it broke off its relationship with the company. In contrast, Coca-Cola entered the market with Georgia, a product developed specifically for this segment of the Japanese market. By leveraging its existing distribution channel, Coca-Cola captured a 40 percent share of the $4 billion a year market for canned coffee in Japan. Nestlé, which failed to enter the market until the 1980s, has only a 4 percent share.

While Nestlé has built businesses from the ground up in many emerging markets, such as Nigeria and China, in others it will purchase local companies if suitable candidates can be found. The company pursued such a strategy in Poland, which it entered in 1994 by purchasing Goplana, the country's second largest chocolate manufacturer. With the collapse of communism and the opening of the Polish market, income levels in Poland have started to rise and so has chocolate consumption. Once a scarce item, the market grew by 8 percent a year throughout the 1990s. To take advantage of this opportunity, Nestlé has pursued a strategy of evolution, rather than revolution. It has kept the top management of the company staffed with locals—as it does in most of its operations around the world—and carefully adjusted Goplana's product line to better match local opportunities. At the same time, it has pumped money into Goplana's marketing, which has enabled the unit to gain share from several other chocolate makers in the country. Still, competition in the market is intense. Eight companies, including several foreign-owned enterprises, such as the market leader, Wedel, which is owned by PepsiCo, are vying for market share, and this has depressed prices and profit margins, despite the healthy volume growth.

Management Structure

Nestlé is a decentralized organization. Responsibility for operating decisions is pushed down to local units, which typically enjoy a high degree of autonomy with regard to decisions involving pricing, distribution, marketing, human resources, and so on. At the same time, the company is organized into seven worldwide strategic business units (SBUs) that have responsibility for high-level strategic decisions and business development. For example, a strategic business unit focuses on coffee and beverages. Another one focuses on confectionery and ice cream. These SBUs engage in overall strategy development, including acquisitions and market entry strategy. In recent years, two-thirds of Nestlé's growth has come from acquisitions, so this is a critical function. Running

in parallel to this structure is a regional organization that divides the world into five major geographical zones, such as Europe, North America, and Asia. The regional organizations assist in the overall strategy development process and are responsible for developing regional strategies (an example would be Nestlé's strategy in the Middle East, which was discussed earlier). Neither the SBU nor regional managers, however, get involved in local operating or strategic decisions on anything other than an exceptional basis.

Although Nestlé makes intensive use of local managers, to knit its diverse worldwide operations together the company relies on its "expatriate army." This consists of about 700 managers who spend the bulk of their careers on foreign assignments, moving from one country to the next. Selected primarily on the basis of their ability, drive, and willingness to live a quasi-nomadic lifestyle, these individuals often work in half a dozen nations during their careers. Nestlé also uses management development programs as a strategic tool for creating an *esprit de corps* among managers. At Rive-Reine, the company's international training center in Switzerland, the company brings together managers from around the world, at different stages in their careers, for specially targeted development programs of two to three weeks' duration. The objective of these programs is to give the managers a better understanding of Nestlé's culture and strategy and to give them access to the company's top management.

The research and development operation has a special place within Nestlé, which is not surprising for a company that was established to commercialize innovative foodstuffs. The R&D function comprises 18 different groups that operate in 11 countries throughout the world. Nestlé spends approximately 1 percent of its annual sales revenue on R&D and has 3,100 employees dedicated to the function. Around 70 percent of the R&D budget is spent on development initiatives. These initiatives focus on developing products and processes that fulfill market needs, as identified by the SBUs, in concert with regional and local managers. For example, Nestlé instant noodle products were originally developed by the R&D group in response to the perceived needs of local operating companies through the Asian region. The company also has longer-term development projects that focus on developing new technological platforms, such as nonanimal protein sources or agricultural biotechnology products.

Discussion Questions

1. Does it make sense for Nestlé to focus its growth efforts on emerging markets? Why?

2. What is the company's strategy with regard to business development in emerging markets? Does this strategy make sense?

3. From an organizational perspective, what is required for this strategy to work effectively?

4. How would you describe Nestlé's strategic posture at the corporate level; is it pursuing a global strategy, a multidomestic strategy, an international strategy, or a transnational strategy?

5. Does this overall strategic posture make sense given the markets and countries that Nestlé participates in? Why?

6. Is Nestlé's management structure and philosophy aligned with its overall strategic posture?

Sources

1. Hall, W. "Strength of Brands Is Key to Success." *Financial Times*, November 30, 1998, p. 2.

2. "How to Conquer China (and the World) with Instant Noodles." *The Economist*, June 17, 1995.

3. Lorenz, C. "Sugar Daddy." *Financial Times*, April 20, 1994, p. 19.

4. Michaels, D. "Chocolate Giants Worldwide Find Themselves Sweet on Polish Market." *The Wall Street Journal*, December 12, 1997.

5. Nestlé. "Key Facts and History." At http://www.nestle.com.

6. Rapoport, C. "Nestlé's Brand Building Machine." *Fortune*, September 19, 1994, p. 147.

7. Steinmetz, G., and T. Parker-Rope. "All Over the Map." *The Wall Street Journal*, September 26, 1996, p. R4.

8. Sullivan, M. "Nestlé Is Looking to Coffee Market in Russia for Sales." *The Wall Street Journal*, August 7, 1998, p. B7A.

FORD 2000

Introduction

Alex Trotman, newly named CEO of Ford, made a proclamation in November 1993: "The top priority is to keep doing what we've been doing."[1] No one really believed him. Trotman had made a career of doing the unexpected. When top management refused him a transfer from Britain in 1969, he bought his own ticket to Dearborn, Michigan, and talked his way into a job at headquarters, alias the Glass House. At 61, Trotman holds a master's degree in business although he never attended college. He has spent years working his way up through Ford's management, primarily on the production side in Europe.

The skeptics were right. It did not take long for Trotman to shake things up. Three weeks after being named CEO, Trotman attended a meeting of senior managers at Ford's London office. The subject of the meeting was to review the success of consolidating the developing of power trains, the main components of engines and transmissions. Trotman asked the managers if it was possible to expand this idea to the entire company, not just engines and transmissions. Could Ford tear down its highly segmented regional structure and create one global system? Trotman gave a team of senior managers six weeks to determine if such an idea was feasible.

The Rationale for Restructuring

There were several motivating factors behind the need for restructuring. Under the previous system, there was massive duplication of processes in both North America and Europe. According to the company, this raised annual costs by at least $3 billion.[2] Furthermore, Ford's average new-car development time was much longer than its competitors', approximately six years as compared to Toyota's three. Its competitors had more profits per car and higher pretax margins. Trotman also saw the need to refocus the company in order to efficiently enter emerging markets in China, Russia, and Latin America.

Thus, Ford 2000 was born. With the ultimate goal to become "the best automaker in the world," Trotman announced the most massive reorganization of the company in its 91-year history on April 1, 1994. The specific directives included:

- Be faster and more efficient developing new models.
- Expand the range of products and fill in gaps.
- Match the Japanese cost advantage and improve profitability.

- Reduce the time it takes to make a vehicle.
- Follow Toyota's lead of selling the same model around the world.[3]

The finer points of Ford 2000 were hammered out by a team of 150 executives. Led by Bob Transou, who engineered the more efficient power train process, the team devised ways for the company to streamline itself. The team itself was a direct contrast to Ford's old corporate culture. It was housed in a war room, a large open area filled with small desks and cubicles, with no private offices. The idea was to put all the decision makers in one place and force them to hash out decisions on the spot, rather than waste months passing around memos. All the team members had delegated their other responsibilities to completely dedicate their efforts to planning the reorganization. Everyone worked in their shirtsleeves, so it was impossible to distinguish vice presidents from underlings. This informal atmosphere was not an accident. Transou "wanted people to leave their corporate credentials at the door."[4]

The team had the blessing of top management, but it still had some history to overcome. Ford's last attempt at building a global car, the Mondeo, which eventually became the Ford Contour, the Mercury Mystique, and the Mondeo, took almost seven years to develop and cost $6 billion. Industry analysts doubted that Ford would ever recoup those development costs through sales. The team's challenge was to incorporate the lessons learned from the Mondeo into its new reorganization plan. The underlying objective was to lay the groundwork for a decade's worth of products all built from a common design and with great economies of scale.

Ford 2000

Ford 2000's initial imperative was to consolidate the North American and European operations. On January 1, 1995, the first part of Ford 2000 was implemented. Ford of Europe and Ford North America merged to form Ford Automotive Operations (FAO). (To give a frame of reference for the scale of this merger, Ford of Europe and Ford North America combine to be a $94 billion business. The Nabisco–RJR Reynolds merger was approximately $24 billion.) The new organization was divided into five vehicle program centers. Each vehicle program center (VPC) was to be responsible for the development, manufacture, marketing, and profitability of its specific Ford vehicles, no matter where they are sold.

The vehicle program centers are divided into small- and medium-sized front-wheel-drive cars, large front-

wheel-drive cars, rear-wheel-drive cars, and light and commercial trucks. Europe kept control of the development of small and medium cars because of its obvious expertise. Dearborn in the United States handles the rest. Although Europe only got one out of the five new VPCs, the European center has responsibility for developing vehicles in market segments that hold the biggest potential from Ford's global strategy and are expected to account for around 50 percent of world car sales by the next decade.

Each VPC has the capability to alter its product to suit regional markets. The formidable task of each VPC is to make everything under the hood the same and everything that has to do with taste and local regulations different and to do this in a cost-efficient manner. As Trotman puts it, "Even with under-the-skin components that may be identical, the design and feel of our vehicles can be made very different to suit local tastes."[5]

Ford believes the new organization will be successful, particularly with quicker adaptation to shifting customer demands. New-product time cycles were targeted to be uniformly under three years by 2000. Plant changeovers for new "global" models produced at various locations around the world are scheduled to follow each other in weeks, not months.[6] Extensive investment in computers and videoconferencing technology has been made to facilitate the process. Ford, with the help of the consulting firm Logica, has created its own Worldwide Integrated Purchasing System (WIPS). All of Ford's purchasing activities, which represent over 100,000 separate parts worth $40 billion, are on the workload management system.[7]

Organization Structure

What does the new Ford look like? The new Ford is a matrix organization (see Figure 1). Most employees report to two or more managers, one within a vehicle center team and one within a functional discipline such as finance or manufacturing. Instead of being temporarily assigned to work on a new Taurus, a brake engineer is now permanently assigned to a team to help develop a specific car for individual countries. Career development is the responsibility of the functional managers, while performance evaluation is the duty of the vehicle program team leader. By shifting the performance evaluation to the vehicle team leader, Ford wants to change the loyalties of its employees from their functional area to the car they are helping to build. This goal has been further reinforced by the co-location of people with their vehicle program teams.

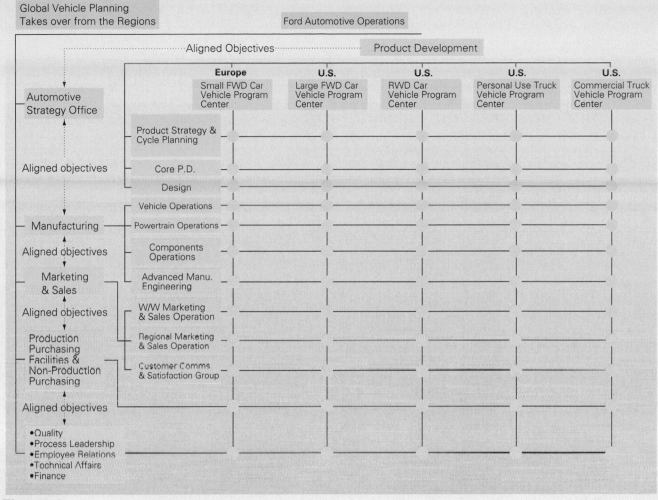

Figure 1

Ford's New Global Matrix Structure

Source: The Ford Motor Company.

Ford has learned lessons from other failed matrix organizations and has built in safeguards. They include:

- Making doubly sure that objectives are agreed on between the vehicle centers and the functional side of the organization.
- Specifying clearly the respective roles and responsibilities of individuals toward each side of the matrix.
- Changing appraisal and reward systems accordingly.
- Appointing only senior executives who have shown they can work collaboratively.
- Training everyone in the art of developing a cooperative matrix perspective, which largely replaces the need for policing.
- Introducing much more intensive and open communication.[8]

Transou hopes to make the matrix system work by ensuring that the structure includes accountability. "You need accountability," says Transou. "Those that have not succeeded with matrix management did not understand that. Without accountability it is always someone else's fault. There are excuses. There are no excuses in Ford 2000; it is very clear where responsibility is."[9]

Above the VPCs, decision making will be centralized through the creation of a global profit center for all automotive operations. Ed Hogenlocker, president of FAO, claims, "By centralizing decision making, we can take the broadest possible view of market opportunities, and we can develop products to serve multiple markets, vastly increasing the return on every product development dollar."[10]

Ford was attempting not only to change how it did business, but also its corporate culture. The Ford 2000 program trimmed the layers of management from 10 to 7 to destroy the delaying bureaucracy and facilitate the matrix system. Ford offered early retirement to a relatively small number of senior officials, including executives, managers, and professionals, approximately 15 percent of the top 2,500. "It'll be a leaner, hopefully much more efficient, faster, more nimble company than it is today and the management structure will reflect and cause it," Trotman said in 1994.[11]

Trotman conducted the reorganization in a very disciplined and principled manner to maximize the probability for success. Primarily, he got the entire company involved in the process. Although the team headed by Transou did much of the planning, it got hundreds of other employees in on the act. The principle was simple: Get the people who will have to live with changes involved in making the changes.[12]

Ford made a great effort to keep all its employees and the public informed of changes. Its public relations department published a weekly faxed newspaper, ran an electronic bulletin board, and broadcast a weekly in-house television show to keep everyone informed of the latest developments. It also held numerous employee meetings.

Ford expected confusion among its employees and attempted to manage it. Hundreds of careers were sidetracked as Ford flattened its hierarchy. In addition, Ford of Europe, which was once an autonomous unit, lost a significant amount of control. There was a notable fear by some European employees that FAO may ultimately stand for "For Americans Only." To ease these fears, members of the reorganization team made presentations to explain how the new organization would work.

Conclusion

Mr. Trotman set an eight-month schedule for revamping Ford. Most multinationals in other industries have taken a decade to shift their organizations gradually to global structures. To some observers, Ford chose a strange time to reorganize. Ford reported record earnings of $5.3 billion for fiscal year 1994 on top of record revenues of $128 billion. Trotman defended this criticism by saying that concentrating on change and improvement is a lot easier when times are good. "Now is the right time for such a change. The tools are there—computers and communications—and we have a strong balance sheet. If you make big changes when times are difficult, expediency often takes precedence."[13]

The benefits of the reorganization could be tremendous. Ford anticipated savings of up to $5 billion a year.[14] The reconstruction also created a more efficient Ford with fewer, global suppliers. Ford estimated that by cutting suppliers of everything but auto parts from 50,000 in 1995 to 5,000 by 1997, it would save $1 billion a year.[15]

Ultimately, the new Ford will have the flexibility to forcefully enter emerging markets. But real dangers are involved. Ford can potentially make itself too global by producing cars that cannot be cost effectively altered to meet local tastes. Can the global cars be kept affordable?

Discussion Questions

1. What other possible obstacles might Ford encounter as a global organization?

2. How important is the new matrix system in the success or failure of Ford 2000?

3. What did Trotman forget in the restructuring?

4. What other efficiencies might also be byproducts of Ford 2000?

5. How successful do you think this program will be in preparing Ford to enter emerging markets? What will be the key factors for success in entering these markets?

Notes

1. J. B. Treece, "Ford: Alex Trotman's Daring Strategy," *Business Week*, April 3, 1995, pp. 94–104.

2. K. Done, "Ford Maps Out a Global Ambition," *Financial Times*, April 3, 1995, p. 9.

3. A. Chamberlain, "Major Shakeup at Ford," *Toronto Star*, April 21, 1994, p. C1.

4. D. Sedgwick, "Ford's Redesigners," *Detroit News*, June 26, 1994, p. 1.

5. Done, "Ford Maps Out a Global Ambition."

6. E. Heinrich, "Ford Takes Historic Gamble," *Financial Post*, August 27, 1994, p. 8

7. "Logica Assists Ford Motor Company," *Business Wire*, May 9, 1995.

8. C. Lorenz, "Ford's Global Matrix Gamble," *Financial Times*, December 16, 1994, p. 14.

9. Done, "Ford Maps Out a Global Ambition."

10. Lorenz, "Ford's Global Matrix Gamble."

11. J. Szczensy, "Ford Exec Ranks to Be Halved," *Oakland Press*, October 15, 1994, p. 20.

12. D. Sedgwick, "Fixing Ford," *Detroit News*, September 18, 1994, p. D1.

13. "The World Car," *The Economist*, July 23, 1994, p. 69.

14. A. Lorenz, "Ford Drives to Win World Leadership, *Sunday Times*, January 1, 1995.

15. Treece, "Ford: Alex Trotman's Daring Strategy."

Orient Foods Ltd.: Business Development in China*

> If Ray Kroc [of McDonald's] were born Chinese, he would not have cooked burgers. He would have given them rice bowls in a spotless and clean environment at a good value.
>
> *Gil Hastings, 1995*

The Orient Foods office in Beijing hummed with activity. The staff was busy putting the final touches on the business plan, which was to be submitted for consideration to the Beijing city government the following day. Gil Hastings, the founder of the company, was optimistic. During the last year he had worked hard to turn his ideas into a real business. While owning and operating his own company had been a lifelong dream, he never imagined that it would be so far from his home in Ohio. Now it looked like he would make his first sale in the capital of China. But there was still a long way to go. Once the plan was approved by the city government, the real work of building a plant and operating a business would get started.

Gil Hastings

Gil Hastings had always been a high achiever. He was an outstanding scholar and athlete as a teenager. His passion for boxing made him the Golden Gloves boxing champion for the state of Ohio. He earned his MBA from Wharton and studied at the London School of Economics. He started his career at Procter & Gamble doing sales and brand management. Next, he went to work for PepsiCo, where he was soon promoted to vice president and regional general manager for Kentucky Fried Chicken, first in the South Central and then the Northeastern United States. This experience with modern food delivery systems would prove to be very helpful in China.

Gil later left PepsiCo to join Citibank Asia as a senior vice president for marketing & sales, bringing his consumer marketing experience to the banking industry. Based in Singapore, Gil successfully managed 34 businesses spread across 17 countries, with a sales force of 2,000, annual sales of over $1 billion, and a marketing budget of over $100 million. Gil's rise had been meteoric. At Citibank, Gil reported directly to the bank's worldwide chairman as part of a key task force driving Citibank's worldwide restructuring and performance improvement efforts.

In 1992, Gil was asked to join Hutchinson Whampoa Limited, one of Hong Kong's premier trading conglomerates to become the chief marketing and operations executive. In his position, Gil worked closely with the conglomerate's owner, Mr. Li Ka-Shing. In 1993, Gil started a project to research fast-food opportunities in China. Hutchinson had pursued a number of infrastructure investments in China, but now was eager to profit from China's burgeoning market for consumer goods. In China's main cities of Beijing, Guangzhou, and Shanghai, middle class had emerged. Small nuclear families, the result of China's one-child policy, still enjoyed subsidies for housing and welfare and had a large percentage of disposable income. Hutchinson asked Gil to research fast-food opportunities for 60 days and to come up with a product and business concept for China.

Researching the Chinese Fast-Food Market

Gil began personally visiting markets in Beijing, Shanghai, and Guangzhou. While he was armed with books about business in China, he relied more on his food industry experience to decipher what markets and products offered the most opportunity. In visiting retail food outlets, he was startled to find people eating food that was of poor quality and served in suspicious hygienic environments.

> For a culture that is absolutely passionate about food, I was dumbfounded at the quality that they were forced to consume. Chinese people are probably more passionate about food than any other culture on the planet, but the options in China are either very expensive or they are slop. By slop I mean food of a non-nutritious, unhygienic, poorly prepared kind. That was amazing to me. As we probed into it and did some research, we were also surprised by many people's assumption that consumers didn't mind the terrible quality, and that there was no huge latent consumer demand in China for higher quality

*This case was developed by Tim Meade, MBA student, with the advice of Professor Richard Moxon, as the basis for class discussion. The authors appreciate greatly the cooperation of the executives from the company described in the case. All names used in the case are fictional. Copyright © 1995 by Tim Meade and Richard W. Moxon.

food. But actually, we felt that Chinese expectations with regard to food were higher than in the West. It was just that they could not get it.

By the early 1990s, many of the West's well-known fast-food companies were already established in China. Kentucky Fried Chicken was the first American company to invest, with its first restaurant opening in Beijing in late 1987. Since then KFC had expanded to six outlets in Beijing, four in Shanghai, and others scattered among smaller cities such as Xian, Tianjin, and Dalian. Other companies soon followed, including Dairy Queen, Pizza Hut, and Japan's Yoshinoya. Most of these products were accepted enthusiastically by Chinese consumers, although they mostly enjoyed them as a novelty, visiting on special occasions such as weekends, family outings, or dates. None of the foreign companies was dominant in the fast-food market.

Gil looked at the operations of foreign fast-food companies and came up with what he thought was a better idea. In designing his concept for China, he was wary of what he called the "shoehorn approach."

> Most US and European companies that enter China are used to taking the concept, getting out the big shoehorn, and squeezing their concept to fit China, maybe tweaking it just a little here and there. But if you believe the premise that China is going to be a major global economy, then you should be doing real marketing. There are 12 billion consumers. You should go find out what they want and then give it to them, not try to jam your own concept down their throats. So the trick is to go in and do some research. It's much better to find the need in China and try to fill it instead of trying to convince the Chinese of a need that they may not feel.

What Gil found out was that there was a huge need for affordable food appealing to the Chinese palate. Virtually all the existing international fast-food enterprises in China served Western-style food. It seemed to Gil that no company had taken the time and effort to ask Chinese consumers if they would prefer Chinese-style products. Even well-known Hong Kong fast-food companies, with experience in Chinese-style products, were not aggressively pursuing the mainland Chinese market. Gil decided that there must be opportunities to fill this void.

> Palates don't change usually after the age of 12, so you have a huge population that is not going to eat burgers as a regular meal. If Ray Kroc were born Chinese, he would not have cooked burgers. He would have given them rice bowls in a spotless and clean environment at a good value.

The one foreign company that was selling Chinese fast food was California Beef Noodle King. The company was founded by a Chinese-American who main-

tained control by selling a mixture of spices and seasonings to his franchisees. The firm had succeeded in establishing close to 50 franchises in northeast China, and its products appealed to the Chinese palate. But like many foreign companies in China, it had seen its concept and trademark copied and abused. By 1994, while consumers still lined up for beef noodles, the company's reputation had suffered. From the point of view of the Chinese consumer, California Beef Noodle King was just another local fast-food company.

The entry of McDonald's to China in 1990 had elevated competition in fast food to a new level. By that time, KFC's outlets were starting to show wear and tear from three years of serving millions of customers. Like many businesses in China, KFC was facing challenges in maintaining its international standards of cleanliness and appearance. In contrast, everything about McDonald's was top grade, and the company seemed to have spared no expense in outfitting its restaurants. In Beijing, McDonald's first outlet was located at possibly the most prestigious intersection in the city, within walking distance of Tiananmen Square and right across from the Beijing Hotel. McDonald's was able to offer consumers a clean and pleasant environment, including air conditioning and high-quality lighting and music, international standards in product quality and taste, and courteous and friendly service. McDonald's established a standard that customers learned to appreciate and eventually, demand from other companies. In fact, some foreigners in China joked that McDonald's was the only restaurant in Beijing where you could have decent Western food that was not too expensive. By 1994, McDonald's had many outlets in Beijing.

While McDonald's was very successful in China, most people could not afford to visit its restaurants even once a week. An average meal such as a Big Mac, drink, and fries cost over $2, while the average salary for people in Beijing was just over $100 per month. One reason for the high cost was that many inputs had to be imported. Although China had made great leaps in food technology, finding high-quality local sources was still a challenge. KFC had a minority share of a chicken farm in Beijing, while McDonald's convinced its traditional suppliers such as Simplot to come to China to upgrade potato and lettuce supplies. However, their Western-style menus still forced these companies to import a substantial amount of their inputs, driving up their costs. Gil Hastings hoped to be able to offer more affordable meals. To do so, he would have to find the most competitive Chinese suppliers of protein, vegetables, starch, and seasonings.

Like many foreign companies operating in China, McDonald's focused its marketing on children. Advertising catered to children, promising fun and happiness, and McDonald's installed playrooms and birthday rooms in all its restaurants. McDonald's realized that China's children influenced many of the purchase decisions within the family. China's one-child policy had resulted in the "Little Emperor Syndrome," where these only children were overindulged by their parents and relatives. Gil recognized the importance of the children's market, but he was also aware the products offered by American fast-food companies were not as well accepted by older consumers. On his trips to McDonald's and KFC, he saw children eating hamburgers, fried chicken, and apple pies, but he saw relatively few parents consuming these products. This was one more reason to come up with a concept and product that appealed directly to Chinese palates.

As Gil concluded his initial market research, he became convinced that as China changed, its consumers would demand more choices, especially in the fast-food industry. He concluded that there was not going to be just one successful fast-food restaurant in China; there were going to 50. Much of what McDonald's or KFC offered had nothing to do with the food. It was convenient, it was fast, it was a pleasant and clean environment and it was affordable. But it was hard to find a Chinese food restaurant with these characteristics.

Striking Off on His Own

Sixty days after starting his research, Gil presented to Hutchinson Whampoa his idea for a fast-food business serving products appealing to the Chinese palate. By the time of Gil's presentation, however, Hutchinson had decided that it was going to put a hold temporarily on all new projects. The company had expanded at a rapid pace, and many of the existing businesses demanded more attention. Gil explained:

> They chose not to put any money in new ventures because of pressures on other business. I was kicked upstairs in effect and made the chief marketing operating officer for Hutchinson Whampoa, working for Simon Murray. I agreed to this with the proviso that we would get another run at food when things loosened up more at the company.

While Gil continued to work hard for Hutchinson Whampoa, in the back of his mind he was eager to pursue the Chinese fast-food venture. When his boss and mentor, Simon Murray, decided to leave the company to join Deutsche Bank, Gil decided that it was time to strike out on his own.

> Simon Murray decided to leave in August 1993. I had continued to pursue the fast-food idea and decided that the best way was to do it on my own. Simon also urged me to

become an entrepreneur and volunteered to be one of the investors in the project.

Without the need to report to anyone else, Gil was free to define the business concept according to his own analysis and research. The marketing concept was simple—fast-food restaurants serving affordable, Chinese-style products in an efficient, clean, and pleasant environment. In short, it was Chinese products served in a Western manner. The operational concept was equally simple. The company would centrally cook products that would be quick-frozen before shipment to retail outlets. Such heat-and-serve foods were becoming standard in the Western food industry and practiced by firms such as Taco Bell. Gil explained the reasoning behind this idea:

> I know from my food experience in the United States that you should not be preparing anything on site anymore. The first reason is consistency. The second reason is asset turnover—equipment utilization in most fast-food restaurants in America is about 20 percent. If you centralize your equipment, you can run it for two shifts and get your equipment utilization up to about 80 percent. A third reason is rental space. In the US there is usually not a problem with rent, but in China the rents are exorbitant.

While the major business opportunity of interest to Gil was retail fast food, he also realized that this was not likely to be highly favored by the Chinese government. So he was alert to other opportunities that might curry government support. Early in his research, Gil attended a Beijing trade exposition. There he met Zhang Zi Li, a Beijing city government official. Gil explained to Zhang that he was researching the food retailing business in China and asked if there were any areas where China needed assistance and development. Zhang thought over Gil's question before answering:

> Actually, in China we have found it difficult to develop and upgrade our school lunches. With both parents now working, people have less time to prepare meals. On the other hand, some children are eating more non-nutritious food and are growing fat as a result. We realize that we need to improve our school lunch service in order to solve these problems.

Gil listened with interest and told the official that he would make it a point to research opportunities for cooperation in this area. Although he had only recently been exposed to business in China, he learned quickly that in order to receive support from the government for your business, it was important to identify an area where your business could help China. He would later recall:

> China asked for our help on developing a school lunch program. From day one, we have been trying to help China

on that issue. It's an emotional issue for China; they have been trying to solve it for over a decade. They recognize the link between nutrition and IQ development as well as physical development.

Gil decided to aggressively pursue the development of a school lunch program. He felt that this would not only contribute to China, but also had the potential to provide valuable experience and to develop a reputation. The entire institutional market—schools, factories, and other organizations—offered great opportunity with very little competition. Maybe a reputation in this field could be leveraged into the retail fast-food business.

Finding Investors and Partners

Rounding up investors turned out to be easy. Simon Murray became one of them, as well as a director of the company. Gil also got the attention of a well-known Hong Kong venture capital company that had helped finance the entry to Asia of companies such as McDonald's and IKEA.

It took all of three seconds to convince them to invest. They understood fast food, they understood Asia, and they understood what it takes. It became obvious that if you could take the most recent developments in US fast food and tailor a menu to the Chinese, you could be successful. This was not going to be *gweilo* (foreign) food; we would have Chinese master chefs that understand the implications of a cook-chill process. So they saw the opportunities. They also came up with the name of Orient Foods. We were surprised to find that no one had registered such a name in Hong Kong.

With one key investor interested, Gil set out to find a partner who could bring technology, skills, and food industry experience to the venture. Although he had plenty of management experience from his days at PepsiCo, Gil needed a partner who could execute his concept. He was looking for a company experienced in cook-chill-reheat processing, and that also understood Chinese foods.

I discovered Ling Ling foods by word of mouth within the food industry. They are one of the few companies on the planet that knows how to do it. They are doing a preprepared, cook-freeze-thaw product sold out of delicatessens in American supermarkets. You reheat the food at home and it tastes as good as freshly made.

Ling Ling was based in New Jersey and sold its products to supermarkets in New York, New Jersey, and Philadelphia. The company had no experience in China. Gil's first meeting with Ling Ling was memorable:

At the meeting here I was one American guy, living in Hong Kong, meeting with 13 members of the Ling family in a Chinese restaurant in Chinatown, in New York City, where the American guy explained the China opportunity to the overseas Chinese in Chinatown. It was an interesting meeting; in fact, a little bizarre. But they bought into the project as an investment partner.

With the key investors in place, Gil's next decision was whether to also seek a Chinese partner to form a joint venture or to establish the project as a wholly foreign-owned enterprise. Twenty years since China first permitted foreign firms to invest, most American firms still operated with joint ventures, often being persuaded to do so by the Chinese government. Gil was convinced, however, that complete foreign ownership was crucial to the success of his venture.

Initially, I was considering a JV but then, after consulting with a number of potential partners, I started to have some second thoughts. Joint ventures run into problems on the partner side. The Chinese expect to participate fully in most aspects of the company, including building the business, which might involve changing the concept. We thought that for this concept to work, it would require laser-beam focus in order to maintain its integrity.

As far as Gil could find out, there were no wholly foreign-owned enterprises (WFOE) in the food industry in China. Even McDonald's and KFC were joint ventures in their retail businesses. Approval of such a project would be unprecedented. It was obvious that the company would have to take a "give and take" approach to the business application. China would not approve a WFOE in the food-industry without Orient Foods becoming a contributor to the development of the food processing industry in China.

Gil felt that the idea of the school lunch program offered the best hope for convincing the government of his contribution. Gil began developing a network of nutrition experts in Hong Kong and the United States and started working with a variety of Chinese government organizations in the areas of nutrition and child welfare. These efforts received broad support. Malnutrition and obesity were recent phenomena in China. China had tried on its own to resolve the school lunch problem, but it was unable to develop meals that were both affordable and nutritious. As a result, the government was receptive to assistance. This made Gil optimistic that a WFOE application could be approved.

The ownership plan for Orient Foods included the Hong Kong venture capital firm at 40 percent, Simon Murray's investment at 10 percent, Ling Ling at 30 percent, and Gil Hastings with the remaining 20 percent.

Building the Start-up Organization

After formally establishing Orient Foods in Hong Kong, Gil began working to put together a management team. He defined his own role to be the company architect and entrepreneur. He would design and adapt strategies that would result in a successful business concept. He would also continue to seek funding from investment banks in Hong Kong and the United States. By nature, Gil was aggressive, and for this business he felt that he needed to implement his plans as fast as possible so as to preempt competition and establish the brand while this was still relatively inexpensive. He often talked about the difference in costs between building a brand in the United States and Asia:

> In the States, it is estimated that building a successful brand costs at least $100 million. In Asia, the costs can be as little as $10 million. Now is the time to build a brand, while the market is still underdeveloped.

While Gil was the entrepreneur, he knew that he needed strong managers to refine and implement the business plan. His first hire would be a manager to be in charge of operations in Beijing. This person would have to find factory space, develop contacts with potential customers, and make the right government connections to ensure the success of the business application. While studying Chinese in Hong Kong, his teacher helped introduce him to the person he would hire for this job.

> My teacher heard that we were doing food in China and said that maybe her mother could help. I asked where her mother lived and she said "New Jersey." "OK, maybe I should meet with her," I said. "She doesn't speak English." "Hmm . . ." But I thought, "Why not? I have a terrific Mandarin teacher, so I'll give it a shot." So I met with her mother, Margaret Zhang, found out she was a terrific lady who was very driven, and hired her as our Beijing manager. From the first meeting in December, we have been on a rocket sled.

Margaret Zhang brought strong discipline, an iron will, and a commanding presence to the company. Born in Beijing before 1949, trained as a classical pianist, and with a traditional education, she was well-suited to building and managing contacts with government officials. She had emigrated first to Hong Kong where she worked in an import-export business and then to the United States where she finished raising her children. She and her husband set up a business importing cookware from China to department stores in the United States. After her children had grown, Margaret was

looking for an opportunity to return to China to participate in the expanding economic opportunities. Gil liked her drive and loyalty, two qualities he saw as necessary to executing his vision. As he would do for all employees, he designed for her a performance-based compensation package.

While Margaret worked on the business license, Gil relied on Ling Ling to come up with a design and equipment recommendations for a pilot kitchen. Willie Ling, the youngest of the 13 Ling siblings, made his first trip to Beijing in March 1994 to commence work on the project. Like Gil, Willie brought a "get it done" attitude to Orient Foods. He had worked in the food industry since his early 20s, when he quit school to begin his own restaurant supply business. Later he was marketing manager for a major hotel and casino in Atlantic City before he rejoined the family business. Willie eventually earned a certificate in food science. He was looking for some new challenges at the time that Gil approached Ling Ling, and with his entrepreneurial spirit, Willie was a natural choice to be the plant manager for Orient Foods. He and Gil complemented each other. Gil worried about the big picture, the grand design, while Willie knew how to take Gil's ideas and put them into action.

Learning by Doing: The Pilot Kitchen and Product Testing

In December 1993, Margaret moved to Beijing to begin working for Orient Foods. Her hotel room was the Orient Foods unofficial office in Beijing. Her first responsibilities were to develop the application for a business license and to find a location for a pilot kitchen where Orient Foods could begin testing its concept. This dual-track approach contrasted with how most companies approached a start-up in China. Most firms first worked on the license and then proceeded to execution. Orient Foods sought to move on both fronts simultaneously. This strategy echoed Gil's belief that in China, the most effective way of learning is by doing.

> Our vision was pretty well all set, we were going to be doing 1 million plus meals a day retail by the end of this decade, and the business model was decided. Once the vision is there, then the trick is to learn by doing. We pushed the learning envelope continuously by just throwing ourselves forward. "Just go, do it, learn" was our motto.
>
> The degrees of freedom on attack are almost 360. The degrees of freedom on defense are almost always very limited. The point is to always move quickly, learn by doing, and just keep going forward. Thus, we took on quite a bit

of risk but kept always being on the attack. The second aspect of this approach is sort of a corollary, to learn in very small increments and very rapidly. That way you fail a lot, but you fail quick and small. No matter what, you know you are going to fail in China, it's just a question of what investment multiple.

Rather than setting up a big factory, we decided that we would set up a pilot kitchen and evolve it into a pilot factory and eventually into our first factory. This would allow us to get experience with the menu, product development, and production simultaneously almost from day one. We had the plant development running almost in parallel with the approval for our business license. The result was we put up a pilot kitchen within three months of starting in China.

When Willie Ling arrived to face Beijing's cold winter and fierce winds, Margaret had identified a professional school that was willing to rent out a room that could be converted into a pilot kitchen. Orient Foods was entering China at a time when all local Chinese organizations, whether they were commercial, political, or educational, were having to *xia hai* (literally "dive into the big sea") and become economically self-sufficient in line with the recently proclaimed "socialist market economy." Schools were receiving less government support and were experimenting with various approaches to earn money. Some government officials introduced Margaret to a school where students from all over China learned home economics, including hygiene and basic food processing skills. They were willing to rent out a kitchen that was no longer in use. While the kitchen was in bad shape, Willie could see that with some repair and new equipment this could serve as Orient Foods' first pilot kitchen, where they could cook products for market testing. The school officials agreed to permit Orient to employ some of its students on a part-time basis. In return for the use of the kitchen, the school officials held out for a verbal commitment that once Orient Foods had a business license, it would upgrade its commitment to the school. Orient hoped that cooperation with the school could eventually turn the pilot plant into a training center.

It took just three weeks to secure equipment suppliers and a construction team to transform the rented kitchen space from an unsanitary, dark, and dingy room to a well-lit, clean, and comfortable pilot kitchen. By this time, Gil, Willie, and Margaret had communicated Orient's "get it done" philosophy to the company's burgeoning staff in Beijing. Sourcing most equipment and food inputs locally, the young office staff quickly learned about suppliers for raw materials and food processing equipment. Knowledge about which local inputs were

competitive, and which should be imported, would be useful later when Orient began work on a large-scale factory. While the staff shopped for freezers, cutting tables, and sinks, Willie started to visit Beijing's numerous public markets and food wholesalers to see what products were available. Working night and day with construction teams that were also new to the business of food factories, Orient completed refurbishing the kitchen within its target of three weeks. The tight deadline was designed to impress the investors, who were anxious to see tangible progress.

With a pilot kitchen and a staff in place, Willie called on his 13 years of food service experience to develop products for testing. Working with Gil, the two came up with a number of Chinese-style Western products for the initial tests, all products to be served over rice. (The Chinese government bureau responsible for school lunches had a policy that all lunches must include rice). They decided to test a variety of chicken products, a chili concept, and two types of pork dishes.

The first round of taste tests were held in June 1994 at the pilot kitchen. Working with a market research company based in Singapore, Willie and his staff, assisted by some of the students from the professional school, cooked up over 200 servings of six products. The market research company brought in a variety of samplers, from adults to schoolchildren. The results were encouraging. Consumers perceived the products as new and different, and all products had high purchase intent. In some test categories, Orients products had higher appeal than McDonald's or KFC. The results only confirmed Gil's original thesis that there was strong demand for fast-food products appealing to the Chinese palate. The initial tests would be followed by another round of testing three months later. Meanwhile, Gil used these first results in his presentations to investors, and Margaret was busy finding organizations interested in Orient's institutional feeding program.

Submitting the Application

By July of 1994, Orient had completed its feasibility study and had found factory space in the northern part of the city near the airport. The local government at that site introduced them to an empty grain storage facility that had been built by a Japanese company for a business that never materialized. The grain storage space could be converted to a food processing factory. The local government had also agreed to sponsor Orient's business application to the Beijing city authorities. Orient's staff in Beijing and Hong Kong had also prepared the company's articles of association and the other materials needed for the business license application. Figure 1 contains a list of the materials that were required.

Everything was ready for submission, but the question remained as to whether the Ministry of Foreign Trade and Economic Cooperation (MOFTEC) would approve an application for a WFOE in the retail food business. One of the biggest obstacles was the export requirement, according to which a WFOE in this business should export 50 percent of its output. But how could the company export ready-to-serve meals? While a consultant had told them that the government was not stringent in this policy, Orient's target of 15 percent exports would probably seem low.

> To Beijing's MOFTEC, approving us as a wholly foreign-owned business would require somebody in the bureaucracy to take a personal risk. This was not impossible, but in order to do so they would need a powerful justification. Unfortunately, our initial application did not provide enough ammunition.

Within 24 hours of submitting the application, Orient received word that its application could not be approved in its present form, and that even with a 50 percent export commitment, the chances of approval were slim. Officials reminded Orient that other food firms were joint ventures and wondered why Orient was entitled to special privileges.

Perplexed and frustrated, Gil and Willie sat down to come up with a solution. Willie suggested that maybe Orient could export sauces, perhaps to Ling Ling in the United States or to food wholesalers in Hong Kong and Southeast Asia. Gil liked the idea, but doubted that the volume would ever reach 50 percent of plant output. After all, their goal for the core business were aggressive—a million meals per day by the year 2000. They decided, nevertheless, to go ahead and include the 50 percent goal in their application.

Our feeling was let's first get this approved, and then we will find a solution to the export requirement.

Although MOFTEC officials were urging Orient to consider the JV option, Gil was intent on getting WFOE approval. He asked Margaret to seek advice from some government officials and to let them know that Orient's school lunch was the reason they deserved WFOE status. Working through the nutrition education bureau, Margaret was able to bring their situation to an important Beijing city official.

> We probably would not have been approved, but then we wrote a letter to a Vice Party Secretary in Beijing who is a bit of a visionary on school lunches. We said that for us to develop a school lunch program that is tailored to China's needs, we need to be a wholly foreign-owned enterprise. This way, we could develop quickly and protect the integrity of the concept. He wrote back with a letter of support, which he also sent to MOFTEC. He stated that our concept would help future generations of Chinese and should be approved. Within 24 hours we were approved.

Data from the successful business license application is included in Figure 2, and a timeline for the project up to the summer of 1994 is shown in Figure 3.

As Gil Hastings reflected on his experience in the Orient Foods project so far and began thinking about the next steps, he concluded:

> There are two strategies. One is to have a vision and continue to work against the vision. The second is to learn by doing. My philosophy is that you can not study your way to success in China. That is absolutely impossible. That does not mean to skip the research. Just do it quickly.

There was bound to be a lot more learning as Orient Foods actually launched its new venture.

Figure 1

Required Items for Orient Foods Business License Application

1. Application for the Establishment of a Wholly Foreign-Owned Enterprise in Beijing, China
2. Feasibility Study of Orient Foods Ltd.
3. Articles of Association of Orient Foods Ltd.
4. Lease Contract between the Sponsoring Party and Orient Foods Ltd.
5. Written Notice of Commission of Foreign Trade & Economic Cooperation of Sponsoring County
6. Approval Notice for the Name Registration of the Foreign Invested Enterprise
7. Certificate of Approval for the Establishment of a Wholly Foreign-Owned Enterprise in China

Business Scope

a. China sourcing and export of food products.

b. Production, distribution, and retail/restaurant sales of food products.

c. Consulting in nutritional and food commercial systems.

Scale of Production

Large-scale/mass production.

Capacity up to 6 million kg. per year.

Total Amount of Investment

US $ 3,500,000.

Amount of Registered Capital

US $2,450,000.

Project Conditions

a. *Scope*

Production and sale of specially prepared nutritious food.

b. *Production scale*

Maximum 20,000 kg. of food per day.

c. *Raw materials and their sources*

60 percent to be sourced in China.

40 percent imported from United States (packaging, hygiene chemicals, and selected spices).

d. *Product uses*

Food for human consumption/nourishment.

e. *Market for sales*

Local residents, workers, schools, institutions, international tourists, and export markets.

f. *Export ratio*

Gradually to achieve 50 percent.

g. *Plan for the balancing of foreign exchange expenditures and receipts*

Materials to be sourced 60 percent locally.

Exports will exceed imports, creating a foreign exchange surplus.

h. *Staff and workers*

Total	153
Foreign staff and workers	4
Management personnel	6
Technical personnel	7
Workers	136

(continued)

Figure 2

Project Characteristics: Excerpts from the Business License Application

Discussion Questions

1. Evaluate Orient Foods' product market concept (Chinese-style prepared food delivered with Western professionalism, institutional feeding). How powerful is this concept? How feasible? Will Chinese consumers accept it?

2. Do you think that Orient Foods will be able to compete successfully in China? Why?

3. Evaluate Orient Foods' operational concept (centralized food preparation, some vertical integration). Does this make sense in the Chinese context?

4. Does Orient Foods' "learning by doing" approach to business development in China make sense? Why?

5. Do you think that Gil Hastings adopted the right approach in his dealings with Chinese government authorities?

Schedule of Construction

a. Year One
- Completion and fit out of 2,160-square-meter manufacturing plant.
- Completion and fit out of retail outlets/kiosks.

b. Year Two
- Addition of 50 retail points (restaurants/kiosks).

Quantity of Production Planned

a. Year 1—1,500,000 kg.

b. Year 2—3,000,000 kg.

c. Year 3—4,500,000 kg.

Training Plan for Chinese Staff and Workers

a. Orient Foods will establish a full food preparation & production training facility.

b. All workers will receive training prior to working on production line.

c. Ongoing training will be provided to all workers for full development in production techniques.

d. Workers will receive training in high-technology food preparation equipment from the United States and Europe.

e. Workers will be trained in nutritional aspects of food technology.

f. Workers will be trained in mass production/fast-food cooking and food preparation techniques.

g. Workers will be trained in hygiene and safety standards in food production/preparation and handling.

h. Workers will be trained in freezing and chilling techniques for mass production of food.

i. Workers will receive training in high-technology packaging techniques.

j. Workers will be trained in high technology food distribution techniques.

Term of Operation of the Wholly Foreign-Owned Enterprise

30 years

Figure 2 (concluded)

Figure 3

Timeline of Orient Foods Project

March 1993: Gil Hastings begins researching retail food opportunities in China for Hutchinson Whampoa Ltd.

May 1993: Gil presents his findings for a Chinese fast-food business to Hutchinson Whampoa management.

June 1993: Hutchinson Whampoa announces that it will not pursue any new business ventures for three months.

September 1993: Gil leaves Hutchinson Whampoa to pursue Orient Foods venture.

November 1993: Orient Foods incorporation.

December 1993: Margaret Zhang moves to Beijing and opens Orient Foods office.

March 1994: Orient signs rent contract for first pilot factory.

April 1994: Orient completes refurbishing of pilot factory.

June 1994: First round of taste tests.

August 1994: Orient is awarded a business license by the Ministry of Foreign Trade and Economic Cooperation for a Wholly Foreign-Owned Enterprise.

KENTUCKY FRIED CHICKEN: LATIN AMERICAN STRATEGY*

Introduction

Kentucky Fried Chicken Corporation (KFC) was the world's largest chicken restaurant chain and third largest fast-food chain. KFC held over 55 percent of the US market in terms of sales and operated over 10,200 restaurants worldwide in 1998. It opened 376 new restaurants in 1997 (more than one restaurant a day) and operated in 79 countries. One of the first fast-food chains to go international during the late 1960s, KFC has developed one of the world's most recognizable brands.

Japan, Australia, and the United Kingdom accounted for the greatest share of KFC's international expansion during the 1970s and 1980s. During the 1990s, KFC turned its attention to other international markets that offered significant opportunities for growth. China, with a population of over 1 billion, and Europe, with a population roughly equal to the United States, offered such opportunities. Latin America also offered a unique opportunity because of the size of its markets, its common language and culture, and its geographical proximity to the United States. Mexico was of particular interest because of the North American Free Trade Agreement (NAFTA), a free trade zone between Canada, the United States, and Mexico that went into effect in 1994.

Before 1990, KFC expanded into Latin America primarily through company-owned restaurants in Mexico and Puerto Rico. Company-owned restaurants gave KFC greater control over its operations than franchised or licensed restaurants. By 1995, KFC had also established company-owned restaurants in Venezuela and Brazil. In addition, it had established franchised units in numerous Caribbean countries. During the early 1990s, KFC shifted to a two-tiered strategy in Latin America. First, it established 29 franchised restaurants in Mexico following enactment of Mexico's new franchise law in 1990. This allowed KFC to expand outside of its company restaurant base in Mexico City, Guadalajara, and Monterrey. KFC was one of many US fast-food, retail, and hotel chains to begin franchising in Mexico following the new franchise law. Second, KFC began an aggressive franchise building program in South America. By 1998, it was operating franchised restaurants in 32 Latin American countries. Much of this growth was in Brazil, Chile, Colombia, Ecuador, and Peru.

Company History

Fast-food franchising was still in its infancy in 1952 when Harland Sanders began his travels across the United States to speak with prospective franchisees about his "Colonel Sanders Recipe Kentucky Fried Chicken." By 1960, "Colonel" Sanders had granted KFC franchises to over 200 take-home retail outlets and restaurants across the United States. He had also succeeded in establishing a number of franchises in Canada. By 1963, the number of KFC franchises had risen to over 300 and revenues had reached $500 million.

By 1964, at the age of 74, the Colonel had tired of running the day-to-day operations of his business and was eager to concentrate on public relations issues. Therefore, he sought out potential buyers, eventually deciding to sell the business to two Louisville businessmen—Jack Massey and John Young Brown, Jr.—for $2 million. The Colonel stayed on as a public relations man and goodwill ambassador for the company.

During the next five years, Massey and Brown concentrated on growing KFC's franchise system across the United States. In 1966, they took KFC public and the company was listed on the New York Stock Exchange. By the late 1960s, a strong foothold had been established in the United States, and Massey and Brown turned their attention to international markets. In 1969, a joint venture was signed with Mitsuoishi Shoji Kaisha, Ltd., in Japan, and the rights to operate 14 existing KFC franchises in England were acquired. Subsidiaries were also established in Hong Kong, South Africa, Australia, New Zealand, and Mexico. By 1971, KFC had 2,450 franchises and 600 company-owned restaurants worldwide and was operating in 48 countries.

Heublein, Inc.

In 1971, KFC entered negotiations with Heublein, Inc., to discuss a possible merger. The decision to seek a merger candidate was partially driven by Brown's desire to pursue other interests, including a political career (Brown was elected governor of Kentucky in 1977). Several months later, Heublein acquired KFC. Heublein was in the business of producing vodka, mixed cocktails, dry gin, cordials, beer, and other alcoholic beverages. However, Heublein had little experience in the restau-

---

*This case was written by Jeffrey A. Krug, an assistant professor of international business at the University of Illinois at Urbana-Champaign. He was previously manager of planning and analysis for Latin America at Kentucky Fried Chicken Corporation in Louisville.

rant business. Conflicts quickly erupted between Colonel Sanders, who continued to act in a public relations capacity, and Heublein management. Colonel Sanders became increasingly distraught over quality control issues and restaurant cleanliness. By 1977, new restaurant openings had slowed to about 20 per year. Few restaurants were being remodeled, and service quality had declined.

In 1977, Heublein sent in a new management team to redirect KFC's strategy. A "back-to-the-basics" strategy was immediately implemented. New unit construction was discontinued until existing restaurants could be upgraded and operating problems eliminated. Restaurants were refurbished, an emphasis was placed on cleanliness and service, marginal products were eliminated, and product consistency was reestablished. By 1982, KFC had succeeded in establishing a successful strategic focus and was again aggressively building new units.

R.J. Reynolds Industries, Inc.

In 1982, R.J. Reynolds Industries, Inc., (RJR) merged Heublein into a wholly owned subsidiary. The merger with Heublein represented part of RJR's overall corporate strategy of diversifying into unrelated businesses, including energy, transportation, food, and restaurants. RJR's objective was to reduce its dependence on the tobacco industry, which had driven RJR sales since its founding in North Carolina in 1875. Sales of cigarettes and tobacco products, while profitable, were declining because of reduced consumption in the United States. This was mainly the result of an increased awareness among Americans about the negative health consequences of smoking.

RJR had no more experience in the restaurant business than did Heublein. However, it decided to take a hands-off approach to managing KFC. Whereas Heublein had installed its own top management at KFC headquarters, RJR left KFC management largely intact, believing that existing KFC managers were better qualified to operate KFC's businesses than were its own managers. In doing so, RJR avoided many of the operating problems that plagued Heublein. This strategy paid off for RJR as KFC continued to expand aggressively and profitably under RJR ownership. In 1985, RJR acquired Nabisco Corporation for $4.9 billion. Nabisco sold a variety of well-known cookies, crackers, cereals, confectioneries, snacks, and other grocery products. The merger with Nabisco represented a decision by RJR to concentrate its diversification efforts on the consumer foods industry. It subsequently divested many of its nonconsumer food businesses. RJR sold KFC to PepsiCo one year later.

PepsiCo, Inc.

PepsiCo first entered the restaurant business in 1977 when it acquired Pizza Hut's 3,200-unit restaurant system. Taco Bell was merged into a division of PepsiCo in 1978. The restaurant business complemented PepsiCo's consumer product orientation. The marketing of fast food followed many of the same patterns as the marketing of soft drinks and snack foods. Therefore, PepsiCo believed that its management skills could be easily transferred among its three business segments. This was compatible with PepsiCo's practice of frequently moving managers among its business units as a way of developing future top executives. PepsiCo's restaurant chains also provided an additional outlet for the sale of Pepsi soft drinks. Pepsi-Cola soft drinks and fast-food products could also be marketed together in the same television and radio segments, thereby providing higher returns for each advertising dollar. To complete its diversification into the restaurant segment, PepsiCo acquired Kentucky Fried Chicken Corporation from RJR-Nabisco for $841 million in 1986. The acquisition of KFC gave PepsiCo the leading market share in chicken (KFC), pizza (Pizza Hut), and Mexican food (Taco Bell), three of the four largest and fastest-growing segments within the US fast-food industry.

PepsiCo's strategy of diversifying into three distinct but related markets—soft drinks, snack foods, and fast-food restaurants—created one of the world's largest consumer products companies and a portfolio of some of the world's most recognizable brands. Between 1990 and 1996, PepsiCo grew at an annual rate of over 10 percent, surpassing $31 billion in sales in 1996. However, PepsiCo's sales growth masked troubles in its fast-food businesses. Operating margins (profit as a percent of sales) at Pepsi-Cola and Frito Lay averaged 12 and 17 percent between 1990 and 1996, respectively. During the same period, margins at KFC, Pizza Hut, and Taco Bell fell from an average of over 8 percent in 1990 to a little more than 4 percent in 1996. Declining margins in the fast-food chains reflected increasing maturity in the US fast-food industry, more intense competition among US fast-food competitors, and the aging of KFC and Pizza Hut's restaurant base. As a result, PepsiCo's restaurant chains absorbed nearly one-half of PepsiCo's annual capital spending during the 1990s. However, they generated less than one-third of PepsiCo's cash flows. Therefore, cash was diverted from PepsiCo's soft drink and snack food businesses to its restaurant businesses. This reduced PepsiCo's return on assets, made it more difficult to compete effectively with Coca-Cola, and hurt its stock price. In 1997, PepsiCo spun off its restaurant businesses into a new company called Tricon Global Restaurants, Inc. (see Table 1). The new company was based in KFC's headquarters in Louisville, Kentucky.

Table 1

Tricon Global Restaurants, Inc., Organizational Chart (1998)

Fast-Food Market

Because of the aggressive pace of new restaurant construction in the United States during the 1970s and 1980s, opportunities to expand domestically through new restaurant construction in the 1990s were limited. Restaurant chains that did build new restaurants found that the higher cost of purchasing prime locations resulted in immense pressure to increase annual per restaurant sales, in order to cover higher initial investment costs. Many restaurants began to expand into international markets as an alternative to continued domestic expansion. In contrast to the US market, international markets offered large customer bases with comparatively little competition. However, only a few US restaurant chains had defined aggressive strategies for penetrating international markets by 1998.

Three restaurant chains that had established aggressive international strategies were McDonald's, KFC, and Pizza Hut. McDonald's operated the largest number of restaurants. In 1998, it operated 23,132 restaurants in 109 countries (10,409 restaurants were located outside of the United States). In comparison, KFC, Pizza Hut, and Taco Bell together operated 29,712 restaurants in 79, 88, and 17 countries, respectively (9,126 restaurants were located outside of the United States). Of these four chains, KFC operated the greatest percentage of its restaurants (50 percent) outside of the United States. McDonald's, Pizza Hut, and Taco Bell operated 45, 31, and 2 percent of their units outside the United States. KFC opened its first restaurant outside of the United

States in the late 1950s. By the time PepsiCo acquired KFC in 1986, KFC was already operating restaurants in 55 countries. KFC's early expansion abroad, its strong brand name, and managerial experience in international markets gave it a strong competitive advantage vis-à-vis other fast-food chains that were investing abroad for the first time.

Table 2 shows Hotels' 1994 list of the world's 30 largest fast-food restaurant chains (Hotels discontinued reporting these data after 1994). Seventeen of the 30 largest restaurant chains (ranked by number of units) were headquartered in the United States. There were a number of possible explanations for the relative scarcity of fast-food restaurant chains outside the United States. First, the United States represented the largest consumer market in the world, accounting for over one-fifth of the world's gross domestic product (GDP). Therefore, the United States was the strategic focus of the largest restaurant chains. Second, Americans were more quick to accept the fast-food concept. Many other cultures had strong culinary traditions that were difficult to break down. Europeans, for example, had histories of frequenting more mid-scale restaurants, where they spent several hours in a formal setting enjoying native dishes and beverages. While KFC was again building restaurants in Germany by the late 1980s, it previously failed to penetrate the German market, because Germans were not accustomed to takeout food or to ordering food over the counter. McDonald's had greater success penetrating the German market, because it made a number of changes in its menu and operating procedures, in order to better

Table 2

The World's 30 Largest Fast-Food Chains (Year-end 1993, ranked by number of countries)

	Franchise	Location	Units	Countries
1	Pizza Hut	Dallas, Texas	10,433	80
2	McDonald's	Oak Brook, Illinois	23,132	70
3	KFC	Louisville, Kentucky	9,033	68
4	Burger King	Miami, Florida	7,121	50
5	Baskin Robbins	Glendale, California	3,557	49
6	Wendy's	Dublin, Ohio	4,168	38
7	Domino's Pizza	Ann Arbor, Michigan	5,238	36
8	TCBY	Little Rock, Arkansas	7,474	22
9	Dairy Queen	Minneapolis, Minnesota	5,471	21
10	Dunkin' Donuts	Randolph, Massachusetts	3,691	21
11	Taco Bell	Irvine, California	4,921	20
12	Arby's	Fort Lauderdale, Florida	2,670	18
13	Subway Sandwiches	Milford, Connecticut	8,477	15
14	Sizzler International	Los Angeles, California	681	14
15	Hardee's	Rocky Mount, North Carolina	4,060	12
16	Little Caesar's	Detroit, Michigan	4,600	12
17	Popeye's Chicken	Atlanta, Georgia	813	12
18	Denny's	Spartanburg, South Carolina	1,515	10
19	A&W Restaurants	Livonia, Michigan	707	9
20	T.G.I. Friday's	Minneapolis, Minnesota	273	8
21	Orange Julius	Minneapolis, Minnesota	480	7
22	Church's Fried Chicken	Atlanta, Georgia	1,079	6
23	Long John Silver's	Lexington, Kentucky	1,464	5
24	Carl's Jr.	Anaheim, California	649	4
25	Loterria	Tokyo, Japan	795	4
26	Mos Burger	Tokyo, Japan	1,263	4
27	Skylark	Tokyo, Japan	1,000	4
28	Jack in the Box	San Diego, California	1,172	3
29	Quick Restaurants	Berchem, Belgium	876	3
30	Taco Time	Eugene, Oregon	300	3

Sources: *Hotels*, May 1994; 1994 PepsiCo, Inc., annual report.

appeal to German culture. For example, German beer was served in all of McDonald's German restaurants. KFC had more success in Asia and Latin America, where chicken was a traditional dish.

Aside from cultural factors, international business carried risks not present in the US market. Long distances between headquarters and foreign franchises often made it difficult to control the quality of individual restaurants. Large distances also caused servicing and support problems. Transportation and other resource costs were higher than in the domestic market. In addition, time, cultural, and language differences increased communication and operational problems. Therefore, it was reasonable to expect US restaurant chains to expand domestically as long as they achieved corporate profit and growth objectives. As the US market became saturated, and companies gained expertise in interna-

tional markets, more companies could be expected to turn to profitable international markets as a means of expanding restaurant bases and increasing sales, profits, and market share.

International Operations

Much of the early success of the top 10 fast-food chains in the United States was the result of aggressive building strategies. Chains were able to discourage competition by building in low population areas that could support only a single fast-food chain. McDonald's was particularly successful as it was able to quickly expand into small towns across the United States, thereby preempting other fast-food chains. It was equally important to beat a competitor into more largely populated areas where location was of prime importance. KFC's early entry into international markets placed it in a strong position to benefit from international expansion as the US market became saturated. In 1997, 50 percent of KFC's restaurants were located outside of the United States. While 364 new restaurants were opened outside of the United States in 1997, only 12 new restaurants were added to the US system. Most of KFC's international expansion was through franchises, though some restaurants were licensed to operators or jointly operated with a local partner. Expansion through franchising was an important strategy for penetrating international markets, because franchises were owned and operated by local entrepreneurs with a deeper understanding of local language, culture, and customs, as well as local law, financial markets, and marketing characteristics. Franchising was particularly important for expansion into smaller countries such as the Dominican Republic, Grenada, Bermuda, and Suriname, which could support only a single restaurant. Costs were prohibitively high for KFC to operate company-owned restaurants in these smaller markets. Of the 5,117 KFC restaurants located outside of the United States in 1997, 68 percent were franchised, while 22 percent were company-owned, and 10 percent were licensed restaurants or joint ventures.

In larger markets such as Japan, China, and Mexico, there was a stronger emphasis on building company-owned restaurants. By coordinating purchasing, recruiting and training, financing, and advertising, fixed costs could be spread over a large number of restaurants and lower prices on products and services could be negotiated. KFC was also better able to control product and service quality. In order to take advantage of economies of scale, Tricon Global Restaurants managed all of the international units of its KFC, Pizza Hut, and Taco Bell chains through its Tricon International division located in Dallas, Texas. This enabled Tricon Global Restaurants to leverage its strong advertising expertise, international experience, and restaurant management experience across all its KFC, Pizza Hut, and Taco Bell restaurants.

Latin American Strategy

KFC's primary market presence in Latin America during the 1980s was in Mexico, Puerto Rico, and the Caribbean. KFC established subsidiaries in Mexico and Puerto Rico, from which it coordinated the construction and operation of company-owned restaurants. A third subsidiary in Venezuela was closed because of the high fixed costs associated with running the small subsidiary. Franchises were used to penetrate other countries in the Caribbean whose market size prevented KFC from profitably operating company restaurants. KFC relied exclu-

sively on the operation of company-owned restaurants in Mexico through 1989. While franchising was popular in the United States, it was virtually unknown in Mexico until 1990, mainly because of the absence of a law protecting patents, information, and technology transferred to the Mexican franchise. In addition, royalties were limited. As a result, most fast-food chains opted to invest in Mexico using company-owned units.

In 1990, Mexico enacted a new law that provided for the protection of technology transferred into Mexico. Under the new legislation, the franchiser and franchisee were free to set their own terms. Royalties were also allowed under the new law. Royalties were taxed at a 15 percent rate on technology assistance and know-how and 35 percent for other royalty categories. The advent of the new franchise law resulted in an explosion of franchises in fast-food, services, hotels, and retail outlets. In 1992, franchises had an estimated $750 million in sales in over 1,200 outlets throughout Mexico. Prior to passage of Mexico's franchise law, KFC limited its Mexican operations primarily to Mexico City, Guadalajara, and Monterrey. This enabled KFC to better coordinate operations and minimize costs of distribution to individual restaurants. The new franchise law gave KFC and other fast-food chains the opportunity to expand their restaurant bases more quickly into more rural regions of Mexico, where responsibility for management could be handled by local franchisees.

After 1990, KFC altered its Latin American strategy in a number of ways. First, it opened 29 franchises in Mexico to complement its company-owned restaurant base. It then expanded its company-owned restaurants into the Virgin Islands and reestablished a subsidiary in Venezuela. Third, it expanded its franchise operations into South America. In 1990, a franchise was opened in Chile, and in 1993, a franchise was opened in Brazil. Franchises were subsequently established in Colombia, Ecuador, Panama, and Peru, among other South American countries. A fourth subsidiary was established in Brazil, in order to develop company-owned restaurants. Brazil was Latin America's largest economy and McDonald's primary Latin American investment location. By June 1998, KFC operated 438 restaurants in 32 Latin American countries. By comparison, McDonald's operated 1,091 restaurants in 28 countries in Latin America.

Table 3 shows the Latin American operations of KFC and McDonald's. KFC's early entry into Latin America during the 1970s gave it a leadership position in Mexico and the Caribbean. It had also gained an edge in Ecuador and Peru, countries where McDonald's had not yet developed a strong presence. McDonald's focused its Latin American investment in Brazil, Argentina, and Uruguay, countries where KFC had little or no presence.

	KFC Company Restaurants	KFC Franchised Restaurants	KFC Total Restaurants	McDonald's
Argentina	—	—	—	131
Bahamas	—	10	10	3
Barbados	—	7	7	—
Brazil	6	2	8	480
Chile	—	29	29	27
Colombia	—	19	19	18
Costa Rica	—	5	5	19
Ecuador	—	18	18	2
Jamaica	—	17	17	7
Mexico	128	29	157	131
Panama	—	21	21	20
Peru	—	17	17	5
Puerto Rico and Virgin Islands	67	—	67	115
Trinidad and Tobago	—	27	27	3
Uruguay	—	—	—	18
Venezuela	6	—	6	53
Other	—	30	30	59
Total	207	231	438	1,091

Sources: Tricon Global Restaurants, Inc.; McDonald's, 1997 annual report.

Table 3

Latin America Restaurant Count (as of December 31, 1997)

McDonald's was also strong in Venezuela. Both KFC and McDonald's were strong in Chile, Colombia, Panama, and Puerto Rico.

Economic Environment and the Mexican Market

Mexico was KFC's strongest market in Latin America. While McDonald's had aggressively established restaurants in Mexico since 1990, KFC retained the leading market share. Because of its close proximity to the United States, Mexico was an attractive location for US trade and investment. Mexico's population of 98 million people was approximately one-third as large as the United States and represented a large market for US companies. In comparison, Canada's population of 30.3 million people was only one-third as large as Mexico's. Mexico's close proximity to the United States meant that transportation costs from the United States to Mexico were significantly lower than to Europe or Asia. This increased the competitiveness of US goods in comparison with European and Asian goods, which had to be transported to Mexico across the Atlantic or Pacific Ocean at substantial cost.

The United States was, in fact, Mexico's largest trading partner. Over 75 percent of Mexico's imports came from the United States, while 84 percent of its exports were to the United States (see Table 4). Many US firms invested in Mexico in order to take advantage of lower wage rates. By producing goods in Mexico, US goods could be shipped back into the United States for sale or shipped to third markets at lower cost.

While the US market was critically important to Mexico, Mexico still represented a small percentage of overall US trade and investment. Since the early 1900s, the portion of US exports to Latin America had declined. Instead, US exports to Canada and Asia, where economic growth outpaced growth in Mexico, increased more quickly. Canada was the largest importer of US goods. Japan was the largest exporter of goods to the United States, with Canada a close second. US investment in Mexico was also small, mainly because of past government restrictions on foreign investment. Most US foreign investment was in Europe, Canada, and Asia.

The lack of US investment in and trade with Mexico during this century was mainly the result of Mexico's long history of restricting trade and foreign direct

Table 4

Mexico's Major Trading Partners (percent of total exports and imports)

	1992		1994		1996	
	Exports	Imports	Exports	Imports	Exports	Imports
United States	81.1	71.3	85.3	71.8	84.0	75.6
Japan	1.7	4.9	1.6	4.8	1.4	4.4
Germany	1.1	4.0	0.6	3.9	0.7	3.5
Canada	2.2	1.7	2.4	2.0	1.2	1.9
Italy	0.3	1.6	0.1	1.3	1.2	1.1
Brazil	0.9	1.8	0.6	1.5	0.9	0.8
Spain	2.7	1.4	1.4	1.7	1.0	0.7
Other	10.0	13.3	8.0	13.0	9.6	12.0
% Total	100.0	100.0	100.0	100.0	100.0	100.0
Value ($M)	46,196	62,129	60,882	79,346	95,991	89,464

Source: International Monetary Fund, *Direction of Trade Statistics Yearbook*, 1997.

investment. The Institutional Revolutionary Party (PRI), which came to power in Mexico during the 1930s, had historically pursued protectionist economic policies, in order to shield Mexico's economy from foreign competition. Many industries were government-owned or controlled and many Mexican companies focused on producing goods for the domestic market without much attention to building export markets. High tariffs and other trade barriers restricted imports into Mexico and foreign ownership of assets in Mexico was largely prohibited or heavily restricted.

Additionally, a dictatorial and entrenched government bureaucracy, corrupt labor unions, and a long tradition of anti-Americanism among many government officials and intellectuals reduced the motivation of US firms for investing in Mexico. The nationalization of Mexico's banks in 1982 led to higher real interest rates and lower investor confidence. Afterward, the Mexican government battled high inflation, high interest rates, labor unrest, and lost consumer purchasing power. Investor confidence in Mexico, however, improved after 1988, when Carlos Salinas de Gortari was elected president. Following his election, Salinas embarked on an ambitious restructuring of the Mexican economy. He initiated policies to strengthen the free market components of the economy, lowered top marginal tax rates to 36 percent (down from 60 percent in 1986), and eliminated many restrictions on foreign investment. Foreign firms can now buy up to 100 percent of the equity in many Mexico firms. Foreign ownership of Mexican firms was previously limited to 49 percent.

Privatization

The privatization of government-owned companies came to symbolize the restructuring of Mexico's economy. In 1990, legislation was passed to privatize all government-run banks. By the end of 1992, over 800 of

some 1,200 government-owned companies had been sold, including Mexicana and AeroMexico, the two largest airline companies in Mexico, and Mexico's 18 major banks. However, more than 350 companies remained under government ownership. These represented a significant portion of the assets owned by the state at the start of 1988. Therefore, the sale of government-owned companies, in terms of asset value, was moderate. A large percentage of the remaining government-owned assets were controlled by government-run companies in certain strategic industries such as steel, electricity, and petroleum. These industries had long been protected by government ownership. As a result, additional privatization of government-owned enterprises until 1993 was limited. However, in 1993, President Salinas opened up the electricity sector to independent power producers, and Petroleos Mexicanos (Pemex), the state-run petrochemical monopoly, initiated a program to sell many of its nonstrategic assets to private and foreign buyers.

North American Free Trade Agreement

Before 1989, Mexico levied high tariffs on most imported goods. In addition, many other goods were subjected to quotas, licensing requirements, and other non-tariff trade barriers. In 1986, Mexico joined the General Agreement on Tariffs and Trade (GATT), a world trade organization designed to eliminate barriers to trade among member nations. As a member of GATT, Mexico was obligated to apply its system of tariffs to all member nations equally. As a result of its membership in GATT, Mexico dropped tariff rates on a variety of imported goods. In addition, import license requirements were dropped for all but 300 imported items. During President Salinas's administration, tariffs were reduced from an average of 100 percent on most items to an average of 11 percent.

Table 5

Selected Economic Data for
Canada, the United States,
and Mexico

Annual Change (%)	1993	1994	1995	1996	1997
GDP Growth					
Canada	3.3	4.8	5.5	4.1	—
United States	4.9	5.8	4.8	5.1	5.9
Mexico	21.4	13.3	29.4	38.2	—
Real GDP Growth					
Canada	2.2	4.1	2.3	1.2	—
United States	2.2	3.5	2.0	2.8	3.8
Mexico	2.0	4.5	−6.2	5.1	—
Inflation					
Canada	1.9	0.2	2.2	1.5	1.6
United States	3.0	2.5	2.8	2.9	2.4
Mexico	9.7	6.9	35.0	34.4	20.6
Depreciation against $US					
Canada (C$)	4.2	6.0	−2.7	0.3	4.3
Mexico (NP)	−0.3	71.4	43.5	2.7	3.6

Source: International Monetary Fund, *International Financial Statistics*, 1998.

On January 1, 1994, the North American Free Trade Agreement (NAFTA) went into effect. The passage of NAFTA, which included Canada, the United States, and Mexico, created a trading bloc with a larger population and gross domestic product than the European Union. All tariffs on goods traded among the three countries were scheduled to be phased out. NAFTA was expected to be particularly beneficial for Mexican exporters because reduced tariffs made their goods more competitive in the United States compared to goods exported to the United States from other countries. In 1995, one year after NAFTA went into effect, Mexico posted its first balance of trade surplus in six years. Part of this surplus was attributed to reduced tariffs resulting from the NAFTA agreement. However, the peso crisis of 1995, which lowered the value of the peso against the dollar, increased the price of goods imported into Mexico and lowered the price of Mexican products exported to the United States. Therefore, it was still too early to assess the full effects of the NAFTA agreement.

Foreign Exchange and the Mexican Peso Crisis of 1995

Between 1982 and 1991, a two-tiered exchange rate system was in force in Mexico. The system consisted of a controlled rate and a free market rate. A controlled rate was used for imports, foreign debt payments, and conversion of export proceeds. An estimated 70 percent of all foreign transactions were covered by the controlled rate. A free market rate was used for other transactions. In 1989, President Salinas instituted a policy of allowing the peso to depreciate against the dollar by one peso per day. The result was a grossly overvalued peso. This lowered the price of imports and led to an increase in imports of over 23 percent in 1989. At the same time, Mexican exports became less competitive on world markets.

In 1991, the controlled rate was abolished and replaced with an official free rate. In order to limit the range of fluctuations in the value of the peso, the government fixed the rate at which it would buy or sell pesos. A floor (the maximum price at which pesos could be purchased) was Mex$3,056.20 and remained fixed. A ceiling (the maximum price at which the peso could be sold) was established at Mex$3,056.40 and allowed to move upward by Mex$0.20 a day. In 1993, a new currency, called the new peso, was issued with three fewer zeros. The new currency was designed to simplify transactions and to reduce the cost of printing currency.

When Ernesto Zedillo became Mexico's president in December 1994, one of his objectives was to continue the stability of prices, wages, and exchange rates achieved by ex-president Carlos Salinas de Gortari during his five-year tenure as president. However, Salinas had achieved stability largely on the basis of price, wage, and foreign exchange controls. While giving the appearance of stability, an overvalued peso continued to encourage imports, which exacerbated Mexico's balance of trade deficit. Mexico's government continued to use foreign reserves to finance its balance of trade deficits. According to the Banco de Mexico, foreign currency reserves fell from $24 billion in January 1994 to $5.5 billion in January 1995. Anticipating a devaluation of the peso, investors began to move capital into US dollar investments. In order to relieve pressure on the peso, Zedillo announced on December 19, 1994, that the peso would be allowed to depreciate by an additional 15 percent per year against the dollar compared to the maximum allowable depreciation of 4 percent per year established during the Salinas administration. Within two days, continued pressure on the peso forced Zedillo to allow the peso to float freely against the dollar. By mid-January 1995, the peso had lost 35 percent of its value against the dollar and the Mexican stock market plunged 20 percent. By November 1995, the peso had depreciated from 3.1 pesos per dollar to 7.3 pesos per dollar.

The continued devaluation of the peso resulted in higher import prices, higher inflation, destabilization within the stock market, and higher interest rates. Mexico struggled pay its dollar-based debts. In order to thwart a possible default by Mexico, the US government, International Monetary Fund, and World Bank pledged $24.9 billion in emergency loans. Zedillo then announced an emergency economic package called the *pacto* that included reduced government spending, increased sales of government-run businesses, and a freeze on wage increases.

Labor Problems

One of KFC's primary concerns in Mexico was the stability of labor markets. Labor was relatively plentiful and wages were low. However, much of the work force was relatively unskilled. KFC benefited from lower labor costs, but labor unrest, low job retention, high absenteeism, and poor punctuality were significant problems. Absenteeism and punctuality were partially cultural. However, problems with worker retention and labor unrest were also the result of workers' frustration over the loss of their purchasing power due to inflation and government controls on wage increases. Absenteeism remained high at approximately 8 to 14 percent of the labor force, though it was declining because of job security fears. Turnover continued to be a problem and ran at between 5 and 12 percent per month. Therefore, employee screening and internal training were important issues for firms investing in Mexico.

Higher inflation and the government's freeze on wage increases led to a dramatic decline in disposable income after 1994. Further, a slowdown in business activity, brought about by higher interest rates and lower government spending, led many businesses to lay off workers. By the end of 1995, an estimated 1 million jobs had been lost as a result of the economic crisis sparked by the peso devaluation. As a result, industry groups within Mexico called for new labor laws giving them more freedom to hire and fire employees and increased flexibility to hire part-time rather than full-time workers.

Risks and Opportunities

The peso crisis of 1995 and resulting recession in Mexico left KFC managers with a great deal of uncertainty regarding Mexico's economic and political future. KFC had benefited from economic stability between 1988 and 1994. Inflation was brought down, the peso was relatively stable, labor unrest was relatively calm, and Mexico's new franchise law had enabled KFC to expand into rural areas using franchises rather than company-owned restaurants. By the end of 1995, KFC had built 29 franchises in Mexico. The foreign exchange crisis of 1995 had severe implications for US firms operating in Mexico. The devaluation of the peso resulted in higher inflation and capital flight out of Mexico. Capital flight reduced the supply of capital and led to higher interest rates. In order to reduce inflation, Mexico's government instituted an austerity program that resulted in lower disposable income, higher unemployment, and lower demand for products and services.

Another problem was Mexico's failure to reduce restrictions on US and Canadian investment in a timely fashion. Many US firms experienced problems getting required approvals for new ventures from the Mexican government. A good example was United Parcel Service (UPS), which sought government approval to use large trucks for deliveries in Mexico. Approvals were delayed, forcing UPS to use smaller trucks. This put UPS at a competitive disadvantage vis-á-vis Mexican companies. In many cases, UPS was forced to subcontract delivery work to Mexican companies that were allowed to use larger, more cost-efficient trucks. Other US companies, such as Bell Atlantic and TRW, faced similar problems. TRW, which signed a joint venture agreement with a Mexican partner, had to wait 15 months longer than anticipated before the Mexican government released rules on how it could receive credit data from banks. TRW claimed that the Mexican government slowed the approval process in order to placate several large Mexican banks.

A final area of concern for KFC was increased political turmoil in Mexico during the last several years. On January 1, 1994, the day NAFTA went into effect, rebels (descendants of the Mayans) rioted in the southern Mexican province of Chiapas on the Guatemalan border. After four days of fighting, Mexican troops had driven the rebels out of several towns earlier seized by the rebels. Around 150—mostly rebels—were killed. The uprising symbolized many of the fears of the poor in Mexico. While ex-President Salinas's economic programs had increased economic growth and wealth in Mexico, many of Mexico's poorest felt that they had not benefited. Many of Mexico's farmers, faced with lower tariffs on imported agricultural goods from the United

States, felt that they might be driven out of business because of lower-priced imports. Therefore, social unrest among Mexico's Indians, farmers, and the poor could potentially unravel much of the economic success achieved in Mexico during the past five years.

Further, ex-President Salinas's hand-picked successor for president was assassinated in early 1994 while campaigning in Tijuana. The assassin was a 23-year-old mechanic and migrant worker believed to be affiliated with a dissident group upset with the PRI's economic reforms. The possible existence of a dissident group raised fears of political violence in the future. The PRI quickly named Ernesto Zedillo, a 42-year-old economist with little political experience, as its new presidential candidate. Zedillo was elected president in December 1994. Political unrest was not limited to Mexican officials and companies. In October 1994, between 30 and 40 masked men attacked a McDonald's restaurant in the tourist section of Mexico City to show their opposition to California's Proposition 187, which would have curtailed benefits to illegal aliens (primarily from Mexico). The men threw cash registers to the floor, cracked them open, smashed windows, overturned tables, and spray-painted slogans on the walls such as "No to Fascism" and "Yankee Go Home."

KFC faced a variety of issues in Mexico and Latin America in 1998. Before 1995, few restaurants had been opened in South America. However, KFC was now aggressively building new restaurants in the region. KFC halted openings of franchised restaurants in Mexico and all restaurants opened since 1995 were company-owned. KFC was more aggressively building restaurants in South America, which remained largely unpenetrated by KFC through 1995. Of greatest importance was Brazil, where McDonald's had already established a strong market share position. Brazil was Latin America's largest economy and a largely untapped market for KFC. The danger in ignoring Mexico was that a conservative investment strategy could jeopardize its market share lead over McDonald's in a large market where KFC had long enjoyed enormous popularity.

Discussion Questions

1. What are the benefits of franchising versus company-owned restaurants for a company such as KFC?

2. Describe KFC's investment strategy in Latin America.

3. Why is Mexico an attractive market?

4. What are the major strategic issues for KFC in Mexico?

5. What are KFC's major strategic alternatives internationally?

BUSINESS OPERATIONS

Chapter Fifteen
Exporting, Importing, and Countertrade

Chapter Sixteen
Global Manufacturing and Materials Management

Chapter Seventeen
Global Marketing and R&D

Chapter Eighteen
Global Human Resource Management

Chapter Nineteen
Accounting in the International Business

Chapter Twenty
Financial Management in the International Business

EXPORTING, IMPORTING, AND COUNTERTRADE

Artais Weather Check

Artais Weather Check, Inc., is a small Ohio-based company that manufactures an automated weather observation system, or AWOS, for small airports. Artais's AWOS system records runway conditions such as wind speed, direction, and temperature and converts the data into a voice message for pilots. Only three other companies besides Artais have been certified by the US Federal Aviation Administration (FAA) to produce the equipment, and Artais dominates the market in the United States with a share of over 80 percent.

Despite its dominant market share in the United States, Artais gets the majority of its $8 million in annual revenues from foreign markets. Within the United States, the market for automated weather observation systems is small. Although there are 18,000 public and private airports in the country, the largest have round-the-clock human weather watchers, while most of the smaller airports cannot afford the $45,000 to $60,000 required to install an AWOS. Thus, the prospects for growth in the United States seem to be limited to sales of about 75 systems per year nationwide.

To continue to grow the company's revenues, Artais has increasingly looked toward export sales. From slow beginnings in the late 1980s, exports have surged to account for close to two-thirds of the company's total revenues. However, to get foreign orders, Artais has had to deal with frustrations it never encountered at home. The first problem it came up against was one of name recognition. Although Artais is well known within the United States, the company found that its name recognition was close to zero overseas. Another problem involves subsidized competition; according to Artais, its main competitors in some foreign markets are subsidized by their governments to protect jobs. Artais has also found that it needs to customize its products for foreign markets. To sell in Egypt, for example, its system had to be reprogrammed to relay weather information in Arabic as well as English. International customers also require that spare parts be located close by and that Artais employees install the equipment and provide on-site training, all of which raises the costs of doing business.

Political factors have also had a major impact on the outcome of some deals. For example, after working hard to secure a deal in Romania, Artais unexpectedly saw the deal fall through at the last moment. Instead, the deal went to a German competitor. According to some locals, the Romanian government, eager to improve trading relations with the European Union, gave the job to Artais's German competitor in an attempt to curry favor with the trading bloc's most powerful member.

Despite problems such as these, Artais has sold systems to airports in Taiwan, China, Ecuador, Saudi Arabia, and Egypt. Artais has found that such overseas contracts can be more lucrative than its domestic sales because of all the extras, such as spare parts, installation fees, and training. For the basic AWOS, the value of the foreign contracts has ranged from $200,000 to $2 million, compared with $45,000 to $60,000 in the United States. Building on this success, Artais in 1995 introduced a new system designed to detect low-level wind shears. The new system, which costs $350,000 per unit, was designed for the market outside the United States. According to company representatives, Artais is disregarding the US market because of the cost and time involved in meeting specifications established by the FAA. Systems built to FAA specifications can cost $1 million a unit, which is beyond the reach of many foreign buyers. The first two sales of the new system were to Saudi Arabia in 1995. The company believes that in time 20 percent of its annual sales will come from the wind-shear system, all of which will be generated overseas. In addition, the company believes that the bulk of revenues for its basic AWOS will continue to be generated overseas.

http://www.faa.gov

Sources: S. N. Mehta, "Enterprise: Artais Finds That Smallness Isn't a Handicap in Global Market," *The Wall Street Journal*, June 23, 1994, p. B2; and R. Carter, "Artais' New System to Help Airlines Harness the Wind," *Columbus Dispatch*, August 28, 1995, p. 8.

CHAPTER OUTLINE

ARTAIS WEATHER CHECK

INTRODUCTION

THE PROMISE AND PITFALLS OF EXPORTING

IMPROVING EXPORT PERFORMANCE
An International Comparison
Information Sources
Utilizing Export Management
  Companies
Exporting Strategy

EXPORT AND IMPORT FINANCING
Lack of Trust
Letter of Credit
Draft
Bill of Lading
A Typical International Trade
  Transaction

EXPORT ASSISTANCE
Export–Import Bank
Export Credit Insurance

COUNTERTRADE
The Growth of Countertrade
Types of Countertrade
The Pros and Cons of Countertrade

CHAPTER SUMMARY

CRITICAL DISCUSSION QUESTIONS

DOWNEY'S SOUP

Introduction

In the previous chapter, we reviewed exporting from a strategic perspective. We considered exporting as just one of a range of strategic options for profiting from international expansion. In this chapter, we are more concerned with the "nuts and bolts" of exporting (and importing). We take the choice of strategy as a given and look instead at how to export.

As we can see from the opening case, exporting is not an activity just for large multinational enterprises; many small firms such as Artais have benefited significantly from the moneymaking opportunities of exporting. In the United States, for example, small firms with less than 500 employees sold $186 billion to customers in other countries in 1997. Although small firms account for only 30 percent of the value of the nation's exports, they represent 96 percent of all firms involved in exporting.[1] The situation is similar in several other nations. In Germany, for example, companies with less than 500 employees account for about 30 percent of that nation's exports.[2]

Evidence suggests that the volume of export activity in the world economy, by firms of all sizes, is likely to increase in the near future. One reason is that exporting has become easier. The gradual decline in trade barriers under the umbrella of GATT and now the WTO (see Chapter 5) along with regional economic agreements such as the European Union and the North American Free Trade Agreement (see Chapter 8) have significantly increased export opportunities. At the same time, the advent of modern communications and transportation technologies has alleviated the logistical problems associated with exporting. Firms are increasingly using fax machines, the World Wide Web, international 800 numbers, and international air express services to reduce the costs of exporting. Consequently, it is no longer unusual to find small companies such as Artais that are thriving as exporters.

Nevertheless, exporting remains a challenge for many firms. While large multinational enterprises have long been conversant with the steps that must be taken to export successfully, smaller enterprises can find the process intimidating. The firm wishing to export must identify foreign market opportunities, avoid a host of unanticipated problems that are often associated with doing business in a foreign market, familiarize itself with the mechanics of export and import financing, learn where it can get financing and export credit insurance, and learn how it should deal with foreign exchange risk. The whole process is made more problematic by the fact that many countries' currencies are not freely convertible. As a result, there is the problem of arranging payment for exports to countries with weak currencies. This brings us to the complex topic of countertrade, by which payment for exports is received in goods and services rather than money. In this chapter, we will discuss all these issues with the exception of foreign exchange risk, which was covered in Chapter 9. We open the chapter by considering the promise and pitfalls of exporting.

The Promise and Pitfalls of Exporting

The great promise of exporting is that huge revenue and profit opportunities are to be found in foreign markets for most firms in most industries. Artais had a very solid competitive position in the United States, including an 80 percent share of the US market for automated weather observing systems, but that was insufficient to guarantee continued strong growth in revenues and profits. The company found that the opportunities for growth in foreign markets can more than make up for any lack of opportunities in the United States. What is true for Artais is also true for a large number of other enterprises of all sizes based in many other countries. The international market is normally so much larger than the firm's domestic market, that exporting is nearly always a way of increasing the revenue and profit base of a company.

Despite the obvious opportunities associated with exporting, studies have shown that while many large firms tends to be *proactive* about seeking opportunities for profitable exporting, systematically scanning foreign markets to see where the opportunities lie for leveraging their technology, products, and marketing skills in foreign countries, many medium-sized and small firms are very *reactive*.[3] Typically, such reactive firms do not even consider exporting until their domestic market is saturated and the emergence of excess productive capacity at home forces them to look for growth opportunities in foreign markets. Also, many small and medium-sized firms tend to wait for the world to come to them, rather than going out into the world to seek opportunities. Even when the world does comes to them, they may not respond. An example is MMO Music Group, which makes sing-along tapes for karaoke machines. Foreign sales accounted for about 15 percent of MMO's revenues of $8 million in the mid-1990s, but the firm's CEO admits that this figure would probably have been much higher had he paid attention to building international sales during the 1980s and early 1990s. At that time, unanswered faxes and phone messages from Asia and Europe piled up while he was trying to manage the burgeoning domestic side of the business. By the time MMO did turn its attention to foreign markets, other competitors had stepped into the breach and MMO found it tough going to build export volume.[4]

MMO's experience is common, and it suggests a need for firms to become more proactive about seeking export opportunities. One reason more firms are not proactive is that they are unfamiliar with foreign market opportunities; they simply do not know how big the opportunities actually are or where they might lie. Simple ignorance of the potential opportunities is a huge barrier to exporting.[5] Also, many would-be exporters are often intimidated by the complexities and mechanics of exporting to countries where business practices, language, culture, legal systems, and currency are all very different from the home market. This combination of unfamiliarity and intimidation probably explains why exporters still account for only a tiny percentage of US firms, less than 2 percent according to the Small Business Administration.[6]

To make matters worse, many neophyte exporters have run into significant problems when first trying to do business abroad and this has soured them on future exporting ventures. Common pitfalls include poor market analysis, a poor understanding of competitive conditions in the foreign market, a failure to customize the product offering to the needs of foreign customers, lack of an effective distribution program, and a poorly executed promotional campaign in the foreign market.[7] Neophyte exporters tend to underestimate the time and expertise needed to cultivate business in foreign countries.[8] Few realize the amount of management resources that have to be dedicated to this activity. Many foreign customers require face-to-face negotiations on their home turf. An exporter may have to spend months learning about a country's trade regulations, business practices, and mores before a deal can be closed.

Exporters often face voluminous paperwork, complex formalities, and many potential delays and errors. According to a UN report on trade and development, a typical international trade transaction may involve 30 different parties, 60 original documents, and 360 document copies, all of which have to be checked, transmitted, reentered into various information systems, processed, and filed. The United Nations has calculated that the time involved in preparing documentation, along with the costs of common errors in paperwork, often amounts to 10 percent of the final value of goods exported.[9]

Improving Export Performance

There are a number of ways in which inexperienced exporters can gain information about foreign market opportunities and avoid some of the common pitfalls that tend to discourage and frustrate novice exporters. In this section, we look at some information sources that exporters can utilize to increase their knowledge of foreign market opportunities, we consider the pros and cons of utilizing export management companies (EMCs) to assist in the export process, and we review various exporting strategies that can increase the probability of successful exporting. We begin, however, with a look at how several nations try to assist domestic firms in the export process.

An International Comparison

One big impediment to exporting is the simple lack of knowledge of the opportunities available. Often there are many markets for a firm's product, but because they are in countries separated from the firm's home base by culture, language, distance, and time, the firm does not know of them. The problem of identifying export opportunities is made even more complex by the fact that 180 countries with widely differing cultures compose the world of potential opportunities. Faced with such complexity and diversity, it is not surprising that firms sometimes hesitate to seek export opportunities.

The way to overcome ignorance is to collect information. In Germany, one of the world's most successful exporting nations, trade associations, government agencies, and commercial banks gather information, helping small firms identify export opportunities. A similar function is provided by the Japanese Ministry of International Trade and Industry (MITI), which is always on the lookout for export opportunities. In addition, many Japanese firms are affiliated in some way with the *sogo shosha*, Japan's great trading houses. The *sogo shosha* have offices all over the world, and they proactively, continuously seek export opportunities for their affiliated companies large and small.[10] The great advantage of German and Japanese firms is that they can draw on the large reservoirs of experience, skills, information, and other resources of their respective export-oriented institutions.

Unlike their German and Japanese competitors, many US firms are relatively blind when they seek export opportunities; they are information disadvantaged. In part, this difference reflects historical differences. Both Germany and Japan have long made their living as trading nations, whereas until recently the United States has been a relatively self-contained continental economy in which international trade played a minor role. This is changing; both imports and exports now play a much greater role in the US economy than they did 20 years ago. However, the United States has not yet evolved an institutional structure for promoting exports similar to that of either Germany or Japan.

Information Sources

Despite institutional disadvantages, US firms can increase their awareness of export opportunities. The most comprehensive source of information is the US Department of Commerce and its district offices all over the country. Within that department are two organizations dedicated to providing businesses with intelligence and assistance for attacking foreign markets: the International Trade Administration and the United States and Foreign Commercial Service Agency.

These agencies provide the potential exporter with a "best prospects" list, which gives the names and addresses of potential distributors in foreign markets along with businesses they are in, the products they handle, and their contact person. In addition, the Department of Commerce has assembled a "comparison shopping service" for 14 countries that are major markets for US exports. For a small fee, a firm can receive a customized market research survey on a product of its choice. This survey provides information on marketability, the competition, comparative prices, distribution channels, and names of potential sales representatives. Each study is conducted on-site by an officer of the Department of Commerce.

The Department of Commerce also organizes trade events that help potential exporters make foreign contacts and explore export opportunities. The department organizes exhibitions at international trade fairs, which are held regularly in major cities worldwide. The department also has a matchmaker program, in which department representatives accompany groups of US businesspeople abroad to meet with qualified agents, distributors, and customers.

In addition to the Department of Commerce, nearly every state and many large cities maintain active trade commissions whose purpose is to promote exports. Most of these provide business counseling, information gatherings, technical assistance, and financing. Unfortunately, many have fallen victim to budget cuts or to turf battles for political and financial support with other export agencies.

A number of private organizations are also beginning to gear up to provide more assistance to would-be exporters. Commercial banks and major accounting firms are more willing to assist small firms in starting export operations than they were a decade ago. In addition, large multinationals that have been successful in the global arena are typically more than willing to discuss opportunities overseas with the owners or managers of small firms.[11]

Utilizing Export Management Companies

One way for first-time exporters to identify the opportunities associated with exporting and to avoid many of the associated pitfalls is to hire an **export management company** (EMC). EMCs are export specialists who act as the export marketing department or international department for their client firms. EMCs normally accept two types of export assignments. They start up exporting operations for a firm with the understanding that the firm will take over operations after they are well established. In another type, start-up services are performed with the understanding that the EMC will have continuing responsibility for selling the firm's products. Many EMCs specialize in serving firms in particular industries and in particular areas of the world. Thus, one EMC may specialize in selling agricultural products in the Asian market, while another may focus on exporting electronics products to Eastern Europe.

In theory, the advantage of EMCs is that they are experienced specialists who can help the neophyte exporter identify opportunities and avoid common pitfalls. A good EMC will have a network of contacts in potential markets, have multilingual employees, have a good knowledge of different business mores, and be fully conversant with the ins and outs of the exporting process and with local business regulations. However, studies have revealed that there is a large variation in the quality of EMCs.[12] While some perform their functions very well, others appear to add little value to the exporting company. Therefore, it is important for an exporter to review carefully a number of EMCs and to check references from an EMC's past clients. One drawback of relying on EMCs is that the company can fail to develop its own exporting capabilities in-house.

Exporting Strategy

In addition to using EMCs, a firm can reduce the risks associated with exporting if it is careful about its choice of exporting strategy. A few guidelines can help firms improve their odds of success. For example, one of the most successful exporting firms in the world, the Minnesota Mining and Manufacturing Co. (3M), has built its export success on three main principles—enter on a small scale to reduce risks, add additional product lines once the exporting operations start to become successful, and hire locals to promote the firm's products (3M's export strategy is profiled in the accompanying Management Focus). Another successful exporter, Red Spot Paint, emphasizes the importance of cultivating personal relationships when trying to build an export business (see the Management Focus at the end of this section).

The probability of exporting successfully can be increased dramatically by taking a handful of simple strategic steps. First, particularly for the novice exporter, it helps to hire an EMC or at least an experienced export consultant to help with the identification of opportunities and navigate through the web of paperwork and regulations so often involved in exporting. Second, it often makes sense to initially focus on one market, or a handful of markets. The idea is to learn about what is required to succeed

MANAGEMENT FOCUS
Exporting Strategy at 3M

http://www.mmm.com

The Minnesota Mining and Manufacturing Co. (3M), which makes over 40,000 products including tape, sandpaper, medical products, and the ever-present Post-it Notes, is one of the world's great multinational operations. In 1997, 52 percent of the firm's $15.1 billion in revenues were generated outside the United States. Although the bulk of these revenues came from foreign-based operations, 3M remains a major exporter with $1.5 billion in exports. The company often uses its exports to establish an initial presence in a foreign market, only building foreign production facilities once sales volume rises to a level where local production is justified.

The export strategy is built around simple principles. One is known as "FIDO," which stands for First In (to a new market) Defeats Others. The essence of FIDO is to gain an advantage over other exporters by getting into a market first and learning about that country and how to sell there before others do. A second principle is "make a little, sell a little," which is the idea of entering on a small scale with a very modest investment and pushing one basic product, such as reflective sheeting for traffic signs in Russia or scouring pads in Hungary. Once 3M believes it has learned enough about the market to reduce the risks of failure to reasonable levels, it adds additional products.

A third principle at 3M is to hire local employees to sell the firm's products. The company normally sets up a local sales subsidiary to handle its export activi-

ties in a country. It then staffs this subsidiary with local hires because it believes they are likely to have a much better idea of how to sell in their own country than American expatriates. Because of the implementation of this principle, just 160 of 3M's 39,500 foreign employees are US expatriates.

Another common practice at 3M is to formulate global strategic plans for the export and eventual overseas production of its products. Within the context of these plans, 3M gives local managers considerable autonomy to find the best way to sell the product within their country. Thus, when 3M first exported its Post-it Notes in 1981 it planned to "sample the daylights" out of the product, but it also told local managers to find the best way of doing this. Local managers hired office cleaning crews to pass out samples in Britain and Germany; in Italy, office products distributors were used to pass out free samples; while in Malaysia, local managers employed young women to go from office to office handing out samples of the product. In typical 3M fashion, when the volume of Post-it Notes was sufficient to justify it, exports from the United States were replaced by local production. Thus, 3M found it worthwhile by 1984 to set up production facilities in France to produce Post-it Notes for the European market.

Sources: R. L. Rose, "Success Abroad," *The Wall Street Journal,* March 29, 1991, p. A1; T. Eiben, "US Exporters Keep on Rolling," *Fortune,* June 14, 1994, pp. 128–131; and 3M's Web site at http://www.mmm.com.

in those markets, before moving on to other markets. The firm that enters many markets at once runs the risk of spreading its limited management resources too thin. The result of such a "shotgun approach" to exporting may be a failure to become established in any one market. Third, as with 3M, it often makes sense to enter a foreign market on a small scale to reduce the costs of any subsequent failure. Most importantly, entering on a small scale provides the time and opportunity to learn about the foreign country before making significant capital commitments to that market. Fourth, the exporter needs to recognize the time and managerial commitment involved in building export sales and should hire additional personnel to oversee this activity. Fifth, in many countries, it is important to devote a lot of attention to building strong and enduring relationships with local distributors and/or customers (see the Management Focus on Red Spot Paint for an example). Sixth, as 3M often does, it is important to hire local personnel to help the firm establish itself in a foreign market.

MANAGEMENT FOCUS
Red Spot Paint & Varnish

http://www.redspot.com

Established in 1903 and based in Evansville, Indiana, Red Spot Paint & Varnish Company is in many ways typical of the companies that can be found in the small towns of America's heartland. The closely held company, whose CEO Charles Storms is the great-grandson of the founder, has 500 employees and annual sales of close to $90 million. The company's main product is paint for plastic components used in the automobile industry. Red Spot products are seen on automobile bumpers, wheel covers, grills, head-lamps, instrument panels, door inserts, radio buttons, and other components. Unlike many other companies of a similar size and location, however, Red Spot has a thriving international business. International sales (which include exports and local production by licensees) now account for between 15 percent and 25 percent of revenue in any one year, and Red Spot does business in about 15 foreign countries.

Red Spot has long had some international sales and won an export award in the early 1960s. To further its international business in the late 1980s, Red Spot hired a Central Michigan University professor, Bryan Williams. Williams, who was hired because of his foreign-language skills (he speaks German, Japanese, and some Chinese), was the first employee at Red Spot whose exclusive focus was international marketing and sales. His first challenge was the lack of staff skilled in the business of exporting. He found that it was difficult to build an international business without in-house expertise in the basic mechanics of exporting. According to Williams, Red Spot needed people who understood the nuts

and bolts of exporting—letters of credit, payment terms, bills of lading, and so on. As might be expected for a business based in the heartland of America, there was not a ready supply of such individuals in the local vicinity. It took Williams several years to solve this problem. Now Red Spot has a full-time staff of two who have been trained in the principles of exporting and international operations.

A second problem that Williams encountered was the clash between the quarter-to-quarter mentality that frequently pervades management practice in the United States and the long-term perspective that is often necessary to build a successful international business. Williams has found that building long-term personal relationships with potential foreign customers is often the key to getting business. When foreign customers visit Evansville, Williams often invites them home for dinner. His young children even started calling one visitor from Hong Kong "uncle." Even with such efforts, however, the business may not come quickly. Meeting with potential foreign customers yields no direct business 90 percent of the time, although Williams points out that it often yields benefits in terms of competitive information and relationship building. He has found that perseverance pays. For example, Williams and Storms called on a major German automobile parts manufacturer for seven years before finally landing some business from the company.

Sources: R. L. Rose and C.Quintanilla, "More Small U.S. Firms Take up Exporting with Much Success," *The Wall Street Journal,* December 20, 1996, p. A1, A10; and interview with Bryan Williams of Red Spot Paint.

Local people are likely to have a much greater sense of how to do business in a given country than a manager from an exporting firm who has previously never set foot in that country.

Finally, it is important for the exporter to keep the option of local production in mind. Once exports build up to a sufficient volume to justify cost-efficient local production, the exporting firm should consider establishing production facilities in the foreign market. Such localization helps foster good relations with the foreign country and can lead to greater market acceptance. Exporting is often not an end in itself, but merely a step on the road toward establishment of foreign production (again, 3M provides us with an example of this philosophy).

Export and Import Financing

Mechanisms for financing exports and imports have evolved over the centuries in response to a problem that can be particularly acute in international trade: the lack of trust that exists when one must put faith in a stranger. In this section, we examine the financial devices that have evolved to cope with this problem in the context of international trade: the letter of credit, the draft (or bill of exchange), and the bill of lading. Then we will trace the 14 steps of a typical export–import transaction.

Lack of Trust

Firms engaged in international trade have to trust someone they may have never seen, who lives in a different country, who speaks a different language, who abides by (or does not abide by) a different legal system, and who could be very difficult to track down if he or she defaults on an obligation. Consider a US firm exporting to a distributor in France. The US businessman might be concerned that if he ships the products to France before he receives payment for them from the French businesswoman, she might take delivery of the products and not pay him for them. Conversely, the French importer might worry that if she pays for the products before they are shipped, the US firm might keep the money and never ship the products or might ship defective products. Neither party to the exchange completely trusts the other. This lack of trust is exacerbated by the distance between the two parties—in space, language, and culture—and by the problems of using an underdeveloped international legal system to enforce contractual obligations.

Due to the (quite reasonable) lack of trust between the two parties, each has his or her own preferences as to how they would like the transaction to be configured. To make sure he is paid, the manager of the US firm would prefer the French distributor to pay for the products before he ships them (see Figure 15.1). Alternatively, to ensure she receives the products, the French distributor would prefer not to pay for them until they arrive (see Figure 15.2). Thus, each party has a different set of preferences. Unless there is some way of establishing trust between the parties, the transaction might never take place.

The problem is solved by using a third party trusted by both—normally a reputable bank—to act as an intermediary. What happens can be summarized as follows (see Figure 15.3). First, the French importer obtains the bank's promise to pay on her behalf, knowing the US exporter will trust the bank. This promise is known as a **letter of credit.** Having seen the letter of credit, the US exporter now ships the products to France. Title to the products is given to the bank in the form of a document called a **bill of lading.** In return, the US exporter tells the bank to pay for the products, which the bank does. The document for requesting this payment is referred to as a **draft.** The bank, having paid for the products, now passes the title on to the French importer, whom the bank trusts. At that time or later, depending on their agreement, the importer reimburses the bank. In the remainder of this section, we will examine how this system works in more detail.

Letter of Credit

A letter of credit, abbreviated as L/C, stands at the center of international commercial transactions. Issued by a bank at the request of an importer, the letter of credit states that the bank will pay a specified sum of money to a beneficiary, normally the exporter, on presentation of particular, specified documents.

Consider again the example of the US exporter and the French importer. The French importer applies to her local bank, say the Bank of Paris, for the issuance of a letter of credit. The Bank of Paris then undertakes a credit check of the importer. If the Bank of Paris is satisfied with her creditworthiness, it will issue a letter of credit. However, the Bank of Paris might require a cash deposit or some other form of collateral from her first. In addition, the Bank of Paris will charge the importer a fee for this

Figure 15.1

Preference of the US Exporter

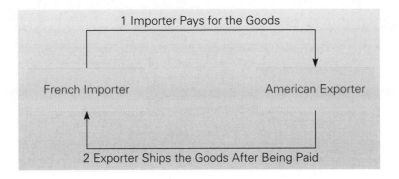

Figure 15.2

Preference of the French Importer

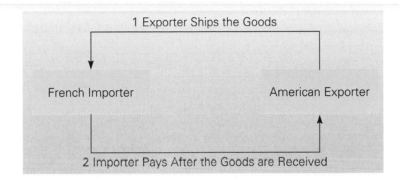

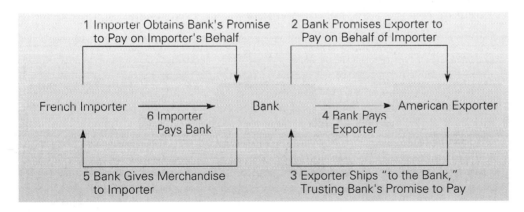

Figure 15.3

The Use of a Third Party

service. Typically this amounts to between 0.5 percent and 2 percent of the value of the letter of credit, depending on the importer's creditworthiness and the size of the transaction. (As a rule, the larger the transaction, the lower the percentage.)

Let us assume the Bank of Paris is satisfied with the French importer's creditworthiness and agrees to issue a letter of credit. The letter states that the Bank of Paris will pay the US exporter for the merchandise as long as it is shipped in accordance with specified instructions and conditions. At this point, the letter of credit becomes a financial contract between the Bank of Paris and the US exporter. The Bank of Paris then sends the letter of credit to the US exporter's bank, say the Bank of New York. The Bank of New York tells the exporter that it has received a letter of credit and that he can ship the merchandise. After the exporter has shipped the merchandise, he draws a draft against the Bank of Paris in accordance with the terms of the letter of credit, attaches the required documents, and presents the draft to his own bank, the Bank of New York, for payment. The Bank of New York then forwards the letter of credit and associated documents to the Bank of Paris. If all of the terms and conditions contained in the letter of credit have been complied with, the Bank of Paris will honor the draft and will send payment to the Bank of New York. When the Bank of New York receives the funds, it will pay the US exporter.

As for the Bank of Paris, once it has transferred the funds to the Bank of New York, it will collect payment from the French importer. Alternatively, the Bank of Paris may allow the importer some time to resell the merchandise before requiring payment. This is not unusual, particularly when the importer is a distributor and not the final consumer of the merchandise, since it helps the importer's cash flow position. The Bank of Paris will treat such an extension of the payment period as a loan to the importer and will charge an appropriate rate of interest.

The great advantage of this system is that both the French importer and the US exporter are likely to trust reputable banks, even if they do not trust each other. Once the U.S. exporter has seen a letter of credit, he knows that he is guaranteed payment and will ship the merchandise. Also, an exporter may find that having a letter of credit will facilitate obtaining pre-export financing. For example, having seen the letter of credit, the Bank of New York might be willing to lend the exporter funds to process and prepare the merchandise for shipping to France. This loan may not have to be repaid until the exporter has received his payment for the merchandise. As for the French importer, the great advantage of the letter of credit arrangement is that she does not have to pay out funds for the merchandise until the documents have arrived and unless all conditions stated in the letter of credit have been satisfied. The drawback for the importer is the fee she must pay the Bank of Paris for the letter of credit. In addition, since the letter of credit is a financial liability against her, it may reduce her ability to borrow funds for other purposes.

Draft

A draft, sometimes referred to as a bill of exchange, is the instrument normally used in international commerce to effect payment. A draft is simply an order written by an exporter instructing an importer, or an importer's agent, to pay a specified amount of money at a specified time. In the example of the US exporter and the French importer, the exporter writes a draft that instructs the Bank of Paris, the French importer's agent, to pay for the merchandise shipped to France. The person or business initiating the draft is known as the maker (in this case, the US exporter). The party to whom the draft is presented is known as the drawee (in this case, the Bank of Paris).

International practice is to use drafts to settle trade transactions. This differs from domestic practice in which a seller usually ships merchandise on an open account, followed by a commercial invoice that specifies the amount due and the terms of payment. In domestic transactions, the buyer can often obtain possession of the merchandise without signing a formal document acknowledging his or her obligation to pay. In contrast, due to the lack of trust in international transactions, payment or a formal promise to pay is required before the buyer can obtain the merchandise.

Drafts fall into two categories, sight drafts and time drafts. A sight draft is payable on presentation to the drawee. A time draft allows for a delay in payment—normally 30, 60, 90, or 120 days. It is presented to the drawee, who signifies acceptance of it by writing or stamping a notice of acceptance on its face. Once accepted, the time draft becomes a promise to pay by the accepting party. When a time draft is drawn on and accepted by a bank, it is called a banker's acceptance. When it is drawn on and accepted by a business firm, it is called a trade acceptance.

Time drafts are negotiable instruments; that is, once the draft is stamped with an acceptance, the maker can sell the draft to an investor at a discount from its face value. Imagine the agreement between the US exporter and the French importer calls for the exporter to present the Bank of Paris (through the Bank of New York) with a time draft requiring payment 120 days after presentation. The Bank of Paris stamps the time draft with an acceptance. Imagine further that the draft is for $100,000.

The exporter can either hold onto the accepted time draft and receive $100,000 in 120 days or he can sell it to an investor, say the Bank of New York, for a discount from the face value. If the prevailing discount rate is 7 percent, the exporter could receive $96,500 by selling it immediately (7 percent per annum discount rate for 120 days for $100,000 equals $3,500, and $100,000 – $3,500 = $96,500). The Bank of New York would then collect the full $100,000 from the Bank of Paris in 120 days. The exporter might sell the accepted time draft immediately if he needed the funds to finance merchandise in transit and/or to cover cash flow shortfalls.

Bill of Lading

The third key document for financing international trade is the bill of lading. The bill of lading is issued to the exporter by the common carrier transporting the merchandise. It serves three purposes: it is a receipt, a contract, and a document of title. As a receipt, the bill of lading indicates that the carrier has received the merchandise described on the face of the document. As a contract, it specifies that the carrier is obligated to provide a transportation service in return for a certain charge. As a document of title, it can be used to obtain payment or a written promise of payment before the merchandise is released to the importer. The bill of lading can also function as collateral against which funds may be advanced to the exporter by its local bank before or during shipment and before final payment by the importer.

A Typical International Trade Transaction

Now that we have reviewed the elements of an international trade transaction, let us see how the process works in a typical case, sticking with the example of the US exporter and the French importer. The typical transaction involves 14 steps (see Figure 15.4). The steps are enumerated here.

1. The French importer places an order with the US exporter and asks the American if he would be willing to ship under a letter of credit.
2. The US exporter agrees to ship under a letter of credit and specifies relevant information such as prices and delivery terms.
3. The French importer applies to the Bank of Paris for a letter of credit to be issued in favor of the US exporter for the merchandise the importer wishes to buy.
4. The Bank of Paris issues a letter of credit in the French importer's favor and sends it to the US exporter's bank, the Bank of New York.
5. The Bank of New York advises the US exporter of the opening of a letter of credit in his favor.
6. The US exporter ships the goods to the French importer on a common carrier. An official of the carrier gives the exporter a bill of lading.
7. The US exporter presents a 90-day time draft drawn on the Bank of Paris in accordance with its letter of credit and the bill of lading to the Bank of New York. The US exporter endorses the bill of lading so title to the goods is transferred to the Bank of New York.
8. The Bank of New York sends the draft and bill of lading to the Bank of Paris. The Bank of Paris accepts the draft, taking possession of the documents and promising to pay the now-accepted draft in 90 days.
9. The Bank of Paris returns the accepted draft to the Bank of New York.
10. The Bank of New York tells the US exporter that it has received the accepted bank draft, which is payable in 90 days.

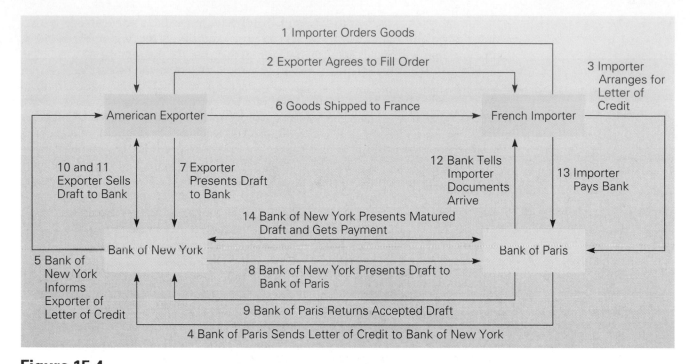

Figure 15.4

A Typical International Trade Transaction

11. The exporter sells the draft to the Bank of New York at a discount from its face value and receives the discounted cash value of the draft in return.

12. The Bank of Paris notifies the French importer of the arrival of the documents. She agrees to pay the Bank of Paris in 90 days. The Bank of Paris releases the documents so the importer can take possession of the shipment.

13. In 90 days, the Bank of Paris receives the importer's payment, so it has funds to pay the maturing draft.

14. In 90 days, the holder of the matured acceptance (in this case, the Bank of New York) presents it to the Bank of Paris for payment. The Bank of Paris pays.

Export Assistance

Prospective U.S. exporters can draw on two forms of government-backed assistance to help finance their export programs. They can get financing aid from the Export–Import Bank and export credit insurance from the Foreign Credit Insurance Association.

Export–Import Bank

The Export–Import Bank, often referred to as Eximbank, is an independent agency of the US government. Its mission is to provide financing aid that will facilitate exports, imports, and the exchange of commodities between the United States and other countries. Eximbank pursues this mission with various loan and loan-guarantee programs.

Eximbank guarantees repayment of medium and long-term loans US commercial banks make to foreign borrowers for purchasing US exports. The Eximbank guarantee makes the commercial banks more willing to lend cash to foreign enterprises.

Eximbank also has a direct lending operation under which it lends dollars to foreign borrowers for use in purchasing US exports. In some cases, it grants loans that commercial banks would not if it sees a potential benefit to the United States in doing so. The foreign borrowers use the loans to pay US suppliers and repay the loan to Eximbank with interest.

Export Credit Insurance

For reasons outlined earlier, exporters clearly prefer to get letters of credit from importers. However, at times an exporter who insists on a letter of credit is likely to lose an order to one who does not require a letter of credit. Thus, particularly when the importer is in a strong bargaining position and able to play competing suppliers off against each other, an exporter may have to forgo a letter of credit.[13] The lack of a letter of credit exposes the exporter to the risk that the foreign importer will default on payment. The exporter can insure against this possibility by buying export credit insurance. If the customer defaults, the insurance firm will cover a major portion of the loss.

In the United States, export credit insurance is provided by the Foreign Credit Insurance Association (FCIA), an association of private commercial institutions operating under the guidance of the Export–Import Bank. The FCIA provides coverage against commercial risks and political risks. Losses due to commercial risk result from the buyer's insolvency or payment default. Political losses arise from actions of governments that are beyond the control of either buyer or seller.

Countertrade

Countertrade is an alternative means of structuring an international sale when conventional means of payment are difficult, costly, or nonexistent. We first encountered countertrade in Chapter 9 in our discussion of currency convertibility. There we noted that many currencies are not freely convertible into other currencies. A government may restrict the convertibility of its currency to preserve its foreign exchange reserves so they can be used to service international debt commitments and purchase crucial imports.[14] This is problematic for exporters. Nonconvertibility implies that the exporter may not be able to be paid in his or her home currency; and few exporters would desire payment in a currency that is not convertible. Countertrade is often the solution. Countertrade denotes a whole range of barterlike agreements; its principle is to trade goods and services for other goods and services when they cannot be traded for money. Some examples of countertrade are:

- An Italian company that manufactures power generating equipment, ABB SAE Sadelmi SpA, was awarded a 720 million baht ($17.7 million) contract by the Electricity Generating Authority of Thailand. The contract specified that the company had to accept 218 million baht ($5.4 million) of Thai farm products as part of the payment.
- Saudi Arabia agreed to buy 10 747 jets from Boeing with payment in crude oil, discounted at 10 percent below posted world oil prices.
- General Electric won a contract for a $150 million electric generator project in Romania by agreeing to market $150 million of Romanian products in markets to which Romania did not have access.
- The Venezuelan government negotiated a contract with Caterpillar under which Venezuela would trade 350,000 tons of iron ore for Caterpillar earthmoving equipment.

- Albania offered such items as spring water, tomato juice, and chrome ore in exchange for a $60 million fertilizer and methanol complex.
- Philip Morris ships cigarettes to Russia, for which it receives chemicals that can be used to make fertilizer. Philip Morris ships the chemicals to China, and in return, China ships glassware to North America for retail sale by Philip Morris.[15]

The Growth of Countertrade

In the modern era, countertrade arose in the 1960s as a way for the Soviet Union and the communist states of Eastern Europe, whose currencies were generally nonconvertible, to purchase imports. During the 1980s, the technique grew in popularity among many developing nations that lacked the foreign exchange reserves required to purchase necessary imports. Today, reflecting their own shortages of foreign exchange reserves, many of the successor states to the former Soviet Union and the Eastern European Communist nations are engaging in countertrade to purchase their imports. Consequently, according to some estimates, more than 20 percent of world trade by value in 1998 was in the form of countertrade, up from only 2 percent in 1975.[16] There was a notable increase in the volume of countertrade after the Asian financial crisis of 1997. That crisis left many Asian nations with little hard currency with which they could finance international trade. In the tight monetary regime that followed the crisis in 1997, many Asian firms found it very difficult to get access to export credits to finance their own international trade. Consequently, they turned to the only option available to them—countertrade.

Given the importance of countertrade as a means of financing world trade, prospective exporters will have to engage in this technique from time to time to gain access to international markets. The governments of developing nations sometimes insist on a certain amount of countertrade.[17] For example, all foreign companies contracted by Thai state agencies for work costing more than 500 million baht ($12.3 million) are required to accept at least 30 percent of their payment in Thai agricultural products. Between 1994 and mid-1998 foreign firms purchased 21 billion baht ($517 million) in Thai goods under countertrade deals.[18]

Types of Countertrade

With its roots in the simple trading of goods and services for other goods and services, countertrade has evolved into a diverse set of activities that can be categorized as five distinct types of trading arrangements: barter, counterpurchase, offset, switch trading, and compensation or buyback.[19] Figure 15.5 summarizes the popularity of each of these arrangements as indicated in a survey of multinational corporations. Many countertrade deals involve not just one arrangement, but elements of two or more.

Barter

Barter is the direct exchange of goods and/or services between two parties without a cash transaction. Although barter is the simplest arrangement, it is not common. Its problems are twofold. First, if goods are not exchanged simultaneously, one party ends up financing the other for a period. Second, firms engaged in barter run the risk of having to accept goods they do not want, cannot use, or have difficulty reselling at a reasonable price. For these reasons, barter is viewed as the most restrictive countertrade arrangement. It is primarily used for one-time-only deals in transactions with trading partners who are not creditworthy or trustworthy.

Counterpurchase

Counterpurchase is a reciprocal buying agreement. It occurs when a firm agrees to purchase a certain amount of materials back from a country to which a sale is made. Suppose a US firm sells some products to China. China pays the US firm in dollars, but in exchange, the US firm agrees to spend some of its proceeds from the sale on textiles pro-

Figure 15.5

Countertrade Practice

Source: Reprinted from "The Do's and Don'ts of International Countertrade," by J. R. Carter and J. Gagne, *Sloan Management Review*, Spring 1988, pp. 31–37, Table 2, by permission of the publisher. Copyright 1998 by Sloan Management Association. All rights reserved.

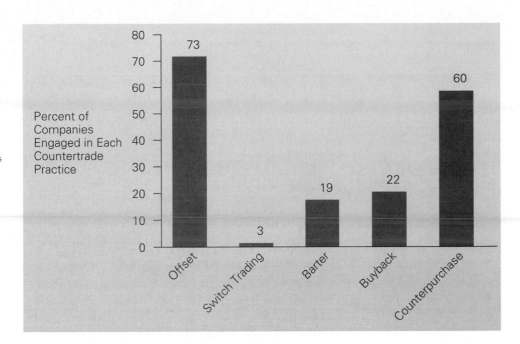

duced by China. Thus, although China must draw on its foreign exchange reserves to pay the US firm, it knows it will receive some of those dollars back because of the counterpurchase agreement. In one counterpurchase agreement, Rolls-Royce sold jet parts to Finland. As part of the deal, Rolls-Royce agreed to use some of the proceeds from the sale to purchase Finnish-manufactured TV sets that it would then sell in Great Britain.

Offset

Offset is similar to counterpurchase insofar as one party agrees to purchase goods and services with a specified percentage of the proceeds from the original sale. The difference is that this party can fulfill the obligation with any firm in the country to which the sale is being made. From an exporter's perspective, this is more attractive than a straight counterpurchase agreement because it gives the exporter greater flexibility to choose the goods that it wishes to purchase.

Switch Trading

Switch trading refers to the use of a specialized third-party trading house in a countertrade arrangement. When a firm enters a counterpurchase or offset agreement with a country, it often ends up with what are called counterpurchase credits, which can be used to purchase goods from that country. Switch trading occurs when a third-party trading house buys the firm's counterpurchase credits and sells them to another firm that can better use them. For example, a US firm concludes a counterpurchase agreement with Poland for which it receives some number of counterpurchase credits for purchasing Polish goods. The US firm cannot use and does not want any Polish goods, however, so it sells the credits to a third-party trading house at a discount. The trading house finds a firm that can use the credits and sells them at a profit.

In one example of switch trading, Poland and Greece had a counterpurchase agreement that called for Poland to buy the same US-dollar value of goods from Greece that it sold to Greece. However, Poland could not find enough Greek goods that it required, so it ended up with a dollar-denominated counterpurchase balance in Greece that it was unwilling to use. A switch trader bought the right to 250,000 counterpurchase dollars from Poland for $225,000 and sold them to a European sultana (grape) merchant for $235,000, who used them to purchase sultanas from Greece.

Compensation or Buybacks

A buyback occurs when a firm builds a plant in a country—or supplies technology, equipment, training, or other services to the country—and agrees to take a certain percentage of the plant's output as partial payment for the contract. For example, Occidental Petroleum negotiated a deal with the former Soviet Union under which Occidental would build several ammonia plants in the Soviet Union and as partial payment receive ammonia over a 20-year period.

The Pros and Cons of Countertrade

The main attraction of countertrade is that it can give a firm a way to finance an export deal when other means are not available. Given the problems that many developing nations have in raising the foreign exchange necessary to pay for imports, countertrade may be the only option available when doing business in these countries. Even when countertrade is not the only option for structuring an export transaction, many countries prefer countertrade to cash deals. Thus, if a firm is unwilling to enter a countertrade agreement, it may lose an export opportunity to a competitor that is willing to make a countertrade agreement.

But the drawbacks of countertrade agreements are substantial. Other things being equal, all firms would prefer to be paid in hard currency. Countertrade contracts may involve the exchange of unusable or poor-quality goods that the firm cannot dispose of profitably. For example, a few years ago, one US firm got burned when 50 percent of the television sets it received in a countertrade agreement with Hungary were defective and could not be sold. In addition, even if the goods it receives are of high quality, the firm still needs to dispose of them profitably. To do this, countertrade requires the firm to invest in an in-house trading department dedicated to arranging and managing countertrade deals. This can be expensive and time consuming.

Given these drawbacks, countertrade is most attractive to large, diverse multinational enterprises that can use their worldwide network of contacts to dispose of goods acquired in countertrading. The masters of countertrade are Japan's giant trading firms, the *sogo shosha,* who use their vast networks of affiliated companies to profitably dispose of goods acquired through countertrade agreements. The trading firm of Mitsui & Company, for example, has about 120 affiliated companies in almost every sector of the manufacturing and service industries. If one of Mitsui's affiliates receives goods in a countertrade agreement that it cannot consume, Mitsui & Company will normally be able to find another affiliate that can profitably use them. Firms affiliated with one of Japan's *sogo shosha* often have a competitive advantage in countries where countertrade agreements are preferred.

Western firms that are large, diverse, and have a global reach (e.g., General Electric, Philip Morris, and 3M) have similar profit advantages from countertrade agreements. Indeed, 3M has established its own trading company—3M Global Trading, Inc.—to develop and manage the company's international countertrade programs. Unless there is no alternative, small and medium-sized exporters should probably try to avoid countertrade deals because they lack the worldwide network of operations that may be required to profitably utilize or dispose of goods acquired through them.[20]

Chapter Summary

In this chapter, we examined the steps that firms must take to establish themselves as exporters. This chapter made the following points:

1. One big impediment to exporting is ignorance of foreign market opportunities.

2. Neophyte exporters often become discouraged or frustrated with the exporting process because they encounter many problems, delays, and pitfalls.

3. The way to overcome ignorance is to gather information. In the United States, a number of institu-

tions, most important of which is the US Department of Commerce, can help firms gather information and in the matchmaking process. Export management companies can also help an exporter to identify export opportunities.

4. Many of the pitfalls associated with exporting can be avoided if a company hires an experienced export management company, or export consultant, and if it adopts the appropriate export strategy.

5. Firms engaged in international trade must do business with people they cannot trust and people who may be difficult to track down if they default on an obligation. Due to the lack of trust, each party to an international transaction has a different set of preferences regarding the configuration of the transaction.

6. The problems arising from lack of trust between exporters and importers can be solved by using a third party that is trusted by both, normally a reputable bank.

7. A letter of credit is issued by a bank at the request of an importer. It states that the bank promises to pay a beneficiary, normally the exporter, on presentation of documents specified in the letter.

8. A draft is the instrument normally used in international commerce to effect payment. It is an order written by an exporter instructing an importer, or an importer's agent, to pay a specified amount of money at a specified time.

9. Drafts are either sight drafts or time drafts. Time drafts are negotiable instruments.

10. A bill of lading is issued to the exporter by the common carrier transporting the merchandise. It serves as a receipt, a contract, and a document of title.

11. US exporters can draw on two types of government-backed assistance to help finance their exports: loans from the Export–Import Bank and export credit insurance from the FCIA.

12. Countertrade includes a whole range of barterlike agreements. It is primarily used when a firm exports to a country whose currency is not freely convertible and who may lack the foreign exchange reserves required to purchase the imports.

13. The main attraction of countertrade is that it gives a firm a way to finance an export deal when other means are not available. A firm that insists on being paid in hard currency may be at a competitive disadvantage vis-à-vis one that is willing to engage in countertrade.

14. The main disadvantage of countertrade is that the firm may receive unusable or poor-quality goods that cannot be disposed of profitably.

Critical Discussion Questions

1. A firm based in Washington state wants to export a shipload of finished lumber to the Philippines. The would-be importer cannot get sufficient credit from domestic sources to pay for the shipment but insists that the finished lumber can quickly be resold in the Philippines for a profit. Outline the steps the exporter should take to effect this export to the Philippines.

2. You are the assistant to the CEO of a small textile firm that manufactures high-quality, premium-priced, stylish clothing. The CEO has decided to see what the opportunities are for exporting and has asked you for advice as to the steps the company should take. What advice would you give to the CEO?

3. An alternative to using a letter of credit is export credit insurance. What are the advantages and disadvantages of using export credit insurance rather than a letter of credit for exporting (a) A luxury yacht from California to Canada, and (b) machine tools from New York to the Ukrainian Republic?

4. How do you explain the popularity of countertrade? Under what scenarios might its popularity increase still further by the year 2005? Under what scenarios might its popularity decline by the year 2005?

CLOSING CASE   Downey's Soup

Downey's is an Irish tavern in Philadelphia created over 20 years ago by Jack Downey. Over the years, the fortunes of the restaurant have wavered, but the strength of some favorite menu items has helped it survive economic downturns. In particular, the lobster bisque soup has met with increasing popularity, but Downey's efforts to market it have been sporadic. Never did Downey imagine that his lobster bisque would someday be the cause of an international trade dispute.

Unbeknown to Downey, the Japanese have a strong penchant for lobster. When the Philadelphia office of the Japanese External Trade Organization (Jetro) asked Downey to serve his lobster bisque at a minitrade show in 1991, he began to think about mass production of his soups. The Japanese loved the lobster bisque. They gave Downey a strong impression that the soup would sell very well in Japan. At the time, Downey did not have a formal product line but that seemed to be only a minor obstacle.

After the trade show, Michael Fisher, executive vice president for the newly formed Downey Foods Inc., was sent on an all-expenses-paid 10-day marketing trip to Japan by Jetro. (Jetro sponsors approximately 60 Americans for similar trips each year.) Although interest expressed by the food brokers and buyers he met seemed to be more polite than enthusiastic, he did get an initial order for 1,000 cases of the lobster bisque. The only condition placed by the buyer was to have the salt content reduced to comply with local Japanese tastes. Both Jetro and Fisher considered this initial order the beginning of rich export relationship with Japan.

Fisher contracted a food processor in Virginia, adapted the recipe for the new salt content, and shipped the soup to Japan in short order. Visions of expanded sales in Japan were quickly dashed as the cases of soup were detained at customs. Samples were sent to a government laboratory and eventually denied entry for containing polysorbate, an emulsifying and antifoaming agent used by food processors. Though it is considered harmless in the United States, polysorbate is not on Jetro's list of 347 approved food additives.

Fisher and Downey did not give up. They reformulated the soup to improve the taste and comply with Jetro's additive regulations. They had the soup tested and certified by a Japanese-approved lab, the Oregon Department of Agriculture's Export Service Center, to meet all Japanese standards. Then, in the fall of 1993, they sent another 1,000 cases to Japan.

The soup was denied entry again. Japanese officials said the expiration date on the Oregon tests had passed, so they retested the cans. Traces of polysorbate were found. A sample from that shipment was sent back to Oregon, and it passed. Two identical cans of soup were sent back to Japan and tested. They failed. Back in Oregon, a sample of the same shipment was tested again and no traces of polysorbate were found.

Japanese officials refused to allow the soup into Japan anyway. By this time, Downey's had been paid $20,000 that it could not afford to give back. "It stunned the customer," says Fisher. "But it stunned me a lot more. I was counting on dozens of reorders."

Fisher filed appeals with the US Embassy in Tokyo to no avail. "It became a bureaucratic/political issue," says

Fisher. "There was a face-saving problem. The Japanese had rejected the soup twice. There was no way they could reverse the decision."

The final irony came when a New York-based Japanese trader sent a few cases of Downey's regular (no reduced salt content) lobster bisque to Japan. This shipment sailed through customs without a problem.

Where was Jetro when Downey's soups were stalled in customs? Fisher thought he had everything covered. He followed the advice of Jetro, adjusted the soups to meet Japanese palates, and had them tested to meet Japanese food standards. Apparently, Jetro failed to inform Fisher of the apparent need for a local partner to sell and distribute in Japan. Most food companies have trouble getting into Japan, whether large or small. Agricultural products are one of the most difficult things to get into the Japanese market.

Jetro's agricultural specialist, Tatsuya Kajishima, contradicts the claim that Japan is hostile to food imports by stating the following statistic: 30 percent of Japan's food imports come from the United States. Further, Japan is the fourth largest importer of America's soups to the tune of $6.5 million worth of soup purchased in 1993. Most of these sales came from Campbell's Soup Co.

Although this venture was not particularly profitable for Downey Foods Inc., the company has been able to redirect its research and development efforts to build its domestic product line. Through its local broker, Santucci Associates, Downey Foods attracted the attention of Liberty Richter Inc., a national distributor of gourmet and imported food items.

http://www.jetro.go.jp/top/index.html

Source: Case written by Mureen Kibelsted and Charles Hill from original research by Mureen Kibelsted.

Case Discussion Questions

1. Did Downey Foods' export opportunity occur as a result of proactive action by Downey or was its strategy reactive?

2. Why did Downey experience frustrations when trying to export to Japan? What actions might Downey take to improve its prospects of succeeding in the Japanese market?

3. You have been hired by Downey Foods to develop an exporting strategy for the firm. What steps do you think Downey should take to increase the volume of its exports?

Notes

1. J. Landers, "Small Firms Learning the Ways of Global Trade," *Dallas Morning News*, August 17, 1998, p. 1D; and J. Norman, "Small Businesses Have Big Role in Export Field," *Orange County Register*, April 27, 1998, p. D15.

2. W. J. Holstein, "Why Johann Can Export, but Johnny Can't," *Business Week*, November 4, 1991, pp. 64–65.

3. S. T.Cavusgil, "Global Dimensions of Marketing," in *Marketing*, ed. P. E. Murphy and B. M. Enis (Glenview, IL: Scott, Foresman, 1985), pp. 577–99.

4. S. M. Mehta,"Enterprise: Small Companies Look to Cultivate Foreign Business," *The Wall Street Journal*, July 7, 1994, p. B2.

5. W. Pavord and R. Bogart, "The Dynamics of the Decision to Export," *Akron Business and Economic Review*, 1975, pp. 6–11.

6. J. Norman, "Small Businesses Have Big Role in Export Field."

7. A. O. Ogbuehi and T. A. Longfellow, "Perceptions of U.S. Manufacturing Companies Concerning Exporting," *Journal of Small Business Management*, October 1994, pp. 37–59.

8. R. W. Haigh, "Thinking of Exporting?" *Columbia Journal of World Business* 29 (December 1994), pp. 66–86.

9. F. Williams," The Quest for More Efficient Commerce," *Financial Times*, October 13, 1994, p. 7.

10. M. Y. Yoshino and T. B. Lifson, *The Invisible Link* (Cambridge, MA: MIT Press, 1986).

11. L. W. Tuller, *Going Global* (Homewood, IL: Business One-Irwin, 1991).

12. Haigh, "Thinking of Exporting?"

13. For a review of the conditions under which a buyer has power over a supplier, see M. E. Porter, *Competitive Strategy* (New York: Free Press, 1980).

14. *Exchange Agreements and Exchange Restrictions* (Washington, DC: International Monetary Fund, 1989).

15. J. R. Carter and J. Gagne, "The Do's and Don'ts of International Countertrade," *Sloan Management Review*, Spring 1988, pp. 31–37; and W. Maneerungsee, "Countertrade: Farm Goods Swapped for Italian Electricity," *Bangkok Post*, July 23, 1998.

16. Estimate from the American Countertrade Association at http://freedonia.tpusa.com/infosrc/aca/.

17. Carter and Gagne, "The Do's and Dont's of International Countertrade."

18. Maneerungsee, "Countertrade: Farm Goods Swapped for Italian Electricity."

19. For details, see Carter and Gagne, "Do's and Dont's," and J. F. Hennart, "Some Empirical Dimensions of Countertrade," *Journal of International Business Studies*, 1990, pp. 240–60.

20. D. J. Lecraw, "The Management of Countertrade: Factors Influencing Success," *Journal of International Business Studies*, Spring 1989, pp. 41–59.

CHAPTER SIXTEEN

GLOBAL MANUFACTURING AND MATERIALS MANAGEMENT

Li & Fung

Established in 1906, Hong Kong-based Li & Fung is now one of the largest multinational trading companies in the developing world, with annual sales of about $2 billion. The company, which is still run by the grandson of the founder, Victor Fung, does not see itself as a traditional trading enterprise. Rather, it sees itself as an expert in supply chain management for its 350 or so customers. These customers are a diverse group and include clothing retailers and consumer electronics companies. Li & Fung takes orders from customers and then sifts through its network of 7,000 independent suppliers located in 26 countries to find the right manufacturing enterprises to produce the product for customers at the most attractive combination of cost and quality. Attaining this goal frequently requires Li & Fung to break up the value chain and disperse different productive activities to manufacturers located in different countries depending on an assessment of factors such as labor costs, trade barriers, transportation costs, and so on. Li & Fung then coordinates the whole process, managing the logistics and arranging for the shipment of the finished product to the customer.

Typical of its customers is The Limited, Inc., a large US-based chain of retail clothing stores. The Limited outsources much of its manufacturing and logistics functions to Li & Fung. The process starts when The Limited comes to Li & Fung with designer sketches of clothes for the next fashion season. Li & Fung takes the basic product concepts and researches the market to find the right kind of yarn, dye, buttons, and so on, then assembles these into prototypes that The

Limited can inspect. Once The Limited has settled on a prototype, it will give Li & Fung an order and ask for delivery within five weeks. The short time between an order and requested delivery is necessitated by the rapid rate of product obsolescence in the fashion clothing industry (personal computer manufacturers also live with very compressed product life cycles).

With order in hand, Li & Fung distributes the various aspects of the overall manufacturing process to different producers depending on their capabilities and costs. For example, Li & Fung might decide to purchase yarn from a Korean company but have it woven and dyed in Taiwan. So Li & Fung will arrange for the yarn to be picked up from Korea and shipped to Taiwan. The Japanese might have the best zippers and buttons, but they manufacture them mostly in China. So Li & Fung will go to YKK, a big Japanese zipper manufacturer, and order the right zippers from their Chinese plants. Then Li & Fung might decide that due to constraints imposed by export quotas and labor costs, the best place to make the final garments might be in Thailand. So everything will be shipped to Thailand. In addition, because The Limited, like many retail customers, needs quick delivery, Li & Fung might divide the order across five factories in Thailand. Five weeks after the order has been received, the garments will arrive on the shelves of The Limited, all looking like they came from one factory, with colors perfectly matched. The result is a product that may have a label that says "Made in Thailand," but is a global product.

To better serve the needs of its customers, Li & Fung is divided into numerous small, customer-focused divisions. There is a theme store division that serves a handful of customers such as Warner Brothers and Rainforest Café, there is a division for The Limited, and another for Gymboree, a US-based children's clothing store. Walk into one of these divisions, such as the Gymboree division, and you will see that every one of the 40 or so people in the division is focused solely on meeting Gymboree's needs. On every desk is a computer with a direct software link to Gymboree. The staff is organized into specialized teams in areas such as design, technical support, merchandising, raw material purchasing, quality assurance, and shipping. These teams also have direct electronic links to dedicated staff in Li & Fung's branch offices in various countries where Gymboree buys in volume, such as China, Indonesia, and the Philippines. Thus, Li & Fung uses information systems to manage, coordinate, and control the globally dispersed design, production, and shipping process to ensure that the time between receipt of an order and delivery is minimized, as are overall costs.

http://www.limited.com

Sources: J. Magretta, "Fast, Global, and Entrepreneurial: Supply Chain Management Hong Kong Style," *Harvard Business Review*, September–October 1998, p. 102–114; J. Ridding, "A Multinational Trading Group with Chinese Characteristics," *Financial Times*, November 7, 1997, p. 16; J. Ridding, "The Family in the Frame," *Financial Times*, October 28, 1996, p. 12; and J. Lo, "Second Half Doubts Shadow Li & Fung Strength in Interims," *South China Morning Post*, August 27, 1998, p. 3.

CHAPTER OUTLINE

LI & FUNG

INTRODUCTION

STRATEGY, MANUFACTURING, AND MATERIALS MANAGEMENT

WHERE TO MANUFACTURE
Country Factors
Technological Factors
Product Factors
Locating Manufacturing Facilities

THE STRATEGIC ROLE OF FOREIGN FACTORIES

MAKE-OR-BUY DECISIONS
The Advantages of Make
The Advantages of Buy
Trade-offs
Strategic Alliances with Suppliers

COORDINATING A GLOBAL MANUFACTURING SYSTEM
The Power of Just-in-Time
The Role of Organization
The Role of Information Technology

CHAPTER SUMMARY

CRITICAL DISCUSSION QUESTIONS

TIMBERLAND

Introduction

In the opening case, Li & Fung deals with a number of issues that many other firms competing in today's global economy also have had to deal with. To serve the needs of its customers, Li & Fung has to decide how best to distribute manufacturing activities among operations based in various countries so as to minimize costs, produce products that have an acceptable level of quality, and do so in a timely manner. Li & Fung scans its global network of some 7,000 suppliers located in 26 countries to make these decisions, weighing factors such as labor costs, trade barriers, transportation costs, and product quality, and only then deciding what should be produced where and in what quantities. Li & Fung often unbundles the value chain associated with producing a product, dispersing various parts of the chain to different locations depending on an assessment of the value that can be created by performing an activity in a particular location. Li & Fung must then coordinate and control the globally dispersed value chain so that it minimizes the time between receipt of an order and delivery of the finished product.

In this chapter, we look at the problems that Li & Fung and many other enterprises are facing and at the various solutions. We will be concerned with answering three central questions:

- Where in the world should productive activities be located?
- How much production should be performed in-house and how much should be out-sourced to foreign suppliers?
- What is the best way to coordinate a globally dispersed supply chain?

We will examine each of the three questions posed above in turn. We begin, however, by reviewing how the information covered in this chapter fits into the "big picture" of global strategy that we introduced in Chapter 12.

Strategy, Manufacturing, and Materials Management

In Chapter 12, we introduced the concept of the value chain and discussed a number of value creation activities, including production, marketing, materials management, R&D, human resources, and information systems. In this chapter we will focus on two of these activities—production and materials management—and attempt to clarify how they might be performed internationally to (1) lower the costs of value creation and (2) add value by better serving customer needs. We will discuss the contributions of information technology to these activities. In later chapters, we will look at other value creation activities in this international context (marketing, R&D, and human resource management).

In Chapter 12, we defined production as "the activities involved in creating a product." We used the term *production* to denote both service and manufacturing activities, since one can produce a service or produce a physical product. In this chapter, we focus more on manufacturing than on service activities, so we will use the term *manufacturing* rather than production. We defined **materials management** as "the activity that controls the transmission of physical materials through the value chain, from procurement through production and into distribution." Materials management includes **logistics,** which refers to the procurement and physical transmission of material through the supply chain, from suppliers to customers. Manufacturing and materials management are closely linked, since a firm's ability to perform its manufacturing function efficiently depends on a continuous supply of high-quality material inputs, for which materials management is responsible.

The manufacturing and materials management functions of an international firm have a number of important strategic objectives.[1] Two important objectives shared by

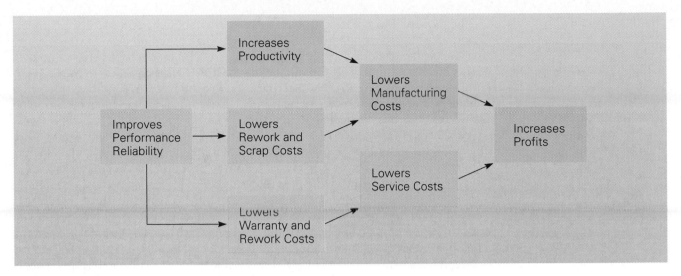

Figure 16.1

The Relationship between Quality and Costs

Source: Reprinted from "What Does Product Quality Really Mean?" by David A. Garvin, *Sloan Management Review* 26 (Fall 1984), Figure 1, p. 37, by permission of the publisher. Copyright 1984 by Sloan Management Review Association. All rights reserved.

both manufacturing and materials management are to *lower costs* and to *simultaneously increase product quality* by eliminating defective products from both the supply chain and the manufacturing process.[2]

These two objectives are not independent of each other. As illustrated in Figure 16.1, the firm that improves its quality control will also reduce its costs of value creation. Improved quality control reduces costs in three ways:

- Productivity increases because time is not wasted manufacturing poor-quality products that cannot be sold. This saving leads to a direct reduction in unit costs.
- Increased product quality means lower rework and scrap costs.
- Greater product quality means lower warranty and rework costs.

The effect is to lower the costs of value creation by reducing both manufacturing and service costs.

The main management technique that companies are utilizing to boost their product quality is **total quality management** (TQM). TQM is a management philosophy that takes as its central focus the need to improve the quality of a company's products and services. The TQM concept was developed by a number of American consultants such as the late W. Edward Deming, Joseph Juran, and A.V. Feigenbaum.[3] Deming identified a number of steps that should be part of any TQM program. He argued that management should embrace the philosophy that mistakes, defects, and poor-quality materials are not acceptable and should be eliminated. He suggested that the quality of supervision should be improved by allowing more time for supervisors to work with employees and by providing them with the tools they need to do the job. Deming recommended that management should create an environment in which employees will not fear reporting problems or recommending improvements. He believed that work standards should be defined not only as numbers or quotas, but also should include some notion of quality to promote the production of defect-free output. He argued that management has the responsibility to train employees in new skills to keep pace with changes in the workplace. In addition, he believed that achieving better quality requires the commitment of everyone in the company.

The growth of international standards has also focused greater attention on the importance of product quality. In Europe, for example, the European Union requires that the quality of a firm's manufacturing processes and products be certified under a quality standard known as **ISO 9000** before the firm is allowed access to the EU marketplace. Although the ISO 9000 certification process has proved to be a somewhat bureaucratic and costly process for many firms, it does focus management attention on the need to improve the quality of products and processes.[4]

In addition to the objectives of lowering costs and improving quality, two other objectives have particular importance in international businesses. First, manufacturing and materials management must be able to accommodate demands for local responsiveness. As we saw in Chapter 12, demands for local responsiveness arise from national differences in consumer tastes and preferences, infrastructure, distribution channels, and host-government demands. Demands for local responsiveness create pressures to decentralize manufacturing activities to the major national or regional markets in which the firm does business.

Second, manufacturing and materials management must be able to respond quickly to shifts in customer demand. In recent years time-based competition has grown more important.[5] When consumer demand is prone to large and unpredictable shifts, the firm that can adapt most quickly to these shifts will gain an advantage. As we shall see, both manufacturing and materials management play critical roles here. This issue surfaced in the opening case. One of Li & Fung's core competencies is its ability to respond to customer needs in a timely manner by ensuring that products arrive just when they are needed, not too late or too soon (which would mean the customer would have to bear the costs of storing the inventory until it was needed).

Where to Manufacture

An essential decision facing an international firm is *where to locate its manufacturing activities* to achieve the twin goals of minimizing costs and improving product quality. For the firm contemplating international production, a number of factors must be considered. These factors can be grouped under three broad headings: country factors, technological factors, and product factors.[6]

Country Factors

We reviewed country-specific factors in some detail earlier in the book and we will not dwell on them here. Political economy, culture, and relative factor costs differ from country to country. In Chapter 4, we saw that due to differences in factor costs, certain countries have a comparative advantage for producing certain products. In Chapters 2 and 3, we saw how differences in political economy and national culture influence the benefits, costs, and risks of doing business in a country. Other things being equal, a firm should locate its various manufacturing activities where the economic, political, and cultural conditions, including relative factor costs, are conducive to the performance of those activities. In Chapter 12, we referred to the benefits derived from such a strategy as location economies. We argued that one result of the strategy is the creation of a global web of value creation activities.

Of course, other things are not equal. Other country factors that impinge on location decisions include formal and informal trade barriers (see Chapter 5) and rules and regulations regarding foreign direct investment (see Chapter 7). For example, although relative factor costs may make a country look attractive as a location for performing a manufacturing activity, regulations prohibiting foreign direct investment may eliminate this option. Similarly, a consideration of factor costs might suggest that a firm should source production of a certain component from a particular country, but trade barriers could make this uneconomical.

Another country factor is expected future movements in its exchange rate (see Chapters 9 and 10). Adverse changes in exchange rates can quickly alter a country's attractiveness as a manufacturing base. Currency appreciation can transform a low-cost location into a high-cost location. Many Japanese corporations had to grapple with this problem during the 1990s. The relatively low value of the yen on foreign exchange markets between 1950 and 1980 helped strengthen Japan's position as a low-cost location for manufacturing. Between 1980 and the mid-1990s, however, the yen's steady appreciation against the dollar increased the dollar cost of products exported from Japan, making Japan less attractive as a manufacturing location. In response, many Japanese firms moved their manufacturing offshore to lower-cost locations in East Asia.

Technological Factors

The technology we are concerned with in this subsection is manufacturing technology—the technology that performs specific manufacturing activities. The type of technology a firm uses in its manufacturing can be pivotal in location decisions. For example, because of technological constraints, in some cases it is feasible to perform certain manufacturing activities in only one location and serve the world market from there. In other cases, the technology may make it feasible to perform an activity in multiple locations. Three characteristics of a manufacturing technology are of interest here: the level of its fixed costs, its minimum efficient scale, and its flexibility.

Fixed Costs

As we noted in Chapter 12, in some cases the fixed costs of setting up a manufacturing plant are so high that a firm must serve the world market from a single location or from a very few locations. For example, it can cost more than $1 billion to set up a plant to manufacture semiconductor chips. Given this, serving the world market from a single plant sited at a single (optimal) location makes sense.

But a relatively low level of fixed costs can make it economical to perform a particular activity in several locations at once. One advantage of this is that the firm can better accommodate demands for local responsiveness. Manufacturing in multiple locations may also help the firm avoid becoming too dependent on one location. Being too dependent on one location is particularly risky in a world of floating exchange rates.

Minimum Efficient Scale

The concept of economies of scale tells us that as plant output expands, unit costs decrease. The reasons include the greater utilization of capital equipment and the productivity gains that come with specialization of employees within the plant.[7] However, beyond a certain level of output, few additional scale economies are available. Thus, the "unit cost curve" declines with output until a certain output level is reached, at which point further increases in output realize little reduction in unit costs. The level of output at which most plant-level scale economies are exhausted is referred to as the minimum efficient scale of output. This is the scale of output a plant must operate at to realize all major plant-level scale economies (see Figure 16.2).

The implications of this concept are as follows: The larger the minimum efficient scale of a plant, the greater the argument for centralizing production in a single location or a limited number of locations. Alternatively, when the minimum efficient scale of production is relatively low, it may be economical to manufacture a product at several locations. As in the case of low fixed costs, the advantages are allowing the firm to accommodate demands for local responsiveness or to hedge against currency risk by manufacturing the same product in several locations.

Figure 16.2

A Typical Unit Cost Curve

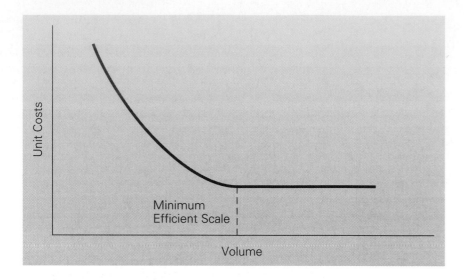

Flexible Manufacturing (Lean Production)

Central to the concept of economies of scale is the idea that the best way to achieve high efficiency, and hence low unit costs, is through the mass production of a standardized output. The trade-off implicit in this idea is one between unit costs and product variety. Producing greater product variety from a factory implies shorter production runs, which in turn implies an inability to realize economies of scale. Increasing product variety makes it difficult for a company to increase its manufacturing efficiency and thus reduce its unit costs. According to this logic, the way to increase efficiency and drive down unit costs is to limit product variety and produce a standardized product in large volumes.

This view of manufacturing efficiency has been challenged by the recent rise of flexible manufacturing technologies. The term *flexible manufacturing technology*—or **lean production** as it is often called—covers a range of manufacturing technologies that are designed to (*a*) reduce setup times for complex equipment, (*b*) increase utilization of individual machines through better scheduling, and (*c*) improve quality control at all stages of the manufacturing process.[8] Flexible manufacturing technologies allow a company to produce a wider variety of end products at a unit cost that at one time could be achieved only through the mass production of a standardized output. The term **mass customization** has been coined to describe this ability.[9] Mass customization implies that a firm may be able to customize its product range to suit the needs of different customer groups without bearing a cost penalty. Research suggests that the adoption of flexible manufacturing technologies may increase efficiency and lower unit costs relative to what can be achieved by the mass production of a standardized output.[10]

Flexible manufacturing technologies vary in their sophistication and complexity. One famous example of a flexible manufacturing technology, Toyota's production system, is relatively unsophisticated, but it has been credited with making Toyota the most efficient auto company in the world. Toyota's flexible manufacturing system was developed by one of the company's engineers, Ohno Taiichi. After working at Toyota for five years and visiting Ford's US plants, Ohno became convinced that the mass production philosophy for making cars was flawed. He saw numerous problems with the mass production system, including the following.

First, long production runs created massive inventories that had to be stored in large warehouses. This was expensive, both because of the cost of warehousing and because inventories tied up capital in unproductive uses. Second, if the initial machine settings were wrong, long production runs resulted in the production of a large number of defects (i.e., waste). Third, the mass production system was unable to accommodate consumer preferences for product diversity.

In response, Ohno looked for ways to make shorter production runs economical. He developed a number of techniques designed to reduce setup times for production equipment (a major source of fixed costs). By using a system of levers and pulleys, he reduced the time required to change dies on stamping equipment from a full day in 1950 to 3 minutes by 1971. This made small production runs economical, which allowed Toyota to respond better to consumer demands for product diversity. Small production runs also eliminated the need to hold large inventories, thereby reducing warehousing costs. Furthermore, small product runs and the lack of inventory meant that defective parts were produced only in small numbers and entered the assembly process immediately. This reduced waste and helped trace defects back to their source to fix the problem. In sum, Ohno's innovations enabled Toyota to produce a more diverse product range at a lower unit cost than was possible with conventional mass production.[11]

Flexible machine cells are another common flexible manufacturing technology. A flexible machine cell is a grouping of various types of machinery, a common materials handler, and a centralized cell controller (computer). Each cell normally contains four to six machines capable of performing a variety of operations. The typical cell is dedicated to the production of a family of parts or products. The settings on machines are computer controlled. This allows each cell to switch quickly between the production of different parts or products.

Improved capacity utilization and reductions in work in progress and waste are major efficiency benefits of flexible machine cells. Improved capacity utilization arises from the reduction in setup times and from the computer-controlled coordination of production flow between machines, which eliminates bottlenecks. The tight coordination between machines also reduces work-in-progress inventory (e.g., stockpiles of partly finished products). Reductions in waste arise from the ability of computer-controlled machinery to identify how to transform inputs into outputs while producing a minimum of unusable waste material. As a consequence of all these factors, while a freestanding machine might be in use 50 percent of the time, the same machines when grouped into a cell can be used more than 80 percent of the time and produce the same end product with half the waste. This increases efficiency and results in lower costs.

The efficiency benefits of installing flexible manufacturing technology can be dramatic. For example, after introduction of a flexible manufacturing system, General Electric's locomotive operations reduced the time it took to produce locomotive motor frames from 16 days to 16 hours. Similarly, after it introduced a flexible manufacturing system, Fireplace Manufacturers Inc., one of the country's largest fireplace businesses, reduced scrap left from the manufacturing process by 60 percent, increased inventory turnover threefold, and increased labor productivity by more than 30 percent.[12]

As these examples make clear, flexible manufacturing technologies can improve a company's efficiency. Not only do flexible manufacturing technologies allow companies to lower costs, but they also enable companies to customize products to the demands of small consumer groups—and to do so at a cost that at one time could be achieved only by mass producing a standardized output. Thus, they help a company increase customer responsiveness. Most important for an international business, flexible manufacturing technologies can help the firm customize products for different national markets. The importance of this advantage cannot be overstated. When flexible manufacturing technologies are available, a firm can manufacture products customized to various national markets at a single factory sited at the optimal location. And it can do this without absorbing a significant cost penalty. Thus, companies no longer need to establish manufacturing facilities in each major national market to provide products that satisfy specific consumer tastes and preferences, part of the rationale for a multidomestic strategy (Chapter 12).

Summary

A number of technological factors support the economic arguments for concentrating manufacturing facilities in a few choice locations or even in a single location. Other things being equal, when

- Fixed costs are substantial,
- The minimum efficient scale of production is high, and/or
- Flexible manufacturing technologies are available,

the arguments for concentrating production at a few choice locations are strong. This is true even when substantial differences in consumer tastes and preferences exist between national markets, since flexible manufacturing technologies allow the firm to customize products to national differences at a single facility. Alternatively, when

- Fixed costs are low,
- The minimum efficient scale of production is low, and
- Flexible manufacturing technologies are not available,

the arguments for concentrating production at one or a few locations are not as compelling. In such cases, it may make more sense to manufacture in each major market in which the firm is active if this helps the firm better respond to local demands. This holds only if the increased local responsiveness more than offsets the cost disadvantages of not concentrating manufacturing. With the advent of flexible manufacturing technologies, such a strategy is becoming less attractive. In sum, technological factors are making it feasible, and necessary, for firms to concentrate their manufacturing facilities at optimal locations. Trade barriers and transportation costs are probably the major brakes on this trend.

Product Factors

Two product features affect location decisions. The first is the product's *value-to-weight* ratio because of its influence on transportation costs. Many electronic components and pharmaceuticals have high value-to-weight ratios; they are expensive and they do not weigh very much. Thus, even if they are shipped halfway around the world, their transportation costs account for a very small percentage of total costs. Given this, other things being equal, there is great pressure to manufacture these products in the optimal location and to serve the world market from there. The opposite holds for products with low value-to-weight ratios. Refined sugar, certain bulk chemicals, paints, and petroleum products all have low value-to-weight ratios; they are relatively inexpensive products that weigh a lot. Accordingly, when they are shipped long distances, transportation costs account for a large percentage of total costs. Thus, other things being equal, there is great pressure to manufacture these products in multiple locations close to major markets to reduce transportation costs.

The other product feature that can influence location decisions is whether the product serves **universal needs,** needs that are the same all over the world. Examples include many industrial products (e.g., industrial electronics, steel, bulk chemicals) and modern consumer products (e.g., handheld calculators and personal computers). Since there are few national differences in consumer taste and preference for such products, the need for local responsiveness is reduced. This increases the attractiveness of concentrating manufacturing at an optimal location.

Locating Manufacturing Facilities

There are two basic strategies for locating manufacturing facilities: concentrating them in the optimal location and serving the world market from there, and decentralizing them in various regional or national locations that are close to major markets. The appropriate strategic choice is determined by the various country,

Table 16.1

Location Strategy and Manufacturing

	Favored Manufactured Strategy	
	Concentrated	Decentralized
Country factors		
Differences in political economy	Substantial	Few
Differences in culture	Substantial	Few
Differences in factor costs	Substantial	Few
Trade barriers	Few	Many
Technological factors		
Fixed costs	High	Low
Minimum efficient scale	High	Low
Flexible manufacturing technology	Available	Not available
Product factors		
Value-to-weight ratio	High	Low
Serves universal needs	Yes	No

technological, and product factors we have discussed in this section, and are summarized in Table 16.1. As can be seen, concentration of manufacturing makes most sense when:

- Differences between countries in factor costs, political economy, and culture have a substantial impact on the costs of manufacturing in various countries.
- Trade barriers are low.
- Important exchange rates are expected to remain relatively stable.
- The production technology has high fixed costs, a high minimum efficient scale, or a flexible manufacturing technology exists.
- The product's value-to-weight ratio is high.
- The product serves universal needs.

Alternatively, decentralization of manufacturing is appropriate when:

- Differences between countries in factor costs, political economy, and culture do not have a substantial impact on the costs of manufacturing in various countries.
- Trade barriers are high.
- Volatility in important exchange rates is expected.
- The production technology has low fixed costs, low minimum efficient scale, and flexible manufacturing technology is not available.
- The product's value-to-weight ratio is low.
- The product does not serve universal needs (that is, significant differences in consumer tastes and preferences exist between nations).

In practice, location decisions are seldom clear cut. For example, it is not unusual for differences in factor costs, technological factors, and product factors to point toward concentrated manufacturing while a combination of trade barriers and volatile exchange rates points toward decentralized manufacturing. This is probably the case in the world automobile industry. Although the availability of flexible manufacturing and cars' relatively high value-to-weight ratios suggest concentrated manufacturing, the combination of formal and informal trade barriers and the uncertainties of the world's current floating exchange rate regime (see Chapter 10) have inhibited firms' ability to pursue this strategy.

Map 16.1

The Ford Fiesta Production Network in Europe

Source: Peter Dicken, *Global Shift* (New York: The Guilford Press, 1992), p. 300.

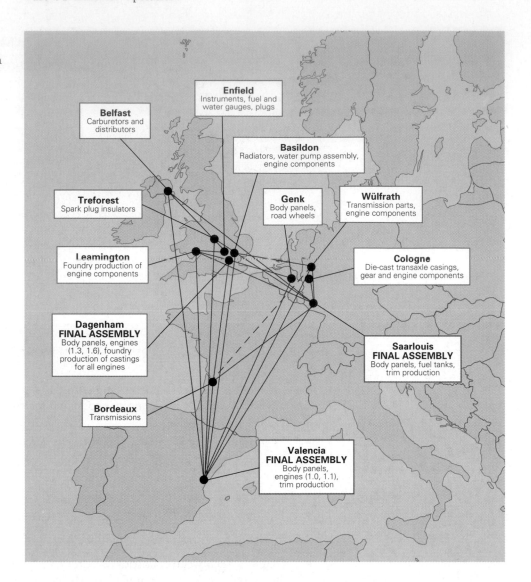

For these reasons, Honda is establishing "top-to-bottom" manufacturing operations in its three major markets: Japan, North America, and Western Europe. Honda can treat Western Europe as a single market because of the European Community's success in removing trade barriers and stabilizing exchange rates in the member countries.

Another auto company that treats Western Europe as a single market is Ford. Map 16.1 shows how Ford of Europe dispersed the various manufacturing activities for its Fiesta to different locations in Western Europe. (This figure shows the geographical pattern of only the network within Ford; independent component suppliers are not shown.) Some components are single sourced to take advantage of economies of scale. For example, all carburetors are supplied by the Belfast plant; all transmissions are built at Bordeaux; Basildon supplies radiator assemblies; Treforest makes spark plugs. Final assembly operations are performed at three locations: Dagenham in Great Britain, Saarlouis in Germany, and Valencia in Spain. Ford reasons that it can better customize the product to local needs by doing this. In addition, it can make up for shortfalls of production at one location by shipping cars from one of the other locations. The result is a complex network of cross-border flows of finished vehicles and components. Presumably, Ford locates the various activities in particular locations because it believes these are the most favorable locations for performing those activities.

The Strategic Role of Foreign Factories

Whatever the rationale behind establishing a foreign manufacturing facility, the strategic role of foreign factories can evolve over time.[13] Initially, many foreign factories are established where labor costs are low. Their strategic role typically is to produce labor-intensive products at as low a cost as possible. For example, beginning in the 1970s, many US firms in the computer and telecommunications equipment businesses established factories across Southeast Asia to manufacture electronic components, such as circuit boards and semiconductors, at the lowest possible cost. They located their factories in countries such as Malaysia, Thailand, and Singapore precisely because each of these countries offered an attractive combination of low labor costs, adequate infrastructure, and a favorable tax and trade regime. Initially, the components produced by these factories were designed elsewhere and the final product would be assembled elsewhere. Over time, however, the strategic role of some of these factories has expanded; they have become important centers for the design and final assembly of products for the global marketplace. An example is Hewlett-Packard's (HP) operation in Singapore. Originally established as a low-cost location for the production of circuit boards, the facility has become the center for the design and final assembly of portable ink-jet printers for the global marketplace (see the accompanying Management Focus).

Such upward migration in the strategic role of foreign factories arises because many foreign factories upgrade their own capabilities.[14] This improvement comes from two sources. First, pressure from the center to improve a factory's cost structure and/or customize a product to the demands of consumers in a particular nation can start a chain of events that ultimately leads to development of additional capabilities at that factory. For example, to meet centrally mandated directions to drive down costs, engineers at HP's Singapore factory argued that they needed to redesign products so they could be manufactured at a lower cost. This led to the establishment of a design center in Singapore. As this design center proved its worth, HP management realized the importance of co-locating design and manufacturing operations. They increasingly transferred more design responsibilities to the Singapore factory. In addition, the Singapore factory ultimately became the center for the design of products tailored to the needs of the Asian market. This too made good strategic sense because it meant products were being designed by engineers who were close to the Asian market and probably had a good understanding of the needs of that market, as opposed to engineers located in the United States.

A second source of improvement in the capabilities of a foreign factory can be the increasing abundance of advanced factors of production in the nation in which the factory is located. Many nations that were considered economic backwaters a generation ago have been experiencing rapid economic development during the 1980s and 1990s. Their communications and transportation infrastructures and the education level of the population have improved. While these countries once lacked the advanced infrastructure required to support sophisticated design, development, and manufacturing operations, this is often no longer the case. This has made it much easier for factories based in these nations to take on a greater strategic role.

Because of such developments many international businesses are moving away from a system in which their foreign factories were viewed as nothing more than low-cost manufacturing facilities and toward one where foreign factories are viewed as globally dispersed centers of excellence. In this new model, foreign factories take the lead role for the design and manufacture of products to serve important national or regional markets or even the global market. The development of such dispersed centers of excellence is consistent with the concept of a transnational strategy, which we introduced in Chapter 12. A major aspect of a transnational strategy is a belief in global learning—the idea that valuable knowledge does not reside just in a firm's

MANAGEMENT FOCUS
Hewlett-Packard in Singapore

http://www.hp.com

In the late 1960s, Hewlett-Packard company was looking around Asia for a low-cost location to produce electronic components that were to be manufactured using labor-intensive processes. The company looked at several Asian locations but eventually settled on Singapore, opening its first factory there in 1970. Although Singapore did not have the lowest labor costs in the region, costs were low relative to North America. Plus, the Singapore location had several important benefits that could not be found at many other locations in Asia. The education level of the local work force was high. English was widely spoken. The government of Singapore seemed stable and committed to economic development, and the city-state had one of the better-developed infrastructures in the region, including good communications and transportation networks and a rapidly developing industrial and commercial base. HP also extracted favorable terms from the Singapore government with regard to taxes, tariffs, and subsidies.

To begin with, the plant manufactured only basic components. The combination of low labor costs and a favorable tax regime helped to make this plant profitable early. In 1973, HP transferred the manufacture of one of its basic handheld calculators from the United States to Singapore. The objective was to reduce manufacturing costs, which the Singapore factory was quickly able to do. Increasingly confident in the capability of the Singapore factory to handle entire products, as opposed to just components, HP's management transferred other products to Singapore over the next few years including keyboards, solid-state displays, and integrated circuits. However, all of these products were still designed, developed, and initially produced in the United States.

The plant's status shifted in the early 1980s when HP embarked on a worldwide campaign to boost product quality and reduce costs. HP transferred the production of its HP41C handheld calculator to Singapore. The managers at the Singapore plant were given the goal of substantially reducing manufacturing costs. They argued that this could be achieved only if they were allowed to redesign the product so

it could be manufactured at a lower overall cost. HP's central management agreed, and 20 engineers from the Singapore facility were transferred to the United States for one year to learn how to design application-specific integrated circuits. They then brought this expertise back to Singapore and set about redesigning the HP41C.

The results were a huge success. By redesigning the product, the Singapore engineers reduced manufacturing costs for the HP41C by 50 percent. Using this newly acquired capability for product design, the Singapore facility then set about redesigning other products it produced. HP's corporate managers were so impressed with the progress made at the factory, they transferred production of the entire calculator line to Singapore in 1983. This was followed by the partial transfer of ink-jet production to Singapore in 1984 and keyboard production in 1986. In all cases, the facility redesigned the products and often reduced unit manufacturing costs by more than 30 percent. The initial development and design of all these products, however, still occurred in the United States.

In the late 1980s and early 1990s, the Singapore plant started to take on added responsibilities, particularly in the ink-jet printer business. In 1990, the factory was given the job of redesigning an HP ink-jet printer for the Japanese market. Although the initial product redesign was a market failure, the managers at Singapore pushed to be allowed to try again, and in 1991 they were given the job of redesigning HP's DeskJet 505 printer for the Japanese market. This time the redesigned product was a success, garnering significant sales in Japan. Emboldened by this success, the plant has continued to take on additional design responsibilities. Today, it is viewed as a "lead plant" within HP's global network, with primary responsibility not just for manufacturing, but also for the development and design of a family of small ink-jet printers targeted at the Asian market.

Sources: K. Ferdows, "Making the Most of Foreign Factories," *Harvard Business Review,* March–April 1997, pp. 73–88; and "Hewlett-Packard: Singapore," *Harvard Business School,* case # 694-035.

domestic operations; it may also be found in its foreign subsidiaries. Foreign factories that upgrade their capabilities over time are creating valuable knowledge that might benefit the whole corporation.

For the manager of an international business, the important point to remember is that foreign factories can improve their capabilities over time, and this can be of immense strategic benefit to the firm. Rather than viewing foreign factories simply as sweatshops where unskilled labor churns out low-cost goods, managers need to view them as potential centers of excellence and to encourage and foster attempts by their local managers to upgrade the capabilities of their factories and, thereby, enhance their strategic standing within the corporation.

Make-or-Buy Decisions

International businesses frequently face **sourcing decisions,** decisions about whether they should make or buy the component parts that go into their final product. Should the firm vertically integrate to manufacture its own component parts or should it outsource them, or buy them from independent suppliers? Make-or-buy decisions are important factors of many firms' manufacturing strategies. In the automobile industry, for example, the typical car contains more than 10,000 components, so automobile firms constantly face make-or-buy decisions. Ford of Europe, for example, produces only about 45 percent of the value of the Fiesta in its own plants. The remaining 55 percent, mainly accounted for by component parts, come from independent suppliers. In the athletic shoe industry, the make-or-buy issue has been taken to an extreme with companies such as Nike and Reebok having no involvement in manufacturing; all production has been outsourced, primarily to manufacturers based in low-wage countries.

Make-or-buy decisions pose plenty of problems for purely domestic businesses but even more problems for international businesses. These decisions in the international arena are complicated by the volatility of countries' political economies, exchange rate movements, changes in relative factor costs, and the like. In this section, we examine the arguments for making components and for buying them, and we consider the trade-offs involved in these decisions. Then we discuss strategic alliances as an alternative to manufacturing component parts within the company.

The Advantages of Make

The arguments that support making component parts in-house—vertical integration—are fourfold. Vertical integration may be associated with lower costs, facilitate investments in highly specialized assets, protect proprietary product technology, and facilitate the scheduling of adjacent processes.

Lower Costs

It may pay a firm to continue manufacturing a product or component part in-house if the firm is more efficient at that production activity than any other enterprise. Boeing, for example, recently undertook a very detailed review of its make-or-buy decisions with regard to commercial jet aircraft (for details see the accompanying Management Focus). It decided that although it would outsource the production of some component parts, it would keep the production of aircraft wings in-house. Its rationale was that Boeing has a core competence in the production of wings, and it is more efficient at this activity than any other comparable enterprise in the world. Therefore, it makes little sense for Boeing to outsource this particular activity.

Facilitating Specialized Investments

We first encountered the concept of specialized assets in Chapter 6 when we looked at the economic theory of vertical foreign direct investment. A variation of that concept explains why firms might want to make their own components rather than buy them.[15] The argument is that when one firm must invest in specialized assets to supply another, mutual dependency is created. In such circumstances, each party fears the other will abuse the relationship by seeking more favorable terms.

Imagine Ford of Europe has developed a new, high-performance, high-quality, and uniquely designed carburetor. The carburetor's increased fuel efficiency will help sell Ford cars. Ford must decide whether to make the carburetor in-house or to contract out the manufacturing to an independent supplier. Manufacturing these uniquely designed carburetors requires investments in equipment that can be used only for this purpose; it cannot be used to make carburetors for any other auto firm. Thus, investment in this equipment constitutes an investment in specialized assets.

Let us first examine this situation from the perspective of an independent supplier who has been asked by Ford to make this investment. The supplier might reason that once it has made the investment, it will become dependent on Ford for business since Ford is the only possible customer for the output of this equipment. The supplier perceives this as putting Ford in a strong bargaining position and worries that once the specialized investment has been made, Ford might use this to squeeze down prices for the carburetors. Given this risk, the supplier declines to make the investment in specialized equipment.

Now take the position of Ford. Ford might reason that if it contracts out production of these carburetors to an independent supplier, it might become too dependent on that supplier for a vital input. Because specialized equipment is required to produce the carburetors, Ford cannot easily switch its orders to other suppliers who lack that equipment. (It would face high switching costs.) Ford perceives this as increasing the bargaining power of the supplier and worries that the supplier might use its bargaining strength to demand higher prices.

Thus, the mutual dependency that outsourcing would create makes Ford nervous and scares away potential suppliers. The problem here is lack of trust. Neither party completely trusts the other to play fair. Consequently, Ford might reason that the only safe way to get the new carburetors is to manufacture them itself. It may be unable to persuade any independent supplier to manufacture them. Thus, Ford decides to make rather than buy.

In general, we can predict that when substantial investments in specialized assets are required to manufacture a component, the firm will prefer to make the component internally rather than contract it out to a supplier. A growing amount of empirical evidence supports this prediction.[16]

Proprietary Product Technology Protection

Proprietary product technology is technology unique to a firm. If it enables the firm to produce a product containing superior features, proprietary technology can give the firm a competitive advantage. The firm would not want this technology to fall into the hands of competitors. If the firm contracts out the manufacture of components containing proprietary technology, it runs the risk that those suppliers will expropriate the technology for their own use or that they will sell it to the firm's competitors. Thus, to maintain control over its technology, the firm might prefer to make such component parts in-house. An example of a firm that has made such decisions is given in the accompanying Management Focus, which looks at make-or-buy decisions at Boeing. While Boeing has decided to outsource a number of important components that go toward the production of an aircraft, it has explicitly decided not to outsource the manufacture of wings and cockpits because it believes that doing so would give away key technology to potential competitors.

Improved Scheduling

The weakest argument for vertical integration is that production cost savings result from it because it makes planning, coordination, and scheduling of adjacent processes easier.[17] This is particularly important in firms with just-in-time inventory systems

MANAGEMENT FOCUS
Make-or-Buy Decisions at the Boeing Company
http://www.boeing.com

The Boeing Company is the world's largest manufacturer of commercial jet aircraft with a 55 to 60 percent share of the global market. Despite its large market share, in recent years Boeing has found it tough going competitively. The company's problems are twofold. First, Boeing faces a very aggressive competitor in Europe's Airbus Industrie. The dogfight between Boeing and Airbus for market share has enabled major airlines to play the two companies off against each other in an attempt to bargain down the price for commercial jet aircraft. Second, several of the world's major airlines have gone through some very rough years during the 1990s, and many now lack the financial resources required to purchase new aircraft. Instead, they are holding onto their used aircraft for much longer than has typically been the case. Thus, while the typical service life of a Boeing 737 was once reckoned to be about 15 years, many airlines are now making the aircraft last as long as 25 years. This translates into lower orders for new aircraft. Confronted with this new reality, Boeing has concluded that the only way it can persuade cash-starved airlines to replace their used airlines with new aircraft is if it prices very aggressively.

Thus, Boeing has had to face up to the fact that its ability to raise prices for commercial jet aircraft, which was once quite strong, has now been severely limited. Falling prices might even be the norm. If prices are under pressure, the only way Boeing can continue to make a profit is if it also drives down its cost structure. With this in mind, in the early part of the 1990s, Boeing undertook a companywide review of its make-or-buy decisions. The objective was to identify activities that could be outsourced to subcontractors, both in the United States and abroad to drive down production costs.

When making these decisions, Boeing applied a number of criteria. First, Boeing looked at the *basic economics* of the outsourcing decision. The central issue here was whether an activity could be performed more cost-effectively by an outside manufacturer or by Boeing. Second, Boeing considered the *strategic risk* associated with outsourcing an activity. Boeing decided that it would not outsource any activity that it deemed to be part of its long-term competitive advantage. For example, the company decided not to outsource the production of wings because it believed that doing so might give away valuable technology to potential competitors. Third, Boeing looked at the *operational risk* associated with outsourcing an activity. The basic objective was to make sure Boeing did not become too dependent on a single outside supplier for critical components. Boeing's philosophy is to hedge operational risk by purchasing from two or more suppliers. Finally, Boeing considered whether it made sense to outsource certain activities to a supplier in a given country to help secure orders for commercial jet aircraft from that country. This practice is known as *offsetting*, and it is common in many industries. For example, Boeing decided to outsource the production of certain components to China. This decision was influenced by the fact that current forecasts suggest the Chinese will purchase over $100 billion worth of commercial jets over the next 20 years. Boeing's hope is that pushing some subcontracting work China's way will help it gain a larger share of this market than its global competitor, Airbus.

One of the first decisions to come out of this process was a decision to outsource the production of insulation blankets for 737 and 757 aircraft to suppliers in Mexico. Insulation blankets are wrapped around the inside of the fuselage of an aircraft to keep the interior warm at high altitudes. Boeing has traditionally made these blankets in-house, but it found that it can save $50 million per year by outsourcing production to a Mexican supplier. In total, Boeing reckons that outsourcing cut its cost structure by $500 million per year between 1994 and 1997. By the time the outsourcing is complete, the amount of an aircraft that Boeing builds will have been reduced from 52 percent to 48 percent.

Source: Based on interviews between Charles Hill and senior management personnel at Boeing.

(which we discuss later in the chapter). In the 1920s, for example, Ford profited from tight coordination and scheduling made possible by backward vertical integration into steel foundries, iron ore shipping, and mining. Deliveries at Ford's foundries on the Great Lakes were coordinated so well that ore was turned into engine blocks within 24 hours. This substantially reduced Ford's production costs by eliminating the need to hold excessive ore inventories.

For international businesses that source worldwide, scheduling problems can be exacerbated by the time and distance between the firm and its suppliers. This is true whether the firms use their own subunits as suppliers or use independent suppliers. Ownership is not the issue here. As we see in the closing case, Timberland may achieve tight scheduling with its globally dispersed parts suppliers without vertical integration. Thus, although this argument for vertical integration is often made, it is not compelling.

The Advantages of Buy

The advantages of buying component parts from independent suppliers are that it gives the firm greater flexibility, it can help drive down the firm's cost structure, and it may help the firm to capture orders from international customers.

Strategic Flexibility

The great advantage of buying component parts from independent suppliers is that the firm can maintain its flexibility, switching orders between suppliers as circumstances dictate. This is particularly important internationally, where changes in exchange rates and trade barriers can alter the attractiveness of supply sources. One year Hong Kong might be the lowest-cost source for a particular component, and the next year, Mexico may be.

Sourcing component parts from independent suppliers can also be advantageous when the optimal location for manufacturing a product is beset by political risks. Under such circumstances, foreign direct investment to establish a component manufacturing operation in that country would expose the firm to political risks. The firm can avoid many of these risks by buying from an independent supplier in that country, thereby maintaining the flexibility to switch sourcing to another country if a war, revolution, or other political change alters that country's attractiveness as a supply source.

However, maintaining strategic flexibility has its downside. If a supplier perceives the firm will change suppliers in response to changes in exchange rates, trade barriers, or general political circumstances, that supplier might not be willing to make specialized investments in plant and equipment that would ultimately benefit the firm.

Lower Costs

Although vertical integration is often undertaken to lower costs, it may have the opposite effect. When this is the case, outsourcing may lower the firm's cost structure. Vertical integration into the manufacture of component parts increases an organization's scope, and the resulting increase in organizational complexity can raise a firm's cost structure. There are three reasons for this.

First, the greater the number of subunits in an organization, the greater are the problems of coordinating and controlling those units. Coordinating and controlling subunits requires top management to process large amounts of information about subunit activities. The greater the number of subunits, the more information top management must process and the harder it is to do well. Theoretically, when the firm becomes involved in too many activities, headquarters management will be unable to effectively control all of them, and the resulting inefficiencies will more than offset any advantages derived from vertical integration.[18] This can be particularly serious in an international business, where the problem of controlling subunits is exacerbated by distance and differences in time, language, and culture.

Second, the firm that vertically integrates into component part manufacture may find that because its internal suppliers have a captive customer in the firm, they lack an incentive to reduce costs. The fact that they do not have to compete for orders with other suppliers may result in high operating costs. The managers of the supply operation may be tempted to pass on cost increases to other parts of the firm in the form of higher transfer prices, rather than looking for ways to reduce those costs.

Third, leading on from the previous point, vertically integrated firms have to determine appropriate prices for goods transferred to subunits within the firm. This is a challenge in any firm, but it is even more complex in international businesses. Different tax regimes, exchange rate movements, and headquarters' ignorance about local conditions all increase the complexity of transfer pricing decisions. This complexity enhances internal suppliers' ability to manipulate transfer prices to their advantage, passing cost increases downstream rather than looking for ways to reduce costs.

The firm that buys its components from independent suppliers can avoid all these problems and the associated costs. The firm that sources from independent suppliers has fewer subunits to control. The incentive problems that occur with internal suppliers do not arise when independent suppliers are used. Independent suppliers know they must continue to be efficient if they are to win business from the firm. Also, because independent suppliers' prices are set by market forces, the transfer pricing problem does not exist. In sum, the bureaucratic inefficiencies and resulting costs that can arise when firms vertically integrate backward and manufacture their own components are avoided by buying component parts from independent suppliers.

Offsets

Another reason for outsourcing some manufacturing to independent suppliers based in other countries is that it may help the firm capture more orders from that country. As noted in the Management Focus on Boeing, the practice of offsets is common in the commercial aerospace industry. For example, before Air India places a large order with Boeing, the Indian government might ask Boeing to push some subcontracting work toward Indian manufacturers. This kind of quid pro quo is not unusual in international business, and it affects far more than just the aerospace industry. Representatives of the US government have repeatedly urged Japanese automobile companies to purchase more component parts from US suppliers in order to partially offset the large volume of automobile exports from Japan to the United States.

Trade-offs

Trade-offs are involved in make-or-buy decisions. The benefits of manufacturing components in-house seem to be greatest when highly specialized assets are involved, when vertical integration is necessary for protecting proprietary technology, or when the firm is simply more efficient than external suppliers at performing a particular activity.

When these conditions are not present, the risk of strategic inflexibility and organizational problems suggest that it may be better to contract out component part manufacturing to independent suppliers. Since issues of strategic flexibility and organizational control loom even larger for international businesses than purely domestic ones, an international business should be particularly wary of vertical integration into component part manufacture. In addition, some outsourcing in the form of *offsets* may help a firm gain larger orders in the future.

Strategic Alliances with Suppliers

Several international businesses have tried to reap some of the benefits of vertical integration without the associated organizational problems by entering strategic alliances with essential suppliers. For example, in recent years we have seen an alliance between Kodak and Canon, under which Canon builds photocopiers for sale by Kodak, and an alliance between Apple and Sony, under which Sony builds laptop computers for Apple. By these alliances, Kodak and Apple have committed themselves to long-term relationships with these suppliers, which have encouraged the suppliers to undertake specialized investments. Recall from our earlier discussion that a lack of trust inhibits suppliers from making specialized investments to supply a firm with inputs. Strategic alliances build trust between the firm and its suppliers. Trust is built when a firm makes a credible commitment to continue purchasing from a supplier on reasonable terms. For example, the firm may invest money in a supplier—perhaps by taking a minority shareholding—to signal its intention to build a productive, mutually beneficial long-term relationship.

This kind of arrangement between the firm and its parts suppliers was pioneered in Japan by large auto companies such as Toyota. Many Japanese automakers have cooperative relationships with their suppliers that go back for decades. In these relationships, the auto companies and their suppliers collaborate on ways to increase value-added by, for example, implementing just-in-time inventory systems or cooperating in the design of component parts to improve quality and reduce assembly costs. These relationships have been formalized when the auto firms acquired minority shareholdings in many of their essential suppliers to symbolize their desire for long-term cooperative relationships with them. At the same time, the relationship between the firm and each essential supplier remains market mediated and terminable if the supplier fails to perform up to standard. By pursuing such a strategy, the Japanese automakers capture many of the benefits of vertical integration, particularly those arising from investments in specialized assets, without suffering the organizational problems that come with formal vertical integration. The parts suppliers also benefit from these relationships because since they grow with the firm they supply and they share in its success. Because of these strategies, Toyota manufactures only 27 percent of its component parts in-house, compared to 48 percent at Ford and 67 percent at GM. Of these three firms, Toyota appears to spend the least on component parts, suggesting it has captured many of the benefits that induced Ford and GM to vertically integrate.[19]

In general, the trends toward just-in-time systems (JIT), computer-aided design (CAD), and computer-aided manufacturing (CAM) seem to have increased pressures for firms to establish long-term relationships with their suppliers. JIT, CAD, and CAM systems all rely on close links between firms and their suppliers supported by substantial specialized investment in equipment and information systems hardware. To get a supplier to agree to adopt such systems, a firm must make a credible commitment to an enduring relationship with the supplier—it must build trust with the supplier. It can do this within the framework of a strategic alliance.

Alliances are not all good. Like formal vertical integration, a firm that enters long-term alliances may limit its strategic flexibility by the commitments it makes to its alliance partners. As we saw in Chapter 14 when we considered alliances between competitors, a firm that allies itself with another firm risks giving away key technological know-how to a potential competitor.

Coordinating a Global Manufacturing System

Materials management, which encompasses *logistics*, embraces the activities necessary to get materials to a manufacturing facility, through the manufacturing process, and out through a distribution system to the end user.[20] The twin objectives of materials management are to achieve this at the lowest possible cost and in a way that best serves customer needs, thereby lowering the costs of value creation and helping the firm establish a competitive advantage through superior customer service.

The potential for reducing costs through more efficient materials management is enormous. For the typical manufacturing enterprise, material costs account for between 50 and 70 percent of revenues, depending on the industry. Even a small reduction in these costs can have a substantial impact on profitability. According to one estimate, for a firm with revenues of $1 million, a return on investment rate of 5 percent, and materials costs that are 50 percent of sales revenues, a $15,000 increase in total profits could be achieved either by increasing sales revenues 30 percent or by reducing materials costs by 3 percent.[21] In a saturated market, it would be much easier to reduce materials costs by 3 percent than to increase sales revenues by 30 percent.

Materials management is a major undertaking in a firm with a globally dispersed manufacturing system and global markets. Consider the example of Bose Corporation, which is presented in the accompanying Management Focus. Bose purchases component parts from suppliers scattered over North America, Europe, and the Far East. It assembles its high-fidelity speakers in Massachusetts and ships them to customers the world over. Bose's materials management function must coordinate the flow of component parts so they arrive at the assembly plant just in time to enter the production system. Then it must oversee the timely distribution of finished speakers to customers around the globe. These tasks are complicated by the vast distances involved and by the fact that component parts and finished products are shipped across national borders, where they must pass customs. As explained in the Management Focus, from time to time Bose must interrupt the normal supply chain to accelerate the delivery of essential components to respond to sudden upsurges in demand for Bose's products.

The Power of Just-in-Time

Pioneered by Japanese firms during the 1950s and 60s, just-in-time inventory systems now play a major role in most manufacturing firms. The basic philosophy behind just-in-time (JIT) systems is to economize on inventory holding costs by having materials arrive at a manufacturing plant just in time to enter the production process and not before. The major cost saving comes from speeding up inventory turnover; this reduces inventory holding costs, such as warehousing and storage costs.

In addition to the cost benefits, JIT systems can also help firms improve product quality. Under a JIT system, parts enter the manufacturing process immediately; they are not warehoused. This allows defective inputs to be spotted right away. The problem can then be traced to the supply source and fixed before more defective parts are produced. Under a more traditional system, warehousing parts for months before they are used allows many defective parts to be produced before a problem is recognized.

The drawback of a JIT system is that it leaves a firm without a buffer stock of inventory. Although buffer stocks are expensive to store, they can tide a firm over shortages brought about by disruption among suppliers (such as a labor dispute). Buffer stocks can also help a firm respond quickly to increases in demand. However, there are ways around these limitations. To reduce the risks associated with depending on one supplier for an important input, some firms source these inputs from several suppliers. As for responding quickly to increases in consumer demand, the experience of Bose Corporation shows that it is possible to do this while maintaining a JIT system, even if it involves shipping component parts by air rather than overland or by ship (see the Management Focus).

The Role of Organization

As the number and dispersion of domestic and foreign markets and sources grow, the number and complexity of organizational linkages increase correspondingly. In a multinational enterprise, the challenge of managing the costs associated with purchases, currency exchange, inbound and outbound transportation, production,

Figure 16.3

Potential Materials
Management Linkages

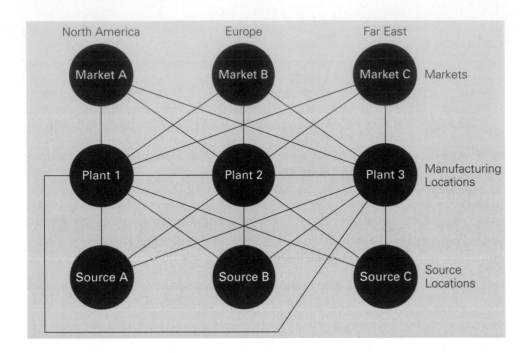

inventory, communication, expediting, tariffs and duties, and overall administration is massive. Figure 16.3 shows the linkages that might exist for a firm that sources, manufactures, and sells internationally. Each linkage represents a flow of materials, capital, information, decisions, and people. The firm must figure out the best organization to achieve tight coordination of the various stages of the value creation process.

A major requirement seems to be to legitimize materials management by separating it out as a function and giving it equal weight, in organizational terms, with other more traditional functions such as manufacturing, marketing, and R&D. According to materials management specialists, purchasing, production, and distribution are not separate activities but three aspects of one basic task: controlling the flow of materials and products from sources of supply through manufacturing and distribution into the hands of customers.

Despite the apparent cost and quality control advantages of having a separate materials management function, all firms do not operate with such a function.[22] Those that do not include many firms in which purchasing costs, inventories, and customer service levels are important, interdependent aspects of establishing competitive advantage. Such firms typically operate with a traditional organizational structure similar to the one in Figure 16.4a. In such an organization, purchasing, production planning and control, and distribution are not integrated. Planning and control are part of the manufacturing function, while distribution is part of the marketing function. Such companies will be unable to establish materials management as a major strength and consequently may face higher costs. Figure 16.4b shows the structure of a typical organization in which materials management is a separate function. Purchasing, planning and control, and distribution are integrated within the materials management function. Such an arrangement allows the firm to transform materials management into an important strength.

Having established the legitimacy of materials management, the next dilemma is determining the best structure in a multinational enterprise. In practice, authority is either centralized or decentralized.[23] Under a centralized solution, most materials

MANAGEMENT FOCUS
Materials Management at Bose
http://www.bose.com

Bose Corporation manufactures some of the world's best high-fidelity speakers. The Massachusetts corporation annually generates about $300 million in revenues. Its worldwide esteem is evidenced by the fact that Bose speakers are best-sellers in Japan, the world leader in consumer electronics. Bose's core competence is its electronic engineering skills, but the company attributes much of its business success to tightly coordinated materials management.

Bose purchases most of its electronic and nonelectronic components from independent suppliers scattered around North America, the Far East, and Europe. Roughly 50 percent of its purchases are from foreign suppliers, the majority of them in the Far East. Bose attempts to coordinate this globally dispersed supply chain so that material holding and transportation costs are minimized. This requires component parts to arrive at Bose's Massachusetts assembly plant just in time to enter the production process. But Bose must remain responsive to customer demands, which requires the company to respond quickly to an increase in customer demand for certain speakers. If it does not, it can lose a big order to competitors. Since Bose does not want to hold extensive inventories at its Massachusetts plant, this need for responsiveness requires Bose's globally dispersed supply chain to respond rapidly to increased demand for component parts.

Responsibility for coordinating the supply chain to meet both objectives—minimizing transportation and inventory holding costs and yet responding quickly to customer demands—falls on Bose's materials management function. This function achieves coordination by means of a sophisticated logistics operation. Most of Bose's imports from the Far East come via ships to the West Coast and then across North America to its Massachusetts plant via train. Most of the company's exports also move by ocean freight, but Bose does not hesitate to use airfreight when goods are needed in a hurry. To control this supply chain, Bose has a long-standing relationship

with W. N. Procter, a Boston-based freight forwarder and customs broker. Procter handles customs clearance and shipping from suppliers to Bose. Procter provides Bose up-to-the-minute electronic data interchange (EDI) capabilities, which gives it the ability to track parts as they move through its global supply chain. Whenever a shipment leaves a supplier, it is entered in this "ProcterLink" system. Bose is then able to fine-tune its production scheduling so supplies enter the production process just in time. ProcterLink is more than a simple tracking system, however. The EDI system also allows Bose to run simulations that allow its logistics managers to examine a variety of factors, such as the effect of duties on the cost of goods sold.

Procter provides several other services to Bose, such as selecting overseas agents who can help move goods out of the Far East. Procter's well-established network of overseas contacts is especially useful when shipments must be expedited through foreign customs. Moreover, Procter is electronically linked in the US customs system, which allows it to clear freight electronically as much as five days before a ship arrives at a US port or hours before an international airfreight shipment arrives. This can get goods to Bose's manufacturing plant several days sooner.

Just how well this system can work was demonstrated when a Japanese customer doubled its order for Bose speakers. Bose needed to gear up its manufacturing immediately, but many of the essential components were far from Massachusetts. Using ProcterLink, Bose located the needed parts in its supply chain, pulled them out of the normal delivery chain, and airfreighted them to the manufacturing line to satisfy the accelerated schedule. Consequently, Bose was able to fill the doubled order for its Japanese customer.

Sources: P. Bradley, "Global Sourcing Takes Split Second Timing," *Purchasing*, July 20, 1989, pp. 52–58; and S. Greenblat, "Continuous Improvement in Supply Chain Management," *Chief Executive*, 1993, June, pp. 40–44.

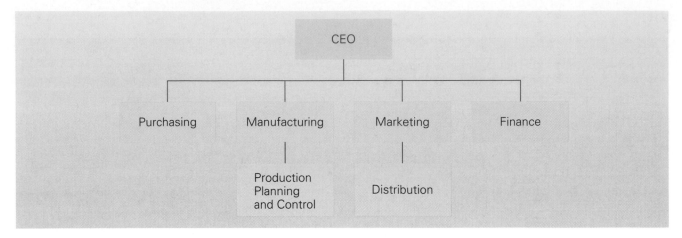

Figure 16.4A

Traditional Organizational Structure

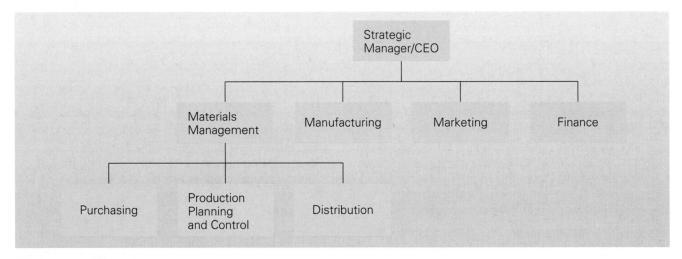

Figure 16.4B

Organization Structure with Materials Management at Separate Function

management decisions are made at the corporate level, which can ensure efficiency and adherence to overall corporate objectives. This is the case at Bose Corporation, for example. In large, complex organizations with many manufacturing plants, however, a centralized materials management function may become overloaded and unable to perform its task effectively. In such cases, a decentralized solution is needed.

A decentralized solution delegates most materials management decisions to the level of individual manufacturing plants within the firm, although corporate headquarters retains responsibility for overseeing the function. The great advantage of decentralizing is that it allows plant-level materials management groups to develop the knowledge and skills needed for interacting with foreign suppliers that are important to their particular plant. This can lead to better decision making. The disadvantage is that a lack of coordination between plants can result in less than optimal global sourcing. It can also lead to duplication of materials management efforts. These disadvantages can be attenuated, however, by information systems that enable headquarters to coordinate the various plant-level materials management groups.

The Role of Information Technology

As we saw in the Management Focus on Bose Corporation, information systems play a crucial role in modern materials management. By tracking component parts as they make their way across the globe toward an assembly plant, information systems enable a firm to optimize its production scheduling according to when components are expected to arrive. By locating component parts in the supply chain precisely, good information systems allow the firm to accelerate production when needed by pulling key components out of the regular supply chain and having them flown to the manufacturing plant.

Firms increasingly use electronic data interchange to coordinate the flow of materials into manufacturing, through manufacturing, and out to customers. EDI systems require computer links between a firm, its suppliers, and its shippers. Sometimes customers also are integrated into the system. These electronic links are then used to place orders with suppliers, to register parts leaving a supplier, to track them as they travel toward a manufacturing plant, and to register their arrival. Suppliers typically use an EDI link to send invoices to the purchasing firm. One consequence of an EDI system is that suppliers, shippers, and the purchasing firm can communicate with each other with no time delay, which increases the flexibility and responsiveness of the whole supply system. A second consequence is that much of the paperwork between suppliers, shippers, and the purchasing firm is eliminated. Good EDI systems can help a firm decentralize materials management decisions to the plant level by giving corporate-level managers the information they need for coordinating and controlling decentralized materials management groups.

Chapter Summary

This chapter explained how efficient manufacturing and materials management functions can improve an international business's competitive position by lowering the costs of value creation and by performing value creation activities in such ways that customer service is enhanced and value-added maximized. We looked closely at three issues central to international manufacturing and materials management: where to manufacture, what to make and what to buy, and how to coordinate a globally dispersed manufacturing and supply system. This chapter made the following points:

1. The choice of an optimal manufacturing location must consider country factors, technological factors, and product factors.

2. Country factors include the influence of factor costs, political economy, and national culture on manufacturing costs.

3. Technological factors include the fixed costs of setting up manufacturing facilities, the minimum effi-

cient scale of production, and the availability of flexible manufacturing technologies.

4. Product factors include the value-to-weight ratio of the product and whether the product serves universal needs.

5. Location strategies either concentrate or decentralize manufacturing. The choice should be made in light of country, technological, and product factors. All location decisions involve trade-offs.

6. Foreign factories can improve their capabilities over time, and this can be of immense strategic benefit to the firm. Managers need to view foreign factories as potential centers of excellence and to encourage and foster attempts by local managers to upgrade factory capabilities.

7. An essential issue in many international businesses is determining which component parts should be manufactured in-house and which should be outsourced to independent suppliers.

8. Making components in-house facilitates investments in specialized assets and helps the firm protect its proprietary technology. It may improve scheduling between adjacent stages in the value chain, also. In-house production also makes sense if the firm is an efficient, low-cost producer of a technology.

9. Buying components from independent suppliers facilitates strategic flexibility and helps the firm avoid the organizational problems associated with extensive vertical integration. Outsourcing might also be employed as part of an "offset" policy, which is designed to win more orders for the firm from a country by pushing some subcontracting work to that country.

10. Several firms have tried to attain the benefits of vertical integration and avoid its associated organizational problems by entering long-term strategic alliances with essential suppliers.

11. Although alliances with suppliers can give a firm the benefits of vertical integration without dispensing entirely with the benefits of a market relationship, alliances have drawbacks. The firm that enters a strategic alliance may find its strategic flexibility limited by commitments to alliance partners.

12. Materials management encompasses all the activities that move materials to a manufacturing facility, through the manufacturing process, and out through a distribution system to the end user. The materials management function is complicated in an international business by distance, time, exchange rates, custom barriers, and other things.

13. Just-in-time systems generate major cost savings from reduced warehousing and inventory holding costs. In addition, JIT systems help the firm spot defective parts and remove them from the manufacturing process quickly, thereby improving product quality.

14. For a firm to establish a good materials management function, it needs to legitimize materials management within the organization. It can do this by giving materials management equal footing with other functions in the firm.

15. Information technology, particularly electronic data interchange, plays a major role in materials management. EDI facilitates the tracking of inputs, allows the firm to optimize its production schedule, allows the firm and its suppliers to communicate in real time, and eliminates the flow of paperwork between a firm and its suppliers.

Critical Discussion Questions

1. An electronics firm is considering how best to supply the world market for microprocessors used in consumer and industrial electronic products. A manufacturing plant costs approximately $500 million to construct and requires a highly skilled work force. The total value of the world market for this product over the next 10 years is estimated to be between $10 and $15 billion. The tariffs prevailing in this industry are currently low. Should the firm adopt a concentrated or decentralized manufacturing strategy? What kind of location(s) should the firm favor for its plant(s)?

2. A chemical firm is considering how best to supply the world market for sulfuric acid. A manufacturing plant costs approximately $20 million to construct and requires a moderately skilled work force. The total value of the world market for this product over the next 10 years is estimated to be between $20 and $30 billion. The tariffs prevailing in this industry are moderate. Should the firm favor concentrated manufacturing or decentralized manufacturing? What kind of location(s) should the firm seek for its plant(s)?

3. A firm must decide whether to make a component part in-house or to contract it out to an independent supplier. Manufacturing the part requires a nonrecoverable investment in specialized assets. The most efficient suppliers are located in countries with currencies that many foreign exchange analysts expect to appreciate substantially over the next decade. What are the pros and cons of (a) manufacturing the component in-house and (b) outsourcing manufacture to an independent supplier? Which option would you recommend? Why?

4. Explain how an efficient materials management function can help an international business compete more effectively in the global marketplace.

CLOSING CASE   Timberland

Timberland, a New Hampshire-based manufacturer of rugged, high-quality shoes is one of the world's fastest-growing companies. From small beginnings in the late 1970s, Timberland has grown into a global business with sales of $797 million in 1997. The company's global expansion began in 1979 when an Italian distributor walked into the then small US outfitter and expressed an interest in shoe #100-81, a hand-sewn moccasin with a lug sole. The Italian thought the shoe would sell well in Italy—land of high-style Gucci shoes. He was right; Timberland quickly became a phenomenon in Italy where Timberland shoes often sold for a 60 percent premium over prices in the United States. Expansion into other countries followed, and by the mid-1990s Timberland was generating 50 percent of its sales from 50 foreign countries, including Italy, Germany, France, Britain, and Japan.

Ignored during this rapid growth phase, however, was any attempt to build a tightly managed and coordinated global manufacturing and logistics system. By the early 1990s, Timberland was confronted with an extremely complex global manufacturing and logistics network. To take advantage of lower wage costs outside the United States, the company had established manufacturing facilities in the Dominican Republic and Puerto Rico (by 1997, 27 percent of its shoes were made at these locations). Timberland had also found it cost-efficient to source footwear and apparel from independent suppliers based in dozens of other low-wage countries in Asia, Europe, and Latin America. At the same time, Timberland's distribution network had grown to serve consumers in over 50 countries. To complicate things further, the average shipment of footwear to retailers was for less than 12 pairs of each type of shoe, which made for an enormous volume of individual shipments to track.

Timberland found that its logistics systems was breaking down under the strains imposed by rapid volume growth, a globally dispersed supply and distribution chain, and a large volume of individual shipments. The company simply lacked the information systems required to coordinate and control its dispersed production and distribution network. No common information systems linked suppliers, Timberland, and retailers. Nor was there any attempt to consolidate shipments from different regions of the world in order to realize shipping economies. Products were shipped from six countries in Southeast Asia to the United States and Europe, as opposed to being consolidated at one location and then shipped.

In the mid-1990s, Timberland decided to reorganize its global logistics system by streamlining its logistics information pipeline first and then its cargo pipeline. The information challenge was to come up with a system that would enable Timberland to track a product from the factory to its final destination. As Timberland's director of distribution explains it: "At every link in the chain, you can make a decision about cargo that would make it flow better, but only if you have the information about the product and the ability to communicate with that location in real time to direct the product." For example, when a product leaves the factory, Timberland can in theory direct a freight forwarder to send the product by air or by ocean carrier, depending on the urgency of the shipment. When a shipment lands in, say, Los Angeles, it can be shipped to a distribution center or shipped directly to a customer, again depending on need. These kinds of choices, however, can be made only if Timberland has the requisite information systems. Until 1994, the company lacked such systems.

The company developed the required information system in conjunction with ACS, a freight forwarder, and The Rockport Group, a software house. To simplify its system at the level of physical distribution and to make implementation of its information systems easier, Timberland moved rapidly toward consolidated regional warehousing. Timberland had separate warehouses in a dozen Asian countries, several in the United States, and three in Europe. Under the new system, sources in Asia feed into one warehouse. The company also switched to single continental distribution centers in North America and Europe. By centralizing its warehousing at three locations, the company can better track where the product is located so that it can be routed quickly and flexibly to where it is needed. The result should be a dramatic improvement in Timberland's ability to deliver products to customers exactly when they need them, as opposed to delivering products too late or too soon. By consolidating warehousing, Timberland can consolidate shipments from a region into one transoceanic shipment, which should enable the company to negotiate much better shipping rates.

http://www.timberland.com

Sources: P. Buxbaum, "Timberland's New Spin on Global Logistics," *Distribution*, May 1994, pp. 33–36; A. E. Serwer, "Will Timberland Grow Up?" *Fortune*, May 29, 1995, p. 24; M. Tedeschi, "Timberland Vows to Get on the Ball," *Footwear News*, May 22, 1995, p. 2; and *Timberland Annual Report, 1997*.

Case Discussion Questions

1. What caused Timberland's logistical problems in the 1990s? What do you think were the competitive and financial consequences of these problems?

2. What was the key to solving Timberland's logistical problems? Why? What are the consequences of this

solution likely to be for Timberland's competitive position and financial performance?

3. Timberland makes almost no products in the United States. Instead, it manufactured some products in the Dominican Republic and Puerto Rico, while outsourcing the remaining products from third-party manufacturers. Explain the probable thinking behind this strategy. Why does the company not outsource all its production? Why does the company make shoes in the Dominican Republic and Puerto Rico, but not the United States?

Notes

1. B. C. Arntzen, G. G. Brown, T. P. Harrison, and L. L.Trafton, "Global Supply Chain Management at Digital Equipment Corporation," *Interfaces* 25 (1995), pp. 69–93.

2. D. A. Garvin, "What Does Product Quality Really Mean," *Sloan Management Review* 26 (Fall 1984), pp. 25–44.

3. For general background information, see "How to Build Quality," *The Economist*, September 23, 1989, pp. 91–92; A. Gabor, *The Man Who Discovered Quality* (New York: Penguin, 1990); and P. B. Crosby, *Quality is Free* (New York: Mentor, 1980).

4. M. Saunders, "US Firms Doing Business in Europe Have Options in Registering for ISO 9000 Quality Standards," *Business America*, June 14, 1993, p. 7.

5. G. Stalk and T. M. Hout, *Competing Against Time* (New York: Free Press, 1990).

6. M. A. Cohen and H. L. Lee," Resource Deployment Analysis of Global Manufacturing and Distribution Networks," *Journal of Manufacturing and Operations Management* 2 (1989), pp. 81–104.

7. For a review of the technical arguments, see D. A. Hay and D. J. Morris, *Industrial Economics: Theory and Evidence* (Oxford: Oxford University Press, 1979). See also C. W. L. Hill and G. R. Jones, *Strategic Management: An Integrated Approach* (Boston: Houghton Mifflin, 1995).

8. See P. Nemetz and L. Fry, "Flexible Manufacturing Organizations: Implications for Strategy Formulation," *Academy of Management Review* 13 (1988), pp. 627–38; N. Greenwood, *Implementing Flexible Manufacturing Systems* (New York: Halstead Press, 1986); and J. P. Womack, D. T. Jones, and D. Roos, *The Machine That*

Changed the World (New York: Rawson Associates, 1990).

9. J. H. Gilmore and B. J. Pine II, "The Four Faces of Mass Customization," *Harvard Business Review*, January–February 1997, pp. 91–101.

10. Womack, Jones, and Roos, *The Machine That Changed the World*.

11. M. A. Cusumano, *The Japanese Automobile Industry* (Cambridge, MA: Harvard University Press, 1989); T. Ohno, *Toyota Production System* (Cambridge, MA: Productivity Press, 1990); and Womack, Jones, and Roos, *The Machine That Changed the World*.

12. J. D. Goldhar and D. Lei, "The Shape of Twenty-First Century Global Manufacturing," *Journal of Business Strategy*, March–April 1991, pp. 37–41; "Factories that Turn Nuts into Bolts," *U.S. News and World Report*, July 14, 1986, pp. 44–45; and J. Kotkin, "The Great American Revival," *Inc.*, February 1988, pp. 52–63.

13. K. Ferdows, "Making the Most of Foreign Factories," *Harvard Business Review*, March–April 1997, pp. 73–88.

14. This argument represents a simple extension of the dynamic capabilities research stream in the strategic management literature. See D. J. Teece, G. Pisano, and A. Shuen, "Dynamic Capabilities and Strategic Management," *Strategic Management Journal*, 18 (1997), pp. 509–33.

15. The material in this section is based primarily on the transaction cost literature of vertical integration; for example, O. E. Williamson, *The Economic Institutions of Capitalism* (New York: The Free Press, 1985).

16. For a review of the evidence, see Williamson, *The Economic Institutions of Capitalism*.

17. A. D. Chandler, *The Visible Hand* (Cambridge, MA: Harvard University Press, 1977).

18. For a review of these arguments, see C. W. L. Hill and R. E. Hoskisson, "Strategy and Structure in the Multiproduct Firm," *Academy of Management Review* 12 (1987), pp. 331–41.

19. C. W. L. Hill, "Cooperation, Opportunism, and the Invisible Hand," *Academy of Management Review* 15 (1990), pp. 500–13.

20. See R. Narasimhan and J. R. Carter, "Organization, Communication and Coordination of International Sourcing," *International Marketing Review* 7 (1990), pp. 6–20, and Arntzen, Brown, Harrison, and Trafton, "Global Supply Chain Management at Digital Equipment Corporation."

21. H. F. Busch, "Integrated Materials Management," *IJPD & MM* 18 (1990), pp. 28–39.

22. J. G. Miller and P. Gilmour, "Materials Managers: Who Needs Them?" *Harvard Business Review*, July–August 1979, pp. 57–67.

23. Narasimhan and Carter, "Organization, Communication and Coordination of International Sourcing."

Chapter Seventeen

Global Marketing and R&D

Procter & Gamble in Japan: From Marketing Failure to Success

Procter & Gamble (P&G), the large US consumer products company, has a well-earned reputation as one of the world's best marketers. With its 80-plus major brands, P&G generates more than $37 billion in annual revenues worldwide. Along with Unilever, P&G is a dominant global force in laundry detergents, cleaning products, and personal care products. P&G expanded abroad after World War II by exporting its brands and marketing policies to Western Europe, initially with considerable success. Over the next 30 years, this policy of developing new products and marketing strategies in the United States and then transferring them to other countries became entrenched. Although some adaptation of marketing policies to accommodate country differences was pursued, it was minimal.

The first signs that this policy was no longer effective emerged in the 1970s, when P&G suffered a number of major setbacks in Japan. By 1985, after 13 years in Japan, P&G was still losing $40 million a year there. It had introduced disposable diapers in Japan and at one time had commanded an 80 percent share of the market, but by the early 1980s it held a miserable 8 percent. Three large Japanese consumer products companies were dominating the market. P&G's diapers, developed in the United States, were too bulky for the tastes of Japanese consumers. Kao, a Japanese company, had developed a line of trim-fit diapers that appealed more to Japanese tastes. Kao introduced its product with a marketing blitz and was quickly rewarded with a 30 percent share of the market. P&G realized it would have to modify its diapers if it were to compete in Japan. It did, and the company now has a 30 percent share of the Japanese market. Plus, P&G's trim-fit diapers have become a best-seller in the United States.

P&G had a similar experience in marketing education in the Japanese laundry detergent market. In the early 1980s, P&G introduced its Cheer laundry detergent in Japan. Developed in the United States, Cheer was promoted in Japan with the US marketing message—Cheer works in all temperatures and produces lots of rich suds. But many Japanese consumers wash their clothes in cold water, which made the claim of working in all temperatures irrelevant. Also, many Japanese add fabric softeners to their water, which reduces detergents' sudsing action, so Cheer did not suds up as advertised. After a disastrous launch, P&G knew it had to adapt its marketing message. Cheer is now promoted as a product that works effectively in cold water with fabric softeners added, and it is one of P&G's best-selling products in Japan.

P&G's experience with disposable diapers and laundry detergents in Japan forced the company to rethink its product development and marketing philosophy. The company now admits that its US-centered way of doing business no longer works. Since the late 1980s, P&G has been delegating more responsibility for new-product development and marketing to its major subsidiaries in Japan and Europe. The company is more responsive to local differences in consumer tastes and preferences and more willing to admit that good new products can be developed outside the United States.

Evidence that this new approach is working can again be found in the company's activities in Japan. Until 1995, P&G did not sell dish soap in Japan. By 1998, it had Japan's best-selling brand, Joy, which now has a 20 percent share of Japan's $400 million market for dish soap. It made major inroads against the products of two domestic firms, Kao and Lion Corp., each of which marketed multiple brands and controlled nearly 40 percent of the market before P&G's entry. P&G's success with Joy was due to its ability to develop a product formula that was specifically targeted at the unmet needs of Japanese consumers, to the design of a packaging format that appealed to retailers, and to the development of a compelling advertising campaign.

In researching the market in the early 1990s, P&G discovered an odd habit: Japanese homemakers, one after another, squirted out excessive amounts of detergent onto dirty dishes, a clear sign of dissatisfaction with existing products. On further inspection, P&G found that this behavior resulted from the changing eating habits of Japanese consumers. The Japanese are consuming more fried food, and existing dish soaps did not effectively remove grease. Armed with this knowledge, P&G researchers in Japan went to work to create a highly concentrated soap formula based on a new technology developed by the company's scientists in Europe that was highly effective in removing grease. The company also designed a novel package for the product. The packaging of existing products had a clear weakness; the long-necked bottles wasted space on supermarket shelves. P&G's dish soap containers were compact cylinders that took less space in stores, warehouses, and delivery trucks. This improved the efficiency of distribution and allowed supermarkets to use their shelf space more effectively, which made them receptive to stocking Joy. P&G also devoted considerable attention to developing an advertising campaign for Joy. P&G's ad agency, Dentsu Inc., created commercials in which a famous comedian dropped in on homemakers unannounced with a camera crew to test Joy on the household's dirty dishes. The camera homed in on a patch of oil in a pan full of water. After a drop of Joy, the oil dramatically disappeared.

With the product, packaging, and advertising strategy carefully worked out, P&G launched Joy throughout Japan in March 1996. The product almost immediately gained a 10 percent market share. Within three months the product's share had increased to 15 percent, and by year-end it was close to 18 percent. Because of strong demand, P&G was also able to raise prices as were the retailers that stocked the product, all of which translated into fatter margins for the retailers and helped consolidate Joy's position in the market.

http://www.pg.com

Sources: G. de Jonquieres and C. Bobinski, "Wash and Get into a Lather in Poland," *Financial Times*, May 28, 1992, p. 2; "Perestroika in Soapland," *The Economist*, June 10, 1989, pp. 69–71; "After Early Stumbles P&G Is Making Inroads Overseas," *The Wall Street Journal*, February 6, 1989, p. B1; C. A. Bartlett and S. Ghoshal, *Managing across Borders: The Transnational Solution* (Boston, MA: Harvard Business School Press, 1989); and N. Shirouzu, "P&G's Joy Makes an Unlikely Splash in Japan," *The Wall Street Journal*, December 10, 1997, p. B1.

Introduction

In the previous chapter, we looked at the roles of global manufacturing and materials management in an international business. In this chapter, we continue our focus on specific business functions by examining the roles of marketing and research and development (R&D) in an international business. We focus on how marketing and R&D can be performed so they will reduce the costs of value creation and add value by better serving customer needs.

In Chapter 12, we spoke of the tension existing in most international businesses between the needs to reduce costs and at the same time to respond to local conditions, which tends to raise costs. This tension has been a persistent theme in most chapters since then, and it continues to be in this chapter. A global marketing strategy that views the world's consumers as similar in their tastes and preferences is consistent with the mass production of a standardized output. By mass producing a standardized output, the firm can realize substantial unit cost reductions from experience curve and other scale economies. But ignoring country differences in consumer tastes and preferences can lead to failure. Thus, an international business's marketing function needs to determine when product standardization is appropriate and when it is not. Similarly, the firm's R&D function needs to be able to develop globally standardized products when appropriate as well as products customized to local requirements.

We consider marketing and R&D within the same chapter because of their close relationship. A critical aspect of the marketing function is identifying gaps in the market so that new products can be developed to fill those gaps. Developing new products requires R&D; thus, the linkage between marketing and R&D. New products should be developed with market needs in mind, and only marketing can define those needs for R&D personnel. Moreover, only marketing can tell R&D whether to produce globally standardized or locally customized products. Academic research has long maintained that a major factor of success for new-product introductions is the closeness of the relationship between marketing and R&D. The closer the linkage, the greater the success rate.[1]

The opening case illustrates some of the issues that we will be debating in this chapter. Many of P&G's problems in Japan were caused by a failure to tailor its marketing strategy to the specific demands of the Japanese marketplace. P&G learned from its experience with disposable diapers and laundry detergent that a marketing approach that works in one context won't necessarily work in another. The company's subsequent success with Joy drives home the point that in many consumer product markets, it is important to customize the product offering, packaging, and advertising message to the specific needs of consumers in that country. Joy was developed by Procter & Gamble's R&D staff in Kobe, Japan, specifically to meet the evolving needs of Japanese consumers. This illustrates the benefits of locating R&D activities close to the market for the product when that market demands a customized product offering.

But it would be wrong to generalize too much from this case. For other firms in other industries, it may make sense to pursue a global strategy, producing a standardized product for global consumption, and using the same basic market message to sell that product worldwide. Some product markets are truly global in their reach. The market for semiconductor chips, for example, is a global market where consumers demand the same standardized product worldwide so a global marketing strategy, supported by a global R&D strategy, might make sense.

In this chapter, we examine the roles of marketing and R&D in international businesses. We begin by reviewing the debate on the globalization of markets. Then we discuss the issue of market segmentation. Next, we look at four elements that constitute a firm's marketing mix: product attributes, distribution strategy, communication strategy, and pricing strategy. The **marketing mix** is the set of choices the firm offers to its targeted markets. Many firms vary their marketing mix from country to country depending on differences in national culture, economic development, product standards, distribution channels, and so on. The chapter closes with a look at new-product development in an international business and at the implications of this for the organization of the firm's R&D function.

The Globalization of Markets?

In a now-famous *Harvard Business Review* article, Theodore Levitt wrote lyrically about the globalization of world markets.[2] Levitt's arguments have become something of a lightning rod in the debate about the extent of globalization. According to Levitt:

> A powerful force drives the world toward a converging commonalty, and that force is technology. It has proletarianized communication, transport, and travel. The result is a new commercial reality—the emergence of global markets for standardized consumer products on a previously unimagined scale of magnitude.
>
> Gone are accustomed differences in national or regional preferences... The globalization of markets is at hand. With that, the multinational commercial world nears its end, and so does the multinational corporation. The multinational corporation operates in a number of countries and adjusts its products and practices to each—at high relative costs. The global corporation operates with resolute consistency—at low relative cost—as if the entire world were a single entity; it sells the same thing in the same way everywhere.
>
> Commercially, nothing confirms this as much as the success of McDonald's from the Champs Elysees to the Ginza, of Coca-Cola in Bahrain and Pepsi-Cola in Moscow, and of rock music, Greek salad, Hollywood movies, Revlon cosmetics, Sony television, and Levi's jeans everywhere.
>
> Ancient differences in national tastes or modes of doing business disappear. The commonalty of preference leads inescapably to the standardization of products, manufacturing, and the institutions of trade and commerce.

This is eloquent and evocative writing, but is Levitt correct? The rise of global media such as MTV (see the accompanying Management Focus) and CNN, and the ability of such media to help shape a global culture, would seem to lend weight to Levitt's argument. If Levitt is correct, his argument has major implications for the marketing strategies pursued by international business. However, the current consensus

MANAGEMENT FOCUS
MTV Rocks the World

In a world where there are still major differences in the tastes, preferences, and purchasing habits of consumers in different countries, no group is more homogenous than those in their teens and early 20s. Whether they live in Los Angeles or London, Tokyo or Prague, Rio de Janeiro or Sydney, young adults the world over wear baggy jeans and Doc Martens, listen to the music of Fiona Apple, drink Coke or Pepsi, and eat at McDonald's. Increasingly, they also watch MTV, the music channel owned by Viacom.

MTV has been singled out by many observers as a major cause of the global homogenization of teen culture and also as a major beneficiary. Both charges are probably true. Introduced in the United States in the late 1970s, MTV is now the most widely distributed cable network in the world. MTV currently broadcasts in 85 countries and has a global audience in the 12- to 34-year-old age category. By mid-1998 the channel reached an impressive 80 million households in the United States and Canada, but it is outside of North America that most of the recent growth has occurred. MTV Europe, which was established in 1987, is now received by over 80 million households across the continent. In Asia, over 50 million households receive MTV Asia, and the number is growing exponentially. And in Central and South America, where MTV launched its service in 1994, 30 million households received the channel by mid-1998.

MTV is keenly aware of the concerns and interest of those in their teens and early 20s, and its global program strategy reflects this. As in the United States, its international services broadcast news and socially conscious programming of interest to the target audience the world over, such as features on global warming, the destruction of the rain forests, and AIDS. The guts of MTV, however, is its music programming. Initially, MTV's music programming was dominated by US and British artists; and MTV broadcast Anglo-American music to the rest of the world. It was thanks to MTV that grunge rock became a global phenomenon, and teens from Italy to Japan came to know Seattle not as the home of Boeing or Microsoft, but as the birthplace of grunge. Increasingly, however, MTV is championing little-known artists from other parts of the world, and it has shown that it has the power to make them international stars. MTV Europe helped discover the Swedish pop group Ace of Base in 1992. Its global programming of the group's single and video, *All That She Wants,* gave it a top 10 hit in Britain, Germany, Italy, and the United States. Thanks to MTV Asia, one of the best-selling albums of 1993 in India was by Cheb Khaled singing in his native Algerian. In Japan, the Swedish "gothic rock" guitarist Yngwie Malmsteen has become a huge star, in part due to promotion by MTV Japan. And for heavily anticipated new

among academics seems to be that Levitt overstates his case.[3] Although Levitt may have a point when it comes to many basic industrial products, such as steel, bulk chemicals, and semiconductor chips, globalization seems to be the exception rather than the rule in many consumer goods markets and industrial markets. Even a firm such as McDonald's, which Levitt holds up as the archetypal example of a consumer products firm that sells a standardized product worldwide, modifies its menu from country to country in light of local consumer preferences.[4] And as we saw in the opening case, although Procter & Gamble may sell dish soap, disposable diapers, and laundry detergent worldwide, and although it may use the same brand names worldwide (e.g., Pampers for diapers), it still customizes the final product offering and marketing strategy to the conditions that pertain in individual national markets.

Levitt is probably correct to assert that modern transportation and communications technologies, such as MTV, are facilitating a convergence of the tastes and preferences of consumers in the more advanced countries of the world. The popularity of sushi in Los Angeles, hamburgers in Tokyo, and grunge rock almost everywhere, support this. In the long run, such technological forces may lead to the evolution of a global culture. At present, however, the continuing persistence of cultural and eco-

http://www.mtv.com

albums by big international stars, MTV stages what it calls "planetary premieres," airing a new video in 24 hours in all 80 plus countries that it covers.

This worldwide marketing reach has made MTV a premier conduit for many companies hoping to profit from the globalization of teen culture. MTV's roster of 200 major advertisers includes Levi Strauss, Procter & Gamble, Johnson & Johnson, Apple Computer, and Pepsi-Cola. According to Donald Holdsworth, head of sales and marketing for Pepsi-Cola International, "MTV not only has broad global coverage, it's also targeted exactly at that segment we want to reach: teenagers." MTV President Tom Freston argues that marketing to those in their teens and early 20s through global communications media such as MTV is becoming increasingly important for many global consumer products companies. He sees music as the most global of communications media; "you could argue that this is a business even more global than movies, because music is more pervasive than any other form of culture." Due to this pervasiveness, MTV is a natural communications conduit for advertisers trying to build a global brand. Today it is still difficult to sell the same products to 35-year-olds in different countries. They prefer traditional food and fashion. In part that's because they didn't bond with international brands as teenagers. But MTV's Freston

believes that because of media such as MTV, this generation is different; they are becoming more homogenized in their tastes and preferences.

However, while the international success of MTV is a testament to the global convergence of tastes and preferences among those in their teens and early 20s in different countries, it is easy to overstate the importance of such globalization. Although music is, as MTV President Freston notes, the most pervasive and global form of culture, important differences still exist in the tastes and preferences of teens in different nations. MTV may have helped to turn Yngwie Malmsteen into a big star in Japan, but there is no sign that this Swedish master of "gothic rock" is going to break into the US market. Even in one of the most global of industries—the music industry—and even among the most homogenous group in the world—teenagers—product standardization has its limits, and national differences in tastes and preferences are still of major importance.

Sources: S. Tully, "Teens: The Most Global Market of All," *Fortune*, May 16, 1994, pp. 90–97; M. Robichaux, "Leave It to Beavis," *The Wall Street Journal*, February 8, 1995, p. A1; A. Rawsthorn, MTV Makes the Big Record Groups Dance to Its Tune," *Financial Times*, July 7, 1995, p. 17; M. Cox, "Global Entertainment: We Are the World," *The Wall Street Journal*, March 26, 1993, p. 17; and Viacom's Web site at http://www.viacom.com

nomic differences between nations acts as a major brake on any trend toward global consumer tastes and preferences. In addition, trade barriers and differences in product and technical standards also constrain a firm's ability to sell a standardized product to a global market. We discuss the sources of these differences in subsequent sections when we look at how products must be altered from country to country. Levitt's globally standardized markets seem a long way off in many industries.

Market Segmentation

Market segmentation refers to identifying distinct groups of consumers whose purchasing behavior differs from others in important ways. Markets can be segmented in numerous ways: by geography, demography (sex, age, income, race, education level, etc.), social-cultural factors (social class, values, religion, lifestyle choices), and psychological factors (personality). Because different segments exhibit different patterns of purchasing behavior, firms often adjust their marketing mix from segment to segment. Thus, the precise design of a product, the pricing strategy, the distribution channels used and the choice of communication strategy may all be varied from segment to segment. The goal is to optimize the fit between the purchasing behavior of consumers in a given segment and the marketing mix, thereby maximizing sales to that segment. Automobile companies, for example, use a different marketing mix to sell cars to different socioeconomic segments. Thus, Toyota uses its Lexus division to sell high-priced luxury cars to high-income consumers, while selling its entry-level models, such as the Toyota Corolla, to lower-income consumers. Similarly, personal computer manufacturers will offer different computer models, embodying different combinations of product attributes and price points, precisely to appeal to consumers from different market segments (e.g., business users and home users).

When managers in an international business consider market segmentation in foreign countries, they need to be cognizant of two main issues—the differences between countries in the structure of market segments, and the existence of segments that transcend national borders. The structure of market segments may differ significantly from country to country. An important market segment in a foreign country may have no parallel in the firm's home country, and vice versa. The firm may have to develop a unique marketing mix to appeal to the unique purchasing behavior of a unique segment in a given country. For example, a research project published in 1998 identified a segment of consumers in China in the 45-to-55 age range that has few parallels in other countries.[5] This group came of age during China's violent and repressive Cultural Revolution in the late 1960s and early 1970s. The values of this group have been shaped by their experiences during the Cultural Revolution. They tend to be highly sensitive to price and respond negatively to new products and most forms of marketing. The existence of this group implies that firms doing business in China may need to customize their marketing mix to address the unique values and purchasing behavior of the group. The existence of such a unique segment constrains the ability of firms to standardize their global marketing strategy.

In contrast, the existence of market segments that transcend national borders clearly enhances the ability of an international business to view the global marketplace as a single entity and pursue a global strategy, selling a standardized product worldwide, and using the same basic marketing mix to help position and sell that product in a variety of national markets. For a segment to transcend national borders, consumers in that segment must have some compelling similarities along important dimensions—such as age, values, lifestyle choices—and those similarities must translate into similar purchasing behavior. Although such segments exist in certain industrial markets, they are rare in consumer markets. However, one emerging global segment that is attracting the attention of international marketers of consumer goods is the so-called global-teen segment. As noted in the Management Focus on MTV, the global media are paving the way for a global teen segment. Evidence that such a segment exists comes from a study of the cultural attitudes and purchasing behavior of more than 6,500 teenagers in 26 countries.[6] The findings suggest that teens around the world are increasingly living parallel lives that share many common values. It follows that they are likely to purchase the same kind of consumer goods and for the same reasons. Even here though, marketing specialists argue that some customization in the marketing mix to account for differences across countries is required.

Product Attributes

A product can be viewed as a bundle of attributes.[7] For example, the attributes that make up a car include power, design, quality, performance, fuel consumption, and comfort; the attributes of a hamburger include taste, texture, and size; a hotel's attributes include atmosphere, quality, comfort, and service. Products sell well when their attributes match consumer needs (and when their prices are appropriate). BMW cars sell well to people who have high needs for luxury, quality, and performance, precisely because BMW builds those attributes into its cars. If consumer needs were the same the world over, a firm could simply sell the same product worldwide. However, consumer needs vary from country to country depending on culture and the level of economic development. A firm's ability to sell the same product worldwide is further constrained by countries' differing product standards. In this section, we review each of these issues and discuss how they influence product attributes.

Cultural Differences

We discussed countries' cultural differences in Chapter 3. Countries differ along a whole range of dimensions, including social structure, language, religion, and education. And as alluded to in Chapter 2, these differences have important implications for marketing strategy. For example, "hamburgers" do not sell well in Islamic countries, where the consumption of ham is forbidden by Islamic law. The most important aspect of cultural differences is probably the impact of tradition. Tradition is particularly important in foodstuffs and beverages. For example, reflecting differences in traditional eating habits, the Findus frozen food division of Nestlé, the Swiss food giant, markets fish cakes and fish fingers in Great Britain, but beef bourguignon and coq au vin in France and vitèllo con funghi and braviola in Italy. In addition to its normal range of products, Coca-Cola in Japan markets Georgia, a cold coffee in a can, and Aquarius, a tonic drink, which appeal to traditional Japanese tastes.

For historical and idiosyncratic reasons, a range of other cultural differences exist between countries. For example, scent preferences differ from one country to another. S. C. Johnson Wax, a manufacturer of waxes and polishes, encountered resistance to its lemon-scented Pledge furniture polish among older consumers in Japan. Careful market research revealed that the polish smelled similar to a latrine disinfectant used widely in Japan in the 1940s. Sales rose sharply after the scent was adjusted.[8] In another example, Cheetos, the bright orange and cheesy-tasting snack from PepsiCo's Frito-Lay unit, do not have a cheese taste in China. Chinese consumers generally do not like the taste of cheese because it has never been part of traditional cuisine and because many Chinese are lactose-intolerant.[9]

There is some evidence of the trends Levitt talked about. Tastes and preferences are becoming more cosmopolitan. Coffee is gaining ground against tea in Japan and Great Britain, while American-style frozen dinners have become popular in Europe (with some fine-tuning to local tastes). Taking advantage of these trends, Nestlé has found that it can market its instant coffee, spaghetti bolognese, and Lean Cuisine frozen dinners in essentially the same manner in both North America and Western Europe. However, there is no market for Lean Cuisine dinners in most of the rest of the world, and there may never be. A calorie-conscious Asian is difficult to find. Although some cultural convergence has occurred, particularly among the advanced industrial nations of North America and Western Europe, Levitt's global culture is still a long way off.

Economic Differences

Just as important as differences in culture are differences in the level of economic development. We discussed the extent of country differences in economic development in Chapter 2. Consumer behavior is influenced by the level of economic development of a country. Firms based in highly developed countries such as the United States tend to build a lot of extra performance attributes into their products. These extra attributes are not usually demanded by consumers in less developed nations, where the preference is for more basic products. Thus, cars sold in less developed nations typically lack many of the features found in the West, such as air-conditioning, power steering, power windows, radios, and cassette players. For most consumer durables, product reliability may be a more important attribute in less developed nations, where such a purchase may account for a major proportion of a consumer's income, than it is in advanced nations.

Contrary to Levitt's suggestions, consumers in the most developed countries are often not willing to sacrifice their preferred attributes for lower prices. Consumers in the most advanced countries often shun globally standardized products that have been developed with the lowest common denominator in mind. They are willing to pay more for products that have additional features and attributes customized to their tastes and preferences. For example, demand for top-of-the-line four-wheel-drive sport utility vehicles, such as Chrysler's Jeep, Ford's Explorer, and Toyota's Land Cruiser, is almost totally restricted to the United States. This is due to a combination of factors, including the high income level of US consumers, the country's vast distances, the relatively low cost of gasoline, and the culturally grounded "outdoor" theme of American life.

Product and Technical Standards

Even with the forces that are creating some convergence of consumer tastes and preferences among advanced, industrialized nations, Levitt's vision of global markets may still be a long way off because of national differences in product and technological standards.

Differing government-mandated product standards can rule out mass production and marketing of a standardized product. For example, Caterpillar, the US construction equipment firm, manufactures backhoe-loaders for all of Europe in Great Britain. These tractor-type machines have a bucket in front and a digger at the back. Several special parts must be built into backhoe-loaders that will be sold in Germany: a separate brake attached to the rear axle, a special locking mechanism on the backhoe operating valve, specially positioned valves in the steering system, and a lock on the bucket for traveling. These extras account for 5 percent of the total cost of the product in Germany.[10] The European Union is trying to harmonize such divergent product standards among its member nations. If the EU is successful, the need to customize products will be reduced within the boundaries of the EU.

Differences in technical standards also constrain the globalization of markets. Some of these differences result from idiosyncratic decisions made long ago, rather than from government actions, but their long-term effects are nonetheless profound. For example, video equipment manufactured for sale in the United States will not play videotapes recorded on equipment manufactured for sale in Great Britain, Germany, and France (and vice versa). Different technical standards for frequency of television signals emerged in the 1950s that require television and video equipment to be customized to prevailing standards. RCA stumbled in the 1970s when it failed to account for this in its marketing of TVs in Asia. Although several Asian countries adopted the US standard, Singapore, Hong Kong, and Malaysia adopted the British standard. People who bought RCA TVs in those countries could receive a picture but no sound![11]

Distribution Strategy

A critical element of a firm's marketing mix is its distribution strategy, the means it chooses for delivering the product to the consumer. The way the product is delivered is determined by the firm's entry strategy, which we discussed in Chapter 14. In this section, we examine a typical distribution system, discuss how its structure varies between countries, and look at how appropriate distribution strategies vary from country to country.

A Typical Distribution System

Figure 17.1 illustrates a typical distribution system consisting of a channel that includes a wholesale distributor and a retailer. If the firm manufactures its product in the particular country, it can sell directly to the consumer, to the retailer, or to the wholesaler. The same options are available to a firm that manufactures outside the country. Plus, this firm may decide to sell to an import agent, who then deals with the wholesale distributor, the retailer, or the consumer. The factors that determine the firm's choice of channel are considered later in this section.

Figure 17.1

A Typical Distribution System

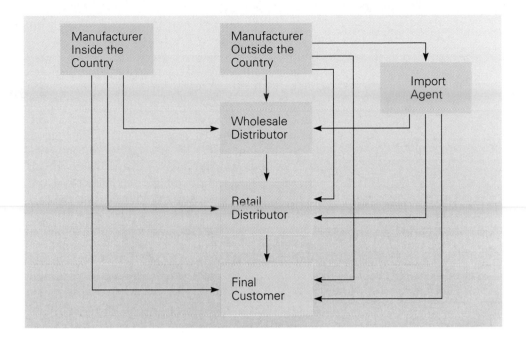

Differences between Countries

The three main differences between distribution systems are retail concentration, channel length, and channel exclusivity.

Retail Concentration

In some countries, the retail system is very concentrated, but it is fragmented in others. In a concentrated system, a few retailers supply most of the market. A fragmented system is one in which there are many retailers, no one of which has a major share of the market. In Germany, for example, four retail chains control 65 percent of the market for food products. In neighboring Italy, retail distribution is fragmented, with no chain controlling more than 2 percent of the market.

Many of the differences in concentration are rooted in history and tradition. In the United States, the importance of the automobile and the relative youth of many urban areas have resulted in a retail system centered around large stores or shopping malls to which people can drive. This has facilitated system concentration. Japan's much greater population density together with the large number of urban centers that grew up before the automobile have yielded a more fragmented retail system of many small stores that serve local neighborhoods and to which people frequently walk. In addition, the Japanese legal system protects small retailers. Small retailers can block the establishment of a large retail outlet by petitioning their local government.

There is a tendency for greater retail concentration in developed countries. Three factors that contribute to this are the increases in car ownership, number of households with refrigerators and freezers, and number of two-income households. All of these factors have changed shopping habits and facilitated the growth of large retail establishments sited away from traditional shopping areas.

Channel Length

Channel length refers to the number of intermediaries between the producer (or manufacturer) and the consumer. If the producer sells directly to the consumer, the channel is very short. If the producer sells through an import agent, a wholesaler, and a retailer, a long channel exists. The choice of a short or long channel is primarily a strategic decision for the producing firm. However, some countries have longer distribution channels than others. The most important determinant of channel length is the degree to which the retail system is fragmented. Fragmented retail systems tend to promote the growth of wholesalers to serve retailers, which lengthens channels.

The more fragmented the retail system, the more expensive it is for a firm to make contact with each individual retailer. Imagine a firm that sells toothpaste in a country where there are 50,000 small retailers. To sell directly to the retailers, the firm would have to build a huge sales force. This would be very expensive, particularly since each sales call would yield a very small order. But suppose there are 50 wholesalers in the country who supply retailers not only with toothpaste but also with all other personal care and household products. Because these wholesalers carry a wide range of products, they get bigger orders with each sales call, making it worthwhile for them to deal directly with the retailers. Accordingly, it makes economic sense for the firm to sell to the wholesalers and the wholesalers to deal with the retailers.

Because of such factors, countries with fragmented retail systems also tend to have long channels of distribution. The classic example is Japan, where there are often two or three layers of wholesalers between the firm and retail outlets. In countries such as Great Britain, Germany, and the United States where the retail system is far more concentrated, channels are much shorter. When the retail sector is very concentrated, it makes sense for the firm to deal directly with retailers, cutting out wholesalers. A relatively small sales force is required to deal with a concentrated retail sector, and the orders generated from each sales call can be large. Such circumstances tend to prevail in the United States, where large food companies sell directly to supermarkets rather than going through wholesale distributors.

Channel Exclusivity

An exclusive distribution channel is one that is difficult for outsiders to access. For example, it is often difficult for a new firm to get access to shelf space in US supermarkets. This occurs because retailers tend to prefer to carry the products of long-established manufacturers of foodstuffs with national reputations rather than gamble on the products of unknown firms. The exclusivity of a distribution system varies between countries. Japan's system is often held up as an example of a very exclusive system. In Japan, relationships between manufacturers, wholesalers, and retailers often go back decades. Many of these relationships are based on the understanding that distributors will not carry the products of competing firms. In return, the distributors are guaranteed an attractive markup by the manufacturer. As many US and European manufacturers have learned, the close ties that result from this arrangement can make access to the Japanese market very difficult. But, as the opening case illustrates, it is possible to break into the Japanese market with a new consumer product, as Procter & Gamble did recently with its Joy brand of dish soap. P&G was able to overcome a tradition of exclusivity for two reasons. First, after a decade of lackluster economic performance, Japan is changing. In their search for profits, retailers are far more willing than they have been historically to violate the old norms of exclusivity. Second, P&G has been in Japan long enough and has a broad enough portfolio of consumer products to give it considerable leverage with distributors, enabling it to push new products out through the distribution channel.

Choosing a Distribution Strategy

A choice of distribution strategy determines which channel the firm will use to reach potential consumers. Should the firm try to sell directly to the consumer or should it go through retailers; should it go through a wholesaler; should it use an import agent? The optimal strategy is determined by the relative costs and benefits of each alternative. The relative costs and benefits of each alternative vary from country to country, depending on the three factors we have just discussed: retail concentration, channel length, and channel exclusivity.

Because each intermediary in a channel adds its own markup to the products, there is generally a critical link between channel length, the final selling price, and the firm's profit margin. The longer a channel, the greater is the aggregate markup, and the higher the price that consumers are charged for the final product. To ensure that prices do not get too high due to markups by multiple intermediaries, a firm might be forced to operate with lower profit margins. Thus, if price is an important competitive weapon, and if the firm does not want to see its profit margins squeezed, other things being equal, the firm would prefer to use a shorter channel.

However, the benefits of using a longer channel often outweigh these drawbacks. As we have seen, one benefit of a longer channel is that it cuts selling costs when the retail sector is very fragmented. Thus, it makes sense for an international business to use longer channels in countries where the retail sector is fragmented and shorter channels in countries where the retail sector is concentrated.

Another benefit of using a longer channel is market access—the ability to enter an exclusive channel. Import agents may have long-term relationships with wholesalers, retailers, and/or important consumers and thus be better able to win orders and get access to a distribution system. Similarly, wholesalers may have long-standing relationships with retailers and be better able to persuade them to carry the firm's product than the firm itself would.

Import agents are not limited to independent trading houses; any firm with a strong local reputation could serve as well. For example, to break down channel exclusivity and gain greater access to the Japanese market, in 1991 and 1992, Apple Computer signed distribution agreements with five large Japanese firms including business equipment giant Brother Industries, stationery leader Kokuyo, Mitsubishi, Sharp, and Minolta. These firms use their own long-established distribution relationships with consumers, retailers, and wholesalers to push Apple Macintosh computers through the Japanese distribution system. As a result, Apple's share of the Japanese market increased from less than 1 percent in 1988 to 6 percent in 1991, and 13 percent by 1994.[12]

If such an arrangement is not possible, the firm might want to consider other, less traditional alternatives to gaining market access. Frustrated by channel exclusivity in Japan, some foreign manufacturers of consumer goods have attempted to sell directly to Japanese consumers using direct mail and catalogs. REI, a retailer of outdoor clothing and equipment based in the northwestern United States, had trouble persuading Japanese wholesalers and retailers to carry its products. So instead it began a direct-mail campaign in Japan that is proving very successful.

Communication Strategy

Another critical element in the marketing mix is communicating the attributes of the product to prospective customers. A number of communications channels are available to a firm, including direct selling, sales promotion, direct marketing, and advertising. A firm's communications strategy is partly defined by its choice of channel. Some firms rely primarily on direct selling, others on point-of-sale promotions or direct marketing, others on mass advertising; still others use several channels simultaneously to communicate their message to prospective customers. In this section, we will look first at the barriers to international communication. Then we will survey the various factors that determine which communications strategy is most appropriate in a particular country. After that we discuss global advertising.

Barriers to International Communications

International communication occurs whenever a firm uses a marketing message to sell its products in another country. The effectiveness of a firm's international communication can be jeopardized by three potentially critical variables: cultural barriers, source effects, and noise levels.

Cultural Barriers

Cultural barriers can make it difficult to communicate messages across cultures. We discussed some sources and consequences of cultural differences between nations in Chapter 3 and in the previous section of this chapter. Due to cultural differences, a message that means one thing in one country may mean something quite different in another. For example, when Procter & Gamble promoted its Camay soap in Japan in 1983 it ran into unexpected trouble. In a TV commercial, a Japanese man walked into the bathroom while his wife was bathing. The woman began telling her husband all about her new soap, but the husband, stroking her shoulder, hinted that suds were not on his mind. This ad had been very popular in Europe, but it flopped in Japan because it is considered very bad manners there for a man to intrude on his wife.[13] Benetton, the Italian clothing manufacturer and retailer, is another firm that has run into cultural problems with its advertising. The company launched a worldwide advertising campaign in 1989 with the theme "United Colors of Benetton" that had won awards in France. One of its ads featured a black woman breast-feeding a white baby, and another one showed a black man and a white man handcuffed together. Benetton was surprised when the ads were attacked by US civil rights groups for promoting white racial domination. Benetton withdrew its ads and fired its advertising agency, Eldorado of France.

The best way for a firm to overcome cultural barriers is to develop cross-cultural literacy (see Chapter 3). In addition, it should use local input, such as a local advertising agency, in developing its marketing message. If the firm uses direct selling rather than advertising to communicate its message, it should develop a local sales force whenever possible. Cultural differences limit a firm's ability to use the same marketing message the world over. What works well in one country may be offensive in another.

Source Effects

Source effects occur when the receiver of the message (the potential consumer in this case) evaluates the message based on the status or image of the sender. Source effects can be damaging for an international business when potential consumers in a target country have a bias against foreign firms. For example, a wave of "Japan bashing" swept the United States in 1992. Worried that US consumers might view its products negatively, Honda responded by creating ads that emphasized the US content of its cars to show how "American" the company had become. Many international businesses try to counter negative source effects by deemphasizing their foreign origins. When British Petroleum acquired Mobil Oil's extensive network of US gas stations, it changed its name to BP, diverting attention away from the fact that one of the biggest operators of gas stations in the United States is a British firm.

Source effects are not always negative. French wine, Italian clothes, and German luxury cars benefit from nearly universal positive source effects. In such cases, it may pay a firm to emphasize its foreign origins. In Japan, for example, there is strong demand for high-quality foreign goods, particularly those from Europe. It has become chic to carry a Gucci handbag, sport a Rolex watch, drink expensive French wine, and drive a BMW.

Noise Levels

Noise tends to reduce the probability of effective communication. Noise refers to the amount of other messages competing for a potential consumer's attention, and this too varies across countries. In highly developed countries such as the United States, noise is extremely high. Fewer firms vie for the attention of prospective customers in developing countries, and the noise level is lower.

Push versus Pull Strategies

The main decision with regard to communications strategy is the choice between a push strategy and a pull strategy. A push strategy emphasizes personal selling rather than mass media advertising in the promotional mix. Although very effective as a promotional tool, personal selling requires intensive use of a sales force and is relatively costly. A pull strategy depends more on mass media advertising to communicate the marketing message to potential consumers.

Although some firms employ only a pull strategy and others only a push strategy, still other firms combine direct selling with mass advertising to maximize communication effectiveness. Factors that determine the relative attractiveness of push and pull strategies include product type relative to consumer sophistication, channel length, and media availability.

Product Type and Consumer Sophistication

A pull strategy is generally favored by firms in consumer goods industries that are trying to sell to a large segment of the market. For such firms, mass communication has cost advantages, and direct selling is rarely used. But a push strategy is favored by firms that sell industrial products or other complex products. Direct selling allows the firm to educate potential consumers about the features of the product. This may not be necessary in advanced nations where a complex product has been in use for some time, where the product's attributes are well understood, and where consumers are sophisticated. However, customer education may be very important when consumers have less sophistication toward the product, which can be the case in developing nations or in advanced nations when a complex product is being introduced.

Channel Length

The longer the distribution channel, the more intermediaries there are that must be persuaded to carry the product for it to reach the consumer. This can lead to inertia in the channel, which can make entry very difficult. Using direct selling to push a product through many layers of a distribution channel can be very expensive. In such circumstances, a firm may try to pull its product through the channels by using mass advertising to create consumer demand—once demand is created, intermediaries will feel obliged to carry the product.

In Japan, products often pass through two, three, or even four wholesalers before they reach the final retail outlet. This can make it difficult for foreign firms to break into the Japanese market. Not only must the foreigner persuade a Japanese retailer to carry her product, but she may also have to persuade every intermediary in the chain to carry the product. Mass advertising may be one way to break down channel resistance in such circumstances.

Media Availability

A pull strategy relies on access to advertising media. In the United States, a large number of media are available, including print media (newspapers and magazines) and electronic media (television and radio). The rise of cable television in the United States has facilitated extremely focused advertising (e.g., MTV for teens and young adults, Lifetime for women, ESPN for sports enthusiasts). With a few exceptions such as Canada and Japan, this level of media sophistication is not found outside the United States. Even many advanced nations have far fewer electronic media available for advertising. In Scandinavia, for example, no commercial television or radio stations existed in 1987; all electronic media were state owned and carried no commercials, although this has now changed with the advent of satellite television deregulation. In many developing nations, the situation is even more restrictive because mass media of all types are typically more limited. A firm's ability to use a pull strategy is limited in some countries by media availability. In such circumstances, a push strategy is more attractive.

Media availability is limited by law in some cases. Few countries allow advertisements for tobacco and alcohol products on television and radio, though they are usually permitted in print media. When the leading Japanese whiskey distiller, Suntory, entered the US market, it had to do so without television, its preferred medium. The firm spends about $50 million annually on television advertising in Japan.

The Push–Pull Mix

The optimal mix between push and pull strategies depends on product type and consumer sophistication, channel length, and media sophistication. Push strategies tend to be emphasized:

- For industrial products and/or complex new products.
- When distribution channels are short.
- When few print or electronic media are available.

Pull strategies tend to be emphasized:

- For consumer goods.
- When distribution channels are long.
- When sufficient print and electronic media are available to carry the marketing message.

Global Advertising

In recent years, largely inspired by the work of visionaries such as Theodore Levitt, there has been much discussion about the pros and cons of standardizing advertising worldwide. One of the most successful standardized campaigns has been Philip Morris's promotion of Marlboro cigarettes. The campaign was instituted in the 1950s, when the brand was repositioned, to assure smokers that the flavor would be unchanged by the addition of a filter. The campaign theme of "Come to where the flavor is. Come to Marlboro country" was a worldwide success. Marlboro built on this when it introduced "the Marlboro man," a rugged cowboy smoking his Marlboro while riding his horse through the great outdoors. This ad proved successful in almost every major market around the world, and it helped propel Marlboro to the top of the world market share table.

For Standardized Advertising

The support for global advertising is threefold. First, it has significant economic advantages. Standardized advertising lowers the costs of value creation by spreading the fixed costs of developing the advertisements over many countries. For example, Levi Strauss paid an advertising agency $550,000 to produce a series of TV commercials. By reusing this series in many countries, rather than developing a series for each country, the company enjoyed significant cost savings. Similarly, Coca-Cola's advertising agency, McCann-Erickson, claims to have saved Coca-Cola $90 million over 20 years by using certain elements of its campaigns globally.

Second, there is the concern that creative talent is scarce and so one large effort to develop a campaign will produce better results than 40 or 50 smaller efforts.

A third justification for a standardized approach is that many brand names are global. With the substantial amount of international travel today and the considerable overlap in media across national borders, many international firms want to project a single brand image to avoid confusion caused by local campaigns. This is particularly important in regions such as Western Europe, where travel across borders is almost as common as travel across state lines in the United States.

Against Standardized Advertising

There are two main arguments against globally standardized advertising. First, as we have seen repeatedly in this chapter and in Chapter 3, cultural differences between nations are such that a message that works in one nation can fail miserably in another. For a detailed example of this phenomenon, see the accompanying Management Focus on Polaroid. Due to cultural diversity, it is extremely difficult to develop a single advertising theme that is effective worldwide. Messages directed at the culture of a given country may be more effective than global messages.

MANAGEMENT FOCUS
Global Advertising at Polaroid

http://www.polaroid.com

Polaroid introduced its SX-70 instant camera in Europe in the mid-1970s with the same marketing strategy, TV commercials, and print ads it had used in North America. Polaroid's headquarters believed the camera served a universal need—the pleasure of instant photography—and the communication strategy should thus be the same the world over. The television commercials featured testimonials of personalities well known in the United States, but few of these personalities were known in Europe and managers of Polaroid's European operations pointed this out to headquarters. Unperturbed by these concerns, headquarters management set strict guidelines to discourage deviation from the global plan. The European personnel were proved correct. The testimonials by "unknown" personalities left consumers cold, and the commercials failed to raise awareness of Polaroid's instant camera. Even though the camera later became successful in Europe, local management believes the misguided introductory campaign did not help its performance.

The lesson was remembered a decade later when Polaroid's European management launched a pan-European program to reposition Polaroid's instant photography from the "party camera" platform to a serious, "utilitarian" platform. This time headquarters did not assume it had the answers. Instead, it looked for inspiration in the various advertising practices of its European subsidiaries, and it found it in the strategy of one of its smallest subsidiaries in Switzerland. With considerable

success, the Swiss subsidiary had promoted the functional uses of instant photography as a means of communicating with family and friends. A task force was set up to test this concept in other markets. The tests showed that the Swiss strategy was transferable and that it produced the desired impact. Thus was born Europe's "Learn to Speak Polaroid" campaign, one of the firm's most successful advertising efforts. Non-European subsidiaries, including those in Japan and Australia, liked the strategy so much that they adopted it too.

What made this campaign different from the SX-70 campaign a decade earlier was the decentralized decision making. Instead of headquarters imposing on Europe an advertising campaign developed in the United States, the European subsidiaries developed their own campaign. Equally important, even after the pan-European program was adopted, European managers had the freedom to adapt the campaign to local tastes and needs. For example, where tests showed that the "Learn to Speak Polaroid" tag did not convey the intended meaning in the local language, the subsidiary was free to change it. By adopting this approach, Polaroid reaped some of the benefits of standardized advertisements while customizing its message to local conditions when that proved necessary.

Source: Reprinted by permission of the *Harvard Business Review*. From "Beware the Pitfalls of Global Marketing," by Kamran Kashani, Sept.–Oct. 1989. Copyright © 1989 by the President and Fellows of Harvard College; all rights reserved.

Second, advertising regulations may block implementation of standardized advertising. For example, Kellogg could not use a television commercial it produced in Great Britain to promote its cornflakes in many other European countries. A reference to the iron and vitamin content of its cornflakes was not permissible in the Netherlands, where claims relating to health and medical benefits are outlawed. A child wearing a Kellogg T-shirt had to be edited out of the commercial before it could be used in France, because French law forbids the use of children in product endorsements. The key line, "Kellogg's makes their cornflakes the best they have ever been," was disallowed in Germany because of a prohibition against competitive claims.[14] Similarly, American Express ran afoul of regulatory authorities in Germany when it launched a promotional scheme that had proved very successful in other countries. The scheme advertised the offer of "bonus points" every time American

Express cardholders used their cards. According to the advertisements, these "bonus points" could be used toward air travel with three airlines and hotel accommodations. American Express was charged with breaking Germany's competition law, which prevents an offer of free gifts in connection with the sale of goods, and the firm had to withdraw the advertisements at considerable cost.[15]

Dealing with Country Differences

Some firms are experimenting with capturing some benefits of global standardization while recognizing differences in countries' cultural and legal environments. A firm may select some features to include in all its advertising campaigns and localize other features. By doing so, it may be able to save on some costs and build international brand recognition and yet customize its advertisements to different cultures.

This is what Polaroid did with the "Learn to Speak Polaroid" campaign (see the Management Focus for details). Pepsi-Cola used a similar approach in a 1980s advertising campaign. The company wanted to use modern music to connect its products with local markets. Pepsi hired US singer Tina Turner and rock stars from six countries to team up in singing and performing the Pepsi-Cola theme song in a big rock concert. The commercials are customized for each market by showing Turner with the rock stars from that country. Except for the footage of the local stars, all the commercials are identical. By shooting the commercials all at once, Pepsi saved on production costs. The campaign was extended to 30 countries, which relieved the local subsidiaries or bottlers of having to develop their own campaigns.[16]

Pricing Strategy

International pricing strategy is an important component of the overall international marketing mix. In this section, we look at three aspects of international pricing strategy. First, we examine the case for pursuing price discrimination, charging different prices for the same product in different countries. Second, we look at what might be called strategic pricing. Third, we review some regulatory factors, such as government-mandated price controls and antidumping regulations, that limit a firm's ability to charge the prices it would prefer in a country.

Price Discrimination

Price discrimination exists whenever consumers in different countries are charged different prices for the same product. Price discrimination involves charging whatever the market will bear; in a competitive market, prices may have to be lower than in a market where the firm has a monopoly. Price discrimination can help a company maximize its profits. It makes economic sense to charge different prices in different countries.

Two conditions are necessary for profitable price discrimination. First, the firm must be able to keep its national markets separate. If it cannot do this, individuals or businesses may undercut its attempt at price discrimination by engaging in arbitrage. Arbitrage occurs when an individual or business capitalizes on a price differential for a firm's product between two countries by purchasing the product in the country where prices are lower and reselling it in the country where prices are higher. For example, many automobile firms have long practiced price discrimination in Europe. A Ford Escort once cost $2,000 more in Germany than it did in Belgium. This policy broke down when car dealers bought Escorts in Belgium and drove them to Germany, where they sold them at a profit for slightly less than Ford was selling Escorts in Germany. To protect the market share of its German auto dealers, Ford had to bring its German prices into line with those being charged in Belgium. Ford could not keep these markets separate.

However, Ford still practices price discrimination between Great Britain and Belgium. A Ford car can cost up to $3,000 more in Great Britain than in Belgium. In this

Figure 17.2

Elastic and Inelastic
Demand Curves

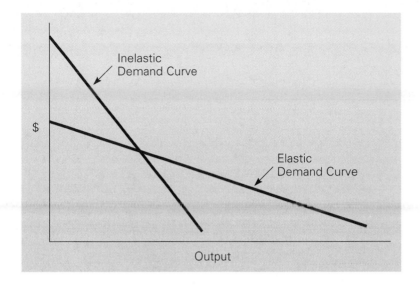

case, arbitrage has not been able to equalize the price, because right-hand-drive cars are sold in Great Britain and left-hand-drive cars in the rest of Europe. Because there is no market for left-hand-drive cars in Great Britain, Ford has been able to keep the markets separate.

The second necessary condition for profitable price discrimination is different price elasticities of demand in different countries. The price elasticity of demand is a measure of the responsiveness of demand for a product to changes in price. Demand is said to be elastic when a small change in price produces a large change in demand; it is said to be inelastic when a large change in price produces only a small change in demand. Figure 17.2 illustrates elastic and inelastic demand curves. Generally, for reasons that will be explained shortly, a firm can charge a higher price in a country where demand is inelastic.

The Determinants of Demand Elasticity

The elasticity of demand for a product in a given country is determined by a number of factors, of which income level and competitive conditions are the two most important. Price elasticity tends to be greater in countries with low income levels. Consumers with limited incomes tend to be very price conscious; they have less to spend, so they look much more closely at price. Thus, price elasticities for products such as television sets are greater in countries such as India, where a television set is still a luxury item, than in the United States, where it is considered a necessity.

In general, the more competitors there are, the greater consumers' bargaining power will be and the more likely consumers will be to buy from the firm that charges the lowest price. Thus, many competitors cause high elasticity of demand. In such circumstances, if a firm raises its prices above those of its competitors, consumers will switch to the competitors' products. The opposite is true when a firm faces few competitors. When competitors are limited, consumers' bargaining power is weaker and price is less important as a competitive weapon. Thus, a firm may charge a higher price for its product in a country where competition is limited than in a country where competition is intense.

Profit Maximizing under Price Discrimination

For those readers with some grasp of economic logic, we can offer a more formal presentation of the above argument. (Readers unfamiliar with basic economic terminology may want to skip this subsection.) Figure 17.3 shows the situation facing a firm that sells the same product in only two countries, Japan and the United States. The

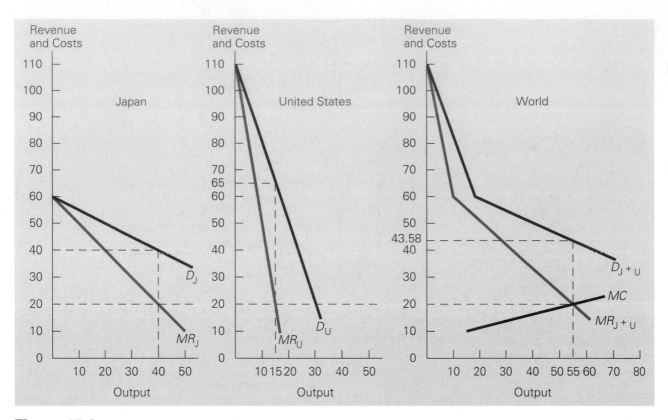

Figure 17.3

Price Discrimination

Japanese market is very competitive, so the firm faces an elastic demand curve (D_J) and marginal revenue curve (MR_J). The US market is not competitive, so there the firm faces an inelastic demand curve (D_U) and marginal revenue curve (MR_U). Also shown in the figure are the firm's total demand curve (D_{J+U}), total marginal revenue curve (MR_{J+U}), and marginal cost curve (MC). The total demand curve is simply the summation of the demand facing the firm in Japan and the United States, as is the total marginal revenue curve.

To maximize profits, the firm must produce at the output where MR = MC. In Figure 17.3, this implies an output of 55 units. If the firm does not practice price discrimination, it will charge a price of $43.58 to sell an output of 55 units. Thus, without price discrimination, the firm's total revenues are

$$\$43.58 \times 55 = \$2,396.90.$$

Look what happens when the firm decides to engage in price discrimination. It will still produce 55 units, since that is where MR = MC. However, the firm must now allocate this output between the two countries to take advantage of the difference in demand elasticity. Proper allocation of output between Japan and the United States can be determined graphically by drawing a line through their respective graphs at $20 to indicate that $20 is the marginal cost in each country (see Figure 17.3). To maximize profits, prices are now set in each country at that level where the marginal revenue for that country equals marginal costs. In Japan, this is a price of $40, and the firm sells 40 units. In the United States, the optimal price is $65, and it sells 15 units. Thus, reflecting the different competitive conditions, the price charged in the United States is over 50 percent more than the price charged in Japan. Look at what happens to total revenues. With price discrimination, the firm earns revenues of

$$\$40 \times 40 \text{ units} = \$1,600$$

in Japan and

$$\$65 \times 15 \text{ units} = \$975$$

in the United States. By engaging in price discrimination, the firm can earn total revenues of

$$\$1,600 + \$975 = \$2,575,$$

which is \$178.10 more than the \$2,396.90 it earned before. Price discrimination pays!

Strategic Pricing

The concept of strategic pricing has three aspects, which we will refer to as predatory pricing, multipoint pricing, and experience curve pricing. Both predatory pricing and experience curve pricing may be in violation of antidumping regulations. After we review predatory and experience curve pricing, we will look at antidumping rules and other regulatory policies.

Predatory Pricing

Predatory pricing is the use of price as a competitive weapon to drive weaker competitors out of a national market. Once the competitors have left the market, the firm can raise prices and enjoy high profits. For such a pricing strategy to work, the firm must normally have a profitable position in another national market, which it can use to subsidize aggressive pricing in the market it is trying to monopolize. Many Japanese firms have been accused of pursuing this strategy. The argument runs similarly to this: Because the Japanese market is protected from foreign competition by high informal trade barriers, Japanese firms can charge high prices and earn high profits at home. They then use these profits to subsidize aggressive pricing overseas, with the goal of driving competitors out of those markets. Once this has occurred, so it is claimed, the Japanese firms then raise prices. Matsushita has been accused of using this strategy to enter the US TV market. As one of the major TV producers in Japan, Matsushita earned high profits at home. It then used these profits to subsidize the losses it made in the United States during its early years there, when it priced low to increase its market penetration. Ultimately, Matsushita became the world's largest manufacturer of TVs.[17]

Multipoint Pricing Strategy

Multipoint pricing becomes an issue when two or more international businesses compete against each other in two or more national markets. For example, multipoint pricing is an issue for Kodak and Fuji Photo because both companies compete against each other in different national markets for film products around the world. **Multipoint pricing** refers to the fact a firm's pricing strategy in one market may have an impact on its rivals' pricing strategy in another market. Aggressive pricing in one market may elicit a competitive response from a rival in another market. In the case of Kodak and Fuji, Fuji launched an aggressive competitive attack against Kodak in the American company's home market in January 1997, cutting prices on multiple-roll packs of 35mm film by as much as 50 percent.[18] This price cutting resulted in a 28 percent increase in shipments of Fuji color film during the first six months of 1997, while Kodak's shipments dropped by 11 percent. This attack created a dilemma for Kodak; the company did not want to start price discounting in its largest and most profitable market. Kodak's response was to aggressively cut prices in Fuji's largest market, Japan. This strategic response recognized the interdependence between Kodak and Fuji and the fact that they compete against each other in many different nations. Fuji responded to Kodak's counterattack by pulling back from its aggressive stance in the United States.

The Kodak story illustrates an important aspect of multipoint pricing—aggressive pricing in one market may elicit a response from rivals in another market. The firm needs to consider how its global rivals will respond to changes in its pricing strategy before making those changes. A second aspect of multipoint pricing arises when two or more global companies focus on particular national markets and launch vigorous price wars in those markets in an attempt to gain market dominance. In the Brazil market for disposable diapers, two US companies, Kimberly-Clark Corp. and Procter & Gamble, entered a price war as each struggled to establish dominance in the market.[19] As a result, the cost of disposable diapers fell from $1 per diaper in 1994 to 33 cents per diaper in 1997, while several other competitors, including indigenous Brazilian firms, were driven out of the market. Kimberly-Clark and Procter & Gamble are engaged in a global struggle for market share and dominance, and Brazil is one of their battlegrounds. Both companies can afford to engage in this behavior, even though it reduces their profits in Brazil, because they have profitable operations elsewhere in the world that can subsidize these losses.

Pricing decisions around the world need to be centrally monitored. It is tempting to delegate full responsibility for pricing decisions to the managers of various national subsidiaries, thereby reaping the benefits of decentralization (see Chapter 13 for a discussion). However, because pricing strategy in one part of the world can elicit a competitive response in another part, central management needs to at least monitor and approve pricing decisions in a given national market, and local managers need to recognize that their actions can affect competitive conditions in other countries.

Experience Curve Pricing

We first encountered the experience curve in Chapter 12. As a firm builds its accumulated production volume over time, unit costs fall due to "experience effects." Learning effects and economies of scale underlie the experience curve. Price comes into the picture because aggressive pricing (along with aggressive promotion and advertising) can build accumulated sales volume rapidly and thus move production down the experience curve. Firms further down the experience curve have a cost advantage vis-à-vis firms further up the curve.

Many firms pursuing an experience curve pricing strategy on an international scale price low worldwide in attempting to build global sales volume as rapidly as possible, even if this means taking large losses initially. Such a firm believes that several years in the future, when it has moved down the experience curve, it will be making substantial profits and have a cost advantage over its less-aggressive competitors.

Regulatory Influences on Prices

The ability to engage in either price discrimination or strategic pricing may be limited by national or international regulations. Most important, a firm's freedom to set its own prices is constrained by antidumping regulations and competition policy.

Antidumping Regulations

Both predatory pricing and experience curve pricing can run afoul of antidumping regulations. Dumping occurs whenever a firm sells a product for a price that is less than the cost of producing it. Most regulations, however, define dumping more vaguely. For example, a country is allowed to bring antidumping actions against an importer under Article 6 of GATT as long as two criteria are met: sales at "less than fair value" and "material injury to a domestic industry." The problem with this terminology is that it does not indicate what is a fair value. The ambiguity has led some to argue that selling abroad at prices below those in the country of origin, as opposed to below cost, is dumping.

Such logic led the Bush administration to place a 25 percent duty on imports of Japanese light trucks in 1988. The Japanese manufacturers protested that they were not selling below cost. Admitting that their prices were lower in the United States than in Japan, they argued that this simply reflected the intensely competitive nature of the US market (i.e., different price elasticities). In a similar example, the European Commission found Japanese exporters of dot-matrix printers to be violating dumping regulations. To correct what they saw as dumping, the EU placed a 47 percent import duty on imports of dot-matrix printers from Japan and required that the import duty be passed on to European consumers as a price increase.[20]

Antidumping rules set a floor under export prices and limit firms' ability to pursue strategic pricing. The rather vague terminology used in most antidumping actions suggests that a firm's ability to engage in price discrimination also may be challenged under antidumping legislation.

Competition Policy

Most industrialized nations have regulations designed to promote competition and to restrict monopoly practices. These regulations can be used to limit the prices a firm can charge in a given country. For example, during the 1960s and 70s, the Swiss pharmaceutical manufacturer Hoffmann-LaRoche had a monopoly on the supply of Valium and Librium tranquilizers. The company was investigated in 1973 by the British Monopolies and Mergers Commission, which is responsible for promoting fair competition in Great Britain. The commission found that Hoffmann-LaRoche was overcharging for its tranquilizers and ordered the company to reduce its prices 35 to 40 percent. Hoffmann-LaRoche maintained unsuccessfully that it was merely engaging in price discrimination. Similar actions were later brought against Hoffmann-LaRoche by the German cartel office and by the Dutch and Danish governments.[21]

Configuring the Marketing Mix

There are many reasons a firm might vary aspects of its marketing mix from country to country to take into account local differences in culture, economic conditions, competitive conditions, product and technical standards, distribution systems, government regulations, and the like. Such differences may require variation in product attributes, distribution strategy, communications strategy, and pricing strategy. The cumulative effect of these factors makes it rare for a firm to adopt the same marketing mix worldwide.

For example, financial services is often thought of as an industry where global standardization of the marketing mix is the norm. However, while a financial services company such as American Express may sell the same basic charge card service worldwide, utilize the same basic fee structure for that product, and adopt the same basic global advertising message ("never leave home without it"), differences in national regulations still mean that it has to vary aspects of its communications strategy from country to country (as pointed out earlier, the promotional strategy it had developed in the United States was illegal in Germany). Similarly, while McDonald's is often thought of as the quintessential example of a firm that sells the same basic standardized product worldwide, in reality it varies one important aspect of its marketing mix—its menu—from country to country. McDonald's also varies its distribution strategy. In Canada and the United States most McDonald's are located in areas that are easily accessible by car, whereas in more densely populated and less automobile-reliant societies of the world—such as Japan and Great Britain—location decisions are driven by the accessibility of a restaurant to pedestrian traffic. Because countries typically still differ along one or more of the dimensions discussed above, some customization of the marketing mix is normal.

However, there are often significant opportunities for standardization along one or more elements of the marketing mix. Firms may find that it is possible and desirable to standardize their global advertising message and/or core product attributes to realize substantial cost economies. They may find it desirable to customize their distribution and pricing strategy to take advantage of local differences. In reality, the "customization versus standardization" debate is not an all or nothing issue; it frequently makes sense to standardize some aspects of the marketing mix, and customize others, depending on conditions in various national marketplaces. An explicit example, that of Castrol Oil, is given in the accompanying Management Focus. Castrol sells a standardized product worldwide—lubricating oil—yet it varies other aspects of its marketing mix from country to country, depending on economic conditions, competitive conditions, and distribution systems. Decisions about what to customize and what to standardize should be driven by a detailed examination of the costs and benefits of doing so for each element in the marketing mix.

New Product Development

Firms that successfully develop and market new products can earn enormous returns. Example include Du Pont, which has produced a steady stream of successful innovations such as cellophane, nylon, Freon, and Teflon (nonstick pans); Sony, whose successes include the Walkman and the compact disk; Merck, the drug company that during the 1980s produced seven major new drugs; 3M, which has applied its core competency in tapes and adhesives to developing a wide range of new products; Intel, which has consistently managed to lead in the development of innovative microprocessors to run personal computers; and Cisco Systems, which developed the routers that sit at the hubs of internet connections, directing the flow of digital traffic.

In today's world, competition is as much about technological innovation as anything else. The pace of technological change has accelerated since the Industrial Revolution in the 18th century, and it continues to do so today. The result has been a dramatic shortening of product life cycles. Technological innovation is both creative and destructive.[22] An innovation can make established products obsolete overnight. But an innovation can also make a host of new products possible. Witness recent changes in the electronics industry. For 40 years before the early 1950s, vacuum valves were a major component in radios and then in record players and early computers. The advent of transistors destroyed the market for vacuum valves, but at the same time it created new opportunities connected with transistors. Transistors took up far less space than vacuum valves, creating a trend toward miniaturization that continues today. The transistor held its position as the major component in the electronics industry for just a decade. Microprocessors were developed in the 1970s and the market for transistors declined rapidly. The microprocessor created yet another set of new-product opportunities—handheld calculators (which destroyed the market for slide rules), compact disk players (which destroyed the market for analog record players), personal computers (which destroyed the market for typewriters), to name a few.

This "creative destruction" unleashed by technological change makes it critical that a firm stay on the leading edge of technology, lest it lose out to a competitor's innovations. As we explain in the next subsection, this not only creates a need for the firm to invest in R&D, but it also requires the firm to establish R&D activities at those locations where expertise is concentrated. As we shall see, leading-edge technology on its own is not enough to guarantee a firm's survival. The firm must also apply that technology to developing products that satisfy consumer needs, and it must design the product so that it can be manufactured in a cost-effective manner. To do that, the firm needs to

MANAGEMENT FOCUS
Castrol Oil
http://www.burmah-castrol.com

Castrol is the lubricants division of the British chemical, oil, and gas concern, Burmah Castrol. In Europe and in the United States where Castrol has a 15 percent share of the do-it-yourself lubricants market, Castrol targets motorists who want to cosset their engine by paying a bit more for Castrol's high-margin GTX brand, rather than a standard lubricant. This differentiated positioning strategy is supported by sponsoring Formula 1 racing and the Indy car series in the United States, and by heavy spending on television and in automobile magazines in both Europe and the United States.

Some of Castrol's most notable successes in recent years, however, have been in the developing nations of Asia where Castrol reaps only one-sixth of its sales, but over one-quarter of its operating profits. In Vietnam, automobiles are still relatively rare, so Castrol has targeted motorcycle owners. Castrol's strategy is to target people who want to take care of their new motorcycles. The long-term goal is to build brand loyalty, so that when automobile ownership becomes common in Vietnam, as Castrol believes it will, former motorcycle owners will stick with Castrol when they trade up to cars. This strategy has already worked in Thailand. Castrol has held the leading share of the motorcycle market in Thailand since the early 1980s, and it now holds the leading share in that country's rapidly growing automobile market.

Unlike its practice in more developed countries, Castrol's communications strategy in Vietnam does not focus on television and glossy print media (since there is relatively little of either in Vietnam). Rather, Castrol focuses on building consumer awareness though extensive use of billboards, car stickers, and some 4,000 signboards at Vietnam's ubiquitous roadside garages and motorcycle cleaning shops. Castrol also developed a unique slogan that has a rhythmic quality in Vietnamese *"Dau nhot tot nhat"* (best quality lubricants) and sticks in consumers' minds. Castrol's researchers say the slogan is now recognized by a remarkable 99 percent of people in Ho Chi Minh City.

As elsewhere, Castrol has adopted a premium pricing strategy in Vietnam, which is consistent with the company's attempt to build a global brand image of high quality. Castrol oil costs about $1.5 per liter in Vietnam, about three times as much as the price of cheaper oil imported from Taiwan and Thailand. Despite the high price of its product, Castrol claims it is gaining share in Vietnam as its branding strategy wins converts.

Castrol has had to tailor its distribution strategy to Vietnam's unique conditions. In most countries where it operates, Castrol divides the country into regions and has a single distributor in each region. In Vietnam, however, Castrol will often have two distinct distributors in a region—one to deal with state-owned customers, of which there are still many in this Communist country, and one to deal with private customers. Castrol acknowledges the system is costly, but says it is the only way to operate in a country where there is still some tension between state and private entities.

Sources: V. Mallet, "Climbing the Slippery Slope," *Financial Times*, July 28, 1994, p. 7; and A. Bolger, "Growth by Successful Targeting," *Financial Times*, June 21, 1994, p. 27.

build close links between R&D, marketing, and manufacturing. This is difficult enough for the domestic firm, but it is even more problematic for the international business competing in an industry where consumer tastes and preferences differ from country to country. With all of this in mind, we move on to examine locating R&D activities and building links between R&D, marketing, and manufacturing.

The Location of R&D

By and large, ideas for new products are stimulated by the interactions of scientific research, demand conditions, and competitive conditions. Other things being equal, the rate of new product development seems to be greater in countries where:

- More money is spent on basic and applied research and development.
- Underlying demand is strong.

- Consumers are affluent.
- Competition is intense.[23]

Basic and applied research and development discovers new technologies and then commercializes them. Strong demand and affluent consumers create a potential market for new products. Intense competition between firms stimulates innovation as the firms try to beat their competitors and reap potentially enormous first-mover advantages that result from successful innovation.

For most of the post-World War II period, the country that ranked highest on these criteria was the United States. The United States devoted a greater proportion of its gross domestic product (GDP) to R&D than any other country did. Its scientific establishment was the largest and most active in the world. US consumers were the most affluent, the market was large, and competition among US firms was brisk. Due to these factors, the United States was the market where most new products were developed and introduced. Accordingly, it was the best location for R&D activities; it was where the action was.

Over the past 20 years, things have been changing fast. The US monopoly on new-product development has weakened considerably. Although US firms are still at the leading edge of many new technologies, Japanese and European firms are also strong players, with companies such as Sony, Sharp, Ericsson, Nokia, and Philips NV driving product innovation in their respective industries. Both Japan and Germany are now devoting a greater proportion of their GDP to nondefense R&D than is the United States.[24] In addition, both Japan and the European Union are large, affluent markets, and the wealth gap between them and the United States is closing.

While it is no longer appropriate to consider the United States the lead market, it is questionable if any country is. To succeed today, it is often necessary to simultaneously introduce new products in all major industrialized markets. Because leading-edge research is now carried out in many locations around the world, the argument for centralizing R&D activity in the United States is now much weaker than it was two decades ago. (It used to be argued that centralized R&D eliminated duplication.) Much leading-edge research is now occurring in Japan and Europe. Dispersing R&D activities to those locations allows a firm to stay close to the center of leading-edge activity to gather scientific and competitive information and to draw on local scientific resources.[25] This may result in some duplication of R&D activities, but the cost disadvantages of duplication are outweighed by the advantages of dispersion.

For example, to expose themselves to the research and new-product development work being done in Japan, many US firms have set up satellite R&D centers in Japan. Kodak's $65 million R&D center in Japan employs approximately 200 people. The company hired about 100 professional Japanese researchers and directed the lab to concentrate on electronic imaging technology. US firms that have established R&D facilities in Japan include Corning, Texas Instruments, IBM, Digital Equipment, Procter & Gamble, Upjohn, Pfizer, Du Pont, and Monsanto.[26] The National Science Foundation (NSF) has documented a sharp increase in the proportion of total R&D spending by US firms that is now done abroad. According to NSF data, between 1985 and 1993, the amount of funds committed to foreign R&D soared ninefold, while R&D spending in the United States remained essentially flat.[27] Thus, for example, Motorola now has 14 dedicated R&D facilities located in seven countries, and Bristol-Myers Squibb has 12 facilities in six countries. At the same time, to internationalize their own research and gain access to US research talent, the NSF reports that many European and Japanese firms are investing in US-based research facilities.

Integrating R&D, Marketing, and Production

Although a firm that is successful at developing new products may earn enormous returns, new-product development is very risky with a high failure rate. One study of product development in 16 companies in the chemical, drug, petroleum, and electronics industries suggested that only about 20 percent of R&D projects result in commercially successful products or processes.[28] Another in-depth case study of product development in three companies (one in chemicals and two in drugs) reported that about 60 percent of R&D projects reached technical completion, 30 percent were commercialized, and only 12 percent earned an economic profit that exceeded the company's cost of capital.[29] Similarly, a study by the consulting division of Booz, Allen & Hamilton found that over one-third of 13,000 consumer and industrial products introduced between 1976 and 1981 failed to meet company-specific financial and strategic performance criteria.[30] A more recent study found that 45 percent of new products did not meet their profitability goals.[31] This evidence suggests that many R&D projects do not result in a commercial product, and that between 33 percent and 60 percent of all new products that do reach the marketplace fail to generate an adequate economic return. Two well-publicized product failures are Apple Computer's Newton, a personal digital assistant, and Sony's Betamax format in the video player and recorder market.

The reasons for such high failure rates are various and include development of a technology for which there is only limited demand, failure to adequately commercialize promising technology, and inability to manufacture a new product cost effectively. Firms can avoid such mistakes by insisting on tight cross-functional coordination and integration between three core functions involved in the development of new products: R&D, marketing, and production.[32] Tight cross-functional integration between R&D, production, and marketing can help a company to ensure that

1. Product development projects are driven by customer needs.
2. New products are designed for ease of manufacture.
3. Development costs are kept in check.
4. Time to market is minimized.

Close integration between R&D and marketing is required to ensure that product development projects are driven by the needs of customers. A company's customers can be a primary source of new-product ideas. Identification of customer needs, particularly unmet needs, can set the context within which successful product innovation occurs. As the point of contact with customers, the marketing function of a company can provide valuable information in this regard. Integration of R&D and marketing are crucial if a new product is to be properly commercialized. Without integration of R&D and marketing, a company runs the risk of developing products for which there is little or no demand.

Integration between R&D and production can help a company design products with manufacturing requirements in mind. Designing for manufacturing can lower costs and increase product quality. Integrating R&D and production can also help lower development costs and speed products to market. If a new product is not designed with manufacturing capabilities in mind, it may prove too difficult to build. Then the product will have to be redesigned, and both overall development costs and the time it takes to bring the product to market may increase significantly. Making design changes during product planning could increase overall development costs by 50 percent and add 25 percent to the time it takes to bring the product to market.[33] Many quantum product innovations require new processes to manufacture them, which makes it all the more important to achieve close integration between R&D and production. Minimizing time to market and development costs may require the simultaneous development of new products and new processes.[34]

Cross-Functional Teams

One way to achieve cross-functional integration is to establish cross-functional product development teams composed of representatives from R&D, marketing, and production. Because these functions may be located in different countries, the team will sometimes have a multinational membership. The objective of a team should be to take a product development project from the initial concept development to market introduction. A number of attributes seem to be important for a product development team to function effectively and meet all its development milestones.[35]

First, the team should be led by a "heavyweight" project manager who has high status within the organization and who has the power and authority required to get the financial and human resources the team needs to succeed. The "heavyweight" leader should be dedicated primarily, if not entirely, to the project. The leader should be someone who believes in the project (a champion), and who is skilled at integrating the perspectives of different functions and at helping personnel from different functions and countries work together for a common goal. The leader should also be able to act as an advocate of the team to senior management.

Second, the team should be composed of at least one member from each key function. The team members should have a number of attributes, including an ability to contribute functional expertise, high standing within their function, a willingness to share responsibility for team results, and an ability to put functional and national advocacy aside. It is generally preferable if core team members are 100 percent dedicated to the project for its duration. This assures their focus in on the project, not on the ongoing work of their function.

Third, the team members should be physically co-located if possible to create a sense of camaraderie and to facilitate communication. This presents problems if the team members are drawn from facilities in different nations. One solution is to transfer key individuals to one location for the duration of a product development project. Fourth, the team should have a clear plan and clear goals, particularly with regard to critical development milestones and development budgets. The team should have incentives to attain those goals, such as receiving pay bonuses when major development milestones are hit. Fifth, each team needs to develop its own processes for communication and conflict resolution. For example, one product development team at Quantum Corporation, a California-based manufacturer of disk drives for personal computers, instituted a rule that all major decisions would be made and conflicts resolved at meetings that were held every Monday afternoon. This simple rule helped the team meet its development goals. In this case, it was also common for team members to fly in from Japan, where the product was to be manufactured, to the US development center for the Monday morning meetings.[36]

Implications for the International Business

The need to integrate R&D and marketing to adequately commercialize new technologies poses special problems in the international business, since commercialization may require different versions of a new product to be produced for different countries. We saw an example of this in the opening case, which described how Procter & Gamble's R&D center in Kobe, Japan, developed a dish soap formula specifically for the Japanese market. To do this, the firm must build close links between its R&D centers and its various country operations. A similar argument applies to the need to integrate R&D and production, particularly in those international businesses that have dispersed production activities to different locations around the globe depending on a consideration of relative factor costs and the like.

Integrating R&D, marketing, and production in an international business may require R&D centers in North America, Asia, and Europe that are linked by formal and informal integrating mechanisms with marketing operations in each country in their regions and with the various manufacturing facilities. In addition, the international business may have to establish cross-functional teams whose members are dispersed around the globe. This complex endeavor requires the company to utilize the formal and informal integrating mechanisms that we discussed in Chapter 13 to knit its far-flung operations together so they can produce new products in an effective and timely manner.

While there is no one best model for allocating product development responsibilities to various centers, one solution adopted by many international businesses involves establishing a global network of R&D centers. Within this model, fundamental research is undertaken at **basic research centers** around the globe. These centers are normally located in regions or cities where valuable scientific knowledge is being created and where there is a pool of skilled research talent (e.g., Silicon Valley in the United States, Cambridge in England, Kobe in Japan). These centers are the innovation engines of the firm. Their job is to develop the basic technologies that become new products.

These technologies are picked up by R&D units attached to global product divisions and are used to generate new products to serve the global marketplace. At this level, emphasis is placed on commercialization of the technology and design for manufacturing. If further customization is needed so the product appeals to the tastes and preferences of consumers in individual markets, such redesign work will be done by an R&D group based in a subsidiary in that country or at a regional center that customizes products for several countries in the region.

Consider the case of Hewlett-Packard (HP).[37] HP has four basic research centers. They are located in Palo Alto, California; Bristol, England; Haifa, Israel; and Tokyo, Japan. These labs are the seedbed for technologies that ultimately become new products and businesses. They are the company's innovation engines. The Palo Alto center, for example, pioneered HP's thermal ink-jet technology. The products are developed by R&D centers associated with HP's global product divisions. Thus, the Consumer Products Group, which has its worldwide headquarters in San Diego, California, designs, develops, and manufactures a range of imaging products using HP-pioneered thermal ink-jet technology. Subsidiaries might then customize the product so that it best matches the needs of important national markets. HP's subsidiary in Singapore, for example, is responsible for the design and production of thermal ink-jet printers for Japan and other Asian markets. This subsidiary takes products originally developed in San Diego and redesigns them for the Asian market. In addition, the Singapore subsidiary has taken the lead from San Diego in the design and development of certain portable thermal ink-jet printers. HP delegated this responsibility to Singapore because this subsidiary has built important competencies in the design and production of thermal ink-jet products, so it has become the best place in the world to undertake this activity.

Microsoft offers a similar example. The company has basic research sites in Redmond, Washington (its headquarters); Cambridge, England; and Silicon Valley, California. Staff at these research sites work on the fundamental problems that underlie the design of future products. For example, a group at Redmond is working on natural language recognition software, while another works on artificial intelligence. These research centers don't produce new products; rather, they produce the technology that is used to enhance existing products or help produce new products. The products are produced by dedicated product groups (e.g., desktop operating systems, applications). Customization of the products to match the needs of local markets is sometimes carried out at local subsidiaries. Thus, the Chinese subsidiary in Singapore will do some basic customization of programs such as Microsoft Office, adding Chinese characters and customizing the interface.

Chapter Summary

This chapter discussed the marketing and R&D functions in international business. A persistent theme of the chapter is the tension that exists between the need to reduce costs and the need to be responsive to local conditions, which raises costs. This chapter made the following points:

1. Theodore Levitt has argued that, due to the advent of modern communications and transport

technologies, consumer tastes and preferences are becoming global, which is creating global markets for standardized consumer products. However, this position is regarded as extreme by many commentators, who argue that substantial differences still exist between countries.

2. Market segmentation refers to the process of identifying distinct groups of consumers whose purchasing behavior differs from each other in important

ways. Managers in an international business need to be aware of two main issues relating to segmentation—the extent to which there are differences between countries in the structure of market segments, and the existence of segments that transcend national borders.

3. A product can be viewed as a bundle of attributes. Product attributes need to be varied from country to country to satisfy different consumer tastes and preferences.

4. Country differences in consumer tastes and preferences are due to differences in culture and economic development. In addition, differences in product and technical standards may require the firm to customize product attributes from country to country.

5. A distribution strategy decision is an attempt to define the optimal channel for delivering a product to the consumer.

6. Significant country differences exist in distribution systems. In some countries, the retail system is concentrated; in others, it is fragmented. In some countries, channel length is short; in others, it is long. Access to distribution channels is difficult to achieve in some countries.

7. A critical element in the marketing mix is communication strategy, which defines the process the firm will use in communicating the attributes of its product to prospective customers.

8. Barriers to international communication include cultural differences, source effects, and noise levels.

9. A communication strategy is either a push strategy or a pull strategy. A push strategy emphasizes personal selling, and a pull strategy emphasizes mass media advertising. Whether a push strategy or a pull strategy is optimal depends on the type of product, consumer sophistication, channel length, and media availability.

10. A globally standardized advertising campaign, which uses the same marketing message all over the world, has economic advantages, but it fails to account for differences in culture and advertising regulations.

11. Price discrimination exists when consumers in different countries are charged different prices for the same product. Price discrimination can help a firm maximize its profits. For price discrimination to be effective, the national markets must be separate and their price elasticities of demand must differ.

12. Predatory pricing is the use of profit gained in one market to support aggressive pricing in another market to drive competitors out of that market.

13. Multipoint pricing refers to the fact a firm's pricing strategy in one market may affect rivals' pricing strategies in another market. Aggressive pricing in one market may elicit a competitive response from a rival in another market that is important to the firm.

14. Experience curve pricing is the use of aggressive pricing to build accumulated volume as rapidly as possible to quickly move the firm down the experience curve.

15. New-product development is a high-risk, potentially high-return activity. To build a competency in new-product development, an international business must do two things: (1) disperse R&D activities to those countries where new products are being pioneered and (2) integrate R&D with marketing and manufacturing.

16. Achieving tight integration among R&D, marketing, and manufacturing requires the use of cross-functional teams.

Critical Discussion Questions

1. Imagine you are the marketing manager for a US manufacturer of disposable diapers. Your firm is considering entering the Brazilian market. Your CEO believes the advertising message that has been effective in the United States will suffice in Brazil. Outline some possible objections to this. Your CEO also believes that the pricing decisions in Brazil can be delegated to local managers. Why might she be wrong?

2. Within 20 years, we will have seen the emergence of enormous global markets for standardized consumer products. Do you agree with this statement? Justify your answer.

3. You are the marketing manager of a food products company that is considering entering the South Korean market. The retail system in South Korea tends to be very fragmented. Also, retailers and wholesalers tend to have long-term ties with South Korean food companies, which makes access to distribution channels difficult. What distribution strategy would you advise the company to pursue? Why?

4. Price discrimination is indistinguishable from dumping. Discuss the accuracy of this statement.

5. You work for a company that designs and manufactures personal computers. Your company's R&D center is in North Dakota. The computers are manufactured under contract in Taiwan. Marketing strategy is delegated to the heads of three regional groups: a North American group (based in Chicago), a European group (based in Paris), and an Asian group (based in Singapore). Each regional group develops the marketing approach within its region. In order of importance, the largest markets for your products are North America, Germany, Britain, China, and Australia. Your company is experiencing problems in its product development and commercialization process. Products are late to market, the manufacturing quality is poor, and costs are higher than projected, and market acceptance of new products is less then hoped for. What might be the source of these problems? How would you fix them?

CLOSING CASE   Nike—The Ugly American?

Nike has always cultivated its rebel image—James Dean in sneakers. Nike was founded in 1972 by Phil Knight, a former university track star, and Bill Bowerman, who had been his coach. In the subsequent quarter of a century, the Beaverton, Oregon, company has grown from a niche supplier of running shoes for hard-core athletes into a global colossus in the athletic footwear and apparel business with sales of $10 billion, 40 percent of which are generated outside its core US market. Three main factors seem to underpin the company's success: the quality and innovation of its products, its sponsorship of key athletes with "star appeal" such as Michael Jordan and Tiger Woods, and its global advertising, which has carved out a strong brand image for the company.

The image of Nike as the cool iconoclastic rebel shines through strongly in its advertising. Tough and gritty, Nike ads urge consumers to damn the consequences and Just Do It!—while wearing Nike gear, of course. In America, the rebel has done extraordinarily well. Nike dominates the market, selling $20 in footwear and apparel per year for every man, woman, and child in the country. But herein lies a problem. The company has been so successful that it is difficult to see how it can continue to grow in the now mature US market. This is not a pleasant thought for an aggressive, ambitious risk-taker like CEO Phil Knight. Knight has set a goal of growing revenues by 15 percent a year, and has focused the company's attentions on international markets where the opportunities for growth seem much greater. In contrast to the saturated US market, annual per capita Nike sales in Japan are $4, in Germany they are $3, and in China just over 2 cents. Knight wants to see foreign sales rise to 50 percent of total sales by 2000 and continue upwards from there.

There is only one problem with this vision. Basketball, for all of its recent global success, is still a fringe sport outside the United States; jogging is a distinctly American passion; and as for baseball and football, don't ask! For Nike to grow its international business, it must focus on the dominant global sport, soccer. But in many countries, soccer is imbued with nationalistic pride, and Nike is American, and Americans aren't very good at soccer. Also, soccer already has its dominant footwear and apparel suppliers, Adidas and Umbro, which have tied up most of the world's top teams and stars in sponsorship deals.

However, Knight and his team don't shy from a challenge. Underdog once more, Nike embarked on an aggressive advertising campaign to build awareness for its brand in the world of soccer. In the spring of 1996, Nike announced its intentions to the world with a series of ads in soccer magazines around the world. "Europe, Asia, and Latin America," the ad screamed, "Barricade your stadiums. Hide your trophies. Invest in some deodorant. As Asia and Latin America have been crushed, so shall Europe...the world has been warned." The world was not amused. The reaction was more along the lines of "who do these Americans think they are, and what's in the gibe about deodorant?" Nike, however, had only just begun.

Next was the TV commercial portraying Satan and his demons playing soccer against a team of Nike endorsers. The ad, which set a company record for cost, ran worldwide. Knight declared the ad his favorite Nike commercial ever, and it was well received in America. But several European broadcasters deemed it too scary and offensive to show in prime time when children were watching. The ad also drew angry letters from viewers. But this was all grist for the mill of the American rebel, so Nike plunged ahead with an ad for British television that featured a French soccer star and perennial "bad boy" proudly detailing how his spitting at a fan and calling his coach a bag of s____ had won him a Nike contract. This ad provoked a scathing editorial against Nike in the newsletter of soccer's governing federation, FIFA. Sepp Blatter, now president of FIFA, condemned an "advertising trend that glorifies violence or bad taste . . . technically clever and futuristic as it may be, such style does nothing to promote values, especially among impressionable youngsters."

What really set anti-American tongues wagging among soccer's ruling establishment, however, was Nike's coup in Brazil. The Brazilian soccer team is legendary, having won a record five World Cups. It is also a vibrant symbol of Brazil's samba culture and a huge source of national pride. Imagine the shock when the loud American waltzed into town with bundles of money and purchased the rights to sponsor Brazil's national team for the next 10 years, pushing aside the existing sponsor, Umbro. The deal, which cost $200 million, commits the Brazilian team to appearances in Nike-produced exhibition matches and community events and requires team members to wear Nike shoes and uniforms sporting the Nike "swoosh" logo. To the soccer establishment, it looked as if the Visigoths had just stormed the high temple of soccer.

While Nike may have alienated soccer's establishment, it is not clear that the same is true of Nike's target market—the youth of the world. The establishment may have hated Nike's Satan soccer ad, but Nike managers tell about a focus audience of teens being mesmerized when French soccer star Mr. Cantona flips up his collar, says "au revoir," and kicks the winning goal through the Devil. As they left the room, the youngsters all flipped their collars and said "au revoir." The kids, apparently, got it!

http://www.nike.com

Sources: M. Sawyer, "Fashion: It's Not Working Out," *The Observer*, May 3, 1998, p. 12; P. Vallely, "Saturday Story," *The Independent*," December 6, 1997, p. 19; and N. Robinson, "Nike Just Does It in Bad Taste," *The Guardian*, November 26, 1996, p. 22.

Case Discussion Questions

1. Is Nike wrong to try to leverage its American rebel image to build brand awareness in the global market for soccer footwear and apparel? What are the potential drawbacks of such an approach?

2. Is Nike's promotional strategy for soccer an example of the ugly American abroad, or is it clever marketing by one of the world's shrewdest promoters?

3. How might Nike alter its marketing approach to woo soccer players over to the Nike brand without generating the negative reaction it has apparently generated among the soccer establishment?

Notes

1. See R. W. Ruekert and O. C. Walker, "Interactions between Marketing and R&D Departments in Implementing Different Business-Level Strategies," *Strategic Management Journal*, 8 (1987), pp. 233–48; and K. B. Clark and S. C. Wheelwright, *Managing New Product and Process Development* (New York: Free Press), 1993.

2. T. Levitt, "The Globalization of Markets," *Harvard Business Review*, May–June 1983, pp. 92–102.

3. For example, see S. P. Douglas and Y. Wind, "The Myth of Globalization," *Columbia Journal of World Business*, Winter 1987, pp. 19–29; and C. A. Bartlett and S. Ghoshal, *Managing across Borders: The Transnational Solution* (Boston, MA: Harvard Business School Press, 1989).

4. "Slow Food," *The Economist*, February 3, 1990, p. 64.

5. J. T. Landry, "Emerging Markets: Are Chinese Consumers Coming of Age?" *Harvard Business Review*, May–June 1998, pp. 17–20.

6. C. Miller, "Teens Seen as the First Truly Global Consumers," *Marketing News*, March 27, 1995, p. 9.

7. This approach was originally developed in K. Lancaster, "A New Approach to Demand Theory," *Journal of Political Economy* 74 (1965), pp. 132–57.

8. V. R. Alden, "Who Says You Can't Crack Japanese Markets?" *Harvard Business Review*, January–February 1987, pp. 52–56.

9. T. Parker-Pope, "Custom Made," *The Wall Street Journal*, September 26, 1996, p. 22.

10. A. Rawthorn, "A Bumpy Ride over Europe's Traditions," *Financial Times*, October 31, 1988, p. 5.

11. "RCA's New Vista: The Bottom Line," *Business Week*, July 4, 1987, p. 44.

12. N. Gross and K. Rebello, "Apple? Japan Can't Say No," *Business Week*, June 29, 1992, pp. 32–33.

13. "After Early Stumbles P&G Is Making Inroads Overseas," *The Wall Street Journal*, February 6, 1989, p. B1.

14. "Advertising in a Single Market," *The Economist*, March 24, 1990, p. 64.

15. D. Waller, "Charged up over Competition Law," *Financial Times*, June 23, 1994, p. 14.

16. J. Lumbin, "Advertising: Tina Turner Helps Pepsi's Global Effort," *New York Times*, March 10, 1986, p. D13.

17. These allegations were made on a PBS "Frontline" documentary telecast in the United States in May 1992.

18. G. Smith and B. Wolverton, "A Dark Moment for Kodak," *Business Week,* August 4, 1997, pp. 30–31.

19. R. Narisette and J. Friedland, "Disposable Income: Diaper Wars of P&G and Kimberly-Clark Now Heat up in Brazil," *The Wall Street Journal,* June 4, 1997, p. A1.

20. "Printers Reflect Pattern of Trade Rows," *Financial Times,* December 20, 1988, p. 3.

21. J. F. Pickering, *Industrial Structure and Market Conduct* (London: Martin Robertson, 1974).

22. The phrase was first used by economist Joseph Schumpeter in *Capitalism, Socialism, and Democracy* (New York: Harper Brothers, 1942).

23. See D. C. Mowery and N. Rosenberg, *Technology and the Pursuit of Economic Growth* (Cambridge, UK: Cambridge University Press, 1989); and M. E. Porter, *The Competitive Advantage of Nations* (New York: The Free Press, 1990).

24. C. Farrell, "Industrial Policy," *Business Week,* April 6, 1992, pp. 70–75.

25. W. Kuemmerle, "Building Effective R&D Capabilities Abroad," *Harvard Business Review,* March–April 1997, pp. 61–70.

26. "When the Corporate Lab Goes to Japan," *New York Times,* April 28, 1991, sec. 3, p. 1.

27. D. Shapley, "Globalization Prompts Exodus," *Financial Times,* March 17, 1994, p. 10.

28. E. Mansfield. "How Economists See R&D," *Harvard Business Review,* November–December, 1981, pp. 98–106.

29. Ibid.

30. Booz, Allen, & Hamilton, "New Products Management for the 1980s," Privately published research report, 1982.

31. A. L. Page, "PDMA's New Product Development Practices Survey: Performance and Best Practices," PDMA 15th Annual International Conference, Boston, October 16, 1991.

32. K. B. Clark and S. C. Wheelwright, *Managing New Product and Process Development* (New York: Free Press, 1993); and M. A. Shilling and C. W. L. Hill, "Managing the New Product Development Process,"*Academy of Management Executive* 12, no. 3 (1998), pp. 67–81.

33. O. Port, "Moving Past the Assembly Line," *Business Week Special Issue: Reinventing America,* 1992, pp. 177–80.

34. K. B. Clark and T. Fujimoto, "The Power of Product Integrity," *Harvard Business Review,* November–December, 1990, pp. 107–18; Clark and Wheelwright, *Managing New Product and Process Development*; S. L. Brown and K. M. Eisenhardt, "Product Development: Past Research, Present Findings, and Future Directions," *Academy of Management Review* 20 (1995), pp. 343–78; and G. Stalk and T. M. Hout, *Competing against Time* (New York: Free Press, 1990).

35. Shilling and Hill, "Managing the New Product Development Process."

36. C. Christensen. "Quantum Corporation—Business and Product Teams," Harvard Business School Case # 9-692-023.

37. Information comes from the company's Web site, and from K. Ferdows, "Making the Most of Foreign Factories," *Harvard Business Review,* March–April 1997, pp. 73–88.

CHAPTER EIGHTEEN

GLOBAL HUMAN RESOURCE MANAGEMENT

Global Human Resource Management at Coca-Cola

The Coca-Cola Company is one of the most successful multinational enterprises. With operations in close to 200 countries and nearly 80 percent of its operating income derived from businesses outside the United States, Coca-Cola is typically perceived as the quintessential global corporation. Coca-Cola, however, likes to think of itself as a "multi-local" company that just happens to be headquartered in Atlanta but could be headquartered anywhere and that presents the Coca-Cola brand with a "local face" in every country where it does business. The philosophy is best summarized by the phrase "think globally, act locally," which captures the essence of Coca-Cola's cross-border management mentality. Coca-Cola grants national businesses the freedom to conduct operations in a manner appropriate to the market. At the same time, the company tries to establish a common mindset that all its employees share.

Coca-Cola manages its global operations through 25 operating divisions that are organized under six regional groups: North America, the European Union, the Pacific Region, the east Europe/Middle East Group, Africa, and Latin America. The corporate human resource management (HRM) function is charged with providing the glue that binds these various divisions and groups into the Coca-Cola family. The corporate HRM function achieves this in two main ways: (1) by propagating a common human resources philosophy within the company, and (2) by developing a group of internationally minded mid-level executives for future senior management responsibility.

The corporate HRM group sees its mission as one of developing and providing the underlying philosophy around which local businesses can develop their own human resource practices. For example, rather than have a standard salary *policy* for all its national operations, Coca-Cola has a common salary *philosophy*—the total compensation package should be competitive with the best companies in the local market. Twice a year the corporate HRM group also conducts a two-week HRM orientation session for the human resource staff from each of its 25 operating divisions. These sessions give an overview of the company's HRM philosophy and talk about how local businesses can translate that philosophy into human resource policies. Coca-Cola has found that information sharing is one of the great benefits of bringing HRM professionals together. For example, tools that have been developed in Brazil to deal with a specific HRM problem might also be useful in Australia. The sessions provide a medium through which HRM professionals can communicate and learn from each other, which facilitates the rapid transfer of innovative and valuable HRM tools from region to region.

As much as possible, Coca-Cola tries to staff its operations with local personnel. To quote one senior executive: "We strive to have a limited number of international people in the field because generally local people are better equipped to do business at their home locations." However, expatriates are needed in the system for two main reasons. One is to fill a need for a specific set of skills that might not exist at a particular location. For example, when Coca-Cola started operations in Eastern Europe, it had to bring in an expatriate from Chicago, who was of Polish descent, to fill the position of finance manager. The second reason for using an expatriate is to improve the employee's own skill base. Coca-Cola believes that because it is a global company, senior managers should have had international exposure.

The corporate HRM group has about 500 high-level managers involved in its "global service program." Coca-Cola characterizes these managers as people who have knowledge of their particular field, plus knowledge of the company, and who can do two things in an international location—add value by the expertise they bring to each assignment and enhance their contribution to the company by having international experience. Of the 500 participants in the program, about 200 move each year. To ease the costs of transfer for these employees, Coca-Cola gives those in its global service program a US-based compensation package. They are paid according to US benchmarks, as opposed to the benchmark prevailing in the country in which they are located. Thus, an Indian manager in this program who is working in Britain will be paid according to US salary benchmarks—and not those prevailing in either India or Britain. An ultimate goal of this program is to build a cadre of internationally minded high-level managers from which the future senior managers of Coca-Cola will be drawn.

http://www.cocacola.com

Sources: D. A. Amfuso, "HR Unites the World of Coca-Cola," *Personnel Journal*, November 1994, pp. 112–20; and S. Foley, "Internationalizing the Cola Wars," *Harvard Business School* Case # 9-794-146.

CHAPTER OUTLINE

GLOBAL HUMAN RESOURCE MANAGEMENT AT COCA-COLA

INTRODUCTION

THE STRATEGIC ROLE OF INTERNATIONAL HRM

STAFFING POLICY
Types of Staffing Policy
The Expatriate Problem

TRAINING AND MANAGEMENT DEVELOPMENT
Training for Expatriate Managers
Repatriation of Expatriates
Management Development and Strategy

PERFORMANCE APPRAISAL
Performance Appraisal Problems
Guidelines for Performance Appraisal

COMPENSATION
National Differences in Compensation
Expatriate Pay

INTERNATIONAL LABOR RELATIONS
The Concerns of Organized Labor
The Strategy of Organized Labor
Approaches to Labor Relations

CHAPTER SUMMARY

CRITICAL DISCUSSION QUESTIONS

GLOBAL HRM AT COLGATE-PALMOLIVE CO.

Introduction

Continuing our survey of specific functions within an international business, this chapter examines international human resource management (HRM). **Human resource management** refers to the activities an organization carries out to use its human resource effectively.[1] These activities include determining the firm's human resource strategy, staffing, performance evaluation, management development, compensation, and labor relations. As the opening case on Coca-Cola makes clear, none of these activities is performed in a vacuum; all are related to the strategy of the firm because, as we will see, HRM has an important strategic component.[2] Through its influence on the character, development, quality, and productivity of the firm's human resources, the HRM function can help the firm achieve its primary strategic goals of reducing the costs of value creation and adding value by better serving customer needs.

The strategic role of HRM is complex enough in a purely domestic firm, but it is more complex in an international business, where staffing, management development, performance evaluation, and compensation activities are complicated by profound differences between countries in labor markets, culture, legal systems, economic systems, and the like (see Chapters 2 and 3). For example,

- Compensation practices may vary from country to country depending on prevailing management customs.
- Labor laws may prohibit union organization in one country and mandate it in another.
- Equal employment legislation may be strongly pursued in one country and not in another.

If it is to build a cadre of international managers, the HRM function must deal with a host of issues related to expatriate managers. (An **expatriate manager** is a citizen of one country who is working abroad in one of the firm's subsidiaries.)

The opening case detailed how Coca-Cola deals with some of these issues. Coca-Cola copes with differences between countries by articulating a common HRM *philosophy*, but by letting each national operation translate this philosophy into HRM specific *policies* that are best suited to their operating environment. Coca-Cola also tries to build a cadre of internationally minded executives through its global service program, which involves the HRM function of identifying and managing the career development of a key group of executives from which future senior management will be selected. Finally, and perhaps most importantly, Coca-Cola sees the HRM function as a vital link in the implementation of its strategic goal of thinking globally and acting locally.

In this chapter, we will look closely at the role of HRM in an international business. We begin by briefly discussing the strategic role of HRM. Then we turn our attention to four major tasks of the HRM function—staffing policy, management training and development, performance appraisal, and compensation policy. We will point out the strategic implications of each of these tasks. The chapter closes with a look at international labor relations and the relationship between the firm's management of labor relations and its overall strategy.

The Strategic Role of International HRM

In Chapter 12, we examined four strategies pursued by international businesses—the multidomestic, the international, the global, and the transnational. Multidomestic firms try to create value by emphasizing local responsiveness; international firms, by transferring core competencies overseas; global firms, by realizing experience curve and location economies; and transnational firms, by doing all these things simultaneously. In Chapter 13, we discussed the organizational requirements for implementing each of these strategies. Table 18.1, identical to Table 13.2, summarizes the relationships between international strategies, structures, and controls.

Structures or controls summarized in Table 18.1 don't mean much if the human resources that support them are not appropriate. Without the right kind of people in place, organizational structure is just a hollow shell. In Chapter 13, we explained that formal and informal structure and controls must be congruent with a firm's strategy for the firm to succeed. Success also requires HRM policies to be congruent with the firm's strategy and with its formal and informal structure and controls. For example, a transnational strategy imposes very different requirements for staffing, management development, and compensation practices than a multidomestic strategy does.

The opening case alluded to the relationship between strategy, structure, and HRM. Like many other consumer products firms, Coca-Cola is trying to become a transnational organization (in some ways, "think globally, act locally" is a good definition of a transnational strategy). As indicated in Table 18.1, firms pursuing a transnational strategy need to build a strong corporate culture and an informal management network for transmitting information within the organization. Through its employee selection, management development, performance appraisal, and compensation policies, the HRM function can help develop these things. For example, Coca-Cola's global service program, by creating a cadre of international managers with experience in various nations, should help to establish an informal management network. In addition, management development programs can build a corporate culture that supports strategic goals. In short, HRM has a critical role to play in implementing strategy. In each section that follows, we will review the strategic role of HRM in some detail.

Staffing Policy

Staffing policy is concerned with the selection of employees for particular jobs. At one level, this involves selecting individuals who have the skills required to do particular jobs. At another level, staffing policy can be a tool for developing and promoting corporate culture.[3] By corporate culture, we mean the organization's norms and value systems. We encountered the concept in Chapter 13 when we discussed the use of "cultural controls" in businesses, noting that strong cultural controls help the firm pursue its strategy. Firms pursuing transnational and global strategies have high needs for a strong unifying culture, and the need is somewhat lower for firms pursuing an international strategy and lowest of all for firms pursuing a multidomestic strategy (see Table 18.1).

In firms pursuing transnational and global strategies, we might expect the HRM function to pay significant attention to selecting individuals who not only have the skills required to perform particular jobs but who also "fit" the prevailing culture of the firm. General Electric, for example, which is positioned toward the transnational end of the strategic spectrum, is not just concerned with hiring people who have the skills required for performing particular jobs; it wants to hire individuals whose behavioral styles, beliefs, and value systems are consistent with those of GE. This is true whether an American is being hired, an Italian, a German, or an Australian and whether the hiring is for a US operation or a foreign operation. The belief is that if employees are predisposed toward the organization's norms and value systems by their personality type, the firm, which has a significant need for integration, will experience fewer problems with performance ambiguity.

The need for integration is substantially lower in a multidomestic firm. There is less performance ambiguity and not the same need for cultural controls. In theory, this means the HRM function can pay less attention to building a unified corporate culture. In multidomestic firms, the culture can be allowed to vary from national

Structure and Controls	International Strategy			
	Multidomestic	**International**	**Global**	**Transnational**
Centralization of operating decisions	Decentralized	Core competency centralized Rest decentralized	Some centralized	Mixed centralized and decentralized Informal matrix
Horizontal differentiation	Worldwide area structure	Worldwide product division	Worldwide product division	Informal matrix
Need for coordination	Low	Moderate	High	Very high
Integrating mechanisms	None	Few	Many	Very many
Performance ambiguity	Low	Moderate	High	Very high
Need for cultural controls	Low	Moderate	High	Very high

Table 18.1

Strategy, Structure, and Control Systems

operation to national operation. (Although, given the questionable viability of a multidomestic strategy in today's world, this might not be the best policy to pursue. Chapter 12 discusses the viability of this strategy.)

Types of Staffing Policy

Research has identified three types of staffing policies in international businesses: the ethnocentric approach, the polycentric approach, and the geocentric approach.[4] We will review each policy and link it to the strategy pursued by the firm. The most attractive staffing policy is probably the geocentric approach, although there are several impediments to adopting it.

The Ethnocentric Approach

An **ethnocentric staffing** policy is one in which all key management positions are filled by parent-country nationals. This practice was very widespread at one time. Firms such as Procter & Gamble, Philips NV, and Matsushita originally followed it. In the Dutch firm Philips, for example, all important positions in most foreign subsidiaries were at one time held by Dutch nationals who were referred to by their non-Dutch colleagues as the Dutch Mafia. In many Japanese and South Korean firms today, such as Toyota, Matsushita, and Samsung, key positions in international operations are still often held by home-country nationals. According to the Japanese Overseas Enterprise Association, in 1996 only 29 percent of foreign subsidiaries of Japanese companies had presidents that were not Japanese. In contrast, 66 percent of the Japanese subsidiaries of foreign companies had Japanese presidents.[5]

Firms pursue an ethnocentric staffing policy for three reasons. First, the firm may believe the host country lacks qualified individuals to fill senior management positions. This argument is heard most often when the firm has operations in less developed countries. Second, the firm may see an ethnocentric staffing policy as the best way to maintain a unified corporate culture. Many Japanese firms, for example, prefer their foreign operations to be headed by expatriate Japanese managers because these managers will have been socialized into the firm's culture while employed in Japan.[6] Procter & Gamble until recently preferred to staff important management positions in its foreign subsidiaries with US nationals who had been socialized into P&G's corporate culture by years of employment in its US operations. Such reasoning tends to predominate when a firm places a high value on its corporate culture.

Third, if the firm is trying to create value by transferring core competencies to a foreign operation, as firms pursuing an international strategy are, it may believe that the best way to do this is to transfer parent-country nationals who have knowledge of that competency to the foreign operation. Imagine what might occur if a firm tried to transfer a core competency in marketing to a foreign subsidiary without supporting the transfer with a corresponding transfer of home-country marketing management personnel. The transfer would probably fail to produce the anticipated benefits because the knowledge underlying a core competency cannot easily be articulated and written down. Such knowledge often has a significant tacit dimension; it is acquired through experience. Just like the great tennis player who cannot instruct others how to become great tennis players simply by writing a handbook, the firm that has a core competency in marketing—or anything else—cannot just write a handbook that tells a foreign subsidiary how to build the firm's core competency anew in a foreign setting. It must also transfer management personnel to the foreign operation to show foreign managers how to become good marketers, for example. The need to transfer managers overseas arises because the knowledge that underlies the firm's core competency resides in the heads of its domestic managers and was acquired through years of experience, not by reading a handbook. Thus, if a firm is to transfer a core competency to a foreign subsidiary, it must also transfer the appropriate managers.

Despite this rationale for pursuing an ethnocentric staffing policy, the policy is now on the wane in most international businesses for two reasons. First, an ethnocentric staffing policy limits advancement opportunities for host-country nationals. This can lead to resentment, lower productivity, and increased turnover among that group. Resentment can be greater still if, as often occurs, expatriate managers are paid significantly more than home-country nationals.

Second, an ethnocentric policy can lead to "cultural myopia," the firm's failure to understand host-country cultural differences that require different approaches to marketing and management. The adaptation of expatriate managers can take a long time, during which they may make major mistakes. For example, expatriate managers may fail to appreciate how product attributes, distribution strategy, communications strategy, and pricing strategy should be adapted to host-country conditions. The result may be costly blunders. In one highly publicized case in the United States, Mitsubishi Motors was sued by the federal Equal Employment Opportunity Commission for allegedly tolerating extensive and systematic sexual harassment in a plant in Illinois. The plant's top management, all Japanese expatriates, denied the charges. The Japanese managers may have failed to realize that behavior that would be viewed as acceptable in Japan was not acceptable in the United States.[7]

The Polycentric Approach

A **polycentric staffing** policy requires host-country nationals to be recruited to manage subsidiaries, while parent-country nationals occupy key positions at corporate headquarters. In many respects, a polycentric approach is a response to the shortcomings of an ethnocentric approach. One advantage of adopting a polycentric approach is that the firm is less likely to suffer from cultural myopia. Host-country managers are unlikely to make the mistakes arising from cultural misunderstandings to which expatriate managers are vulnerable. A second advantage is that a polycentric approach may be less expensive to implement, reducing the costs of value creation. Expatriate managers can be very expensive to maintain.

A polycentric approach also has its drawbacks. Host-country nationals have limited opportunities to gain experience outside their own country and thus cannot progress beyond senior positions in their own subsidiary. As in the case of an ethnocentric policy, this may cause resentment. Perhaps the major drawback with a polycentric approach, however, is the gap that can form between host-country managers and parent-country managers. Language barriers, national loyalties, and a range of cultural differences may isolate the corporate headquarters staff from the various foreign subsidiaries. The lack of management transfers from home to host countries, and vice versa, can exacerbate this isolation and lead to a lack of integration between corporate headquarters and foreign subsidiaries. The result can be a "federation" of largely independent national units with only nominal links to the corporate headquarters. Within such a federation, the coordination required to transfer core competencies or to pursue experience curve and location economies may be difficult to achieve. Thus, although a polycentric approach may be effective for firms pursuing a multidomestic strategy, it is inappropriate for other strategies.

The federation that may result from a polycentric approach can also be a force for inertia within the firm. After decades of pursing a polycentric staffing policy, food and detergents giant Unilever found that shifting from a multidomestic strategic posture to a transnational posture was very difficult. Unilever's foreign subsidiaries had evolved into quasi-autonomous operations, each with its own strong national identity. These "little kingdoms" objected strenuously to corporate headquarters' attempts to limit their autonomy and to rationalize global manufacturing.[8]

The Geocentric Approach

A **geocentric staffing** policy seeks the best people for key jobs throughout the organization, regardless of nationality. There are a number of advantages to this policy. First, it enables the firm to make the best use of its human resources. Second, and perhaps more important, a geocentric policy enables the firm to build a cadre of international executives who feel at home working in a number of cultures. Creation of such a cadre may be a critical first step toward building a strong unifying corporate culture and an informal management network, both of which are required for global and transnational strategies (see Table 18.1).[9] Firms pursuing a geocentric staffing policy may be better able to create value from the pursuit of experience curve and location economies and from the multidirectional transfer of core competencies than firms pursuing other staffing policies. In addition, the multinational composition of the management team that results from geocentric staffing tends to reduce cultural myopia and to enhance local responsiveness. Thus, other things being equal, a geocentric staffing policy seems the most attractive.

A number of problems limit the firm's ability to pursue a geocentric policy. Many countries want foreign subsidiaries to employ their citizens. To achieve this goal, they use immigration laws to require the employment of host-country nationals if they are available in adequate numbers and have the necessary skills. Most countries (including the United States) require firms to provide extensive documentation if they wish to hire a foreign national instead of a local national. This documentation can be time consuming, expensive, and at times futile. A geocentric staffing policy also can be very expensive to implement. There are increased training costs and relocation costs involved in transferring managers from country to country. The company may also need a compensation structure with a standardized international base pay level higher than national levels in many countries. In addition, the higher pay enjoyed by managers placed on an international "fast track" may be a source of resentment within a firm.

Summary

The advantages and disadvantages of the three approaches to staffing policy are summarized in Table 18.2. Broadly speaking, an ethnocentric approach is compatible with an international strategy, a polycentric approach is compatible with a multidomestic strategy, and a geocentric approach is compatible with both global and transnational strategies. (See Chapter 12 for details of the strategies.)

While the staffing policies described here are well known and widely used among both practitioners and scholars of international businesses, recently some critics have claimed that the typology is too simplistic and that it obscures the internal differenti-

Table 18.2

Comparison of Staffing Approaches

Staffing Approach	Strategic Appropriateness	Advantages	Disadvantages
Ethnocentric	International	Overcomes lack of qualified managers in host nation Unified culture Helps transfer core competencies	Produces resentment in host country Can lead to cultural myopia
Polycentric	Multidomestic	Alleviates cultural myopia Inexpensive to implement	Limits career mobility Isolates headquarters from foreign subsidiaries
Geocentric	Global and transnational	Uses human resources efficiently Helps build strong culture and informal management network	National immigration policies may limit implementation Expensive

ation of management practices within international businesses. The critics claim that within some international businesses, staffing policies vary significantly from national subsidiary to national subsidiary; while some are managed on an ethnocentric basis, others are managed in a polycentric or geocentric manner.[10] Other critics note that the staffing policy adopted by a firm is primarily driven by its geographic scope, as opposed to its strategic orientation. Firms that have a very broad geographic scope are the most likely to have a geocentric mind-set.[11] Thus, Coca-Cola, which is involved in about 200 countries, is by this argument more likely to have a geocentric mind-set than a firm that is involved in only 3 countries.

The Expatriate Problem

Two of the three staffing policies we have discussed—the ethnocentric and the geocentric—rely on extensive use of expatriate managers. With an ethnocentric policy, the expatriates are all home-country nationals who are transferred abroad. With a geocentric approach, the expatriates need not be home-country nationals; the firm does not base transfer decisions on nationality. A prominent issue in the international staffing literature is **expatriate failure**—the premature return of an expatriate manager to his or her home country.[12] Here we briefly review the evidence on expatriate failure before discussing a number of ways to minimize the expatriate failure rate.

Expatriate Failure Rates

Expatriate failure represents a failure of the firm's selection policies to identify individuals who will not thrive abroad. The costs of expatriate failure are high. One estimate is that the average cost per failure to the parent firm can be as high as three times the expatriate's annual domestic salary plus the cost of relocation (which is affected by currency exchange rates and location of assignment).[13] Research suggests that between 16 and 40 percent of all American employees sent abroad to developed nations return from their assignments early, and almost 70 percent of employees sent to developing nations return home early.[14] Although detailed data are not available for other nationalities, one suspects that high expatriate failure is a universal problem. Estimates of the costs of each failure run between $250,000 and $1 million.[15] In addition, approximately 30 to 50 percent of American expatriates, whose average annual

Table 18.3

Expatriate Failure Rates

Recall Rate Percent	Percent of Companies
U.S. multinationals	
20–40%	7%
10–20	69
<10	24
European multinationals	
11–15%	3%
6–10	38
<5	59
Japanese multinationals	
11–19%	14%
6–10	10
<5	76

Source: Data from R. L. Tung, "Selection and Training Procedures of U.S., European, and Japanese Multinationals," *California Management Review* 25 (1982), pp. 57–71.

compensation package runs to $250,000, stay at their international assignments but are considered ineffective or marginally effective by their firms.[16] In a seminal study, R. L. Tung surveyed a number of US, European, and Japanese multinationals.[17] Her results, summarized in Table 18.3, suggested that 76 percent of US multinationals experienced expatriate failure rates of 10 percent or more, and 7 percent experienced a failure rate of more than 20 percent. Tung's work also suggests that US-based multinationals experience a much higher expatriate failure rate than either European or Japanese multinationals.

Tung asked her sample of multinational managers to indicate reasons for expatriate failure. For US multinationals, the reasons, in order of importance, were

1. Inability of spouse to adjust.
2. Manager's inability to adjust.
3. Other family problems.
4. Manager's personal or emotional maturity.
5. Inability to cope with larger overseas responsibilities.

Managers of European firms gave only one reason consistently to explain expatriate failure: the inability of the manager's spouse to adjust to a new environment. For the Japanese firms, the reasons for failure were

1. Inability to cope with larger overseas responsibilities.
2. Difficulties with new environment.
3. Personal or emotional problems.
4. Lack of technical competence.
5. Inability of spouse to adjust.

The most striking difference between these lists is that "inability of spouse to adjust" was the top reason for expatriate failure among US and European multinationals but only the number-five reason among Japanese multinationals. Tung comments that this difference is not surprising, given the role and status to which Japanese society traditionally relegates the wife and the fact that most of the Japanese expatriate managers in the study were men.

Since Tung's study, a number of other studies have confirmed that the inability of a spouse to adjust, the inability of the manager to adjust, or other family problems remain major reasons for continuing high levels of expatriate failure. One study by

International Orientation Resources, an HRM consulting firm, found that 60 percent of expatriate failures occur due to these three reasons.[18] The inability of expatriate managers to adjust to foreign postings seems to be caused by a lack of cultural skills on the part of the manager being transferred. According to one HRM management consulting firm, this is because the expatriate selection process at many firms is fundamentally flawed. "Expatriate assignments rarely fail because the person cannot accommodate to the technical demands of the job. Typically, the expatriate selections are made by line managers based on technical competence. They fail because of family and personal issues and lack of cultural skills that haven't been part of the selection process".[19]

The failure of spouses to adjust to a foreign posting seems to be related to a number of factors. Often spouses find themselves in a foreign country without the familiar network of family and friends. Language differences make it difficult for them to make new friends. While this may not be a problem for the manager, who can make friends at work, it can be difficult for the spouse who might feel trapped at home. The problem is often exacerbated by immigration regulations prohibiting the spouse from taking employment. With the recent rise of two-career families in many developed nations, this has become a much more important issue. Recent research suggests that a main reason managers now turn down international assignments is concern over the impact such an assignment might have on their spouse's career.[20] The accompanying Management Focus examines how one large multinational company, Shell International Petroleum, has tried to come to grips with this issue.

Expatriate Selection

One way to reduce expatriate failure rates is by improving selection procedures to screen out inappropriate candidates. In a review of the research on this issue, Mendenhall and Oddou state that a major problem in many firms is that HRM managers tend to equate domestic performance with overseas performance potential.[21] Domestic performance and overseas performance potential are not the same thing. An executive who performs well in a domestic setting may not be able to adapt to managing in a different cultural setting. From their review of the research, Mendenhall and Oddou identified four dimensions that seem to predict success in a foreign posting: self-orientation, others-orientation, perceptual ability, and cultural toughness.

1. *Self-orientation.* The attributes of this dimension strengthen the expatriate's self-esteem, self-confidence, and mental well-being. Expatriates with high self-esteem, self-confidence, and mental well-being were more likely to succeed in foreign postings. Mendenhall and Oddou concluded that such individuals were able to adapt their interests in food, sport, and music; had interests outside of work that could be pursued (e.g., hobbies); and were technically competent.

2. *Others-orientation.* The attributes of this dimension enhance the expatriate's ability to interact effectively with host-country nationals. The more effectively the expatriate interacts with host-country nationals, the more likely he or she is to succeed. Two factors seem to be particularly important here: relationship development and willingness to communicate. Relationship development refers to the ability to develop long-lasting friendships with host-country nationals. Willingness to communicate refers to the expatriate's willingness to use the host-country language. Although language fluency helps, an expatriate need not be fluent to show willingness to communicate. Making the effort to use the language is what is important. Such gestures tend to be rewarded with greater cooperation by host-country nationals.

3. *Perceptual ability.* This is the ability to understand why people of other countries behave the way they do; that is, the ability to empathize. This dimension seems critical for managing host-country nationals. Expatriate managers who lack this ability tend to treat foreign nationals as if they were home-country nationals. As a result,

MANAGEMENT FOCUS
Managing Expatriates at Shell International Petroleum

Shell International is a global petroleum company with joint headquarters in both London and The Hague in the Netherlands. The company employs over 100,000 people, approximately 5,500 of whom are at any one time living and working as expatriates. The expatriates at Shell are a very diverse group, made up of over 70 nationalities and located in more than 100 countries. Shell has long recognized that as a global corporation, the international mobility of its work force is essential to its success. By the early 1990s, however, Shell was finding it harder to recruit key personnel for foreign postings. To discover why, the company in 1993 interviewed more than 200 expatriate employees and their spouses to determine their biggest concerns. The data were then used to construct a survey that was sent to 17,000 current and former expatriate employees, expatriates' spouses, and employees who had declined international assignments.

The survey registered a phenomenal 70 percent response rate, clearly indicating that many employees thought this was an important issue. According to the survey, five issues had the greatest impact on the willingness of an employee to accept an international assignment. In order of importance, these were (1) separation from children during their secondary education (the children of British and Dutch expatriates were often sent to boarding schools in their home countries while their parents worked abroad), (2) harm done to a spouse's career and employment, (3) a failure to recognize and involve a spouse in the relocation decision, (4) a failure to provide adequate information and assistance regarding relocation, and (5) health issues. The underlying message was that the family is the basic unit of expatriation, not the individual, and Shell needed to do more to recognize this.

In 1994, Shell implemented a number of programs designed to address some of these problems. To help with the education of children, Shell built elementary schools for Shell employees where there was a heavy concentration of expatriates. As for secondary school education, it worked with local schools, often providing grants, to help them upgrade their educational offerings. It also offered an education supplement to help expatriates send their children to private schools in the host country (before 1994, it would pay only for a child's boarding school education in its home country).

Helping spouses with their careers is a more vexing problem. According to the survey data, half of the spouses accompanying Shell staff on assignment were employed until the transfer. When expatriated, only 12 percent were able to secure employment, while a further 33 percent wished to be employed. Shell set up a spouse employment center to address the problem. The center provides career counseling and assistance in locating employment opportunities both during and immediately after an international assignment. The company also agreed to reimburse up to 80 percent of the costs of vocational training, further education, or reaccreditation, up to $4,400 per assignment.

Shell also set up a global information and advice network known as "The Outpost" to provide support for families contemplating a foreign posting. The Outpost has its headquarters in The Hague and now runs 40 information centers in more than 30 countries. Staffed by spouses and fully supported by Shell, this network had by 1998 helped more than 1,000 couples prepare for placements overseas. The center recommends schools and medical facilities and provides housing advice and up-to-date information on employment, study, self-employment, and volunteer work.

Sources: E. Smockum, "Don't Forget the Trailing Spouse," *Financial Times,* May 6, 1998, p. 22; V. Frazee, "Tearing Down Roadblocks," *Workforce* 77, no. 2 (1998), pp. 50–54; and C. Sievers, "Expatriate Management," *HR Focus* 75(3)(1998), pp. 75–76.

they may experience significant management problems and considerable frustration. As one expatriate executive from Hewlett-Packard observed, "It took me six months to accept the fact that my staff meetings would start 30 minutes late, and that it would bother no one but me." According to Mendenhall and Oddou, well-adjusted expatriates tend to be nonjudgmental and nonevaluative in interpreting the behavior of host-country nationals and willing to be flexible in their management style, adjusting it as cultural conditions warrant.

4. *Cultural toughness.* This dimension refers to the fact that how well an expatriate adjusts to a particular posting tends to be related to the country of assignment. Some countries are much tougher postings than others because their cultures are more unfamiliar and uncomfortable. For example, many Americans regard Great Britain as a relatively easy foreign posting, and for good reason—the two cultures have much in common. But many Americans find postings in non-Western cultures, such as India, Southeast Asia, and the Middle East, to be much tougher.[22] The reasons are many, including poor health care and housing standards, inhospitable climate, lack of Western entertainment, and language difficulties. Also, many cultures are extremely male dominated and may be particularly difficult postings for female Western managers.

Mendenhall and Oddou note that standard psychological tests can be used to assess the first three of these dimensions, whereas a comparison of cultures can give managers a feeling for the fourth dimension. They contend that these four dimensions, in addition to domestic performance, should be considered when selecting a manager for foreign posting. However, current practice does not conform to Mendenhall and Oddou's recommendations. Tung's research, for example, showed that only 5 percent of the firms in her sample used formal procedures and psychological tests to assess the personality traits and relational abilities of potential expatriates.[23] Research by International Orientation Resources suggests that when selecting employees for foreign assignments, only 10 percent of the 50 Fortune 500 firms they surveyed tested for important psychological traits such as cultural sensitivity, interpersonal skills, adaptability, and flexibility. Instead, 90 percent of the time employees were selected on the basis of their technical expertise, not their cross-cultural fluency.[24]

Mendenhall and Oddou do not address the problem of expatriate failure due to a spouse's inability to adjust. According to a number of other researchers, a review of the family situation should be part of the expatriate selection process (see the Management Focus on Shell for an example).[25] A survey by Windam International, another international HRM management consulting firm, found that spouses were included in preselection interviews for foreign postings only 21 percent of the time, and that only half of them receive any cross-cultural training. The rise of dual-career families has added an additional and difficult dimension to this long-standing problem.[26] Increasingly, spouses wonder why they should have to sacrifice their own career to further that of their partner.[27]

Training and Management Development

Selection is just the first step in matching a manager with a job. The next step is training the manager to do the specific job. For example, an intensive training program might be used to give expatriate managers the skills required for success in a foreign posting. Management development is a much broader concept. It is intended to develop the manager's skills over his or her career with the firm. Thus, as part of a management development program, a manager might be sent on several foreign postings over a number of years to build her cross-cultural sensitivity and experience. At the same time, along with other managers in the firm, she might attend management education programs at regular intervals.

Historically, most international businesses have been more concerned with training than with management development. Plus, they tended to focus their training efforts on preparing home-country nationals for foreign postings. Recently, however, the shift toward greater global competition and the rise of transnational firms have changed this. It is increasingly common for firms to provide general management development programs in addition to training for particular posts. In many international businesses, the explicit purpose of these management development programs is strategic. Management development is seen as a tool to help the firm achieve its strategic goals.

With this distinction between training and management development in mind, we first examine the types of training managers receive for foreign postings. Then we discuss the connection between management development and strategy in the international business.

Training for Expatriate Managers

Earlier in the chapter we saw that the two most common reasons for expatriate failure were the inability of a manager's spouse to adjust to a foreign environment and the manager's own inability to adjust to a foreign environment. Training can help the manager and spouse cope with both these problems. Cultural training, language training, and practical training all seem to reduce expatriate failure. We discuss each of these kinds of training here.[28] Despite the usefulness of these kinds of training, evidence suggests that many managers receive no training before they are sent on foreign postings. One study found that only about 30 percent of managers sent on one- to five-year expatriate assignments received training before their departure.[29]

Cultural Training

Cultural training seeks to foster an appreciation for the host country's culture. The belief is that understanding a host country's culture will help the manager empathize with the culture, which will enhance her effectiveness in dealing with host-country nationals. It has been suggested that expatriates should receive training in the host country's culture, history, politics, economy, religion, and social and business practices.[30] If possible, it is also advisable to arrange for a familiarization trip to the host country before the formal transfer, as this seems to ease culture shock. Given the problems related to spouse adaptation, it is important that the spouse, and perhaps the whole family, be included in cultural training programs.

Language Training

English is the language of world business; it is quite possible to conduct business all over the world using only English. For example, at ABB Group, a Swiss electrical equipment giant, the company's top 13 managers hold frequent meetings in different countries. Because they share no common first language, they speak only English, a foreign tongue to all but one.[31] Despite the prevalence of English, however, an exclusive reliance on English diminishes an expatriate manager's ability to interact with host-country nationals. As noted earlier, a willingness to communicate in the language of the host country, even if the expatriate is far from fluent, can help build rapport with local employees and improve the manager's effectiveness. Despite this, J. C. Baker's study of 74 executives of US multinationals found that only 23 believed knowledge of foreign languages was necessary for conducting business abroad.[32] Those firms that did offer foreign language training for expatriates believed it improved their employees' effectiveness and enabled them to relate more easily to a foreign culture, which fostered a better image of the firm in the host country.

Practical Training

Practical training is aimed at helping the expatriate manager and family ease themselves into day-to-day life in the host country. The sooner a routine is established, the better are the prospects that the expatriate and her family will adapt successfully. One critical need is for a support network of friends for the expatriate. Where an expatriate community exists, firms often devote considerable effort to ensuring the new expatriate family is quickly integrated into that group. The expatriate community can be a useful source of support and information and can be invaluable in helping the family adapt to a foreign culture.

Repatriation of Expatriates

A largely overlooked but critically important issue in the training and development of expatriate managers is to prepare them for reentry into their home country organization.[33] Repatriation should be seen as the final link in an integrated, circular process that connects good selection and cross-cultural training of expatriate managers with completion of their term abroad and reintegration into their national organization. However, instead of having employees come home to share their knowledge and encourage other high-performing managers to take the same international career track, expatriates too often face a different scenario.[34]

Often when they return home after a stint abroad—where they have typically been autonomous, well-compensated, and celebrated as a big fish in a little pond—they face an organization that doesn't know what they have done for the last few years, doesn't know how to use their new knowledge, and doesn't particularly care. In the worst cases, reentering employees have to scrounge for jobs, or firms will create standby positions that don't use the expatriate's skills and capabilities and fail to make the most of the business investment the firm has made in that individual.

Research illustrates the extent of this problem. According to one study of repatriated employees, 60 to 70 percent didn't know what their position would be when they returned home. Also, 60 percent said their organizations were vague about repatriation, about their new roles, and about their future career progression within the company, while 77 percent of those surveyed took jobs at a lower level in their home organization than in their international assignments.[35] It is small wonder then that 15 percent of returning expatriates leave their firms within a year of arriving home, while 40 percent leave within three years.[36]

The key to solving this problem is good human resource planning. Just as the HRM function needs to develop good selection and training programs for its expatriates, it also needs to develop good programs for reintegrating expatriates back into work life within their home-country organization, and for utilizing the knowledge they acquired while abroad. For an example of the kind of program that might be used, see the accompanying Management Focus that looks at Monsanto's repatriation program.

Management Development and Strategy

Management development programs are designed to increase the overall skill levels of managers through a mix of ongoing management education and rotations of managers through a number of jobs within the firm to give them varied experiences. They are attempts to improve the overall productivity and quality of the firm's management resources.

International businesses increasingly are using management development as a strategic tool. This is particularly true in firms pursuing a transnational strategy, as increasing numbers are. Such firms need a strong unifying corporate culture and informal management networks to assist in coordination and control (see Table 18.2). In addition, transnational firm managers need to be able to detect pressures for local responsiveness, and that requires them to understand the culture of a host country.

Management development programs help build a unifying corporate culture by socializing new managers into the norms and value systems of the firm. In-house company training programs and intense interaction during off-site training can foster esprit de corps—shared experiences, informal networks, perhaps a company language or jargon—as well as develop technical competencies. These training events often include songs, picnics, and sporting events that promote feelings of togetherness.

MANAGEMENT FOCUS
Monsanto's Repatriation Program

http://www.monsanto.com

Monsanto is a global agricultural, chemical, and pharmaceutical company with revenues in excess of $10 billion and 30,000 employees. At any one time, the company will have 100 mid- and higher-level managers on extended postings abroad. Two-thirds of these are Americans who are being posted overseas, while the remainder are foreign nationals being employed in the United States. At Monsanto, managing expatriates and their repatriation begins with a rigorous selection process and intensive cross-cultural training, both for the managers and for their families. As at many other global companies, the idea is to build an internationally minded cadre of highly capable managers who will lead the organization in the future.

One of the strongest features of this program is that employees and their sending and receiving managers, or sponsors, develop an agreement about how this assignment will fit into the firm's business objectives. The focus is on why they are sending people abroad to do the job, and what their contribution to Monsanto will be when they return. Sponsoring managers are expected to be explicit about the kind of job opportunities the expatriates will have once they return home.

Once they arrive back in their home country, expatriate managers meet with cross-cultural trainers during debriefing sessions. They are also given the opportunity to showcase their experiences to their peers, subordinates, and superiors in special information exchanges.

However, Monsanto's repatriation program focuses on more than just business; it also attends to the family's reentry. Monsanto has found that difficulties with repatriation often have more to do with personal and family-related issues than with work-related issues. But the personal matters obviously affect an employee's on-the-job performance, so it is important for the company to pay attention to such issues.

This is why Monsanto offers returning employees an opportunity to work through personal difficulties. About three months after they return home, expatriates meet for three hours at work with several colleagues of their choice. The debriefing session is a conversation aided by a trained facilitator who has an outline to help the expatriate cover all the important aspects of the repatriation. The debriefing allows the employee to share important experiences and to enlighten managers, colleagues, and friends about his or her expertise so others within the organization can use some of the global knowledge.

According to one participant, "It sounds silly, but it's such a hectic time in the family's life, you don't have time to sit down and take stock of what's happening. You're going through the move, transitioning to a new job, a new house, the children may be going to a new school. This is a kind of oasis; a time to talk and put your feelings on the table." Apparently it works; since the program was introduced in 1992, the attrition rate among returning expatriates has dropped sharply.

Source: C. M. Solomon, "Repatriation: Up, Down, or Out?" *Personnel Journal,* January 1995, pp. 28–34.

These rites of integration may include "initiation rites" wherein personal culture is stripped, company uniforms are donned (e.g., T-shirts bearing the company logo), and humiliation is inflicted (e.g., a pie in the face). All these activities aim to strengthen a manager's identification with the company.[37]

Bringing managers together in one location for extended periods and rotating them through different jobs in several countries help the firm build an informal management network. (Chapter 13 explained the importance of such networks in transnational firms.) Consider the Swedish telecommunications company L. M. Ericsson. Interunit cooperation is extremely important at Ericsson, particularly for transferring know-how and core competencies from the parent to foreign subsidiaries, from foreign subsidiaries to the parent, and between foreign subsidiaries. To facilitate cooperation, Ericsson transfers large numbers of people back and forth between headquarters and subsidiaries. Ericsson sends a team of 50 to 100 engineers and managers from one unit to another for a year or two. This establishes a network of interpersonal contacts. This policy is effective for both solidifying a common culture in the company and coordinating the company's globally dispersed operations.[38]

Performance Appraisal

A particularly thorny issue in many international businesses is how best to evaluate its expatriate managers' performance.[39] In this section, we look at this issue and consider some guidelines for appraising expatriate performance.

Performance Appraisal Problems

Unintentional bias makes it difficult to evaluate the performance of expatriate managers objectively. In most cases, two groups evaluate the performance of expatriate managers, host-nation managers and home-office managers, and both are subject to bias. The host-nation managers may be biased by their own cultural frame of reference and expectations. For example, Oddou and Mendenhall report the case of a US manager who introduced participative decision making while working in an Indian subsidiary.[40] The manager subsequently received a negative evaluation from host-country managers because in India, the strong social stratification means managers are seen as experts who should not have to ask subordinates for help. The local employees apparently viewed the US manager's attempt at participatory management as an indication that he was incompetent and did not know his job.

Home-country managers' appraisals may be biased by distance and by their own lack of experience working abroad. Home-office management is often not aware of what is going on in a foreign operation. Accordingly, they tend to rely on hard data in evaluating an expatriate's performance, such as the subunit's productivity, profitability, or market share. Such criteria may reflect factors outside the expatriate manager's control (e.g., adverse changes in exchange rates, economic downturns). Also, hard data do not take into account many less-visible "soft" variables that are also important, such as an expatriate's ability to develop cross-cultural awareness and to work productively with local managers.

Due to such biases, many expatriate managers believe that headquarters management evaluates them unfairly and does not fully appreciate the value of their skills and experience. This could be one reason many expatriates believe a foreign posting does not benefit their careers. In one study of personnel managers in US multinationals, 56 percent of the managers surveyed stated that a foreign assignment is either detrimental or immaterial to one's career.[41]

Guidelines for Performance Appraisal

Several things can reduce bias in the performance appraisal process.[42] First, most expatriates appear to believe more weight should be given to an on-site manager's appraisal than to an off-site manager's appraisal. Due to proximity, an on-site manager is more likely to evaluate the soft variables that are important aspects of an expatriate's performance. The evaluation may be especially valid when the on-site manager is of the same nationality as the expatriate, since cultural bias should be alleviated.

In practice, home-office managers often write performance evaluations after receiving input from on-site managers. When this is the case, most experts recommend that a former expatriate who served in the same location should be involved in the appraisal to help reduce bias. Finally, when the policy is for foreign on-site managers to write performance evaluations, home-office managers should be consulted before an on-site manager completes a formal termination evaluation. This gives the home-office manager the opportunity to balance what could be a very hostile evaluation based on a cultural misunderstanding.

Compensation

Two issues are raised in every discussion of compensation practices in an international business. One is how compensation should be adjusted to reflect national differences in economic circumstances and compensation practices. The other issue is how expatriate managers should be paid.

National Differences in Compensation

Substantial differences exist in the compensation of executives at the same level in various countries. For example, the average CEO of a large public company in the United States made $2.3 million in salary and bonuses in 1996, and this went up to $5.8 million when stock options were included. In 1997, the figure soared to $7.8 million. In comparison, the average pay of foreign executives is much lower. The CEO of a large public Japanese firm, such as Sony or Matsushita, makes $1.2 million to $1.5 million per year. In Europe, when it was announced that Pierre Suard, then the CEO of French-based telecommunications equipment supplier Alcatel Alsthom, made $2.5 million, it sparked a scandal and much hand-wringing about the excesses of executive pay. According to Towers Perrin, an international human relations consulting firm, the average CEO of a firm in the United States, big or small, public or private, made $927,896 in salary and bonuses (excluding stock options) in 1996. By contrast, the average total pay was $600,052 for a French CEO, $558,457 for a Japanese, $512,651 for a German, and $483,815 for a British CEO. These figures underestimate the true differential because many US executives earn considerable sums of money from stock options and grants, while the practice of granting options is still rare in other nations.[43]

These differences in compensation raise a perplexing question for an international business: Should the firm pay executives in different countries according to the prevailing standards in each country, or should it equalize pay on a global basis? The problem does not arise in firms pursuing ethnocentric or polycentric staffing policies. In ethnocentric firms, the issue can be reduced to that of how much home-country expatriates should be paid (which we will consider later). As for polycentric firms, the lack of managers' mobility among national operations implies that pay can and should be kept country-specific. There would seem to be no point in paying executives in Great Britain the same as US executives if they never work side by side.

However, this problem is very real in firms with geocentric staffing policies. A geocentric staffing policy is consistent with a transnational strategy. One aspect of this policy is the need for a cadre of international managers that may include many different nationalities. Should all members of such a cadre be paid the same salary and the same incentive pay? For a US-based firm, this would mean raising the compensation of foreign nationals to US levels, which could be very expensive. If the firm does not equalize pay, it could cause considerable resentment among foreign nationals who are members of the international cadre and work with US nationals. If a firm is serious about building an international cadre, it may have to pay its international executives the same basic salary irrespective of their country of origin or assignment. The accompanying Management Focus contains several examples of how some international businesses have tried to deal with this problem.

Expatriate Pay

The most common approach to expatriate pay is the balance sheet approach. This approach equalizes purchasing power across countries so employees can enjoy the same living standard in their foreign posting that they enjoyed at home. In addition, the approach provides financial incentives to offset qualitative differences between assignment locations.[44] Figure 18.1 shows a typical balance sheet. Note that home-country outlays for the employee are designated as income taxes, housing expenses,

Figure 18.1

A Typical Balance Sheet

Source: C. Reynolds, "Compensation of Overseas Personnel," in *Handbook of Human Resource Administration,* 2nd ed., ed. J. J. Famularo (New York: McGraw-Hill, 1986), p. 51.

Reproduced with permission of the McGraw-Hill companies.

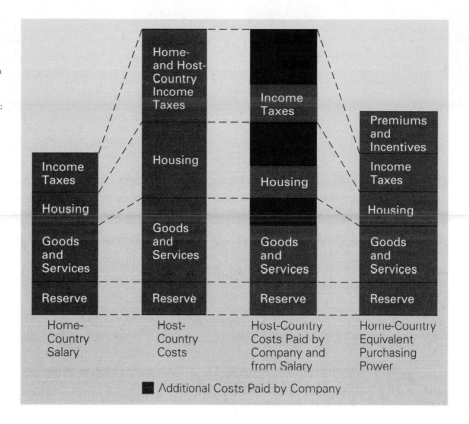

expenditures for goods and services (food, clothing, entertainment, etc.), and reserves (savings, pension contributions, etc.). The balance sheet approach attempts to provide expatriates with the same standard of living in their host countries as they enjoy at home plus a financial inducement (i.e., premium, incentive) for accepting an overseas assignment.

The components of the typical expatriate compensation package are a base salary, a foreign service premium, allowances of various types, tax differentials, and benefits. We shall briefly review each of these components.[45] An expatriate's total compensation package may amount to three times what he or she would cost the firm in a home-country posting. Because of the high cost of expatriates, many firms have reduced their use of them in recent years. However, a firm's ability to reduce its use of expatriates may be limited, particularly if it is pursuing an ethnocentric or geocentric staffing policy.

Base Salary

An expatriate's base salary is normally in the same range as the base salary for a similar position in the home country. The base salary is normally paid in either the home-country currency or in the local currency.

Foreign Service Premium

A foreign service premium is extra pay the expatriate receives for working outside his or her country of origin. It is offered as an inducement to accept foreign postings. It compensates the expatriate for having to live in an unfamiliar country isolated from family and friends, having to deal with a new culture and language, and having to adapt new work habits and practices. Many firms pay foreign service premiums as a percentage of base salary ranging from 10 to 30 percent after tax with 16 percent being the average premium.[46]

MANAGEMENT FOCUS
Executive Pay Policies for Global Managers
http://www.hp.com

A survey of human resource professionals in 45 large US multinational companies undertaken by Organizational Resources Consulting, an international HRM consulting firm, found that all 45 companies viewed differing pay levels and perks as their biggest problem when trying to develop an international work force. The root of the problem is cost; expatriate pay packages that are based on American salaries and needs are increasingly seen as too expensive. To deal with this, many international businesses are trying to develop special pay schemes for their cadre of internationally mobile managers.

Hewlett-Packard transfers about 600 people a year across national borders. Although most of these transferees are on one- to two-year assignments, up to 25 percent are on indefinite assignments. HP ties the pay of short-term transferees to pay scales in their home country, but longer-term HP transferees are quickly switched to the pay scale of their host country and paid according to prevailing local standards. For employees moving from high-pay countries such as Germany to lower-pay countries, such as Spain, HP offers temporary bridging payments to ease the adjustment.

The Minnesota Mining and Manufacturing Co. (3M) has a completely different type of program for longer-term expatriates. The company developed the program because it drastically altered its international organization. In Europe, for example, 3M used to organize its operations on a country-by-country basis. However, 3M has established Europeanwide divisions, so many 3M executives who might have spent their career in one country are now being asked to move, perhaps permanently, to another country.

The 3M program compares net salaries in both the old and new country by subtracting the major costs, such as taxes and housing, from gross pay. The transferred executive then gets whichever pay packet is highest. Thus, when 3M transfers a German executive to France, the German remains on her home-country pay scale. But a British employee transferred to Germany, where salaries are higher, can expect to be switched to the German pay scale. Although the policy considers local housing costs, it doesn't compensate for higher housing costs through a special payment, as many traditional expatriate pay policies did. Any housing subsidy that resulted could last for the rest of an executive's career following a transfer and this would be very expensive.

The large oil company Phillips Petroleum has adopted yet another policy. At Phillips, the policy used to be that when a third-country national, such as a British citizen, was transferred abroad (for example, from Britain to Kuwait), he would be paid in US dollars and his salary would be raised to a level equivalent to that of someone in the United States doing a similar job. This was a very expensive policy given the generally high level of pay prevailing in the United States. Now Phillips has a "third-country nationals program." Under this program, the transferred employee is given generous housing allowances and educational assistance for his children. However, his salary is now pegged to the level prevailing in his home country.

Sources: A. Bennett, "Executive Pay: What's an Expatriate?" *The Wall Street Journal,* April 21, 1994, p. A5; and J. Flynn; "Continental Divide over Executive Pay," *Business Week,* July 3, 1995, pp. 40–41.

Allowances

Four types of allowances are often included in an expatriate's compensation package: hardship allowances, housing allowances, cost-of-living allowances, and education allowances. A hardship allowance is paid when the expatriate is being sent to a difficult location, usually defined as one where such basic amenities as health care, schools, and retail stores are grossly deficient by the standards of the expatriate's home country. A housing allowance is normally given to ensure that the expatriate can afford the same quality of housing in the foreign country as at home. In locations where housing is very expensive (e.g., London, Tokyo), this allowance can be substantial—as much as 10 to 30 percent of the expatriate's total compensation package. A cost-of-living allowance ensures that the expatriate will enjoy the same standard of living in the foreign posting as at home. An education allowance ensures that an expatriate's children receive adequate schooling (by home-country standards). Host-country public schools are sometimes not suitable for an expatriate's children, in which case they must attend a private school.

Taxation

Unless a host country has a reciprocal tax treaty with the expatriate's home country, the expatriate may have to pay income tax to both the home- and host-country governments. When a reciprocal tax treaty is not in force, the firm typically pays the expatriate's income tax in the host country. In addition, firms normally make up the difference when a higher income tax rate in a host country reduces an expatriate's take-home pay.

Benefits

Many firms also ensure that their expatriates receive the same level of medical and pension benefits abroad that they received at home. This can be very costly for the firm, since many benefits that are tax deductible for the firm in the home country (e.g., medical and pension benefits) may not be deductible out of the country.

International Labor Relations

The HRM function of an international business is typically responsible for international labor relations. From a strategic perspective, the key issue in international labor relations is the degree to which organized labor can limit the choices of an international business. A firm's ability to integrate and consolidate its global operations to realize experience curve and location economies can be limited by organized labor, constraining the pursuit of a transnational or global strategy. Prahalad and Doz cite the example of General Motors, which bought peace with labor unions by agreeing not to integrate and consolidate operations in the most efficient manner.[47] In the early 1980s, General Motors made substantial investments in Germany—matching its new investments in Austria and Spain—at the demand of the German metal workers' unions.

One task of the HRM function is to foster harmony and minimize conflict between the firm and organized labor. With this in mind, this section is divided into three parts. First, we review organized labor's concerns about multinational enterprises. Second, we look at how organized labor has tried to deal with these concerns. And third, we look at how international businesses manage their labor relations to minimize labor disputes.

The Concerns of Organized Labor

Labor unions generally try to get better pay, greater job security, and better working conditions for their members through collective bargaining with management. Unions' bargaining power is derived largely from their ability to threaten to disrupt production, either by a strike or some other form of work protest (e.g., refusing to work overtime). This threat is credible, however, only insofar as management has no alternative but to employ union labor.

A principal concern of domestic unions about multinational firms is that the company can counter their bargaining power with the power to move production to another country. Ford, for example, very clearly threatened British unions with a plan to move manufacturing to Continental Europe unless British workers abandoned work rules that limited productivity, showed restraint in negotiating for wage increases, and curtailed strikes and other work disruptions.[48]

Another concern of organized labor is that an international business will keep highly skilled tasks in its home country and farm out only low-skilled tasks to foreign plants. Such a practice makes it relatively easy for an international business to switch production from one location to another as economic conditions warrant. Consequently, the bargaining power of organized labor is once more reduced.

A final union concern arises when an international business attempts to import employment practices and contractual agreements from its home country. When these practices are alien to the host country, organized labor fears the change will reduce its influence and power. This concern has surfaced in response to Japanese multinationals that have been trying to export their style of labor relations to other countries. For example, much to the annoyance of the United Auto Workers (UAW), most Japanese auto plants in the United States are not unionized. As a result, union influence in the auto industry is declining.

The Strategy of Organized Labor

Organized labor has responded to the increased bargaining power of multinational corporations by taking three actions: (1) trying to establish international labor organizations, (2) lobbying for national legislation to restrict multinationals, and (3) trying to achieve international regulations on multinationals through such organizations as the United Nations. These efforts have not been very successful.

In the 1960s, organized labor began to establish international trade secretariats (ITSs) to provide worldwide links for national unions in particular industries. The long-term goal was to be able to bargain transnationally with multinational firms. Organized labor believed that by coordinating union action across countries through an ITS, it could counter the power of a multinational corporation by threatening to disrupt production on an international scale. For example, Ford's threat to move production from Great Britain to other European locations would not have been credible if the unions in various European countries had united to oppose it.

However, the ITSs have had virtually no real success. Although national unions may want to cooperate, they also compete with each other to attract investment from international businesses, and hence jobs for their members. For example, in attempting to gain new jobs for their members, national unions in the auto industry often court auto firms that are seeking locations for new plants. One reason Nissan chose to build its European production facilities in Great Britain rather than Spain was that the British unions agreed to greater concessions than the Spanish unions did. As a result of such competition between national unions, cooperation is difficult to establish.

A further impediment to cooperation has been the wide variation in union structure. Trade unions developed independently in each country. As a result, the structure and ideology of unions tend to vary significantly from country to country, as does the nature of collective bargaining. For example, in Great Britain, France, and Italy many unions are controlled by left-wing socialists, who view collective bargaining through the lens of "class conflict." In contrast, most union leaders in Germany, the Netherlands, Scandinavia, and Switzerland are far more moderate politically. The ideological gap between union leaders in different countries has made cooperation difficult. Divergent ideologies are reflected in radically different views about the role of a union in society and the stance unions should take toward multinationals.

Organized labor has also met with only limited success in its efforts to get national and international bodies to regulate multinationals. Such international organizations as the International Labor Organization (ILO) and the Organization for Economic Cooperation and Development (OECD) have adopted codes of conduct for multinational firms to follow in labor relations. However, these guidelines are not as far-reaching as many unions would like. They also do not provide any enforcement mechanisms. Many researchers report that such guidelines are of only limited effectiveness.[49]

Approaches to Labor Relations

International businesses differ markedly in their approaches to international labor relations. The main difference is the degree to which labor relations activities are centralized or decentralized. Historically, most international businesses have decentralized international labor relations activities to their foreign subsidiaries because labor laws, union power, and the nature of collective bargaining varied so much from country to country. It made sense to decentralize the labor relations function to local managers. The belief was that there was no way central management could effectively handle the complexity of simultaneously managing labor relations in a number of different environments.

Although this logic still holds, there is now a trend toward greater centralized control. This trend reflects international firms' attempts to rationalize their global operations. The general rise in competitive pressure in industry after industry has made it more important for firms to control their costs. Since labor costs account for such a large percentage of total costs, many firms are now using the threat to move production to another country in their negotiations with unions to change work rules and limit wage increases (as Ford did in Europe). Because such a move would involve major new investments and plant closures, this bargaining tactic requires the input of headquarters management. Thus, the level of centralized input into labor relations is increasing.

In addition, there is a growing realization that the way work is organized within a plant can be a major source of competitive advantage. Much of the competitive advantage of Japanese automakers, for example, has been attributed to the use of self-managing teams, job rotation, crosstraining, and the like in their Japanese plants.[50] To replicate their domestic performance in foreign plants, the Japanese firms have tried to replicate their work practices there. This often brings them into direct conflict with traditional work practices in those countries, as sanctioned by the local labor unions, so the Japanese firms have often made their foreign investments contingent on the local union accepting a radical change in work practices. To achieve this, the headquarters of many Japanese firms bargains directly with local unions to get union agreement to changes in work rules before committing to an investment. For example, before Nissan decided to invest in northern England, it got a commitment from British unions to agree to a change in traditional work practices. By its very nature, pursuing such a strategy requires centralized control over the labor relations function.

Chapter Summary

This chapter focused on human resource management in international businesses. HRM activities include human resource strategy, staffing, performance evaluation, management development, compensation, and labor relations. None of these activities is performed in a vacuum; all must be appropriate to the firm's strategy. This chapter made the following points:

1. Firm success requires HRM policies to be congruent with the firm's strategy and with its formal and informal structure and controls.

2. Staffing policy is concerned with selecting employees who have the skills required to perform particular jobs. Staffing policy can be a tool for developing and promoting a corporate culture.

3. An ethnocentric approach to staffing policy fills all key management positions in an international business with parent-country nationals. The policy is congruent with an international strategy. A drawback is that ethnocentric staffing can result in cultural myopia.

4. A polycentric staffing policy uses host-country nationals to manage foreign subsidiaries and parent-country nationals for the key positions at corporate headquarters. This approach can minimize the dangers of cultural myopia, but it can create a gap between home and host-country operations. The policy is best suited to a multidomestic strategy.

5. A geocentric staffing policy seeks the best people for key jobs throughout the organization, regardless of their nationality. This approach is consistent with building a strong unifying culture and informal management network and is well suited to both global and transnational strategies. Immigration policies of national governments may limit a firm's ability to pursue this policy.

6. A prominent issue in the international staffing literature is expatriate failure, defined as the premature return of an expatriate manager to his or her home country. The costs of expatriate failure can be substantial.

7. Expatriate failure can be reduced by selection procedures that screen out inappropriate candidates. The most successful expatriates seem to be those who have high self-esteem and self-confidence, get along well with others, are willing to attempt to communicate in a foreign language, and can empathize with people of other cultures.

8. Training can lower the probability of expatriate failure. It should include cultural training, language training, and practical training, and it should be provided to both the expatriate manager and the spouse.

9. Management development programs attempt to increase the overall skill levels of managers through a mix of ongoing management education and rotation of managers through different jobs within the firm to give them varied experiences. Management development is often used as a strategic tool to build a strong unifying culture and informal management network, both of which support transnational and global strategies.

10. It can be difficult to evaluate the performance of expatriate managers objectively because of unintentional bias. A number of steps can be taken to reduce this bias.

11. Country differences in compensation practices raise a difficult question for an international business: Should the firm pay executives in different countries according to the standards in each country or equalize pay on a global basis?

12. The most common approach to expatriate pay is the balance sheet approach. This approach aims to equalize purchasing power so employees can enjoy the same living standard in their foreign posting that they had at home.

13. A key issue in international labor relations is the degree to which organized labor can limit the choices available to an international business. A firm's ability to pursue a transnational or global strategy can be significantly constrained by the actions of labor unions.

14. A principal concern of organized labor is that the multinational can counter union bargaining power with threats to move production to another country.

15. Organized labor has tried to counter the bargaining power of multinationals by forming international labor organizations. In general, these efforts have not been effective.

Critical Discussion Questions

1. What are the main advantages and disadvantages of the ethnocentric, polycentric, and geocentric approaches to staffing policy? When is each approach appropriate?

2. Research suggests that many expatriate employees encounter problems that limit both their effectiveness in a foreign posting and their contribution to the company when they return home. What are the main causes and consequences of these problems, and how might a firm reduce the occurrence of such problems?

3. What is the link between an international business's strategy and its human resource management policies, particularly with regard to the use of expatriate employees and their pay scale?

4. In what ways can organized labor constrain the strategic choices of an international business? How can an international business limit these constraints?

CLOSING CASE Global HRM at Colgate-Palmolive Co.

Colgate-Palmolive, the $6 billion a year personal products giant, earns nearly two-thirds of its revenues outside the United States. For years Colgate succeeded, as many US multinationals have, by developing products at home and then "throwing them over the wall" to foreign subsidiaries. Each major foreign subsidiary was responsible for local manufacturing and marketing. Senior management positions in these subsidiaries were typically held by Americans, and practically all the company's US-based managers were US citizens.

In the early 1980s, Colgate realized that if it was going to succeed in the rapidly changing international business environment, it would have to develop a more transnational orientation. Its competitors, such as Procter & Gamble, Unilever, and Kao, were trying to become transnational companies, and Colgate needed to follow suit. Becoming a transnational requires developing an international cadre of executive managers who are as at home working in one culture as in another and who have the ability to rise above their ethnocentric perspectives.

As a first step toward building such a team, Colgate began recruiting college graduates in 1987 and putting them through an intensive international training program. The typical recruit holds an MBA from a US university, speaks at least one foreign language, has lived outside the United States, and has strong computer skills and business experience. Over one-quarter of the participants are foreign nationals.

The trainees spend 24 months in a US program. During three-month stints, they learn global business development secrets of, for example, Colgate toothpaste, compiling a guide for introducing a new product or revamping an existing one in various national markets. Participants also receive additional language instruction and take international business trips. When they have completed the program, the participants become associate product managers in the United States or abroad. Unlike most US companies, Colgate does not send foreign-born trainees to their native countries for their initial jobs. Instead, it is more likely that a French national will remain in the United States, a US national will be sent to Germany, and a British national will go to Spain. The foreigners receive the same generous expatriate compensation packages the Americans do, even if they are assigned to their home country. This extra pay can create resentment among locally hired managers of foreign subsidiaries. Colgate is trying to resolve this problem by urging its foreign subsidiaries to send their brightest young managers to the training program.

In addition to the management training program, Colgate has taken a number of other steps to develop its international cadre of managers. In Europe, for example, the company is developing "Euromanagers," managers who have experience working in several European countries. This is a departure from the established practice of having managers spend most (if not all) of their working careers in their home country. Also, Colgate now tries to ensure that project teams contain managers from several different countries.

http://www.colgate.com

Sources: J. S. Lublin, "Managing Globally: Younger Managers Learn Global Skills," *The Wall Street Journal*, March 31, 1992, p. B1; B. Hagerty, "Companies in Europe Seeking Executives Who Can Cross Borders in a Single Bound," *The Wall Street Journal*, January 25, 1991, p. B1; and C.M. Solomon, "Global Operations Demand That HR Re-think Diversity," *Personnel Journal* 73 (1994), pp. 40–50.

Case Discussion Questions

1. What is the relationship between HRM and strategy at Colgate-Palmolive?

2. How might Colgate-Palmolive's international training program improve its economic performance?

3. What potential problems and pitfalls do you see with Colgate-Palmolive's international training program?

Notes

1. P. J. Dowling and R. S. Schuler, *International Dimensions of Human Resource Management* (Boston: PSW-Kent, 1990).

2. J. Millman, M.A. von Glinow, and M. Nathan, "Organizational Life Cycles and Strategic International Human Resource Management in Multinational Companies," *Academy of Management Review* 16 (1991), pp. 318–39.

3. E. H. Schein, *Organizational Culture and Leadership* (San Francisco: Jossey-Bass, 1985).

4. H.V. Perlmutter, "The Tortuous Evolution of the Multinational Corporation," *Columbia Journal of World Business* 4 (1969), pp. 9–18; D. A. Heenan and H. V. Perlmutter, *Multinational Organizational Development* (Reading, MA: Addison-Wesley, 1979); and D. A. Ondrack, "International Human Resources Management in European and North American Firms," *International Studies of Management and Organization* 15 (1985), pp. 6–32.

5. V. Reitman and M. Schuman, "Men's Club: Japanese and Korean Companies Rarely Look Outside for People to Run Their Overseas Operations," *The Wall Street Journal*, September 26, 1996, p. 17.

6. S. Beechler and J. Z. Yang, "The Transfer of Japanese Style Management to American Subsidiaries," *Journal of International Business Studies* 25 (1994), pp. 467–91.

7. Reitman and Schuman, "Men's Club: Japanese and Korean Companies Rarely Look Outside for People to Run Their Overseas Operations."

8. C. A. Bartlett and S. Ghoshal, *Managing across Borders: The Transnational Solution* (Boston, MA: Harvard Business School Press, 1989).

9. S. J. Kobrin, "Geocentric Mindset and Multinational Strategy," *Journal of International Business Studies* 25 (1994), pp. 493–511.

10. P. M. Rosenzweig and N. Nohria, "Influences on Human Resource Management Practices in Multinational Corporations," *Journal of International Business Studies* 25 (1994), pp. 229–51.

11. Kobrin, "Geocentric Mindset and Multinational Strategy."

12. J. S. Black, M. Mendenhall, and G. Oddou, "Towards a Comprehensive Model of International Adjustment," *Academy of Management Review* 16 (1991), pp. 291–317; and J. Shay and T. J. Bruce, "Expatriate Managers," *Cornell Hotel & Restaurant Administration Quarterly*, February 1997, p. 30–40.

13. M. G. Harvey, "The Multinational Corporation's Expatriate Problem: An Application of Murphy's Law," *Business Horizons* 26, 1983, pp. 71–78.

14. Shay and Bruce, "Expatriate Managers."

15. S. Caudron, "Training Ensures Overseas Success," *Personnel Journal*, December 1991, p. 27.

16. Black, Mendenhall, and Oddou, "Towards a Comprehensive Model of International Adjustment."

17. R. L. Tung, "Selection and Training Procedures of U.S., European, and Japanese Multinationals," *California Management Review* 25 (1982), pp. 57–71.

18. C. M. Salomon, "Success Abroad Depends upon More Than Job Skills," *Personnel Journal*, April 1994, pp. 51–58.

19. Ibid.

20. M. Harvey, "Addressing the Dual Career Expatriation Dilemma," *Human Resource Planning* 19, no. 4 (1996), pp. 18–32.

21. M. Mendenhall and G. Oddou, "The Dimensions of Expatriate Acculturation: A Review," *Academy of Management Review* 10 (1985), pp. 39–47.

22. I. Torbiorin, *Living Abroad: Personal Adjustment and Personnel Policy in the Overseas Setting* (New York: John Wiley & Sons, 1982).

23. R. L. Tung, "Selection and Training of Personnel for Overseas Assignments," *Columbia Journal of World Business* 16 (1981), pp. 68–78.

24. Salomon, "Success Abroad Depends upon More Than Job Skills."

25. S. Ronen, "Training and International Assignee," in *Training and Career Development*, ed. I. Goldstein (San Francisco: Jossey-Bass, 1985); and Tung, "Selection and Training of Personnel for Overseas Assignments."

26. Salomon, "Success Abroad Depends upon More Than Job Skills."

27. Harvey, "Addressing the Dual Career Expatriation Dilemma;" and J. W. Hunt, "The Perils of Foreign Postings for Two," *Financial Times*, May 6, 1998, p. 22.

28. Dowling and Schuler, *International Dimensions of Human Resource Management*.

29. Ibid.

30. G. Baliga and J. C. Baker, "Multinational Corporate Policies for Expatriate Managers: Selection, Training, and Evaluation," *Advanced Management Journal*, Autumn 1985, pp. 31–38.

31. C. Rapoport, "A Tough Swede Invades the U.S.," *Fortune*, June 20, 1992, pp. 67–70.

32. J. C. Baker, "Foreign Language and Departure Training in U.S. Multinational Firms," *Personnel Administrator*, July 1984, pp. 68–70.

33. A 1997 study by the Conference Board looked at this in depth. For a summary, see L. Grant, "That Overseas Job Could Derail Your Career," *Fortune*, April 14, 1997, p. 166.

34. J. S. Black and M. E. Mendenhall, *Global Assignments: Successfully Expatriating and Repatriating International Managers* (San Francisco: Jossey-Bass, 1992).

35. Ibid.

36. Figures from the Conference Board study. For a summary, see Grant, "That Overseas Job Could Derail Your Career."

37. S. C. Schneider, "National v. Corporate Culture: Implications for Human Resource Management," *Human Resource Management* 27 (Summer 1988), pp. 231–46.

38. Bartlett and Ghoshal, *Managing across Borders*.

39. See G. Oddou and M. Mendenhall, "Expatriate Performance Appraisal: Problems and Solutions," in *International Human Resource Management*, ed. Mendenhall and Oddou (Boston: PWS-Kent, 1991); Dowling and Schuler, *International Dimensions*; R. S. Schuler and G. W. Florkowski, "International Human Resource Management," in *Handbook for International Management Research* ed. B. J. Punnett and O. Shenkar (Oxford:

Blackwell, 1996); and K. Roth and S. O'Donnell, "Foreign Subsidiary Compensation Strategy: An Agency Theory Perspective," *Academy of Management Journal* 39, no. 3 (1996), pp. 678–703.

40. Oddou and Mendenhall, "Expatriate Performance Appraisal."

41. "Expatriates Often See Little Benefit to Careers in Foreign Stints, Indifference at Home," *The Wall Street Journal*, December 11, 1989, p. B1.

42. Oddou and Mendenhall, "Expatriate Performance Appraisal;" and Schuler and Florkowski, "International Human Resource Management."

43. R. C. Longworth, "US Executives Sit on Top of the World," *Chicago Tribune*, May 31, 1998, p. C1.

44. C. Reynolds, "Compensation of Overseas Personnel," in *Handbook of Human Resource Administration*, ed. J. J. Famularo (New York: McGraw-Hill, 1986).

45. M. Helms, "International Executive Compensation Practices," in *International Human Resource Management*, ed. M. Mendenhall and G. Oddou (Boston: PWS-Kent, 1991).

46. G. W. Latta, "Expatriate Incentives," *HR Focus* 75, no. 3 (March 1998), p. S3.

47. C. K. Prahalad and Y. L. Doz, *The Multinational Mission* (New York: The Free Press, 1987).

48. Ibid.

49. Schuler and Florkowski, "International Human Resource Management."

50. See J. P. Womack, D. T. Jones, and D. Roos, *The Machine that Changed the World* (New York: Rawson Associates, 1990).

CHAPTER NINETEEN

ACCOUNTING IN THE INTERNATIONAL BUSINESS

The Adoption of International Accounting Standards in Germany

A number of major German firms have begun to adopt international accounting standards that reveal far more about their financial performance than hitherto. This represents a major shift away from inscrutable German accounting standards that often hid as much about a company's financial performance as they revealed. The change has been driven by a recognition that German capital markets are too narrow and illiquid to satisfy the future funding requirements of many major German companies. These corporations are realizing that it is in their best interests to get a listing on the New York Stock Exchange (NYSE), the world's largest capital market, as a prelude to issuing equity and raising debt through the New York market.

Historically, German firms have almost never resorted to international capital markets to raise additional equity. Their view was that bank debt was adequate. However, the German market for debt has become expensive, while the possibility of raising additional equity in Germany has been limited by the relatively small and illiquid nature of the German equity market. The move among German firms to raise equity on international capital markets began in the early 1990s when a number of major German firms, including Daimler-Benz, Siemens, and Volkswagen, discretely applied to the US Securities and Exchange Commission (SEC) for a listing. The SEC, however, was not particularly responsive. In the SEC's view, German accounting standards were not comparable to those in the United States and did not provide sufficient information to investors. Among the SEC's objections was the German practice of not disclosing the size of a company's financial reserves and pension fund commitments, as well as the more liberal policy for writing down goodwill in Germany, which tended to overstate a firm's financial performance relative to that which would be reported under US accounting rules.

After the initial rebuff from the SEC, this group of firms fell apart quite rapidly. However, Daimler-Benz announced in 1993 that it had reached an agreement with the SEC and would soon have a listing on the NYSE. To achieve this, Daimler-Benz had to issue two sets of accounts, one that adhered to German standards and another that adhered to US generally accepted accounting principles (GAAP). When Daimler-Benz reported its 1994 financial results, the impact of using different accounting standards was readily apparent. Under German rules, Daimler-Benz reported a profit of over $100 million, but under GAAP, the company reported a $1 billion loss!

Following the lead of Daimler-Benz, several other German firms have announced that they are willing to adopt international accounting standards. International accounting standards are being devised by a London-based committee of leading accountants that was established in 1973. Since 1987, the International Accounting Standards Committee (IASC) has been attempting to harmonize accounting rules that historically have varied significantly from country to country.

The international standards are more forthcoming about financial performance than the German rules. However, they still fall short of the GAAP, primarily because they allow for a looser treatment of goodwill. In March 1995, the pharmaceutical company Schering AG became the first German firm to shift completely to international standards. It was quickly followed by two other major German firms, Bayer AG and Hoechst AG. In 1997, Hoechst became the second German firm to list its shares on the NYSE. To support its listing, Hoechst issued two sets of accounts, one in accordance with IASC principles and one in accordance with GAAP. Under the IASC principles, Hoechst reported profits of $1.2 billion in 1995, and $1.4 billion in 1996. Under the more restrictive GAAP, it lost $40 million in 1995, and $708 million in 1996!

Despite the fact that adhering to GAAP apparently reduces the reported profit of German firms, others seem willing to follow these standards to gain access to the US capital market. For example, Allianz, a large German insurance company, recently adopted IASC principles as a prelude to seeking a listing on the NYSE. Allianz believes such a listing will help it finance acquisitions of other firms in the large US insurance market. Under the IASC principles, Allianz became the first German insurance company to reveal the size of its "hidden reserves"—defined as the difference between the book value of its assets and their current market value. Since insurance companies generally invest the proceeds from insurance premiums in financial assets, such as stocks, and since the value of these assets tends to appreciate as the stock market rises, their market value can be substantial. However, their market value also fluctuates sharply with the value of the stock market, which is why German companies have preferred to keep them secret. In early 1998, the value of Allianz's hidden assets stood at $56.1 billion, but as the company pointed out, a sharp fall in the value of the stock market would cause a comparable fall in the assets. Nevertheless, because US insurance companies always reveal the market value of such assets, Allianz must do so if it is to list its stock on the NYSE.

http://www.nyse.com

Sources: P. Gumbel and G. Steinmetz, "German Firms Shift to More Open Accounting," *The Wall Street Journal*, March 15, 1995, p. C1; "Daimler-Benz: A Capital Suggestion," *The Economist,* April 9, 1994, p. 69; L. Berton, "All Accountants May Soon Speak the Same Language," *The Wall Street Journal*, August 29, 1995, p. A15; R. Atkins, "Allianz Plans to Seek New York Listing," *Financial Times*, May 29, 1998, p. 30; and G. Meek, "Accountants Gather Round Different Standards," *Financial Times*, March 20, 1998, p. 12.

Introduction

Accounting has often been referred to as "the language of business."[1] This language finds expression in profit-and-loss statements, balance sheets, budgets, investment analysis, and tax analysis. Accounting information is the means by which firms communicate their financial position to the providers of capital investors, creditors, and government. It enables the providers of capital to assess the value of their investments or the security of their loans and to make decisions about future resource allocations (see Figure 19.1). Accounting information is also the means by which firms report their income to the government, so the government can assess how much tax the firm owes. It is also the means by which the firm can evaluate its performance, control its internal expenditures, and plan for future expenditures and income. Thus, a good accounting function is critical to the smooth running of the firm.

International businesses are confronted with a number of accounting problems that do not confront purely domestic businesses. The opening case draws attention to one of these problems—the lack of consistency in the accounting standards of different countries. We begin this chapter by looking at the source of these country differences. Then we shift our attention to attempts to establish international accounting and auditing standards—the International Accounting Standards Committee (IASC).

We will examine the problems arising when an international business with operations in more than one country must produce consolidated financial statements. As we will see, these firms face special problems because, for example, the accounts for their operations in Brazil will be in real, in Korea they will be in won, and in Japan they will be in yen. If the firm is based in the United States, it will have to decide what basis to use for translating all these accounts into US dollars. The last

Figure 19.1

Accounting Information
and Capital Flows

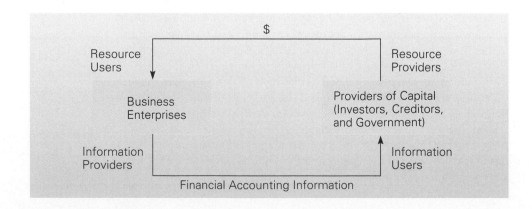

issue we discuss is control in an international business. We touched on the issue of control in Chapter 13 in rather abstract terms. Here we look at control from an accounting perspective.

Country Differences in Accounting Standards

Accounting is shaped by the environment in which it operates. Just as different countries have different political systems, economic systems, and cultures, they also have different accounting systems.[2] In each country, the accounting system has evolved in response to the demands for accounting information.

An example of differences in accounting conventions concerns employee disclosures. In many European countries, government regulations require firms to publish detailed information about their training and employment policies, but there is no such requirement in the United States. Another difference is in the treatment of goodwill. A firm's goodwill is any advantage, such as a trademark or brand name (e.g., the Coca-Cola brand name), that enables a firm to earn higher profits than its competitors. When one company acquires another in a takeover, the value of the goodwill is calculated as the amount paid for a firm above its book value, which is often substantial. Under accounting rules prevailing in many countries, acquiring firms are allowed to deduct the value of goodwill from the amount of *equity* or *net worth* reported on their balance sheet. In the United States, goodwill has to be deducted from the *profits* of the acquiring firm over as much as 40 years (although firms typically write down goodwill much more rapidly). If two equally profitable firms, one German and one American, acquire comparable firms that have identical goodwill, the US firm will report a much lower profit than the German firm, because of differences in accounting conventions regarding goodwill.[3]

Despite attempts to harmonize standards by developing internationally acceptable accounting conventions (more on this later), a myriad of differences between national accounting systems still remain. A study tried to quantify the extent of these differences by comparing various accounting measures and profitability ratios across 22 developed nations, including Australia, Britain, France, Germany, Hong Kong, Japan, Spain, and South Korea.[4] The study found that among the 22 countries, there were 76 differences in the way cost of goods sold was assessed, 65 differences in the assessment of return on assets, 54 differences in the measurement of research and development expenses as a percentage of sales, and 20 differences in the calculation of net profit margin. These differences make it very difficult to compare the financial performance of firms based in different nation-states.

Although many factors can influence the development of a country's accounting system, there appear to be five main variables:[5]

1. The relationship between business and the providers of capital.
2. Political and economic ties with other countries.
3. The level of inflation.
4. The level of a country's economic development.
5. The prevailing culture in a country.

Figure 19.2 illustrates these variables. We will review each in turn.

Relationship between Business and Providers of Capital

The three main external sources of capital for business enterprises are individual investors, banks, and government. In most advanced countries, all three sources are important. In the United States, for example, business firms can raise capital by selling shares and bonds to individual investors through the stock market and the bond market. They can also borrow capital from banks and, in rather limited cases (particularly to support investments in defense-related R&D), from the government. The

Figure 19.2

Determinants of National
Accounting Standards

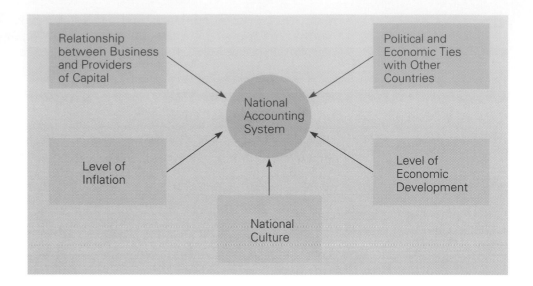

importance of each source of capital varies from country to country. In some countries, such as the United States, individual investors are the major source of capital; in others, banks play a greater role; in still others, the government is the major provider of capital. A country's accounting system tends to reflect the relative importance of these three constituencies as providers of capital.

Consider the case of the United States and Great Britain. Both have well-developed stock and bond markets in which firms can raise capital by selling stocks and bonds to individual investors. Most individual investors purchase only a very small proportion of a firm's total outstanding stocks or bonds. As such, they have no desire to be involved in the day-to-day management of the firms in which they invest; they leave that task to professional managers. But because of their lack of contact with the management of the firms in which they invest, individual investors may not have the information required to assess how well the companies are performing. Because of their small stake in firms, individual investors generally lack the ability to get information on demand from management. The financial accounting system in both Great Britain and the United States evolved to cope with this problem. In both countries, the financial accounting system is oriented toward providing individual investors with the information they need to make decisions about purchasing or selling corporate stocks and bonds.

In countries such as Switzerland, Germany, and Japan, a few large banks satisfy most of the capital needs of business enterprises. Individual investors play a relatively minor role. In these countries, the role of the banks is so important that a bank's officers often have seats on the boards of firms to which it lends capital. In such circumstances, the information needs of the capital providers are satisfied in a relatively straightforward way—through personal contacts, direct visits, and information provided at board meetings. Consequently, although firms still prepare financial reports, because government regulations in these countries mandate some public disclosure of a firm's financial position, the reports tend to contain less information than those of British or US firms. Because banks are the major providers of capital, financial accounting practices are oriented toward protecting a bank's investment. Thus, assets are valued conservatively and liabilities are overvalued (in contrast to US practice) to provide a cushion for the bank in the event of default.

In still other countries, the national government has historically been an important provider of capital, and this has influenced accounting practices. This is the case in France and Sweden, where the national government has often stepped in to make loans or to invest in firms whose activities are deemed in the "national interest." In these countries, financial accounting practices tend to be oriented toward the needs of government planners.

Political and Economic Ties with Other Countries

Similarities in the accounting systems of countries are sometimes due to the countries' close political and/or economic ties. For example, the US system has influenced accounting practices in Canada and Mexico, and since passage of NAFTA, the accounting systems in these three countries seem set to converge on a common set of norms. US-style accounting systems are also used in the Philippines, which was once a US protectorate. Another significant force in accounting worldwide has been the British system. The vast majority of former colonies of the British empire have accounting practices modeled after Great Britain's. Similarly, the European Union has been attempting to harmonize accounting practices in its member countries. The accounting systems of EU members such as Great Britain, Germany, and France are quite different now, but they may all converge on some norm eventually.

Inflation Accounting

In many countries, including Germany, Japan, and the United States, accounting is based on the **historic cost principle.** This principle assumes the currency unit used to report financial results is not losing its value due to inflation. Firms record sales, purchases, and the like at the original transaction price and make no adjustments in the amounts later. The historic cost principle affects accounting most significantly in the area of asset valuation. If inflation is high, the historic cost principle underestimates a firm's assets, so the depreciation charges based on these underestimates can be inadequate for replacing assets when they wear out or become obsolete.

The appropriateness of this principle varies inversely with the level of inflation in a country. The high level of price inflation in many industrialized countries during the 1970s created a need for accounting methods that adjust for inflation. A number of industrialized countries adopted new practices. One of the most far-reaching approaches was adopted in Great Britain in 1980. Called **current cost accounting,** it adjusts all items in a financial statement—assets, liabilities, costs, and revenues—to factor out the effects of inflation. The method uses a general price index to convert historic figures into current values. The standard was not made compulsory, however, and once Great Britain's inflation rate fell in the 1980s, most firms stopped providing the data.

Level of Development

Developed nations tend to have large, complex organizations, whose accounting problems are far more difficult than those of small organizations. Developed nations also tend to have sophisticated capital markets in which business organizations raise funds from investors and banks. These providers of capital require that the organizations they invest in and lend to provide comprehensive reports of their financial activities. The work forces of developed nations tend to be highly educated and skilled and can perform complex accounting functions. For all these reasons, accounting in developed countries tends to be far more sophisticated than it is in less developed countries, where the accounting standards may be fairly primitive.

Culture

A number of academic accountants have argued that the culture of a country has an important impact upon the nature of its accounting system.[6] Using the cultural typologies developed by Hofstede,[7] which we reviewed in Chapter 3, researchers have found that the extent to which a culture is characterized by *uncertainty avoidance* seems to have an impact on accounting systems.[8] **Uncertainty avoidance** refers to the extent to which cultures socialize their members to accept ambiguous situations and tolerate uncertainty. Members of high uncertainty avoidance cultures place a premium on job security, career patterns, retirement benefits, and so on. They also have a strong need for rules and regulations; the manager is expected to issue clear instructions, and subordinates' initiatives are tightly controlled. Lower uncertainty avoidance cultures are characterized by a greater readiness to take risks and less emotional resistance to change. According to Hofstede, countries such as Britain, the United States and Sweden are characterized by low uncertainty avoidance, while countries such as Japan, Mexico, and Greece have higher uncertainty avoidance. Research suggests that countries with low uncertainty avoidance cultures tend to have strong independent auditing professions that audit a firm's accounts to make sure they comply with generally accepted accounting regulations.[9]

Accounting Clusters

Few countries have identical accounting systems. Notable similarities between nations do exist, however, and three groups of countries with similar standards are identified in Map 19.1.[10] One group might be called the British-American-Dutch group. Great Britain, the United States, and the Netherlands are the trendsetters in this group. All these countries have large, well-developed stock and bond markets where firms raise capital from investors. Thus, their accounting systems are tailored to providing information to individual investors. A second group might be called the Europe-Japan group. Firms in these countries have very close ties to banks, which supply a large proportion of their capital needs. Therefore, their accounting practices are geared to the needs of banks. A third group might be the South American group. The countries in this group have all experienced persistent and rapid inflation. Consequently, they have adopted inflation accounting principles.

National and International Standards

The diverse accounting practices discussed in the previous section have been enshrined in national accounting and auditing standards. Accounting standards are rules for preparing financial statements; they define what is useful accounting information. Auditing standards specify the rules for performing an audit—the technical process by which an independent person (the auditor) gathers evidence for determining if financial accounts conform to required accounting standards and if they are also reliable.

Consequences of the Lack of Comparability

An unfortunate result of national differences in accounting and auditing standards is the general lack of comparability of financial reports from one country to another. For example, consider the following:

- Dutch standards favor the use of current values for replacement assets; Japanese law generally prohibits revaluation and prescribes historic cost.
- Capitalization of financial leases is required practice in Great Britain, but it is not practiced in France.
- Research and development costs must be written off in the year they are incurred in the United States, but in Spain they may be deferred as an asset and need not be amortized as long as benefits that will cover them are expected to arise in the future.
- German accountants treat depreciation as a liability, whereas British companies deduct it from assets.

Such differences would not matter much if there was little need for a firm headquartered in one country to report its financial results to citizens of another country. However, as you might recall from Chapter 11, one striking development of the past two decades has been the development of global capital markets. We have seen the growth of both transnational financing and transnational investment.

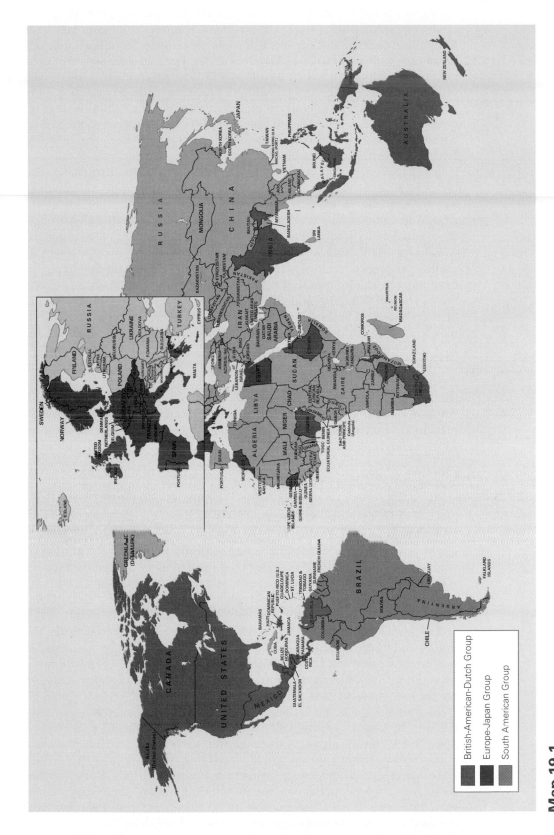

Legend:
- British-American-Dutch Group
- Europe-Japan Group
- South American Group

Map 19.1

Accounting Clusters

Transnational financing occurs when a firm based in one country enters another country's capital market to raise capital from the sale of stocks or bonds. A Danish firm raising capital by selling stock through the London Stock Exchange is an example of transnational financing. As we saw in the opening case, a number of large German firms are increasing their use of transnational financing by gaining listings, and ultimately issuing stock, on the New York Stock Exchange. Transnational investment occurs when an investor based in one country enters the capital market of another nation to invest in the stocks or bonds of a firm based in that country. An investor based in Great Britain buying General Motors stock through the New York Stock Exchange would be an example of transnational investment.

The rapid expansion of transnational financing and investment in recent years has been accompanied by a corresponding growth in transnational financial reporting. For example, in addition to its Danish financial reports, the Danish firm raising capital in London must issue financial reports that serve the needs of its British investors. Similarly, the US firm with a large number of British investors might wish to issue reports that serve the needs of those investors. However, the lack of comparability between accounting standards in different nations can lead to confusion. For example, the Danish firm that issues two sets of financial reports, one set prepared under Danish standards and the other under British standards, may find that its financial position looks significantly different in the two reports, and its investors may have difficulty identifying the firm's true worth. Some examples of the confusion that can arise from this lack of comparability appear in the accompanying Management Focus.

In addition to the problems this lack of comparability gives investors, it can give the firm major headaches. The firm has to explain to its investors why its financial position looks so different in the two accountings. Also, an international business may find it difficult to assess the financial positions of important foreign customers, suppliers, and competitors.

International Standards

Substantial efforts have been made in recent years to harmonize accounting standards across countries. The International Accounting Standards Committee (IASC) is a major proponent of standardization. The IASC is composed of representatives of 106 professional accounting groups in 79 countries. Governed by a 14-member board of representatives from 13 countries plus a representative from the International Federation of Financial Analysts, the IASC is responsible for formulating international accounting standards (IAS). Other areas of interest to the accounting profession worldwide, including auditing, ethical, educational, and public-sector standards, are handled by the International Federation of Accountants (IFAC), which has the same membership.

The IASC was begun in 1973 as an outgrowth of an effort by Canada, the United States, and Great Britain to develop international accounting standards. The IFAC was established in 1977, when it was determined that the IASC did not have the expertise to deal with broader professional issues. The two organizations work closely, but they are operated and funded separately.

By the mid-1990s, the IASC had issued over 30 international accounting standards.[11] To issue a new standard, 75 percent of the 14 members of the board must agree. It can be difficult to get three-quarters agreement, particularly since members come from different cultures and legal systems. To get around this problem, most IASC statements provide two acceptable alternatives. Arthur Wyatt, chairman of the IASC, says, "It's not much of a standard if you have two alternatives, but it's better than having six. If you can get agreement on two alternatives, you can capture the 11 required votes and eliminate some of the less used practices."[12]

Another hindrance to the development of international accounting standards is that compliance is voluntary; the IASC has no power to enforce its standards.

MANAGEMENT FOCUS
http://www.sb.com
Examples of the Consequences of Different Accounting Standards

US-based SmithKline Beckman (SKB) merged with the British company Beecham Group in 1989. After the merger, SKB had quotations on both the London and New York stock exchanges, so it had to prepare financial reports in accordance with both US and British standards. SKB's postmerger earnings, properly prepared in accordance with British accounting standards, were £130 million—quite a bit more than the £87 million reported in SKB's statement prepared in accordance with US accounting standards. The difference resulted primarily from treating the merger as a pooling of assets for British purposes and as a purchase of assets for US purposes. Even more confusing, the differences resulted in a shareholders' equity of £3.5 billion in the United States, but a negative £300 million in Great Britain! Not surprisingly, after these figures were released, SKB's stock was trading 17 percent lower on the London Stock Exchange than on the New York Stock Exchange.

In the mid-1980s, Teletonica, Spain's largest industrial company, was the first company in the world to float a multicountry stock offering simultaneously. In 1990, it reported net income under US accounting standards of 176 billion pesetas, more than twice the 76 billion pesetas it reported under

Spanish accounting standards. The difference was mainly due to an "add-back" of the incremental depreciation on assets carried at historic cost in the United States but reflecting more recent market value in the Spanish report. The effect of this difference on shareholders' equity was in the opposite direction; the equity reported in the US accounts was 15 percent less than the equity reported in the Spanish accounts.

A final example is more hypothetical in nature, but just as revealing. Two college professors set up a computer model to evaluate the reported net profits of an imaginary company with gross operating profits of $1.5 million. This imaginary company operated in three different countries—the United States, Britain, and Australia. The professors found that holding all else equal (such as national differences in interest rates on the firm's debt), when different accounting standards were applied the firm made a net profit of $34,600 in the United States, $260,600 in Britain, and $240,600 in Australia.

Sources: S. F. O'Malley, "Accounting across Borders," *Financial Executive*, March/April 1992, pp. 28–31; and L. Berton, "All Accountants May Soon Speak the Same Language, *The Wall Street Journal*, August 29, 1995, p. A15.

Despite this, support for the IASC and recognition of its standards is growing. Increasingly, the IASC is regarded as an effective voice for defining acceptable worldwide accounting principles. Japan, for example, began requiring financial statements to be prepared on a consolidated basis after the IASC issued its initial standards on the topic. By 1998, the IASC claimed that more than 450 companies around the world currently follow its rules, including Central African Cable from Zimbabwe, Guangshen Railway Company from China, Bayer from Germany, and Microsoft from the United States.

The impact of the IASC standards has probably been least noticeable in the United States because most of the standards issued by the IASC have been consistent with opinions already articulated by the US Financial Accounting Standards Board (FASB). The FASB writes the generally accepted accounting principles by which the financial statements of US firms must be prepared. In sharp contrast, some IASC standards have had a significant impact in many other countries because they eliminated a commonly used alternative.

Another body that promises to have substantial influence on the harmonization of accounting standards, at least within Europe, is the European Union (EU). In accordance with its plans for closer economic and political union, the EU is attempting to harmonize the accounting principles of its 15 member countries. The EU does this by issuing directives that the member states are obligated to incorporate into their own national laws. Because EU directives have the power of law, we might assume the EU has a better chance of achieving harmonization than the IASC does, but the EU is experiencing implementation difficulties. These difficulties arise from the wide variation in accounting practices among EU member countries. Accounting practices in Great Britain, for example, are closer to those of the United States than to those of France or Germany. Despite these difficulties, developments in the EU should be watched closely. If the EU achieves harmonization (in all probability, it eventually will), the accounting principles adopted in the EU could have a major influence on future IASC pronouncements.

In a move that indicates the trend toward adoption of acceptable international accounting standards is accelerating, the IASC hoped to develop by mid-1999 accounting standards for firms seeking stock listings in global markets. Also, the FASB has joined forces with accounting standard setters in Canada, Mexico, and Chile to explore areas in which the four countries can harmonize their accounting standards (Canada, Mexico, and the United States are members of NAFTA, and Chile may join in the near future). The Securities and Exchange Commission also is dropping some of its objections to international standards, which could accelerate their adoption. In 1994, the SEC for the first time accepted three international accounting standards on cash flow data, the effects of hyperinflation, and business combinations for cross-border filings.[13] A taste of what is to come if increasing numbers of international firms jump on the bandwagon and adopt IASC principles can be found in the accompanying Management Focus, which details the impact of adopting these standards on Ciba, the Swiss pharmaceuticals and chemicals group.

Multinational Consolidation and Currency Translation

A consolidated financial statement combines the separate financial statements of two or more companies to yield a single set of financial statements as if the individual companies were really one. Most multinational firms are composed of a parent company and a number of subsidiary companies located in various other countries. Such firms typically issue consolidated financial statements, which merge the accounts of all the companies, rather than issuing individual financial statements for the parent company and each subsidiary. In this section we examine the consolidated financial statements and then look at the related issue of foreign currency translation.

Consolidated Financial Statements

Many firms find it advantageous to organize as a set of separate legal entities (companies). For example, a firm may separately incorporate the various components of its business to limit its total legal liability or to take advantage of corporate tax regulations. Multinationals are often required by the countries in which they do business to set up a separate company. Thus, the typical multinational comprises a parent company and a number of subsidiary companies located in different countries, most of which are wholly owned by the parent. However, although the subsidiaries may be separate legal entities, they are not separate economic entities. Economically, all the companies in a corporate group are interdependent. For example, if the Brazilian subsidiary of a US parent company experiences substantial financial losses that suck up corporate funds, the cash available for investment in that subsidiary, the US parent company, and other subsidiary companies will be

MANAGEMENT FOCUS
Ciba Joins the International Accounting Club

http://www.ciba-aero.com

Switzerland does not have a history of very detailed accounting rules. As a result, published financial statements by major Swiss firms such as Ciba Specialty Chemicals Corp., Roche Group, and Nestlé often obscured as much as they revealed. The standard set of accounts from a Swiss firm was viewed as being very unusual and difficult for international investors to understand and described as being more like a statistical summary than the result of an integrated accounting system.

Swiss firms began to move toward adoption of IASC accounting principles in the early 1990s. The catalyst was increasing interest by foreign investors in the stock of major Swiss corporations. By the early 1990s, up to 40 percent of the stock of many of these firms was owned by foreign investors. As a group these investors were demanding more detailed financial statements that were comparable to those issued by other multinational enterprises.

One of the first firms to respond to these pressures was Ciba, Switzerland's largest pharmaceuticals and chemicals firm and a major multinational enterprise with operations around the globe. In 1993, the company announced that its 1994 financial statements would be in accordance with IASC guidelines. At the same time, it restated its 1992 results in line with IASC guidelines. The effect was to increase post-tax profits by 18 percent while raising inventories, cash, and marketable securities. Ciba's decision was motivated by a desire to appease foreign stockholders, who in 1994 held over one-third of Ciba's stock, and to position itself for the possibility of listings on the London and New York stock markets.

Ciba also decided to use the same international standards for internal financial reporting. Ciba set up a small international team to develop and implement its new system. While there were some preliminary problems in development of the system, including a figure on the insurance value of fixed assets that was off by $690 million, the new system is now running smoothly and seems to have produced several major benefits.

Ciba has discovered large savings as a result of the change, including tighter cash management, more efficient capital investment, a different approach to acquisitions, and more rigid asset management, which has reportedly reduced the value of inventories by 6 percent. The new system also has enabled Ciba to benchmark its performance for the first time against its global competitors.

One big difference between the new and old systems is the move from the arguably more informative current cost accounting method, which Ciba has used for over 25 years and which regularly updates asset values to account for inflation, to historic cost accounting under international standards. However, Ciba's management admits this drawback is not serious given the low inflation rate in Switzerland and given the offsetting gains produced by the switch to a new system.

Sources: A. Jack, "Swiss Group Moves from Night to Day," *Financial Times*, March 30, 1994, p. 22; and L. Berton, "All Accountants May Soon Speak the Same Language," *The Wall Street Journal*, August 29, 1995, p. A15.

limited. Thus, the purpose of consolidated financial statements is to provide accounting information about a group of companies that recognize their economic interdependence.

Transactions among the members of a corporate family are not included in consolidated financial statements; only assets, liabilities, revenues, and expenses with external third parties are shown. By law, however, separate legal entities are required to keep their own accounting records and to prepare their own financial statements. Thus, transactions with other members of a corporate group must be identified in the separate statements so they can be excluded when the consolidated statements are prepared. The process involves adding up the individual assets, liabilities, revenues, and expenses reported on the separate financial statements and then eliminating the intragroup ones. For example, consider these items selected from the individual financial statements of a parent company and one of its foreign subsidiaries:

	Parent	**Foreign Subsidiary**
Cash	$1,000	$ 250
Receivables	3,000*	900
Payables	300	500*
Revenues	7,000†	5,000
Expenses	2,000	3,000†

*Subsidiary owes parent $300.

†Subsidiary pays parent $1,000 in royalties for products licensed from parent.

The $300 receivable that the parent includes on its financial statements and the $300 payable that the subsidiary includes on its statements represent an intragroup item. These items cancel each other out and thus are not included in consolidated financial statements. Similarly, the $1,000 the subsidiary owes the parent in royalty payments is an intragroup item that will not appear in the consolidated accounts. The adjustments are as follows:

			Eliminations		
	Parent	**Subsidiary**	**Debit**	**Credit**	**Consolidated**
Cash	$1,000	$ 250			$ 1,250
Receivables	3,000*	900		$ 300	3,600
Payables	300	500*	$ 300		500
Revenues	7,000†	5,000		1,000	11,000
Expenses	2,000	3,000†	1,000		4,000

*Subsidiary owes parent $300.

†Subsidiary pays parent $1,000 in royalties for products licensed from parent.

Thus, while simply adding the two sets of accounts would suggest that the group of companies has revenues of $12,000 and receivables of $3,900, once intragroup transactions are removed from the picture, these figures drop to $11,000 and $3,600, respectively.

Preparing consolidated financial statements is becoming the norm for multinational firms. Investors realize that without consolidated financial statements, a multinational firm could conceal losses in an unconsolidated subsidiary, thereby hiding the economic status of the entire group. For example, the parent company in our illustration could increase its profit merely by charging the subsidiary company higher royalty fees. Since this has no effect on the group's overall profits, it amounts to little more than window dressing, making the parent company look good. If the parent does not issue a consolidated financial statement, however, the true economic status of the group is obscured by such a practice. With this in mind, the IASC has issued two standards requiring firms to prepare consolidated financial statements, and in most industrialized countries this is now required.

Currency Translation

Foreign subsidiaries of multinational firms normally keep their accounting records and prepare their financial statements in the currency of the country in which they are located. Thus, the Japanese subsidiary of a US firm will prepare its accounts in yen, a Brazilian subsidiary in real, a Korean subsidiary in won, and so on. When a multinational prepares consolidated accounts, it must convert all these financial statements into the currency of its home country. As we saw in Chapter 9, however, exchange rates vary in response to changes in economic circumstances. Companies can use two main methods to determine what exchange rate should be used when translating financial statement currencies—the current rate method and the temporal method.

The Current Rate Method

Under the current rate method, the exchange rate at the balance sheet date is used to translate the financial statements of a foreign subsidiary into the home currency of the multinational firm. Although this may seem logical, it is incompatible with the historic cost principle, which, as we saw earlier, is a generally accepted accounting principle in many countries, including the United States. Consider the case of a US firm that invests $100,000 in a Malaysian subsidiary. Assume the exchange rate at the time is $1 = 5 Malaysian ringgit. The subsidiary converts the $100,000 into ringgit, which gives it 500,000 ringgit. It then purchases land with this money. Subsequently, the dollar depreciates against the ringgit, so that by year-end, $1 = 4 ringgit. If this exchange rate is used to convert the value of the land back into US dollars for preparing consolidated accounts, the land will be valued at $125,000. The piece of land would appear to have increased in value by $25,000, although in reality the increase would be simply a function of an exchange rate change. Thus, the consolidated accounts would present a somewhat misleading picture.

The Temporal Method

One way to avoid this problem is to use the temporal method to translate the accounts of a foreign subsidiary. The temporal method translates assets valued in a foreign currency into the home-country currency using the exchange rate that exists when the assets are purchased. Referring to our example, the exchange rate of $1 = 5 ringgit, the rate on the day the Malaysian subsidiary purchased the land, would be used to convert the value of the land back into US dollars at year-end. However, although the temporal method will ensure the dollar value of the land does not fluctuate due to exchange rate changes, it has its own serious problem. Because the various assets of a foreign subsidiary will in all probability be acquired at different times and because exchange rates seldom remain stable for long, different exchange rates will probably have to be used to translate those foreign assets into the multinational's home currency. Consequently, the multinational's balance sheet may not balance!

Consider the case of a US firm that on January 1, 1999, invests $100,000 in a new Japanese subsidiary. The exchange rate at that time is $1 = ¥100. The initial investment is therefore ¥10 million, and the Japanese subsidiary's balance sheet looks like this on January 1, 1999:

	Yen	**Exchange Rate**	**US Dollars**
Cash	10,000,000	($1 = ¥100)	100,000
Owners' equity	10,000,000	($1 = ¥100)	100,000

Assume that on January 31, when the exchange rate is $1 = ¥95, the Japanese subsidiary invests ¥5 million in a factory (i.e., fixed assets). Then on February 15, when the exchange rate is $1 = ¥90, the subsidiary purchases ¥5 million of inventory. The balance sheet of the subsidiary will look like this on March 1, 1999:

	Yen	**Exchange Rate**	**US Dollars**
Fixed assets	5,000,000	($1 = ¥95)	52,632
Inventory	5,000,000	($1 = ¥90)	55,556
Total	10,000,000		108,187
Owners' equity	10,000,000	($1 = ¥100)	100,000

Although the balance sheet balances in yen, it does not balance when the temporal method is used to translate the yen-denominated balance sheet figures back into dollars. In translation, the balance sheet debits exceed the credits by $8,187. The accounting profession has yet to adopt a satisfactory solution to the gap between debits and credits. The practice currently used in the United States is explained next.

Current US Practice

US-based multinational firms must follow the requirements of Statement 52, "Foreign Currency Translation," issued by the Financial Accounting Standards Board in 1981. Under Statement 52, a foreign subsidiary is classified either as a self-sustaining, autonomous subsidiary or as integral to the activities of the parent company. (A link can be made here with the material on strategy discussed in Chapter 12. Firms pursuing multidomestic and international strategies are most likely to have self-sustaining subsidiaries, whereas firms pursuing global and transnational strategies are most likely to have integral subsidiaries.) According to Statement 52, the local currency of a self-sustaining foreign subsidiary is to be its functional currency. The balance sheet for such subsidiaries is translated into the home currency using the exchange rate in effect at the end of the firm's financial year, whereas the income statement is translated using the average exchange rate for the firm's financial year. But the functional currency of an integral subsidiary is to be US dollars. The financial statements of such subsidiaries are translated at various historic rates using the temporal method (as we did in the example), and the dangling debit or credit increases or decreases consolidated earnings for the period.

Accounting Aspects of Control Systems

Corporate headquarters' role is to control subunits within the organization to ensure they achieve the best possible performance. In the typical firm, the control process is annual and involves three main steps:

1. Head office and subunit management jointly determine subunit goals for the coming year.
2. Throughout the year, the head office monitors subunit performance against the agreed goals.
3. If a subunit fails to achieve its goals, the head office intervenes in the subunit to learn why the shortfall occurred, taking corrective action when appropriate.

The accounting function plays a critical role in this process. Most of the goals for subunits are expressed in financial terms and are embodied in the subunit's budget for the coming year. The budget is the main instrument of financial control. The budget is typically prepared by the subunit, but it must be approved by headquarters management. During the approval process, headquarters and subunit managements debate the goals that should be incorporated in the budget. One function of headquarters management is to ensure a subunit's budget contains challenging but realistic performance goals. Once a budget is agreed to, accounting information systems are used to collect data throughout the year so a subunit's performance can be evaluated against the goals contained in its budget.

In most international businesses, many of the firm's subunits are foreign subsidiaries. The performance goals for the coming year are thus set by negotiation between corporate management and the managers of foreign subsidiaries. According to one survey of control practices within multinational enterprises, the most important criterion for evaluating the performance of a foreign subsidiary is the subsidiary's

Table 19.1

Importance of Financial Criteria Used to Evaluate Performance of Foreign Subsidiaries and Their Managers[*]

Item	Subsidiary	Manager
Return on investment (ROI)	1.9	2.2
Return on equity (ROE)	3.0	3.0
Return on assets (ROA)	2.3	2.3
Return on sales (ROS)	2.1	2.1
Residual income	3.4	3.3
Budget compared to actual sales	1.9	1.7
Budget compared to actual profit	1.5	1.3
Budget compared to actual ROI	2.3	2.4
Budget compared to actual ROA	2.7	2.5
Budget compared to actual ROE	3.1	3.0

[*]Importance of criteria ranked on a scale from: 1 = very important to 5 = unimportant.

Source: F. Choi and I. Czechowicz, "Assessing Foreign Subsidiary Performance: A Multinational Comparison," *Management International Review* 4 (1983), p. 16.

actual profits compared to budgeted profits (see Table 19.1).[14] This is closely followed by a subsidiary's actual sales compared to budgeted sales and its return on investment. The same criteria were also useful in evaluating the performance of the subsidiary managers (see Table 19.1). We will discuss this point later in this section. First, however, we will examine two factors that can complicate the control process in an international business: exchange rate changes and transfer pricing practices.

Exchange Rate Changes and Control Systems

Most international businesses require all budgets and performance data within the firm to be expressed in the "corporate currency," which is normally the home currency. Thus, the Malaysian subsidiary of a US multinational would probably submit a budget prepared in US dollars, rather than Malaysian ringgit, and performance data throughout the year would be reported to headquarters in US dollars. This facilitates comparisons between subsidiaries in different countries, and it makes things easier for headquarters management. However, it also allows exchange rate changes during the year to introduce substantial distortions. For example, the Malaysian subsidiary may fail to achieve profit goals not because of any performance problems, but merely because of a decline in the value of the ringgit against the dollar. The opposite can occur, also, making a foreign subsidiary's performance look better than it actually is.

The Lessard–Lorange Model

According to research by Donald Lessard and Peter Lorange, a number of methods are available to international businesses for dealing with this problem.[15] Lessard and Lorange point out three exchange rates that can be used to translate foreign currencies into the corporate currency in setting budgets and in the subsequent tracking of performance:

- The **initial rate,** the spot exchange rate when the budget is adopted.
- The **projected rate,** the spot exchange rate forecast for the end of the budget period (i.e., the forward rate).
- The **ending rate,** the spot exchange rate when the budget and performance are being compared.

These three exchange rates imply nine possible combinations (see Figure 19.3). Lessard and Lorange ruled out four of the nine combinations as illogical and unreasonable; they are shaded in Figure 19.3. For example, it would make no sense to use

Figure 19.3

Possible Combinations
of Exchange Rates in the
Control Process

		Rate Used to Translate Actual Performance for Comparison with Budget		
		Initial (I)	Projected (P)	Ending (E)
	Initial (I)	(II) Budget at Initial Actual at Initial	(IP) Budget at Intial Actual at Projected	(IE) Budget at Initial Actual at Ending
Rate Used for Translating Budget	Projected (P)	(PI) Budget at Projected Actual at Initial	(PP) Budget at Projected Actual at Projected	(PE) Budget at Projected Actual at Ending
	Ending (E)	(EI) Budget at Ending Actual at Initial	(EP) Budget at Ending Actual at Projected	(EE) Budget at Ending Actual at Ending

the ending rate to translate the budget and the initial rate to translate actual performance data. Any of the remaining five combinations might be used for setting budgets and evaluating performance.

With three of these five combinations—II, PP, and EE—the same exchange rate is used for translating both budget figures and performance figures into the corporate currency. All three combinations have the advantage that a change in the exchange rate during the year does not distort the control process. This is not true for the other two combinations, IE and PE. In those cases, exchange rate changes can introduce distortions. The potential for distortion is greater with IE; the ending spot exchange rate used to evaluate performance against the budget may be quite different from the initial spot exchange rate used to translate the budget. The distortion is less serious in the case of PE because the projected exchange rate takes into account future exchange rate movements.

Of the five combinations, Lessard and Lorange recommend that firms use the projected spot exchange rate to translate both the budget and performance figures into the corporate currency, combination PP. The projected rate in such cases will typically be the forward exchange rate as determined by the foreign exchange market (see Chapter 9 for the definition of forward rate) or some company-generated forecast of future spot rates, which Lessard and Lorange refer to as the **internal forward rate.** The internal forward rate may differ from the forward rate quoted by the foreign exchange market if the firm wishes to bias its business in favor of, or against, the particular foreign currency.

Transfer Pricing and Control Systems

In Chapter 12 we reviewed the various strategies that international businesses pursue. Two of these strategies, the global strategy and the transnational strategy, give rise to a globally dispersed web of productive activities. Firms pursuing these strategies disperse each value creation activity to its optimal location in the world. Thus, a product might be designed in one country, some of its components manufactured in a second country, other components manufactured in a third country, all assembled in a fourth country, and then sold worldwide.

The volume of intrafirm transactions in such firms is very high. The firms are continually shipping component parts and finished goods between subsidiaries in different countries. This poses a very important question: How should goods and services transferred between subsidiary companies in a multinational firm be priced? The price at which such goods and services are transferred is referred to as the **transfer price.**

The choice of transfer price can critically affect the performance of two subsidiaries that exchange goods or services. Consider this example: A French manufacturing subsidiary of a US multinational imports a major component from Brazil. It incorporates this part into a product that it sells in France for the equivalent of $230 per unit. The product costs $200 to manufacture, of which $100 goes to the Brazilian subsidiary to pay for the component part. The remaining $100 covers costs incurred in France. Thus, the French subsidiary earns $30 profit per unit.

	Before Change in Transfer Price	After 20 Percent Increase in Transfer Price
Revenues per unit	$230	$230
Cost of component per unit	100	120
Other costs per unit	100	100
Profit per unit	$ 30	$ 10

Look at what happens if corporate headquarters decides to increase transfer prices by 20 percent ($20 per unit). The French subsidiary's profits will fall by two-thirds from $30 per unit to $10 per unit. Thus, the performance of the French subsidiary depends on the transfer price for the component part imported from Brazil, and the transfer price is controlled by corporate headquarters. When setting budgets and reviewing a subsidiary's performance, corporate headquarters must keep in mind the distorting effect of transfer prices.

How should transfer prices be determined? We discuss this issue in detail in the next chapter. International businesses often manipulate transfer prices to minimize their worldwide tax liability, minimize import duties, and avoid government restrictions on capital flows. For now, however, it is enough to note that the transfer price must be considered when setting budgets and evaluating a subsidiary's performance.

Separation of Subsidiary and Manager Performance

Table 19.1 suggests that in many international businesses, the same quantitative criteria are used to assess the performance of both a foreign subsidiary and its managers. Many accountants, however, argue that although it is legitimate to compare subsidiaries against each other on the basis of return on investment (ROI) or other indicators of profitability, it may not be appropriate to use these for comparing and evaluating the managers of different subsidiaries. Foreign subsidiaries do not operate in uniform environments; their environments have widely different economic, political, and social conditions, all of which influence the costs of doing business in a country and hence the subsidiaries' profitability. Thus, the manager of a subsidiary in an adverse environment that has an ROI of 5 percent may be doing a better job than the manager of a subsidiary in a benign environment that has an ROI of 20 percent. Although the firm might want to pull out of a country where its ROI is only 5 percent, it may also want to recognize the manager's achievement.

Accordingly, it has been suggested that the evaluation of a subsidiary should be kept separate from the evaluation of its manager.[16] The manager's evaluation should consider how hostile or benign the country's environment is for that business. Further, managers should be evaluated in local currency terms after making allowances for those items over which they have no control (e.g., interest rates, tax rates, inflation rates, transfer prices, exchange rates).

Chapter Summary

This chapter focused on financial accounting within the multinational firm. We explained why accounting practices and standards differ from country to country and surveyed the efforts under way to harmonize countries' accounting practices. We discussed the rationale behind consolidated accounts and looked at currency translation. We reviewed several issues related to the use of accounting-based control systems within international businesses. This chapter made the following points:

1. Accounting is the language of business: the means by which firms communicate their financial position to the providers of capital and to governments (for tax purposes). It is also the means by which firms evaluate their own performance, control their expenditures, and plan for the future.

2. Accounting is shaped by the environment in which it operates. Each country's accounting system has evolved in response to the local demands for accounting information.

3. Five main factors seem to influence the type of accounting system a country has: (*i*) the relationship between business and the providers of capital, (*ii*) political and economic ties with other countries, (*iii*) the level of inflation, (*iv*) the level of a country's development, and (*v*) the prevailing culture in a country.

4. National differences in accounting and auditing standards have resulted in a general lack of comparability in countries' financial reports.

5. This lack of comparability has become a problem as transnational financing and transnational investment have grown rapidly in recent decades (a consequence of the globalization of capital markets). Due to the lack of comparability, a firm may have to explain to investors why its financial position looks very different on financial reports that are based on different accounting practices.

6. The most significant push for harmonization of accounting standards across countries has come from the International Accounting Standards Committee (IASC). So far, the IASC's success, while noteworthy, has been limited.

7. Consolidated financial statements provide financial accounting information about a group of companies that recognizes the companies' economic interdependence.

8. Transactions among the members of a corporate family are not included on consolidated financial statements; only assets, liabilities, revenues, and expenses generated with external third parties are shown.

9. Foreign subsidiaries of a multinational firm normally keep their accounting records and prepare their financial statements in the currency of the country in which they are located. When the multinational prepares its consolidated accounts, these financial statements must be translated into the currency of its home country.

10. Under the current rate translation method, the exchange rate at the balance sheet date is used to translate the financial statements of a foreign subsidiary into the home currency. This has the drawback of being incompatible with the historic cost principle.

11. Under the temporal method, assets valued in a foreign currency are translated into the home currency using the exchange rate that existed when the assets were purchased. A problem with this approach is that the multinational's balance sheet may not balance.

12. In most international businesses, the annual budget is the main instrument by which headquarters controls foreign subsidiaries. Throughout the year, headquarters compares a subsidiary's performance against the financial goals incorporated in its budget, intervening selectively in its operations when shortfalls occur.

13. Most international businesses require all budgets and performance data within the firm to be expressed in the corporate currency. This enhances comparability, but it distorts the control process if the relevant exchange rates change between the time a foreign subsidiary's budget is set and the time its performance is evaluated.

14. According to the Lessard–Lorange model, the best way to deal with this problem is to use a projected spot exchange rate to translate both budget figures and performance figures into the corporate currency.

15. Transfer prices also can introduce significant distortions into the control process and thus must be considered when setting budgets and evaluating a subsidiary's performance.

16. Foreign subsidiaries do not operate in uniform environments, and some environments are much tougher than others. Accordingly, it has been suggested that the evaluation of a subsidiary should be kept separate from the evaluation of the subsidiary manager.

Critical Discussion Questions

1. Why do the accounting systems of different countries differ? Why do these differences matter?

2. Why are transactions among members of a corporate family not included in consolidated financial statements?

3. The following are selected amounts from the separate financial statements of a parent company (unconsolidated) and one of its subsidiaries:

	Parent	Subsidiary
Cash	$ 180	$ 80
Receivables	380	200
Accounts payable	245	110
Retained earnings	790	680
Revenues	4,980	3,520
Rent income	0	200
Dividend income	250	0
Expenses	4,160	2,960

Notes:
1. Parent owes subsidiary $70.
2. Parent owns 100 percent of subsidiary. During the year subsidiary paid parent a dividend of $250.
3. Subsidiary owns the building that parent rents for $200.
4. During the year parent sold some inventory to subsidiary for $2,200. It had cost parent $1,500. Subsidiary sold the inventory to an unrelated party for $3,200.

Given this,

a. What is the parent's (unconsolidated) net income?

b. What is the subsidiary's net income?

c. What is the consolidated profit on the inventory that the parent originally sold to the subsidiary?

d. What are the amounts of consolidated cash and receivables?

4. Why might an accounting-based control system provide headquarters management with biased information about the performance of a foreign subsidiary? How can these biases best be corrected?

CLOSING CASE China's Evolving Accounting System

Attracted by its rapid transformation from a socialist planned economy into a market economy, economic annual growth rates of around 12 percent, and a population in excess of 1.2 billion, Western firms over the past 10 years have favored China as a site for foreign direct investment. Most see China as an emerging economic superpower with an economy that will be as large as that of Japan by 2000 and of the US before 2010 if current growth projections hold true.

The Chinese government sees foreign direct investment as a primary engine of China's economic growth. To encourage such investment, the government has offered generous tax incentives to foreign firms that invest in China, either on their own or in a joint venture with a local enterprise. These tax incentives include a two-year exemption from corporate income tax following an investment, plus a further three years during which taxes are paid at only 50 percent of

the standard tax rate. Such incentives when coupled with the promise of China's vast internal market have made the country a prime site for investment by Western firms. However, once established in China, many Western firms find themselves struggling to comply with the complex and often obtuse nature of China's rapidly evolving accounting system.

Accounting in China has traditionally been rooted in information gathering and compliance reporting designed to measure the government's production and tax goals. The Chinese system was based on the old Soviet system, which had little to do with profit or accounting systems created to report financial positions or the results of foreign operations. Although the system is changing rapidly, many problems associated with the old system still remain.

One problem for investors is a severe shortage of accountants, financial managers, and auditors in China, especially those experienced with market economy transactions and international accounting practices. As of 1995, there were only 25,000 accountants in China, far short of the hundreds of thousands that will be needed if China continues on its path toward becoming a market economy. Chinese enterprises, including equity and cooperative joint ventures with foreign firms, must be audited by Chinese accounting firms, which are regulated by the state. Traditionally, many experienced auditors have audited only state-owned enterprises, working through the local province or city authorities and the state audit bureau to report to the government entity overseeing the audited firm. In response to the shortage of accountants schooled in the principles of private sector accounting, several large international auditing firms have established joint ventures with emerging Chinese accounting and auditing firms to bridge the growing need for international accounting, tax, and securities expertise.

A further problem concerns the somewhat halting evolution of China's emerging accounting standards. Current thinking is that China won't simply adopt the international accounting standards specified by the IASC, nor will it use the generally accepted accounting principles of any particular country as its model. Rather, accounting standards in China are expected to evolve in a rather piecemeal fashion, with the Chinese adopting a few standards as they are studied and deemed appropriate for Chinese circumstances.

In the meantime, current Chinese accounting principles, present difficult problems for Western firms. For example, the former Chinese accounting system didn't need to accrue unrealized losses. In an economy where shortages were the norm, if a state-owned company didn't sell its inventory right away, it could store it and use it for some other purpose later. Similarly, accounting principles assumed the state always paid its debts—eventually. Thus, Chinese enterprises don't generally provide for lower-of-cost or market inventory adjustments or the creation of allowance for bad debts, both of which are standard practices in the West.

http://www.china-window.com/window.html

Sources: L. E. Graham and A. H. Carley, "When East Meets West," *Financial Executive*, July/August 1995, pp. 40–45; and K. Theonnes and A. Yeung, "Playing Favorites," *Financial Executive*, July/August 1995, pp. 46–51.

Case Discussion Questions

1. What factors have shaped the accounting system currently in use in China?

2. What problems does the accounting system currently in use in China present to foreign investors in joint ventures with Chinese companies?

3. If the evolving Chinese system does not adhere to IASC standards, but instead to standards that the Chinese government deems appropriate to China's "special situation," how might this affect foreign firms with operations in China?

Notes

1. G. G. Mueller, H. Gernon, and G. Meek, *Accounting: An International Perspective* (Burr Ridge, IL: Richard D. Irwin, 1991).

2. S. J. Gary, "Towards a Theory of Cultural Influence on the Development of Accounting Systems Internationally," *Abacus* 3 (1988), pp. 1–15; and R. S. Wallace, O. Gernon, and H. Gernon, "Frameworks for International Comparative Financial Accounting," *Journal of Accounting Literature* 10 (1991), pp. 209–64.

3. K. M. Dunne and G. A. Ndubizu, "International Acquisition Accounting Method and Corporate Multinationalism," *Journal of International Business Studies* 26 (1995), pp. 361–77.

4. W. A. Wallace and J. Walsh, "Apples to Apples: Profits Abroad," *Financial Executive*, May–June 1995, pp. 28–31.

5. Wallace, Gernon, and Gernon, "Frameworks for International Comparative Financial Accounting."

6. Gary, "Towards a Theory of Cultural Influence on the Development of Accounting Systems Internationally;" and S. B. Salter and F. Niswander, "Cultural Influences on the Development of Accounting Systems Internationally," *Journal of International Business Studies* 26 (1995), pp. 379–97.

7. G. Hofstede, *Culture's Consequences: International Differences in Work Related Values* (Beverly Hills, CA: Sage Publications, 1980).

8. Salter and Niswander, "Cultural Influences on the Development of Accounting Systems Internationally."

9. Ibid.

10. Mueller, Gernon, and Meek, *Accounting: An International Perspective*.

11. P. D. Fleming, "The Growing Importance of International Accounting Standards," *Journal of Accountancy*, September 1991, pp. 100–06; and "Bean Counters, Unite!" *The Economist*, June 10, 1995, pp. 67–68.

12. Fleming, "The Growing Importance of International Accounting Standards."

13. L. Berton, "All Accountants May Soon Speak the Same Language," *The Wall Street Journal*, August 29, 1995, p. A15.

14. F. Choi and I. Czechowicz, "Assessing Foreign Subsidiary Performance: A Multinational Comparison," *Management International Review* 4, 1983, pp. 14–25.

15. D. Lessard and P. Lorange, "Currency Changes and Management Control: Resolving the Centralization/Decentralization Dilemma," *Accounting Review*, July 1977, pp. 628–37.

16. Mueller, Gernon, and Meek, *Accounting: An International Perspective*.

CHAPTER TWENTY

FINANCIAL MANAGEMENT IN THE INTERNATIONAL BUSINESS

Global Treasury Management at Procter & Gamble

With more than 300 brands of paper, detergent, food, health, and cosmetics products sold in over 140 countries and over 60 percent of its almost $40 billion in revenues generated outside the United States, Procter & Gamble is the quintessential example of a global consumer products firm. Despite this global spread, P&G's treasury operations—which embrace investment, financing, money management, and foreign exchange decisions—were quite decentralized until the early 1990s. Essentially, each major international subsidiary managed its own investments, borrowings, and foreign exchange trades, subject only to outside borrowing limits imposed by the international treasury group at P&G's headquarters in Cincinnati.

Today P&G operates with a much more centralized system in which a global treasury management function at corporate headquarters exercises close oversight over the operations of different regional treasury centers around the world. This move was a response in part to the rise in the volume of P&G's international transactions and the resulting increase in foreign exchange exposures. Like many global firms, P&G has been trying to rationalize its global production system to realize cost economies by concentrating the production of certain products at specific locations, as opposed to producing those products in every major country in which it does business. As it has moved in this direction, the number and volume of raw materials and finished products that are being shipped across borders has been growing by leaps and bounds. This has led to a commensurate increase in the size of P&G's foreign exchange exposure, which at any one time now runs into billions of dollars. Also, more than one-third of P&G's foreign exchange exposure is now in nondollar exposures, such as transactions that involve the exchange of rubles into won or sterling into yen.

P&G believes that centralizing the overall management of the resulting foreign exchange transactions can help the company realize a number of important gains. First, because its international subsidiaries often accumulate cash balances in the currency of the country where they are based, P&G now trades currencies between its subsidiaries. By cutting banks out of the process, P&G saves on transaction costs. Second, P&G has found that many of its subsidiaries purchase currencies in relatively small lots of say $100,000. By grouping these lots into larger purchases, P&G can generally get a better price from foreign trade dealers. Third, P&G is pooling foreign exchange risks and purchasing an "umbrella option" to cover the risks associated with various currency positions, which is cheaper than purchasing options to cover each position.

In addition to managing foreign exchange transactions, P&G's global treasury operation arranges for subsidiaries to invest their surplus funds in and to borrow money from other Procter & Gamble entities, instead of from local banks. Subsidiaries that have excess cash lend it to those that need cash, and the global treasury operation acts as a financial intermediary. P&G has cut the number of local banks that it does business with from 450 to about 200. Using intracompany loans instead of loans from local banks lowers the overall borrowing costs, which may result in annual savings on interest payments that run into tens if not hundreds of millions of dollars.

http://www.pg.com

Sources: R. C. Stewart, "Balancing on the Global High Wire," *Financial Executive*, September/October 1995, pp. 35–39; and S. Lipin, F. R. Bleakley, and B. D. Granito, "Portfolio Poker," *The Wall Street Journal*, April 14, 1994, p. A1.

Introduction

As the opening case makes clear, this chapter focuses on financial management in the international business. Included within the scope of financial management are three sets of related decisions:

- *Investment decisions*, decisions about what activities to finance.
- *Financing decisions*, decisions about how to finance those activities.
- *Money management decisions*, decisions about how to manage the firm's financial resources most efficiently.

The opening case describes Procter & Gamble's approach toward these decisions. By managing investing, financing, and money management decisions centrally through its global treasury function, P&G has realized considerable cost economies. These economies help P&G compete more effectively in the global marketplace.

In an international business, investment, financing, and money management decisions are complicated by the fact that countries have different currencies, different tax regimes, different regulations concerning the flow of capital across their borders, different norms regarding the financing of business activities, different levels of economic and political risk, and so on. Financial managers must consider all these factors when deciding which activities to finance, how best to finance those activities, how best to manage the firm's financial resources, and how best to protect the firm from political and economic risks (including foreign exchange risk).

Good financial management can be an important source of competitive advantage. This is implicit in the opening case, where good financial management helps P&G attain cost economies and lower its overall cost structure. For another example, consider FMC, a Chicago-based producer of chemicals and farm equipment. FMC counts on overseas business for 40 percent of its sales. FMC attributes some of its success overseas to aggressive trading in the forward foreign exchange market. By trading in currency futures, FMC can provide overseas customers with stable long-term prices for three years or more, regardless of what happens to exchange rates. Ralph DelZenero, FMC's foreign exchange specialist, says, "Some of our competitors change their prices on a relatively short-term basis depending on what is happening with their own exchange rate . . . We want to provide longer-term pricing as a customer service—they can plan their budgets knowing what the numbers will be—and we can hopefully maintain and build our customer base." FMC also offers its customers the option of paying in any of several currencies as a convenience to them and as an attempt to retain customers. If customers could pay only in dollars, they might give their business to a competitor that offered pricing in a variety of currencies. By adopting this policy, FMC deals with "the hassle of foreign exchange movements," says Mr. DelZenero, so its customers don't have to. By offering customers multicurrency pricing alternatives, FMC implicitly accepts the responsibility of managing foreign exchange risk for its business units that sell overseas. It has set up what amounts to an in-house bank to manage the operation, monitoring currency rates daily and managing its risks on a portfolio basis. This bank handles more than $1 billion in currency transactions annually, which means the company can often beat the currency prices quoted by commercial banks.[1]

Chapter 12 talked about the value chain and pointed out that creating a competitive advantage requires a firm to reduce its costs of value creation and/or add value by improving its customer service. P&G and FMC show how good financial management can help both reduce the costs of creating value and add value by improving customer service. By reducing the firm's cost of capital, eliminating foreign exchange losses, minimizing the firm's tax burden, minimizing the firm's exposure to unnecessarily risky activities, and managing the firm's cash flows and reserves in the most efficient manner, the finance function can reduce the costs of creating value. As the example of FMC illustrates, good financial management can also enhance customer service, thus adding value.

We begin this chapter by looking at investment decisions in an international business. We will be most concerned with the issue of capital budgeting. Our objective is to identify the factors that can complicate capital budgeting decisions in an international business, as opposed to a purely domestic business. Most important, we will discuss how such factors as political and economic risk complicate capital budgeting decisions.

Then we look at financing decisions in an international business, focusing on the financial structure of foreign affiliates—the mix of equity and debt financing. Financial structure norms for firms vary widely from country to country. We will discuss the advantages and disadvantages of localizing the financial structure of a foreign affiliate to make it consistent with the norms of the country in which it is based.

Next we examine money management decisions in an international business. We will look at the objectives of global money management, the various ways businesses can move money across borders, and some techniques for managing the firm's financial resources efficiently.

The chapter closes with a section on managing foreign exchange risk. Foreign exchange risk was discussed in Chapter 9, but there our focus was on how the foreign exchange market works and the forces that determine exchange rate movements. In this chapter, we focus on the various tactics and strategies international businesses use to manage their foreign exchange risk.

Investment Decisions

A decision to invest in activities in a given country must consider many economic, political, cultural, and strategic variables. We have been discussing this issue throughout much of this book. We touched on it in Chapters 2 and 3 when we discussed how the political, economic, legal, and cultural environment of a country can influence the benefits, costs, and risks of doing business there and thus its attractiveness as an investment site. We returned to the issue in Chapter 6 with a discussion of the economic theory of foreign direct investment. We identified a number of factors that determine the economic attractiveness of a foreign investment opportunity. In Chapter 7, we looked at the political economy of foreign direct investment and we considered the role that government intervention can play in foreign investment. In Chapter 12, we pulled much of this material together when we considered how a firm can reduce its costs of value creation and/or increase its value added by investing in productive activities in other countries. We returned to the issue again in Chapter 14 when we considered the various modes for entering foreign markets.

One role of the financial manager in an international business is to try to quantify the various benefits, costs, and risks that are likely to flow from an investment in a given location. This is done by using capital budgeting techniques.

Capital Budgeting

Capital budgeting quantifies the benefits, costs, and risks of an investment. This enables top managers to compare, in a reasonably objective fashion, different investment alternatives within and across countries so they can make informed choices about where the firm should invest its scarce financial resources. Capital budgeting for a foreign project uses the same theoretical framework that domestic capital budgeting uses; that is, the firm must first estimate the cash flows associated with the project over time. In most cases, the cash flows will be negative at first, because the firm will be investing heavily in production facilities. After some initial period, however, the cash flows will become positive as investment costs decline and revenues grow. Once the cash flows have been estimated, they must be discounted to determine their net present value using an appropriate discount rate. The most commonly used discount rate is either the firm's cost of capital or some other required rate of return. If the net present value of the discounted cash flows is greater than zero, the firm should go ahead with the project.[2]

Although this might sound quite straightforward, capital budgeting is in practice a very complex and imperfect process. Among the factors complicating the process for an international business are these:

1. A distinction must be made between cash flows to the project and cash flows to the parent company.
2. Political and economic risks, including foreign exchange risk, can significantly change the value of a foreign investment.
3. The connection between cash flows to the parent and the source of financing must be recognized.

We look at the first two of these issues in this section. Discussion of the connection between cash flows and the source of financing is postponed until the next section, where we discuss the source of financing.

Project and Parent Cash Flows

A theoretical argument exists for analyzing any foreign project from the perspective of the parent company because cash flows to the project are not necessarily the same thing as cash flows to the parent company. The project may not be able to remit all its cash flows to the parent for a number of reasons. For example, cash flows may be blocked from repatriation by the host-country government, they may be taxed at an unfavorable rate, or the host government may require a certain percentage of the cash flows generated from the project be reinvested within the host nation. While these restrictions don't affect the net present value of the project itself, they do affect the net present value of the project to the parent company because they limit the cash flows that can be remitted to it from the project.

When evaluating a foreign investment opportunity, the parent should be interested in the cash flows it will receive—as opposed to those the project generates—because those are the basis for dividends to stockholders, investments elsewhere in the world, repayment of worldwide corporate debt, and so on. Stockholders will not perceive blocked earnings as contributing to the value of the firm, and creditors will not count them when calculating the parent's ability to service its debt.

But the problem of blocked earnings is not as serious as it once was. The worldwide move toward greater acceptance of free market economics (discussed in Chapter 2) has reduced the number of countries in which governments are likely to prohibit the affiliates of foreign multinationals from remitting cash flows to their parent companies. In addition, as we will see later in the chapter, firms have a number of options for circumventing host-government attempts to block the free flow of funds from an affiliate.

Adjusting for Political and Economic Risk

When analyzing a foreign investment opportunity, the company must consider the political and economic risks that stem from the foreign location. We will discuss these before looking at how capital budgeting methods can be adjusted to take risks into account.

Political Risk

We initially encountered the concept of **political risk** in Chapter 2. There we defined it as the likelihood that political forces will cause drastic changes in a country's business environment that hurt the profit and other goals of a business enterprise. Political risk tends to be greater in countries experiencing social unrest or disorder and countries where the underlying nature of the society makes the likelihood of social unrest high. When political risk is high, there is a high probability that a change will occur in the country's political environment that will endanger foreign firms there.

In extreme cases, political change may result in the expropriation of foreign firms' assets. This occurred to US firms after the Iranian revolution of 1979. Social unrest may also result in economic collapse, which can render worthless a firm's assets. This has occurred to many foreign companies' assets as a result of the bloody war following the breakup of the former Yugoslavia. In less extreme cases, political changes may result in increased tax rates, the imposition of exchange controls that limit or block a subsidiary's ability to remit earnings to its parent company, the imposition of price controls, and government interference in existing contracts. The likelihood of any of these events impairs the attractiveness of a foreign investment opportunity.

Many firms devote considerable attention to political risk analysis and to quantifying political risk. For example, Union Carbide, the US multinational chemical giant, has an elaborate procedure for incorporating political risk into its strategic planning and capital budgeting process.[3] *Euromoney* magazine publishes an annual "country risk rating," which incorporates assessments of political and other risks (see Table 20.1 and the associated description). The problem with all attempts to forecast political risk, however, is that they try to predict a future that can only be guessed at—and in many cases, the guesses are wrong. Few people foresaw the 1979 Iranian revolution, the collapse of communism in Eastern Europe, or the dramatic breakup of the Soviet Union, yet all these events have had a profound impact on the business environments of the countries involved. This is not to say that political risk assessment is without value, but it is more art than science.

Economic Risk

Like political risk, we first encountered the concept of **economic risk** in Chapter 2. There we defined it as the likelihood that economic mismanagement will cause drastic changes in a country's business environment that hurt the profit and other goals of a business enterprise. In practice, the biggest problem arising from economic mismanagement seems to be inflation. Historically, many governments have expanded their domestic money supply in misguided attempts to stimulate economic activity. The result has often been too much money chasing too few goods, resulting in price inflation. As we saw in Chapter 9, price inflation is reflected in a drop in the value of a country's currency on the foreign exchange market. This can be a serious problem for a foreign firm with assets in that country because the value of the cash flows it receives from those assets will fall as the country's currency depreciates on the foreign exchange market. The likelihood of this occurring decreases the attractiveness of foreign investment in that country.

There have been many attempts to quantify countries' economic risk and long-term movements in their exchange rates. *Euromoney's* annual country risk rating (Table 20.1) incorporates an assessment of economic risk in its calculation of each country's overall level of risk. As we saw in Chapter 9, there have been extensive empirical studies of the relationship between countries' inflation rates and their currencies' exchange rates. These studies show that there is a long-run relationship between a country's relative inflation rates and changes in exchange rates. However, the relationship is not as close as theory would predict; it is not reliable in the short run and is not totally reliable in the long run. So, as with political risk, any attempts to quantify economic risk must be tempered with some healthy skepticism.

Risk and Capital Budgeting

In analyzing a foreign investment opportunity, the additional risk that stems from its location can be handled in at least two ways. The first method is to treat all risk as a single problem by increasing the discount rate applicable to foreign projects in countries where political and economic risks are perceived as high. Thus, for example, a

Rank													
Sep 98	Dec 97	Change Sept–Dec		Total score	Political risk	Economic performance	Debt indicators	Debt in default or rescheduled	Credit ratings	Access to bank finance	Access to short-term finance	Access to capital markets	Discount on forfeiting
			Weighting:	100	25	25	10	10	10	5	5	5	5
1	2	1	Luxembourg	98.90	24.76	25.00	10.00	10.00	10.00	5.00	5.00	5.00	4.14
2	1	–1	United States	97.85	24.97	22.88	10.00	10.00	10.00	5.00	5.00	5.00	5.00
3	6	3	Germany	97.06	24.89	22.21	10.00	10.00	10.00	5.00	5.00	5.00	4.96
4	3	–1	Netherlands	96.92	24.84	22.57	10.00	10.00	10.00	5.00	5.00	5.00	4.50
5	10	5	Austria	96.79	24.19	22.65	10.00	10.00	10.00	5.00	5.00	5.00	4.95
6	7	1	Switzerland	96.43	25.00	21.45	10.00	10.00	10.00	5.00	5.00	5.00	4.99
7	11	4	France	95.87	24.22	21.69	10.00	10.00	10.00	5.00	5.00	5.00	4.96
8	4	–4	Norway	95.83	22.91	23.03	10.00	10.00	10.00	5.00	5.00	5.00	4.89
9	5	–4	United Kingdom	95.01	25.00	20.04	10.00	10.00	10.00	5.00	5.00	5.00	4.97
10	12	2	Ireland	94.87	23.02	22.61	10.00	10.00	9.57	5.00	5.00	5.00	4.66
11	9	–2	Denmark	94.67	23.74	21.91	10.00	10.00	9.36	5.00	5.00	5.00	4.66
12	13	1	Finland	94.52	22.54	22.47	10.00	10.00	9.57	5.00	5.00	5.00	4.93
13	14	1	Belgium	94.25	23.72	21.01	10.00	10.00	9.57	5.00	5.00	5.00	4.95
14	15	1	Sweden	93.39	23.25	21.49	10.00	10.00	8.72	5.00	5.00	5.00	4.93
15	8	–7	Canada	93.02	22.98	21.21	10.00	10.00	8.94	5.00	5.00	5.00	4.89
16	19	3	Spain	92.01	22.24	21.33	10.00	10.00	9.15	5.00	4.64	5.00	4.64
17	20	3	New Zealand	91.34	22.23	19.86	10.00	10.00	9.36	5.00	5.00	5.00	4.89
18	22	4	Italy	91.10	21.66	20.57	10.00	10.00	8.94	5.00	5.00	5.00	4.93
19	17	–2	Australia	90.91	22.60	20.51	10.00	10.00	8.72	5.00	5.00	5.00	4.07
20	21	1	Portugal	90.73	21.76	21.34	10.00	10.00	8.94	5.00	4.64	5.00	4.04
21	16	–5	Singapore	89.17	23.29	19.24	10.00	10.00	9.68	5.00	4.64	4.30	3.02
22	24	2	Iceland	89.03	21.38	21.17	10.00	10.00	7.77	5.00	4.64	5.00	4.07
23	18	–5	Japan	88.02	23.39	15.85	10.00	10.00	10.00	5.00	5.00	5.00	3.79
24	23	–1	Taiwan	86.49	22.28	19.52	10.00	10.00	8.72	5.00	4.64	3.30	3.02
25	26	1	Cyprus	81.92	18.69	18.22	10.00	10.00	7.45	5.00	4.64	5.00	2.92
26	47	21	Malta	81.75	19.84	21.94	10.00	10.00	6.81	5.00	4.64	0.00	3.52
27	32	5	Greece	79.61	18.03	18.01	10.00	10.00	4.89	5.00	4.64	5.00	4.04
28	27	–1	United Arab Emirates	79.38	19.20	17.51	10.00	10.00	6.81	5.00	4.02	3.30	3.54
29	28	–1	Kuwait	77.70	18.34	17.50	10.00	10.00	6.38	5.00	4.40	2.72	3.36
30	31	1	Chile	76.60	18.56	17.29	8.63	10.00	5.96	5.00	3.75	3.40	4.02
31	33	2	Israel	76.06	17.22	15.96	10.00	10.00	6.17	5.00	4.35	3.77	3.59
32	25	–7	Hong Kong	75.75	19.32	16.20	10.00	10.00	7.02	5.00	5.00	3.21	0.00
33	37	4	Slovenia	74.49	17.56	17.34	9.57	10.00	6.38	3.04	3.45	3.58	3.56
34	34	0	Saudi Arabia	73.68	17.43	15.20	10.00	10.00	4.26	5.00	4.64	3.68	3.47
35	41	6	Qatar	72.68	16.77	14.53	10.00	10.00	4.89	5.00	4.64	3.30	3.54
36	42	6	Bahrain	71.97	15.77	16.52	10.00	10.00	3.62	5.00	4.64	3.06	3.36
37	43	6	Oman	71.47	16.74	14.23	10.00	10.00	4.57	5.00	4.64	3.11	3.18
38	48	10	Poland	71.11	17.60	18.45	9.50	10.00	4.47	0.22	3.21	3.87	3.79
39	45	6	Hungary	71.06	17.16	17.84	8.02	10.00	4.68	3.58	2.44	4.06	3.29
40	44	4	Czech Republic	71.01	17.58	16.99	9.34	10.00	5.96	1.14	3.15	3.96	2.88
41	39	–2	China	67.26	17.08	16.32	9.65	10.00	5.96	0.01	2.68	2.83	2.74
42	30	–12	South Korea	64.47	15.11	14.06	10.00	10.00	3.62	5.00	3.87	2.26	0.55
43	52	9	Tunisia	63.43	15.43	15.16	8.86	10.00	4.26	0.10	3.45	3.02	3.15
44	58	14	Uruguay	62.88	13.06	17.42	9.19	10.00	4.26	0.05	3.33	2.74	2.83
45	56	11	Colombia	62.85	13.31	13.68	8.59	10.00	4.26	3.09	3.51	3.11	3.29
46	99	53	Trinidad & Tobago	61.99	17.74	16.52	9.02	10.00	3.62	0.00	3.21	1.89	0.00
47	50	3	Mexico	61.75	14.25	15.16	8.38	10.00	2.98	1.69	3.48	3.30	2.51
48	54	6	Argentina	61.33	13.73	15.58	8.36	10.00	2.77	1.05	4.17	3.40	2.29
49	62	13	Egypt	61.22	14.83	15.01	9.12	9.93	4.04	0.00	2.50	2.64	3.15
50	46	–4	South Africa	61.09	14.96	13.26	9.53	10.00	3.62	0.07	3.51	3.40	2.74
51	60	9	Estonia	61.08	13.52	15.88	9.95	10.00	5.32	0.00	2.01	2.49	1.92
52	63	11	Botswana	59.85	15.90	19.05	9.81	10.00	0.00	0.00	3.51	1.58	0.00
53	35	–18	Malaysia	59.70	15.25	12.47	9.28	10.00	4.47	3.22	3.51	1.51	0.00
54	51	–3	Thailand	59.24	14.00	12.26	9.05	10.00	3.83	4.23	2.98	2.26	0.64

Table 20.1

Euromoney Magazine's Country Risk Ratings

Rank													
Sep 98	Dec 97	Change Sept–Dec		Total score	Political risk	Economic performance	Debt indicators	Debt in default or rescheduled	Credit ratings	Access to bank finance	Access to short-term finance	Access to capital markets	Discount on forfeiting
			Weighting:	100	25	25	10	10	10	5	5	5	5
55	57	2	Philippines	58.42	13.69	14.54	9.04	10.00	3.62	1.30	3.33	2.17	0.73
56	69	13	Morocco	57.90	13.10	14.04	8.42	10.00	3.30	0.12	3.10	2.94	2.88
57	64	7	Latvia	57.65	12.65	13.99	9.92	10.00	4.89	0.00	2.01	2.26	1.92
58	61	3	Slovak Republic	57.35	13.11	13.08	9.17	10.00	4.04	1.66	2.22	2.60	1.46
59	53	–6	India	57.11	14.46	13.86	9.05	10.00	3.30	0.14	1.67	2.17	2.47
60	68	8	Costa Rica	56.28	13.48	16.94	9.16	10.00	2.98	0.00	3.15	0.57	0.00
61	59	–2	Turkey	56.22	13.48	13.72	8.86	10.00	1.49	1.35	3.21	2.64	1.46
62	70	8	Lithuania	56.20	11.60	14.21	9.79	10.00	3.83	0.30	2.01	2.55	1.92
63	66	3	Jordan	55.15	12.89	15.21	8.09	9.33	2.34	0.00	1.79	2.45	3.04
64	114	50	Dominican Republic	54.80	16.82	14.34	9.30	9.93	1.70	0.00	2.32	0.38	0.00
65	86	21	Jamaica	54.38	16.36	12.56	8.22	10.00	2.34	0.00	2.92	1.98	0.00
66	72	6	Croatia	54.29	11.97	13.65	9.61	5.59	4.26	1.87	1.64	2.83	2.88
67	65	–2	El Salvador	53.03	10.95	14.53	9.45	10.00	3.62	0.00	3.21	1.27	0.00
68	73	5	Lebanon	53.01	11.13	10.65	9.47	10.00	2.13	1.73	1.06	2.02	3.02
69	36	–33	Brunei	52.79	20.55	0.00	10.00	10.00	0.00	5.00	4.40	2.83	0.00
70	67	–3	Brazil	52.56	11.69	12.92	8.57	9.98	1.91	1.70	1.55	2.83	1.42
71	55	–16	Panama	51.40	12.56	16.44	8.55	3.35	4.26	0.59	3.48	2.17	0.00
72	75	3	Peru	50.43	10.89	14.51	8.37	7.25	2.66	0.16	2.62	2.04	1.92
73	76	3	Guatemala	49.37	9.31	13.97	9.45	10.00	2.98	0.00	3.10	0.57	0.00
74	131	57	St. Lucia	48.04	18.78	6.59	9.67	10.00	0.00	0.00	2.62	0.38	0.00
75	81	6	Paraguay	47.83	10.10	13.03	9.64	10.00	1.70	0.07	2.92	0.38	0.00
76	71	–5	Venezuela	47.33	9.83	11.66	8.87	10.00	1.91	0.39	2.86	1.81	0.00
77	38	–39	Mauritius	47.32	15.44	0.00	9.30	10.00	4.89	0.27	3.51	1.98	1.92
78	84	6	Bolivia	47.16	11.26	12.88	8.03	8.83	2.02	0.91	2.08	1.13	0.00
79	87	8	Papua New Guinea	47.15	10.48	12.22	9.05	10.00	0.00	2.16	2.86	0.38	0.00
80	80	0	Fiji	46.91	11.32	13.10	9.87	10.00	0.00	0.00	2.62	0.00	0.00
81	82	1	Kazakhstan	46.73	7.50	12.02	9.64	10.00	2.55	1.66	1.56	1.79	0.00
82	74	–8	Romania	46.25	10.27	9.60	9.41	10.00	2.13	0.05	1.98	1.36	1.46
83	83	0	Sri Lanka	45.65	10.53	12.64	9.06	10.00	0.00	0.00	2.38	1.04	0.00
84	40	–44	Bahamas	44.89	19.02	12.79	0.00	0.00	6.17	0.00	4.64	2.26	0.00
85	79	–6	Ghana	44.87	10.61	11.18	7.89	9.86	0.00	2.57	2.38	0.38	0.00
86	100	14	Ecuador	44.84	8.13	12.35	8.27	9.97	1.70	0.00	2.92	1.51	0.00
87	77	–10	Vietnam	43.97	10.11	11.04	8.33	9.91	1.70	0.00	1.96	0.91	0.00
88	49	–39	Indonesia	43.56	8.89	8.49	8.18	10.00	0.21	3.97	2.50	1.32	0.00
89	110	21	Iran	43.26	10.74	9.66	9.92	10.00	0.00	0.00	1.16	0.23	1.55
90	95	5	Zimbabwe	43.22	9.40	9.81	8.50	10.00	0.00	1.25	3.21	1.04	0.00
91	90	–1	Uganda	43.00	7.85	14.09	8.65	10.00	0.00	0.00	2.02	0.38	0.00
92	97	5	Côte d'Ivoire	42.71	8.73	11.37	6.41	9.78	0.00	2.61	2.68	1.13	0.00
93	101	8	Bulgaria	42.30	9.40	10.30	7.95	9.98	1.38	0.43	1.55	1.32	0.00
94	98	4	Gabon	42.26	8.66	13.72	8.53	8.47	0.00	0.00	2.50	0.38	0.00
95	106	11	Senegal	42.24	7.74	13.31	8.60	9.78	0.00	0.00	2.44	0.38	0.00
96	93	3	Bangladesh	41.45	8.24	11.55	9.04	10.00	0.00	0.00	2.38	0.23	0.00
97	89	–8	Barbados	41.43	16.21	6.90	0.00	10.00	3.62	0.00	3.57	1.13	0.00
98	96	–2	Kenya	40.97	8.96	10.47	8.20	10.00	0.00	0.00	2.32	1.02	0.00
99	103	4	Syria	40.58	9.43	9.23	8.11	10.00	0.00	0.00	1.25	0.28	2.29
100	108	8	Mali	40.47	7.96	11.94	7.91	9.91	0.00	0.00	2.38	0.38	0.00
101	158	57	Guyana	40.44	13.24	11.24	6.53	7.62	0.00	0.00	1.43	0.38	0.00
102	136	34	Honduras	40.32	8.37	10.86	7.66	9.79	0.00	1.06	2.20	0.38	0.00
103	111	8	Algeria	39.64	9.38	10.25	8.20	8.47	0.00	0.00	1.96	1.02	0.37
104	143	39	St. Vincent & Grenadines	39.41	17.47	0.00	8.71	10.00	0.00	0.00	2.86	0.38	0.00
105	92	–13	Uzbekistan	39.03	5.55	10.62	9.75	10.00	0.00	0.00	1.55	1.56	0.00
106	91	–15	Nepal	38.80	9.61	6.90	9.11	10.00	0.00	0.00	2.80	0.38	0.00
107	102	–5	Yemen	38.73	8.30	10.19	8.30	10.00	0.00	0.00	1.56	0.38	0.00

(continued)

Table 20.1

(continued)

Rank													
Sep 98	Dec 97	Change Sept–Dec		Total score	Political risk	Economic performance	Debt indicators	Debt in default or rescheduled	Credit ratings	Access to bank finance	Access to short-term finance	Access to capital markets	Discount on forfeiting
			Weighting:	100	25	25	10	10	10	5	5	5	5
108	161	53	Haiti	38.16	7.39	10.16	9.22	9.97	0.00	0.00	1.43	0.00	0.00
109	162	53	Grenada	37.76	15.25	0.00	9.52	10.00	0.00	0.00	2.62	0.38	0.00
110	146	36	Dominica	37.75	15.51	0.00	9.24	10.00	0.00	0.00	2.62	0.38	0.00
111	148	37	Mongolia	37.71	7.09	10.31	9.04	10.00	0.00	0.00	0.89	0.38	0.00
112	105	−7	Burkina Faso	37.71	5.99	10.70	9.07	9.52	0.00	0.00	2.14	0.28	0.00
113	137	24	Ethiopia	37.51	5.42	13.88	6.40	10.00	0.00	0.00	1.43	0.38	0.00
114	29	−85	Bermuda	37.38	21.53	0.00	0.00	0.00	8.94	0.00	4.64	2.26	0.00
115	112	−3	Benin	37.33	3.77	13.41	8.86	8.88	0.00	0.00	2.02	0.38	0.00
116	142	26	Azerbaijan	37.28	5.00	10.43	9.89	10.00	0.00	0.00	0.89	1.06	0.00
117	128	11	Madagascar	36.83	8.04	9.02	8.32	10.00	0.00	0.00	1.07	0.38	0.00

Euromoney Risk Assessment	_Euromoney's_ assessment of country risk uses three categories. These are analytical indicators, 40%; credit indicators, 20%; and market indicators, 40%. These offer a broad but sensitive evaluation of the relative risks faced by exposure in these countries.
Analytical Indicators	This 40% is made up of political risk, 20%; economic risk, 10%; and economic indicators, 10%. Political risk is a measure of stability and the potential fallout from any instability. The economic indicators consist of three key ratios: the debt-service-to-export ratio as a measure of liquidity, and balance-of-payments-to-GNP and external-debt-to-GNP as measures of solvency. As these are historical, the prospective view of economic performance to 1993 is used to gauge economic risk.
Credit Indicators	This 20% is made up of payment record, 15%, and ease of rescheduling, 5%. Ease of rescheduling indicates a country's general creditworthiness in the face of temporary liquidity problems.
Market Indicators	This 40% consists of access to bond markets (FRN, straight, and Yankee), 15%; availability of short-term finance, 10%; and access to and discount available on forfeiting, 15%. Bond market access is fine-tuned by considering access to syndicated loans, credit ratings, and secondary market spreads. The attitudes of the market to countries will incorporate analytical and credit indicators, but its favor can be crucial to sustaining a country's economy as well as maintaining liquidity for its sovereign debt in the secondary markets.

Source: _Euromoney_, December 1998.

Table 20.1

(concluded)

firm might apply a 6 percent discount rate to potential investments in Great Britain, the United States, and Germany, reflecting those countries' economic and political stability, and it might use a 20 percent discount rate for potential investments in Russia, reflecting the political and economic turmoil in that country. The higher the discount rate, the higher the projected net cash flows must be for an investment to have a positive net present value.

Adjusting discount rates to reflect a location's riskiness seems to be fairly widely practiced. For example, a study of large US multinationals found that 49 percent of them routinely added a premium percentage for risk to the discount rate they used in evaluating potential foreign investment projects.[4] However, critics of this method argue that it penalizes early cash flows too heavily and does not penalize distant cash flows enough.[5] They point out that if political or economic collapse were expected in the near future, the investment would not occur anyway. (This is borne out today in the case of Russia; Western companies are not investing there because they perceive the imminent danger of political and economic collapse.) So for any investment decisions, the political and economic risk being assessed is not of immediate possibilities, but rather at some distance in the future. Accordingly, it can be argued that rather than using a higher discount rate to evaluate such risky projects, which penalizes early cash flows too heavily, it is better to revise future cash flows from the project downward to reflect the possibility of adverse political or economic changes sometime in the future. Surveys of actual practice within multinationals suggest that the practice of revising future cash flows downward is almost as popular as that of revising the discount rate upward.[6]

Financing Decisions

When considering its options for financing a foreign investment, an international business must consider two factors. The first is how the foreign investment will be financed. If external financing is required, the firm must decide whether to borrow from sources in the host country or elsewhere. The second factor is how the financial structure of the foreign affiliate should be configured.

Source of Financing

If the firm is going to seek external financing for a project, it will want to borrow funds from the lowest-cost source of capital available. As we saw in Chapter 11, firms increasingly are turning to the global capital market to finance their investments. The cost of capital is typically lower in the global capital market, by virtue of its size and liquidity, than in many domestic capital markets, particularly those that are small and relatively illiquid. Thus, for example, a US firm making an investment in Denmark may finance the investment by borrowing through the London-based eurobond market rather than the Danish capital market.

However, host-country government restrictions may rule out this option. The governments of many countries require, or at least prefer, foreign multinationals to finance projects in their country by local debt financing or local sales of equity. In countries where liquidity is limited, this raises the cost of capital used to finance a project. Thus, in capital budgeting decisions, the discount rate must be adjusted upward to reflect this. However, this is not the only possibility. In Chapter 8, we saw that some governments court foreign investment by offering foreign firms low-interest loans, lowering the cost of capital. Accordingly, in capital budgeting decisions, the discount rate should be revised downward in such cases.

In addition to the impact of host-government policies on the cost of capital and financing decisions, the firm may wish to consider local debt financing for investments in countries where the local currency is expected to depreciate on the foreign exchange market. The amount of local currency required to meet interest payments and retire principal on local debt obligations is not affected when a country's currency depreciates. However, if foreign debt obligations must be served, the amount of local currency required to do this will increase as the currency depreciates, and this effectively raises the cost of capital. (We looked at this issue in Chapter 11 when we considered foreign exchange risk and the cost of capital.) Thus, although the initial cost of capital may be greater with local borrowing, it may be better to borrow locally if the local currency is expected to depreciate on the foreign exchange market.

Financial Structure

There is a quite striking difference in the financial structures of firms based in different countries. By financial structure we mean the mix of debt and equity used to finance a business. It is well known, for example, that Japanese firms rely far more on debt financing than do most US firms. Table 20.2 reproduces the results of a study comparing debt ratios for 677 firms in nine industries in 23 countries.[7] As can be seen, there is wide variation in the average debt ratios of firms based in different countries. The average debt ratio of firms based in Italy, for example, is more than double that of firms based in Singapore.

	Alcoholic Beverages	Auto-mobiles	Chemicals	Electrical	Foods	Iron & Steel	Nonferrous Metals	Paper	Textiles	Country Mean
Singapore		.22		.57	.28	.28	.38			.34
Malaysia	.20	.60	.41		.30	.38	.30	.77	.69	.37
Argentina		.42		.44	.35	.32				.38
Australia	.29	.50	.52	.51	.45	.53	.34	.48	.54	.46
Chile			.33	.28	.70	.48	.50	.47		.46
Mexico	.18		.47	.57	.59	.53	.47	.47		.47
South Africa	.59	.50	.51		.46	.53	.32	.42	.69	.50
Brazil		.66	.48	.53	.57	.61		.37		.54
United Kingdom	.45	.73	.50	.60	.55	.51	.57	.56	.52	.55
United States	.51	.58	.55	.54	.56	.54	58	.58	.50	.55
Benelux	.41	.62	.60	.51	.64	.61	.49	.65	.54	.56
Canada	.55		.45	.52		.69	.61	.68		.58
India	.08	.75	.55			.49	.69	.74	.48	.60
Switzerland				.63	.54	.64				.60
Germany		.57	.56	.66	.49	.60	.70	.70	.65	.62
Denmark	.66		.47	.74	.69	.52	.61	.74		.63
Spain		.59	.64	.45	.66	.82	.70	.85	.43	.64
Sweden	.79	.75	.67	.67	.63	.67	.64	.61	.60	.68
France	.56	.67	.72	.72	.78	.73	.67	.74	.74	.71
Finland	.40	.82	.71	.73	.77	.73	.72	.76	.82	.72
Pakistan		.87	.87				.72	.66	.70	.72
Norway			.76	.67	.79	.62		.82	.75	.74
Italy		.49	.65	.79	.85	.87	.86	.77	.83	.76
Industry mean	.49	.58	.56	.59	.62	.61	.58	.63	.70	

Note: Debt ratio is defined as total debt divided by total assets at book value.

Source: W. S. Sekely and J. M. Collins, "Cultural Influences on International Capital Structure," *Journal of International Business Studies* 19 (1988), p. 91.

Table 20.2

Debt Ratios for Selected Industrial Countries

It is not clear why the financial structure of firms should vary so much across countries. One possible explanation is that different tax regimes determine the relative attractiveness of debt and equity in a country. For example, if dividends are taxed highly, a preference for debt financing over equity financing would be expected. However, according to recent empirical research, country differences in financial structure do not seem related in any systematic way to country differences in tax structure.[8] Another possibility is that these country differences may reflect cultural norms.[9] This explanation may be valid, although the mechanism by which culture influences capital structure has not yet been explained.

The interesting question for the international business is whether it should conform to local capital structure norms. Should a US firm investing in Italy adopt the higher debt ratio typical of Italian firms for its Italian subsidiary, or should it stick with its more conservative practice? There are few good arguments for conforming to local norms. One advantage claimed for conforming to host-country debt norms is that management can more easily evaluate its return on equity relative to local competitors in the same industry. However, this seems a weak rationale for what is an important decision. Another point often made is that conforming to higher host-country debt norms can improve the image of foreign affiliates that have been operating with too little debt and thus appear insensitive to local monetary policy. Just how important this point is, however, has not been established. The best recommendation is that an international business should adopt a financial structure for each foreign affiliate that minimizes its cost of capital, irrespective of whether that structure is consistent with local practice.

Global Money Management: The Efficiency Objective

Money management decisions attempt to manage the firm's global cash resources—its working capital—most efficiently. This involves minimizing cash balances and reducing transaction costs.

Minimizing Cash Balances

For any given period, a firm must hold certain cash balances. This is necessary for serving any accounts and notes payable during that period and as a contingency against unexpected demands on cash. The firm does not sit on its cash reserves. It typically invests them in money market accounts so it can earn interest on them. However, it must be able to withdraw its money from those accounts freely. Such accounts typically offer a relatively low rate of interest. In contrast, the firm could earn a higher rate of interest if it could invest its cash resources in longer-term financial instruments (e.g., six-month certificates of deposit). The problem with longer-term instruments, however, is that the firm cannot withdraw its money before the instruments mature without suffering a financial penalty.

Thus, the firm faces a dilemma. If it invests its cash balances in money market accounts (or the equivalent), it will have unlimited liquidity but earn a relatively low rate of interest. If it invests its cash in longer-term financial instruments (certificates of deposit, bonds, etc.), it will earn a higher rate of interest, but liquidity will be limited. In an ideal world, the firm would have minimal liquid cash balances. We will see later in the chapter that by managing its total global cash reserves through a centralized depository (as opposed to letting each affiliate manage its own cash reserves), an international business can reduce the amount of funds it must hold in liquid accounts and thereby increase its rate of return on its cash reserves.

Reducing Transaction Costs

Transaction costs are the cost of exchange. Every time a firm changes cash from one currency into another currency it must bear a transaction cost—the commission fee it pays to foreign exchange dealers for performing the transaction. Most banks also charge a **transfer fee** for moving cash from one location to another; this is another transaction cost. The commission and transfer fees arising from intrafirm transactions can be substantial; according to the United Nations, 40 percent of international trade involves transactions between the different national subsidiaries of transnational corporations. As we will see later in the chapter, multilateral netting can reduce the number of transactions between the firm's subsidiaries, thereby reducing the total transactions costs arising from foreign exchange dealings and transfer fees.

Global Money Management: The Tax Objective

Different countries have different tax regimes. Table 20.3 illustrates top corporate income tax rates for countries that are members of the Organization of Economic Cooperation and Development (OECD).[10] The top tax rate varies from a high near 60 percent in Germany to a low of 25 percent in Finland. The picture is much more complex than the one presented in Table 20.3. For example, in Germany and Japan, the tax rate is lower on income distributed to stockholders as dividends (36 and 35 percent, respectively), whereas in France the tax on profits distributed to stockholders is higher (42 percent).

Table 20.3

OECD Corporate Income
Tax Rates

Country	Top Tax Rate (%)
Australia	33
Austria	34
Belgium	40.17
Canada	44.3
Denmark	34
Finland	25
France	33.33
Germany	58.95/46.13
Greece	40
Iceland	33
Ireland	40
Italy	52.2
Japan	51.6
Luxembourg	40.29
Mexico	34
Netherlands	35
New Zealand	33
Norway	28
Portugal	39.6
Spain	35
Sweden	28
Switzerland	28.5
Turkey	42.8
United Kingdom	33
United States	40

Source: Organization of Economic Cooperation and Development.

Many nations follow the worldwide principle that they have the right to tax income earned outside their boundaries by entities based in their country.[11] Thus, the US government can tax the earnings of the German subsidiary of an enterprise incorporated in the United States. Double taxation occurs when the income of a foreign subsidiary is taxed both by the host-country government and by the parent company's home government. However, double taxation is mitigated to some extent by tax credits, tax treaties, and the deferral principle.

A **tax credit** allows an entity to reduce the taxes paid to the home government by the amount of taxes paid to the foreign government. A **tax treaty** between two countries is an agreement specifying what items of income will be taxed by the authorities of the country where the income is earned. For example, a tax treaty between the United States and Germany may specify that a US firm need not pay tax in Germany on any earnings from its German subsidiary that are remitted to the United States in the form of dividends. A **deferral principle** specifies that parent companies are not taxed on foreign source income until they actually receive a dividend.

For the international business with activities in many countries, the various tax regimes and the tax treaties have important implications for how the firm should structure its internal payments system among the foreign subsidiaries and the parent company. As we will see in the next section, the firm can use transfer prices and fronting loans to minimize its global tax liability. In addition, the form in which income is remitted from a foreign subsidiary to the parent company (e.g., royalty payments versus dividend payments) can be structured to minimize the firm's global tax liability.

Some firms use **tax havens** such as the Bahamas and Bermuda to minimize their tax liability. A tax haven is a country with an exceptionally low, or even no, income tax. International businesses avoid or defer income taxes by establishing a wholly owned, nonoperating subsidiary in the tax haven. The tax haven subsidiary owns the common stock of the operating foreign subsidiaries. This allows all transfers of funds from foreign operating subsidiaries to the parent company to be funneled through the tax haven subsidiary. The tax levied on foreign source income by a firm's home government, which might normally be paid when a dividend is declared by a foreign subsidiary, can be deferred under the deferral principle until the tax haven subsidiary pays the dividend to the parent. This dividend payment can be postponed indefinitely if foreign operations continue to grow and require new internal financing from the tax haven affiliate. For US-based enterprises, however, US regulations tax US shareholders on the firm's overseas income when it is earned, regardless of when the parent company in the United States receives it. This regulation eliminates US-based firms' ability to use tax haven subsidiaries to avoid tax liabilities in the manner just described.

Moving Money across Borders: Attaining Efficiencies and Reducing Taxes

Pursuing the objectives of utilizing the firm's cash resources most efficiently and minimizing the firm's global tax liability requires the firm to be able to transfer funds from one location to another around the globe. International businesses use a number of techniques to transfer liquid funds across borders. These include dividend remittances, royalty payments and fees, transfer prices, and fronting loans. Some firms rely on more than one of these techniques to transfer funds across borders—a practice known as **unbundling.** By using a mix of techniques to transfer liquid funds from a foreign subsidiary to the parent company, unbundling allows an international business to recover funds from its foreign subsidiaries without piquing host-country sensitivities with large "dividend drains."

A firm's ability to select a particular policy is severely limited when a foreign subsidiary is part-owned either by a local joint venture partner or by local stockholders. Serving the legitimate demands of the local co-owners of a foreign subsidiary may limit the firm's ability to impose the kind of dividend policy, royalty payment schedule, or transfer pricing policy that would be optimal for the parent company.

Dividend Remittances

Payment of dividends is probably the most common method by which firms transfer funds from foreign subsidiaries to the parent company. The dividend policy typically varies with each subsidiary depending on such factors as tax regulations, foreign exchange risk, the age of the subsidiary, and the extent of local equity participation. For example, the higher the rate of tax levied on dividends by the host-country government, the less attractive this option becomes relative to other options for transferring liquid funds. With regard to foreign exchange risk, firms sometimes require foreign subsidiaries based in "high-risk" countries to speed up the transfer of funds to the parent through accelerated dividend payments. This moves corporate funds out of a country whose currency is expected to depreciate significantly. The age of a foreign subsidiary influences dividend policy in that older subsidiaries tend to remit a higher proportion of their earnings in dividends to the parent, presumably because a subsidiary has fewer capital investment needs as it matures. Local equity participation is a factor because local co-owners' demands for dividends must be recognized.

Royalty Payments and Fees

Royalties represent the remuneration paid to the owners of technology, patents, or trade names for the use of that technology or the right to manufacture and/or sell products under those patents or trade names. It is common for a parent company to charge its foreign subsidiaries royalties for the technology, patents, or trade names it has transferred to them. Royalties may be levied as a fixed monetary amount per unit of the product the subsidiary sells or as a percentage of a subsidiary's gross revenues.

A fee is compensation for professional services or expertise supplied to a foreign subsidiary by the parent company or another subsidiary. Fees are sometimes differentiated into "management fees" for general expertise and advice and "technical assistance fees" for guidance in technical matters. Fees are usually levied as fixed charges for the particular services provided.

Royalties and fees have certain tax advantages over dividends, particularly when the corporate tax rate is higher in the host country than in the parent's home country. Royalties and fees are often tax-deductible locally (because they are viewed as an expense), so arranging for payment in royalties and fees will reduce the foreign subsidiary's tax liability. If the foreign subsidiary compensates the parent company by dividend payments, local income taxes must be paid before the dividend distribution, and withholding taxes must be paid on the dividend itself. Although the parent can often take a tax credit for the local withholding and income taxes it has paid, part of the benefit can be lost if the subsidiary's combined tax rate is higher than the parent's.

Transfer Prices

In any international business, there are normally a large number of transfers of goods and services between the parent company and foreign subsidiaries and between foreign subsidiaries. This is particularly likely in firms pursuing global and transnational strategies because these firms are likely to have dispersed their value creation activities to various "optimal" locations around the globe (see Chapter 12). As noted in Chapter 19, the price at which goods and services are transferred between entities within the firm is referred to as the **transfer price.**[12]

Transfer prices can be used to position funds within an international business. For example, funds can be moved out of a particular country by setting high transfer prices for goods and services supplied to a subsidiary in that country and by setting low transfer prices for the goods and services sourced from that subsidiary. Conversely, funds can be positioned in a country by the opposite policy: setting low transfer prices for goods and services supplied to a subsidiary in that country and setting high transfer prices for the goods and services sourced from that subsidiary. This movement of funds can be between the firm's subsidiaries or between the parent company and a subsidiary.

Benefits of Manipulating Transfer Prices

At least four gains can be derived by manipulating transfer prices.

1. The firm can reduce its tax liabilities by using transfer prices to shift earnings from a high-tax country to a low-tax one.
2. The firm can use transfer prices to move funds out of a country where a significant currency devaluation is expected, thereby reducing its exposure to foreign exchange risk.
3. The firm can use transfer prices to move funds from a subsidiary to the parent company (or a tax haven) when financial transfers in the form of dividends are restricted or blocked by host-country government policies.

4. The firm can use transfer prices to reduce the import duties it must pay when an ad valorem tariff is in force—a tariff assessed as a percentage of value. In this case, low transfer prices on goods or services being imported into the country are required. Since this lowers the value of the goods or services, it lowers the tariff.

Problems with Transfer Pricing

Significant problems are associated with pursuing a transfer pricing policy. Few governments like it.[13] When transfer prices are used to reduce a firm's tax liabilities or import duties, most governments feel they are being cheated of their legitimate income. Similarly, when transfer prices are manipulated to circumvent government restrictions on capital flows (e.g., dividend remittances), governments perceive this as breaking the spirit—if not the letter—of the law. A number of governments limit international businesses' ability to manipulate transfer prices in the manner described. The United States has strict regulations governing transfer pricing practices. According to Section 482 of the Internal Revenue Code, the Internal Revenue Service (IRS) can reallocate gross income, deductions, credits, or allowances between related corporations to prevent tax evasion or to reflect more clearly a proper allocation of income. Under the IRS guidelines and subsequent judicial interpretation, the burden of proof is on the taxpayer to show that the IRS has been arbitrary or unreasonable in reallocating income. The correct transfer price, according to the IRS guidelines, is an arm's-length price—the price that would prevail between unrelated firms in a market setting. Such a strict interpretation of what is a correct transfer price theoretically limits a firm's ability to manipulate transfer prices to achieve the benefits we have discussed. In reality, however, transfer pricing is still widely practiced, as indicated in the accompanying Management Focus which looks at transfer pricing in the United States and Japan.

Another problem associated with transfer pricing is related to management incentives and performance evaluation.[14] Transfer pricing is inconsistent with a policy of treating each subsidiary in the firm as a profit center. When transfer prices are manipulated by the firm and deviate significantly from the arm's-length price, the subsidiary's performance may depend as much on transfer prices as it does on other pertinent factors, such as management effort. A subsidiary told to charge a high transfer price for a good supplied to another subsidiary will appear to be doing better than it actually is, while the subsidiary purchasing the good will appear to be doing worse. Unless this is recognized when performance is being evaluated, serious distortions in management incentive systems can occur. For example, managers in the selling subsidiary may be able to use high transfer prices to mask inefficiencies, while managers in the purchasing subsidiary may become disheartened by the effect of high transfer prices on their subsidiary's profitability.

Despite these problems, research suggests that many international businesses do not use arm's-length pricing but instead use some cost-based system for pricing transfers among their subunits (typically cost plus some standard markup). A survey of 164 US multinational firms found that 35 percent of the firms used market-based prices, 15 percent used negotiated prices, and 65 percent used a cost-based pricing method. (The figures add up to more than 100 percent because some companies use more than one method.)[15] Only market and negotiated prices could reasonably be interpreted as arm's-length prices. The opportunity for price manipulation is much greater with cost-based transfer pricing.

Although a firm may be able to manipulate transfer prices to avoid tax liabilities or circumvent government restrictions on capital flows across borders, this does not mean the firm should do so. Since the practice often violates at least the spirit of the law in many countries, the ethics of engaging in transfer pricing are dubious at best.

MANAGEMENT FOCUS
Transfer Pricing in the United States and Japan

http://www.toshiba.com

According to testimony given at hearings held by the US House Ways and Means Oversight subcommittee in July 1990, foreign-based multinationals, through elaborate transfer pricing schemes, underpaid the US government by as much as $35 billion during the 1980s. Japanese companies were cited as the principal offenders, followed by German, Canadian, and British companies. Toyota, Toshiba, Sony, Mitsubishi, Fuji Bank, and Siemens AG were among the foreign multinationals cited for abusing the US tax code. Yamaha, the Japanese motorcycle manufacturer, for example, paid just $123 in US taxes one year, and the IRS claimed it should have paid more than $27 million!

One scheme foreign-based multinationals were using to pay little or no taxes was charging US subsidiaries for inflated or nonexisting freight, insurance, interest, and other expenses. In one example, a Japanese multinational was accused of double-billing its US subsidiary for insurance on motorcycle inventory. In another case, US officials testified that a foreign automaker charged its US subsidiary $15 interest per vehicle even though interest payments were not required under the distribution agreement. Foreign multinationals argued that they have done nothing wrong.

As multinationals' use of transfer pricing has come under increasing scrutiny in the United States, other countries seem likely to scrutinize US multinationals more closely in response.

Japan started to hit back after 1992 at US multinationals doing business in that country, accusing several of manipulating transfer prices to avoid tax liabilities. Japan's high corporate tax rates make it a tempting target for firms trying to minimize their tax liability through transfer pricing. On average, firms pay about 50 percent of their yearly earnings to the government in Japan, compared to 41 percent in the United States and 33 percent in Britain. In the financial year ending June 1996, Japan's National Tax Administration filed claims against 50 foreign firms for alleged transfer pricing, demanding back taxes totaling ¥54.8 billion ($492 million). The agency filed only 80 transfer pricing claims during the previous eight years, totaling ¥140 billion.

Firms accused of manipulating transfer prices to reduce their tax liability in Japan often face a large bill. In 1994, Coca-Cola's Japanese unit announced it would contest a claim for back taxes amounting to some $140 million. The Japanese unit of Goodyear Tire & Rubber Co. was hit for roughly ¥600 million, and Japanese tax officials claimed ¥800 million from Procter & Gamble. In each case, the firms involved indicated they would contest the claims of the tax authorities in Japan.

Sources: E. Neumann, "Washington Escalates the Transfer Pricing War," *Business International Money Report*, July 23, 1990, p. 277–79; and R. Steiner, "Japan's Tax Man Leans on Foreign Firms," *The Wall Street Journal*, November 25, 1996, p. A15.

Fronting Loans

A **fronting loan** is a loan between a parent and its subsidiary channeled through a financial intermediary, usually a large international bank. In a direct intrafirm loan, the parent company lends cash directly to the foreign subsidiary, and the subsidiary repays it later. In a fronting loan, the parent company deposits funds in an international bank, and the bank then lends the same amount to the foreign subsidiary. Thus, a US firm might deposit $100,000 in a London bank. The London bank might then lend that $100,000 to an Indian subsidiary of the firm. From the bank's point of view, the loan is risk free because it has 100 percent collateral in the form of the parent's deposit. The bank "fronts" for the parent, hence the name. The bank makes a profit by paying the parent company a slightly lower interest rate on its deposit than it charges the foreign subsidiary on the borrowed funds.

Firms use fronting loans for two reasons. First, fronting loans can circumvent host-country restrictions on the remittance of funds from a foreign subsidiary to the parent company. A host government might restrict a foreign subsidiary from repaying a loan to its parent in order to preserve the country's foreign exchange reserves, but it is less

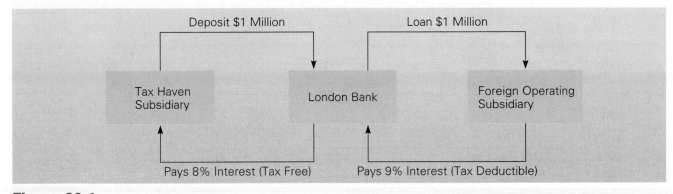

Figure 20.1

An Example of the Tax Aspects of a Fronting Loan

likely to restrict a subsidiary's ability to repay a loan to a large international bank. To stop payment to an international bank would hurt the country's credit image, whereas halting payment to the parent company would probably have a minimal impact on its image. Consequently, international businesses sometimes use fronting loans when they want to lend funds to a subsidiary based in a country with a fairly high probability of political turmoil that might lead to restrictions on capital flows (i.e., where the level of political risk is high).

A fronting loan can also provide tax advantages. For example, a tax haven (Bermuda) subsidiary that is 100 percent owned by the parent company deposits $1 million in a London-based international bank at 8 percent interest. The bank lends the $1 million to a foreign operating subsidiary at 9 percent interest. The country where the foreign operating subsidiary is based taxes corporate income at 50 percent (see Figure 20.1).

Under this arrangement, interest payments net of income tax will be as follows:

1. The foreign operating subsidiary pays $90,000 interest to the London bank. Deducting these interest payments from its taxable income results in a net after-tax cost of $45,000 to the foreign operating subsidiary.
2. The London bank receives the $90,000. It retains $10,000 for its services and pays $80,000 interest on the deposit to the Bermuda subsidiary.
3. The Bermuda subsidiary receives $80,000 interest on its deposit tax free.

The net result is that $80,000 in cash has been moved from the foreign operating subsidiary to the tax haven subsidiary. Because the foreign operating subsidiary's after-tax cost of borrowing is only $45,000, the parent company has moved an additional $35,000 out of the country by using this arrangement. If the tax haven subsidiary had made a direct loan to the foreign operating subsidiary, the host government may have disallowed the interest charge as a tax-deductible expense by ruling that it was a dividend to the parent disguised as an interest payment.

Techniques for Global Money Management

We now look at two money management techniques firms use in attempting to manage their global cash resources in the most efficient manner: centralized depositories and multilateral netting.

Centralized Depositories

Every business needs to hold some cash balances for servicing accounts that must be paid and for insuring against unanticipated negative variation from its projected cash flows. The critical issue for an international business is whether each foreign subsidiary should hold its own cash balances or whether cash balances should be held at a centralized depository. In general, firms prefer to hold cash balances at a centralized depository for three reasons.

First, by pooling cash reserves centrally, the firm can deposit larger amounts. Cash balances are typically deposited in liquid accounts, such as overnight money market accounts. Because interest rates on such deposits normally increase with the size of the deposit, by pooling cash centrally, the firm should be able to earn a higher interest rate than it would if each subsidiary managed its own cash balances.

Second, if the centralized depository is located in a major financial center (e.g., London, New York, or Tokyo), it should have access to information about good short-term investment opportunities that the typical foreign subsidiary would lack. Also, the financial experts at a centralized depository should be able to develop investment skills and know-how that managers in the typical foreign subsidiary would lack. Thus, the firm should make better investment decisions if it pools its cash reserves at a centralized depository.

Third, by pooling its cash reserves, the firm can reduce the total size of the cash pool it must hold in highly liquid accounts, which enables the firm to invest a larger amount of cash reserves in longer-term, less liquid financial instruments that earn a higher interest rate. For example, a US firm has three foreign subsidiaries—one in Spain, one in Italy, and one in Germany. Each subsidiary maintains a cash balance that includes an amount for dealing with its day-to-day needs plus a precautionary amount for dealing with unanticipated cash demands. The firm's policy is that the total required cash balance is equal to three standard deviations of the expected day-to-day-needs amount. The three-standard-deviation requirement reflects the firm's estimate that, in practice, there is a 99.87 percent probability that the subsidiary will have sufficient cash to deal with both day-to-day and unanticipated cash demands. Cash needs are assumed to be normally distributed in each country and independent of each other (e.g., cash needs in Germany do not affect cash needs in Italy).

The individual subsidiaries' day-to-day cash needs and the precautionary cash balances they should hold are as follows (in millions of dollars):

	Day-to-Day Cash Needs (A)	One Standard Deviation (B)	Required Cash Balance (A + 3 × B)
Spain	$10	$1	$13
Italy	6	2	12
Germany	12	3	21
Total	$28	$6	$46

Thus, the Spanish subsidiary estimates that it must hold $10 million to serve its day-to-day needs. The standard deviation of this is $1 million, so it is to hold an additional $3 million as a precautionary amount. This gives a total required cash balance of $13 million. The total of the required cash balances for all three subsidiaries is $46 million.

Now consider what might occur if the firm decided to maintain all three cash balances at a centralized depository in London. Because variances are additive when probability distributions are independent of each other, the standard deviation of the combined precautionary account would be:

$$\sqrt{(\$1,000,000^2 + 2,000,000^2 + 3,000,000^2)}$$
$$= \sqrt{14,000,000}$$
$$= \$3,741,657$$

Therefore, if the firm used a centralized depository, it would need to hold $28 million for day-to-day needs plus (3 × $3,741,657) as a precautionary amount, or a total cash balance of $39,224,972. In other words, the firm's total required cash balance would be reduced from $46 million to $39,224,972, a saving of $6,775,028. This is cash that could be invested in less liquid, higher-interest accounts or in tangible assets. The saving arises simply due to the statistical effects of summing the three independent, normal probability distributions.

However, a firm's ability to establish a centralized depository that can serve short-term cash needs might be limited by government-imposed restrictions on capital flows across borders (e.g., controls put in place to protect a country's foreign exchange reserves). Also, the transaction costs of moving money into and out of different currencies can limit the advantages of such a system. Despite this, many firms hold at least their subsidiaries' precautionary cash reserves at a centralized depository, having each subsidiary hold its own day-to-day-needs cash balance. The globalization of the world capital market and the general removal of barriers to the free flow of cash across borders (particularly among advanced industrialized countries) are two trends likely to increase the use of centralized depositories.

Multilateral Netting

Multilateral netting allows a multinational firm to reduce the transaction costs that arise when many transactions occur between its subsidiaries. These transaction costs are the commissions paid to foreign exchange dealers for foreign exchange transactions and the fees charged by banks for transferring cash between locations. The volume of such transactions is likely to be particularly high in a firm that has a globally dispersed web of interdependent value creation activities. Netting reduces transaction costs by reducing the number of transactions.

Multilateral netting is an extension of **bilateral netting.** Under bilateral netting, if a French subsidiary owes a Mexican subsidiary $6 million and the Mexican subsidiary simultaneously owes the French subsidiary $4 million, a bilateral settlement will be made with a single payment of $2 million from the French subsidiary to the Mexican subsidiary, the remaining debt being canceled.

Under **multilateral netting,** this simple concept is extended to the transactions between multiple subsidiaries within an international business. Consider a firm that wants to establish multilateral netting among four European subsidiaries based in Germany, France, Spain, and Italy. These subsidiaries all trade with each other, so at the end of each month a large volume of cash transactions must be settled. Figure 20.2a shows how the payment schedule might look at the end of a given month. Figure 20.2b is a payment matrix that summarizes the obligations among the subsidiaries.

Figure 20.2a

Cash Flows before Multilateral Netting

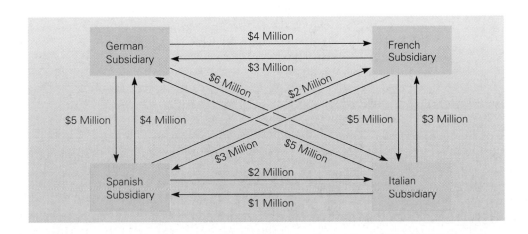

Receiving Subsidiary	Paying Subsidiary				Total Receipts	Net Receipts* (payments)
	Germany	**France**	**Spain**	**Italy**		
Germany	—	$ 3	$4	$5	$12	($3)
France	$ 4	—	2	3	9	(2)
Spain	5	3	—	1	9	1
Italy	6	5	2	—	13	4
Total payments	$15	$11	$8	$9		

*Net receipts = Total payments − Total receipts.

Figure 20.2b

Calculation of Net Receipts (all amounts in millions)

Figure 20.2c

Cash Flows after Multilateral Netting

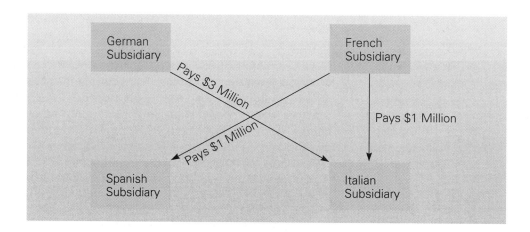

Note that $43 million needs to flow among the subsidiaries. If the transaction costs (foreign exchange commissions plus transfer fees) amount to 1 percent of the total funds to be transferred, this will cost the parent firm $430,000. However, this amount can be reduced by multilateral netting. Using the payment matrix (Figure 20.2b), the firm can determine the payments that need to be made among its subsidiaries to settle these obligations. Figure 20.2c shows the results. By multilateral netting, the transactions depicted in Figure 20.2a are reduced to just three; the German subsidiary pays $3 million to the Italian subsidiary, and the French subsidiary pays $1 million to the Spanish subsidiary and $1 million to the Italian subsidiary. The total funds that flow among the subsidiaries are reduced from $43 million to just $5 million, and the transaction costs are reduced from $430,000 to $50,000, a savings of $380,000 achieved through multilateral netting.

Managing Foreign Exchange Risk

The nature of foreign exchange risk was discussed in Chapter 9. There we described how changes in exchange rates alter the profitability of trade and investment deals, how forward exchange rates and currency swaps enable firms to insure themselves to some degree against foreign exchange risk, and how relative inflation rates determine exchange rate movements. In this section, we focus on the various strategies international businesses use to manage their foreign exchange risk. Buying forward, the strategy most discussed in Chapter 9, is just one of these. We will examine the types of foreign exchange exposure, the tactics and strategies firms adopt in attempting to minimize their exposure to foreign exchange risk, and things firms can do to develop policies for managing foreign exchange risk.

Types of Foreign Exchange Exposure

When we speak of **foreign exchange exposure,** we are referring to the risk that future changes in a country's exchange rate will hurt the firm. As we saw in Chapter 9, changes in foreign exchange values often affect the profitability of international trade and investment deals. Foreign exchange exposure is normally broken into three categories: transaction exposure, translation exposure, and economic exposure. Each is explained here.

Transaction Exposure

Transaction exposure is typically defined as the extent to which the income from individual transactions is affected by fluctuations in foreign exchange values. Such exposure includes obligations for the purchase or sale of goods and services at previously agreed prices and the borrowing or lending of funds in foreign currencies. Suppose a US company has just contracted to import laptop computers from Japan. When the shipment arrives in 30 days, the company must pay the Japanese supplier ¥200,000 for each computer. The dollar/yen spot exchange rate today is $1 = ¥120. At this rate, each laptop computer would cost the importer $1,667 (i.e., 200,000/120 = 1,667). The importer knows it can sell each computer for $2,000 on the day the shipment arrives, so as the exchange rate stands, the US company expects to make a gross profit of $333 on every computer it sells (2,000 − 1,667). If the dollar depreciates against the yen over the next 30 days, say to $1 = ¥95, the U.S. company will still have to pay the Japanese company ¥200,000 per computer, but in dollar terms that would be $2,105 per laptop computer—more than the computers could be sold for. A depreciation in the value of the dollar against the yen from $1 = ¥120 to $1 = ¥95 would transform this profitable transaction into an unprofitable one.

Translation Exposure

Translation exposure is the impact of currency exchange rate changes on the reported consolidated results and balance sheet of a company. This issue was discussed in Chapter 19 when we looked at currency translation practices. Translation exposure is basically concerned with the present measurement of past events. The resulting accounting gains or losses are said to be unrealized—they are "paper" gains and losses—but they are still important. Consider a US firm with a subsidiary in Mexico. If the value of the Mexican peso depreciates significantly against the dollar, as it did during the early 1990s, this would substantially reduce the dollar value of the Mexican subsidiary's equity. In turn, this would reduce the total dollar value of the firm's equity reported in its consolidated balance sheet. This would raise the apparent leverage of the firm (its debt ratio), which could increase the firm's cost of borrowing and restrict its access to the capital market. Thus, translation exposure can have a very negative impact on a firm.

Economic Exposure

Economic exposure is the extent to which a firm's future international earning power is affected by changes in exchange rates. Economic exposure is concerned with the long-run effect of changes in exchange rates on future prices, sales, and costs. This is distinct from transaction exposure, which is concerned with the effect of exchange rate changes on individual transactions, most of which are short-term affairs that will be executed within a few weeks or months. Consider the effect of the wide swings in the value of the dollar on many US firms' international competitiveness during the 1980s. The rapid rise in the value of the dollar on the foreign exchange market in the early 1980s hurt the price competitiveness of many US producers in world markets. US manufacturers that relied heavily on exports (such as Caterpillar) saw their export volume and world market share plunge. The reverse phenomenon has occurred since the mid-1980s, when the dollar has declined against most major currencies. The fall in the value of the dollar between 1985 and 1995 increased the price competitiveness of US manufacturers in world markets and helped produce an export boom in the United States.

Tactics and Strategies for Reducing Foreign Exchange Risk

A number of strategies and tactics can help firms reduce their foreign exchange exposure. The tactics, which include buying forward and the use of leading and lagging, are best suited to alleviating transaction exposure and translation exposure. The strategies addressing the configuration of a firm's assets across countries are best suited to reducing economic exposure.

Reducing Transaction and Translation Exposure

A number of tactics can help firms minimize their transaction and translation exposure. These tactics primarily protect short-term cash flows from adverse changes in exchange rates. We discussed two of these tactics in Chapter 9, buying forward and using currency swaps. They are important sources of insurance against the short-term effects of foreign exchange exposure. (For details, return to Chapter 9.)

In addition to buying forward and using swaps, firms can minimize their foreign exchange exposure through leading and lagging payables and receivables—that is, collecting and paying early or late depending on expected exchange rate movements. A **lead strategy** involves attempting to collect foreign currency receivables early when a foreign currency is expected to depreciate and paying foreign currency payables before they are due when a currency is expected to appreciate. A **lag strategy** involves delaying collection of foreign currency receivables if that currency is expected to appreciate and delaying payables if the currency is expected to depreciate. Leading and lagging involves accelerating payments from weak-currency to strong-currency countries and delaying inflows from strong-currency to weak-currency countries.

Lead and lag strategies can be difficult to implement, however. The firm must be in a position to exercise some control over payment terms. Firms do not always have this kind of bargaining power, particularly when they are dealing with important customers who are in a position to dictate payment terms. Also, because lead and lag strategies can put pressure on a weak currency, many governments limit leads and lags. For example, some countries set 180 days as a limit for receiving payments for exports or making payments for imports.

Several other tactics that can reduce transaction and translation exposure have already been discussed in this chapter. We have explained that:

- Transfer prices can be manipulated to move funds out of a country whose currency is expected to depreciate.
- Local debt financing can provide a hedge against foreign exchange risk.
- It may make sense to accelerate dividend payments from subsidiaries based in countries with weak currencies.
- Capital budgeting techniques can be adjusted to deflect the negative impact of adverse exchange rate movements on the current net value of a foreign investment.

Reducing Economic Exposure

Reducing economic exposure requires strategic choices that go beyond the realm of financial management. The key to reducing economic exposure is to distribute the firm's productive assets to various locations so the firm's long-term financial well-

MANAGEMENT FOCUS
http://www.blackanddecker.com

How Black & Decker Hedges against Economic Exposure

Black & Decker is one of the few multinationals actively managing its economic risk. The key to Black & Decker's strategy is flexible sourcing. In response to foreign exchange movements, Black & Decker can move production from one location to another to offer the most competitive pricing.

Black & Decker manufactures in more than a dozen locations around the world—in Europe, Australia, Brazil, Mexico, and Japan. More than 50 percent of the company's productive assets are based outside North America. Although each of Black & Decker's factories focuses on one or two products to achieve economies of scale, there is considerable overlap. On average, the company runs its factories at no more than 80 percent capacity, so most are able to switch rapidly from producing one product to producing another or to add a product. This allows a factory's production to be changed in response to foreign exchange movements. For example, as the dollar depreciated during the latter half of the 1980s,

the amount of imports into the United States from overseas subsidiaries was reduced, and the amount of exports from US subsidiaries to other locations was increased.

According to the company, the ability to move production in response to changes in foreign exchange movements is a source of competitive advantage. Black & Decker enjoys a much better long-term competitive position than one of its most significant competitors in the power tool business, Japan's Makita Electric Works, Ltd., because 90 percent of Makita's operations are located in Japan, and it exports heavily to the United States. Although Makita may benefit when the yen is depreciating, its margins are vulnerable during periods of yen strength. Black & Decker, in contrast, is not so vulnerable to appreciations in the value of the dollar.

Source: S. Arterian, "How Black & Decker Defines Exposure," *Business International Money Report,* December 18, 1989, pp. 404, 405, 409.

being is not severely affected by adverse changes in exchange rates. The post-1985 trend by Japanese automakers to establish productive capacity in North America and Western Europe can partly be seen as a strategy for reducing economic exposure (it is also a strategy for reducing trade tensions). Before 1985, most Japanese automobile companies concentrated their productive assets in Japan. However, the rise in the value of the yen on the foreign exchange market has transformed Japan from a low-cost to a high-cost manufacturing location over the past 10 years. In response, Japanese auto firms have moved many of their productive assets overseas to ensure their car prices will not be unduly affected by further rises in the value of the yen. In general, reducing economic exposure necessitates that the firm ensure its assets are not too concentrated in countries where likely rises in currency values will lead to damaging increases in the foreign prices of the goods and services they produce. An example of how Black & Decker has pursued strategies for reducing its economic exposure is given in the accompanying Management Focus.

Developing Policies for Managing Foreign Exchange Exposure

The firm needs to develop a mechanism for ensuring it maintains an appropriate mix of tactics and strategies for minimizing its foreign exchange exposure. Although there is no universal agreement as to the components of this mechanism, a number of common themes stand out.[16] First, central control of exposure is needed to protect resources efficiently and ensure that each subunit adopts the correct mix of tactics and strategies. Many companies have set up in-house foreign exchange centers. Although such centers may not be able to execute all foreign exchange deals—particularly in large, complex multinationals where myriad transactions may be pursued simultaneously—they should at least set guidelines for the firm's subsidiaries to follow.

Second, firms should distinguish between, on one hand, transaction and translation exposure and, on the other, economic exposure. Many companies seem to focus on reducing their transaction and translation exposure and pay scant attention to economic exposure, which may have more profound long-term implications.[17] Firms need to develop strategies for dealing with economic exposure (see the Management Focus about Black & Decker).

Third, the need to forecast future exchange rate movements cannot be overstated, though, as we saw in Chapter 9, this is a tricky business. No model comes close to perfectly predicting future movements in foreign exchange rates. The best that can be said is that in the short run, forward exchange rates provide reasonable predictions of exchange rate movements, and in the long run, fundamental economic factors—particularly relative inflation rates—should be watched because they influence exchange rate movements. Some firms attempt to forecast exchange rate movements in-house; others rely on outside forecasters. However, all such forecasts are imperfect attempts to predict the future.

Fourth, firms need to establish good reporting systems so the central finance function (or in-house foreign exchange center) can regularly monitor the firm's exposure positions. Such reporting systems should enable the firm to identify any exposed accounts, the exposed position by currency of each account, and the time periods covered.

Finally, on the basis of the information it receives from exchange rate forecasts and its own regular reporting systems, the firm should produce monthly foreign exchange exposure reports. These reports should identify how cash flows and balance sheet elements might be affected by forecasted changes in exchange rates. The reports can then be used by management as a basis for adopting tactics and strategies to hedge against undue foreign exchange risks.

Unfortunately, some of the largest and most sophisticated firms don't take such precautionary steps, exposing themselves to very large foreign exchange risks. In 1990, the treasury department of the British food company Allied-Lyons apparently entered the forward foreign exchange market, not so much to hedge against future currency movements as to profit from placing large speculative bets that currencies would move one way or another. Unfortunately for Allied-Lyons, its treasury department made the incorrect speculative bets and it incurred losses of $240 million. Similarly, Showa Shell Sekiyu, the Royal Dutch/Shell group's Japanese affiliate, revealed in February 1993 that its treasury department had incurred some $1 billion in unrealized foreign exchange losses.[18]

Chapter Summary

This chapter was concerned with financial management in the international business. We discussed how investment decisions, financing decisions, and money management decisions are complicated by the fact that different countries have different currencies, different tax regimes, different levels of political and economic risk, and so on. Financial managers must account for all of these factors when deciding which activities to finance, how best to finance those activities, how best to manage the firm's financial resources, and how best to protect the firm from political and economic risks (including foreign exchange risk). This chapter made the following points:

1. When using capital budgeting techniques to evaluate a potential foreign project, a distinction must be made between cash flows to the project and cash flows to the parent. The two will not be the same thing when a host-country government blocks the repatriation of cash flows from a foreign investment.

2. When using capital budgeting techniques to evaluate a potential foreign project, the firm needs to recognize the specific risks arising from its foreign location. These include political risks and economic risks (including foreign exchange risk).

3. Political and economic risks can be incorporated into the capital budgeting process either by using a higher discount rate to evaluate risky projects or by forecasting lower cash flows for such projects.

4. The cost of capital is typically lower in the global capital market than in domestic markets. Consequently, other things being equal, firms prefer to finance their investments by borrowing from the global capital market.

5. Borrowing from the global capital market may be restricted by host-government regulations or demands. In such cases, the discount rate used in capital budgeting must be revised upward to reflect this.

6. The firm may want to consider local debt financing for investments in countries where the local currency is expected to depreciate.

7. The principal objectives of global money management are to utilize the firm's cash resources in the most efficient manner and to minimize the firm's global tax liabilities.

8. Firms use a number of techniques to transfer funds across borders, including dividend remittances, royalty payments and fees, transfer prices, and fronting loans.

9. Dividend remittances are the most common method used for transferring funds across borders, but royalty payments and fees have certain tax advantages over dividend remittances.

10. The manipulation of transfer prices is sometimes used by firms to move funds out of a country to minimize tax liabilities, hedge against foreign exchange risk, circumvent government restrictions on capital flows, and reduce tariff payments.

11. However, manipulating transfer prices in this manner runs counter to government regulations in many countries, it may distort incentive systems within the firm, and it has ethically dubious foundations.

12. Fronting loans involves channeling funds from a parent company to a foreign subsidiary through a

third party, normally an international bank. Fronting loans can circumvent host-government restrictions on the remittance of funds and provide certain tax advantages.

13. By holding cash at a centralized depository, the firm may be able to invest its cash reserves more efficiently. It can reduce the total size of the cash pool that it needs to hold in highly liquid accounts, thereby freeing cash for investment in higher-interest-bearing (less liquid) accounts or in tangible assets.

14. Multilateral netting reduces the transaction costs arising when a large number of transactions occur between a firm's subsidiaries in the normal course of business.

15. The three types of exposure to foreign exchange risk are transaction exposure, translation exposure, and economic exposure.

16. Tactics that insure against transaction and translation exposure include buying forward, using currency swaps, leading and lagging payables and receivables, manipulating transfer prices, using local debt financing, accelerating dividend payments, and adjusting capital budgeting to reflect foreign exchange exposure.

17. Reducing a firm's economic exposure requires strategic choices about how the firm's productive assets are distributed around the globe.

18. To manage foreign exchange exposure effectively, the firm must exercise centralized oversight over its foreign exchange hedging activities, recognize the difference between transaction exposure and economic exposure, forecast future exchange rate movements, establish good reporting systems within the firm to monitor exposure positions, and produce regular foreign exchange exposure reports that can be used as a basis for action.

Critical Discussion Questions

1. How can the finance function of an international business improve the firm's competitive position in the global marketplace?

2. What actions can a firm take to minimize its global tax liability? On ethical grounds, can such actions be justified?

3. You are the CFO of a US firm whose wholly owned subsidiary in Mexico manufactures component parts for your US assembly operations. The subsidiary has been financed by bank borrowings in

the United States. One of your analysts told you that the Mexican peso is expected to depreciate by 30 percent against the dollar on the foreign exchange markets over the next year. What actions, if any, should you take?

4. You are the CFO of a Canadian firm that is considering building a $10 million factory in Russia to produce milk. The investment is expected to produce net cash flows of $3 million each year for the next 10 years, after which the investment will

have to close down because of technological obsolescence. Scrap values will be zero. The cost of capital will be 6 percent if financing is arranged through the eurobond market. However, you have an option to finance the project by borrowing funds from a Russian bank at 12 percent. Analysts tell you that due to high inflation in Russia, the

Russian ruble is expected to depreciate against the Canadian dollar. Analysts also rate the probability of violent revolution occurring in Russia within the next 10 years as high. How would you incorporate these factors into your evaluation of the investment opportunity? What would you recommend the firm do?

CLOSING CASE   Motorola's Global Cash Management System

A multinational corporation with operating companies in more than 80 countries and sales in excess of $23 billion, Motorola is one of the world's leading providers of wireless communications equipment, semiconductors, and advanced electronics systems and services. Separate Motorola companies act autonomously and trade with each other on an arm's-length basis, often across national borders. Historically, each operating company managed its own payments with other Motorola subsidiaries and with independent suppliers and executed its own foreign exchange dealings. By the mid-1990s, however, Motorola had built a global cash management system that not only managed transactions between Motorola operating companies, but also between Motorola companies and key suppliers.

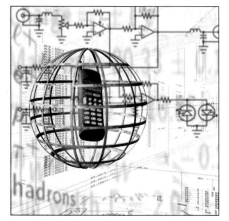

The evolution of Motorola's global cash management system dates to 1976 when the company decided to develop a foreign currency netting system for transactions between Motorola companies. The objective of this system was to achieve cost savings by reducing both cash flows and the amount of foreign exchange deals required to execute cross-border payments. Under this system, all foreign currency transactions between Motorola companies are managed with a single payment or invoice from a London-based treasury management center to each Motorola company once every week. Figures C.1, C.2, and C.3 show how this system reduces organizational complexity, while the follow-

ing table gives a numerical example using the exchange rates detailed in Figure C3.

Using the table, the net payments for each operating company can be easily calculated. Specifically,

Company A (£550 – £50 = £500).

Company B ($100 – $140 = –$40).

Company C (¥10,000 – ¥125,000 = –¥115,000).

Company D (Kr200 – Kr400 = –Kr200).

Before netting, the total amount of cash flows was the sum of all payments, which in dollar terms amounted to $1,320. The netted cash for each company is the sum of its payables less the sum of its receivables. In local currency, company A will receive £500, B will pay $40, C will pay ¥115,000, and D will pay Kr200. The netted cash flow in dollars is now $1,000. The center receives three different types of currencies, makes one payment to company A, and has a neutral cash position.

The benefits of this system are a reduction in cash flows and in the volume of foreign exchange dealings. Moving from localized treasury management to one centralized system realized an estimated annual financial saving from lower transaction costs (bank fees and foreign exchange commissions) of about $6.5 million. However, this figure does not include administrative

Accounts Receivable

Accounts Payable	Company A (£)	Company B ($)	Company C (¥)	Company D (Kr)	Total Payable
Company A	0	$100	0	0	
Company B	£50	0	0	Kr200	$140
Company C	£500	0	0	0	¥125,000
Company D	0	0	¥10,000	0	Kr400
Total receivable	£550	$100	¥10,000	Kr200	

Figure C.1

Prenetting Information
Flows

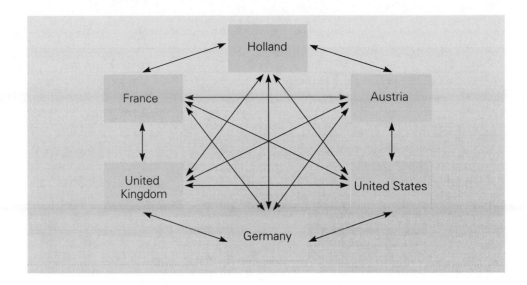

Figure C.2

Postnetting Information
Flows

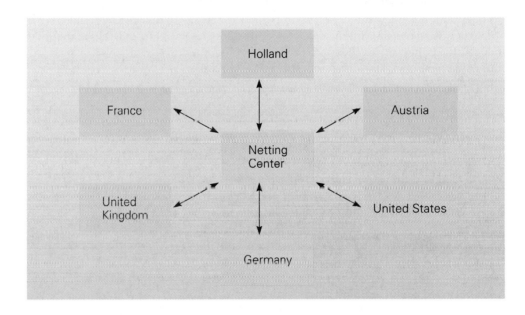

Figure C.3

Schematic Model of
Currency Netting

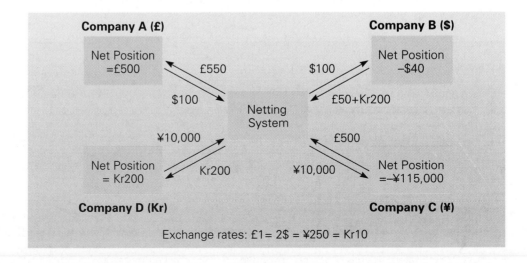

gains from more streamlined operations, which while more difficult to quantify, are also probably quite substantial.

Motorola's success at implementing this system is attributed to a number of factors. First, senior management had the foresight to become committed to this initiative at a very early stage. Management saw the system, and the information technology systems required to support it, as a source of strategic advantage. This was helpful in overcoming the normal resistance of operating managers to changes that take away some of their autonomy. Second, Motorola had already made substantial investments in building an information technology backbone to share manufacturing and logistics data between operating companies. Once this system was built, it could easily be extended to incorporate the data required for global treasury management. Third, Motorola took a gradual approach to implementing the system, which helped the company to perfect it before implementing it organizationwide. A few sites were chosen as prototypes. After they had been integrated into the system and operating difficulties had been overcome, the inclusion of other sites proceeded smoothly. As a result, the number of participating Motorola entities rose from 38 in 1983 to 106 by the early 1990s.

Once the internal cash management system was working smoothly, Motorola extended the system to embrace key suppliers and customers. Extending the system was in principle relatively straightforward. Each week, the Motorola netting center collects data from each Motorola entity detailing payments that have to be made to suppliers. The global treasury function executes the required foreign exchange transactions, initiates payment orders, and advises Motorola companies of their net positions. After netting incoming payments with outgoing payments and combining common currencies, an approximate foreign exchange position is reached in which surplus currencies are sold and deficit currencies are purchased. The transaction value is approximately $100 million per week.

These payments are all handled by Citibank, which uses its own global information systems network to transfer funds between the various entities involved in the Motorola system, whether they are Motorola companies or independent vendors. Making this system work requires close electronic links between Motorola and Citibank, compatible information systems, a shared vision as to the purpose of the system, and ongoing cooperation between Motorola and Citibank to improve and manage the global flow of money.

As a result of this system, the net cash flow in 1991 between Motorola operating companies was $2.4 billion, a reduction of $2.38 billion from the value of payments settled in 1991. Without netting, Motorola would have had to engage in foreign exchange transactions valued at $4.3 billion. With netting, foreign exchange transactions were reduced to about $1.3 billion, which equates to annual direct savings in transaction costs of around $6.5 million.

http://www.mot.com

Sources: C. P. Holland, G. Lockett, J.-M. Richard, and I. Blackman, "The Evolution of a Global Cash Management System," *Sloan Management Review*, Fall 1994, pp. 37–47; and B. Ettorre, "How Motorola Closes Its Books in Two Days," *Management Review*, March 1995, pp. 84–89.

Case Discussion Questions

1. What are the strategic benefits to Motorola of the global cash management system described in this case?

2. How important is the relationship between Citibank and Motorola to the development, implementation, and smooth functioning of this system?

3. What factors helped Motorola to implement this system in a company where treasury operations had been decentralized to various national operations?

Notes

1. L. Quinn, "Currency Futures Trading Helps Firms Sharpen Competitive Edge," *Crain's Chicago Business*, March 2, 1992, p. 20.

2. For details of capital budgeting techniques, see R. A. Brealy and S. C. Myers, *Principles of Corporate Finance* (New York: McGraw-Hill, 1988).

3. For details, see E. G. Roberts, "Country Risk Assessment: The Union Carbide Experience," in *Global Risk Assessment, Book 3*, ed. J. Rogers (Riverside, CA: Global Risk Assessments, 1988).

4. J. C. Backer and L. J. Beardsley, "Multinational Companies' Use of Risk Evaluation and Profit Measurement for Capital Budgeting Decisions," *Journal of Business Finance*, Spring 1973, pp. 34–43.

5. For example, see D. K. Eiteman, A. I. Stonehill, and M. H. Moffett, *Multinational Business Finance* (Reading, MA: Addison-Wesley, 1922).

6. M. Stanley and S. Block, "An Empirical Study of Management and Financial Variables Influencing Capital Budgeting Decisions for Multinational Corporations in

the 1980s," *Management International Review* 23 (1983), pp. 61–71.

7. W. S. Sekely and J. M. Collins, "Cultural Influences on International Capital Structure," *Journal of International Business Studies*, Spring 1988, pp. 87–100.

8. J. Collins and W. S. Sekely, "The Relationship of Headquarters, Country, and Industry Classification to Financial Structure," *Financial Structure*, Autumn 1983, pp. 45–51; and J. Rutterford, "An International Perspective on the Capital Structure Puzzle," *Midland Corporate Finance Journal*, Fall 1985, p. 72.

9. Sekely and Collins, "Cultural Influences on International Capital Structure."

10. S. C. Ruchelman, "Cross Border Targets," *Financial Times*, February 24, 1995, p. 10.

11. "Taxing Questions," *The Economist*, May 22, 1993, p. 73.

12. S. Crow and E. Sauls, "Setting the Right Transfer Price," *Management Accounting*, December 1994, pp. 41–47.

13. J. Kelly, "Administrators Prepare for a More Efficient Future," *Financial Times Survey: World Taxation*, February 24, 1995, p. 9.

14. S. Crow and E. Sauls, "Setting the Right Transfer Price."

15. M. F. Al-Eryani, P. Alam, and S. Akhter, "Transfer Pricing Determinants of U.S. Multinationals," *Journal of International Business Studies*, September 1990, pp. 409–25.

16. For details on how various firms manage their foreign exchange exposure, see the articles contained in the special foreign exchange issue of *Business International Money Report*, December 18, 1989, pp. 401–12.

17. Ibid.

18. T. Corrigan, "Corporate Treasury Management," *Financial Times*, November 2, 1993, p. 31.

CASES

Starbucks Corporation: Going Global

Steinway & Sons: Global
Competition and Entry into China

STARBUCKS CORPORATION: GOING GLOBAL*

Starbucks Corporation is a Seattle, Washington-based coffee company. It roasts and sells whole bean coffees and coffee drinks through a national chain of retail outlets/restaurants. Originally only a seller of packaged, premium, roasted coffees, the bulk of the company's revenues now comes from its coffee bars where people can purchase beverages and pastries in addition to coffee by the pound. Starbucks is credited with changing the way Americans view coffee, and its success has attracted the attention of investors nationwide.

Starbucks has consistently been one of the fastest growing companies in the United States with over 1,006 retail outlets in 1996. Over a five-year period starting in 1991, net revenues increased at a compounded annual growth rate of 61 percent. In fiscal 1996, net revenues increased 50 percent to $696 million from $465 million for the same period the previous year. Net earnings rose 61 percent to $42 million from the previous year's $26 million. Sales for Starbucks have been continuing to grow steadily, and the company is still a darling of investors with a PE ratio of 58.

To continue to grow at a rapid pace, the firm's senior executives have been considering international expansion. Specifically, they are interested in Japan and other Asian countries, where Starbucks has had little or no presence. Japan, the world's third largest coffee consumer after the United States and Germany, represented both a challenge and a huge opportunity to the firm. To explore what changes in Starbucks strategy were required, and the questions that might arise during expansion, this case looks at the firm's entry strategy into Japan and the nature of issues facing the firm during early 1997.

The Company Background

In 1971, three Seattle entrepreneurs—Jerry Baldwin, Zev Siegl, and Gordon Bowker—started selling whole-bean coffee in Seattle's Pike Place Market. They named their store Starbucks, after the first mate in *Moby Dick*. By 1982, the business had grown to five stores, a small roasting facility, and a wholesale business selling coffee to local restaurants. At the same time, Howard Schultz had been working as Vice President of US operations for Hammarplast, a Swedish housewares company in New York, marketing coffeemakers to a number of retailers,

including Starbucks. Through selling to Starbucks, Schultz was introduced to the three founders, who then recruited him to bring marketing savvy to the company. Schultz, 29 and recently married, was eager to leave New York. He joined Starbucks as manager of retail sales and marketing.

A year later, Schultz visited Verona, Italy, for the first time on a buying trip. As he strolled through the piazzas of Milan one evening, he was inspired by a vision. He noticed that coffee was an integral part of the romantic culture in Italy; Italians start their day at an espresso bar, and later in the day return with their friends. There are 200,000 coffee bars in Italy, and about 1,500 in Milan alone. Schultz believed that given the chance, Americans would pay good money for a premium cup of coffee and a stylish, romantic place to enjoy it. Enthusiastic about his idea, Schultz returned to tell Starbucks' owners of his plan for a national chain of cafes stylized on the Italian coffee bar. The owners, however, were less enthusiastic and did not want to be in the restaurant business. Undaunted, Schultz wrote a business plan, videotaped dozens of Italian coffee bars, and began looking for investors. By April 1985 he had opened his first coffee bar, Il Giornale (named after the Italian newspaper), where he served Starbucks coffee. Following Il Giornale's immediate success, Schultz opened a second coffee bar in Seattle, and then a third in Vancouver. In 1987, the owners of Starbucks agreed to sell to Schultz for $4 million. The Il Giornale coffee bars took on the name of Starbucks.

Convinced that Starbucks would one day be in every neighborhood in America, Schultz focused on expansion. In 1987 he entered Chicago, four years later he opened in Los Angeles, and in 1993 he entered the District of Columbia. Additionally, he hired executives away from corporations such as PepsiCo. At first, the company's losses almost doubled, to $1.2 million from fiscal 1989 to 1990 as overhead and operating expenses ballooned with the expansion. Starbucks lost money for three years running, and the stress was hard on Schultz, but he stuck to his conviction not to "sacrifice long-term integrity and values for short-term profit."[1] In 1991 sales shot up 84 percent, and the company turned profitable. In 1992 Schultz took the firm public at $17 a share.

Always believing that market share and name recognition are critical to the company's success, Schultz con-

*This case was prepared by Melissa Schilling and Assistant Professor Suresh Kotha, both from the University of Washington, Business School of Administration, as the basis for class discussion rather than to illustrate either effective or ineffective handling of an administrative situation. Copyright © 1997 Kotha & Schilling. All rights reserved.

tinued to expand the business rather aggressively. Notes Schultz, "There is no secret sauce here. Anyone can do it." To stop potential copycats, he opened 100 new stores in 1993, and another 145 in 1994. Additionally, he acquired the Coffee Connection, a 25-store Boston chain in 1994.

Everywhere Starbucks has opened, customers have flocked to pay upwards of $1.85 for a cup of coffee (latte). Currently, the firm operates stores in most of the major metropolitan areas in the United States and Canada, including Seattle; New York; Chicago; Boston; Los Angeles; San Francisco; San Diego; Austin; Dallas; Houston; San Antonio; Las Vegas; Philadelphia; Pittsburgh; Cincinnati; Minneapolis; Portland; Atlanta; Baltimore; Washington, D.C.; Denver; Toronto; and Vancouver, B.C. Its mail-order business serves customers throughout the United States. Enthusiastic financial analysts predict that Starbucks could top $1 billion by the end of the decade (see Appendix A).

In 1996, Starbucks employed approximately 16,600 individuals, including approximately 15,000 in retail stores and regional offices, and the remainder in the firm's administrative, sales, real estate, direct response, roasting, and warehousing operations. Only 5 of the firm's stores (located in Vancouver, British Columbia) out of a total of 929 company-operated stores in North America were unionized. Starbucks has never experienced a strike or work stoppage. Management was confident that its relationship with its employees was excellent.

Market and Competition

Americans have a reputation for buying the cheapest coffee beans available. Most American coffee buyers have to fight growers to keep them from just showing them the culls. Much of the canned coffee on American supermarket shelves is made from the robusta bean—considered to be the lowest quality coffee bean and the highest in caffeine content. Japanese, German, and Italian buyers, in contrast, are known for buying the best beans, primarily Arabica. There are many different types and grades of Arabica and robusta beans, though for years Americans have treated them as a generic commodity.[2]

The US Coffee Industry

US coffee consumption peaked in 1962. At that time Americans were drinking an average of 3.1 cups per day. However, from the 1960s to the 1980s coffee consumption declined, bottoming out at an average con-

sumption of 1.8 cups per day, or $6.5 billion annually. Over the past decade, coffee demand has been stagnant, with growth only occurring in some of the specialty coffees (see Figures 1a, 1b, and 1c). Whereas three-fourths of all Americans were regular coffee drinkers in the 1960s, today only half of the US population consumes coffee.[3]

There has been a marked consumer trend toward more healthful fare, causing overall coffee consumption to decline. Although the coffee industry had expected decaffeinated coffee brands to increase, decaffeinated sales in the grocery stores have been steadily dropping, making decaffeinated coffee one of the fastest-declining categories in the supermarket.[4] Industry observers note that many consumers are disappointed with the flavor of decaffeinated coffees and have opted to give up coffee entirely. Demand for better tasting coffees has also hurt the instant coffee market, with sales of instant coffee declining too. While the instant coffee technology impressed consumers following its introduction in 1939, younger coffee consumers appear to be spurning instants.

The Growth of the Gourmet Segment

The more faithful coffee drinkers have turned to the gourmet decaffeinated coffees, specialty flavors, and whole bean coffees. According to the Specialty Coffee Association of America (SCAA), the gourmet coffee segment grew by more than 30 percent each year for the past three years. The SCAA predicts that by 1999 specialty coffee will capture about 30 percent of the market (up from 17 percent in 1988) for combined retail sales of $5 billion. Also by 1999, the number of espresso bars and cafes is expected to grow to more than 10,000, up from 4,500 in 1994, and 1,000 in 1989.

Sales of specialty coffee have climbed steadily. For instance, in 1969 the retail sales volume of specialty coffee totaled just under $45 million. However, sales grew to more than $2.0 billion in 1994. During 1994, the specialty coffee segment represented about 19 percent of all coffee sold. This figure was up from 10 percent in 1983. However, by 1996 about 30 percent of all coffee drinkers consumed specialty coffees. This amounted to a customer base of approximately 35 million people in the United States. Today, specialty coffees such as espressos and lattes have become so popular that they are being offered in drive-through cafes and coffee stands throughout many parts of the United States.[5]

Some analysts attribute the explosive growth in specialty coffees to the poor economy. They note that as people scale back in other areas, they still need their "minor" indulgences. Although many people cannot

	1985	1986	1987	1988	1989	1990	1991	1992	1993	1994	1995
*Total coffee**	1.83	1.74	1.76	1.67	1.75	1.73	1.75	NA	1.87	NA	1.67
By sex:											
Male	1.91	1.80	1.89	1.86	1.85	1.86	1.92	NA	2.11	NA	1.81
Female	1.76	1.68	1.64	1.50	1.66	1.60	1.59	NA	1.64	NA	1.54
By age:											
10–19 years	0.12	0.09	0.11	0.14	0.11	0.16	0.12	NA	0.15	NA	0.16
20–29 years	1.24	1.06	0.99	0.94	0.99	0.96	0.83	NA	0.89	NA	0.69
30–59 years	2.65	2.43	2.56	2.35	2.46	2.34	2.40	NA	2.62	NA	2.35
60 plus	2.20	2.40	2.18	2.17	2.30	2.32	2.44	NA	2.38	NA	2.11

NA=not available.

*Average number of cups per day.

Source: *National Coffee Association of U.S.A. 1995 report.*

Figure 1a

US Consumption of Coffee and Other Beverages

Figure 1b

US Specialty Coffee Consumption (% of the population drinking)

	1993	1995	Male[*]	Female[*]
Espresso	0.6%	0.9%	0.9%	0.9%
Cappuccino	1.1%	1.2%	0.7%	1.6%
Latte	0.5%	0.4%	0.3%	0.5%

[*]Based on 1995 figures.

Source: *National Coffee Association of U.S.A. 1995 report.*

Figure 1c

US Consumption in Gallons

	1990	1991	1992	1993	1994[e]	1995[p]
Soft drinks	47.6	47.8	48	49	50.6	51
Coffee[*]	26.2	26.6	26.5	25.4	23.4	21.2
Beer	24	23.3	23	22.9	22.6	22.5
Milk	19.4	19.4	19.1	18.9	18.9	18.8
Tea[*]	7	6.7	6.8	6.9	7.1	7.4
Bottled water	8	8	8.2	8.8	9.2	9.6
Juices	7.1	7.6	7.1	7	7	7
Powdered Drinks	5.7	5.9	5.8	5.5	5.4	5.3
Wine	2	1.9	2	1.7	1.7	1.6
Distilled spirits	1.5	1.4	1.3	1.3	1.3	1.3
Total	148.5	148.5	147.8	147.4	147.2	145.7

[*]Coffee and tea data are based on a three-year moving average to counterbalance inventory swings, thereby portraying consumption more realistically.

e=Estimates, p=Projected.

Source: John C. Maxwell, Jr., *Beverage Industry Annual Manual 1995/1997.*

afford a luxury car, they can still afford a luxury coffee.[6] Despite this growth, some analysts anticipate trouble on the horizon for the specialty coffee business. As evidence, they cite several indicators. For instance:

- In many markets some of the smaller coffeehouses have closed due to excessive competition.

- In Los Angeles, the city council (in response to complaints about rowdy late-night patrons) was considering an ordinance that would require coffeehouses open past midnight to obtain a license. This move, suggest analysts, is a sign that the coffee business is maturing.

- The cost of coffee beans is expected to rise in the near future, tightening margins for coffee merchants. Coffee farmers are switching to more profitable fruit and vegetable crops, reducing the world's supply of coffee beans.

Competition for the Gourmet Segment

Starbucks faces two main competitive arenas—retail beverages and coffee beans. Starbucks whole bean coffees compete directly against specialty coffees sold at retail through supermarkets, specialty retailers, and a growing number of specialty coffee stores. According to senior executives at Starbucks, supermarkets pose the greatest competitive challenge in the whole bean coffee market, in part because supermarkets offer customers the convenience of not having to make a separate trip to "a Starbucks store." A number of nationwide coffee manufacturers, such as Kraft General Foods, Procter & Gamble, and Nestlé, are distributing premium coffee products in supermarkets, and these products serve as substitutes for Starbucks coffees. Additionally, regional specialty coffee companies also sell whole bean coffees in supermarkets.

Starbucks' coffee beverages compete directly against all restaurant and beverage outlets that serve coffee and a growing number of espresso stands, carts, and stores. Both the company's whole bean coffees and its coffee beverages compete indirectly against all other coffees on the market. Starbucks executives believe that their customers choose among retailers primarily on the basis of quality and convenience, and, to a lesser extent, on price.

Starbucks competes for whole bean coffee sales with franchise operators and independent specialty coffee stores in both the United States and Canada. There are a number of competing specialty coffee retailers. One specialty coffee retailer that has grown to considerable size is Second Cup, a Canadian franchiser with stores primarily in Canada. In 1996 there were 235 Second Cup stores in Canada. Second Cup also owns Gloria Jean's Coffee Bean and Brother's Gourmet, both franchisers of specialty coffee stores that are primarily located in malls in the United States. Gloria Jean's, founded in 1979, operated 249 retail stores with about $125 million in annual sales in 1996. Brother's Gourmet is a Florida-based coffee chain with almost 250 franchisee-owned locations in the Chicago area.

Seattle's Best Coffee (SBC) competes fiercely with Starbucks on Starbucks' own turf, Seattle. This firm is following Starbucks' lead in national expansion. However, unlike Starbucks, SBC sells franchise rights to its stores in order to expand rapidly with limited capital. SBC takes advantage of Starbucks' market presence by waiting for Starbucks to invest in consumer education. Then, once customers are familiar with the concept of gourmet coffees, SBC enters that market. In following this approach, the firm has had an easier time finding franchisees. SBC intends to operate 500 stores by 1999.

Starbucks also competes with established suppliers in its specialty sales and direct response (mail order) businesses, many of whom have greater financial and marketing resources than Starbucks has. Lately, competition for suitable sites to locate stores has also become intense. Starbucks competes against restaurants, specialty coffee stores, other stores offering coffee stands within them (e.g., bookstores, clothing retailers, kitchenware retailers) and even espresso carts for attractive locations. In many metropolitan areas a single square block may have four or five different coffee beverage stores. This level of competition prompted Brother's Gourmet Coffee to abandon its 1995 expansion plans after it determined that the market was almost saturated and that Starbucks was already in all of their markets. Finally, the firm also competes for qualified personnel to operate its retail stores.

The Starbucks Legacy

In establishing Starbucks' unique approach to competition, Schultz had four companies in mind as role models: Nordstrom, Home Depot, Microsoft, and Ben & Jerry's. Nordstrom, a national chain of upscale department stores based in Seattle, provided a role model for service and is part of the reason that each employee must receive at least 24 hours of training. Home Depot, the home improvement chain, was Schultz's guideline for managing high growth. Microsoft gave Schultz the inspiration for employee ownership, resulting in Starbucks' innovative Bean Stock Plan. And Ben & Jerry's was his role model for philanthropy; Starbucks sponsors community festivals, donates money to CARE for health and literacy programs in coffee-growing countries, and donates to charity any packages of coffee beans that have been open a week.

Schultz's goal is to "establish Starbucks as the premier purveyor of the finest coffee in the world while maintaining uncompromising principles as we grow." He has since articulated six guiding principles to measure the appropriateness of the firm's decisions (see Figure 2).

Securing the Finest Raw Materials

Starbucks coffee quality begins with bean procurement. Although many Americans were raised on a commodity-like coffee composed of Arabica beans mixed with less-expensive filler beans, Starbucks coffee is strictly

Figure 2

Starbucks Mission
Statement and Guiding
Principles

Mission Statement:

To establish Starbucks as the premier purveyor of the finest coffee in the world while maintaining our uncompromising principles as we grow.

The following six guiding principles will help us measure the appropriateness of our decisions:

- Provide a great work environment and treat each other with respect and dignity.
- Embrace diversity as an essential component in the way we do business.
- Apply the highest standards of excellence to the purchasing, roasting, and fresh delivery of our coffee.
- Develop enthusiastically satisfied customers all of the time.
- Contribute positively to our communities and our environment.
- Recognize that profitability is essential to our future success.

Source: http://www.starbucks.com/company/?sid=&&.

Arabica, and the company ensures that only the highest quality beans are used. Dave Olsen, the company's senior vice president and chief coffee procurer, scours mountain trails in Indonesia, Kenya, Guatemala, and elsewhere in search of Starbucks' premium bean. His standards are demanding and he conducts exacting experiments in order to get the proper balance of flavor, body, and acidity. He tests the coffees by "cupping" them, a process similar to wine tasting that involves inhaling the steam ("the strike" and "breaking the crust"), tasting the coffee, and spitting it out ("aspirating" and "expectorating").[7]

From the company's inception, it has worked on developing relationships with the countries from which it buys coffee beans. Traditionally, most of the premium coffee beans were bought by Europeans and Japanese. Olsen has sometimes had to convince coffee growers that it is worth growing premium coffees—especially since American coffee buyers are notorious purchasers of the "dregs" of the coffee beans. In 1992 Starbucks set a new precedent by outbidding European buyers for the exclusive Narino Supremo bean crop.[8] Starbucks collaborated with a mill in the tiny town of Pasto, located on the side of the Volcano Galero. There they set up a special operation to single out the particular Narino Supremo bean, and Starbucks guaranteed to purchase the entire yield. This enabled Starbucks to be the exclusive purveyor of Narino Supremo, purportedly one of the best coffees in the world.[9]

Vertical Integration

Roasting of the coffee bean is close to an art form at Starbucks. The company currently operates three roasting and distribution facilities: two in the Seattle area, and one in East Manchester Township, York County,

Pennsylvania. In the Seattle area, the company leases approximately 92,000 square feet in one building located in Seattle, Washington, and owns an additional roasting plant and distribution facility of approximately 305,000 square feet located in Kent, Washington.

Roasters are promoted from within the company and trained for over a year, and it is considered quite an honor to be chosen. The coffee is roasted in a powerful gas-fired drum roaster for 12 to 15 minutes while roasters use their sight, smell, hearing, and computers to judge when beans are perfectly done. The color of the beans is even tested in an Agtron blood-cell analyzer, with the whole batch being discarded if the sample is not deemed perfect.

The Starbucks Experience

According to Schultz, "We're not just selling a cup of coffee, we are providing an experience." As Americans reduce their alcohol consumption, Schultz hopes to make coffee bars their new destination. In order to create American coffee enthusiasts with the dedication of their Italian counterparts, Starbucks provides a seductive atmosphere in which to imbibe. Its stores are distinctive and sleek, yet comfortable. Though the sizes of the stores and their formats vary from small to full-size restaurants, most are modeled after the Italian coffee bars where regulars sit and drink espresso with their friends.

Starbucks stores tend to be located in high-traffic locations such as malls, busy street corners, and even grocery stores. They are well-lit and feature plenty of light cherry wood. Further, sophisticated artwork hangs on the walls. The people who prepare the coffee are referred to as *baristas*, Italian for bartender. And jazz or opera music plays softly in the background. The stores range from 200 to 4,000 square feet, with new units tending to range from 1,500 to 1,700 square feet. In 1995, the average cost of opening a new unit (including equipment, inventory, and leasehold improvements) was about $377,000. The firm employs a staff of over 100 people whose job is to plan, design, and build the unique interiors and displays. The Starbucks interiors have inspired a slew of imitators.

Location choices so far have been easy; Starbucks opens its cafes in those cities where its direct mail business is strong. By tracking addresses of mail order customers to find the highest concentration in a city, Starbucks can ensure that its new stores have a ready audience. Although this would normally imply cannibalizing mail order sales, mail order revenues have continued to increase.

The packaging of the firm's products is also distinctive. In addition to prepared Italian beverages such as lattes, mochas, and cappuccinos, the retail outlets/restaurants offer coffee by-the-pound, specialty mugs, and home espresso-making machines. *Biscotti* is available in glass jars on the counter. Many of the firm's stores offer light lunch fare including sandwiches and salads, and an assortment of pastries, bottled waters, and juices. Notes George Reynolds, a former senior vice president for marketing:

> [Starbucks'] goal is to make a powerful aesthetic statement about the quality and integrity of their products, reaffirming through their visual identity the commitment they feel to providing the very best product and service for customers.

The company has also developed unique strategies for its products in new markets; for instance, for its passport promotion, customers receive a frequent buyer bonus stamp in their "passport" every time they purchase a half-pound of coffee. Each time a customer buys a different coffee, Starbucks also validates their "World Coffee Tour." Once a customer has collected 10 stamps, he receives a free half-pound of coffee. The passport also contains explanations of each type of coffee bean and country of origin.

Despite the attention to store environment and coffee quality, Starbucks' effort at bringing a premium coffee and Italian-style beverage experience to the American market could have been lost on consumers had the company not invested in consumer education. Starbucks employees spend a good portion of their time instructing customers on Starbucks' global selection of coffee and the different processes by which the beverages are produced. Employees are also encouraged to help customers make decisions about beans, grind, and coffee/espresso machines and to instruct customers on home brewing. Starbucks' consumer education is credited with defining the American espresso market, paving the way for other coffee competitors.[10]

Building a Unique Culture

While Starbucks enforces almost fanatical standards about coffee quality and service, the policy at Starbucks toward employees is laid-back and supportive. They are encouraged to think of themselves as partners in the business. Schultz believes that happy employees are the key to competitiveness and growth:

> We can't achieve our strategic objectives without a work force of people who are immersed in the same commitment as management. Our only sustainable advantage is the quality of our work force. We're building a national retail company by creating pride in—and stake in—the outcome of our labor.[11]

Schultz is also known for his sensitivity to the well-being of employees. Recently when an employee had come to tell Schultz that he had AIDS, he reassured him that he could work as long as he wanted to, and when he left, the firm would continue his health insurance. After the employee left the room, Schultz reportedly sat down and wept. He attributes such concern for employees to memories of his father:

> My father struggled a great deal and never made more than $20,000 a year, and his work was never valued, emotionally or physically, by his employer. . . . This was an injustice. . . . I want our employees to know we value them.

A recent article on the firm in *Fortune* points out:

> Starbucks has instituted all sorts of mechanisms for its Gen X-ers to communicate with headquarters: E-mail, suggestion cards, regular forums. And it acts quickly on issues that are supposedly important to young kids today, like using recycling bins and improving living conditions in coffee-growing countries. To determine the extent to which Starbucks has truly identified and addressed the inner needs of twentysomethings would require several years and a doctorate. But anecdotally, the company appears to be right on the money.[12]

On a practical level, Starbucks promotes an empowered employee culture through employee training, employee benefits programs, and an employee stock ownership plan.

Employee Training

Each employee must have at least 24 hours of training. Notes *Fortune*:

> Not unlike the cultural blitz of personal computing, Starbucks has created one of the great marketing stories of recent history, and it's just getting started. The company manages to imprint its obsession with customer service on 20,000 milk-steaming, shot-pulling employees. It turns tattooed kids into managers of $800,000-a-year cafes. It

successfully replicates a perfectly creamy caffe latte in stores from Seattle to St. Paul. There is some science involved, and one of its primary labs happens to be Starbucks' employee training program.[13]

Classes cover everything from coffee history to a seven-hour workshop called "Brewing the Perfect Cup at Home." This workshop is one of five classes that all employees (called partners) must complete during their first six weeks with the company. This workshop focuses on the need to educate the customer in proper coffeemaking techniques.

Store managers (who have gone through facilitation workshops and are certified by the company as trainers) teach the classes. The classes teach the employees to make decisions that will enhance customer satisfaction without requiring manager authorization. For example, if a customer comes into the store complaining about how her beans were ground, the employee is authorized to replace them on the spot. While most restaurants use on-the-job training, Starbucks holds bar classes where employees practice taking orders and preparing beverages in a company training room. This allows employees to hone their skills in a low-stress environment, and also protects Starbucks' quality image by allowing only experienced baristas to serve customers.[14] Reports *Fortune:*

> It's silly, soft-headed stuff, though basically, of course, it's true. Maybe some of it sinks in. Starbucks is a smashing success, thanks in large part to the people who come out of these therapy-like training programs. Annual barista turnover at the company is 60 percent compared with 140 percent for hourly workers in the fast-food business. "I don't have a negative thing to say," says Kim Sigeman, who manages the store in Emeryville, California, of her four years with the company. She seems to mean it.[15]

Employee Benefits

Starbucks offers its benefits package to both part-time and full-time employees with dependent coverage available. Dependent coverage is also extended to same-sex partners. The package includes medical, dental, vision and short-term disability insurance, as well as paid vacation, paid holidays, mental health/chemical dependency benefits, an employee assistance program, a 401(k) savings plan, and a stock option plan. They also offer career counseling and product discounts.[16]

Schultz believes that without these benefits, people do not feel financially or spiritually tied to their jobs. He argues that stock options and the complete benefits package increase employee loyalty and encourage attentive service to the customer.[17] Notes Bradley Honeycutt, the company's vice president, HR services and international: "[Our] part-timers are on the front line with our

customers. If we treat them right, we feel they will treat [the customers] well."[18] Sharon Elliot, HR senior vice president, offers another explanation: "Most importantly, this is the right thing to do. It's a basic operating philosophy of our organization."

Despite the increased coverage, Starbucks' health care costs are well within the national average, running around $150 per employee per month. This may be due, in part, to the fact that its employees are relatively young, resulting in lower claims. Half of the management at Starbucks is under 50, and retail employees tend to be much younger. Starbucks is betting on the increases in premiums being largely offset by lower training costs due to the lower attrition rate. Comments *Fortune:*

> It has become boilerplate public relations for corporations to boast about how much they value their people. But Starbucks really does treat its partners astonishingly well. The pay—between $6 and $8 an hour—is better than that of most entry-level food service jobs. The company offers health insurance to all employees, even part-timers.... Walk into just about any Starbucks, and you'll see that these are fairly soft hands: Some 80 percent of the partners are white, 85 percent have some college education beyond high school, and the average age is 26.

The Bean Stock Plan

Employee turnover is also discouraged by Starbucks' stock option plan known as the Bean Stock Plan. Implemented in August of 1991, the plan made Starbucks the only private company to offer stock options unilaterally to all employees. After one year, employees may join a 401(k) plan. There is a vesting period of five years; it starts one year after the option is granted, then vests the employee at 20 percent every year. In addition, every employee receives a new stock-option award each year, and a new vesting period begins. This plan required getting an exemption from the Securities and Exchange Commission, since any company with more than 500 shareholders has to report its financial performance publicly—a costly process that reveals valuable information to competitors.

The option plan did not go uncontested by the venture capitalists and shareholders on the board. Craig Foley, a director and managing partner of Chancellor Capital Management Inc. (the largest shareholder before the public offering), noted that, "Increasing the shareholders substantially dilutes our interest. We take that very seriously." In the end he and others were won over by a study conducted by the company that revealed the positive relationship between employee ownership and productivity rates, and a scenario analysis of how many employees would be vested. Foley conceded that "the grants are tied to overachieving. If you just come to work and do your job, that isn't as attractive as if you beat the numbers."[19]

Since the Bean Stock Plan was put into place, enthusiastic employees have been suggesting ways to save money and increase productivity. The strong company culture has also served as a levy against pilferage; Starbucks inventory shrinkage is less than half of 1 percent.

In 1995 Starbucks demonstrated that its concern for employee welfare extended beyond the US borders. After a human-rights group leafleted the stores complaining that Guatemalan coffee pickers received less than $3 a day, Starbucks became the first agricultural commodity importer to implement a code for minimal working conditions and pay for foreign subcontractors.[20] The company's guidelines call for overseas suppliers to pay wages and benefits that "address the basic needs of workers and their families" and to only allow child labor when it does not interrupt required education.[21] This move has set a precedent for other importers of agricultural commodities.

Leveraging the Brand

Multiple Channels of Distribution

While Starbucks has resisted offering its coffee in grocery stores, it has found a variety of other distribution channels for its products. Besides its stand-alone stores, Starbucks has set up cafes and carts in hospitals, banks, office buildings, supermarkets, and shopping centers. In 1992 Starbucks signed a deal with Nordstrom to serve Starbucks coffee exclusively in all of its stores. Nordstrom also named Starbucks as the exclusive coffee supplier for its restaurants, employee lunchrooms, and catering operations. As of 1992, Nordstrom was operating 62 restaurants and 48 espresso bars. A year later, Barnes & Noble initiated an agreement with Starbucks to implement a "cafe-in-a-bookshop" plan.

Other distribution agreements have included office coffee suppliers, hotels, and airlines. Office coffee is a large segment of the coffee market. Associated Services (an office coffee supplier) provides Starbucks coffee exclusively to the 5,000 northern California businesses it services. Sheraton Hotel has also signed an agreement to serve Starbucks coffee. In 1995 Starbucks signed a deal with United Airlines to provide Starbucks coffee to United's nearly 75 million passengers a year.[22]

While Starbucks is the largest and best-known of the coffeehouse chains and its presence is very apparent in metropolitan areas, the firm's estimates indicate that only 1 percent of the US population has tried its products. Through these distribution agreements and the new product partnerships it is establishing, Starbucks hopes to capture more of the US market.

Brand Extensions

In 1995, Starbucks launched a line of packaged and prepared teas in response to growing demand for tea houses and packaged tea. Tea is a highly profitable beverage for restaurants to sell, costing only 2 cents to 4 cents a cup to produce.[23]

Starbucks coffee is not sold in grocery stores, but its name is making its way onto grocery shelves via a carefully planned series of joint ventures.[24] An agreement with PepsiCo Inc. brought a bottled version of Starbucks Frappuccino (a cold, sweetened coffee drink) to store shelves in August of 1996. A similar product released a year before, called Mazagran, was a failure and was pulled from the shelves; however, both Starbucks and PepsiCo had higher hopes for Frappuccino.[25] Starbucks also has an agreement with Washington-based Redhook Ale Brewery to make a product called Double Black Stout, a coffee-flavored stout. In another 50-50 partnership, Dreyers' Grand Ice Cream Inc. distributes seven quart-products and two bar-products of Starbucks coffee ice cream.

Other partnerships by the company are designed to form new product associations with coffee. For instance, Starbucks has collaborated with Capitol Records Inc. to produce two Starbucks jazz CDs, available only in Starbucks stores. Starbucks is also opening tandem units with Bruegger's Bagel Bakeries and had bought a minority stake in Noah's New York Bagels in 1995. This minority stake has since been sold.

International Expansion

From the beginning, Schultz has professed a strict growth policy. Although many other coffeehouses or espresso bars are franchised, Starbucks owns all of its stores outright with the exception of license agreements in airports.[26] Despite over 300 calls a day from willing investors, Schultz feels it is important to the company's integrity to own its stores. Further, rather than trying to capture all the potential markets as soon as possible, Starbucks goes into a market and tries to completely dominate it before setting its sights on further expansion. As Alstead points out, "Starbucks hopes to achieve the same density in all of its markets that they have achieved in Seattle, Vancouver, and Chicago."

In 1996, the firm opened 307 stores (including four replacement stores), converted 19 Coffee Connection stores to Starbucks, and closed one store. In 1997, Starbucks intends to open at least 325 new stores and enter at least three major new markets in North America including Phoenix, Arizona, and Miami, Florida. Moreover, Schultz plans to have 2,000 stores by the year 2000.

Some analysts believe that the US coffee-bar market may be reaching saturation. They point to the fact that there have been some consolidations, as bigger players snap up some of the smaller coffee bar competitors.[27] Further, they note that Starbucks' store base is also maturing, leading to a slowdown in the growth of unit volume and firm profitability. Higher coffee costs have also cut into margins, intensifying the competition in what has now become a crowded market. Recognizing this, Starbucks has turned its attention to foreign markets for continued growth. Notes Schultz, "We are looking at the Asia-Pacific region as the focus of our international business."

Expansion into Asian Markets

In 1996 the firm invested $1.5 million and established a subsidiary called Starbucks Coffee International Inc. The focus of this subsidiary will be on penetrating the Asia-Pacific region. According to Kathie Lindemann, the director of international operations at Starbucks:

> We are not overlooking Europe and South America as areas for future expansion. But, we feel that expanding into these regions is more risky than Asia. The Asia-Pacific region we feel has much more potential for us. It is full of emerging markets. Also consumers' disposable income is increasing as their countries' economies grow. Most important of all, people in these countries are open to Western lifestyles.

This international subsidiary consists of 12 managers located primarily in Seattle, Washington. Together these managers are responsible for: the developing of new businesses internationally, financing and planning of international stores, managing international operations and logistics, merchandising in international markets, and, finally, for the training and developing of Starbucks' international managers. Since its establishment, this subsidiary has been responsible for opening Starbucks coffeehouses in Hawaii, Japan, and Singapore.

Lindemann, commenting on Starbucks' approach to Asian markets, notes:

> At Starbucks we don't like the concept of franchising. Therefore, we decided to work with partners in Japan and other Asian countries. Our approach to international expansion is to focus on the partnership first, country second. Partnership is everything in Asia. We rely on the local connection to get everything up and working. The key is finding the right local partners to negotiate local regulations and other issues.

When asked to list the criteria by which Starbucks chose partners in Asia, Lindemann highlights six points:

> We look for partners who share our values, culture, and goals about community development. We are trying to align ourselves with people, or companies, with plenty of

experience. We are primarily interested in partners who can guide us through the process of starting up in a foreign location. We look for firms with: (1) similar philosophy to ours in terms of shared values, corporate citizenship, and commitment to be in the business for the long haul, (2) multi-unit restaurant experience, (3) financial resources to expand the Starbucks concept rapidly to prevent imitators, (4) strong real estate experience with knowledge about how to pick prime real estate locations, (5) knowledge of the retail market, and (6) the availability of the people to commit to our project.

Entry into Japan

In October 1995, Starbucks entered into a joint venture with a Tokyo-based Sazaby Inc. This firm was expected to help Starbucks open 12 new stores in Japan by the end of 1997. This joint venture, amounting to 250 million yen ($2.33 million) in capitalization, is equally owned by Starbucks Coffee International and Sazaby. The Tokyo-based Sazaby, often recognized as a leader in bringing unique goods to the people of Japan, operates upscale retail and restaurant chains throughout Japan. Commenting on this joint venture, the president of Starbucks International, Howard Behar, notes:

> This powerful strategic alliance, which combines two major lifestyle companies, will provide the Japanese consumer a new and unique specialty coffee experience. . . . We look at this venture as though we're starting all over again, and in many ways, we are.

With Sazaby's assistance the firm opened two stores in Tokyo in September of 1996. The first outlet was in Tokyo's posh Ginza shopping district. The Ginza store was planned so that Japanese customers can have the same "Starbucks experience" offered in US stores. The firm's second store was located in Ochanomizu, a student area cluttered with colleges, bookstores, and fast-food restaurants. Starbucks hopes that students and office workers in the neighborhood will come in to grab a cup of coffee and a light snack. At both stores customers can eat in the store or take out their purchases.

The food-and-drink menus in the firm's Japanese coffeehouses are similar to those in the United States. The firm offers 15 types of beverages, snacks such as cookies and sandwiches, coffee beans, and novelty goods such as coffee mugs and T-shirts. The firm's single-shot-short latte costs 280 yen in Tokyo (about $2.50, a price that is roughly 50 cents more than in the United States). According to an August 1996 industry report, a cup of coffee in Tokyo cost about 399 yen, on average, in August 1996.

Although the Japanese are not used to Italian-style coffee beverages, Starbucks executives believe that Japanese consumers are ready to embrace the Starbucks

Figure 3

Japan Consumer
Preferences*

	1980	1985	1990	1994
Instant coffee	57.6%	59.2%	50.6%	45.4%
Regular coffee	33.3%	29.4%	33.1%	37.4%
Canned coffee	9.1%	11.4%	13.1%	17.3%
Total (cups per week)	7.4	9.02	9.52	10.36
Place of Consumption†				
Home	55.8%	58.3%	56.6%	54.7%
Coffee shop	24.6%	11.6%	8.9%	8.0%
Work/school	15.4%	21.8%	23.9%	26.4%
Other	4.2%	8.3%	10.6%	10.9%

*Based on a survey from October 20 through November 7, 1994, by the All Japan Coffee Association. The survey reported that men aged between 25 and 39 years consumed the most coffee at 16 cups per week and girls between 12 and 17 years consumed the least at 3 cups.

†Source: *Tea & Coffee Trade Journal*, August 1995.

Figure 4

Canned Coffee Sales in
Japan (US $ millions)

	Market Share	1991	1992	1993	1994	1995
Coca-Cola	40%	2,718	2,396	2,635	2,899	3,189
UCC	12	653	718	790	869	965
Pokka	11	599	658	724	797	877
Daido	10	544	599	658	724	797
Nestlé	7	381	419	461	507	558
Others	20	1,089	1,198	1,317	1,449	1,594
Total	100%	5,445	6,990	6,589	7,248	7,972

Canned coffee accounts for approximately 40% of total beverage sales in Japan, including soft drinks.

Source: *Advertising Age*, 1996.

concept. A report in *The Wall Street Journal* suggests that breaking into the Japanese market may not be easy (see Figures 3 and 4):

The Japanese haven't developed a taste for espresso drinks like latte and caffe mocha; they drink a lot of instant coffee or ready-to-drink coffee in cans, as well as American-style hot coffee. Moreover, the Japanese coffee market may be saturated with many coffee shops and vending machines serving hot coffees. Coca-Cola alone has more than 800,000 vending machines that sell canned coffee.[30]

Similarly, a report in the *Nikkei Weekly* points out:

Though Japan is the world's third largest coffee consumer, its coffee shops constitute a declining industry, with high operating costs knocking many small operators out of business. In 1992, there were 115,143 coffee shops in Japan, according to the latest government survey available. That figure is nearly 30 percent less than the peak in 1982.[31]

Japan's coffee core revolves around the *kissaten*, a relatively formal sit-down coffeehouse. According to the All Japan Coffee Association, while US and German consumers consumed 18.1 and 10 million bags of coffee

in 1994, respectively, the Japanese consumed 6.1 million coffee bags (one bag of coffee contains 60 kilograms of coffee beans).

Despite the absolute size of the Japanese coffee market, knowledgeable analysts note that Starbucks is likely to face stiff competition and retaliation from well-established players in Japan. Two of Japan's well-established coffee chains are the Doutor Coffee Company and the Pronto Corp.

Started in 1980, Doutor Coffee Company is Japan's leading coffee-bar chain. In 1996, it had over 466 shops in and around Tokyo. At times, the consumers refer to this firm as the McDonald's of coffeehouses since it provides a limited menu and emphasizes self-service. In Doutor's shops seating is limited and counters are provided where customers can stand while they consume their beverages. The focus is on speed of service and quick turnover of customers. The average customer stay in a Doutor coffee shop is about 10 minutes, about one-third the stay in a typical *kissaten*. Close to 90 percent of the Doutor's coffeehouses are operated by franchisees, while the remaining 10 percent are operated directly by Doutor. A standard cup of coffee at Doutor costs 180 yen. The firm serves other refreshments, such as juice, sandwiches, and pastries. It is reported that nearly 10 million customers per month visit Doutor coffeehouses. The firm has five shops in Ginza, the location where Starbucks opened its first store.[32]

Pronto Corp. is Japan's second largest coffee-bar chain. The firm opened its first shop in Tokyo in 1987. In 1996, it operated over 95 outlets, most of them in Tokyo. The firm's coffeehouses serve coffee and light snacks during the day, and at night they switch to neighborhood bar-type operations, serving alcoholic drinks and light meals. At Pronto, a standard cup of coffee costs 160 yen. Reacting to Starbucks' entry into Japan, Seiji Honna, president of Pronto Corp., notes: "For the past few years, we've had this nightmare scenario that espresso drinks are going to swallow up Japan's coffee market. . . . And we won't know how to make a good cup of espresso. . . . [And now Starbucks' entry], if they really mean business, I think they'll probably put some of us out of business."[33]

But he goes on to comment:

I don't think that the opening of the first Starbucks store in Japan would immediately be a threat to our

business...But Starbucks could become a strong competitor if it is able to gain consumer recognition in the next three years or so. In order to do so, Starbucks will need to have about 30 to 50 stores in the Tokyo area.[34]

Yuji Tsunoda, president of Starbucks Coffee Japan Ltd., indicates the company intends to have 100 directly owned coffee bars in major Japanese cities in the next five years.

According to Kazuo Sunago, an analyst from Japan's leading advertising firm Dentsu Inc., Japanese coffee bars lack the creativity to stop a firm like Starbucks from making inroads in the Japanese coffee market.

As traditional mom-and-pop coffee shops die off, big chains are looking for more attractive formats...But they are like a dry lake bed—void of new ideas. That's why the whole industry is stirred up about Starbucks.[35]

Comments Alstead: "The issue facing Starbucks is how, as we expand geographically and through expanding channels, will we be able maintain the Starbucks' culture."

1971	Starbucks Coffee opens its first store in the Pike Place Market—Seattle's legendary, open-air farmer's market.
1982	Howard Schultz joins Starbucks as director of retail operations and marketing. Starbucks begins providing coffee to fine restaurants and espresso bars in Seattle.
1983	Schultz travels to Italy, where he's impressed with the popularity of espresso bars. Milan, a city the size of Philadelphia, hosts 1,500 of these bars.
1984	Schultz convinces the original founders of Starbucks to test the coffee bar concept in a new Starbucks store on the corner of 4th and Spring in downtown Seattle. Overwhelmingly successful, this experiment is the genesis for a company that Schultz will found in 1985.
1985	Schultz founds Il Giomale, offering brewed coffee and espresso beverages made from Starbucks coffee beans.
1987	In August, with the backing of local investors, Il Giomale acquires the Seattle assets of Starbucks and changes its name to Starbucks Corporation. The company has fewer then 100 employees and opens its first stores in Chicago and Vancouver, B.C. **Starbucks store total = 17**
1988	Starbucks introduces mail order catalog, offering mail order service in all 50 states. **Starbucks store total = 33**
1989	Opens first Portland, Oregon, store in Pioneer Courthouse Square. **Starbucks store total = 55**
1990	Starbucks expands corporate headquarters in Seattle and builds a new roasting plant. **Starbucks store total = 84**
1991	Starbucks opens first stores in Los Angeles, California. Announces Starbucks' commitment to establish a long-term relationship with CARE, the international relief and development organization, and introduces CARE coffee sampler.
	Becomes the first US privately owned company in history to offer a stock option program, Bean Stock, that includes part-time employees. **Starbucks store total = 116**
1992	Starbucks opens first stores in San Francisco, San Diego, Orange County, and Denver. Specialty Sales and Marketing Division awarded Nordstrom's national coffee account. Completes initial public offering, with common stock being traded on the NASDAQ National Market System. **Starbucks store total =165**
1993	Opens premier East Coast market: Washington, D.C., Specialty Sales and Marketing Division begins relationship with Barnes & Noble, Inc., as national account. Opens second roasting plant located in Kent, Washington. **Starbucks store total = 275**

Appendix A

Starbucks Corporation—A Brief History

1994 Opens first stores in Minneapolis, Boston, New York, Atlanta, Dallas, and Houston. Specialty Sales and Marketing Division awarded ITT/Sheraton Hotel's national coffee account.

The Coffee Connection, Inc., becomes wholly-owned subsidiary of Starbucks Corporation in June.

Starbucks announces partnership with PepsiCo to develop ready-to-drink coffee-based beverages.

Completes offering of additional 6,025,000 shares of common stock at $28.50 per share.

Schultz receives Business Enterprise Trust Award recognizing the company's innovative benefits plan. **Starbucks store total = 425**

1995 Starbucks opens first stores in Pittsburgh, Las Vegas, San Antonio, Philadelphia, Cincinnati, Baltimore, and Austin. Specialty Sales and Marketing Division begins relationship with United Airlines.

Starbucks and Redhook Ale Brewery introduced Double Black Stout—a new dark-roasted malt beer with the aromatic and flavorful addition of coffee.

Acquires minority interest in Noah's New York Bagels, Inc.

Starbucks stores begin serving Frappuccino blended beverages, a line of low fat, creamy, iced coffee beverages.

Starbucks opens state-of-the-art roasting facility in York, Pennsylvania, serving East Coast markets.

Announces alliance with Chapters Inc. to operate coffee bars inside Chapters' superstores in Canada.

Announces partnership with Star Markets to open Starbucks retail locations within Star Market stores.

Develops framework for a code of conduct as part of a long-term strategy to improve conditions in coffee origin countries.

Starbucks Coffee International signs agreement with Sazaby Inc., a Japanese retailer and restaurateur, to form a joint venture partnership that develop Starbucks retail stores in Japan. The joint venture is called Starbucks Coffee Japan, Ltd.

Forms long-term joint venture with Dreyer's Grand Ice Cream, Inc., to develop revolutionary line of coffee ice creams. **Starbucks store total = 676**

1996 Opens first stores in Rhode Island, Idaho, North Carolina, Arizona, Utah, and Toronto, Ontario. Specialty Sales and Marketing Division awarded Westin Hotel's national coffee account.

Starbucks Coffee Japan, Ltd., opens first location outside North America in the Ginza District, Tokyo, Japan. Announces plans to develop 10 to 12 additional stores in the Tokyo metropolitan area over the next 18 months.

Starbucks Coffee International signs agreement forming Coffee Partners Hawaii, which will develop Starbucks retail locations in Hawaii.

First Starbucks store in Honolulu opens at Kalala Mall.

Starbucks Coffee International signs licensing agreement with Bonstar Pte. Ltd. to open stores in Singapore.

First Licensed Singapore location opens at Liat Towers.

Direct Response Division reaches over 7 million America Online (AOL) customers through Caffe Starbucks, a marketplace channel store that offers select Starbucks catalog products.

Announces that all Coffee Connection locations in the Boston area will become Starbucks stores during fiscal 1996.

Announces development agreement with three leading digital media companies—Digital Brands, Inc., Watts-Silverstein & Associates, and Cyberstruction, Inc.—to develop a wide-ranging on-line strategy.

Unveils prototype store at Comdex Convention and Trade Show, Las Vegas, with Intel Corp., showcasing some of the technologies Starbucks will be testing over the next year in several stores.

Forms licensing arrangement with ARAMARK Corp. to put licensed Starbucks operations at various locations operated by ARAMARK.

Starbucks and Dreyer's Grand Ice Cream, Inc., introduce six flavors of Starbucks ice cream and Starbucks ice cream bars, available in grocery stores across the United States. Starbucks ice cream quickly becomes the number one brand of coffee ice cream in the United States.

North American Coffee Partnership (between Starbucks and PepsiCo) announces a bottled version of Starbucks' popular Frappuccino blended beverage will be sold in supermarkets, convenience stores, and other retail points of distribution on the West Coast.

(continued)

Appendix A

(Continued)

Starbucks commemorates the first anniversary of the Blue Note Blend coffee and CD with Blue Note 2, an encore collection of jazz from the Blue Note Records label. The Blue Note Blend coffee also returns for a limited engagement in the company's coffee lineup.

Celebrates the company's 25th anniversary with marketing program featuring the art, music, and culture of 1971, the year Starbucks was born. **Starbucks store total = 1,100**

1997   First Starbucks locations open in Florida, Michigan, and Wisconsin.

Starbucks Coffee International opens first location in the Philippines.

Starbucks forms alliance with eight companies to enable the gift of over 320,000 new books for children through the All Books for Children holiday book buy.

Starbucks tests the sale of whole bean and ground coffee in Chicago-area supermarkets.

Starbucks successfully converts approximately $165 million of its 4.25% convertible subordinated debentures to common stock.

The Starbucks Foundation is launched through an initial contribution from Starbucks chairman and CEO Howard Schultz. The nonprofit foundation will support philanthropic efforts in the communities where Starbucks partners and customers live, work and play.

Starbucks Specialty Sales & Marketing Division awarded Canadian Airlines' national coffee account. **Starbucks location total = 1,412.**

1998   Starbucks opens first locations in New Orleans, St. Louis, Kansas City, and Portland, Maine.

Starbucks Coffee International opens first locations in Taiwan, Thailand, and New Zealand.

Starbucks introduces two new tea-based beverages: Chai Tea Latte, a sweet and spicy combination of black tea and milk, and Tiazzi blended juiced tea, a refreshing mixture of tea, fruit juice, and ice.

Starbucks acquires Seattle Coffee Company, the United Kingdom's leading specialty coffee company. In September, Starbucks Coffee Company (UK) Limited opens its first location in London and announces that all Seattle Coffee Company locations will be renamed during the course of 1999.

Starbucks introduces Milder Dimensions, a family of new lighter and milder-tasting premium coffee blends.

Starbucks forms a joint venture partnership with Earvin "Magic" Johnson's Johnson Development Corp. to develop Starbucks Coffee locations in underserved, inner-city urban neighborhoods throughout the United States.

Starbucks introduces coffee to supermarkets in 10 additional U.S. markets. Following the success of this program, Starbucks forms a long-term licensing agreement with Kraft Foods to accelerate growth of the Starbucks brand into the grocery channel across the United States.

For the second year in a row, Starbucks named one of the "100 Best Companies to Work For" in *Fortune* magazine. **Starbucks current location total = approx. 1,900.**

Appendix A

(Concluded)

Discussion Questions

1. What is the source of Starbucks' competitive success in the United States?

2. How vulnerable do you think Starbucks is to competition from imitators?

3. What is the logic behind Starbucks' strategy of expanding into international markets? Why is it important for the company to do this?

4. What is Starbucks' approach to entering international markets? What are the pros and cons of this approach?

5. Traditionally Starbucks has stayed away from a franchising strategy. Is this wise, particularly in the context of an international expansion strategy?

6. What challenges does Starbucks face in establishing a presence in Asia in general and Japan in particular? How successful do you think the company will be given the strategic choices it has made?

Notes

1. *Success*, April 1993.

2. *Chicago Tribune*, July 1, 1993.

3. According to the *Berkeley Wellness Letter*, a newsletter from the University of California, 53 percent of all coffee in the United States is consumed at breakfast. Further, 11 percent of the US population drinks decaf coffee, and 10 percent drinks instant coffee. Of the people who drink instant coffee most are over the age 55.

4. *The Wall Street Journal*, February 25, 1993. According to the National Coffee Association, brewed coffee

accounted for 85 percent of all coffee consumed in the United States during 1995. This was followed by espresso-based drinks (14 percent) and express coffee (1 percent).

5. Espresso, despite its potent flavor, is lower in caffeine than the canned coffees offered in supermarkets. It is made with Arabica beans that are lower in caffeine content, and the brewing method yields less caffeine per cup.

6. *The Wall Street Journal*, February 25, 1993.

7. *Sacramento Bee*, April 28, 1993.

8. This Colombian coffee bean crop is very small and grows only in the high regions of the Cordillera mountain range. For years, the Narino beans were guarded zealously by Western Europeans who prized their colorful and complex flavor. They were usually used for upgrading blends. Starbucks was determined to make them available for the first time as a pure varietal. This required breaking Western Europe's monopoly over the beans by convincing the Colombian growers that it intended to use "the best beans for a higher purpose."

9. *Canada Newswire*, March 1, 1993.

10. Though *Consumer Reports* rated Starbucks coffee as burnt and bitter, Starbucks customers felt otherwise and most of Starbucks' early growth can be attributed to enthusiastic word-of-mouth advertising. The typical Starbucks customer is highly proficient in the science of coffee beans and brewing techniques. The coffee bars even have their own dialect; executives from downtown Seattle businesses line up in force to order "tall-skinny-double mochas" and "2% short no-foam lattes."

11. *Inc.*, January 1993.

12. *Fortune*, December 9, 1996.

13. Ibid.

14. *Training*, June 1995.

15. *Fortune*, December 9, 1996.

16. The decision to offer benefits even to part-time employees (who represent roughly two-thirds of Starbucks' 10,000 employees) has gained a great deal of attention in the press. According to a Hewitt Associates L.L.C. survey of more than 500 employers, only 25 percent of employers offer medical coverage to employees working less than 20 hours a week. It was difficult to get insurers to sign Starbucks up since they did not understand why Starbucks would want to cover part-timers.

17. *Inc.*, January 1993.

18. *Business Insurance*, March 27, 1995, p. 6.

19. *Inc.*, January 1993.

20. *The Wall Street Journal*, April 4, 1995.

21. *The Wall Street Journal*, October 23, 1995.

22. In the past, one interesting outlet for Starbucks coffee was Starbucks' deal with Smith Brothers, one of the Northwest's oldest dairies. Smith Brothers used to sell Starbucks coffee on its home delivery routes. The idea for the alliance actually came from the dairy, a supplier for Starbucks. Management at Smith Brothers began to wonder if Starbucks' rapid growth might prompt it to look for other dairies to supply its milk. A report in the Seattle *Times* (November 6, 1992) noted that Carl Keller, sales manager for Smith Brothers, got the idea that "Maybe if we were a good customer of theirs, it would be more difficult for them to leave us." In 1992, Smith delivered 1,000 pounds of coffee beans a week. The coffee was sold at the same price as in Starbucks' retail stores, and the only complaint has been that Smith does not carry all 30 varieties. The company no longer sells coffee through Smith Brothers.

23. *Nations Restaurant News*, July 10, 1995.

24. According to Troy Alstead, "We are evaluating whether to offer our coffee in grocery stores, and we have done some private labeling of Starbucks coffee for Costco." The Specialty Coffee Association of America predicts that by 1999, supermarkets will account for 63 percent of all coffee sold in America. This will be followed by gourmet stores (14%), mass market (11%), mail order (8%), and other (8%).

25. Coke and Nestlé have signed a similar agreement to produce single-serving cold coffee drinks in specialty flavors such as French vanilla, mocha, and café au lait to compete with the Starbucks product.

26. Airports often grant exclusive concessions contracts to a single provider (e.g., Host Marriott). Since Starbucks wanted to tap these markets, it negotiated licensing arrangements with Marriott to run Starbucks stands in the airports that Marriott has under contract.

27. *Washington Post*, August 1, 1995.

28. The Hawaii entry is based on a joint venture with The MacNaugton Group, a real estate development firm that has been responsible for the successful introduction of several well-known mainland firms such as Sports Authority, Office Max, and Eagle Hardware stores into the Hawaiian Islands. Using this joint venture, the firm plans to develop approximately 30 stores throughout the Hawaiian Islands over the next three to four years. Starbucks' entry into Singapore is based on a licensing agreement with Bonvests Holdings Limited, a firm that is involved in property and hotel development, investment, related management services, waste management and building maintenance services, food and beverage retailing, and marketing of branded luxury products in Singapore. Under this agreement (completed in December 1996), 10 Starbucks coffee stores are expected to be opened within the first 12 to 15 months.

29. *Puget Sound Business Journal*, June 21–27, 1996.

30. *The Wall Street Journal*, September 4, 1996

31. *Nikkei Weekly*, September 23, 1996.

32. According to a report in the *Nihon Keizai Shimbum* (June 18, 1988), Doutor is good at segmenting the coffee market. For instance, the firm has a coffee shop for just about every taste and service level. The low-end shops are located near train stations and busy areas where people are in a hurry. In residential locations the firm operates Cafe Colorado where people can sit and chat for a while. The price of coffee in Cafe Colorado is double that in the firm's inexpensive coffeehouses. The firm also caters to more upscale customers via Cafe Doutor, where the ambiance is more elegant and the coffee price is much higher.

33. According to a report in *The Wall Street Journal,* Honna spent time last year gathering intelligence on Starbucks' method in the United States. He reportedly visited, incognito, more than 20 Starbucks coffee shops along the West Coast.

34. Reuters World Service, August 1, 1996.

35. *The Wall Street Journal*, September 4, 1996.

STEINWAY & SONS: GLOBAL COMPETITION AND ENTRY INTO CHINA

A Steinway is a Steinway. . . . There is no such thing as a "better" Steinway. Each and every Steinway is *the best Steinway*.

—*Theodore Steinway*

Bruce Stevens sat in the chair where Henry Z. Steinway, the last of the Steinway family dynasty, once sat. Across the table from him was Bob Dove, the firm's executive vice president. They were discussing issues concerning the growing size of the Chinese market and Steinway & Sons' strategy to enter this market.

The 1990s was a period of change for the music industry. Foreign competition in the mid-priced upright piano market was intense. In addition to well-entrenched players from Japan (Yamaha and Kawai), two South Korean firms (Young Chang and Samick) were emerging as strong competitors. Moreover, Yamaha and Young Chang had already established a presence in China. Forecasts indicated that the future market for pianos will be concentrated in Asia.

This case discusses Steinway & Sons' history, the evolution of its value system, and the current market conditions facing the firm. It highlights the issues faced by Steinway & Sons as its top management formulates its strategy toward the growing Chinese piano market.

Company Background

The Steinway Family Years—1853 to 1971

Steinway & Sons was founded in 1853 by Henry E. Steinway, Sr., and his sons, Henry, Jr., Charles, and William. In 1854 the firm entered and won its first competition. A year later it won first prize at the American Institute Fair in New York. By 1860 Steinway & Sons had built a manufacturing facility at 52nd Street and Fourth (now Park) Avenue, on the site now occupied by the Waldorf Astoria Hotel. Here 350 men produced 30 square pianos and 5 grands per week. In 1864 the firm opened a showroom on 14th Street. In 1865 sales topped $1 million.

From the beginning, piano building at Steinway & Sons was a family affair. Each of the Steinway sons concentrated on gaining expertise in a different aspect of piano manufacturing: William was a "bellyman" who installed the piano soundboards; Henry, Jr., focused on piano "finishing"; and Charles concentrated on "voicing" the piano. By 1854 the Steinways were employers, and the family members had become managers. Henry, Sr., was in charge overall, while

This case was prepared by Suresh Kotha, University of Washington and Roger Dunbar, Stern School of Business. The authors would like to acknowledge the assistance of Joseph H. Alhadeff (Stern MBA, 1995), Gerald Tennenbaum (Stern MBA, 1995), and Professor Xavier Martin (Stern). This case is intended to be used as a basis for class discussion rather than as an illustration of either effective or ineffective handling of the situation. Throughout the case, the authors quote from interviews conducted with company executives.

Henry, Jr., focused on research and development, Charles managed the plant, and William took care of marketing.

Music historians consider the competition at the 1867 Paris Exhibition as the turning point in the piano industry because it was there that the "American" system of cast-iron frames, heavier strings, solid construction, and more powerful tone took the competitive honors from European pianos. The jury report gave the Steinway piano a slight edge over the other major US manufacturer, Chickering & Sons, due to its expression, delicate shading, and a variety of accentuations.

With this recognition, Steinway's domestic piano sales and exports grew rapidly, requiring greater production capacity. In 1870, under William's leadership, the firm purchased 400 acres of remote farmland in Astoria, Queens, with the idea of moving the factory from Manhattan. By 1873 the new factory was operating, and Steinway-sponsored employee housing, transport, and other facilities were built. Two years later the firm opened a showroom in London. Ten years later, to avoid US labor issues and build a global presence, the firm built a factory in Hamburg, Germany. Pianos manufactured there were marketed in Europe and exported to the rest of the world. Today, these two factories remain the firm's only manufacturing centers.

In the 1870s, low-cost piano producers were a significant competitive threat. Conflict emerged between William and Theodore concerning the best way to respond. (C. F. Theodore was the fourth son of the founder and had joined the firm following his brothers' deaths in 1865.) The choice was to continue to emphasize class and high quality, as William favored, or to make inexpensive models, as advocated by Theodore. William's view won out. Ever since, the firm has remained steadfast in its focus on the high-end segment of the market.

At the turn of the century, the public developed an interest in player pianos. Steinway & Sons, however, showed no interest in these add-on technologies. Sales of player pianos plummeted after radio broadcasting began in 1920. In contrast, Steinway's sales continued to climb. They were supported by extensive advertising and a generous sponsorship program that deployed 600 Steinways to support concert artists.

Successive generations of Steinways sought to follow the founder's advice: "We provide customers with the highest quality instrument and services, consistent with Steinway's reputation for excellence, by building the finest piano in the world and selling it at a reasonable profit." This approach was threatened when the US economy entered a depression in the 1930s and the firm's survival was at stake. To market pianos to people of more modest means with smaller homes, Steinway developed and introduced two new models, the 5-foot, 1-inch "baby grand" and a 40-inch upright. At the outbreak of World War II, production was stopped. When piano making resumed in 1946, the television set was at the center of the American home. The task of rebuilding Steinway & Sons fell to Henry Z. Steinway, a fourth-generation Steinway, who took over the responsibility for manufacturing. His brother John took over promotions and marketing. To help consolidate the firm financially, Henry Z. sold Steinway Hall on 57th Street in Manhattan (the company's showroom) and leased back the lower two floors. In the 1960s new competition emerged from Asia. Yamaha and Kawai began exporting thousands of pianos to the United States. A Yamaha piano sold for about one-half the price of the equivalent Steinway model. By the early 1970s, the Japanese threat raised doubts about the future of Steinway & Sons and the entire US piano industry. Henry Z. decided to sell:

> Among the active family members, none were getting younger. And no young Steinways were interested in the firm. In the mid-20s, two stockholder managers could get in a room and do anything they wanted. With the depression, shares were diluted bringing many new owners. The New York factory was located in an area hostile to manufacturing. Other piano makers had moved South to where they appreciated manufacturers. If we chose to move, we needed lots of capital.

In 1972 the firm was sold and merged into the CBS Musical Instruments Division. Henry Z. observed:

> Japan represents both an opportunity and a menace. As the largest market in the world for new pianos, having surpassed the US, possibly Steinway could enter that market effectively with the aid of CBS. Conversely, free from restraints imposed by antitrust legislation in the US, one huge company [Yamaha] has the avowed purpose of overcoming Steinway. Why CBS and not General Motors or U.S. Steel? CBS wanted us at a price we thought right. More importantly, we thought CBS could and would handle our product in the right way.

The CBS Years—1972 to 1985

CBS increased capital spending from $100,000 annually to between $1 and 2 million. Workers received the medical and retirement benefits of other CBS employees. These were a big improvement over what had been provided previously. To facilitate continuity, Henry Z. remained president. Nevertheless, concerns soon arose. According to industry reports:

> Once CBS entered upon its own period of decline, Steinway was plagued by bureaucratic confusion, changing

strategies,and parades of efficiency experts. There were four Steinway presidents in [16 years]."Quality control" slipped. . . . There were pianists who began to say that the Steinway was no longer a great instrument; the market for half-century-old rebuilt Steinway boomed.[1]

Recalling the top management changes under CBS, Henry Z. Steinway observed:

Each new [division] president wanted to do something different. It was like riding a different horse every six months—first it was quality, then it was volume, then it was automation. The firm was drifting from one program to another. Also, I got so many memos from the parent corporation [CBS Musical Instruments Division] that after a while, I simply ignored them. I also thought it was rather amusing that I reported to the head of the division in California who, in turn, reported to a guy at the [CBS] headquarters just a few blocks from our offices in Manhattan.

Further, CBS often showed little regard or understanding for Steinway's established traditions. Steinway tradition, for example, encouraged workers to bring their relatives to work for the firm. Steinway believed this was a good way of preserving established skills and also encouraged loyalty and a reliable, motivated work force. Under CBS, however, such nepotism was strictly forbidden. Annoyed, Henry Z. retired from the firm in 1980. During the early 1980s, under the fourth CBS president, quality revived, and the firm introduced a new upright. This new 52-inch piano was aimed at institutions and music schools. Then CBS decided to divest all of its music businesses. The *Smithsonian* magazine reported:

That announcement alone nearly completed what earlier sloppiness and mismanagement could not. . . . In 1985, the year of the sale, Steinway was earning $8 million on $60 million in revenues. The sale, involving at least 18 interested parties, dragged out over a period of 10 months. There were rumors that the factory would be sold for its real estate value. CBS claimed to be concerned over the future of the company, but finally it needed cash to fend off attempts to take it over. And so CBS sold Steinway & Sons in haste, along with three other musical instrument companies, for less than $50 million—a much smaller sum than was offered earlier by serious devotees of the instrument.[2]

This brought morale among Steinway workers to an all-time low.

The Birmingham Years—1985 to 1995

CBS sold Steinway & Sons and the rest of its musical instruments division in December 1985 to John and Robert Birmingham, two brothers from Boston who had made their fortune through a family-owned heating-oil

business. The Steinway work force, which had just survived the uncertainty and confusion of the CBS years, was not predisposed to trust strangers.

Lloyd Meyers, the last CBS president, had tried to organize a leveraged buyout. Following the firm's acquisition, he left, as did the chief financial officer. Bruce Stevens became president. The sales force, which had been managed by a two-day-a-week manager, was placed under Frank Mazurco, a long-time Steinway district sales manager. The number of US dealers was reduced from 152 to 92. Bruce established a program to strengthen the ties between Steinway & Sons and its dealers. A formal five-day program for technicians was established to provide hands-on training at the New York and Germany plants. Additionally, the firm instituted a three-year strategic planning process. To instill more "discipline" into manufacturing, top management replaced the factory manager with Daniel Koenig, a manufacturing engineer who had spent 21 years at GE.

Under Koenig, the firm introduced state-of-the-art machines for manufacturing such components as hammers so that tolerances could be brought within carefully established limits. The whole "action-mechanism" department was reorganized and moved into a single location. New programs, such as statistical process control, were introduced. Engineers were hired and provided with state-of-the-art computer-aided design technology. The goal was to document the design and manufacturing process using old Steinway drawings, many of which dated back to the turn of the century.

These changes were viewed as controversial by some employees, music critics, and other followers of the firm. They observed that the changes top management had introduced to increase efficiency were working to the detriment of Steinway's historical tradition of craftsmanship and quality. Steinway management countered by arguing that employing a modern, scientific approach to manufacturing was not a break with, but a continuation of, Steinway traditions.

In 1991 Steinway & Sons introduced a new line—the Boston Pianos—designed to compete in the mid-range $10,000 piano market. This line was designed by Steinway & Sons and manufactured at Kawai's factory in Japan. According to Bruce Stevens:

Steinway dealers had suggested that a logical step-up strategy to a Steinway piano was needed. The availability of many competent lower-priced pianos made making a Steinway sale to a novice pianist harder to justify. We decided that a new line of mid-priced pianos was necessary.

Steinway dealers now had a piano they could offer to compete against similarly priced pianos made by Yamaha, Young Chang, Kawai, and Samick. Currently, the Boston line includes four grand piano models ranging in length from 5 feet, 4 inches to 7 feet, 2 inches, as well as four upright models ranging in height from 44 to 52 inches. The line does not include a full-size concert grand. As they were originally intended strictly as an export from Japan, Boston pianos sell for 25 percent more than Japanese domestic pianos.

According to John Birmingham perhaps the most important ingredient that the new owners brought to Steinway was their attitude. Noted John:

> We did not purchase the company to move it and make a fortune in real estate, or to silkscreen Steinway t-shirts, or to go public and make a killing on the stock offering. It was our intention to operate the Steinway piano business in a vigorous and creative way. Our guiding principle has been to guard and nurture the quality and integrity of the Steinway piano.

During the Birminghams' tenure, worker morale was gradually reestablished. Discussions between management and workers evolved so appropriate modernization of technical equipment occurred while respect for the unique aspects of the craft mode of production associated with a Steinway piano was maintained. In 1995 one of the firm's harshest critics from the New York Times acknowledged the following:

> A recent tour of the Steinway's factory in Queens showed an apparently serious effort to improve the instrument. The final stages of manufacture receive more attention than they did a few years ago. Outside technicians have also reported improvements in Steinways, a heartening sign.[3]

Enter Selmer Company, 1995

In 1995 Steinway & Sons was purchased by the Selmer Company, for nearly $100 million. This Elkhart, Indiana, firm had manufacturing facilities in La Grange, Illinois; Cleveland, Ohio; and Monroe, North Carolina. The Steinway & Sons management team installed by the Birminghams remained intact and in charge. Commenting on the merger, Dana Messina, an investment banker and a controlling shareholder of Selmer's parent corporation, noted:

> The combination of Steinway and Selmer is an exciting opportunity for both of the companies and their employees. Our extensive investigation has made it clear that Steinway's New York factory today produces excellent instruments of a quality unequaled in many years, and the Steinways made in the company's Hamburg factory continue to dominate the European and Asian concert scene. . . . We intend to continue the mission of producing great instruments that has been pursued by Steinway.

The new owners made an IPO stock offering to raise $60 million in August 1996.

The Steinway Legacy

There are two fundamentals in understanding the origins of the Steinway legacy: technical innovation and marketing. Around 1800 the piano's identity was still in a formative stage, but by the 1850s, the instrument's basic structure had been defined. Taking the basic structure as a given, the Steinways improved the piano and, ultimately, the entire industry.

Building Technical Capabilities

In 1850 producers were working to make piano performance more reliable and louder. New piano works by romantic composers had appeared, and they demanded a broader range of tones. In addition, larger concert halls were being built. These developments served to establish a need for pianos with a louder tone. The general objective of Steinway & Sons' efforts was to develop reliable pianos that offered a more powerful tone.

Experimentation at Steinway & Sons was done primarily by two of the founder's sons, Henry, Jr., and Theodore. These Steinway brothers experimented and developed theories about improvements to both the design and the manufacture of pianos. In 1911 Alfred Dolge described Theodore's approach as follows:

> Step-by-step he invaded the fields of modern science, investigating and testing different kinds of wood in order to ascertain why one kind or another was best adapted for piano construction, then taking up the study of metallurgy, to find a proper alloy for casting iron plates which would stand the tremendous strain of 75,000 pounds of the new concert-grand piano that was already born in his mind, calling chemistry to his aid to establish the scientific basis for felts, glue, varnish oils—in short, nothing in the realm of science having any bearing on piano construction was overlooked.[4]

Over a 50-year period starting in 1857, the firm obtained 58 patents for various innovations to piano design. At international exhibitions in Europe, the Steinways proudly showed off their new methods and basked in the resulting acclaim. One consequence was that their methods were copied widely, especially in Europe. By the 1870s, the "Steinway system" was well recognized, and, by the end of the century, it became the de facto industry standard.

During the mid-19th century, new industrial technologies emerged to cause a revolution in piano manufacturing. Steinway & Sons was at the forefront of these developments, implementing innovative and unique approaches to piano manufacturing. At their large facility, opened in 1860, they standardized various parts of the piano to facilitate volume manufacturing, refitting, and servicing. Though the firm used increased mechanization to produce standardized components, it retained a "craft" approach for other components and for assembling pianos. The combination of the mechanized technologies and individual craft skills quickly became a hallmark of the Steinway approach to manufacturing pianos.

Building Reputation

From the beginning, Steinway & Sons faced intense competition from rivals such as Chickering & Sons and Mason & Hamlin in the United States, and Erard and Broadwood in Europe. Facing this competition, the firm sought to highlight not only the unique construction of the Steinway piano but also its superior sound.

To do this, the firm entered its pianos in contests that compared manufacturers' products. In 1854, for example, the firm exhibited a square piano at the Metropolitan Fair held in Washington, D.C., and received a prize medal. A year later Steinway & Sons entered the American Institute Fair at the Crystal Palace in New York and the judges awarded it first prize from among 19 competitors.

> [Steinway & Sons'] great triumph came at the great fair of the American Institute in New York in 1855, where their overstrung square piano with full iron frame created a sensation in the piano world. As a result their business expanded so rapidly that in 1859 the erection of that mammoth factory on Fifty-Third Street and Fourth Avenue, New York, became a necessity.[5]

To gain international recognition, Steinway & Sons, along with 130 other manufacturers, entered the International Exhibition held at the Crystal Palace in London in 1862. Steinway & Sons was recognized as the best American manufacturer and was awarded a major prize. The main prize went to Broadwood. In 1867 the firm entered the Paris Exposition, along with 178 other firms. Both Steinway and Chickering were awarded gold medals there.

Winning by Not Competing

At the major manufacturers' competition held in Vienna in 1873, around two-thirds of the pianos exhibited were built according to the Steinway system. Steinway & Sons itself did not compete, however, having reached an agreement with Chickering not to do so to avoid continuation of the shrill accusations that had arisen between the two rivals after the Paris Exposition. With the competition over, however, the judges issued a statement regretting that "Steinway & Sons, the celebrated inaugurators of the new piano-making system,

had chosen not to exhibit." From the standpoint of enhancing its reputation for making a superior piano, Steinway & Sons "won" in Vienna by not competing.

Industry rivalries also persuaded Steinway & Sons and 15 other piano-making firms from the eastern United States to boycott the 1893 World's Fair held in Chicago. As expected, W. W. Kimball, a Chicago piano manufacturer, won the highest award. At the time, however, Steinway & Sons was promoting a US tour of the Polish virtuoso, Ignace Jan Paderewski. Paderewski was invited to play at the exhibition's inauguration, but only if he would play on a piano entered in the competition. Paderewski countered that he could only play on a piano he was used to playing. The organizers relented and Paderewski played his Steinway. Again, unfolding events enabled Steinway & Sons to enhance their reputation by not competing.

A Steinway Is a Steinway

Steinway & Sons always sought to establish a reputation for itself as the firm that built the best piano for musicians, especially concert artists. It also sought to establish itself as being a contributor, supporter, and leader in the cultural arts. As Dolge noted:

> They never relaxed in letting the public know that they manufactured a fine piano. William Steinway, with far-seeing judgment, was not satisfied only to use printer's ink with telling effect, but he also began to educate the public to appreciate good music. Steinway Hall was erected, the Theodore Thomas orchestra generously supported, and the greatest piano virtuosos from Rubinstein to Joseffy engaged for concerts, not only in New York but in all large cities of the United States and Canada[7]

Steinway Hall, designed and built by William Steinway in 1866, was the largest concert hall in New York City. Notes Dolge:

> The opening of this hall was the inauguration of a new era in the musical life of America. Anton Rubenstein, Annette Essipoff, Teresa Carreno, Fannie Bloomfield-Zeisler, Rafael Joseffy, Eugene D'Albert, Leopold Damrosch and Anto Seidl made their bows to select audiences from the platform of Steinway Hall. William Steinway knew that the American people needed musical education. He provided it.[8]

Concert artist endorsements was another method used by Steinway & Sons to convince the public that its pianos were superior. Initially, the effort at Steinway & Sons was largely opportunistic and informal. However, the benefits of more large-scale efforts were recognized as a result of the 215-concert US tour in 1872 by the virtuoso Anton Rubinstein, who was sponsored by Steinway & Sons. Rubinstein and his Steinway dazzled audiences. In 1891 the Steinway-sponsored concert tour of Ignace Jan Paderewski was also a great success. Paderewski cleared an unprecedented $200,000 from his tour, and the promotional value to Steinway & Sons was immeasurable.

These concerts, the artists involved, and the sponsor all received extensive press coverage and acclaim. In 1912 Charles Steinway, the president of Steinway & Sons, observed, "It was without doubt the most effective of all advertising methods we employed, since it not only made the piano and its maker widely known, but assisted in laying the foundation for a broad national culture."

Though Steinway & Sons never offered to reduce the price of its pianos, it sought endorsements from New York's social elite.[9] To this and other groups the firm presented itself as offering a high-quality product worthy of a high price. Today, the Steinway pianos are priced the highest in the industry. Often, this price is nearly double that of an equivalent Yamaha, the firm's most competitive rival in the United States.

Steinway & Sons has consistently emphasized its commitment to the cultural enrichment of the nation and the world. The firm's promotions argue, for example, that the act of buying a piano is not the same as the act of buying a Steinway. Buying a Steinway is depicted as an indication of appreciation for high cultural taste and, hence, a sign of high achievement. The firm also built upon its international presence. Dolge noted:

> Having established the fame of his piano in America beyond dispute, William [Steinway] looked for other worlds to conquer, and opened a branch house in the city of London about the year 1875. Steinway Hall in London was formally opened in 1876. In 1880 Hamburg factories were started, to supply the ever-growing European Trade.[10]

The Hamburg facility was established primarily to challenge the domination of European piano markets by companies such as Bechstein, Bluthner, and Ibach. At the time, the firm was the only piano maker that served all well-known concert artists in every major city in America and in Europe. According to D. W. Fostle, an author and keyboard expert, "A Steinway piano soon became recognized as an admired cultural icon in any refined home, a necessary element on any prominent concert stage, and part of the necessary baggage of any prominent pianist."[11]

Building a Marketing Approach

Like its competitors, Steinway & Sons originally sought out and paid for endorsements from prominent concert artists. Over time, however, Steinway and other firms ceased paying for endorsements. Concert artists, however, still chose to endorse the Steinway piano over others. Today, more than 90 percent of all classical music concerts featuring a piano soloist are performed on a Steinway concert grand piano.[12] This endorsement has remained stable for many decades. Music schools and conservatories such as Juilliard, Oberlin, and Indiana University have always showed a great fondness for Steinways. Steinway & Sons sought to be associated with high culture, style, status, and class. In 1855 the firm started advertising daily in the *New York Times*. Gradually, Steinway & Sons moved to much more extensive advertising campaigns.

> To the astonishment and chagrin of the older and more conservative houses in the piano trade, William [Steinway] started an aggressive and heretofore unheard-of advertising campaign. As a competent judge he knew that his factories turned out the best pianos that could possibly be made, and he was bent not only on letting the world know it, but on making the world believe it, as he did. This was revolutionary, even shocking, but William persisted until he carried his point.[13]

Steinway as an Investment

In 1900 Steinway & Sons hired N. W. Ayer & Son, the oldest full-service advertising agency in the country, to promote Steinway pianos. Ayer & Son emphasized that many potential Steinway buyers not only were interested in music but also were greatly interested in class and status. Their interest in owning a Steinway would increase if the class and status associated with the Steinway name were emphasized.

Systematically, the firm broadened the message in its promotions. The firm's advertising emphasized, for example, that one did not "buy" but "invested" in a Steinway, that there was no such thing as a better Steinway for a Steinway was the best, that owning a Steinway was more important than being able to play it, and that a Steinway piano was always made just a little bit better than was necessary. Steinway advertising was targeted to emphasize family values, the contributions to art and music of Steinway & Sons, Steinway's technical excellence, or some combination of these. Forging a link with the arts community, the firm commissioned paintings showing famous artists and composers, past and present, linked to the Steinway piano. The timeless excellence of a Steinway was emphasized.

> The commission and use of modern art in Steinway ads of the 1920s was an extension of the advertising style that the New York firm had employed for decades...[W]ith Steinway the association was natural. However much another product's image was improved by its proximity to art, it remained a mere product. The Steinway itself became art.[14]

In the 1920s the program to make sure that all out-standing concert artists used a Steinway grew to include more than 600 supported artists. With a consistent and overwhelming advertising message and its US competition in retreat, the firm convinced the public that a Steinway was the only "artistic" piano.[15]

According to *Forbes*, a Steinway piano outperforms Mercedes-Benz automobiles, powerboats, wine, and gold as luxury items for investment. A Steinway created between 1929 and 1958 is now worth nearly six times its original cost; for those dating from 1959 to 1978 the factor of appreciation currently stands at nearly three times. Piano rebuilders are known to scour the world in search of old Steinways because, regardless of its age or neglect, a Steinway grand can often be restored to its original magnificence.

The 1970s and 1980s saw new competition emerge from Asian competitors. Of particular interest was Yamaha's announced intention to overtake the status associated with a Steinway. Yamaha's president claimed this would be done by promoting Yamaha's sound quality and tone along with the status and class associated with the Yamaha name. Despite Yamaha's avowed threat to overtake the status of Steinway & Sons, the firm's reputation as producer of the best-sounding piano has remained pretty much intact. In 1991 Dolge noted:

> Just as a most masterful copy of a Raphael or Correggio will ever be only a copy and far from the original, so it has proved impossible to produce a piano equal to the Steinway piano, even though the Steinways were copied to the minutest detail. No art product can be duplicated by copying.

Manufacturing Steinways

Manufacturing a Steinway piano is a labor-intensive and time-consuming process. A Steinway concert grand piano is one of the world's most complex pieces of hand-built machinery. It consists of more than 12,000 parts and requires about a year to complete. Approximately 300 craftspeople have a hand in its development.

The 44,000-square-foot manufacturing facility manufactured about 67 percent of Steinway pianos sold in 1995. This facility consists of many linked buildings that house the factory and Steinway's offices. In 1985, 260 direct workers and 61 nondirect workers were involved in manufacturing pianos. The production workers are represented by Local 102 of the United Furniture Workers, a small two-company local that has bargained with Steinway management for decades. In 1986 wages averaged approximately $9 per hour ($12 including fringes). About 25 percent of the skilled artisans are paid via

piece rates, while other workers are paid on a straight-time basis. Throughout the factory, there are workers who represent families that have been with the firm for generations. Currently, the work force has a multinational cast of first-generation immigrants. More than 17 languages are spoken in the factory.

The factory is part lumber mill, part fine-cabinet works, part manual-crafts assembly line, and part studio for industrial artisans working an art acquired through many years of apprenticeship. Although the buildings have undergone significant changes over the years, the piano-making operations have hardly changed in the last century.

Lumber Mill

The mill, the factory's lumber yard, carries approximately 1.5 million board feet of select woods (costing approximately $2 million) such as hard rock maple and sitka spruce. Twice a year, the firm's wood technologist, Warren Albrecht, goes to Canada and the American Northwest to identify wood of sufficient quality and grain to be used by Steinway. These woods are air-dried in the open for about 18 months and then kiln-dried using recently installed computer-controlled equipment. Reduction of the wood's moisture content through drying is essential for the instrument's acoustics. Through years of trial and error, the firm has managed to establish ideal moisture content and drying times for each of the instrument's various wooden components. It is here, via the world's finest woods, that the foundation of what eventually becomes a Steinway piano begins.

M-Bending Operations

This operation focuses on the piano's rim (the curved sideboard giving grand pianos their shape and support). A concert grand's rim requires a 22-foot-long, three-and-one-half-inch-wide board of hard rock maple. Because boards of this length rarely occur in nature, thin slats of maple laminates (18 layers thick) are glued together to form the piece. When bent, this wooden piece forms the piano's familiar outer and the hidden inner rim that extends below the sound board and frame. Steinway's processes for bending the inner and outer board remain unique in the industry. According to Henry Z. Steinway, it is this process that provides the instrument with greater strength and durability.

The rim-bending room consists of eight piano-shaped forms of steel whose perimeters are fitted with screws and clamps. With the glue holding the 18 layers of laminates still wet, the piece is manually pressed against the form and secured by iron pinions.[16] The bent rim is then heated by high-frequency radio waves. Although the rim is technically ready in minutes for the next process, it remains in the iron form for 24 hours. Once removed, the piece is stacked in a humidity-controlled environment for 10 weeks. This curing period ensures that the rim retains its bent form. Following the waiting period, the rim is planed, sanded, and cross-braced and then the key bed and pin block are inserted. Slowly the rim is transformed into a unitary piano case.

The Sounding Board Assembly

In another part of the factory, highly skilled woodworkers create the piano's sounding board. The sounding board consists of 20 spruce boards, selected from the same lot of wood, meticulously cleared of any imperfections. These boards are matched for grain and color and glued along their lengths. Once glued, the board is thinned in certain places and tapered toward the ends. By the application of support ribs to its underside, the board is also slightly crowned. Then a bridge, the clefshaped support for the strings, is affixed.

The Action Mechanism

The guts of the piano consists of the keys and the action. Together, they constitute the mechanism by which the act of depressing the key causes the corresponding hammer to strike the string and return to its original resting place.[17] Once assembled, the actions are mated with the piano's keys and the entire key-action assembly mechanism is regulated to ensure proper movement. After being regulated, the key-action assembly is moved to another part of the factory, where the keys are weighted to ensure they provide the appropriate touch and recoil. Proper touch and recoil result in the piano's "even feel," an important trait of the legendary Steinway experience. The mechanism is then fitted into a piano case. The foundation that supports the key-action assembly is the spruce key bed.

The Final Assembly

The joining of the piano case and an iron plate to support the strings is carried out in the factory's "belly" room. The bellying process involves attaching the iron plate and the sounding board to the inner rim of the piano case. This process takes up to eight hours over the course of two days. During this process, the sounding board is securely affixed to the piano case using a special hot glue that ensures a good seal between the board and the piano case. The board installation process is critical for the proper resonance of the strings, and multiple measurements are taken to ensure a proper fit.

Once the hot glue sets and the clamps holding the board in place are removed, the cast-iron plate is lowered into the case. Accurate installation of the plate ensures the proper bearing of the bridge, which then helps maintain the right pressure on the piano's strings. Too little or too much pressure results in an instrument that sounds weak or muffled. With the sounding board and iron-plate installation complete, the piano is ready for stringing.

The stringing process involves the hammering of pins into a pin block underneath the iron plate and the insertion of about 243 strings. After the instrument is strung, it passes through a "banger," which mechanically pounds every key about 8,000 times within a 45-minute period. This "aging" process ensures that the sound notes emanating from the instrument are stable. The instrument is then regulated to ensure its moving parts (the key-action mechanism) interact properly.

The Steinway piano comes in flat and glossy finishes. The flat finish is the trademark of the Queens factory, and the glossy finish is typical of the Hamburg factory. Each piano receives five coats of lacquer prior to the insertion of the sounding board and iron plate, but it is not truly finished until the time of shipment. Once assembled, pianos are polished and rubbed in a manually intensive process.

The Tone-Regulating Department

Many of the sound-related operations are carried out in the tone-regulating department by a group considered to include Steinway's most skilled technicians. Highly skilled artisans (as the firm prefers to call them) optimize the final tone of the piano and do all the fine-tuning. For the concert grands, this process can take as long as a week per piano.

Tuning involves adjusting the piano strings to get the proper tonal quality, and "voicing" entails final adjustments to the shape of the hammer, the feel of the felt, and the movement and position of actions. With the personality or voice of the piano exposed, final adjustments are completed to optimize the instrument's sound qualities. The time taken to complete this process varies from 8 to 24 hours. Variations in the production process are accommodated during the tuning and voicing processes and contribute to the distinctive sound of each Steinway piano. Given the nature of the craft production process, each step is contingent upon the success of the previous steps, and there is little room for error. Each piano sounds and feels different. The firm encourages prospective buyers to play several pianos and then to pick the one they think sounds best.

By the time a piano is assembled, strung, tuned, and voiced, it has gone through 25 to 30 checkpoints. The workers responsible for sounding board placement, stringing, and tone adjustment and other big jobs often sign their work. According to one Steinway tuner, "It's an aspiration of everybody to be immortal, and so, like an artist who signs his painting, I sign the piano. I put into the piano the best of myself."[18] In the 1980s John Steinway observed:

> A Steinway is a Steinway only because we don't cut any corners. My great-grandfather started that 135 years ago. I often say we're probably thickheaded and stubborn; we stick to our principles. But it works.[19]

Arthur Loesser has chronicled the history of the piano and describes the sound of Steinway's concert grand piano most eloquently:

> The end result of the Steinway effort was a tone-producing tool of matchless strength and sensitiveness...It was a marvelous kind of sound for the music that people loved then: thick, thundering piles of chord, booming batteries of octaves, and sizzling double jets of arpeggios. But the single Steinway tone, struck gently and held, also worked its ineffable spell, taking an endless, yearning time to die.[20]

In 1986 the total direct-labor costs for a grand piano averaged between $1,350 and $2,050, and for vertical pianos, between $600 and $800. The material costs for a grand piano averaged between $1,900 and $3,600, and for upright pianos, between $1,200 and $2,200. The firm produced 2,698 pianos in 1994.

Historically, grand pianos have accounted for the bulk of Steinway's production. Steinway offers eight models of the grand pianos that range in length from five feet, one inch for a baby grand to nine feet for the largest concert-style piano. Grand pianos are at the premium end of the piano market in terms of quality and price, with Steinway's grands dominating the high end of the market. Retail prices range from $27,600 to $101,200 in the United States.

The Market and Competition

According to a 1990 survey conducted by the Gallup Organization for the American Music Conference, slightly more than 4 in 10 (43 percent) US households contained at least one amateur instrumental musician. The survey reported that about 42 million music-making households exist in the United States. However, this represented a drop from 46 percent in 1985. About 44 percent of piano players were male, and 56 percent were female.

Generally, players were under the age of 35 (the median age was 28). Among musical instruments, piano and the guitar topped the survey's list, with about 40 percent of players choosing the piano and 17 percent the guitar. Amateur musicians came from households that had a higher median income level ($45,860) than the total population ($37,640) and were headed by an adult with more than a high school education.[21]

Domestic Competition

In the 1960s US piano manufacturers were first confronted with Japanese piano imports. The Japanese firms offered high-quality pianos at a much lower price than US manufacturers. By 1968 two Japanese firms, Yamaha and Kawai, were selling 10,000 units annually. Together they captured 5 percent of US upright piano sales and 28 percent of US grand piano sales.

The 1980s saw further significant change in the US piano market. Yamaha introduced the first all-digital synthesizer, which could effectively produce a range of high-quality sounds. Yahama's introduction of the synthesizer effectively undercut the low-end acoustic piano market. In fact, sales of acoustic pianos declined from a high of 233,000 per year at the beginning of the 1980s to 50,000 units annually in 1994. As sales of upright pianos decline, the number of grand pianos sold has increased (see Figure 1 and Table 1).

Although Japan and Korea held 11 percent of the US market in 1980, they held 38 percent of it by 1985. Several US firms have closed, and currently only two US firms, Steinway & Sons and Baldwin, continue to make pianos. Several foreign firms now have US manufacturing facilities. Kawai operates a plant in North Carolina, and Samick has a manufacturing facility in California. Currently, the high-volume producers are located in Japan, Korea, China, and the Soviet Union. Total US production is in third place—at about the same level as that of South Korea.

US Piano Market in 1995

In 1995 the musical instrument industry in the United States generated retail sales of approximately $5.5 billion. The acoustic piano segment, which represents approximately 11 percent of the total musical instrument industry, had retail sales of $598 million in 1995, up 7 percent from 1994.[22] This included an 11 percent increase for grand pianos more than five feet in length. During the period from 1991 to 1995, total dollar sales of grand pianos increased at an average annual rate of more than 7 percent, from $288 million to $372 million. Upright piano dollar sales, in contrast, increased at an average rate of only 1.5 percent during the same period.

Steinway's domestic market share of the grand piano market was approximately 7 percent in 1995. Approximately 90 percent of Steinway's unit sales were made on a wholesale basis, with the remaining 10 percent sold directly by Steinway at one of its five company-owned retail locations. Steinway & Sons operates five retail stores in New York, New Jersey, London, Hamburg, and Berlin. The West 57th Street store in New York City, known as Steinway Hall, is one of the largest and most famous piano stores in the world. Steinway pianos are sold by dealers in 45 states across the country. The firm's

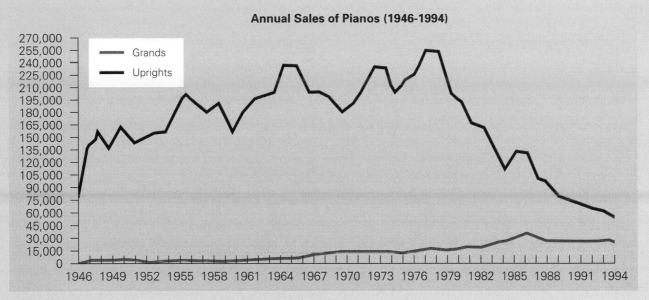

Figure 1

Historical Sales of Steinway & Sons Pianos

	1992			1987		
Product Type	**Firms with Shipments of $100,000 or More**	**Units***	**Value* (mil.)**	**Firms with Shipments of $100,000 or More**	**Units***	**Value* (mil.)**
Verticals, uprights, consoles, 37" or less in height	1	—	—	3	40,900	$38.5
Verticals, uprights, consoles, more than 37" in height	7	53,700†	$84.1†	5	52,100	$75.1
Grand pianos	3	5,500	$53.5	3	7,700	$58.2

*Number of units shipped and value of shipments reported are for all producers in the industry, not just for those with shipments valued at greater than $100,000.

†Represents combined figures for all verticals and upright pianos. Figures for 37" or less are not available separately.

Source: *U.S. Bureau of Census, 1992.*

Table 1

Sales of US Pianos by Product Type—1992 and 1987

leading markets are in and around major metropolitan areas. The two largest regions in terms of sales are California and New York, which together accounted for approximately 20 percent of domestic wholesale revenues in 1995 (see Table 2). The institutional segment of the US piano market, which includes music schools, conservatories, and universities, represented less than 10 percent of Steinway's domestic sales.[23] Steinway's largest dealer accounted for approximately 8 percent of sales in 1995, while the top 15 accounts represented 28 percent of sales.

In 1994 the firm sold 2,698 grand pianos worldwide. (See Table 3 for a history of Steinway's grand piano sales.) During this same year, the firm reported a net income of $3.1 million on sales of $101 million (see Table 4). Approximately 50 percent of Steinway's total sales were in the United States, 37 percent were in Europe, and the remaining 13 percent were in Asia. Steinway's market share in Japan and Korea combined was less than 1 percent. Germany, Switzerland, France, the United Kingdom, and Italy accounted for the

Table 2

Steinway's Top 10 US
Markets, 1994 (000s)

Location	Sales
New York City	$6,007
Los Angeles	2,643
Baltimore/Washington, D.C./Virginia	2,250
Dallas	1,642
Phoenix	1,438
Boston	1,144
San Francisco	1,078
Salt Lake City	848
Minneapolis/St. Paul	793
Detroit	605

Source: Steinway & Sons.

Year	US Grands	Foreign Grands	Total Grands	Year	US Grands	Foreign Grands	Total Grands
1994	1,720	978	2,698	1979	1,815	1,357	3,172
1993	1,631	887	2,518	1978	1,819	1,334	3,153
1992	1,344	917	2,261	1977	1,590	1,372	2,962
1991	1,550	1,438	2,988	1976	1,908	1,241	3,149
1990	2,117	1,459	3,576	1975	1,875	1,160	3,035
1989	2,096	1,385	3,481	1974	2,001	937	2,938
1988	2,144	1,283	3,427	1973	1,919	1,131	3,050
1987	2,144	1,237	3,381	1972	1,809	1,212	3,021
1986	1,763	1,369	3,132	1971	1,540	1,173	2,713
1985	1,337	1,291	2,628	1970	1,470	1,142	2,612
1984	1,876	1,340	3,216	1969	1,806	1,163	2,969
1983	2,036	1,263	3,299	1968	1,932	1,250	3,182
1982	1,677	1,141	2,818	1967	1,603	1,043	2,646
1981	2,041	1,394	3,435	1966	1,770	1,056	2,826
1980	1,897	1,349	3,246	1965	1,659	1,259	2,918

Source: Steinway & Sons.

Table 3

Historical Steinway Unit Sales (1965–1994)

greatest percentage of sales outside the Americas. Steinway's largest European markets were Germany and Switzerland.

Steinway pianos are primarily purchased by affluent individuals with incomes of more than $100,000 per year. The typical customer is more than 45 years old and has a serious interest in music. Steinway's core customer base consists of professional artists and amateur pianists, as well as institutions such as concert halls, conservatories, colleges, universities, and music schools. Customers purchase Steinway pianos either through one of the firm's five retail stores or through independently owned dealerships. More than 90 percent of the firm's piano

sales in the United States are to individuals. In other countries, sales to individuals are a smaller percentage of the total sales.

Baldwin

In 1862 Dwight H. Baldwin, a music teacher, founded this firm as a retail piano business in Cincinnati, Ohio. In 1865 Baldwin hired Lucien Wulsin as a bookkeeper and in 1870 made him a partner. Until his death in 1912, Wulsin shaped the firm's development.

Branch stores were opened in Indianapolis, Indiana; Louisville, Kentucky; and other towns in Ohio. In 1887, when M. Steinert & Company, a Steinway franchisee,

	1990	1991	1992	1993	1994
Income Statement Data					
Net sales	$92,037	$98,816	$89,240	$89,714	$101,896
Gross profit	33,673	35,586	30,759	26,139	31,636
Operating income	10,096	9,124	4,556	1,919	8,795
Income (loss) from continuing operations	3,077	2,753	(2,930)	(3,009)	2,847
Net income (loss)*	3,618	2,825	(10,335)	(3,009)	3,115
Ratio of earnings to fixed charges[#]	2	2	1	**	2
Other Data					
EBITDA[†]	$13,500	$13,535	$9,591	$6,067	$13,068
Nonrecurring charges‡	1,861	2,319	2,532	2,047	1,658
Interest expenses, net	3,448	3,186	3,307	4,390	3,842
Depreciation and amortization§	1,669	2,099	2,675	2,695	2,664
Capital expenditures*	2,451	1,889	1,936	1,237	1,145
Steinway grand pianos sold (in units)	3,558	3,282	2,648	2,245	2,569
Margins					
Gross profit, percentage	37%	36%	44%	29%	31%
EBITDA, percentage	15%	14%	11%	7%	13%
Balance Sheet Data					
Current assets	$68,306	$70,120	$73,300	$56,259	$58,760
Total assets	85,701	87,832	91,784	72,677	76,019
Current liabilities	30,327	32,078	45,602	31,896	32,969
Long-term debt	31,921	29,395	28,715	26,394	25,379
Redeemable equity	3,614	4,227	1,471	1,000	270
Stockholders' equity	9,066	10,606	3,690	767	4,935

*Net loss for the fiscal year ended June 30, 1992, included loss from discontinued operations of $7,405,000 as a result of Steinway's September 14, 1992, disposition of its Gemeinhardt Company, Inc., subsidiary.

[†]EBITDA represents earnings before tax expense (benefit), adjusted to exclude certain nonrecurring charges and charges related to previous ownership, which are not expected to recur. While EBITDA should not be construed as a substitute for operating income or a better indicator of liquidity than cash flow from operating activities, which are determined in accordance with generally accepted accounting principles, it is included herein to provide additional information with respect to the ability of the company to meet its future debt service, capital expenditure, and working capital requirements. EBITDA is not necessarily a measure of the company's ability to fund its cash needs. EBITDA is included herein because management believes that certain investors find it to be a useful tool for measuring the ability to service debt.

‡Nonrecurring charges represent certain costs and expenses primarily consisting of certain executive compensation and benefits and office-related expenses of Steinway which, as a result of the merger, are not expected to recur.

§Depreciation and amortization for the fiscal year ended June 30, 1994, excludes approximately $563,000 of amortization of deferred financing costs written off pursuant to a debt refinancing effected in April 1994. (See note # following.)

*Capital expenditures of Steinway exclude expenditures for additions to the Concert and Artist Piano Bank.

[#]For purposes of this computation, fixed charges consist of interest expense and amortization of deferred financing costs and the estimated portion of rental expense attributable to interest. Earnings consist of income (loss) before taxes plus fixed charges.

**Earnings were inadequate to cover fixed charges by $3,065,000 for the year ended June 30, 1993.

Table 4

Steinway & Sons—Income Statement and Balance Sheet (000s)

opened a retail store in Cincinnati, the Steinways canceled Baldwin's Steinway franchise. Wulsin responded by planning Baldwin's first manufacturing facilities, and production started in Chicago in 1889. To sell Baldwin pianos, Wulsin introduced a dealer consignment program whereby the dealer paid for the piano only after it sold. The company also experimented with installment sales contracts. This combination of consignment selling and installment contracts led to the firm's rapid growth at the turn of the century. Baldwin's successful approach was copied by most other piano manufacturers.

Rapid growth of the firm in the 1950s and the inadequacies of the company's manufacturing facilities in Cincinnati convinced the firm to move south. Eventually five plants were opened—three in Arkansas and one each in Mississippi and Juarez, Mexico. Baldwin's

Table 5

Baldwin Piano & Organ Company (figures in US$, 000s)

This firm is the largest domestic manufacturer of keyboard musical instruments that manufactures or distributes all major product classes of pianos and electronic organs.

	1995	1994	1993
Sales	$122,634	$122,347	$120,658
Net income	3,960	345	4,561
Total assets	101,429	97,460	89,928
Stockholders' equity	54,114	50,154	49,892

Note: The company also manufactures grandfather clocks, wooden cabinets, and printed circuit boards utilized in a wide variety of products outside of the music industry. Musical products and other accounted for 72 percent of 1995 revenues; electronic contracting, 23.2 percent; and financing services, 4.7 percent.

Source: Compact Disclosure Database, 1996.

offering included a line of high-quality grand pianos and a line of relatively inexpensive uprights assembled in the firm's highly automated Arkansas plants.

During the 1970s, the firm transformed itself into a conglomerate—Baldwin-United Corp.—and acquired banks, savings and loans, and insurance companies. However, the acquisitions ran up a sizable debt. Unable to repay the debt, the firm filed for bankruptcy protection in 1983. A year later, R. S. Harrison and Harold Smith led a $55 million leveraged buyout of the company's piano and organ operations and reestablished the firm as a dedicated keyboard manufacturer.

Baldwin has more than 800 dealers in the United States. Its dealership base and broad product line help attract students and other low-end users who generally stay with a Baldwin piano as they upgrade. In 1987 the firm sold 175,000 pianos, a figure well below the 282,000 units it sold a decade earlier. With excess capacity in its Arkansas facility, Baldwin obtained a contract from Yamaha to manufacture the Everett piano line. Actions for Baldwin pianos are assembled at the Juarez plant. In 1995 the firm reported a net income of $3.9 million on sales of $122 million (see Table 5).

Japanese Competitors

In the early part of the century, there was little piano manufacturing in Japan, due to a lack of quality components, impoverished circumstances, and a work force that was uninformed about the subtleties of instrument design and construction. After World War II, however, two Japanese companies, Yamaha and Kawai, quickly became important piano manufacturers. Figures for the 1980s indicate that these two firms together made more pianos than manufacturers in any other nation. In 1954 only 1 percent of Japanese homes owned a piano; currently, more than 20 percent do. In contrast to Steinway & Sons, the Japanese approach to piano manufacture emphasizes automation and assembly-line operations.

Yamaha Corporation

Founded in 1887 as Nippon Gakki, Yamaha's main plants are near Hamamatsu. From the time of its founding, the firm has built pianos.[24] It first exported pianos to the United States in 1960. By the 1970s, Yamaha had developed a strong reputation for making high-quality pianos. In the United States it took significant market share away from US producers. The company uses innovative engineering and automated manufacturing to produce its pianos. The firm markets its pianos worldwide.

In 1987, its centenary year, Yamaha was the world's leading musical instrument maker. It commanded 30 percent of the world piano market, 40 percent of the organ market, and 30 percent of the wind instrument market. Currently, the firm markets a line of grands, uprights, consoles, and studio pianos manufactured in either Georgia in the United States or Hamamatsu in Japan. These pianos are the company's pride. Concert grands represent the measure of its aspirations. Yamaha currently commands around 55 percent of the Japanese piano market.

In 1983 Genichi's son, Hiroshi Kawakami, took over the leadership of Yamaha. Under his direction Yamaha established several close working relationships with other firms in the late 1980s and 1990s. In 1984 Yamaha subcontracted Kemble & Co. of England to make pianos. In 1986 the firm subcontracted Baldwin to make the Everett piano line. In 1988 Yamaha established Tienjin Yamaha Electronic Musical Instruments for production in China. Furthermore, it obtained an option to buy 25 percent of Schimmel Pianofortefabrik in Germany. More recently, Yamaha held a 60 percent ownership of a $10 million joint venture with Jiangzhu Piano, China's largest piano manufacturer, located in Guangzhou, China. In 1996 the joint venture started producing pianos at a monthly rate of 1,300 units. In 1995 the firm reported a net income of $61.6 million on sales of more than $5.5 billion (see Table 6).

Table 6

Yamaha Corporation
(figures in US$, 000s)

The firm's products include pianos, electronic organs, digital musical instruments, wind instruments, and percussion instruments, and audio equipment.

	1995	1994	1993
Sales	$5,576,860	$4,348,744	$4,210,910
Net income	61,665	–38,854	15,913
Total assets	5,327,507	4,518,696	4,151,752
Stockholders' equity	1,702,343	1,424,758	1,353,630

Note: Audio and musical instruments accounted for 61 percent of fiscal 1995 revenues; electronic equipment and metal products, 18 percent; household utensils, 12 percent; and other, including sports goods and housing equipment, 9 percent. The company has 58 consolidated subsidiaries, 26 in Japan and 32 overseas. Overseas sales accounted for 30.5 percent of fiscal revenues.

Source: World Scope Database, 1996.

Table 7

Kawai Musical Instruments
(figures in US$, 000s)

This second-largest musical instruments firm in Japan is also an OEM supplier of pianos to the Boston Piano Co., wholly owned subsidiary of Steinway Musical Properties.

	1995	1994	1993
Sales	$877,742	$881,114	$899,657
Net income	(2,733)	(2,200)	1,180
Total assets	—	—	530,666
Stockholders' equity	—	—	235,114

Note: Pianos accounted for 25 percent of fiscal 1995 revenues; electronic equipment and metal products, 8 percent; other, including musical instruments, 9 percent; metallic parts for electronic instruments, 13 percent; other products, 10 percent; and music schools, 35 percent. Overseas sales accounted for 11 percent of fiscal 1995 revenues.

Source: Japan Company Handbook.

Kawai Musical Instruments

In 1889, while he was an employee of Yamaha, Koichi Kawai, the founder of Kawai Musical Instruments, began his piano research. He developed the first rudimentary assembly line to make pianos. He was the first in Japan to design and build a piano action. Prior to his effort, all Japanese manufacturers had imported their actions from the United States or Germany. Kawai began the production of upright pianos a year after building his first piano action. It was the cost advantage of his domestically produced action that gave him a foothold in the fledgling Japanese market. Soon he began building grand pianos.

In 1955 Koichi's son, Shigeru Kawai, took over as president and he has since overseen the firm's growth and the introduction of modern technology. In 1956 the firm had one plant and 546 employees, and production capacity was 1,776 units. By 1996 Kawai had nine factories and employed over 7,000 people who produced about 100,000 pianos. The firm's main manufacturing center, Ryuyo Grand Piano Facility, opened in 1980, and is known for the efficient methods it has developed to build grand pianos. Kawai emphasizes the engineer-

ing, research and development, quality control, technological innovation, and skill that go into its pianos. Koichi's son, Hirotaki Kawai, is expected to take over leadership of the firm.

In its advertising, Kawai emphasizes the number of institutions and music venues (prominent universities, symphony orchestras, opera companies, music centers, theater companies, churches, music studios, and hotels) around the world that have purchased the Kawai piano. In 1995, however, the firm reported a loss of $2 million on sales of $877 million. This loss was attributed to the lingering economic recession facing firms in Japan (see Table 7).

Korean Competitors

In 1964 the Korean government decided to promote musical-instrument manufacturing. To support this effort, it passed a prohibitive tariff on imported luxury goods such as pianos. Three firms immediately benefited from this protection. They included Samick, which had already established its piano manufacturing facility, Young Chang, which formed a joint venture with

Table 8

Samick Corporation
(figures in US$, 000s)

	1995	1994	1993
Sales	$291,512	$243,287	$254,125
Net income	13,350	225	14,062
Total assets	477,887	474,387	414,575
Stockholders' equity	31,037	26,737	25,000

Note: Pianos accounted for 54.5 percent of fiscal 1995 revenues; guitars, 28.5 percent; amplifiers, 16.8 percent; and other, 0.2 percent.

Yamaha, and Sojin, a division of Daewoo. Industry assessments state that, "despite a harsh environment and a lack of Western musical tradition, Young Chang and Samick made the transformation from primitive manufacturers to global powerhouses in record time. Over the past century, no other manufacturers have come so far so fast."[25] Recently, Hyundai also became an additional Korean piano manufacturer. In the 1990s, with growing labor and raw material shortages, Samick and Young Chang have shifted their production to locations with either lower costs or better access to raw materials or markets.

Samick

Established in 1958 by Hyo Ick Lee, Samick has grown into the world's largest producer of pianos, with its main plant in Inchon. The firm produced 18,000 grand pianos in 1995. Samick pianos feature cabinets designed by Kenneth Benson and incorporate a high-tension, imperial-German scale. In making its pianos, Samick makes extensive use of computer-controlled equipment to shape parts and perform finishing operations.

In 1989 Samick Music Corporation, a wholly owned subsidiary of Samick, opened an 85,000-square-foot facility in California to assemble upright pianos. In 1991 monthly production at the facility had reached 325 units. While case parts were American, all actions, backs, and hardware were imported by Samick.

Recently, Samick opened parts-producing facilities in Indonesia and China. Components and subassemblies from these plants are then shipped to the firm's main plant at Inchon for assembly. These new facilities have allowed Samick to hold costs down and minimize price increases. Samick offers the best warranty in the industry—10 years on the piano, plus a lifetime warranty on the iron plate, the sounding board, and the pin block. In 1995 the firm reported a net income of $13 million on sales of $292 million (see Table 8). At the end of 1996, Samick filed for bankruptcy protection due to financial difficulties.

Young Chang

Young Chang was founded by three brothers. Jai-Sup Kim had studied engineering, Jai-Young Kim had studied finance at New York University, and Jai-Chang Kim had studied music. In 1956 they began to produce pianos in a small storefront in Seoul, South Korea. They also secured distribution rights to Yamaha pianos in South Korea. In 1962 they became the first musical instrument manufacturer in South Korea and in 1964 they built their first assembly plant in Seoul.

In 1967 they entered into a partnership with Yamaha Corporation, receiving technical assistance to acquire the production skills necessary to create instruments capable of competing with those made in Japan, the United States, and Europe. In 1971 they began exporting. In 1975 Yamaha and Young Chang parted ways, and in the next year Young Chang opened its second factory in Inchon, which was expanded in the late 1980s. In 1979 Young Chang America was established.

Young Chang's economies of scale, in combination with its advanced manufacturing processes, have resulted in one of the best price/value offerings in the market today. With an annual production capacity of 200,000 pianos, Young Chang is also the largest piano manufacturer in the world. The firm produces around 110,000 units annually, including 13,000 grand pianos. It holds more than 50 percent of the expanding Korean market (around 150,000 units per year) and currently has more than 4,000 employees. It offers a complete line of upright and grand pianos, as well as guitars. The firm sees piano manufacturing as a totally integrated activity and has facilities for making all the significant parts of a piano.

In 1990 Young Chang acquired Kurzweil, a music keyboard manufacturer, for $20 million. In 1993 Young Chang acquired its own timber mill in Tacoma, Washington for $32 million. It opened a $40 million production facility in Tienjin, China, with an annual production capacity of 60,000 units in 1995. As J. S. Kim observes:

> In the short term, our balance sheet would look stronger if we were to stay out of China. But it is obvious that the future for the piano industry is in China, and companies not willing to make the investment are in great jeopardy.

The firm anticipates that the Chinese market will eventually be the world's largest. In 1995 the firm reported a net income of $9.6 million on sales of $262 million (see Table 9).

Table 9

Young Chang (figures in U.S.$, 000s)

This firm produces pianos, guitars, electronic organs, and other musical instruments. The company has six subsidiaries, two each in the United States and China, and one each in Canada and Germany.

	1995	1994*	1993
Sales	$262,158	$258,489	$225,716
Net income	965	8,209	3,368
Stockholders' equity	131,818	135,698	126,536
Total assets	302,437	292,172	233,889

*In 1994 export sales accounted for 37 percent of total revenues. Acoustic and digital pianos accounted for 80 percent of fiscal 1995 revenues; synthesizers, 5.5 percent; guitars, 2 percent; and other, 12.5 percent.

Source: World Scope Database, 1996.

European Competitors

Although German piano manufacturers make high-quality, high-priced pianos, they have been severely tested by the low-priced Asian competitors. As a consequence of this competition, the number of German piano makers has fallen from several hundred to around 10. All surviving firms faced financial difficulties in the 1990s. In 1995 total annual production in Germany was more than 20,000 units, with 20 percent being grand pianos. Bechstein Gruppe, the manufacturer of Bechstein and Zimmerman pianos, had annual sales of around DM30 million. Recently, the group has been working its way out of bankruptcy protection.

Other firms included Bluthner of Leipzig, which produced about 400 pianos annually with 50 percent marked for export, and Schimmel in Braunschweig, which has held around 11 percent of the German market. Schimmel has a close relationship with Yamaha, which has marketed Schimmel pianos in Japan. Steinway & Sons of Hamburg produces around 1,000 grands and 200 uprights annually and exports around 300 grand pianos to Japan.

While English firms were world-renowned piano manufacturers during Steinway's formative years, today there is little piano making in England. The manufacturing that does occur involves subcontracting from non-British makers. The most prominent is Kemble Co., a firm that employs 100 people and makes pianos for Yamaha (Japan) and Scheidmeyer (Germany).

In Austria, Bösendorfer continues to make a limited number of high-end concert grands and upright pianos for its parent, Kimball International. Until recently, Kimball was a US domestic piano maker with a single plant in Indiana. This facility, however, closed in 1995.

Significant numbers of pianos are made in the former Soviet Union. Few of these pianos have appeared in the United States. Recently, some imports have started to appear. Perhaps the best-known brand is the Belarus piano from Borisov.

Issues Facing Steinway's Management

Domestic grand piano sales increased 12 percent from 1992 to 1995. This increased growth was largely attributable to economic recovery in the United States as well as increased marketing efforts by the major piano producers.

Growing Importance of China

Industry forecasts indicate that the future market for pianos will be concentrated in Japan, Korea, and China. Bruce Stevens acknowledged that:

> Although the Steinway piano has an excellent reputation in Asia and is the piano of choice in virtually every Japanese concert venue, Steinway has not historically focused significant selling or marketing efforts in these markets.

According to Bob Dove, however, the situation was changing:

> The Boston piano currently has around 5 percent of the Japanese market in terms of units and a higher percentage, about 8 percent, in terms of value (since the Boston line is more expensive than your average piano). We are optimistic about future sales of both Boston and Steinway pianos in Japan. We believe the Boston piano is significantly better than that offered by competitors at similar prices.

The recent ownership changes and the growth of Asian markets had increased Steinway's interest in finding ways to find advantage in these developing situations. Bob Dove said:

> The merger of Steinway & Sons with the Selmer Company and its woodwind and band instruments has introduced a number of new strategic possibilities. The future demand for the band instruments made by Selmer is predictable

from demographic data, peaking as larger cohorts of children enter high school. So this gives the new company a predictable source of demand for its products. So far as growth is concerned, pianos are important, and there is no doubt that growth in demand for pianos will occur mainly in Asia and so this is the current focus of company attention. . . . There are also other instruments that have high-quality standards and which have high sales and growth rates, e.g., guitars. These may be areas which offer new opportunities for the enlarged firm. Finally, the Steinway brand name, itself, is unsurpassed in terms of its positive reputation. In the future, this, too, could be used in a number of different ways.

Additionally, the developing situation in China was intriguing. Estimates indicated that the Chinese domestic production of pianos had risen from 43,000 units in 1987 to more than 100,000 units in 1994. The Chinese government's policy of one child per family has encouraged parents to spend more money on their children. This, many observers believe, may keep unsatisfied demand for pianos relatively high. Moreover, children in school are being taught to appreciate music, and this will have a positive impact on demand. In 1994 there were four main piano-producing centers in China, including Beijing (30,000 units), Shanghai, Guangzhou (50,000 units), and Yingkuo in Liaoning Province. In 1996 Tienjin in North China also became a center of acoustic piano production when Young Chang established a plant there. Dove, however, was skeptical:

All expect that China will be the world's largest market for pianos. However, since the price of pianos is currently set very low [the average price of a piano in China was around $1,100], the reported levels of untapped demand there are probably a bit illusory. Further, there are already large piano-making facilities in China such as Young Chang's and Yamaha's factories. It is not clear there is a need for additional production capacity.

Although the demand at current prices far outstrips supply, it is uncertain how an increase in prices might affect demand. Bob Dove believes that Steinway's current approach is appropriate:

Given the emphasis on culture in China, the country's rapidly growing income levels, the small families, and the interest parents have in their children, one can expect the usual developments to occur so far as piano penetration is concerned. But this takes time, and people don't start off their interest in music by buying a Steinway. Rather, they work up to a Steinway. We already have an active Steinway dealership in Hong Kong, and this firm has opened a branch in Shanghai. Currently [therefore], we should be just watching to see how things develop.

Moreover, he is optimistic about other Asian markets:

Other Southeast Asian countries like Japan, South Korea, Hong Kong, Taiwan, and Singapore have already achieved higher general wealth levels and have meaningful piano penetration into homes. These countries, therefore, should be more immediate targets for both the Steinway and Boston lines of pianos.

Among the proposals Steinway & Sons is considering is the possibility of building a plant in Asia, perhaps in China. This new facility could help service the demand for pianos in Asian markets. Dove commented:

Ideally, because quality is such an important issue and the desire to "do the job right" is so strong, it would be better for all Steinways to be built in one place. Perhaps standardized and mass-produced components could be supplied from different sources and could reduce costs, but for assembly and to do the other processes involving specialist skills, it would be better to have the Steinway piano built in a single place.

Irrespective of the approach the firm decides to pursue with respect to China and other Asian markets, Dove commented that:

In considering what to do, Steinway & Sons has to remember two things. First, the company has built up a tremendous brand name and enjoys an unsurpassed reputation for quality. So first, anything we do must be consistent with the idea that we are the "keepers of the flame." Second, as Henry Z. Steinway said, "Capital loves growth." To generate growth, we also have to know where we are adding value.

Discussion Questions

1. How has Steinway managed to earn a reputation as the world's leading producer of high-quality pianos? What are the most important sources of success?

2. To what extent is Steinway's approach unique in this industry?

3. What are the firm's practices that provide it with a competitive advantage? How sustainable is Steinway's success in the face of intense foreign competition?

4. Can the firm's practices be transferred successfully to the Chinese piano market?

5. What are some of the options facing Bruce Stevens as he contemplates entering the Chinese market?

Notes

1. E. Rothstein, "To Make a Piano It Takes More Than Tools," *Smithsonian*, November 1988.
2. Ibid.
3. E. Rothstein, "Made in the USA, Once Gloriously, Now Precariously," *New York Times*, May 28, 1995.
4. A. Dolge, *Pianos and Their Makers* (Covina, CA: Covina Publishing Company, 1911), p. 303.

5. Ibid.

6. Both Chickering and Steinway attempted to depict the results of the Paris Exposition as confirming they (not their rival) were the leading US piano manufacturer. This competition escalated into a notorious series of claims and counterclaims as each firm claimed additional endorsements and awards in their efforts to convince the public that it was they who had "really won" in Paris.

7. Dolge, *Pianos and Their Makers*, p. 174

8. Ibid., p. 309.

9. As judges, newspaper proprietors, music publishers, teachers, clergy, music critics, and others prominent in New York social or cultural circles indicated they'd like to buy a Steinway, the firm offered them generous credit terms to encourage the purchase. By having a Steinway in influential New York homes, Steinway & Sons calculated its status by association tended to grow.

10. Dolge, *Pianos and Their Makers*, p. 309.

11. D. Fostle, *The Steinway Saga* (New York: Scribner, 1995).

12. Currently, the Concert Artists' Department maintains a bank of 330 Steinway concert-grand pianos spread about 160 cities. Once an artist achieves sufficient stature to be considered eligible by Steinway & Sons to receive concert service, he or she is offered the opportunity to use Steinway pianos for all performances. The only expense to the artist is the cost of hauling the piano to the recital hall.

13. Dolge, *Pianos and Their Makers*, p. 309.

14. C. H. Roell, *The Piano in America, 1890–1940* (Chapel Hill: The University of North Carolina Press, 1989), p. 180.

15. The firm's ads necessarily were—and are—devoted to maintaining an appeal to a minority audience of high culture that has not been swept into mass society. Hence the promotion of a Steinway as art. According to the classical pianist Jose Feghali, "Steinways are a work of art, if they weren't, we wouldn't be playing them . . . You can walk into a room with 10 pianos and it's like playing 10 different instruments."

16. To prevent damage and facilitate conductivity, a brass strap equal to the length of the piece is placed on the exterior side. The wet glue, along with the wood's slightly elevated moisture content, permits the laminates that formed the wooden piece to slide against each other just enough to permit bending.

17. The piano key covers are made from a mock ivory polymer, in deference to the ban on ivory imports. The action consists of 17 different wooden parts including machined wooden parts, Brazilian deer hide, felt-covered maple hammers, metal pins, and Teflon impregnated wool bushings. The components of the action are milled on the third floor and then assembled on the second floor. The design of the actions, much like the rest of the piano, only works if all of the milled parts fit together perfectly. Employees are trained to determine the exact fit and also to spot problems through visual and physical inspection of the action components.

18. "Steinway's Key . . . One at a Time," *Associated Press International*, 1985.

19. Ibid.

20. Quoted in R. Ratcliffe, *Steinway & Sons* (San Francisco: Chronicle Books, 1985), p. 102.

21. American Music Conference, *Music USA, 1991*, pp. 2143.

22. The US acoustic piano market consisted of two important segments—grands and uprights. Grand pianos are larger and give a louder, more resonant sound. The grands were more expensive, and the market for such pianos was generally smaller than that for uprights, and fewer firms were involved in their manufacture.

23. Steinway provides restoration services and sells piano parts from its New York, London, Berlin, and Hamburg locations. It also provides tuning and regulating services. Restoration, repair, tuning, and regulating services are important because they lead to potential new customers. In 1995 restoration services and piano parts accounted for approximately 7 percent of revenue, with gross margins of approximately 29 percent.

24. In 1950 Genichi Kawakami took over the leadership of the firm from his father. In 1953 Genichi toured the United States and Western Europe and was struck by the emphasis being placed on recreational products and the waning interest in musical instruments. He returned home, determined to stimulate an interest in musical instruments in Japan and opened a chain of franchised music schools, which have since graduated 4 million students. There are currently 10,000 franchised schools, and many of these schools have a showroom for Yamaha instruments on the ground floor.

25. *The Music Trades*, January 1991.

GLOSSARY

A

absolute advantage   A country has an absolute advantage in the production of a product when it is more efficient than any other country at producing it.

ad valorem tariff   A tariff levied as a proportion of the value of an imported good.

administrative trade policies   Administrative policies, typically adopted by government bureaucracies, that can be used to restrict imports or boost exports.

Andean Pact   A 1969 agreement between Bolivia, Chile, Ecuador, Colombia, and Peru to establish a customs union.

antidumping policies   Designed to punish foreign firms that engage in dumping and thus protect domestic producers from unfair foreign competition.

antidumping regulations   Regulations designed to restrict the sale of goods for less than their fair market price.

arbitrage   The purchase of securities in one market for immediate resale in another to profit from a price discrepancy.

ASEAN (Association of South East Asian Nations)   Formed in 1967, an attempt to establish a free trade area between Brunei, Indonesia, Malaysia, the Philippines, Singapore, and Thailand.

B

balance-of-payments accounts   National accounts that track both payments to and receipts from foreigners.

banking crisis   A loss of confidence in the banking system that leads to a run on banks, as individuals and companies withdraw their deposits.

barriers to entry   Factors that make it difficult or costly for firms to enter an industry or market.

barter   The direct exchange of goods or services between two parties without a cash transaction.

basic research centers   Centers for fundamental research located in regions where valuable scientific knowledge is being created; they develop the basic technologies that become new products.

bilateral netting   Settlement in which the amount one subsidiary owes another can be canceled by the debt the second subsidiary owes the first.

bill of exchange   An order written by an exporter instructing an importer, or an importer's agent, to pay a specified amount of money at a specified time.

bill of lading (or draft)   A document issued to an exporter by a common carrier transporting merchandise. It serves as a receipt, a contract, and a document of title.

Bretton Woods   A 1944 conference in which representatives of 40 countries met to design a new international monetary system.

bureaucratic controls   Achieving control through establishment of a system of rules and procedures.

C

capital account   In the balance of payments, records transactions involving the purchase or sale of assets.

capital controls   Restrictions on cross-border capital flows that segment different stock markets; limit amount of a firm's stock a foreigner can own; and limit a citizen's ability to invest outside the country.

CARICOM   An association of English-speaking Caribbean states that are attempting to establish a customs union.

caste system   A system of social stratification in which social position is determined by the family into which a person is born, and change in that position is usually not possible during an individual's lifetime.

centralized depository   The practice of centralizing corporate cash balances in a single depository.

channel length   The number of intermediaries that a product has to go through before it reaches the final consumer.

civil law system   A system of law based on a very detailed set of written laws and codes.

class consciousness   A tendency for individuals to perceive themselves in terms of their class background.

class system   A system of social stratification in which social status is determined by the family into which a person is born and by subsequent socioeconomic achievements. Mobility between classes is possible.

collectivism   An emphasis on collective goals as opposed to individual goals.

COMECON   Now-defunct economic association of Eastern European communist states headed by the former Soviet Union.

command economy   An economic system where the allocation of resources, including determination of what goods and services should be produced, and in what quantity, is planned by the government.

common law system   A system of law based on tradition, precedent, and custom. When law courts interpret common law, they do so with regard to these characteristics.

common market   A group of countries committed to (1) removing all barriers to the free flow of goods, services, and factors of production between each other and (2) the pursuit of a common external trade policy.

674

communist totalitarianism A version of collectivism advocating that socialism can be achieved only through a totalitarian dictatorship.

communists Those who believe socialism can be achieved only through revolution and totalitarian dictatorship.

comparative advantage The theory that countries should specialize in the production of goods and services they can produce most efficiently. A country is said to have a comparative advantage in the production of such goods and services.

competition policy Regulations designed to promote competition and restrict monopoly practices.

constant returns to specialization The units of resources required to produce a good are assumed to remain constant no matter where one is on a country's production possibility frontier.

controlling interest A firm has a controlling interest in another business entity when it owns more than 50 percent of that entity's voting stock.

copyright Exclusive legal rights of authors, composers, playwrights, artists, and publishers to publish and dispose of their work as they see fit.

core competence Firm skills that competitors cannot easily match or imitate.

counterpurchase A reciprocal buying agreement.

countertrade The trade of goods and services for other goods and services.

cross-cultural literacy Understanding how the culture of a country affects the way business is practiced.

cross-licensing agreement An arrangement in which a company licenses valuable intangible property to a foreign partner and receives a license for the partner's valuable knowledge; reduces risk of licensing.

cultural controls Achieving control by persuading subordinates to identify with the norms and value systems of the organization (self-control).

culture The complex whole that includes knowledge, belief, art, morals, law, custom, and other capabilities acquired by a person as a member of society.

currency board Means of controlling a country's currency.

currency crisis Occurs when a speculative attack on the exchange value of a currency results in a sharp depreciation in the value of the currency or forces authorities to expend large volumes of international currency reserves and sharply increase interest rates to defend the prevailing exchange rate.

currency speculation Involves short-term movement of funds from one currency to another in hopes of profiting from shifts in exchange rates.

currency swap Simultaneous purchase and sale of a given amount of foreign exchange for two different value dates.

currency translation Converting the financial statements of foreign subsidiaries into the currency of the home country.

current account In the balance of payments, records transactions involving the export or import of goods and services.

current account deficit The current account of the balance of payments is in deficit when a country imports more goods and services than it exports.

current account surplus The current account of the balance of payments is in surplus when a country exports more goods and services than it imports.

current cost accounting Method that adjusts all items in a financial statement to factor out the effects of inflation.

current rate method Using the exchange rate at the balance sheet date to translate the financial statements of a foreign subsidiary into the home currency.

customs union A group of countries committed to (1) removing all barriers to the free flow of goods and services between each other and (2) the pursuit of a common external trade policy.

D

D'Amato Act Act passed in 1996, similar to the Helms-Burton Act, aimed at Libya and Iran.

deferral principle Parent companies are not taxed on the income of a foreign subsidiary until they actually receive a dividend from that subsidiary.

democracy Political system in which government is by the people, exercised either directly or through elected representatives.

deregulation Removal of government restrictions concerning the conduct of a business.

diminishing returns to specialization Applied to international trade theory, the more of a good that a country produces, the greater the units of resources required to produce each additional item.

dirty-float system A system under which a country's currency is nominally allowed to float freely against other currencies, but in which the government will intervene, buying and selling currency, if it believes that the currency has deviated too far from its fair value.

draft See **bill of lading.**

drawee The party to whom a bill of lading is presented.

dumping Selling goods in a foreign market for less than their cost of production or below their "fair" market value.

E

eclectic paradigm Argument that combining location-specific assets or resource endowments and the firm's own unique assets often requires FDI; it requires the firm to establish production facilities where those foreign assets or resource endowments are located.

e-commerce Conducting business on-line through the Internet.

economic exposure The extent to which a firm's future international earning power is affected by changes in exchange rates.

economic risk The likelihood that events, including economic mismanagement, will cause drastic changes in a country's business environment that adversely affect the profit and other goals of a particular business enterprise.

economic union A group of countries committed to (1) removing all barriers to the free flow of goods, services, and factors of production between each other, (2) the adoption of a common currency, (3) the harmonization of tax rates, and (4) the pursuit of a common external trade policy.

economies of scale Cost advantages associated with large-scale production.

ecu A basket of EU currencies that serves as the unit of account for the EMS.

efficient market A market where prices reflect all available information.

ending rate The spot exchange rate when budget and performance are being compared.

ethical systems Cultural beliefs about what is proper behavior and conduct.

ethnocentric behavior Behavior that is based on the belief in the superiority of one's own ethnic group or culture; often shows disregard or contempt for the culture of other countries.

ethnocentric staffing A staffing approach within the MNE in which all key management positions are filled by parent-country nationals.

eurobonds A bond placed in countries other than the one in whose currency the bond is denominated.

eurocurrency Any currency banked outside its country of origin.

eurodollar Dollar banked outside the United States.

European Free Trade Association (EFTA) A free trade association including Norway, Iceland, and Switzerland.

European Monetary System (EMS) EU system designed to create a zone of monetary stability in Europe, control inflation, and coordinate exchange rate policies of EU countries.

European Union (EU) An economic group of 15 European nations: Austria, Belgium, Denmark, Finland, France, Germany, Great Britain, Greece, the Netherlands, Ireland, Italy, Luxembourg, Portugal, Spain, and Sweden. Established as a customs union, it is now moving toward economic union. (Formerly the European Community.)

exchange rate The rate at which one currency is converted into another.

exchange rate mechanism (ERM) Mechanism for aligning the exchange rates of EU currencies against each other.

exclusive channels A distribution channel that outsiders find difficult to access.

expatriate failure The premature return of an expatriate manager to the home country.

expatriate manager A national of one country appointed to a management position in another country.

experience curve Systematic production cost reductions that occur over the life of a product.

experience curve pricing Aggressive pricing designed to increase volume and help the firm realize experience curve economies.

export management company Export specialists who act as an export marketing department for client firms.

Export-Import Bank (Eximbank) Agency of the US government whose mission is to provide aid in financing and facilitate exports and imports.

exporting Sale of products produced in one country to residents of another country.

externalities Knowledge spillovers.

externally convertible currency Nonresidents can convert their holdings of domestic currency into foreign currency, but the ability of residents to convert the currency is limited in some way.

F

factor endowments A country's endowment with resources such as land, labor, and capital.

factors of production Inputs into the productive process of a firm, including labor, management, land, capital, and technological know-how.

Financial Accounting Standards Board (FASB) The body that writes the generally accepted accounting principles by which the financial statements of US firms must be prepared.

financial structure Mix of debt and equity used to finance a business.

first-mover advantages Advantages accruing to the first to enter a market.

first-mover disadvantages Disadvantages associated with entering a foreign market before other international businesses.

Fisher Effect Nominal interest rates (i) in each country equal the required real rate of interest (r) and the expected rate of inflation over the period of time for which the funds are to be lent (I). That is, $i = r + I$.

fixed exchange rates A system under which the exchange rate for converting one currency into another is fixed.

fixed-rate bond Offers a fixed set of cash payoffs each year until maturity, when the investor also receives the face value of the bond in cash.

flexible machine cells Flexible manufacturing technology in which a grouping of various machine types, a common materials handler, and a centralized cell controller produce a family of products.

flexible manufacturing technologies Manufacturing technologies designed to improve job scheduling, reduce setup time, and improve quality control.

floating exchange rates A system under which the exchange rate for converting one currency into another is continuously adjusted depending on the laws of supply and demand.

flow of foreign direct investment The amount of foreign direct investment undertaken over a given time period (normally one year).

folkways Routine conventions of everyday life.

foreign bonds Bonds sold outside the borrower's country and denominated in the currency of the country in which they are issued.

Foreign Corrupt Practices Act US law regulating behavior regarding the conduct of international business in the taking of bribes and other unethical actions.

foreign debt crisis Situation in which a country cannot service its foreign debt obligations, whether private-sector or government debt.

foreign direct investment (FDI) Direct investment in business operations in a foreign country.

foreign exchange exposure The risk that future changes in a country's exchange rate will hurt the firm.

foreign exchange market A market for converting the currency of one country into that of another country.

foreign exchange risk The risk that changes in exchange rates will hurt the profitability of a business deal.

foreign portfolio investment (FPI) Investments by individuals, firms, or public bodies (e.g., national and local governments) in foreign financial instruments (e.g., government bonds, foreign stocks).

forward exchange When two parties agree to exchange currency and execute a deal at some specific date in the future.

forward exchange rate The exchange rates governing forward exchange transactions.

franchising A specialized form of licensing in which the franchiser sells intangible property to the franchisee and insists on rules to conduct the business.

free trade The absence of barriers to the free flow of goods and services between countries.

free trade area A group of countries committed to removing all barriers to the free flow of goods and services between each other, but pursuing independent external trade policies.

freely convertible currency A country's currency is freely convertible when the government of that country allows both residents and nonresidents to purchase unlimited amounts of foreign currency with the domestic currency.

fronting loans A loan between a parent company and a foreign subsidiary that is channeled through a financial intermediary.

fundamental analysis Draws on economic theory to construct sophisticated econometric models for predicting exchange rate movements.

G

gains from trade The economic gains to a country from engaging in international trade.

General Agreement on Tariffs and Trade (GATT) International treaty that committed signatories to lowering barriers to the free flow of goods across national borders and led to the WTO.

geocentric staffing A staffing policy where the best people are sought for key jobs throughout an MNE, regardless of nationality.

global learning The flow of skills and product offerings from foreign subsidiary to home country and from foreign subsidiary to foreign subsidiary.

global matrix structure Horizontal differentiation proceeds along two dimensions: product divisions and areas.

global strategy Strategy focusing on increasing profitability by reaping cost reductions from experience curve and location economies.

global web When different stages of value chain are dispersed to those locations around the globe where value added is maximized or where costs of value creation are minimized.

globalization Trend away from distinct national economic units and toward one huge global market.

globalization of markets Moving away from an economic system in which national markets are distinct entities, isolated by trade barriers and barriers of distance, time, and culture, and toward a system in which national markets are merging into one global market.

globalization of production Trend by individual firms to disperse parts of their productive processes to different locations around the globe to take advantage of differences in cost and quality of factors of production.

gold par value The amount of currency needed to purchase one ounce of gold.

gold standard The practice of pegging currencies to gold and guaranteeing convertibility.

gross domestic product (GDP) The market value of a country's output attributable to factors of production located in the country's territory.

gross fixed capital formation Summarizes the total amount of capital invested in factories, stores, office buildings, and the like.

gross national product (GNP) The market value of all the final goods and services produced by a national economy.

group An association of two or more individuals who have a shared sense of identity and who interact with each other in structured ways on the basis of a common set of expectations about each other's behavior.

H

Heckscher-Ohlin theory Countries will export those goods that make intensive use of locally abundant factors of production and import goods that make intensive use of locally scarce factors of production.

hedge fund Investment fund that not only buys financial assets (stocks, bonds, currencies) but also sells them short.

Helms-Burton Act Act passed in 1996 that allowed Americans to sue foreign firms that use Cuban property confiscated from them after the 1959 revolution.

historic cost principle Accounting principle founded on the assumption that the currency unit used to report financial results is not losing its value due to inflation.

home country The source country for foreign direct investment.

horizontal differentiation The division of the firm into subunits.

horizontal foreign direct investment Foreign direct investment in the same industry abroad as a firm operates in at home.

host country Recipient country of inward investment by a foreign firm.

human development index An attempt by the United Nations to assess the impact of a number of factors on the quality of human life in a country.

human resource management Activities an organization conducts to use its human resources effectively.

I

import quota A direct restriction on the quantity of a good that can be imported into a country.

individualism An emphasis on the importance of guaranteeing individual freedom and self-expression.

individualism versus collectivism Theory focusing on the relationship between the individual and his or her fellows. In individualistic societies, the ties between individuals are loose and individual achievement is highly valued. In societies where collectivism is emphasized, ties between individuals are tight, people are born into collectives, such as extended families, and everyone is supposed to look after the interests of his or her collective.

inefficient market One in which prices do not reflect all available information.

infant industry argument New industries in developing countries must be temporarily protected from international competition to help them reach a position where they can compete on world markets with the firms of developed nations.

inflows of FDI Flow of foreign direct investment into a country.

initial rate The spot exchange rate when a budget is adopted.

innovation Development of new products, processes, organizations, management practices, and strategies.

integrating mechanisms Mechanisms for achieving coordination between subunits within an organization.

intellectual property Products of the mind, ideas (e.g., books, music, computer software, designs, technological know-how). Intellectual property can be protected by patents, copyrights, and trademarks.

internal forward rate A company-generated forecast of future spot rates.

internalization theory Marketing imperfection approach to foreign direct investment.

International Accounting Standards Committee (IASC) Organization of representatives of 106 professional accounting organizations from 79 countries that is attempting to harmonize accounting standards across countries.

international business Any firm that engages in international trade or investment.

international division Division responsible for a firm's international activities.

International Fisher Effect For any two countries, the spot exchange rate should change in an equal amount but in the opposite direction to the difference in nominal interest rates between countries.

International Monetary Fund (IMF) International institution set up to maintain order in the international monetary system.

international strategy Trying to create value by transferring core competencies to foreign markets where indigenous competitors lack those competencies.

international trade Occurs when a firm exports goods or services to consumers in another country.

ISO 9000 Certification process that requires certain quality standards that must be met.

J

joint venture A cooperative undertaking between two or more firms.

just-in-time (JIT) Logistics systems designed to deliver parts to a production process as they are needed, not before.

L

lag strategy Delaying the collection of foreign currency receivables if that currency is expected to appreciate, and delaying payables if that currency is expected to depreciate.

late-mover advantage Benefits enjoyed by a company that is late to enter a new market, such as consumer familiarity with the product or knowledge gained about a market.

law of one price In competitive markets free of transportation costs and barriers to trade, identical products sold in different countries must sell for the same price when their price is expressed in the same currency.

lead market Market where products are first introduced.

lead strategy Collecting foreign currency receivables early when a foreign currency is expected to depreciate, and paying foreign currency payables before they are due when a currency is expected to appreciate.

lean production systems Flexible manufacturing technologies pioneered at Toyota and now used in much of the automobile industry.

learning effects Cost savings from learning by doing.

legal risk The likelihood that a trading partner will opportunistically break a contract or expropriate intellectual property rights.

legal system System of rules that regulate behavior and the processes by which the laws of a country are enforced and through which redress of grievances is obtained.

Leontief paradox The empirical finding that, in contrast to the predictions of the Heckscher-Ohlin theory, US exports are less capital intensive than US imports.

letter of credit Issued by a bank, indicating that the bank will make payments under specific circumstances.

licensing Occurs when a firm (the licensor) licenses the right to produce its product, use its production processes, or use its brand name or trademark to another firm (the licensee). In return for giving the licensee these rights, the licensor collects a royalty fee on every unit the licensee sells.

local content requirement A requirement that some specific fraction of a good be produced domestically.

location economies Cost advantages from performing a value creation activity at the optimal location for that activity.

location-specific advantages Advantages that arise from using resource endowments or assets that are tied to a particular foreign location and that a firm finds valuable to combine with its own unique assets (such as the firm's technological, marketing, or management know-how).

logistics The procurement and physical transmission of material through the supply chain, from suppliers to customers.

M

Maastricht Treaty Treaty agreed to in 1991, but not ratified until January 1, 1994, that committed the 12 member states of the European Community to a closer economic and political union.

maker Person or business initiating a bill of lading (draft).

managed-float system System under which some currencies are allowed to float freely, but the majority are either managed by government intervention or pegged to another currency.

management networks A network of informal contact between individual managers.

market economy The allocation of resources is determined by the invisible hand of the price system.

market imperfections Imperfections in the operation of the market mechanism.

market makers Financial service companies that connect investors and borrowers, either directly or indirectly.

market power Ability of a firm to exercise control over industry prices or output.

market segmentation Identifying groups of consumers whose purchasing behavior differs from others in important ways.

marketing mix Choices about product attributes, distribution strategy, communication strategy, and pricing strategy that a firm offers its targeted markets.

masculinity versus femininity Theory of the relationship between gender and work roles. In masculine cultures, sex roles are sharply differentiated and traditional "masculine values" such as achievement and the effective exercise of power determine cultural ideals. In feminine cultures, sex roles are less sharply distinguished, and little differentiation is made between men and women in the same job.

mass customization The production of a wide variety of end products at a unit cost that could once be achieved only through mass production of a standardized output.

materials management The activity that controls the transmission of physical materials through the value chain, from procurement through production and into distribution.

mercantilism An economic philosophy advocating that countries should simultaneously encourage exports and discourage imports.

MERCOSUR Pact between Argentina, Brazil, Paraguay, and Uruguay to establish a free trade area.

minimum efficient scale The level of output at which most plant-level scale economies are exhausted.

MITI Japan's Ministry of International Trade and Industry.

mixed economy Certain sectors of the economy are left to private ownership and free market mechanisms, while other sectors have significant government ownership and government planning.

money management Managing a firm's global cash resources efficiently.

Moore's Law The power of microprocessor technology doubles and its costs of production fall in half every 18 months.

moral hazard Arises when people behave recklessly because they know they will be saved if things go wrong.

mores Norms seen as central to the functioning of a society and to its social life.

multidomestic strategy Emphasizing the need to be responsive to the unique conditions prevailing in different national markets.

Multilateral Agreement on Investment (MAI) An agreement that would make it illegal for signatory states to discriminate against foreign investors; would have liberalized rules governing FDI between OECD states.

multilateral netting A technique used to reduce the number of transactions between subsidiaries of the firm, thereby reducing the total transaction costs arising from foreign exchange dealings and transfer fees.

multinational enterprise (MNE) A firm that owns business operations in more than one country.

multipoint competition Arises when two or more enterprises encounter each other in different regional markets, national markets, or industries.

multipoint pricing Occurs when a pricing strategy in one market may have an impact on a rival's pricing strategy in another market.

N

new trade theory The observed pattern of trade in the world economy may be due in part to the ability of firms in a given market to capture first-mover advantages.

nonconvertible currency A currency is not convertible when both residents and nonresidents are prohibited from converting their holdings of that currency into another currency.

norms Social rules and guidelines that prescribe appropriate behavior in particular situations.

North American Free Trade Agreement (NAFTA) Free trade area between Canada, Mexico, and the United States.

O

oligopoly An industry composed of a limited number of large firms.

Organization for Economic Cooperation and Development (OECD) A Paris-based intergovernmental organization of "wealthy" nations whose purpose is to provide its 29 member states with a forum in which governments can compare their experiences, discuss the problems they share, and seek solutions that can then be applied within their own national contexts.

outflows of FDI Flow of foreign direct investment out of a country.

output controls Achieving control by setting goals for subordinates, expressing these goals in terms of objective criteria, and then judging performance by a subordinate's ability to meet these goals.

P

Paris Convention for the Protection of Industrial Property International agreement to protect intellectual property; signed by 96 countries.

patent Grants the inventor of a new product or process exclusive rights to the manufacture, use, or sale of that invention.

performance ambiguity Occurs when the causes of good or bad performance are not clearly identifiable.

personal controls Achieving control by personal contact with subordinates.

pioneering costs Costs an early entrant bears that later entrants avoid, such as the time and effort in learning the rules, failure due to ignorance, and the liability of being a foreigner.

political economy The study of how political factors influence the functioning of an economic system.

political risk The likelihood that political forces will cause drastic changes in a country's business environment that will adversely affect the profit and other goals of a particular business enterprise.

political system System of government in a nation.

polycentric staffing A staffing policy in an MNE in which host-country nationals are recruited to manage subsidiaries in their own country, while parent-country nationals occupy key positions at corporate headquarters.

positive-sum game A situation in which all countries can benefit even if some benefit more than others.

power distance Theory of how a society deals with the fact that people are unequal in physical and intellectual capabilities. High power distance cultures are found in countries that let inequalities grow over time into inequalities of power and wealth. Low power distance cultures are found in societies that try to play down such inequalities as much as possible.

predatory pricing Reducing prices below fair market value as a competitive weapon to drive weaker competitors out of the market ("fair" being cost plus some reasonable profit margin).

price discrimination The practice of charging different prices for the same product in different markets.

price elasticity of demand A measure of how responsive demand for a product is to changes in price.

privatization The sale of state-owned enterprises to private investors.

product life-cycle theory The optimal location in the world to produce a product changes as the market for the product matures.

production Activities involved in creating a product.

projected rate The spot exchange rate forecast for the end of the budget period.

property rights Bundle of legal rights over the use to which a resource is put and over the use made of any income that may be derived from that resource.

pull strategy A marketing strategy emphasizing mass media advertising as opposed to personal selling.

purchasing power parity (PPP) An adjustment in gross domestic product per capita to reflect differences in the cost of living.

push strategy A marketing strategy emphasizing personal selling rather than mass media advertising.

R

regional economic integration Agreements among countries in a geographic region to reduce and ultimately remove tariff and nontariff barriers to the free flow of goods, services, and factors of production between each other.

relatively efficient market One in which few impediments to international trade and investment exist.

representative democracy A political system in which citizens periodically elect individuals to represent them in government.

right-wing totalitarianism A political system in which political power is monopolized by a party, group, or individual that generally permits individual economic freedom but restricts individual political freedom, including free speech, often on the grounds that it would lead to the rise of communism.

royalties Remuneration paid to the owners of technology, patents, or trade names for the use of same.

S

short selling Occurs when an investor places a speculative bet that the value of a financial asset will decline, and profits from that decline.

sight draft A draft payable on presentation to the drawee.

Single European Act A 1997 act, adopted by members of the European Community, that committed member countries to establishing an economic union.

Smoot-Hawley Tariff Enacted in 1930 by the US Congress, this tariff erected a wall of barriers against imports into the United States.

social democrats Those committed to achieving socialism by democratic means.

social mobility The extent to which individuals can move out of the social strata into which they are born.

social strata Hierarchical social categories.

social structure The basic social organization of a society.

socialism A political philosophy advocating substantial public involvement, through government ownership, in the means of production and distribution.

society Group of people who share a common set of values and norms.

sogo shosha Japanese trading companies; a key part of the *keiretsu*, the large Japanese industrial groups.

sourcing decisions Whether a firm should make or buy component parts.

specialized asset An asset designed to perform a specific task, whose value is significantly reduced in its next-best use.

specific tariff Tariff levied as a fixed charge for each unit of good imported.

spot exchange rate The exchange rate at which a foreign exchange dealer will convert one currency into another that particular day.

staffing policy Strategy concerned with selecting employees for particular jobs.

state-directed economy An economy in which the state plays a proactive role in influencing the direction and magnitude of private sector investments.

stock of foreign direct investment The total accumulated value of foreign-owned assets at a given time.

strategic alliances Cooperative agreements between two or more firms.

strategic commitment A decision that has a long-term impact and is difficult to reverse, such as entering a foreign market on a large scale.

strategic trade policy Government policy aimed at improving the competitive position of a domestic industry and/or domestic firm in the world market.

strategy Actions managers take to attain the firm's goals.

Structural Impediments Initiative A 1990 agreement between the United States and Japan aimed at trying to decrease nontariff barriers restricting imports into Japan.

subsidy Government financial assistance to a domestic producer.

swaps The simultaneous purchase and sale of a given amount of foreign exchange for two different value dates.

systematic risk Movements in a stock portfolio's value that are attributable to macroeconomic forces affecting all firms in an economy, rather than factors specific to an individual firm (unsystematic risk).

T

tariff A tax levied on imports.

tax credit Allows a firm to reduce the taxes paid to the home government by the amount of taxes paid to the foreign government.

tax haven A country with exceptionally low, or even no, income taxes.

tax treaty Agreement between two countries specifying what items of income will be taxed by the authorities of the country where the income is earned.

technical analysis Uses price and volume data to determine past trends, which are expected to continue into the future.

temporal method Translating assets valued in a foreign currency into the home currency using the exchange rate that existed when the assets were originally purchased.

theocratic totalitarianism A political system in which political power is monopolized by a party, group, or individual that governs according to religious principles.

time draft A promise to pay by the accepting party at some future date.

time-based competition Competing on the basis of speed in responding to customer demands and developing new products.

timing of entry Entry is early when a firm enters a foreign market before other foreign firms and late when a firm enters after other international businesses have established themselves.

total quality management Management philosophy that takes as its central focus the need to improve the quality of a company's products and services.

totalitarianism Form of government in which one person or political party exercises absolute control over all spheres of human life and opposing political parties are prohibited.

trade creation Trade created due to regional economic integration; occurs when high-cost domestic producers are replaced by low-cost foreign producers in a free trade area.

trade deficit See **current account deficit.**

trade diversion Trade diverted due to regional economic integration; occurs when low-cost foreign suppliers outside a free trade area are replaced by higher-cost foreign suppliers in a free trade area.

trade surplus See **current account surplus.**

trademark Designs and names, often officially registered, by which merchants or manufacturers designate and differentiate their products.

transaction costs The costs of exchange.

transaction exposure The extent to which income from individual transactions is affected by fluctuations in foreign exchange values.

transfer fee A bank charge for moving cash from one location to another.

transfer price The price at which goods and services are transferred between subsidiary companies of a corporation.

translation exposure The extent to which the reported consolidated results and balance sheets of a corporation are affected by fluctuations in foreign exchange values.

transnational corporation A firm that tries to simultaneously realize gains from experience curve economies, location economies, and global learning, while remaining locally responsive.

transnational financial reporting The need for a firm headquartered in one country to report its results to citizens of another country.

transnational strategy Plan to exploit experience-based cost and location economies, transfer core competencies with the firm, and pay attention to local responsiveness.

Treaty of Rome The 1957 treaty that established the European Community.

tribal totalitarianism A political system in which a party, group, or individual that represents the interests of a particular tribe (ethnic group) monopolizes political power.

turnkey project A project in which a firm agrees to set up an operating plant for a foreign client and hand over the "key" when the plant is fully operational.

U

unbundling Relying on more than one financial technique to transfer funds across borders.

uncertainty avoidance Extent to which cultures socialize members to accept ambiguous situations and to tolerate uncertainty.

universal needs Needs that are the same all over the world, such as steel, bulk chemicals, and industrial electronics.

V

value creation Performing activities that increase the value of goods or services to consumers.

values Abstract ideas about what a society believes to be good, right, and desirable.

vehicle currency A currency that plays a central role in the foreign exchange market (e.g., the US dollar and Japanese yen).

vertical differentiation The centralization and decentralization of decision-making responsibilities.

vertical foreign direct investment Foreign direct investment in an industry abroad that provides input into a firm's domestic operations, or foreign direct investment into an industry abroad that sells the outputs of a firm's domestic operations.

vertical integration Extension of a firm's activities into adjacent stages of productions (i.e., those providing the firm's inputs or those that purchase the firm's outputs).

voluntary export restraint (VER) A quota on trade imposed from the exporting country's side, instead of the importer's; usually imposed at the request of the importing country's government.

W

wholly owned subsidiary A subsidiary in which the firm owns 100 percent of the stock.

World Bank International institution set up to promote general economic development in the world's poorer nations.

World Trade Organization (WTO) The organization that succeeded the General Agreement on Tariffs and Trade (GATT) as a result of the successful completion of the Uruguay round of GATT negotiations.

worldwide area structure Business organizational structure under which the world is divided into areas.

worldwide product division structure Business organizational structure based on product divisions that have worldwide responsibility.

Z

zero-sum game A situation in which an economic gain by one country results in an economic loss by another.

INDEXES

URL Index

Organization Index

Name Index

Subject Index

Scale: 1 to 125,000,000

Note: All world maps are Robinson projection.